# Evolution, Diversity and Ecology

## Units 4, 5, and 8

Selected Materials from

# BIOLOGY

Ninth Edition

**Kenneth A. Mason**
Purdue University

**Jonathan B. Losos**
Harvard University

**Susan R. Singer**
Carleton College

*based on the work of*

**Peter H. Raven**
Director, Missouri Botanical Gardens;
Engelmann Professor of Botany
Washington Universtiy

**George B. Johnson**
Professor Emeritus of Biology
Washington University

 **Learning Solutions**

Boston   Burr Ridge, IL   Dubuque, IA   New York   San Francisco   St. Louis
Bangkok   Bogotá   Caracas   Lisbon   London   Madrid
Mexico City   Milan   New Delhi   Seoul   Singapore   Sydney   Taipei   Toronto

The McGraw·Hill Companies

Evolution, Diversity and Ecology
Units 4, 5, and 8
Selected Material from
Biology, Ninth Edition

This book is a McGraw-Hill Learning Solutions textbook and contains select material from *Biology*, Ninth Edition by Peter H. Raven, George B. Johnson, Kenneth A. Mason, Jonathan B. Losos, and Susan R. Singer. Copyright © 2011, 2008 by The McGraw-Hill Companies, Inc. Reprinted with permission of the publisher. Many custom published texts are modified versions or adaptations of our best-selling textbooks. Some adaptations are printed in black and white to keep prices at a minimum, while others are in color.

1 2 3 4 5 6 7 8 9 0 DOW DOW 12 11 10

ISBN-13: 978-0-07-739717-3
ISBN-10: 0-07-739717-7

*Learning Solutions Specialist: Shirley Grall*
*Production Editor: Kelly Heinrichs*
*Printer/Binder: RR Donnelley*

# Brief Contents

# About the Authors

Pictured left to right: Susan Rundell Singer, Jonathan Losos, Kenneth Mason

**Kenneth Mason** is a lecturer at the University of Iowa where he teaches introductory biology. He was formerly at Purdue University where for 6 years he was responsible for the largest introductory biology course on campus and collaborated with chemistry and physics faculty on an innovative new course supported by the National Science Foundation that combined biology, chemistry, and physics. Prior to Purdue, he was on the faculty at the University of Kansas for 11 years, where he did research on the genetics of pigmentation in amphibians, publishing both original work and reviews on the topic. While there he taught a variety of courses, was involved in curricular issues, and wrote the lab manual for an upper division genetics laboratory course. His latest move to the University of Iowa was precipitated by his wife's being named president of the University of Iowa.

**Jonathan Losos** is the Monique and Philip Lehner Professor for the Study of Latin America in the Department of Organismic and Evolutionary Biology and curator of herpetology at the Museum of Comparative Zoology at Harvard University. Losos's research has focused on studying patterns of adaptive radiation and evolutionary diversification in lizards. The recipient of several awards, including the prestigious Theodosius Dobzhanksy and David Starr Jordan Prizes, and the Edward Osborne-Wilson Naturalist Award. Losos has published more than 100 scientific articles.

**Susan Rundell Singer** is the Laurence McKinley Gould Professor of the Natural Sciences in the department of biology at Carleton College in Northfield, Minnesota, where she has taught introductory biology, plant biology, genetics, plant development, and developmental genetics for 23 years. Her research interests focus on the development and evolution of flowering plants. Singer has authored numerous scientific publications on plant development, contributed chapters to developmental biology texts, and is actively involved with the education efforts of several professional societies. She received the American Society of Plant Biology's Excellence in Teaching Award, serves on the National Academies Board on Science Education, and chaired the National Research Council study committee that produced *America's Lab Report*.

# Committed To Excellence

This edition continues the evolution of the new Raven & Johnson's *Biology*. The author team is committed to continually improving the text, keeping the student and learning foremost. We have an improved design and updated pedagogical features to complement the new art program and completely revised content of the transformative eighth edition of *Biology*. This latest edition of the text maintains the clear, accessible, and engaging writing style of past editions while maintaining the clear emphasis on evolution and scientific inquiry that made this a leading textbook for students majoring in biology. This emphasis on the organizing power of evolution is combined with a modern integration of the importance of cellular and molecular biology and genomics to offer our readers a text that is student-friendly while containing current content discussed from the most modern perspective.

We are committed to producing the best possible text for both student and faculty. Lead author, Kenneth Mason (University of Iowa) has taught majors biology at three different major public universities for more than 15 years. Jonathan Losos (Harvard University) is at the cutting edge of evolutionary biology research and has taught evolutionary biology to both biology majors and nonmajors students. Susan Rundell Singer (Carleton College) has been deeply involved in science education policy issues on a national level.

The extensive nature of the revision for the eighth edition allowed the incorporation of the most current possible content throughout. This has been continued in the ninth edition. Here we provide a more consistent approach to concepts so that the reader is not buried in detail in one chapter and left wondering how something works in another. In all chapters, we provide a modern perspective emphasizing the structure and function of macromolecules and the evolutionary process that has led to this structure and function.

This modern approach is illustrated with two examples. First, genomics are not given one chapter and otherwise ignored. Instead, results from the analysis of genomes are presented in context across the text. It is important that these results are provided in the context of our traditional approaches and not just lumped into a single chapter. We do not ignore the unique features of this approach and therefore provide two chapters devoted to genomics and to genome evolution.

A second example is expanded coverage of noncoding RNA. It is hard to believe how rapidly miRNA have moved from a mere curiosity to a major topic in gene expression. We have included both new text and graphics on this important topic. The results from complete genome sequencing have highlighted this important category of RNA that was largely ignored in past texts.

The revised physiology unit has been further updated to strengthen the evolutionary basis for understanding this section. The single chapter on circulation and respiration has been broken into two to provide a more reasonable amount of material for the student in each chapter. The coverage of temperature regulation has also been moved to the introductory chapter 43: The Animal Body and Principles of Regulation to provide a concrete example of regulation. All of this should enhance readability for the student as well as integrate this material even closer with the rest of the text.

The entire approach throughout the text is to emphasize important biological concepts. This conceptual approach is supported by an evolutionary perspective and an emphasis on scientific inquiry. Rather than present only dry facts, our conceptual view combines an emphasis on scientific inquiry.

## Our Consistent Themes

It is important to have consistent themes that organize and unify a text. A number of themes are used throughout the book to unify the broad-ranging material that makes up modern biology. This begins with the primary goal of this textbook to provide a comprehensive understanding of evolutionary theory and the scientific basis for this view. We use an experimental framework combining both historical and contemporary research examples to help students appreciate the progressive and integrated nature of science.

### Biology Is Based on an Understanding of Evolution

When Peter Raven and George Johnson began work on *Biology* in 1982 they set out to write a text that presented biology the way they taught in their classrooms—as the product of evolution. We bear in mind always that all biology "only makes sense in the light of evolution;" so this text is enhanced by a consistent evolutionary theme that is woven throughout the text, and we have enhanced this theme in the ninth edition.

The enhanced evolutionary thread can be found in obvious examples such as the two chapters on molecular evolution, but can also be seen throughout the text. As each section considers the current state of knowledge, the "what" of biological phenomenon, they also consider how each system may have arisen by evolution, the "where it came from" of biological phenomenon.

We added an explicit phylogenetic perspective to the understanding of animal form and function. This is most obvious in the numerous figures containing phylogenies in the form and function chapters. The diversity material is s<br>ed by the most up-to-date approach to phyloge

animals and plants. Together these current approaches add even more evolutionary support to a text that set the standard for the integration of evolution in biology.

Our approach allows evolution to be dealt with in the context in which it is relevant. The material throughout this book is considered not only in terms of present structure and function, but how that structure and function may have arisen via evolution by natural selection.

## Biology Uses the Methods of Scientific Inquiry

Another unifying theme within the text is that knowledge arises from experimental work that moves us progressively forward. The use of historical and experimental approaches throughout allow the student not only to see where the field is now, but more importantly, how we arrived here. The incredible expansion of knowledge in biology has created challenges for authors in deciding what content to keep, and to what level an introductory text should strive. We have tried to keep as much historical context as possible and to provide this within an experimental framework consistently throughout the text.

We use a variety of approaches to expose the student to scientific inquiry. We use our new Scientific Thinking figures to walk through an experiment and its implications. These figures always use material that is relevant to the story being told. Data are also provided throughout the text, and other figures illustrate how we arrived at our current view of the topics that make up the different sections. Students are provided with Inquiry Questions to stimulate thinking about the material throughout the book. The questions often involve data that are presented in figures, but are not limited to this approach, also leading the student to question the material in the text as well.

## Biology Is an Integrative Science

The explosion of molecular information has reverberated throughout all areas of biological study. Scientists are increasingly able to describe complicated processes in terms of the interaction of specific molecules, and this knowledge of life at the molecular level has illuminated relationships that were previously unknown. Using this cutting-edge information, we more strongly connect the different areas of biology in this edition.

One example of this integration concerns the structure and function of biological molecules—an emphasis of modern biology. This edition brings that focus to the entire book, using this as a theme to weave together the different aspects of content material with a modern perspective. Given the enormous amount of information that has accumulated in recent years, this emphasis on structure and function provides a necessary thread integrating these new perspectives into the fabric of the traditional biology text.

Although all current biology texts have added a genomics chapter, our text was one of the first to do so. This chapter has been updated, and we have added a chapter on the evolution of genomes. More importantly, the results from the analysis of genomes and the proteomes they encode have been added throughout the book wherever this information is relevant. This allows a more modern perspective throughout the book rather than limiting it to a few chapters. Examples, for instance, can be found in the diversity chapters, where classification of some organisms were updated based on new findings revealed by molecular techniques.

This systems approach to biology also shows up at the level of chapter organization. We introduce genomes in the genetics section in the context of learning about DNA and genomics. We then come back to this topic with an entire chapter at the end of the evolution unit where we look at the evolution of genomes, followed by a chapter on the evolution of development, which leads into our unit on the diversity of organisms.

Similarly, we introduce the topic of development with a chapter in the genetics section, return to it in the evolution unit, and dedicate chapters to it in both the plant and animal units. This layering of concepts is important because we believe that students best understand evolution, development, physiology, and ecology when they can reflect on the connections between the microscopic and macroscopic levels of organization.

We're excited about how we moved the previous high-quality textbook forward in a significant way for a new generation of students. All of us have extensive experience teaching undergraduate biology, and we've used this knowledge as a guide in producing a text that is up to date, beautifully illustrated, and pedagogically sound for the student. We've also worked to provide clear explicit learning objectives, and more closely integrate the text with its media support materials to provide instructors with an excellent complement to their teaching.

*Ken Mason, Jonathan Losos, Susan Rundell Singer*

> This chapter covers one of the fastest-progressing fields in biology. It must cover fundamental topics as well as a wide variety of real and potential applications of the technology. The chapter does all of this well. There is good continuity from one section to the next, which I find important to make the text "readable."
>
> *Michael Lentz*
> *University of North Florida*

# Committed To Excellence

This edition continues the evolution of the new Raven & Johnson's *Biology*. The author team is committed to continually improving the text, keeping the student and learning foremost. We have an improved design and updated pedagogical features to complement the new art program and completely revised content of the transformative eighth edition of *Biology*. This latest edition of the text maintains the clear, accessible, and engaging writing style of past editions while maintaining the clear emphasis on evolution and scientific inquiry that made this a leading textbook for students majoring in biology. This emphasis on the organizing power of evolution is combined with a modern integration of the importance of cellular and molecular biology and genomics to offer our readers a text that is student-friendly while containing current content discussed from the most modern perspective.

We are committed to producing the best possible text for both student and faculty. Lead author, Kenneth Mason (University of Iowa) has taught majors biology at three different major public universities for more than 15 years. Jonathan Losos (Harvard University) is at the cutting edge of evolutionary biology research and has taught evolutionary biology to both biology majors and nonmajors students. Susan Rundell Singer (Carleton College) has been deeply involved in science education policy issues on a national level.

The extensive nature of the revision for the eighth edition allowed the incorporation of the most current possible content throughout. This has been continued in the ninth edition. Here we provide a more consistent approach to concepts so that the reader is not buried in detail in one chapter and left wondering how something works in another. In all chapters, we provide a modern perspective emphasizing the structure and function of macromolecules and the evolutionary process that has led to this structure and function.

This modern approach is illustrated with two examples. First, genomics are not given one chapter and otherwise ignored. Instead, results from the analysis of genomes are presented in context across the text. It is important that these results are provided in the context of our traditional approaches and not just lumped into a single chapter. We do not ignore the unique features of this approach and therefore provide two chapters devoted to genomics and to genome evolution.

A second example is expanded coverage of noncoding RNA. It is hard to believe how rapidly miRNA have moved from a mere curiosity to a major topic in gene expression. We have included both new text and graphics on this important topic. The results from complete genome sequencing have highlighted this important category of RNA that was largely ignored in past texts.

The revised physiology unit has been further updated to strengthen the evolutionary basis for understanding this section. The single chapter on circulation and respiration has been broken into two to provide a more reasonable amount of material for the student in each chapter. The coverage of temperature regulation has also been moved to the introductory chapter 43: The Animal Body and Principles of Regulation to provide a concrete example of regulation. All of this should enhance readability for the student as well as integrate this material even closer with the rest of the text.

The entire approach throughout the text is to emphasize important biological concepts. This conceptual approach is supported by an evolutionary perspective and an emphasis on scientific inquiry. Rather than present only dry facts, our conceptual view combines an emphasis on scientific inquiry.

## Our Consistent Themes

It is important to have consistent themes that organize and unify a text. A number of themes are used throughout the book to unify the broad-ranging material that makes up modern biology. This begins with the primary goal of this textbook to provide a comprehensive understanding of evolutionary theory and the scientific basis for this view. We use an experimental framework combining both historical and contemporary research examples to help students appreciate the progressive and integrated nature of science.

### Biology Is Based on an Understanding of Evolution

When Peter Raven and George Johnson began work on *Biology* in 1982 they set out to write a text that presented biology the way they taught in their classrooms—as the product of evolution. We bear in mind always that all biology "only makes sense in the light of evolution;" so this text is enhanced by a consistent evolutionary theme that is woven throughout the text, and we have enhanced this theme in the ninth edition.

The enhanced evolutionary thread can be found in obvious examples such as the two chapters on molecular evolution, but can also be seen throughout the text. As each section considers the current state of knowledge, the "what" of biological phenomenon, they also consider how each system may have arisen by evolution, the "where it came from" of biological phenomenon.

We added an explicit phylogenetic perspective to the understanding of animal form and function. This is most obvious in the numerous figures containing phylogenies in the form and function chapters. The diversity material is supported by the most up-to-date approach to phylogenies of both animals and plants. Together these current approaches add even more evolutionary support to a text that set the standard for the integration of evolution in biology.

Our approach allows evolution to be dealt with in the context in which it is relevant. The material throughout this book is considered not only in terms of present structure and function, but how that structure and function may have arisen via evolution by natural selection.

## Biology Uses the Methods of Scientific Inquiry

Another unifying theme within the text is that knowledge arises from experimental work that moves us progressively forward. The use of historical and experimental approaches throughout allow the student not only to see where the field is now, but more importantly, how we arrived here. The incredible expansion of knowledge in biology has created challenges for authors in deciding what content to keep, and to what level an introductory text should strive. We have tried to keep as much historical context as possible and to provide this within an experimental framework consistently throughout the text.

We use a variety of approaches to expose the student to scientific inquiry. We use our new Scientific Thinking figures to walk through an experiment and its implications. These figures always use material that is relevant to the story being told. Data are also provided throughout the text, and other figures illustrate how we arrived at our current view of the topics that make up the different sections. Students are provided with Inquiry Questions to stimulate thinking about the material throughout the book. The questions often involve data that are presented in figures, but are not limited to this approach, also leading the student to question the material in the text as well.

## Biology Is an Integrative Science

The explosion of molecular information has reverberated throughout all areas of biological study. Scientists are increasingly able to describe complicated processes in terms of the interaction of specific molecules, and this knowledge of life at the molecular level has illuminated relationships that were previously unknown. Using this cutting-edge information, we more strongly connect the different areas of biology in this edition.

One example of this integration concerns the structure and function of biological molecules—an emphasis of modern biology. This edition brings that focus to the entire book, using this as a theme to weave together the different aspects of content material with a modern perspective. Given the enormous amount of information that has accumulated in recent years, this emphasis on structure and function provides a necessary thread integrating these new perspectives into the fabric of the traditional biology text.

Although all current biology texts have added a genomics chapter, our text was one of the first to do so. This chapter has been updated, and we have added a chapter on the evolution of genomes. More importantly, the results from the analysis of genomes and the proteomes they encode have been added throughout the book wherever this information is relevant. This allows a more modern perspective throughout the book rather than limiting it to a few chapters. Examples, for instance, can be found in the diversity chapters, where classification of some organisms were updated based on new findings revealed by molecular techniques.

This systems approach to biology also shows up at the level of chapter organization. We introduce genomes in the genetics section in the context of learning about DNA and genomics. We then come back to this topic with an entire chapter at the end of the evolution unit where we look at the evolution of genomes, followed by a chapter on the evolution of development, which leads into our unit on the diversity of organisms.

Similarly, we introduce the topic of development with a chapter in the genetics section, return to it in the evolution unit, and dedicate chapters to it in both the plant and animal units. This layering of concepts is important because we believe that students best understand evolution, development, physiology, and ecology when they can reflect on the connections between the microscopic and macroscopic levels of organization.

We're excited about how we moved the previous high-quality textbook forward in a significant way for a new generation of students. All of us have extensive experience teaching undergraduate biology, and we've used this knowledge as a guide in producing a text that is up to date, beautifully illustrated, and pedagogically sound for the student. We've also worked to provide clear explicit learning objectives, and more closely integrate the text with its media support materials to provide instructors with an excellent complement to their teaching.

*Ken Mason, Jonathan Losos, Susan Rundell Singer*

This chapter covers one of the fastest-progressing fields in biology. It must cover fundamental topics as well as a wide variety of real and potential applications of the technology. The chapter does all of this well. There is good continuity from one section to the next, which I find important to make the text "readable."

*Michael Lentz*
*University of North Florida*

# Cutting Edge Science

*Changes to the Ninth Edition*

## Part I: The Molecular Basis of Life

The material in this section does not change much with time. However, we have updated it to make it more friendly to the student. The student is introduced to the pedagogical features that characterize the book here: learning objectives with various levels of cognitive difficulty, scientific thinking figures, and an integrated approach to guide the student through complex material.

In chapter 1, the idea of emergent properties has been clarified and material added to emphasize the nonequilibrium nature of biology. This will help introduce students to the fundamental nature of biological systems and prepare them for the rest of the book.

## Part II: Biology of the Cell

The overall organization of this section was retained, but material on cell junctions and cell-to-cell interactions was moved from chapter 9 to chapter 4, where it forms a natural conclusion to cell structure. Within chapter 4 microsome/peroxisome biogenesis was clarified to complete the picture of cell structure. The nature of trans fats is clarified, a subject students are likely to have been exposed to but not understand. A brief discussion of the distribution of lipids in different membranes was also added.

**Chapter 7**—The organization of chapter 7 was improved for greater clarity. ATP structure and function is introduced earlier, and the opening summary section covering all of respiration was removed. This allows the information to unfold in a way that is easier to digest. A new analogy was added for the mechanism of ATP synthase to make this difficult enzyme more approachable.

**Chapter 8**—The section on bacterial photosynthesis was completely rewritten for clarity and accuracy. In addition to the emphasis we always had on the experimental history of photosynthesis, the scientific thinking figures for chapters 7 and 8 are complementary and cross referenced to reinforce how we accumulate evidence for complex phenomenon such as chemiosmosis.

**Chapter 9**—The removal of the cell junction material keeps the focus of chapter 9 on signaling through receptors, making this difficult topic more accessible. The distribution of G protein-coupled receptor genes in humans and mouse was updated.

**Chapter 10**—The discussion of bacterial cell division was updated again to reflect the enormous change in our view of this field. The organization of the chapter was tightened, by combining mitosis and cytokinesis as M phase. Not only is this a consensus view in the field, it simplifies the overall organization for greater clarity.

## Part III: Genetic and Molecular Biology

The overall organization of this section remains the same. The splitting of transmission genetics into two chapters allows students to first be introduced to general principles, then tie these back to the behavior of chromosomes and the more complex topics related to genetic mapping.

Content changes in the molecular genetics portion of this section are intended to do two things: (1) update material that is the most rapidly changing in the entire book, and (2) introduce the idea that RNA plays a much greater role now than appreciated in the past. The view of RNA has undergone a revolution that is underappreciated in introductory textbooks. This has led to a complete updating of the section in chapter 16 on small RNAs complete with new graphics to go with the greatly expanded and reorganized text. This new section should both introduce students to exciting new material and organize it so as to make it coherent with the rest of the chapter. The new material is put into historical context and updated to distinguish between siRNA and miRNA, and the mechanisms of RNA silencing. Material on the classical bacterial operons trp and lac was also refined for greater clarity.

**Chapter 11**—The information on meiotic cohesins and protection of cohesins during meiosis I was clarified and updated. This is critical for students to understand how meiosis actually works as opposed to memorizing a series of events.

**Chapter 12**—The second example of epistasis, which did not have graphical support in the eighth edition, was removed. This allows the remaining example to be explored in greater detail. The organization of the explication of Mendel's principles was tightened to improve clarity.

**Chapter 14**—Material on the eukaryotic replisome was updated and the graphics for this refined from the last edition. Archaeal replication proteins are also introduced to give the student a more complete view of replication.

**Chapter 15**—Has been tightened considerably. The example of sickle cell anemia was moved from chapter 13 to 15, where it fits more naturally in a discussion of how mutations affect gene function.

**Chapter 17**—Our goal is to help students apply what they've learned about molecular biology to answering important biological questions. This chapter has been revised to balance newer technologies with approaches that continue to be used in both the research and education communities. RNAi applications to diseases like macular degeneration and next-generation sequencing technology are introduced by building on what the student already knows about DNA replication, transcription, and PCR.

**Chapter 18**—Our book is unique in having two chapters on genomes. The first extends the molecular unit to the scale of whole genomes, and chapter 24 focuses

committed t

on comparative genomics after students have learned about evolution. This organization is core to our full integration of evolution throughout the book. Chapter 18 has been revised to demonstrate the broad relevance of genomics, from understanding the evolution of speech to identifying the source of the 2001 anthrax attacks.

**Chapter 19**—The material on stem cells was completely rewritten and updated. The content was reorganized to put it into an even more solid historical context using the idea of nuclear reprogramming, and how this led to both the cloning of mammals and embryonic stem cells. New information on induced pluripotent stem cells is included to keep this as current as possible. This topic is one that is of general interest and is another subject about which students have significant misinformation. We strove to provide clear, well-organized information.

## Part IV: Evolution

The evolution chapters were updated with new examples. A strong emphasis on the role of experimental approaches to studying evolutionary phenomena has been maintained and enhanced.

**Chapter 20**—The various processes that can lead to evolutionary change within populations are discussed in detail. Notably, these processes are not considered in isolation, but explored through how they interact.

**Chapter 21**—This chapter presents a state-of-the-art discussion of the power of natural selection to produce evolutionary change and the ever-increasing documentation in the fossil record of evolutionary transitions through time. It also discusses a variety of phenomena that only make sense if evolution has occurred and concludes with a critique of arguments posed against the existence of evolution.

**Chapter 22**—The process of speciation and evolutionary diversification is considered in this chapter. It includes current disagreements on how species are identified and how speciation operates.

**Chapter 23**—An up-to-date discussion of not only how phylogenies are inferred, but their broad and central role in comparative biology is the focus of chapter 23.

**Chapter 24**—This chapter has been revised to incorporate the rapidly growing number of fully sequenced genomes in a conceptual manner. We included the paradigm-changing findings that noncoding DNA plays a critical role in regulating DNA expression. This chapter and chapter 25 illustrate how we integrate both evolution and molecular biology throughout our text.

**Chapter 25**—With updated examples we explore the changing perspectives on the evolution of development. Specifically, the field is shifting away from the simplified view that changes in regulatory regions of genes are responsible for the evolution of form.

## Part V: Diversity of Life on Earth

In revising the diversity chapters (protist, plants, and fungi) our emphasis was on integrating an evolutionary theme. The fungi chapter was restructured to reflect the current phylogenies while keeping species that are familiar to instructors at the fore. While competitors have two plant diversity chapters, we have one. We integrated the diversity of flowers and pollination strategies, as well as fruit diversity into the plant unit to enable students to fully appreciate morphological diversity because they have already learned about plant structure and development.

**Chapter 26**—This chapter has been updated so instructors have the option of using it as a stand-alone diversity chapter if their syllabus is too crowded to include the extensive coverage of diversity in the unit. Endosymbiosis has been consolidated in this chapter (moving some of the content from chapter 4).

**Chapter 27**—Material on archaeal viruses was added to incorporate this area of active research that is often ignored. The approach to HIV drug treatments was completely redone with revised strategies and updated graphics. The discussions of prions and viroids were also revised.

**Chapter 28**—All health statistics in chapter 28 were updated, including information on TB, HIV and STDs. A discussion on archaeal photosynthesis was added to the section on microbial metabolism.

**Chapter 30**—Findings of several plant genome projects informed the revision of the plant chapter. The remarkable desiccation tolerance of moss is emphasized in a Scientific Thinking figure exploring the genes involved in desiccation tolerance. New findings on correlations between the rate of pollen tube growth and the origins of the angiosperms have also been integrated into the chapter.

**Chapter 31**—Since the previous edition, much has been learned about the evolution of fungi, fundamentally changing relationships among groups. We revised the fungal phylogenies in this chapter to conform with the current understanding of fungal evolution, while contextualizing the older taxonomic groupings that may be more familiar to some readers.

**Chapters 32–34**—These chapters have been completely overhauled to emphasize the latest understanding, synthesizing molecular and morphological information, on the phylogeny of animals. We refocused these chapters to emphasize the differences in major morphological, behavioral, and ecological features that differentiate the major animal groups, placing a strong emphasis on understanding the organism in the context of its environment. Chapter 32 is an overview, which could be used as a standalone chapter, setting the stage for Chapters 33 on non-coelomate animals and Chapter 34 on coelomates.

**Chapter 35**—This chapter on vertebrates was revised to incorporate current ideas on vertebrate phylogeny and to emphasize the phylogenetic approach to understanding evolutionary diversification.

## Part VI: Plant Form and Function

As with the animal unit we incorporated an evolutionary theme. In the Scientific Thinking figures, as well as the text, we challenge the students to combine morphological, developmental, and molecular approaches to asking questions about plants. The goal is to help students integrate their conceptual understanding over multiple levels of organization. In addition, most of the questions at the end of the chapter are new.

**Chapter 36**—The section on leaf development has been updated to include a molecular analysis of the role of a key gene, *UNIFOLIATA*, in compound leaf development.

**Chapter 39**—Throughout the unit we included relevant examples to illustrate core concepts in plant biology. Here we added information about the effect of pH on germination and included a Scientific Thinking figure to more fully engage the student in considering pH effects in an agricultural context. The discussion of elevated $CO_2$ levels and increased temperatures on plant growth was updated. The very complex interactions affecting carbon and nitrogen content in plants is addressed at the level of plant and cell physiology. In addition, they are discussed at the ecosystem level later in the text in a more coherent presentation of the effects of climate change.

**Chapter 41**—The section of phytochrome was reorganized and updated. The emphasis is on guiding the student away from the historic examples of morphological responses to different day lengths to a clear, coherent understanding of how red and far red light affect the conformation of phytochrome and the signaling pathway it affects.

## Part VII: Animal Form and Function

Several organizational changes were made to this section to enhance overall coherence. The entire section was reinterpreted with the intent of better integrating evolution into all topics. The material on temperature regulation was moved from chapter 50 (8E) to the introductory chapter 43. This both provides an illustrative example to the introduction to homeostasis and removes a formerly artificial combination of temperature control and osmotic control. Respiration and circulation were made into separate chapters (49 and 50), allowing for greater clarity and removing an overly long chapter that was a barrier to understanding.

**Chapter 44**—The material on synaptic plasticity was rewritten with new graphics added. And in chapter 46 the addition of learning objectives and our integrated pedagogical tools make a complex topic more approachable. A new Scientific Thinking figure was added as well.

**Chapter 51**—The osmotic regulation material in this chapter is more coherent as a separate section without the temperature regulation material.

**Chapter 52**—This chapter was reorganized and restructured to emphasize the existence of innate versus adaptive immunity. This replaces the old paradigm of nonspecific versus specific immunity. This reorganization and new material also emphasize the evolutionary basis of innate immunity, which exists in invertebrates and vertebrates.

**Chapter 54**—The material on organizer function was updated. The Scientific Thinking figure uses molecular approaches introduced in part III and a figure that was already in the chapter. This figure is much more pedagogically useful in this repurposing than as a static figure and illustrates the use of these figures.

## Part VIII: Ecology and Behavior

The ecology chapters have been revised with a particular focus on providing up-to-date information on current environmental issues, both in terms of the problems that exist and the potential action that can be taken to ameliorate them.

**Chapter 55**—Completely revised with a strong emphasis on neuroethological approaches to understanding behavioral patterns, this chapter emphasizes modern molecular approaches to the study of behavior.

**Chapter 56**—Considers the ecology of individuals and populations and includes up-to-date discussion of human population growth.

**Chapter 57**—The ecology of communities is discussed in the context of the various ecological processes that mediate interactions between co-occurring species. With updated examples, chapter 57 illustrates how different processes can interact, as well as emphasizing the experimental approach to the study of ecology.

**Chapter 58**—This chapter focuses on the dynamics of ecosystems. It has been updated to emphasize current understanding of the how ecosystems function.

**Chapter 59**—The chapter has been extensively updated to provide the latest information on factors affecting the environment and human health with a clear focus on the biosphere and current environmental threats.

**Chapter 60**—And finally, chapter 60 considers conservation biology, emphasizing the causes of species endangerment and what can be done. Data and examples provide the latest information and thinking on conservation issues.

# Committed to Preparing Students for the Future

## Understand Biology With the Help of . . .

### Integrated Learning Outcomes

Each section begins with specific Learning Outcomes that represent each major concept. At the end of each section, Learning Outcomes Reviews serve as a check to help students confirm their understanding of the concepts in that section. Questions at the end of the Learning Outcomes Review ask students to think critically about what they have read.

> Any opportunity to identify "learning outcomes" is a welcome addition; we are forced more and more to identify these in learning assessments. I would use these as a guide for students to understand the minimum material they are expected to learn from each section.
>
> *Michael Lentz*
> *University of North Florida*

### In Print and Online

The online eBook in Connect Plus™ provides students with clear understanding of concepts through a media-rich experience. Embedded animations bring key concepts to life. Also, the ebook provides an interactive experience with the Learning Outcome Review questions.

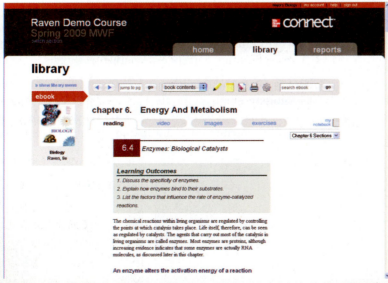

# www.ravenbiology.com

## Companion Website

Students can enhance their understanding of the concepts with the rich study materials available to at www.ravenbiology.com. This open access website provides self-study options with chapter pretest quizzes to assess current understanding, animations that highlight topics students typically struggle with and textbook images that can be used for notetaking and study.

## A Consistent and Instructional Visual Program

The author team collaborated with a team of medical and scientific illustrations to create the unsurpassed visual program. Focusing on consistency, accuracy, and instructional value, they created an art program that is intimately connected with the text narrative. The resulting realistic, 3-D illustrations will stimulate student interest and help instructors teach difficult concepts.

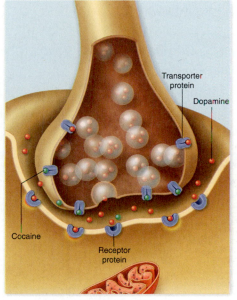

**Figure 44.18** How cocaine alters events at the synapse.
When cocaine binds to the dopamine transporters, it prevents reuptake of dopamine so the neurotransmitter survives longer in the synapse and continues to stimulate the postsynaptic cell. Cocaine thus acts to intensify pleasurable sensations.

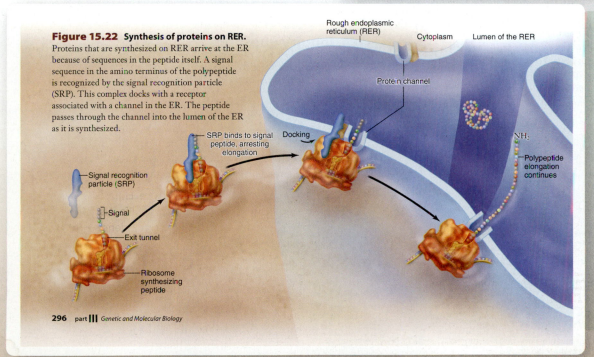

**Figure 15.22** Synthesis of proteins on RER.
Proteins that are synthesized on RER arrive at the ER because of sequences in the peptide itself. A signal sequence in the amino terminus of the polypeptide is recognized by the signal recognition particle (SRP). This complex docks with a receptor associated with a channel in the ER. The peptide passes through the channel into the lumen of the ER as it is synthesized.

Signal recognition particle (SRP)
Signal
Exit tunnel
Ribosome synthesizing peptide
SRP binds to signal peptide, arresting elongation
Docking
Rough endoplasmic reticulum (RER)
Cytoplasm
Lumen of the RER
Protein channel
NH₂
Polypeptide elongation continues

**296** part III *Genetic and Molecular Biology*

The art is quite good! The colors are well saturated and the figures are clear and often compelling, particularly in showing the molecular complexity of these molecules and cells.

*Susan J Stamler*
*College of DuPage*

## Apply Your Knowledge With...

### NEW Scientific Thinking Art

**Key illustrations** in every chapter highlight how the frontiers of knowledge are pushed forward by a combination of hypothesis and experiment. These figures begin with a hypothesis, then show how it makes explicit predictions, tests these by experiment and finally demonstrates what conclusions can be drawn, and where this leads. These provide a consistent framework to guide the student in the logic of scientific inquiry. Each illustration concludes with open-ended questions to promote scientific inquiry.

> Knowing how scientists solve problems, and then using this knowledge to solve a problem (as an example) drives home the concept of induction and deduction — I applaud this highly!
>
> *Marc LaBella*
> *Ocean County College*

### SCIENTIFIC THINKING

**Hypothesis:** *The plasma membrane is fluid, not rigid.*

**Prediction:** *If the membrane is fluid, membrane proteins may diffuse laterally.*

**Test:** *Fuse mouse and human cells, then observe the distribution of membrane proteins over time by labeling specific mouse and human proteins.*

Mouse cell

Human cell

Fuse cells

Allow time for mixing to occur

Intermixed membrane proteins

**Result:** *Over time, hybrid cells show increasingly intermixed proteins.*

**Conclusion:** *At least some membrane proteins can diffuse laterally in the membrane.*

**Further Experiments:** *Can you think of any other explanation for these observations? What if newly synthesized proteins were inserted into the membrane during the experiment? How could you use this basic experimental design to rule out this or other possible explanations?*

**Figure 5.4** Test of membrane fluidity.

### SCIENTIFIC THINKING

**Hypothesis:** *There are positive regulators of cell division.*

**Prediction:** *Frog oocytes are arrested in $G_2$ of meiosis I. They can be induced to mature (undergo meiosis) by progesterone treatment. If maturing oocytes contain a positive regulator of cell division, injection of cytoplasm should induce an immature oocyte to undergo meiosis.*

**Test:** *Oocytes are induced with progesterone, then cytoplasm from these maturing cells is injected into immature oocytes.*

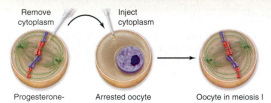

Remove cytoplasm

Inject cytoplasm

Progesterone-treated oocyte

Arrested oocyte

Oocyte in meiosis I

**Result:** *Injected oocytes progress $G_2$ from into meiosis I.*

**Conclusion:** *The progesterone treatment causes production of a positive regulator of maturation: Maturation Promoting Factor (MPF).*

**Prediction:** *If mitosis is driven by positive regulators, then cytoplasm from a mitotic cell should cause a $G_1$ cell to enter mitosis.*

**Test:** *M phase cells are fused with $G_1$ phase cells, then the nucleus from the $G_1$ phase cell is monitored microscopically.*

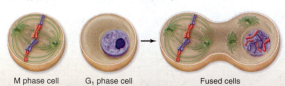

M phase cell

$G_1$ phase cell

Fused cells

**Conclusion:** *Cytoplasm from M phase cells contains a positive regulator that causes a cell to enter mitosis.*

**Further Experiments:** *How can both of these experiments be rationalized? What would be the next step in characterizing these factors?*

**Figure 10.16** Discovery of positive regulator of cell division.

### Inquiry question

**?** Based only on amino acid sequence, how would you recognize an integral membrane protein?

### Inquiry Questions

Questions that challenge students to think about and engage in what they are reading at a more sophisticated level.

# Synthesize and Tie It All Together With . . .

### End-of-Chapter Conceptual Assessment Questions

Thought-provoking questions at the end of each chapter tie the concepts together by asking the student to go beyond the basics to achieve a higher level of cognitive thinking.

I think that the end-of-chapter summary and review questions are thorough and written well. I very much like the way that they are categorized into understanding, application, and synthesizing. I use these types of questions on my exams. So I think that these end-of-chapter questions can be used as homework or in class work to help prepare students for exams.

*Dr. Sharon K. Bullock*
*UNC Charlotte*

---

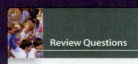

## Review Questions

### UNDERSTAND

1. What property distinguished Mendel's investigation from previous studies?
   a. Mendel used true-breeding pea plants.
   b. Mendel quantified his results.
   c. Mendel examined many different traits.
   d. Mendel examined the segregation of traits.

2. The $F_1$ generation of the monohybrid cross purple ($PP$) × white ($pp$) flower pea plants should
   a. all have white flowers.
   b. all have a light purple or blended appearance.
   c. all have purple flowers.
   d. have (¾) purple flowers, and ¼ white flowers.

3. The $F_1$ plants from the previous question are allowed to self-fertilize. The phenotypic ratio for the $F_2$ should be
   a. all purple.          c.  3 purple:1 white.
   b. 1 purple:1 white.     d.  3 white:1 purple.

4. Which of the following is *not* a part of Mendel's five-element model?
   a. Traits have alternative forms (what we now call alleles).
   b. Parents transmit discrete traits to their offspring.
   c. If an allele is present it will be expressed.
   d. Traits do not blend.

5. An organism's _____ is/are determined by its
   a. genotype; phenotype    c.  alleles; phenotype
   b. phenotype; genotype    d.  genes; alleles

6. Phenotypes like height in humans, which show a continuous distribution, are usually the result of
   a. an alteration of dominance for multiple alleles of a single gene.
   b. the presence of multiple alleles for a single gene.
   c. the action of one gene on multiple phenotypes.
   d. the action of multiple genes on a single phenotype.

### APPLY

1. A dihybrid cross between a plant with long smooth leaves and a plant with short hairy leaves produces a long smooth $F_1$. If this $F_1$ is allowed to self-cross to produce an $F_2$, what would you predict for the ratio of $F_2$ phenotypes?
   a. 9 long smooth:3 long hairy:3 short smooth:1 short smooth
   b. 9 long smooth:3 long hairy:3 short smooth:1 short hairy
   c. 9 short hairy:3 long hairy:3 short smooth:1 long smooth
   d. 1 long smooth:1 long hairy:1 short smooth:1 short hairy

2. Consider a long smooth $F_2$ plant from the previous question. This plant's genotype
   a. must be homozygous for both long alleles and hairy alleles.
   b. must be heterozygous at both the leaf length gene, and the leaf hair gene.
   c. can only be inferred by another cross.
   d. cannot be determined by any means.

3. What is the probability of obtaining an individual with the genotype $Bb$ from a cross between two individuals with the genotype $Bb$?
   a. ½          c.  ⅛
   b. ¼          d.  0

4. What is the probability of obtaining an individual with the genotype $CC$ from a cross between two individuals with the genotypes $CC$ and $Cc$?
   a. ½          c.  ⅛
   b. ¼          d.  ¹⁄₁₆

5. You discover a new variety of plant with color varieties of purple and white. When you intercross these, the $F_1$ is a lighter purple. You consider that this may be an example of blending and self-cross the $F_1$. If Mendel is correct, what would you predict for the $F_2$?
   a. 1 purple:2 white:1 light purple
   b. 1 white:2 purple:1 light purple
   c. 1 purple:2 light purple:1 white
   d. 1 light purple:2 purple:1 white

6. Mendel's model assumes that each trait is determined by a single factor with alternate forms. We now know that this is too simplistic and that
   a. a single gene may affect more than one trait.
   b. a single trait may be affected by more than one gene.
   c. a single gene always affects only one trait, but traits may be affected by more than one gene.
   d. a single gene can affect more than one trait, and traits may be affected by more than one gene.

### SYNTHESIZE

1. Create a Punnett square for the following crosses and use this to predict phenotypic ratio for dominant and recessive traits. Dominant alleles are indicated by uppercase letters and recessive are indicated by lowercase letters. For parts b and c, predict ratios using probability and the product rule.
   a. A monohybrid cross between individuals with the genotype $Aa$ and $Aa$
   b. A dihybrid cross between two individuals with the genotype $AaBb$
   c. A dihybrid cross between individuals with the genotype $AaBb$ and $aabb$

2. Explain how the events of meiosis can explain both segregation and independent assortment.

3. In mice, there is a yellow strain that when crossed yields 2 yellow:1 black. How could you explain this observation? How could you test this with crosses?

4. In mammals, a variety of genes affect coat color. One of these is a gene with mutant alleles that results in the complete loss of pigment, or albinism. Another controls the type of dark pigment with alleles that lead to black or brown colors. The albinistic trait is recessive, and black is dominant to brown. Two black mice are crossed and yield 9 black:4 albino:3 brown. How would you explain these results?

### ONLINE RESOURCE

www.ravenbiology.com

Understand, Apply, and Synthesize—enhance your study with animations that bring concepts to life and practice tests to assess your understanding. Your instructor may also recommend the interactive eBook, individualized learning tools, and more.

**238**  part **III**  *Genetic and Molecular Biology*

---

## Integrated Study Quizzes

Study quizzes have been integrated into the Connect Plus ebook for students to assess their understanding of the information presented in each section. End of chapter questions are linked to the answer section of the text to provide for easy study. The notebook feature allows students to collect and manage notes and highlights from the ebook to create a custom study guide.

## McGraw-Hill Connect Biology

**Connect Biology™** is a web-based assignment and assessment platform that gives students the means to better connect with their coursework, with their instructors, and with the important concepts that they will need to know for success now and in the future.

With Connect Biology you can deliver assignments, quizzes, and tests online. A robust set of questions and activities are presented and tied to the textbook's learning objectives. As an instructor, you can edit existing questions and author entirely new problems. Track individual student performance — by question, assignment, or in relation to the class overall — with detailed grade reports. Integrate grade reports easily with Learning Management Systems (LMS) such as WebCT and Blackboard. And much more.

ConnectPlus™ Biology provides students with all the advantages of Connect™ Biology, plus 24/7 access to an eBook. This media-rich version of the book includes animations, videos, and inline assessments placed appropriately throughout the chapter. Connect Plus Biology allows students to practice important skills at their own pace and on their own schedule. By purchasing eBooks from McGraw-Hill students can save as much as 50% on selected titles delivered on the most advanced eBook platforms available. Contact your McGraw-Hill sales representative to discuss eBook packaging options.

## Powerful Presentation Tools

Everything you need for outstanding presentation in one place!

- **FlexArt Image PowerPoints** — including every piece of art that has been sized and cropped specifically for superior presentations as well as labels that you can edit, flexible art that can be picked up and moved, tables, and photographs

- **Animation PowerPoints** — Numerous full-color animations illustrating important processes. Harness the visual impact of concepts in motion by importing these slides into classroom presentations or online course materials

- **Lecture PowerPoints** — with fully embedded animations

- **Labeled and unlabeled JPEG images** — Full-color digital files of all illustrations, which can be readily incorporated into presentations, exams, or custom-made classroom materials

## Presentation Center

In addition to the images from your book, this **online digital library** contains photos, artwork, animations, and other media from an array of McGraw-Hill textbooks that can be used to create customized lectures, visually enhance tests and quizzes, and make compelling course websites or attractive printed support materials.

## Quality Test Bank

All questions have been written to fully align with the Learning Outcomes and content of the text. Provided within a computerized test bank powered by McGraw-Hill's flexible electronic testing program **EZ Test Online**, instructors can create paper and online tests or quizzes in this easy to use program! A new tagging scheme allows you to sort questions by difficulty level, topic, and section. Imagine being able to create and access your test or quiz anywhere, at any time, without installing the testing software. Now, with EZ Test Online, instructors can select questions from multiple McGraw-Hill test banks or author their own, and then either print the test for paper distribution or give it online.

# Active Learning Exercises

Supporting biology faculty in their efforts to make introductory courses more active and student-centered is critical to improving undergraduate biological education. Active learning can broadly be described as strategies and techniques in which students are engaged in their own learning, and is typically characterized by the utilization of higher order critical thinking skills. The use of these techniques is critical to biological education because of their powerful impact on students' learning and development of scientific professional skills.

Active leaning strategies are highly valued and have been shown to:

- Help make content relevant
- Be particularly adept at addressing common misconceptions
- Help students to think about their own learning (metacognition)
- Promote meaningful learning of content by emphasizing application
- Foster student interest in science

**Guided Activities** have been provided for instructors to use in their course for both in-class and out-of-class activities. The Guided Activities make it easy for you to incorporate active learning into your course and are flexible to fit your specific needs.

# Flexible Delivery Options

Raven et al Biology is available in many formats in addition to the traditional textbook so that instructors and students have more choices when deciding which format best suits their needs.

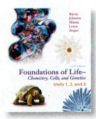  

- **Foundations of Life — Chemistry, Cells and Genetics**
  ISBN: 0-07-739750-9
  Units 1, 2 and 3

- **Evolution, Diversity and Ecology**
  ISBN: 0-07-739717-7
  Units 4, 5 and 8

- **Plants and Animals**
  ISBN: 0-07-739751-7
  Units 6 and 7

Also available, customized versions for all of your course needs. You're in charge of your course, so why not be in control of the content of your textbook? At McGraw-Hill Custom Publishing, we can help you create the ideal text — the one you've always imagined— quickly and easily. With more than 20 years of experience in custom publishing, we're experts. But at McGraw-Hill we're also innovators, leading the way with new methods and means of creating simplified value-added custom textbooks.

The options are never-ending when you work with McGraw-Hill. You already know what will work best for you and your students. And here, you can choose it.

# Laboratory Manuals

**Biology Laboratory Manual, Ninth Edition**
Vodopich and Moore
ISBN: 0-07-338306-6

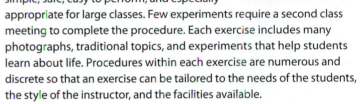

This laboratory manual is designed for an introductory course for biology majors with a broad survey of basic laboratory techniques. The experiments and procedures are simple, safe, easy to perform, and especially appropriate for large classes. Few experiments require a second class meeting to complete the procedure. Each exercise includes many photographs, traditional topics, and experiments that help students learn about life. Procedures within each exercise are numerous and discrete so that an exercise can be tailored to the needs of the students, the style of the instructor, and the facilities available.

**Biological Investigations Lab Manual, Ninth Edition**
Dolphin
ISBN: 0-07-338305-8

This independent lab manual can be used for a one- or two-semester majors' level general biology lab and can be used with any majors' level general biology textbook. The labs are investigative and ask students to use more critical thinking and hands-on learning. The author emphasizes investigative, quantitative, and comparative approaches to studying the life sciences.

# Focus on Evolution

**Understanding Evolution, Seventh Edition**
Rosenbaum and Volpe
ISBN: 0-07-338323-6

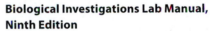

As an introduction to the principles of evolution, this paperback text is ideally suited as a main text for general evolution or as a supplement for general biology, genetics, zoology, botany, anthropology, or any life science course that utilizes evolution as the underlying theme of all life.

# Committed to Quality

## 360° Development Process

McGraw-Hill's 360° Development Process is an ongoing, never-ending, education-oriented approach to building accurate and innovative print and digital products. It is dedicated to continual large-scale and incremental improvement, driven by multiple user feedback loops and checkpoints. This is initiated during the early planning stages of our new products, intensifies during the development and production stages, then begins again after publication in anticipation of the next edition.

This process is designed to provide a broad, comprehensive spectrum of feedback for refinement and innovation of our learning tools, for both student and instructor. The 360° Development Process includes market research, content reviews, course- and product-specific symposia, accuracy checks, and art reviews. We appreciate the expertise of the many individuals involved in this process.

### Contributing Authors

**Active Learning Exercises**

Frank Bailey, Middle Tennessee State University

Steve Howard, Middle Tennessee State University

Michael Rutledge, Middle Tennessee State University

**Chapter Contributors**

Daphne Fautin, University of Kansas

Shelley Jansky, University of Wisconsin, Madison

Stephanie Pandolfi, Wayne State University

James Traniello, Boston University

**Instructor's Manual**

Mark Hens, University of North Carolina, Charlotte

**Integrated eBook Study Guide**

David Bos, Purdue University

Koy Miskin, Purdue University

Kathleen Broomall, Miami University, Oxford

**Test Bank**

Brian Bagatto, University of Akron

Tom Sasek, University of Louisiana at Monroe

Stephanie Pandolfi, Wayne State University

**Connect Content Contributors**

Susan Hengeveld, Indiana University

Salvatore Tavormina, Austin Community College

Scott Cooper, University of Wisconsin, LaCrosse

Brian Shmaefsky, Lone Star College

Phil Gibson, Oklahoma University

Morris Maduro, University of California, Riverside

Matt Neatrour, Northern Kentucky University

Leslie Jones, Valdosta State

Lynn Preston, Tarrant County College

**Website**

Tom Pitzer, Florida International University

Marceau Ratard, Delgado Community College

Amanda Rosenzweig, Delgado Community College

**Instructor Media**

Mark Browning, Purdue University

Brenda Leady, University of Toledo

### Digital Board of Advisors

We are indebted to the valuable advice and direction of an outstanding group of advisors, led by Melissa Michael, University of Illinois at Urbana-Champaign. Other board members include:

Randy Phillis, University of Massachusetts

John Merrill, Michigan State

Russell Borski, North Carolina State

Deb Pires, University of California, Los Angeles

Bill Wischusen, Louisiana State University

David Scicchitano, New York City University

Michael Rutledge, Middle Tennessee State

Lynn Preston, Tarrant County College

Karen Gerhart, University of California, Davis

Jean Heitz, University of Wisconsin, Madison

Mark Lyford, University of Wyoming

### General Biology Symposia

Every year McGraw-Hill conducts several General Biology Symposia, which are attended by instructors from across the country. These events are an opportunity for editors from McGraw-Hill to gather information about the needs and challenges of instructors teaching the major's biology course. It also offers a forum for the attendees to exchange ideas and experiences with colleagues they might not have otherwise met. The feedback we have received has been invaluable and has contributed to the development of Biology and its supplements. A special thank you to recent attendees:

Sylvester Allred  *Northern Arizona University*

Michael Bell  *Richland College*

Arlene Billock  *University of Louisiana Lafayette*

Stephane Boissinot  *Queens College, the City University of New York*

David Bos  *Purdue University*

Scott Bowling  *Auburn University*

Jacqueline Bowman  *Arkansas Technical University*

Arthur Buikema  *Virginia Polytechnic Institute*

Anne Bullerjahn  *Owens Community College*

Helaine Burstein  *Ohio University*

Raymond Burton  *Germanna Community College*

Peter Busher  *Boston University*

Richard Cardullo  *University of California — Riverside*

Jennifer Ciaccio  *Dixie State College*

Anne Barrett Clark  *Binghamton University*

Allison Cleveland  *University of South Florida, Tampa*

Jennifer Coleman   *University of Massachusetts, Amherst*
Sehoya Cotner   *University of Minnesota*
Mitch Cruzan   *Portland State University*
Laura DiCaprio   *Ohio University*
Kathyrn Dickson   *California State College, Fullerton*
Cathy Donald-Whitney   *Collin County Community College*
Stanley Faeth   *Arizona State University*
Donald French   *Oklahoma State University*
Douglas Gaffin   *University of Oklahoma*
Karen Gerhart   *University of California, Davis*
Cynthia Giffen   *University of Wisconsin — Madison*
William Glider   *University of Nebraska, Lincoln*
Christopher Gregg   *Louisiana State University*
Stan Guffey   *The University of Tennessee*
Bernard Hauser   *University of Florida, Gainesville*
Jean Heitz   *Unversity of Wisconsin — Madison*
Mark Hens   *University of North Carolina, Greensboro*
Albert Herrera   *University of Southern California*

Ralph James Hickey   *Miami University of Ohio, Oxford*
Brad Hyman   *University of California — Riverside*
Kyoungtae Kim   *Missouri State University*
Sherry Krayesky   *University of Louisiana, Lafayette*
Jerry Kudenov   *University of Alaska Anchorage*
Josephine Kurdziel   *University of Michigan*
Ellen Lamb   *University of North Carolina — Greensboro*
Brenda Leady   *University of Toledo*
Graeme Lindbeck   *Valencia Community College*
Susan Meiers   *Western Illinois University*
Michael Meighan   *University of California, Berkeley*
John Mersfelder   *Sinclair Community College*
Melissa Michael   *University of Illinois at Urbana-Champaign*
Leonore Neary   *Joliet Junior College*
Shawn Nordell   *Saint Louis University*
John Osterman   *University of Nebraska—Lincoln*
Stephanie Pandolfi   *Wayne State University*
C.O. Patterson   *Texas A&M University*

Nancy Pencoe   *State University of West Georgia*
Roger Persell   *Hunter College*
Marius Pfeiffer   *Tarrant County College NE*
Steve Phelps   *University of Florida*
Debra Pires   *University of California, Los Angeles*
Eileen Preston   *Tarrant County College NW*
Rajinder Ranu   *Colorado State University*
Marceau Ratard   *Delgado Community College City Park*
Melanie Rathburn   *Boston University*
Robin Richardson   *Winona State University*
Amanda Rosenzweig   *Delgado Community College — City Park*
Laurie Russell   *Saint Louis University*
Connie Russell   *Angelo State University*
David Scicchitano   *New York University*
Timothy Shannon   *Francis Marion University*
Brian Shmaefsky   *Lone Star College — Kingwood*
Richard Showman   *University of South Carolina*
Robert Simons   *University of California, Los Angeles*

Steve Skarda   *Linn Benton Community College*
Steven D. Skopik   *University of Delaware*
Phillip Sokolove   *University of Maryland*
Brad Swanson   *Central Michigan University*
David Thompson   *Northern Kentucky University*
Maureen Tubbola   *St. Cloud State University*
Ashok Upadhyaya   *University of South Florida, Tampa*
Anthony Uzwiak   *Rutgers University*
Rani Vajravelu   *University of Central Florida*
Gary Walker   *Appalachian State University*
Pat Walsh   *University of Delaware*
Elizabeth Weiss-Kuziel   *University of Texas at Austin*
Holly Williams   *Seminole Community College*
David Williams   *Valencia Community College, East Campus*
Michael Windelspecht   *Appalachian State University*
Mary Wisgirda   *San Jacinto College, South Campus*
Jay Zimmerman   *St. John's University*

## 9th Edition Reviewers

Tamarah Adair   *Baylor University*
Gladys Alexandre-Jouline   *University of Tennessee at Knoxville*
Gregory Andraso   *Gannon University*
Jorge E. Arriagada   *St. Cloud State University*
David Asch   *Youngstown State University*
Jeffrey G. Baguley   *University of Nevada — Reno*
Suman Batish   *Temple University*
Donald Baud   *University of Memphis*
Peter Berget   *Carnegie Mellon University*
Randall Bernot   *Ball State University*
Deborah Bielser   *University of Illinois— Champaign*
Wendy Binder   *Loyola Marymount University*
Todd A. Blackledge   *University of Akron*
Andrew R. Blaustein   *Oregon State University*
Dennis Bogyo   *Valdosta State University*
David Bos   *Purdue University*
Robert Boyd   *Auburn University*
Graciela Brelles-Marino   *California State Polytechnic University—Pomona*
Joanna Brooke   *DePaul University*
Roxanne Brown   *Blinn College*
Mark Browning   *Purdue University*
Cedric O. Buckley   *Jackson State University*
Arthur L. Buikema, Jr.   *Virginia Tech*
Sharon Bullock   *UNC — Charlotte*
Lisa Burgess   *Broward College*
Scott Carlson   *Luther College*
John L. Carr   *University of Louisiana — Monroe*
Laura Carruth   *Georgia State University*
Dale Cassamatta   *University of North Florida*
Peter Chabora   *Queens College—CUNY*

Tien-Hsien Chang   *Ohio State University*
Genevieve Chung   *Broward College*
Cynthia Church   *Metropolitan State College of Denver*
William Cohen   *University of Kentucky*
James Collins   *Kilgore College*
Joanne Conover   *University of Connecticut*
Iris Cook   *Westchester Community College*
Erica Corbett   *Southeastern Oklahoma State University*
Robert Corin   *College of Staten Island — CUNY*
William G. R. Crampton   *University of Central Florida*
Scott Crousillac   *Louisiana State University—Baton Rouge*
Karen A. Curto   *University of Pittsburgh*
Denise Deal   *Nassau Community College*
Philias Denette   *Delgado Community College*
Mary Dettman   *Seminole Community College—Oviedo*
Ann Marie DiLorenzo   *Montclair State University*
Ernest DuBrul   *University of Toledo*
Richard Duhrkopf   *Baylor University*
Susan Dunford   *University of Cincinnati*
Andrew R. Dyer   *University of South Carolina — Aiken*
Carmen Eilertson   *Georgia State University*
Richard P. Elinson   *Duquesne University*
William L. Ellis   *Pasco-Hernando Community College*
Seema Endley   *Blinn College*
Gary Ervin   *Mississippi State University*
Karl Fath   *Queens College — CUNY*

Zen Faulkes   *The University of Texas — Pan American*
Myriam Feldman   *Lake Washington Technical College*
Melissa Fierke   *State University of New York*
Gary L. Firestone   *University of California — Berkeley*
Jason Flores   *UNC — Charlotte*
Markus Friedrich   *Wayne State University*
Deborah Garrity   *Colorado State University*
Christopher Gee   *University of North Carolina-Charlotte*
John R. Geiser   *Western Michigan University*
J.P. Gibson   *University of Oklahoma*
Matthew Gilg   *University of North Florida*
Teresa Golden   *Southeastern Oklahoma State University*
Venkat Gopalan   *Ohio State University*
Michael Groesbeck   *Brigham Young University*
Theresa Grove   *Valdosta State University*
David Hanson   *University of New Mexico*
Paul Hapeman   *University of Florida*
Nargess Hassanzadeh-Kiabi   *California State University— Los Angeles*
Stephen K. Herbert   *University of Wyoming*
Hon Ho   *State University of New York at New Paltz*
Barbara Hunnicutt   *Seminole Community College*
Steve Huskey   *Western Kentucky University*

Cynthia Jacobs   *Arkansas Tech University*
Jason B. Jennings   *Southwest Tennessee Community College*
Frank J. Jochem   *Florida International University—Miami*
Norman Johnson   *University of Massachusetts*
Gregory A. Jones   *Santa Fe Community College*
Jerry Kaster   *University of Wisconsin— Milwaukee*
Mary Jane Keith   *Wichita State University*
Mary Kelley   *Wayne State University*
Scott Kight   *Montclair State University*
Wendy Kimber   *Stevenson University*
Jeff Klahn   *University of Iowa*
David S. Koetje   *Calvin College*
Olga Kopp   *Utah Valley University*
John C. Krenetsky   *Metropolitan State College of Denver*
Patrick J. Krug   *California State University — LA*
Robert Kurt   *Lafayette College*
Marc J. LaBella   *Ocean County College*
Ellen S. Lamb   *University of North Carolina — Greensboro*
David Lampe   *Duquesne University*
Grace Lasker   *Lake Washington Technical College*
Kari Lavalli   *Boston University*
Shannon Erickson Lee   *California Sate University- Northridge*
Zhiming Liu   *Eastern New Mexico University*
J. Mitchell Lockhart   *Valdosta State University*
David Logan   *Clark Atlanta University*

Thomas A. Lonergan  *University of New Orleans*
Andreas Madlung  *University of Puget Sound*
Lynn Mahaffy  *University of Delaware*
Jennifer Marcinkiewicz  *Kent State University*
Henri Maurice  *University of Southern Indiana*
Deanna McCullough  *University of Houston—Downtown*
Dean McCurdy  *Albion College*
Richard Merritt  *Houston Community College—Northwest*
Stephanie Miller  *Jefferson State Community College*
Thomas Miller  *University of California, Riverside*
Hector C. Miranda, Jr.  *Texas Southern University*
Jasleen Mishra  *Houston Community College*
Randy Mogg  *Columbus State Community College*
Daniel Moon  *University of North Florida*
Janice Moore  *Colorado State University*
Richard C. Moore  *Miami University*
Juan Morata  *Miami Dade College—Wolfson*
Ellyn R. Mulcahy  *Johnson County Community College*
Kimberlyn Nelson  *Pennsylvania State University*
Howard Neufeld  *Appalachian State University*
Jacalyn Newman  *University of Pittsburgh*
Margaret N. Nsofor  *Southern Illinois University—Carbondale*
Judith D. Ochrietor  *University of North Florida*
Robert O'Donnell  *SUNY—Geneseo*
Olumide Ogunmosin  *Texas Southern University*

Nathan O. Okia  *Auburn University—Montgomery*
Stephanie Pandolfi  *Michigan State University*
Peter Pappas  *County College of Morris*
J. Payne  *Bergen Community College*
Andrew Pease  *Stevenson University*
Craig Peebles  *University of Pittsburgh*
David G. Pennock  *Miami University*
Beverly Perry  *Houston Community College*
John S. Peters  *College of Charleston, SC*
Stephanie Toering Peters  *Wartburg College*
Teresa Petrino-Lin  *Barry University*
Susan Phillips  *Brevard Community College—Palm Bay*
Paul Pillitteri  *Southern Utah University*
Thomas Pitzer  *Florida International University—Miami*
Uwe Pott  *University of Wisconsin—Green Bay*
Nimala Prabhu  *Edison State College*
Lynn Preston  *Tarrant County College—NW*
Kelli Prior  *Finger Lakes Community College*
Penny L. Ragland  *Auburn Montgomery*
Marceau Ratard  *Delgado Community College*
Michael Reagan  *College of St. Benedict/St. John's University*
Nancy A. Rice  *Western Kentucky University*
Linda Richardson  *Blinn College*
Amanda Rosenzweig  *Delgado Community College*
Cliff Ross  *University of North Florida*
John Roufaiel  *SUNY—Rockland Community College*
Kenneth Roux  *Florida State University*
Ann E. Rushing  *Baylor University*

Sangha Saha  *Harold Washington College*
Eric Saliim  *North Carolina Central University*
Thomas Sasek  *University of Louisiana—Monroe*
Leena Sawant  *Houston Community College*
Emily Schmitt  *Nova Southeastern University*
Mark Schneegurt  *Wichita State University*
Brenda Schoffstall  *Barry University*
Scott Schuette  *Southern Illinois University*
Pramila Sen  *Houston Community College*
Bin Shuai  *Wichita State University*
Susan Skambis  *Valencia Community College*
Michael Smith  *Western Kentucky University*
Ramona Smith  *Brevard Community College*
Nancy G. Solomon  *Miami University*
Sally K. Sommers Smith  *Boston University*
Melissa Spitler  *California State University—Northridge*
Ashley Spring  *Brevard Community College*
Moira Van Staaden  *Bowling Green State University*
Bruce Stallsmith  *University of Alabama—Huntsville*
Susan Stamler  *College of DuPage*
Nancy Staub  *Gonzaga University*
Stanley Stevens  *University of Memphis*
Ivan Still  *Arkansas Tech University*
Gregory W. Stunz  *Texas A&M University—Corpus Christi*
Ken D. Sumida  *Chapman University*
Rema Suniga  *Ohio Northern University*

Bradley Swanson  *Central Michigan University*
David Tam  *University of North Texas*
Franklyn Tan Te  *Miami Dade College—Wolfson*
William Terzaghi  *Wilkes University*
Melvin Thomson  *University of Wisconsin—Parkside*
Martin Tracey  *Florida International University*
James Traniello  *Boston University*
Bibit Halliday Traut  *City College of San Francisco*
Alexa Tullis  *University of Puget Sound*
Catherine Ueckert  *Northern Arizona University*
Mark VanCura  *Cape Fear CC/University of NC Pembroke*
Charles J. Venglarik  *Jefferson State Community College*
Diane Wagner  *University of Alaska—Fairbanks*
Maureen Walter  *Florida International University*
Wei Wan  *Texas A&M University*
James T. Warren, Jr.  *Penn State Erie*
Delon Washo-Krupps  *Arizona State University*
Frederick Wasserman  *Boston University*
Raymond R. White  *City College of San Francisco*
Stephen W. White  *Ozarks Technical Community College*
Kimberlyn Williams  *California State University-San Bernardino*
Martha Comstock Williams  *Southern Polytechnic State University*
David E. Wolfe  *American River College*
Amber Wyman  *Finger Lakes Community College*
Robert D. Young, Jr.  *Blinn College*

## Previous Edition Reviewers and Contributors

### Art Review Panel
David K. Asch  *Youngstown State University*
Karl J. Aufderheide  *Texas A&M University*
Brian Bagatto  *University of Akron*
Andrew R. Blaustein  *Oregon State University*
Nancy Maroushek Boury  *Iowa State University*
Mark Browning  *Purdue University*
Jeff Carmichael  *University of North Dakota*
Wes Colgan III  *Pikes Peak Community College*
Karen A. Curto  *University of Pittsburgh*
Donald Deters  *Bowling Green State University*
Ernest F. DuBrul  *University of Toledo*
Ralph P. Eckerlin  *Northern Virginia Community College*
Julia Emerson  *Amherst College*
Frederick B. Essig  *University of South Florida*
Sharon Eversman  *Montana State University, Bozeman*
Barbara A. Frase  *Bradley University*
T. H. Frazzetta  *University of Illinois, Urbana—Champaign*
Douglas Gaffin  *University of Oklahoma*
John R. Geiser  *Western Michigan University*

Gonzalo Giribet  *Harvard University*
John Graham  *Bowling Green State University*
Susan E. Hengeveld  *Indiana University*
Richard Hill  *Michigan State University*
David Julian  *University of Florida*
Pamela J. Lanford  *University of Maryland, College Park*
James B. Ludden  *College of DuPage*
Duncan S. MacKenzie  *Texas A&M University*
Patricia Mire  *University of Louisiana, Lafayette*
Janice Moore  *Colorado State University*
Jacalyn S. Newman  *University of Pittsburgh*
Robert Newman  *University of North Dakota*
Nicole S. Obert  *University of Illinois, Urbana-Champaign*
David G. Oppenheimer  *University of Florida*
Ellen Ott-Reeves  *Blinn College, Bryan*
Laurel Bridges Roberts  *University of Pittsburgh*
Deemah N. Schirf  *The University of Texas, San Antonio*
Mark A. Sheridan  *North Dakota State University*
Richard Showman  *University of South Carolina*

Phillip Snider Jr.  *Gadsden State Community College*
Nancy G. Solomon  *Miami University*
David Tam  *University of North Texas*
Marty Tracey  *Florida International University*
Michael J. Wade  *Indiana University*
Jyoti R. Wagle  *Houston Community College System, Central*
Andy Wang  *The University of Iowa*
Cindy Martinez Wedig  *University of Texas, Pan American*
Elizabeth A. Weiss  *University of Texas, Austin*
C. B. Wolfe  *The University of North Carolina, Charlotte*

### End-of-Chapter Pedagogy and Inquiry Contributors
Arthur Buikema  *Virginia Polytechnic Institute*
Merri Lynn Casem  *California State University-Fullerton*
Mark Lyford  *University of Wyoming*
Peter Niewiarowski  *University of Akron*
Thomas Pitzer  *Florida International University*
Laurel Roberts  *University of Pittsburgh*
Michael Windelspecht  *Appalachian State University*

### Reviewers and Accuracy Checkers
Barbara J. Abraham  *Hampton University*
Richard Adler  *University of Michigan, Dearborn*
Sylvester Allred  *Northern Arizona University*
Steven M. Aquilani  *Delaware County Community College*
Jonathan W. Armbruster  *Auburn University*
Gregory A. Armstrong  *The Ohio State University*
Jorge E. Arriagada  *St. Cloud State University*
David K. Asch  *Youngstown State University*
Brian Bagatto  *University of Akron*
Garen Baghdasarian  *Santa Monica College*
Anita Davelos Baines  *The University of Texas, Pan American*
Ronald A. Balsamo Jr.  *Villanova University*
Michael Bartlett  *Portland State University*
Vernon W. Bauer  *Francis Marion University*
James E. Baxter  *Ohlone College*
George W. Benz  *Middle Tennessee State University*

Gerald K. Bergtrom   *University of Wisconsin, Milwaukee*
Arlene G. Billock   *University of Louisiana, Lafayette*
Catherine S. Black   *Idaho State University*
Michael W. Black   *California Polytechnic State University*
Robert O. Blanchard   *University of New Hampshire*
Andrew R. Blaustein   *Oregon State University*
Mary A. Bober   *Santa Monica College*
Nancy Maroushek Boury   *Iowa State University*
M. Deane Bowers   *University of Colorado*
Scott A. Bowling   *Auburn University*
Benita A. Brink   *Adams State College*
Anne Bullerjahn   *Owens Community College*
Ray D. Burkett   *Southwest Tennessee Community College*
Helaine Burstein   *Ohio University*
Scott Burt   *Truman State University*
Carol T. Burton   *Bellevue Community College*
Jennifer Carr Burtwistle   *Northeast Community College*
Jorge Busciglio   *University of California, Irvine*
Pat Calie   *Eastern Kentucky University*
Christy A. Carello   *The Metropolitan State College of Denver*
Michael Carey   *University of Scranton*
Jeff Carmichael   *University of North Dakota*
Michael J. Carlisle   *Trinity Valley Community College*
John H. Caruso   *University of New Orleans*
Thomas T. Chen   *University of Connecticut*
Cynthia Church   *The Metropolitan State College of Denver*
Linda T. Collins   *University of Tennessee, Chattanooga*
Scott T. Cooper   *University of Wisconsin, La Crosse*
Joe R. Cowles   *Virginia Tech*
Nigel M. Crawford   *University of California, San Diego*
James Crowder   *Brookdale Community College*
Karen A. Curto   *University of Pittsburgh*
Bela Dadhich   *Delaware County Community College*
Lydia B. Daniels   *University of Pittsburgh*
Terry Davin   *Penn Valley Community College*
Joseph S. Davis   *University of Florida*
Neta Dean   *Stony Brook University*
Kevin W. Dees   *Wharton County Junior College*
D. Michael Denbow   *Virginia Tech*
Donald Deters   *Bowling Green State University*
Hudson DeYoe   *University of Texas, Pan American*
Randy DiDomenico   *University of Colorado*
Nd Dikeocha   *College of the Mainland*
Robert S. Dill   *Bergen Community College*
Diane M. Dixon   *Southeastern Oklahoma State University*
Kevin Dixon   *University of Illinois*
John S. Doctor   *Duquesne University*
Ernest F. DuBrul   *University of Toledo*
Charles Duggins Jr.   *University of South Carolina*

Richard P. Elinson   *Duquesne University*
Johnny El-Rady   *University of South Florida*
Frederick B. Essig   *University of South Florida*
David H. Evans   *University of Florida*
Guy E. Farish   *Adams State College*
Daphne G. Fautin   *University of Kansas*
Bruce E. Felgenhauer   *University of Louisiana, Lafayette*
Carolyn J. Ferguson   *Kansas State University*
Teresa G. Fischer   *Indian River Community College*
Irwin Forseth   *University of Maryland*
Gail Fraizer   *Kent State University*
Barbara A. Frase   *Bradley University*
Sylvia Fromherz   *University of Northern Colorado*
Phillip E. Funk   *DePaul University*
Caitlin R. Gabor   *Texas State University, San Marcos*
Purti P. Gadkari   *Wharton County Junior College*
John R. Geiser   *Western Michigan University*
Frank S. Gilliam   *Marshall University*
Miriam S. Golbert   *College of the Canyons*
Scott A. Gordon   *University of Southern Indiana*
John S. Graham   *Bowling Green State University*
David A. Gray   *California State University, Northridge*
William F. Hanna   *Massasoit Community College*
Kyle E. Harms   *Louisiana State University*
Kerry D. Heafner   *University of Louisiana, Monroe*
Susan E. Hengeveld   *Indiana University*
Charles Henry   *University of Connecticut, Storrs*
Peter Heywood   *Brown University*
Juliana G. Hinton   *McNeese State University*
Margaret L. Horton   *University of North Carolina, Greensboro*
James Horwitz   *Palm Beach Community College*
Laura A. Houston   *Montgomery College*
Feng Sheng Hu   *University of Illinois*
Allen N. Hunt   *Elizabethtown Community and Technical College*
David C. Jarrell   *University of Mary Washington*
Jennifer L. Jeffery   *Wharton County Junior College*
William Jeffery   *University of Maryland, College Park*
Lee Johnson   *The Ohio State University*
Craig T. Jordan   *The University of Texas, San Antonio*
Ronald L. Jones   *Eastern Kentucky University*
Robyn Jordan   *University of Louisiana, Monroe*
Walter S. Judd   *University of Florida*
David Julian   *University of Florida*
Daniel Kainer   *Montgomery College*
Ronald C. Kaltreider   *York College of Pennsylvania*
Thomas C. Kane   *University of Cincinnati*
Donald A. Kangas   *Truman State University*
William J. Katembe   *Delta State University*
Steven J. Kaye   *Red Rocks Community College*

Stephen R. Kelso   *University of Illinois, Chicago*
Nancy S. Kirkpatrick   *Lake Superior State University*
John Z. Kiss   *Miami University*
John C. Krenetsky   *The Metropolitan State College of Denver*
Karin E. Krieger   *University of Wisconsin, Green Bay*
David T. Kurjiaka   *University of Arizona*
Arlene T. Larson   *University of Colorado, Denver*
Peter Lavrentyev   *University of Akron*
Laura G. Leff   *Kent State University*
Michael R. Lentz   *University of North Florida*
Harvey Liftin   *Broward Community College*
Yue J. Lin   *St. John's University*
Amy Litt   *New York Botanical Garden*
Christopher R. Little   *The University of Texas, Pan American*
James Long   *Boise State University*
James O. Luken   *Coastal Carolina University*
Dennis J. Lye   *Northern Kentucky University*
P. T. Magee   *University of Minnesota, Minneapolis*
Richard Malkin   *University of California, Berkeley*
Mark D. Mamrack   *Wright State University*
Kathleen A. Marrs   *Indiana University Purdue University, Indianapolis*
Diane L. Marshall   *University of New Mexico*
Paul B. Martin   *St. Philip's College*
Peter J. Martinat   *Xavier University, Los Angeles*
Joel Maruniak   *University of Missouri*
Patricia Matthews   *Grand Valley State University*
Robin G. Maxwell   *The University of North Carolina, Greensboro*
Brenda S. McAdory   *Tennessee State University*
Nael A. McCarty   *Georgia Institute of Technology*
Brock R. McMillan   *Minnesota State University, Mankato*
Kay McMurry   *The University of Texas, Austin*
Elizabeth McPartlan   *De Anza College*
Brad Mehrtens   *University of Illinois, Urbana—Champaign*
Michael Meighan   *University of California, Berkeley*
Douglas Meikle   *Miami University*
Allen F. Mensinger   *University of Minnesota, Duluth*
Wayne B. Merkley   *Drake University*
Catherine E. Merovich   *West Virginia University*
Frank J. Messina   *Utah State University*
Brian T. Miller   *Middle Tennessee State University*
Sarah L. Milton   *Florida Atlantic University*
Subhash Minocha   *University of New Hampshire*
Hector C. Miranda Jr.   *Texas Southern University*
Patricia Mire   *University of Louisiana, Lafayette*
Robert W. Morris   *Widener University*
Satyanarayana Swamy Mruthinti   *State University of West Georgia*

Richard L. Myers   *Southwest Missouri State University*
Monica Marquez Nelson   *Joliet Junior College*
Jacalyn S. Newman   *University of Pittsburgh*
Harry Nickla   *Creighton University*
Richard A. Niesenbaum   *Muhlenberg College*
Kris M. Norenberg   *Xavier University, Louisiana*
Deborah A. O'Dell   *University of Mary Washington*
Sharman D. O'Neill   *University of California, Davis*
Cynthia P. Paul   *University of Michigan, Dearborn*
John S. Peters   *College of Charleston*
Jay Phelan   *University of California, Los Angeles*
Gregory W. Phillips   *Blinn College*
Thomas R. Pitzer   *Florida International University*
Gregory J. Podgorski   *Utah State University*
Alan Prather   *Michigan State University*
Mitch Price   *The Pennsylvania State University*
Carl Quertermus   *State University of West Georgia*
Shana Rapoport   *California State University, Northridge*
Kim Raun   *Wharton County Junior College*
Robert S. Rawding   *Gannon University*
Jill D. Reid   *Virginia Commonwealth University*
Linda R. Richardson   *Blinn College*
Robin K. Richardson   *Winona State University*
Carolyn Roberson   *Roane State Community College*
Kenneth R. Robinson   *Purdue University*
Kenneth H. Roux   *Florida State University*
Charles L. Rutherford   *Virginia Tech University*
Margaret Saha   *College of William and Mary*
Thomas Sasek   *University of Louisiana, Monroe*
Bruce M. Saul   *Augusta State University*
Deemah N. Schirf   *The University of Texas, San Antonio*
Christopher J. Schneider   *Boston University*
Timothy E. Shannon   *Francis Marion University*
Rebecca Sheller   *Southwestern University*
Mark A. Sheridan   *North Dakota State University*
Richard Showman   *University of South Carolina*
Michéle Shuster   *New Mexico State University*
William Simcik   *Tomball College, a North Harris Community College*
Rebecca B. Simmons   *University of North Dakota*
Phillip Snider Jr.   *Gadsden State Community College*
Thomas E. Snowden   *Florida Memorial College*
Dianne Snyder   *Augusta State University*
Farah Sogo   *Orange Coast College*
Nancy G. Solomon   *Miami University*
Kathryn H. Sorensen   *American River College*
Kevin N. Sorensen   *Snow College*

Bruce Stallsmith  *University of Alabama, Huntsville*
Patricia Steinke  *San Jacinto College*
Jacqueline J. Stevens  *Jackson State University*
John W. Stiller  *East Carolina University*
Antony Stretton  *University of Wisconsin, Madison*
Brett W. Strong  *Palm Beach Community College*
Gregory W. Stunz  *Texas A&M University, Corpus Christi*
Cynthia A. Surmacz  *Bloomsburg University*
Yves S. H. Tan  *Cabrillo College*
Sharon Thoma  *University of Wisconsin, Madison*
Anne M. S. Tokazewski  *Burlington County College*
Marty Tracey  *Florida International University*

Terry M. Trier  *Grand Valley State University*
Marsha R. Turell  *Houston Community College*
Linda Tyson  *Santa Fe Community College*
Rani Vajravelu  *University of Central Florida*
Jim Van Brunt  *Rogue Community College*
Judith B. Varelas  *University of Northern Colorado*
Neal J. Voelz  *St. Cloud State University*
Janice Voltzow  *University of Scranton*
Jyoti R. Wagle  *Houston Community College System, Central*
Charles Walcott  *Cornell University*
Randall Walikonis  *University of Connecticut*
Eileen Walsh  *Westchester Community College*

Steven A. Wasserman  *University of California, San Diego*
R. Douglas Watson  *University of Alabama, Birmingham*
Cindy Martinez Wedig  *University of Texas, Pan American*
Richard Weinstein  *Southern New Hampshire University*
Elizabeth A. Weiss  *University of Texas, Austin*
William R. Wellnitz  *Augusta State University*
Jonathan F. Wendel  *Iowa State University*
Sue Simon Westendorf  *Ohio University*
Vernon Lee Wiersema  *Houston Community College, Southwest*
Judy Williams  *Southeastern Oklahoma State University*
Lawrence R. Williams  *University of Houston*

Robert Winning  *Eastern Michigan University*
C. B. Wolfe  *The University of North Carolina, Charlotte*
Clarence C. Wolfe  *Northern Virginia Community College*
Eric Vivien Wong  *University of Louisville*
Gene K. Wong  *Quinnipiac University*
Denise Woodward  *The Pennsylvania State University*
Richard P. Wunderlin  *University of South Florida*
Douglas A. Wymer  *The University of West Alabama*
Lan Xu  *South Dakota State University*
H. Randall Yoder  *Lamar University*
Kathryn G. Zeiler  *Red Rocks Community College*
Scott D. Zimmerman  *Missouri State University*
Henry G. Zot  *University of West Georgia*

## International Reviewers

Mari L. Acevedo  *University of Puerto Rico, Arecibo*
Heather Addy  *University of Calgary*
Heather E. Allison  *University of Liverpool*
David Backhouse  *University of New England*
Andrew Bendall  *University of Guelph*
Tony Bradshaw  *Oxford Brookes University*
D. Bruce Campbell  *Okanagan College*
Clara E. Carrasco  *University of Puerto Rico, Ponce*
Ian Cock  *Griffith University*
Margaret Cooley  *University of New South Wales*
R. S. Currah  *University of Alberta*

Logan Donaldson  *York University*
Theo Elzenga  *University of Groningen*
Neil Haave  *University of Alberta, Augustana*
Louise M. Hafner  *QUT*
Clare Hasenkampf  *University of Toronto, Scarborough*
Annika F. M. Haywood  *Memorial University of Newfoundland*
Rong-Nan Huang  *National Central University*
William Huddleston  *University of Calgary*
Wendy J. Keenleyside  *University of Guelph*
Chris Kennedy  *Simon Fraser University*

Alex Law  *Nanyang Technical University, Singapore*
Richard C. Leegood  *University of Sheffield*
R. W. Longair  *University of Calgary*
Thomas H. MacRae  *Dalhousie University*
Rolf W. Matthewes  *Simon Fraser University*
R. Ian Menz  *Flinders University*
Todd C. Nickle  *Mount Royal College*
Kirsten Poling  *University of Windsor*
Jim Provan  *Queen's University Belfast*
Roberto Quinlan  *York University*
Elsa I. Colón Reyes  *University of Puerto Rico, Aguadilla Campus*
Richard Roy  *McGill University*

Liliane Schoofs  *Katholicke Universiteit Leuren*
Joan Sharp  *Simon Fraser University*
Julie Smit  *University of Windsor*
Nguan Soon Tan  *Nanyang Technological University*
Fleur Tiver  *University of South Australia*
Llinil Torres-Ojeda  *University of Puerto Rico, Aguadilla Campus*
Han A. B. Wösten  *University of Utrecht*
H. H. Yeoh  *National University of Singapore*
Dr. Khaled Abou-Aisha  *German University in Cairo*

# A Note From the Authors

A revision of this scope relies on the talents and efforts of many people working behind the scenes and we have benefited greatly from their assistance.

Jody Larson, our developmental copyeditor, labored many hours and provided countless suggestions for improving the organization and clarity of the text. She has made a tremendous contribution to the quality of the final product.

We were fortunate to again work with Electronic Publishing Services to update the art program and improve the layout of the pages. Our close collaboration resulted in a text that is pedagogically effective as well as more beautiful than any other biology text on the market.

We have the continued support of our McGraw-Hill team. Developmental editors Rose Koos and Lisa Bruflodt kept the authors on track during the development process. Sheila Frank, project manager, and David Hash, designer, ensured our text was on time and elegantly designed. Patrick Reidy, marketing manager and many more people behind the scenes have all contributed to the success or our text.

Throughout this edition we have had the support of spouses and children, who have seen less of us than they might have liked because of the pressures of getting this revision completed. They have adapted to the many hours this book draws us away from them, and, even more than us, looked forward to its completion.

As with every edition, acknowledgments would not be complete without thanking the generations of students who have used the many editions of this text. They have taught us as least as much as we have taught them, and their questions and suggestions continue to improve the text and supplementary materials.

Finally, we need to thank our reviewers and contributors. Instructors from across the country are continually invited to share their knowledge and experience with us through reviews and focus groups. The feedback we received shaped this edition, resulting in new chapters, reorganization of the table of contents, and expanded coverage in key areas. Several faculty members were asked to provide preliminary drafts of chapters to ensure that the content was as up to date and accurate as possible, and still others were asked to provide chapter outlines and assessment questions. All of these people took time out of their already busy lives to help us build a better edition of Biology for the next generation of introductory biology students, and they have our heartfelt thanks.

# Contents

Part **IV** Evolution

*Chapter* **20**

# Genes Within Populations

## Chapter Outline

## Introduction

*No other human being is exactly like you (unless you have an identical twin). Often the particular characteristics of an individual have an important bearing on its survival, on its chances to reproduce, and on the success of its offspring. Evolution is driven by such factors, as different alleles rise and fall in populations. These deceptively simple matters lie at the core of evolutionary biology, which is the topic of this chapter and chapters 21 through 25.*

## 20.1 Genetic Variation and Evolution

### Learning Outcomes

1. *Define* evolution *and* population genetics.
2. *Explain the difference between evolution by natural selection and the inheritance of acquired characteristics.*

Genetic variation, that is, differences in alleles of genes found within individuals of a population, provides the raw material for natural selection, which will be described shortly. Natural populations contain a wealth of such variation. In plants, insects, and vertebrates, many genes exhibit some level of variation. In this chapter, we explore genetic variation in natural populations and consider the evolutionary forces that cause allele frequencies in natural populations to change.

The word *evolution* is widely used in the natural and social sciences. It refers to how an entity—be it a social system, a gas, or a planet—changes through time. Although development of the modern concept of evolution in biology can be traced to Darwin's landmark work, *On the Origin of Species*, the first five editions of his book never actually used the term. Rather, Darwin used the phrase "descent with modification."

Although many more complicated definitions have been proposed, Darwin's words probably best capture the essence of biological evolution: Through time, species accumulate differences; as a result, descendants differ from their ancestors. In this way, new species arise from existing ones.

## Many processes can lead to evolutionary change

You have already learned about the development of Darwin's ideas in chapter 1. Darwin was not the first to propose a theory of evolution. Rather, he followed a long line of earlier philosophers and naturalists who deduced that the many kinds of organisms around us were produced by a process of evolution.

Unlike his predecessors, however, Darwin proposed natural selection as the mechanism of evolution. Natural selection produces evolutionary change when some individuals in a population possess certain inherited characteristics and then produce more surviving offspring than individuals lacking these characteristics. As a result, the population gradually comes to include more and more individuals with the advantageous characteristics. In this way, the population evolves and becomes better adapted to its local circumstances.

A rival theory, championed by the prominent biologist Jean-Baptiste Lamarck, was that evolution occurred by the **inheritance of acquired characteristics.** According to Lamarck, changes that individuals acquired during their lives were passed on to their offspring. For example, Lamarck proposed that ancestral giraffes with short necks tended to stretch their necks to feed on tree leaves, and this extension of the neck was passed on to subsequent generations, leading to the long-necked giraffe (figure 20.1*a*). In Darwin's theory, by contrast, the variation is not created by experience, but is the result of preexisting genetic differences among individuals (figure 20.1*b*).

One way to monitor how populations change through time is to look at changes in the frequencies of alleles of a gene from one generation to the next. Natural selection, by favoring individuals with certain alleles, can lead to change in such *allele frequencies*, but it is not the only process that can do so. Allele frequencies can also change when mutations occur repeatedly, changing one allele to another, and when migrants bring alleles into a population. In addition, when populations are small, the frequencies of alleles can change randomly as the result of chance events. Often, natural selection overwhelms the effects of these other processes, but as you will see later in this chapter, this is not always the case.

Evolution can result from any process that causes a change in the genetic composition of a population. We cannot talk about evolution, therefore, without also considering **population genetics,** the study of the properties of genes in populations.

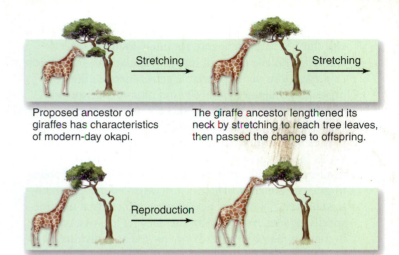

*a.* Lamarck's theory: acquired variation is passed on to descendants.

Some individuals born happen to have longer necks due to genetic differences.

Individuals pass on their traits to next generation.

Over many generations, longer-necked individuals are more successful, perhaps because they can feed on taller trees, and pass the long-neck trait on to their offspring.

*b.* Darwin's theory: natural selection or genetically-based variation leads to evolutionary change.

**Figure 20.1** **Two ideas of how giraffes might have evolved long necks.**

## Populations contain ample genetic variation

It is best to start by looking at the genetic variation present among individuals within a species. This is the raw material available for the selective process.

As you saw in chapter 12, a natural population can contain a great deal of genetic variation. How much variation usually occurs? Humans are representative of most—but not all—species in that human populations contain substantial amounts of genetic variation. For example:

1. **Genes that influence blood groups.** Chemical analysis has revealed the existence of more than 30 blood group genes in humans, in addition to the ABO locus. At least

one third of these genes are routinely found in several alternative allelic forms in human populations. In addition to these, more than 45 variable genes encode other proteins in human blood cells and plasma that are not considered blood groups. In short, many genetically variable genes are present in this one system alone.

2. **Genes that influence enzymes.** Alternative alleles of genes specifying particular enzymes are easy to distinguish by measuring how fast the alternative proteins migrate in an electrical field (a process called *electrophoresis*— see chapter 17). A great deal of variation exists at enzyme-specifying loci. About 5% of the enzyme loci of a typical human are heterozygous: If you picked an individual at random, and in turn selected one of the enzyme-encoding genes of that individual at random, the chances are 1 in 20 (5%) that the gene you selected would be heterozygous in that individual.

Considering the entire genome, it is fair to say that all humans are different from one another except for identical twins. This is also true of other organisms, except for those that reproduce asexually. In nature, genetic variation is the rule.

### Enzyme polymorphism

Many loci in a particular population have more than one allele at frequencies significantly greater than would occur due to mutation alone. Researchers refer to such a locus as **polymorphic** (figure 20.2). The extent of such variation within natural popula-

tions was not even suspected a few decades ago, when modern techniques such as protein electrophoresis made it possible to examine enzymes and other proteins directly.

We now know that most populations of insects and plants are polymorphic at more than half of their enzyme-encoding loci, that is, the loci have more than one allele occurring at a frequency greater than 5%. Vertebrates are somewhat less polymorphic. Heterozygosity, the probability that a randomly selected gene will be heterozygous in a randomly selected individual, is about 15% in *Drosophila* and other invertebrates, between 5% and 8% in vertebrates, and around 8% in outcrossing plants (values of heterozygosity tend to be lower than the proportion of loci that are polymorphic because for loci that are polymorphic, many individuals within the population will be homozygous). These high levels of genetic variability provide ample supplies of raw material for evolution.

### DNA sequence polymorphism

The advent of gene technology has made it possible to assess genetic variation even more directly by sequencing the DNA itself. For example, when the *ADH* genes (which encode for alcohol dehydrogenase) of 11 *Drosophila melanogaster* individuals were sequenced, scientists found 43 variable sites, only 1 of which had been detected by protein electrophoresis.

Numerous other studies of variation at the DNA level have confirmed these findings: Abundant variation exists in both the coding regions of genes and in their nontranslated introns—considerably more variation than we can detect by examining enzymes with electrophoresis.

**Figure 20.2 Polymorphic variation.** This natural population of loosestrife, *Lythrum salicaria*, exhibits considerable variation in flower color. Individual differences are inherited and passed on to offspring.

## 20.2 Changes in Allele Frequency

**Learning Outcomes**

1. *Explain the Hardy–Weinberg principle.*
2. *Describe the characteristics of a population that is in Hardy–Weinberg equilibrium.*
3. *Demonstrate how the operation of evolutionary processes can be detected.*

Genetic variation within natural populations was a puzzle to Darwin and his contemporaries in the mid-1800s. The way in which meiosis produces genetic segregation among the progeny of a hybrid had not yet been discovered. And, although Mendel performed his experiments during this same time period, his work was largely unknown. Selection, scientists then thought, should always favor an optimal form, and so tend to eliminate variation. Moreover, the theory of *blending inheritance*—in which offspring were expected to be phenotypically intermediate relative to their parents—was widely accepted. If blending inheritance were correct, then the effect of any new genetic variant would quickly be diluted to the point of disappearance in subsequent generations.

## The Hardy–Weinberg principle allows prediction of genotype frequencies

Following the rediscovery of Mendel's research, two people in 1908 solved the puzzle of why genetic variation persists—Godfrey H. Hardy, an English mathematician, and Wilhelm Weinberg, a German physician. These workers were initially confused about why, after many generations, a population didn't come to be composed solely of individuals with the dominant phenotype. The conclusion they independently came to was that the original proportions of the genotypes in a population will remain constant from generation to generation, as long as the following assumptions are met:

1. No mutation takes place.
2. No genes are transferred to or from other sources (no immigration or emigration takes place).
3. Random mating is occurring.
4. The population size is very large.
5. No selection occurs.

Because the genotypes' proportions do not change, they are said to be in **Hardy–Weinberg equilibrium.**

### The Hardy–Weinberg equation with two alleles: A binomial expansion

In algebraic terms, the Hardy–Weinberg principle is written as an equation. Consider a population of 100 cats in which 84 are black and 16 are white. The frequencies of the two phenotypes would be 0.84 (or 84%) black and 0.16 (or 16%) white. Based on these phenotypic frequencies, can we deduce the underlying frequency of genotypes?

If we assume that the white cats are homozygous recessive for an allele we designate as $b$, and the black cats are either homozygous dominant $BB$ or heterozygous $Bb$, we can calculate the **allele frequencies** of the two alleles in the population from the proportion of black and white individuals, assuming that the population is in Hardy–Weinberg equilibrium.

Let the letter $p$ designate the frequency of the $B$ allele and the letter $q$ the frequency of the alternative allele. Because there are only two alleles, $p$ plus $q$ must always equal 1 (that is, the total population). In addition, we know that the sum of the three genotype frequencies must also equal 1. If the frequency of the $B$ allele is $p$, then the probability that an individual will have two $B$ alleles is simply the probability that each of its alleles is a $B$. The probability of two events happening independently is the product of the probability of each event; in this case, the probability that the individual received a $B$ allele from its father is $p$, and the probability the individual received a $B$ allele from its mother is also $p$, so the probability that both happened is $p * p = p^2$ (figure 20.3). By the same reasoning, the probability that an individual will have two $b$ alleles is $q^2$.

What about the probability that an individual will be a heterozygote? There are two ways this could happen: The individual could receive a $B$ from its father and a $b$ from its mother, or vice versa. The probability of the first case is $p * q$ and the probability of the second case is $q * p$. Because the result in either case is that the individual is a heterozygote, the probability of that outcome is the sum of the two probabilities, or $2pq$.

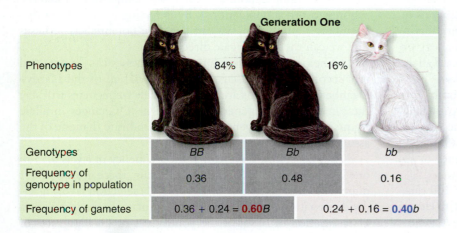

| | Generation One | | |
|---|---|---|---|
| Phenotypes | 84% | 16% | |
| Genotypes | $BB$ | $Bb$ | $bb$ |
| Frequency of genotype in population | 0.36 | 0.48 | 0.16 |
| Frequency of gametes | $0.36 + 0.24 = 0.60B$ | $0.24 + 0.16 = 0.40b$ | |

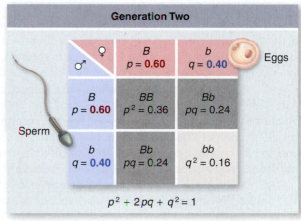

| Generation Two | | |
|---|---|---|
| ♂ / ♀ | $B$ $p = 0.60$ | $b$ $q = 0.40$ Eggs |
| $B$ $p = 0.60$ | $BB$ $p^2 = 0.36$ | $Bb$ $pq = 0.24$ |
| Sperm $b$ $q = 0.40$ | $Bb$ $pq = 0.24$ | $bb$ $q^2 = 0.16$ |
| | $p^2 + 2pq + q^2 = 1$ | |

**Figure 20.3  The Hardy–Weinberg equilibrium.** In the absence of factors that alter them, the frequencies of gametes, genotypes, and phenotypes remain constant generation after generation.

### Inquiry question

**?** If all white cats died, what proportion of the kittens in the next generation would be white?

So, to summarize, if a population is in Hardy–Weinberg equilibrium with allele frequencies of $p$ and $q$, then the probability that an individual will have each of the three possible genotypes is $p^2 + 2pq + q^2$. You may recognize this as the *binomial expansion*:

$$(p + q)^2 = p^2 + 2pq + q^2$$

Finally, we may use these probabilities to predict the distribution of genotypes in the population, again assuming that the population is in Hardy–Weinberg equilibrium. If the probability that any individual is a heterozygote is $2pq$, then we would expect the proportion of heterozygous individuals in the population to be $2pq$; similarly, the frequency of $BB$ and $bb$ homozygotes would be expected to be $p^2$ and $q^2$.

Let us return to our example. Remember that 16% of the cats are white. If white is a recessive trait, then this means that such individuals must have the genotype $bb$. If the frequency of this genotype is $q^2 = 0.16$ (the frequency of white cats), then $q$ (the frequency of the $b$ allele) = 0.4. Because $p + q = 1$, therefore, $p$, the frequency of allele $B$, would be $1.0 - 0.4 = 0.6$ (remember, the frequencies must add up to 1). We can now easily calculate the expected **genotype frequencies**: homozygous dominant $BB$ cats would make up the $p^2$ group, and the value of $p^2 = (0.6)^2 = 0.36$, or 36 homozygous dominant $BB$ individuals in a population of 100 cats. The heterozygous cats have the $Bb$ genotype and would have the frequency corresponding to $2pq$, or $(2 * 0.6 * 0.4) = 0.48$, or 48 heterozygous $Bb$ individuals.

### Using the Hardy–Weinberg equation to predict frequencies in subsequent generations

The Hardy–Weinberg equation is another way of expressing the Punnett square described in chapter 12, with two alleles assigned frequencies, $p$ and $q$. Figure 20.3 allows you to trace genetic reassortment during sexual reproduction and see how it affects the frequencies of the $B$ and $b$ alleles during the next generation.

In constructing this diagram, we have assumed that the union of sperm and egg in these cats is random, so that all combinations of $b$ and $B$ alleles occur. The alleles are therefore mixed randomly and are represented in the next generation in proportion to their original occurrence. Each individual egg or sperm in each generation has a 0.6 chance of receiving a $B$ allele ($p = 0.6$) and a 0.4 chance of receiving a $b$ allele ($q = 0.4$).

In the next generation, therefore, the chance of combining two $B$ alleles is $p^2$, or 0.36 (that is, 0.6 * 0.6), and approximately 36% of the individuals in the population will continue to have the $BB$ genotype. The frequency of $bb$ individuals is $q^2$ (0.4 * 0.4) and so will continue to be about 16%, and the frequency of $Bb$ individuals will be $2pq$ (2 * 0.6 * 0.4), or on average, 48%.

Phenotypically, if the population size remains at 100 cats, we would still see approximately 84 black individuals (with either $BB$ or $Bb$ genotypes) and 16 white individuals (with the $bb$ genotype). Allele, genotype, and phenotype frequencies have remained unchanged from one generation to the next, despite the reshuffling of genes that occurs during meiosis and sexual reproduction. Dominance and recessiveness of alleles can therefore be seen only to affect how an allele is expressed in an individual and not how allele frequencies will change through time.

## Hardy–Weinberg predictions can be applied to data to find evidence of evolutionary processes

The lesson from the example of black and white cats is that if all five of the assumptions listed earlier hold true, the allele and genotype frequencies will not change from one generation to the next. But in reality, most populations in nature will not fit all five assumptions. The primary utility of this method is to determine whether some evolutionary process or processes are operating in a population and, if so, to suggest hypotheses about what they may be.

Suppose, for example, that the observed frequencies of the $BB$, $bb$, and $Bb$ genotypes in a different population of cats were 0.6, 0.2, and 0.2, respectively. We can calculate the allele frequencies for $B$ as follows: 60% (0.6) of the cats have two $B$ alleles, 20% have one, and 20% have none. This means that the average number of $B$ alleles per cat is 1.4 [(0.6 × 2) + (0.2 × 1) + (0.2 × 0) = 1.4]. Because each cat has two alleles for this gene, the frequency is 1.4/2.0 = 0.7. Similarly, you should be able to calculate that the frequency of the $b$ allele = 0.3.

If the population were in Hardy–Weinberg equilibrium, then, according to the equation earlier in this section, the frequency of the $BB$ genotype would be $0.7^2 = 0.49$, lower than it really is. Similarly, you can calculate that there are fewer heterozygotes and more $bb$ homozygotes than expected; then clearly, the population is not in Hardy–Weinberg equilibrium.

What could cause such an excess of homozygotes and deficit of heterozygotes? A number of possibilities exist, including (1) natural selection favoring homozygotes over heterozygotes, (2) individuals choosing to mate with genetically similar individuals (because $BB * BB$ and $bb * bb$ matings always produce homozygous offspring, but only half of $Bb * Bb$ produce heterozygous offspring, such mating patterns would lead to an excess of homozygotes), or (3) an influx of homozygous individuals from outside populations (or conversely, emigration of heterozygotes to other populations). By detecting a lack of Hardy–Weinberg equilibrium, we can generate potential hypotheses that we can then investigate directly.

The operation of evolutionary processes can be detected in a second way. As discussed previously, if all of the Hardy–Weinberg assumptions are met, then allele frequencies will stay the same from one generation to the next. Changes in allele frequencies between generations would indicate that one of the assumptions is not met.

Suppose, for example, that the frequency of $b$ was 0.53 in one generation and 0.61 in the next. Again, there are a number of possible explanations: For example, (1) selection favoring individuals with $b$ over $B$, (2) immigration of $b$ into the population or emigration of $B$ out of the population, or (3) high rates of mutation that more commonly occur from $B$ to $b$ than vice versa. Another possibility is that the population is a small one, and that the change represents the random fluctuations that result because, simply by chance, some individuals pass on more of their genes than others. We will discuss how each of these processes is studied in the rest of the chapter.

## 20.3 Five Agents of Evolutionary Change

The five assumptions of the Hardy–Weinberg principle also indicate the five agents that can lead to evolutionary change in populations. They are mutation, gene flow, nonrandom mating, genetic drift in small populations, and the pressures of natural selection. Any one of these may bring about changes in allele or genotype proportions.

## Mutation changes alleles

Mutation from one allele to another can obviously change the proportions of particular alleles in a population. Mutation rates are generally so low that they have little effect on the Hardy–Weinberg proportions of common alleles. A typical gene mutates about once per 100,000 cell divisions. Because this rate is so low, other evolutionary processes are usually more important in determining how allele frequencies change.

Nonetheless, mutation is the ultimate source of genetic variation and thus makes evolution possible (figure 20.4a). It is important to remember, however, that the likelihood of a particular mutation occurring is not affected by natural selection; that is, mutations do not occur more frequently in situations in which they would be favored by natural selection.

## Gene flow occurs when alleles move between populations

**Gene flow** is the movement of alleles from one population to another. It can be a powerful agent of change. Sometimes gene flow is obvious, as when an animal physically moves from one place to another. If the characteristics of the newly arrived individual differ from those of the animals already there, and if the newcomer is adapted well enough to the new area to survive and mate successfully, the genetic composition of the receiving population may be altered.

Other important kinds of gene flow are not as obvious. These subtler movements include the drifting of gametes or the immature stages of plants or marine animals from one place to another (figure 20.4b). Pollen, the male gamete of flowering plants, is often carried great distances by insects and other animals that visit flowers. Seeds may also blow in the wind or be carried by animals to new populations far from their place of

| Mutation | Gene Flow | Nonrandom Mating | Genetic Drift | Selection |
|---|---|---|---|---|
| 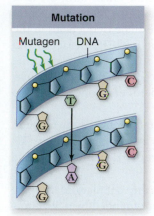 |  | 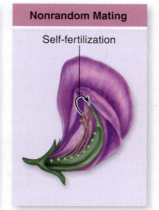 |  |  |

*a.* The ultimate source of variation. Individual mutations occur so rarely that mutation alone usually does not change allele frequency much.

*b.* A very potent agent of change. Individuals or gametes move from one population to another.

*c.* Inbreeding is the most common form. It does not alter allele frequency but reduces the proportion of heterozygotes.

*d.* Statistical accidents. The random fluctuation in allele frequencies increases as population size decreases.

*e.* The only agent that produces *adaptive* evolutionary changes.

**Figure 20.4 Five agents of evolutionary change.** *a.* Mutation, **(b)** gene flow, **(c)** nonrandom mating, **(d)** genetic drift, and **(e)** selection.

origin. In addition, gene flow may also result from the mating of individuals belonging to adjacent populations.

Consider two populations initially different in allele frequencies: In population 1, $p = 0.2$ and $q = 0.8$; in population 2, $p = 0.8$ and $q = 0.2$. Gene flow will tend to bring the rarer allele into each population. Thus, allele frequencies will change from generation to generation, and the populations will not be in Hardy–Weinberg equilibrium. Only when allele frequencies reach 0.5 for both alleles in both populations will equilibrium be attained. This example also indicates that gene flow tends to homogenize allele frequencies among populations.

## Nonrandom mating shifts genotype frequencies

Individuals with certain genotypes sometimes mate with one another more commonly than would be expected on a random basis, a phenomenon known as *nonrandom mating* (figure 20.4c). **Assortative mating,** in which phenotypically similar individuals mate, is a type of nonrandom mating that causes the frequencies of particular genotypes to differ greatly from those predicted by the Hardy–Weinberg principle.

Assortative mating does not change the frequency of the individual alleles, but rather increases the proportion of homozygous individuals because phenotypically similar individuals are likely to be genetically similar and thus are also more likely to produce offspring with two copies of the same allele. This is why populations of self-fertilizing plants consist primarily of homozygous individuals.

By contrast, **disassortative mating,** in which phenotypically different individuals mate, produces an excess of heterozygotes.

## Genetic drift may alter allele frequencies in small populations

In small populations, frequencies of particular alleles may change drastically by chance alone. Such changes in allele frequencies occur randomly, as if the frequencies were drifting from their values. These changes are thus known as **genetic drift** (figure 20.4d). For this reason, a population must be large to be in Hardy–Weinberg equilibrium.

If the gametes of only a few individuals form the next generation, the alleles they carry may by chance not be representative of the parent population from which they were drawn, as illustrated in figure 20.5. In this example, a small number of individuals are removed from a bottle containing many. By chance, most of the individuals removed are green, so the new population has a much higher population of green individuals than the parent generation had.

A set of small populations that are isolated from one another may come to differ strongly as a result of genetic drift, even if the forces of natural selection are the same for both. Because of genetic drift, sometimes harmful alleles may increase in frequency in small populations, despite selective disadvantage, and favorable alleles may be lost even though they are selectively advantageous. It is interesting to realize that humans have lived in small groups for much of the course of their

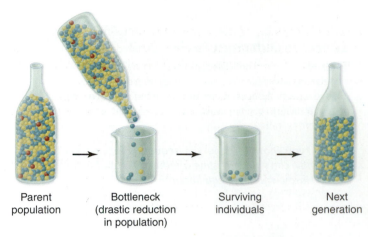

**Figure 20.5 Genetic drift: a bottleneck effect.** The parent population contains roughly equal numbers of green and yellow individuals and a small number of red individuals. By chance, the few remaining individuals that contribute to the next generation are mostly green. The bottleneck occurs because so few individuals form the next generation, as might happen after an epidemic or a catastrophic storm.

evolution; consequently, genetic drift may have been a particularly important factor in the evolution of our species.

Larger populations also experience the effect of genetic drift, but to a lesser extent than smaller populations—the magnitude of genetic drift is inversely related to population size. However, large populations may have been much smaller in the past, and genetic drift may have greatly altered allele frequencies at that time. Imagine a population containing only two alleles of a gene, $B$ and $b$, in equal frequency (that is, $p = q = 0.50$). In a large Hardy–Weinberg population, the genotype frequencies are expected to be 0.25 $BB$, 0.50 $Bb$, and 0.25 $bb$. If only a small sample of individuals produces the next generation, large deviations in these genotype frequencies can occur simply by chance.

Suppose, for example, that four individuals form the next generation, and that by chance they are two $Bb$ heterozygotes and two $BB$ homozygotes—that is, the allele frequencies in the next generation would be $p = 0.75$ and $q = 0.25$. In fact, if you were to replicate this experiment 1000 times, each time randomly drawing four individuals from the parental population, then in about 8 of the 1000 experiments, one of the two alleles would be missing entirely.

This result leads to an important conclusion: Genetic drift can lead to the loss of alleles in isolated populations. Alleles that initially are uncommon are particularly vulnerable (see figure 20.5).

Although genetic drift occurs in any population, it is particularly likely in populations that were founded by a few individuals or in which the population was reduced to a very small number at some time in the past.

### The founder effect

Sometimes one or a few individuals disperse and become the founders of a new, isolated population at some distance from their place of origin. These pioneers are not likely to carry all the alleles present in the source population. Thus, some alleles may be lost from the new population, and others may change drastically in frequency. In some cases, previously rare alleles in the source population may be a significant fraction of the new population's genetic endowment. This phenomenon is called the **founder effect.**

Founder effects are not rare in nature. Many self-pollinating plants start new populations from a single seed. Founder effects have been particularly important in the evolution of organisms on distant oceanic islands, such as the Hawaiian and Galápagos Islands. Most of the organisms in such areas probably derive from one or a few initial founders. Although rare, such events are occasionally observed, such as when a mass of vegetation carrying several iguanas washed up on the shore of the Caribbean island of Anguilla in 1996, leading to the establishment of a population that still occurs there to this day.

In a similar way, isolated human populations begun by relatively few individuals are often dominated by genetic features characteristic of their founders. Amish populations in the United States, for example, have unusually high frequencies of a number of conditions, such as polydactylism (the presence of a sixth finger).

### The bottleneck effect

Even if organisms do not move from place to place, occasionally their populations may be drastically reduced in size. This may result from flooding, drought, epidemic disease, and other natural forces, or from changes in the environment. The few surviving individuals may constitute a random genetic sample of the original population (unless some individuals survive specifically because of their genetic makeup). The resulting alterations and loss of genetic variability have been termed the **bottleneck effect.**

The genetic variation of some living species appears to be severely depleted, probably as the result of a bottleneck effect in the past. For example, the northern elephant seal, which breeds on the western coast of North America and nearby islands, was nearly hunted to extinction in the nineteenth century and was reduced to a single population containing perhaps

no more than 20 individuals on the island of Guadalupe off the coast of Baja, California (figure 20.6). As a result of this bottleneck, the species has lost almost all of its genetic variation, even though the seal populations have rebounded and now number in the tens of thousands and breed in locations as far north as near San Francisco.

Any time a population becomes drastically reduced in numbers, such as in endangered species, the bottleneck effect is a potential problem. Even if population size rebounds, the lack of variability may mean that the species remains vulnerable to extinction—a topic we will return to in chapter 59.

## Selection favors some genotypes over others

As Darwin pointed out, some individuals leave behind more progeny than others, and the rate at which they do so is affected by phenotype and behavior. We describe the results of this process as **selection** (see figure 20.4e). In *artificial selection*, a breeder selects for the desired characteristics. In *natural selection*, environmental conditions determine which individuals in a population produce the most offspring.

For natural selection to occur and to result in evolutionary change, three conditions must be met:

1. **Variation must exist among individuals in a population.** Natural selection works by favoring individuals with some traits over individuals with alternative traits. If no variation exists, natural selection cannot operate.
2. **Variation among individuals must result in differences in the number of offspring surviving in the next generation.** This is the essence of natural selection. Because of their phenotype or behavior, some individuals are more successful than others in producing offspring. Although many traits are phenotypically variable, individuals exhibiting variation do not always differ in survival and reproductive success.
3. **Variation must be genetically inherited.** For natural selection to result in evolutionary change, the selected differences must have a genetic basis. Not all variation has a genetic basis—even genetically identical individuals may be phenotypically quite distinctive if they grow up in different environments. Such environmental effects are

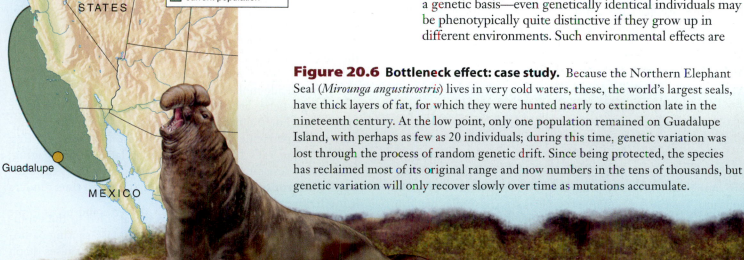

**Figure 20.6 Bottleneck effect: case study.** Because the Northern Elephant Seal (*Mirounga angustirostris*) lives in very cold waters, these, the world's largest seals, have thick layers of fat, for which they were hunted nearly to extinction late in the nineteenth century. At the low point, only one population remained on Guadalupe Island, with perhaps as few as 20 individuals; during this time, genetic variation was lost through the process of random genetic drift. Since being protected, the species has reclaimed most of its original range and now numbers in the tens of thousands, but genetic variation will only recover slowly over time as mutations accumulate.

(Map legend: population in 1890, reduced to inhabiting Guadalupe only; current population)

UNITED STATES

Guadalupe

MEXICO

common in nature. In many turtles, for example, individuals that hatch from eggs laid in moist soil are heavier, with longer and wider shells, than individuals from nests in drier areas.

When phenotypically different individuals do not differ genetically, then differences in the number of their offspring will not alter the genetic composition of the population in the next generation, and thus, no evolutionary change will have occurred.

It is important to remember that natural selection and evolution are not the same—the two concepts often are incorrectly equated. Natural selection is a process, whereas evolution is the historical record, or outcome, of change through time. Natural selection (the process) can lead to evolution (the outcome), but natural selection is only one of several processes that can result in evolutionary change. Moreover, natural selection can occur without producing evolutionary change; only if variation is genetically based will natural selection lead to evolution.

### Selection to avoid predators

The result of evolution driven by natural selection is that populations become better adapted to their environment. Many of the most dramatic documented instances of adaptation involve genetic changes that decrease the probability of capture by a predator. The caterpillar larvae of the common sulphur butterfly *Colias eurytheme* usually exhibit a pale green color, providing excellent camouflage against the alfalfa plants on which they feed. An alternative bright yellow color morph is kept at very low frequency because this color renders the larvae highly visible on the food plant, making it easier for bird predators to see them (see figure 20.4*e*).

One of the most dramatic examples of background matching involves ancient lava flows in the deserts of the American Southwest. In these areas, the black rock formations produced when the lava cooled contrast starkly with the surrounding bright glare of the desert sand. Populations of many species of animals occurring on these rocks—including lizards, rodents, and a variety of insects—are dark in color, whereas sand-dwelling populations in surrounding areas are much lighter (figure 20.7).

Predation is the likely cause for these differences in color. Laboratory studies have confirmed that predatory birds such as owls are adept at picking out individuals occurring on backgrounds to which they are not adapted.

### Selection to match climatic conditions

Many studies of selection have focused on genes encoding enzymes, because in such cases the investigator can directly assess the consequences to the organism of changes in the frequency of alternative enzyme alleles.

Often investigators find that enzyme allele frequencies vary with latitude, so that one allele is more common in northern populations, but is progressively less common at more southern locations. A superb example is seen in studies of a fish, the mummichog (*Fundulus heteroclitus*), which ranges along the eastern coast of North America. In this fish, geographic variation occurs in allele frequencies for the gene that produces the enzyme lactate dehydrogenase, which catalyzes the conversion of pyruvate to lactate (see section 7.8).

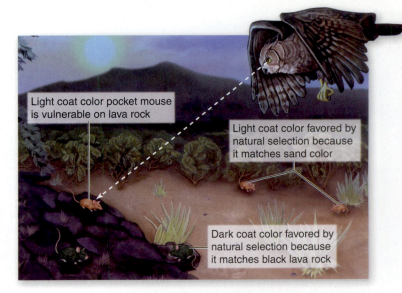

**Figure 20.7 Pocket mice from the Tularosa Basin of New Mexico whose color matches their background.** Black lava formations are surrounded by desert, and selection favors coat color in pocket mice that matches their surroundings. Genetic studies indicate that the differences in coat color are the result of small differences in the DNA of alleles of a single gene.

*Labels in figure:*
- Light coat color pocket mouse is vulnerable on lava rock
- Light coat color favored by natural selection because it matches sand color
- Dark coat color favored by natural selection because it matches black lava rock

Biochemical studies show that the enzymes formed by these alleles function differently at different temperatures, thus explaining their geographic distributions. The form of the enzyme more frequent in the north is a better catalyst at low temperatures than is the enzyme from the south. Moreover, studies indicate that at low temperatures, individuals with the northern allele swim faster, and presumably survive better, than individuals with the alternative allele.

### Selection for pesticide and microbial resistance

A particularly clear example of selection in natural populations is provided by studies of pesticide resistance in insects. The widespread use of insecticides has led to the rapid evolution of resistance in more than 500 pest species. The cost of this evolution, in terms of crop losses and increased pesticide use, has been estimated at $3–8 billion per year.

In the housefly, the resistance allele at the *pen* gene decreases the uptake of insecticide, whereas alleles at the *kdr* and *dld-r* genes decrease the number of target sites, thus decreasing the binding ability of the insecticide (figure 20.8). Other alleles enhance the ability of the insects' enzymes to identify and detoxify insecticide molecules.

Single genes are also responsible for resistance in other organisms. For example, Norway rats are normally susceptible to the pesticide warfarin, which diminishes the clotting ability of the rat's blood and leads to fatal hemorrhaging. However, a resistance allele at a single gene reduces the ability of warfarin to bind to its target enzyme and thus renders it ineffective.

Selection imposed by humans has also led to the evolution of resistance to antibiotics in many disease-causing pathogens. For example, *Staphylococcus aureus*, which causes staph infections, was initially treated by penicillin. However, within four years of mass-production of the drug, evolutionary change

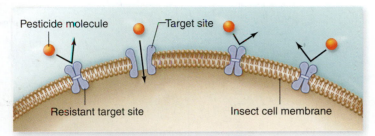

*a.* Insect cells with resistance allele at *pen* gene: decreased uptake of the pesticide.

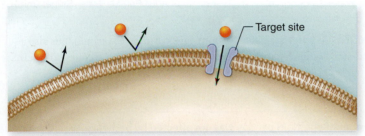

*b.* Insect cells with resistance allele at *kdr* gene: decreased number of target sites for the pesticide.

**Figure 20.8 Selection for pesticide resistance.** Resistance alleles at genes such as *pen* and *kdr* allow insects to be more resistant to pesticides. Insects that possess these resistance alleles have become more common through selection.

in *S. aureus* modified an enzyme so that it would attack penicillin and render it inactive. Since that time, several other drugs have been developed to attack the microbe, and each time resistance has evolved. As a result, staph infections have re-emerged as a major health threat.

---

### Learning Outcomes Review 20.3

Five factors can bring about deviation from the predicted Hardy–Weinberg genotype frequencies. Of these, only selection regularly produces adaptive evolutionary change, but the genetic constitution of populations, and thus the course of evolution, can also be affected by mutation, gene flow, nonrandom mating, and genetic drift.

- ■ *How do each of these processes cause populations to vary from Hardy-Weinberg equilibrium?*

---

## 20.4 Fitness and Its Measurement

### Learning Outcomes

1. *Define evolutionary fitness.*
2. *Explain the different components of fitness.*
3. *Demonstrate how the success of different phenotypes can be compared by calculating their relative fitness.*

---

Selection occurs when individuals with one phenotype leave more surviving offspring in the next generation than individuals with an alternative phenotype. Evolutionary biologists quantify reproductive success as **fitness,** the number of surviving offspring left in the next generation.

Fitness is a relative concept; the most fit phenotype is simply the one that produces, on average, the greatest number of offspring.

### A phenotype with greater fitness usually increases in frequency

Suppose, for example, that in a population of toads, two phenotypes exist: green and brown. Suppose, further, that green toads leave, on average, 4.0 offspring in the next generation, but brown toads leave only 2.5. By custom, the most fit phenotype is assigned a fitness value of 1.0, and other phenotypes are expressed as relative proportions. In this case, the fitness of the green phenotype would be 4.0/4.0 = 1.000, and the fitness of the brown phenotype would be 2.5/4.0 = 0.625. The difference in fitness would therefore be 1.000 – 0.625 = 0.375. A difference in fitness of 0.375 is quite large; natural selection in this case strongly favors the green phenotype.

If differences in color have a genetic basis, then we would expect evolutionary change to occur; the frequency of green toads should be substantially greater in the next generation. Further, if the fitness of two phenotypes remained unchanged, we would expect alleles for the brown phenotype eventually to disappear from the population.

### Inquiry question

Why might the frequency of green toads not increase in the next generation, even if color differences have a genetic basis?

### Fitness may consist of many components

Although selection is often characterized as "survival of the fittest," differences in survival are only one component of fitness.

Even if no differences in survival occur, selection may operate if some individuals are more successful than others in attracting mates. In many territorial animal species, for example, large males mate with many females, and small males rarely get to mate. Selection with respect to mating success is termed *sexual selection*; we describe this topic more fully in the discussion of behavioral biology in chapter 54.

In addition, the number of offspring produced per mating is also important. Large female frogs and fish lay more eggs than do smaller females, and thus they may leave more offspring in the next generation.

Fitness is therefore a combination of survival, mating success, and number of offspring per mating. Selection favors phenotypes with the greatest fitness, but predicting fitness from a single component can be tricky because traits favored for one component of fitness may be at a disadvantage for others. As an example, in water striders, larger females lay more eggs per day

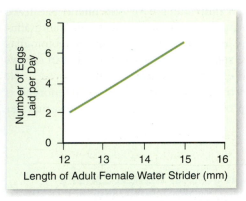 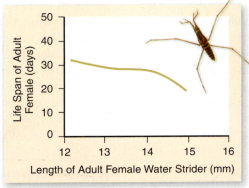 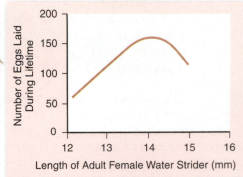

**Figure 20.9 Body size and egg-laying in water striders.** Larger female water striders lay more eggs per day (left panel), but also survive for a shorter period of time (center panel). As a result, intermediate-sized females produce the most offspring over the course of their entire lives and thus have the highest fitness (right panel).

**Inquiry question**

❓ What evolutionary change in body size might you expect? If the number of eggs laid per day was not affected by body size, would your prediction change?

(figure 20.9). Thus, natural selection at this stage favors large size. However, larger females also die at a younger age and thus have fewer opportunities to reproduce than smaller females. Overall, the two opposing directions of selection cancel each other out, and the intermediate-sized females leave the most offspring in the next generation.

### Learning Outcomes Review 20.4

Fitness is defined by an organism's reproductive success relative to other members of its population. This success is determined by how long it survives, how often it mates, and how many offspring it produces per mating. Relative fitness assigns numerical values to different phenotypes relative to the most fit phenotype.

- **■** *Is one of these factors always the most important in determining reproductive success? Explain.*

## 20.5 Interactions Among Evolutionary Forces

### Learning Outcomes

1. *Discuss how evolutionary processes can work simultaneously, but in opposing ways.*
2. *Evaluate what determines the evolutionary outcome when multiple processes are operating simultaneously.*

The amount of genetic variation in a population may be determined by the relative strength of different evolutionary processes. Sometimes these processes act together, and in other cases they work in opposition.

### Mutation and genetic drift may counter selection

In theory, if allele $B$ mutates to allele $b$ at a high enough rate, allele $b$ could be maintained in the population, even if natural selection strongly favored allele $B$. In nature, however, mutation rates are rarely high enough to counter the effects of natural selection.

The effect of natural selection also may be countered by genetic drift. Both of these processes may act to remove variation from a population. But selection is a nonrandom process that operates to increase the representation of alleles that enhance survival and reproductive success, whereas genetic drift is a random process in which any allele may increase. Thus, in some cases, drift may lead to a decrease in the frequency of an allele that is favored by selection. In some extreme cases, drift may even lead to the loss of a favored allele from a population.

Remember, however, that the magnitude of drift is inversely related to population size; consequently, natural selection is expected to overwhelm drift, except when populations are very small.

### Gene flow may promote or constrain evolutionary change

Gene flow can be either a constructive or a constraining force. On one hand, gene flow can spread a beneficial mutation that arises in one population to other populations. On the other hand, gene flow can impede adaptation within a population by the continual flow of inferior alleles from other populations.

Consider two populations of a species that live in different environments. In this situation, natural selection might favor different alleles—$B$ and $b$—in the two populations. In the absence of other evolutionary processes such as gene flow, the frequency of $B$ would be expected to reach 100% in one population and 0% in the other. However, if gene flow occurred between the two populations, then the less favored allele would continually be reintroduced into each population. As a result, the frequency of the alleles in the populations would reflect a balance between the rate at which gene flow brings the inferior allele into a population, and the rate at which natural selection removes it.

A classic example of gene flow opposing natural selection occurs on abandoned mine sites in Great Britain. Although mining activities ceased hundreds of years ago, the concentration of metal ions in the soil is still much greater than in surrounding areas. Large concentrations of heavy metals are generally toxic to plants, but alleles at certain genes confer the ability to grow on soils high in heavy metals. The ability to tolerate heavy metals comes at a price, however; individuals with the resistance allele exhibit lower growth rates on nonpolluted soil. Consequently, we would expect the resistance allele to occur with a frequency of 100% on mine sites and 0% elsewhere.

Heavy-metal tolerance has been studied intensively in the slender bent grass *Agrostis tenuis*, in which the resistance allele occurs at intermediate levels in many areas (figure 20.10). The explanation relates to the reproductive system of this grass, in which pollen, the floral equivalent of sperm, is dispersed by the wind. As a result, pollen grains—and the alleles they carry—can move great distances, leading to levels of gene flow between mine sites and unpolluted areas high enough to counteract the effects of natural selection.

In general, the extent to which gene flow can hinder the effects of natural selection should depend on the relative

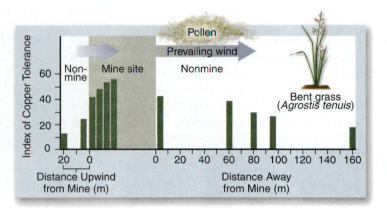

**Figure 20.10** **Degree of copper tolerance in grass plants on and near ancient mine sites.** Individuals with tolerant alleles have decreased growth rates on unpolluted soil. Thus, we would expect copper tolerance to be 100% on mine sites and 0% on non-mine sites. However, prevailing winds blow pollen containing nontolerant alleles onto the mine site and tolerant alleles beyond the site's borders. The amount of pollen received decreases with distance, which explains the changes in levels of tolerance. The index of copper tolerance is calculated as the growth rate of a plant on soil with high concentrations of copper relative to growth rate on soils with low levels of copper; the higher the index, the more tolerant the plant is of heavy metal pollution.

**Inquiry question**

? Would you expect the frequency of copper tolerance to be affected by distance from the mine site?

strengths of the two processes. In species in which gene flow is generally strong, such as in birds and wind-pollinated plants, the frequency of the allele less favored by natural selection may be relatively high. In more sedentary species that exhibit low levels of gene flow, such as salamanders, the favored allele should occur at a frequency near 100%.

**Learning Outcomes Review 20.5**

Allele frequencies sometimes reflect a balance between opposing processes. Gene flow, for example, may increase some alleles while natural selection decreases them. Where several processes are involved, observed frequencies depend on the relative strength of the processes.

■ *Under what circumstances might evolutionary processes operate in the same direction, and what would be the outcome?*

## 20.6 Maintenance of Variation

**Learning Outcomes**

1. *Define frequency-dependent selection, oscillating selection, and heterozygote advantage.*
2. *Explain how these processes affect the amount of genetic variation in a population.*

In the previous pages, natural selection has been discussed as a process that removes variation from a population by favoring one allele over others at a gene locus. However, in some circumstances, selection can do exactly the opposite and actually maintain population variation.

### Frequency-dependent selection may favor either rare or common phenotypes

In some circumstances, the fitness of a phenotype depends on its frequency within the population, a phenomenon termed **frequency-dependent selection.** This type of selection favors certain phenotypes depending on how commonly or uncommonly they occur.

#### Negative frequency-dependent selection

In negative frequency-dependent selection, rare phenotypes are favored by selection. Assuming a genetic basis for phenotypic variation, such selection will have the effect of making rare alleles more common, thus maintaining variation.

Negative frequency-dependent selection can occur for many reasons. For example, it is well known that animals or people searching for something form a "search image." That is, they become particularly adept at picking out certain objects. Consequently, predators may form a search image for common prey phenotypes. Rare forms may thus be preyed upon less frequently.

An example is fish predation on an insect, the water boatman, which occurs in three different colors. Experiments indicate that each of the color types is preyed upon disproportionately when it is the most common one; fish eat more of the common-colored insects than would occur by chance alone (figure 20.11).

Another cause of negative frequency dependence is resource competition. If genotypes differ in their resource requirements, as occurs in many plants, then the rarer genotype will have fewer competitors. When the different resource types are equally abundant, the rarer genotype will be at an advantage relative to the more common genotype.

### Positive frequency-dependent selection

Positive frequency-dependent selection has the opposite effect; by favoring common forms, it tends to eliminate variation from a population. For example, predators don't always select common individuals. In some cases, "oddballs" stand out from the rest and attract attention (figure 20.12).

The strength of selection should change through time as a result of frequency-dependent selection. In negative frequency-dependent selection, rare genotypes should become increasingly common, and their selective advantage will decrease correspondingly. Conversely, in positive frequency dependence, the rarer a genotype becomes, the greater the chance it will be selected against.

**Figure 20.12 Positive frequency-dependent selection.** In some cases, rare individuals stand out from the rest and draw the attention of predators; thus, in these cases, common phenotypes have the advantage (positive frequency-dependent selection).

## In oscillating selection, the favored phenotype changes as the environment changes

In some cases, selection favors one phenotype at one time and another phenotype at another time, a phenomenon called **oscillating selection.** If selection repeatedly oscillates in this fashion, the effect will be to maintain genetic variation in the population.

One example, discussed in chapter 21, concerns the medium ground finch of the Galápagos Islands. In times of drought, the supply of small, soft seeds is depleted, but there are still enough large seeds around. Consequently, birds with big bills are favored. However, when wet conditions return, the ensuing abundance of small seeds favors birds with smaller bills.

Oscillating selection and frequency-dependent selection are similar because in both cases the form of selection changes through time. But it is important to recognize that they are not the same: In oscillating selection, the fitness of a phenotype does not depend on its frequency; rather, environmental changes lead to the oscillation in selection. In contrast, in frequency-dependent selection, it is the change in frequencies themselves that leads to the changes in fitness of the different phenotypes.

## In some cases, heterozygotes may exhibit greater fitness than homozygotes

If heterozygotes are favored over homozygotes, then natural selection actually tends to maintain variation in the population. This **heterozygote advantage** favors individuals with copies of both alleles, and thus works to maintain both alleles in the population. Some evolutionary biologists believe that heterozygote advantage is pervasive and can explain the high levels of polymorphism observed in natural populations. Others, however, believe that it is relatively rare.

The best documented example of heterozygote advantage is sickle cell anemia, a hereditary disease affecting hemoglobin in humans. Individuals with sickle cell anemia exhibit symptoms of severe anemia and abnormal red blood cells that are irregular

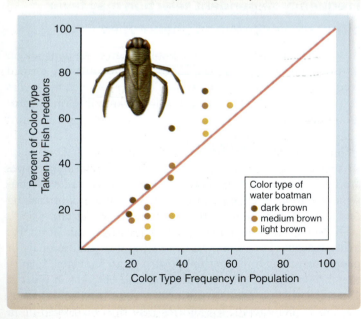

**SCIENTIFIC THINKING**

**Question:** *Does negative frequency-dependent selection maintain variation in a population?*

**Hypothesis:** *Fish may disproportionately capture water boatmen (a type of aquatic insect) with the most common color.*

**Experiment:** *Place predatory fish in different aquaria with the different frequencies of the color types in each aquarium.*

**Result:** *Fish prey disproportionately on the common color in each aquarium. The rare color in each aquarium generally survives best.*

Color type of water boatman
- dark brown
- medium brown
- light brown

*y-axis: Percent of Color Type Taken by Fish Predators*
*x-axis: Color Type Frequency in Population*

**Figure 20.11 Frequency-dependent selection.**

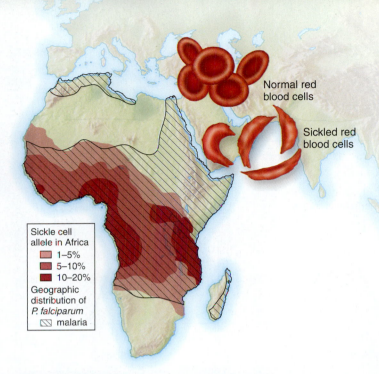

Normal red
blood cells

Sickled red
blood cells

Sickle cell
allele in Africa
- 1–5%
- 5–10%
- 10–20%
Geographic
distribution of
*P. falciparum*
- malaria

**Figure 20.13** **Frequency of sickle cell allele and distribution of *Plasmodium falciparum* malaria.** The red blood cells of people homozygous for the sickle cell allele collapse into sickled shapes when the oxygen level in the blood is low. The distribution of the sickle cell allele in Africa coincides closely with that of *P. falciparum* malaria.

in shape, with a great number of long, sickle-shaped cells (figure 20.13). Chapter 13 discusses why the sickle cell mutation (*S*) causes red blood cells to sickle.

The average incidence of the *S* allele in central African populations is about 0.12, far higher than that found among African Americans. From the Hardy–Weinberg principle, you can calculate that 1 in 5 central African individuals is heterozygous at the *S* allele, and 1 in 100 is homozygous and develops the fatal form of the disorder. People who are homozygous for the sickle cell allele almost never reproduce because they usually die before they reach reproductive age.

Why, then, is the *S* allele not eliminated from the central African population by selection rather than being maintained at such high levels? As it turns out, one of the leading causes of illness and death in central Africa, especially among young children, is malaria. People who are heterozygous for the sickle cell allele (and thus do not suffer from sickle cell anemia) are much less susceptible to malaria. The reason is that when the parasite that causes malaria, *Plasmodium falciparum*, enters a red blood cell, it causes extremely low oxygen tension in the cell, which leads to sickling in cells of individuals either homozygous or heterozygous for the sickle cell allele (but not in individuals that do not have the sickle cell allele). Such cells are quickly filtered out of the bloodstream by the spleen, thus eliminating the parasite. (The spleen's filtering effect is what leads to anemia in persons homozygous for the sickle cell allele because large numbers of red blood cells become sickle-shaped and are removed; in the case of heterozygotes, only those cells containing the *Plasmodium* parasite sickle, whereas the remaining cells are not affected, and thus anemia does not occur.)

Consequently, even though most homozygous recessive individuals die at a young age, the sickle cell allele is maintained at high levels in these populations because it is associated with resistance to malaria in heterozygotes and also, for reasons not yet fully understood, with increased fertility in female heterozygotes. Figure 20.13 shows the overlap between regions where sickle cell anemia is found and where malaria is prevalent.

For people living in areas where malaria is common, having the sickle cell allele in the heterozygous condition has adaptive value (see figure 20.13). Among African Americans, however, many of whose ancestors have lived for many generations in a country where malaria is now essentially absent, the environment does not place a premium on resistance to malaria. Consequently, no adaptive value counterbalances the ill effects of the disease; in this nonmalarial environment, selection is acting to eliminate the *S* allele. Only 1 in 375 African Americans develops sickle cell anemia, far fewer than in central Africa.

### Learning Outcomes Review 20.6

Selection can maintain variation within populations in a number of ways. Negative frequency-dependent selection tends to favor rare phenotypes. Oscillating selection favors different phenotypes at different times. In some cases, heterozygotes have a selective advantage that may act to retain deleterious alleles.

■ *How would genetic variation in a population change if heterozygotes had the lowest fitness?*

## 20.7 Selection Acting on Traits Affected by Multiple Genes

### Learning Outcomes
1. **Define and contrast disruptive, stabilizing, and directional selection.**
2. **Explain the evolutionary outcome of each of these types of selection.**

In nature, many traits—perhaps most—are affected by more than one gene. The interactions between genes are typically complex, as you saw in chapter 12. For example, alleles of many different genes play a role in determining human height (see figure 12.11). In such cases, selection operates on all the genes, influencing most strongly those that make the greatest contribution to the phenotype. How selection changes the population depends on which genotypes are favored.

### Disruptive selection removes intermediates

In some situations, selection acts to eliminate intermediate types, a phenomenon called **disruptive selection** (figure 20.14*a*). A clear example is the different beak sizes of the African black-bellied

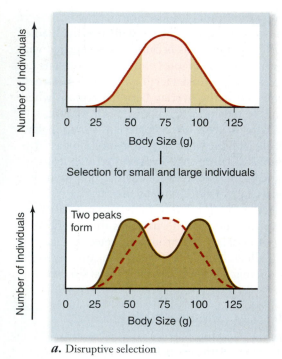

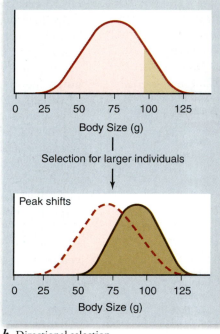

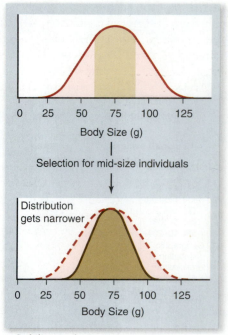

*a.* Disruptive selection    *b.* Directional selection    *c.* Stabilizing selection

**Figure 20.14 Three kinds of selection.** The top panels show the populations before selection has occurred (under the solid red line). Within the population, those favored by selection are shown in light brown. The bottom panels indicate what the populations would look like in the next generation. The dashed red lines are the distribution of the original population and the solid, dark brown lines are the true distribution of the population in the next generation. *a.* In disruptive selection, individuals in the middle of the range of phenotypes of a certain trait are selected against, and the extreme forms of the trait are favored. *b.* In directional selection, individuals concentrated toward one extreme of the array of phenotypes are favored. *c.* In stabilizing selection, individuals with midrange phenotypes are favored, with selection acting against both ends of the range of phenotypes.

seedcracker finch *Pyrenestes ostrinus* (figure 20.15). Populations of these birds contain individuals with large and small beaks, but very few individuals with intermediate-sized beaks.

As their name implies, these birds feed on seeds, and the available seeds fall into two size categories: large and small. Only large-beaked birds can open the tough shells of large seeds, whereas birds with the smaller beaks are more adept at handling small seeds. Birds with intermediate-sized beaks are at a disadvantage with both seed types—they are unable to open large seeds and too clumsy to efficiently process small seeds. Consequently, selection acts to eliminate the intermediate phenotypes, in effect partitioning (or "disrupting") the population into two phenotypically distinct groups.

## Directional selection eliminates phenotypes on one end of a range

When selection acts to eliminate one extreme from an array of phenotypes, the genes promoting this extreme become less frequent in the population and may eventually disappear. This form of selection is called **directional selection** (see figure 20.14*b*). Thus, in the *Drosophila* population illustrated in figure 20.16, eliminating flies that move toward light causes the population over time to contain fewer individuals with alleles promoting such behavior. If you were to pick an individual at random from a later generation of flies, there is a smaller chance that the fly

**SCIENTIFIC THINKING**

**Question:** *Does disruptive selection promote differences in beak size in the African Black-bellied Seedcracker Finches (Pyrenestes ostrinus)?*

**Field Study:** *Capture, measure, and release birds in a population. Follow the birds through time to determine how long each lives.*

**Result:** *Large- and small-beaked birds have higher survival rates than birds with intermediate-sized beaks.*

**Interpretation:** *What would happen if the distribution of seed size and hardness in the environment changed?*

**Figure 20.15 Disruptive selection for large and small beaks.** Differences in beak size in the black-bellied seedcracker finch of west Africa are the result of disruptive selection.

would spontaneously move toward light than if you had selected a fly from the original population. Artificial selection has changed the population in the direction of being less attracted to light. Directional selection often occurs in nature when the environment changes; one example is the widespread evolution of pesticide resistance discussed earlier in this chapter.

## Stabilizing selection favors individuals with intermediate phenotypes

When selection acts to eliminate both extremes from an array of phenotypes, the result is to increase the frequency of the already common intermediate type. This form of selection is called **stabilizing selection** (see figure 20.14c). In effect, selection is operating to prevent change away from this middle range of values. Selection does not change the most common phenotype of the population, but rather makes it even more common by eliminating extremes. Many examples are known. In humans, infants with intermediate weight at birth have the highest survival rate (figure 20.17). In ducks and chickens, eggs of intermediate weight have the highest hatching success.

### Learning Outcomes Review 20.7

In disruptive selection, intermediate forms of a trait diminish; in stabilizing selection, intermediates increase, whereas in disruptive selection they decrease. Directional selection shifts frequencies toward one end or the other and may eventually eliminate alleles entirely.

- *How does directional selection differ from frequency-dependent selection?*

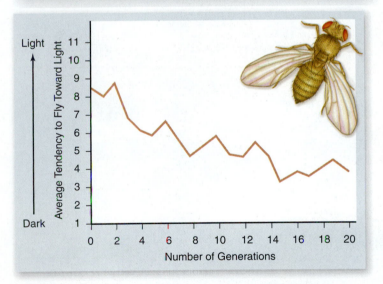

**Figure 20.16 Directional selection for negative phototropism in** *Drosophila.* Flies that moved toward light were discarded, and only flies that moved away from light were used as parents for the next generation. This procedure was repeated for 20 generations, producing substantial evolutionary change.

### Inquiry question

**?** What would happen if after 20 generations, experimenters started keeping flies that moved toward the light and discarded the others?

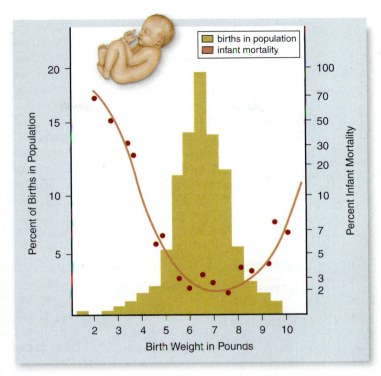

**Figure 20.17 Stabilizing selection for birth weight in humans.** The death rate among babies (red curve; right y-axis) is lowest at an intermediate birth weight; both smaller and larger babies have a greater tendency to die than those around the most frequent weight (tan area; left y-axis) of between 7 and 8 pounds. Recent medical advances have reduced mortality rates for small and large babies.

### Inquiry question

**?** As improved medical technology leads to decreased infant mortality rates, how would you expect the distribution of birth weights in the population to change?

## 20.8 Experimental Studies of Natural Selection

### Learning Outcome

1. *Explain how experiments can be used to test evolutionary hypotheses.*

To study evolution, biologists have traditionally investigated what has happened in the past, sometimes many millions of years ago. To learn about dinosaurs, a paleontologist looks at dinosaur fossils. To study human evolution, an anthropologist looks at human fossils and, increasingly, examines the "family tree" of mutations that have accumulated in human DNA over millions of years. In this traditional approach, evolutionary biology is similar to astronomy and history, relying on observation rather than experimentation to examine ideas about past events.

Nonetheless, evolutionary biology is not entirely an observational science. Darwin was right about many things, but one area in which he was mistaken concerns the pace at which evolution occurs. Darwin thought that evolution occurred at a very slow, almost imperceptible pace. But in recent years many case studies have demonstrated that in some circumstances, evolutionary change can occur rapidly. Consequently, experimental studies can be devised to test evolutionary hypotheses.

Although laboratory studies on fruit flies and other organisms have been common for more than 50 years, scientists have only recently started conducting experimental studies of evolution in nature. One excellent example of how observations of the natural world can be combined with rigorous experiments in the lab and in the field concerns research on the guppy, *Poecilia reticulata*.

## Guppy color variation in different environments suggests natural selection at work

The guppy is a popular aquarium fish because of its bright coloration and prolific reproduction. In nature, guppies are found in small streams in northeastern South America and in many mountain streams on the nearby island of Trinidad. One interesting feature of several of the streams is that they have waterfalls. Amazingly, guppies and some other fish are capable of colonizing portions of the stream above the waterfall.

The killifish is a particularly good colonizer; apparently on rainy nights, it will wriggle out of the stream and move through the damp leaf litter. Guppies are not so proficient, but they are good at swimming upstream. During flood seasons, rivers sometimes overflow their banks, creating secondary channels that move through the forest. On these occasions, guppies may be able to swim upstream in the secondary channels and invade the pools above waterfalls.

By contrast, some species are not capable of such dispersal and thus are only found in streams below the first waterfall. One species whose distribution is restricted by waterfalls is the pike cichlid, a voracious predator that feeds on other fish, including guppies.

Because of these barriers to dispersal, guppies can be found in two very different environments. In pools just below the waterfalls, predation by the pike cichlid is a substantial risk, and rates of survival are relatively low. But in similar pools just above the waterfall, the only predator present is the killifish, which rarely preys on guppies.

Guppy populations above and below waterfalls exhibit many differences. In the high-predation pools, guppies exhibit drab coloration. Moreover, they tend to reproduce at a younger age and attain relatively smaller adult sizes. Male fish above the waterfall, in contrast, are colorful (figure 20.18), mature later, and grow to larger sizes.

These differences suggest the operation of natural selection. In the low-predation environment, males display gaudy colors and spots that they use to court females. Moreover, larger males are most successful at holding territories and mating with females, and larger females lay more eggs. Thus, in the absence of predators, larger and more colorful fish may have produced more offspring, leading to the evolution of those traits.

In pools below the waterfall, natural selection would favor different traits. Colorful males are likely to attract the attention of the pike cichlid, and high predation rates mean that most fish live short lives. Individuals that are more drab and shunt energy into early reproduction, rather than growth to a larger size, are therefore likely to be favored by natural selection.

## Experimentation reveals the agent of selection

Although the differences between guppies living above and below the waterfalls suggest evolutionary responses to differences in the strength of predation, alternative explanations are possible. Perhaps, for example, only very large fish are capable of crawling past the waterfall to colonize pools. If this were the case, then a founder effect would occur in which the new population was established solely by individuals with genes for large size. The only way to rule out such alternative possibilities is to conduct a controlled experiment.

### The laboratory experiment

The first experiments were conducted in large pools in laboratory greenhouses. At the start of the experiment, a group of

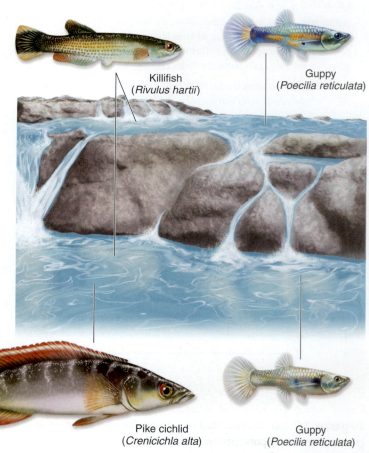

Killifish
(*Rivulus hartii*)

Guppy
(*Poecilia reticulata*)

Pike cichlid
(*Crenicichla alta*)

Guppy
(*Poecilia reticulata*)

**Figure 20.18 The evolution of protective coloration in guppies.** In pools below waterfalls where predation is high, male guppies are drab in color. In the absence of the highly predatory pike cichlid (*Crenicichla alta*) in pools above waterfalls, male guppies are much more colorful and attractive to females. The killifish is also a predator, but it only rarely eats guppies. The evolution of these differences in guppies can be experimentally tested.

2000 guppies was divided equally among 10 large pools. Six months later, pike cichlids were added to four of the pools and killifish to another four, with the remaining two pools left to serve as "no-predation" controls.

Fourteen months later (which corresponds to 10 guppy generations), the scientists compared the populations. The guppies in the killifish and control pools were indistinguishable—brightly colored and large. In contrast, the guppies in the pike cichlid pools were smaller and drab in coloration (figure 20.19).

These results established that predation can lead to rapid evolutionary change, but do these laboratory experiments reflect what occurs in nature?

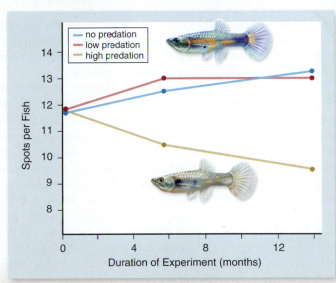

**Figure 20.19 Evolutionary change in spot number.** Guppy populations raised for 10 generations in low-predation or no-predation environments in laboratory greenhouses evolved a greater number of spots, whereas selection in more dangerous environments, such as the pools with the highly predatory pike cichlid, led to less conspicuous fish. The same results are seen in field experiments conducted in pools above and below waterfalls.

**? Inquiry question**

How do these results depend on the manner by which the guppy predators locate their prey?

### The field experiment

To find out whether the laboratory results were an accurate reflection of natural processes, the scientists located two streams that had guppies in pools below a waterfall, but not above it. As in other Trinidadian streams, the pike cichlid was present in the lower pools, but only the killifish was found above the waterfalls.

The scientists then transplanted guppies to the upper pools and returned at several-year intervals to monitor the populations. Despite originating from populations in which predation levels were high, the transplanted populations rapidly evolved the traits characteristic of low-predation guppies: they matured late, attained greater size, and had brighter colors. The control populations in the lower pools, by contrast, continued to be drab and to mature early and at a smaller size. Laboratory analysis confirmed that the variations between the populations were the result of genetic differences.

These results demonstrate that substantial evolutionary change can occur in less than 12 years. More generally, these studies indicate how scientists can formulate hypotheses about how evolution occurs and then test these hypotheses in natural conditions. The results give strong support to the theory of evolution by natural selection.

**Learning Outcome Review 20.8**

Although much of evolutionary theory is derived from observation, experiments are sometimes possible in natural settings. Studies have revealed that traits can shift in populations in a relatively short time. The data obtained from evolutionary experiments can be used to refine theoretical assumptions.

■ *What experiments could you design to test other examples of natural selection, such as the evolution of pesticide resistance or background color matching?*

## 20.9 The Limits of Selection

**Learning Outcomes**

1. Define pleiotropy and epistasis.
2. Explain how these phenomena may affect the evolutionary response to selective pressure.

Although selection is the most powerful of the principal agents of genetic change, there are limits to what it can accomplish. These limits result from multiple phenotypic effects of alleles, lack of genetic variation upon which selection can act, and interactions between genes.

### Genes have multiple effects

Alleles often affect multiple aspects of a phenotype (the phenomenon of *pleiotropy*; see chapter 12). These multiple effects tend to set limits on how much a phenotype can be altered.

For example, selecting for large clutch size in chickens eventually leads to eggs with thinner shells that break more easily. For this reason, we could never produce chickens that lay eggs twice as large as the best layers do now. Likewise, we cannot produce gigantic cattle that yield twice as much meat as our leading breeds, or corn with an ear at the base of every leaf, instead of just at the bases of a few leaves.

## Evolution requires genetic variation

Over 80% of the gene pool of the thoroughbred horses racing today goes back to 31 ancestors from the late eighteenth century. Despite intense directional selection on thoroughbreds, their performance times have not improved for more than 50 years (figure 20.20). Decades of intense selection presumably have removed variation from the population at a rate greater than mutation can replenish it, such that little genetic variation now remains, and evolutionary change is not possible.

In some cases, phenotypic variation for a trait may never have had a genetic basis. The compound eyes of insects are made up of hundreds of visual units, termed ommatidia (described in chapter 34). In some individuals, the left eye contains more ommatidia than the right. In other individuals, the right eye contains more than the left (figure 20.21). However, despite intense selection experiments in the laboratory, scientists have never been able to produce a line of fruit flies that consistently has more ommatidia in the left eye than in the right.

The reason is that separate genes do not exist for the left and right eyes. Rather, the same genes affect both eyes, and differences in the number of ommatidia result from differences

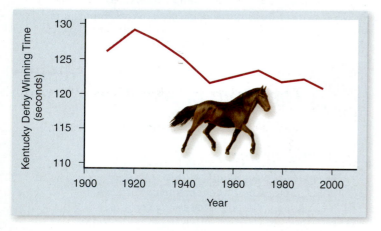

**Figure 20.20** **Selection for increased speed in racehorses is no longer effective.** Kentucky Derby winning speeds have not improved significantly since 1950.

**? Inquiry question**

What might explain the lack of change in winning speeds?

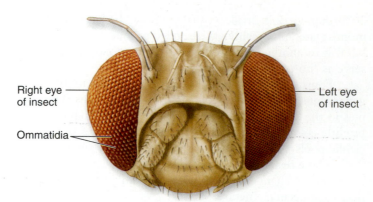

**Figure 20.21** **Phenotypic variation in insect ommatidia.** In some individuals, the number of ommatidia in the left eye is greater than the number in the right.

that occur as the eyes are formed in the development process. Thus, despite the existence of phenotypic variation, no underlying genetic variation is available for selection to favor.

## Gene interactions affect fitness of alleles

As discussed in chapter 12, *epistasis* is the phenomenon in which an allele for one gene may have different effects, depending on alleles present at other genes. Because of epistasis, the selective advantage of an allele at one gene may vary from one genotype to another. If a population is polymorphic for a second gene, then selection on the first gene may be constrained because different alleles are favored in different individuals of the same population.

Studies on bacteria illustrate how selection on alleles for one gene can depend on which alleles are present at other genes. In *E. coli*, two biochemical pathways exist to break down gluconate, each using enzymes produced by different genes. One gene produces the enzyme 6-PGD, for which there are several alleles. When the common allele for the second gene, which codes for the other biochemical pathway, is present, selection does not favor one allele over another at the 6-PGD gene. In some *E. coli*, however, an alternative allele at the second gene occurs that is not functional. The bacteria with this alternative allele are forced to rely only on the 6-PGD pathway, and in this case, selection favors one 6-PGD allele over another. Thus, epistatic interactions exist between the two genes, and the outcome of natural selection on the 6-PGD gene depends on which alleles are present at the second gene.

### Learning Outcomes Review 20.9

In pleiotropy, a single gene affects multiple traits; in epistasis, interaction between alleles of different genes affects a single trait. Both these conditions can constrain the effects of natural selection.

■ *How can epistasis and pleiotropy constrain the evolutionary response to natural selection?*

# Chapter Review

## 20.1 Genetic Variation and Evolution

### Many processes can lead to evolutionary change.

Darwin proposed that evolution of species occurs by the process of natural selection. Other processes can also lead to evolutionary change.

### Populations contain ample genetic variation.

For a population to be able to evolve, it must contain genetic variation. DNA testing shows that natural populations generally have substantial variation.

## 20.2 Changes in Allele Frequency (figure 20.3)

### The Hardy–Weinberg principle allows prediction of genotype frequencies.

Hardy–Weinberg equilibrium exists when observed genotype frequencies match the prediction from calculated frequencies. It occurs only when evolutionary processes are not acting to shift the distribution of alleles or genotypes in the population .

### Hardy–Weinberg predictions can be applied to data to find evidence of evolutionary processes.

If genotype frequencies are not in Hardy–Weinberg equilibrium, then evolutionary processes must be at work.

## 20.3 Five Agents of Evolutionary Change (figure 20.4)

### Mutation changes alleles.

Mutations are the ultimate source of genetic variation. Because mutation rates are low, mutation usually is not responsible for deviations from Hardy–Weinberg equilibrium.

### Gene flow occurs when alleles move between populations.

Gene flow is the migration of new alleles into a population. It can introduce genetic variation and can homogenize allele frequencies between populations.

### Nonrandom mating shifts genotype frequencies.

Assortative mating, in which similar individuals tend to mate, increases homozygosity; disassortative mating increases the frequency of heterozygotes.

*not allele frequencies but H-W predicts for genotype as well*

### Genetic drift may alter allele frequencies in small populations.

Genetic drift refers to random shifts in allele frequency. Its effects may be severe in small populations.

### Selection favors some genotypes over others.

For natural selection to occur, genetic variation must exist, it must result in differential reproductive success, and it must be inheritable.

## 20.4 Fitness and Its Measurement

### A phenotype with greater fitness usually increases in frequency.

Fitness is defined as the reproductive success of an individual. Relative fitness refers to the success of one genotype relative to others in a population. Usually, the genotype with highest relative fitness increases in frequency in the next generation.

### Fitness may consist of many components.

Reproductive success is determined by how long an individual survives, how often it mates, and how many offspring it has per reproductive event.

## 20.5 Interactions Among Evolutionary Forces

### Mutation and genetic drift may counter selection.

In theory, a high rate of mutation could oppose natural selection, but this rarely happens. Genetic drift also can work counter to natural selection.

### Gene flow may promote or constrain evolutionary change.

Gene flow can spread a beneficial mutation to other populations, but it can also impede adaptation due to influx of alleles with low fitness in a population's environment.

## 20.6 Maintenance of Variation

### Frequency-dependent selection may favor either rare or common phenotypes.

Negative frequency-dependent selection favors rare phenotypes and maintains variation within a population. Positive frequency-dependent selection favors the common phenotype and leads to decreased variation.

### In oscillating selection, the favored phenotype changes as the environment changes.

If environmental change is cyclical, selection would favor first one phenotype, then another, maintaining variation.

### In some cases, heterozygotes may exhibit greater fitness than homozygotes.

Heterozygote advantage favors individuals with both alleles.

## 20.7 Selection Acting on Traits Affected by Multiple Genes (figure 20.13)

### Disruptive selection removes intermediates.

When intermediate phenotypes are at a disadvantage, a population may exhibit a bimodal trait distribution. *two peaks*

### Directional selection eliminates phenotypes at one end of a range.

Directional selection tends to shift the mean value of the population toward the favored end of the distribution.

### Stabilizing selection favors individuals with intermediate phenotypes.

Stabilizing selection eliminates both extremes and increases the frequency of an intermediate type. The population may have the same mean value, but with decreased variation.

## 20.8 Experimental Studies of Natural Selection

### The hypothesis that natural selection leads to evolutionary change can be tested experimentally.

### Guppy color variation in different environments suggests natural selection at work.

### Experimentation reveals the agent of selection.

Guppies in natural populations subject to different predators were shown to undergo color change over generations.

## 20.9 The Limits of Selection

### Genes have multiple effects.

Pleiotropic genes, which have multiple effects, set limits on how much a phenotype can be altered. Even if one affected trait is favored, other affected traits may not be.

### Evolution requires genetic variation.

Intense selection pressure may remove genetic variation.

### Gene interactions affect fitness of alleles.

In epistasis, fitness of one allele may vary depending on the genotype of a second gene.

## Review Questions

### UNDERSTAND

1. Assortative mating
   a. affects genotype frequencies expected under Hardy–Weinberg equilibrium.
   b. affects allele frequencies expected under Hardy–Weinberg equilibrium.
   c. has no effect on the genotypic frequencies expected under Hardy–Weinberg equilibrium because it does not affect the relative proportion of alleles in a population.
   d. increases the frequency of heterozygous individuals above Hardy–Weinberg expectations.

2. When the environment changes from year to year and different phenotypes have different fitness in different environments
   a. natural selection will operate in a frequency-dependent manner.
   b. the effect of natural selection may oscillate from year to year, favoring alternative phenotypes in different years.
   c. genetic variation is not required to get evolutionary change by natural selection.
   d. none of the above.

3. Many factors can limit the ability of natural selection to cause evolutionary change, including
   a. a conflict between reproduction and survival as seen in Trinidadian guppies.
   b. lack of genetic variation.
   c. pleiotropy.
   d. all of the above.

4. Stabilizing selection differs from directional selection because
   a. in the former, phenotypic variation is reduced but the average phenotype stays the same, whereas in the latter both the variation and the mean phenotype change.
   b. the former requires genetic variation, but the latter does not.
   c. intermediate phenotypes are favored in directional selection.
   d. none of the above.

5. Founder effects and bottlenecks are
   a. expected only in large populations.
   b. mechanisms that increase genetic variation in a population.
   c. two different modes of natural selection.
   d. forms of genetic drift.

6. *Relative fitness*
   a. refers to the survival rate of one phenotype compared to that of another.
   b. is the physical condition of an individual's siblings and cousins.
   c. refers to the reproductive success of a phenotype.
   d. is none of the above.

7. For natural selection to result in evolutionary change
   a. variation must exist in a population.
   b. reproductive success of different phenotypes must differ.
   c. variation must be inherited from one generation to the next.
   d. all of the above.

### APPLY

1. In a population of red (dominant allele) or white flowers in Hardy–Weinberg equilibrium, the frequency of red flowers is 91%. What is the frequency of the red allele?
   a. 9%          c. 91%
   b. 30%         d. 70%

2. Genetic drift and natural selection can both lead to rapid rates of evolution. However,
   a. genetic drift works fastest in large populations.
   b. only drift leads to adaptation.
   c. natural selection requires genetic drift to produce new variation in populations.
   d. both processes of evolution can be slowed by gene flow.

3. What would happen to average birth weight if over the next several years advances in medical technology reduced infant mortality rates of large babies to equal that for intermediate-sized babies (see the following figure, red line). Assume that differences in birth weight have a genetic basis.
   a. Over time, average birth weight would only increase.
   b. Over time, average birth weight would only decrease.
   c. Both a and b.
   d. None of the above.

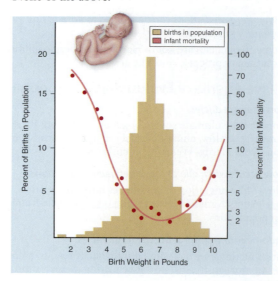

### SYNTHESIZE

1. In Trinidadian guppies a combination of elegant laboratory and field experiments builds a very compelling case for predator-induced evolutionary changes in color and life history traits. It is still possible, though not likely, that there are other differences between the sites above and below the falls aside from whether predators are present. What additional studies could strengthen the interpretation of the results?

2. On large, black lava flows in the deserts of the southwestern United States, populations of many types of animals are composed primarily of black individuals. By contrast, on small lava flows, populations often have a relatively high proportion of light-colored individuals. How can you explain this difference?

3. Based on a consideration of how strong artificial selection has helped eliminate genetic variation for speed in thoroughbred horses, we are left with the question of why, for many traits like speed (continuous traits), there is usually abundant genetic variation. This is true even for traits we know are under strong selection. Where does genetic variation ultimately come from, and how does the rate of production compare with the strength of natural selection? What other mechanisms can maintain and increase genetic variation in natural populations?

Chapter

# 21

# The Evidence for Evolution

## Chapter Outline

## Introduction

As we discussed in chapter 1, when Darwin proposed his revolutionary theory of evolution by natural selection, little actual evidence existed to bolster his case. Instead, Darwin relied on observations of the natural world, logic, and results obtained by breeders working with domestic animals. Since his day, however, the evidence for Darwin's theory has become overwhelming.

The case is built upon two pillars: first, evidence that natural selection can produce evolutionary change, and second, evidence from the fossil record that evolution has occurred. In addition, information from many different areas of biology—fields as different as anatomy, molecular biology, and biogeography—is only interpretable scientifically as being the outcome of evolution.

# 21.1 The Beaks of Darwin's Finches: Evidence of Natural Selection

### Learning Outcomes

1. Describe how the species of Darwin's finches have adapted to feed in different ways.
2. Explain how climatic variation drives evolutionary change in the medium ground finch.

As you learned in the preceding chapter, a variety of processes can produce evolutionary change. Most evolutionary biologists, however, agree with Darwin's thinking that natural selection is the primary process responsible for evolution. Although we cannot travel back through time, modern-day evidence allows us to test hypotheses about how evolution proceeds and confirms the power of natural selection as an agent of evolutionary change. This evidence comes from both the field and the laboratory and from both natural and human-altered situations.

Darwin's finches are a classic example of evolution by natural selection. When he visited the Galápagos Islands off the coast of Ecuador in 1835, Darwin collected 31 specimens of finches from three islands. Darwin, not an expert on birds, had trouble identifying the specimens, believing by examining their bills that his collection contained wrens, "gross-beaks," and blackbirds.

Upon Darwin's return to England, ornithologist John Gould informed Darwin that his collection was in fact a closely related group of distinct species, all similar to one another except for their bills. In all, 14 species are now recognized.

## Galápagos finches exhibit variation related to food gathering

The diversity of Darwin's finches is illustrated in figure 21.1. The ground finches feed on seeds that they crush in their powerful beaks; species with smaller and narrower bills such as the warbler finch eat insects. Other species include fruit and bud eaters, and species that feed on cactus fruits and the insects they attract; some populations of the sharp-beaked ground finch even include "vampires" that sometimes creep up on seabirds and use their sharp beaks to pierce the seabirds' skin and drink their blood. Perhaps most remarkable are the tool users, woodpecker finches that pick up a twig, cactus spine, or leaf stalk, trim it into shape with their bills, and then poke it into dead branches to pry out grubs.

The correspondence between the beaks of the finch species and their food source suggested to Darwin that natural selection had shaped them. In *The Voyage of the Beagle*, Darwin wrote, "Seeing this gradation and diversity of structure in one small, intimately related group of birds, one might really fancy that from an original paucity of birds in this archipelago, one species has been taken and modified for different ends."

Woodpecker finch (*Cactospiza pallida*)

Large ground finch (*Geospiza magnirostris*)

Cactus finch (*Geospiza scandens*)

Warbler finch (*Certhidea olivacea*)

Vegetarian tree finch (*Platyspiza crassirostris*)

**Figure 21.1 Darwin's finches.** These species show differences in bills and feeding habits among Darwin's finches. This diversity arose when an ancestral finch colonized the islands and diversified into habitats lacking other types of small birds. The bills of several species resemble those of different families of birds on the mainland. For example, the warbler finch has a beak very similar to warblers, to which it is not closely related.

## Modern research has verified Darwin's selection hypothesis

Darwin's observations suggest that differences among species in beak size and shape have evolved as the species adapted to use different food resources, but can this hypothesis be tested? In chapter 20, you read that the theory of evolution by natural selection requires that three conditions be met:

1. Variation must exist in the population.
2. This variation must lead to differences among individuals in lifetime reproductive success.
3. Variation among individuals must be genetically transmissible to the next generation.

The key to successfully testing Darwin's proposal proved to be patience. For more than 30 years, starting in 1973, Peter and Rosemary Grant of Princeton University and their students have studied the medium ground finch, *Geospiza fortis*, on a tiny island in the center of the Galápagos called Daphne Major. These finches feed preferentially on small, tender seeds, produced in abundance by plants in wet years. The birds resort to larger, drier seeds, which are harder to crush, only when small seeds become depleted during long periods of dry weather, when plants produce few seeds.

The Grants quantified beak shape among the medium ground finches of Daphne Major by carefully measuring beak depth (height of beak, from top to bottom, at its base) on individual birds. Measuring many birds every year, they were able to assemble for the first time a detailed portrait of evolution in action. The Grants found that not only did a great deal of variation in beak depth exist among members of the population, but the average beak depth changed from one year to the next in a predictable fashion.

During droughts, plants produced few seeds, and all available small seeds were quickly eaten, leaving large seeds as the major remaining source of food. As a result, birds with deeper, more powerful beaks survived better, because they were better able to break open these large seeds. Consequently, the average beak depth of birds in the population increased the next year. Then, when normal rains returned, average beak depth of the population decreased to its original size (figure 21.2*a*).

Conversely, in particularly wet years, plants flourished, producing an abundance of small seeds; as a result, small-beaked birds were favored, and beak depth decreased greatly.

Could these changes in beak dimension reflect the action of natural selection? An alternative possibility might be that the changes in beak depth do not reflect changes in gene frequencies, but rather are simply a response to diet—for example, perhaps crushing large seeds causes a growing bird to develop a larger beak.

To rule out this possibility, the Grants measured the relation of parent beak size to offspring beak size, examining many broods over several years. The depth of the beak was very similar between parents and offspring regardless of environmental conditions (figure 21.2*b*), suggesting that the differences among individuals in beak size reflect genetic differences, and therefore that the year-to-year changes in average beak depth represent evolutionary change resulting from natural selection.

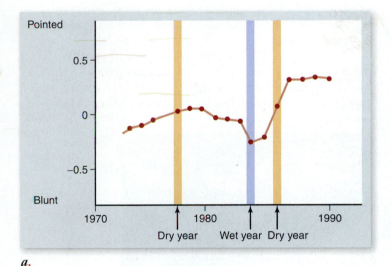

a.

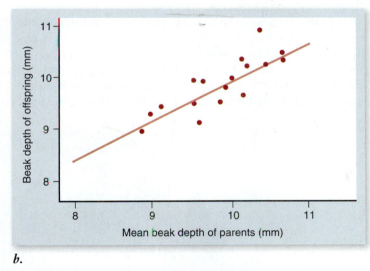

b.

**Figure 21.2** **Evidence that natural selection alters beak shape in the medium ground finch (*Geospiza fortis*).** *a.* In dry years, when only large, tough seeds are available, the mean beak depth increases. In wet years, when many small seeds are available, mean beak depth decreases. *b.* Beak depth is inherited from parents to offspring.

### Inquiry question

**?**  Suppose a bird with a large bill mates with a bird with a small bill. Would the bills of the pair's offspring tend to be larger or smaller than the bills of offspring from a pair of birds with medium-sized bills?

# 21.2 Peppered Moths and Industrial Melanism: More Evidence of Selection

When the environment changes, natural selection often may favor different traits in a species. One classic example concerns the peppered moth, *Biston betularia*. Adults come in a range of shades, from light gray with black speckling (hence the name "peppered" moth) to jet black (melanic).

Extensive genetic analysis has shown that the moth's body color is a genetic trait that reflects different alleles of a single gene. Black individuals have a dominant allele, one that was present but very rare in populations before 1850. From that time on, dark individuals increased in frequency in moth populations near industrialized centers until they made up almost 100% of these populations.

Biologists soon noticed that in industrialized regions where the dark moths were common, the tree trunks were darkened almost black by the soot of pollution, which also killed many of the light-colored lichens on tree trunks.

## Light-colored moths decreased in polluted areas

Why did dark moths gain a survival advantage around 1850? In 1896, an amateur moth collector named J. W. Tutt proposed what became the most commonly accepted hypothesis explaining the decline of the light-colored moths. He suggested that peppered forms were more visible to predators on sooty trees that have lost their lichens. Consequently, birds ate the peppered moths resting on the trunks of trees during the day. The black forms, in contrast, had an advantage because they were camouflaged (figure 21.3).

Although Tutt initially had no evidence, British ecologist Bernard Kettlewell tested the hypothesis in the 1950s by releasing equal numbers of dark and light individuals into two sets of woods: one near heavily polluted Birmingham, and the other in unpolluted Dorset. Kettlewell then set up lights in the woods to attract moths to traps to see how many of both kinds of moths survived. To evaluate his results, he had marked the released moths with a dot of paint on the underside of their wings, where birds could not see it.

In the polluted area near Birmingham, Kettlewell recaptured only 19% of the light moths, but 40% of the dark ones. This indicated that dark moths had a far better chance of surviving in these polluted woods, where tree trunks were dark. In the relatively unpolluted Dorset woods, Kettlewell recovered 12.5% of the light moths but only 6% of the dark ones. This result indicated that where the tree trunks were still light-colored, light moths had a much better chance of survival.

Kettlewell later solidified his argument by placing moths on trees and filming birds looking for food. Sometimes the birds actually passed right over a moth that was the same color as its background.

Kettlewell's finding that birds more frequently detect moths whose color does not match their background has subsequently been confirmed in eight separate field studies, with a variety of experimental designs and corrections for deficiencies

**Figure 21.3 Tutt's hypothesis explaining industrial melanism.** These photographs show preserved specimens of the peppered moth *(Biston betularia)* placed on trees. Tutt proposed that the dark melanic variant of the moth is more visible to predators on unpolluted trees *(left)*, while the light "peppered" moth is more visible to predators on bark blackened by industrial pollution *(right)*.

in Kettlewell's initial design. These results, combined with the recapture studies, provide strong evidence for the action of natural selection and implicate birds as the agent of selection in the case of the peppered moth.

## When environmental conditions reverse, so does selection pressure

In industrialized areas throughout Eurasia and North America, dozens of other species of moths have evolved in the same way as the peppered moth. The term **industrial melanism** refers to the phenomenon in which darker individuals come to predominate over lighter ones. In the second half of the 20th century, with the widespread implementation of pollution controls, the trend toward melanism began reversing for many species of moths throughout the northern continents.

In England, the air pollution that promoted industrial melanism began to reverse following enactment of the Clean Air Act in 1956. Beginning in 1959, the *Biston* population at Caldy Common outside Liverpool has been sampled each year. The frequency of the melanic (dark) form has dropped from a high of 93% in 1959 to a low of 15% in 1995 (figure 21.4).

The drop correlates well with a significant drop in air pollution, particularly with a lowering of the levels of sulfur dioxide and suspended particulates, both of which act to darken trees. The drop is consistent with a 15% selective disadvantage acting against moths with the dominant melanic allele.

Interestingly, the same reversal of melanism occurred in the United States. Of 576 peppered moths collected at a field station near Detroit from 1959 to 1961, 515 were melanic, a frequency of 89%. The American Clean Air Act, passed in 1963, led to significant reductions in air pollution. Resampled in 1994, the Detroit field station peppered moth population had only 15% melanic moths (see figure 21.4). The moth populations in Liverpool and Detroit, both part of the same natural experiment, exhibit strong evidence for natural selection.

## The agent of selection may be difficult to pin down

Although the evidence for natural selection in the case of the peppered moth is strong, Tutt's hypothesis about the agent of selection is currently being reevaluated. Researchers have noted that the recent selection against melanism does not appear to correlate with changes in tree lichens.

At Caldy Common, the light form of the peppered moth began to increase in frequency long before lichens began to reappear on the trees. At the Detroit field station, the lichens never changed significantly as the dark moths first became dominant and then declined over a 30-year period. In fact, investigators have not been able to find peppered moths on Detroit trees at all, whether covered with lichens or not. Some evidence suggests the moths rest on leaves in the treetops during the day, but no one is sure. Could poisoning by pollution rather than predation by birds be the agent of natural selection on the moths? Perhaps—but to date, only predation by birds is backed by experimental evidence.

Researchers supporting the bird predation hypothesis point out that a bird's ability to detect moths may depend less on

**Figure 21.4 Selection against melanism.** The red circles indicate the frequency of melanic *Biston betularia* moths at Caldy Common in England, sampled continuously from 1959 to 1995. Green diamonds indicate frequencies of melanic *B. betularia* in Michigan from 1959 to 1962 and from 1994 to 1995.

### Inquiry question

**?** What can you conclude from the fact that the frequency of melanic moths decreased to the same degree in the two locations?

the presence or absence of lichens, and more on other ways in which the environment is darkened by industrial pollution. Pollution tends to cover all objects in the environment with a fine layer of particulate dust, which tends to decrease how much light surfaces reflect. In addition, pollution has a particularly severe effect on birch trees, which are light in color. Both effects would tend to make the environment darker, and thus would favor darker moths by protecting them from predation by birds.

Despite this uncertainty over the agent of selection, the overall pattern is clear. Kettlewell's experiments established indisputably that selection favors dark moths in polluted habitats and light moths in pristine areas. The increase and subsequent decrease in the frequency of melanic moths, correlated with levels of pollution independently on two continents, demonstrates clearly that this selection drives evolutionary change.

The current reconsideration of the agent of natural selection illustrates well the way in which scientific progress is achieved: Hypotheses, such as Tutt's, are put forth and then tested. If rejected, new hypotheses are formulated, and the process begins anew.

### Learning Outcomes Review 21.2

Natural selection has favored the dark form of the peppered moth in areas subject to severe air pollution, perhaps because on darkened trees they are less easily seen by moth-eating birds. As pollution has abated, selection has in turn shifted to favor the light form. Although selection is clearly occurring, further research is required to understand whether predation by birds is the agent of selection.

■ *How would you test the idea that predation by birds is the agent of selection on moth coloration?*

# 21.3 Artificial Selection: Human-Initiated Change

## Learning Outcomes

1. Contrast the processes of artificial and natural selection.
2. Explain what artificial selection demonstrates about the power of natural selection.

Humans have imposed selection upon plants and animals since the dawn of civilization. Just as in natural selection, artificial selection operates by favoring individuals with certain phenotypic traits, allowing them to reproduce and pass their genes on to the next generation. Assuming that phenotypic differences are genetically determined, this directional selection should lead to evolutionary change, and indeed it has.

Artificial selection, imposed in laboratory experiments, agriculture, and the domestication process, has produced substantial change in almost every case in which it has been applied. This success is strong proof that selection is an effective evolutionary process.

## Experimental selection produces changes in populations

With the rise of genetics as a field of science in the 1920s and 1930s, researchers began conducting experiments to test the hypothesis that selection can produce evolutionary change. A favorite subject was the laboratory fruit fly, *Drosophila melanogaster*. Geneticists have imposed selection on just about every conceivable aspect of the fruit fly—including body size, eye color, growth rate, life span, and exploratory behavior—with a consistent result: Selection for a trait leads to strong and predictable evolutionary response.

In one classic experiment, scientists selected for fruit flies with many bristles (stiff, hairlike structures) on their abdomens. At the start of the experiment, the average number of bristles was 9.5. Each generation, scientists picked out the 20% of the population with the greatest number of bristles and allowed them to reproduce, thus establishing the next generation. After 86 generations of this directional selection, the average number of bristles had quadrupled, to nearly 40! In another experiment, fruit flies in one population were selected for high numbers of bristles, while fruit flies in the other cage were selected for low numbers of bristles. Within 35 generations, the populations did not overlap at all in range of variation (figure 21.5).

Similar experiments have been conducted on a wide variety of other laboratory organisms. For example, by selecting for rats that were resistant to tooth decay, in less than 20 generations scientists were able to increase the average time for onset of decay from barely over 100 days to greater than 500 days.

## Agricultural selection has led to extensive modification of crops and livestock

Familiar livestock, such as cattle and pigs, and crops, such as corn and strawberries, are greatly different from their wild an-

**SCIENTIFIC THINKING**

**Question:** *Can artificial selection lead to substantial evolutionary change?*

**Hypothesis:** *Strong directional selection will quickly lead to a large shift in the mean value of the population.*

**Experiment:** *In one population, every generation pick out the 20% of the population with the most bristles and allow them to reproduce to form the next generation. In the other population, do the same with the 20% with the fewest number of bristles.*

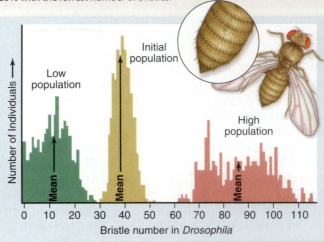

**Result:** *After 35 generations, mean number of bristles has changed substantially in both populations.*

**Interpretation:** *Note that at the end of the experiment, the range of variation lies outside the range seen in the initial population. Selection can move a population beyond its original range because mutation and recombination continuously introduce new variation into populations.*

**Figure 21.5 Artificial selection can lead to rapid and substantial evolutionary change.**

**Inquiry question**

**?** What would happen if, within a population, both small and large individuals were allowed to breed, but middle-sized ones were not?

cestors (figure 21.6). These differences have resulted from generations of human selection for desirable traits, such as greater milk production and larger corn ear size.

An experiment with corn demonstrates the ability of artificial selection to rapidly produce major change in crop plants. In 1896, agricultural scientists began selecting for the oil content of corn kernels, which initially was 4.5%. Just as in the fruit fly experiments, the top 20% of all individuals were allowed to reproduce. By 1986, at which time 90 generations had passed, average oil content of the corn kernels had increased approximately 450%.

## Domesticated breeds have arisen from artificial selection

Human-imposed selection has produced a great variety of breeds of cats, dogs (figure 21.7), pigeons, and other domestic animals. In some cases, breeds have been developed for particular purposes. Greyhound dogs, for example, resulted from

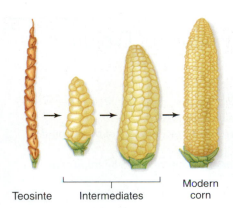

**Figure 21.6 Corn looks very different from its ancestor.** Teosinte, which can be found today in a remote part of Mexico, is very similar to the ancestor of modern corn. Artificial selection has transformed it into the form we know today.

Teosinte    Intermediates    Modern corn

**Figure 21.8 Domesticated foxes.** After 40 years of selectively breeding the tamest individuals, artificial selection has produced silver foxes that are not only as friendly as domestic dogs, but also exhibit many physical traits seen in dog breeds.

selection for maximal running ability, resulting in an animal with long legs, a long tail for balance, an arched back to increase stride length, and great muscle mass. By contrast, the odd proportions of the ungainly dachshund resulted from selection for dogs that could enter narrow holes in pursuit of badgers. In other cases, varieties have been selected primarily for their appearance, such as the many colorful breeds of pigeons or cats.

Domestication also has led to unintentional selection for some traits. In recent years, as part of an attempt to domesticate the silver fox, Russian scientists have chosen the most docile animals in each generation and allowed them to reproduce. Within 40 years, most foxes were exceptionally tame, not only allowing themselves to be petted, but also whimpering to get attention and sniffing and licking their caretakers (figure 21.8). In many respects, they had become no different from domestic dogs.

It was not only their behavior that changed, however. These foxes also began to exhibit other traits seen in some dog breeds, such as different color patterns, floppy ears, curled tails, and shorter legs and tails. Presumably, the genes responsible for docile behavior either affect these traits as well or are closely linked to the genes for these other traits (the phenomena of pleiotropy and linkage, which are discussed in chapters 12 and 13).

### Can selection produce major evolutionary changes?

Given that we can observe the results of selection operating over a relatively short time, most scientists think that natural selection is the process responsible for the evolutionary changes documented in the fossil record. Some critics of evolution accept that selection can lead to changes within a species, but contend that such changes are relatively minor in scope and not equivalent to the substantial changes documented in the fossil record. In other words, it is one thing to change the number of bristles on a fruit fly or the size of an ear of corn, and quite another to produce an entirely new species.

This argument does not fully appreciate the extent of change produced by artificial selection. Consider, for example, the existing breeds of dogs, all of which have been produced since wolves were first domesticated, perhaps 10,000 years ago. If the various dog breeds did not exist and a paleontologist found fossils of animals similar to dachshunds, greyhounds, mastiffs, and chihuahuas, there is no question that they would be considered different species. Indeed, the differences in size and shape exhibited by these breeds are greater than those between members of different genera in the family Canidae—such as coyotes, jackals, foxes, and wolves—which have been evolving separately for 5 to 10 million years. Consequently, the claim that artificial selection produces only minor changes is clearly incorrect. If selection operating over a period of only 10,000 years can produce such substantial differences, it should be powerful enough, over the course of many millions of years, to produce the diversity of life we see around us today.

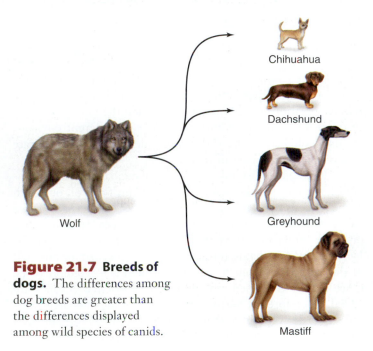

Chihuahua

Dachshund

Greyhound

Wolf

**Figure 21.7 Breeds of dogs.** The differences among dog breeds are greater than the differences displayed among wild species of canids.

Mastiff

### Learning Outcomes Review 21.3

In artificial selection, humans choose which plants or animals to mate in an attempt to conserve desirable traits. Rapid and substantial results can be obtained over a very short time, often in a few generations. From this we can see that natural selection is capable of producing major evolutionary change.

■ *In what circumstances might artificial selection fail to produce a desired change?*

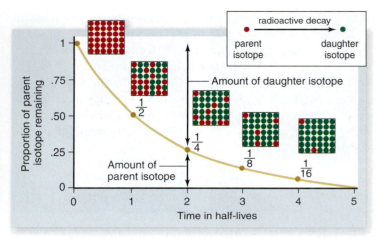

**Figure 21.9 Radioactive decay.** Radioactive elements decay at a known rate, called their half-life. After one half-life, one half of the original amount of parent isotope has transformed into a nonradioactive daughter isotope. After each successive half-life, one half of the remaining amount of parent isotope is transformed.

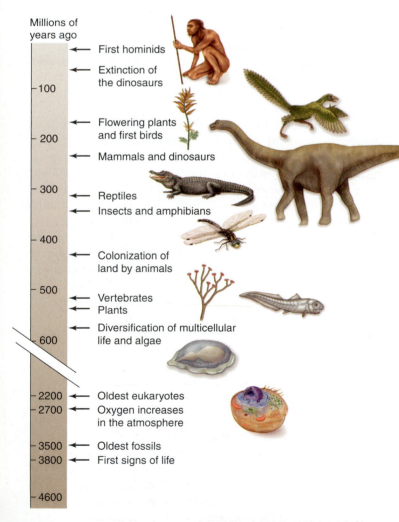

**Figure 21.10 History of evolutionary change as revealed by the fossil record.**

**Learning Outcomes**

1. **Describe how fossils are formed.**
2. **Explain the importance of the discovery of transitional fossils.**
3. **Name the evolutionary trends revealed by study of horse evolution.**

The most direct evidence that evolution has occurred is found in the fossil record. Today we have a far more complete understanding of this record than was available in Darwin's time.

Fossils are the preserved remains of once-living organisms. They include specimens preserved in amber, Siberian permafrost, and dry caves, as well as the more common fossils preserved as rocks.

Rock fossils are created when three events occur. First, the organism must become buried in sediment; then, the calcium in bone or other hard tissue must mineralize; and finally, the surrounding sediment must eventually harden to form rock.

The process of fossilization occurs only rarely. Usually, animal or plant remains decay or are scavenged before the process can begin. In addition, many fossils occur in rocks that are inaccessible to scientists. When they do become available, they are often destroyed by erosion and other natural processes before they can be collected. As a result, only a very small fraction of the species that have ever existed (estimated by some to be as many as 500 million) are known from fossils. Nonetheless, the fossils that have been discovered are sufficient to provide detailed information on the course of evolution through time.

## The age of fossils is estimated by rates of radioactive decay

By dating the rocks in which fossils occur, we can get an accurate idea of how old the fossils are. In Darwin's day, rocks were dated by their position with respect to one another (*relative dating*); rocks in deeper strata are generally older. Knowing the relative positions of sedimentary rocks and the rates of erosion of different kinds of sedimentary rocks in different environments, geologists of the 19th century derived a fairly accurate idea of the relative ages of rocks.

Today, geologists take advantage of radioactive decay to establish the age of rocks (*absolute dating*). Many types of rock, such as the igneous rocks formed when lava cools, contain radioactive elements such as uranium-238. These isotopes transform at a precisely known rate into nonradioactive forms. For example, for $U^{238}$ the *half-life* (that is, the amount of time needed for one-half of the original amount to be transformed) is 4.5 billion years. Once a rock is formed, no additional radioactive isotopes are added. Therefore, by measuring the ratio of the radioactive isotope to its derivative, "daughter" isotope (figure 21.9), geologists can determine the age of the rock. If a fossil is found between two layers of rock, each of which can be dated, then the age at which the fossil formed can be determined.

## Fossils present a history of evolutionary change

When fossils are arrayed according to their age (figure 21.10), from oldest to youngest, they often provide evidence of successive evolutionary change. At the largest scale, the fossil record documents the course of life through time, from the origin of first prokaryotic and then eukaryotic organisms, through the evolution of fishes, the rise of land-dwelling organisms, the reign of the dinosaurs, and on to the origin of humans. In addition, the fossil record shows the waxing and waning of biological diversity through time, such as the periodic mass extinctions that have reduced the number of living species.

## Fossils document evolutionary transition

Given the low likelihood of fossil preservation and recovery, it is not surprising that there are gaps in the fossil record. Nonetheless, intermediate forms are often available to illustrate how the major transitions in life occurred.

Undoubtedly the most famous of these is the oldest known bird, *Archaeopteryx* (meaning "ancient feather") which lived around 165 million years ago (figure 21.11). This specimen is clearly intermediate between birds and dinosaurs. Its feathers, similar in many respects to those of birds today, clearly reveal that it is a bird. Nonetheless, in many other respects—for example, possession of teeth, a bony tail, and other anatomical characteristics—it is indistinguishable from some carnivorous dinosaurs. Indeed, it is so similar to these dinosaurs that several specimens lacking preserved feathers were misidentified as dinosaurs and lay in the wrong natural history museum cabinet for several decades before the mistake was discovered!

*Archaeopteryx* reveals a pattern commonly seen in intermediate fossils—rather than being intermediate in every trait, such fossils usually exhibit some traits like their ancestors and others like their descendants. In other words, traits evolve at different rates and different times; expecting an intermediate form to be intermediate in every trait would not be correct.

The first *Archaeopteryx* fossil was discovered in 1859, the year Darwin published *On the Origin of Species*. Since then, paleontologists have continued to fill in the gaps in the fossil record. Today, the fossil record is far more complete, particularly among the vertebrates; fossils have been found linking all the major groups.

Recent years have seen spectacular discoveries, closing some of the major remaining gaps in our understanding of vertebrate evolution. For example, a four-legged aquatic mammal was discovered only recently that provides important insights concerning the evolution of whales and dolphins from land-dwelling, hoofed ancestors (figure 21.12). Similarly, a fossil snake with legs has shed light on the evolution of snakes, which are descended from lizards that gradually

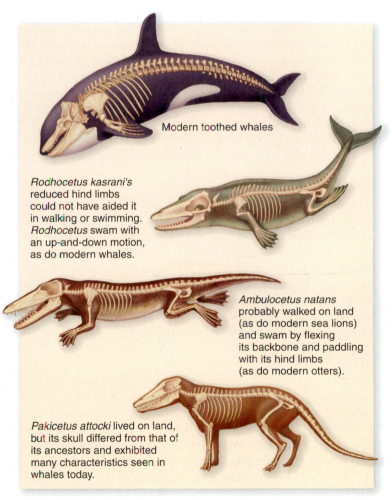

Modern toothed whales

*Rodhocetus kasrani's* reduced hind limbs could not have aided it in walking or swimming. *Rodhocetus* swam with an up-and-down motion, as do modern whales.

*Ambulocetus natans* probably walked on land (as do modern sea lions) and swam by flexing its backbone and paddling with its hind limbs (as do modern otters).

*Pakicetus attocki* lived on land, but its skull differed from that of its ancestors and exhibited many characteristics seen in whales today.

**Figure 21.12 Whale "missing links."** The recent discoveries of *Ambulocetus*, *Rodhocetus*, and *Pakicetus* have filled in the gaps between whales and their hoofed mammal ancestors. The features of *Pakicetus* illustrate that intermediate forms are not intermediate in all characteristics; rather, some traits evolve before others. In the case of the evolution of whales, changes occurred in the skull prior to evolutionary modification of the limbs. All three fossil forms occurred in the Eocene period, 45–55 MYA.

**Figure 21.11 Fossil of *Archaeopteryx*, the first bird.** The remarkable preservation of this specimen reveals soft parts usually not preserved in fossils; the presence of feathers makes clear that *Archaeopteryx* was a bird, despite the presence of many dinosaurian traits.

became more and more elongated with the simultaneous reduction and eventual disappearance of the limbs. In chapter 35, we discuss the most recent such discovery, *Tiktaalik*, a species that bridged the gap between fish and the first amphibians.

On a finer scale, evolutionary change within some types of animals is known in exceptional detail. For example, about 200 million years ago (MYA), oysters underwent a change from small, curved shells to larger, flatter ones, with progressively flatter fossils seen in the fossil record over a period of 12 million years. A host of other examples illustrate similar records of successive change. The demonstration of this successive change is one of the strongest lines of evidence that evolution has occurred.

## The evolution of horses is a prime example of evidence from fossils

One of the most studied cases in the fossil record concerns the evolution of horses. Modern-day members of the family Equidae include horses, zebras, donkeys, and asses, all of which are large, long-legged, fast-running animals adapted to living on open grasslands. These species, all classified in the genus *Equus*, are the last living descendants of a long lineage that has produced 34 genera since its origin in the Eocene period, approximately 55 MYA. Examination of these fossils has provided a particularly well-documented case of how evolution has proceeded through adaptation to changing environments.

### The first horse

The earliest known members of the horse family, species in the genus *Hyracotherium*, didn't look much like modern-day horses at all. Small, with short legs and broad feet, these species occurred in wooded habitats, where they probably browsed on leaves and herbs and escaped predators by dodging through openings in the forest vegetation. The evolutionary path from these diminutive creatures to the workhorses of today has involved changes in a variety of traits, including size, toe reduction, and tooth size and shape (figure 21.13).

### Changes in size

The first species of horses were as big as a large house cat or a medium-sized dog. By contrast, modern equids can weigh more than 500 kg. Examination of the fossil record reveals that horses changed little in size for their first 30 million years, but since then, a number of different lineages have exhibited rapid and substantial increases. However, trends toward decreased size were also exhibited in some branches of the equid evolutionary tree.

### Toe reduction

The feet of modern horses have a single toe enclosed in a tough, bony hoof. By contrast, *Hyracotherium* had four toes on its front feet and three on its hind feet. Rather than hooves, these toes were encased in fleshy pads like those of dogs and cats.

Examination of fossils clearly shows the transition through time: a general increase in length of the central toe, develop-

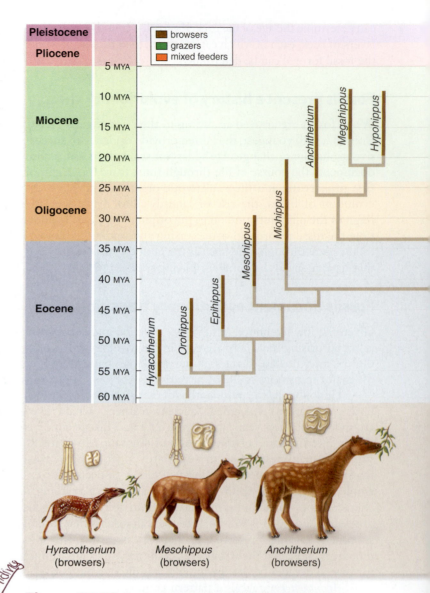

Hyracotherium (browsers)    Mesohippus (browsers)    Anchitherium (browsers)

**Figure 21.13 Evolutionary change in body size of horses.** Lines indicate evolutionary relationships of the horse family. Horse evolution is more like a bush than a single-trunk tree; diversity was much greater in the past than it is today. In general, there has been a trend toward larger size, more complex molar teeth, and fewer toes, but this trend has exceptions. For example, a relatively recent form, *Nannippus*, evolved in the opposite direction, toward decreased size.

### Inquiry question

? Why might the evolutionary line leading to *Nannippus* have experienced an evolutionary decrease in body size?

ment of the bony hoof, and reduction and loss of the other toes (see figure 21.13). As with body size, these trends occurred concurrently on several different branches of the horse evolutionary tree and were not exhibited by all lineages.

At the same time as toe reduction was occurring, these horse lineages were evolving changes in the length and skeletal structure of their limbs, leading to animals capable of running long distances at high speeds.

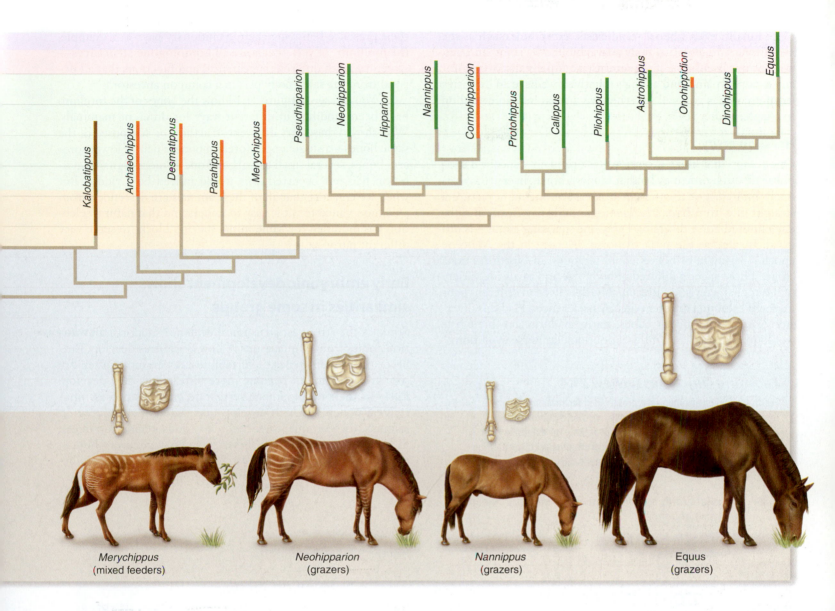

*Merychippus*
(mixed feeders)

*Neohipparion*
(grazers)

*Nannippus*
(grazers)

*Equus*
(grazers)

### Tooth size and shape

The teeth of *Hyracotherium* were small and relatively simple in shape. Through time, horse teeth have increased greatly in length and have developed a complex pattern of ridges on their molars and premolars. The effect of these changes is to produce teeth better capable of chewing tough and gritty vegetation, such as grass, which tends to wear teeth down.

Accompanying these changes have been alterations in the shape of the skull that strengthened the skull to withstand the stresses imposed by continual chewing. As with body size, evolutionary change has not been constant through time. Rather, much of the change in tooth shape has occurred within the past 20 million years, and changes have not been constant among all horse lineages.

All of these changes may be understood as adaptations to changing global climates. In particular, during the late Miocene and early Oligocene epochs (approximately 20 to 25 mya), grasslands became widespread in North America, where much of horse evolution occurred. As horses adapted to these habitats, high-speed locomotion probably became more important to escape predators. By contrast, the greater flexibility provided by multiple toes and shorter limbs, which was advantageous for ducking through complex forest vegetation, was no longer beneficial. At the same time, horses were eating grasses and other vegetation that contained more grit and other hard substances, thus favoring teeth and skulls better suited for withstanding such materials.

### Evolutionary trends

For many years, horse evolution was held up as an example of constant evolutionary change through time. Some even saw in the record of horse evolution evidence for a progressive, guiding force, consistently pushing evolution in a single direction. We now know that such views are misguided, and that the course of evolutionary change over millions of years is rarely so simple.

Rather, the fossils demonstrate that even though overall trends have been evident in a variety of characteristics, evolutionary change has been far from constant and uniform through time. Instead, rates of evolution have varied widely, with long periods of little observable change and some periods of great change. Moreover, when changes happen, they often occur simultaneously in different lineages of the horse evolutionary tree.

Finally, even when a trend exists, exceptions, such as the evolutionary decrease in body size exhibited by some lineages, are not uncommon. These patterns are usually discovered for any group of plants and animals for which we have an extensive fossil record, as you will see when we discuss human evolution in chapter 35.

### Horse diversity

One reason that horse evolution was originally conceived of as linear through time may be that modern horse diversity is relatively limited. For this reason it is easy to mentally picture a straight line from *Hyracotherium* to modern-day *Equus*. But today's limited horse diversity—only one surviving genus—is unusual. In fact, at the peak of horse diversity in the Miocene epoch, 13 genera of horses could be found in North America alone. These species differed in body size and in a wide variety of other characteristics. Presumably, they lived in different habitats and exhibited different dietary preferences. Had this diversity existed to modern times, early evolutionary biologists would likely have had a different outlook on horse evolution.

#### Learning Outcomes Review 21.4

Fossils form when an organism is preserved in a matrix such as amber, permafrost, or rock. They can be used to construct a record of major evolutionary transitions over long periods of time. The extensive fossil record for horses provides a detailed view of evolutionary diversification of this group, although trends are not constant and uniform and may include exceptions.

■ *Why might rates and direction of evolutionary change vary through time?*

## 21.5 Anatomical Evidence for Evolution

#### Learning Outcomes

1. *Explain the evolutionary significance of homologous and vestigial structures.*
2. *Describe how patterns of early development provide evidence for evolution.*

Much of the power of the theory of evolution is its ability to provide a sensible framework for understanding the diversity of life. Many observations from throughout biology simply cannot be understood in any meaningful way except as a result of evolution.

### Homologous structures suggest common derivation

As vertebrates have evolved, the same bones have sometimes been put to different uses. Yet the bones are still recognizable, their presence betraying their evolutionary past. For example, the forelimbs of vertebrates are all **homologous structures**—structures with different appearances and functions that all derived from the same body part in a common ancestor.

You can see in figure 21.14 how the bones of the forelimb have been modified in different ways for different mammals. Why should these very different structures be composed of the same bones—a single upper forearm bone, a pair of lower forearm bones, several small carpals, and one or more digits? If evolution had not occurred, this would indeed be a riddle. But when we consider that all of these animals are descended from a common ancestor, it is easy to understand that natural selection has modified the same initial starting blocks to serve very different purposes.

### Early embryonic development shows similarities in some groups

Some of the strongest anatomical evidence supporting evolution comes from comparisons of how organisms develop. Embryos of different types of vertebrates, for example, often are similar early on, but become more different as they develop. Early in their development vertebrate embryos possess pharyngeal pouches, which develop into different structures. In humans, for example, they become various glands and ducts; in fish, they turn into gill slits. At a later stage, every human embryo has a long tail, the vestige of which we carry to adulthood as the coccyx at the end of our spine. Human fetuses

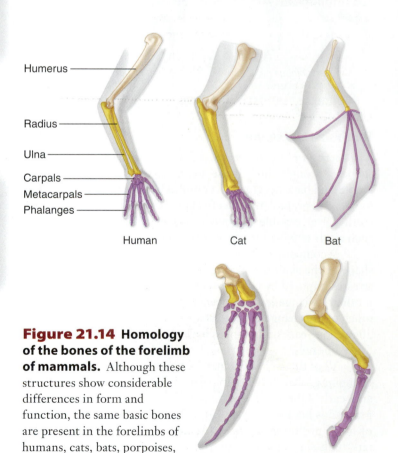

**Figure 21.14 Homology of the bones of the forelimb of mammals.** Although these structures show considerable differences in form and function, the same basic bones are present in the forelimbs of humans, cats, bats, porpoises, and horses.

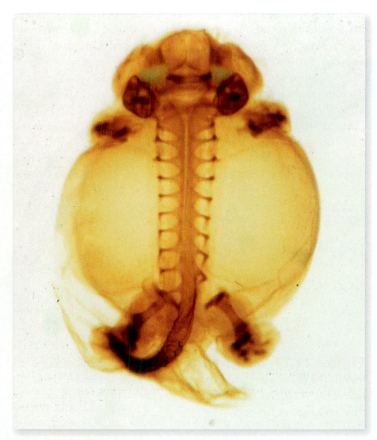

**Figure 21.15 Developmental features reflect evolutionary ancestry.** Some species of frogs have lost the tadpole stage. Nonetheless, tadpole features first appear and then disappear during development in the egg.

even possess a fine fur (called *lanugo*) during the fifth month of development.

Similarly, although most frogs go through a tadpole stage, some species develop directly and hatch out as little, fully-formed frogs. However, the embryos of these species still ex-

hibit tadpole features, such as the presence of a tail, which disappear before the froglet hatches (figure 21.15).

These relict developmental forms suggest strongly that our development has evolved, with new instructions modifying ancestral developmental patterns. We will return to the topic of embryonic development and evolution in chapter 25.

## Some structures are imperfectly suited to their use

Because natural selection can only work on the variation present in a population, it should not be surprising that some organisms do not appear perfectly adapted to their environments. For example, most animals with long necks have many neck vertebrae for enhanced flexibility: Geese have up to 25, and plesiosaurs, the long-necked reptiles that patrolled the seas during the age of dinosaurs, had as many as 76. By contrast, almost all mammals have only 7 neck vertebrae, even the giraffe. In the absence of variation in vertebrae number, selection led to an evolutionary increase in vertebra size to produce the long neck of the giraffe.

An excellent example of an imperfect design is the eye of vertebrate animals, in which the photoreceptors face backward, toward the wall of the eye (figure 21.16*a*). As a result, the nerve fibers extend not backward, toward the brain, but forward into the eye chamber, where they slightly obstruct light. Moreover, these fibers bundle together to form the optic nerve, which exits through a hole at the back of the eye, creating a blind spot.

By contrast, the eye of mollusks—such as squid and octopuses—are more optimally designed: The photoreceptors face forward, and the nerve fibers exit at the back, neither obstructing light nor creating a blind spot (figure 21.16*b*).

Such examples illustrate that natural selection is like a tinkerer, working with whatever material is available to craft a workable solution, rather than like an engineer, who can design

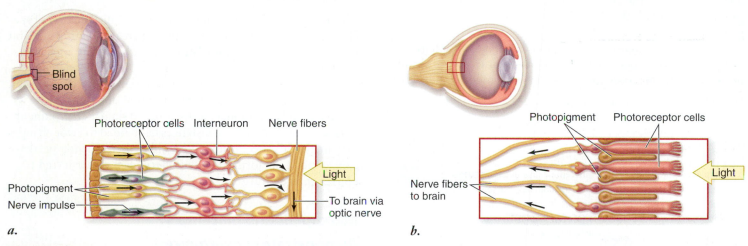

*a.*                    *b.*

**Figure 21.16 The eyes of vertebrates and mollusks.** *a*. Photoreceptors of vertebrates point backward, whereas (*b*) those of mollusks face forward. As a result, vertebrate nerve fibers pass in front of the photoreceptor; and where they bundle together and exit the eye, a blind spot is created. Mollusks' eyes have neither of these problems.

and build the best possible structure for a given task. Workable, but imperfect, structures such as the vertebrate eye are an expected outcome of evolution by natural selection.

## Vestigial structures can be explained as holdovers from the past

Many organisms possess **vestigial structures** that have no apparent function, but resemble structures their ancestors possessed. Humans, for example, possess a complete set of muscles for wiggling their ears, just like many other mammals do. Although these muscles allow other mammals to move their ears to pinpoint sounds such as the movements or growl of a predator, they have little purpose in humans other than amusement.

As other examples, boa constrictors have hip bones and rudimentary hind legs. Manatees (a type of aquatic mammal often referred to as "sea cows") have fingernails on their fins, which evolved from legs. Blind cave fish, which never see the light of day, have small, nonfunctional eyes. Figure 21.17 illustrates the skeleton of a baleen whale, which contains pelvic bones, as other mammal skeletons do, even though such bones serve no known function in the whale.

The human vermiform appendix is apparently vestigial; it represents the degenerate terminal part of the cecum, the blind pouch or sac in which the large intestine begins. In other mammals, such as mice, the cecum is the largest part of the large intestine and functions in storage—usually of bulk cellulose in herbivores. Although some functions have been suggested, it is difficult to assign any current function to the human vermiform appendix. In many respects, it can be a dangerous organ: appendicitis, which results from infection of the appendix, can be fatal.

It is difficult to understand vestigial structures such as these as anything other than evolutionary relicts, holdovers from the past. However, the existence of vestigial structures argues strongly for the common ancestry of the members of the groups that share them, regardless of how different those groups have subsequently become.

All of these anatomical lines of evidence—homology, development, and imperfect and vestigial structures—are readily understandable as a result of descent with modification, that is, evolution.

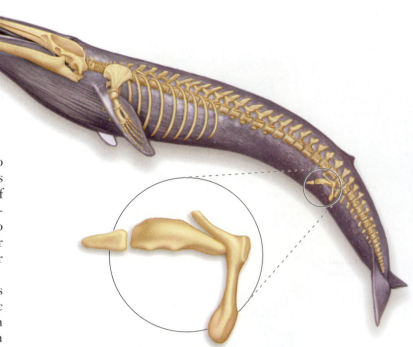

**Figure 21.17 Vestigial structures.** The skeleton of a whale reveals the presence of pelvic bones. These bones resemble those of other mammals, but are only weakly developed in the whale and have no apparent function.

## 21.6 Convergent Evolution and the Biogeographical Record

### Learning Outcomes

1. Explain the principle of convergent evolution.
2. Demonstrate how the biogeographical distribution of plant and animal species on islands provides evidence of evolutionary diversification.

**Biogeography,** the study of the geographic distribution of species, reveals that different geographical areas sometimes exhibit groups of plants and animals of strikingly similar appearance, even though the organisms may be only distantly related.

It is difficult to explain so many similarities as the result of coincidence. Instead, natural selection appears to have favored parallel evolutionary adaptations in similar environments. Because selection in these instances has tended to favor changes that made the two groups more alike, their phenotypes have converged. This form of evolutionary change is referred to as **convergent evolution.**

### Marsupials and placentals demonstrate convergence

In the best known case of convergent evolution, two major groups of mammals—marsupials and placentals—have evolved in very similar ways in different parts of the world. Marsupials

### Learning Outcomes Review 21.5

Comparisons of the anatomy of different living animals often reveal evidence of shared ancestry. In cases of homology, the same organ has evolved to carry out different functions. In other cases, an organ is still present, usually in diminished form, even though it has lost its function altogether; such an organ or structure is termed vestigial.

- *How might homologous and vestigial structures be explained other than as a result of evolutionary descent with modification?*

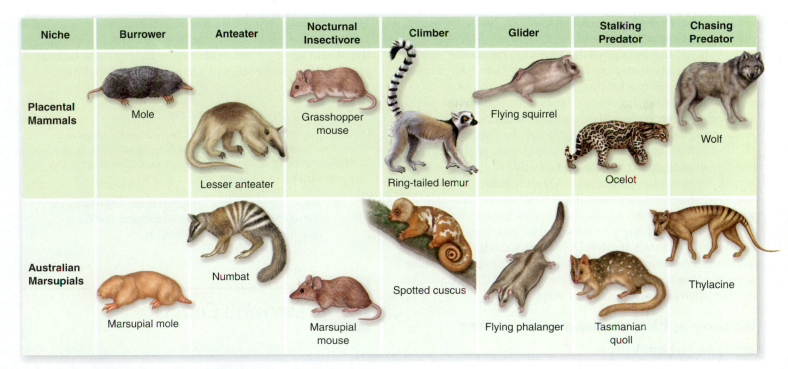

| Niche | Burrower | Anteater | Nocturnal Insectivore | Climber | Glider | Stalking Predator | Chasing Predator |
|---|---|---|---|---|---|---|---|
| Placental Mammals | Mole | Lesser anteater | Grasshopper mouse | Ring-tailed lemur | Flying squirrel | Ocelot | Wolf |
| Australian Marsupials | Marsupial mole | Numbat | Marsupial mouse | Spotted cuscus | Flying phalanger | Tasmanian quoll | Thylacine |

**Figure 21.18 Convergent evolution.** Many marsupial species in Australia resemble placental mammals occupying similar ecological niches elsewhere in the rest of the world. Marsupials evolved in isolation after Australia separated from other continents.

are a group in which the young are born in a very immature condition and held in a pouch until they are ready to emerge into the outside world. In placentals, by contrast, offspring are not born until they can safely survive in the external environment (with varying degrees of parental care).

Australia separated from the other continents more than 70 million years ago; at that time, both marsupials and placental mammals had evolved, but in different places. In particular, only marsupials occurred in Australia. As a result of this continental separation, the only placental mammals in Australia today are bats and a few colonizing rodents (which arrived relatively recently), and Australia is dominated by marsupials.

What are the Australian marsupials like? To an astonishing degree, they resemble the placental mammals living today on the other continents (figure 21.18). The similarity between some individual members of these two sets of mammals argues strongly that they are the result of convergent evolution, similar forms having evolved in different, isolated areas because of similar selective pressures in similar environments.

## Convergent evolution is a widespread phenomenon

When species interact with the environment in similar ways, they often are exposed to similar selective pressures, and they therefore frequently develop the same evolutionary adaptations. Consider, for example, fast-moving marine predators (figure 21.19). The hydrodynamics of moving through water require a streamlined body shape to minimize friction. It is no coincidence that dolphins, sharks, and tuna—among the fastest of marine species—have all evolved to have the same basic shape. We can infer as well that ichthyosaurs—marine reptiles that lived during the Age of the Dinosaurs—exhibited a similar lifestyle.

Island trees exhibit a similar phenomenon. Most islands are covered by trees (or were until the arrival of humans). Careful inspection of these trees, however, reveals that they are not closely related to the trees with which we are familiar. Although they have all the characteristics of trees, such as being tall and having a tough outer covering, in many cases island trees are members of plant families that elsewhere exist only as flowers,

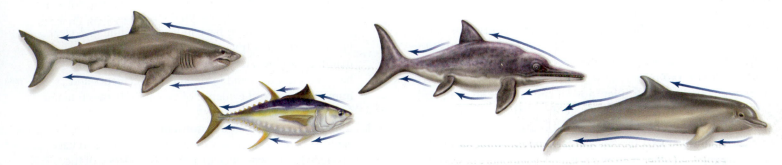

**Figure 21.19 Convergence among fast-swimming predators.** Fast movement through water requires a streamlined body form, which has evolved numerous times.

chapter **21** *The Evidence for Evolution*

shrubs, or other small bushes. For example, on many islands, the native trees are members of the sunflower family.

Why do these plants evolve into trees on islands? Probably because seeds from trees rarely make it to isolated islands. As a result, those species that do manage to colonize distant islands face an empty ecological landscape upon arrival. In the absence of other treelike plants, natural selection often would favor individual plants that could capture the most sunlight for photosynthesis, and the result is the evolution of similar treelike forms on islands throughout the world.

Convergent evolution is even seen in humans. People in most populations stop producing lactase, the enzyme that digests milk, some time in childhood. However, individuals in African and European populations that raise cattle produce lactase throughout their lives. DNA analysis indicates that this has been accomplished by the incorporation of different mutations in Africa and Europe, which indicates that the populations have independently acquired this adaptation.

## Biogeographical studies provide further evidence of evolution

Darwin made several important observations during his voyage around the world. He noted that islands often are missing plants and animals common on continents, such as frogs and land mammals. Accidental human introductions have proved that these species can survive if they are released on islands, so lack of suitable habitat is not the cause. In addition, those species that are present on islands often have diverged from their continental relatives and sometimes—as with Darwin's finches and the island trees just discussed—occupy ecological niches used by other species on continents. Lastly, island species usually are more closely related to species on nearby continents, even though the environment there is often not very similar to that on island.

Darwin deduced the explanation for these phenomena. Many islands have never been connected to continental areas. The species that occur there arrived by dispersing across the water; dispersal from nearby areas is more likely than from more distant sources, though long-distance colonization does occur occasionally. Some species, those that can fly, float, or swim are more likely to get to the island than others. Some, like frogs, are particularly vulnerable to dehydration in saltwater and have almost no chance of island colonization.

The absence of some types of plants and animals provides opportunity to those that do arrive; as a result, colonizers often evolve into many species exhibiting great ecological and morphological diversity.

Geographic proximity is not always a good predictor of evolutionary relationships, however. Earth's continents have not always been where they are today; rather, continents are constantly moving because of the process known as *continental drift*. Although the pace is slow, on the order of several centimeters per year, the configuration of the continents can, and has, changed considerably over geologic time. As a result, closely related species that at one time occurred near each other may now be separated by thousands of miles. Many examples occur on the southern continents, which were last united as the supercontinent Gondwana more than 100 million years ago.

One such example is the southern beech tree, which is found in Chile, and also in Australia and New Zealand. In cases such as this, Earth's history and evolutionary history must be considered jointly to make sense of geographical distributions.

### Learning Outcomes Review 21.6

Convergence is the evolution of similar forms in different lineages when exposed to similar selective pressures. The biogeographical distribution of species often reflects the outcome of evolutionary diversification with closely related species in nearby areas.

■ *Why does convergent evolution occur and why might species occupying similar environments in different localities sometimes not exhibit it?*

## 21.7 Darwin's Critics

### Learning Outcomes

1. *Characterize the criticisms of evolutionary theory and list counterarguments that can be made.*
2. *Distinguish between hypothesis and theory in scientific usage.*

In the century and a half since he proposed it, Darwin's theory of evolution by natural selection has become nearly universally accepted by biologists, but has been a source of controversy among some members of the general public. Here we discuss seven principle objections that critics raise to the teaching of evolution as biological fact, along with some answers that scientists present in response.

1. **Evolution is not solidly demonstrated.** "Evolution is just a theory," Darwin's critics point out, as though *theory* meant a lack of knowledge, or some kind of guess.

   Scientists, however, use the word *theory* in a very different sense than the general public does. Theories are the solid ground of science—that about which we are most certain. Few of us doubt the theory of gravity because it is "just a theory."

2. **There are no fossil intermediates.** "No one ever saw a fin on the way to becoming a leg," critics claim, pointing to the many gaps in the fossil record in Darwin's day.

   Since that time, however, many fossil intermediates in vertebrate evolution have indeed been found. A clear line of fossils now traces the transition between hoofed mammals and whales, between reptiles and mammals, between dinosaurs and birds, and between apes and humans. The fossil evidence of evolution between major forms is compelling.

3. **The intelligent design argument.** "The organs of living creatures are too complex for a random process to have produced—the existence of a clock is evidence of the existence of a clockmaker."

Evolution by natural selection is not a random process. Quite the contrary, by favoring those variations that lead to the highest reproductive fitness, natural selection is a nonrandom process that can construct highly complex organs by incrementally improving them from one generation to the next.

For example, the intermediates in the evolution of the mammalian ear can be seen in fossils, and many intermediate "eyes" are known in various invertebrates. These intermediate forms arose because they have value—being able to detect light slightly is better than not being able to detect it at all. Complex structures such as eyes evolved as a progression of slight improvements. Moreover, inefficiencies of certain designs, such as the vertebrate eye and the existence of vestigial structures, do not support the idea of an intelligent designer.

4. **Evolution violates the Second Law of Thermodynamics.** "A jumble of soda cans doesn't by itself jump neatly into a stack—things become more disorganized due to random events, not more organized."

Biologists point out that this argument ignores what the second law really says: Disorder increases in a closed system, which the Earth most certainly is not. Energy continually enters the biosphere from the Sun, fueling life and all the processes that organize it.

5. **Proteins are too improbable.** "Hemoglobin has 141 amino acids. The probability that the first one would be leucine is 1/20, and that all 141 would be the ones they are by chance is $(1/20)^{141}$, an impossibly rare event."

This argument illustrates a lack of understanding of probability and statistics—probability cannot be used to argue backwards. The probability that a student in a classroom has a particular birthdate is 1/365; arguing this way, the probability that everyone in a class of 50 would have the birthdates that they do is $(1/365)^{50}$, and yet there the class sits, all with their actual birthdates.

6. **Natural selection does not imply evolution.** "No scientist has come up with an experiment in which fish evolve into frogs and leap away from predators."

Can we extrapolate from our understanding that natural selection produces relatively small changes that are observable in populations *within* species to explain the major differences observed *between* species? Most biologists who have studied the problem think so. The differences between breeds produced by artificial selection—such as chihuahuas, mastiffs, and greyhounds—are more distinctive than the differences between some wild species, and laboratory selection experiments sometimes create forms that cannot interbreed and thus would in nature be considered different species. Thus, production of radically different forms has indeed been observed, repeatedly. To object that evolution still does not explain really major differences, such as those between fish and amphibians, simply takes us back to point number 2. These changes take millions of years, and they are seen clearly in the fossil record.

7. **The irreducible complexity argument.** Because each part of a complex cellular mechanism such as blood clotting is essential to the overall process, the intricate machinery of the cell cannot be explained by evolution from simpler stages.

What's wrong with this argument is that each part of a complex molecular machine evolves as part of the whole system. Natural selection can act on a complex system because at every stage of its evolution, the system functions. Parts that improved function are added. Subsequently, other parts may be modified or even lost, so that parts that were not essential when they first evolved become essential. In this way, an "irreducible complex" structure can evolve by natural selection. The same process works at the molecular level.

For example, snake venom initially evolved as enzymes to increase the ability of snakes to digest large prey items, which were captured by biting the prey and then constricting them with coils. Subsequently, the digestive enzymes evolved to become increasingly lethal. Rattlesnakes kill large prey by injecting them with venom, letting them go, and then tracking them down and eating them after they die. To do so, they have evolved extremely toxic venom, highly modified syringelike front teeth, and many other characteristics. Take away the fangs or the venom and the rattlesnakes can't feed—what initially evolved as nonessential parts are now indispensable; irreducible complexity has evolved by natural selection.

The mammalian blood clotting system similarly has evolved from much simpler systems. The core clotting system evolved at the dawn of the vertebrates more than 500 million years ago, and it is found today in primitive fishes such as lampreys. One hundred million years later, as vertebrates continued to evolve, proteins were added to the clotting system, making it sensitive to substances released from damaged tissues. Fifty million years later, a third component was added, triggering clotting by contact with the jagged surfaces produced by injury. At each stage, as the clotting system evolved to become more complex, its overall performance came to depend on the added elements. Thus, blood clotting has become "irreducibly complex" as the result of Darwinian evolution.

Statements that various structures could not have been built by natural selection have repeatedly been made over the past 150 years. In many cases, after detailed scientific study, the likely path by which such structures have evolved has been discovered.

---

### Learning Outcomes Review 21.7

Darwin's theory of evolution is controversial to some in the general public. Objections are often based on a misunderstanding of the theory. In scientific usage, a hypothesis is an educated guess, whereas a theory is an explanation that fits available evidence and has withstood rigorous testing.

■ *Suppose someone suggests that humans originally came from Mars. Would this be a hypothesis or a theory, and how could it be tested?*

# Chapter Review

## 21.1 The Beaks of Darwin's Finches: Evidence of Natural Selection

### Galápagos finches exhibit variation related to food gathering.

The correspondence between beak shape and its use in obtaining food suggested to Darwin that finch species had diversified and adapted to eat different foods.

### Modern research has verified Darwin's selection hypothesis.

Natural selection acts on variation in beak morphology, favoring larger-beaked birds during extended droughts and smaller-beaked birds during long periods of heavy rains.

Because this variation is heritable, evolutionary change occurs in the frequencies of beak sizes in subsequent generations.

## 21.2 Peppered Moths and Industrial Melanism: More Evidence of Selection

### Light-colored moths decreased in polluted areas.

In polluted areas where soot built up on tree trunks, the dark-colored form of the peppered moth became more common. In unpolluted areas, light-colored forms remained predominant.

Experiments suggested that predation by birds was the cause; light-colored moths stand out on dark trunks, and vice-versa.

### When environmental conditions reverse, so does selection pressure.

In the last 40 years, pollution has decreased in many areas and the frequency of light-colored moths has rebounded.

### The agent of selection may be difficult to pin down.

Recent research has questioned whether bird predation is the agent of selection. Regardless, the observation that the dark-colored form has increased during times of pollution and then declined as pollution abates indicates that natural selection has acted on moth coloration.

## 21.3 Artificial Selection: Human-Initiated Change
(see figure 21.5)

### Experimental selection produces changes in populations.

Laboratory experiments in directional selection have shown that substantial evolutionary change can occur in these controlled populations.

### Agricultural selection has led to extensive modification of crops and livestock.

### Domesticated breeds have arisen from artificial selection.

Crop plants and domesticated animal breeds are often substantially different from their wild ancestors.

If artificial selection can rapidly create substantial change, then it is reasonable to assume that natural selection could have created the Earth's diversity of life over millions of years.

## 21.4 Fossil Evidence of Evolution

### The age of fossils is estimated by rates of radioactive decay.

Specimens become fossilized in different ways. Fossils in rock can be dated by calculating the extent of radioactive decay based on half-lives of known isotopes.

### Fossils present a history of evolutionary change.

### Fossils document evolutionary transition.

The history of life on Earth can be traced through the fossil record. In recent years, new fossil discoveries have provided more detailed understanding of major evolutionary transitions.

### The evolution of horses is a prime example of evidence from fossils.

The fossil record indicates that horses have evolved from small, forest-dwelling animals to the large and fast plains-dwelling species alive today.

Over the course of 50 million years, evolution has not been constant and uniform. Rather, change has been rapid at some times, slow at others. Although a general trend toward increase in size is evident, some species evolved to smaller sizes.

## 21.5 Anatomical Evidence for Evolution

### Homologous structures suggest common derivation.

Homologous structures may have different appearances and functions even though derived from the same common ancestral body part.

### Early embryonic development shows similarities in some groups.

Embryonic development shows similarity in developmental patterns among species whose adult phenotypes are very different.

Species that have lost a feature that was present in an ancestral form often develop and then lose that feature during embryological development.

### Some structures are imperfectly suited to their use.

Natural selection can influence only the variation present in a population; because of this, evolution often results in workable, but imperfect structures, such as the vertebrate eye.

### Vestigial structures can be explained as holdovers from the past.

The existence of vestigial structures supports the concept of common ancestry among organisms that share them.

## 21.6 Convergent Evolution and the Biogeographical Record

### Marsupials and placentals demonstrate convergence.

Convergent evolution may occur in species or populations exposed to similar selective pressures. Marsupial mammals in Australia have converged upon features of their placental counterparts elsewhere.

### Convergent evolution is a widespread phenomenon.

Examples include hydrodynamic streamlining in marine species and the evolution of tree species on islands from ancestral forms that were not treelike.

### Biogeographical studies provide further evidence of evolution.

Island species usually are closely related to species on nearby continents even if the environments are different. Early island colonizers often evolve into diverse species because other, competing species are scarce.

## 21.7 Darwin's Critics

Darwin's theory of evolution by natural selection is almost universally accepted by biologists. Many criticisms have been made both historically and recently, but most stem from a lack of understanding of scientific principles, the theory's actual content, or the time spans involved in evolution.

## Review Questions

### UNDERSTAND

1. Artificial selection is different from natural selection because
   a. artificial selection is not capable of producing large changes.
   b. artificial selection does not require genetic variation.
   c. natural selection cannot produce new species.
   d. breeders (people) choose which individuals reproduce based on desirability of traits.

2. Gaps in the fossil record
   a. demonstrate our inability to date geological sediments.
   b. are expected since the probability that any organism will fossilize is extremely low.
   c. have not been filled in as new fossils have been discovered.
   d. weaken the theory of evolution.

3. The evolution of modern horses (*Equus*) is best described as
   a. the constant change and replacement of one species by another over time.
   b. a complex history of lineages that changed over time, with many going extinct.
   c. a simple history of lineages that have always resembled extant horses.
   d. none of these.

4. Homologous structures
   a. are structures in two or more species that originate as the same structure in a common ancestor.
   b. are structures that look the same in different species.
   c. cannot serve different functions in different species.
   d. must serve different functions in different species.

5. Convergent evolution
   a. is an example of stabilizing selection.
   b. depends on natural selection to independently produce similar phenotypic responses in different species or populations.
   c. occurs only on islands.
   d. is expected when different lineages are exposed to vastly different selective environments.

6. Darwin's finches are a noteworthy case study of evolution by natural selection because evidence suggests
   a. they are descendants of many different species that colonized the Galápagos.
   b. they radiated from a single species that colonized the Galápagos.
   c. they are more closely related to mainland species than to one another.
   d. none of the above.

7. The possession of fine fur in 5-month human embryos indicates
   a. that the womb is cold at that point in pregnancy.
   b. humans evolved from a hairy ancestor.
   c. hair is a defining feature of mammals.
   d. some parts of the embryo grow faster than others.

### APPLY

1. In Darwin's finches,
   a. occurrence of wet and dry years preserves genetic variation for beak size.
   b. increasing beak size over time proves that beak size is inherited.
   c. large beak size is always favored.
   d. all of the above.

2. Artificial selection experiments in the laboratory such as in figure 21.5 are an example of
   a. stabilizing selection.
   b. negative frequency-dependent selection.
   c. directional selection.
   d. disruptive selection.

3. Convergent evolution is often seen among species on different islands because
   a. island populations are usually smaller and more affected by genetic drift.
   b. disruptive selection occurs commonly on islands.
   c. island species are usually most closely related to species in similar habitats elsewhere.
   d. when islands are first colonized, many ecological resources are unused, allowing descendants of a colonizing species to diversify and adapt to many different parts of the environment.

### SYNTHESIZE

1. What conditions are necessary for evolution by natural selection?

Refer to figure 21.2 for the following two questions.

2. Explain how data shown in figure 21.2*a* and *b* relate to the conditions identified by you in question 1.

3. On figure 21.2*b*, draw the relationship between offspring beak depth and parent beak depth, assuming that there is no genetic basis to beak depth in the medium ground finch.

4. Refer to figure 21.5, artificial selection in the laboratory. In this experiment, one population of *Drosophila* was selected for low numbers of bristles and the other for high numbers. Note that not only did the means of the populations change greatly in 35 generations, but also all individuals in both experimental populations lie outside the range of the initial population. What would the result of this experiment have been if only flies with high numbers of bristles were allowed to breed?

5. The ancestor of horses was a small, many-toed animal that lived in forests, whereas today's horses are large animals with a single hoof that live on open plains. A series of intermediate fossils illustrate how this transition has occurred, and for this reason, many old treatments of horse evolution portrayed it as a steady increase through time in body size accompanied by a steady decrease in toe number. Why is this interpretation incorrect?

### ONLINE RESOURCE

**www.ravenbiology.com**

Understand, Apply, and Synthesize—enhance your study with animations that bring concepts to life and practice tests to assess your understanding. Your instructor may also recommend the interactive eBook, individualized learning tools, and more.

Chapter 22

# The Origin of Species

## Chapter Outline

## Introduction

*Although Darwin titled his book* On the Origin of Species, *he never actually discussed what he referred to as that "mystery of mysteries"—how one species gives rise to another. Rather, his argument concerned evolution by natural selection; that is, how one species evolves through time to adapt to its changing environment. Although an important mechanism of evolutionary change, the process of adaptation does not explain how one species becomes another, a process we call* speciation. *As we shall see, adaptation may be involved in the speciation process, but it does not have to be.*

*Before we can discuss how one species gives rise to another, we need to understand exactly what a species is. Even though the definition of a species is of fundamental importance to evolutionary biology, this issue has still not been completely settled and is currently the subject of considerable research and debate.*

## 22.1 The Nature of Species and the Biological Species Concept

### Learning Outcomes

1. *Distinguish between the biological species concept and the ecological species concept.*
2. *Define the two kinds of reproductive isolating mechanisms.*
3. *Describe the relationship of reproductive isolating mechanisms to the biological species concept.*

Any concept of a species must account for two phenomena: the distinctiveness of species that occur together at a single locality, and the connection that exists among different populations belonging to the same species.

### Sympatric species inhabit the same locale but remain distinct

Put out birdfeeders on your balcony or in your back yard, and you will attract a wide variety of birds (especially if you include different kinds of foods). In the midwestern United States, for example, you might routinely see cardinals, blue jays, downy woodpeckers, house finches—even hummingbirds in the summer.

Although it might take a few days of careful observation, you would soon be able to readily distinguish the many different species. The reason is that species that occur together (termed **sympatric**) are distinctive entities that are phenotypically different, utilize different parts of the habitat, and behave differently. This observation is generally true not only for birds, but also for most other types of organisms.

Occasionally, two species occur together that appear to be nearly identical. In such cases, we need to go beyond visual similarities. When other aspects of the phenotype are examined, such as the mating calls or the chemicals exuded by each species, they usually reveal great differences. In other words, even though we might have trouble distinguishing them, the organisms themselves have no such difficulties.

### Populations of a species exhibit geographic variation

Within a single species, individuals in populations that occur in different areas may be distinct from one another. Such groups of distinctive individuals may be classified as **subspecies** (the vague term *race* has a similar connotation, but is no longer commonly used). In areas where these populations occur close to one another, individuals often exhibit combinations of features characteristic of both populations (figure 22.1). In other words, even though geographically distant populations may appear distinct, they are usually connected by intervening populations that are intermediate in their characteristics.

### The biological species concept focuses on the ability to exchange genes

What can account for both the distinctiveness of sympatric species and the connectedness of geographically separate populations of the same species? One obvious possibility is that each species exchanges genetic material only with other members of its species. If sympatric species commonly exchanged genes, which they generally do not, we might expect such species to rapidly lose their distinctions, as the gene pools (that is, all of the alleles present in a species) of the different species became homogenized. Conversely, the ability of geographically distant populations of a single species to share genes through the process of gene flow may keep these populations integrated as members of the same species.

Based on these ideas, in 1942 the evolutionary biologist Ernst Mayr set forth the **biological species concept**, which defines *species* as ". . . groups of actually or potentially interbreeding natural populations which are reproductively isolated from other such groups."

In other words, the biological species concept says that a species is composed of populations whose members mate with each other and produce fertile offspring—or would do so if they came into contact. Conversely, populations whose members do not mate with each other or who cannot produce fertile offspring are said to be **reproductively isolated** and, therefore, are members of different species.

What causes reproductive isolation? If organisms cannot interbreed or cannot produce fertile offspring, they clearly belong to different species. However, some populations that are considered separate species can interbreed and produce fertile offspring,

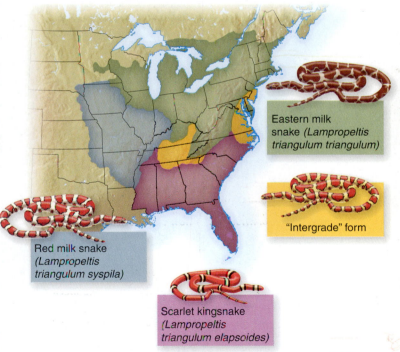

Eastern milk snake (*Lampropeltis triangulum triangulum*)

"Intergrade" form

Red milk snake (*Lampropeltis triangulum syspila*)

Scarlet kingsnake (*Lampropeltis triangulum elapsoides*)

**Figure 22.1 Geographic variation in the milk snake, *Lampropeltis triangulum.*** Although subspecies appear phenotypically quite distinctive from one another, they are connected by populations that are phenotypically intermediate.

but they ordinarily do not do so under natural conditions. They are still considered reproductively isolated in that genes from one species generally will not enter the gene pool of the other.

Table 22.1 summarizes the steps at which barriers to successful reproduction may occur. Such barriers are termed reproductive isolating mechanisms because they prevent genetic exchange between species. We will discuss examples of these next, beginning with those that prevent the formation of zygotes, which are called **prezygotic isolating mechanisms.** Mechanisms that prevent the proper functioning of zygotes after they form are called **postzygotic isolating mechanisms.**

## Prezygotic isolating mechanisms prevent the formation of a zygote

Mechanisms that prevent formation of a zygote include ecological or environmental isolation, behavioral isolation, temporal isolation, mechanical isolation, and prevention of gamete fusion.

### Ecological isolation

Even if two species occur in the same area, they may utilize different portions of the environment and thus not hybridize because they do not encounter each other. For example, in India, the ranges of lions and tigers overlapped until about 150 years ago. Even so, there were no records of natural hybrids. Lions stayed mainly in the open grassland and hunted in groups called prides; tigers tended to be solitary creatures of the forest (figure 22.2). Because of their ecological and behavioral differences, lions and tigers rarely came into direct contact with each other, even though their ranges overlapped over thousands of square kilometers.

In another example, the ranges of two toads, *Bufo woodhousei* and *B. americanus*, overlap in some areas. Although these two species can produce viable hybrids, they usually do not interbreed because they utilize different portions of the habitat for breeding. *B. woodhousei* prefers to breed in streams, and *B. americanus* breeds in rainwater puddles.

Similar situations occur among plants. Two species of oaks occur widely in California: the valley oak, *Quercus lobata*, and the scrub oak, *Q. dumosa*. The valley oak, a graceful deciduous tree that can be as tall as 35 m, occurs in the fertile soils of open grassland on gentle slopes and valley floors. In contrast, the scrub oak is an evergreen shrub, usually only 1 to 3 m tall, which often forms the kind of dense scrub known as chaparral. The scrub oak is found on steep slopes in less fertile soils. Hybrids between these different oaks do occur and are fully fertile, but they are rare. The sharply distinct habitats of their parents limit their occurrence together, and there is little intermediate habitat where the hybrids might flourish.

| TABLE 22.1 | Reproductive Isolating Mechanisms | |
|---|---|---|
| **Mechanism** | | **Description** |
| *PREZYGOTIC ISOLATING MECHANISMS* | | |
| Geographic isolation | | Species occur in different areas, which are often separated by a physical barrier, such as a river or mountain range. |
| Ecological isolation | | Species occur in the same area, but they occupy different habitats and rarely encounter each other. |
| Behavioral isolation | | Species differ in their mating rituals. |
| Temporal isolation | | Species reproduce in different seasons or at different times of the day. |
| Mechanical isolation | | Structural differences between species prevent mating. |
| Prevention of gamete fusion | | Gametes of one species function poorly with the gametes of another species or within the reproductive tract of another species. |
| *POSTZYGOTIC ISOLATING MECHANISMS* | | |
| Hybrid inviability or infertility | | Hybrid embryos do not develop properly, hybrid adults do not survive in nature, or hybrid adults are sterile or have reduced fertility. |

**Figure 22.2 Lions and tigers are ecologically isolated.**
The ranges of lions and tigers overlap in India. However, lions and tigers do not hybridize in the wild because they utilize different portions of the habitat. Lions live in open grassland, whereas tigers are solitary animals that live in the forest. Hybrids, such as this tiglon, have been successfully produced in captivity, but hybridization does not occur in the wild.

**Figure 22.3 Differences in courtship rituals can isolate related bird species.** These Galápagos blue-footed boobies select their mates only after an elaborate courtship display. This male is lifting his feet in a ritualized high-step that shows off his bright blue feet. The display behavior of the two other species of boobies that occur in the Galápagos is very different, as is the color of their feet.

### Behavioral isolation

Chapter 54 describes the often elaborate courtship and mating rituals of some groups of animals. Related species of organisms such as birds often differ in their courtship rituals, which tends to keep these species distinct in nature even if they inhabit the same places (figure 22.3). For example, mallard and pintail ducks are perhaps the two most common freshwater ducks in North America. In captivity, they produce completely fertile hybrid offspring, but in nature they nest side by side and only rarely hybridize.

Sympatric species avoid mating with members of the wrong species in a variety of ways; every mode of communication imaginable appears to be used by some species. Differences in visual signals, as just discussed, are common; however, other types of animals rely more on other sensory modes for communication. Many species, such as frogs, birds, and a variety of insects, use sound to attract mates. Predictably, sympatric species of these animals produce different calls. Similarly, the "songs" of lacewings are produced when they vibrate their abdomens against the surface on which they are sitting, and sympatric species produce different vibration patterns (figure 22.4).

Other species rely on the detection of chemical signals, called **pheromones.** The use of pheromones in moths has been particularly well studied. When female moths are ready to mate, they emit a pheromone that males can detect at great distances. Sympatric species differ in the pheromone they produce: Either they use different chemical compounds, or, if using the same compounds the proportions used are different. Laboratory studies indicate that males are remarkably adept at distinguishing the pheromones of their own species from those of other species or even from synthetic compounds similar, but not identical, to that of their own species.

Some species even use electroreception. African and South Asian electric fish independently have evolved specialized organs in their tails that produce electrical discharges and electroreceptors on their skins to detect them. These discharges are used to communicate in social interactions; field experiments indicate that males can distinguish between signals produced by their own and other species, probably on the basis of differences in the timing of the electrical pulses.

### Temporal isolation

*Lactuca graminifolia* and *L. canadensis,* two species of wild lettuce, grow together along roadsides throughout the southeastern United States. Hybrids between these two species are easily made experimentally and are completely fertile. But these hybrids are rare in nature because *L. graminifolia* flowers in early spring and *L. canadensis* flowers in summer. When their blooming periods overlap, as happens occasionally, the two species do form hybrids, which may become locally abundant.

Many species of closely related amphibians have different breeding seasons that prevent hybridization. For example, five species of frogs of the genus *Rana* occur together in most of the eastern United States, but hybrids are rare because the peak breeding time is different for each of them.

### Mechanical isolation

Structural differences prevent mating between some related species of animals. Aside from such obvious features as size, the structure of the male and female copulatory organs may be incompatible. In many insect and other arthropod groups, the sexual organs, particularly those of the male, are so diverse that they are used as a primary basis for distinguishing species.

Similarly, flowers of related species of plants often differ significantly in their proportions and structures. Some of these differences limit the transfer of pollen from one plant species to another. For example, bees may carry the pollen of one species on a certain place on their bodies; if this area does not come into

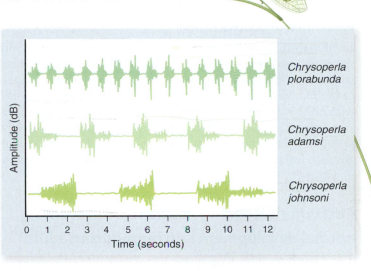

**Figure 22.4 Differences in courtship song of sympatric species of lacewings.** Lacewings are small insects that rely on auditory signals produced by moving their abdomens to vibrate the surface on which they are sitting to attract mates. As these recordings indicate, the vibration patterns produced by sympatric species differ greatly. Females, which detect the calls as they are transmitted through solid surfaces such as branches, are able to distinguish calls of different species and only respond to individuals producing their own species' call.

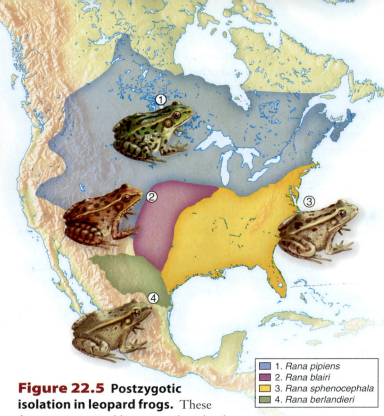

**Figure 22.5 Postzygotic isolation in leopard frogs.** These four species resemble one another closely in their external features. Their status as separate species first was suspected when hybrids between some pairs of these species were found to produce defective embryos in the laboratory. Subsequent research revealed that the mating calls of the four species differ substantially, indicating that the species have both pre- and postzygotic isolating mechanisms.

1. *Rana pipiens*
2. *Rana blairi*
3. *Rana sphenocephala*
4. *Rana berlandieri*

contact with the receptive structures of the flowers of another plant species, the pollen is not transferred.

### Prevention of gamete fusion

In animals that shed gametes directly into water, the eggs and sperm derived from different species may not attract or fuse with one another. Many land animals may not hybridize successfully because the sperm of one species functions so poorly within the reproductive tract of another that fertilization never takes place. In plants, the growth of pollen tubes may be impeded in hybrids between different species. In both plants and animals, isolating mechanisms such as these prevent the union of gametes, even following successful mating.

## Postzygotic isolating mechanisms prevent normal development into reproducing adults

All of the factors we have discussed so far tend to prevent hybridization. If hybrid matings do occur and zygotes are produced, many factors may still prevent those zygotes from developing into normally functioning, fertile individuals.

As you saw in chapter 19, development is a complex process. In hybrids, the genetic complements of two species may be so different that they cannot function together normally in embryonic development. For example, hybridization between sheep and goats usually produces embryos that die in the earliest developmental stages.

The leopard frogs (*Rana pipiens* complex) of the eastern United States are a group of similar species, assumed for a long time to constitute a single species (figure 22.5). Careful examination, however, revealed that although the frogs appear similar, successful mating between them is rare because of problems that occur as the fertilized eggs develop. Many of the hybrid combinations cannot be produced even in the laboratory.

Examples of this kind, in which similar species have been recognized only as a result of hybridization experiments, are common in plants. Sometimes the hybrid plant embryos can be removed at an early stage and grown in an artificial medium. When these hybrids are supplied with extra nutrients or other supplements that compensate for their weakness or inviability, they may complete their development normally.

Even when hybrids survive the embryo stage, they may still not develop normally. If the hybrids are less physically fit than their parents, they will almost certainly be eliminated in nature. Even if a hybrid is vigorous and strong, as in the case of the mule, which is a hybrid between a female horse and a male donkey, it may still be sterile and thus incapable of contributing to succeeding generations.

Hybrids may be sterile because the development of sex organs is abnormal, because the chromosomes derived from the respective parents cannot pair properly during meiosis, or due to a variety of other causes.

## The biological species concept does not explain all observations

The biological species concept has proved to be an effective way of understanding the existence of species in nature. Nonetheless, it fails to take into account all observations, leading some biologists to propose alternative species concepts.

One criticism of the biological species concept concerns the extent to which all species truly are reproductively isolated. By definition, under the biological species concept, species should not interbreed and produce fertile offspring. But in recent years, biologists have detected much greater amounts of interspecies hybridization than was previously thought to occur between populations that seem to coexist as distinct biological entities.

Botanists have always been aware that plant species often undergo substantial amounts of hybridization. More than 50% of California plant species included in one study, for example, were not well defined by genetic isolation. This coexistence without genetic isolation can be long-lasting: Fossil data show that balsam poplars and cottonwoods have been phenotypically distinct for 12 million years, but they also have routinely produced hybrids throughout this time. Consequently, many botanists have long felt that the biological species concept applies only to animals.

New evidence, however, increasingly indicates that hybridization is not all that uncommon in animals, either. In recent years, many cases of substantial hybridization between animal species have been documented. One recent survey indicated that almost 10% of the world's 9500 bird species are known to have hybridized in nature.

The Galápagos finches provide a particularly well-studied example. Three species on the island of Daphne Major—the medium ground finch, the cactus finch, and the small ground finch—are clearly distinct morphologically, and they occupy different ecological niches. Studies over the past 20 years by Peter and Rosemary Grant found that, on average, 2% of the medium ground finches and 1% of the cactus ground finches mated with other species every year. Furthermore, hybrid offspring appeared to be at no disadvantage in terms of survival or subsequent reproduction. This is not a trivial amount of genetic exchange, and one might expect to see the species coalesce into one genetically variable population—but the species are maintaining their distinctiveness.

Hybridization is not rampant throughout the animal world, however. Most bird species do not hybridize, and probably even fewer experience significant amounts of hybridization. Still, hybridization is common enough to cast doubt on whether reproductive isolation is the only force maintaining the integrity of species.

### Natural selection and the ecological species concept

An alternative hypothesis proposes that the distinctions among species are maintained by natural selection. The idea is that each species has adapted to its own specific part of the environment. Stabilizing selection, described in chapter 20, then maintains the species' adaptations. Hybridization has little effect because alleles introduced into one species' gene pool from other species are quickly eliminated by natural selection.

You probably recall from chapter 20 that the interaction between gene flow and natural selection can have many outcomes. In some cases, strong selection can overwhelm any effects of gene flow—but in other situations, gene flow can prevent populations from eliminating less successful alleles from a population.

As a general explanation, then, an ecological species concept is not likely to have any fewer exceptions than does the biological species concept, although it might prove to be a more successful description for certain types of organisms or habitats.

### Other weaknesses of the biological species concept

The biological species concept has been criticized for other reasons as well. For example, it can be difficult to apply the concept to populations that are geographically separated in nature. Because individuals of these populations do not encounter each other, it is not possible to observe whether they would interbreed naturally.

Although experiments can determine whether fertile hybrids can be produced, this information is not enough. Many species that coexist without interbreeding in nature will readily hybridize in the artificial settings of the laboratory or zoo. Consequently, evaluating whether such populations constitute different species is ultimately a judgment call. In addition, the concept is more limited than its name would imply. Many organisms are asexual and reproduce without mating. Reproductive isolation therefore has no meaning for such organisms.

For these reasons, a variety of other ideas have been put forward to establish criteria for defining species. Many of these are specific to a particular type of organism, and none has universal applicability. In reality, there may be no single explanation for what maintains the identity of species. Given the incredible variation evident in plants, animals, and microorganisms in all

aspects of their biology, it would not be surprising to find that different processes are operating in different organisms.

In addition, some scientists have turned from emphasizing the processes that maintain species distinctions to examining the evolutionary history of populations. These genealogical species concepts are currently a topic of great debate and are discussed further in chapter 23.

### Learning Outcomes Review 22.1

Species are populations of organisms that are distinct from other, co-occurring species, and are interconnected geographically. The biological species concept therefore defines species based on their ability to interbreed. Reproductive isolating mechanisms prevent successful interbreeding between species. The ecological species concept relies on adaptation and natural selection as a force for maintaining separation of species.

■ *How does the ability to exchange genes explain why sympatric species remain distinct and geographic populations of one species remain connected?*

## 22.2 Natural Selection and Reproductive Isolation

### Learning Outcomes

1. *Define reinforcement in the context of reproductive isolation.*
2. *Explain the possible outcomes when two populations that are partially reproductively isolated become sympatric.*

One of the oldest questions in the field of evolution is: How does one ancestral species become divided into two descendant species (a process termed cladogenesis)? If species are defined by the existence of reproductive isolation, then the process of speciation is identical to the evolution of reproductive isolating mechanisms.

### Selection may reinforce isolating mechanisms

The formation of species is a continuous process, and as a result, two populations may only be partially reproductively isolated. For example, because of behavioral or ecological differences, individuals of two populations may be more likely to mate with members of their own population, and yet between-population matings may still occur. If mating occurs and fertilization produces a zygote, postzygotic barriers may also be incomplete: developmental problems may result in lower embryo survival or reduced fertility, but some individuals may survive and reproduce.

What happens when two populations come into contact thus depends on the extent to which isolating mechanisms have already evolved. If isolating mechanisms have not evolved at all,

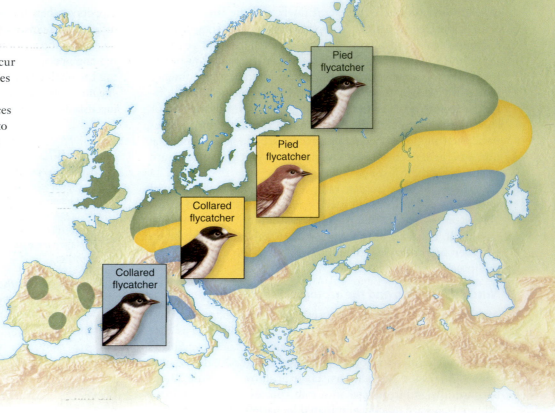

**Figure 22.6** **Reinforcement in European flycatchers.** The pied flycatcher (*Ficedula hypoleuca*) and the collared flycatcher (*F. albicollis*) appear very similar when they occur alone. However, in places where the two species occur sympatrically (indicated by the yellow color on the map), they have evolved differences in color and pattern, which allow individuals to choose mates from their own species and thus avoid hybridizing.

Pied flycatcher

Pied flycatcher

Collared flycatcher

Collared flycatcher

then the two populations will interbreed freely, and whatever other differences have evolved between them should disappear over the course of time, as genetic exchange homogenizes the populations. Conversely, if the populations are completely reproductively isolated, then no genetic exchange will occur, and the two populations will remain different species.

### How reinforcement can complete the speciation process

The intermediate state, in which reproductive isolation has partially evolved but is not complete, is perhaps the most interesting situation. If the hybrids are partly sterile, or not as well adapted to the existing habitats as their parents, they will be at a disadvantage. Selection would favor any alleles in the parental populations that prevented hybridization, because individuals that did not engage in hybridization would produce more successful offspring.

The result would be the continual improvement of prezygotic isolating mechanisms until the two populations were completely reproductively isolated. This process is termed **reinforcement** because initially incomplete isolating mechanisms are reinforced by natural selection until they are completely effective.

An example of reinforcement is provided by pied and collared flycatchers. Throughout much of eastern and central Europe, these two bird species are geographically separated **(allopatric)** and are very similar in color (figure 22.6). However, in the Czech Republic and Slovakia, the two species occur together and occasionally hybridize, producing offspring that usually have very low fertility. At those sites, the species have evolved to look very different from each other, and birds prefer to mate with individuals with their own species' coloration. In contrast, birds from the allopatric populations prefer the allopatric color pattern. As a consequence of the color differences

where the species are sympatric the rate of hybridization is extremely low. These results indicate that when populations of the two species came into contact, natural selection led to the evolution of differences in color patterns, resulting in the evolution of behavioral, prezygotic isolation.

### How gene flow may counter speciation

Reinforcement is not inevitable, however. When incompletely isolated populations come together, gene flow immediately begins to occur between them. Although hybrids may be inferior, they are not completely inviable or infertile—if they were, the species would already be completely reproductively isolated. When these surviving hybrids reproduce with members of either population, they will serve as a conduit of genetic exchange from one population to the other, and the two populations will tend to lose their genetic distinctiveness. Thus, a race ensues: Can complete reproductive isolation evolve before gene flow erases the differences between the populations? Experts disagree on the likely outcome, but many consider reinforcement to be the much less common outcome.

---

**Learning Outcomes Review 22.2**

Natural selection may favor the evolution of increased prezygotic reproductive isolation between sympatric populations. This phenomenon is termed reinforcement, and it may lead to populations becoming completely reproductively isolated. In contrast, however, genetic exchange between populations may decrease genetic differences among populations, thus preventing speciation from occurring.

- *How might the initial degree of reproductive isolation affect the probability that reinforcement will occur when two populations come into sympatry?*

# The Role of Genetic Drift and Natural Selection in Speciation

## Learning Outcomes

1. Describe the effects of genetic drift on a population.
2. Explain how genetic drift and natural selection can lead to speciation.

What role does natural selection play in the speciation process? Certainly, the process of reinforcement is driven by natural selection, favoring the evolution of complete reproductive isolation. But reinforcement may not be common. In situations other than reinforcement, does natural selection play a role in the evolution of reproductive isolating mechanisms?

## Random changes may cause reproductive isolation

As mentioned in chapter 20, populations may diverge for purely random reasons. Genetic drift in small populations, founder effects, and population bottlenecks all may lead to changes in traits that cause reproductive isolation.

For example, in the Hawaiian Islands, closely related species of *Drosophila* often differ greatly in their courtship behavior. Colonization of new islands by these fruit flies probably involved a founder effect, in which one or a few flies—perhaps only a single pregnant female—was blown by strong winds to the new island. Changes in courtship behavior between ancestor and descendant populations may be the result of such founder events.

Given enough time, any two isolated populations will diverge because of genetic drift (remember that even large populations experience drift, but at a lower rate than in small populations). In some cases, this random divergence may affect traits responsible for reproductive isolation, and speciation may occur.

## Adaptation can lead to speciation

Although random processes may sometimes be responsible, in many cases natural selection probably plays a role in the speciation process. As populations of a species adapt to different circumstances, they likely accumulate many differences that may lead to reproductive isolation. For example, if one population of flies adapts to wet conditions and another to dry ones, then natural selection will favor a variety of corresponding differences in physiological and sensory traits. These differences may promote ecological and behavioral isolation and may cause any hybrids the two populations produce to be poorly adapted to either habitat.

Selection might also act directly on mating behavior. Male *Anolis* lizards, for example, court females by extending a colorful flap of skin, called a *dewlap*, located under their throats (figure 22.7). The ability of one lizard to see the dewlap of another lizard depends not only on the color of the dewlap, but on the environment in which the lizards occur. A light-colored dewlap, for example, is most effective in reflecting light in a dim forest, whereas dark colors are more apparent in the bright glare of open habitats. As a result, when these lizards occupy new habitats, natural selection favors evolutionary change in dewlap color because males whose dewlaps cannot be seen will attract few mates. But the lizards also distinguish members of their own species from other species by the color of the dewlap. Adaptive change in mating signals in new environments could therefore have the incidental consequence of producing reproductive isolation from populations in the ancestral environment.

Laboratory scientists have conducted experiments on fruit flies and other fast-reproducing organisms in which they isolate populations in different laboratory chambers and measure how much reproductive isolation evolves. These experiments indicate that genetic drift by itself can lead to some degree of reproductive isolation, but in general, reproductive isolation evolves more rapidly when the populations are forced to adapt to different laboratory environments (such as temperature or food type). Although natural selection in the experiment does not directly favor traits because they lead to reproductive isolation, the incidental effect of adaptive divergence is that populations in different environments become reproductively isolated. For this reason, some biologists believe that the term *isolating mechanisms* is misguided, because it implies that the traits evolved specifically for the purpose of genetically isolating a species, which in most cases—except reinforcement—is probably incorrect.

### Learning Outcomes Review 22.3

Genetic drift refers to randomly generated changes in a population's genetic makeup. Isolated populations will eventually diverge because of genetic drift. Adaptation to different environments may also lead to populations becoming reproductively isolated from each other.

- *How is the evolution of reproductive isolation in populations adapting to different environments different from the process of reinforcement?*

**Figure 22.7 Dewlaps of different species of Caribbean *Anolis* lizards.** Males use their dewlaps in both territorial and courtship displays. Coexisting species almost always differ in their dewlaps, which are used in species recognition. Darker-colored dewlaps, such as those of the two species on the left, are easier to see in open habitats, whereas lighter-colored dewlaps, like those of the two species on the right, are more visible in shaded environments.

*a.*                    *b.*                                    *c.*

**Figure 22.8 Populations can become geographically isolated for a variety of reasons.** *a.* Colonization of remote areas by one or a few individuals can establish populations in a distant place. *b.* Barriers to movement can split an ancestral population into two isolated populations. *c.* Extinction of intermediate populations can leave the remaining populations isolated from one another.

## 22.4 *The Geography of Speciation*

### Learning Outcomes

1. Compare and contrast sympatric and allopatric speciation.
2. Explain the conditions required for sympatric speciation to occur.

Speciation is a two-part process. First, initially identical populations must diverge, and second, reproductive isolation must evolve to maintain these differences. The difficulty with this process, as we have seen, is that the homogenizing effect of gene flow between populations is constantly acting to erase any differences that may arise, either by genetic drift or natural selection. Gene flow only occurs between populations that are in contact, however, and populations can become geographically isolated for a variety of reasons (figure 22.8). Consequently, evolutionary biologists have long recognized that speciation is much more likely in geographically isolated populations.

### Allopatric speciation takes place when populations are geographically isolated

Ernst Mayr was the first biologist to demonstrate that geographically separated, or *allopatric*, populations appear much more likely to have evolved substantial differences leading to speciation. Marshalling data from a wide variety of organisms and localities, Mayr made a strong case for allopatric speciation as the primary means of speciation.

For example, the little paradise kingfisher varies little throughout its wide range in New Guinea, despite the great variation in the island's topography and climate. By contrast, isolated populations on nearby islands are strikingly differ-

ent from one another and from the mainland population (figure 22.9). Thus, geographic isolation seems to have been an important prerequisite for the evolution of differences between populations.

Many other examples indicate that speciation can occur under allopatric conditions. Because we would expect isolated populations to diverge over time, by either drift or selection,

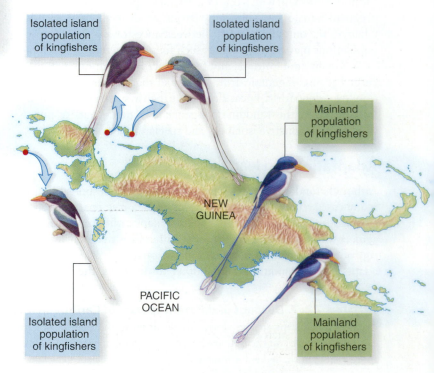

**Figure 22.9 Phenotypic differentiation in the little paradise kingfisher *Tanysiptera hydrocharis* in New Guinea.** Isolated island populations *(left)* are quite distinctive, showing variation in tail feather structure and length, plumage coloration, and bill size, whereas kingfishers on the mainland *(right)* show little variation.

this result is not surprising. Rather, the more intriguing question becomes: Is geographic isolation *required* for speciation to occur?

## Sympatric speciation occurs without geographic separation

For decades, biologists have debated whether one species can split into two at a single locality, without the two new species ever having been geographically separated. Investigators have suggested that this sympatric speciation could occur either instantaneously or over the course of multiple generations. Although most of the hypotheses suggested so far are highly controversial, one type of instantaneous sympatric speciation is known to occur commonly, as the result of polyploidy.

### Instantaneous speciation through polyploidy

Instantaneous sympatric speciation occurs when an individual is born that is reproductively isolated from all other members of its species. In most cases, a mutation that would cause an individual to be greatly different from others of its species would have many adverse pleiotropic side effects, and the individual would not survive. One exception often seen in plants, however, occurs through the process of **polyploidy,** which produces individuals that have more than two sets of chromosomes.

Polyploid individuals can arise in two ways. In **autopolyploidy,** all of the chromosomes may arise from a single species. This might happen, for example, due to an error in cell division that causes a doubling of chromosomes. Such individuals, termed *tetraploids* because they have four sets of chromosomes, can self fertilize or mate with other tetraploids, but cannot mate and produce fertile offspring with normal diploids. The reason is that the tetraploid species produce "diploid" gametes that produce triploid offspring (having three sets of chromosomes) when combined with haploid gametes from normal diploids. Triploids are sterile because the odd number of chromosomes prevent proper pairing during meiosis.

A more common type of polyploid speciation is **allopolyploidy,** which may happen when two species hybridize (figure 22.10). The resulting offspring, having one copy of the chromosomes of each species, is usually infertile because the chromosomes do not pair correctly in meiosis. However, such individuals are often otherwise healthy, can reproduce asexually, and can even become fertile through a variety of events. For example, if the chromosomes of such an individual were to spontaneously double, as just described, the resulting tetraploid would have two copies of each set of chromosomes. Consequently, pairing would no longer be a problem in meiosis. As a result, such tetraploids would be able to interbreed, and a new species would have been created.

It is estimated that about half of the approximately 260,000 species of plants have a polyploid episode in their history, including many of great commercial importance, such as bread wheat, cotton, tobacco, sugarcane, bananas, and potatoes. Speciation by polyploidy is also known to occur in a variety of animals, including insects, fish, and salamanders, although much more rarely than in plants.

### Sympatric speciation by disruptive selection

Some investigators believe that sympatric speciation can occur over the course of multiple generations through the process of disruptive selection. As noted in chapter 20, disruptive selection can cause a population to contain individuals exhibiting two different phenotypes.

One might think that if selection is strong enough, these two phenotypes would evolve over a number of generations into different species. But before the two phenotypes could become different species, they would have to evolve reproductive isolating mechanisms. Initially, the two phenotypes would not

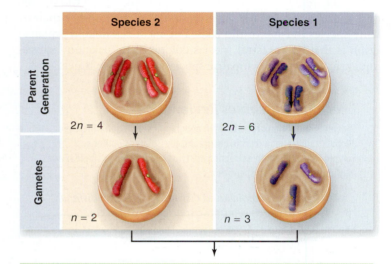

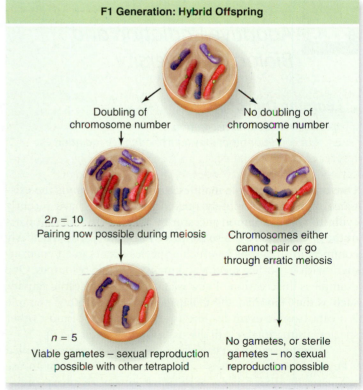

**Figure 22.10 Allopolyploid speciation.** Hybrid offspring from parents with different numbers of chromosomes often cannot reproduce sexually. Sometimes, the number of chromosomes in such hybrids doubles to produce a tetraploid individual that can undergo meiosis and reproduce with similar tetraploid individuals.

*(margin note: hot [over "not"]; gene flow)*

be reproductively isolated at all, and genetic exchange between individuals of the two phenotypes would tend to prevent genetic divergence in mating preferences or other isolating mechanisms. As a result, the two phenotypes would be retained as polymorphisms within a single population. For this reason, most biologists consider sympatric speciation of this type to be a rare event.

In recent years, however, a number of cases have appeared that are difficult to interpret in any way other than as sympatric speciation. For example, Lake Barombi Mbo in Cameroon is an extremely small and ecologically homogeneous lake, with no opportunity for within-lake isolation. Nonetheless, 11 species of closely related cichlid fish occur in the lake; all of the species are more closely related evolutionarily to one another than to any species outside of the lake. The most reasonable explanation is that an ancestral species colonized the lake and subsequently underwent sympatric speciation multiple times.

### Learning Outcomes Review 22.4

Sympatric speciation occurs without geographic separation, whereas allopatric speciation occurs in geographically isolated populations. Polyploidy and disruptive selection are two ways by which a single species may undergo sympatric speciation.

■ *How do polyploidy and disruptive selection differ as ways in which sympatric speciation can occur?*

## 22.5 Adaptive Radiation and Biological Diversity

### Learning Outcomes

1. **Describe adaptive radiation.**
2. **List conditions that may lead to adaptive radiation.**

One of the most visible manifestations of evolution is the existence of groups of closely related species that have recently evolved from a common ancestor by adapting to different parts of the environment. These **adaptive radiations** are particularly common in situations in which a species occurs in an environment with few other species and many available resources. One example is the creation of new islands through volcanic activity, such as the Hawaiian and Galápagos Islands. Another example is a catastrophic event leading to the extinction of most other species, a situation we will discuss soon in greater detail.

Adaptive radiation can also result when a new trait, called a **key innovation,** evolves within a species allowing it to use resources or other aspects of the environment that were previously inaccessible. Classic examples of key innovation leading to adaptive radiation are the evolution of lungs in fish and of wings in birds and insects, both of which allowed descendant species to diversify and adapt to many newly available parts of the environment.

Adaptive radiation requires both speciation and adaptation to different habitats. A classic model postulates that a species colonizes multiple islands in an archipelago. Speciation subsequently occurs allopatrically, and then the newly arisen species colonize other islands, producing multiple species per island (figure 22.11).

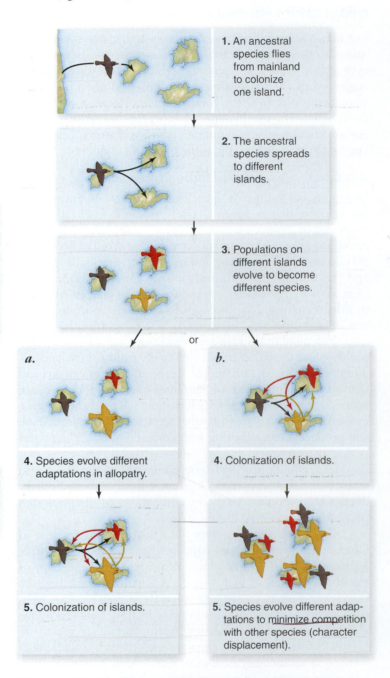

1. An ancestral species flies from mainland to colonize one island.

2. The ancestral species spreads to different islands.

3. Populations on different islands evolve to become different species.

or

a.

4. Species evolve different adaptations in allopatry.

5. Colonization of islands.

b.

4. Colonization of islands.

5. Species evolve different adaptations to minimize competition with other species (character displacement).

**Figure 22.11 Classic model of adaptive radiation on island archipelagoes.** *(1)* An ancestral species colonizes an island in an archipelago. Subsequently, the population colonizes other islands *(2),* after which the populations on the different islands speciate in allopatry *(3).* Then some of these new species colonize other islands, leading to local communities of two or more species. Adaptive differences can either evolve when species are in allopatry in response to different environmental conditions *(a)* or as the result of ecological interactions between species *(b)* by the process of character displacement.

Adaptation to new habitats can occur either during the allopatric phase, as the species respond to different environments on the different islands, or after two species become sympatric. In the latter case, this adaptation may be driven by the need to minimize competition for available resources with other species. Populations on different islands evolve to become different species. In this process, termed **character displacement**, natural selection in each species favors those individuals that use resources not used by the other species. Because those individuals will have greater fitness, whatever traits cause the differences in resource use will increase in frequency (assuming that a genetic basis exists for these differences), and, over time, the species will diverge (figure 22.12).

An alternative possibility is that adaptive radiation occurs through repeated instances of sympatric speciation, producing a suite of species adapted to different habitats. As discussed earlier such scenarios are hotly debated.

In the following sections we discuss four exemplary cases of adaptive radiation.

## SCIENTIFIC THINKING

**Question:** *Does competition for resources cause character displacement?*

**Hypothesis:** *Competition with similar species will cause natural selection to promote evolutionary divergence.*

**Experiment:** *Place a species of fish in a pond with another, similar fish species and measure the form of selection. As a control, place a population of the same species in a pond without the second species. Note that the size of food that these fish eat is related to the size of the fish.*

**Result:** *In the pond with two species, directional selection favors those individuals which have phenotypes most dissimilar from the other species, and thus are most different in resource use. Directional selection does not occur in the control population.*

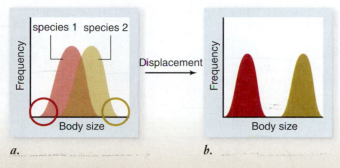

*a.* *b.*

**Interpretation:** *Would you expect character displacement to occur if resources were unlimited?*

**Figure 22.12 Character displacement.** *a.* Two species are initially similar and thus overlap greatly in resource use, as might happen if the two species were similar in size (in many species, body size and food size are closely related). Individuals in each species that are most different from the other species (circled) will be favored by natural selection, because they will not have to compete with the other species. For example, the smallest individuals of one species and the largest of the other would not compete with the other species for food and thus would be favored. *b.* As a result, the species will diverge in resource use and minimize competition between the species.

**Inquiry question**

? How would the scenario for adaptive radiation differ depending on whether speciation is allopatric? What is the relationship between character displacement and sympatric speciation?

## Hawaiian *Drosophila* exploited a rich, diverse habitat

More than 1000 species in the fly genus *Drosophila* occur on the Hawaiian Islands. New species of *Drosophila* are still being discovered in Hawaii, although the rapid destruction of the native vegetation is making the search more difficult.

Aside from their sheer number, Hawaiian *Drosophila* species are unusual because of their incredible diversity of morphological and behavioral traits (figure 22.13). Evidently, when their ancestors first reached these islands, they encountered many "empty" habitats that other kinds of insects and other animals occupied elsewhere. As a result, the species have adapted to all manners of fruit fly life and include predators, parasites, and herbivores, as well as species specialized for eating the detritus in leaf litter and the nectar of flowers. The larvae of various species live in rotting stems, fruits, bark, leaves, or roots, or feed on sap. No comparable diversity of *Drosophila* species is found anywhere else in the world.

The great diversity of Hawaiian species is a result of the geological history of these islands. New islands have continually arisen from the sea in this region. As they have done so, they appear to have been invaded successively by the various *Drosophila* groups present on the older islands. New species thus have evolved as new islands have been colonized.

In addition, the Hawaiian Islands are among the most volcanically active islands in the world. Periodic lava flows often have created patches of habitat within an island surrounded by a "sea" of barren rock. These land islands are termed *kipukas*. *Drosophila* populations isolated in these kipukas often undergo speciation. In these ways, rampant speciation combined with ecological opportunity has led to an unparalleled diversity of insect life.

*a.* *b.*

**Figure 22.13 Hawaiian *Drosophila*.** The hundreds of species that have evolved on the Hawaiian Islands are extremely variable in appearance, although genetically almost identical. *a. Drosophila heteroneura. b. Drosophila digressa.*

## Darwin's finch species adapted to use different food types

The diversity of Darwin's finches on the Galápagos Islands was first mentioned in chapter 21. Presumably, the ancestor of Darwin's finches reached these islands before other land birds, and many of the types of habitats that other types of birds use on the mainland were unoccupied.

As the new arrivals moved into these vacant ecological niches and adopted new lifestyles, they were subjected to many different sets of selective pressures. Under these circumstances, and aided by the geographic isolation afforded by the many islands of the Galápagos archipelago, the ancestral finches rapidly split into a series of diverse populations, some of which evolved into separate species. These species now occupy many different habitats on the Galápagos Islands, which are comparable to the habitats several distinct groups of birds occupy on the mainland. As illustrated in figure 22.14, the 14 species fall into four groups:

1. **Ground finches.** There are six species of *Geospiza* ground finches. Most of the ground finches feed on seeds. The size of their bills is related to the size of the seeds they eat. Some of the ground finches feed primarily on cactus flowers and fruits, and they have a longer, larger, and more pointed bill than the others.

2. **Tree finches.** There are five species of insect-eating tree finches. Four species have bills suitable for feeding on insects. The woodpecker finch has a chisel-like beak. This unusual bird carries around a twig or a cactus spine, which it uses to probe for insects in deep crevices.

3. **Vegetarian finch.** The very heavy bill of this species is used to wrench buds from branches.

4. **Warbler finches.** These unusual birds play the same ecological role in the Galápagos woods that warblers play on the mainland, searching continuously over the leaves and branches for insects. They have slender, warblerlike beaks.

Recently, scientists have examined the DNA of Darwin's finches to study their evolutionary history. These studies suggest that the deepest branches in the finch evolutionary tree lead to warbler finches, which implies that warbler finches were among the first types to evolve after colonization of the islands. All of the ground species are closely related to one another, as are all of the tree finches. Nonetheless, within each group, species differ in beak size and other attributes, as well as in resource use.

Field studies, conducted in conjunction with those discussed in chapter 21, demonstrate that ground species compete for resources; the differences between species likely resulted from character displacement as initially similar species diverged to minimize competitive pressures.

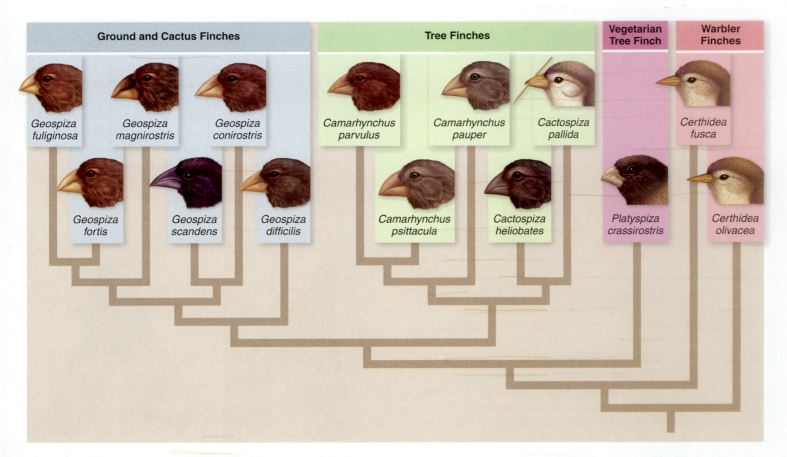

**Figure 22.14 An evolutionary tree of Darwin's finches.** This evolutionary tree, derived from examination of DNA sequences, suggests that warbler finches are an early offshoot. Ground and tree finches subsequently diverged, and then species within each group specialized to use different resources. Recent studies have shown, surprisingly, that the two warbler finches are not each other's closest relatives. Rather, *Certhidea fusca* is more closely related to the remaining Darwin's finches than it is to *C. olivacea*.

## Lake Victoria cichlid fishes diversified very rapidly

Lake Victoria is an immense, shallow, freshwater sea about the size of Switzerland in the heart of equatorial East Africa. Until recently, the lake was home to an incredibly diverse collection of over 450 species of cichlid fishes.

### Geologically recent radiation

The cluster of cichlid species appears to have evolved recently and quite rapidly. By sequencing the cytochrome *b* gene in many of the lake's fish, scientists have been able to estimate that the first cichlids entered Lake Victoria only 200,000 years ago.

Dramatic changes in water level encouraged species formation. As the lake rose, it flooded new areas and opened up new habitats. Many of the species may have originated after the lake dried down 14,000 years ago, isolating local populations in small lakes until the water level rose again.

### Cichlid diversity

Cichlids are small, perchlike fishes ranging from 5 to 25 centimeters (cm) in length, and the males come in endless varieties of colors. The ecological and morphological diversity of these fish is remarkable, particularly given the short span of time over which they have evolved.

We can gain some sense of the vast range of types by looking at how different species eat. There are mud biters, algae scrapers, leaf chewers, snail crushers, zooplankton eaters, insect eaters, prawn eaters, and fish eaters. Snail shellers pounce on slow-crawling snails and spear their soft parts with long, curved teeth before the snail can retreat into its shell. Scale scrapers rasp slices of scales off other fish. There are even cichlid species that are "pedophages," eating the young of other cichlids.

Cichlid fish have a remarkable key innovation that may have been instrumental in their evolutionary radiation: They carry a second set of functioning jaws (figure 22.15). This trait occurs in many other fish, but in cichlids it is greatly enlarged. The ability of these second jaws to manipulate and process food has freed the oral jaws to evolve for other purposes, and the result has been the incredible diversity of ecological roles filled by these fish.

### Abrupt extinction in the last several decades

Recently, much of the cichlid diversity has disappeared. In the 1950s, the Nile perch, a large commercial fish with a voracious appetite, was introduced to Lake Victoria. Since

**Figure 22.15 Cichlid fishes of Lake Victoria.** These fishes have evolved adaptations to use a variety of different habitats. The enlarged second set of jaws located in the throat of these fish has provided evolutionary flexibility, allowing oral jaws to be modified in many ways.

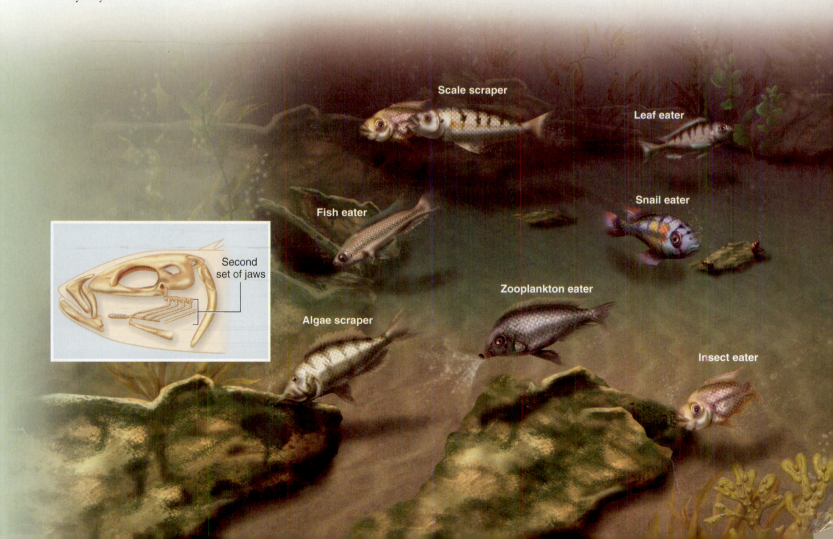

then, it has spread through the lake, eating its way through the cichlids.

By 1990, many of the open-water cichlid species had become extinct, as well as others living in rocky shallow regions. Over 70% of all the named Lake Victoria cichlid species had disappeared, as well as untold numbers of species that had yet to be described. We will revisit the story of Lake Victoria when we discuss conservation biology in chapter 59.

## New Zealand alpine buttercups underwent speciation in glacial habitats

Adaptive radiations such as those we have described in Hawaiian *Drosophila*, Galápagos finches, and cichlid fishes seem to have been favored by periodic isolation. A clear example of the role periodic isolation plays in species formation can be seen in the alpine buttercups that grow among the glaciers of New Zealand (figure 22.16).

More species of alpine buttercups grow on the two main islands of New Zealand than in all of North and South America combined. The evolutionary mechanism responsible for this diversity is recurrent isolation associated with the recession of glaciers.

The 14 species of alpine buttercups occupy five distinctive habitats within glacial areas:

- *snowfields*—rocky crevices among outcrops in permanent snowfields at 2130- to 2740-m elevation;
- *snowline fringe*—rocks at lower margin of snowfields between 1220 and 2130 m;
- *stony debris*—slopes of exposed loose rocks at 610 to 1830 m;
- *sheltered situations*—shaded by rock or shrubs at 305 to 1830 m; and
- *boggy habitats*—sheltered slopes and hollows, poorly drained tussocks at elevations between 760 and 1525 m.

Buttercup speciation and diversification have been promoted by repeated cycles of glacial advance and retreat. As the glaciers retreat up the mountains, populations become isolated on mountain peaks, permitting speciation (see figure 22.16). In the next glacial advances, these new species can expand throughout the mountain range, coming into contact with their close relatives. In this way, one initial species could give rise to many descendants. Moreover, on isolated mountaintops during glacial retreats, species have

snowfield      snowline fringe      stony debris      sheltered      boggy

*a.*

Glaciers recede →

Glaciation →

Glaciers link alpine zones into one continuous range.

Mountain populations become isolated, permitting divergence and speciation.

Alpine zones are reconnected. Separately evolved species come back into contact.

*b.*

**Figure 22.16 New Zealand alpine buttercups (genus *Ranunculus*).** Periodic glaciation encouraged species formation among alpine buttercups in New Zealand. *a.* Fourteen species of alpine *Ranunculus* grow among the glaciers and mountains of New Zealand. *b.* The formation of extensive glaciers during the Pleistocene epoch linked the alpine zones *(white)* of many mountains together. When the glaciers receded, these alpine zones were isolated from one another, only to become reconnected with the advent of the next glacial period. During periods of isolation, populations of alpine buttercups diverged in the isolated habitats.

convergently evolved to occupy similar habitats; these distantly related but ecologically similar species have then been brought back into contact in subsequent glacial advances.

## 22.6 The Pace of Evolution

We have discussed the manner in which speciation may occur, but we haven't yet considered the relationship between speciation and the evolutionary change that occurs within a species. Two hypotheses, *gradualism* and *punctuated equilibrium*, have been advanced to explain the relationship.

### Gradualism is the accumulation of small changes

For more than a century after the publication of *On the Origin of Species*, the standard view was that evolution occurred very slowly. Such change would be nearly imperceptible from generation to generation, but would accumulate such that, over the course of thousands and millions of years, major changes could occur. This view is termed **gradualism** (figure 22.17*a*).

### Punctuated equilibrium is long periods of stasis followed by relatively rapid change

Gradualism was challenged in 1972 by paleontologists Niles Eldredge of the American Museum of Natural History in New York and Stephen Jay Gould of Harvard University, who argued that species experience long periods of little or no evolutionary change (termed **stasis**), punctuated by bursts

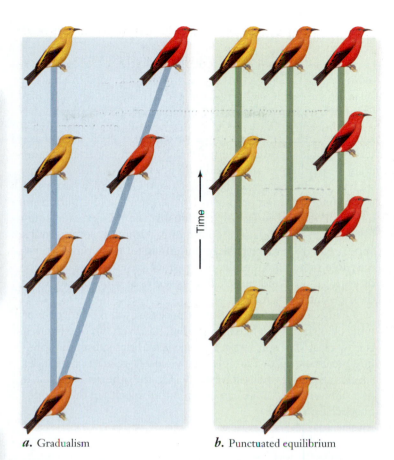

*a.* Gradualism     *b.* Punctuated equilibrium

**Figure 22.17  Two views of the pace of macroevolution.** *a.* Gradualism suggests that evolutionary change occurs slowly through time and is not linked to speciation, whereas *(b)* punctuated equilibrium surmises that phenotypic change occurs in bursts associated with speciation, separated by long periods of little or no change.

of evolutionary change occurring over geologically short time intervals. They called this phenomenon **punctuated equilibrium** (figure 22.17*b*) and argued that these periods of rapid change occurred only during the speciation process.

Initial criticism of the punctuated equilibrium hypothesis focused on whether rapid change could occur over short periods of time. As we have seen in the last two chapters, however, when natural selection is strong, rapid and substantial evolutionary change can occur. A more difficult question involves the long periods of stasis: Why would species exist for thousands, or even millions, of years without changing?

Although a number of possible reasons have been suggested, most researchers now believe that a combination of stabilizing and oscillating selection is responsible for stasis. If the environment does not change over long periods of time, or if environmental changes oscillate back and forth, then stasis may occur for long periods. One factor that may enhance this stasis is the ability of species to shift their ranges; for example, during the ice ages, when the global climate cooled, the geographic ranges of many species shifted southward, so that the species continued to experience similar environmental conditions.

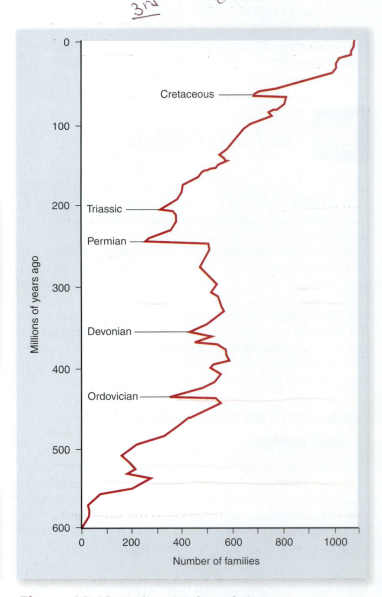

## Inquiry question

**?** Why would changes in geographic ranges promote evolutionary stasis?

## Evolution may include both types of change

Eldredge and Gould's proposal prompted a great deal of research. Some well-documented groups, such as African mammals, clearly have evolved gradually, not in spurts. Other groups, such as marine bryozoa, seem to show the irregular pattern of evolutionary change predicted by the punctuated equilibrium model. It appears, in fact, that gradualism and punctuated equilibrium are two ends of a continuum. Although some groups appear to have evolved solely in a gradual manner and others only in a punctuated mode, many other groups show evidence of both gradual and punctuated episodes at different times in their evolutionary history.

The idea that speciation is necessarily linked to phenotypic change has not been supported, however. On one hand, it is now clear that speciation can occur without substantial phenotypic change. For example, many closely-related salamander species are nearly indistinguishable. On the other, it is also clear that phenotypic change can occur within species in the absence of speciation.

### Learning Outcomes Review 22.6

Gradualism is the accumulation of almost imperceptible changes that eventually results in major differences. Punctuated equilibrium proposes that long periods of stasis are interrupted (punctuated) by periods of rapid change. Evidence for both gradualism and punctuated equilibrium has been found in different groups. Stasis refers to a period in which little or no evolutionary change occurs. Stasis may result from stabilizing or oscillating selection.

■ *Could evolutionary change be punctuated in time (that is, rapid and episodic), but not linked to speciation?*

## 22.7 Speciation and Extinction Through Time

### Learning Outcomes

1. *Describe the pattern of species diversity through time.*
2. *Define mass extinction and identify when major mass extinctions have occurred.*

Biological diversity has increased vastly since the Cambrian period, but the trend has been far from consistent. After a rapid rise, diversity reached a plateau for about 200 million years, but since then has risen steadily. Because changes in the number of species reflect the rate of origin of new species relative to the rate at which existing species disappear, this long-term trend reveals that speciation has, in general, surpassed extinction.

Nonetheless, speciation has not always outpaced extinction. In particular, interspersed in the long-term increase in species diversity have been a number of sharp declines, termed **mass extinctions.**

## Five mass extinctions have occurred in the distant past

Five major mass extinctions have been identified, the most severe one occurring at the end of the Permian period, approximately 250 million years ago (figure 22.18). At that time, more than half of all plant and animal families and as much as 96% of all species may have perished.

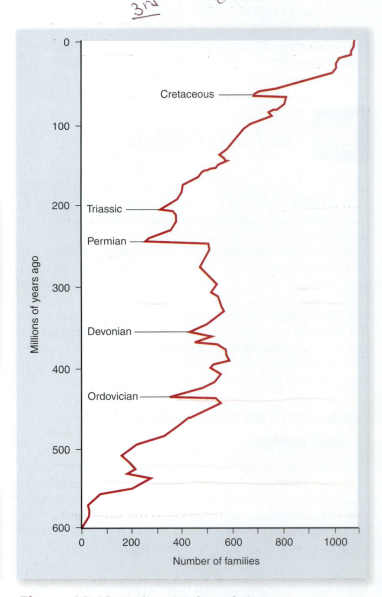

**Figure 22.18 Biodiversity through time.** The taxonomic diversity of families of marine animals has increased since the Cambrian period, although occasional dips have occurred. The fossil record is most complete for marine organisms because they are more readily fossilized than terrestrial species. Families are shown, rather than species, because many species are known from only one specimen, thus introducing error into estimates of the time of extinction. Arrows indicate the five major mass extinction events.

The most famous and well-studied extinction, although not as drastic, occurred at the end of the Cretaceous period (65 million years ago), at which time the dinosaurs and a variety of other organisms went extinct. Recent findings have supported the hypothesis that this extinction event was triggered when a large asteroid slammed into Earth, perhaps causing global forest fires and obscuring the Sun for months by throwing particles into the air. The cause of other mass extinction events is less certain. Some scientists suggest that asteroids may have played a role in at least some of the other mass extinction events; other hypotheses implicate global climate change and other causes.

One important result of mass extinctions is that not all groups of organisms are affected equally. For example, in the extinction at the end of the Cretaceous, not only dinosaurs, but also marine and flying reptiles, and ammonites (a type of mollusk) went extinct. Marsupials, flowering plants, birds, and some forms of plankton were greatly reduced in diversity. In contrast, turtles, crocodilians, and amphibians seemed to have been unscathed. Why some groups were harder hit than others is not clear, but one hypothesis suggests that survivors were those animals that could shelter underground or in water, and that could either scavenge or required little food in the cool temperatures that resulted from the blockage of sunlight.

A consequence of mass extinctions is that previously dominant groups may perish, thus changing the course of evolution. This is certainly true of the Cretaceous extinction. During the Cretaceous period, placental mammals were a minor group composed of species that were mostly no larger than a house cat. When the dinosaurs, which had dominated the world for more than 100 million years, disappeared at the end of this period, the placental mammals underwent a significant adaptive radiation. It is humbling to think that humans might never have arisen had that asteroid not struck Earth 65 million years ago.

As the world around us illustrates today, species diversity does rebound after mass extinctions, but this recovery is not rapid. Examination of the fossil record indicates that rates of speciation do not immediately increase after an extinction pulse, but rather take about 10 million years to reach their maximum. The cause of this delay is not clear, but it may result because it takes time for ecosystems to recover and for the processes of speciation and adaptive diversification to begin. Consequently, species diversity may require 10 million years, or even much longer, to attain its previous level.

## A sixth extinction is underway

The number of species in the world in recent times is greater than it has ever been. Unfortunately, that number is decreasing at an alarming rate due to human activities (see chapter 59).

Some estimate that as much as one-fourth of all species will become extinct in the near future, a rate of extinction not seen on Earth since the Cretaceous mass extinction. Moreover, the rebound in species diversity may be even slower than following previous mass extinction events because, instead of the ecologically impoverished, but energy-rich environment that existed after previous mass extinction events, a large proportion of the world's resources will be taken up already by human activities, leaving few resources available for adaptive radiation.

### Learning Outcomes Review 22.7

The number of species has increased through time, although not at a constant rate. Five major extinction events have substantially, though briefly, reduced the number of species. Diversity rebounds, but the recovery is not rapid, and the groups making up that diversity are not the same as those that existed before the extinction event. Unfortunately, humans are currently causing a sixth mass extinction event.

■ *In what ways are the current mass extinction event different from those that have occurred in the past?*

## Chapter Review

### 22.1 The Nature of Species and the Biological Species Concept

**Sympatric species inhabit the same locale but remain distinct.**
Most sympatric species are readily distinguishable phenotypically and ecologically. Others can usually be identified by careful study.

**Populations of a species exhibit geographic variation.**
Populations that differ greatly in phenotype or ecologically are usually connected by geographically intermediate populations.

**The biological species concept focuses on the ability to exchange genes.**
Biological species are generally defined as populations that interbreed, or have the potential to do so, and produce fertile offspring. Reproductive isolating mechanisms prevent genetic exchange between species.

**Prezygotic isolating mechanisms prevent the formation of a zygote.**
Prezygotic isolating mechanisms prevent a viable zygote from being created. These mechanisms include ecological, behavioral, temporal, and mechanical isolation.

**Postzygotic isolating mechanisms prevent normal development into reproducing adults.**
Postzygotic isolating mechanisms prevent a zygote from developing into a viable and fertile individual.

**The biological species concept does not explain all observations.**
The ecological species concept, one alternative explanation, focuses on the role of natural selection and differences among species in their ecological requirements.

In reality, no one species concept can explain all the diversity of life.

## 22.2 Natural Selection and Reproductive Isolation

**Selection may reinforce isolating mechanisms.**

Populations may evolve complete reproductive isolation in allopatry. If populations that have evolved only partial reproductive isolation come into contact, natural selection can lead to increased reproductive isolation, a process termed "reinforcement."

Alternatively, genetic exchange between the populations can lead to homogenization and thus prevent speciation from occurring.

## 22.3 The Role of Genetic Drift and Natural Selection in Speciation

**Random changes may cause reproductive isolation.**

In small populations, genetic drift may cause populations to diverge; the differences that evolve may cause the populations to become reproductively isolated.

**Adaptation can lead to speciation.**

Adaptation to different situations or environments may incidentally lead to reproductive isolation. In contrast to reinforcement, these differences are not directly favored by natural selection because they prevent hybridization.

Natural selection can directly select for traits that increase reproductive isolation.

## 22.4 The Geography of Speciation (see figure 22.9)

**Allopatric speciation takes place when populations are geographically isolated.**

Allopatric, or geographically isolated, populations are much more likely to evolve into separate species because no gene flow occurs between them. Most speciation probably occurs in allopatry.

**Sympatric speciation occurs without geographic separation.**

Sympatric speciation can occur in two ways. One is polyploidy, which instantly creates a new species. Disruptive selection also can cause one species to divide into two, but scientists debate how commonly it occurs.

## 22.5 Adaptive Radiation and Biological Diversity

Adaptive radiation occurs when a species finds itself in a new or suddenly changed environment with many resources and few competing species (see figure 22.11).

The evolution of a new trait that allows individuals to use previously inaccessible parts of the environment, termed a "key innovation," may also trigger an adaptive radiation.

**Hawaiian Drosophila exploited a rich, diverse habitat.**

At least 1000 species of Hawaiian *Drosophila* have been identified.

**Darwin's finch species adapted to use different food types.**

Fourteen species in four genera have evolved to exploit four different habitats based on type of food.

**Lake Victoria cichlid fishes diversified very rapidly.**

Cichlids underwent rapid radiation to form 300 species, although today more than 70% of these species are now extinct.

**New Zealand alpine buttercups underwent speciation in glacial habitats.**

Periodic isolation by glaciers has led to 14 species in distinct habitats.

## 22.6 The Pace of Evolution

**Gradualism is the accumulation of small changes.**

Historically, scientists took the view that speciation occurred gradually through very small cumulative changes.

**Punctuated equilibrium is long periods of stasis followed by relatively rapid change.**

The punctuated equilibrium hypothesis contends that not only is change rapid and episodic, but that it is only associated with the speciation process.

**Evolution may include both types of change.**

Scientists generally agree that evolutionary change occurs on a continuum, with gradualism and punctuated change being the extremes.

## 22.7 Speciation and Extinction Through Time

In general, the number of species have increased through time (see figure 22.18).

**Five mass extinctions have occurred in the distant past.**

Mass extinctions have led to dramatic decreases in species diversity, which takes millions of years to recover. Five such mass extinctions have occurred in the distant past due to asteroids hitting the Earth and global climate change, among other events.

**A sixth mass extinction is underway.**

Humans are currently causing a sixth mass extinction.

## Review Questions

### UNDERSTAND

1. Prezygotic isolating mechanisms include all of the following except
   a. hybrid sterility.
   b. courtship rituals.
   c. habitat separation.
   d. seasonal reproduction.

2. Reproductive isolation is
   a. a result of individuals not mating with each other.
   b. a specific type of postzygotic isolating mechanism.
   c. required by the biological species concept.
   d. none of the above.

3. Problems with the biological species concept include the fact that
   a. many species reproduce asexually.
   b. postzygotic isolating mechanisms decrease hybrid viability.
   c. prezygotic isolating mechanisms are extremely rare.
   d. all of these.

4. Allopatric speciation
   a. is less common than sympatric speciation.
   b. involves geographic isolation of some kind.
   c. is the only kind of speciation that occurs in plants.
   d. requires polyploidy.

5. Gradualism and punctuated equilibrium are

   a. two ends of the continuum of the rate of evolutionary change over time.
   b. mutually exclusive views about how all evolutionary change takes place.
   c. mechanisms of reproductive isolation.
   d. none of the above.

6. During the history of life on Earth

   a. there have been major extinction events.
   b. species diversity has steadily increased.
   c. species diversity has stayed relatively constant.
   d. extinction rates have been completely offset by speciation rates.

7. Speciation by allopolyploidy

   a. takes a long time.
   b. is common in birds.
   c. leads to reduced numbers of chromosomes.
   d. occurs after hybridization between two species.

8. Adaptive radiation

   a. is the result of enriched uranium used in power plants.
   b. is the evolution of closely related species adapted to use different parts of the environment.
   c. results from genetic drift.
   d. is the outcome of stabilizing selection favoring the maintenance of adaptive traits.

## APPLY

1. Leopard frogs from different geographic populations of the *Rana pipiens* complex

   a. are members of a single species because they look very similar to one another.
   b. are different species shown to have pre- and postzygotic isolating mechanisms.
   c. frequently interbreed to produce viable hybrids.
   d. are genetically identical due to effective reproductive isolation.

2. If reinforcement is weak and hybrids are not completely infertile,

   a. genetic divergence between populations may be overcome by gene flow.
   b. speciation will occur 100% of the time.
   c. gene flow between populations will be impossible.
   d. the speciation will be more likely than if hybrids were completely infertile.

3. Natural selection can

   a. enhance the probability of speciation.
   b. enhance reproductive isolation.
   c. act against hybrid survival and reproduction.
   d. do all of these.

4. Character displacement

   a. arises through competition and natural selection, favoring divergence in resource use.
   b. arises through competition and natural selection, favoring convergence in resource use.

   c. does not promote speciation.
   d. reduced speciation rates in Galápagos finches.

5. Hybridization between incompletely isolated populations

   a. always leads to reinforcement due to the inferiority of hybrids.
   b. can serve as a mechanism for preserving gene flow between populations, thus preventing speciation.
   c. only occurs in plants.
   d. never affects rates of speciation.

6. Natural selection can lead to speciation

   a. by causing small populations to diverge more than large populations.
   b. because the evolutionary changes that two populations acquire while adapting to different habitats may have the effect of making them reproductively isolated.
   c. by favoring the same evolutionary change in multiple populations.
   d. by favoring intermediate phenotypes.

## SYNTHESIZE

1. Natural selection can lead to the evolution of prezygotic isolating mechanisms, but not postzygotic isolating mechanisms? Explain.

2. If there is no universally accepted definition of a species, what good is the term? Will the idea of and need for a "species concept" be eliminated in the future?

3. Refer to figure 22.6. In Europe, pied and collared flycatchers are dissimilar in sympatry, but very similar in allopatry, consistent with character divergence in coloration. In this case, there is no competition for ecological resources as in other cases of character divergence discussed. How might this example work?

4. Refer to figure 22.14. *Geospiza fuliginosa* and *Geospiza fortis* are found in sympatry on at least one island in the Galápagos and in allopatry on several islands in the same archipelago. Compare your expectations about degree of morphological similarity of the two species in these two contexts, given the hypothesis that competition for food played a large role in the adaptive radiation of this group. Would your expectations be the same for a pair of finch species that are not as closely related? Explain.

## ONLINE RESOURCE

**www.ravenbiology.com**

Understand, Apply, and Synthesize—enhance your study with animations that bring concepts to life and practice tests to assess your understanding. Your instructor may also recommend the interactive eBook, individualized learning tools, and more.

Chapter 23

# Systematics and the Phylogenetic Revolution

## Chapter Outline

## Introduction

*All organisms share many biological characteristics. They are composed of one or more cells, carry out metabolism and transfer energy with ATP, and encode hereditary information in DNA. Yet, there is also a tremendous diversity of life, ranging from bacteria and amoebas to blue whales and sequoia trees. For generations, biologists have tried to group organisms based on shared characteristics. The most meaningful groupings are based on the study of evolutionary relationships among organisms. New methods for constructing evolutionary trees and a sea of molecular sequence data are leading to improved evolutionary hypotheses to explain life's diversification.*

## 23.1 Systematics

### Learning Outcomes

1. Understand what a phylogeny represents.
2. Explain why phenotypic similarity does not necessarily indicate close evolutionary relationship.

One of the great challenges of modern science is to understand the history of ancestor–descendant relationships that unites all forms of life on Earth, from the earliest single-celled organisms to the complex organisms we see around us today. If the fossil record were perfect, we could trace the evolutionary history of species and examine how each arose and proliferated; however, as discussed in chapter 21, the fossil record is far from complete. Although it answers many questions about life's diversification, it leaves many others unsettled.

Consequently, scientists must rely on other types of evidence to establish the best hypothesis of evolutionary relationships. Bear in mind that the outcomes of such studies *are* hypotheses, and as such, they require further testing. All hypotheses may be disproved by new data, leading to the formation of better, more accurate scientific ideas.

The reconstruction and study of evolutionary relationships is called **systematics.** By looking at the similarities and differences between species, systematists can construct an evolutionary tree, or **phylogeny,** which represents a hypothesis about patterns of relationship among species.

## Branching diagrams depict evolutionary relationships

Darwin envisioned that all species were descended from a single common ancestor, and that the history of life could be depicted as a branching tree (figure 23.1). In Darwin's view, the twigs of the tree represent existing species. As one works down the tree, the joining of twigs and branches reflects the pattern of common ancestry back in time to the single common ancestor of all life. The process of descent with modification from common ancestry results in all species being related in this branching, hierarchical fashion, and their evolutionary history can be depicted using branching diagrams or phylogenetic trees. Figure 23.1b shows how evolutionary relationships are depicted with a branching diagram. Humans and chimpanzees

are descended from a common ancestor and are each other's closest living relative (the position of this common ancestor is indicated by the node labeled 1). Humans, chimps, and gorillas share an older common ancestor (node 2), and all great apes share a more distant common ancestor (node 3).

One key to interpreting a phylogeny is to look at how recently species share a common ancestor, rather than looking at the arrangement of species across the top of the tree. If you compare the three versions of the phylogeny of figure 23.1b, you can see that the relationships are the same: Regardless of where they are positioned, chimpanzees and humans are still more closely related to each other than to any other species.

Moreover, even though humans are placed next to gibbons in version 1 of figure 23.1b, the pattern of relationships still indicates that humans are more closely related (that is, share a more recent common ancestor) with gorillas and orangutans than with gibbons. Phylogenies are also sometimes displayed on their side, rather than upright figure 23.1b (version 3), but this arrangement also does not affect its interpretation.

## Similarity may not accurately predict evolutionary relationships

We might expect that the greater the time since two species diverged from a common ancestor, the more different they would be. Early systematists relied on this reasoning and constructed phylogenies based on overall similarity. If, in fact,

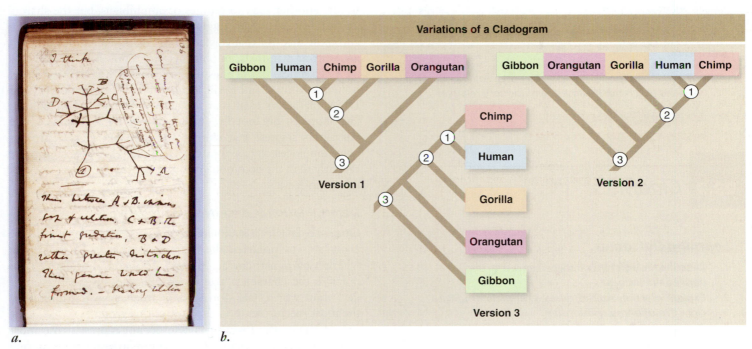

**Figure 23.1** **Phylogenies depict evolutionary relationships.** *a.* A drawing from one of Darwin's notebooks, written in 1837 as he developed his ideas that led to *On the Origin of Species.* Darwin viewed life as a branching process akin to a tree, with species on the twigs, and evolutionary change represented by the branching pattern displayed by a tree as it grows. *b.* An example of a phylogeny. Humans and chimpanzees are more closely related to each other than they are to any other living species. This is apparent because they share a common ancestor (the node labeled 1) that was not an ancestor of other species. Similarly, humans, chimpanzees, and gorillas are more closely related to one another than any of them is to orangutans because they share a common ancestor (node 2) that was not ancestral to orangutans. Node 3 represents the common ancestor of all apes. Note that these three versions convey the same information despite the differences in arrangement of species and orientation.

species evolved at a constant rate, then the amount of divergence between two species would be a function of how long they had been diverging, and thus phylogenies based on degree of similarity would be accurate. As a result, we might think that chimps and gorillas are more closely related to each other than either is to humans.

But as chapter 22 revealed, evolution can occur very rapidly at some times and very slowly at others. In addition, evolution is not unidirectional—sometimes species' traits evolve in one direction, and then back the other way (a result of oscillating selection; see chapter 20). Species invading new habitats are likely to experience new selective pressures and may change greatly; those staying in the same habitats as their ancestors may change only a little. For this reason, similarity is not necessarily a good predictor of how long it has been since two species shared a common ancestor.

A second fundamental problem exists as well: Evolution is not always divergent. In chapter 21, we discussed convergent evolution, in which two species independently evolve the same features. Often, species evolve convergently because they use similar habitats, in which similar adaptations are favored. As a result, two species that are not closely related may end up more similar to each other than they are to their close relatives. Evolutionary reversal, the process in which a species re-evolves the characteristics of an ancestral species, also has this effect.

### Learning Outcomes Review 23.1

Systematics is the study of evolutionary relationships. Phylogenies, or phylogenetic trees, are graphic representations of relationships among species. Similarity of organisms alone does not necessarily correlate with their relatedness because evolutionary change is not constant in rate and direction.

■ *Why might a species be most phenotypically similar to a species that is not its closest evolutionary relative?*

## 23.2 Cladistics

### Learning Outcomes

1. *Describe the difference between ancestral and derived similarities.*
2. *Explain why only shared, derived characters indicate close evolutionary relationship.*
3. *Demonstrate how a cladogram is constructed.*

Because phenotypic similarity may be misleading, most systematists no longer construct their phylogenetic hypotheses solely on this basis. Rather, they distinguish similarity among species that is inherited from the most recent common ancestor of an entire group, which is called **derived,** from similarity that arose prior to the common ancestor of the group, which is termed *ancestral*. In this approach, termed **cladistics,** only **shared**

derived characters are considered informative in determining evolutionary relationships.

## The cladistic method requires that character variation be identified as ancestral or derived

To employ the method of cladistics, systematists first gather data on a number of characters for all the species in the analysis. Characters can be any aspect of the phenotype, including morphology, physiology, behavior, and DNA. As chapters 18 and 24 show, the revolution in genomics should soon provide a vast body of data that may revolutionize our ability to identify and study character variation.

To be useful, the characters should exist in recognizable **character states.** For example, consider the character "teeth" in amniote vertebrates (namely birds, reptiles, and mammals; see chapter 35). This character has two states: presence in most mammals and reptiles and absence in birds and a few other groups such as turtles.

### Examples of ancestral versus derived characters

The presence of hair is a shared derived feature of mammals (figure 23.2); in contrast, the presence of lungs in mammals is an ancestral feature because it is also present in amphibians and reptiles (represented by a salamander and a lizard) and therefore presumably evolved prior to the common ancestor of mammals (see figure 23.2). The presence of lungs, therefore, does not tell us that mammal species are all more closely related to one another than to reptiles or amphibians, but the shared, derived feature of hair suggests that all mammal species share a common ancestor that existed more recently than the common ancestor of mammals, amphibians, and reptiles.

To return to the question concerning the relationships of humans, chimps, and gorillas, a number of morphological and DNA characters exist that are derived and shared by chimps and humans, but not by gorillas or other great apes. These characters suggest that chimps and humans diverged from a common ancestor (see figure 23.1b, node 1) that existed more recently than the common ancestor of gorillas, chimps, and humans (node 2).

### Determination of ancestral versus derived

Once the data are assembled, the first step in a manual cladistic analysis is to **polarize** the characters—that is, to determine whether particular character states are ancestral or derived. To polarize the character "teeth," for example, systematists must determine which state—presence or absence—was exhibited by the most recent common ancestor of this group.

Usually, the fossils available do not represent the most recent common ancestor—or we cannot be confident that they do. As a result, the method of *outgroup comparison* is used to assign character polarity. To use this method, a species or group of species that is closely related to, but not a member of, the group under study is designated as the **outgroup.** When the group under study exhibits multiple character states, and one of those states is exhibited by the outgroup, then that state is considered to be ancestral and other states are considered to be derived. However, outgroup species also evolve from their

| Traits: Organism | Jaws | Lungs | Amniotic Membrane | Hair | No Tail | Bipedal |
|---|---|---|---|---|---|---|
| Lamprey | 0 | 0 | 0 | 0 | 0 | 0 |
| Shark | 1 | 0 | 0 | 0 | 0 | 0 |
| Salamander | 1 | 1 | 0 | 0 | 0 | 0 |
| Lizard | 1 | 1 | 1 | 0 | 0 | 0 |
| Tiger | 1 | 1 | 1 | 1 | 0 | 0 |
| Gorilla | 1 | 1 | 1 | 1 | 1 | 0 |
| Human | 1 | 1 | 1 | 1 | 1 | 1 |

a.

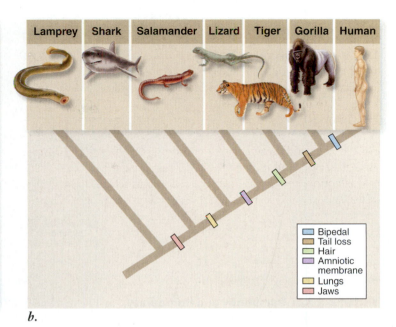

b.

**Figure 23.2 A cladogram.** *a.* Morphological data for a group of seven vertebrates are tabulated. A "1" indicates possession of the derived character state, and a "0" indicates possession of the ancestral character state (note that the derived state for character "no tail" is the absence of a tail; for all other traits, absence of the trait is the ancestral character state). *b.* A tree, or cladogram, diagrams the relationships among the organisms based on the presence of derived characters. The derived characters between the cladogram branch points are shared by all organisms above the branch points and are not present in any below them. The outgroup (in this case, the lamprey) does not possess any of the derived characters.

ancestors, so the outgroup species will not always exhibit the ancestral condition.

Polarity assignments are most reliable when the same character state is exhibited by several different outgroups. In the preceding example, teeth are generally present in the nearest outgroups of amniotes—amphibians and fish— as well as in many species of amniotes themselves. Consequently, the presence of teeth in mammals and reptiles is considered ancestral, and their absence in birds and turtles is considered derived.

### Construction of a cladogram

Once all characters have been polarized, systematists use this information to construct a **cladogram,** which depicts a hypothesis of evolutionary relationships. Species that share a common ancestor, as indicated by the possession of shared derived characters, are said to belong to a **clade.** Clades are thus evolutionary units and refer to a common ancestor and all of its descendants. A derived character shared by clade members is called a **synapomorphy** of that clade. Figure 23.2b illustrates that a simple cladogram is a nested set of clades, each characterized by its own synapomorphies. For example, amniotes are a clade for which the evolution of an amniotic membrane is a synapomorphy. Within that clade, mammals are a clade, with hair as a synapomorphy, and so on.

Ancestral states are also called **plesiomorphies,** and shared ancestral states are called **symplesiomorphies.** In contrast to synapomorphies, symplesiomorphies are not informative about phylogenetic relationships.

Consider, for example, the character state "presence of a tail," which is exhibited by lampreys, sharks, salamanders, lizards,

and tigers. Does this mean that tigers are more closely related to—and shared a more recent common ancestor with—lizards and sharks than to apes and humans, their fellow mammals? The answer, of course, is no: Because symplesiomorphies reflect character states inherited from a distant ancestor, they do not imply that species exhibiting that state are closely related.

### Homoplasy complicates cladistic analysis

In real-world cases, phylogenetic studies are rarely as simple as the examples we have shown so far. The reason is that in some cases, the same character has evolved independently in several species. These characters would be categorized as shared derived characters, but they would be false signals of a close evolutionary relationship. In addition, derived characters may sometimes be lost as species within a clade re-evolve to the ancestral state.

**Homoplasy** refers to a shared character state that has not been inherited from a common ancestor exhibiting that character state. Homoplasy can result from convergent evolution or from evolutionary reversal. For example, adult frogs do not have a tail. Thus, absence of a tail is a synapomorphy that unites not only gorillas and humans, but also frogs. However, frogs have neither an amniotic membrane nor hair, both of which are synapomorphies for clades that contain gorillas and humans.

In cases such as this, when there are conflicts among the characters, systematists rely on the **principle of parsimony,** which favors the hypothesis that requires the fewest assumptions. As a result, the phylogeny that requires the fewest evolutionary events is considered the best hypothesis of phylogenetic

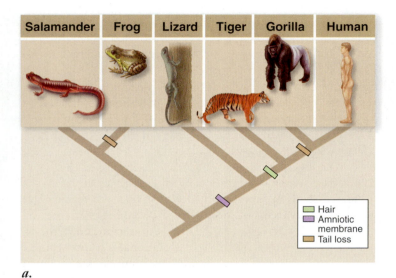

a.

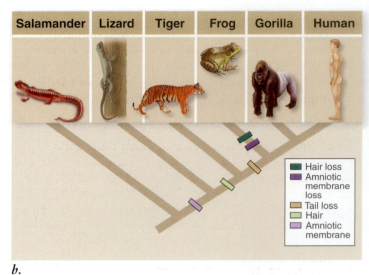

b.

**Figure 23.3 Parsimony and homoplasy.** *a.* The placement of frogs as closely related to salamanders requires that tail loss evolved twice, an example of homoplasy. *b.* If frogs are closely related to gorillas and humans, then tail loss only had to evolve once. However, this arrangement would require two additional evolutionary changes: Frogs would have had to have lost the amniotic membrane and hair (alternatively, hair could have evolved independently in tigers and the clade of humans and gorillas; this interpretation would require two evolutionary changes in the hair character, just like the interpretation shown in the figure, in which hair evolved only once, but then was lost in frogs). Based on the principle of parsimony, the cladogram that requires the fewest number of evolutionary changes is favored; in this case the cladogram in *(a)* requires four changes, whereas that in *(b)* requires five, so *(a)* is considered the preferred hypothesis of evolutionary relationships.

relationships (figure 23.3). In the example just stated, therefore, grouping frogs with salamanders is favored because it requires only one instance of homoplasy (the multiple origins of taillessness), whereas a phylogeny in which frogs were most closely related to humans and gorillas would require two homoplastic evolutionary events (the loss of both amniotic membranes and hair in frogs).

The examples presented so far have all involved morphological characters, but systematists increasingly use DNA sequence data to construct phylogenies because of the large number of characters that can be obtained through sequencing. Cladistics analyzes sequence data in the same manner as any

other type of data: Character states are polarized by reference to the sequence of an outgroup, and a cladogram is constructed that minimizes the amount of character evolution required (figure 23.4).

## Other phylogenetic methods work better than cladistics in some situations

If characters evolve from one state to another at a slow rate compared with the frequency of speciation events, then the principle of parsimony works well in reconstructing

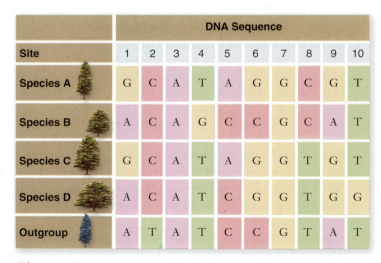

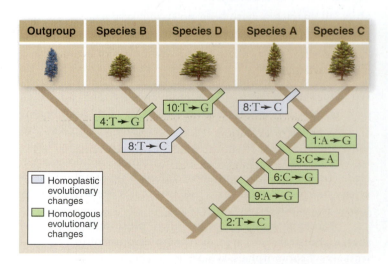

**Figure 23.4 Cladistic analysis of DNA sequence data.** Sequence data are analyzed just like any other data. The most parsimonious interpretation of the DNA sequence data requires nine evolutionary changes. Each of these changes is indicated on the phylogeny. Change in site 8 is homoplastic: Species A and B independently evolved from thymine to cytosine at that site.

evolutionary relationships. In this situation, the principle's underlying assumption—that shared derived similarity is indicative of recent common ancestry—is usually correct. In recent years, however, systematists have realized that some characters evolve so rapidly that the principle of parsimony may be misleading.

### Rapid rates of evolutionary change and homoplasy

Of particular interest is the rate at which some parts of the genome evolve. As discussed in chapter 18, some stretches of DNA do not appear to have any function. As a result, mutations that occur in these parts of the DNA are not eliminated by natural selection, and thus the rate of evolution of new character states can be quite high in these regions as a result of genetic drift.

Moreover, because only four character states are possible for any nucleotide base (A, C, G, or T), there is a high probability that two species will independently evolve the same derived character state at any particular base position. If such homoplasy dominates the character data set, then the assumptions of the principle of parsimony are violated, and as a result, phylogenies inferred using this method are likely to be inaccurate.

> ### ? Inquiry question
>
> Why do high rates of evolutionary change and a limited number of character states cause problems for parsimony analyses?

### Statistical approaches

Because evolution can sometimes proceed rapidly, systematists in recent years have been exploring other methods based on statistical approaches, such as maximum likelihood, to infer phylogenies. These methods start with an assumption about the rate at which characters evolve and then fit the data to these models to derive the phylogeny that best accords (i.e., "maximally likely") with these assumptions.

One advantage of these methods is that different assumptions of rate of evolution can be used for different characters. If some DNA characters evolve more slowly than others—for example, because they are constrained by natural selection—then the methods can employ different models of evolution for the different characters. This approach is more effective than parsimony in dealing with homoplasy when rates of evolutionary changes are high.

### The molecular clock

In general, cladograms such as the one in figure 23.2 only indicate the order of evolutionary branching events; they do not contain information about the timing of these events. In some cases, however, branching events can be timed, either by reference to fossils, or by making assumptions about the rate at which characters change. One widely used but controversial method is the **molecular clock,** which states that the rate of evolution of a molecule is constant through time. In this model, divergence in DNA can be used to calculate the times at which branching events have occurred. To make such estimates, the timing of one or more divergence events must be confidently estimated. For example, the fossil record may indicate that two clades diverged from a common ancestor at a particular time.

Alternatively, the timing of separation of two clades may be estimated from geological events that likely led to their divergence, such as the rise of a mountain that now separates the two clades. With this information, the amount of DNA divergence separating two clades can be divided by the length of time separating the two clades, which produces an estimate of the rate of DNA divergence per unit of time (usually, per million years). Assuming a molecular clock, this rate can then be used to date other divergence events in a cladogram.

Although the molecular clock appears to hold true in some cases, in many others the data indicate that rates of evolution have not been constant through time across all branches in an evolutionary tree. For this reason, evolutionary dates derived from molecular data must be treated cautiously. Recently, methods have been developed to date evolutionary events without assuming that molecular evolution has been clocklike. These methods hold great promise for providing more reliable estimates of evolutionary timing.

> ### Learning Outcomes Review 23.2
>
> In cladistics, derived character states are distinguished from ancestral character states, species are grouped based on shared derived character states. Derived characters are determined from comparison to a group known to be closely related, termed an outgroup. A clade contains all descendants of a common ancestor. A cladogram is a hypothetical representation of evolutionary relationships based on derived character states. Homoplasies may give a false picture of relationships.
>
> - *Why is cladistics more successful at inferring phylogenetic relationships in some cases than in others?*

## 23.3 Systematics and Classification

> ### Learning Outcomes
>
> 1. *Differentiate among monophyletic, paraphyletic, and polyphyletic groups.*
> 2. *Explain the meaning of the phylogenetic species concept and why it is controversial.*

Whereas systematics is the reconstruction and study of evolutionary relationships, **classification** refers to how we place species and higher groups—genus, family, class, and so forth—into the taxonomic hierarchy (a topic we discuss in greater detail in chapter 26).

### Current classification sometimes does not reflect evolutionary relationships

Systematics and traditional classification are not always congruent; to understand why, we need to consider how species may be grouped based on their phylogenetic relationships. A **monophyletic** group includes the most recent common ancestor of the group and all of its descendants. By definition, a clade is a monophyletic group. A **paraphyletic** group includes the most recent common ancestor of the group, but not all its descendants, and a **polyphyletic** group does not include the most recent common ancestor of all members of the group (figure 23.5).

Taxonomic hierarchies are based on shared traits, and ideally they should reflect evolutionary relationships. Traditional taxonomic groups, however, do not always fit well with new understanding of phylogenetic relationships. For example, birds have historically been placed in the class Aves, and

### Figure 23.5
**Monophyletic, paraphyletic, and polyphyletic groups.**

*a.* A monophyletic group consists of the most recent common ancestor and all of its descendants. For example, the name "Archosaurs" is given to the monophyletic group that includes a crocodile, *Stegosaurus, Tyrannosaurus, Velociraptor*, and a hawk.
*b.* A paraphyletic group consists of the most recent common ancestor and some of its descendants. For example, some, but not all, taxonomists traditionally give the name "dinosaurs" to the paraphyletic group that includes *Stegosaurus, Tyrannosaurus*, and *Velociraptor*. This group is paraphyletic because one descendant of the most recent ancestor of these species, the bird, is not included in the group. Other taxonomists include birds within the Dinosauria because *Tyrannosaurus* and *Velociraptor* are more closely related to birds than to other dinosaurs. *c.* A polyphyletic group does not contain the most recent common ancestor of the group. For example, bats and birds could be classified in the same group, which we might call "flying vertebrates," because they have similar shapes, anatomical features, and habitats. However, their similarities reflect convergent evolution, not common ancestry.

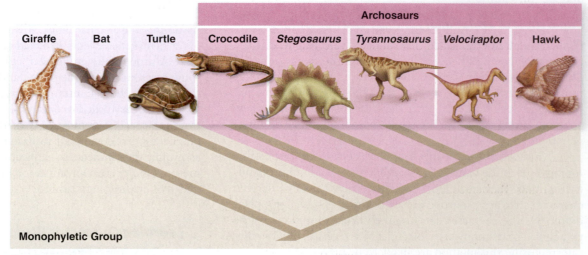

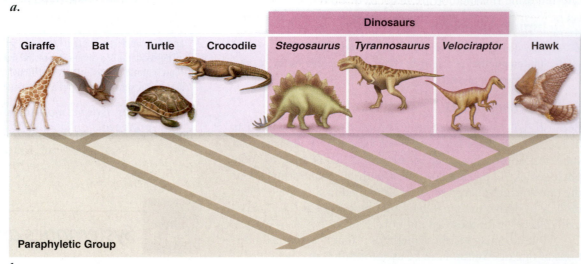

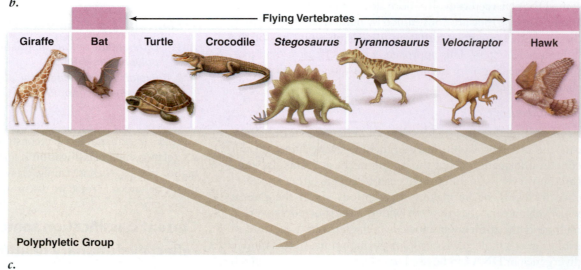

### Inquiry question

? Based on this phylogeny, are there any alternatives to convergence to explain the presence of wings in birds and bats? What types of data might be used to test these hypotheses?

dinosaurs have been considered part of the class Reptilia. But recent phylogenetic advances make clear that birds evolved from dinosaurs. The last common ancestor of all birds and a dinosaur was a meat-eating dinosaur (see figure 23.5).

Therefore, having two separate monophyletic groups, one for birds and one for reptiles (including dinosaurs and crocodiles, as well as lizards, snakes, and turtles), is not possible based on phylogeny. And yet the terms Aves and Reptilia are so familiar and well established that suddenly referring to birds as a type of dinosaur, and thus a type of reptile, is difficult for some. Nonetheless, biologists increasingly refer to birds as a type of dinosaur and hence a type of reptile.

Situations like this are not uncommon. Another example concerns the classification of plants. Traditionally, three major groups were recognized: green algae, bryophytes, and vascular plants (figure 23.6). However, recent research reveals that neither the green algae nor the bryophytes constitute monophyletic groups. Rather, some bryophyte groups are more closely related to vascular plants than they are to other bryophytes, and some green algae are more closely related to bryophytes and vascular plants than they are to other green algae. As a result, systematists no longer recognize green algae or bryophytes as evolutionary groups, and the classification system has been changed to reflect evolutionary relationships.

## The phylogenetic species concept focuses on shared derived characters

In the preceding chapter, you read about a number of different ideas concerning what determines whether two populations belong to the same species. The biological species concept (BSC) defines species as groups of interbreeding populations that are reproductively isolated from other groups. In recent years, a phylogenetic perspective has emerged and has been applied to the question of species concepts. Advocates of the **phylogenetic species concept (PSC)** propose that the term *species* should be applied to groups of populations that have been evolving independently of other groups of populations. Moreover, they suggest that phylogenetic analysis is the way to identify such species. In this view, a species is a population or set of populations characterized by one or more shared derived characters.

This approach solves two of the problems with the BSC that were discussed in chapter 22. First, the BSC cannot be applied to allopatric populations because scientists cannot determine whether individuals of the populations would interbreed and produce fertile offspring if they ever came together. The PSC solves this problem: Instead of trying to predict what will happen in the future if allopatric populations ever come into contact, the PSC looks to the past to determine whether a population (or groups of populations) has evolved independently for a long enough time to develop its own derived characters.

Second, the PSC can be applied equally well to both sexual and asexual species, in contrast to the BSC, which deals only with sexual forms.

## The PSC also has drawbacks

The PSC is controversial, however, for several reasons. First, some critics contend that it will lead to the recognition of every slightly differentiated population as a distinct species. In Missouri, for example, open, desert-like habitat patches called glades are distributed throughout much of the state. These glades contain a variety of warmth-loving species of plants and animals that do not occur in the forests that separate the glades. Glades have been isolated from one another for a few thousand years, allowing enough time for populations on each glade to evolve differences in some rapidly evolving parts of the genome. Does that mean that each of the hundreds, if not thousands, of Missouri glades contains its own species of lizards, grasshoppers, and scorpions? Some scientists argue that if one takes the PSC to its logical extreme, that is exactly what would result.

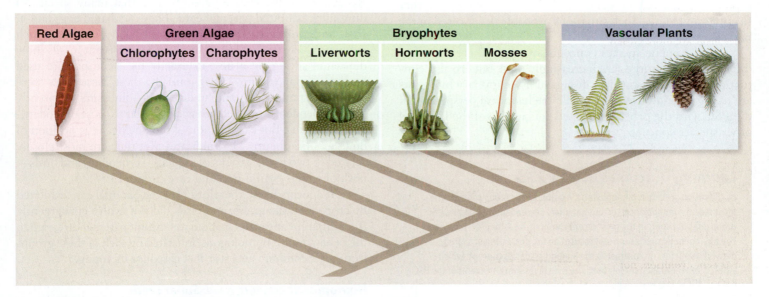

**Figure 23.6 Phylogenetic information transforms plant classification.** The traditional classification included two groups that we now realize are not monophyletic: the green algae and bryophytes. For this reason, plant systematists have developed a new classification of plants that does not include these groups (discussed in chapter 30).

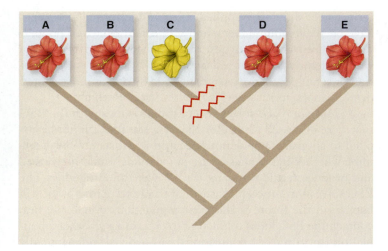

**Figure 23.7 Paraphyly and the phylogenetic species concept.** The five populations initially were all members of the same species, with their historical relationships indicated by the cladogram. Then, population C evolved in some ways to become greatly differentiated ecologically and reproductively from the other populations. By all species concepts, this population would qualify as a different species. However, the remaining four species do not form a clade; they are paraphyletic because population C has been removed and placed in a different species. This scenario may occur commonly in nature, but most versions of the phylogenetic species concept do not recognize paraphyletic species.

A second problem is that species may not always be monophyletic, contrary to the definition of some versions of the phylogenetic species concept. Consider, for example, a species composed of five populations, with evolutionary relationships like those indicated in figure 23.7. Suppose that population C becomes isolated and evolves differences that make it qualify as a species by any concept (for example, reproductively isolated, ecologically differentiated). But this distinction would mean that the remaining populations, which might still be perfectly capable of exchanging genes, would be paraphyletic, rather than monophyletic. Such situations probably occur often in the natural world.

Phylogenetic species concepts, of which there are many different permutations, are increasingly used, but are also contentious for the reasons just discussed. Evolutionary biologists are trying to find ways to reconcile the historical perspective of the PSC with the process-oriented perspective of the BSC and other species concepts.

### Learning Outcomes Review 23.3

By definition, a clade is monophyletic. A paraphyletic group contains the most recent common ancestor, but not all its descendants; a polyphyletic group does not contain the most recent common ancestor of all members. The phylogenetic species concept focuses on the possession of shared derived characters, in contrast to the biological species concept, which emphasizes reproductive isolation. The PSC solves some problems of the BSC but has difficulties of its own.

■ *Under the biological species concept, is it possible for a species to be polyphyletic?*

### Learning Outcomes

1. *Explain the concept of homoplasy.*
2. *Describe how phylogenetic trees can reveal the existence of homoplasy.*
3. *Discuss how a phylogenetic tree can indicate the timing of species diversification.*

Phylogenies not only provide information about evolutionary relationships among species, but they are also indispensable for understanding how evolution has occurred. By examining the distribution of traits among species in the context of their phylogenetic relationships, much can be learned about how and why evolution may have proceeded. In this way, phylogenetics is the basis of all comparative biology.

## Homologous features are derived from the same ancestral source; homoplastic features are not

In chapter 21, we pointed out that homologous structures are those that are derived from the same body part in a common ancestor. Thus, the forelegs of a dolphin (flipper) and of a horse (leg) are homologous because they are derived from the same bones in an ancestral vertebrate. By contrast, the wings of birds and those of dragonflies are homoplastic structures because they are derived from different ancestral structures. Phylogenetic analysis can help determine whether structures are homologous or homoplastic.

### Homologous parental care in dinosaurs, crocodiles, and birds

Recent fossil discoveries have revealed that many species of dinosaurs exhibited parental care. They incubated eggs laid in nests and took care of growing baby dinosaurs, many of which could not have fended for themselves. Some recent fossils show dinosaurs sitting on a nest in exactly the same posture used by birds today (figure 23.8a)! Initially, these discoveries were treated as remarkable and unexpected—dinosaurs apparently had independently evolved behaviors similar to those of modern-day organisms. But examination of the phylogenetic position of dinosaurs (see figure 23.5) indicates that they are most closely related to two living groups of animals—crocodiles and birds—both of which exhibit parental care (figure 23.8b).

It appears likely, therefore, that the parental care exhibited by crocodiles, dinosaurs, and birds did not evolve convergently from different ancestors that did not exhibit parental care; rather, the behaviors are homologous, inherited by each of these groups from their common ancestor that cared for its young.

### Homoplastic convergence: Saber teeth and plant conducting tubes

In other cases, by contrast, phylogenetic analysis can indicate that similar traits have evolved independently in different

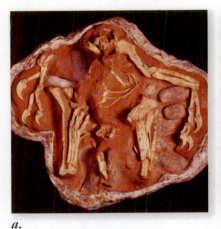

a.

b.

**Figure 23.8 Parental care in dinosaurs and crocodiles** *a.* Fossil dinosaur incubating its eggs. This remarkable fossil of *Oviraptor* shows the dinosaur sitting on its nest of eggs just as chickens do today. Not only is the dinosaur squatting on the nest, but its forelimbs are outstretched, perhaps to shade the eggs. *b.* Crocodile exhibiting parental care. Female crocodilians build nests and then remain nearby, guarding them, while the eggs incubate. When they are ready to hatch, the baby crocodiles vocalize; females respond by digging up the eggs and carrying the babies to the water.

clades. This convergent evolution from different ancestral sources indicates that such traits represent homoplasies. As one example, the fossil record reveals that extremely elongated canine teeth (saber teeth) occurred in a number of different groups of extinct carnivorous mammals. Although how these teeth were actually used is still debated, all saber-toothed carnivores had body proportions similar to those of cats, which suggests that these different types of carnivores all evolved into a similar predatory lifestyle. Examination of the saber-toothed character state in a phylogenetic context reveals that it most likely evolved independently at least three times (figure 23.9).

## SCIENTIFIC THINKING

**Question:** *How many times have saber teeth evolved in carnivores?*

**Hypothesis:** *Saber teeth are homologous and have only evolved once in carnivores (or, conversely, saber teeth are convergent and have evolved multiple times in carnivores).*

**Phylogenic Analysis:** *Examine the distribution of saber teeth on a phylogeny of carnivores, and use parsimony to infer the history of saber tooth evolution (note that not all branches within marsupials and placentals are shown on the phylogeny).*

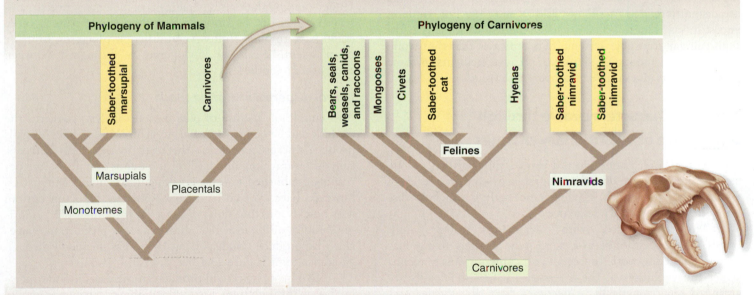

**Result:** *Saber teeth have evolved at least three times in mammals: once within marsupials, once in felines, and at least once in nimravids.*

**Interpretation:** *Note that it is possible that saber teeth evolved twice in nimravids, but another possibility that requires the same number of evolutionary changes (and thus is equally parsimonious) is that saber teeth evolved only once in the ancestor of nimravids and then were subsequently lost in one group of nimravids.*

**Figure 23.9 Distribution of saber-toothed mammals.** Saber teeth have evolved at least three times in mammals: once within marsupials, once in felines, and at least once in a now-extinct group of catlike carnivores called nimravids. It is possible that the condition evolved twice in nimravids, but another possibility that requires the same number of evolutionary changes (and thus is equally parsimonious) is that saber teeth evolved only once in the ancestor of nimravids and then were subsequently lost in one group of nimravids (not all of the branches within marsupials and placentals are shown).

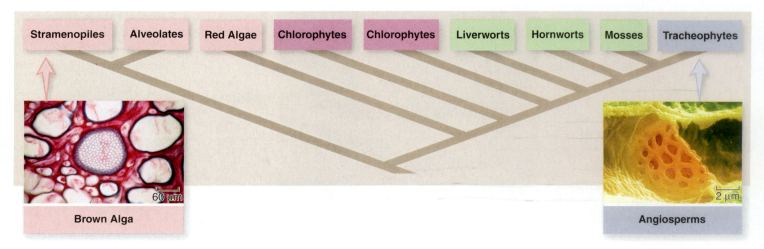

Stramenopiles | Alveolates | Red Algae | Chlorophytes | Chlorophytes | Liverworts | Hornworts | Mosses | Tracheophytes

Brown Alga

60 µm

Angiosperms

2 µm

**Figure 23.10 Convergent evolution of conducting tubes.** Sieve tubes, which transport hormones and other substances throughout the plant, have evolved in two distantly related plant groups (brown algae are stramenopiles and angiosperms are tracheophytes).
© Dr. Richard Kessel & Dr. Gene Shih/Visuals Unlimited

Conducting tubes in plants provide a similar example. The tracheophytes, a large group of land plants discussed in chapter 30, transport photosynthetic products, hormones, and other molecules over long distances through elongated, tubular cells that have perforated walls at the end. These structures are stacked upon each other to create a conduit called a sieve tube. Sieve tubes facilitate long-distance transport that is essential for the survival of tall plants on land.

Most members of the brown algae, which includes kelp, also have sieve elements (see figure 23.10 for a comparison of the sieve plates in brown algae and angiosperms) that aid in the rapid transport of materials. The land plants and brown algae are distantly related (see figure 23.10), and their last common ancestor was a single-celled organism that could not have had a multicellular transport system. This indicates that the strong structural and functional similarity of sieve elements in these plant groups is an example of convergent evolution.

## Complex characters evolve through a sequence of evolutionary changes

Most complex characters do not evolve, fully formed, in one step. Rather, they are often built up, step-by-step, in a series of evolutionary transitions. Phylogenetic analysis can help discover these evolutionary sequences.

Modern-day birds—with their wings, feathers, light bones, and breastbone—are exquisitely adapted flying machines. Fossil discoveries in recent years now allow us to reconstruct the evolution of these features. When the fossils are arranged phylogenetically, it becomes clear that the features characterizing living birds did not evolve simultaneously. Figure 23.11 shows how the features important to flight evolved sequentially, probably over a long period of time, in the ancestors of modern birds.

One important finding often revealed by studies of the evolution of complex characters is that the initial stages of a character evolved as an adaptation to some environmental selective pressure different from that for which the character is currently adapted. Examination of figure 23.11 reveals that the first feathery structures evolved deep in the theropod phylogeny, in animals with forearms clearly not modified for flight. Therefore, the initial feather-like structures must have evolved for some other reason, perhaps serving as insulation or decoration. Through time, these structures have become modified to the extent that modern feathers produce excellent aerodynamic performance.

## Phylogenetic methods can be used to distinguish between competing hypotheses

Understanding the causes of patterns of biological diversity observed today can be difficult because a single pattern often could have resulted from several different processes. In many cases, scientists can use phylogenies to distinguish between competing hypotheses.

### Larval dispersal in marine snails

An example of this use of phylogenetic analysis concerns the evolution of larval forms in marine snails. Most species of snails produce microscopic larvae that drift in the ocean currents, sometimes traveling hundreds or thousands of miles before becoming established and transforming into adults. Some species, however, have evolved larvae that settle to the ocean bottom very quickly and thus don't disperse far from their place of origin. Studies of fossil snails indicate that the proportion of species that produce nondispersing larvae has increased through geological time (figure 23.12).

Two processes could produce an increase in nondispersing larvae through time. First, if evolutionary change from dispersing to nondispersing occurs more often than change in the opposite direction, then the proportion of species that are nondispersing would increase through time.

Alternatively, if species that are nondispersing speciate more frequently, or become extinct less frequently, than dispersing species, then through time the proportion of nondispersers would also increase (assuming that the descendants of nondispersing species also were nondispersing). This latter case is a reasonable hypothesis because nondispersing species

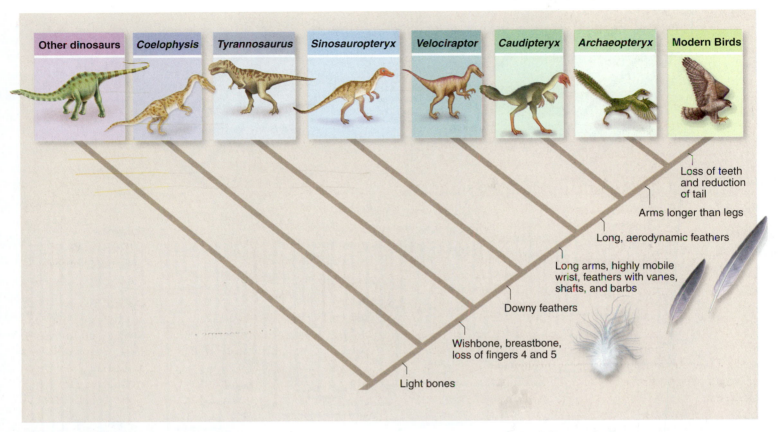

| Other dinosaurs | Coelophysis | Tyrannosaurus | Sinosauropteryx | Velociraptor | Caudipteryx | Archaeopteryx | Modern Birds |

Loss of teeth and reduction of tail

Arms longer than legs

Long, aerodynamic feathers

Long arms, highly mobile wrist, feathers with vanes, shafts, and barbs

Downy feathers

Wishbone, breastbone, loss of fingers 4 and 5

Light bones

**Figure 23.11** **The evolution of birds.** The traits we think of as characteristic of modern birds have evolved in stages over many millions of years.

From Richard O. Prum and Alan H. Brush, "The Evolutionary Origin and Diversification of Feathers," *Quarterly Review of Biology*, September 2002. Reprinted with permission of the University of Chicago Press.

probably have lower amounts of gene flow than dispersing species, and thus might more easily become geographically isolated, increasing the likelihood of allopatric speciation (see chapter 22).

These two processes would result in different phylogenetic patterns. If evolution from a dispersing ancestor to a nondispersing descendant occurred more often than the reverse, then an excess of such changes should be evident in the phylog-

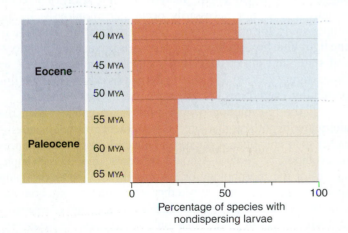

**Figure 23.12** **Larvae dispersal.** Increase through time in the proportion of species whose larvae do not disperse far from their place of birth.

eny, as shown by more dispersing ⟶ nondispersing branch-points in figure 23.13*a*. In contrast, if nondispersing species underwent greater speciation, then clades of nondispersing species would contain more species than clades of dispersing species, as shown in figure 23.13*b*.

Evidence for both processes was revealed in an examination of the phylogeny of marine snails in the genus *Conus*, in which 30% of species are nondispersing (figure 23.13*c*). The phylogeny indicates that possession of dispersing larvae was the ancestral state; nondispersing larvae are inferred to have evolved eight times, with no evidence for evolutionary reversal from nondispersing to dispersing larvae.

At the same time, clades of nondispersing larvae tend to have on average 3.5 times as many species as dispersing larvae, which suggests that in nondispersing species, rates of speciation are higher, rates of extinction are lower, or both.

This analysis therefore indicates that the evolutionary increase in nondispersing larvae through time may be a result both of a bias in the direction in which evolution proceeds plus an increase in rate of diversification (that is, speciation rate minus extinction rate) in nondispersing clades.

The lack of evolutionary reversal is not surprising because when larvae evolve to become nondispersing, they often lose a variety of structures used for feeding while drifting in the ocean current. In most cases, once a structure is lost, it rarely re-evolves, and thus the standard view is that the

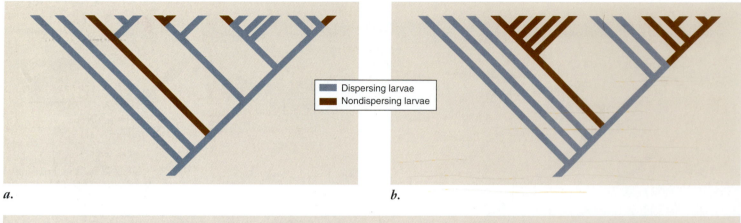

a.

b.

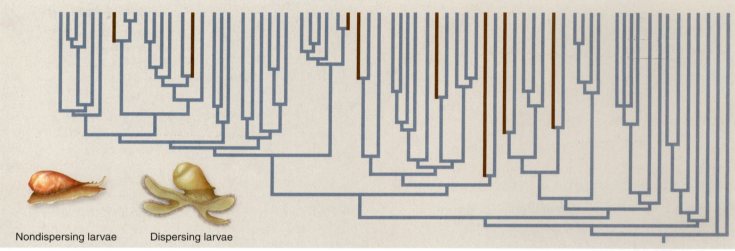

Nondispersing larvae    Dispersing larvae

c.

**Figure 23.13 Phylogenetic investigation of the evolution of nondispersing larvae.** *a.* In this hypothetical example, the evolutionary transition from dispersing to nondispersing larvae occurs more frequently (four times) than the converse (once). By contrast, in *(b)* clades that have nondispersing larvae diversify to a greater extent due to higher rates of speciation or lower rates of extinction (assuming that extinct forms are not shown). *c.* Phylogeny for *Conus*, a genus of marine snails. Nondispersing larvae have evolved eight separate times from dispersing larvae, with no instances of evolution in the reverse direction. This phylogeny does not show all species, however; nondispersing clades contain on average 3.5 times as many species as dispersing clades.

evolution of nondispersing larvae is a one-way street, with few examples of re-evolution of dispersing larvae.

### Loss of the larval stage in marine invertebrates

A related phenomenon in many marine invertebrates is the loss of the larval stage entirely. Most marine invertebrates—in groups as diverse as snails, sea stars, and anemones—pass through a larval stage as they develop. But in a number of different types of organisms, the larval stage is omitted, and the eggs develop directly into adults.

The evolutionary loss of the larval stage has been suggested as another example of a nonreversible evolutionary change because once the larval stages are lost, it is difficult for them to re-evolve—or so the argument goes. A recent study on one group of marine limpets, shelled marine organisms related to snails, shows that this is not necessarily the case. Among these limpets, direct development has evolved many times; however, in three cases, the phylogeny strongly suggests that evolution reversed and a larval stage re-evolved (figure 23.14*a*).

It is important to remember that patterns of evolution suggested by phylogenetic analysis are not always correct—evolution does not necessarily occur parsimoniously. In the limpet study, for example, it is possible that within the clade in the light blue box, presence of a larva was retained as the ancestral state, and direct development evolved independently six times (figure 23.14*b*). Phylogenetic analysis cannot rule out this possibility, even if it is less phylogenetically parsimonious.

If the re-evolution of lost traits seems unlikely, then the alternative hypothesis that direct development evolved six times—rather than only once at the base of the clade, with two instances of evolutionary reversal—should be considered. For example, studies of the morphology or embryology of direct-developing species might shed light on whether such structures are homologous or convergent. In some cases, artificial selection experiments in the laboratory or genetic manipulations can test the hypothesis that it is difficult for lost structures to re-evolve. Conclusions from phylogenetic analyses are always stronger when supported by results of other types of studies.

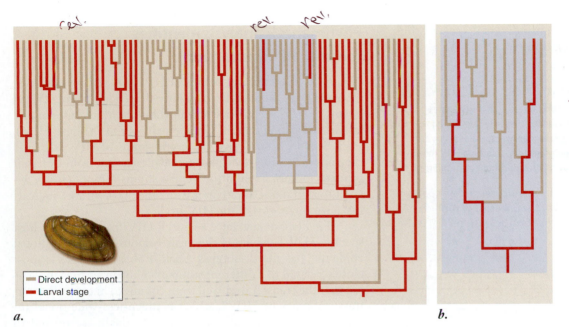

*a.*

Direct development
Larval stage

*b.*

**Figure 23.14 Evolution of direct development in a family of limpets.** *a.* Direct development evolved many times (indicated by beige lines stemming from a red ancestor), and three instances of reversed evolution from direct development to larval development are indicated (red lines from a beige ancestor). *b.* A less parsimonious interpretation of evolution in the clade in the light blue box is that, rather than two evolutionary reversals, six instances of the evolution of development occurred without any evolutionary reversal.

## Phylogenetics helps explain species diversification

One of the central goals of evolutionary biology is to explain patterns of species diversity: Why do some types of plants and animals exhibit more **species richness**—a greater number of species per clade—than others? Phylogenetic analysis can be used both to suggest and to test hypotheses about such differences.

### Species richness in beetles

Beetles (order Coleoptera) are the most diverse group of animals. Approximately 60% of all animal species are insects, and approximately 80% of all insect species are beetles. Among beetles, families that are herbivorous are particularly species-rich.

Examination of the phylogeny provides insight into beetle evolutionary diversification (figure 23.15). Among the Phytophaga, the clade which contains most herbivorous beetle species, the deepest branches belong to beetle families that specialize on conifers. This finding agrees with the fossil record because conifers were among the earliest seed plant groups to evolve. By contrast, the flowering plants (angiosperms) evolved more recently, in the Cretaceous, and beetle families specializing on them have shorter evolutionary branches, indicating their more recent evolutionary appearance.

This correspondence between phylogenetic position and timing of plant origins suggests that beetles have been remarkably conservative in their diet. The family Nemonychidae, for example, appears to have remained specialized on conifers since the beginning of the Jurassic, approximately 210 MYA.

### Phylogenetic explanations for beetle diversification

The phylogenetic perspective suggests factors that may be responsible for the incredible diversity of beetles. The phylogeny for the Phytophaga indicates that it is not the evolution of herbivory itself that is linked to great species richness. Rather, specialization on angiosperms seems to have been a prerequisite for great species diversification. Specialization on angiosperms appears to have arisen five times independently within herbivorous beetles; in each case, the angiosperm-specializing clade is substantially more species-rich than the clade to which it is most closely related (termed a *sister clade)* and which specializes on some other type of plant.

Why specialization on angiosperms has led to great species diversity is not yet clear and is the focus of much current research. One possibility is that this diversity is linked to the great species-richness of angiosperms themselves. With more than 250,000 species of angiosperms, beetle clades specializing on them may have had a multitude

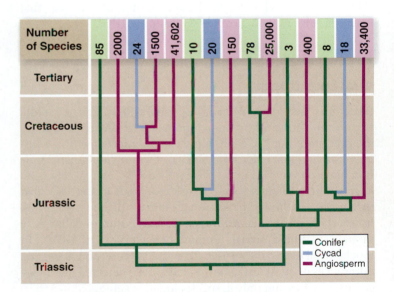

Conifer
Cycad
Angiosperm

**Figure 23.15 Evolutionary diversification of the Phytophaga, the largest clade of herbivorous beetles.** Clades that originated deep in the phylogenetic tree feed on conifers; clades that feed on angiosperms, which evolved more recently, originated more recently. Age of clades is established by examination of fossil beetles.

of opportunities to adapt to feed on individual species, thus promoting divergence and speciation.

### Learning Outcomes Review 23.4

Homologous traits are derived from the same ancestral character states, whereas homoplastic traits are not, even though they may have similar function. Phylogenetic analysis can help determine whether homology or homoplasy has occurred. By correlating phylogenetic branching with known evolutionary events, the timing and cause of diversification can be inferred.

■ **Does the possession of the same character state by all members of a clade mean that the ancestor of that clade necessarily possessed that character state?**

## 23.5 Phylogenetics and Disease Evolution

### Learning Outcome

1. Discuss how phylogenetic analysis can help identify patterns of disease transmission.

The examples so far have illustrated the use of phylogenetic analysis to examine relationships among species. Such analyses can also be conducted on virtually any group of biological entities, as long as evolutionary divergence in these groups occurs by a branching process, with little or no genetic exchange between different groups. No example illustrates this better than recent attempts to understand the evolution of the virus that causes autoimmune deficiency syndrome (AIDS).

### HIV has evolved from a simian viral counterpart

AIDS was first recognized in the early 1980s, and it rapidly became epidemic in the human population. Current estimates are that more than 33 million people are infected with the human immunodeficiency virus (HIV), of whom more than 2 million die each year.

At first, scientists were perplexed about where HIV had originated and how it had infected humans. In the mid-1980s, however, scientists discovered a related virus in laboratory monkeys, termed simian immunodeficiency virus (SIV). In biochemical terms, the viruses are very similar, although genetic differences exist. At last count, SIV has been detected in 36 species of primates, but only in species found in sub-Saharan Africa. Interestingly, SIV—which appears to be transmitted sexually—does not appear to cause any illness in these primates.

Based on the degree of genetic differentiation among strains of SIV, scientists estimate that SIV may have been around for more than a million years in these primates, perhaps providing enough time for these species to adapt to the virus and thus prevent it from having adverse effects.

### Phylogenetic analysis identifies the path of transmission

Phylogenetic analysis of strains of HIV and SIV reveals three clear findings. First, HIV obviously descended from SIV. All strains of HIV are phylogenetically nested within clades of SIV strains, indicating that HIV is derived from SIV (figure 23.16).

Second, a number of different strains of HIV exist, and they appear to represent independent transfers from different primate species. Each of the human strains is more closely related to a strain of SIV than it is to other HIV strains, indicating separate origins of the HIV strains.

Finally, humans have acquired HIV from different host species. HIV-1, which is the virus responsible for the global epidemic, has three subtypes. Each of these subtypes is most closely related to a different strain of chimpanzee SIV, indicating that the transfer occurred from chimps to humans. By contrast, subtypes of HIV-2, which is much less widespread (in some cases known from only one individual), are related to SIV found in West African monkeys, primarily the sooty mangabey (*Cercocebus atys*). Moreover, the subtypes of HIV-2 also appear to represent several independent cross-species transmissions to humans.

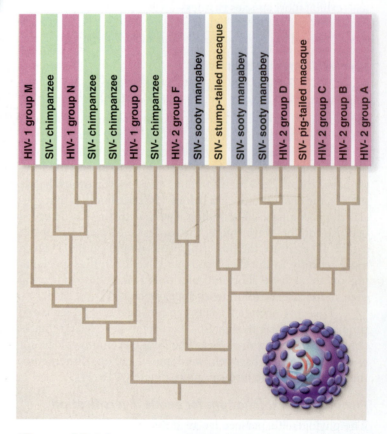

**Figure 23.16 Evolution of HIV and SIV.** HIV has evolved multiple times and from strains of SIV in different primate species (each primate species indicated by a different color). The three-way branching event on the right side of the phylogeny results because the data do not clearly indicate the relationships among the three clades.

### Transmission from other primates to humans

Several hypotheses have been proposed to explain how SIV jumped from chimps and monkeys to humans. The most likely idea is that transmission occurred as the result of blood-to-blood contact that may occur when humans kill and butcher monkeys and apes. Recent years have seen a huge increase in the rate at which primates are hunted for the "bushmeat" market, particularly in central and western Africa. This increase has resulted from a combination of increased human populations desiring ever greater amounts of protein, combined with increased access to the habitats in which these primates live as the result of road building and economic development. The unfortunate result is that population sizes of many primate species, including our closest relatives, are plummeting toward extinction. A second consequence of this hunting is that humans are increasingly brought into contact with bodily fluids of these animals, and it is easy to imagine how during the butchering process, blood from a recently killed animal might enter the human bloodstream through cuts in the skin, perhaps obtained during the hunting process.

### Establishing the crossover time line and location

Where and when did this cross-species transmission occur? HIV strains are most diverse in Africa, and the incidence of HIV is higher there than elsewhere in the world. Combined with the evidence that HIV is related to SIV in African primates, it seems certain that AIDS appeared first in Africa.

As for when the jump from other primates to humans occurred, the fact that AIDS was not recognized until the 1980s suggests that HIV probably arose recently. Descendants of slaves brought to North America from West Africa in the 19th century lacked the disease, indicating that it probably did not occur at the time of the slave trade.

Once the disease was recognized in the 1980s, scientists scoured repositories of blood samples to see whether HIV could be detected in blood samples from the past. The earliest HIV-positive result was found in a sample from 1959, pushing the date of origin back at least two decades. Based on the amount of genetic difference between strains of HIV-1, including the 1959 sample, and assuming the operation of a molecular clock, scientists estimate that the deadly strain of AIDS probably crossed into humans some time before 1940.

### Phylogenies can be used to track the evolution of AIDS among individuals

The AIDS virus evolves extremely rapidly, so much so that different strains can exist within different individuals in a single population. As a result, phylogenetic analysis can be applied to answer very specific questions; just as phylogeny proved useful in determining the source of HIV, it can also pinpoint the source of infection for particular individuals.

This ability became apparent in a court case in Louisiana in 1998, in which a dentist was accused of injecting his former girlfriend with blood drawn from an HIV-infected patient. The dentist's records revealed that he had drawn blood from the patient and had done so in a suspicious manner. Scientists sequenced the viral strains from the victim, the

patient, and from a large number of HIV-infected people in the local community. The phylogenetic analysis clearly demonstrated that the victim's viral strain was most closely related to the patient's (figure 23.17). This analysis, which for the first time established phylogenetics as a legally admissible form of evidence in courts in the United States, helped convict the dentist, who is now serving a 50-year sentence for attempted murder.

### Learning Outcome Review 23.5

Modern phylogenetic techniques and analysis can track the evolution of disease strains, uncovering sources and progression. The HIV virus provides a prime example: Analysis of viral strains has shown that the progression from simian immunodeficiency virus (SIV) into human hosts has occurred several times. Phylogenetic analysis is also used to track the transmission of human disease.

- *Could HIV have arisen in humans and then have been transmitted to other primate species?*

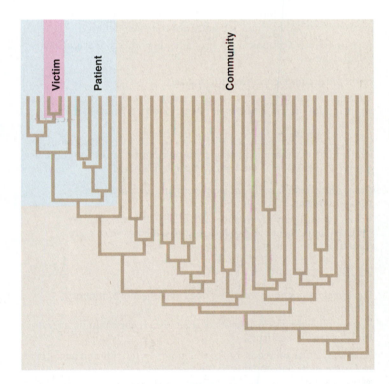

**Figure 23.17 Evolution of HIV strains reveals the source of infection.** HIV mutates so rapidly that a single HIV-infected individual often contains multiple genotypes in his or her body. As a result, it is possible to create a phylogeny of HIV strains and to identify the source of infection of a particular individual. In this case, the HIV strains of the victim clearly are derived from strains in the body of another individual, the patient. Other HIV strains are from HIV-infected individuals in the local community.

### Inquiry question

**?** What would the phylogeny look like if the victim had not gotten HIV from the patient?

# Chapter Review

## 23.1 Systematics

### Branching diagrams depict evolutionary relationships.

Systematics is the study of evolutionary relationships, which are depicted on branching evolutionary trees, called phylogenies.

### Similarity may not accurately predict evolutionary relationships.

The rate of evolution can vary among species and can even reverse direction. Closely related species can therefore be dissimilar in phenotypic characteristics.

Conversely, convergent evolution results in distantly related species being phenotypically similar.

## 23.2 Cladistics

### The cladistic method requires that character variation be identified as ancestral or derived.

Derived character states are those that differ from the ancestral condition.

Character polarity is established using an outgroup comparison in which the outgroup consists of closely related species or a group of species, relative to the group under study.

Character states exhibited by the outgroup are assumed to be ancestral, and other character states are considered derived.

A cladogram is a graphically represented hypothesis of evolutionary relationships.

### Homoplasy complicates cladistic analysis.

Homoplasy refers to a shared character state, such as wings of birds and wings of insects, that has not been inherited from a common ancestor.

Cladograms are constructed based on the principle of parsimony, which indicates that the phylogeny requiring the fewest evolutionary changes is accepted as the best working hypothesis.

### Other phylogenetic methods work better than cladistics in some situations.

When evolutionary change is rapid, other methods, such as statistical approaches and the use of the molecular clock, are sometimes more useful.

## 23.3 Systematics and Classification

### Current classification sometimes does not reflect evolutionary relationships.

A monophyletic group consists of the most recent common ancestor and all of its descendants.

A paraphyletic group consists of the most recent common ancestor and some of its descendants.

A polyphyletic group does not contain the most recent ancestor of the group. Some currently recognized taxa are not monophyletic, such as reptiles, which are paraphyletic with respect to birds.

### The phylogenetic species concept focuses on shared derived characters.

The phylogenetic species concept emphasizes the possession of shared derived characters, whereas the biological species concept focuses on reproductive isolation. Many versions of this concept only recognize species that are monophyletic.

### The PSC (phylogenetic species concept) also has drawbacks.

Among criticisms of the PSC (phylogenetic species concept) are that it subdivides groups too far via impractical distinctions, and that the PSC definition of a group may not always apply as selection proceeds.

## 23.4 Phylogenetics and Comparative Biology

### Homologous features are derived from the same ancestral source; homoplastic features are not.

Homologous structures can be identified by phylogenetic analysis, establishing whether or not different structures have been built from the same ancestral structure.

### Complex characters evolve through a sequence of evolutionary changes.

Most complex features do not evolve in a single step but include stages of transition. They may have begun as an adaptation to a selective pressure different from the one for which the feature is currently adapted.

### Phylogenetic methods can be used to distinguish between competing hypotheses.

Different evolutionary scenarios can be distinguished by phylogenetic analysis. The minimum number of times a trait may have evolved can be established, as well as the direction of trait evolution, the timing, and the cause of diversification.

### Phylogenetics helps explain species diversification.

Questions regarding the causes of species richness may be addressed with phylogenetic analysis.

## 23.5 Phylogenetics and Disease Evolution

### HIV has evolved from a simian viral counterpart.

Phylogenetic methods have indicated that HIV is related to SIV.

### Phylogenetic analysis identifies the path of transmission.

It is clear that HIV has descended from SIV, and that independent transfers from simians to humans have occurred several times. Application of findings has allowed identification of the first occurrence in humans, in 1959.

### Phylogenies can be used to track the evolution of AIDS among individuals.

Even though HIV evolves rapidly, phylogenetic analysis can trace the origin of a current strain to a specific source of infection.

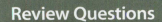
## UNDERSTAND

1. Overall similarity of phenotypes may not always reflect evolutionary relationships
   a. due to convergent evolution.
   b. because of variation in rates of evolutionary change of different kinds of characters.
   c. due to homoplasy.
   d. due to all of the above.

2. Cladistics
   a. is based on overall similarity of phenotypes.
   b. requires distinguishing similarity due to inheritance from a common ancestor from other reasons for similarity.
   c. is not affected by homoplasy.
   d. is none of the above.

3. The principle of parsimony
   a. helps evolutionary biologists distinguish among competing phylogenetic hypotheses.
   b. does not require that the polarity of traits be determined.
   c. is a way to avoid having to use outgroups in a phylogenetic analysis.
   d. cannot be applied to molecular traits.

4. Parsimony suggests that parental care in birds, crocodiles, and some dinosaurs
   a. evolved independently multiple times by convergent evolution.
   b. evolved once in an ancestor common to all three groups.
   c. is a homoplastic trait.
   d. is not a homologous trait.

5. The forelimb of a bird and the forelimb of a rhinoceros
   a. are homologous and symplesiomorphic.
   b. are not homologous but are symplesiomorphic.
   c. are homologous and synapomorphic.
   d. are not homologous but are synapomorphic.

6. In order to determine polarity for different states of a character
   a. there must be a fossil record of the groups in question.
   b. genetic sequence data must be available.
   c. an appropriate name for the taxonomic group must be selected.
   d. an outgroup must be identified.

7. A paraphyletic group includes
   a. an ancestor and all of its descendants.
   b. an ancestor and some of its descendants.
   c. descendants of more than one common ancestor.
   d. all of the above.

8. Sieve tubes and sieve elements are
   a. homoplastic because they have different function.
   b. homologous because they have similar function.
   c. homoplastic because their common ancestor was single-celled.
   d. structures involved in transport within animals.

## APPLY

1. A taxonomic group that contains species that have similar phenotypes due to convergent evolution is
   a. paraphyletic.
   b. monophyletic.
   c. polyphyletic.
   d. a good cladistic group.

2. Rapid rates of character change relative to the rate of speciation pose a problem for cladistics because
   a. the frequency with which distantly related species evolve the same derived character state may be high.
   b. evolutionary reversals may occur frequently.
   c. homoplasy will be common.
   d. all of the above.

3. In a paraphyletic group
   a. all species are more closely related to each other than they are to a species outside the group.
   b. evolutionary reversal is common.
   c. polyphyly also usually occurs.
   d. some species are more closely related to species outside the group than they are to some species within the group.

4. Species recognized by the phylogenetic species concept
   a. sometimes also would be recognized as species by the biological species concept.
   b. are sometimes paraphyletic.
   c. are characterized by symplesiomorphies.
   d. are more frequent in plants than in animals.

## SYNTHESIZE

1. List the synapomorphy and the taxa defined by that synapomorphy for the groups pictured in figure 23.2. Name each group defined by a set of synapomorphies in a way that might be construed as informative about what kind of characters define the group.

2. Identifying "outgroups" is a central component of cladistic analysis. As described on page 458, a group is chosen that is closely related to, but not a part of the group under study. If one does not know the relationships of members of the group under study, how can one be certain that an appropriate outgroup is chosen? Can you think of any approaches that would minimize the effect of a poor choice of outgroup?

3. As noted in your reading, cladistics is a widely utilized method of systematics, and our classification system (taxonomy) is increasingly becoming reflective of our knowledge of evolutionary relationships. Using birds as an example, discuss the advantages and disadvantages of recognizing them as reptiles versus as a group separate and equal to reptiles.

4. Across many species of limpets, loss of larval development and reversal from direct development appears to have occurred multiple times. Under the simple principle of parsimony are changes in either direction merely counted equally in evaluating the most parsimonious hypothesis? If it is much more likely to lose a larval mode than to re-evolve it from direct development, should that be taken into account? If so, how?

5. Birds, pterosaurs (a type of flying reptile that lived in the Cretaceous period), and bats all have modified their forelimbs to serve as wings, but they have done so in different ways. Are these structures homologous? If so, how can they be both homologous and convergent? Do any organisms possess wings that are convergent, but not homologous?

6. In what sense does the biological species concept focus on evolutionary mechanisms and the phylogenetic species concept on evolutionary patterns? Which, if either, is correct?

## ONLINE RESOURCE

**www.ravenbiology.com**

Understand, Apply, and Synthesize—enhance your study with animations that bring concepts to life and practice tests to assess your understanding. Your instructor may also recommend the interactive eBook, individualized learning tools, and more.

# Genome Evolution

## Chapter Outline

## Introduction

*Genomes contain the raw material for evolution, and many clues to evolution are hidden in the ever-changing nature of genomes. As more genomes have been sequenced, the new and exciting field of comparative genomics has emerged and has yielded some surprising results as well as many, many questions. Comparing whole genomes, not just individual genes, enhances our ability to understand the workings of evolution, to improve crops, and to identify the genetic basis of disease so that we might develop more effective treatments with minimal side effects. The focus of this chapter is the role of comparative genomics in enhancing our understanding of genome evolution and how this new knowledge can be applied to improve our lives.*

## 24.1 Comparative Genomics

### Learning Outcomes

1. *Describe the kinds of differences that can be found between genomes.*
2. *Relate timescale to genome evolution.*
3. *Explain why genomes may evolve at different rates.*

A key challenge of modern evolutionary biology is finding a way to link changes in DNA sequences, which we are now able to study in great detail, with the evolution of the complex morphological characters used to construct a traditional phylogeny. Many different genes contribute to complex characters. Making the connection between a specific change in a gene and a modification in a morphological character is particularly difficult.

Comparing genomes (entire DNA sequences) provides a powerful tool for exploring evolutionary divergence among organisms to connect DNA level changes with morphological differences. Genomes are more than instruction books for building and maintaining an organism; they also record the history of life. The growing number of fully sequenced genomes in all kingdoms is leading to a revolution in comparative evolutionary biology (figure 24.1). Genetic differences between species can be explored in a very direct way, examining the footprints on the evolutionary path between different species.

**Saccharomyces cerevisiae**
(baker's yeast)
1996
12.7 Mb
5,805 genes
23.25 μm

**Caenorhabditis elegans**
(a translucent worm)
1998
97 Mb
20,000 genes

**Drosophila melanogaster**
(fruit fly)
1999
120 Mb
21,116 genes

**Arabidopsis thaliana**
(wall cress)
2000
125 Mb
25,498 genes

**Homo sapiens**
(human)
2000
2,500 Mb
22,698 genes

**Mus musculus**
(mouse)
2002
2,600 Mb
37,000 genes

**Fugu rubripes**
(pufferfish)
2002
365 Mb
33,609 genes

**Anopheles gambiae**
(mosquito)
2002
230 Mb
13,749 genes
2500 μm

**Schizosaccharomyces pombe**
(fission yeast)
2002
13.8 Mb
4,824 genes
1.8 μm

**Oryza sativa**
(rice)
2002
430 Mb
43,000 genes

**Plasmodium falciparum**
(malaria parasite)
2002
23 Mb
5,300 genes
1 μm

**Rattus norvegicus**
(rat)
2004
2,718 Mb
23,829 genes

**Pan troglodytes**
(chimpanzee)
2005
3,100 Mb
20,000–25,000 genes

**Zea mays**
(maize)
2008
2,500 Mb
59,000 genes

**Ornithorynchus anatinus**
(duck-billed platypus)
2008
2,200 Mb
18,500 genes

**Bos taurus**
(domestic cow)
2009
2,870 Mb
22,000 genes

**Figure 24.1** Milestones of comparative eukaryotic genomics.

# Evolutionary differences accumulate over long periods

Genomes of viruses and bacteria can evolve in a matter of days, whereas complex eukaryotic species evolve over millions of years. To illustrate this point, we compare four vertebrate genomes: human, tiger pufferfish *(Fugu rubripes)*, mouse *(Mus musculus)*, and chimpanzee *(Pan troglodytes)*.

### Comparison between human and pufferfish genomes

The draft (preliminary) sequence of the tiger pufferfish was completed in 2002; it was only the second vertebrate genome to be sequenced. For the first time, we were able to compare the genomes of two vertebrates: humans and pufferfish. These two animals last shared a common ancestor 450 MYA.

Some human and pufferfish genes have been conserved during evolution, but others are unique to each species. About 25% of human genes have no counterparts in *Fugu*. Also, extensive genome rearrangements have occurred during the 450 million years since the mammal lineage and the teleost fish diverged, indicating a considerable scrambling of gene order. Finally, the human genome is 97% repetitive DNA (chapter 18), but repetitive DNA accounts for less than one-sixth of the *Fugu* sequence.

### Comparison between human and mouse genomes

Later in 2002, a draft sequence of the mouse genome was completed by an international consortium of investigators, allowing for the first time a comparison of two mammalian genomes. In contrast to the human–pufferfish genome comparison, the differences between these two mammalian genomes are miniscule.

The human genome has about 400 million more nucleotides than that of the mouse. A comparison of the genomes reveals that both have about 25,000 genes, and that they share the bulk of them; in fact, the human genome shares 99% of its genes with mice. Humans and mice diverged about 75 MYA, approximately one-sixth of the amount of time that separates humans from pufferfish. There are only 300 genes unique to either human or mouse, constituting about 1% of the genome. Even 450 million years after last sharing a common ancestor, 75% of the genes found in humans have counterparts in pufferfish.

### Comparison between human and chimpanzee genomes

Humans and chimpanzees, *Pan troglodytes*, diverged only about 4.1 MYA, leaving even less time for their genomes to accumulate mutational differences. The chimp genome was sequenced in 2005, providing a comparative window between us and our closest living relative. A 1.5% difference in insertions and deletions (indels) is found between chimps and humans. Comparing chimp and human indels to outgroups can allow a determination of whether the indel was ancestrally present, and thus can identify which species has the derived condition. Fifty-three of the potentially human-specific indels lead to loss-of-function changes that might correlate with some of the traits that distinguish us from chimps, including a larger cranium and lack of body hair. As will be discussed later in this chapter, mutations leading to differences in the patterns of gene expression are particularly important in understanding why chimps are chimps and humans are humans.

Comparisons of single-nucleotide substitutions reveal that only 2.7% of the two genomes have consistent differences in single nucleotides. Mutations in coding DNA are classified into two groups: those that alter the amino acids coded for in the sequence (nonsynonymous changes) and those that do not (synonymous changes). For example, a synonymous mutation that changed UUU to UUC would still code for phenylalanine (use the genetic code in table 15.1 to see if you can identify examples of possible synonymous and nonsynonymous changes).

## Genomes evolve at different rates

A comparison of the mouse and rat genomes reveals a smaller ratio of nonsynonymous to synonymous changes than that seen between humans and chimps. The higher ratio in the primates indicates that fewer nonsynonymous mutations have been removed by natural selection than has occurred in mice and rats. The removal of nonsynonymous codons during evolution is called stabilizing selection. Stabilizing selection prevents change and maintains the same protein structure across species. For 387 human and chimp genes, the rate of nonsynonymous changes was higher than expected. Selection has not been preventing change in protein structure between these genes in human and chimp. Rather, divergent selection has been at work. Comparing these sequences with an outgroup, the macaque, we see that chimps have experienced a higher rate of divergent selection than humans since they last shared a common ancestor.

## Plant, fungal, and animal genomes have unique and shared genes

We now step back farther and consider genomic differences among the eukaryotic kingdoms that diverged long before the examples just discussed. You have already seen that many genes are highly conserved in animals. Are plant genes also highly conserved, and if so, are they similar to animal and fungal genes?

### Comparison between two plant genomes

The first plant genome to be sequenced was *Arabidopsis thaliana*, the wall cress, a tiny member of the mustard family often used as a model organism for studying flowering plant molecular genetics and development. Its genome sequence, largely completed in 2000, revealed 25,948 genes, about as many as humans have, in a genome with a size of only 125 million base-pairs, a 30-fold smaller genome than that of humans.

Rice, *Oryza sativa*, belongs to the grass family, which includes maize (corn), wheat, barley, sorghum, and sugarcane. Unlike most grasses, rice has a relatively small genome of 430 million base-pairs. Its close relative maize, *Zea mays*, has a 60-fold larger genome. Although rice and *Arabidopsis* are distant relatives, they share many genes. More than 80% of the genes found in rice, including duplicates, are also found in *Arabidopsis*. Among the other 20% are genes that may be responsible for some of the physiological and morphological differences between rice and *Arabidopsis*. It is probable that many of the other differences between the two species reflect differences in gene expression, as discussed later in this chapter. (The morphological and physiological distinctions are described in chapter 30.)

## Comparison of plants with animals and fungi

About one-third of the genes in *Arabidopsis* and rice appear to be in some sense "plant" genes—that is, genes not found in any animal or fungal genome sequenced so far. These include the many thousands of genes involved in photosynthesis and photosynthetic anatomy. Few plant genomes have been sequenced to date, however.

Among the remaining genes found in plants are many that are very similar to those found in animal and fungal genomes, particularly the genes involved in basic intermediary metabolism, in genome replication and repair, and in transcription and protein synthesis. Prior to the availability of whole-genome sequences, assessment of the extent of genetic similarity and difference among diverse organisms had been difficult at best.

### Learning Outcomes Review 24.1

Genomes vary in number of similar genes, arrangement of genes, total number of base pairs, and base-pair differences. Closely related organisms such as humans and chimps exhibit highly similar genomes.

- *Would you expect a high degree of similarity between genomes of a bony fish, such as a swordfish, and a cartilaginous fish, such as a shark? What genes might be different?*

## 24.2 Whole-Genome Duplications

### Learning Outcomes

1. *Differentiate between autopolyploidy and allopolyploidy.*
2. *Explain why most crosses between two species do not result in a new polyploid species.*
3. *Explain why the genome of a polyploid is not identical to the sum of the two parental genomes.*

Polyploidy (three or more chromosome sets) can give rise to new species, as you learned in chapter 22. Polyploidy can result from either genome duplication in one species or from hybridization of two different species. In autopolyploids, the genome of one species is duplicated through a meiotic error, resulting in four copies of each chromosome. Allopolyploids result from the hybridization and subsequent duplication of the genomes of two different species (figure 24.2). The origins of wheat, illustrated in figure 24.3, involve two successive allopolyploid events.

### Ancient and newly created polyploids guide studies of genome evolution

Two avenues of research have lead to intriguing insights into genome alterations following polyploidization. The first method studies ancient polyploids, called **paleopolyploids.**

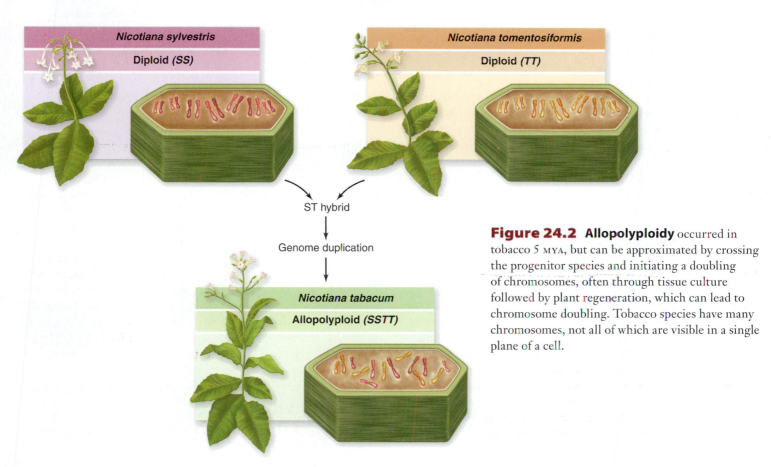

**Figure 24.2 Allopolyploidy** occurred in tobacco 5 MYA, but can be approximated by crossing the progenitor species and initiating a doubling of chromosomes, often through tissue culture followed by plant regeneration, which can lead to chromosome doubling. Tobacco species have many chromosomes, not all of which are visible in a single plane of a cell.

**Figure 24.3 Evolutionary history of wheat.** Domestic wheat arose in southwestern Asia in the hilly country of what is now Iraq. This region contains a rich assembly of grasses of the genus *Triticum*. Domestic wheat (*T. aestivum*) is a polyploid species of *Triticum* that arose through two so-called allopolyploid events. (1) Two different diploid genomes, symbolized here as *AA* and *BB*, hybridized to form an *AB* species hybrid; the species were so different that A and B chromosomes could not pair in meiosis, so the *AB* hybrid was sterile. However, in some plants the chromosome number spontaneously doubled due to a failure of chromosomes to separate in meiosis, producing a fertile tetraploid species, *AABB*. This wheat (durum semolina) is used in the production of pasta. (2) In a similar fashion, the tetraploid species *AABB* hybridized much more recently, within the last 10,000 years, with a different diploid species, with genome *CC*. The second hybridization produced, after another doubling event, the hexaploid *T. aestivum*, *AABBCC*. This bread wheat is one of the most important food plants in the world. Not all chromosomes appear in a single plane of any cell.

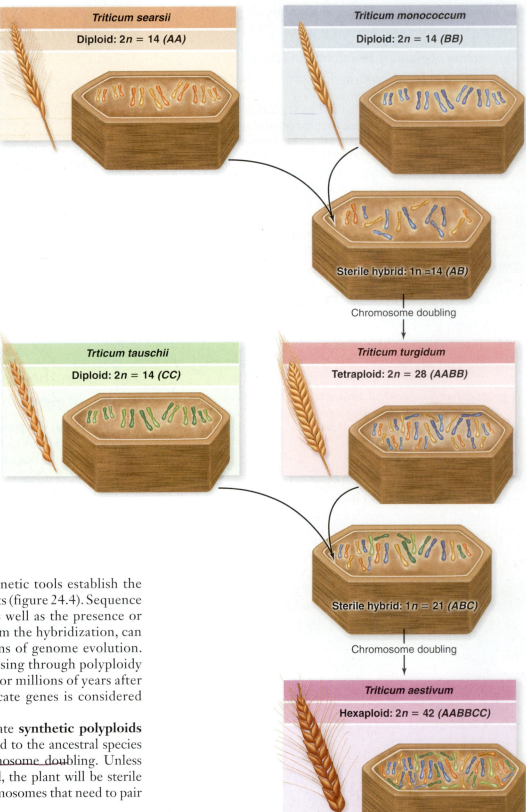

Sequence comparisons and phylogenetic tools establish the time and patterns of polyploidy events (figure 24.4). Sequence divergence between homologues, as well as the presence or absence of duplicated gene pairs from the hybridization, can be used for historical reconstructions of genome evolution. All copies of duplicate gene pairs arising through polyploidy are not necessarily found thousands or millions of years after polyploidization. The loss of duplicate genes is considered later in this section.

The second approach is to create **synthetic polyploids** by crossing plants most closely related to the ancestral species and then chemically inducing chromosome doubling. Unless the hybrid genome becomes doubled, the plant will be sterile because it will lack homologous chromosomes that need to pair during metaphase I of meiosis.

Because meiosis requires an even number of chromosome sets, species with ploidy levels that are multiples of two can reproduce sexually. However, meiosis would be a disaster in a 3*n* organism such as asexually propagated commercial bananas since three sets of chromosomes can't be evenly divided between two cells. Triploid bananas are seedless. The aborted ovules appear as the little brown dots in the center of any cross section of a banana.

### Inquiry question

**?** Sketch out what would happen in meiosis in a 3*n* banana cell, referring back to chapter 11 if necessary.

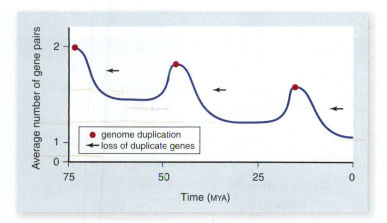

**Figure 24.4 Sequence comparisons of numerous genes in a polyploid genome tell us how long ago allopolyploidy or autopolyploidy events occurred.** Complex analyses of sequence divergence among duplicate gene pairs and presence or absence of duplicate gene pairs provide information about when both genome duplication and gene loss occurred. The graph reveals multiple polyploidy events over evolutionary time.

**Inquiry question**

**?** Why is there a decrease in the number of duplicate genes after multiple rounds of polyploidization?

In the following sections we examine further the effect of polyploidization on genomes. Plant examples have been selected to illustrate key points in this section because polyploidization occurs more frequently in plants. The somewhat surprising findings, however, are not limited to the plant kingdom.

## Evidence of ancient polyploidy is found in plant genomes

Polyploidy has occurred numerous times in the evolution of the flowering plants (figure 24.5). The legume clade that includes the soybean (*Glycine max*), the plant *Medicago trunca-*

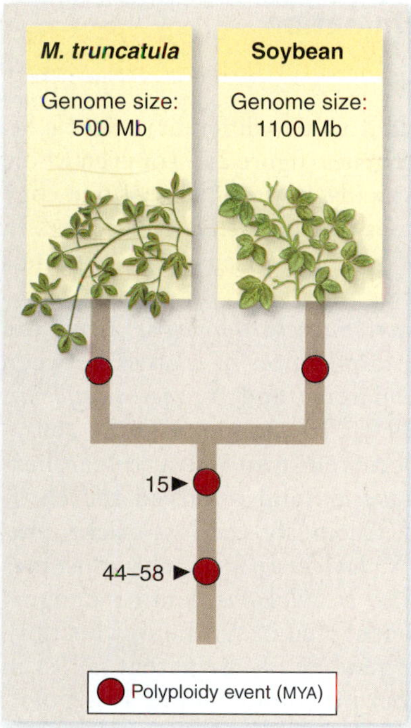

**Figure 24.6**
**Genome downsizing.** Genome downsizing must have occurred in *M. truncatula.*

*tula* (a forage legume often used in research), and the garden pea *(Pisum sativum)* underwent a major polyploidization event 44 to 58 MYA and again 15 MYA (figure 24.6).

A quick comparison of the genomes of soybean and *M. truncatula* reveal a huge difference in genome size. In addition to increasing genome size through polyploidization, genomes like *M. trunculata* definitely downsized over evolutionary time as well. The total size of a genome cannot be explained solely on the basis of polyploidization.

A number of independent whole-genome duplications in plants cluster around 65 MYA, coinciding with a mass extinction event caused by a catastrophic change due to an asteroid impact or increased volcanic activity. Polyploids may have had a better chance of surviving the extinction event with increased genes and alleles available for selection.

**Figure 24.5**
**Polyploidy has occurred numerous times in the evolution of the flowering plants.**

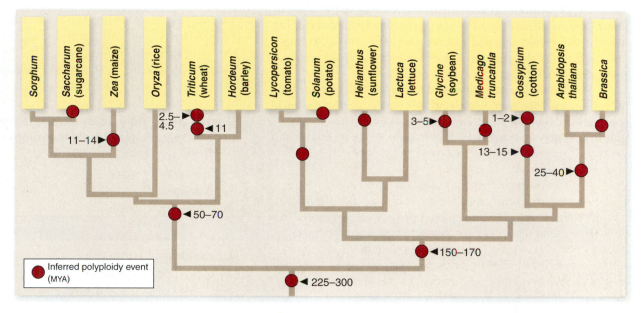

## Polyploidy induces elimination of duplicated genes

Formation of an allopolyploid from two different species is often followed by a rapid loss of genes (figure 24.7) or even whole chromosomes. In some polyploids, however, loss of one copy of many duplicated genes arises over a much longer period. In some species a great deal of gene loss occurs in the first few generations after polyploidization.

Modern tobacco, *Nicotiana tabacum* arose from the hybridization and genome duplication of a cross between *Nicotiana sylvestris* (female parent) and *N. tomentosiformis* (male parent) (see figure 24.2). To complement the analysis based on a cross that occurred over 5 MYA, researchers constructed synthetic *N. tabacum* and observed the chromosome loss that followed. Curiously, the loss of chromosomes is not even. More *N. tomentosiformis* chromosomes were jettisoned than those of *N. sylvestris*. Similar unequal chromosome loss has been observed in synthetic wheat hybrids, in which 13% of the genome of one parent is lost in contrast to 0.5% of the other parental genome. It is possible that different rates of genome replication could explain the differential loss, as is true for synthetic human–mouse hybrid cultured cells.

## Polyploidy can alter gene expression

A striking discovery is the change in gene expression that occurs in the early generations after polyploidization. Some of this may be connected to an increase in the methylation of cytosines in the DNA. Methylated genes cannot be transcribed, as described in chapter 16. Simply put, polyploidization can lead to a short-term silencing of some genes. In subsequent generations, there is a decrease in methylation.

## Transposons jump around following polyploidization

Barbara McClintock, in her Nobel Prize-winning work on transposable (mobile) genetic elements, referred to these jumping DNA regions as *controlling elements*. She hypothesized that transposons could respond to genome shock and jump into a new position in the genome. Depending on where the transposon moved, new phenotypes could emerge.

Recent work on transposon activity following hybridization supports McClintock's hypothesis. Again, during the early generations following a polyploidization event, new transposon insertions occur because of unusually active transposition.

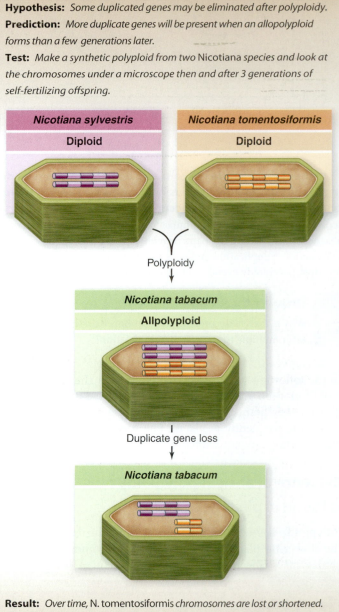

**SCIENTIFIC THINKING**

**Hypothesis:** *Some duplicated genes may be eliminated after polyploidy.*

**Prediction:** *More duplicate genes will be present when an allopolyploid forms than a few generations later.*

**Test:** *Make a synthetic polyploid from two Nicotiana species and look at the chromosomes under a microscope then and after 3 generations of self-fertilizing offspring.*

Nicotiana sylvestris — Diploid

Nicotiana tomentosiformis — Diploid

Polyploidy

Nicotiana tabacum — Allopolyploid

Duplicate gene loss

Nicotiana tabacum

**Result:** *Over time, N. tomentosiformis chromosomes are lost or shortened.*

**Conclusion:** *Chromosomes and genes are preferentially eliminated following polyploidy.*

**Further Experiments:** *Why might the chromosomes and genes of one species be preferentially eliminated? How could you test your explanation?*

**Figure 24.7 Polyploidy may be followed by the unequal loss of duplicate genes from the combined genomes.**

These new insertions may cause gene mutations, changes in gene expression, and chromosomal rearrangements, all of which provide additional genetic variation on which evolution might act.

### Learning Outcomes Review 24.2

Autopolyploids arise from duplication of a species' genome; allopolyploids occur from hybridization between two species. Unless the number of chromosomes doubles, an allopolyploid will likely be sterile because of lack of homologous pairs at meiosis. Polyploidization can lead to major changes in genome structure, including loss of genes, alteration of gene expression, increased transposon hopping, and chromosomal rearrangements. Polyploidy is considered important in generation of biodiversity and adaptation, especially in plants.

■ *What would be the result if a synthetic autopolyploid eliminated one of four duplicate chromosomes?*

## 24.3 Evolution Within Genomes

### Learning Outcomes

1. *Define the terms segmental duplication, genome rearrangement, and pseudogene.*
2. *Explain why horizontal gene transfer can complicate evolutionary hypotheses.*

From individual genes to whole chromosomes, duplications of portions of genomes contribute to evolution. Duplications provide opportunities for genes with the same function to diverge because a "backup pair" of genes is in place. After duplication, one gene can lose function, because the duplicate compensates for it. The mutated gene is not selected against because another functioning gene, not just an allele, exists. The duplicated gene can also diverge and acquire new functions because a backup copy exists.

### Individual chromosomes may be duplicated

**Aneuploidy** refers to the duplication or loss of an individual chromosome rather than of an entire genome. Failure of a pair of homologous chromosomes or sister chromatids to separate during meiosis is the most common way that aneuploids occur.

In general, plants are better able to tolerate aneuploidy than animals, but the explanation for this difference is elusive.

### DNA segments may be duplicated

One of the greatest sources of novel traits in genomes is duplication of segments of DNA. Two genes within an organism that have arisen from the duplication of a single gene in an ancestor are called paralogues. In contrast, orthologues reflect the conservation of a single gene from a common ancestor.

When a gene duplicates, the most likely fates of the duplicate gene are (1) losing function through subsequent mutation, (2) gaining a novel function through subsequent mutation, and (3) having the total function of the ancestral gene partitioned into the two duplicates. Gene families grow through gene duplication. In reality, however, most duplicate genes lose function.

How then can researchers claim that gene duplication is a major evolutionary force for gene innovation, that is, genes gaining new function? One piece of the answer can be found by noting where gene duplication is most likely to occur in the genome. In humans, the highest rates of duplication have occurred in the three most gene-rich chromosomes of the genome. The seven chromosomes with the fewest genes also show the least amount of duplication. (Remember, having fewer genes does not mean that there is less total DNA.)

Even more compelling, certain types of human genes appear to be more likely to be duplicated: growth and development genes, immune system genes, and cell-surface receptors. About 5% of the human genome consists of segmental duplications (figure 24.8). Finally, and important, gene duplication is thought to be a major evolutionary force for gene innovation because the duplicated genes are found to have different patterns of gene expression (see chapter 25 for examples). For example, the two duplicated copies may be expressed in different or overlapping sets of tissues or organs during development.

Segmental duplications may account for differences between human and chimp. Species-specific segmental duplications tend to contain genes that are differentially expressed between the species. This is true for genes expressed in liver, kidney, or heart. A simple explanation is that there are more copies of the gene being expressed, but experimental evidence shows that it is more likely that the regulatory DNA near the duplicate is different.

**Figure 24.8 Segmental duplication on the human Y chromosome.** Each orange region has 98% sequence similarity with a sequence on a different human chromosome. Each dark blue region has 98% sequence similarity with a sequence elsewhere on the Y chromosome.

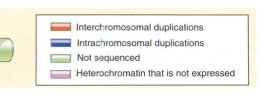

Interchromosomal duplications
Intrachromosomal duplications
Not sequenced
Heterochromatin that is not expressed

## Genomes may become rearranged

Humans have one fewer chromosome than chimpanzees, gorillas, and orangutans (figure 24.9). It's not that we have lost a chromosome. Rather, at some point in time, two midsized ape chromosomes fused to make what is now human chromosome 2, the second largest chromosome in our genome.

The fusion leading to human chromosome 2 is an example of the sort of genome reorganization that has occurred in many species. Rearrangements like this can provide evolutionary clues, but they are not always definitive proof of how closely related two species are.

Consider the organization of known orthologues shared by humans, chickens, and mice. One study estimated that 72 chromosome rearrangements had occurred since the chicken and human last shared a common ancestor. This number is substantially less than the estimated 128 rearrangements between chicken and mouse, or 171 between mouse and human.

This does not mean that chickens and humans are more closely related than mice and humans or mice and chickens. What these data actually show is that chromosome rearrangements have occurred at a much lower frequency in the lineages that led to humans and to chickens than in the lineages leading to mice. Chromosomal rearrangements in mouse ancestors seem to have occurred at twice the rate seen in the human line. These different rates of change help counter the notion that humans existed hundreds of millions of years ago.

Genomes that have undergone relatively slow chromosome change are the most helpful in reconstructing the hypothetical genomes of ancestral vertebrates. If regions of chromosomes have changed little in distantly related vertebrates over the last 300 million years, then we can reasonably infer that the common ancestor of these vertebrates had genomic similarities.

Variation in the organization of genomes is as intriguing as gene sequence differences. Chromosome rearrangements are common, yet over long segments of chromosomes, the linear order of mouse and human genes is the same—the common ancestral sequence has been preserved in both species. This **conservation of synteny** (see chapter 18) was anticipated from earlier gene-mapping studies, and it provides strong evidence that evolution actively shapes the organization of the eukaryotic genome. As seen in figure 24.10, the conservation of synteny allows researchers to more readily locate a gene in a different species using information about synteny, thus underscoring the power of a comparative genomic approach.

## Gene inactivation results in pseudogenes

The loss of gene function is another important way genomes evolve. Consider the olfactory receptor (OR) genes that are responsible for our sense of smell. These genes code for receptors that bind odorants, initiating a cascade of signaling events that eventually lead to our perception of scents.

Gene inactivation seems to be the best explanation for our reduced sense of smell relative to that of the great apes and other mammals. Mice have about 1500 OR genes, the largest mammalian gene family. Mice have about 50% more OR genes than humans. Only 20% of the mouse OR genes are pseudogenes, in contrast to about 60% in humans, which are inactive **pseudogenes** (sequences of DNA that are very similar to functional genes but that do not produce a functional product because they have premature stop codons, missense mutations, or deletions that prevent the production of an active protein). In contrast, half the chimpanzee and gorilla OR genes function effectively, and over 95% of New World monkey OR genes and probably all mouse OR genes are working quite well. The most likely explanation for these differences is that humans came to rely on other senses, reducing the selection pressure against loss of OR gene function by random mutation.

An older question about the possibility of positive selection for OR genes in chimps was resolved with the completion of the chimp genome. A careful analysis indicated that both humans and chimps are gradually losing OR genes to pseudogenes and that there is no evidence to support positive selection for any of the OR genes in the chimp.

**Figure 24.9** **Living great apes.** All living great apes, with the exception of humans, have a haploid chromosome number of 24. Humans have not lost a chromosome; rather, two smaller chromosomes fused to make a single chromosome.

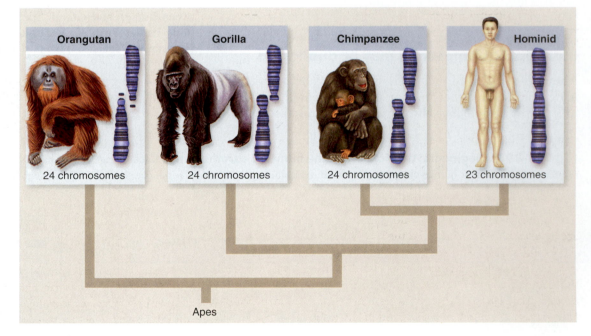

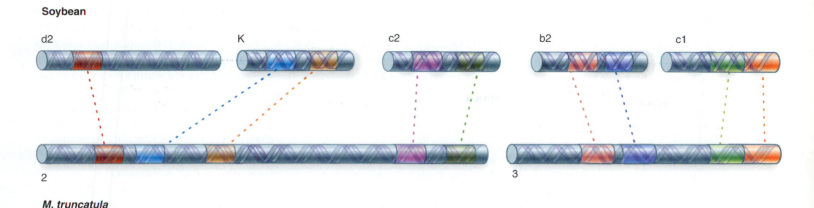

**Soybean**

d2　　　　　　K　　　　　　c2　　　　　　b2　　　　　　c1

2　　　　　　　　　　　　　　　　　　　　　3

*M. truncatula*

**Figure 24.10** **Synteny and gene identification.** Genes sequenced in the model legume, *Medicago truncatula*, can be used to identify homologous genes in soybean, *Glycine max*, because large regions of the genomes are syntenic as illustrated for some of the linkage groups (chromosomes) of the two species. Regions of the same color represent homologous genes.

## Rearranged DNA can acquire new functions

Errors in meiosis that rearrange parts of genes most often create pseudogenes, but occasionally a broken piece of a gene can end up in a new spot in the genome where it acquires a new function. One of the most intriguing examples occurred within a family of fish in the suborder Notothenioidae found in the Antarctic ocean. These fish are called icefish because they survive the frigid temperatures in the Antarctic, in part because of a protein in their blood that works like antifreeze. Reconstructing evolutionary history using comparative genomics reveals that 9 bp of a gene coding for a digestive enzyme evolved to encode part of an antifreeze protein. The series of errors that gave rise to the new protein persisted only because the change coincided with a massive cooling of the Antarctic waters. Natural selection acted on this mutation over millions of years.

## Horizontal gene transfer complicates matters

Evolutionary biologists build phylogenies on the assumption that genes are passed from generation to generation, a process called **vertical gene transfer (VGT)**. Hitchhiking genes from other species, a process referred to as **horizontal gene transfer (HGT)** and sometimes called *lateral gene transfer*, can lead to phylogenetic complexity. HGT was likely most prevalent very early in the history of life, when the boundaries between individual cells and species seem to have been less firm than they are now and DNA more readily moved among different organisms. Although earlier in the history of life, gene swapping between species was rampant, HGT continues today in prokaryotes and eukaryotes. An intriguing example of more recent HGT between moss and a flowering plant is described in chapter 26.

### Gene swapping in early lineages

The extensive gene swapping among early organisms has caused many researchers to reexamine the base of the tree of life. Early phylogenies based on ribosomal RNA (rRNA) sequences indicate that an early prokaryote gave rise to two major domains: the Bacteria and the Archaea. From one of these lineages, the domain Eukarya emerged; its organelles originated as unicellular organisms engulfed specialized prokaryotes.

This rRNA phylogeny is being revised as more microbial genomes are sequenced. By 2009, the Microbial Genome Program of the U.S. Department of Energy had sequenced 485 microbial genomes and 30 microbial communities. With new sequencing technology, microbial genomes can be sequenced in less than a day. Phylogenies built with rRNA sequences suggest that the domain Archaea is more closely related to the Eukarya than to the Bacteria. But as more microbial genomes are sequenced, investigators find bacterial and archaeal genes showing up in the same organism! The most likely conclusion is that organisms swapped genes, even absorbing DNA obtained from a food source. Perhaps the base of the tree of life is better viewed as a web than a branch (figure 24.11).

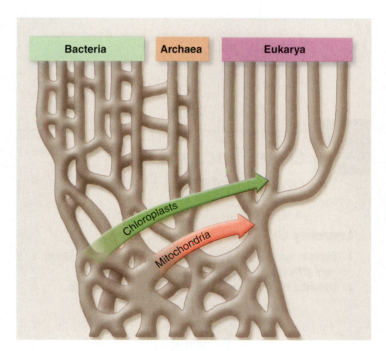

**Figure 24.11** **Horizontal gene transfer.** Early in the history of life, organisms may have freely exchanged genes beyond multiple endosymbiotic events. To a lesser extent, this transfer continues today. The tree of life may be more like a web or a net.

### Gene swapping evidence in the human genome

Let's move closer to home and look at the human genome, which is riddled with foreign DNA, often in the form of transposons. The many transposons of the human genome provide a paleontological record over several hundred million years.

Comparisons of versions of a transposon that has duplicated many times allow researchers to construct a "family tree" to identify the ancestral form of the transposon. The percent of sequence divergence found in duplicates allows an estimate of the time at which that particular transposon originally invaded the human genome. In humans, most of the DNA hitchhiking seems to have occurred millions of years ago in very distant ancestor genomes.

Our genome carries many more ancient transposons than genomes of *Drosophila*, *C. elegans*, and *Arabidopsis*. One explanation for the observed low level of transposons in *Drosophila* is that fruit flies somehow eliminate unnecessary DNA from their genome 75 times faster than humans do. Our genome has simply hung on to hitchhiking DNA more often.

The human genome has had minimal transposon activity in the past 50 million years; mice, by contrast, are continuing to acquire new transposable elements. This difference may explain in part the more rapid change in chromosome organization in mice than in humans.

---

#### Learning Outcomes Review 24.3

In segmental duplication, part of a chromosome and the genes it contains are duplicated. In genome rearrangement, segments of chromosomes may change places or chromosomes may fuse with one another. Pseudogenes have become inactivated in the course of evolution but still persist in the genome. All these changes have evolutionary consequences. Horizontal gene transfer has led to an unexpected mixing of genes among organisms, creating many phylogenetic questions.

■ *How would you determine whether a gene was a pseudogene or an example of horizontal gene transfer?*

---

## 24.4 Gene Function and Expression Patterns

#### Learning Outcomes

1. *Explain how species with nearly identical genes can look very different.*
2. *Describe the action of the FOXP2 gene across species.*

Gene function can be inferred by comparing genes in different species. You saw earlier that the function of 1000 human genes was understood once the mouse genome was sequenced. One of the major puzzles arising from comparative genomics is that organisms with very different forms can share so many conserved genes in their genomic toolkit.

The best explanation for why a mouse develops into a mouse and not a human is that the same or similar genes are expressed at different times, in different tissues, and in different amounts and combinations. For example, the cystic fibrosis gene (cystic fibrosis transmembrane conductance regulator, *CFTR*), which has been identified in both species and affects a chloride ion channel, illustrates this point. Defects in the human *CFTR* gene cause especially devastating effects in the lungs, but mice with the mutant *CFTR* gene do not have lung symptoms. Possibly variations in expression of *CFTR* between mouse and human explain the difference in lung symptoms when *CFTR* is defective.

### Chimp and human gene transcription patterns differ

Humans and chimps diverged from a common ancestor only about 4.1 MYA—too little time for much genetic differentiation to evolve, but enough for significant morphological and behavioral differences to have developed. Sequence comparisons indicate that chimp DNA is 98.7% identical to human DNA. If just the gene sequences encoding proteins are considered, the similarity increases to 99.2%. How could two species differ so much in body and behavior, and yet have almost equivalent sets of genes?

One potential answer to this question is based on the observation that chimp and human genomes show very different patterns of gene transcription activity, at least in brain cells. Investigators used microarrays containing up to 18,000 human genes to analyze RNA isolated from cells in the fluid extracted from several regions of living brains of chimps and humans. (See figure 18.10 for a summary of this technique.) The RNA was linked with a fluorescent tag and then incubated with the microarray under conditions that allow the formation of DNA–RNA hybrids if the sequences are complementary. If the transcript of a particular gene is present in the cells, then the microarray spot corresponding to that gene lights up under UV light. The more copies of the RNA, the more intense the signal.

Because the chimp genome is so similar to that of humans, the microarray detects the activity of chimp genes reasonably well. Although the same genes were transcribed in chimp and human brain cells, the patterns and levels of transcription varied. Much of the difference between human and chimp brains lies in which genes are transcribed, and when and where that transcription occurs.

---

#### Inquiry question

**?** You are given a microarray of ape genes and RNA from both human and ape brain cells. Using the experimental technique described for comparison of humans and chimps, what would you expect to find in terms of genes being transcribed? What about levels of transcription?

---

Posttranscriptional differences may also play a role in building distinct organisms from similar genomes. As research continues to push the frontiers of proteomics and functional genomics, a more detailed picture of the subtle differences in the developmental and physiological processes of closely related species will be revealed. The integration of development and genome evolution is explored in depth in the following chapter.

## Speech is uniquely human: An example of complex expression

Development of human culture is closely tied to the capacity to control the larynx and mouth to produce speech. Humans with a single point mutation in the transcription factor gene *FOXP2* have impaired speech and grammar but not impaired language comprehension.

The *FOXP2* gene is also found in chimpanzees, gorillas, orangutans, rhesus macaques, and even the mouse, yet none of these mammals speak (figure 24.12). The gene is expressed in areas of the brain that affect motor function, including the complex coordination needed to create words.

FOXP2 protein in mice and humans differs by only three amino acids. There is only a single amino acid difference between mouse and chimp, gorilla, and rhesus macaque, which all have identical amino acid sequences for FOXP2. Two more amino acid differences exist between humans and the sequence shared by chimp, gorilla, and macaques. The difference of only two amino acids between human and other primate FOXP2 appears to have made it possible for language to arise. Evidence points to strong selective pressure for the two *FOXP2* mutations that allow brain, larynx, and mouth to coordinate to produce speech.

Is it possible that two amino acid changes lead to speech, language, and ultimately human culture? This box of mysteries will take a long time to unpack, but hints indicate that the changes are linked to signaling and gene expression. The two

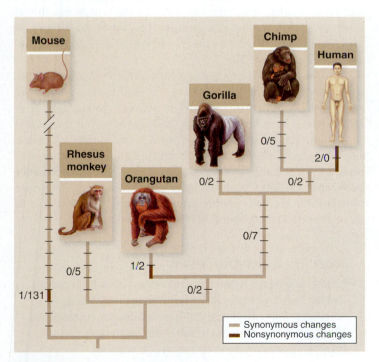

**Figure 24.12 Evolution of *FOXP2*.** Comparisons of synonymous and nonsynomous changes in mouse and primate *FOXP2* genes indicate that changing two amino acids in the gene corresponds to the emergence of human language. Black bars represent synonymous changes and gray bars represent nonsynonymous changes.

altered amino acids may change the ability of FOXP2 transcription factor to be phosphorylated. One way signaling pathways operate is through activation or inactivation of an existing transcription factor by phosphorylation.

Comparative genomics efforts are now extending beyond primates. A role for *FOXP2* in songbird singing and vocal learning has been proposed. Mice communicate via squeaks, with lost young mice emitting high-pitched squeaks. *FOXP2* mutations leave mice squeakless. For both mice and songbirds, it is a stretch to claim that *FOXP2* is a language gene—but it likely is needed in the neuromuscular pathway to make sounds.

### Learning Outcomes Review 24.4

To understand functional differences between genes shared by species, one must look beyond sequence similarity. Alterations in the time and place of gene expression can lead to marked differences in phenotype. As an example, the FOXP2 factor appears to be involved in sound production in mice, chimps, gorillas, macaques, and humans, and only very small differences may have led to human speech.

■ *How can a single-nucleotide difference in a gene lead to a noticeably different phenotype? Give examples.*

## 24.5 Nonprotein-Coding DNA and Regulatory Function

### Learning Outcome

1. *Describe the role of nonprotein-coding DNA.*

So far, we have primarily compared genes that code for proteins. As more genomes are sequenced, we learn that much of the genome is composed of nonprotein-coding DNA (ncDNA). The repetitive DNA is often retrotransposon DNA, contributing to as much as 30% of animal genomes and 40 to 80% of plant genomes. (Refer to chapter 18 for more information on repetitive DNA in genomes.)

Perhaps the most unexpected finding in comparing the mouse and human genomes lies in the similarities between the repetitive DNA, mostly retrotransposons, in the two species. This DNA does not code for proteins. Retrotransposon DNA in both species shows that it has independently ended up in comparable regions of the genome.

At first glance it appeared that all this extra DNA was "junk" DNA, DNA just along for the ride. But it is beginning to look like this ncDNA may have more of a function than was previously assumed. If the DNA had no function, differences should begin to accumulate in mouse and human as mutations occur and occasionally become fixed due to genetic drift. The fact that the "junk" regions are so conserved in mouse and human indicates that, in fact, mutations are being selected out to maintain some function, thus keeping them similar. Hence, these regions of DNA must have some function. The point is that the differences in the "junk" DNA between mouse and human are too small to have resulted from genetic drift.

The possibility that this DNA is rich in regulatory RNA sequences is being actively investigated. RNAs that are not translated can play several roles, including silencing other genes. Small RNAs can form double-stranded RNA with complementary mRNA sequences, blocking translation. They can also participate in the targeted degradation of RNAs. For details on other possible functions of ncDNA, refer to chapter 16.

In one study, researchers collected almost all of the RNA transcripts made by mouse cells taken from every tissue. Although most of the transcripts coded for mouse proteins, as many as 4280 could not be matched to any known mouse protein. This finding suggests that a large part of the transcribed genome consists of genes that do not code for proteins—that is, transcripts that function as RNA. Perhaps this function can explain why a single retrotransposon can cause heritable differences in coat color in mice.

### Learning Outcome Review 24.5

DNA that does not code for protein may regulate gene expression, often through its RNA transcript. Nonprotein-coding sequences can be found in retrotransposon-rich regions of the genome.

- ■ *How would you determine whether RNA produced by a nonprotein-coding gene has a regulatory function?*

## 24.6 Genome Size and Gene Number

### Learning Outcome

1. *Explain why genome size and gene number do not correlate.*

Genome size was a major factor in selecting which genomes would be sequenced first. Practical considerations led to the choice of organisms with relatively small genomes. Considering genome size, the original gene count for the human genome was estimated at 100,000 genes.

As sequence data were analyzed, the predicted number of genes started to decrease. A very different picture emerged. Our genome has only 25% of the 100,000 anticipated genes, approximately the same number of genes as the tiny *Arabidopsis* plant. Humans have nine times the amount of DNA found in the $3.65 \times 10^8$ bp-pufferfish genome, but about the same number of genes. Keep in mind that the number of genes may not correspond to the number of proteins. For example, alternative splicing (see chapter 16) can produce multiple, distinct transcripts from a single gene.

### Noncoding DNA inflates genome size

Why do humans have so much extra DNA? Much of it appears to be in the form of introns, noncoding segments within a gene's sequence, that are substantially bigger than those in pufferfish. The *Fugu* genome has only a handful of "giant" genes containing long introns; studying them should provide insight into the evolutionary forces that have driven the change in genome size during vertebrate evolution.

As described earlier, large expanses of retrotransposon DNA contribute to the differences in genome size from one species to another. Although part of the genome, ncDNA does not contain genes in the usual sense. As another example, *Drosophila* exhibits less ncDNA than *Anopheles*, although the evolutionary force driving this reduction in noncoding regions is unclear. The number of genes are not correlated with genome size.

### Plants have widely varying genome size

Plants have an even greater range of genome sizes. As much as a 200-fold difference has been found, yet all these plants weigh in with about 30,000 to 59,000 genes. Tulips for example, have 170 times more DNA than *Arabidopsis*.

Both rice and *Arabidopsis* have higher *copy numbers* for gene families (multiple slightly divergent copies of a gene) than are seen in animals or fungi, suggesting that these plants have undergone numerous episodes of polyploidy, segmental duplication, or both during the 150 to 200 million years since rice and *Arabidopsis* diverged from a common ancestor.

Whole-genome duplication is insufficient to explain the size of some genomes. Wheat and rice are very closely related and have similar gene content, and yet the wheat genome is 40 times larger than the rice genome. This difference cannot be explained solely by the fact that bread wheat is a hexaploid (*6n*) and rice is a diploid (*2n*).

Now that the rice genome is fully sequenced, attention has shifted to sequencing the other cereal grains, especially maize and wheat, both of which apparently contain lots of repetitive DNA, which has increased their DNA content, but not necessarily their gene content. Comparisons between the rice, maize, and wheat genomes should provide clues about the genome of their common ancestor and the dynamic evolutionary balance between opposing forces that increase genome size (polyploidy, transposable element proliferation, and gene duplication) and those that decrease genome size (mutational loss).

### Learning Outcome Review 24.6

Increases or decreases in genome size do not correlate with the number of genes. Evidently DNA content is not the same as gene content. Polyploidy in plants does not by itself explain differences in genome size. Often a greater amount of DNA is explained by the presence of introns and nonprotein-coding sequences than by gene duplicates.

- ■ *How might a genome with a small number of genes and a small number of total base pairs evolve into a genome with the same small number of genes and a thousand-fold larger genome?*

# 24.7 Genome Analysis and Disease Prevention and Treatment

**Learning Outcomes**

1. *Describe how comparative genomics can reveal the genetic basis for disease.*
2. *Explain how genome comparisons between a pathogen and its host can aid drug development.*

Comparisons among individual human genomes continue to provide information on genetic disease detection and the best course of treatment. An even broader array of possibilities arises when comparisons are made among species. There are advantages to comparing both closely and distantly related pairs of species, as well as comparing the genomes of a pathogen and its host. Examples of the benefits of each type of genome comparison follow.

## Distantly related genomes offer clues for causes of disease

Sequences that are conserved between humans and puffer-fish provide valuable clues for understanding the genetic basis of many human diseases. Amino acids critical to protein function tend to be preserved over the course of evolution, and changes at such sites within genes are more likely to cause disease.

It is difficult to distinguish functionally conserved sites when comparing human proteins with those of other mammals because not enough time has elapsed for sufficient changes to accumulate at nonconserved sites. A promising exception is the duck-billed platypus (*Ornithorhynchus anatinus*), which diverged from other mammals about 166 MYA and whose genome provides clues to the evolution of the immune system. Because the pufferfish genome is only distantly related to humans, conserved sequences are far more easily distinguished than even in the platypus.

## Closely related organisms enhance medical research

It is much easier to design experiments to identify gene function in an experimental system like the mouse than it is in humans. Comparing mouse and human genomes quickly revealed the function of 1000 previously unidentified human genes. The effects of these genes can be studied in mice, and the results can be used in potential treatments for human diseases.

A draft of the rat genome has been completed, and even more exciting news about the evolution of mammalian genomes may emerge from comparisons of these species. One of the most exciting aspects of comparing rat and mice genomes is the potential to capitalize on the extensive research on rat physiology, especially heart disease, and the long history of genetics in mice. Linking genes to disease has become much easier.

Humans have been found to contain segmental duplications that are absent in the chimp. Some of these duplications correspond to human disease. These differences can aid medical researchers in developing treatments for genetic disease. For example, some of the regions duplicated only in humans correspond with regions of the human genome that have been implicated in Prader-Willi syndrome and spinal muscular atrophy. Children with Prader-Willi lack muscle tone and struggle with life-threatening obesity because of an insatiable appetite. Spinal muscular atrophy affects all muscles in the body, but especially those nearest the trunk. Affected individuals can have difficulty swallowing and breathing, as well as experiencing weakness in the legs, but ethical issues surrounding chimpanzee research and protection should be of paramount importance.

## Pathogen–host genome differences reveal drug targets

With genome sequences in hand, pharmaceutical researchers are more likely to find suitable drug targets to eliminate pathogens without harming the host. Diseases in many developing countries—including malaria and Chagas disease—have both human and insect hosts. Both these infections are caused by protists (see chapter 29). The value of comparative genomics in drug discovery is illustrated for both malaria and Chagas disease in the following sections.

### Malaria

*Anopheles gambiae*, the malaria-carrying mosquito, along with *Plasmodium falciparum*, the protistan parasite it transmits, together have an enormous effect on human health, resulting in 1.7 to 2.5 million deaths each year from malaria. The genomes of both *Anopheles* and *Plasmodium* were sequenced in 2002.

*Plasmodium falciparum*, which causes malaria, has a relatively small genome of $2.46 \times 10^7$ bp that proved very difficult to sequence. It has an unusually high proportion of adenine and thymine, making it hard to distinguish one portion of the genome from the next. The project took five years to complete. *P. falciparum* appears to have about 5300 genes, with those of related function clustered together, suggesting that they might share the same regulatory DNA.

*P. falciparum* is a particularly crafty organism that hides from our immune system inside red blood cells, regularly changing the proteins it presents on the surface of the red blood cell. This "cloaking" has made developing a vaccine or other treatment for malaria particularly difficult.

Recently, a link to chloroplast-like structures in *P. falciparum* has raised other possibilities for treatment. An odd subcellular component called the *apicoplast*, found only in *Plasmodium* and its relatives, appears to be derived from a

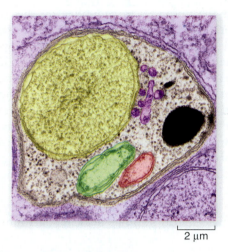

**Figure 24.13** *Plasmodium* **apicoplast.** Drugs targeting enzymes used for fatty acid biosynthesis within *Plasmodium* apicoplasts (colored dark green) offer hope for treating malaria.

chloroplast appropriated from algae engulfed by the parasite's ancestor (figure 24.13).

Analysis of the *Plasmodium* genome reveals that about 12% of all the parasite's proteins, encoded by the nuclear genome, head for the apicoplast. These proteins act there to produce fatty acids. The apicoplast is the only location in which the parasite makes the fatty acids, suggesting that drugs targeted at this biochemical pathway might be very effective against malaria.

Another disease-prevention possibility is to look at chloroplast-specific herbicides, which might kill *Plasmodium* by targeting the chloroplast-derived apicoplast.

### Chagas disease

*Trypanosoma cruzi*, an insect-borne protozoan, kills about 21,000 people in Central and South America each year. As many as 18 million suffer from this infection, called Chagas disease, the symptoms of which include damage to the heart and other internal organs. Genome sequencing of *T. cruzi* was completed in 2005.

A surprising and hopeful finding is that a common core of 6200 genes is shared among *T. cruzi* and two other insect-borne pathogens: *T. brucei* and *Leishmania major*. *T. brucei* causes African sleeping sickness, and *L. major* infections result in lesions of the skin of the limbs and face. These core genes are being considered as possible targets for drug treatments.

Currently, no effective vaccines and only a few drugs with limited effectiveness are available to treat any of these diseases. The genomic similarities may aid not only in targeting drug development, but perhaps also result in a treatment or vaccine that is effective against all three devastating illnesses (figure 24.14).

---

**Learning Outcomes Review 24.7**

DNA sequences conserved over evolutionary time tend to be those critical for protein function and survival. Variations in these conserved sequences may provide clues to diseases with a hereditary component. Knowledge of a pathogenic organism's genome and its differences from a host's genome may allow targeting of drugs and vaccines that affect the invader but leave the host unharmed.

■ *A pathogen makes a critical protein that differs from the human version by only seven amino acids. What approaches might lead to an effective drug against the pathogen? What drawbacks might be encountered?*

---

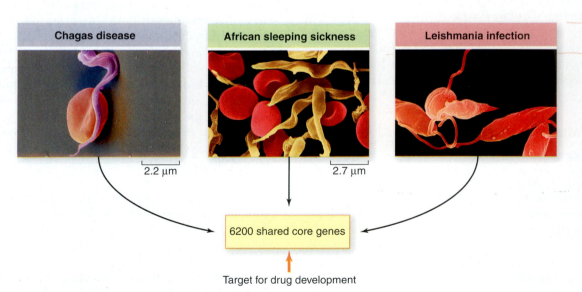

**Figure 24.14 Comparative genomics may aid in drug development.** The organisms that cause Chagas disease, African sleeping sickness, and leishmaniasis, which claim millions of lives in developing nations each year, share 6200 core genes. Drug development targeted at proteins encoded by the shared core genes could yield a single treatment for all three diseases.

## 24.8 Crop Improvement Through Genome Analysis

### Learning Outcome

1. Describe how the genome sequence of one plant can be used to improve a number of crop species.

Farmers and researchers have long relied on genetics for crop improvement. Whole-genome sequences offer even more information for research on artificial selection for crop improvement. Highly conserved genes can be characterized in a model system and then used to identify orthologues in crop species.

### Model plant genomes provide links to genetics of crop plants

*Arabidopsis* is a flowering plant mainly used for experimental purposes, but with no commercial significance. The second plant genome for which a draft sequence has been prepared—rice—is, however, of enormous economic significance. Rice, as mentioned earlier, belongs to the grass family, which includes a number of other important cereal crop plants. Together, these crops provide most of the world's food and animal feed.

Unlike most grasses, rice has a relatively small genome of $4.3 \times 10^8$ bp, in contrast to the maize (corn) genome ($2.5 \times 10^9$ bp) and that of barley (an enormous $4.9 \times 10^9$ bp). Two different subspecies of rice have been sequenced, yielding similar results. The proportion of the rice nuclear genome devoted to repetitive DNA, for example, was 42% in one variety, and 45% in the other.

Genome sequencing is underway for maize and for another model plant, *Medicago truncatula*. *M. truncatula* has a much smaller genome than its close relative, soybean, making it much easier to sequence. Large regions of *M. truncatula* DNA are syntenous with soybean DNA, increasing the odds of finding agriculturally important soybean genes using the *M. truncatula* genome (see figure 24.10).

### Beneficial bacterial genes can be located and utilized

Genome sequences of beneficial microbes may also improve crop yield. *Pseudomonas fluorescens* naturally protects plant roots from disease by excreting protective compounds. In 2005, *P. fluorescens* became the first biological control agent to have its genome sequenced. Work on identifying chemical pathways that produce protective compounds should proceed rapidly, given the bacterium's small genome size. Understanding these pathways can lead to more effective methods of protecting crops from disease—for example, isolation of a protective gene (or genes) could lead to being able to insert this beneficial gene into a crop plant's genome, so that the plant could protect itself directly. Bt (*Bacillus thuringiensis*) crops, as described in chapter 17, are one example.

### Learning Outcome Review 24.8

Comparative genomics extends the benefits of sequenced genomes in model plant species to other species important as crops, allowing potential improvement. A growing understanding of microbial genomes may also be used to improve crop yield by allowing targeted protection.

- *One ounce of soybeans contains half as much protein as one ounce of beefsteak. How would you go about increasing the protein content in soybeans?*

## Chapter Review

### 24.1 Comparative Genomics

*Evolutionary differences accumulate over long periods.*
Even distantly related species may often have many genes in common. Changes in DNA codons that do not alter the amino acid specified are termed synonymous changes.

*Genomes evolve at different rates.*
Mouse DNA has apparently mutated twice as fast as human DNA, and insect evolution is even more rapid. Short generation time may be responsible for these rate differences.

*Plant, fungal, and animal genomes have unique and shared genes.*
Plants, animals, and fungi have approximately 70% of their genes in common.

### 24.2 Whole-Genome Duplications

*Ancient and newly created polyploids guide studies of genome evolution.*
Autopolyploidy results from an error in meiosis that leads to a duplicated genome; allopolyploidy is the result of hybridization between species (see figure 24.2).

*Evidence of ancient polyploidy is found in plant genomes.*
Polyploidy has occurred numerous times in the evolution of flowering plants, and downsizing of genomes is common.

*Polyploidy induces elimination of duplicated genes.*
Downsizing of a polyploid genome can be caused by unequal loss of duplicated genes (see figure 24.7).

*Polyploidy can alter gene expression.*

Polyploidization can lead to short-term silencing of genes via methylation of cytosines in the DNA.

*Transposons jump around following polyploidization.*

Transposons become highly active after polyploidization; their insertions into new positions may lead to new phenotypes.

## 24.3 Evolution Within Genomes

*Individual chromosomes may be duplicated.*

Aneuploidy creates problems in gamete formation. It is tolerated better in plants than in animals.

*DNA segments may be duplicated (see figure 24.8).*

Duplicated DNA is common for genes associated with growth and development, immunity, and cell-surface receptors. Paralogues are duplicated ancestral genes; orthologues are conserved ancestral genes.

*Genomes may become rearranged.*

Genomes may be rearranged by moving gene locations within a chromosome or by the fusion of two chromosomes.

Conservation of synteny refers to preservation of long segments of ancestral chromosome sequences identifiable in related species (see figure 24.10).

*Gene inactivation results in pseudogenes.*

Some ancestral genes become inactivated as they acquire mutations and are termed pseudogenes.

*Rearranged DNA can acquire new functions.*

Occasionally part of a gene can end up in a new spot in the genome where its function changes.

*Horizontal gene transfer complicates matters.*

Horizontal gene transfer creates many phylogenetic questions, such as the origins of the three major domains (see figure 24.11).

## 24.4 Gene Function and Expression Patterns

*Chimp and human gene transcription patterns differ.*

Even when species have highly similar genes, expression of these genes may vary greatly. Posttranscriptional differences may also contribute to species differences.

*Speech is uniquely human: An example of complex expression.*

Small evolutionary changes in the FOXP2 protein and its expression may have led to human speech (see figure 24.12).

## 24.5 Nonprotein-Coding DNA and Regulatory Function

Nonprotein-coding sequences are found in retrotransposon-rich regions of the genome. Noncoding DNA may contain regulatory RNA sequences for silencing other genes.

## 24.6 Genome Size and Gene Number

*Noncoding DNA inflates genome size.*

Genome size is most often inflated due to the presence of introns and nonprotein-coding sequences. Genome size does not correlate with the number of genes.

*Plants have widely varying genome size.*

As much as a 200-fold difference in genome size has been found in plants; the number of genes has a narrower range.

## 24.7 Genome Analysis and Disease Prevention and Treatment

*Distantly related genomes offer clues for causes of disease.*

Changes in amino acid sequences of critical proteins are a likely cause of diseases, and these differences can be identified by genome comparison.

*Closely related organisms enhance medical research.*

By comparing related organisms, researchers can focus on genes that cause diseases and devise possible treatments.

*Pathogen–host genome differences reveal drug targets.*

Analysis of the genomes of pathogenic organisms may provide new avenues of treatment and prevention.

## 24.8 Crop Improvement Through Genome Analysis

*Model plant genomes provide links to genetics of crop plants.*

Research on *Arabidopsis* and *Medicago* species may provide insight into improvements in crop production and value.

*Beneficial bacterial genes can be located and utilized.*

Bacterial genes that produce protective compounds may be identified and used to engineer crop plants.

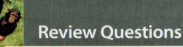

## Review Questions

### UNDERSTAND

1. Humans and pufferfish diverged from a common ancestor about 450 MYA, and these two genomes have
   a. very few of the same genes in common.
   b. all the same genes.
   c. a large proporation of the genes in in common.
   d. no nucleotide divergence.

2. Genome comparisons have suggested that mouse DNA has mutated about twice as fast as human DNA. What is a possible explanation for this discrepancy?
   a. Mice are much smaller than humans.
   b. Mice live in much less sanitary conditions than humans and are therefore exposed to a wider range of mutation-causing substances.
   c. Mice have a smaller genome size.
   d. Mice have a much shorter generation time.

3. Polyploidy in plants
   a. has only arisen once and therefore is very rare.
   b. only occurs naturally when there is a hybridization event between two species.
   c. is common, but never occurs in animals.
   d. is common, and does occur in some animals.

4. Homologous genes in distantly related organisms can often be easily located on chromosomes due to
   a. horizontal gene transfer.
   b. conservation of synteny.
   c. gene inactivation.
   d. pseudogenes.

5. All of the following are believed to contribute to genomic diversity among various species, *except*
   a. gene duplication.
   b. gene transcription.
   c. lateral gene transfer.
   d. chromosomal rearrangements.

6. What is the fate of *most* duplicated genes?
   a. Gene inactivation
   b. Gain of a novel function through subsequent mutation
   c. They are transferred to a new organism using lateral gene transfer.
   d. They become orthologues.

### APPLY

1. Chimp and human DNA whole genome sequences differ by about 2.7%. Determine which of the following explanations is most consistent with the substantial differences in morphology and behavior between the two species.
   a. It must be due largely to gene expression.
   b. It must be due exclusively to environmental differences.
   c. It cannot be explained with current genetic theory.
   d. The differences are caused by random effects during development.

2. You are offered a summer research opportunity to investigate a region of ncDNA in maize. A friend politely smiles and says that only graduate students get to work on the coding regions of DNA. How would you critique your friend's statement?
   a. The friend has a point; ncDNA is "junk" DNA and therefore not very important.
   b. The ncDNA produces protein through mechanisms other than transcription.
   c. Most ncDNA is usually translated.
   d. Often ncDNA produces RNA transcripts that themselves have regulatory function.

3. Analyze the conclusion that the *Medicago truncatula* genome has been downsized relative to its ancestral legume, and circle the evidence that is consistent with this conclusion.
   a. *Medicago* has a proportional decrease in the number of genes.
   b. *Medicago* has a proportional increase in the number of genes.
   c. *Medicago* has an increase in the amount of DNA.
   d. *Medicago* has a decrease in the amount of DNA.

4. Analyze why a herbicide that targets the chloroplast is effective against malaria.
   a. Because *Plasmodium* needs a functional apicoplast
   b. Because the main vector for malaria is a plant
   c. Because mosquitoes require plant leaves for food
   d. Because *Plasmodium* mitochondria are very similar to chloroplasts

### SYNTHESIZE

1. The *FOXP2* gene is associated with speech in humans. It is also found in chimpanzees, gorillas, orangutans, rhesus macaques, and even the mouse, yet none of these mammals speak. Develop a hypothesis that explains why *FOXP2* supports speech in humans but not other mammals.

2. One of the common misconceptions about sequencing projects (especially the high-profile Human Genome Project) is that creating a complete road map of the DNA will lead directly to cures for genetically based diseases. Given the percentage similarity in DNA between humans and chimps, is this simplistic view justified? Explain.

3. How does horizontal gene transfer (HGT) complicate phylogenetic analysis?

### ONLINE RESOURCE

**www.ravenbiology.com**

Understand, Apply, and Synthesize—enhance your study with animations that bring concepts to life and practice tests to assess your understanding. Your instructor may also recommend the interactive eBook, individualized learning tools, and more.

*Chapter* **25**

# Evolution of Development

## Chapter Outline

## Introduction

*How is it that closely related species of frogs can have completely different patterns of development? One frog goes from fertilized egg to adult frog with no intermediate tadpole stage. The sister species has an extra developmental stage neatly slipped in between early development and the formation of limbs—the tadpole stage. The answer to this and other such evolutionary differences in development that yield novel phenotypes are now being investigated with modern genetic and genomic tools. Research findings are accentuating the biological puzzle that many developmental genes are highly conserved, and a tremendous diversity of life shares this basic toolkit of developmental genes. In this chapter, we explore the emerging field of developmental evolution, a field that brings together previously distinct fields of biology.*

---

## 25.1   Overview of Evolutionary Developmental Biology

### Learning Outcomes

1. *Explain how the same gene can produce different morphologies in different species.*
2. *Identify types of genes most likely to affect morphology.*

Ultimately, to explain the differences among species, we need to look at changes in developmental processes. These changes result in a different phenotype and trace back to changes in genes.

Phenotypic diversity could either result from many different genes or be explained by how a smaller set of genes are deployed and regulated. In some cases, changes in the protein-coding region have been implicated in novel phenotypes. In other cases, a conserved set of genes appear to be responsible for the basic body plan of organisms with changes in regulation of gene expression accounting for phenotypic differences. The latter is true for two sea urchin species.

Closely related sea urchins have been discovered that have very distinctive developmental patterns (figure 25.1). The direct-developing urchin never makes a pluteus (free-swimming) larva—it just jumps ahead to its adult form. We could speculate that the two forms have different developmental genes, but it turns out that this is not the case. Instead, the two forms have undergone dramatic changes in patterns of developmental gene expression, even though their adult form is nearly the same. In this case, patterns of expression have changed.

## Highly conserved genes produce diverse morphologies

Transcription factors and genes involved in signaling pathways are responsible for coordination of development. As you saw in chapter 9, key elements of kinase and G protein-signaling pathways are also highly conserved among organisms. Even subtle changes in a signaling pathway can alter the enzyme that is activated or repressed, the transcription factor that is activated or repressed, or the activation or repression of gene expression. Any of these changes can have dramatic effects on the development of an organism.

A relatively small number of gene families, about two dozen, regulate animal and plant development. The developmental roles of several of these families, including *Hox* gene transcription factors, are described in chapter 19.

*Hox* (homeobox) genes appeared before the divergence of plants and animals; in plants, they have a role in shoot growth and leaf development, and in animals they establish body plans. These genes code for proteins with a highly conserved homeodomain that binds to the regulatory region of other genes to activate or repress these genes' expression. *Hox* genes specify when and where genes are expressed.

Another family of transcription factors, *MADS* box genes, are found throughout the eukaryotes. The *MADS* box also codes for a DNA-binding motif. Large numbers of *MADS* box genes establish the body plan of plants, especially the flowers. Although the *MADS* box region is highly conserved, variation exists in other regions of the coding sequence. Later in this chapter, we consider how there came to be so many *MADS* box genes in plants and how such similar genes can have very different functions.

## Developmental mechanisms exhibit evolutionary change

Understanding how development evolves requires integration of knowledge about genes, gene expression, development, and evolution. Either transcription factors or signaling molecules can be modified during evolution, changing the timing or position of gene expression and, as a result, gene function.

### Heterochrony

Alterations in timing of developmental events due to a genetic change are called **heterochrony**. A heterochronic mutation could affect a gene that controls when a plant transitions from the juvenile to the adult stage, at which point it can produce reproductive organs. A mutation in a gene that delays flowering in plants can result in a small plant that flowers quickly rather than requiring months or years of growth.

Most mutations that affect developmental regulatory genes are lethal, but every so often a novel phenotype emerges that persists because of increased fitness. If a mutation leading to early flowering increased the fitness of a plant, the new phenotype will persist. For example, a tundra plant that flowers earlier, enabling it to be fertilized and set seed, could have increased fitness over an individual of the same species that flowers later, just as the short summer comes to a close.

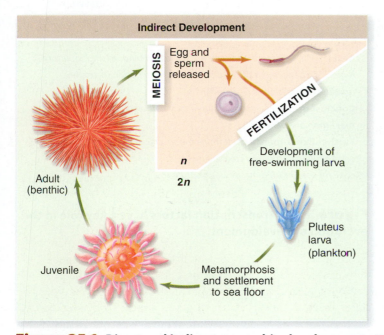

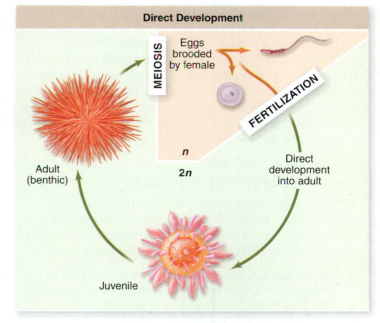

**Figure 25.1** **Direct and indirect sea urchin development.** Phylogenetic analysis shows that indirect development (pluteus larva) was the ancestral state. Direct-developing sea urchins have lost an intermediate stage of development.

## Homeosis

Alternations in the spatial pattern of gene expression can result in **homeosis**. A four-winged *Drosophila* fly is an example of a homeotic mutation in which gene expression patterns shift. Mutations in three genes in the *Bithorax* complex are required to produce this phenotype, which resembles more ancestral insects with four rather than two wings.

The *Drosophila Antennapedia* mutant, which has a leg where an antenna should be, is another example of a homeotic mutation. Mutations in genes such as *Antennapedia* can arise spontaneously in the natural world or by mutagenesis in the laboratory, but their bizarre phenotypes would have little survival value in nature.

### Changes in translated regions of transcription factors

The coding sequence of a gene can contain multiple regions with different functions (figure 25.2). The DNA-binding motifs, exemplified by *MADS* box and *Hox* genes, could be altered so that they no longer bind to their target genes; as a result, that developmental pathway would cease to function. Alternatively, the modified transcription factor might bind to a different target and initiate a new sequence of developmental events.

The regulatory region sequence of a transcription factor must also be considered in the evolution of developmental mechanisms. A sequence change could alter the transcription complex that forms at a regulatory region, resulting in novel expression patterns. Either the time or place of gene expression could be affected, giving rise to heterochrony or homeosis. In this case, the downstream targets might be the same, but the cells that express the target genes or the time at which these target genes are expressed could change.

### Changes in signaling pathways

Coordinating information about neighboring cells and the external environment is essential for successful development. Signaling pathways are essential for cell-to-cell communication. If the structure of a ligand changes, it may no longer bind to its target receptor, or it could bind to a different receptor or no receptor at all. If, as a result of a genetic change, a receptor is produced in a different cell type, a homeotic phenotype may appear. And, as mentioned earlier, small changes in signaling molecules can alter their targets.

The sections that follow use specific examples of the evolution of diverse morphologies. For each example, consider how the mechanism of development has been altered and what the outcome is. Keep in mind that these are the successful examples; most morphological novelties that arise quickly, but do not improve fitness, go extinct.

---

### Learning Outcomes Review 25.1

Highly conserved genes can undergo small changes in their coding or regulatory regions that alter the place or time of gene expression and function, resulting in new body plans. Changes in transcription factors and signaling pathways are the most common source of new morphologies.

■ *Two closely related species of* Drosophila *in Hawaii can be distinguished by the presence of one pair of wings versus two pairs. How would you explain the evolution of this difference?*

---

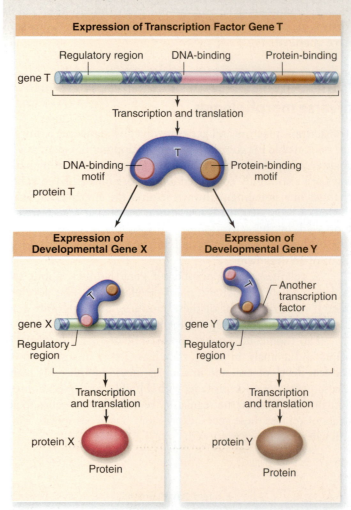

**SCIENTIFIC THINKING**

**Hypothesis:** *A transcription factor can affect the expression of more than one gene.*

**Prediction:** *The protein encoded by a transcription factor gene will have multiple DNA- or protein-binding sites.*

**Test:** *Experimentally identify molecules that bind to the transcription factor.*

**Expression of Transcription Factor Gene T**

Regulatory region   DNA-binding   Protein-binding

gene T

Transcription and translation

DNA-binding motif   T   Protein-binding motif

protein T

**Expression of Developmental Gene X**

gene X
Regulatory region

Transcription and translation

protein X

Protein

**Expression of Developmental Gene Y**

Another transcription factor

gene Y
Regulatory region

Transcription and translation

protein Y

Protein

**Result:** *This transcription factor has a site that binds to the regulatory region of a gene and a site that binds to a transcription factor that regulates expression of a second gene.*

**Conclusion:** *A single transcription factor can regulate the expression of more than one gene.*

**Further Experiments:** *Determine the specific developmental role of each binding domain by creating mutations in regions of the gene that code for specific binding sites in the protein.*

**Figure 25.2 Transcription factors have a key role in the evolution of development.**

# 25.2 One or Two Gene Mutations, New Form

### Learning Outcome

1. **Explain how a small number of mutations can give rise to a new species.**

Here we consider three examples of single gene mutations with altered morphology: (1) wild cabbage, (2) jaw shape in cichlid fish, and (3) bony armor in threespine sticklebacks. In all cases, the change increased fitness in a particular environment at a specific time, leading to selection of the new phenotypes.

## Cauliflower and broccoli began with a stop codon

The species *Brassica oleracea* is particularly fascinating because individual members can have extraordinarily diverse phenotypes. The diversity in form is so great that *B. oleracea* members are divided into subspecies (figure 25.3).

Wild cabbage, kale, tree kale, red cabbage, green cabbage, brussels sprouts, broccoli, and cauliflower are all members of the same species. Some flower early, some late. Some have long stems, others have short ones. Some form a few flowers, and others, like broccoli and cauliflower, initiate many flowers but development of the flowers is arrested. Curiously, these plants with such different appearances are very closely related.

One piece of the puzzle lies with the gene *CAL (Cauliflower)*, which was first cloned in a close *Brassica* relative, *Arabidopsis*. In combination with another mutation, *Apetala1*, *Arabidopsis* plants can be turned from plants with a limited number of simple flowers into miniature broccoli or cauliflower plants with masses of arrested flower meristems or flower buds. These two genes are needed for the transition to making flowers and arose through duplication of a single ancestral gene within the brassica group. When they are absent, meristems continue to make branches, but are delayed in producing flowers.

The *CAL* gene was cloned from large numbers of *B. oleracea* subspecies, and a stop codon, TAG, was found in the middle of the *CAL* coding sequences of broccoli and cauliflower. A phylogenetic analysis of *B. oleracea* coupled with the *CAL* sequence analysis leads to the conclusion that this stop codon appeared after the ancestors of broccoli and cauliflower diverged from other subspecies members, but before broccoli and cauliflower diverged from each other (see figure 25.3).

### Inquiry question

 Knowing that cauliflower and broccoli have a stop codon in the middle of the *CAL* gene-coding sequence, predict the wild-type function of *CAL*. What additional evolutionary events may have occurred since broccoli and cauliflower diverged?

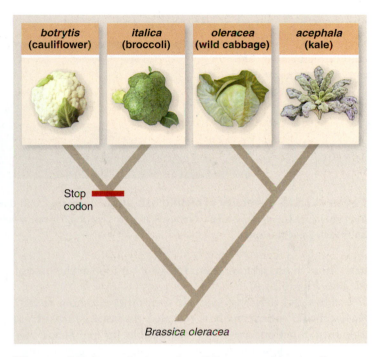

**Figure 25.3 Evolution of cauliflower and broccoli.** A point mutation that converted an amino acid-coding region into a stop codon resulted in the extensive reproductive branching pattern that was artificially selected for in two crop plants that are subspecies of *Brassica oleracea*.

This study points out the importance of having well-documented phylogenies in place to enable the analysis of developmental pattern evolution. A second, somewhat unusual, feature of this example is that the driving selective force for these subspecies was artificial. Wild relatives are still found scattered along the rocky coasts of Spain and the Mediterranean region. The most likely scenario is that humans found a *cal* mutant and selected for that phenotype through cultivation. The large heads of broccoli and cauliflower offer a larger amount of a vegetable material than the wild kale plants and a tasty alternative to *Brassica* leaves.

## Cichlid fish jaws demonstrate morphological diversity

Our second example of how a single gene can change form and function comes from natural selection of cichlid fish in Lake Malawi in East Africa. In less than a few million years, hundreds of species have evolved in the lake from a common ancestor. The rapid speciation of cichlids is discussed in chapter 22.

One explanation for the successful speciation is that different species have acquired different niches based on feeding habits. There are bottom eaters, biters, and rammers. The rammers have particularly long snouts with which to ram their prey; biters have an intermediate snout; and the bottom feeders

**Figure 25.4 Diversity of cichlid fish jaws.** A difference in one gene is responsible for a short snout in *Labeotropheus fuelleborni* and a long snout in *Metriaclima zebra*. Genes that affect jaw length can affect body shape as well because of the constraints the size of the jaw places on muscle development.

have short snouts adapted to scrounging for food at the base of the lake (figure 25.4).

How did these fish acquire such different snout forms? An extensive genetic analysis revealed that two genes, of yet unknown function, are likely responsible for the shape and size of the jaw. The results of crossing long- and short-snouted cichlids indicate the importance of a single gene in determining jaw length and height.

Regulating the length versus the height of the jaw may well be an early and important developmental event. The overall size of the fish and the extent of muscle development both hinge on the form of the jaw. The range of jaw forms appears to have persisted because the cichlids establish unique niches for feeding within the lake.

Our third example underscores the critical link between persistence of a new mutation and increased fitness. The freshwater, threespine stickleback fish, *Gasterousteus aculeatus*, originated after the last ice age from marine populations with bony plates that protect the fish from predators. Freshwater populations, subject to less predation, have lost their bony armor. The *Ectodysplasin (Eda)* gene is one of a few associated with reduced armor in freshwater threespine sticklebacks. The *Eda* allele that causes reduced armor originated about 2 MYA in marine sticklebacks and persists with a frequency of about 1% in marine environments. The frequency is much higher in freshwater populations. To test the fitness of the *Eda* allele in freshwater, marine sticklebacks that were heterozygous for the *Eda* allele were moved to four freshwater environments and allowed to breed. Positive selection for the reduced armor allele was observed and correlated with longer length in juvenile fish, likely because fewer resources were allocated to armor development. Although the reduced armor allele has persisted in marine populations for 2 million years as a rare genetic variant, increased frequency of the allele and phenotype are only seen under adaptive conditions.

### Learning Outcome Review 25.2

Although most mutations are lethal, some confer a fitness advantage. These may consist of very small mutations, such as a change to a single codon, that have large effects on development and morphology.

■ *A cichlid hatches with a much longer jaw than ever observed before. You determine that a mutation is responsible for the extra-long jaw. Is this fish a new species? How would you determine this?*

## 25.3 Same Gene, New Function

### Learning Outcome

1. Explain how a gene could acquire a new function.

In the preceding chapter, we discussed the similarity between human and mouse genomes. If all but 300 of the 20,000 to 25,000 human genes are shared with mice, why are mice and humans so different? Part of the answer is that genes with similar sequences in two different species may work in slightly or even dramatically different ways.

### Ancestral genes may be co-opted for new functions

The evolution of chordates can partially be explained by the co-option of an existing gene for a new function. Ascidians are basal chordates that have a notochord but no vertebrae (chapter 35). The *Brachyury* gene of ascidians encodes a transcription factor, and it is expressed in the developing notochord (figure 25.5).

*Brachyury* is not a novel gene that appeared as vertebrates evolved. It is also found in invertebrates. For example, a mollusk homologue of *Brachyury* is associated with anterior–posterior axis specification. Most likely, an ancestral *Brachyury* gene was co-opted for a new role in notochord development.

*Brachyury* is a member of a gene family with a specific domain, that is, a conserved sequence of base-pairs within the gene. A region of *Brachyury* encodes a protein domain called the **T box,** which is a transcription factor. So, *Brachyury*-encoded protein turns on a gene or genes. The details of which genes are regulated by *Brachyury* are only now being discovered.

In mice and dogs, a mutation in *Brachyury* that prevents the encoded protein from binding to DNA causes a short tail to develop. In some dog breeds it is customary to "bob" (surgically shorten) a puppy's tail. Nonlethal, short-tail mutations are being used to breed dogs like Welsh corgis to avoid bobbing. Humans lack tails, but have wild-type copies of *Brachyury*. Genes in addition to *Brachyury* must be needed to make a tail.

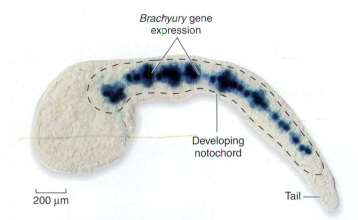

**Figure 25.5 Co-opting a gene for a new function.**
*Brachyury* is a gene found in invertebrates that has been used
for notochord development in this ascidian, a basal chordate. By
attaching the *Brachyury* promoter to a gene with a protein product
that stains blue, it is possible to see that *Brachyury* gene expression
in ascidians is associated with the development of the notochord, a
novel function compared with its function in organisms lacking a
notochord. The orthologue in the nematode *Caenorhabditis elegans*
is important for hind gut and male tail development, but there is no
evidence of a notochord precursor.

How a single genetic toolkit can be used to build an insect, a bird, a bat, a whale, or a human is an intriguing puzzle
for evolutionary developmental biologists, exemplified with
the *Brachyury* gene. One explanation is that *Brachyury* turns on
different genes or combinations of genes in different animals.
Although there are not yet enough data to sort out the details

of *Brachyury*, we can look at limb formation for an explanation
of how such a change could have evolved.

## Limbs have developed through modification of transcriptional regulation

Most tetrapods have four limbs—two hindlimbs and two forelimbs, although two or more limbs have been lost in snakes
and many lizards. The forelimb in a bird is actually the wing.
Our forelimb is the arm. Clearly, these are two very different
structures, but they have a common evolutionary origin. As you
learned in chapter 23, these are termed *homologous structures*.

At the genetic level, humans and birds both express the
*Tbx5* gene in developing forelimb buds. Like *Brachyury*, *Tbx5*
is a member of a transcription factor gene family with T box
domain, that is, a conserved sequence of base-pairs within
the gene. So, *Tbx5*-encoded protein turns on a gene or genes
that are needed to make a limb. Mutations in the human *Tbx5*
gene cause Holt–Oram syndrome, resulting in forelimb and
heart abnormalities.

What seems to have changed as birds and humans evolved
are the genes that are transcribed because of the Tbx5 protein
(figure 25.6). In the ancestral tetrapod, perhaps Tbx5 protein
bound to only one gene and triggered transcription. In humans
and birds, different genes are expressed in response to Tbx5.

*Tbx5* evolution corresponds to changes in the coding
sequence for the Tbx5 protein in different species. But, it
is also possible for changes in noncoding regions of a gene
to alter gene expression during evolution. The *paired-like
homeodomain transcription factor 1* (*pitx1*) is expressed in the
hindlimbs of developing mouse embryos and its homologue

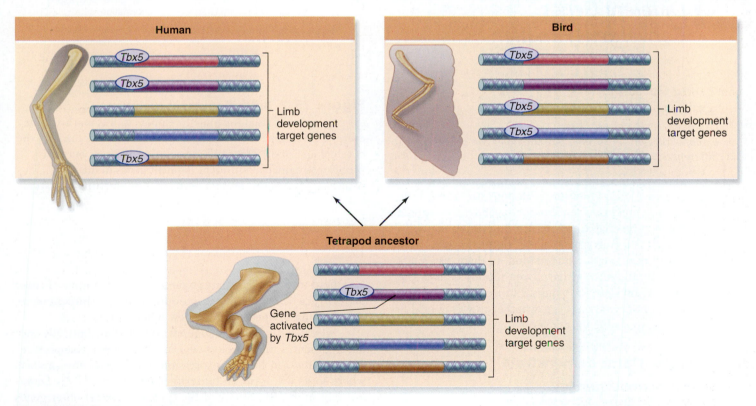

**Figure 25.6** *Tbx5* **regulates wing and arm development.** Wings and arms are very different, but the development of each
depends on *Tbx5*. Why the difference? *Tbx5* turns on different genes in birds and humans.

chapter **25** *Evolution of Development*

is expressed in the pelvic region of the ninespine stickleback fish *(Pungitius pungitius)*. Much like *Brachyury* gene evolution, *pitx1* was co-opted for a new function in tetrapods. Within the sticklebacks, *pitx1* gene expression is different in marine and freshwater populations of the same species, yet the pitx1 proteins in both populations have identical amino acid sequences. The explanation for the difference can be found in the regulatory regions of the gene that are not translated into protein.

Marine sticklebacks have skeletal armor, including spines, in the pelvic region that protects them from predatory fish. Isolated populations in freshwater have lost the pelvic skeletal armor and do not express *pitx1* in the pelvic region. Loss of gene expression, rather than a change in the protein structure of this transcription factor accounts for the morphological differences between the marine and freshwater sticklebacks.

## Learning Outcome Review 25.3

During the long course of evolution, genes have been co-opted for new functions. A change in the protein-coding region of a transcription factor can change the genes it can bind to and regulate. A change in the regulatory region of a gene can change where or when that gene is expressed, which can lead to altered morphology.

■ *A marine threespine stickleback fish is mated with a freshwater threespine with reduced armor, and all the offspring have reduced armor. Both populations have identical* pitx1 *coding regions. Could* pitx1 *be the cause of the difference in armor? How could you test this?*

## 25.4 Different Genes, Convergent Function

### Learning Outcomes

1. Differentiate between homologous structures and homoplastic structures.
2. Explain how two very similar morphologies can arise from different developmental pathways.

*Homoplastic structures*, also known as analogous structures, have the same or similar functions, but arose independently—unlike homologous structures that arose once from a common ancestor. Phylogenies reveal convergent events, but the origin of the convergence may not be easily understood. In many cases different developmental pathways have been modified, as is the case with the spots on butterfly wings. In other cases, such as flower shape, it is not always as clear whether the same or different genes are responsible for convergent evolution.

## Insect wing patterns demonstrate homoplastic convergence

Insect wings, especially those of moths and butterflies, have beautiful patterns that can protect them from predation and al-

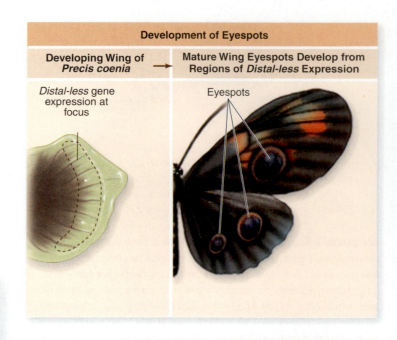

**Development of Eyespots**

| Developing Wing of *Precis coenia* | → | Mature Wing Eyespots Develop from Regions of *Distal-less* Expression |

*Distal-less* gene expression at focus

Eyespots

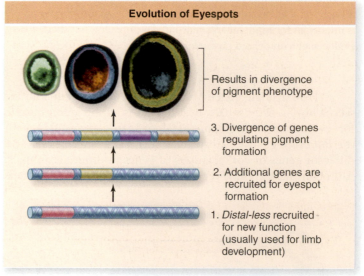

**Evolution of Eyespots**

Results in divergence of pigment phenotype

3. Divergence of genes regulating pigment formation

2. Additional genes are recruited for eyespot formation

1. *Distal-less* recruited for new function (usually used for limb development)

**Figure 25.7 Butterfly eyespot evolution.** The *Distal-less* gene, usually used for limb development, was recruited for eyespot development on butterfly wings. *Distal-less* initiates the development of different colored spots in different butterfly species by regulating different pigment genes in different species. Eyespots can protect butterflies by startling predators.

low them to thermoregulate (figure 25.7). The origins of these patterns are best explained by co-option, the recruitment of existing regulatory programs for new functions.

*Distal-less* is one of the genes co-opted for butterfly spot development. Limb development in insects and arthropods requires *Distal-less*, but the expression of this gene also predicts where spots will form on butterfly wings (figure 27.7). *Distal-less* determines the center of the spot, but several other genes have been co-opted to determine the overall size and pattern of different spots.

Not all insects have co-opted the same sets of genes for these new functions, but all the evolutionary pathways have converged around production of these novel, highly patterned wings.

## Flower shapes also demonstrate convergence

Flowers exhibit two types of symmetry. Looking down on a **radially symmetrical** flower, you see a circle. No matter how you cut that flower, as long as you have a straight line that intersects with the center, you end up with two identical parts. Examples of radially symmetrical flowers are daisies, roses, tulips, and many other flowers.

**Bilaterally symmetrical** flowers have mirror-image halves on each side of a single central axis. If they are cut in any other direction, two nonsimilar shapes result. Plants with bilaterally symmetrical flowers include snapdragons, mints, and peas. Bilaterally symmetrical flowers are attractive to their pollinators, and the shape may have been an important factor in their evolutionary success.

At the crossroads of evolution and development, two questions arise: first, What genes are involved in bilateral symmetry? And second, Are the same genes involved in the numerous, independent origins of asymmetrical flowers?

*Cycloidia (CYC)* is a snapdragon gene responsible for the bilateral symmetry of the flower. Snapdragons with mutations in *CYC* have radially symmetrical flowers (see figure 42.17*b*). Beginning with robust phylogenies, researchers have selected flowers that evolved bilateral symmetry independently from snapdragons and cloned the *CYC* gene. The *CYC* gene in closely related symmetrical flowers has also been sequenced.

Comparisons of the *CYC* gene sequence among phylogenetically diverse flowers indicate that both radial symmetry and bilateral symmetry evolved in multiple ways in flowers. Although radial symmetry is the ancestral condition, some radially symmetrical flowers have a bilaterally symmetrical ancestor. Loss of *CYC* function accounts for the loss of bilateral symmetry in some of these plants.

Gain of bilateral symmetry arose independently among some species because of the *CYC* gene. This change is an example of convergent evolution through mutations of the same gene. In other cases, *CYC* is not clearly responsible for the bilateral symmetry. Other genes also played a role in the convergent evolution of bilaterally symmetrical flowers.

### Learning Outcomes Review 25.4

Homoplastic features have a similar function but different evolutionary origins and are examples of convergent evolution. Homologous features have the same evolutionary origins, but may have a different function. Knowledge of the underlying genes often reveals that a feature thought to be homoplastic has a more common origin than expected.

■ *Both sharks and whales have pectoral fins. Are these features homologous or homoplastic?*

## 25.5 Gene Duplication and Divergence

### Learning Outcome

1. *Describe how duplicated genes could give rise to new functions in an organism.*

You encountered the role of gene duplication in genome evolution in chapter 24. In this section, we explore a specific example of the evolution of development through gene duplication and divergence in flower form.

## Gene duplications of *paleoAP3* led to flowering-plant morphology

Before the flowering plants originated, a *MADS* box gene duplicated, giving rise to genes called *PI* and *paleoAP3*. In ancestral flowering plants, these genes affected stamen development, and this function has been retained. (Stamens are the male reproductive structures of flowering plants.)

The *paleoAP3* gene duplicated to produce *AP3* and an *AP3* duplicate some time after members of the poppy family last shared a common ancestor with the clade of plants called the eudicots (plants like apple, tomato, and *Arabidopsis*). This clade of eudicots is distinguished on the genome level by both the duplication of *paleoAP3* and the origins of a precise pattern of petal development in their last common ancestor (figure 25.8). The phylogenetic inference is that *AP3* gained a role in petal development.

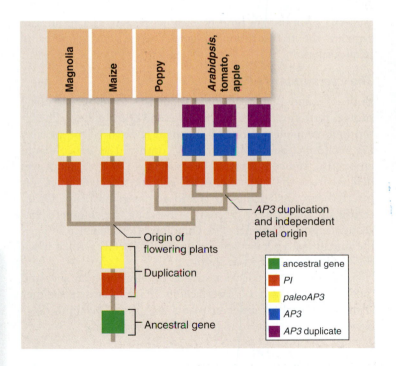

**Figure 25.8** Petal evolution through gene duplication. Two gene duplications resulted in the *AP3* gene in the eudicots that has acquired a role in petal development.

**Figure 25.9** *AP3* **has acquired a domain necessary for petal development.** The *AP3* gene includes MADS box encoding a DNA-binding domain and a highly specific sequence near the C terminus. Without the 3′ region of the *AP3* gene, the *Arabidopsis* plant will not make petals.

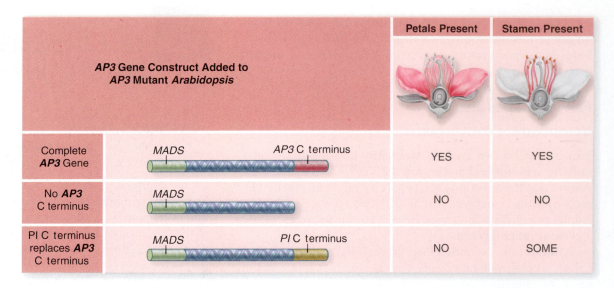

| *AP3* Gene Construct Added to *AP3* Mutant *Arabidopsis* | | Petals Present | Stamen Present |
|---|---|---|---|
| Complete *AP3* Gene | MADS — *AP3* C terminus | YES | YES |
| No *AP3* C terminus | MADS | NO | NO |
| PI C terminus replaces *AP3* C terminus | MADS — *PI* C terminus | NO | SOME |

## Gene divergence of *AP3* altered function to control petal development

Although the occurrence of *AP3* through duplication corresponds with a uniform developmental process for specifying petal development, the correlation could simply be coincidental. Experiments that mix and match parts of the *AP3* and *PI* genes, and then introduce them into *ap3* mutant plants, confirm that the phylogenetic correspondence is not a coincidence. The *ap3* plants do not produce either petals or stamens. A summary of the experiments is shown in figure 25.9.

Earlier in this chapter, the *MADS* box transcription factor gene family was introduced. One region of a *MADS* gene codes for a DNA-binding motif; other regions code for different functions, including protein–protein binding. The PI and AP3 proteins can bind to each other, and, as a result, can regulate the transcription of genes needed for stamen and petal formation.

### The C terminus of AP3

Both AP3 and PI have distinct sequences at the C (carboxy) protein terminus (coded for by the 3′ end of the genes). The C-terminus sequence of the AP3 protein is essential for specifying petal function, and it contains a conserved sequence shared among the eudicots. The *AP3* C-terminus DNA sequence was deleted from the wild-type gene, and the new construct was inserted into *ap3* plants to create a transgenic plant. Other transgenic plants were created by inserting the complete *AP3* sequence into *ap3* plants. The complete *AP3* sequence rescued the mutant, and petals were produced. No petals formed when the C-terminus motif was absent.

*AP3* is also needed for stamen development, an ancestral trait found in *paleoAP3*. Plants lacking *AP3* fail to produce either stamens or petals. Transgenic plants with the C-terminus deletion construct also failed to produce stamens.

### The C terminus of PI

The *pi* mutant phenotype also lacks stamens and petals. To test whether the *PI* C terminus could substitute for the *AP3* C terminus in specifying petal formation, the *PI* C terminus was added to the truncated *AP3* gene. No petals formed, but stamen development was partially rescued. These experiments demonstrate that *AP3* has acquired an essential role in petal development, encoded in a sequence at the 3′ end of the gene.

> **Learning Outcome Review 25.5**
>
> Gene duplication allows divergence that can lead to novel function. In eudicot flowering plants, the *AP3* gene, which arose by duplication from the *paleoAP3* gene, gained a role in petal development in addition to its function in stamen development.
>
> ■ *Suppose duplication of a particular gene proved to be lethal. What changes, if any, would allow this duplication to persist and possibly evolve into a new function?*

## 25.6 Functional Analysis of Genes Across Species

> **Learning Outcome**
>
> 1. Evaluate the limitations of comparative genomics in exploring the evolution of development.

Comparative genomics is amazingly useful for understanding morphological diversity. Limitations exist, however, in the inferences about evolution of development that we can draw from sequence comparison alone. *Functional genomics* includes a range of experiments designed to test the actual function of a gene in different species as explained in chapter 18.

Sequence comparisons among organisms are essential for both phylogenetic and comparative developmental studies. Careful analysis is needed to distinguish paralogues from orthologues. Rapidly evolving research using bioinformatics, which utilizes computer programming to analyze DNA and protein data, leads to hypotheses that can be tested experimentally.

You have already seen how this can work with highly conserved genes such as *Tbx5*. However, a single base mutation can change an active gene into an inactive pseudogene and experiments are necessary to demonstrate the actual function of the gene.

**? Inquiry question**

Explain how functional analysis was used to support the claim that petal development evolved through the acquisition of petal function in the *AP3* gene of *Arabidopsis*.

Tools for functional analysis exist in model systems but need to be developed in other organisms on the tree of life if we are going to piece together evolutionary history. Model systems such as yeast, the flowering plant *Arabidopsis*, the nematode *Caenorhabditis elegans*, *Drosophila*, and the mouse have been selected because they are easy to manipulate in the laboratory, have short life cycles, and have well-delineated genomes. Also, it is possible to visualize gene expression within parts of the organism using labeled markers and to create transgenic organisms that contain and express foreign genes.

**Learning Outcome Review 25.6**

Genomic similarities alone are not enough to determine the function of genes in different species; functional genomics studies whether conserved genes operate in the same way across species utilizing model organisms and genetic engineering.

■ *What tests and techniques were used to demonstrate the AP3 gene's role in petal development?*

## 25.7 Diversity of Eyes in the Natural World: A Case Study

**Learning Outcome**

1. *Explain how the compound eye of a fly, the human eye, and the eyespot of a ribbon worm could have a common evolutionary origin.*

The eye is one of the most complex organs. Biologists have studied it for centuries. Indeed, explaining how such a complicated structure could evolve was one of the great challenges facing Darwin. If all parts of a structure such as an eye are required for proper functioning, how could natural selection build such a structure?

Darwin's response was that even intermediate structures—which provide, for example, the ability to distinguish light from dark—would be advantageous compared with the ancestral state of no visual capability whatsoever, and thus these structures would be favored by natural selection. In this way, by incremental improvements in function, natural selection could build a complicated structure.

### Morphological evidence indicates eyes evolved at least twenty times

Comparative anatomists long have noted that the structures of the eyes of different types of animals are quite different. Consider, for example, the difference in the eyes of a vertebrate, an insect, a mollusk (octopus), and a planarian (figure 25.10). The eyes of these organisms are extremely different in many ways, ranging from compound eyes, to simple eyes, to mere eyespots.

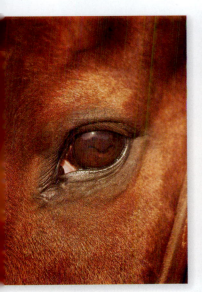

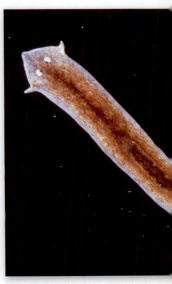

**Figure 25.10 A diversity of eyes.** Morphological and anatomical comparisons of eyes are consistent with the hypothesis of independent, convergent evolution of eyes in diverse species such as flies and humans.

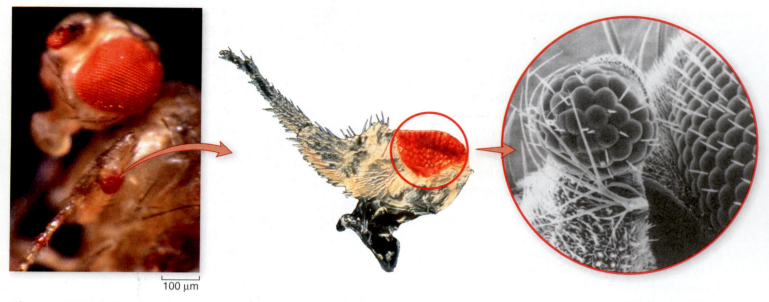

100 μm

**Figure 25.11  Mouse *Pax6* makes an eye on the leg of a fly.** *Pax6* and *eyeless* are functional homologues. The *Pax6* master regulator gene can initiate compound eye development in a fruit fly or simple eye development in a mouse.

Consequently, these eyes are examples of convergent evolution and are homoplastic. For this reason, evolutionary biologists traditionally viewed the eyes of different organisms as having independently evolved, perhaps as many as 20 times. Moreover, this view holds that the most recent common ancestor of all these forms was a primitive animal with no ability to detect light.

## The same gene, *Pax6*, initiates fly and mouse eye development

In the early 1990s, biologists studied the development of the eye in both vertebrates and insects. In each case, a gene was discovered that codes for a transcription factor important in lens formation; the mouse gene was given the name ***Pax6,*** whereas the fly gene was called *eyeless*. A mutation in the *eyeless* gene led to a lack of production of the transcription factor, and thus the complete absence of eye development, giving the gene its name.

When these genes were sequenced, it became apparent that they were highly similar; in essence, the homologous *Pax6* gene was responsible for triggering lens formation in both insects and vertebrates. A stunning demonstration of this homology was conducted by the Swiss biologist Walter Gehring, who inserted the mouse version of the *Pax6* into the genome of a fruit fly, creating a transgenic fly. In this fly, the *Pax6* gene was turned on by regulatory factors in the fly's leg and an eye formed on the leg of the fly (figure 25.11)!

These results were truly shocking to the evolutionary biology community. Insects and vertebrates diverged from a common ancestor more than 500 MYA. Moreover, given the large differences in structure of the vertebrate eye and insect eye, the standard assumption was that the eyes evolved independently, and thus that their development would be controlled by completely different genes. That eye development was affected by the same homologous gene, and that these genes

were so similar that the vertebrate gene seemed to function normally in the insect genome, was completely unexpected.

The *Pax6* story extends to eyeless fish found in caves (figure 25.12). Fish that live in dark caves need to rely on senses other than sight. In cavefish, *Pax6* gene expression is greatly reduced. Eyes start to develop, but then degenerate.

Surface Dweller — Has *Pax6*

*a.*

Cave Dweller — Loss of *Pax6*

*b.*

**Figure 25.12  Cavefish have lost their sight.** Mexican tetras (*Astyanax mexicanus*) have (*a*) surface-dwelling members and (*b*) cave-dwelling members of the same species. The cavefish have very tiny eyes, partly because of reduced expression of *Pax6*.

## Ribbon worms, but not planaria, use *Pax6* for eye development

Recent discoveries have yielded further surprises about the *Pax6* gene. Even the very simple ribbon worm, *Lineus sanguineus*, relies on *Pax6* for development of its eyespots. A *Pax6* homologue has been cloned and has been shown to express at the sites where eyespots develop. In contrast, planarian worms do not rely on *Pax6* for eyespot development.

### Ribbon worm eyespot regeneration

The simple marine ribbon worm evolved later than the flatworm planaria. Just like planaria, ribbon worms can regenerate their head region if it is removed. In an elegant experiment, the head of a ribbon worm was removed, and biologists followed the regeneration of eyespots. At the same time, the expression of the *Pax6* homologue was observed using in situ hybridization.

To observe *Pax6* gene expression, an antisense RNA sequence of the *Pax6* was made and labeled with a color marker. When the regenerating ribbon worms were exposed to the antisense *Pax6* probe, the antisense RNA paired with expressed *Pax6* RNA transcripts and could be seen as colored spots under the microscope (figure 25.13).

### Planarian eyespot regeneration

Similar experiments were tried with planaria species that are phylogenetically related to ribbon worms, but the conclusion was quite different from that in ribbon worms. If a planaria is cut in half lengthwise, it can regenerate its missing half, including the second eyespot, but no *Pax6* gene expression is associated with regenerating the eyespots.

Planaria do have *Pax6*-related genes, but inactivating those genes does not stop eye regeneration (figure 25.14). These *Pax6*-related genes are, however, expressed in the central nervous system. A *Pax6*-responsive element, P3-enhancer, has also been identified and shown to be active in planaria. Perhaps some clues as to the origin of *Pax6*'s role in eye development will be uncovered as comparisons between ribbon worm and planarian eyespot regeneration continue.

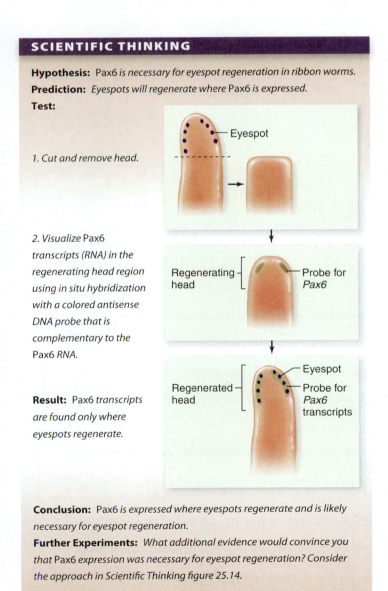

**SCIENTIFIC THINKING**

**Hypothesis:** Pax6 *is necessary for eyespot regeneration in ribbon worms.*

**Prediction:** *Eyespots will regenerate where Pax6 is expressed.*

**Test:**

*1. Cut and remove head.* — Eyespot

*2. Visualize* Pax6 *transcripts (RNA) in the regenerating head region using in situ hybridization with a colored antisense DNA probe that is complementary to the* Pax6 *RNA.*

Regenerating head — Probe for *Pax6*

**Result:** Pax6 *transcripts are found only where eyespots regenerate.*

Regenerated head — Eyespot / Probe for *Pax6* transcripts

**Conclusion:** Pax6 *is expressed where eyespots regenerate and is likely necessary for eyespot regeneration.*

**Further Experiments:** *What additional evidence would convince you that Pax6 expression was necessary for eyespot regeneration? Consider the approach in Scientific Thinking figure 25.14.*

**Figure 25.13** *Pax6* expression correlates with ribbon worm eyespot regeneration.

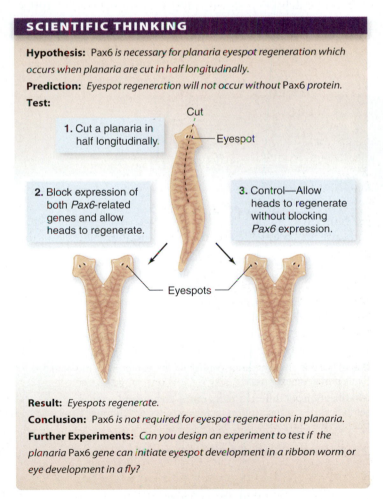

**SCIENTIFIC THINKING**

**Hypothesis:** Pax6 *is necessary for planaria eyespot regeneration which occurs when planaria are cut in half longitudinally.*

**Prediction:** *Eyespot regeneration will not occur without Pax6 protein.*

**Test:**

Cut

**1.** Cut a planaria in half longitudinally. — Eyespot

**2.** Block expression of both *Pax6*-related genes and allow heads to regenerate.

**3.** Control—Allow heads to regenerate without blocking *Pax6* expression.

Eyespots

**Result:** *Eyespots regenerate.*

**Conclusion:** Pax6 *is not required for eyespot regeneration in planaria.*

**Further Experiments:** *Can you design an experiment to test if the planaria Pax6 gene can initiate eyespot development in a ribbon worm or eye development in a fly?*

**Figure 25.14** *Pax6* is not required for planaria eyespot regeneration.

## The initiation of eye development may have evolved just once

Several explanations are possible for these findings. One is that eyes in different types of animals evolved truly independently, as originally believed. But if this is the case, why is *Pax6* so structurally similar and able to play a similar role in so many different groups? Opponents of single evolution of the eye point out that *Pax6* is involved not only in development of the eye, but also in development of the entire forehead region of many organisms. Consequently, it is possible that if *Pax6* had a regulatory role in the forehead of early animals, perhaps it has been independently co-opted time and time again to serve a role in eye development. This role would be consistent with the data on planarians (see figure 25.14).

Many other biologists find this interpretation unlikely. The consistent use of *Pax6* in eye development in so many organisms, the fact that it functions in the same role in each case, and the great similarity in DNA sequence and even functional replaceability suggest to many that *Pax6* acquired its evolutionary role in eye development only a single time, in the common ancestor of all extant organisms that use *Pax6* in eye development.

Given the great dissimilarity among eyes of different groups, how can this be? One hypothesis is that the common ancestor of these groups was not completely blind, as traditionally assumed. Rather, that organism may have had some sort of rudimentary visual system—maybe no more than a pigmented photoreceptor cell, maybe a slightly more elaborate organ that could distinguish light from dark.

Whatever the exact phenotype, the important point is that some sort of basic visual system existed that used *Pax6* in its development. Subsequently, the descendants of this ancestor diversified independently, evolving the sophisticated and complex image-forming eyes exhibited by different animal groups today.

Most evolutionary and developmental biologists today support some form of this hypothesis. Nonetheless, no independent evidence exists that the common ancestor of most of today's animal groups, a primitive form that lived probably more than 500 MYA, had any ability to detect light. The reason for this belief comes not from the fossil record, but from a synthesis of phylogenetic and molecular developmental data.

> ### Learning Outcome Review 25.7
>
> Multidisciplinary approaches can clarify the evolutionary history of the world's biological diversity. The *Pax6* gene and its many homologues indicate that eye development, although highly diverse in outcome, may have a single evolutionary origin.
>
> ■ *Why would mutations leading to defective Pax6 persist in cavefish? If these fish were introduced into a habitat with light, what would you expect to occur?*

## Chapter Review

### 25.1 Overview of Evolutionary Developmental Biology

*Highly conserved genes produce diverse morphologies.*

The *Hox* genes establish body form in animals; *MADS* box genes have a similar function in plants. Changes in these transcription factors and in genes involved in signaling pathways are responsible for new morphologies.

*Developmental mechanisms exhibit evolutionary change.*

Heterochrony refers to alteration of timing of developmental events due to genetic changes; homeosis refers to alterations in the spatial pattern of gene expression.

Modifications of different parts of the coding and regulatory sequences of a transcription factor can alter development and phenotypic expression (see figure 25.2).

### 25.2 One or Two Gene Mutations, New Form

*Cauliflower and broccoli began with a stop codon.*

The wide diversity of cabbage subspecies is due to a simple mutation of one gene (see figure 25.3).

*Cichlid fish jaws demonstrate morphological diversity.*

Jaw and body armor morphology in fish have also been modified by mutations in one or a few genes.

### 25.3 Same Gene, New Function (see figure 25.6)

*Ancestral genes may be co-opted for new functions.*

A single gene may act on different genes or combinations of genes in different species.

*Limbs have developed through modification of transcriptional regulation.*

Species differences in limbs have resulted from evolutionary changes in gene expression and timing of expression.

### 25.4 Different Genes, Convergent Function

*Insect wing patterns demonstrate homoplastic convergence.*

Wing patterns in butterflies have evolved as wing scales developed from ancestral sensory bristles.

*Flower shapes also demonstrate convergence*

Both radial and bilateral symmetry have arisen in multiple ways in flowers, even though radial symmetry is considered ancestral.

## 25.5 Gene Duplication and Divergence

**Gene duplications of paleoAP3 led to flowering-plant morphology.**

Duplication of the *AP3* gene and subsequent divergence produced flower petals, whereas the ancestral form affected only stamen development.

**Gene divergence of AP3 altered function to control petal development.**

Studies have narrowed the active region in *AP3* to the C terminus, which acts differently from the C terminus of the related *PI* gene; only *AP3* can produce petals (see figure 25.9).

## 25.6 Functional Analysis of Genes Across Species

Sequence comparisons are essential for both phylogenetic and comparative development studies, but we can only infer function from this information.

## 25.7 Diversity of Eyes in the Natural World: A Case Study

**Morphological evidence indicates eyes evolved at least twenty times.**

Homoplasy and convergent evolution are supported as explaining the diversity of eyes found in the animal kingdom.

**The same gene, Pax6, initiates fly and mouse eye development.**

Transgenic experiments showed that the *Pax6* gene from a mouse, inserted into the genome of *Drosophila*, could cause development of an eye.

**Ribbon worms, but not planaria, use Pax6 for eye development.**

In planaria, *Pax6* gene expression does not occur even when an eyespot successfully regenerates.

**The initiation of eye development may have evolved just once.**

It appears that at some distant point in evolutionary time, *Pax6* was part of a visual system that later diverged many times.

---

## Review Questions

### UNDERSTAND

1. Heterochrony is
   a. the alteration of the spatial pattern of gene expression.
   b. a change in the relative position of a body part.
   c. a change in the relative timing of developmental events.
   d. a change in a signaling pathway.

2. Vast differences in the phenotypes of organisms as different as fruit flies and humans
   a. must result from differences among many thousands of genes controlling development.
   b. have apparently arisen largely through manipulation of the timing and regulation of expression of probably less than 100 highly conserved genes.
   c. can be entirely explained by heterochrony.
   d. can be entirely explained by homeotic factors.

3. Homoplastic structures
   a. can involve convergence of completely unrelated developmental pathways.
   b. always are morphologically distinct.
   c. are produced by divergent evolution of homologous structures.
   d. are derived from the same structure in a shared common ancestor.

4. *Hox* genes are
   a. found in both plants and animals.
   b. found only in animals.
   c. found only in plants.
   d. only associated with genes in the *MADS* complex.

5. The *Brachyury* and *pictx1* genes in vertebrates and the *Ap3* gene in flowering plants
   a. are examples of *Hox* genes.
   b. are examples of co-opting a gene for a new function.
   c. are homologues for determining the body plan of eukaryotes.
   d. help regulate the formation of appendages.

6. Which of the following statements about *Pax6* is false?
   a. *Pax6* has a similar function in mice and flies.
   b. *Pax6* is involved in eyespot formation in ribbon worms.
   c. *Pax6* is required for eye formation in *Drosophila*.
   d. *Pax6* is required for eyespot formation in planaria.

7. Which of the following statements about *Tbx5* is true?
   a. *Tbx5* is found only in tetrapods.
   b. *Tbx5* is involved in limb development in vertebrates.
   c. *Tbx5* is only found in the ancestors of tetrapods.
   d. *Tbx5* interacts with the same set of genes across different tetrapod species.

8. Homeosis
   a. refers to a maintained and unchanging genetic environment.
   b. is a temporal change in gene expression.
   c. is a spatial change in gene expression.
   d. is not an important genetic mechanism in development.

9. Transcription factors are
   a. genes.
   b. sequences of RNA.
   c. proteins that affect the expression of genes.
   d. none of the above

10. Independently derived mutations of the *CYC* gene in plants
    a. suggests bilateral floral symmetry among all plants is homologous.
    b. establishes that radial floral symmetry is preferred by pollinators.
    c. establishes that radial floral symmetry is derived for all plants.
    d. none of the above

## APPLY

1. Choose the statement that best explains how the Tbx5 protein can be responsible for the development of arms in humans and wings in birds.
    a. Tbx5 is a key component of bone.
    b. Tbx5 is a transcription factor that binds to the promoters of different genes in humans and birds to initiate arm and wing development.
    c. Tbx5 was co-opted from its role in tail development for the role in limb development.
    d. Tbx5 is a signaling molecule involved in the signaling pathway for limb development in both species.

2. Analyze why it was important to create transgenic plants to determine the role of *AP3* in petal formation and choose the most compelling reason.
    a. It provided a functional test of the role of *AP3* in petal development.
    b. Duplication of *AP3* could not be resolved on the phylogeny.
    c. To check if the phylogenetic position of *AP3* is really derived.
    d. Because tests already established the role of *paleoAP3* in stamen development.

3. The *Eda* allele that causes reduced armor originated about 2 MYA in marine stickleback fish and persists with a frequency of about 1% in marine environments. The frequency is much higher in freshwater populations. Apply your understanding of evolution to determine the most likely reason for the difference in *Eda* allele frequency.
    a. There is positive selection for armor in marine environments because fish are more buoyant in salt water.
    b. Fish have many predators in the marine environment and fish with reduced armor have reduced fitness.
    c. There is negative selection for armor in freshwater because building armor is energetically expensive.
    d. Both b and c are valid.

4. In *Drosophila* species, the yellow (*y*) gene is responsible for the patterning of black pigment on the body and the wings. A comparison of two species reveals that one has a black spot on each wing, and the other species lacks black pigmentation on the wing. The sequence of the coding region for *y* is identical in both species. Critique the following explanations and choose the most plausible one.
    a. The protein coded for by the *y* gene has a different structure in species with the black spots than the species without.
    b. The species without black pigmentation on the wing has a mutation in a regulatory region of the *y* gene.
    c. There is a deletion mutation in one of the exons of the *y* gene in the species without black pigment in the wings.
    d. Convergent evolution explains why both species develop black wing spots.

## SYNTHESIZE

1. If the tetrapod ancestor of humans and birds had a single gene that was regulated by Tbx5 transcription factor, propose an evolutionary hypothesis for how several genes are regulated by Tbx5 in humans and birds.

2. From the chapter on evolution of development it would seem that the generation of new developmental patterns would be fairly easy and fast, leading to the ability of organisms to adapt quickly to environmental changes. Construct an explanation for why it can take millions of years, typically, for many of the traits examined to evolve. (Hint: Consider the differences in *Eda* allele frequency in marine and freshwater threespine stickleback fish.)

3. There are several ways in which phenotypic diversity among major groups of organisms can be explained. On one end of the spectrum, such differences could arise out of differences in many genes that control development. On the other end, small sets of genes might differ in how they regulate the expression of various parts of the genome. Evaluate which view represents our current understanding.

4. Critique the argument that eyes have multiple evolutionary origins.

5. Based on the information in figure 25.8, construct an explanation for the evolutionary differences in genes related to *AP3* in maize and tomato. Be sure to consider what happened before and after the two species diverged from a common ancestor.

6. Having read all of this chapter, return to the claim that the difference between direct and indirect development in sea urchins is caused by a change in gene expression, not differences in genes. Starting at the level of DNA sequence, formulate an argument in support of the claim.

## ONLINE RESOURCE

www.ravenbiology.com

Understand, Apply, and Synthesize—enhance your study with animations that bring concepts to life and practice tests to assess your understanding. Your instructor may also recommend the interactive eBook, individualized learning tools, and more.

Chapter **26**

# The Tree of Life

## Chapter Outline

**Part V** Diversity of Life on Earth

## Introduction

*Different life forms descended from the same origin event and have many things in common: they are composed of one or more cells, they carry out metabolism and transfer energy with ATP, and they encode hereditary information in DNA. But living things are also highly diverse, ranging from bacteria and amoebas to blue whales and sequoia trees. Coral reefs, such as the one pictured here, are microcosms of diversity, comprising many life forms and sheltering an enormous array of life. For generations, biologists have tried to group organisms based on shared characteristics. The most meaningful groupings are based on the study of evolutionary relationships among organisms. These phylogenetic approaches and a sea of molecular sequence data are leading to new evolutionary hypotheses to explain life's variety. In this chapter and those that follow in this unit, we explore the diversity of the living world.*

# 26.1 Origins of Life

### Learning Outcomes

1. Explain what qualifies something as "living."
2. Describe different proposals for the origin of life on Earth.

The cell is the basic unit of life, and today all cells come from preexisting cells. But, how can we explain the origins of the tremendous diversity of life on Earth today? The Earth formed as a hot mass of molten rock about 4.5 BYA. As it cooled, much of the water vapor present in Earth's atmosphere condensed into liquid water that accumulated on the surface in chemically rich oceans. One scenario for the origin of life is that it originated in this dilute, hot, smelly soup of ammonia, formaldehyde, formic acid, cyanide, methane, hydrogen sulfide, and organic hydrocarbons. Whether at the oceans' edges, in hydrothermal deep-sea vents, or elsewhere, the consensus among researchers is that life arose spontaneously from these early waters. Although the way in which this happened remains a puzzle, we cannot escape a certain curiosity about the earliest steps that eventually led to the origin of all living things on Earth, including ourselves. How did organisms evolve from the complex molecules that swirled in the early oceans?

## All organisms share fundamental properties of life

Before we can address the origins of life, we must consider what qualifies something as "living." Biologists have found that the following set of properties are common to all organisms on Earth, with heredity playing a particularly key role.

**Cellular organization.** All organisms consist of one or more *cells*—complex, organized assemblages of molecules enclosed within membranes (figure 26.1).

**Sensitivity.** All organisms respond to stimuli—though not always to the same stimuli in the same ways.

**Growth.** All living things assimilate energy and use it to maintain internal order and grow, a process called **metabolism.** Plants, algae, and some bacteria use sunlight to create covalent carbon–carbon bonds from $CO_2$ and $H_2O$ through photosynthesis. This transfer of the energy in covalent bonds is essential to all life on Earth.

**Development.** Both unicellular and multicellular organisms undergo systematic, gene-directed changes as they grow and mature.

**Reproduction.** Organisms reproduce, passing on genes from one generation to the next.

**Regulation.** All organisms have regulatory mechanisms that coordinate internal processes.

**Homeostasis.** All living things maintain relatively constant internal conditions, different from their environment.

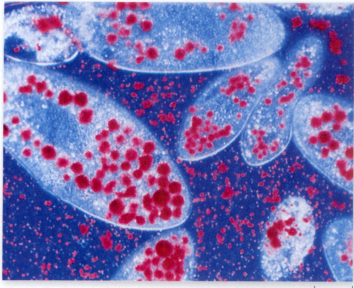

**Figure 26.1 Cellular compartmentalization.** These complex, single-celled organisms called Paramecia are classified as protists. The yeasts, stained red in this photograph, have been consumed and are enclosed within membrane-bounded sacs called digestive vacuoles.

66.7 μm

**Heredity.** All organisms on Earth possess a *genetic system* that is based on the replication of a long, complex molecule called DNA. This mechanism allows for adaptation and evolution over time and is a distinguishing characteristic of living organisms.

Long before there were cells with the properties of life, organic (carbon-based) molecules formed from inorganic molecules. The formation of proteins, nucleic acids, carbohydrates, and lipids were essential, but not sufficient for life. The evolution of cells required early organic molecules to assemble into a functional, interdependent unit.

## Life may have had extraterrestrial origins

Life may not have originated on Earth at all; instead, life may have "infected" Earth from some other planet. This hypothesis, called **panspermia,** proposes that meteors or cosmic dust may have carried significant amounts of complex organic molecules to Earth, kicking off the evolution of life. Hundreds of thousands of meteorites and comets are known to have slammed into the early

**Figure 26.2** The Phoenix lander sent gigabytes of information and tens of thousands of images of Mars' surface back to Earth, providing clues about the possibility of ancient life on Mars.

Earth, and recent findings suggest that at least some may have carried organic materials. Nor is life on other planets ruled out. For example, the discovery of liquid water under the surfaces of Jupiter's ice-shrouded moon Europa and Saturn's moon, Enceladus, as well as suggestions of fossils in rocks from Mars lend some credence to this idea. Enceladus may harbor an ocean of liquid water, raising intriguing questions about whether it is habitable. Plumes of ice and vapor escape its gravitational field and contribute to the outermost ring around Saturn. In 2009, sodium salt was discovered in Saturn's ring that appears to originate from Enceladus. The Mars lander Phoenix confirmed the presence of frozen water on the planet in 2008 (figure 26.2). Analysis of soil samples from the same mission revealed an alkaline soil composed of sodium, magnesium, chloride, potassium, and other chemicals, but many questions remain about the watery environment that might have harbored life.

## Life may have originated on early Earth

### Conditions on early Earth

The more we learn about the Earth's early history, the more likely it seems that Earth's first organisms emerged and lived at very high temperatures. Rubble from the forming solar system slammed into the early Earth beginning about 4.6 BYA, keeping the surface molten hot. As the bombardment slowed down, temperatures dropped. By about 3.8 BYA, ocean temperatures are thought to have dropped to a hot 49° to 88°C (120° to 190°F). Between 3.8 and 3.5 BYA, life first appeared, promptly after the Earth was habitable. Thus, as intolerable as early Earth's infernal temperatures seem to us today, they gave birth to life.

Very few geochemists agree on the exact composition of the early atmosphere. One popular view is that it contained principally carbon dioxide ($CO_2$) and nitrogen gas ($N_2$), along with significant amounts of water vapor ($H_2O$). It is possible that the early atmosphere also contained hydrogen gas ($H_2$) and compounds in which hydrogen atoms were bonded to the other light elements (sulfur, nitrogen, and carbon), producing hydrogen sulfide ($H_2S$), ammonia ($NH_3$), and methane ($CH_4$).

We refer to such an atmosphere as a *reducing atmosphere* because of the ample availability of hydrogen atoms and their electrons. Because a reducing atmosphere would not require as much energy as it would today, it would have made it easier to form the carbon-rich molecules from which life evolved.

Exactly where on Earth life originated is also an open question. Possible locations include the ocean's edge, under frozen oceans, deep in the Earth's crust, within clay, or at deep-sea vents.

### Organic molecules on early Earth

An early attempt to determine what kinds of organic molecules might have been produced on the early Earth was carried out in 1953 by Stanley L. Miller and Harold C. Urey. In what has become a classic experiment, they attempted to reproduce the conditions in the Earth's primitive oceans under a reducing atmosphere. Even if this hypothesis proves incorrect—the jury is still out on this—their experiment is critically important because it ushered in the whole new field of prebiotic chemistry.

To carry out their experiment, Miller and Urey (1) assembled a reducing atmosphere rich in hydrogen and excluding gaseous oxygen; (2) placed this atmosphere over liquid water; (3) maintained this mixture at a temperature somewhat below 100°C; and (4) simulated lightning by bombarding it with energy in the form of sparks (figure 26.3).

They found that within a week, 15% of the carbon originally present as methane gas ($CH_4$) had converted into other simple carbon compounds. Among these compounds were formaldehyde ($CH_2O$) and hydrogen cyanide (HCN). These compounds then combined to form simple molecules, such as formic acid (HCOOH) and urea ($NH_2CONH_2$), and more complex molecules containing carbon–carbon bonds, including the amino acids glycine and alanine.

In similar experiments performed later by other scientists, more than 30 different carbon compounds were identified,

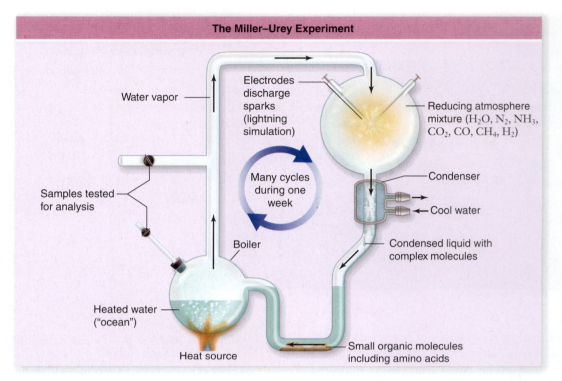

**The Miller–Urey Experiment**

Water vapor

Electrodes discharge sparks (lightning simulation)

Reducing atmosphere mixture ($H_2O$, $N_2$, $NH_3$, $CO_2$, $CO$, $CH_4$, $H_2$)

Condenser

Samples tested for analysis

Many cycles during one week

Cool water

Boiler

Condensed liquid with complex molecules

Heated water ("ocean")

Heat source

Small organic molecules including amino acids

**Figure 26.3** **The Miller–Urey experiment.** The apparatus consisted of a closed tube connecting two chambers. The upper chamber contained a mixture of gases thought to resemble the primitive Earth's atmosphere. Electrodes discharged sparks through this mixture, simulating lightning. Condensers then cooled the gases, causing water droplets to form, which passed into the second heated chamber, the "ocean." Any complex molecules formed in the atmosphere chamber would be dissolved in these droplets and carried to the ocean chamber, from which samples were withdrawn for analysis.

including the amino acids glycine, alanine, glutamic acid, valine, proline, and aspartic acid. As we saw in chapter 3, amino acids are the basic building blocks of proteins, and proteins are one of the major kinds of molecules of which organisms are composed. Other biologically important molecules were also formed in these experiments. For example, hydrogen cyanide contributed to the production of a complex ring-shaped molecule called adenine—one of the bases found in DNA and RNA. Thus, the key molecules of life could have formed in the reducing atmosphere of the early Earth.

## Cells evolved from the functional assembly of organic molecules

Organic molecules can convey information or provide energy to maintain life through metabolism. Although DNA is the hereditary information molecule, RNA can both act as an enzyme used in self-replication (a ribozyme) and may have been the first genetic material.

Many hypotheses for the emergence of metabolic pathways exist. One scenario assumes that primitive organisms were autotrophic, building all the complex organic molecules they require from simple inorganic compounds. For example, glucose may have been synthesized from formaldehyde, $CH_2O$, in the alkaline conditions that could have existed on early Earth. Glycolysis and a version of the Krebs cycle (see chapter 7) that functioned without enzymes are proposed to be the core from which other metabolic pathways emerged. Early autotrophs could have made, stored, and later used glucose as an energy source.

In addition to information and metabolism, cells require membranes. Constraining organic molecules to a physical space within a lipid or protein bubble could lead to an increased concentration of specific molecules. This in turn could increase the probability of metabolic reactions occurring. At some point, these bubbles became living cells with cell membranes and all the properties of life described earlier. As detailed in chapter 28, 3.5-billion-year-old prokaryotic fossils have been identified. For most of the history of life on Earth, these single-celled organisms were the only life forms. Several major evolutionary innovations—eukaryotic cells, sexual reproduction, and multicellularity—contributed to the diverse forms of life on Earth today (figure 26.4). We will continue with an overview of the amazing diversity of life on Earth and the evolutionary relationships among organisms.

### Learning Outcomes Review 26.1

Living organisms consist of one or more cells and are capable of sensing their environment, reproducing, developing, and maintaining their internal processes. Whether the organic molecules necessary for life formed on Earth or formed elsewhere and came to Earth within meteors remains an open question. Although conditions on early Earth cannot be completely reconstructed, it is likely that the temperatures were extreme and that the atmosphere had a very different gaseous composition than it does today.

■ *If you read a news headline claiming that life has been found on Mars, what type of evidence would you require to accept the claim?*

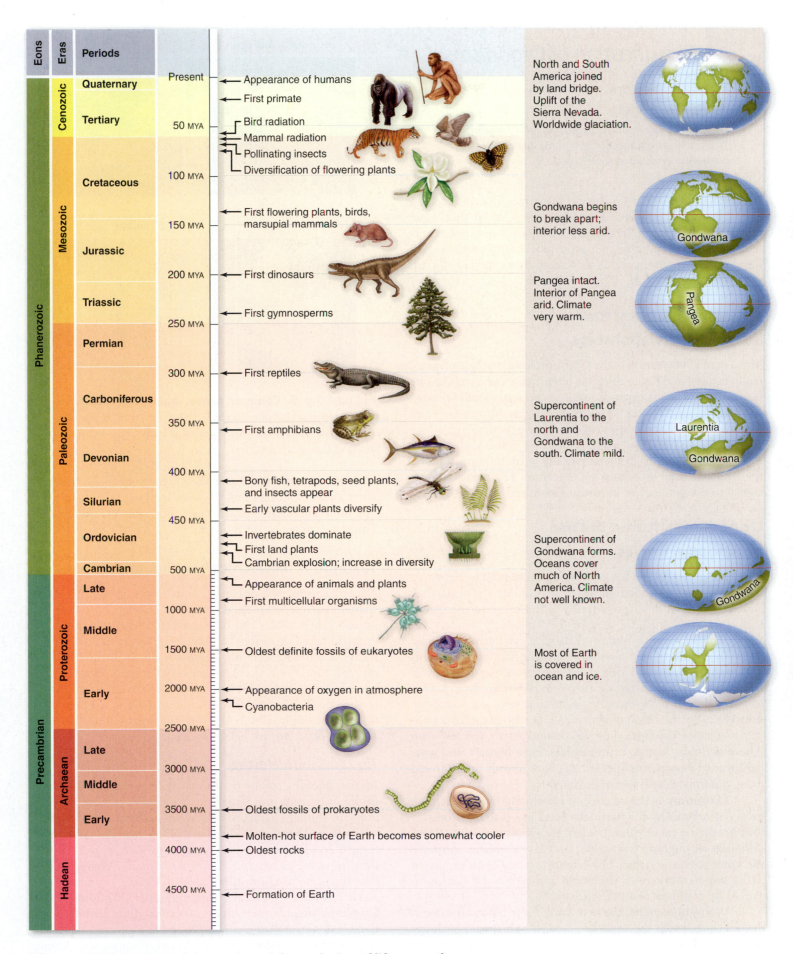

| Eons | Eras | Periods | | |
|------|------|---------|---|---|
| Phanerozoic | Cenozoic | Quaternary | Present | ← Appearance of humans |
| | | | | ← First primate |
| | | Tertiary | 50 MYA | ← Bird radiation |
| | | | | ← Mammal radiation |
| | | | | ← Pollinating insects |
| | | | | ← Diversification of flowering plants |
| | Mesozoic | Cretaceous | 100 MYA | |
| | | | 150 MYA | ← First flowering plants, birds, marsupial mammals |
| | | Jurassic | 200 MYA | ← First dinosaurs |
| | | Triassic | 250 MYA | ← First gymnosperms |
| | Paleozoic | Permian | 300 MYA | ← First reptiles |
| | | Carboniferous | 350 MYA | ← First amphibians |
| | | Devonian | 400 MYA | ← Bony fish, tetrapods, seed plants, and insects appear |
| | | Silurian | | ← Early vascular plants diversify |
| | | Ordovician | 450 MYA | ← Invertebrates dominate |
| | | | | ← First land plants |
| | | Cambrian | 500 MYA | ← Cambrian explosion; increase in diversity |
| Precambrian | Proterozoic | Late | | ← Appearance of animals and plants |
| | | | 1000 MYA | ← First multicellular organisms |
| | | Middle | 1500 MYA | ← Oldest definite fossils of eukaryotes |
| | | Early | 2000 MYA | ← Appearance of oxygen in atmosphere |
| | | | | ← Cyanobacteria |
| | | | 2500 MYA | |
| | Archaean | Late | 3000 MYA | |
| | | Middle | | |
| | | Early | 3500 MYA | ← Oldest fossils of prokaryotes |
| | | | | ← Molten-hot surface of Earth becomes somewhat cooler |
| | Hadean | | 4000 MYA | ← Oldest rocks |
| | | | 4500 MYA | ← Formation of Earth |

North and South America joined by land bridge. Uplift of the Sierra Nevada. Worldwide glaciation.

Gondwana begins to break apart; interior less arid.

Pangea intact. Interior of Pangea arid. Climate very warm.

Supercontinent of Laurentia to the north and Gondwana to the south. Climate mild.

Supercontinent of Gondwana forms. Oceans cover much of North America. Climate not well known.

Most of Earth is covered in ocean and ice.

**Figure 26.4  Geological timescale and the evolution of life on earth.**

# Classification of Organisms

People have known from the earliest times that differences exist between organisms. Early humans learned that some plants could be eaten, but others were poisonous. Some animals could be hunted or domesticated; others were dangerous hunters themselves. In this section, we review formal scientific classification.

## Taxonomy is a quest for identity and relationships

More than 2000 years ago, the Greek philosopher Aristotle formally categorized living things as either plants or animals. The Greeks and Romans expanded this simple system and grouped animals and plants into basic units such as cats, horses, and oaks. Eventually, these units began to be called genera (singular, *genus*), the Latin word for "groups." Starting in the Middle Ages, these names began to be systematically written down in Latin, the language used by scholars at that time. Thus, cats were assigned to the genus *Felis*, horses to *Equus*, and oaks to *Quercus*.

## Linnaeus instituted the use of binomial names

Until the mid-1700s, whenever biologists wanted to refer to a particular kind of organism, which they called a species, they added a series of descriptive terms to the name of the genus; this was a polynomial, or "many names" system.

A much simpler system of naming organisms stemmed from the work of the Swedish biologist Carolus Linnaeus (1707–1778). In the 1750s, Linnaeus used the polynomial names *Apis pubescens, thorace subgriseo, abdomine fusco, pedibus posticis glabris utrinque margine ciliates* to denote the European honeybee. But as a kind of shorthand, he also included a two-part name for the honeybee; he designated it *Apis mellifera.* These two-part names, or **binomials,** have become our standard way of designating species. You have already encountered many binomial names in earlier chapters.

**Taxonomy** is the science of classifying living things. A group of organisms at a particular level in a classification system is called a *taxon* (plural, *taxa*). By agreement among taxonomists throughout the world, no two organisms can have the same scientific name. The scientific name of an organism is the same anywhere in the world and avoids the confusion caused by common names (figure 26.5).

Also by agreement, the first word of the binomial name is the genus to which the organism belongs. This word is always capitalized. The second word refers to the particular species and is not capitalized. The two words together are called the species

**Figure 26.5  Common names make poor labels.** In North America, the common names "bear" and "corn" bring clear images to our minds, but the images are very different for someone living in Europe or Australia.

name (or scientific name) and are written in italics—for example, *Homo sapiens.* Once a genus has been used in the body of a text, it is often abbreviated in later uses. For example, the dinosaur *Tyrannosaurus rex* becomes *T. rex.*

## Taxonomic hierarchies have limitations

Named species are organized into larger groups based on shared characteristics. As discussed in chapter 23, sound evolutionary hypotheses can be constructed when organisms are grouped based on derived characters, not ancestral characters. Early taxonomists were not aware that the distinction between derived and ancestral characters could make a difference; as a result, many hierarchies are now being re-examined. As the phylogenetic and systematic revolution continues, other limitations of the original levels of taxonomic organization, called the *Linnaean taxonomy*, are being revealed.

### The Linnaean hierarchy

In the decades following Linnaeus, taxonomists began to group organisms into larger, more inclusive categories. Genera with similar characters were grouped into a cluster called a **family,** and similar families were placed into the same **order** (figure 26.6). Orders with common properties were placed into the same **class,** and classes with similar characteristics into the same **phylum** (plural, *phyla*). Finally, the phyla were assigned to one of several great groups, the **kingdoms.** These kingdoms include two kinds of prokaryotes (Archaea and Bacteria), a largely unicellular group of eukaryotes (Protista), and three multicellular groups (Fungi, Plantae, and Animalia). As you will see later in this chapter, the protists are not

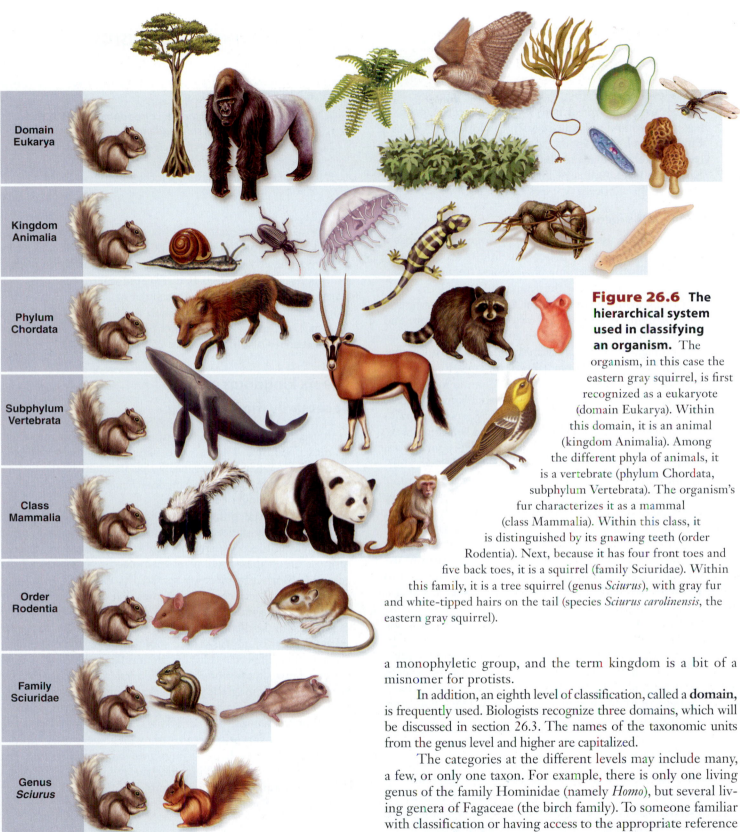

**Figure 26.6** The hierarchical system used in classifying an organism. The organism, in this case the eastern gray squirrel, is first recognized as a eukaryote (domain Eukarya). Within this domain, it is an animal (kingdom Animalia). Among the different phyla of animals, it is a vertebrate (phylum Chordata, subphylum Vertebrata). The organism's fur characterizes it as a mammal (class Mammalia). Within this class, it is distinguished by its gnawing teeth (order Rodentia). Next, because it has four front toes and five back toes, it is a squirrel (family Sciuridae). Within this family, it is a tree squirrel (genus *Sciurus*), with gray fur and white-tipped hairs on the tail (species *Sciurus carolinensis*, the eastern gray squirrel).

Domain Eukarya

Kingdom Animalia

Phylum Chordata

Subphylum Vertebrata

Class Mammalia

Order Rodentia

Family Sciuridae

Genus *Sciurus*

Species *Sciurus carolinensis*

*Sciurus carolinensis*

a monophyletic group, and the term kingdom is a bit of a misnomer for protists.

In addition, an eighth level of classification, called a **domain,** is frequently used. Biologists recognize three domains, which will be discussed in section 26.3. The names of the taxonomic units from the genus level and higher are capitalized.

The categories at the different levels may include many, a few, or only one taxon. For example, there is only one living genus of the family Hominidae (namely *Homo*), but several living genera of Fagaceae (the birch family). To someone familiar with classification or having access to the appropriate reference books, each taxon implies both a set of characteristics and a group of organisms belonging to the taxon.

To return to the example of the European honeybee, we can analyze the bee's taxonomic classification as follows:

1. **Species level:** *Apis mellifera*, meaning honey-bearing bee.
2. **Genus level:** *Apis*, a genus of bees.
3. **Family level:** Apidae, a bee family. All members of this

family are bees—some solitary, some living in colonies as *A. mellifera* does.

4. **Order level:** Hymenoptera, a grouping that includes bees, wasps, ants, and sawflies—all of which have wings with membranes.
5. **Class level:** Insecta, a very large class that comprises animals with three major body segments, three pairs of legs attached to the middle segment, and wings.
6. **Phylum level:** Arthropoda. Animals in this phylum have a hard exoskeleton made of chitin and jointed appendages.
7. **Kingdom level:** Animalia. The animals are multicellular heterotrophs with cells that lack cell walls.

### Limitations of the hierarchy

In chapter 23, we discussed the modern phylogenetic approach, which distinguishes relationships between different species based on evolutionary history. Emerging phylogenies, frequently based on molecular data, reveal that the Linnaean hierarchy is inadequate for recognizing the hierarchical relationships among taxa that result naturally from a history of common ancestory and descent. New evolutionary hypotheses are developing.

One problem with the Linnaean system is that many higher taxonomic ranks are not monophyletic (for example, Reptilia) and therefore do not represent natural groups. A common ancestor and all of its descendants is a natural group that results from descent from a common ancestor, but any other type of group (paraphyletic or polyphyletic) is an artificial group created by taxonomists.

In addition, Linnaean ranks, as currently recognized, are not equivalent in any meaningful way. For example, two families may not represent clades that originated at the same time. One family may have diverged 70 million years before another family, and therefore these families have had vastly different amounts of time to diverge and develop evolutionary adaptations. Two groups that diverged from a common ancestor at the same time may be given different ranks. Thus, comparisons using Linnaean categories may be misleading. It is much better to use hypotheses of phylogenetic relationships in such instances.

One result of all these differences is that families demonstrate different degrees of biological diversity. Here's one example. It is difficult to say that the legume family with 16,000 species represents the same level of taxonomic organization as the cat family with only 36 species. The differences across a single rank, whether it is class, order, or family, limit the usefulness of taxonomic hierarchies in making evolutionary predictions.

### Learning Outcomes Review 26.2

By convention, a species is given a binomial name. The first part of the name identifies the genus, and the second part the individual species. The Linnaean taxonomic hierarchy groups species into genera, then families, orders, classes, phyla, and kingdoms. Traditional classification systems are based on similar traits, but because they include a mix of derived and ancestral traits, they do not necessarily take into account evolutionary relationships.

■ *What can you infer about evolutionary relationships by comparing a taxonomic hierarchy for a squirrel and a fox (refer to figure 26.6)? What questions remain unanswered?*

### Learning Outcomes

1. *List examples showing that the three domains of life are monophyletic, but the six kingdoms are not.*
2. *Distinguish among the characteristics of Eukarya, Archaea, and Bacteria.*
3. *Explain why biologists do not include viruses in the tree of life.*

In this section, we examine the largest groupings of organisms: kingdoms and domains. The earliest classification systems recognized only two kingdoms of living things: animals and plants. But as biologists discovered microorganisms and learned more about other multicellular organisms, they added kingdoms in recognition of certain fundamental differences. The six-kingdom system was first proposed by Carl Woese of the University of Illinois (figure 26.7*b*).

### The six kingdoms are not necessarily monophyletic

In the six-kingdom system, four of the kingdoms consist of eukaryotic organisms. The two most familiar kingdoms, *Animalia* and *Plantae*, contain only organisms that are multicellular during most of their life cycle. The kingdom *Fungi* contains multicellular forms and single-celled yeasts.

Fundamental differences divide these three kingdoms. Plants are mainly stationary, but some have motile sperm; most fungi lack motile cells; animals are mainly motile or mobile. Animals ingest their food, plants manufacture it, and fungi digest and absorb it by means of secreted extracellular enzymes.

The large number of eukaryotes that do not fit in any of the three eukaryotic kingdoms are arbitrarily grouped into a single kingdom called **Protista** (see chapter 29). Most protists are unicellular or, in the case of some algae, have a unicellular phase in their life cycle. This kingdom reflects the current controversy between taxonomic and phylogenetic approaches. The protists are a paraphyletic group, containing several nonmonophyletic adaptive lineages with distinct evolutionary origins.

The remaining two kingdoms, **Archaea** and **Bacteria**, consist of prokaryotic organisms, which are vastly different from all other living things (see chapter 28). Archaea are a diverse group that includes the methanogens and extreme thermophiles, and its members differ from the other prokaryotes—Bacteria.

### The three domains probably are monophyletic

As biologists have learned more about the Archaea, it has become increasingly clear that this group is very different from all other organisms. When the full genomic DNA sequences of an archaean and a bacterium were first compared in 1996,

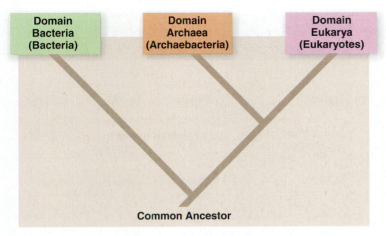

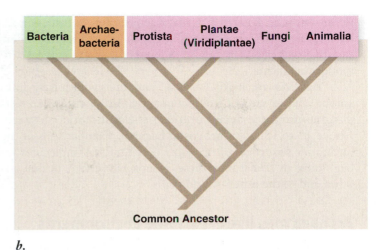

*a.*

*b.*

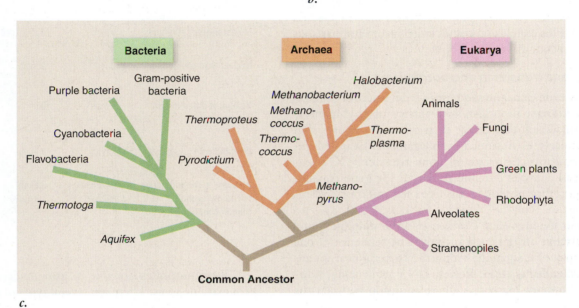

*c.*

**Figure 26.7  Different approaches to classifying living organisms.** *a.* Bacteria and Archaea are so distinct that they have been assigned to separate domains distinct from the Eukarya. Members of the domain Bacteria are thought to have diverged early from the evolutionary line that gave rise to the archaea and eukaryotes. *b.* Eukarya are grouped into four kingdoms, but these, especially the protists, are not necessarily monophyletic groups. *c.* This phylogeny is prepared from rRNA analyses. The base of the tree was determined by examining genes that are duplicated in all three domains, the duplication presumably having occurred in the common ancestor. Archaea and eukaryotes diverged later than bacteria and are more closely related to each other than either is to bacteria. Bases of trees constructed with other traits are often less clear because of horizontal gene transfer (see chapter 24).

the differences proved striking. Archaea are as different from bacteria as bacteria are from eukaryotes.

Recognizing this, biologists are increasingly adopting a classification of living organisms that recognizes three **domains,** a taxonomic level higher than kingdom (figure 26.7*a*). Archaea are in one domain (**Domain Archaea),** bacteria in a second (**Domain Bacteria),** and eukaryotes in the third (**Domain Eukarya).** Phylogenetically each of these domains form a clade.

### Inquiry question

**?  Why would the Archaea be considered a clade?**

In the remainder of this section, we preview the major characteristics of the three domains and viruses. Our current understanding of the "tree of life" is presented in figure 26.7*c*. The

oldest divergences represent the deepest rooted branches in the tree. The archaea and eukaryotes are more closely related to each other than to bacteria and are on a separate evolutionary branch of the tree.

## Bacteria are more numerous than any other organism

The bacteria are the most abundant organisms on Earth. There are more living bacteria in your mouth than there are mammals living on Earth.

Although too tiny to see with the unaided eye, bacteria play critical roles throughout the biosphere. Some extract from the air all the nitrogen used by organisms, and they play key roles in cycling carbon and sulfur. Much of the world's photosynthesis is carried out by bacteria. In contrast, certain bacteria are also responsible for many forms of disease. Understanding bacterial metabolism and genetics is a critical part of modern medicine.

Bacteria are highly diverse, and the evolutionary links among species are not well understood. Although taxonomists disagree about the details of bacterial classification, most recognize 12 to 15 major groups of bacteria. Comparisons of the nucleotide sequences of ribosomal RNA (rRNA) molecules are beginning to reveal how these groups are related to one another and to the other two domains.

## Archaea may live in extreme environments

The archaea seem to have diverged very early from the bacteria and are more closely related to eukaryotes than to bacteria (figure 26.7c). This conclusion comes largely from comparisons of genes that encode ribosomal RNAs.

### Horizontal gene transfer in microorganisms

Comparing whole-genome sequences from microorganisms has led evolutionary biologists to a variety of phylogenetic trees, some of which contradict each other. It appears that during their early evolution, microorganisms swapped genetic information via horizontal gene transfer (HGT), as you learned in chapter 24. The potential for gene transfer makes constructing phylogenetic trees for microorganisms very difficult.

Consider the archaean *Thermotoga*, a thermophile found on Vulcano Island off the coast of Italy. The sequence of one of its RNAs places it squarely within the bacteria near an ancient microbe called *Aquifex*. Recent DNA sequencing, however, fails to support any consistent relationship between the two microbes.

Over the next few years, we can expect to see considerable change in accepted viewpoints as more and more data are brought to bear.

### Archaean characteristics

Although they are a diverse group, all archae share certain key characteristics (table 26.1). Their cell walls lack peptidoglycan (an important component of the cell walls of bacteria); the lipids in the cell membranes of archae have a different structure from those in all other organisms; and archae have distinctive ribosomal RNA sequences. Some of their genes possess introns, unlike those of bacteria. Both archae and eukaryotes lack the peptidoglycan cell wall found in bacteria.

The archae are grouped into three general categories—methanogens, extremophiles, and nonextreme archae—based primarily on the environments in which they live or on their specialized metabolic pathways. The word *extreme* refers to our current environment. When archae first appeared on the scene their now extreme habitats may have been typical.

**Methanogens** obtain their energy by using hydrogen gas ($H_2$) to reduce carbon dioxide ($CO_2$) to methane gas ($CH_4$). They are strict anaerobes, poisoned by even traces of oxygen. They live in swamps, marshes, and the intestines of mammals. Methanogens release about 2 billion tons of methane gas into the atmosphere each year.

| TABLE 26.1 | Features of the Domains of Life | | |
|---|---|---|---|
| | **D O M A I N** | | |
| **Feature** | **Archaea** | **Bacteria** | **Eukarya** |
| Amino acid that initiates protein synthesis | Methionine | Formyl-methionine | Methionine |
| Introns | Present in some genes | Absent | Present |
| Membrane-bounded organelles | Absent | Absent | Present |
| Membrane lipid structure | Branched | Unbranched | Unbranched |
| Nuclear envelope | Absent | Absent | Present |
| Number of different RNA polymerases | Several | One | Several |
| Peptidoglycan in cell wall | Absent | Present | Absent |
| Response to the antibiotics streptomycin and chloramphenicol | Growth not inhibited | Growth inhibited | Growth not inhibited |

**Extremophiles** are able to grow under conditions that seem extreme to us. There are several types of extremophiles:

- Thermophiles, which live in temperatures ranging from 60° to 80°C. Many of these are autotrophs with a sulfur-based metabolism.
- Cold-adapted, which live in glacier ice and alpine lakes.
- Halophiles, which live in very salty environments including the Great Salt Lake and the Dead Sea. These organisms require water with a salinity of 15 to 20%.
- pH-tolerant archaea, growing in highly acidic (pH = 0.7) or highly basic (pH = 11) environments.
- Pressure-tolerant archaea found in the ocean depths. These archaeans require at least 300 atmospheres (atm) of pressure to survive and tolerate up to 800 atm. To experience a pressure of 300 atm (300 times the pressure of our atmosphere) you would need to dive 3000 m below the surface of the ocean (not a good idea unless you were in a deep-sea submersible). The deepest recorded skin dive is 127 m and a 145-m record is reported for SCUBA diving.

**Nonextreme archaea** grow in the same environments bacteria do. As the genomes of archaea have become better known, microbiologists have been able to identify signature sequences of DNA present only in archaea. The newly discovered microbe *Nanoarchaeum equitens* was identified as an archaean based on a signature sequence. This odd Icelandic microbe may have the smallest known genome, only 500 bp.

## Eukaryotes have compartmentalized cells

For at least 1 billion years, prokaryotes ruled the Earth. No other types of organisms existed to eat them or compete with them, and their tiny cells formed the world's oldest fossils. Members of the third great domain of life, the eukaryotes, appear in the fossil record much later, only about 2.5 BYA. But despite the metabolic similarity of eukaryotic cells to prokaryotic cells, their structure and function enabled these cells to be larger, and eventually, allowed multicellular life to evolve.

### Endosymbiosis and the origin of eukaryotes

The hallmark of eukaryotes is complex cellular organization, highlighted by an extensive endomembrane system that subdivides the eukaryotic cell into functional compartments (chapter 4). Not all cellular compartments, however, are derived from the endomembrane system.

With few exceptions, modern eukaryotic cells possess the energy-producing organelles termed *mitochondria*, and photosynthetic eukaryotic cells possess *chloroplasts*, the energy-harvesting organelles. Mitochondria and chloroplasts are both believed to have entered early eukaryotic cells by a process called **endosymbiosis,** which is discussed in more detail in chapter 29 (figure 26.8).

Mitochondria are the descendants of relatives of purple sulfur bacteria and the parasitic *Rickettsia* that were incorporated into eukaryotic cells early in the history of the group. Chloroplasts are derived from cyanobacteria (figure 26.9). As shown in figures 26.8 and 26.9, the red and green algae

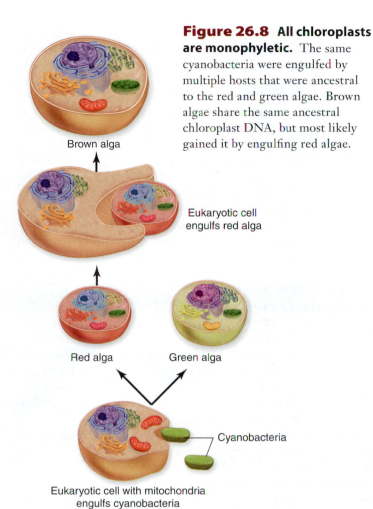

**Figure 26.8 All chloroplasts are monophyletic.** The same cyanobacteria were engulfed by multiple hosts that were ancestral to the red and green algae. Brown algae share the same ancestral chloroplast DNA, but most likely gained it by engulfing red algae.

Brown alga

Eukaryotic cell engulfs red alga

Red alga          Green alga

Cyanobacteria

Eukaryotic cell with mitochondria engulfs cyanobacteria

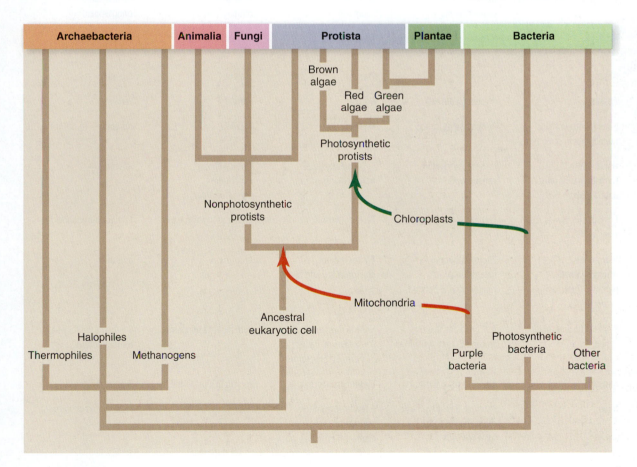

**Figure 26.9 Hypothesis for evolutionary relationships among the six kingdoms of organisms.** The colored lines indicate symbiotic events.

acquired their chloroplasts by directly engulfing a cyanobacterium. The brown algae most likely engulfed red algae to obtain chloroplasts.

## The four kingdoms of eukaryotes

The first eukaryotes were unicellular organisms. A wide variety of unicellular eukaryotes exist today, grouped together in the kingdom Protista (along with some multicellular descendants) on the basis that they do not fit into any of the other three kingdoms of eukaryotes. Fungi, plants, and animals are largely multicellular kingdoms, each a distinct evolutionary line from a single-celled ancestor that would be classified in the kingdom Protista.

Because of the size and ecological dominance of plants, animals, and fungi, and because they are predominantly multicellular, we recognize them as kingdoms distinct from Protista, even though the amount of diversity among the protists is much greater than that within or between the fungi, plants, and animals.

## Key characteristics of the eukaryotes

The characteristics of the six kingdoms are outlined in table 26.2; note that the archaea and bacteria are grouped in the same column. Although eukaryotic organisms are extraordinarily diverse, they share three characteristics that distinguish them from prokaryotes: compartmentalization; multicellularity in many, but not all, eukaryotes; and sexual reproduction.

**Compartmentalization.** Discrete compartments provide evolutionary opportunities for increased specialization

| **TABLE 26.2** | **Characteristics of the Six Kingdoms and Three Domains** | | | | |
|---|---|---|---|---|---|
| | **Archaea and Bacteria** | **Protista** | **Plantae** | **Fungi** | **Animalia** |
| **Cell Type** | Prokaryotic | Eukaryotic | Eukaryotic | Eukaryotic | Eukaryotic |
| **Nuclear Envelope** | Absent | Present | Present | Present | Present |
| **Transcription and Translation** | Occur in same compartment | Occur in different compartments | Occur in different compartments | Occur in different compartments | Occur in different compartments |
| **Histone Proteins Associated with DNA** | Absent | Present | Present | Present | Present |
| **Cytoskeleton** | Absent | Present | Present | Present | Present |
| **Mitochondria** | Absent | Present (or absent) | Present | Present | Present |
| **Chloroplasts** | None (photosynthetic membranes in some types) | Present (some forms) | Present | Absent | Absent |
| **Cell Wall** | Noncellulose (polysaccharide plus amino acids) | Present in some forms, various types | Cellulose and other polysaccharides | Chitin and other noncellulose polysaccharides | Absent |
| **Means of Genetic Recombination, if Present** | Conjugation, transduction, transformation | Fertilization and meiosis | Fertilization and meiosis | Fertilization and meiosis | Fertilization and meiosis |
| **Mode of Nutrition** | Autotrophic (chemosynthetic, photosynthetic) or heterotrophic | Photosynthetic or heterotrophic, or combination of both | Photosynthetic, chlorophylls $a$ and $b$ | Absorption | Ingestion |
| **Motility** | Bacterial flagella, gliding or nonmotile | 9 + 2 cilia and flagella; amoeboid, contractile fibrils | None in most forms; 9 + 2 cilia and flagella in gametes of some forms | Both motile and nonmotile | 9 + 2 cilia and flagella, contractile fibrils |
| **Multicellularity** | Absent | Absent in most forms | Present in all forms | Present in most forms | Present in all forms |
| **Nervous System** | None | Primitive mechanisms for conducting stimuli in some forms | A few have primitive mechanisms for conducting stimuli | None | Present (except sponges), often complex |

within the cell, as we see with chloroplasts and mitochondria. The evolution of a nuclear membrane, not found in prokaryotes, also accounts for increased complexity in eukaryotes. In eukaryotes, RNA transcripts from nuclear DNA are processed and transported across the nuclear membrane into the cytosol, where translation occurs. The physical separation of transcription and translation in eukaryotes adds additional levels of control to the process of gene expression.

**Multicellularity.** The unicellular body plan has been tremendously successful, with unicellular prokaryotes and eukaryotes constituting about half of the biomass on Earth. But a single cell has limits. The evolution of multicellularity allowed organisms to deal with their environments in novel ways through differentiation of cell types into tissues and organs.

True multicellularity, in which the activities of individual cells are coordinated and the cells themselves are in contact, occurs only in eukaryotes and is one of their major characteristics. Bacteria and many protists form colonial aggregates of many cells, but the cells in the aggregates have little differentiation or integration of function.

Other protists—the red, brown, and green algae, for example—have independently attained multicellularity. One lineage of multicellular green algae was the ancestor of the plants (see chapters 29 and 30), and most taxonomists now place its members in the green plant kingdom, the *Viridiplantae*.

The multiple origins of multicellularity are also seen in the fungi and the animals, which arose from unicellular protist ancestors with different characteristics. As you will see in subsequent chapters, the groups that seem to have given rise to each of these kingdoms are still in existence.

**Sexual Reproduction.** Another major characteristic of eukaryotic species as a group is sexual reproduction. Although some interchange of genetic material occurs in bacteria, it is certainly not a regular, predictable mechanism in the same sense that sex is in eukaryotes. Sexual reproduction allows greater genetic diversity through the processes of meiosis and crossing over, as you learned in chapter 13.

In many of the unicellular phyla of protists, sexual reproduction occurs only occasionally. The first eukaryotes were probably haploid; diploids seem to have arisen on a number of separate occasions by the fusion of haploid cells, which then eventually divided by mitosis.

## Viruses are a special case

Viruses possess only a portion of the properties of organisms. Viruses are literally "parasitic" macromolecules, segments of DNA or RNA wrapped in a protein coat. They cannot reproduce on their own, and for this reason they are not considered alive by biologists. They can, however, reproduce within cells, often with disastrous results to the host.

Viruses are currently viewed as detached fragments of the genomes of organisms because of the high degree of similarity found in some viral and eukaryotic genes. Viruses thus present a special classification problem. Because they are not organisms, we cannot logically place them in any of the kingdoms.

Viruses vary greatly in appearance and size. The smallest are only about 17 nanometers (nm) in diameter, and the largest are up to 1000 nm (1 micrometer; μm) in their greatest dimension, barely visible with a light microscope (figure 26.10). Viral morphology is best revealed using the electron microscope.

Biologists first began to suspect the existence of viruses near the end of the 19th century. European scientists were attempting to isolate the infectious agent responsible for hoof-and-mouth disease in cattle, and they concluded that it was smaller than a bacterium. The true nature of viruses was discovered in 1933, when biologist Wendell Stanley prepared an extract of the tobacco mosaic virus (TMV) and attempted to purify it. To his great surprise, the purified TMV preparation precipitated in the form of crystals—the virus was acting like a chemical off the shelf rather than like an organism. Stanley

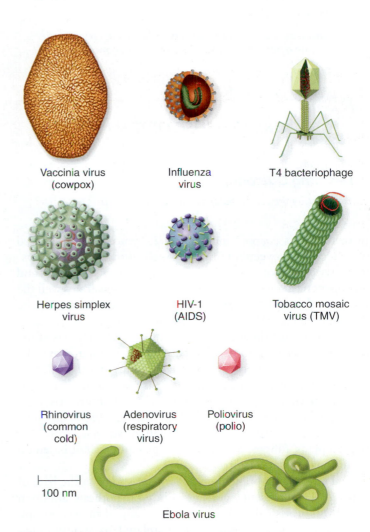

Vaccinia virus (cowpox)

Influenza virus

T4 bacteriophage

Herpes simplex virus

HIV-1 (AIDS)

Tobacco mosaic virus (TMV)

Rhinovirus (common cold)

Adenovirus (respiratory virus)

Poliovirus (polio)

100 nm

Ebola virus

**Figure 26.10 Viral diversity.** Viruses exhibit extensive diversity in shape and size. At the scale these sample viruses are shown, a human hair would be nearly 8 m thick.

concluded that TMV is best regarded as just that—chemical matter rather than a living organism.

Within a few years, scientists disassembled the TMV virus and found that Stanley was right. TMV was not cellular but chemical. Each particle of TMV virus is in fact a mixture of two chemicals: RNA and protein. The TMV virus consists of a tube made of protein with an RNA core. If these two components are separated and then reassembled, the reconstructed TMV particles are fully able to infect healthy tobacco plants.

Because eukaryote diversity is so vast, we next take a brief look at the three kingdoms of the eukaryote domain.

### Learning Outcomes Review 26.3

The six kingdoms are not necessarily based on common lineage; Kingdom Protista, for example, is not a monophyletic group. The three domains, however, do appear to be monophyletic. Bacteria and archaea are tiny but numerous unicellular organisms that lack internal compartmentalization. Eukaryotic cells are highly compartmentalized, and they have acquired mitochondria and chloroplasts by endosymbiosis. Viruses are not organisms classified in the kingdoms of life, but instead are chemical assemblies that can infect cells and replicate within them.

■ *What would be the outcome if a virus infected a cell and became a permanent resident in the cell's genome?*

## 26.4 Making Sense of the Protists

### Learning Outcome

1. Describe the relationships among groups of protists.

In reading this chapter and chapter 23, you may have sensed some tension between traditional classification systems and systems based on evolutionary relationships, such as cladistics and phylogenetic analysis. The kingdom Protista illustrates well the source of this tension. This kingdom is the weakest area of the six-kingdom classification system shown in figure 26.7.

Eukaryotes diverged rapidly in a world that was shifting from anaerobic to aerobic conditions. We may never be able to completely sort out the relationships among different lineages during this major evolutionary transition. Molecular systematics, however, clearly shows that the protists are a paraphyletic group (figure 26.11). Although biologists continue to use the term *protist* as a catchall for any eukaryote that is not a plant, fungus, or animal, this grouping is not based on evolutionary relationships.

The six main branchings of protists, shown at the base of figure 26.11, represent a current working hypothesis, although at least 60 protists do not seem to fit in any of the six groups. Choanoflagellates are most closely related to sponges, and indeed, to all animals. The green algae can be split into two

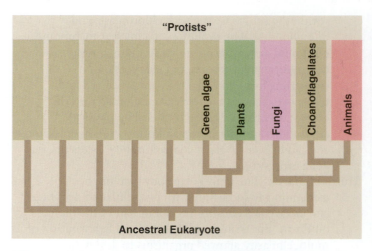

**Figure 26.11 The fall of kingdom Protista.** Systematists have shown that protists as a group are not monophyletic. Note how some lineages are actually more closely related to plants or animals than they are to other protists.

monophyletic groups, one of which gave rise to land plants. Many systematists are calling for a new kingdom called Viridiplantae, or the green plant kingdom, which would include all the green algae (not red or brown algae) and the land plants. Thus, the definition of a plant has been expanded beyond those species that made it onto land. Although the kingdom Protista is in ruins, our understanding of the evolutionary relationships among these early eukaryotes is growing exponentially.

### Learning Outcome Review 26.4

Relationships among organisms in Kingdom Protista, a paraphyletic group, are being clarified by modern methods. Choanoflagellates are most closely related to animals, and green algae may belong in a new kingdom that would include plants. Systematics and cladistics continue to add to our knowledge of these relationships.

■ *How might life have evolved if photosynthesis had not produced atmospheric oxygen?*

## 26.5 Origin of Plants

### Learning Outcomes

1. Describe the evolutionary relationship between algae and plants.
2. Explain how moss genes have come to be found in the genome of a flowering plant.

The origin of land plants from a green algal ancestor has long been recognized as a major evolutionary event. Molecular phylogenetics reveals that land plants arose from an ancestral green alga, and that the evolution of land plants occurred only once, an indication of the incredible challenges involved in the move onto land.

## Molecular phylogenetics has identified the closest living relatives of land plants

The phylogenetic relationships among the algae and the first land plants have been fuzzy and subject to long debate. Cell biology, biochemistry, and molecular systematics have provided surprising new evolutionary hypotheses.

The green algae consist of two monophyletic groups, the *Chlorophyta* and the *Streptophyta* (chapter 30). Land plants are actually members of the Streptophyta, not a separate kingdom. This new phylogenetic information demoted the land plants from constituting a kingdom to being a branch within the algal group Streptophyta. The Streptophyta along with the sister green algal clade, Chlorophyta, are now considered by most to make up the kingdom Viridiplantae. The current phylogeny is shown in figure 26.12.

What was the earliest streptophyte? Conflicting answers have been obtained with different phylogenetic analyses, but growing evidence supports the hypothesis that the scaly, unicellular flagellate Mesostigma (order Mesostigmatales) represents the earliest streptophyte branch.

Which of the Streptophyta clades contains the closest living relative of land plants? The two contenders have been the Charales, with about 300 species, and the Coleochaetales, with about 30 species. Both lineages are freshwater algae, but the Charales are huge compared with the microscopic Coleochaetales. At the moment, the Charales appear to be the sister clade to land plants, with the Coleochaetales the next closest relatives. Charales fossils dating back 420 MYA indicate that the common ancestor of land plants was a relatively complex freshwater alga.

## Horizontal gene transfer occurred in land plants

The shrub *Amborella trichopoda* is the closest living relative to the earliest flowering plants (angiosperms). Its clade is a sister clade to all other flowering plants, yet at least one copy of 20 out of 31 of its known mitochondrial protein genes hopped into the mitochondrial genome from other land plants through horizontal gene transfer (HGT). In addition, three different moss species contributed to the mix (figure 26.13).

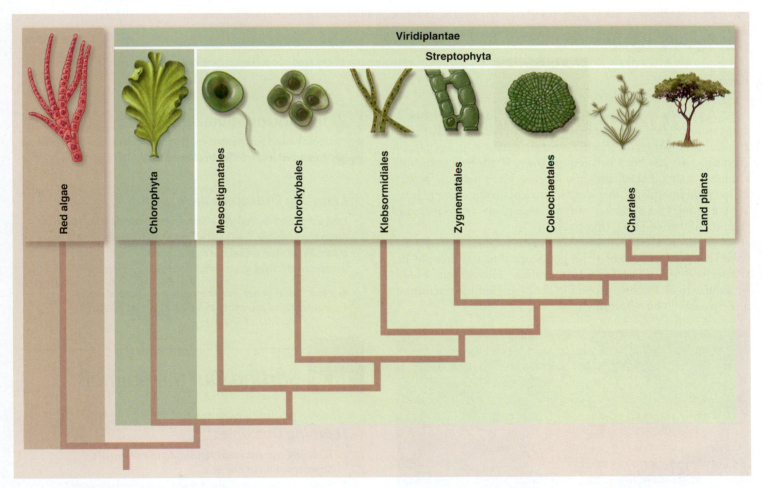

**Figure 26.12** **A new hypothesis for land plant evolution.** Kingdom Plantae (land plants) has been reduced to a clade within the green algal branch Streptophyta, and a new kingdom, Viridiplantae, which includes the green algal branches Chlorophyta and Streptophyta, has been proposed. Within the Streptophyta, the relatively complex Charales are believed to be the sister clade to the land plants. Contrast this phylogeny with the one predicted by the six-kingdom system in figure 26.7b.

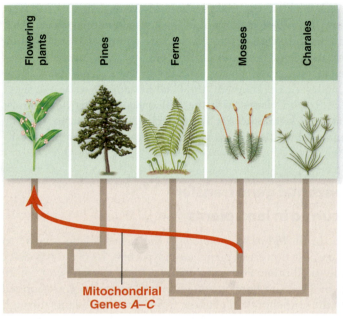

a.

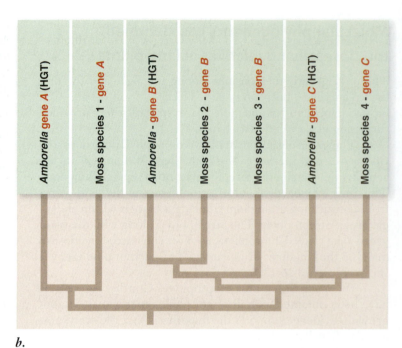

b.

**Figure 26.13** **The flowering plant *Amborella* acquired three moss genes through horizontal gene transfer.** *a.* Phylogenetic relationship of *Amborella* to other land plants. As shown by the arrow connecting moss and the flowering plants, HGT is the only plausible explanation for the presence of moss mitochondrial genes in *Amborella*. *b.* Phylogenetic relationships among the horizontally transferred gene.

**Inquiry question**

**?** Explain why a phylogenetic tree based on comparisons of a single gene could result in an inaccurate evolutionary hypothesis.

*Amborella* is not typical of most extant flowering plants. It is the only existing member of its genus and is native only to the tropical rain forests of New Caledonia, an island group east of Australia that has been isolated for some 70 million years and contains many ancient endemic species. Here parasitic plants called *epiphytes* (plants that derive nutrients from other plants) are common. Close contact with parasitic plants could increase the probability of HGT (figure 26.14).

An open question is whether the moss genes in *Amborella* have functions. About half the genes are intact and could be transcribed and translated into a protein. The protein would be similar to an existing protein in the plant, but its function, if any, remains to be determined.

**Inquiry question**

**?** How would you determine if a moss gene in *Amborella* had a function? (Hint: Refer to chapter 25.)

**Learning Outcomes Review 26.5**

Land plants are now thought to be most closely related to the Streptophyta group of green algae. The Charales appear to be the sister clade to land plants. Not all plant evolution is vertical, however; horizontal gene transfer has apparently mixed genes from distantly related species.

■ *How could genes from moss be transported into a flowering plant, other than via parasitic plants?*

## 26.6 Sorting Out the Animals

**Learning Outcomes**

1. *Describe current ideas regarding the origin of segmentation in animals.*
2. *Explain why insects are termed "flying crustaceans."*
3. *State the evidence for a common ancestor between whales and hippos.*

**Figure 26.14** **Close contact between species can lead to HGT.** Here moss are growing on the base of an *Amborella* leaf with lichens scattered on the rest of the leaf.

Molecular systematics is leading to a revision of our understanding of evolutionary history in all kingdoms, including the animals. Some phylogenies are changing, and others, including mammalian phylogenies, are actually being written for the first time. In this section, we explore three examples: the relationship between annelids and arthropods, relationships within the arthropods, and the discovery of phylogenetic relationships among mammals.

## The origins of segmentation are puzzling

The arthropod phylum is a group of over one million described invertebrates that includes the insects and crustaceans; the annelid phylum, another invertebrate group, contains the segmented worms such as the earthworm. Morphological traits such as segmentation have been used in the past to group arthropods and annelids close together, but comparisons of

rRNA sequences are raising questions about their relationship. As rRNA sequences are obtained, it is becoming increasingly clear that annelids and arthropods are more distantly related than taxonomists previously believed.

### Evolutionary occurrences of segmentation

Distinctions can be made among eukaryote animals on the basis of timing of embryonic development of the mouth and anus. Annelids and arthropods belong to the **protostome** group, in which the mouth develops before the anus. Chordates, including humans, fall into the **deuterostome** group, in which the anus forms first. (You will learn more about these divisions in chapter 33.)

With the addition of newly available molecular traits, annelids and arthropods fell into two distinct protostome branches (figure 26.15): **lophotrochozoans** and **ecdysozoans.**

**SCIENTIFIC THINKING**

**Hypothesis:** *Origins of segmentation can be explained by the duplication of a Hox gene that regulates segmentation.*

**Prediction:** *Duplication of Hox genes will correlate with changes in segmentation patterns.*

**Test:**

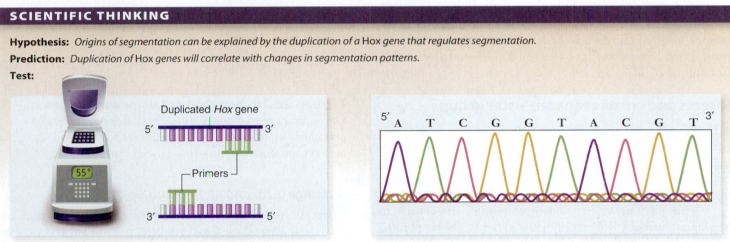

1. *Using primers for the Hox gene of interest and polymerase chain reaction (PCR), amplify the Hox gene of interest. Duplicated genes have nearly identical sequences and will be amplified with the same primer sets.*

2. *Sequence the PCR products and group them based on sequence similarity.*

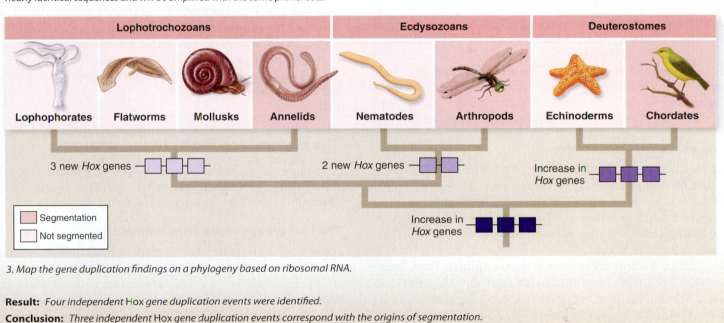

3. *Map the gene duplication findings on a phylogeny based on ribosomal RNA.*

**Result:** *Four independent Hox gene duplication events were identified.*

**Conclusion:** *Three independent Hox gene duplication events correspond with the origins of segmentation.*

**Further Research:** *Explore where the duplicated Hox genes are expressed using in situ hybridization (refer to figure 19.13).*

**Figure 26.15** **Multiple origins of segmentation.**

These two branches have been evolving independently since ancient times. Lophotrochozoans include flatworms, mollusks, and annelids. Two ecdysozoan phyla have been particularly successful: roundworms (nematodes) and arthropods.

In the new protostome phylogeny, annelids and arthropods do not constitute a monophyletic group, as they had in the past. The implication is that segmentation arose twice, not once, in the protostomes, as had been believed originally. Segmentation then arose independently once again in the deuterostomes, specifically in the chordates.

### Molecular details of segmentation

The most likely explanation for the independent appearance of segmentation is that members of the same family of genes were co-opted at least three times. Segmentation is regulated by the *Hox* gene family that contains a homeodomain region (see chapter 19). The *Hox* ancestral genes predate the ecdysozoans and lophotrochozoans. The ancient ancestor of the lophotrochozoans, ecdysozoans, and deuterostomes most likely already had seven *Hox* genes. Some of these genes appear to have evolved a role in segmentation (see figure 26.15).

## Insects and crustaceans are sister groups

Arthropods are the most diverse of all the animal phyla, composed of 80% of all described animal species. Within the arthropods, insects have traditionally been set apart from the crustaceans (such as shrimp, crabs, and lobsters), and grouped instead with the myriapods (centipedes and millipedes).

This phylogeny, still widely employed, dates back to benchmark work by Robert Snodgrass in the 1930s. He pointed out that insects, centipedes, and millipedes are united by several seemingly powerful attributes, including **uniramous** (single-branched) appendages. All crustacean appendages, by contrast, are basically **biramous,** or "two-branched" (figure 26.16), although some of these appendages have become single-branched by reduction in the course of their evolution.

Taxonomists have traditionally assumed a character such as two-branched appendages to be a fundamental one, conserved over the course of evolution, and thus suitable for making taxonomic distinctions. As molecular methods have been developed, however, this assumption has become questionable.

### Hox *genes and appendages*

The patterning of appendages among arthropods is orchestrated by *Hox* genes. A single one of these *Hox* genes, called *Distal-less*, has been shown to initiate development of unbranched limbs in insects and branched limbs in crustaceans. The same *Distal-less* gene is found in many animal phyla, including the vertebrates.

*Distal-less* appears to be necessary to initiate limb development, and it turns on genes that are more directly involved in the development of the limb itself. Evolutionary changes in the genes that *Distal-less* acts on most likely account for differences in limb morphology.

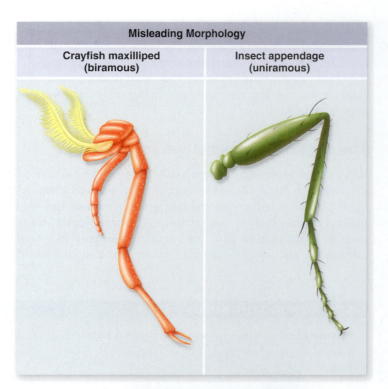

| **Misleading Morphology** | |
| --- | --- |
| Crayfish maxilliped (biramous) | Insect appendage (uniramous) |

**Figure 26.16** Branched and single appendages. Development of a biramous leg in a crustacean (crayfish) and a uniramous leg in an insect are both initiated by the *Distal-less* gene even though their adult morphologies are distinct.

### A change in taxonomic relationship?

In recent years, a mass of accumulating morphological and molecular data has led many taxonomists to suggest new arthropod phylogenies. Hexapods (insects) with their six legs and terrestrial habitat are the closest relatives of crustaceans, not the myriopods. Hexapods and crustaceans form a clade called pancrustacea. But, hexapods likely are not monophyletic, indicating that crustacean ancestors moved onto land multiple times. The relationships among the pancrustacea suggest that hexapods are "flying crustaceans."

These conclusions engender lively discussion since they are in conflict with 150 years of morphology-based phylogenetic inference.

## The mammalian family tree is emerging

In the preceding arthropod examples, our interpretation of evolutionary history has been rewritten. In mammals, however, parts of the phylogeny are just emerging, based on molecular data.

### The four groups of placental mammals

Among the vertebrate classes, mammals are unique because they have mammary glands to feed their young. The majority of mammals—over 90%—are **eutherians,** or **placental mammals** (see chapter 36). There are at least 18 extant orders of eutherians, which are now divided into four major groups (figure 26.17).

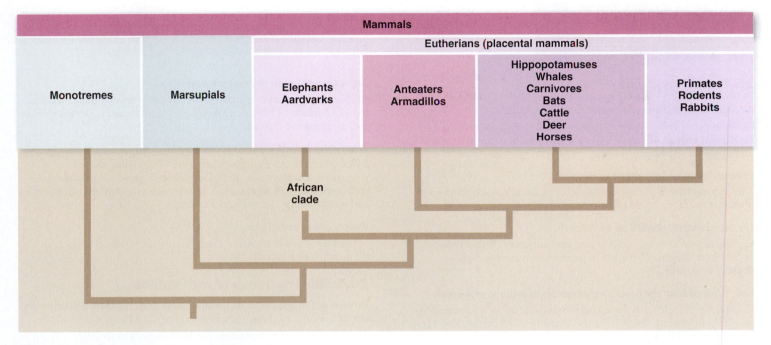

**Figure 26.17** Major groups of mammals.

The first major split occurred between the African clade and the other placental mammals when South America and Africa separated about 100 MYA. Aardvarks and elephants are part of this African lineage, called the Afrotheria, a clade we did not even recognize a decade ago. In South America, anteaters and armadillos soon appeared. Then two other branches arose—one includes ungulates with an even number of toes (camels, llamas, and other artiodactyls), odd-toed ungulates (perissodactyls such as horses and rhinoceros), and carnivores, and the other, primates and rodents. Sorting out the relationships within these branches is an ongoing challenge.

### Whales and hippos

The origin and relationships of whales has been debated for over 200 years. Whales were initially thought to be relatives of pigs based on morphological information from fossils and extant animals, primarily the bones of the skull and shape of the teeth.

DNA sequence data, however, revealed a particularly close relationship between whales and hippopotamuses, suggesting that whales were derived from within the group Artiodactyla. Whales and hippopotamuses appear to be much more closely related than, for example, hippopotamuses and cows. With this new phylogenetic information, the possibility arises that some adaptations to aquatic environments in both species had a common origin. Recent finds of fossil whales with hind limbs have confirmed the artiodactyl origin of whales. Prior to these recent discoveries, no fossil whales with hind limbs had been found, so the key character

uniting whales and artiodactyls, the shape of a bone in the ankle, was not known. A careful analysis of 80 traits in fossil whales and hippos indicated a common, water-loving ancestor existed 50 to 60 MYA belonging to the anthracotheres. The anthracotheres split into two groups. One moved back to an aquatic environment. The other gave rise to at least 37 genera that left a single descendent, the hippopotamus. In this case, molecular data provided insight into whale origins that was later confirmed by fossil evidence.

Understanding evolutionary relationships among organisms does more than provide biologists with a sense of order and a logical way to name organisms. A phylogenetically based taxonomy allows researchers to ask important questions about physiology, behavior, and development using information already known about a related species. This information not only enriches our understanding of how biological complexity evolved, but also provides novel insights that lead to progress in our understanding of the history and origins of important features and functions.

### Learning Outcomes Review 26.6

Molecular systematics has provided new insight into evolutionary relationships of animals. Segmentation likely arose more than once; hexapods are more closely related to crustaceans than to myriapods; and relationships among mammalian groups are still being revised based on molecular data and new fossil finds.

■ *Why might the most closely related living organisms have very different appearances?*

## 26.1 Origins of Life

### All organisms share fundamental properties of life.

Common properties of living things include cellular organization, sensitivity, growth and development, reproduction, regulation and homeostasis, and heredity.

### Life may have had extraterrestrial origins.

The panspermia hypothesis proposes that the organic molecules of life came to Earth inside meteorites.

### Life may have originated on early Earth.

Conditions on the early Earth were very different, with a reducing atmosphere that may have led to formation of carbon-rich, organic molecules.

### Cells evolved from the functional assembly of organic molecules.

Complex molecules may have coalesced inside a space surrounded by a lipid or protein "bubble," a precursor of a cell membrane. Here, reactions could proceed more rapidly.

## 26.2 Classification of Organisms

### Taxonomy is a quest for identity and relationships.

Taxonomy is the science of assigning organisms to a particular level of classification called a taxon. Taxonomic hierarchies are organized by domain, kingdom, phylum, class, order, family, genus, and species (see figure 26.6).

### Linnaeus instituted the use of binomial names.

Carolus Linnaeus devised a system of giving individual species unique names, beginning with the capitalized genus, followed by a species name. These are italicized.

### Taxonomic hierarchies have limitations.

Traditional classifications are limited because they are based on similar traits and do not take into account evolutionary relationships.

## 26.3 Grouping Organisms

### The six kingdoms are not necessarily monophyletic.

The six kingdoms proposed by Woese are not necessarily monophyletic. In particular, Protista is paraphyletic (see figures 26.7 and 26.9).

### The three domains probably are monophyletic.

Domain Eukarya contains the kingdoms Protista, Plantae, Fungi, and Animalia; the other two domains, Bacteria and Archaea, each contain only prokaryotes.

### Bacteria are more numerous than any other organism.

Bacteria are the most abundant and diverse organisms on Earth; they consist of 12 to 15 major groups but their evolutionary links are unclear.

### Archaea may live in extreme environments.

Archaea are prokaryotes that are more closely related to eukaryotes than to bacteria. They are grouped into methanogens, extremophiles, and nonextreme archaea.

### Eukaryotes have compartmentalized cells.

Eukaryote cells have compartmentalized organelles and other structures. Eukaryotes acquired mitochondria and chloroplasts by endosymbiosis (see figure 26.8). Many eukaryotes are multicellular, and most undergo sexual reproduction.

### Viruses are a special case.

Viruses are diverse chemical assemblies that cannot reproduce on their own (see figure 26.10).

## 26.4 Making Sense of the Protists

Protists are divided into six groups, but at least 60 known protists do not fit into any of these groups (see figure 26.11).

A new kingdom, Viridiplantae, has been suggested to include green algae and all aquatic and land plants.

## 26.5 Origin of Plants

### Molecular phylogenetics has identified the closest living relatives of land plants (see figure 26.12).

Green algae consist of two monophyletic groups: Chlorophyta and Streptophyta. The latter group gave rise to land plants.

### Horizontal gene transfer occurred in land plants.

Some land plants show evidence of horizontal gene transfer, such as between the flowering plant *Amborella* and mosses (see figure 26.13).

## 26.6 Sorting Out the Animals

### The origins of segmentation are puzzling.

Phylogeny based on rRNA shows that segmentation in arthropods, annelids, and chordates arose independently at least three times. Evidence points to duplications in *Hox* genes that regulate segmentation as the cause (see figure 26.15).

### Insects and crustaceans are sister groups.

Although previously based on appendages, classification of arthropods has now placed hexapods (insects) as close relatives of crustaceans based on molecular and genetic data.

### The mammalian family tree is emerging.

Mammalian phylogeny continues to be refined as molecular data becomes available. Whales, for example, are most closely related to hippopotamuses, sharing a water-loving common ancestor.

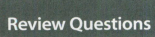
## UNDERSTAND

1. The Miller–Urey experiment demonstrated that
   a. life originated on Earth.
   b. organic molecules could have originated in the early atmosphere.
   c. the early genetic material on the planet was DNA.
   d. the early atmosphere contained large amounts of oxygen.

2. Which of the following properties of life would have to be significantly different for an organism that evolved on a planet located far from its sun?
   a. Homeostasis
   b. Reproduction
   c. Growth
   d. Sensitivity

3. Analyze a key limitation of the Linnaean system of classification.

4. Identify which of the following would not belong to the domain Eukarya.
   a. Photosynthetic plants
   b. Multicellular fungi
   c. Thermophilic archaea
   d. Multicellular animals

5. Explain which of the kingdoms presented the greatest challenge to the acceptance of a six-kingdom system.

6. Identify which of the following statements is false and correct the statement.
   a. Brown and red algae are not closely related phylogenetically.
   b. Chloroplasts in brown and red algae are monophyletic.
   c. Brown algae gained chloroplasts by engulfing green algae (endosymbiosis).
   d. None of the above statements are false.

7. Which of the following events occurred first in eukaryotic evolution?
   a. Endosymbiosis and mitochondria evolution
   b. Endosymbiosis and chloroplast evolution
   c. Compartmentalization and formation of the nucleus
   d. Formation of multicellular organisms

8. Given your understanding of phylogenetics, where would you place viruses in the tree of life?
   a. Archaea
   b. Fungi
   c. Bacteria
   d. None of the above

## APPLY

1. As a researcher you discover a new species that is eukaryotic, motile, possesses a cell wall made of chitin, but lacks any evidence of a nervous system. Choose the kingdom of life that best aligns with this new species.

2. Kingdom Plantae is being replaced by a new kingdom named Viridiplantae. Choose the evidence that justifies this change.
   a. Molecular phylogenetics
   b. Newly discovered fossils
   c. Biochemical differences
   d. All of the above

3. Based on information in this chapter, choose which areas of research in plant biology have the greatest potential to increase our understanding of land plant evolution.
   a. Photosynthetic pigments
   b. Chloroplast endosymbiosis
   c. Horizontal gene transfer
   d. Changes in cell wall composition

4. You are given access to a database of *Hox* gene sequences from a very large number of animals. Choose which topic you could explore with your sequences from an evolutionary perspective.
   a. Multicellularity
   b. Sexual reproduction
   c. Cellular compartmentalization
   d. Segmentation

5. Molecular evidence and morphological evidence do not always produce the same evolutionary hypotheses. Consider the morphological evidence for arthropod evolution and evaluate how it aligns with the conclusions drawn from the molecular evidence. Choose the aspect of morphological evidence for arthropod evolution that has been refuted by molecular evidence.
   a. Protostome and deuterostome classification
   b. Limb morphology and development
   c. Metamorphosis
   d. Development of eyes

6. Choose the most compelling evidence supporting the claim that the whale is the closest relative of the hippopotamus.
   a. Morphological information from fossils
   b. Morphological information from hippopotamuses
   c. Morphological evidence from carnivores
   d. DNA sequence data

## SYNTHESIZE

1. The conditions on Mars, Jupiter's moon Europa, and Saturn's moon Titan mimic those that are believed to have occurred on the early Earth. Yet, these places are also different from our early planet. For example, both Europa and Titan are located far from the Sun. Suppose that someday in the future scientists discover bacteria on these moons that are very similar biochemically to the early bacteria on Earth. Explain how this information would support the theory of panspermia. What if the life was biochemically different?

2. Construct a phylogeny that includes arthropods, hexapods, crustaceans, echinoderms, nematodes, mollusks, and annelids based on evidence in this chapter.

3. You are part of a research team that has recently discovered evidence of a single-celled prokaryotic organism on Mars. As you begin your study of the organism, you wish to use a species from Earth as a comparison. Propose which domain of life you should obtain your reference species from and defend your choice.

4. In the past, classification has relied primarily on the evolution of morphological characteristics. Modern approaches are relying more heavily on molecular analysis. Defend the claim that molecular approaches are very important in developing evolutionary hypotheses.

## ONLINE RESOURCE

**www.ravenbiology.com**

Mc Graw Hill **connect** |BIOLOGY

Understand, Apply, and Synthesize—enhance your study with animations that bring concepts to life and practice tests to assess your understanding. Your instructor may also recommend the interactive eBook, individualized learning tools, and more.

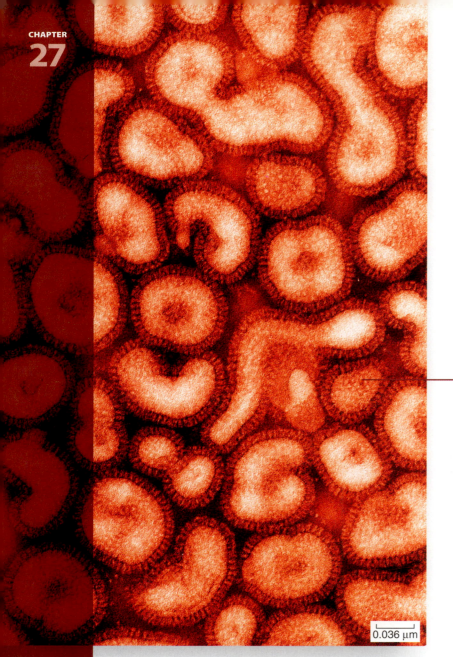

0.036 μm

Chapter **27**

# Viruses

## Chapter Outline

**27.1**   The Nature of Viruses

**27.2**   Bacteriophage: Bacterial Viruses

**27.3**   Human Immunodeficiency Virus (HIV)

**27.4**   Other Viral Diseases

**27.5**   Prions and Viroids: Subviral Particles

## W Introduction

*We begin our exploration of the diversity of life with viruses. Viruses are genetic elements enclosed in protein; they are not considered organisms since they lack many of the features associated with life, including cellular structure, and independent metabolism or replication. For this reason viral particles are not called viral cells, but virions, and they are generally not described as living or dead but as active or inactive. Because of their disease-producing potential, however, viruses are important biological entities. The virus particles pictured here are responsible for causing influenza—flu for short. In the flu season of 1918 to 1919, an influenza pandemic killed approximately 20 to 50 million people worldwide, twice as many as were killed in combat during World War I. Other viruses cause such diseases as AIDS, SARS, and hemorrhagic fever, and some cause certain forms of cancer.*

*For more than four decades, viral studies have been thoroughly intertwined with those of genetics and molecular biology. Classic studies using viruses that infect bacteria (known as* bacteriophage*) have led to the discovery of restriction enzymes and the identification of nucleic acid, not protein, as the hereditary material. Currently, viruses are one of the principal tools used to experimentally carry genes from one organism to another. Applications of this technology could include treating genetic illnesses and fighting cancer.*

## 27.1 The Nature of Viruses

**Learning Outcomes**

1.  Describe the different structures found in viruses.
2.  Understand the basic mechanism of viral replication.

All viruses have the same basic structure—a core of nucleic acid surrounded by protein. This structure lacks cytoplasm, and it is not a cell. Individual viruses contain only a single type of nucleic acid, either DNA or RNA. The DNA or RNA genome may be linear or circular; single-stranded or double-stranded.

RNA viruses may be segmented, with multiple RNA molecules within a virion, or nonsegmented, with a single RNA molecule. Viruses are classified, in part, by the nature of their genomes: RNA viruses, DNA viruses, or retroviruses.

### Viruses are strands of nucleic acids encased in a protein coat

Nearly all viruses form a protein sheath, or **capsid,** around their nucleic acid core (figure 27.1). The capsid is composed of one to a few different protein molecules repeated many times. The repeating units are called capsomeres.

In several viruses, specialized enzymes are stored with the nucleic acid, inside the capsid. One example is reverse transcriptase, which is required for retroviruses to complete their cycle and is not found in the host. This enzyme is needed early in the infection process and is carried within each virion.

Many animal viruses have an *envelope* around the capsid that is rich in proteins, lipids, and glycoprotein molecules. The lipids found in the envelope are derived from the host cell; however, the proteins found in a viral envelope are generally virally encoded.

### Viral hosts include virtually every kind of organism

Viruses occur as obligate intracellular parasites in every kind of organism that has been investigated for their presence. Viruses infect fungal cells, bacterial cells, and protists as well as cells of plants and animals; however, each type of virus can replicate in only a very limited number of cell types. A virus that infects bacteria would be ill-equipped to infect a human or plant cell.

The suitable cells for a particular virus are collectively referred to as its **host range.** Once inside a multicellular host, many viruses also exhibit **tissue tropism,** targeting only a specific set of cells. For example, rabies virus grows within neurons, and hepatitis virus replicates within liver cells. Once inside a host cell, some viruses, such as the highly dangerous Ebola virus, wreak havoc on the cells they infect; others produce little or no damage. Still other viruses remain dormant until a specific signal or event triggers their expression.

As one example, a person can get chicken pox as a child, recover, and develop the disease shingles decades later. Both chicken pox and shingles are caused by the same virus, varicella zoster. This virus can remain dormant, or *latent,* for years. Stresses to the immune system may trigger an outbreak of shingles in people who have had chicken pox in the past. This is caused by the same virus, but the infection may be called herpes zoster because the virus is actually a herpes virus.

Any given organism may often be susceptible to more than one kind of virus. This observation suggests that many more kinds of viruses may exist than there are kinds of organisms—perhaps trillions of different viruses. Only a few thousand viruses have been described at this point.

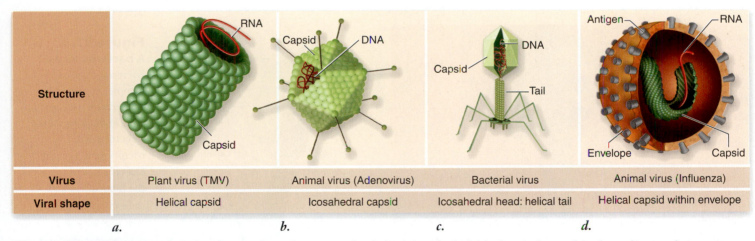

| Structure | | | | |
|---|---|---|---|---|
| **Virus** | Plant virus (TMV) | Animal virus (Adenovirus) | Bacterial virus | Animal virus (Influenza) |
| **Viral shape** | Helical capsid | Icosahedral capsid | Icosahedral head: helical tail | Helical capsid within envelope |
| | *a.* | *b.* | *c.* | *d.* |

**Figure 27.1 Structure of virions.** Viruses are characterized as helical, icosahedral, binal, or polymorphic, depending on their symmetry. *a.* The capsid may have helical symmetry such as the tobacco mosaic virus (TMV). TMV infects plants and consists of 2130 identical protein molecules *(green)* that form a cylindrical coat around the single strand of RNA *(red).* *b.* The capsid of icosahedral viruses has 20 facets made of equilateral triangles. These viruses can come in many different sizes all based on the same basic shape. *c.* Bacteriophage come in a variety of shapes, but binal symmetry is exclusively seen in phages such as the T4 phage of *E. coli.* This form of symmetry is characterized by an icosahedral head, which contains the viral genome, and a helical tail. *d.* Viruses can also have an envelope surrounding the capsid such as the influenza virus. This gives the virus a polymorphic shape. This virus has eight RNA segments, each within a helical capsid.

## Viruses replicate by taking over host machinery

An infecting virus can be thought of as a set of instructions, not unlike a computer program. A cell is normally directed by chromosomal DNA-encoded instructions, just as a computer's operation is controlled by the instructions in its operating system. A virus is simply a set of instructions, the viral genome, that can trick the cell's replication and metabolic enzymes into making copies of the virus. Computer viruses get their name because they perform similar actions, taking over a computer and directing its activities. Like a computer with a virus, a cell with a virus is often damaged by infection.

Viruses can reproduce only when they enter cells. When they are outside of a cell, viral particles are called *virions* and are metabolically inert. Viruses lack ribosomes and the enzymes necessary for protein synthesis and most, if not all of the enzymes for nucleic acid replication. Inside cells, the virus hijacks the transcription and translation systems to produce viral proteins from *early genes*, which are the genes in the viral genome expressed first. This is followed by the expression of *middle genes* and eventually *late genes*. This cascade of gene expression leads to replication of viral nucleic acid and production of viral capsid proteins. The late genes generally code for proteins important in assembly and release of viral particles from a host cell.

## Most viruses come in two simple shapes

Most viruses have an overall structure that is either *helical* or *icosahedral*. Helical viruses, such as the tobacco mosaic virus in figure 27.1a, have a rodlike or threadlike appearance. Icosahedral viruses have a soccer ball shape, the geometry of which is revealed only under the highest magnification with an electron microscope.

The **icosahedron** is a structure with 20 equilateral triangular facets. Most animal viruses are icosahedral in basic struc-

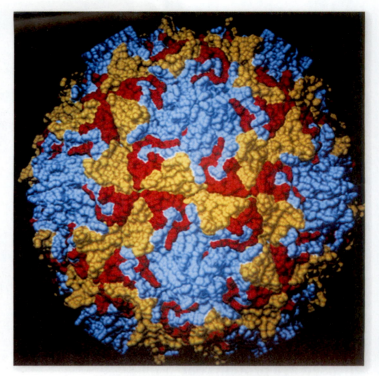

**Figure 27.2  Icosahedral virion.** The poliovirus has icosahedral symmetry. The capsid is formed from multiple copies of four different proteins shown in different colors. (One protein is internal and cannot be seen.)

ture (figure 27.1b). The icosahedron is the basic design of the geodesic dome, and it is the most efficient symmetrical arrangement that subunits can take to form a shell with maximum internal capacity (figure 27.2).

Some viruses, such as the T-even bacteriophage shown in figure 27.3, are complex. Complex viruses have a *binal*, or

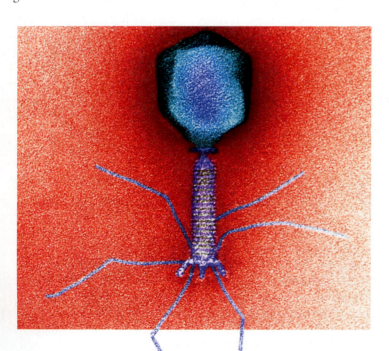

*a.*

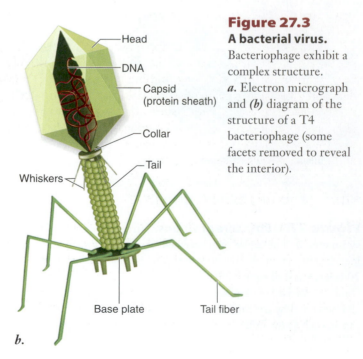

**Figure 27.3 A bacterial virus.** Bacteriophage exhibit a complex structure. *a.* Electron micrograph and *(b)* diagram of the structure of a T4 bacteriophage (some facets removed to reveal the interior).

Head
DNA
Capsid (protein sheath)
Collar
Tail
Whiskers
Base plate
Tail fiber

*b.*

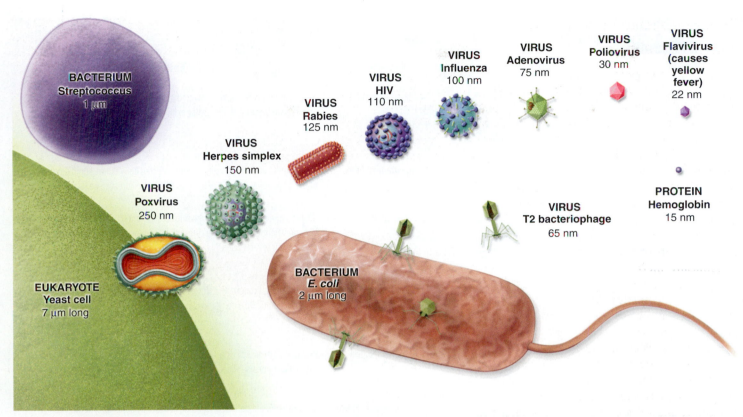

**Figure 27.4** **Viruses vary in size and shape.** Note the dramatic differences in the size of a eukaryotic yeast cell, prokaryotic bacterial cells, and the many different viruses.

two-fold, symmetry that is not either purely icosahedral or helical. The T-even phage shown has a head structure that is an elongated icosahedron. A collar connects the head to a hollow tube with helical symmetry that ends in a complex baseplate with tail fibers. Although animal viruses do not have this binal symmetry, some, such as the poxviruses, do have a complex multilayered capsid structure. Some enveloped viruses, such as influenza, are *polymorphic*, having no distinctive symmetry.

Viruses also vary greatly in size. As shown in figure 27.4, the very smallest viruses, such as the poliovirus, have actually been synthesized in a lab using nothing more than sequence data and a machine capable of synthesizing nucleic acids from nucleotides. The larger viruses, such as the poxviruses, generally carry more genes, have more complex structures, and tend to have a very short cycle time between entry of viral particles and release of newly formed virions.

## Viral genomes exhibit great variation

Viral genomes vary greatly in both type of nucleic acid and number of strands (table 27.1). Some viruses, including those that cause flu, measles, and AIDS, possess RNA genomes. Most RNA viruses are single-stranded and are replicated and assembled in the cytosol of infected eukaryotic cells. RNA virus replication is error-prone, leading to high rates of mutation. This makes them difficult targets for the host immune system, vaccines, and antiviral drugs.

In single-stranded RNA viruses, if the genome has the same base sequence as the mRNA used to produce viral proteins, then the genomic RNA can serve as the mRNA. Such viruses are called *positive-strand viruses*. In contrast, if the genome is complementary to the viral mRNA, then the virus is called a *negative-strand virus*.

A special class of RNA viruses, called *retroviruses*, have an RNA genome that is reverse-transcribed into DNA by the enzyme *reverse transcriptase*. The DNA fragments produced by reverse transcription are often integrated into a host's chromosomal DNA. *Human immunodeficiency virus (HIV)*, the agent that causes *acquired immune deficiency syndrome (AIDS)*, is a retrovirus. (We describe HIV in detail later on.)

Other viruses, such as the viruses causing smallpox and herpes, have DNA genomes. Most DNA viruses are double-stranded, and their DNA is replicated in the nucleus of eukaryotic host cells.

---

**Learning Outcomes Review 27.1**

Viruses have a very simple structure that includes a nucleic acid genome encased in a protein coat. Viruses replicate by taking over a host's cell systems and are thus obligate intracellular parasites. Viruses show diverse genomes that are composed of DNA or RNA, which may be single- or double-stranded; most DNA viruses are double-stranded.

■ *Why can't viruses replicate outside of a cell?*

**TABLE 27.1**

## Important Human Viral Diseases

| Disease | Pathogen | | Genome | Vector/Epidemiology |
|---------|----------|---|--------|---------------------|
| Chicken pox | Varicella-zoster virus | | Double-stranded DNA | Spread through contact with infected individuals. No cure. Rarely fatal. Vaccine approved in U.S. in early 1995. May exhibit latency leading to shingles. |
| Hepatitis B (viral) | Hepadnavirus | | Double-stranded DNA | Highly infectious through contact with infected body fluids. Approximately 1% of U.S. population infected. Vaccine available. No cure. Can be fatal. |
| Herpes | Herpes simplex virus | | Double-stranded DNA | Blisters; spread primarily through skin-to-skin contact with cold sores/blisters. Very prevalent worldwide. No cure. Exhibits latency—the disease can be dormant for several years. |
| Mononucleosis | Epstein–Barr virus | | Double-stranded DNA | Spread through contact with infected saliva. May last several weeks; common in young adults. No cure. Rarely fatal. |
| Smallpox | Variola virus | | Double-stranded DNA | Historically a major killer; the last recorded case of smallpox was in 1977. A worldwide vaccination campaign wiped out the disease completely. |
| AIDS | HIV | | (+) Single-stranded RNA (two copies) | Destroys immune defenses, resulting in death by opportunistic infection or cancer. For the year 2007, WHO estimated that 33.2 million people are living with AIDS, with an estimated 4.1 million new HIV infections and an estimated 2.8 million deaths. |
| Polio | Enterovirus | | (+) Single-stranded RNA | Acute viral infection of the CNS that can lead to paralysis and is often fatal. Prior to the development of Salk's vaccine in 1954, 60,000 people a year contracted the disease in the U.S. alone. |
| Yellow fever | Flavivirus | | (+) Single-stranded RNA | Spread from individual to individual by mosquito bites; a notable cause of death during the construction of the Panama Canal. If untreated, this disease has a peak mortality rate of 60%. |
| Ebola | Filoviruses | | (−) Single-stranded RNA | Acute hemorrhagic fever; virus attacks connective tissue, leading to massive hemorrhaging and death. Peak mortality is 50–90% if untreated. Outbreaks confined to local regions of central Africa. |
| Influenza | Influenza viruses | | (−) Single-stranded RNA (eight segments) | Historically a major killer (20–50 million died during 18 months in 1918–1919); wild Asian ducks, chickens, and pigs are major reservoirs. The ducks are not affected by the flu virus, which shuffles its antigen genes while multiplying within them, leading to new flu strains. Vaccines are available. |
| Measles | Paramyxoviruses | | (−) Single-stranded RNA | Extremely contagious through contact with infected individuals. Vaccine available. Usually contracted in childhood, when it is not serious; more dangerous to adults. |
| SARS | Coronavirus | | (−) Single-stranded RNA | Acute respiratory infection; an emerging disease, can be fatal, especially in the elderly. Commonly infected animals include bats, foxes, skunks, and raccoons. Domestic animals can be infected. |
| Rabies | Rhabdovirus | | (−) Single-stranded RNA | An acute viral encephalomyelitis transmitted by the bite of an infected animal. Fatal if untreated. Commonly infected animals include bats, foxes, skunks, and raccoons. Domestic animals can be infected. |

Bacteriophage (both singular and plural) are viruses that infect bacteria. They are diverse, both structurally and functionally, and are united solely by their occurrence in bacterial hosts. Many of these types of bacteriophage, called *phage* for short, are large and complex, with relatively large amounts of DNA and proteins.

*E. coli*-infecting viruses were among the first bacteriophage to be discovered and are still some of the best studied. Some of these viruses that infect *E. coli* have been named as members of a "T" series (T1, T2, and so forth); others have been given different types of names. To illustrate the diversity of these viruses, T3 and T7 phage are icosahedral and have short tails. In contrast, the so-called T-even phage (T2, T4, and T6) have an icosahedral head, a capsid that consists primarily of three proteins, a connecting neck with a collar and long "whiskers," a long tail, and a complex base plate (see figure 27.3).

## Archaeal viruses have diverse morphologies

Archaeal viruses were initially thought to be similar to bacterial viruses, but recent evidence argues against this. Surveys of viruses in several extreme environments dominated by archaeal species have uncovered an unexpected diversity of viral forms. In addition to the viral types described in the previous section, viruses with a two-tailed structure, with a bottle-shaped structure, and with a spindle-shaped structure have all been observed. All of these viruses have double-stranded DNA genomes, and most appear to be unrelated to any bacteriophage. The characterization of these viruses is in the early stages, so we will not discuss them further.

## Bacterial viruses exhibit two reproductive cycles

During the process of bacterial infection by phage T4, at least one of the tail fibers of the phage—they are normally held near the phage head by the "whiskers"—contacts proteins of the host bacterial cell wall. The other tail fibers set the phage perpendicular to the surface of the bacterium and bring the base plate into contact with the cell surface.

### Contact with the host

Different phages may target different parts of the outer surface of a bacterial cell. This first step is called *attachment*, or *adsorption*. The next step, release of the phage genome into the host, is best understood in the binal phage, such as T4. Once contact is established, the tail contracts, and the tail tube passes through an opening that appears in the base plate, piercing the bacterial cell wall. The contents of the head, the DNA genome, are then injected into the host cytoplasm. This step is called *penetration*, or *injection*.

Once inside the bacterial cell a phage may immediately take over the cell's replication and protein synthesis enzymes to synthesize viral components. This is the *synthesis* phase. Once the components are made, they are assembled **(assembly)** and mature virus particles are *released*, either through the action of enzymes that lyse the host cell or by budding through the host cell wall.

The time between adsorption and the formation of new viral particles is called an *eclipse period* because if a cell is lysed at this point, few if any active virions can be released.

### The lytic cycle

When a virus lyses the infected host cell in which it is replicating, the reproductive cycle is referred to as a **lytic cycle** (figure 27.5, *left*). The basic steps of a lytic bacteriophage cycle are similar to those of a nonenveloped animal virus. The T-series bacteriophage are all **virulent,** or **lytic, phage,** multiplying within infected cells and eventually lysing (rupturing) them.

### The lysogenic cycle

In contrast to the rather simple lytic cycles, some bacteriophage do not immediately kill the cells they infect, instead they integrate their nucleic acid into the genome of the infected host cell. This integration gives them a distinct advantage; integration allows a virus to be replicated along with the host cell's DNA as the host divides. These viruses are called **temperate,** or **lysogenic, phage.** The DNA segment that is integrated into a host cell's genome is called a *prophage*, and the resulting cell is called a *lysogen*.

Among the bacteriophage that do this is the binal phage lambda (λ) of *E. coli*. Lambda may be the best studied biological particle; the complete sequence of its 48,502 bases has been determined. At least 23 proteins are associated with the development and maturation of phage λ, and other enzymes are involved in integrating this virus into the host genome.

When phage λ infects a cell, the early events constitute a genetic switch that will determine whether the virus will replicate and destroy the cell or become a lysogen and be passively replicated with the cell's genome. This lysis/lysogeny "decision" depends on the expression of early genes. Early on, two regulatory proteins are produced that will compete for binding to sites on the phage's DNA. Depending on which protein "wins" either the genes necessary for replication of the genome will be expressed beginning the lytic cycle, or the enzymes necessary for integrating the viral genome into the chromosome will be expressed and the **lysogenic cycle** initiated (figure 27.5, *right*).

A lysogenic phage has the expression of its genome repressed (see chapter 16) by one of the two viral regulatory proteins mentioned earlier. This is not a permanent state, however; in times of cell stress, the prophage can be derepressed, and the enzymes necessary for excision of the genome expressed. The viral genome then is in the same state as the initial stage of infection, and the lytic cycle can commence, leading to formation of viral particles and lysis of the cell.

The switch from a lysogenic prophage to a lytic cycle is called induction because it requires turning on the gene expression necessary for the lytic cycle. It can be stimulated in

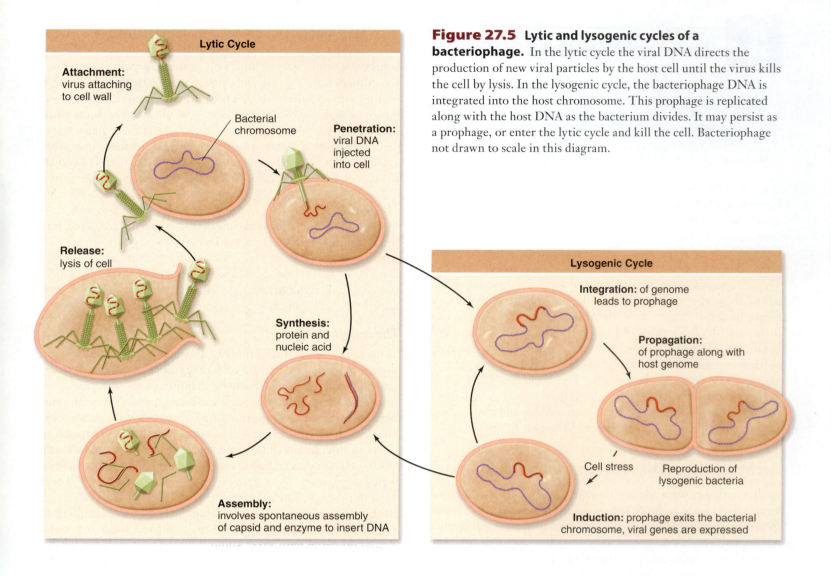

**Lytic Cycle**

**Attachment:** virus attaching to cell wall

Bacterial chromosome

**Penetration:** viral DNA injected into cell

**Release:** lysis of cell

**Synthesis:** protein and nucleic acid

**Assembly:** involves spontaneous assembly of capsid and enzyme to insert DNA

**Lysogenic Cycle**

**Integration:** of genome leads to prophage

**Propagation:** of prophage along with host genome

Cell stress

Reproduction of lysogenic bacteria

**Induction:** prophage exits the bacterial chromosome, viral genes are expressed

**Figure 27.5 Lytic and lysogenic cycles of a bacteriophage.** In the lytic cycle the viral DNA directs the production of new viral particles by the host cell until the virus kills the cell by lysis. In the lysogenic cycle, the bacteriophage DNA is integrated into the host chromosome. This prophage is replicated along with the host DNA as the bacterium divides. It may persist as a prophage, or enter the lytic cycle and kill the cell. Bacteriophage not drawn to scale in this diagram.

the laboratory by stressors such as starvation or ultraviolet radiation. The molecular events of induction take advantage of host proteins that respond to stress to produce a protease that can destroy the repressor protein that is keeping the viral genome silent. The normal function of this protease is to degrade a host repressor that controls DNA repair genes. The two repressor proteins are similar enough that both are degraded by the protease.

## Bacteriophage can contribute genes to the host genome

During the integrated portion of a lysogenic reproductive cycle, a few viral genes may be expressed at the same time as host cell genes. Sometimes the expression of these genes has an important effect on the host cell, altering it in novel ways. When the phenotype or characteristics of the lysogenic bacterium is altered by the prophage, the alteration is called **phage conversion.**

### *Phage conversion of the cholera-causing bacterium*

The bacterium *Vibrio cholerae* usually exists in a harmless form, but a second, disease-causing form also occurs. In this latter form, the bacterium is responsible for the deadly disease cholera, but how the bacteria changed from harmless to deadly was not known until recently.

Research now shows that a lysogenic bacteriophage that infects *V. cholerae* introduces into the host bacterial cell a gene that codes for the cholera toxin. This gene, along with the rest of the phage genome, becomes incorporated into the bacterial chromosome. The toxin gene is expressed along with the other host genes, thereby converting the benign bacterium to a disease-causing agent.

The receptors used by this toxin-encoding phage are pili (hairlike projections) found on the outer surface of *V. cholerae* (chapter 28); in recent experiments, it was determined that mutant bacteria that did not have pili were resistant to infection by the bacteriophage. This discovery has important implications in efforts to develop vaccines against cholera, which have been unsuccessful up to this point. Phage conversion could change any pili-expressing, nontoxigenic *V. cholerae* into a toxin-producing, potentially deadly form.

Another example involved in human disease is the toxin found in *Corynebacterium diphtheriae*. This toxin is the product of phage conversion, as are the changes to the outer surface of certain infectious *Salmonella* species.

A diverse array of viruses occurs among animals. A good way to gain a general idea of the characteristics of these viruses is to look at one animal virus in detail. Here we examine the virus responsible for a comparatively new and fatal viral disease, *acquired immune deficiency syndrome (AIDS)*.

## AIDS is caused by HIV

The disease now known as AIDS was first reported in the United States in 1981, although a few dozen people in the United States had likely died of AIDS prior to that time and had not been diagnosed. Frozen plasma samples and estimates based on evolutionary speed and current diversity of HIV strains trace the origins of HIV in the human population to Africa in the 1950s. It was not long before the infectious agent, a retrovirus, was identified by laboratories in France. Study of HIV revealed it to be closely related to a chimpanzee virus (simian immunodeficiency virus, SIV), suggesting a recent host expansion to humans from chimpanzees in central Africa.

Infected humans have varying degrees of resistance to HIV. Some have little resistance to infection and rapidly progress from having HIV-positive status to developing AIDS and eventually die. Others, even after repeated exposure, fail to become HIV-positive or may become HIV-positive without developing AIDS.

A relatively recent hypothesis to explain this great variability in susceptibility is genetic variation among these groups due to the selective pressure put on the human population by the smallpox virus (variola major) over the centuries. Because of successful vaccination and immunization, smallpox has been eradicated from the human population; however, before its eradication, it caused billions of deaths worldwide.

In order for smallpox to infect a cell, the cell must have a receptor protein in its plasma membrane that the virus can bind to. Individuals with mutated receptors would have been more resistant to smallpox and would have passed their genes on to their offspring. It has been suggested that one of the receptors used by HIV, CCR5, is also a receptor for smallpox. It is known that people resistant to HIV infection have a mutation in the CCR5 gene. The historical appearance and distribution of this mutation in human populations correlates with the historical distribution of smallpox. The AIDS epidemic is discussed further in chapter 52.

## HIV infection compromises the host immune system

In AIDS patients, HIV primarily targets **CD4⁺ cells,** particularly T-helper cells. **T-Helper cells** are responsible for mounting the immune response against foreign invaders, and their action is described more fully in chapter 52.

HIV infects and kills the CD4⁺ cells until very few are left. Without these crucial immune system cells, the body cannot mount a defense against invading bacteria or viruses. AIDS patients die of infections that a healthy person could fight off. These diseases, called *opportunistic infections*, normally do not cause disease and are part of the progression from HIV infection to having AIDS.

Clinical symptoms typically do not begin to develop until after a long latency period, generally 8 to 10 years after the initial infection with HIV. Some individuals, however, may develop symptoms in as few as two years. During latency, HIV particles are not in circulation, but the virus can be found integrated within the genome of macrophages and CD4⁺ T cells as a provirus (equivalent to a prophage in bacteria).

### HIV testing

HIV tests do not test for the presence of circulating virus but rather for the presence of antibody against HIV. Because only those people exposed to HIV in their bloodstream at one time or another would have anti-HIV antibodies, this screening provides an effective way to determine whether further testing is needed to confirm HIV-positive status.

### The spread of AIDS

Although carriers of HIV have no clinical symptoms during the long latency period, they are apparently fully infectious, which makes the spread of HIV very difficult to control. The reason HIV remains hidden for so long seems to be that its infection cycle continues throughout the 8- to 10-year latency period without doing serious harm to the infected person because of an effective immune response. Eventually, however, a random mutational event in the virus or a failure of the immune response allows the virus to quickly overcome the immune defense, beginning the course of AIDS.

# HIV infects key immune-system cells

The way in which HIV infects humans provides a good example of how animal viruses replicate (figure 27.6). Most other viral infections follow a similar course, although the details of entry and replication differ in individual cases.

## Attachment

When HIV is introduced into the human bloodstream, the virus particles circulate throughout the body but only infect CD4+ cells. Most other animal viruses are similarly narrow in their requirements; hepatitis goes only to the liver, and rabies to the brain. This tissue tropism is determined by the proteins found on a cell surface and on a viral surface.

For example, the common cold virus uses the ICAM-1 membrane protein as a receptor to enter cells. ICAM-1 is a protein that is up-regulated (increased) in times of immune activation and stress. So, the more inflammation and stress in an area, the more receptors exist for the virus to enter a cell and continue the disease process.

How does a virus such as HIV recognize a target cell? Recall from chapter 4 that every kind of cell in the human body has a specific array of cell-surface glycoprotein markers that serve to identify them to other, similar cells. Invading viruses take advantage of this to bind to specific cell types. Each HIV particle possesses a glycoprotein called gp120 on its surface that precisely fits the cell-surface marker protein CD4 on the surfaces of the immune system macrophages and T cells. Macrophages, another type of white blood cell, are infected first. Because macrophages commonly interact with CD4+ T cells, this may be one way that the T cells

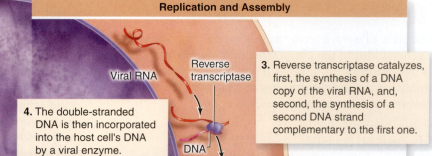

**Figure 27.6** **The HIV infection cycle.** The cycle begins and ends with free HIV particles present in the bloodstream of its human host. These free viruses infect white blood cells that have CD4 receptors, cells called CD4+ cells.

**Attachment**

Envelope

HIV

gp120 glycoprotein

**1.** The gp120 glycoprotein on the surface of HIV attaches to CD4 and one of two coreceptors on the surface of a CD4+ cell.

**Entry into CD4+ Cells**

**2.** The viral contents enter the cell by endocytosis.

Ruptured capsid

CD4+ cell

Viral RNA

Nucleus

CCR5 or CXCR4 coreceptor
CD4 receptor

**Replication and Assembly**

Viral RNA

Reverse transcriptase

**3.** Reverse transcriptase catalyzes, first, the synthesis of a DNA copy of the viral RNA, and, second, the synthesis of a second DNA strand complementary to the first one.

DNA

**4.** The double-stranded DNA is then incorporated into the host cell's DNA by a viral enzyme.

Host cell's DNA

Double-stranded DNA

Transcription

RNA

Virus exits by budding.

**5.** Transcription of the DNA results in the production of RNA. This RNA can serve as the genome for new viruses or can be translated to produce viral proteins.

Ribosome

Assembly

**6.** Complete HIV particles are assembled and HIV buds out of the cell. As the disease progresses HIV-infected T-helper cells, but not macrophages, are killed by a poorly understood mechanism.

are infected. Several coreceptors also significantly affect the likelihood of viral entry into cells, including the CCR5 receptor, which is mutated in HIV-immune individuals.

### Entry of virus

After docking onto the CD4 receptor of a cell, HIV requires a coreceptor such as CCR5, to pull itself across the cell membrane. After gp120 binds to CD4, it goes through a conformational change that allows it to then bind the coreceptor. Receptor binding is thought to ultimately result in fusion of the viral and target cell membranes and entry of the virus through a fusion pore. The coreceptor, CCR5, is hypothesized to have been used by the smallpox virus as was mentioned earlier.

### Replication

Once inside the host cell, the HIV particle sheds its protective coat. This leaves viral RNA floating in the cytoplasm, along with the reverse transcriptase enzyme that was also within the virion. Reverse transcriptase synthesizes a double strand of DNA complementary to the virus RNA, often making mistakes and introducing new mutations. This double-stranded DNA then enters the nucleus along with a viral enzyme that incorporates the viral DNA into the host cell's DNA. After a variable period of dormancy the HIV provirus directs the host cell's machinery to produce many copies of the virus.

As is the case with most enveloped viruses, HIV does not directly rupture and kill the cells it infects. Instead, the new viruses are released from the cell by *budding*, a process much like exocytosis. HIV synthesizes large numbers of viruses in this way, challenging the immune system over a period of years. In contrast, naked viruses, those lacking an envelope, generally lyse the host cell in order to exit. Some enveloped viruses may produce enzymes that damage the host cell enough to kill it or may produce lytic enzymes as well.

### Evolution of HIV during infection

During an infection, HIV is constantly replicating and mutating. The reverse transcriptase enzyme is less accurate than DNA polymerases, leading to a high mutation rate. Eventually, by chance, variants in the gene for gp120 arise that cause the gp120 protein to alter its second-receptor partner. This new form of gp120 protein will bind to a different second receptor, for example CXCR4, instead of CCR5. During the early phase of an infection, HIV primarily targets immune cells with the CCR5 receptor. Eventually the virus mutates to infect a broader range of cells. Ultimately, infection results in the destruction and loss of critical T-helper cells.

This destruction of T cells blocks the body's immune response and leads directly to the onset of AIDS, with cancers and opportunistic infections free to invade the defenseless victim. Most deaths due to AIDS are not a direct result of HIV, but are from other diseases that normally do not harm a host with a normal immune system.

## AIDS treatment targets different phases of the HIV life cycle

The federal Food and Drug Administration (FDA) currently lists 32 antiretroviral drugs that are used in AIDS therapy. These target four aspects of the HIV life cycle: viral entry, genome replication, integration of viral DNA, and maturation of HIV proteins (figure 27.7). Of these, the vast majority are

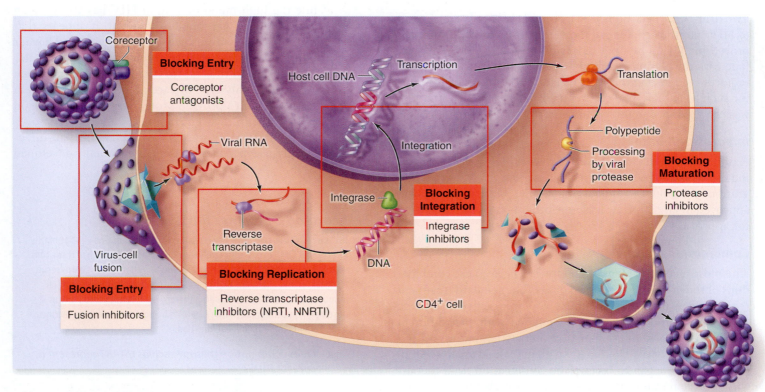

**Figure 27.7** **Viral targets for therapeutic drugs.** A simplified version of the HIV infection cycle is shown with the steps targeted for drug intervention. Four parts of the life cycle have been targeted: viral entry, genome replication, integration of the genome, and maturation of viral proteins. NRTI, nucleoside reverse transcriptase inhibitor; NNRTI, nonnucleoside reverse transcriptase inhibitor.

inhibitors of the replication enzyme, reverse transcriptase, and the protease that is involved in maturation of proteins. Only two drugs block viral entry: one that blocks the fusion of virus with the cell membrane, and one that blocks the chemokine coreceptor CCR5. A single drug has also been approved that targets the integrase protein that integrates the viral genome into a chromosome.

### Reverse transcriptase inhibitors

The first drug licensed for clinical use was AZT, a reverse transcriptase inhibitor. This class of drugs falls into two categories: nucleotide or nucleoside reverse transcriptase inhibitors (NRTI) such as AZT, and nonnucleoside reverse transcriptase inhibitors (NNRTI). These drugs are selective for HIV (or other retroviruses) because reverse transcriptase is not a cellular enzyme. So although the NRTI drugs affect cellular enzymes, they inhibit reverse transcriptase at much lower doses. More than 17 RT inhibitors are currently approved by FDA.

### Protease inhibitors

The second class of drugs discovered to be effective in AIDS treatment were the protease inhibitors. These drugs target a protease that cleaves a polyprotein into the smaller proteins necessary for viral replication and assembly. Some of these drugs are actually a good example of the concept of rational drug design. Drug designers started with the protease enzyme, then targeted drugs at transition state analogues of this enzyme. There are now more than 10 of these drugs that have received FDA approval.

### Blocking viral entry

Two drugs have been approved by the FDA that block the entry of HIV into the cell. One of these, the fusion inhibitor, was approved in 2003. The drug blocks the fusion of the viral envelope with the plasma membrane of a target cell. This entry also requires recognizing the CD4 receptor protein, and a coreceptor such as CCR5. The coreceptor blocker is a new drug that was just approved in mid-2007.

### Integrase inhibitors

A number of companies have been working on drugs targeting the viral integrase protein. This protein catalyzes the integration reaction of the viral genome. One of these was approved in late 2007. At least one other is currently in testing for approval.

### Combination therapy

The most successful form of therapy has been to use combinations of the previously discussed drugs. The standard treatment regimen consists of a minimum of three active drugs: an NNRTI or protease inhibitor combined with two different NRTIs. This form of combination therapy has entirely eliminated the HIV virus from many patients' bloodstreams. All of these patients began to receive the combination drug therapy within three months of contracting the virus, before their bod-

ies had an opportunity to develop tolerance to any single drug. Widespread use of this *combination therapy*, otherwise known as *highly active antiretroviral therapy (HAART)* has cut the U.S. AIDS death rate by three-fourths since its introduction in the mid-1990s.

Unfortunately, this sort of combination therapy does not appear to actually eliminate HIV from the body. Although the virus disappears from the bloodstream, traces of it can still be detected in the patient's lymph tissue. When combination therapy is discontinued, virus levels in the bloodstream once again rise.

In addition to the search for new drugs to add to the mix of HAART, much effort has been put into simplifying the drug regimens. The more complex the regimen of drugs, the less likely that patients will stick with it. Thus drugs have been developed that combine two NRTIs into one dose, for example.

## Vaccine development for HIV has been unsuccessful

A large amount of effort has been put toward developing an anti-HIV vaccine. Thus far, this has been totally unsuccessful. A recent large-scale international HIV vaccine trial was halted when an early examination of data indicated that the vaccine was essentially useless for preventing infection or lowering viral load. This has led to a retooling of clinical trials to have periodic examination of data instead of waiting for endpoints, but has not helped in terms of the vaccine itself. This vaccine was a subunit vaccine in which a specific HIV protein was engineered into an adenovirus vector.

While the high mutation rate of HIV has always been seen as a problem for vaccine development, it appears that the reason for vaccine failures may be more basic, and harder to surmount. A vaccine needs to produce a strong cellular immune response, and thus far no trial HIV subunit vaccine has done this. The only type of vaccine in an animal system that has been shown to provide protection against infection was a vaccine made from attenuated SIV. Unfortunately over time, the attenuated virus was able to mutate into an infective virus, and the experimental animals eventually developed simian AIDS.

### Learning Outcomes Review 27.3

HIV is a retrovirus that enters cells via membrane fusion. The virus primarily infects host CD4+ T cells, ultimately resulting in massive death of these cells, which thereby compromises the host's immune system. Most deaths result from cancer and infections that typically do not harm hosts with normal immune systems. Combination drug therapy is a treatment modality in developed countries, and much research is being done to develop vaccines or to find agents that can prevent infection.

■ *Does combination therapy such as HAART represent a cure for AIDS?*

## 27.4 Other Viral Diseases

### Learning Outcomes

1. Explain why we need a new vaccine each year for influenza.
2. Illustrate where emerging viruses come from.

Humans have known and feared diseases caused by viruses for thousands of years. Among the diseases that viruses cause (see table 27.1) are influenza, smallpox, hepatitis, yellow fever, polio, AIDS, and SARS. In addition, viruses have been implicated in some cancers including leukemias. Viruses not only cause many human diseases, but also cause major losses in agriculture, forestry, and the productivity of natural ecosystems.

### The flu is caused by influenza virus

Perhaps the most lethal virus in human history has been the influenza virus. As mentioned earlier, some 20 to 50 million people worldwide died of flu within 18 months in 1918 and 1919.

#### Types and subtypes

Flu viruses are enveloped segmented RNA viruses that infect animals. An individual flu virus resembles a rod studded with spikes composed of two kinds of protein. The three general "types" of flu virus are distinguished by their capsid protein, which surrounds the viral RNA segments and is different for each type: **Type A flu virus** causes most of the serious flu epidemics in humans and also occurs in mammals and birds. Type B and type C viruses are restricted to humans and rarely cause serious health problems.

Different strains of flu virus, called subtypes, differ in their protein spikes. One of these proteins, hemagglutinin (H), aids the virus in gaining access to the cell interior. The other, neuraminidase (N), helps the daughter viruses break free of the host cell once virus replication has been completed.

Parts of the H molecule contain "hotspots" that display an unusual tendency to change as a result of mutation of the viral RNA during imprecise replication. Point mutations cause changes in these spike proteins in 1 of 100,000 viruses during the course of each generation. These highly variable segments of the H molecule are targets against which the body's antibodies are directed. These constantly changing H-molecule regions improve the reproductive capacity of the virus and hinder our ability to make effective vaccines.

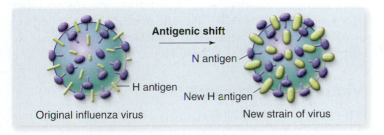

Original influenza virus
Antigenic shift
N antigen
H antigen
New H antigen
New strain of virus

Because of accumulating changes in the H and N molecules, different flu vaccines are required to protect against different subtypes. Type A flu viruses are currently classified into 13 distinct *H subtypes* and 9 distinct *N subtypes*, each of which requires a different vaccine to protect against infection. Thus, the type A virus that caused the 1918 influenza pandemic (that is, worldwide epidemic) has type 1H and type 1N and is designated A(H1N1).

#### The importance of recombination

The greatest problem in combating flu viruses arises not through mutation, but through recombination. Viral RNA segments are readily reassorted by genetic recombination when two different subtypes simultaneously infect the same cell. This may put together novel combinations of H and N spikes unrecognizable by human antibodies specific for the old configuration.

Viral recombination of this kind seems to have been responsible for the three major flu pandemics that occurred in the 20th century, by producing drastic shifts in H–N combinations. The "Spanish flu" of 1918, A(H1N1), killed 20–50 million people worldwide. The Asian flu of 1957, A(H2N2), killed over 100,000 Americans. The Hong Kong flu of 1968, A(H3N2), infected 50 million people in the United States alone, of whom 70,000 died.

#### Origin of new strains

It is no accident that new strains of flu usually originate in the Far East. The most common hosts of influenza virus are ducks, chickens, and pigs, which in Asia often live in close proximity to each other and to humans. Pigs are subject to infection by both bird and human strains of the virus, and individual animals are often simultaneously infected with multiple strains. This creates conditions favoring genetic recombination between strains, producing new combinations of H and N subtypes.

The Hong Kong flu, for example, arose from recombination between A(H3N8) from ducks and A(H2N2) from humans. The new strain of influenza, in this case A(H3N2), then passed back to humans, causing a pandemic in 1968-69.

In 1997, a form of avian influenza, A(H5N1), was discovered that could infect humans. Avian influenza, or "bird flu," is highly contagious and deadly among domestic bird populations, and it is now clear that this H5N1 strain is transmitted between domestic birds, which live in close contact with humans, and wild birds that have worldwide migratory patterns. This new influenza variant has caused much concern because, while the number of infections worldwide is low, the mortality rate in these rare infections has been around 50%. However, these infections all appear to be transmitted from birds to humans, and it does not appear to spread by human-to-human contact.

While H5N1 captured the interest of the press worldwide, another viral reassortment occurred that has resulted in an actual pandemic. An A(H1N1) virus was isolated that appears to be the result of reassortment of human A(H3N2) and pig A(H1N1). Epidemiological studies indicate that this virus first appeared in an outbreak of influenza in Veracruz, Mexico.

The virus has since spread worldwide with the WHO raising the event to pandemic status in May, 2009. As of September, 2009, more than 300,000 cases have been reported worldwide. Fortunately, as of this writing, the pathogenicity of this virus is low, with a mortality rate of around 1.5%.

## New viruses emerge by infecting new hosts

Sometimes viruses that originate in one organism pass to another, thus expanding their host range. Often, this expansion is deadly to the new host. HIV, for example, is thought to have arisen in chimpanzees and relatively recently passed to humans. Influenza is fundamentally a bird virus. Viruses that originate in one organism and then pass to another and cause disease are called **emerging viruses.** They represent a considerable threat in an age when airplane travel potentially allows infected individuals to move about the world quickly, spreading an infection.

### Hantavirus

An emerging virus caused a sudden outbreak of a deadly pneumonia in the southwestern United States in 1993. This disease was traced to a species of **hantavirus** and was called the *sin nombre,* or *no-name, virus.* Hantavirus is a single-stranded RNA virus associated with rodents. This virus was eventually traced to deer mice. The deer mouse hantavirus is transmitted to humans through fecal and urine contamination in areas of human habitation. Controlling the deer mouse population has limited the disease.

### Hemorrhagic fever: Ebola

Sometimes the origin of an emerging virus is unknown, making an outbreak more difficult to control. Among the most lethal of emerging viruses are a collection of filamentous viruses arising in central Africa that cause severe hemorrhagic fever. With lethality rates in excess of 50%, these so-called **filoviruses** are among the most lethal infectious diseases known. One, **Ebola virus** (figure 27.8), has exhibited lethality rates in excess of 90% in isolated outbreaks in central Africa. The outbreak of Ebola virus in the summer of 1995 in Zaire killed 245 people out of 316 infected—a mortality rate of 78%. A recent (2004) outbreak of Ebola in Yambio, southern Sudan, caused 17 infections

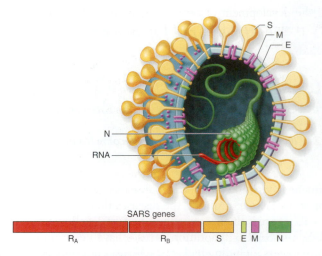

**Figure 27.9  SARS coronavirus.**  The 29,751-nucleotide SARS genome is composed of RNA and contains six principal genes: $R_A$ and $R_B$, replicases; S, spike proteins; E, envelope glycoproteins; M, membrane glycoprotein; N, nucleocapsid protein.

and 7 deaths. This outbreak was rapidly contained by isolating patients from family members as soon as symptoms appeared. The natural host of Ebola is unknown.

### SARS

A recently emerged species of coronavirus (figure 27.9) was responsible for the 2003 worldwide outbreak of **severe acute respiratory syndrome (SARS),** a respiratory infection with pneumonia-like symptoms that is fatal in over 8% of cases. When the 29,751-nucleotide RNA genome of the SARS coronavirus was sequenced, it proved to be a completely new form of coronavirus, not closely related to any of the three previously described forms.

Virologists suspect that the SARS coronavirus most likely came from civets (a weasel-like mammal) and possibly other wild animals that live in China and are eaten as delicacies. If the SARS virus indeed exists in natural populations, future outbreaks will be difficult to prevent without an effective vaccine. Recent data have implicated bats as the natural reservoir for SARS virus. The significance of this finding for control of the virus is unclear at present.

Genome sequences have been analyzed from SARS patients at various stages of the outbreak, and these analyses indicate that the virus's mutation rate is low, in marked contrast to HIV, another RNA virus. The stable genome of the SARS virus should make development of a SARS vaccine practical. The lessons learned from developing antiviral agents against other RNA viruses, such as HIV and influenza have helped develop drugs to treat SARS. Several anti-SARS agents and vaccines are currently being tested in laboratories across the world.

## Viruses can cause cancer

Through epidemiological studies and research, scientists have established a link between some viral infections and the subsequent development of cancer. Examples include the association between chronic hepatitis B infections and the development of liver cancer,

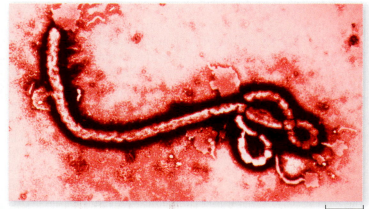

0.3 μm

**Figure 27.8  The Ebola virus.**  This virus, with a fatality rate that can exceed 90%, appears sporadically in central Africa. The natural host of the virus currently is unknown.

and the development of cervical carcinoma following infections with certain strains of human papillomaviruses (HPV).

Viruses may contribute to about 15% of all human cancer cases worldwide. They are capable of altering the growth properties of human cells they infect by triggering the expression of cancer-causing genes called oncogenes (see chapter 10). Changes in the normal function of these genes leads to cancer.

These changes can occur because viral proteins interfere with the regulation of oncogene expression. Alternatively, the integration of a viral genome into a host chromosome may disrupt a gene required to control the cell cycle. Viruses themselves may encode these oncogenes as well. Virus-induced cancer involves complex interactions with cellular genes and requires a series of events in order to develop. The association of viruses with some forms of cancer has led to research on vaccine development for the prevention of these cancers. In June 2006, the FDA approved the use of a new HPV vaccine in women and young girls from the age of 11 to prevent cervical cancer.

### Learning Outcomes Review 27.4

Many types of viruses have caused disease in humans for as long as we have recorded history. Some of these, such as influenza, have caused pandemics responsible for millions of deaths worldwide. Recombination is common in the influenza virus, making natural immunity and development of vaccines problematic. Emerging diseases can occur when viruses switch hosts, that is, jump from another species to humans. Hantavirus, Ebola, and SARS all fall into this category. Virus infection has also been linked to the development of certain cancers.

■ *Why does the effectiveness of flu shots vary from year to year?*

## 27.5 Prions and Viroids: Subviral Particles

### Learning Outcomes

1. *Explain why prion replication was a "heretical" concept.*
2. *Describe the mechanism of prion transmission.*

For decades, scientists have been fascinated by a peculiar group of fatal brain diseases. These diseases have an unusual property: Years and often decades pass after infection before the disease is detected in infected individuals. The brains of infected individuals develop numerous small cavities as neurons die, producing a marked spongy appearance. Called *transmissible spongiform encephalopathies (TSEs)*, these diseases include scrapie in sheep; bovine spongiform encephalopathy (BSE), or "mad cow" disease in cattle; chronic wasting disease in deer and elk; and kuru, Creutzfeldt–Jakob disease (CJD), and variant Creutzfeldt–Jakob disease (vCJD) in humans.

TSEs can be transmitted experimentally by injecting infected brain tissue into a recipient animal's brain. TSEs can also spread via tissue transplants and, apparently, tainted food. The disease kuru was once common in the Fore people of Papua New Guinea, because they practiced ritual cannibalism, eating the brains of infected individuals. Mad cow disease spread widely among the cattle herds of England in the 1990s because cows were fed bonemeal prepared from sheep and cattle carcasses to increase the protein content of their diet. Like the Fore, the British cattle were eating the tissue of cattle that had died of the disease.

In the years following the outbreak of BSE, there has been a significant increase in CJD incidence in England. Some cases appear to be genetic. Mysteriously, patients with no family history of CJD were being diagnosed with the disease. This led to the discovery of a new form of CJD called variant CJD, or vCJD, that is acquired from eating meat of BSE-infected animals. Concern exists that vCJD may be transmitted from person to person through blood products, similar to the transmission of HIV through blood and blood products.

### Prion replication was a heretical suggestion

In the 1960s, British researchers Tikvah Alper and John Stanley Griffith noted that infectious TSE preparations remained infectious even after exposure to radiation that would destroy DNA or RNA. They suggested that the infectious agent was a protein. They speculated that the protein could sometimes misfold, and then catalyze other proteins to do the same, the misfolding spreading like a chain reaction. This "heretical" suggestion was not accepted by the scientific community, because it violated a key tenet of molecular biology: Only DNA or RNA act as hereditary material, transmitting information from one generation to the next.

### Evidence has accumulated that prions cause TSEs

In the early 1970s, physician Stanley Prusiner began to study TSEs. Try as he might, Prusiner could find no evidence of nucleic acids or viruses in the infectious TSE preparations. He concluded, as Alper and Griffith had, that the infectious agent was a *protein*, which in a 1982 paper he named a **prion**, for "proteinaceous infectious particle."

Prusiner went on to isolate a distinctive prion protein, and to amass evidence that prions play a key role in triggering TSEs. Every host tested to date expresses a normal prion protein (PrP$^c$) in their cells. The disease-causing prions are the same protein, but folded differently (PrP$^{sc}$). These misfolded proteins have been shown in vitro to serve as a template for normal PrP to misfold. The misfolded PrP proteins are very resistant to degradation, making it possible for them to pass through the acidic digestive tract intact and therefore to be transmitted by ingesting tainted food.

Experimental evidence has accumulated to support this idea. Injection of prions with different abnormal conformations into hosts leads to the same abnormal conformations as the parent prions. Mice genetically engineered to lack PrP$^c$ are

**Hypothesis:** *Normal cellular PrP protein is required for scrapie infection.*

**Prediction:** *Infection of mice lacking PrP with scrapie agent should not lead to scrapie.*

**Test:** *Construct "knockout" mice with PrP deleted. Inject PrP knockout mice, and control mice with normal PrP, with brain homogenates from scrapie infected mice.*

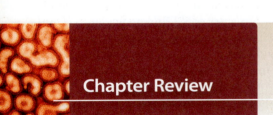

Scrapie infected mouse

Brain homogenate

**PrP deletion mouse**

**Control mouse**

Mice live normal life span. Brain appears normal.

Mice die of neurological disorder. Brain sections show characteristic damage.

**Result:** *All control mice died with scrapie like neurological damage. Periodic sacrifice and histological examination showed normal disease progress. None of the PrP knockout mice showed any sign of neurological disorder.*

**Conclusion:** *Normal PrP protein is necessary for productive infection by scrapie infectious particle.*

**Further Experiments:** *What kind of experiment would conclusively prove that the infectious agent of scrapie is a misfolded PrP protein?*

**Figure 27.10** Demonstration that normal prion protein is necessary for scrapie infectivity.

immune to TSE infection (figure 27.10). If brain tissue with the prion protein is grafted into the mice, the grafted tissue—but not the rest of the brain—can then be infected with TSE. However, infectious PrP has not been generated in vitro in quantities that would produce disease in nature. The mechanism of pathogenesis also remains controversial.

Prions have also been found in yeast and other fungi. Three different "genes" that behave in a nonmendelian fashion have all been shown to be prions in yeast. There has been greater progress in the in vitro conversion of normal cellular proteins to the prion form in the yeast system.

## Viroids are infectious RNA with no protein coat

**Viroids** are tiny, naked molecules of circular RNA, only a few hundred nucleotides long, that are important infectious disease agents in plants. A recent viroid outbreak killed over 10 million coconut palms in the Philippines. Despite their small size, viroids autonomously replicate without a helper virus, although they obviously use host proteins. Despite being nucleic acids, the important information they carry appears to be in their three-dimensional structure. There are also some intriguing hints that they might use the plant siRNA machinery to affect gene expression.

### Learning Outcomes Review 27.5

Prions and viroids are smaller and simpler than viruses. Prions are infectious particles that do not seem to contain any nucleic acid. They appear to be misfolded proteins that cause related cellular proteins to also misfold. Prions are the causative agent of TSEs. Viroids are infectious RNAs that are implicated in some plant diseases.

■ *If prions are infectious proteins, then what is the form of genetic information that they carry?*

## Chapter Review

### 27.1 The Nature of Viruses

**Viruses are strands of nucleic acids encased in a protein coat.**

Viral genomes can consist of either DNA or RNA and can be classified as DNA viruses, RNA viruses, or retroviruses.

Most viruses have a protein sheath or capsid around their nucleic acid core. Many animal viruses have an envelope around the capsid composed of proteins that are virally encoded, lipids from the host cell, and glycoproteins.

Some viruses also have enzymes inside their capsid that are important in early infection.

**Viral hosts include virtually every kind of organism.**

Each virus has a limited host range, and many also exhibit tissue tropism.

**Viruses replicate by taking over host machinery.**

Viruses are obligate intracellular parasites lacking ribosomes and proteins needed for replication. Viruses take over host machinery and direct their own nucleic acid and protein synthesis.

**Most viruses come in two simple shapes.**

Viruses vary in size and come in two simple shapes: helical (rodlike) or icosahedral (spherical) (see figures 27.1 and 27.4).

### Viral genomes exhibit great variation.

The DNA or RNA viral genome may be linear or circular, single- or double-stranded. RNA viruses may have multiple RNA molecules (segmented), or only one RNA molecule (nonsegmented). Retroviruses contain RNA that is transcribed into DNA by reverse transcriptase.

## 27.2 Bacteriophage: Bacterial Viruses

### Archaeal viruses have diverse morphologies.

### Bacterial viruses exhibit two reproductive cycles.

The lytic cycle kills the host cell, whereas the lysogenic cycle incorporates the virus into the host genome as a prophage (see figure 27.5). A cell containing a prophage is called a lysogen.

The prophage can be induced by DNA damage and other environmental cues to reenter the lytic cycle.

For most phage, steps in infection include attachment, injection of DNA (penetration), macromolecular synthesis, assembly of new phage, and release of progeny phage.

### Bacteriophage can contribute genes to the host genome.

Phage conversion occurs when foreign DNA is contributed to the host by a bacterial virus.

## 27.3 Human Immunodeficiency Virus (HIV)

### AIDS is caused by HIV.

Human immunodeficiency virus (HIV) causes acquired immunodeficiency syndrome (AIDS) (see figure 27.6).

### HIV infection compromises the host immune system.

HIV specifically targets macrophages and CD4+ cells, a type of helper T-lymphocyte cell. With the loss of these cells the body cannot fight off opportunistic infections, which ultimately lead to death.

### HIV infects key immune-system cells.

The viral glycoprotein gp120 precisely fits on the cell-surface marker protein CD4+ on macrophages and T cells. When HIV attaches to two receptors, CD4+ and CCR5, receptor-mediated endocytosis is activated, bringing the HIV particle into the cell.

Once inside the cell, the protective coat is shed, releasing viral RNA and reverse transcriptase into the cytoplasm. Reverse transcriptase makes double-stranded DNA complementary to the viral RNA. This DNA may be incorporated into the host DNA as a provirus.

Replicated viruses are budded off the host cell by exocytosis.

HIV has a high mutation rate because the reverse transcriptase enzyme is much less accurate than DNA polymerases. Mutations lead to an altered glycoprotein gp120, which now binds instead to the CXCR4 receptor found only on the surface of CD4+ cells. Incorporation of the altered HIV particle leads to a rapid decline in T cells and immune response.

### AIDS treatment targets different phases of the HIV life cycle.

Drugs target reverse transcriptase, a protease involved in protein maturation, viral entry, and the integration of the genome. Most approved drugs are reverse transcriptase and protease inhibitors.

Combination drug therapy using nucleoside analogues and protease inhibitors eliminates HIV from the bloodstream but not totally from the body.

### Vaccine development for HIV has been unsuccessful.

Successful vaccines must elicit a strong immune response, and attempts to create immunity against a specific HIV subunit have failed. Attenuated viruses in animal tests have also proved capable of mutating into infectious forms.

## 27.4 Other Viral Diseases

### The flu is caused by influenza virus.

One of the most lethal viruses in human history is type A influenza virus. Influenza can also infect other mammals and birds.

Genes in influenza viruses undergo recombination frequently, so they are not recognized by antibodies against past infections. Each year the composition of flu vaccines must be changed.

### New viruses emerge by infecting new hosts.

Viruses can extend their host range by jumping to another species. Examples include hantavirus, hemorrhagic fever, and SARS (see figure 27.9).

### Viruses can cause cancer.

Viruses have been linked to formation of cancers, including liver cancer and cervical papillomas.

## 27.5 Prions and Viroids: Subviral Particles

### Prion replication was a heretical suggestion.

Prions are proteinaceous infectious particles consisting of a misfolded form of a protein. This misfolding catalyzes a chain reaction of misfolding in normal proteins, causing disease.

### Evidence has accumulated that prions cause TSEs (see figure 27.10).

TSE disease-causing prions (PrP$^{sc}$) are the same protein as the normal version (PrP$^{c}$) but misfolded.

### Viroids are infectious RNA with no protein coat.

Viroids are circular, naked molecules of RNA that infect plants. They use host protein to replicate.

## Review Questions

### UNDERSTAND

1. The reverse transcriptase enzyme is active in which class of viruses?
   a. Positive-strand RNA viruses
   b. Double-stranded DNA viruses
   c. Retroviruses
   d. Negative-strand RNA viruses

2. Which of the following is not part of a virus?
   a. Capsid
   b. Ribosomes
   c. Genetic material
   d. All of the above are found in viruses.

3. Which of the following is common in animal viruses but not in bacteriophage?

   a. DNA
   b. Capsid
   c. Envelope
   d. Icosahedral shape

4. Which of the following would not be part of the life cycle of a lytic virus?

   a. Macromolecular synthesis
   b. Attachment to host cell
   c. Assembly of progeny virus
   d. Integration into the host genome

5. A process by which a virus may change a benign bacteria into a virulent strain is called

   a. induction.
   b. phage conversion.
   c. lysogeny.
   d. replication.

6. Prior to entry, the _____ glycoprotein of the HIV virus recognizes the _____ receptor on the surface of the macrophage.

   a. CCR5; gp120
   b. CXCR4; CCR5
   c. CD4; CCR5
   d. gp120; CD4

7. The use of multiple drugs in HAART to treat AIDS has

   a. completely removed the virus from infected individuals.
   b. reduced the viral level in the bloodstream to undetectable levels.
   c. been a complete failure.
   d. been supplanted by the new HIV vaccine.

## APPLY

1. The varying degrees of resistance to HIV in populations has been suggested to be related to the patterns of smallpox outbreaks over human history. This explanation hinges on

   a. the similarity in the genomes of the two viruses.
   b. the fact that both viruses use reverse transcriptase.
   c. both viruses using the same receptor to bind to host cells.
   d. the fact that both viruses compromise the immune system.

2. The idea of a protein that was an infectious agent was heretical because

   a. proteins are not that important in cells.
   b. proteins are not the informational molecules in cells.
   c. the function of proteins does not depend on their structure.
   d. proteins require nucleic acids for their function.

3. Bacterial viruses and animal viruses are similar in that they both

   a. have only DNA as genetic material.
   b. have only RNA as genetic material.
   c. require host functions for some aspect of their life cycle.
   d. do not require any host proteins.

4. The drugs used against HIV in AIDS therapy are not effective against the flu because

   a. HIV is an RNA virus and influenza is a DNA virus.
   b. HIV is a DNA virus and influenza is an RNA virus.
   c. the two viruses have different sized genomes.
   d. the proteins targeted by HIV drugs are not found in influenza.

5. Phage conversion in which viruses add genes to a bacterial cell can be considered to be a form of

   a. standard inheritance.
   b. horizontal gene transfer.
   c. vertical gene transfer.
   d. parasitism.

6. According to the prion hypothesis, the infectious agent for scrapie must have "genetic" information in

   a. the sequence of amino acids in the scrapie protein.
   b. the sequence of bases in the scrapie gene.
   c. the three-dimensional structure of the scrapie prion.
   d. all of the above.

7. The difficulty designing a single flu vaccine that will work forever is that influenza

   a. is an RNA virus.
   b. is a DNA virus.
   c. both mutates and can be recombined to form new viruses.
   d. infects only humans.

8. The SARS outbreak is an example of

   a. a virus jumping from one species to another.
   b. mutation of a virus that only infects humans.
   c. how viruses can disable the human immune system.
   d. two viruses combining to form a new virus.

## SYNTHESIZE

1. *E. coli* lysogens derived from infection by phage λ can be induced to form progeny viruses by exposure to radiation. The inductive event is the destruction of a repressor protein that keeps the prophage genome unexpressed. What might be the normal role of the protein that recognizes and destroys the λ repressor?

2. Most biologists believe that viruses evolved following the origin of the first cells. Defend or critique this concept.

3. Much effort has been expended to produce a vaccine for HIV. To date, this has not been successful. Why has this been such a difficult task? Are any other viruses equally resistant to a vaccine, and are the reasons the same? Why do you think that we could make a vaccine against the smallpox virus that allowed us to completely eradicate this virus?

4. What do we mean by the term "emerging virus"? How is this a medical problem, and what is a recent example?

5. How might phage λ be used to transfer *E. coli* genes between different bacterial cells? Could this be used to transfer any gene?

## ONLINE RESOURCE

**www.ravenbiology.com**

Understand, Apply, and Synthesize—enhance your study with animations that bring concepts to life and practice tests to assess your understanding. Your instructor may also recommend the interactive eBook, individualized learning tools, and more.

Chapter 28

# Prokaryotes

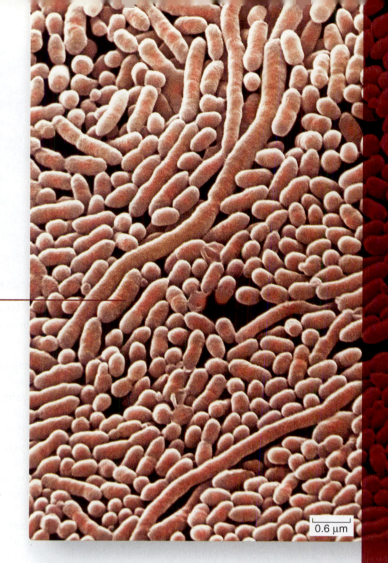

0.6 μm

## Chapter Outline

## Introduction

*One of the hallmarks of living organisms is their cellular organization. You learned earlier that living things come in two basic cell types: prokaryotes and eukaryotes. To review, prokaryotes lack the membrane-bounded nucleus found in all eukaryotes, and they also have a much less complex cellular structure, lacking many of the organelles seen in eukaryotes (chapter 4). Prokaryotes are considerably smaller and more numerous than their eukaryotic counterparts. If we examined a human being closely, we would discover that for every single cell of the human body there are approximately 10 prokaryotic cells—and there are trillions of human cells.*

*Prokaryotic microbes play an important role in global ecology as well. Most biologists think prokaryotes were the first organisms to evolve. The diversity of eukaryotic organisms that currently live on Earth could not exist without prokaryotes because they make possible many of the essential functions of ecosystems. Prokaryotic photosynthesis, for example, is thought to have been the source for the oxygen in the ancient Earth's atmosphere, and it still contributes significantly to oxygen production today. An understanding of prokaryotes is essential to understanding all life on Earth, past and present.*

# *The First Cells*

### Learning Outcomes

1. *Explain the evidence for the earliest cells.*
2. *Describe possible pathways of carbon fixation by early life forms.*

As no human was present at the formation of life, we are left with indirect evidence for the earliest life-forms. The most direct evidence we have are fossils, but these can be difficult to interpret, especially since we are looking for microscopic evidence of life. We also can analyze the composition of carbon-containing rocks to look for signs of life acting on organic material, as indicated by a change in isotopic ratios. Finally, we can look for the presence of organic chemicals, which are of biological origin.

## Microfossils indicate that the first cells were probably prokaryotic

Evidence of life in the form of microfossils is difficult both to find and to interpret. Rocks older than 3 billion years are rarely unchanged by geologic action over time. Two main formations of 3.5- to 3.8-billion-year-old rocks have been found that are mostly intact: the Kaapvaal craton in South Africa and the Pilbara craton in western Australia. (A *craton* is a rock layer of undisturbed continental crust.) Structures have been found in each of these formations and others that are interpreted to be biological in origin. Although this interpretation has been controversial, the accumulation of evidence over time favors these structures as being true fossil cells.

Microfossils are fossilized forms of microscopic life. Many microfossils are small (1–2 μm in diameter) and appear to be single-celled, lack external appendages, and have little evidence of internal structure (figure 28.1). Thus, microfossils seem to resemble present-day prokaryotes.

The currently oldest microfossils are 3.5 billion years old. The claim that these microfossils are the remains of liv-

**Figure 28.2** **Stromatolites.** Mats of bacterial cells that trap mineral deposits and form the characteristic dome shapes seen here.

ing organisms is supported by isotopic data (described shortly) and by spectroscopic analysis that indicates they do contain complex carbon molecules. Whether these microscopic structures are true fossil cells is still controversial, and the identity of the prokaryotic groups represented by the various microfossils is still unclear. Arguments have been made for various bacteria, including cyanobacteria (described later on) being the microfossils in question, but definitive interpretation is difficult.

In addition to these microfossils, indirect evidence for ancient life can be found in the form of sedimentary deposits called **stromatolites.** These structures are commonly interpreted as a combination of sedimentary deposits and precipitated material that are held in place by mats of microorganisms. The microorganisms that make up the mats are thought to be cyanobacteria. Formations of stromatolites are as old as 2.7 billion years. Because relatively modern stromatolites are also known, the formation and biological nature of these structures is less contentious (figure 28.2).

## Isotopic data indicate that carbon fixation is an ancient process

Another way to ask when life began is to look for the signature of living systems in the geological record. Living systems alter their environments, and sometimes this change can be detected. The most obvious change is that living systems are selective in the isotopes of carbon in compounds they use. Living organisms incorporate carbon-12 into their cells before any other carbon isotope, and thus they can alter the ratios of these isotopes in the atmosphere. They also have a higher level of carbon-12 in their fossilized bodies than does the nonorganic rock around them.

Much work has been done on dating and analyzing carbon compounds in the oldest rocks, looking for signatures of life. Although this work is controversial, it has been argued that carbon signatures indicate carbon fixation, the incorporation of inorganic carbon into organic form, was active as long as 3.8 BYA.

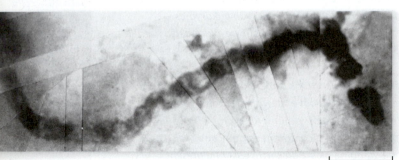

10 μm

**Figure 28.1** **Evidence of bacterial fossils.** Rocks approximately 3.5 billion years old to 1 billion years old have tiny fossils resembling bacterial cells embedded within them.

The ancient fixation of carbon happened via four possible pathways. The most common pathway for carbon fixation is the Calvin cycle (see chapter 8). This is the pathway used by cyanobacteria, algae, and modern land plants that perform oxygenic photosynthesis using two photosystems. The Calvin cycle is also active in green and purple sulfur bacteria that perform anoxygenic photosynthesis using a single photosystem. This anoxygenic form of photosynthesis could account for ancient carbon fixation.

To date, the entire Calvin cycle has not been demonstrated in the domain Archaea, although the key enzyme for this pathway has been identified in a few archaeal isolates. Instead, some archaea use a reductive version of the Krebs cycle (see chapter 7). This pathway of carbon fixation is also used by some lithotrophic bacteria, which derive energy from the oxidation of inorganic compounds, and by the green sulfur bacteria. Two other pathways may also occur in the lithotrophs, archaea, and the green nonsulfur bacteria. Evidence suggests that the ability to fix carbon has evolved multiple times over the course of evolution.

## Some hydrocarbons found in ancient rocks may have biological origins

Another way to look for evidence of ancient life is to look for organic molecules, which are clearly of biological origin; such molecules are called *biomarkers*. Although the process sounds simple, it has proved difficult to find such markers. One type of biomarker molecule is hydrocarbons, which are derived from the fatty acid tails of lipids. These can be analyzed for their carbon isotope ratios to indicate biological origin. The analysis of extractable hydrocarbons from the Pilbara formation in Australia found lipids that are indicative of cyanobacteria as long ago as 2.7 billion years. The search for definitive chemical markers for living systems in the oldest rocks and in meteorites is an area of intense interest.

Arguments for the oldest microfossils have been supported by analysis of the carbon isotope ratios in carbonaceous material from the same formations. If these fossils indeed represent living cells, it implies that life was much more abundant 3.5 BYA than previously thought. Although much of this work is still being debated, it pushes the possible origin of life back well beyond 3.5 BYA.

### Learning Outcomes Review 28.1

Evidence for the earliest cells exists in microfossils. The earliest microfossils are controversial, but they are at least 3.5 billion years old. Other evidence for early life includes isotopic ratios that are skewed by biological activity. The Calvin cycle and a reductive version of the Krebs cycle, as well as other pathways, appear to have led to carbon fixation in ancient life. Some hydrocarbons appear to be biomarkers and may therefore also indicate ancient life forms.

■ *When we are looking for life on Mars, what kind of evidence would be the most convincing?*

# 28.2 Prokaryotic Diversity

### Learning Outcomes

1. **Differentiate among archaea, bacteria, and eukarya.**
2. **Describe the basic features of bacteria and archaea.**
3. **Explain classification methods for prokaryotes.**

Although thousands of different kinds of prokaryotes are currently recognized, many thousands more await proper identification. New molecular techniques have allowed scientists to identify and study microorganisms without culturing them. As a result, microbiologists have discovered thousands of new species that were never discovered or characterized because they could not be maintained in culture.

It is estimated that only between 1 and 10% of all prokaryotic species are known and characterized, leaving between 90 and 99% unknown and undescribed. Every place microbiologists look, new species are being discovered, often altering the way we think about prokaryotes. In the 1970s and 1980s, a new type of prokaryote was identified and analyzed that eventually led to the division of prokaryotes into two groups: the *Archaea* (formerly called Archaebacteria) and the *Bacteria* (sometimes also called Eubacteria).

Archaea and bacteria are the oldest, structurally simplest, and most abundant forms of life. They are also the only organisms with prokaryotic cellular organization. Prokaryotes were abundant for over a billion years before eukaryotes appeared in the world. Early photosynthetic bacteria (cyanobacteria) altered the Earth's atmosphere by producing oxygen, which stimulated extreme bacterial and eukaryotic diversity.

Prokaryotes are ubiquitous and live everywhere eukaryotes do; they are also able to thrive in places no eukaryote could live. Bacteria and archaea have been found in deep-sea caves, volcanic rims, and deep within glaciers. Some of the extreme environments in which prokaryotes can be found would be lethal to any other life-form.

Many archaea are *extremophiles*. They live in hot springs that would cook other organisms, in hypersaline environments that would dehydrate other cells, and in atmospheres rich in otherwise-toxic gases such as methane or hydrogen sulfide. They have even been recovered living beneath 435 m of ice in Antarctica!

These harsh environments may be similar to the conditions present on the early Earth when life first began. It is likely that prokaryotes evolved to dwell in these harsh conditions early on and have retained the ability to exploit these areas as the rest of the atmosphere has changed.

## Prokaryotes are fundamentally different from eukaryotes

Prokaryotes differ from eukaryotes in numerous important features. These differences represent some of the most fundamental distinctions that separate any groups of organisms.

**Unicellularity.** With a few exceptions prokaryotes are fundamentally single-celled). In some types, individual cells adhere to one another within a matrix and form filaments; however, the cells retain their individuality. Cyanobacteria, in particular, are likely to form such associations, but their cytoplasm is not directly interconnected, as is often the case in multicellular eukaryotes. These filaments do have a common cell wall, however, making it difficult to isolate single cells.

  In their natural environments, most bacteria appear to be capable of forming a complex community of different species called a **biofilm.** Although not a multicellular organism, a biofilm is more resistant to antibiotics, dessication, and other environmental stressors than is a simple colony of a single type of microbe, such as a laboratory culture.

**Cell size.** As new species of prokaryotes are discovered, investigators are finding that the size of prokaryotic cells varies tremendously, by as much as five orders of magnitude. The largest bacterial cells currently characterized are from *Thiomargarita namibia*. A single cell from this species is up to 750 μm across, which is visible to the naked eye and is roughly the size of the eye of a bumblebee. Most prokaryotic cells, however, are only 1 μm or less in diameter, whereas most eukaryotic cells are well over 10 times bigger. This generality is misleading, however, because there are very small eukaryotes as well as very large prokaryotes.

**Chromosomes.** Eukaryotic cells have a membrane-bounded nucleus containing linear chromosomes made up of both nucleic acids and histone proteins. Prokaryotes do not have membrane-bounded nuclei; instead they usually have a single circular chromosome made up of DNA and histonelike proteins in a *nucleoid* region of the cell. An exception to this single chromosome includes *Vibrio cholerae*, which has two circular chromosomes. Prokaryotic cells often have accessory DNA molecules called plasmids as well. Plasmids are genetic elements that can sometimes be transferred between prokaryotic cells.

**Cell division and genetic recombination.** Cell division in eukaryotes takes place by mitosis and involves spindles made up of microtubules. Cell division in prokaryotes takes place mainly by binary fission (see chapter 10), which is also a form of asexual reproduction. True sexual reproduction occurs only in eukaryotes and involves the production of haploid gametes that fuse to form a diploid zygote that grows to adulthood, producing more gametes and starting the cycle over again (see chapter 11).

  Despite their asexual mode of reproduction, prokaryotes do have mechanisms that lead to the transfer of genetic material and generation of genetic diversity. These mechanisms are collectively called *horizontal gene transfer* and are not a form of reproduction.

**Internal compartmentalization.** In eukaryotes, the enzymes for cellular respiration are packaged in mitochondria. In prokaryotes, the corresponding enzymes are not packaged separately, but instead are bound to the cell membranes or are in the cytosol. The cytoplasm of prokaryotes, unlike that of eukaryotes, contains no internal compartments and no membrane-bounded organelles. Ribosomes are found in both prokaryotes and eukaryotes, but differ significantly in structure. (See chapter 4 for a review of cell structure.)

**Flagella.** Prokaryotic flagella are simple in structure, composed of a single fiber of the protein flagellin. Eukaryotic flagella and cilia are complex, having a 9 + 2 structure of microtubules (see figure 4.23). Bacterial flagella also function differently, being rigid and spinning like propellers, whereas eukaryotic flagella have a whiplike motion (described in more detail later and in figure 28.8).

**Metabolic diversity.** Only one kind of photosynthesis occurs in eukaryotes, and it involves the release of oxygen. Photosynthetic bacteria have two basic patterns of photosynthesis: *oxygenic*, producing oxygen, and *anoxygenic*, nonoxygen producing. Anoxygenic photosynthesis involves the formation of products such as sulfur and sulfate instead of oxygen.

  Prokaryotic cells can also be *chemolithotrophic*, meaning that they use the energy stored in chemical bonds of inorganic molecules to synthesize carbohydrates; eukaryotes are not capable of this metabolic process.

## Despite similarities, bacteria and archaea differ fundamentally

Archaea and bacteria are similar in that both have a prokaryotic cellular structure, but they vary considerably at the biochemical and molecular levels. They differ in four key areas: plasma membranes, cell walls, DNA replication, and gene expression.

**Plasma membranes.** All prokaryotes have plasma membranes with a fluid mosaic architecture (see chapter 5). The plasma membranes of archaea differ from both bacteria and eukaryotes. Archaean membrane lipids are composed of glycerol linked to hydrocarbon chains by ether linkages, not the ester linkages seen in bacteria and eukaryotes (figure 28.3*a*). These hydrocarbons may also be branched, and they may be organized as tetraethers that form a monolayer instead of a bilayer (figure 28.3*b*).

  In the case of some hyperthermophiles, the majority of the membrane may be this tetraether monolayer. This structural feature is part of what allows these archaeans to withstand high temperatures.

**Cell wall.** Both kinds of prokaryotes typically have cell walls covering the plasma membrane that strengthen the cell. The cell walls of bacteria are constructed, minimally, of **peptidoglycan,** which is formed from carbohydrate polymers linked together by peptide cross-bridges. The peptide cross-bridges also contain D-amino acids, which are never found in cellular protein. The cell walls of archaea lack peptidoglycan, although some have **pseudomurein,** which is similar to peptidogylcan in structure and function. This wall layer is also a carbohydrate polymer with peptide cross-bridges, but the carbohydrates are different, and the peptide cross-bridge

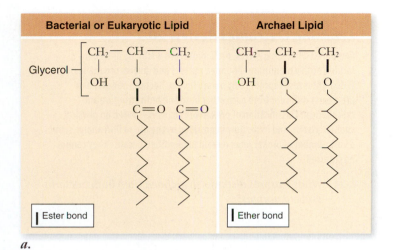
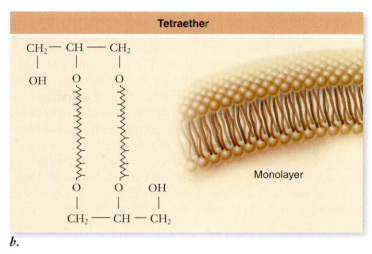

a.                                    b.

**Figure 28.3** **Archaea membrane lipids.** *a.* Archaea membrane lipids are formed on a glycerol skeleton similar to bacterial and eukaryotic lipids, but the hydrocarbon chains are connected to the glycerol by ether linkages not ester linkages. The hydrocarbons can also be branched and even contain rings. *b.* These lipids can also form as tetraethers instead of diethers. The tetraether forms a monolayer as it includes two polar regions connected by hydrophobic hydrocarbons.

structure also differs. Other archaeal cell walls have been found to be composed of a variety of proteins and carbohydrates, making generalizations difficult.

**DNA replication.** Although both archaea and bacteria have a single replication origin, the nature of this origin and the proteins that act there are quite different. Archaeal initiation of DNA replication is more similar to that of eukaryotes (see chapter 14).

**Gene expression.** The machinery used for gene expression also differs between archaea and bacteria. The archaea may have more than one RNA polymerase, and these enzymes more closely resemble the eukaryotic RNA polymerases than they do the single bacterial RNA polymerase. Some of the translation machinery is also more similar to that of eukaryotes (see chapter 15).

## Most prokaryotes have not been characterized

Prokaryotes are not easily classified according to their forms, and only recently has enough been learned about their biochemical and metabolic characteristics to develop a satisfactory overall classification scheme comparable to that used for other organisms.

### Early classification characteristics

Early systems for classifying prokaryotes relied on differential stains such as the Gram stain and differences in the observable phenotype of the organism. Key characteristics once used in classifying prokaryotes were

1. photosynthetic or nonphotosynthetic
2. motile or nonmotile
3. unicellular or colony-forming or filamentous
4. formation of spores or division by transverse binary fission
5. importance as human pathogens or not

### Molecular approaches to classification

With the development of genetic and molecular approaches, prokaryotic classifications may help reflect true evolutionary relatedness. Molecular approaches include

1. the analysis of the amino acid sequences of key proteins
2. the analysis of nucleic acid–base sequences by establishing the percent of guanine (G) and cytosine (C)
3. nucleic acid hybridization, which is essentially the mixing of single-stranded DNA from two species and determining the amount of base-pairing (closely related species will have more bases pairing)
4. gene and RNA sequencing, especially looking at ribosomal RNA
5. whole-genome sequencing

The three-domain, or Woese, system of phylogeny (figure 28.4) relies on all of these molecular methods, but emphasizes the comparison of rRNA sequences to establish the evolutionary relatedness of all organisms. The rRNA sequences were chosen for their high degree of evolutionary

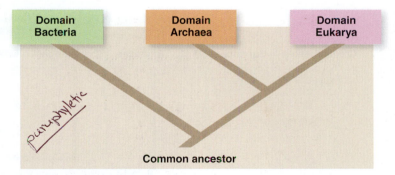

**Figure 28.4** **The three domains of life.** The two prokaryotic domains, Archaea and Bacteria, are not closely related, though both are prokaryotes. In many ways (see text), archaea more closely resemble eukaryotes than bacteria. This tree is based on rRNA sequences.

conservation to ask questions about these most ancient splits in the tree of life.

Based on these sorts of molecular data, several groupings of prokaryotes have been proposed. The most widely accepted is that presented in *Bergey's Manual of Systematic Bacteriology*, second edition, which is being published in 5 volumes, 3 of which have been completed (figure 28.5). At the same time, large scale sequencing of randomly sampled collections of bacteria show an incredible amount of diversity. While it has always been challenging to assign bacteria to species, these new data indicate that the vast majority of bacteria have never been cultured and studied in any detail. The field is in a state of flux as attempts are made to define the nature of bacterial species.

### Learning Outcomes Review 28.2

Compared with eukaryotyes, prokaryotes are distinctly different, lacking both a membrane-bounded nucleus and diverse organelles. Prokaryotes also reproduce by binary fission. Bacteria and archaea are clearly different from each other based on both structure and metabolism. Classification of prokaryotes had been based on physical characteristics, and it has now been aided by the use of DNA analysis; but a vast number of prokaryotes remain unidentified because they cannot be cultured.

■ **What features distinguish archaea from both bacteria and eukaryotes?**

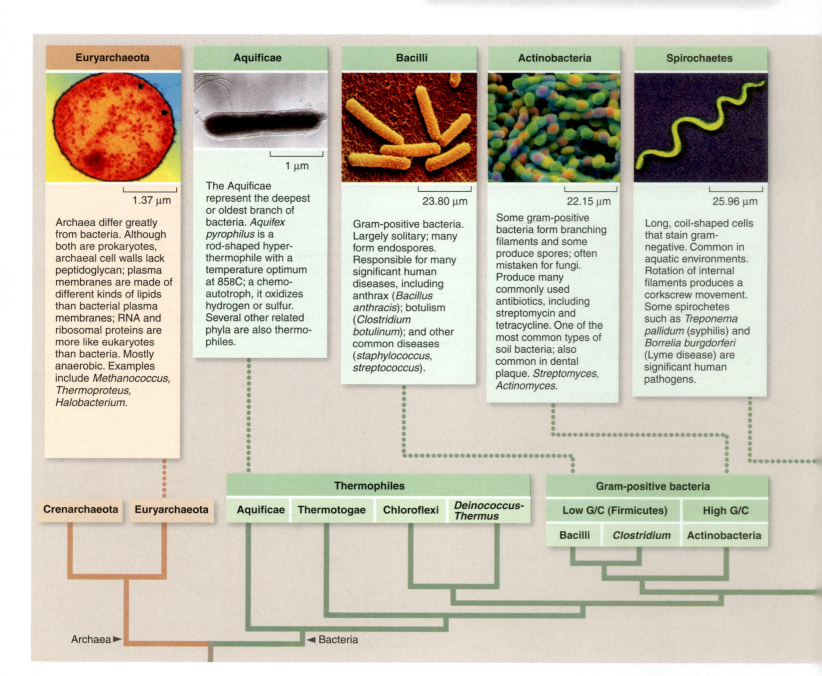

**Figure 28.5** **Some major clades of prokaryotes.** The classification adopted here is that of *Bergey's Manual of Systematic Bacteriology*, second edition, 2001. G/C refers to %G/C in genome.

# 28.3 Prokaryotic Cell Structure

## Learning Outcomes

1. Describe the general features common to all prokaryotic cells.
2. Explain the differences between gram-positive and gram-negative bacterial cells.
3. Describe the features that distinguish different kinds of prokaryotic cells.

Prokaryotic cells are relatively simple, but they can be categorized based on cell shape. They also have some variations in structure that give them different staining properties for certain dyes. Other features are found in some types of cells but not in others.

## Prokaryotes have three basic forms: rods, cocci, and spirals

Although it is an oversimplification, it is useful to divide bacteria based on easily definable morphologies. Most prokaryotes exhibit one of three basic shapes: rod-shaped, often called a

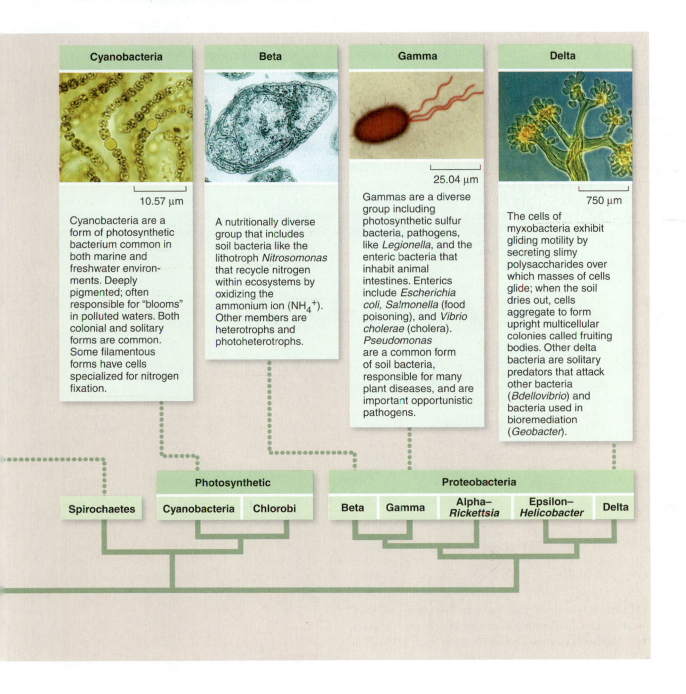

**Cyanobacteria**

10.57 µm

Cyanobacteria are a form of photosynthetic bacterium common in both marine and freshwater environments. Deeply pigmented; often responsible for "blooms" in polluted waters. Both colonial and solitary forms are common. Some filamentous forms have cells specialized for nitrogen fixation.

**Beta**

A nutritionally diverse group that includes soil bacteria like the lithotroph *Nitrosomonas* that recycle nitrogen within ecosystems by oxidizing the ammonium ion ($NH_4^+$). Other members are heterotrophs and photoheterotrophs.

**Gamma**

25.04 µm

Gammas are a diverse group including photosynthetic sulfur bacteria, pathogens, like *Legionella*, and the enteric bacteria that inhabit animal intestines. Enterics include *Escherichia coli*, *Salmonella* (food poisoning), and *Vibrio cholerae* (cholera). *Pseudomonas* are a common form of soil bacteria, responsible for many plant diseases, and are important opportunistic pathogens.

**Delta**

750 µm

The cells of myxobacteria exhibit gliding motility by secreting slimy polysaccharides over which masses of cells glide; when the soil dries out, cells aggregate to form upright multicellular colonies called fruiting bodies. Other delta bacteria are solitary predators that attack other bacteria (*Bdellovibrio*) and bacteria used in bioremediation (*Geobacter*).

| Spirochaetes | Photosynthetic | | Proteobacteria | | | | |
|---|---|---|---|---|---|---|---|
| | Cyanobacteria | Chlorobi | Beta | Gamma | Alpha–*Rickettsia* | Epsilon–*Helicobacter* | Delta |

*bacillus* (plural, *bacilli*); *coccus* (plural, *cocci*), spherical- or ovoid-shaped; and *spirillum* (plural, *spirilla*), long and helical-shaped; these bacteria are also called *spirochetes*.

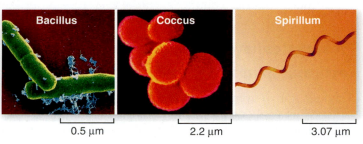

0.5 μm    2.2 μm    3.07 μm

© Dr. Richard Kessel & Dr. Gene Shih/Visuals Unlimited

The bacterial cell wall is the single most important contributor to cell shape. Bacteria that normally lack cell walls, such as the mycoplasmas, do not have a set shape.

As diverse as their shapes may be, prokaryotic cells also have many different methods to move through their environment. A *flagellum* or several flagella may be found on the outer surface of many prokaryotic cells. These structures are used to propel the organisms in a fluid environment. Some rod-shaped and spherical bacteria form colonies, adhering end-to-end after they have divided, forming chains. Some bacterial cells change into stalked structures or grow long, branched filaments. Some filamentous bacteria are capable of a gliding motion on solid surfaces, often combined with rotation around a longitudinal axis.

## Prokaryotes have a tough cell wall and other external structures

The prokaryotic cell wall is often complex, consisting of many layers. Minimally it consists of peptidoglycan, a polymer unique to bacteria. This polymer forms a rigid network of polysaccharide strands cross-linked by peptide side chains. It is an important structure because it maintains the shape of the cell and protects the cell from swelling and rupturing in hypotonic solutions, which are most commonly found in the environment. The archaea do not possess peptidoglycan, but some have a similar structure called pseudomurein, or pseudopeptidoglycan.

### Gram-positive and gram-negative bacteria

Two types of bacteria can be identified using a staining process called the **Gram stain**, hence their names. **Gram-positive** bacteria have a thicker peptidoglycan wall and stain a purple color, whereas the more common **gram-negative** bacteria contain less peptidoglycan and do not retain the purple-colored dye. These gram-negative bacteria can be stained with a red counterstain and then appear dark pink (figure 28.6).

In the gram-positive bacteria, the peptidoglycan forms a thick, complex network around the outer surface of the cell. This network also contains lipoteichoic and teichoic acid, which protrudes from the cell wall. In the gram-negative bacteria, a thin layer of peptidoglycan is sandwiched between the plasma membranes and a second outer membrane (figure 28.7). The outer membrane contains large molecules

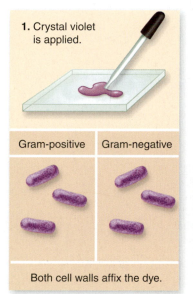

1. Crystal violet is applied.

Gram-positive | Gram-negative

Both cell walls affix the dye.

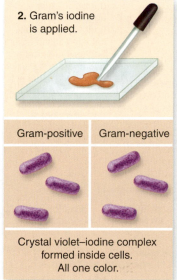

2. Gram's iodine is applied.

Gram-positive | Gram-negative

Crystal violet–iodine complex formed inside cells. All one color.

3. Alcohol wash is applied.

Gram-positive | Gram-negative

Alcohol dehydrates thick PG layer trapping dye complex. | Alcohol has minimal effect on thin PG layer.

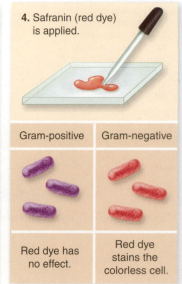

4. Safranin (red dye) is applied.

Gram-positive | Gram-negative

Red dye has no effect. | Red dye stains the colorless cell.

*a.*

**Figure 28.6 The Gram stain.** *a.* The thick peptidoglycan (PG) layer encasing gram-positive bacteria traps crystal violet dye, so the bacteria appear purple in a gram-stained smear (named after Hans Christian Gram—Danish bacteriologist, 1853–1938—who developed the technique). Because gram-negative bacteria have much less peptidoglycan (located between the plasma membrane and an outer membrane), they do not retain the crystal violet dye and so exhibit the red counterstain (usually a safranin dye). *b.* A micrograph showing the results of a Gram stain with both gram-positive and gram-negative cells.

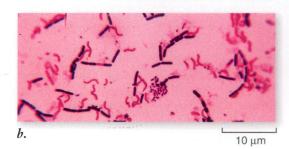

*b.*    10 μm

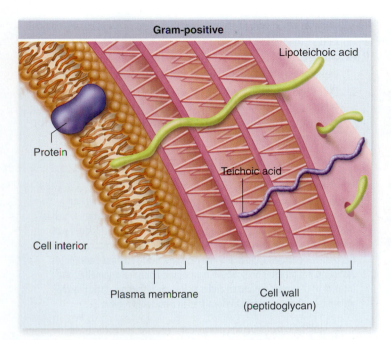

**Gram-positive**

Lipoteichoic acid

Protein

Teichoic acid

Cell interior

Plasma membrane

Cell wall
(peptidoglycan)

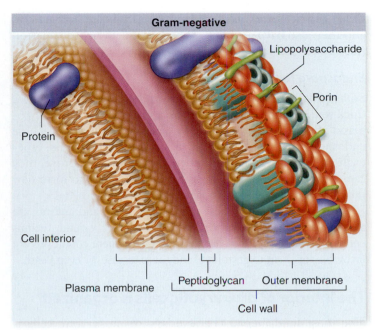

**Gram-negative**

Lipopolysaccharide

Porin

Protein

Cell interior

Plasma membrane

Peptidoglycan

Outer membrane

Cell wall

**Figure 28.7** **The structure of gram-positive and gram-negative cell walls.** The gram-positive cell wall is much simpler, composed of a thick layer of cross-linked peptidoglycan chains. Molecules of lipoteichoic acid and teichoic acid are also embedded in the wall and exposed on the surface of the cell. The gram-negative cell wall is composed of multiple layers. The peptidoglycan layer is thinner than in gram-positive bacteria and is surrounded by an additional membrane composed of lipopolysaccharide. Porin proteins form aqueous pores in the outer membrane. The space between the outer membrane and peptidoglycan is called the periplasmic space.

of **lipopolysaccharide,** lipids with polysaccharide chains attached. The outer membrane layer makes gram-negative bacteria resistant to many antibiotics that interfere with cell-wall synthesis in gram-positive bacteria. For example, penicillin acts to inhibit the cross-linking of peptidoglycan in a gram-positive cell wall, killing growing bacterial populations.

### S-layer

In some bacteria and archaea, an additional protein or glycoprotein layer forms a rigid paracrystalline surface called an *S-layer* outside of the peptidoglycan or outer membrane layers of gram-positive and gram-negative bacteria, respectively. Among the archaea, the S-layer is almost universal and can be found outside of a pseudopeptidoglycan layer or, in contrast to the bacteria, may be the only rigid layer surrounding the cell. The functions of S-layers are diverse and variable but often involve adhesion to surfaces or protection.

### The capsule

In some bacteria, an additional gelatinous layer, the **capsule,** surrounds the other wall layers. A capsule enables a prokaryotic cell to adhere to surfaces and to other cells, and, most important, to evade an immune response by interfering with recognition by phagocytic cells. Therefore, a capsule often contributes to the ability of bacteria to cause disease.

### Bacterial flagella and pili

Many kinds of prokaryotes have slender, rigid, helical flagella composed of the protein **flagellin** (figure 28.8). These flagella range from 3 to 12 μm in length and are very thin—only 10 to 20 nm thick. They are anchored in the cell wall and spin like a propeller, moving the cell through a liquid environment.

Bacterial cells that have lost the genes for flagellin are not able to swim.

**Pili** (singular, *pilus*) are other hairlike structures that occur on the cells of some gram-negative prokaryotes. They are shorter than prokaryotic flagella and about 7.5 to 10 nm

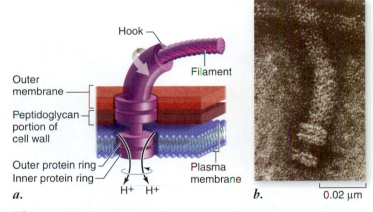

Hook

Filament

Outer membrane

Peptidoglycan portion of cell wall

Outer protein ring

Inner protein ring

Plasma membrane

H+ H+

*a.*

*b.*

0.02 μm

**Figure 28.8** **The flagellar motor of a gram-negative bacterium.** *a.* A protein filament, composed of the protein flagellin, is attached to a protein rod that passes through a sleeve in the outer membrane and through a hole in the peptidoglycan layer to rings of protein anchored in the cell wall and plasma membrane, like rings of ball bearings. The rod rotates when the inner protein ring attached to the rod turns with respect to the outer ring fixed to the cell wall. The inner ring is an H+ ion channel, a proton pump that uses the flow of protons into the cell to power the movement of the inner ring past the outer one. The membrane wall anchor of the flagellum is called the basal body. *b.* Electron micrograph of bacterial flagellum.

thick. Pili are more important in adhesion than movement, and they also have a role in exchange of genetic information (discussed later).

### Endospore formation

Some prokaryotes are able to form **endospores,** developing a thick wall around their genome and a small portion of the cytoplasm when they are exposed to environmental stress. These endospores are highly resistant to environmental stress, especially heat, and when environmental conditions improve, they can germinate and return to normal cell division to form new individuals after decades or even centuries.

The bacteria that cause tetanus, botulism, and anthrax are all capable of forming spores. With a puncture wound, tetanus endospores may be driven deep into the skin where conditions are favorable for them to germinate and cause disease, or even death.

## The interior of prokaryotic cells is organized

The most fundamental characteristic of prokaryotic cells is their simple interior organization. Prokaryotic cells lack the extensive functional compartmentalization seen within eukaryotic cells, but they do have the following structures:

**Internal membranes.** Many prokaryotes possess invaginated regions of the plasma membrane that function in respiration or photosynthesis (figure 28.9).

**Nucleoid region.** Prokaryotes lack nuclei and generally do not possess linear chromosomes. Instead, their genes are encoded within a single double-stranded ring of DNA that is highly condensed to form a visible region of the cell known as the **nucleoid region.** Many prokaryotic cells also possess plasmids, which as described earlier are small, independently replicating circles of DNA. Plasmids contain only a few genes, and although these genes may

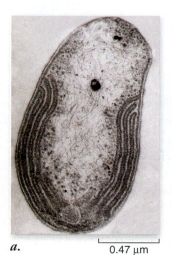 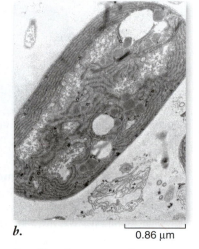

*a.* 0.47 µm    *b.* 0.86 µm

**Figure 28.9 Prokaryotic cells often have complex internal membranes.** *a.* This aerobic bacterium exhibits extensive respiratory membranes (long dark curves that hug the cell wall) within its cytoplasm not unlike those seen in mitochondria. *b.* This cyanobacterium has thylakoid-like membranes (ripple-like shapes along the edges and in the center) that provide a site for photosynthesis.

confer a selective advantage, they are not essential for the cell's survival.

**Ribosomes.** Prokaryotic ribosomes are smaller than those of eukaryotes and differ in protein and RNA content. Antibiotics such as tetracycline and chloramphenicol can tell the difference, however—they bind to prokaryotic ribosomes and block protein synthesis, but they do not bind to eukaryotic ribosomes.

### Learning Outcomes Review 28.3

The three basic shapes of prokaryotes are rod-shaped, spherical, and spiral-shaped. Bacteria have a cell wall containing peptidoglycan, which is the basis for the Gram stain. Gram-positive bacteria have a thick cell wall, relative to gram-negative species. Many also have an external capsule. Some bacteria have flagella and pili. Some can form heat-resistant endospores. Although prokaryotes do not have membrane-bounded organelles, the interior of the cell is organized and may include infolding of the plasma membrane. Prokaryotic DNA is localized in a nucleoid region.

■ *What would be the simplest method to determine whether two bacteria belong to the same species?*

## 28.4 Prokaryotic Genetics

### Learning Outcomes

1. *Contrast the mechanisms of DNA exchange in prokaryotes.*
2. *Explain genetic mapping in E. coli.*
3. *Describe how genetics explains the spread of antibiotic resistance.*

In sexually reproducing populations, traits are transferred vertically from parent to child. Prokaryotes do not reproduce sexually, but they can exchange DNA between different cells. This horizontal gene transfer occurs when genes move from one cell to another by **conjugation,** requiring cell-to-cell contact, or by means of viruses *(transduction)*. Some species of bacteria can also pick up genetic material directly from the environment *(transformation)*.

All of these processes have been observed in archaea, but the study of archaeal genetics is still in its infancy because of the difficulty in culturing most species. We concentrate here on bacterial systems, primarily *E. coli*, which has been studied extensively.

### Conjugation depends on the presence of a conjugative plasmid

Plasmids may encode functions that can confer an advantage to the cell, such as antibiotic resistance, on which natural selection can operate—but they are not required for normal function. In some cases, plasmids can be transferred from one cell to another via conjugation. The best known plasmid capable of transfer is called the **F plasmid,** for fertility factor; cells containing F plasmids are termed **F⁺** cells, and cells that lack the F plasmid

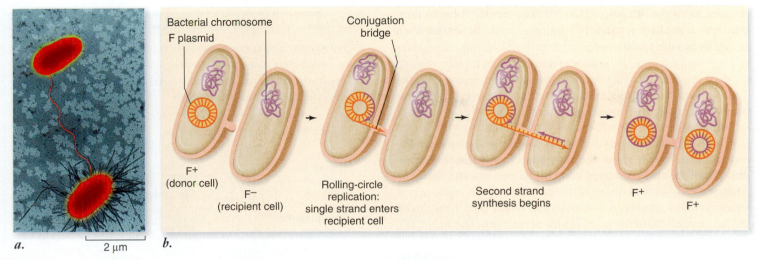

*a.*   *b.*

**Figure 28.10**  **Conjugation bridge and transfer of F plasmid between F⁺ and F⁻ cell.**  *a.* The electron micrograph shows two *E. coli* cells caught in the act of conjugation. The connection between the cells is the extended F pilus. *b.* F⁻ cells are converted to F⁺ cells by the transfer of the F plasmid. The cells are joined by a conjugation bridge and the plasmid is replicated in the donor cell, displacing one parental strand. The displaced strand is transferred to the recipient cell then replicated. After successful transfer, the recipient cell becomes an F⁺ cell capable of expressing genes for the F pilus and acting as a donor.

are F⁻ cells. The F plasmid occurs in *E. coli* and, like all plasmids, acts as an independent genetic entity that nevertheless depends on the cell for replication. Studies involving the F plasmid were critical to our current understanding of bacterial genetics and the organization of the *E. coli* chromosome.

### F plasmid transfer

The F plasmid contains a DNA replication origin and several genes that promote its transfer to other cells. These genes encode protein subunits that assemble on the surface of the bacterial cell, forming a hollow pilus that is necessary for the transfer process (figure 28.10*a*).

First, the F plasmid binds to a site on the interior of the F⁺ cell just beneath the pilus, now called a *conjugation bridge*. Then, by a process called *rolling-circle replication*, the F plasmid begins to copy its DNA at the binding point. As it is replicated, the displaced single strand of the plasmid passes into the other cell. There, a complementary strand is added, creating a new, stable F plasmid (figure 28.10*b*).

### Recombination between the F plasmid and host chromosome

The F plasmid can integrate into the host chromosome by recombining with it (see chapter 13). The molecular events in this process are similar to events during meiosis in eukaryotes when crossing over (recombination) exchanges material between chromosomes. This process is also called homologous recombination. In the case of the F plasmid and the *E. coli* chromosome, a single recombination event between two circles produces a larger circle, consisting of the chromosome and the integrated plasmid. This integration is actually mediated by host-encoded proteins, but it takes advantage of regions in the F plasmid called insertion sequences (IS) that also exist in the *E. coli* chromosome. These IS elements are actually transposable elements that probably moved from the chromosome to the F plasmid.

When the F plasmid is integrated into the chromosome, the cell is called an **Hfr cell** for high frequency of recombination (figure 28.11), because now transfer by the F plasmid will include chromosomal DNA. The site on the F plasmid where transfer initiates is located in the middle of the integrated plasmid, so that the entire chromosome would have to be transferred to also

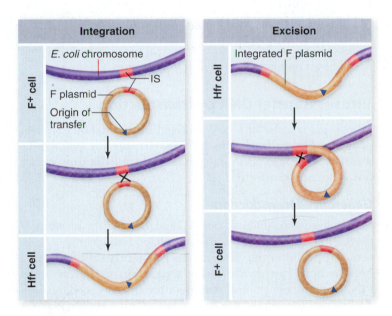

**Figure 28.11**  **Integration and excision of F plasmid.** The F plasmid contains short insertion sequences (IS) that also exist in the chromosome. This allows the plasmid to pair with the chromosome, and a single recombination event between two circles leads to a larger circle. This integrates the plasmid into the chromosome, creating an Hfr cell, as shown on the left. The process is reversible because the IS sequences in the integrated plasmid can pair, and now a recombination event will return the two circles and convert the Hfr back to an F⁺ cell as shown on the right.

transfer all of the integrated plasmid. The transfer of the entire chromosome takes around 100 minutes, and the conjugation bridge is usually broken before that time. This leads to transfer of portions of donor chromosome that can then replace regions of the recipient chromosome by homologous recombination. This occurs by *two* recombination events between the linear piece and the circular chromosome, similar to a double crossover in eukaryotic meiosis.

Geneticists have taken advantage of this process to map the order of genes in the *E. coli* chromosome. Genes close to the origin of transfer are transferred early in the process, and those far from the origin are transferred later. If the process of mating is experimentally interrupted at different times, then gene order can be mapped based on time of entry of each gene (figure 28.12). The entry of genes can be detected by using a donor with wild-type alleles that can replace mutant alleles in the recipient by homologous recombination as described. These experiments have shown that the *E. coli* chromosome is indeed circular, and the genetic map is therefore circular. The units of the map are minutes, and the entire map is 100 minutes long.

The F plasmid can also excise itself by reversing the integration process. In this case, the IS elements bounding the integrated plasmid pair and now a single recombination event will restore the two circles (see figure 28.11). If excision is inaccurate, the F plasmid can pick up some chromosomal DNA in the process. This creates what is called an F plasmid that can then be transferred rapidly and in its entirety to another cell. In this case, the cell already has the same genetic material in its chromosome as that carried by the F'. This makes the cell a **partial diploid**, sometimes called a **merodiploid**. Merodiploids can be used to determine if new isolated mutations are alleles of known genes. This is done by using wild types of alleles of known genes of the F' plasmid to provide normal function heterozygous to unknown mutant alleles in the chromosome.

## Viruses transfer DNA by transduction

Horizontal transfer of DNA can also be mediated by bacteriophage. In **generalized transduction,** virtually any gene can be transferred between cells; in **specialized transduction,** only a few genes are transferred.

### Generalized transduction

Generalized transduction can be thought of as an accident of the biology of some types of lytic phage (see chapter 27). In these viruses, after the viral genome is replicated and the phage head is constructed, the phage packaging machinery stuffs DNA into the phage head until no more fits, so-called headfull packaging. Sometimes the phage begins with bacterial DNA instead of phage DNA and packages this DNA into a phage head (figure 28.13). When this viral particle goes on to infect another cell, it injects the bacterial DNA into the infected cell instead of viral DNA. This DNA can then be incorporated into the recipient chromosome by homologous recombination. Similar to transfer by Hfr cells described earlier, two recombination events are necessary to integrate the linear piece of DNA into the circular chromosome (see figure 28.13).

Generalized transduction has also been used for mapping purposes in *E. coli*, although the logic is different from that in

**Hypothesis:** *Conjugation using Hfr strains involves the linear transfer of information from donor to recipient cell.*

**Prediction:** *If there is a linear transfer of information, then different markers should appear in a time sequence.*

**Test:** *Mating strains are agitated at time points to break the conjugation bridge, then plated to determine genotype.*

Mating interrupted by agitation in blender

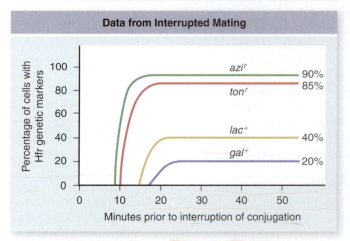

**Data from Interrupted Mating**

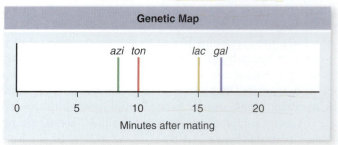

**Genetic Map**

**Result:** *The different genes from the donor strain appear in a linear time sequence.*

**Conclusion:** *The transfer of genetic information is linear. This sequence can be used to construct a genetic map ordering the genes on the chromosomes.*

**Further Experiments:** *Can other methods of DNA exchange also be used for genetic mapping?*

**Figure 28.12 Interrupted mating experiment allows construction of genetic map.**

conjugation. In transduction, the closer together two genes are, the more likely it is that they will be transferred in a single transduction event. This can be expressed mathematically as the *cotransduction frequency*. Correlation of maps from the two

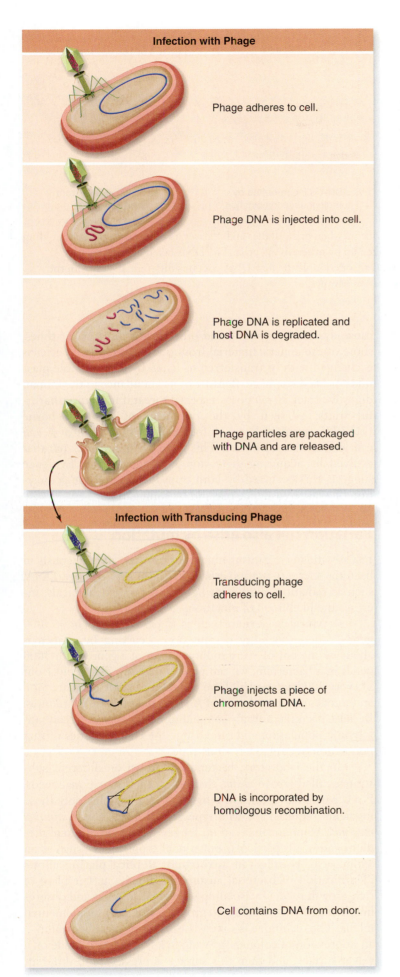

**Infection with Phage**

Phage adheres to cell.

Phage DNA is injected into cell.

Phage DNA is replicated and host DNA is degraded.

Phage particles are packaged with DNA and are released.

**Infection with Transducing Phage**

Transducing phage adheres to cell.

Phage injects a piece of chromosomal DNA.

DNA is incorporated by homologous recombination.

Cell contains DNA from donor.

**Figure 28.13 Transduction by generalized transducing phage.** When some phage infect cells, they degrade the host DNA into pieces. When the phage package their DNA, they can package host DNA in place of phage DNA to produce a transducing phage as shown on the top. When a transducing phage infects a cell, it injects host DNA that can then be integrated into the host genome by homologous recombination. With a linear piece of DNA, it requires two recombination events, which replace the chromosomal DNA with the transducing DNA as shown on the bottom. If the new allele is different from the old, the cell's phenotype will change.

methods allows an empirical conversion between cotransduction frequency and minutes in the genetic map.

### Specialized transduction

Specialized transduction is limited to phage that exhibit a lysogenic life cycle (see chapter 27). The prototype for this is phage λ from *E. coli*. When λ infects a cell and its genome integrates into the host chromosome, it does not destroy the cell but is passed on by cell division. This integration event is similar to the integration of the F plasmid, except that in the case of λ the recombination is a site-specific event mediated by phage-encoded proteins.

In this lysogenic state, the phage is called a prophage and it is dormant. The prophage encodes the functions necessary to eventually excise itself and undergo lytic growth, leading to the death of the cell. If this excision event is imprecise, it may take some chromosomal DNA with it, in the process making a specialized transducing phage. These phage carry both phage genes and chromosomal genes, unlike generalized transducing phage that carry only chromosomal DNA.

Because the phage head can carry only as much DNA as is found in the phage genome, imprecise excision results in deletion of phage genes. Thus specialized transducing phage may be defective if genes necessary for phage growth are lost in the process.

Specialized transducing phage particles can then integrate into the chromosome, just like wild-type phage, also making the cell diploid for the genes carried by the phage. Phage particles that can integrate as prophages may become trapped in the host genome if the genes necessary for excision become defective by mutation or are lost. The *E. coli* genome contains a number of such cryptic prophage, some of which encode functions important to the cell and must now be considered part of the host genome.

## Transformation is the uptake of DNA directly from the environment

Transformation is a naturally occurring process in some species, such as the bacteria that were studied by Frederick Griffith (see chapter 14). Griffith discovered the process despite not knowing what chemical component was transferred. Transformation occurs when one bacterial cell has died and ruptured,

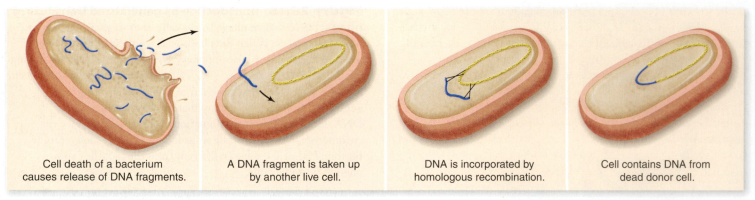

| Cell death of a bacterium causes release of DNA fragments. | A DNA fragment is taken up by another live cell. | DNA is incorporated by homologous recombination. | Cell contains DNA from dead donor cell. |

**Figure 28.14** **Natural transformation.** Natural transformation occurs when one cell dies and releases its contents to the surrounding environment. The DNA is usually fragmented, and small pieces can be taken up by other, living cells. The DNA taken up can replace chromosomal DNA by homologous recombination as in conjugation and transduction. If the new DNA contains different alleles from the chromosome, the phenotype of the cell changes, possibly providing a selective advantage.

spilling its fragmented DNA into the surrounding environment. This DNA can be taken up by another cell and incorporated into its genome, thereby transforming it (figure 28.14). When the uptake occurs under natural conditions, it is termed natural transformation. Some species of both gram-positive and gram-negative bacteria exhibit natural transformation, although the mechanisms seem to differ between the groups.

The proteins involved in the process of natural transformation are all encoded by the bacterial chromosome. The implication is that natural transformation may be the only one of the mechanisms of DNA exchange that evolved as part of normal cellular machinery. The transfer of chromosomal DNA by either conjugation or transduction can be thought of as accidents of plasmid or phage biology, respectively.

Transformation is also important in molecular cloning, but *E. coli* does not exhibit natural transformation. When transformation is accomplished in the laboratory it is called artificial transformation. Artificial transformation is useful for cloning and DNA manipulation (see chapter 17).

## Antibiotic resistance can be transferred by resistance plasmids

Some conjugative plasmids pick up antibiotic resistance genes, becoming resistance plasmids, or **R plasmids.** The rapid transfer of newly acquired, antibiotic resistance genes by plasmids has been an important factor in the appearance of the resistant strains of the pathogen *Staphylococcus aureus* discussed in the next section.

The means by which resistance plasmids acquire antibiotic resistance genes is often through transposable elements, which were described in chapter 18. These elements can move from chromosome to chromosome or from plasmid to chromosome and back again, and they can transfer antibiotic resistance genes in the process. If a conjugative plasmid picks up these genes, then the bacterium carrying it has a selective advantage in the presence of those antibiotics.

An important example in terms of human health involves the Enterobacteriaceae, the family of bacteria to which the common intestinal bacterium *E. coli* belongs. This family contains many pathogenic bacteria, including the organisms that cause dysentery, typhoid, and other major diseases. At times, some of the genetic material from these pathogenic species is exchanged with or transferred to *E. coli* by transmissible plasmids or bacteriophage. Because of its abundance in the human digestive tract, *E. coli* poses a special threat if it acquires harmful traits, as seen by the outbreaks of the food-borne O157:H7 strain of *E. coli*. Infection with this strain of *E. coli* can lead to serious illness. This is a new strain of *E. coli* that evolved by acquiring genes for pathogenic traits. Evidence suggests this occurred by both transduction and the acquisition of a large virulence plasmid by conjugation.

## Variation can also arise by mutation

Just as with any organism, mutations can arise spontaneously in bacteria. Certain factors, especially those that damage DNA, such as radiation, ultraviolet light, and various chemicals, increase the likelihood of mutation.

A typical bacterium such as *E. coli* contains about 5000 genes. The probability of mutation occurring by chance is about in one out of every million copies of a gene. With 5000 genes in a bacterium, we can predict that approximately 1 out of every 200 bacteria will have a mutation. With adequate food and nutrients, a population of *E. coli* can double in 20 minutes. Because bacteria multiply so rapidly, mutations can spread rapidly in a population and can change the characteristics of that population in a relatively short time.

In the laboratory, bacteria are grown on different substrates, called *growth media*, that reflect their nutritional needs. For a particular species, the medium that contains only those nutrients required for wild-type growth is termed a *minimal medium*. A mutant that can no longer survive on minimal medium and needs particular nutritional supplements, such as an amino acid, is called an **auxotroph. Replica plating** allows identification of bacterial auxotrophs from a master plate of rich growth media by isolating individual colonies and observing their growth (or failure to grow) on different supplemented media. The technique is somewhat like using a rubber stamp—an impression of colonies growing in a Petri plate is made on a velvet surface, and then this surface is pressed onto different media in other plates. The impression contains many thousands if not millions of cells from each colony—and each colony has grown from a single cell. In this way, a bacterium with a highly specific mutation can be isolated, identified, and grown.

The ability of prokaryotes to change rapidly in response to new challenges often has adverse effects on humans. A number of antibiotic-resistant strains of the bacterium *Staphylococcus aureus* (termed methicillin-resistant *Staphylococcus aureus*, or MRSA) had been known in hospital settings for some time. More recently these have been observed in infections out of the hospital setting, so-called community acquired MRSA.

Of most concern among these strains is **vancomycin-resistant *Staphylococcus aureus*** (VRSA). This appears to have arisen rapidly by mutation and is alarming because vancomycin is the drug of last resort, making these strains and the infections they cause very difficult to stop. *Staphylococcus* infections, or "staph" infections for short, provide an excellent example of the way in which mutation and intensive selection can bring about rapid change in bacterial populations.

### Learning Outcomes Review 28.4

Prokaryotic DNA exchange is horizontal, from donor cell to recipient cell. DNA can be exchanged by conjugation via plasmids, by transduction via viruses, and by transformation through the direct uptake of DNA from the environment. These forms of DNA exchange can be used experimentally to map genes. Variation in prokaryotes also arises by mutation. Extensive use of antibiotics has lead to selection for resistant organisms. Resistance genes can be transferred, rapidly spreading resistance.

■  *How does transfer of genetic information in bacteria differ from eukaryotic sex?*

## 28.5 Prokaryotic Metabolism

### Learning Outcomes

1. Describe the different ways that prokaryotes acquire energy and carbon.
2. Explain how bacterial proteins can cause disease in humans.

The variation seen in prokaryotes manifests itself most noticeably in biochemical rather than morphological diversity. Wide variation has been found in the types of metabolism prokaryotes exhibit, especially in the means by which they acquire energy and carbon.

### Prokaryotes acquire carbon and energy in four basic ways

Prokaryotes have evolved many mechanisms to acquire the energy and carbon they need for growth and reproduction. Many are *autotrophs* that obtain their carbon from inorganic $CO_2$.

Other prokaryotes are *heterotrophs* that obtain at least some of their carbon from organic molecules, such as glucose. Depending on the method by which they acquire energy, autotrophs and heterotrophs are categorized as follows:

**Photoautotrophs.** Many bacteria carry out photosynthesis, using the energy of sunlight to build organic molecules from carbon dioxide. The **cyanobacteria** use chlorophyll *a* as the key light-capturing pigment and $H_2O$ as an electron donor, releasing oxygen gas as a by-product. They are therefore oxygenic, and their method of photosynthesis is very similar to that found in algae and plants.

Other bacteria use bacteriochlorophyll as their light-capturing pigment and $H_2S$ as an electron donor, leaving elemental sulfur as the by-product. These bacteria do not produce oxygen (anoxygenic) and have a simpler method of photosynthesis. These are the purple and green sulfur bacteria.

Archaeal species also carry out photosynthesis, the simplest form known. This involves a single protein, bacteriorhodopsin, that uses energy from light to translocate protons across a membrane. This then provides a proton motive force for ATP synthesis. Recent surveys of microbial diversity in marine ecosystems using DNA sequencing have found a new relative of the rhodopsin family called proteorhodopsin. First found in a bacterial species, these proteorhodopsins are quite widespread, found in bacterial, archaeal, and even algal species. This raises the possibility that photosynthesis in marine systems may be more widespread and complex than previously thought.

**Chemolithoautotrophs.** Some prokaryotes obtain energy by oxidizing inorganic substances. Nitrifiers, for example, oxidize ammonia or nitrite to obtain energy, producing the nitrate that is taken up by plants. This process is called **nitrification,** and it is essential in terrestrial ecosystems because plants primarily absorb nitrogen in the form of nitrate.

Other chemolithoautotrophs oxidize sulfur, hydrogen gas, and other inorganic molecules. On the dark ocean floor at depths of 2500 m, entire ecosystems subsist on prokaryotes that oxidize hydrogen sulfide as it escapes from thermal vents.

**Photoheterotrophs.** The so-called purple and green nonsulfur bacteria use light as their source of energy but obtain carbon from organic molecules, such as carbohydrates or alcohols that have been produced by other organisms.

**Chemoheterotrophs.** The majority of prokaryotes obtain both carbon atoms and energy from organic molecules. These include decomposers and most pathogens. Human beings and all nonphotosynthetic eukaryotes are chemoheterotrophs as well.

### Some bacteria can attack other cells directly

Invading pathogens of the genera *Yersinia* can introduce proteins directly into host cells by a specialized form of secretion. (*Yersinia pestis* is the bacterial species responsible for bubonic plague.) Most proteins secreted by gram-negative bacteria have special signal sequences that allow them to pass through the bacterium's double membrane. The proteins secreted by *Yersinia* lacked a key signal sequence that two known secretion mechanisms require for transport. The proteins must therefore have been secreted by means of a third type of system, which researchers called the *type III system*. This kind of system acts like a kind of molecular syringe allowing the pathogen to inject proteins directly into the cytoplasm of host cells.

As more bacterial species are studied, the genes coding for the type III system are turning up in other gram-negative animal pathogens, and even in more distantly related plant pathogens. The genes seem more closely related to one another than are the bacteria. Furthermore, the genes are similar to those that code for bacterial flagella.

These proteins are used to transfer other virulence proteins, such as toxins, into nearby eukaryotic cells. Given the similarity of the type III genes to the genes that code for flagella, the transfer proteins may form a flagellum-like structure that shoots virulence proteins into the host cells. Once in the eukaryotic cells, the virulence proteins affect the host's response to the pathogen.

In *Yersinia*, proteins secreted by the type III system are injected into macrophages; the proteins disrupt signals that tell the macrophages to engulf bacteria. *Salmonella* and *Shigella* use their type III proteins to enter the cytoplasm of eukaryotic cells, and thus they are protected from the immune system of their host. The proteins secreted by certain strains of *E. coli* alter the cytoskeleton of nearby intestinal eukaryotic cells, resulting in a bulge onto which the bacterial cells can tightly bind.

## Bacteria are costly plant pathogens

Although the majority of commercially relevant plant pathogens are fungi, many diseases of plants are associated with particular heterotrophic bacteria. Almost every kind of plant is susceptible to one or more kinds of bacterial disease, including blights, soft rots, and wilts. Fire blight, which destroys pear and apple trees and related plants, is a well-known example of bacterial disease.

The early symptoms of these plant diseases vary, but they are commonly manifested as spots of various sizes on the stems, leaves, flowers, or fruits. Most bacteria that cause plant diseases are members of the group of rod-shaped gram-negative bacteria known as pseudomonads.

### Learning Outcomes Review 28.5

Prokaryotes exhibit amazing metabolic diversity with both autotrophic and heterotrophic species. Photoautotrophs use light as an energy source; chemolithoautotrophs oxidize inorganic compounds. Photoheterotrophs use light as an energy source and organic compounds as carbon sources. Chemoheterotrophs use organic compounds for both energy and carbon. Bacterial animal pathogens attack host cells with toxic proteins that disrupt the host's immune response, among other effects.

■ **Why is metabolism a better way than morphology to characterize prokaryotes?**

### Learning Outcomes
1. *Describe common human bacterial pathogens.*
2. *Explain how bacteria can cause ulcers.*
3. *Identify sexually transmitted diseases caused by bacteria.*

In the early 20th century, before the discovery and widespread use of antibiotics, infectious diseases killed nearly 20% of all U.S. children before they reached the age of five. Sanitation and antibiotics considerably improved the situation. In recent years, however, we have seen the appearance or reappearance of many bacterial diseases, including cholera, leprosy, tetanus, bacterial pneumonia, whooping cough, diphtheria, and Lyme disease (table 28.1). Members of the genus *Streptococcus* are associated with scarlet fever, rheumatic fever, pneumonia, "flesh-eating disease," and other infections. Tuberculosis, another bacterial disease, is still a leading cause of death in humans worldwide.

Bacteria have many different methods to spread through a susceptible population. Tuberculosis and many other bacterial diseases of the respiratory tract are mostly spread through the air in droplets of mucus or saliva. Diseases such as typhoid fever, paratyphoid fever, and bacillary dysentery are spread by fecal contamination of food or water. Lyme disease and Rocky Mountain spotted fever are spread to humans by tick vectors.

## Tuberculosis has infected humans for all of recorded history

Tuberculosis (TB) has been a scourge to humanity for thousands of years. There is evidence that peoples from ancient Egypt and pre-Columbian South America died from TB; the TB bacillus (*Mycobacterium tuberculosis*) has been identified in prehistoric mummies. TB afflicts the respiratory system, thwarts the immune system, and is easily transmitted from person to person through the air.

### The spread of tuberculosis

Currently, about one-third of all people worldwide are regularly exposed to *Mycobacterium tuberculosis*. An estimated 9.27 million new cases were diagnosed, and 1.8 million deaths occurred in 2007. In 2006, the World Health Organization reported the incidence of TB falling in five of six WHO regions, but the numbers continue to rise in Africa driven by the spread of HIV.

Since the mid-1980s, the United States has experienced a resurgence of TB. This peaked in the mid-1990s and has been declining since, although the rate of decline is leveling off. The latest statistics from the CDC indicate 13,300 TB cases in 2007, down from 13,754 cases in 2006.

### Tuberculosis treatment

Most TB patients are placed on multiple, expensive antibiotics for six to twelve months. Alarming outbreaks of **multidrug-resistant**

TABLE 28.1    Important Human Bacterial Diseases

| Disease | Pathogen | Vector/Reservoir | Epidemiology |
|---|---|---|---|
| Anthrax | Bacillus antbracis | Animals, including processed skins | Bacterial infection that can be transmitted through contact or ingestion. Rare except in sporadic outbreaks. May be fatal. |
| Botulism | Clostridium botulinum | Improperly prepared food | Contracted through ingestion or contact with wound. Produces acute toxic poison; can be fatal. |
| Chlamydia | Chlamydia trachomatis | Humans, sexually transmitted disease (STD) | Urogenital infections with possible spread to eyes and respiratory tract. Increasingly common over past 20 years. |
| Cholera | Vibrio cholerae | Human feces, plankton | Causes severe diarrhea that can lead to death by dehydration; 50% peak mortality rate if untreated. A major killer in times of crowding and poor sanitation; over 100,000 died in Rwanda in 1994 outbreak. |
| Dental caries | Streptococcus mutans, Streptococcus sabrinus | Humans | A dense collection of these bacteria on the surface of teeth leads to secretion of acids that destroy minerals in tooth enamel; sugar alone does not cause caries. |
| Diphtheria | Corynebacterium diphtheriae | Humans | Acute inflammation and lesions of respiratory mucous membranes. Spread through respiratory droplets. Vaccine available. |
| Gonorrhea | Neisseria gonorrhoeae | Humans only | STD, on the increase worldwide. Usually not fatal. |
| Hansen disease (leprosy) | Mycobacterium leprae | Humans, feral armadillos | Chronic infection of the skin; worldwide incidence about 10–12 million, especially in southeast Asia. Spread through contact with infected individuals. |
| Lyme disease | Borrelia burgdorferi | Ticks, deer, small rodents | Spread through bite of infected tick. Lesion followed by malaise, fever, fatigue, pain, stiff neck, and headache. |
| Peptic ulcers | Helicobacter pylori | Humans | Originally thought to be caused by stress or diet, most peptic ulcers now appear to be caused by this bacterium; good news for ulcer sufferers because it can be treated with antibiotics. |
| Plague | Yersinia pestis | Fleas of wild rodents: rats and squirrels | Killed one-fourth of the population of Europe in the 14th century; endemic in wild rodent populations of the western United States today. |
| Pneumonia | Streptococcus, Mycoplasma, Chlamydia, Haemophilus | Humans | Acute infection of the lungs; often fatal without treatment. Vaccine for streptococcal pneumonia available. |
| Tuberculosis | Mycobacterium tuberculosis | Humans | An acute bacterial infection of the lungs, lymph, and meninges. Its incidence is on the rise, complicated by the development of new strains of the bacterium that are resistant to antibiotics. |
| Typhoid fever | Salmonella typhi | Humans | A systemic bacterial disease of worldwide incidence. Fewer than 500 cases a year are reported in the United States. Spread through contaminated water or foods (such as improperly washed fruits and vegetables). Vaccines are available for travelers. |
| Typhus | Rickettsia typhi | Lice, rat fleas, humans | Historically a major killer in times of crowding and poor sanitation; transmitted from human to human through the bite of infected lice and fleas. Peak untreated mortality rate of 70%. |

(MDR) strains of TB have occurred, however, in the United States and worldwide. These MDR strains are resistant to most of the best available anti-TB medications. MDR TB is of particular concern because it requires much more time and is more expensive to treat. Also, it is more likely to prove fatal.

This spread of MDR TB is likely due to the extremely long course of antibiotics required to treat the disease. Patients often quit taking the antibiotics before completing the course, setting up conditions in their bodies to allow drug-resistant bacteria to thrive.

The basic principles of TB treatment and control are to make sure all patients complete a full course of medication, so that all of the bacteria causing the infection are killed and drug-resistant strains do not develop. Great efforts are being made to ensure that high-risk individuals who are infected but not yet sick receive preventive therapy under observation. Such programs are approximately 90% effective in reducing the likelihood of developing active TB and spreading it to others. These efforts are having an effect, since the disease is on the decline in the United States, decreasing by 3.3% from 2006 to 2007.

## Bacterial biofilms are involved in tooth decay

Bacteria and other organisms may form mixed cultures on certain surfaces that are extremely difficult to treat. On teeth, this biofilm, or plaque, consists largely of bacterial cells surrounded by a polysaccharide matrix. Most of the bacteria in plaque are filaments of rod-shaped cells classified as various species of *Actinomyces*, which extend out perpendicular to the surface of the tooth. Many other bacterial species are also present in plaque.

Tooth decay, or dental caries, is caused by the bacteria present in the plaque, which persist especially in places that are difficult to reach with a toothbrush. Diets that are high in simple sugars are especially harmful to teeth because certain bacteria, notably *Streptococcus sobrinus* and *S. mutans*, ferment the sugars to lactic acid. This acid production reduces the pH in the area around the plaque, breaking down the structure of the hydroxyapatite that makes tooth enamel hard. As the enamel degenerates, the remaining soft matrix of the tooth becomes vulnerable to bacterial attack.

## Bacteria can cause ulcers

Bacteria can also be the cause of disease states that on the surface appear to have no infectious basis. Peptic ulcer disease is due to craterlike lesions in the gastrointestinal tract that are exposed to peptic acid. Ulcers can be caused by drugs, such as nonsteroidal anti-inflammatory drugs, and also by some tumors of the pancreas that cause an oversecretion of peptic acid. In 1982, a bacterium named *Campylobacter pylori* (now named *Helicobacter pylori*) was isolated from gastric juices. Over the years evidence has accumulated that this bacterium is actually the causative agent in the majority of cases of peptic ulcer disease.

Antibiotic therapy can now eliminate *H. pylori*, treating the cause of the disease, and not just the symptoms. The discovery of the action of this bacterial species illustrates how even disease states that appear to be unrelated to infectious disease may actually be caused by cryptic (unknown) infection.

## Many sexually transmitted diseases are bacterial

A number of bacteria cause sexually transmitted diseases (STDs), three particularly important examples of which are gonorrhea, syphilis, and chlamydia (figure 28.15).

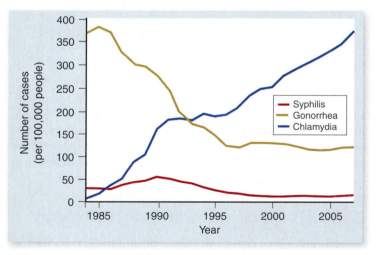

**Figure 28.15** **Trends in sexually transmitted diseases in the United States.**

### Inquiry question

**?** How is it possible for the incidence of one STD (chlamydia) to rise as another (gonorrhea) falls?

### Gonorrhea

*Gonorrhea* is one of the most prevalent communicable diseases in North America. Caused by the bacterium *Neisseria gonorrhoeae*, gonorrhea can be transmitted through sexual intercourse or any other sexual contact in which body fluids are exchanged, such as oral or anal intercourse. It can also pass from mother to baby during delivery through the birth canal.

The incidence of gonorrhea has been on the decline in the United States, but it remains a serious threat worldwide. Of particular concern is the appearance of antibiotic-resistant strains of *N. gonorrhoeae*.

### Syphilis

*Syphilis*, a very destructive STD, was once prevalent and deadly but is now less common due to the advent of blood-screening procedures and antibiotics. Syphilis is caused by a spirochete bacterium, *Treponema pallidum*, transmitted during sexual intercourse or through direct contact with an open syphilis chancre sore. The bacterium can also be transmitted from a mother to her fetus, often causing damage to the heart, eyes, and nervous system of the baby.

Once inside the body, the disease progresses in four distinct stages. The first, or primary stage, is characterized by the appearance of a small, painless, often unnoticed sore called a *chancre*. The chancre resembles a blister and occurs at the location where the bacterium entered the body about three weeks following exposure. This stage of the disease is highly infectious, and an infected person may unwittingly transmit the disease to others. This sore heals without treatment in approximately four weeks, deceptively indicating a "cure" of the disease, although the bacterium remains in the body.

The second stage of syphilis, or secondary syphilis, is marked by a rash, a sore throat, and sores in the mouth. The bacteria can be transmitted at this stage through kissing or contact with an open sore. Commonly at this point, the disease enters the third stage, a latent period. This latent stage of syphilis is symptomless and may last for several years. At this point, the person is no longer infectious, but the bacteria are still present in the body, attacking the internal organs.

The final stage of syphilis is the most debilitating, as the damage done by the bacteria in the third stage becomes evident. Sufferers at this stage of syphilis experience heart disease, mental deficiency, and nerve damage, which may include loss of motor functions or blindness.

### Chlamydia

*Chlamydia* is caused by an unusual bacterium. *Chlamydia trachomatis* is genetically a bacterium but is an obligate intracellular parasite, much like a virus in this respect. It is susceptible to antibiotics but it depends on its host to replicate its genetic material. The bacterium is transmitted through vaginal, anal, or oral intercourse with an infected person.

Chlamydia is called the "silent STD" because women usually experience no symptoms until after the infection has become established. In part because of this symptomless nature, the incidence of chlamydia has skyrocketed, increasing from 142 cases per 100,000 population in 1988 to 544 cases per 100,000 population in 2007.

The effects of an established chlamydia infection on the female body are extremely serious. Chlamydia can cause pelvic inflammatory disease (PID), which can lead to sterility and sometimes death.

It has recently been established that infection of the male or female reproductive tract by chlamydia can cause heart disease. Chlamydiae produce a peptide similar to one produced by cardiac muscle. As the body's immune system tries to fight off the infection, it recognizes and reacts to this peptide. The similarity between the bacterial and cardiac peptides confuses the immune system, and T cells attack cardiac muscle fibers, inadvertently causing inflammation of the heart and other problems.

Within the last few years, two types of tests for chlamydia have been developed. The treatment for the disease is antibiotics, usually tetracycline, which can penetrate the eukaryotic plasma membrane to attack the bacterium. Any woman who experiences the symptoms associated with this STD or who is at risk of developing an STD should be tested for the presence of the chlamydia bacterium; otherwise, her fertility may be at risk.

### Learning Outcomes Review 28.6

Many human diseases are due to bacterial infection, including tuberculosis, streptococcal and staphylococcal infection, and sexually transmitted diseases. The causative agent of most peptic ulcers is *Helicobacter pylori,* an inhabitant of the digestive tract. Bacteria are responsible for many STDs, including gonorrhea, syphilis, and chlamydia. In many cases symptoms of infection disappear although the disease is still present, and all can have serious consequences if untreated, especially for women.

■ *Why is infection by most pathogens not fatal?*

## 28.7 Beneficial Prokaryotes

### Learning Outcomes

1. *Recognize the role of prokaryotes in the global cycling of elements.*
2. *Describe examples of bacterial/eukaryote symbiosis.*
3. *Explain how bacteria can be used for bioremediation.*

Prokaryotes were largely responsible for creating the current properties of the atmosphere and the soil through billions of years of their activity. Today, they still affect the Earth and human life in many important ways.

## Prokaryotes are involved in cycling important elements

Life on Earth is critically dependent on the cycling of chemical elements between organisms and the physical environments in which they live—that is, between the living and nonliving elements of ecosystems. Prokaryotes, algae, and fungi play many key roles in this chemical cycling, a process discussed in detail in chapter 58.

### Decomposition

The carbon, nitrogen, phosphorus, sulfur, and other atoms of biological systems all have come from the physical environment, and when organisms die and decay, these elements all return to it. The prokaryotes and fungi that carry out the decomposition portion of chemical cycles, releasing a dead organism's atoms to the environment, are called *decomposers.*

### Fixation

Other prokaryotes play important roles in fixation, the other half of chemical cycles, helping to return elements from inorganic forms to organic forms that heterotrophic organisms can use.

**Carbon.** The role of photosynthetic prokaryotes in fixing carbon is obvious. The organic compounds that plants, algae, and photosynthetic prokaryotes produce from $CO_2$ pass up through food chains to form the bodies of all the ecosystem's heterotrophs. Ancient cyanobacteria are thought to have added oxygen to the Earth's atmosphere as a by-product of their photosynthesis. Modern photosynthetic prokaryotes continue to contribute to the production of oxygen.

**Nitrogen.** Less obvious, but no less critical to life, is the role of prokaryotes in recycling nitrogen. The nitrogen in the Earth's atmosphere is in the form of $N_2$ gas. A triple covalent bond links the two nitrogen atoms and is not easy to break. Among the Earth's organisms, only a very few species of prokaryotes are able to accomplish this feat, reducing $N_2$ to ammonia ($NH_3$), which is used to build amino acids and other nitrogen-containing biological molecules. When the organisms that contain these molecules die, decomposers return nitrogen to the soil as ammonia. This is then converted to nitrate ($NO^{3-}$) by nitrifying bacteria, making nitrogen available for plants. The nitrate can also be converted back into molecular nitrogen by *denitrifiers* that return the nitrogen to the atmosphere, completing the cycle.

To fix atmospheric nitrogen, prokaryotes employ an enzyme complex called nitrogenase, encoded by a set of genes called *nif* ("nitrogen fixation") genes. The nitrogenase complex is extremely sensitive to oxygen and is found in a wide range of free-living prokaryotes.

In aquatic environments, nitrogen fixation is carried out largely by cyanobacteria such as *Anabaena,* which forms long chains of cells. Because the nitrogen fixation process is strictly anaerobic, individual cyanobacteria cells may develop into *heterocysts,* specialized nitrogen-fixing cells impermeable to oxygen.

In soil, nitrogen fixation occurs in the roots of plants that harbor symbiotic colonies of nitrogen-fixing bacteria. These associations include *Rhizobium* (a genus of proteobacteria; see figure 28.5) with legumes, *Frankia* (an actinomycete) with many woody shrubs, and *Anabaena* with water ferns.

## Prokaryotes may live in symbiotic associations with eukaryotes

Many prokaryotes live in symbiotic association with eukaryotes. **Symbiosis** refers to the ecological relationship between different species that live in direct contact with each other. The symbiotic association of nitrogen-fixing bacteria with plant roots is an example of *mutualism*, a form of symbiosis in which both parties benefit. The bacteria supply the plant with useful nitrogen, and the plant supplies the bacteria with sugars and other organic nutrients (see chapter 39).

Many bacteria live symbiotically within the digestive tracts of animals, providing nutrients to their hosts. Cattle and other grazing mammals are unable to digest cellulose in the grass and plants they eat because they lack the required cellulase enzyme. Colonies of cellulase-producing bacteria inhabiting the gut allow cattle to digest their food (see chapter 48 for a fuller account). Similarly, humans maintain large colonies of bacteria in the large intestine that produce vitamins—particularly $B_{12}$ and K—that the body cannot make.

Many bacteria inhabit the outer surfaces of animals and plants without doing damage. These associations are examples of *commensalism*, in which one organism (the bacterium) receives benefits while the animal or plant is neither benefited nor harmed.

*Parasitism* is a form of symbiosis in which one member (in this case, the bacterium) benefits, and the other (the infected animal or plant) is harmed. Infection might be considered a form of parasitism.

## Bacteria are used in genetic engineering

Because the genetic code is universal, a gene from a human can be inserted into a bacterial cell, and the bacterium produces a human protein. The use of bacteria in genetic engineering was discussed in chapter 17, and it is a large part of modern molecular biology.

In addition to the production of pharmaceutical agents such as insulin, discussed in chapter 17, applying genetic engineering methods to produce improved strains of bacteria for commercial use holds promise for the future. Bacteria are now widely used as "biofactories" in the commercial production of a variety of enzymes, vitamins, and antibiotics. Immense cultures of bacteria, often genetically modified to enhance performance, are used to produce commercial acetone and other industrially important compounds.

## Bacteria can be used for bioremediation

The use of organisms to remove pollutants from water, air, and soil is called *bioremediation*. The normal functioning of sewage treatment plants depends on the activity of microorganisms. In sewage treatment plants, the solid matter from raw sewage is broken down by bacteria and archaea naturally present in the sewage. The end product, methane gas ($CH_4$) is often used as an energy source to heat the treatment plant.

Biostimulation, that is, the addition of nutrients such as nitrogen and phosphorus sources, has been used to encourage the growth of naturally occurring microbes that can degrade crude oil spills. This approach was used successfully to clean up the Alaskan shoreline after the crude oil spill of the Exxon Valdez in 1998. Similarly, biostimulation has been used to encourage the growth of naturally occurring microbial flora in contaminated groundwater. Current efforts include those concentrated on the use of endogenous microbes such as *Geobacter* (see figure 28.5) to eliminate radioactive uranium from groundwater contaminated during the cold war.

Chlorinated compounds released into the environment by a variety of sources are another serious pollutant. Some bacteria can actually use these compounds for energy by performing reductive dehalogenation that is linked to electron transport, a process termed *halorespiration*. Although still at the development stage, the use of such bacteria to remove halogenated compounds from toxic waste holds great promise.

### Learning Outcomes Review 28.7

Prokaryotes are vital to ecosystems for both recycling elements and fixation, or making elements available in organic form. Bacteria are involved in fixation of both carbon and nitrogen and are the only organisms that can fix nitrogen. These nitrogen-fixing bacteria may live in symbiotic association with plants. Bacteria are a key component of waste treatment, and they are also being used in bioremediation to remove toxic compounds introduced into the environment.

■ *Does the information about nitrogen fixation shed any light on the practice of crop rotation?*

## Chapter Review

### 28.1 The First Cells

*Microfossils indicate that the first cells were probably prokaryotic.*
The oldest microfossils are 3.5 billion years old. Stromatolites, a combination of sedimentary deposits and precipitated materials, are as old as 2.7 billion years.

*Isotopic data indicate that carbon fixation is an ancient process.*
Relatively higher levels of carbon-12 in fossils compared with neighboring rocks indicate the action of ancient carbon fixation.

*Some hydrocarbons found in ancient rocks may have biological origins.*
Biomarkers such as lipids indicate that cyanobacteria are at least 2.7 billion years old.

### 28.2 Prokaryotic Diversity

*Prokaryotes are fundamentally different from eukaryotes.*
Prokaryotic features include unicellularity, small circular DNA, division by binary fission, lack of internal compartmentalization, a singular flagellum, and metabolic diversity.

**Despite similarities, bacteria and archaea differ fundamentally.**

Bacteria and archaea differ in four key areas: plasma membranes, cell walls, DNA replication, and gene expression.

Archaeal lipids have ether instead of ester linkages and can form tetraether monolayers. The cell walls of bacteria contain peptidoglycans, but those of archaea do not.

Both bacteria and archaea DNA have a single replication origin, but the origin and the replication proteins are different. Archaeal initiation of DNA replication and RNA polymerases are more like those of eukaryotes.

**Most prokaryotes have not been characterized.**

Nine clades of prokaryotes have been found so far, but many bacteria have not been studied (see figure 28.5).

## 28.3 Prokaryotic Cell Structure

**Prokaryotes have three basic forms: rods, cocci, and spirals.**

**Prokaryotes have a tough cell wall and other external structures.**

Bacteria are classified as gram-positive or gram-negative based on the Gram stain (see figure 28.6). Gram-positive bacteria have a thick peptidoglycan layer in the cell wall that contains teichoic acid (see figure 28.7). Gram-negative bacteria have a thin peptidoglycan layer and an outer membrane containing lipopolysaccharides in their cell wall (see figure 28.7).

Some bacteria have a gelatinous layer, the capsule, enabling the bacterium to adhere to surfaces and evade an immune response.

Many bacteria have a slender, rigid, helical flagellum composed of flagellin, which can rotate to drive movement (see figure 28.8). Some bacteria have hairlike pili that have roles in adhesion and exchange of genetic information.

Some bacteria form highly resistant endospores in response to environmental stress.

**The interior of prokaryotic cells is organized.**

In prokaryotes, invaginated regions of the plasma membrane function in respiration and photosynthesis. The nucleoid region contains a compacted circular DNA with no bounding membrane.

Prokaryotic ribosomes are smaller than those of eukaryotes and some antibiotics work by binding to these ribosomes, blocking protein synthesis.

## 28.4 Prokaryotic Genetics

**Conjugation depends on the presence of a conjugative plasmid.**

DNA can be exchanged by conjugation (see figure 28.10), which depends on the presence of conjugative plasmids like the F plasmid in *E coli*. The F$^+$ donor cell transfers the F plasmid to the F$^-$ recipient cell.

The F plasmid can also integrate into the bacterial genome. Excision may be imprecise, so that the F plasmid carries genetic information from the host.

**Viruses transfer DNA by transduction (see figure 28.13).**

Generalized transduction occurs when viruses package host DNA and transfer it on subsequent infection. Specialized transduction is limited to lysogenic phage.

**Transformation is the uptake of DNA directly from the environment (see figure 28.14).**

Transformation occurs when cells take up DNA from the surrounding medium. It can be induced artificially in the laboratory.

**Antibiotic resistance can be transferred by resistance plasmids.**

R plasmids have played a significant role in the appearance of strains resistant to antibiodies, such as *S. aureus* and *E. coli* O157:H7.

**Variation can also arise by mutation.**

Mutations can occur spontaneously in bacteria due to radiation, UV, and various chemicals.

## 28.5 Prokaryotic Metabolism

**Prokaryotes acquire carbon and energy in four basic ways.**

Photoautotrophs carry out photosynthesis and obtain carbon from carbon dioxide. Chemolithoautotrophs obtain energy by oxidizing inorganic substances. Photoheterotrophs use light for energy but obtain carbon from organic molecules. Chemoheterotrophs, the largest group, obtain carbon and energy from organic molecules.

**Some bacteria can attack other cells directly.**

Some bacteria release proteins through their cell walls, and these proteins may transfer other, virulent proteins into eukaryotic cells.

**Bacteria are costly plant pathogens.**

Gram-negative bacteria known as pseudomonads are responsible for most plant diseases.

## 28.6 Human Bacterial Disease (see table 28.1)

Bacterial diseases are spread through mucus or saliva droplets, contaminated food and water, and insect vectors.

**Tuberculosis has infected humans for all of recorded history.**

Tuberculosis continues to be a major public health problem. Treatment requires a long course of antibiotics.

**Bacterial biofilms are involved in tooth decay.**

**Bacteria can cause ulcers.**

Most stomach ulcers are caused by infection with *Helicobacter pylori*.

**Many sexually transmitted diseases are bacterial.**

The potentially dangerous sexually transmitted diseases gonorrhea, syphilis, and chlamydia are caused by bacteria.

## 28.7 Beneficial Prokaryotes

**Prokaryotes are involved in cycling important elements.**

Prokaryotes are involved in the recycling of carbon and nitrogen; only bacteria can fix nitrogen.

**Prokaryotes may live in symbiotic associations with eukaryotes.**

**Bacteria are used in genetic engineering.**

Genetically engineered prokaryotes can be used to produce human pharmaceutical agents and other useful products.

**Bacteria can be used for bioremediation.**

# Review Questions

## UNDERSTAND

1. Which of the following would be an example of a biomarker?
   a. A microfossil found in a meteorite
   b. A hydrocarbon found in an ancient rock layer
   c. An area that is high in carbon-12 concentration in a rock layer
   d. A newly discovered formation of stromatolites

2. A cell that can use energy from the sun, and $CO_2$ as a carbon source is a
   a. photoautotroph.        c. photoheterotroph.
   b. chemoautotroph.        d. chemoheterotroph.

3. Gram-positive (+) and gram-negative (–) bacteria are characterized by differences in
   a. the cell wall: gram+ have peptidoglycan, gram– have pseudo-peptidoglycan.
   b. the plasma membrane: gram+ have ester-linked lipids, gram– have ether-linked lipids.
   c. the cell wall: gram+ have a thick layer of peptidoglycan and gram– have an outer membrane.
   d. chromosomal structure: gram+ have circular chromosomes, gram– have linear chromosomes.

4. Which of the following characteristics is unique to the archaea?
   a. A fluid mosaic model of plasma membrane structure
   b. The use of an RNA polymerase during gene expression
   c. Ether-linked phospholipids
   d. A single origin of DNA replication

5. The horizontal transfer of DNA using a plasmid is an example of
   a. generalized transduction.
   b. binary fission.
   c. transformation.
   d. conjugation.

6. The disease tuberculosis is
   a. caused by a bacterial pathogen.
   b. an emerging disease that is now worldwide.
   c. caused by a viral pathogen.
   d. not treatable with antibiotics.

7. Prokaryotes participate in the global cycling of
   a. proteins and nucleic acids.
   b. carbon and nitrogen.
   c. carbohydrates and lipids.
   d. all of the above.

## APPLY

1. Which of the following is typically not associated with a prokaryote?
   a. Horizontal transfer of genetic information
   b. A lack of internal compartmentalization
   c. Multiple, linear chromosomes
   d. A cell size of 1 μm

2. The mechanisms of DNA exchange in prokaryotes share the feature of
   a. vertical transmission of information.
   b. horizontal transfer of information.
   c. requiring cell contact.
   d. the presence of a plasmid in one cell.

3. The cell wall in both gram-positive and gram-negative cells is
   a. composed of phospholipids.
   b. a target for antibiotics that affect peptidoglycan synthesis.
   c. composed of peptidoglycan.
   d. surrounded by a membrane.

4. The three domains of life
   a. represent variations of the same basic cell type.
   b. include two different basic cell types.
   c. consist of three different basic cell types.
   d. describe current cells but say nothing about their history.

5. Ulcers and tooth decay do not appear related, but in fact both
   a. are due to eating particular kinds of foods.
   b. are caused by viral infection.
   c. are caused by environmental factors.
   d. can be due to bacterial infection.

6. Bacteria lack independent internal membrane systems, but are able to perform photosynthesis and respiration, both of which use membranes. They are able to perform these functions because
   a. they actually have internal membranes, but only for these functions.
   b. invaginations of the plasma membrane can provide an internal membrane surface.
   c. they take place outside of the cell between the membrane and the cell wall.
   d. they use protein-based structures to take the place of internal membraes.

7. Plants cannot fix nitrogen, yet some plants do not need nitrogen from the soil. This is because
   a. of a symbiotic association with a bacterium that can fix nitrogen.
   b. these plants are the exceptions that can fix nitrogen.
   c. they have been infected by a parasitic virus that can fix nitrogen.
   d. they are able to obtain nitrogen from the air.

## SYNTHESIZE

1. If a new form of carbon fixation was discovered that was not biased toward carbon-12, would this affect our analysis of the earliest evidence for life?

2. Frederick Griffith's experiments (see chapter 14) played an important role in showing that DNA is the genetic material. Griffith showed that dead virulent bacteria mixed with live nonvirulent bacteria could cause pneumonia in mice. Live rough bacteria could also be cultured from the infected mice. The difference between the two strains is a polysaccharide capsule found in the smooth strain. Given what you have learned in this chapter, how would you explain these observations?

3. In the 1960s, it was common practice to prescribe multiple antibiotics to fight bacterial infections. It is also often the case that patients do not always take the entire "course" of their antibiotics. Antibiotic resistance genes are often found on conjugative plasmids. How do these factors affect the evolution of antibiotic resistance and of resistance to multiple antibiotics in particular?

4. Soil-based nitrogen-fixing bacteria appear to be highly vulnerable to exposure to UV radiation. Suppose that the ozone level continues to be depleted, what are the long-term effects on the planet?

Chapter 29

# Protists

## Chapter Outline

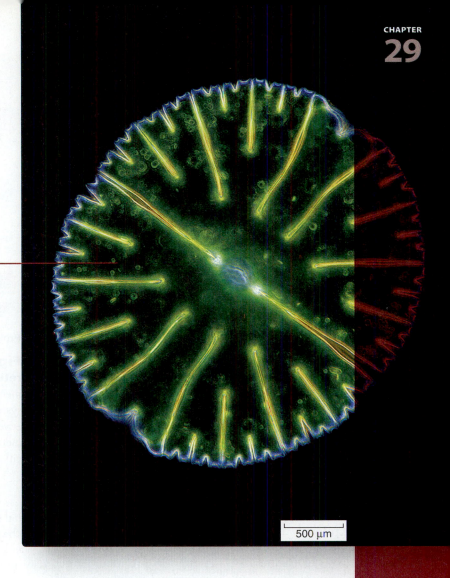

500 μm

## Introduction

*For more than half of the long history of life on Earth, all life was microscopic. The biggest organisms that existed for over 2 billion years were single-celled bacteria fewer than 6 μm thick. These prokaryotes lacked internal membranes, except for invaginations of surface membranes in photosynthetic bacteria.*

*The first evidence of a different kind of organism is found in tiny fossils in rock 1.5 billion years old. These fossil cells are much larger than bacteria (up to 10 times larger) and contain internal membranes and what appear to be small, membrane-bounded structures. The complexity and diversity of form among these single cells is astonishing. The step from relatively simple to quite complex cells marks one of the most important events in the evolution of life, the appearance of a new kind of organism, the eukaryote. Eukaryotes that are clearly not animals, plants, or fungi have been lumped together and called protists.*

# 29.1 Eukaryotic Origins and Endosymbiosis

## Learning Outcomes

1. List the defining features of eukaryotes.
2. Define endosymbiosis and explain how it relates to the evolution of mitochondria and chloroplasts.
3. Explain why mitosis is not believed to have evolved all at once.

Eukaryotic cells are distinguished from prokaryotes by the presence of a cytoskeleton and compartmentalization that includes a nuclear envelope and organelles. The exact sequence of events that led to large, complex eukaryotic cells is unknown, but several key events are agreed upon. Loss of a rigid cell wall allowed membranes to fold inward, increasing surface area. Membrane flexibility also made it possible for one cell to engulf another.

## Fossil evidence dates the origins of eukaryotes

Indirect chemical traces hint that eukaryotes may go as far back as 2.7 billion years, but no fossils as yet support such an early appearance. In rocks about 1.5 billion years old, we begin to see the first microfossils that are noticeably different in appearance from the earlier, simpler forms, none of which were more than 6 μm in diameter (figure 29.1). These cells are much larger than those of prokaryotes and have internal membranes and thicker walls.

These early fossils mark a major event in the evolution of life: A new kind of organism had appeared. These new cells are called eukaryotes, from the Greek words meaning "true nucleus," because they possess an internal structure called a nucleus. All organisms other than prokaryotes are eukaryotes.

**Figure 29.1 Early eukaryotic fossil.** Fossil algae that lived in Siberia 1 BYA.

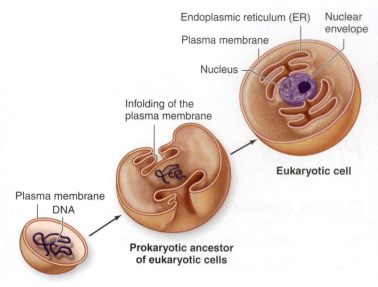

**Figure 29.2 Origin of the nucleus and endoplasmic reticulum.** Many prokaryotes today have infoldings of the plasma membrane (see also figure 27.6). The eukaryotic internal membrane system, called the endoplasmic reticulum (ER), and the nuclear envelope may have evolved from such infoldings of the plasma membrane, encasing the DNA of prokaryotic cells that gave rise to eukaryotic cells.

In the sections that follow, the origins of eukaryotic internal structure are considered. Keep in mind that, as discussed in chapter 24, horizontal gene transfer occurred frequently while eukaryotic cells were evolving. Eukaryotic cells evolved not only through horizontal gene transfer, but through infolding of membranes and engulfing other cells. Today's eukaryotic cell is the result of cutting and pasting of DNA and organelles from different species.

## The nucleus and ER arose from membrane infoldings

Many prokaryotes have infoldings of their outer membranes extending into the cytoplasm that serve as passageways to the surface. The network of internal membranes in eukaryotes is called the endoplasmic reticulum (ER), and the nuclear envelope, an extension of the ER network that isolates and protects the nucleus, is thought to have evolved from such infoldings (figure 29.2).

## Mitochondria evolved from engulfed aerobic bacteria

Bacteria that live within other cells and perform specific functions for their host cells are called *endosymbiotic bacteria*. Their widespread presence in nature led biologist Lynn Margulis in the early 1970s to champion the theory of endosymbiosis, which was first proposed by Konstantin

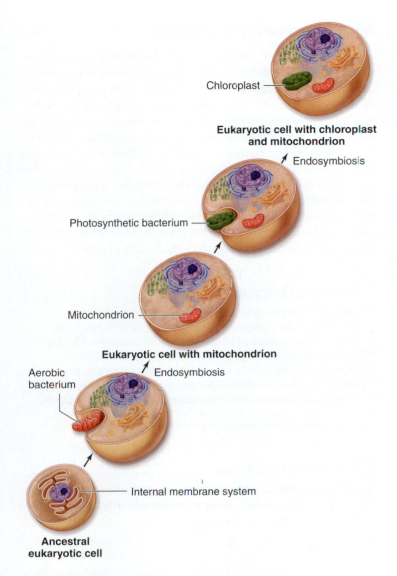

Chloroplast

**Eukaryotic cell with chloroplast and mitochondrion**

↗ Endosymbiosis

Photosynthetic bacterium

Mitochondrion

**Eukaryotic cell with mitochondrion**

Aerobic bacterium    ↗ Endosymbiosis

Internal membrane system

**Ancestral eukaryotic cell**

**Figure 29.3  The theory of endosymbiosis.** Scientists propose that ancestral eukaryotic cells, which already had an internal system of membranes, engulfed aerobic bacteria, which then became mitochondria in the eukaryotic cell. Chloroplasts also originated this way, with eukaryotic cells engulfing photosynthetic bacteria.

Mereschkowsky in 1905. Endosymbiosis means living together in close association.

Endosymbiosis, a concept that is now widely accepted, suggests that a critical stage in the evolution of eukaryotic cells involved endosymbiotic relationships with prokaryotic organisms. According to this theory, energy-producing bacteria may have come to reside within larger bacteria, eventually evolving into what we now know as mitochondria (figure 29.3). Possibly the original host cell was anaerobic with hydrogen-dependent metabolic pathways. The symbiont had a form of respiration that produced $H_2$. The host depended on the symbiont for $H_2$ under anaerobic conditions and was able later to adapt to an $O_2$-rich atmosphere using the symbiont's respiratory pathways.

## Chloroplasts evolved from engulfed photosynthetic bacteria

Photosynthetic bacteria may have come to live within other larger bacteria, leading to the evolution of chloroplasts, the photosynthetic organelles of plants and algae (see figure 29.3). The history of chloroplast evolution is an example of the care that must be taken in phylogenetic studies. All chloroplasts are likely derived from a single line of cyanobacteria, but the organisms that host these chloroplasts are not monophyletic. This apparent paradox is resolved by considering the possibility of secondary, and even tertiary endosymbiosis. Figure 26.8 explains how red and green algae both obtained their chloroplasts by engulfing photosynthetic cyanobacteria. The brown algae most likely obtained their chloroplasts by engulfing one or more red algae, a process called **secondary endosymbiosis** (figure 29.4). (As mentioned, green algae are considered in the following chapter even though they are protists.)

A phylogenetic tree based only on chloroplast gene sequences from red and green algae reveals an incredibly close evolutionary relationship. This tree is misleading, however, because it is not possible to tell just from these data how

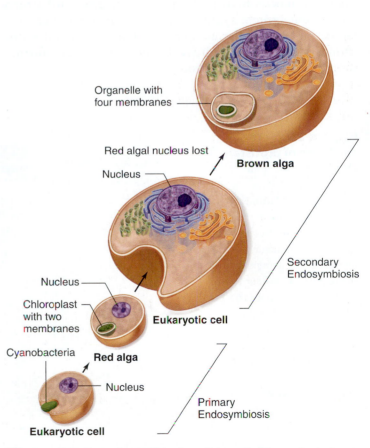

Organelle with four membranes

Red algal nucleus lost

Nucleus

**Brown alga**

Nucleus

Chloroplast with two membranes

**Eukaryotic cell**

Cyanobacteria    **Red alga**

Nucleus

Secondary Endosymbiosis

Primary Endosymbiosis

**Eukaryotic cell**

**Figure 29.4  Endosymbiotic origins of chloroplasts in red and brown algae.**

much the two algal lines had diverged at the time they engulfed the same line of cyanobacteria. Morphological and chemical traits are more helpful than chloroplast gene sequences in sorting out red and green algal relations. More data and analyses are still needed to confirm the position of red algae in figure 29.5.

## Endosymbiosis is supported by a range of evidence

The fact that we now witness so many symbiotic relationships lends general support to the endosymbiotic theory. Even stronger support comes from the observation that present-day organelles such as mitochondria and chloroplasts contain their own DNA, which is remarkably similar to the DNA of bacteria in size and character. During the billion and a half years in which mitochondria have existed as endosymbionts within eukaryotic cells, most of their genes have been transferred to the chromosomes of the host cells—but not all. Each mitochondrion still has its own genome, a circular, closed molecule of DNA similar to that found in bacteria, on which are located genes encoding the essential proteins of oxidative metabolism. These genes are transcribed within the mitochondrion, using mitochondrial ribosomes that are smaller than those of eukaryotic cells, very much like bacterial ribosomes in size and structure. Many antibiotics that inhibit protein synthesis in bacteria also inhibit protein synthesis in mitochondria and chloroplasts, but not in the cytoplasm. Chloroplasts and mitochondria replicate via binary fission, not mitosis, further supporting bacterial origins.

## Mitosis evolved in eukaryotes

The mechanisms of mitosis and cytokinesis, now so common among eukaryotes, did not evolve all at once. Traces of very different, and possibly intermediate, mechanisms survive today in some of the eukaryotes. In fungi and in some groups of protists, for example, the nuclear membrane does not dissolve, as it does in plants, animals, and most other protists, and mitosis is confined to the nucleus. When mitosis is complete in these organisms, the nucleus divides into two daughter nuclei, and only then does the rest of the cell divide. We do not know whether mitosis without nuclear membrane dissolution represents an intermediate step on the evolutionary journey, or simply a different way of solving the same problem. We cannot see the interiors of dividing cells well enough in fossils to be able to trace the history of mitosis.

### Learning Outcomes Review 29.1

Eukaryotes are organisms that contain a nucleus and other membrane-bounded organelles. Endoplasmic reticulum and the nuclear membrane are believed to have evolved from infoldings of the outer membranes. According to the endosymbiont theory, mitochondria and chloroplasts evolved from engulfed bacteria that remained intact. Mitochondria, chloroplasts, and centrioles have their own DNA, which is similar to that of prokaryotes. Mitosis did not evolve all at once; different mechanisms persist in different organisms.

■ *What evidence supports the endosymbiont theory?*

### Inquiry question

**?** How could you distinguish between primary and secondary endosymbiosis by looking at micrographs of cells with chloroplasts?

**Figure 29.5 The challenge of protistan classification.** Our understanding of the evolutionary relationships among protists is currently in flux. The most recent data support seven major, monophyletic groups within the protists. Consider this a working model, not fact. The green algae (Chlorophyta) are not truly monophyletic in that another branch, Streptophyta, gave rise to the land plants. Protist lineages are shaded in blue.

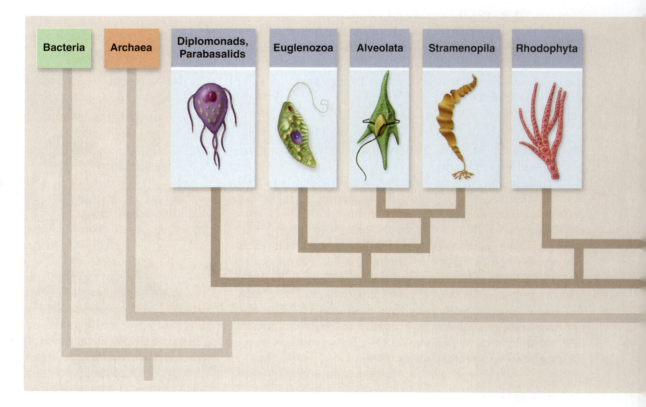

## 29.2 Defining Protists

### Learning Outcomes

1. Describe the feature that distinguishes protists from other eukaryotes.
2. Define monophyletic.
3. Describe the various kinds of protist cell surfaces.
4. List the two main means of locomotion used by protists.
5. Distinguish between phototrophs, phagotrophs, and osmotrophs.

*Protists* are the most diverse of the four kingdoms in the domain Eukarya. Protists are united on the basis of a single negative characteristic: They are eukaryotes that are not fungi, plants, or animals. In all other respects, they vary considerably, with no uniting features. Many are unicellular, but numerous colonial and multicellular groups also exist. Most are microscopic, but some are as large as trees. They represent all symmetries and exhibit all types of nutrition. The origin of eukaryotes, which began with ancestral protists, is among the most significant events in the evolution of life.

### Protista is not monophyletic

One of the most important statements we can make about the kingdom Protista is that it is paraphyletic and not a kingdom at all; as a matter of convenience, single-celled eukaryotic organisms have typically been grouped together and called protists. This lumps 200,000 different and only distantly related forms together. The "single-kingdom" classification of the Protista is artificial and not representative of any evolutionary relationships. You may be wondering why biologists continue to refer to the protista as a kingdom and why we have a chapter devoted to the protists. While we wait for the evolutionary relationships among protists to be sorted out, lumping the protists together allows us to explore the biology of a number of fascinating eukaryotes that might otherwise disappear from the pages of your textbook.

### Monophyletic clades have been identified among the protists

Applications of a variety of molecular methods are providing insights into the relationships among protists. Many questions about how to classify the protists are being addressed with these techniques. Are protists best considered as several different kingdoms, each of equal rank with animals, plants, and fungi? Are some of the protists actually members of other kingdoms? While these questions continue to be debated, new information is becoming available concerning which organisms among the protists are most likely to be monophyletic.

In this chapter, we group the 15 major protist phyla into seven major monophyletic groups, based on our current understanding of phylogeny (figure 29.5). Although these lineages may change, this approach allows us to examine groups with many shared traits. Keep in mind that about 60 of the protist lineages cannot yet be placed on the tree of life with any confidence! Protists exemplify the challenges and excitement of the revolutionary changes in taxonomy and phylogeny we explored in chapter 26. Understanding the evolution of protists is key to understanding the origins of plants, fungi, and animals.

Because green algae and land plants form a monophyletic clade, the green algae are explored in more detail in the following chapter on plant diversity. The characteristics of green algae and land plants are best understood when considered in concert because of their shared evolutionary history. The remaining six monophyletic clades that are loosely called protists are examined in this chapter.

### Protist cell surfaces vary widely

Protists possess a varied array of cell surfaces. Some protists, such as amoebas, are surrounded only by their plasma membrane. All other protists have a plasma membrane with an extracellular matrix (ECM) deposited on the outside of the membrane. Some ECMs form strong cell walls; for instance, diatoms and foraminifera secrete glassy shells of silica.

Many protists with delicate surfaces are capable of surviving unfavorable environmental conditions. How do they manage to survive so well? They form cysts, which are dormant forms with resistant outer coverings in which cell metabolism is more or less completely shut down. Not all cysts are so sturdy, however. Vertebrate parasitic amoebas, for example, form cysts that are quite resistant to gastric acidity, but will not tolerate desiccation or high temperature.

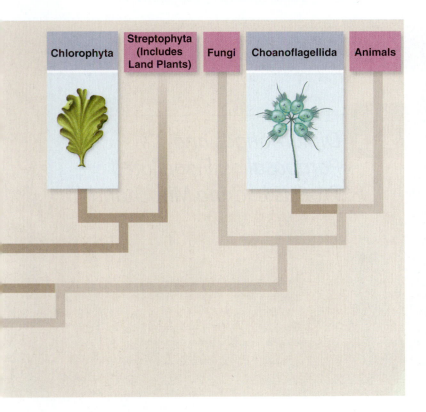

| Chlorophyta | Streptophyta (Includes Land Plants) | Fungi | Choanoflagellida | Animals |

## Protists have several means of locomotion

Movement in protists is also accomplished by diverse mechanisms. Protists move chiefly by either flagellar rotation or pseudopodial movement. Many protists wave one or more flagella to propel themselves through the water, and others use banks of short, flagella-like structures called cilia to create water currents for their feeding or propulsion. Pseudopods (Greek, meaning "false feet") are the chief means of locomotion among amoebas, whose pseudopods are large, blunt extensions of the cell body called lobopodia. Other related protists extend thin, branching protrusions called filopodia. Still other protists extend long, thin pseudopods called axopodia supported by axial rods of microtubules. Axopodia can be extended or retracted. Because the tips can adhere to adjacent surfaces, the cell can move by a rolling motion, shortening the axopodia in front and extending those in the rear.

## Protists have a range of nutritional strategies

Protists can be heterotrophic or autotrophic. Some autotrophic protists are photosynthetic and are called **phototrophs.** Others are heterotrophs that obtain energy from organic molecules synthesized by other organisms.

Among the heterotrophic protists are some called *phagotrophs*, which ingest visible particles of food by pulling them into intracellular vesicles called food vacuoles or phagosomes. Lysosomes fuse with the food vacuoles, introducing enzymes that digest the food particles within. Digested molecules are absorbed across the vacuolar membrane.

Protists that ingest food in soluble form are called *osmotrophs*. Another example of the protists' tremendous nutritional flexibility is seen in *mixotrophs*, protists that are both phototrophic and heterotrophic.

## Protists reproduce asexually and sexually

Protists typically reproduce asexually, although some have an obligate sexual reproductive phase and others undergo sexual reproduction at times of stress, including food shortages.

### Asexual reproduction

**Asexual reproduction** involves mitosis, but the process often differs from the mitosis in multicellular animals. For example, the nuclear membrane often persists throughout mitosis, with the microtubular spindle forming within it.

In some species, a cell simply splits into nearly equal halves after mitosis. Sometimes the daughter cell is considerably smaller than its parent and then grows to adult size—a type of cell division called **budding.** In *schizogony*, common among some protists, cell division is preceded by several nuclear divisions. This allows cytokinesis to produce several individuals almost simultaneously.

### Sexual reproduction

Most eukaryotic cells also possess the ability to reproduce sexually, something prokaryotes cannot do at all. Meiosis (see chapter 11) is a major evolutionary innovation that arose in ancestral protists and allows for the production of haploid cells from diploid cells. Sexual reproduction is the process of producing offspring by fertilization, the union of two haploid cells. The great advantage of sexual reproduction is that it allows for frequent genetic recombination, which generates the variation that is the starting point of evolution. Not all eukaryotes reproduce sexually, but most have the capacity to do so. The evolution of meiosis and sexual reproduction contributed to the tremendous explosion of diversity among the eukaryotes.

## Protists are the bridge to multicellularity

Diversity was also promoted by the development of *multicellularity*. Some single eukaryotic cells began living in association with others, in colonies. Eventually, individual members of the colony began to assume different duties, and the colony began to take on the characteristics of a single individual. Multicellularity has arisen many times among the eukaryotes. Practically every organism big enough to be seen with the unaided eye, including all animals and plants, is multicellular. The great advantage of multicellularity is that it fosters specialization; some cells devote all of their energies to one task, other cells to another. Few innovations have had as great an influence on the history of life as the specialization made possible by multicellularity.

### Learning Outcomes Review 29.2

A monophyletic group is one in which all members have a single common ancestor. Protista is paraphyletic, however, so it is not really a kingdom. The major protist phyla have been grouped into seven major monophyletic groups. All protists have plasma membranes, but other cell-surface components, such as deposited extracellular material (ECM), are highly variable. Protists mainly use flagella or pseudopodial movement to propel themselves. Phototrophic protists carry out photosynthesis; phagotrophs ingest food particles; and osmotrophs ingest dissolved nutrients. Sexual reproduction is common, but asexual reproduction also occurs in many groups. Multicellular organisms likely arose from colonial protists.

- **Why is Kingdom Protista considered to be a paraphyletic group?**
- **What would be the advantage of movement by pseudopodia?**

## 29.3 Diplomonads and Parabasalids: Flagellated Protists Lacking Mitochondria

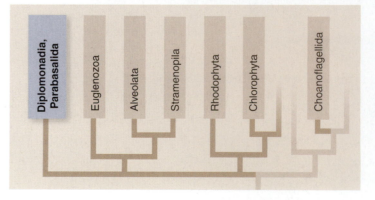

What was the first eukaryote like? We cannot be sure, but the *diplomonads* and the *parabasalids* likely had early eukaryotic ancestors. Although these groups have similar features, their differences put them into separate clades.

## Diplomonads have two nuclei

Diplomonads are unicellular and move with flagella. This group lacks mitochondria, but has two nuclei. *Giardia intestinalis* is an example of a diplomonad (figure 29.6). *Giardia* is a parasite that can pass from human to human via contaminated water and cause diarrhea. Mitochondrial genes are found in their nuclei, leading to the conclusion that *Giardia* evolved from aerobes. Electron micrographs of *Giardia* cells stained with mitochondrial-specific antibodies reveal degenerate mitochondria. Thus, *Giardia* is unlikely to represent an early protist.

## Parabasalids have undulating membranes

Parabasalids contain an intriguing array of species. Some live in the gut of termites and digest cellulose, the main component of the termite's wood-based diet. The symbiotic relationship is one layer more complex because these parabasalids have a symbiotic relationship with bacteria that also aid in the digestion of cellulose. The persistent activity of these three symbiotic organisms from three different kingdoms can lead to the collapse of a home built of wood or recycle tons of fallen trees in a forest. Another parabasalid, *Trichomonas vaginalis*, causes a sexually transmitted disease in humans.

Parabasalids have undulating membranes that assist in locomotion (figure 29.7). Like diplomonads, parabasalids also

**Figure 29.6** *Giardia intestinalis.* This parasitic diplomonad lacks a mitochondrion.

0.62 μm

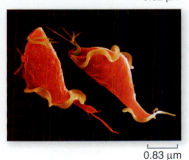

**Figure 29.7** **Undulating membrane characteristic of parabasalids.** Vaginitis can be caused by this parasite species, *Trichomonas vaginalis.*

0.83 μm

use flagella to move and lack mitochondria. The lack of mitochondria in both groups is now believed to be a derived rather than an ancestral trait.

### Learning Outcomes Review 29.3

The ancestors of diplomonads and parabasalids are likely to be among the earliest eukaryotes. Diplomonads lack mitochondria but may contain mitochondrial genes. They are unicellular, have two nuclei, and move with flagella; an example is *Giardia*. Parabasalids also lack mitochondria and use flagella and undulating membranes for locomotion; an example is *Trichomonas*.

■ *In what type of habitat would it be useful to use undulating membranes for locomotion?*

## 29.4 Euglenozoa: A Diverse Group in Which Some Members Have Chloroplasts

### Learning Outcomes

1. *Explain why Euglenozoa cannot be classified as either plants or animals.*
2. *Describe the distinguishing feature of kinetoplastids.*

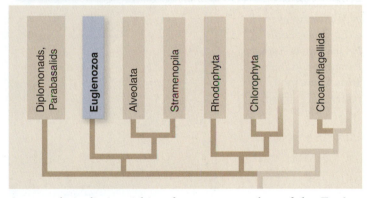

Among their distinguishing features, a number of the *Euglenozoa* have acquired chloroplasts through endosymbiosis. None of the algae are closely related to Euglenozoa, a reminder that endosymbiosis is widespread.

## Euglenoids are free-living eukaryotes with anterior flagella

**Euglenoids** diverged early and were among the earliest free-living eukaryotes to possess mitochondria. Euglenoids clearly illustrate the impossibility of distinguishing "plants" from "animals" among the protists. About one-third of the approximately 40 genera of euglenoids have chloroplasts and are fully autotrophic; the others lack chloroplasts, ingest their food, and are heterotrophic.

Some euglenoids with chloroplasts may become heterotrophic in the dark; the chloroplasts become small and nonfunctional. If they are put back in the light, they may become green within a few hours. Photosynthetic euglenoids may sometimes feed on dissolved or particulate food.

Individual euglenoids range from 10 to 500 μm long and vary greatly in form. Interlocking proteinaceous strips arranged in a helical pattern form a flexible structure called the *pellicle*, which lies within the plasma membrane of the euglenoids. Because its pellicle is flexible, a euglenoid is able to change its shape.

Reproduction in this phylum occurs by mitotic cell division. The nuclear envelope remains intact throughout the process of mitosis. No sexual reproduction is known to occur in this group.

### Euglena, the best known euglenoid

In *Euglena* (figure 29.8), the genus for which the phylum is named, two flagella are attached at the base of a flask-shaped opening called the *reservoir*, which is located at the anterior end of the cell. One of the flagella is long and has a row of very fine, short, hairlike projections along one side. A second, shorter flagellum is located within the reservoir but does not emerge from it. Contractile vacuoles collect excess water from all parts of the organism and empty it into the reservoir, which apparently helps regulate the osmotic pressure within the organism. The stigma, which also occurs in the green algae (phylum Chlorophyta), helps these photosynthetic organisms move toward light.

Cells of *Euglena* contain numerous small chloroplasts. These chloroplasts, like those of the green algae and plants, contain chlorophylls *a* and *b*, together with carotenoids. Although the chloroplasts of euglenoids differ somewhat in structure from those of green algae, they probably had a common origin. *Euglena's* photosynthetic pigments are light-sensitive (figure 29.9). It seems likely that euglenoid chloroplasts ultimately evolved from a symbiotic relationship through ingestion of green algae. Recent phylogenetic evidence indicates that *Euglena* had multiple origins within the Euglenoids, and the concept of a single *Euglena* genus is now being debated.

## Kinetoplastids are parasitic

A second major group within the Euglenozoa is the *kinetoplastids*. The name kinetoplastid refers to a unique, single mitochondrion in each cell. The mitochondria have two types of DNA: minicircles and maxicircles. (Remember that prokaryotes have circular DNA, and mitochondria had prokaryotic origins.) This mitochondrial DNA is responsible for very rapid glycolysis and also for an unusual kind of editing of the RNA by guide RNAs encoded in the minicircles.

### Trypanosomes: Disease-causing kinetoplastids

Parasitism has evolved multiple times within the kinetoplastids. Trypanosomes are a group of kinetoplastids that cause many serious human diseases, the most familiar being trypanosomiasis, also known as African sleeping sickness, which causes extreme lethargy and fatigue (figure 29.10).

Leishmaniasis, which is transmitted by sand flies, is a trypanosomic disease that causes skin sores and in some cases can affect internal organs, leading to death. About 1.5 million new cases are reported each year. The rise in leishmaniasis in South America correlates with the move of infected individuals from rural to urban environments, where there is a greater chance of spreading the parasite.

Chagas disease is caused by *Trypanosoma cruzi*. At least 90 million people, from the southern United States to Argentina, are at risk of contracting *T. cruzi* from small wild mammals that carry the parasite and can spread it to other mammals and humans through skin contact with urine and feces. Blood transfusions have also increased the spread of the infection. Chagas disease can lead to severe cardiac and digestive problems in humans and domestic animals, but it appears to be tolerated in the wild mammals.

Control is especially difficult because of the unique attributes of these organisms. For example, tsetse fly-transmitted trypanosomes have evolved an elaborate genetic mechanism for repeatedly changing the antigenic nature of their protective glycoprotein coat, thus dodging the antibodies their hosts produce against them (see chapter 52). Only a single one out of some 1000 variable-surface glycoprotein (VSG) genes is expressed at a time. A VSG gene is usually duplicated and moved to 1 of about 20 expression sites near the telomere where it is transcribed. Only one expression site is transcribed at a time.

**Figure 29.8**
**Euglenoids.**
*a.* Micrograph of *Euglena gracilis.*
*b.* Diagram of *Euglena.* Paramylon granules are areas where food reserves are stored.

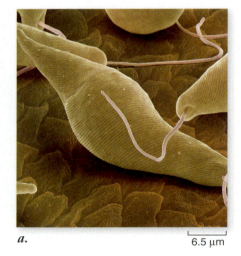
*a.*                                          6.5 μm

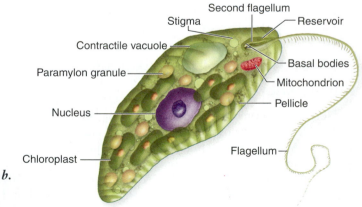

Second flagellum
Stigma
Reservoir
Contractile vacuole
Basal bodies
Paramylon granule
Mitochondrion
Pellicle
Nucleus
Flagellum
Chloroplast
*b.*

**Hypothesis:** Euglena *cells do not retain photosynthetic pigments in a dark environment.*

**Prediction:** *Photosynthetic pigments will be degraded when light-grown* Euglena *cells are transferred to the dark and new pigment will not be produced.*

**Test:** *Grow* Euglena *under normal light conditions. Transfer the culture to two flasks. Take a sample from each flask and measure the amount of photosynthetic pigments in each. Maintain one flask in the light and transfer the other to the dark. After several days, extract the photosynthetic pigments from each flask, and compare amounts with each other and with initial levels.*

Grow culture of *Euglena* under light.

Partition into two flasks.

Take a sample from each flask and quantify photosynthetic pigment.

Put one flask in dark, and expose the other to light.

Allow growth for several days.

Quantify photosynthetic pigment in each flask.

**Result:** *Photosynthetic pigment levels are lower in the dark-grown flask than in the light-grown one. Pigment levels in the dark-grown flask are lower than at the beginning of the experiment. Pigment levels in the light-grown flask are unchanged.*

**Conclusion:** *The hypothesis is supported. Maintenance of* Euglena *in the dark resulted in a loss of photosynthetic pigment. Pigments were degraded in the dark-grown flask.*

**Further Experiments:** *Transfer dark-grown flasks back to the light and measure changes in pigment levels over time. Are original pigment levels restored after growth in light?*

**Figure 29.9** **Effect of light on *Euglena* photosynthetic pigments.**

In the guts of the flies that spread them, trypanosomes are noninfective. When they are ready to transfer to the skin or bloodstream of their host, trypanosomes migrate to the salivary glands and acquire the thick coat of glycoprotein antigens that protect them from the host's antibodies. Later, when they are taken up by a tsetse fly, the trypanosomes again shed their coats.

The production of vaccines against such a system is complex, but tests are under way. Releasing sterilized flies to impede the reproduction of populations is another technique being tried to control the fly population. Traps made of dark cloth and scented like cows, but poisoned with insecticides, have likewise proved effective.

The recent sequencing of the genomes of the three kinetoplastids described earlier revealed a core of common genes in all three, as described in chapter 24. The devastating toll of all three on human life could be alleviated by the development of a single drug targeted at one or more of the core proteins shared by the three parasites.

---

**Learning Outcomes Review 29.4**

The Euglenozoa were among the earliest protists to contain mitochondria. This group contains phototrophs and heterotrophs. Some members have chloroplasts that remain nonfunctional unless light is present, and some phototrophs may feed if food particles are present. The kinetoplastids contain a single mitochondrion with two types of DNA and the ability to edit RNA with RNA guides. Trypanosomes are disease-causing kinetoplastids.

■  *How does a contractile vacuole regulate osmotic pressure in a Euglena cell?*

---

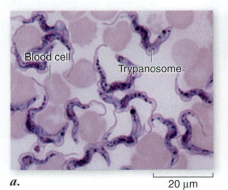

Blood cell

Trypanosome

*a.*                    20 μm

*b.*

**Figure 29.10** **A kinetoplastid.**
*a. Trypanosoma* among red blood cells. The nuclei (dark-staining bodies), anterior flagella, and undulating, changeable shape of the trypanosomes are visible in this photomicrograph. *b.* The tsetse fly, shown here sucking blood from a human arm, can carry trypanosomes.

# 29.5 Alveolata: Protists with Submembrane Vesicles

### Learning Outcomes

1. Identify the distinguishing feature of the members of Alveolata.
2. Describe the swimming motion of a dinoflagellate.
3. Explain the function of the apical complex in Apicomplexans.

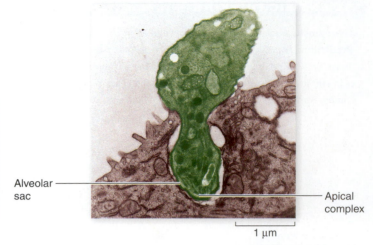

Alveolar sac — Apical complex

1 µm

**Figure 29.11** **Alveoli are a continuum of vesicles just below the plasma membrane of dinoflagellates, apicomplexans, and ciliates.** The apical complex of apicomplexans forces the parasite into host cells.

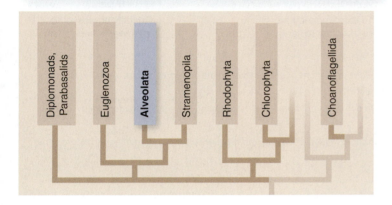

Diplomonads, Parabasalids | Euglenozoa | Alveolata | Stramenopila | Rhodophyta | Chlorophyta | Choanoflagellida

Members of the **Alveolata** include the *dinoflagellates*, *apicomplexans*, and *ciliates*, all of which have a common lineage but diverse modes of locomotion. One common trait is the presence of flattened vesicles called alveoli (hence the name alveolata) stacked in a continuous layer below their plasma membranes (figure 29.11). The alveoli may function in membrane transport, similar to Golgi bodies.

## Dinoflagellates are photosynthesizers with distinctive features

Most dinoflagellates are photosynthetic unicells with two flagella. Dinoflagellates live in both marine and freshwater environments. Some dinoflagellates are luminous and contribute to the twinkling or flashing effects seen in the sea at night, especially in the tropics.

The flagella, protective coats, and biochemistry of dinoflagellates are distinctive, and the dinoflagellates do not appear to be directly related to any other phylum. Plates made of a cellulose-like material, often encrusted with silica, encase the dinoflagellate cells (figure 29.12). Grooves at the junctures of these plates usually house the flagella, one encircling the cell like a belt, and the other perpendicular to it. By beating in their grooves, these flagella cause the dinoflagellate to spin as it moves.

Most dinoflagellates have chlorophylls *a* and *c*, in addition to carotenoids, so that in the biochemistry of their chloroplasts, they resemble the diatoms and the brown algae. Possibly this lineage acquired such chloroplasts by forming endosymbiotic relationships with members of those groups.

### Red tide: Overgrowth of dinoflagellates

The poisonous and destructive "red tides" that occur frequently in coastal areas are often associated with great population explosions, or "blooms," of dinoflagellates, whose pigments color the water (figure 29.13). Red tides have a profound, detrimental effect on the fishing industry worldwide. Some 20 species of dinoflagellates produce powerful toxins that inhibit the diaphragm and cause respiratory failure in many vertebrates. When the toxic dinoflagellates are abundant, many fishes, birds, and marine mammals may die.

Although sexual reproduction does occur under starvation conditions, dinoflagellates reproduce primarily by asexual cell division. Asexual cell division relies on a unique form of mitosis in which the permanently condensed chromosomes divide within a permanent nuclear envelope. After the numerous chromosomes duplicate, the nucleus divides into two daughter nuclei.

Also, the dinoflagellate chromosome is unique among eukaryotes in that the DNA is not generally complexed with

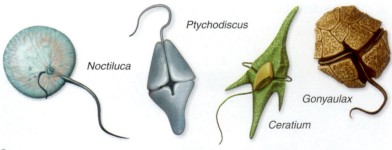

*Ptychodiscus*

*Noctiluca*

*Gonyaulax*

*Ceratium*

**Figure 29.12** **Some dinoflagellates.** *Noctiluca*, which lacks the heavy cellulose armor characteristic of most dinoflagellates, is one of the bioluminescent organisms that cause the waves to sparkle in warm seas. In the other three genera, the shorter, encircling flagellum is seen in its groove, with the longer one projecting away from the body of the dinoflagellate. (Not drawn to scale.)

## Apicomplexans include the malaria parasite

Apicomplexans are spore-forming parasites of animals. They are called apicomplexans because of a unique arrangement of fibrils, microtubules, vacuoles, and other cell organelles at one end of the cell, termed an *apical complex* (see figure 29.11). The apical complex is a cytoskeletal and secretory complex that enables the apicomplexan to invade its host. The best known apicomplexan is the malarial parasite *Plasmodium*. (The use of the genome sequence of the parasite and the mosquito that carries it is discussed in chapter 24.)

### Plasmodium and malaria

*Plasmodium* glides inside the red blood cells of its host with amoeboid-like contractility. Like other apicomplexans, *Plasmodium* has a complex life cycle involving sexual and asexual phases and alternation between different hosts, in this case mosquitoes (*Anopheles gambiae*) and humans (figure 29.14). Even though *Plasmodium* has mitochondria, it grows best in a low-$O_2$, high-$CO_2$ environment.

Efforts to eradicate malaria have focused on (1) eliminating the mosquito vectors; (2) developing drugs to poison the parasites that have entered the human body; and (3) developing vaccines. From the 1940s to the 1960s, wide-scale applications of dichlorodiphenyltrichloroethane (DDT) killed mosquitoes in the United States, Italy, Greece, and certain areas of Latin America. For a time, the worldwide elimination of malaria appeared possible. But this hope was soon crushed by the development of DDT-resistant mosquitoes in many regions. Furthermore, the use of DDT has had serious

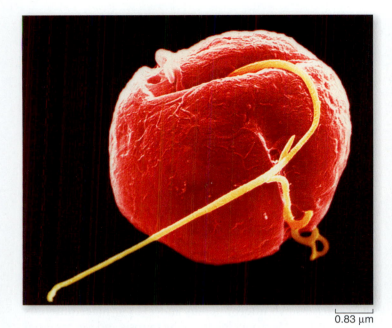

**Figure 29.13  Red tide.** Although small in size, huge populations of dinoflagellates, including this *Gymnopodium* species, can color the sea red and release toxins into the water.

0.83 μm

histone proteins. In all other eukaryotes, the chromosomal DNA is complexed with histones to form nucleosomes, structures that represent the first order of DNA packaging in the nucleus (chapter 10). How dinoflagellates maintain distinct chromosomes with a small amount of histones remains a mystery.

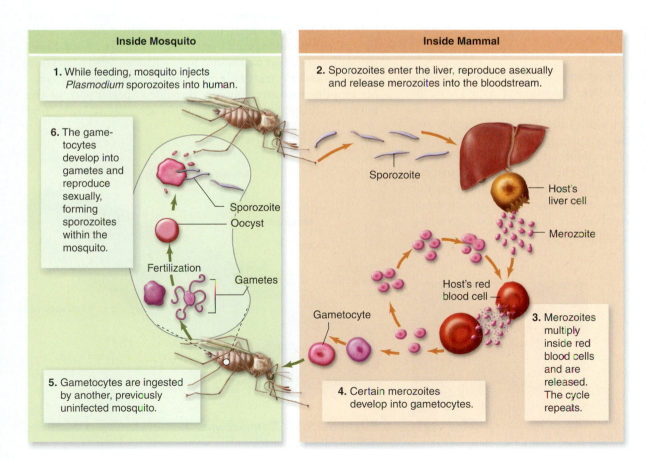

**Inside Mosquito**

**Inside Mammal**

1. While feeding, mosquito injects *Plasmodium* sporozoites into human.

2. Sporozoites enter the liver, reproduce asexually and release merozoites into the bloodstream.

6. The gametocytes develop into gametes and reproduce sexually, forming sporozoites within the mosquito.

Sporozoite

Oocyst

Fertilization

Gametes

Sporozoite

Host's liver cell

Merozoite

Host's red blood cell

Gametocyte

3. Merozoites multiply inside red blood cells and are released. The cycle repeats.

5. Gametocytes are ingested by another, previously uninfected mosquito.

4. Certain merozoites develop into gametocytes.

**Figure 29.14**
**The life cycle of *Plasmodium*.**
*Plasmodium*, the apicomplexan that causes malaria, has a complex life cycle that alternates between mosquitoes and mammals.

## Figure 29.15
**Gregarine entering a cell.**

200 μm

environmental consequences. In addition to the problems with resistant strains of mosquitoes, strains of *Plasmodium* have appeared that are resistant to the drugs historically used to kill them, including quinine.

An experimental vaccine containing a surface protein of one malaria-causing parasite, *P. falciparum*, seems to induce the immune system to defend against future infections. In tests, six out of seven vaccinated people did not get malaria after being bitten by mosquitoes that carried *P. falciparum*. Many are hopeful that this new vaccine may be able to fight malaria. (Chapter 24 contains a discussion of the genome sequences of both *Plasmodium* and its mosquito vector.)

### Gregarines

Gregarines are another group of apicomplexans that use their distinctive apical complex to attach themselves in the intestinal epithelium of arthropods, annelids, and mollusks. Most of the gregarine body, aside from the apical complex, is in the intestinal cavity, and nutrients appear to be obtained through the apicomplex attachment to the cell (figure 29.15).

### Toxoplasma

Using its apical complex, *Toxoplasma gondii* invades the epithelial cells of the human gut. Most individuals infected with the parasite mount an immune response, preventing any permanent damage. In the absence of a fully functional immune system, however, *Toxoplasma* can damage brain (figure 29.16), heart, and skeletal tissues, in addition to gut and lymph tissue, during extended infections. Individuals with AIDS are particularly susceptible to *Toxoplasma* infection. If a pregnant women touches a cat litter box, *Toxoplasma* parasites from the cat can, if ingested, cross the placental barrier and harm the developing fetus with an immature immune system.

## Figure 29.16
**Micrograph of a cyst filled with *Toxoplasma*.**
*Toxoplasma* can enter the brain and form cysts filled with slowly replicating parasites.

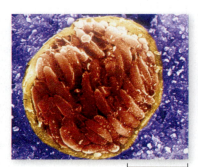

10 μm

## Ciliates are characterized by their mode of locomotion

As the name indicates, most ciliates feature large numbers of cilia (tiny beating hairs). These heterotrophic, unicellular protists are 10 to 3000 μm long. Their cilia are usually arranged either in longitudinal rows or in spirals around the cell. Cilia are anchored to microtubules beneath the plasma membrane (see chapter 5), and they beat in a coordinated fashion. In some groups, the cilia have specialized functions, becoming fused into sheets, spikes, and rods that may then function as mouths, paddles, teeth, or feet.

The ciliates have a pellicle, a tough but flexible outer covering, that enables them to squeeze through or move around obstacles.

### Micronucleus and macronucleus

All known ciliates have two different types of nuclei within their cells: a small **micronucleus** and a larger **macronucleus** (figure 29.17). Macronuclei divide by mitosis and are essential for the physiological function of the well-known ciliate *Paramecium*. The micronucleus of some individuals of *Tetrahymena pyriformis*, a common laboratory species, was experimentally removed in the 1930s, and their descendants continue to reproduce asexually to this day! *Paramecium*, however, is not immortal. The cells divide asexually for about 700 generations and then die if sexual reproduction has not occurred. The micronucleus in ciliates is evidently needed only for sexual reproduction.

### Vacuoles

Ciliates form vacuoles for ingesting food and regulating water balance. Food first enters the gullet, which in *Paramecium* is lined with cilia fused into a membrane (see figure 29.17). From the gullet, the food passes into food vacuoles, where enzymes and hydrochloric acid aid in its digestion. Afterward, the vacuole empties its waste contents through a special pore in the pellicle called the *cytoproct*, which is essentially an exocytotic

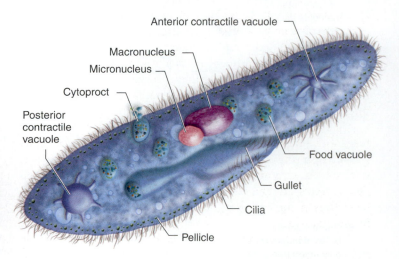

Anterior contractile vacuole

Macronucleus

Micronucleus

Cytoproct

Posterior contractile vacuole

Food vacuole

Gullet

Cilia

Pellicle

**Figure 29.17** *Paramecium.* The main features of this ciliate include cilia, two nuclei, and numerous specialized organelles.

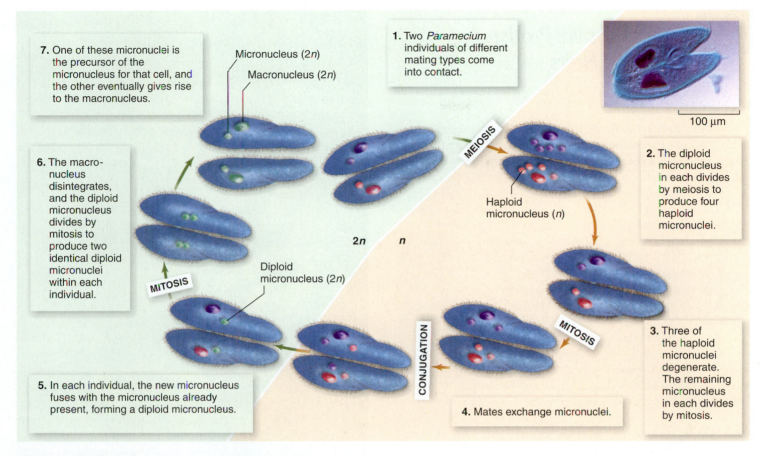

**7.** One of these micronuclei is the precursor of the micronucleus for that cell, and the other eventually gives rise to the macronucleus.

Micronucleus (2n)

Macronucleus (2n)

**1.** Two *Paramecium* individuals of different mating types come into contact.

100 µm

MEIOSIS

**6.** The macro-nucleus disintegrates, and the diploid micronucleus divides by mitosis to produce two identical diploid micronuclei within each individual.

Haploid micronucleus (n)

**2.** The diploid micronucleus in each divides by meiosis to produce four haploid micronuclei.

2n    n

MITOSIS

Diploid micronucleus (2n)

MITOSIS

CONJUGATION

**3.** Three of the haploid micronuclei degenerate. The remaining micronucleus in each divides by mitosis.

**5.** In each individual, the new micronucleus fuses with the micronucleus already present, forming a diploid micronucleus.

**4.** Mates exchange micronuclei.

**Figure 29.18 Life cycle of *Paramecium*.** In sexual reproduction, two mature cells fuse in a process called conjugation.

vesicle that appears periodically when solid particles are ready to be expelled.

The contractile vacuoles, which regulate water balance, periodically expand and contract as they empty their contents to the outside of the organism.

### Conjugation: Exchange of micronuclei

Like most ciliates, *Paramecium* undergoes a sexual process called conjugation, in which two individual cells remain attached to each other for up to several hours (figure 29.18).

Paramecia have multiple mating types. Only cells of two different genetically determined mating types can conjugate. Meiosis in the micronuclei produces several haploid micronuclei, and the two partners exchange a pair of their micronuclei through a cytoplasmic bridge between them.

In each conjugating individual, the new micronucleus fuses with one of the micronuclei already present in that individual, resulting in the production of a new diploid micronucleus. After conjugation, the macronucleus in each cell disintegrates, and the new diploid micronucleus undergoes mitosis, thus giving rise to two new identical diploid micronuclei in each individual.

One of these micronuclei becomes the precursor of the future micronuclei of that cell, while the other micronucleus undergoes multiple rounds of DNA replication, becoming the new macronucleus. This complete segregation of the genetic

material is unique to the ciliates and makes them ideal organisms for the study of certain aspects of genetics.

### "Killer" strains

*Paramecium* strains that kill other, sensitive strains of *Paramecium* long puzzled researchers. Initially, killer strains were believed to have genes coding for a substance toxic to sensitive strains. The true source of the toxin turned out to be an endosymbiotic bacterium in the "killer" strains. If this bacterium is engulfed by a "nonkiller" strain, the toxin is released, and the sensitive *Paramecium* dies.

### Learning Outcomes Review 29.5

All members of the Alveolata contain flattened vesicles called alveoli. Dinoflagellates have pairs of flagella arranged perpendicular to each other, which causes them to swim with a spinning motion. Blooms of dinoflagellates cause red tides. Apicomplexans are animal parasites that produce a structure called an apical complex, which is composed of cytoskeleton and secretory structures and aids in penetrating their host. The ciliates are unicellular, heterotrophic protists with cilia used for feeding and propulsion.

■ *What would be a major difficulty in finding a poison to fight the malaria-causing protist Plasmodium?*

## 29.6 Stramenopila: Protists with Fine Hairs

### Learning Outcomes

1. *Describe the characteristic features of the Stramenopila.*
2. *Describe the composition of the unique shells of diatoms.*
3. *Explain how the oomycetes are distinguished from other protists.*

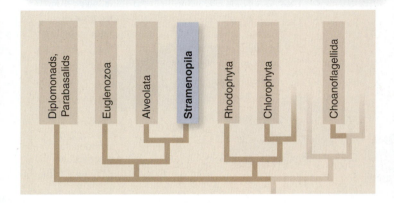

*Stramenopiles* include *brown algae*, *diatoms*, and the *oomycetes* (water molds). The name *stramenopila* refers to unique, fine hairs (figure 29.19) found on the flagella of members of this group, although a few species have lost their hairs during evolution.

### Brown algae include large seaweeds

Brown algae are the most conspicuous seaweeds in many northern regions (figure 29.20). The life cycle of the brown algae is marked by an alternation of generations between a multicellular sporophyte (diploid) and a multicellular gametophyte (haploid) (figure 29.21). Some sporophyte cells go through meiosis and produce spores. These spores germinate and undergo mitosis to produce the large individuals we recognize, such as the

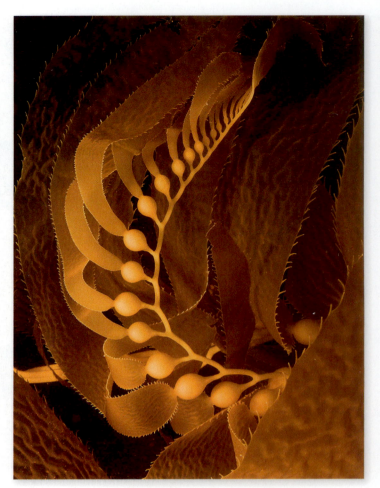

**Figure 29.20 Brown alga.** The giant kelp, *Macrocystis pyrifera*, grows in relatively shallow water along the coasts throughout the world and provides food and shelter for many different kinds of organisms.

kelps. The gametophytes are often much smaller, filamentous individuals, perhaps a few centimeters in width.

Even in an aquatic environment, transport can be a challenge for the very large brown algal species. Distinctive transport cells that stack one upon the other enhance transport within some species (see figure 23.10). However, even though the large kelp look like plants, it is important to realize that they do not contain the complex tissues such as xylem that are found in plants.

### Diatoms are unicellular organisms with double shells

Diatoms, members of the phylum Chrysophyta, are photosynthetic, unicellular organisms with unique double shells made of opaline silica, which are often strikingly marked (figure 29.22). The shells of diatoms are like small boxes with lids, one half of the shell fitting inside the other. Their chloroplasts, containing chlorophylls *a* and *c*, as well as carotenoids, resemble those of the brown algae and dinoflagellates. Diatoms produce a unique carbohydrate called chrysolaminarin.

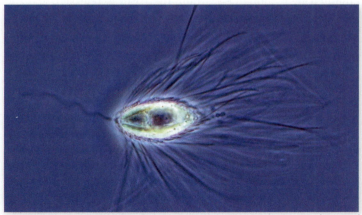

20 μm

**Figure 29.19 Stramenopiles have very fine hairs on their flagella.**

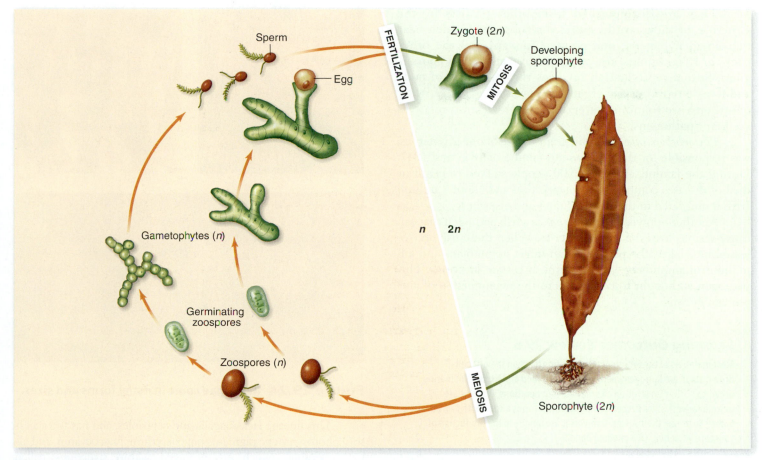

**Figure 29.21** **Life cycle of *Laminaria,* a brown alga.** Multicellular haploid and diploid stages are found in this life cycle, although the male and female gametophytes are quite small.

Some diatoms move by using two long grooves, called *raphes*, which are lined with vibrating fibrils (figure 29.23). The exact mechanism is still being unraveled and may involve the ejection of mucopolysaccharide streams from the raphe that propel the diatom. Pencil-shaped diatoms can slide back and forth over each other, creating an ever-changing shape.

## Oomycetes, the "water molds," have some pathogenic members

All oomycetes are either parasites or saprobes (organisms that live by feeding on dead organic matter). At one time, these organisms were considered fungi, which is the origin of the term *water mold* and why their name contains -*mycetes*.

86 μm

**Figure 29.22** **Diatoms.** These different radially symmetrical diatoms have unique silica, two-part shells.

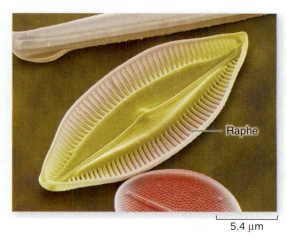

5.4 μm

**Figure 29.23** **Diatom raphe are lined with fibrils that aid in locomotion.**

They are distinguished from other protists by the structure of their motile spores, or zoospores, which bear two unequal flagella, one pointed forward and the other backward. Zoospores are produced asexually in a sporangium. Sexual reproduction involves the formation of male and female reproductive organs that produce gametes. Most oomycetes are found in water, but their terrestrial relatives are plant pathogens.

*Phytophthora infestans,* which causes late blight of potatoes, was responsible for the Irish potato famine of 1845 and 1847. During the famine, about 400,000 people starved to death or died of diseases complicated by starvation and about 2 million Irish immigrated to the United States and elsewhere.

Another oomycete, *Saprolegnia,* is a fish pathogen that can cause serious losses in fish hatcheries. When these fish are released into lakes, the pathogen can infect amphibians and kill millions of amphibian eggs at a time at certain locations. This pathogen is thought to contribute to the phenomenon of amphibian decline.

**Figure 29.24** **Red algae come in many forms and sizes.**

### Learning Outcomes Review 29.6

Most members of the Stramenopila have fine hairs on their flagella. Brown algae are large seaweeds that provide food and habitat for marine organisms. They undergo an alternation of generations. Diatoms are unicellular with silica in their cell walls, which forms a shell with two halves. Some can propel themselves. Oomycetes are unique in the production of zoospores that bear two unequal flagella.

- ■ *How could you distinguish between the sporophyte and the gametophyte of a brown alga?*

## 29.7 Rhodophyta: Red Algae

### Learning Outcomes

1. *List the major characteristics of red algae.*
2. *Describe how humans use red algae.*

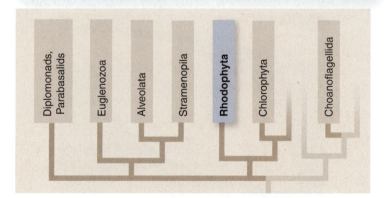

**Rhodophyta,** the red algae, range in size from microscopic organisms to *Schizymenia borealis* with blades as long as 2 m (figure 29.24). Sushi rolls are wrapped in nori, a red alga. Red algal polysaccharides are used commercially to thicken ice cream and cosmetics.

This lineage lacks flagella and centrioles, and has the accessory photosynthetic pigments phycoerythrin, phycocyanin, and allophycocyanin, which are arranged within structures called *phycobilisomes.* They reproduce using alternation of generations.

The origin of the over 7000 species of Rhodophyta has been a source of controversy. Evidence supporting very early eukaryotic origins and a common ancestry with green algae has been considered. Molecular comparisons of the chloroplasts in red and green algae support a single endosymbiotic origin for both.

Comparisons of the nuclear DNA coding for the large subunit of RNA polymerase II from two red algae, a green alga, and another protist support the conclusion that the Rhodophyta emerged before the evolutionary lineage that led to plants, animals, and fungi.

How can we reconcile the data from plastid and nuclear DNA? The host cells and the cyanobacterial symbionts probably did not follow congruent evolutionary pathways. The host cell that gave rise to red algae may have been distinct from the one that gave rise to plants. One possibility is that different host cells engulfed the same bacterial symbiont. Tentatively, we will treat Rhodophyta and Chlorophyta (the green algae; see chapter 30) as sister clades based on the substantial amount of chloroplast data.

### Learning Outcomes Review 29.7

Red algae vary greatly in size and produce accessory pigments that may give them a red color. They lack centrioles and flagella, and they reproduce using an alternation of generations. Humans use red algae as a food and a thickening agent. The evolutionary origin of red algae is a subject of controversy.

- ■ *Why would you expect to get different results from analysis of nuclear DNA versus plastid DNA?*

## 29.8 Choanoflagellida: Possible Animal Ancestors

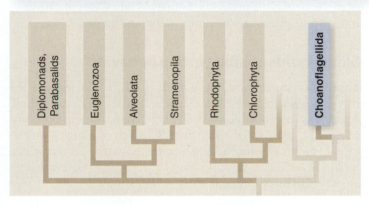

*Choanoflagellates* are most like the common ancestor of the sponges and, indeed, all animals. Choanoflagellates have a single emergent flagellum surrounded by a funnel-shaped, contractile collar composed of closely placed filaments, a structure that is exactly matched in the sponges, which are animals. These protists feed on bacteria strained out of the water by their collar. Colonial forms resemble freshwater sponges (figure 29.25).

The close relationship of choanoflagellates to animals was further demonstrated by the strong homology between a surface receptor (a tyrosine kinase receptor) found in choanoflagellates and sponges. This surface receptor initiates a signaling pathway involving phosphorylation (see chapter 9).

**Figure 29.25** Colonial choanoflagellates resemble their close animal relatives, the sponges.

33 µm

## 29.9 Protists Without a Clade

Many protists remain to be placed on the tree of life. The following examples are of particular importance to human health and the environment.

### Amoebas are paraphyletic

So far, we have organized the protists based on their closest relatives. Some lineages vary tremendously if you consider just a single trait. For example, the stramenopiles include autotrophic, marine algae, and terrestrial plant pathogens. As seen in chapter 25, it is also possible for unrelated organisms to acquire similar traits. That is the case with amoebas, which have similar cell morphology, but are not monophyletic.

#### Rhizopoda: True amoebas

Amoebas move from place to place by means of their pseudopods. Pseudopods are flowing projections of cytoplasm that extend and pull the amoeba forward or engulf food particles. An amoeba puts a pseudopod forward and then flows into it (figure 29.26). Microfilaments of actin and myosin similar to those found in muscles are associated with these movements. The pseudopods can form at any point on the cell body so that it can move in any direction.

#### Actinopoda: Radiolarians

The pseudopods of amoeboid cells give them truly amorphous bodies. One group, however, has more distinct structures. Members of the phylum Actinopoda, often called *radiolarians*, secrete glassy exoskeletons made of silica. These skeletons give the unicellular organisms a distinct shape, exhibiting either bilateral or radial symmetry. The shells of different species form many elaborate and beautiful shapes, with pseudopods extruding outward

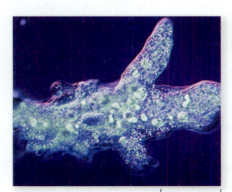

**Figure 29.26** *Amoeba proteus.* The projections are pseudopods; an amoeba moves by flowing into them.

62.5 µm

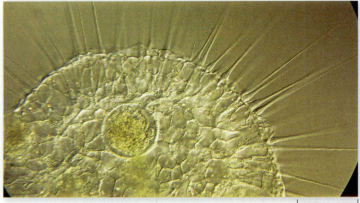

**Figure 29.27** *Actinosphaerium* with needle-like pseudopods.

33.3 μm

along spiky projections of the skeleton (figure 29.27). Microtubules support these cytoplasmic projections.

## Foraminifera fossils created huge limestone deposits

Members of the phylum Foraminifera are heterotrophic marine protists. They range in diameter from about 20 μm to several centimeters. They resemble tiny snails and can form 3-m-deep layers in marine sediments. Characteristic of the group are pore-studded shells (called *tests*) composed of organic materials usually reinforced with grains of calcium carbonate, sand, or even plates from shells of echinoderms or spicules (minute needles of calcium carbonate) from sponge skeletons.

Depending on the building materials they use, foraminifera may have shells of very different appearance. Some of them are brilliantly colored red, salmon, or yellow-brown.

Most foraminifera live in sand or are attached to other organisms, but two families consist of free-floating planktonic organisms. Their tests may be single-chambered, but are more often multichambered, and they sometimes have a spiral shape resembling that of a tiny snail. Thin cytoplasmic projections called *podia* emerge through openings in the tests (figure 29.28).

Podia are used for swimming, gathering materials for the tests, and feeding. Foraminifera eat a wide variety of small organisms.

The life cycles of foraminifera are extremely complex, involving alternation between haploid and diploid generations. Foraminifera have contributed massive accumulations of their tests to the fossil record for more than 200 million years. Because of the excellent preservation of their tests and the striking differences among them, forams are very important as geological markers. The pattern of occurrence of different forams is often used as a guide in searching for oil-bearing strata. Limestones all over the world, including the famous White Cliffs of Dover in southern England, are often rich in forams (figure 29.29).

## Slime molds exhibit "group behavior"

**Slime molds** originated at least three distinct times, and the three lineages are very distantly related. Like water molds, these organisms were once considered fungi. We will explore two lineages: the plasmodial slime molds, which are huge, single-celled, multinucleate, oozing masses, and the cellular slime molds, in which single cells combine and differentiate, creating an early model of multicellularity.

### Plasmodial slime molds

Plasmodial slime molds stream along as a **plasmodium,** a non-walled, multinucleate mass of cytoplasm that resembles a moving mass of slime (figure 29.30). This form is called the *feeding phase*, and the plasmodia may be orange, yellow, or another color.

Plasmodia show a back-and-forth streaming of cytoplasm that is very conspicuous, especially under a microscope. They are able to pass through the mesh in cloth or simply to flow around or through other obstacles. As they move, they engulf and digest bacteria, yeasts, and other small particles of organic matter.

A multinucleated *Plasmodium* cell undergoes mitosis synchronously, with the nuclear envelope breaking down, but only at late anaphase or telophase. Centrioles are absent.

8.3 μm

**Figure 29.28** **A representative of the foraminifera.** Podia, thin cytoplasmic projections, extend through pores in the calcareous test, or shell, of this living foram.

**Figure 29.29** **White Cliffs of Dover.** The limestone that forms these cliffs is composed almost entirely of fossil shells of protists, including foraminifera.

## UNDERSTAND

1. Fossil evidence of eukaryote dates back to *Hemitrichia serpula*
   - a. 2.5 BYA.
   - c. 2.5 MYA.
   - b. 1.5 BYA.
   - d. 1.5 MYA.

2. DNA is not found in this organelle.
   - a. Endoplasmic reticulum
   - b. Nucleus
   - c. Chloroplast
   - d. Centriole
   - e. Mitochondrion

3. The products of budding are
   - a. two cells of equal size.
   - b. two cells, one of which is smaller than the other.
   - c. many cells of equal size.
   - d. many cells of variable size.

4. Both diplomonads and parabasalids
   - a. contain chloroplasts.
   - b. have multinucleate cells.
   - c. lack mitochondria.
   - d. have silica in their cell walls.

5. Trypanosomes are examples of
   - a. euglenoids.
   - c. parabasilids.
   - b. diplomonads.
   - d. kinetoplastids.

6. The function of the apical complex in Apicomplexans is to
   - a. propel the cell through water.
   - b. penetrate host tissue.
   - c. absorb food.
   - d. detect light.

7. If a cell contains a pellicle, it
   - a. can change shape readily.
   - b. is shaped like a sphere.
   - c. is shaped like a torpedo.
   - d. must have a contractile vacuole.

8. Stramenopila are
   - a. tiny flagella.
   - c. small hairs on flagella.
   - b. large cilia.
   - d. pairs of large flagella.

9. Choose all of the following that exhibit an alternation of multicellular generations.
   - a. Dinoflagellates
   - c. Red algae
   - b. Brown algae
   - d. Diatoms

10. Choose all of the following that are photosynthetic.
    - a. Diatoms
    - c. Apicomplexans
    - b. Ciliates
    - d. Dinoflagellates

11. Which is most likely the ancestor of animals?
    - a. Trypanosomes
    - c. Ciliates
    - b. Diplomonads
    - d. Choanoflagellates

12. When food is scarce, cells of this organism communicate with each other to form a multicellular slug.
    - a. Cellular slime molds
    - c. Foraminifera
    - b. True amoebas
    - d. Diatoms

## APPLY

1. Analyze the following statements and choose the one that most accurately supports the endosymbiotic theory.
   - a. Mitochondria rely on mitosis for replication.
   - b. Chloroplasts contain DNA but translation does not occur in chloroplasts.
   - c. Vacuoles have double membranes.
   - d. Antibiotics that inhibit protein synthesis in bacteria can have the same effect on mitochondria.

2. Determine which feature of the choanoflagellates was likely the most significant for the evolution of animals?
   - a. Flagellum with a funnel-shaped, contractile collar also found in sponges
   - b. A tyrosine kinase receptor on the surface of choanoflagellates that has strong homology to fungi
   - c. A colonial form that resembles some fungi
   - d. Eyespots that are similar to ribbonworms

3. Examine the life cycle of cellular slime molds, and determine which feature affords the greatest advantage for surviving food shortages.
   - a. Cellular slime molds produce spores when starved.
   - b. Cellular slime molds are saprobes.
   - c. A diet of bacteria ensures there will never be a shortage of food.
   - d. Cellular slime molds use cAMP to guide each other to food sources.

## SYNTHESIZE

1. Modern taxonomic treatments rely heavily on phylogenetic data to classify organisms. In the past, taxonomists often used a morphological species concept, in which species were defined based on similarities in growth form. Give an example to show how a morphological species concept would group a set of protists differently than a phylogenetic species concept would.

2. Three methods have been used to try to eradicate malaria. One is to eliminate the mosquito vectors of the parasite, a second is to kill the parasites after they entered the human body, and the third is to develop a vaccine against the parasite, allowing the human immune system to provide protection from the disease. Which do you suppose is the most promising in the long run? Why? Think about both the biology of the disease and the efficacy of carrying out each of the methods on a large scale.

3. Design an experiment to demonstrate that cells of cellular slime molds are attracted to cyclic-AMP. Then, design a follow-up experiment to determine whether they are always attracted to cAMP or only when resources are scarce.

## ONLINE RESOURCE

**www.ravenbiology.com**

Understand, Apply, and Synthesize—enhance your study with animations that bring concepts to life and practice tests to assess your understanding. Your instructor may also recommend the interactive eBook, individualized learning tools, and more.

*Chapter* 30

# Green Plants

## Chapter Outline

## Introduction

*Colonization of land by plants fundamentally altered the history of life on Earth. A terrestrial environment offers abundant $CO_2$ and solar radiation for photosynthesis. But for at least 500 million years, the lack of water and higher ultraviolet (UV) radiation on land confined green algal ancestors to an aquatic environment. Evolutionary innovations for reproduction, structural support, and prevention of water-loss are key in the story of plant adaptation to land. The evolutionary shift on land to life cycles dominated by a diploid generation masks recessive mutations arising from higher UV exposure. As a result, larger numbers of alleles persist in the gene pool, creating greater genetic diversity. Numerous evolutionary solutions to terrestrial challenges have resulted in over 300,000 species of plants dominating all terrestrial communities today, from forests to alpine tundra and from agricultural fields to deserts. Plants affect almost every aspect of our lives, from improving environmental quality to providing pharmaceuticals, food, fuels, building materials, and clothing. This chapter explores the evolutionary history and strategies of the green plants.*

## 30.1 Defining Plants

### Learning Outcomes

1. *Explain the relationship between the different algae clades and plants.*
2. *Describe the haplodiplontic life cycle.*
3. *Distinguish between a sporophyte and a gametophyte.*
4. *Identify two major environmental challenges for land plants and associated adaptations.*

As you saw in chapter 26, the phylogenetic revolution has completely altered our definition of a plant. We now know that all green algae and the land plants shared a common ancestor a little over 1 BYA, and the two groups are now recognized as a kingdom or crown group referred to as the Viridiplantae, or simply, the green plants. DNA sequence data are consistent with the claim that a single individual gave rise to all plants. Thus, plants are all members of the Viridiplantae, extending an older definition of plants to include the green algae.

Plants are photoautotrophic, but not all photoautotrophs are members of the Viridiplantae. The definition of a plant is broad, but it excludes the red and brown algae. All algae—red, brown, and green—shared a primary endosymbiotic event 1.5 BYA. But sharing an ancestral chloroplast lineage is not the same as being monophyletic. Red and green algae last shared a common ancestor about 1.4 BYA. Brown algae became photosynthetic through endosymbiosis with a eukaryotic red alga that had itself already acquired a photosynthetic cyanobacterium, as described in the preceding chapter.

Plants are also not fungi, which are more closely related to metazoan animals (see chapter 32). Fungi, however, were essential to the colonization of land by plants, enhancing plants' nutrient uptake from the soil.

## Land plants evolved from freshwater algae

Some saltwater algae evolved to thrive in a freshwater environment. Just a single species of freshwater green algae gave rise to the entire terrestrial plant lineage, from mosses through the flowering plants (angiosperms). Given the incredibly harsh conditions of life on land, it is not surprising that all land plants share a single common ancestor. Exactly what this ancestral alga was is still a mystery, but close relatives, members of the charophytes, exist in freshwater lakes today.

The green algae split into two major clades: the chlorophytes, which never made it to land, and the charophytes, which are sister to all the land plants (figure 30.1). Land plants, although diverse, have certain characteristics in common. Unlike the charophytes, land plants have multicellular haploid and diploid stages. Diploid embryos are also land plant innovations.

Over time, the trend has been toward more embryo protection and a smaller haploid stage in the life cycle.

## Land plants have adapted to terrestrial life

Unlike their freshwater ancestors, most land plants have only limited amounts of water available. As an adaptation to living on land, most plants are protected from desiccation—the tendency of organisms to lose water to the air—by a waxy surface material called the cuticle that is secreted onto their exposed surfaces. The cuticle is relatively impermeable, preventing water loss. This solution, however, limits the gas exchange essential for respiration and photosynthesis. Gas diffusion into and out of a plant occurs through tiny mouth-shaped openings called **stomata** (singular, *stoma*), which allows water to diffuse out at the same time. Chapter 36 describes how stomata can be closed at times to limit water loss.

Moving water within plants is a challenge that increases with plant size. Members of the land plants can be distinguished based on the presence or absence of **tracheids,** specialized cells that facilitate the transport of water and minerals (see chapter 36). Tracheophytes have specialized transport cells called tracheids and have evolved highly efficient transport systems: water-conducting xylem and food-conducting phloem strands of tissues in their stems, roots, and leaves. Some plants that grow in aquatic environments, including water lilies, have tracheids. Aquatic tracheophytes had terrestrial ancestors that adapted back to a watery environment.

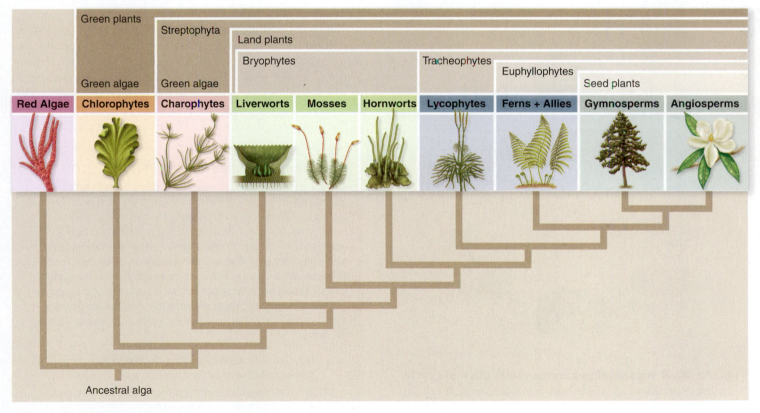

**Figure 30.1  Green plant phylogeny.**

Terrestrial plants are exposed to higher intensities of UV irradiation than aquatic algae, increasing the chance of mutation. Diploid genomes mask the effect of a single, deleterious allele. All land plants have both haploid and diploid generations, and the evolutionary shift toward a dominant diploid generation allows for greater genetic variability to persist in terrestrial plants.

Most multicellular Viridiplantae have haplodiplontic life cycles. Many multicellular green algae and all land plants have haplodiplontic life cycles and undergo mitosis after both gamete fusion and meiosis. The result is a multicellular haploid individual and a multicellular diploid individual—unlike in the human life cycle, in which gamete fusion directly follows meiosis. Humans have a **diplontic** life cycle, meaning that only the diploid stage is multicellular; by contrast, the land plant life cycle is **haplodiplontic,** having multicellular haploid and diploid stages.

## The haplodiplontic cycle produces alternation of generations

The basic haplodiplontic cycle is summarized in figure 30.2. Many brown, red, and green algae are also haplodiplontic. Humans produce gametes via meiosis, but land plants actually produce gametes by *mitosis* in a multicellular, haploid individual. The diploid generation, or **sporophyte,** alternates with the haploid generation, or **gametophyte.** Sporophyte means "spore plant," and gametophyte means "gamete plant." These terms indicate the kinds of reproductive cells the respective generations produce.

The diploid sporophyte produces haploid spores (not gametes) by meiosis. Meiosis takes place in structures called sporangia, where diploid **spore mother cells (sporocytes)** undergo meiosis, each producing four haploid **spores.** Spores

are the first cells of the gametophyte generation. Spores divide by mitosis, producing a multicellular, haploid gametophyte.

The haploid gametophyte is the source of gametes. When the gametes fuse, the zygote they form is diploid and is the first cell of the next sporophyte generation. The zygote grows into a diploid sporophyte by mitosis and produces sporangia in which meiosis ultimately occurs.

## The relative sizes of haploid and diploid generations vary

All land plants are haplodiplontic; however, the haploid generation consumes a much larger portion of the life cycle in mosses and ferns than it does in gymnosperms and angiosperms. In mosses, liverworts, and ferns, the gametophyte is photosynthetic and free-living. When you look at mosses, what you see is largely gametophyte tissue; the sporophytes are usually smaller, brownish or yellowish structures attached to the tissues of the gametophyte. In other plants, the gametophyte is usually nutritionally dependent on the sporophyte. When you look at a gymnosperm or angiosperm, such as most trees, the largest, most visible portion is a sporophyte.

Although the sporophyte generation can get very large, the size of the gametophyte is limited in all plants. The gametophyte generation of mosses produces gametes at its tips. The egg is stationary, and sperm lands near the egg in a droplet of water. If the moss were the height of a sequoia, not only would vascular tissue be needed for conduction and support, but the sperm would have to swim up the tree! In contrast, the small gametophyte of the fern develops on the forest floor where gametes can meet. Tree ferns are especially abundant in Australia; the haploid spores the sporophyte trees produce fall to the ground and develop into gametophytes.

Having completed an overview of plant life cycles, we next consider the major plant groups within Viridiplantae. As we proceed, you will see a reduction of the gametophyte from group to group, a loss of multicellular **gametangia** (structures in which gametes are produced), and increasing specialization for life on land, including the remarkable structural adaptations of the flowering plants, which are the dominant plants today.

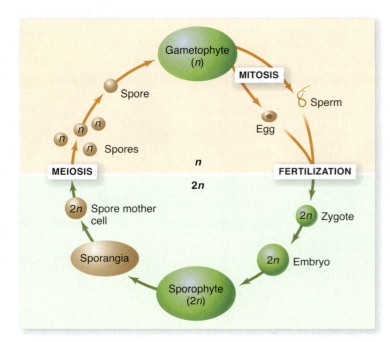

**Figure 30.2 A generalized multicellular plant life cycle.** Note that both haploid and diploid individuals can be multicellular. Also, spores are produced by meiosis, while gametes are produced by mitosis.

### Learning Outcomes Review 30.1

All algae acquired chloroplasts necessary for photosynthesis, but green algae diverged from red algae after that event. A single freshwater green alga successfully invaded land; its descendants eventually developed reproductive strategies, conducting systems, stomata, and cuticles as adaptations. Green plants (Viridiplantae) include all green algae and the land plants. Most plants have a haplodiplontic life cycle, a haploid form alternates with a diploid form in a single organism. Diploid sporophytes produce haploid spores by meiosis. Each spore can develop into a haploid gametophyte by mitosis; the gametophyte form produces haploid gametes, again by mitosis. When the gametes fuse, the diploid sporophyte is formed once more.

■  *How would you distinguish a small aquatic tracheophyte from a freshwater alga?*

■  *What distinguishes gamete formation in plants from gamete formation in humans?*

## 30.2 Chlorophytes and Charophytes: Green Algae

### Learning Outcomes

1. Explain why chlorophytes are considered close relatives of land plants.
2. Explain why charophytes are considered the closest relatives of land plants.

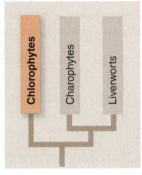

Green algae have two distinct lineages: the chlorophytes, discussed here, and another lineage, the **streptophytes**, that gave rise to the land plants (see figure 30.1). The chlorophytes are of special interest here because of their unusual diversity and lines of specialization. The chlorophytes have an extensive fossil record dating back 900 million years. Modern chlorophytes closely resemble land plants, especially in their chloroplasts, which are biochemically similar to those of the plants. They contain chlorophylls *a* and *b*, as well as carotenoids.

### Chlorophytes can be unicellular

Early green algae probably resembled *Chlamydomonas reinhardtii*, diverging from land plants over 1 BYA (figure 30.3). Individuals are microscopic (usually less than 25 μm long), green, and rounded, and they have two flagella at the anterior end. They are soil dwellers that move rapidly in water by beating their flagella in opposite directions. Most individuals of *Chlamydomonas* are haploid. *Chlamydomonas* reproduces asexually as well as sexually, but because it is always unicellular the life cycle is not haplodiplontic (see figure 30.3).

Several lines of evolutionary specialization have been derived from organisms such as *Chlamydomonas, including* the evolution of nonmotile, unicellular green algae. *Chlamydomonas* is capable of retracting its flagella and settling down as an immobile unicellular organism if the pond in which it lives dries out. Some common algae found in soil and bark, such as *Chlorella*, are essentially like *Chlamydomonas* in this trait, but they do not have the ability to form flagella.

Genome-sequencing projects are providing new insights into the evolution of the Viridiplantae. A comparison of the 6968 protein families predicted by the *Chlamydomonas* genome were compared with a red algal genome and two streptophyte genomes (moss and *Arabidopsis*). Of these proteins, 172 are found only in the Viridiplantae. Comparing these conserved proteins in the green plants will provide new information about the evolution of the green plants.

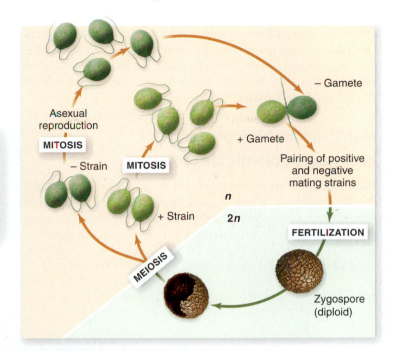

### Figure 30.3
*Chlamydomonas* **life cycle.**
This single-celled chlorophyte has both asexual and sexual reproduction. Unlike multicellular green plants, gamete fusion is not followed by mitosis. © Dr. Richard Kessel & Dr. Gene Shih/Visuals Unlimited

### Colonial chlorophytes have some cell specialization

Multicellularity arose many times in the eukaryotes. Colonial chlorophytes provide examples of cellular specialization, an aspect of multicellularity. A line of specialization from cells like those of *Chlamydomonas* concerns the formation of motile, colonial organisms. In these genera of green algae, the *Chlamydomonas*-like cells retain some of their individuality.

The most elaborate of these organisms is *Volvox* (figure 30.4), a hollow sphere made up of a single layer of

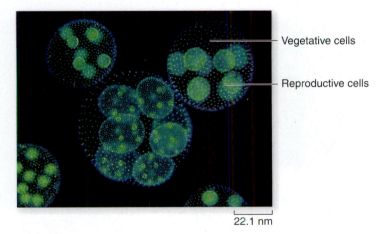

**Figure 30.4** *Volvox.* This chlorophyte forms a colony where some cells specialize for reproduction.

500 to 60,000 individual cells, each cell having two flagella. Only a small number of the cells are reproductive. Some reproductive cells may divide asexually, bulge inward, and give rise to new colonies that initially remain within the parent colony. Others produce gametes.

## Multicellular chlorophytes can have haplodiplontic life cycles

Haplodiplontic life cycles are found in some chlorophytes and the streptophytes, which include both charophytes and land plants. *Ulva*, a multicellular chlorophyte, has identical gametophyte and sporophyte generations that consist of flattened sheets two cells thick (figure 30.5). Unlike the charophytes, none of the ancestral chlorophytes gave rise to land plants.

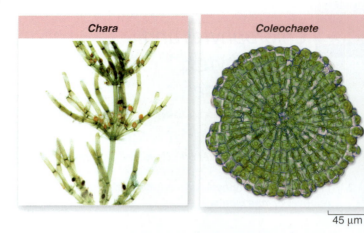

**Figure 30.6** *Chara,* a member of the Charales, and *Coleochaete*, a member of the Coleochaetales, represent the two clades most closely related to land plants.

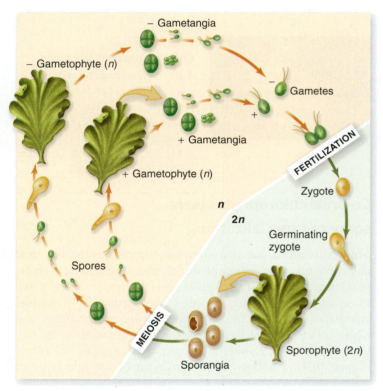

**Figure 30.5** Life cycle of *Ulva*. This chlorophyte alga has a haplodiplontic life cycle. The gametophyte and sporophyte are multicellular and identical in appearance.

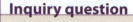

**Inquiry question**

? Are *Ulva* gametes formed by meiosis? Explain your response.

## Charophytes are the closest relatives to land plants

**Charophytes,** a clade of streptophytes, are also green algae, and they are distinguished from chlorophytes by their close phylogenetic relationship to the land plants. Charophytes have haplontic life cycles, indicating that the evolution of a diplontic embryo and haplodiplontic life cycle occurred after the move onto land.

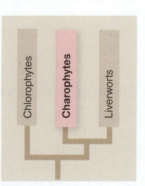

Identifying which of the charophyte clades is sister (most closely related) to the land plants puzzled biologists for a long time. The charophyte algae fossil record is scarce. Currently, the molecular evidence from rRNA and DNA sequences favors the charophytes as the green algal clade in the streptophytes.

The two candidate Charophyta clades have been the Charales, with about 300 species, and the Coleochaetales, with about 30 species (figure 30.6). Both lineages are primarily freshwater algae, but the Charales are huge, relative to the microscopic Coleochaetales. Both clades have similarities to land plants. *Coleochaete* and its relatives have cytoplasmic linkages between cells called *plasmodesmata*, which are found in land plants. The species *Chara* in the Charales undergoes mitosis and cytokinesis like land plant cells. Sexual reproduction in both relies on a large, nonmotile egg and flagellated sperm. These gametes are more similar to those of land plants than many charophyte relatives. Both charophyte clades form green mats around the edges of freshwater ponds and marshes. One species must have successfully inched its way onto land through adaptations to drying.

## 30.3 Bryophytes: Dominant Gametophyte Generation

Bryophytes are the closest living descendants of the first land plants. Plants in this group are also called nontracheophytes because they lack the derived transport cell called a *tracheid*.

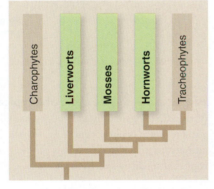

Fossil evidence and molecular systematics can be used to reconstruct early terrestrial plant life. Water and gas availability were limiting factors. These plants likely had little ability to regulate internal water levels and likely tolerated desication, traits found in most extant mosses, although some are aquatic.

Algae, including the Charales, lack roots. Fungi and early land plants cohabitated, and the fungi formed close associations with the plants that enhanced water uptake. The tight symbiotic relationship between fungi and plants, called **mycorrhizal associations,** are also found in many existing bryophytes. More information on mycorrhizal fungi is found in chapter 31.

### Bryophytes are unspecialized but successful in many environments

The approximately 24,700 species of bryophytes are simple but highly adapted to a diversity of terrestrial environments, even deserts. Most bryophytes are small; few exceed 7 cm in height. Bryophytes have conducting cells other than tracheids for water and nutrients. The tracheid is a derived trait that characterizes the tracheophytes, all land plants but the bryophytes.

Bryophytes are sometimes called nonvascular plants, but *nontracheophyte* is a more accurate term because they do have conducting cells of different types.

Scientists now agree that bryophytes consist of three quite distinct clades of relatively unspecialized plants: liverworts, mosses, and hornworts. Their gametophytes are photosynthetic and are more conspicuous than the sporophytes. Sporophytes are attached to the gametophytes and depend on them nutritionally in varying degrees. Some of the sporophytes are completely enclosed within gametophyte tissue; others are not and usually turn brownish or straw-colored at maturity. Like ferns and certain other vascular (tracheophyte) plants, bryophytes require water (such as rainwater) to reproduce sexually, tracing back to their aquatic origins. It is not surprising that they are especially common in moist places, both in the tropics and temperate regions.

### Liverworts are an ancient phylum

The Old English word *wyrt* means "plant" or "herb." Some common liverworts (phylum Hepaticophyta) have flattened gametophytes with lobes resembling those of liver—hence the name "liverwort." Although the lobed liverworts are the best known representatives of this phylum, they constitute only about 20% of the species (figure 30.7). The other 80% are leafy and superficially resemble mosses. The gametophytes are prostrate instead of erect, and the rhizoids are one-celled.

Some liverworts have air chambers containing upright, branching rows of photosynthetic cells, each chamber having a pore at the top to facilitate gas exchange. Unlike stomata, the pores are fixed open and cannot close.

Sexual reproduction in liverworts is similar to that in mosses. Lobed liverworts may form gametangia in umbrella-like structures. Asexual reproduction occurs when lens-shaped pieces of tissue that are released from the gametophyte grow to form new gametophytes.

Female gametophyte

**Figure 30.7 A common liverwort, *Marchantia* (phylum Hepaticophyta).** The microscopic sporophytes are formed by fertilization within the tissues of the umbrella-shaped structures that arise from the surface of the flat, green, creeping gametophyte.

## Mosses have rhizoids and water-conducting tissue

Unlike other bryophytes, the gametophytes of mosses typically consist of small, leaflike structures (not true leaves, which contain vascular tissue) arranged spirally or alternately around a stemlike axis (figure 30.8); the axis is anchored to its substrate by means of rhizoids. Each rhizoid consists of several cells that absorb water, but not nearly the volume of water that is absorbed by a vascular plant root.

Moss leaflike structures have little in common with leaves of vascular plants, except for the superficial appearance of the green, flattened blade and slightly thickened midrib that runs lengthwise down the middle. Only one cell layer thick (except at the midrib), they lack vascular strands and stomata, and all the cells are haploid.

Water may rise up a strand of specialized cells in the center of a moss gametophyte axis. Some mosses also have specialized food-conducting cells surrounding those that conduct water.

### Moss reproduction

Multicellular gametangia are formed at the tips of the leafy gametophytes (figure 30.9). Female gametangia (**archegonia**) may develop either on the same gametophyte as the male gametangia (**antheridia**) or on separate plants. A single egg is produced in the swollen lower part of an archegonium, whereas numerous sperm are produced in an antheridium.

When sperm are released from an antheridium, they swim with the aid of flagella through a film of dew or rainwater to the archegonia. One sperm (which is haploid) unites with an egg (also haploid), forming a diploid zygote. The zygote divides by mitosis and develops into the sporophyte, a slender, basal stalk with a swollen capsule, the *sporangium*, at its tip. As the

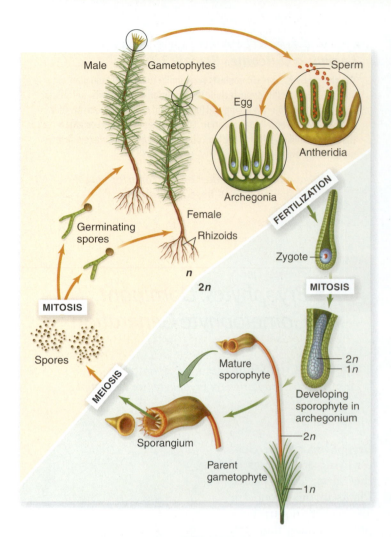

**Figure 30.9 Life cycle of a typical moss.** The majority of the life cycle of a moss is in the haploid state. The leafy gametophyte is photosynthetic, but the smaller sporophyte is not and is nutritionally dependent on the gametophyte. Water is required to carry sperm to the egg.

sporophyte develops, its base is embedded in gametophyte tissue, its nutritional source.

The sporangium is often cylindrical or club-shaped. Spore mother cells within the sporangium undergo meiosis, each producing four haploid spores. In many mosses at maturity, the top of the sporangium pops off, and the spores are released. A spore that lands in a suitable damp location may germinate and grow, using mitosis, into a threadlike structure, which branches to form rhizoids and "buds" that grow upright. Each bud develops into a new gametophyte plant consisting of a leafy axis.

### Moss distribution

In the Arctic and the Antarctic, mosses are the most abundant plants. The greatest diversity of moss species, however, is found in the tropics. Many mosses are able to withstand prolonged periods of drought, although mosses are not common in deserts.

Most mosses are highly sensitive to air pollution and are rarely found in abundance in or near cities or other areas with high levels of air pollution. Some mosses, such as the peat mosses (*Sphagnum*), can absorb up to 25 times their weight in

**Figure 30.8 A hair-cup moss, *Polytrichum* (phylum Bryophyta).** The leaflike structures belong to the gametophyte. Each of the yellowish-brown stalks with a capsule, or sporangium, at its summit is a sporophyte.

water and are valuable commercially as a soil conditioner or as a fuel when dry.

## The moss genome

Moss plants can survive extreme water loss—an adaptive trait in the early colonization of land that has been lost from vegetative tissues of tracheophytes (figure 30.10). Desication toler-

**SCIENTIFIC THINKING**

**Hypothesis:** *Desiccation tolerance genes in moss and flowering plants first appeared in a common ancestor.*

**Prediction:** *The late embryogenesis abundant (LEA) protein gene, a desiccation tolerance gene, from flowering plants will be expressed in moss plants when they experience severe water loss.*

**Test:** *Isolate RNA from moss plants that have not been water stressed (control), have been dehydrated to 84% water loss, and have been dehydrated to 95% water loss. Load a gel with equal amounts of RNA from each treatment. Probe the gel with a cDNA sequence for the LEA gene that is labeled.*

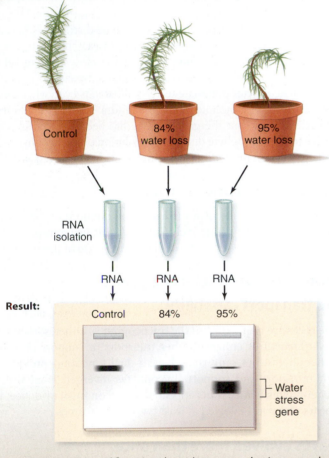

Control

84% water loss

95% water loss

RNA isolation

RNA    RNA    RNA

**Result:**

Control    84%    95%

Water stress gene

**Conclusion:** *Moss and flowering plants share a gene that is expressed under water stress conditions.*

**Further Experiments:** *Are other stress genes shared by bryophytes and flowering plants? Repeat the experiment with other stress-induced genes.*

**Figure 30.10** Moss and flowering plants share desication tolerance genes.

Photosynthetic sporophyte

**Figure 30.11** Hornworts (phylum Anthocerotophyta). Hornwort sporophytes are seen in this photo. Unlike the sporophytes of other bryophytes, most hornwort sporophytes are photosynthetic.

ance and phylogenetic position were among the traits that led researchers to sequence the genome of the moss *Physcomitrella patens* as being the first streptophyte that is not a seed plant. Although the moss genome is a single genome bracketed by *Chlamydomonas* and the flowering plant *Arabidopsis*, many evolutionary hints are hidden within it. Evidence indicates the loss of genes associated with a watery life, including flagellar arms, which have completely vanished in the flowering plants. Genes associated with tolerance of terrestrial stresses, including temperature and water availability, are absent in *Chlamydomonas* and present in moss. The genome data add rich sets of traits to be used in phylogenetic analyses.

## Hornworts developed stomata

The origin of hornworts (phylum Anthocerotophyta) is a puzzle. They are most likely among the earliest land plants, yet the earliest hornwort fossil spores date from the Cretaceous period (65 to 145 MYA), when angiosperms were emerging.

The small hornwort sporophytes resemble tiny green broom handles or horns, rising from filmy gametophytes usually less than 2 cm in diameter (figure 30.11). The sporophyte base is embedded in gametophyte tissue, from which it derives some of its nutrition. However, the sporophyte has stomata to regulate gas exchange, is photosynthetic, and provides much of the energy needed for growth and reproduction. Hornwort cells usually have a single large chloroplast.

### Learning Outcome Review 30.3

The bryophytes exhibit adaptations to terrestrial life. Moss adaptations include rhizoids to anchor the moss body and to absorb water, and water-conducting tissues. Mosses are found in a variety of habitats, and some can survive droughts. Hornworts developed stomata that can open and close to regulate gas exchange.

■ *What might account for the abundance of mosses in the Arctic and Antarctic?*

## 30.4 Tracheophyte Plants: Roots, Stems, and Leaves

### Learning Outcomes

1. Explain the evolutionary significance of tracheids.
2. Analyze the claim that roots, stems, and leaves are evolutionary innovations unique to tracheophytes.

The first tracheophytes with a relatively complete record belonged to the phylum Rhyniophyta. We are not certain what the earliest of these vascular plants looked like, but fossils of *Cooksonia* provide some insight into their characteristics (figure 30.12).

*Cooksonia*, the first known vascular land plant, appeared in the late Silurian period about 420 MYA, but is now extinct. It was successful partly because it encountered little competition as it spread out over vast tracts of land. The plants were only a few centimeters tall and had no roots or leaves. They consisted of little more than a branching axis, the branches forking evenly and expanding slightly toward the tips. They were **homosporous** (producing only one type of spore). Sporangia formed at branch tips. Other ancient vascular plants that followed evolved more complex arrangements of sporangia.

### Vascular tissue allows for distribution of nutrients

*Cooksonia* and the other early plants that followed it became successful colonizers of the land by developing efficient water- and food-conducting systems called *vascular tissues*. These tissues con-

Sporangia

**Figure 30.12** *Cooksonia*, **the first known vascular land plant.** This fossil represents a plant that lived some 420 MYA. *Cooksonia* belongs to phylum Rhyniophyta, consisting entirely of extinct plants. Its upright, branched stems, which were no more than a few centimeters tall, terminated in sporangia, as seen here. It probably lived in moist environments such as mudflats, had a resistant cuticle, and produced spores typical of vascular plants.

sist of strands of specialized cylindrical or elongated cells that form a network throughout a plant, extending from near the tips of the roots, through the stems, and into true leaves, defined by the presence of vascular tissue in the blade. One type of vascular tissue, **xylem,** conducts water and dissolved minerals upward from the roots; another type of tissue, **phloem,** conducts sucrose and hormones throughout the plant. Vascular tissue enables enhanced height and size in the tracheophytes. It develops in the sporophyte, but (with a few exceptions) not in the gametophyte. (Vascular tissue structure is discussed more fully in chapter 38.) A cuticle and stomata are also characteristic of vascular plants.

 **Inquiry question**

Explain why tracheophytes may have had a selective advantage during the evolution of land plants.

### Tracheophytes include seven extant phyla grouped in three clades

Three clades of vascular plants exist today: (1) lycophytes (club mosses), (2) pterophytes (ferns and their relatives), and (3) seed plants. Advances in molecular systematics have changed the way we view the evolutionary history of vascular plants. Whisk ferns and horsetails were long believed to be distinct phyla that were transitional between bryophytes and vascular plants. Phylogenetic evidence now shows they are the closest living relatives to ferns, and they are grouped as pterophytes.

Tracheophytes dominate terrestrial habitats everywhere, except for the highest mountains and the tundra. The haplodiplontic life cycle persists, but the gametophyte has been reduced in size relative to the sporophyte during the evolution of tracheophytes. A similar reduction in multicellular gametangia has occurred as well.

### Stems evolved prior to roots

Fossils of early vascular plants reveal stems, but no roots or leaves. The earliest vascular plants, including *Cooksonia*, had transport cells in their stems, but the lack of roots limited the size of these plants.

### Roots provide structural support and transport capability

True roots are found only in the tracheophytes. Other, somewhat similar structures enhance either transport or support in non-tracheophytes, but only roots have a dual function—providing both transport and support. Lycophytes diverged from other tracheophytes before roots appeared, based on fossil evidence. It appears that roots evolved at least two separate times.

### Leaves evolved more than once

Leaves increase surface area of the sporophyte, enhancing photosynthetic capacity. Lycophytes have single vascular strands supporting relatively small leaves called lycophylls. True leaves, called euphylls, are found only in ferns and seed plants, having distinct origins from lycophylls (figure 30.13). Lycophylls may have resulted from vascular tissue penetrating small, leafy protuberances on stems. Euphylls most likely arose from branching stems that became webbed with leaf tissue.

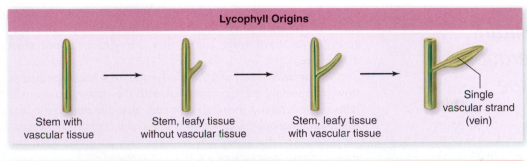

### Lycophyll Origins

Stem with vascular tissue → Stem, leafy tissue without vascular tissue → Stem, leafy tissue with vascular tissue → Single vascular strand (vein)

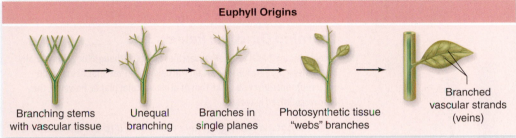

### Euphyll Origins

Branching stems with vascular tissue → Unequal branching → Branches in single planes → Photosynthetic tissue "webs" branches → Branched vascular strands (veins)

**Figure 30.13 Evolution of leaves.**

About 400 million years separates the appearance of vascular tissue and the wide euphyll leaf—a curiously large amount of time. The current hypothesis is that a 90% drop in atmospheric $CO_2$ 360 MYA allowed for the increase in leaf size because of an increase in the number of stomata on a leaf. Large, horizontal leaves capture 200% more radiation than thin, axial leaves. Although beneficial for photosynthesis, larger leaves correspondingly increase leaf temperature, which can be lethal. Stomatal openings in the leaf enhance the movement of water out of the leaf, thereby cooling it. The density of stomata on leaf surfaces correlates with $CO_2$ concentration, as the stomatal openings are essential for gas exchange. As the atmospheric $CO_2$ levels dropped, plants could not obtain sufficient $CO_2$ for photosynthesis. In the low-$CO_2$ atmosphere, natural selection favored plants with higher stomatal densities. Higher stomatal densities favored larger leaves with a photosynthetic advantage that did not overheat. Leaves up to 120 mm wide

and 160 mm long have been identified in the fossil record from that time period.

## Seeds are another innovation in some phyla

Seeds are highly resistant structures well suited to protecting a plant embryo from drought and to some extent from predators. In addition, almost all seeds contain a supply of food for the young plant. Lycophytes and pterophytes do not have seeds.

Fruits in the flowering plants (angiosperms) add a layer of protection to seeds and attract animals that assist in seed dispersal, expanding the potential range of the species. Flowers allow plants to secure the benefits of wide outcrossing in promoting genetic diversity. Before moving on to the specifics of lycophytes and pterophytes, review the evolutionary history of terrestrial innovations in the land plants illustrated in figure 30.14. The advantages conferred by seeds have led to the current dominance of seed plants in terrestrial environments.

### Learning Outcomes Review 30.4

Most tracheophytes have well-developed vascular tissues, including tracheids, that enable efficient delivery of water and nutrients throughout the organism. They also exhibit specialized roots, stems, leaves, cuticles, and stomata. Many produce seeds, which protect and nourish embryos.

■ *Why would vascular tissue be prevalent in the sporophyte, but not the gametophyte, generation?*

**Figure 30.14 Land plant innovations.**

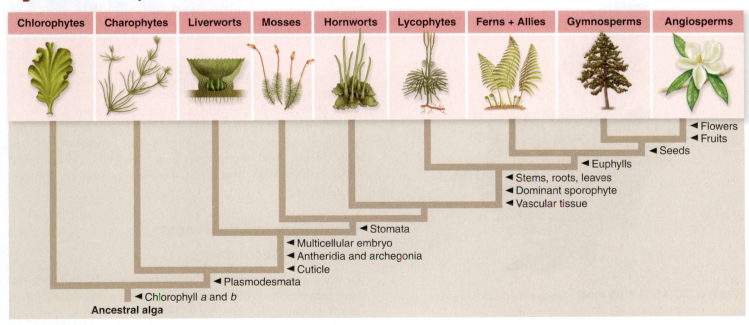

Chlorophytes | Charophytes | Liverworts | Mosses | Hornworts | Lycophytes | Ferns + Allies | Gymnosperms | Angiosperms

◄ Flowers
◄ Fruits
◄ Seeds
◄ Euphylls
◄ Stems, roots, leaves
◄ Dominant sporophyte
◄ Vascular tissue
◄ Stomata
◄ Multicellular embryo
◄ Antheridia and archegonia
◄ Cuticle
◄ Plasmodesmata
◄ Chlorophyll *a* and *b*
Ancestral alga

# 30.5 Lycophytes: Dominant Sporophyte Generation and Vascular Tissue

## Learning Outcome

1. **Explain features that differentiate lycophytes from bryophytes.**

The earliest vascular plants lacked seeds. Members of four phyla of living vascular plants also lack seeds, as do at least three other phyla known only from fossils. As we explore the adaptations of the vascular plants, we focus on both reproductive strategies and the advantages of increasingly complex transport systems.

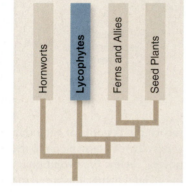

The lycophytes (club mosses) are relic species of an ancient past when vascular plants first evolved (figure 30.15). They are the sister group to all vascular plants. Several genera of club mosses, some of them treelike, became extinct about 270 MYA. Today, club mosses are worldwide in distribution but are most abundant in the tropics and moist temperate regions.

Members of the 12 to 13 genera and about 1150 living species of club mosses superficially resemble true mosses, but once their internal vascular structure and reproductive pro-cesses became known, it was clear that they are unrelated to mosses. The sporophyte stage is the dominant (obvious) stage; sporophytes have leafy stems that are seldom more than 30 cm long.

*Selaginella moellendorffii* is a lycophyte whose genome is now being analyzed. Comparisons with the moss genome will help us understand more about genes that are important in a dominant sporophyte generation and in the evolution of vascular tissue. Are the genes new or were they co-opted from the gametophyte generation?

## Learning Outcome Review 30.5

Lycophytes are basal to all other vascular plants. Although they superficially resemble bryophytes, they contain tracheid-based vascular tissues, and their reproductive cycle is like that of other vascular plants; however, they lack vascularized leaves.

■ **What events might have contributed to the extinction of large club mosses 270 MYA?**

# 30.6 Pterophytes: Ferns and Their Relatives

## Learning Outcomes

1. **List the features exhibited by pterophytes.**
2. **Contrast pterophyte and moss sporophytes.**

The phylogenetic relationships among ferns and their near relations are still being sorted out. A common ancestor gave rise to two clades: One clade diverged to produce a line of ferns and horsetails; the other diverged to yield another line of ferns and whisk ferns—ancient-looking plants.

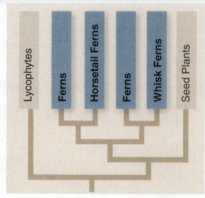

Whisk ferns and horsetails are close relatives of ferns. Like lycophytes and bryophytes, they all form antheridia and archegonia. Free water is required for the process of fertilization, during which the sperm, which have flagella, swim to and unite with the eggs. In contrast, most seed plants have nonflagellated sperm.

## Whisk ferns lost their roots and leaves secondarily

In whisk ferns, which occur in the tropics and subtropics, the sporophytic generation consist merely of evenly forking green stems without roots (figure 30.16). The two or three species of

**Figure 30.15 A club moss.** *Selaginella moellendorffii's sporophyte generation* grows on moist forest floors.

## Figure 30.16

**A whisk fern.** Whisk ferns have no roots or leaves. The green, photosynthetic stems have yellow sporangia attached.

## Figure 30.17

**A horsetail, *Equisetum telmateia*.** This species forms two kinds of erect stems; one is green and photosynthetic, and the other, which terminates in a spore-producing "cone," is mostly light brown.

the genus *Psilotum* do, however, have tiny, green, spirally arranged flaps of tissue lacking veins and stomata. Another genus, *Tmesipteris*, has more leaflike appendages. Currently, systematists believe that whisk ferns lost leaves and roots when they diverged from others in the fern lineage.

Given the simple structure of whisk ferns, it was particularly surprising to discover that they are monophyletic with ferns. The gametophytes of whisk ferns are essentially colorless and are less than 2 mm in diameter, but they can be up to 18 mm long. They form symbiotic associations with fungi, which furnish their nutrients. Some develop elements of vascular tissue and have the distinction of being the only gametophytes known to do so.

## Horsetails have jointed stems with brushlike leaves

The 15 living species of horsetails are all homosporous. They constitute a single genus, *Equisetum*. Fossil forms of *Equisetum* extend back 300 million years to an era when some of their relatives were treelike. Today, they are widely scattered around the world, mostly in damp places. Some that grow among the coastal redwoods of California may reach a height of 3 m, but most are less than a meter tall (figure 30.17).

Horsetail sporophytes consist of ribbed, jointed, photosynthetic stems that arise from branching underground *rhizomes* with roots at their nodes. A whorl of nonphotosynthetic, scalelike leaves emerges at each node. The hollow stems have silica deposits in the epidermal cells of the ribs, and the interior parts of the stems have two sets of vertical, tubular canals. The larger outer canals, which alternate with the ribs, contain air, while the smaller inner canals opposite the ribs contain water. Horsetails are also called scouring rushes because pioneers of the American West used them to scrub pans.

## Ferns have fronds that bear sori

**Ferns** are the most abundant group of seedless vascular plants, with about 11,000 living species. Recent research indicates that they may be the closest relatives to the seed plants.

The fossil record indicates that ferns originated during the Devonian period about 350 MYA and became abundant and varied in form during the next 50 million years. Their apparent ancestors were established on land as much as 375 MYA. Rainforests and swamps of lycopsid and fern trees growing in the Eastern United States and Europe over 300 MYA formed the coal currently being mined. Today, ferns flourish in a wide range of habitats throughout the world; however, about 75% of the species occur in the tropics.

The conspicuous sporophytes may be less than a centimeter in diameter (as in small aquatic ferns such as *Azolla*), or more than 24 m tall, with leaves up to 5 m or longer in the tree ferns (figure 30.18). The sporophytes and the much smaller

## Figure 30.18

**A tree fern (phylum Pterophyta) in the forests of Malaysia.** The ferns are by far the largest group of seedless vascular plants.

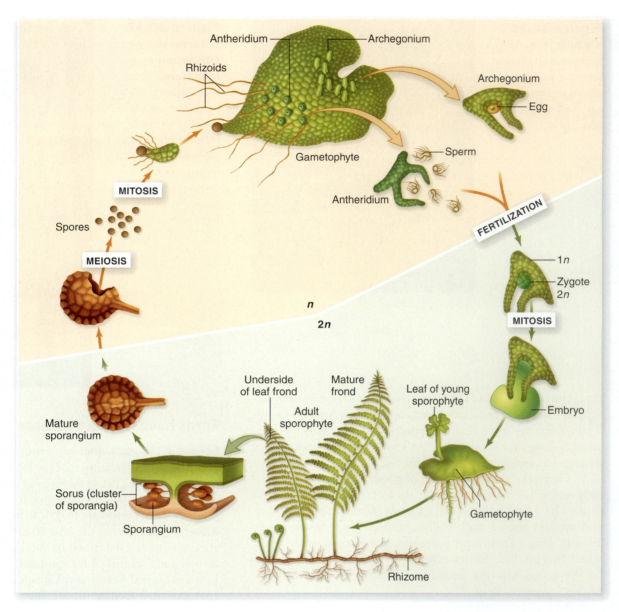

**Figure 30.19** **Life cycle of a typical fern.** Both the gametophyte and sporophyte are photosynthetic and can live independently. Water is necessary for fertilization. Sperm are released on the underside of the gametophyte and swim in moist soil to neighboring gametophytes. Spores are dispersed by wind.

gametophytes, which rarely reach 6 mm in diameter, are both photosynthetic.

The fern life cycle (figure 30.19) differs from that of a moss primarily in the much greater development, independence, and dominance of the fern's sporophyte. The fern sporophyte is structurally more complex than the moss sporophyte, having vascular tissue and well-differentiated roots, stems, and leaves. The gametophyte, however, lacks the vascular tissue found in the sporophyte.

### Fern morphology

Fern sporophytes, like horsetails, have rhizomes. Leaves, referred to as *fronds*, usually develop at the tip of the rhizome as tightly rolled-up coils ("fiddleheads") that unroll and expand (figure 30.20). Fiddleheads are considered a delicacy in several cuisines, but some species contain secondary compounds linked to stomach cancer.

Many fronds are highly dissected and feathery, making the ferns that produce them prized as ornamental garden plants. Some ferns, such as *Marsilea*, have fronds that resemble a four-

leaf clover, but *Marsilea* fronds still begin as coiled fiddleheads. Other ferns produce a mixture of photosynthetic fronds and nonphotosynthetic reproductive fronds that tend to be brownish in color.

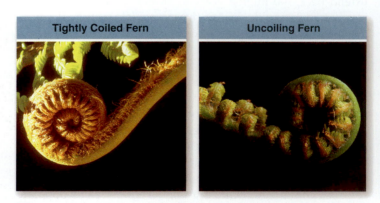

**Figure 30.20** **Fern "fiddlehead."** Fronds develop in a coil and slowly unfold on ferns, including the tree fern fronds in these photos.

## Fern reproduction

Ferns, produce distinctive sporangia, usually in clusters called **sori** (singular, *sorus*), typically on the underside of the fronds. Sori are often protected during their development by a transparent, umbrella-like covering. (At first glance, one might mistake the sori for an infection on the plant.) Diploid spore mother cells in each sporangium undergo meiosis, producing haploid spores.

At maturity, the spores are catapulted from the sporangium by a snapping action, and those that land in suitable damp locations may germinate, producing gametophytes that are often heart-shaped, are only one cell layer thick (except in the center), and have rhizoids that anchor them to their substrate. These rhizoids are not true roots because they lack vascular tissue, but they do aid in transporting water and nutrients from the soil. Flask-shaped archegonia and globular antheridia are produced on either the same or a different gametophyte. The multicellular archegonia provide some protection for the developing embryo.

The sperm formed in the antheridia have flagella, with which they swim toward the archegonia when water is present, often in response to a chemical signal secreted by the archegonia. One sperm unites with the single egg toward the base of an archegonium, forming a zygote. The zygote then develops into a new sporophyte, completing the life cycle (see figure 30.19).

The developing fern embryo has substantially more protection from the environment than a charophyte zygote, but it cannot enter a dormant phase to survive a harsh winter the way a seed plant embryo can. Although extant ferns do not produce seeds, seed fern fossils have been found that date back 365 million years. The seed ferns are not actually pterophytes, but gymnosperms. Of the seven tracheophyte phyla (table 30.1), only two—gymnosperms and angiosperms—produce seeds.

### Learning Outcomes Review 30.6

Ferns and their relatives have a large and conspicuous sporophyte with vascular tissue. Many have well-differentiated roots, stems, and leaves (fronds). The gametophyte generation is small and lacks vascular tissue.

■ *What would be the advantage of silica deposits in stems, as is found in horsetails?*

| TABLE 30.1 | The Seven Phyla of Extant Vascular Plants | | | |
|---|---|---|---|---|
| **Phylum** | **Examples** | | **Key Characteristics** | **Approximate Number of Living Species** |
| S E E D L E S S   V A S C U L A R   P L A N T S | | | | |
| Lycophyta | Club mosses | | Homosporous or heterosporous. Sperm motile. External water necessary for fertilization. About 12–13 genera. | 1150 |
| Pterophyta | Ferns | | Primarily homosporous (a few heterosporous). Sperm motile. External water necessary for fertilization. Leaves uncoil as they mature. Sporophytes and virtually all gametophytes are photosynthetic. About 365 genera. | 11,000 |
| | Horsetails | | Homosporous. Sperm motile. External water necessary for fertilization. Stems ribbed, jointed, either photosynthetic or nonphotosynthetic. Leaves scalelike, in whorls; nonphotosynthetic at maturity. One genus. | 15 |
| | Whisk ferns | | Homosporous. Sperm motile. External water necessary for fertilization. No differentiation between root and shoot. No leaves; one of the two genera has scalelike extensions and the other leaflike appendages. | 6 |

(Continued on next page)

TABLE 30.1 | The Seven Phyla of Extant Vascular Plants, *continued*

| Phylum | Examples | | Key Characteristics | Approximate Number of Living Species |
|---|---|---|---|---|
| *S E E D   P L A N T S* | | | | |
| Coniferophyta | Conifers (including pines, spruces, firs, yews, redwoods, and others) | | Heterosporous seed plants. Sperm not motile; conducted to egg by a pollen tube. Leaves mostly needlelike or scalelike. Trees, shrubs. About 50 genera. Many produce seeds in cones. | 601 |
| Cycadophyta | Cycads | | Heterosporous. Sperm flagellated and motile but confined within a pollen tube that grows to the vicinity of the egg. Palmlike plants with pinnate leaves. Secondary growth slow compared with that of the conifers. Ten genera. Seeds in cones. | 206 |
| Gnetophyta | Gnetophytes | | Heterosporous. Sperm not motile; conducted to egg by a pollen tube. The only gymnosperms with vessels. Trees, shrubs, vines. Three very diverse genera (*Ephedra, Gnetum, Welwitschia*). | 65 |
| Ginkgophyta | *Ginkgo* | | Heterosporous. Sperm flagellated and motile but conducted to the vicinity of the egg by a pollen tube. Deciduous tree with fan-shaped leaves that have evenly forking veins. Seeds resemble a small plum with fleshy, foul-smelling outer covering. One genus. | 1 |
| Anthophyta | Flowering plants (angiosperms) | | Heterosporous. Sperm not motile; conducted to egg by a pollen tube. Seeds enclosed within a fruit. Leaves greatly varied in size and form. Herbs, vines, shrubs, trees. About 14,000 genera. | 250,000 |

## 30.7 *The Evolution of Seed Plants*

### Learning Outcomes

1. *List the evolutionary advantages of seeds.*
2. *Distinguish between pollen and sperm in seed plants.*

The history of the land plants is replete with evolutionary innovations allowing the ancestors of aquatic algae to colonize the harsh and varied terrestrial terrains. Early innovations made survival on land possible, later followed by an explosion of plant life that continues to change the land and atmosphere, and support terrestrial animal life. Seed-producing plants have come to dominate the terrestrial landscape over the last several hundred million years. Much of the remarkable success of seed plants, both gymnosperms and angiosperms, can be attributed to the evolution of the seed, an innovation that protects and provides food for delicate embryos. Seeds allow embryos to "stop the clock" and germinate after a harsh winter or extremely dry season has passed.

Fruits, a later innovation, enhanced the dispersal of embryos across a broader landscape.

Seed plants, which have additional embryo protection, first appeared about 305 to 465 MYA and were the ancestors of gymnosperms and angiosperms. Seed plants appear to have evolved from spore-bearing plants known as **progymnosperms.** Progymnosperms shared several features with modern gymnosperms, including secondary vascular tissues (which allow for an increase in girth later in development). Some progymnosperms had leaves. Their reproduction was very simple, and it is not certain which particular group of progymnosperms gave rise to seed plants.

### The seed protects the embryo

From an evolutionary and ecological perspective, the seed represents an important advance. The embryo is protected by an extra layer or two of sporophyte tissue called the **integument,** creating the **ovule** (figure 30.21). Within the ovule, the megasporangium divides meiotically, producing a haploid megaspore. The megaspore produces the egg that combines with the sperm, resulting in the zygote. Seeds also contain a food supply for the developing embryo.

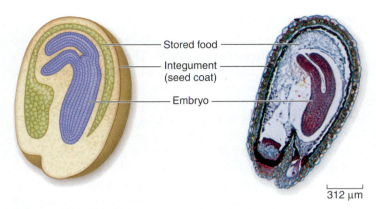

**Figure 30.21 Cross-section of an ovule.**

During development, the integuments harden to produce the seed coat. In addition to protecting the embryo from drought, the seed can be easily dispersed. Perhaps even more significantly, the presence of seeds introduces into the life cycle a dormant phase that allows the embryo to survive until environmental conditions are favorable for further growth.

### A pollen grain is the male gametophyte

Seed plants produce two kinds of gametophytes—male and female—each of which consists of just a few cells. Pollen grains, multicellular male gametophytes, are conveyed to the egg in the female gametophyte by wind or by a pollinator. In some seed plants, the sperm moves toward the egg through a growing **pollen tube.** This eliminates the need for external water. In contrast to the seedless plants, the whole male gametophyte, rather than just the sperm, moves to the female gametophyte.

A female gametophyte forms within the protection of the integuments, collectively forming the ovule. In angiosperms, the ovules are completely enclosed within additional diploid sporophyte tissue. The ovule and the surrounding, protective tissue are called the ovary. The ovary develops into the fruit.

**Learning Outcomes Review 30.7**

A common ancestor that had seeds gave rise to the gymnosperms and the angiosperms. Seeds protect the embryo, aid in dispersal, and can allow for an extended pause in the life cycle. Seed plants produce male and female gametophytes; the male gametophyte is a pollen grain, which is carried to the female gametophyte by wind or other means. The sperm is within the pollen grain.

■ *Why is water not essential for fertilization in seed plants?*

## 30.8 Gymnosperms: Plants with "Naked Seeds"

### Learning Outcomes

1. Describe the distinguishing features of a gymnosperm.
2. List the four groups of living gymnosperms.

Seeds distinguish the gymnosperms from the pterophytes. There are four groups of living **gymnosperms,** namely coniferophytes, cycadophytes, gnetophytes, and ginkgophytes, all of which lack the flowers and fruits of angiosperms. In all of them, the ovule, which becomes a seed, rests exposed on a scale (a modified shoot or leaf) and is not completely enclosed by sporophyte tissues at the time of pollination. The name *gymnosperm* literally means "naked seed." Although the ovules are naked at the time of pollination, the seeds of gymnosperms are sometimes enclosed by other sporophyte tissues by the time they are mature.

Details of reproduction vary somewhat in gymnosperms, and their forms vary greatly. For example, cycads and *Ginkgo* have motile sperm, whereas conifers and gnetophytes have sperm with no flagella. All sperm are carried within a pollen tube. The female cones range from tiny, woody structures weighing less than 25 g and having a diameter of a few millimeters, to massive structures produced in some cycads, weighing more than 45 kg and growing to lengths of more than a meter.

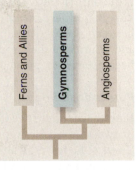

### Conifers are the largest gymnosperm phylum

The most familiar gymnosperms are **conifers** (phylum Coniferophyta), which include pines (figure 30.22), spruces, firs, cedars, hemlocks, yews, larches, cypresses, and others. The coastal redwood (*Sequoia sempervirens*), a conifer native to northwestern California and southwestern Oregon, is the tallest living vascular plant; it may attain a height of nearly 100 m (300 ft). Another conifer, the bristlecone pine (*Pinus longaeva*) of the White Mountains of California, is the oldest living tree; one specimen is 4900 years of age.

Conifers are found in the colder temperate and sometimes drier regions of the world. Various species are sources of timber, paper, resin, taxol (used to treat cancer), and other economically important products.

### Pines are an exemplary conifer genus

More than 100 species of pines exist today, all native to the northern hemisphere, although the range of one species does extend a

**Figure 30.22 Conifers.** Longleaf pines, *Pinus palustris,* in Florida are representative of the Coniferophyta, the largest phylum of gymnosperms.

little south of the equator. Pines and spruces, which belong to the same family, are members of the vast coniferous forests that lie between the arctic tundra and the temperate deciduous forests and prairies to their south. During the past century, pines have been extensively planted in the southern hemisphere.

## Pine morphology

Pines have tough, needlelike leaves produced mostly in clusters of two to five. Among the conifers, only pines have clustered leaves. The leaves, which have a thick cuticle and recessed stomata, represent an evolutionary adaptation for retarding water loss. This strategy is important because many of the trees grow in areas where the topsoil is frozen for part of the year, making it difficult for the roots to obtain water.

The leaves and other parts of the sporophyte have canals into which surrounding cells secrete resin. The resin deters insect and fungal attacks. The resin of certain pines is harvested commercially for its volatile liquid portion, called *turpentine*, and for the solid *rosin*, which is used on bowed stringed instruments. The wood of pines lacks some of the more rigid cell types found in other trees, and it is considered a "soft" rather than a "hard" wood. The thick bark of pines is an adaptation for surviving fires and subzero temperatures. Some cones actually depend on fire to open them, releasing seeds to reforest burned areas.

## Reproductive structures

All seed plants produce two types of spores that give rise to two types of gametophytes (figure 30.23). The male gametophytes (pollen grains) of pines develop from microspores, which are produced in male cones that develop in clusters of 30 to 70, typically at the tips of the lower branches; there may be hundreds of such clusters on any single tree.

The male pine cones generally are 1 to 4 cm long and consist of small, papery scales arranged in a spiral or in whorls. A pair of microsporangia form as sacs within each scale. Numerous microspore mother cells in the microsporangia undergo meiosis, each becoming four microspores. The microspores develop into four-celled pollen grains with a pair of air sacs that give them added buoyancy when released into the air. A single cluster of male pine cones may produce more than a million pollen grains.

Female pine cones typically are produced on the upper branches of the same tree that produces male cones. Female cones are larger than male cones, and their scales become woody.

Two ovules develop toward the base of each scale. Each ovule contains a megasporangium called the **nucellus**. The nucellus itself is completely surrounded by a thick layer of cells called the integument that has a small opening (the **micropyle**) toward one end. One of the layers of the integument later

**Figure 30.23**
**Life cycle of a typical pine.** The male and female gametophytes are dramatically reduced in size in these plants. Wind generally disperses the male gametophyte (pollen), which produces sperm. Pollen tube growth delivers the sperm to the egg on the female cone. Additional protection for the embryo is provided by the integument, which develops into the seed coat.

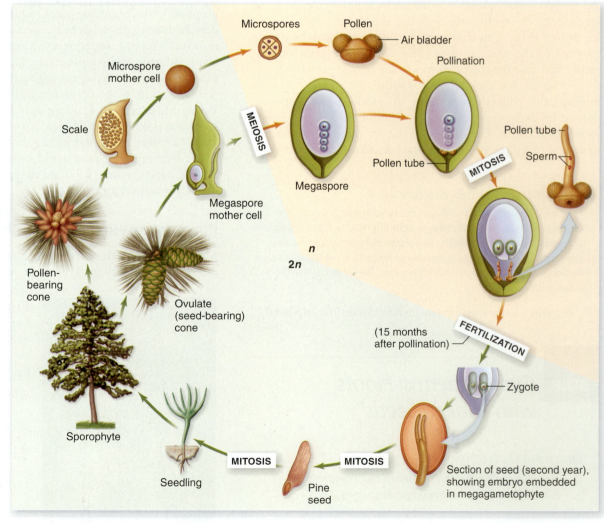

becomes the seed coat. A single megaspore mother cell within each megasporangium undergoes meiosis, becoming a row of four megaspores. Three of the megaspores break down, but the remaining one, over the better part of a year, slowly develops into a female gametophyte. The female gametophyte at maturity may consist of thousands of cells, with two to six archegonia formed at the micropylar end. Each archegonium contains an egg so large it can be seen without a microscope.

### Fertilization and seed formation

Female cones usually take two or more seasons to mature. At first they may be reddish or purplish in color, but they soon turn green, and during the first spring, the scales spread apart. While the scales are open, pollen grains carried by the wind drift down between them, some catching in sticky fluid oozing out of the micropyle. The pollen grains within the sticky fluid are slowly drawn down through the micropyle to the top of the nucellus, and the scales close shortly thereafter.

The archegonia and the rest of the female gametophyte are not mature until about a year later. While the female gametophyte is developing, a pollen tube emerges from a pollen grain at the bottom of the micropyle and slowly digests its way through the nucellus to the archegonia. During growth of the pollen tube, one of the pollen grain's four cells, the *generative cell*, divides by mitosis, with one of the resulting two cells dividing once more. These last two cells function as sperm. The germinated pollen grain with its two sperm is the mature male gametophyte, a very limited haploid phase compared with fern gametophytes.

About 15 months after pollination, the pollen tube reaches an archegonium and discharges its contents into it. One sperm unites with the egg, forming a zygote. The other sperm and cells of the pollen grain degenerate. The zygote develops into an embryo within the seed. After dispersal and germination of the seed, the young sporophyte of the next generation develops into a tree.

## Cycads resemble palms, but are not flowering plants

**Cycads** (phylum Cycadophyta) are slow-growing gymnosperms of tropical and subtropical regions. The sporophytes of most of the 100 known species resemble palm trees (figure 30.24*a*) with trunks that can attain heights of 15 m or more. Unlike palm trees, which are flowering plants, cycads produce cones and have a life cycle similar to that of pines.

The female cones, which develop upright among the leaf bases, are huge in some species and can weigh up to 45 kg. The sperm of cycads, although formed within a pollen tube, are released within the ovule to swim to an archegonium. These sperm are the largest sperm cells among all living organisms. Several species of cycads are facing extinction in the wild and soon may exist only in botanical gardens.

## Gnetophytes have xylem vessels

There are three genera and about 65 living species of gnetophytes (phylum Gnetophyta). They are the only gymnosperms with vessels in their xylem. **Vessels** are a particularly efficient conducting cell type that is a common feature in angiosperms.

The members of the three genera differ greatly from one another in form. One of the most bizarre of all plants is *Welwitschia*, which occurs in the Namib and Mossamedes deserts of southwestern Africa (figure 30.24*b*). The stem is shaped like a large, shallow cup that tapers into a taproot below the surface. It has two strap-shaped, leathery leaves that grow continuously from their base, splitting as they flap in the wind. The reproductive structures of *Welwitschia* are conelike, appear toward the bases of the leaves around the rims of the stems, and are produced on separate male and female plants.

More than half of the gnetophyte species are in the genus *Ephedra*, which is common in arid regions of the western United States and Mexico. Species are found on every continent except Australia. The plants are shrubby, with stems that superficially resemble those of horsetails, being jointed and having tiny, scale-like leaves at each node. Male and female reproductive structures may be produced on the same or different plants.

The drug ephedrine, widely used in the treatment of respiratory problems, was in the past extracted from Chinese species of *Ephedra*, but it has now been largely replaced with synthetic preparations (pseudoephedrine). Because ephedrine found in herbal remedies for weight loss was linked to strokes and heart attacks, it was withdrawn from the market in April of 2004. Sales restrictions were placed on pseudoephedrine-containing products in 2006 because it can be used to manufacture the illegal drug methamphetamine.

**Figure 30.24** **Three phyla of gymnosperms.** *a.* A cycad, *Cycas circinalis*. *b. Welwitschia mirabilis* represents one of the three genera of gnetophytes. *c.* Maidenhair tree, *Ginkgo biloba*, the only living representative of the phylum Ginkgophyta.

The best known species of the third genus, *Gnetum*, is a tropical tree, but most species are vinelike. All species have broad leaves similar to those of angiosperms. One *Gnetum* species is cultivated in Java for its tender shoots, which are cooked as a vegetable.

## Only one species of the ginkgophytes remains extant

The fossil record indicates that members of the ginkgophytes (phylum Ginkgophyta) were once widely distributed, particularly in the northern hemisphere; today, only one living species, *Ginkgo biloba*, remains (figure 30.24c). This tree, which sheds its leaves in the fall, was first encountered by Europeans in cultivation in Japan and China; it apparently no longer exists in the wild.

Like the sperm of cycads, those of *Ginkgo* have flagella. The ginkgo is **dioecious**—that is, the male and female reproductive structures are produced on separate trees. The fleshy outer coverings of the seeds of female ginkgo plants exude the foul smell of rancid butter, caused by the presence of butyric and isobutyric acids. As a result, male plants vegetatively propagated from shoots are preferred for cultivation. Because of its beauty and resistance to air pollution, *Ginkgo* is commonly planted along city streets.

### Learning Outcomes Review 30.8

Gymnosperms are mostly cone-bearing seed plants. In gymnosperms, the ovules are not completely enclosed by sporophyte tissue at pollination, and thus have "naked seeds." The four groups of gymnosperms are conifers, cycads, gnetophytes, and ginkgophytes.

■ **What adaptation do conifers exhibit to capture wind-borne pollen?**

## 30.9 Angiosperms: The Flowering Plants

### Learning Outcomes

1. List the defining features of angiosperms.
2. Describe the roles of some animals in the angiosperm life cycle.
3. Explain double fertilization and its outcome.

The 270,000 known species of flowering plants are called **angiosperms** because their ovules, unlike those of gymnosperms, are enclosed within diploid tissues at the time of pollination. The *carpel*, a modified leaf that encapsulates seeds, develops into the fruit, a unique angiosperm feature (figure 30.25). Although some gymnosperms, including the yew (*Taxus* spp.), have fleshlike tissue around their seeds, it is of a different origin and not a true fruit.

### Angiosperm origins are a mystery

The origins of the angiosperms puzzled even Darwin (he referred to their origin as an "abominable mystery"). Recent fossil pollen and plants accompanied by molecular sequence data have provided exciting clues about basal angiosperms, indicating origins as early as 145 to 208 MYA.

In the remote Liaoning province of China, a complete angiosperm fossil that is at least 125 million years old has been found (figure 30.26). The fossil may represent a new, basal, and

**Figure 30.25**
**Evolution of fruit.** Unlike gymnosperms, the ovule of angiosperms is surrounded by diploid tissue derived from leaves. This tissue is called the carpel and develops into the fruit. The leaf origins of carpels are still visible in the pea pod.

Ovules
(seeds)

Carpel
(fruit)

Ovules

Cross section

Modified leaf with ovules

Folding of leaf protects ovules

Fusion of leaf margins

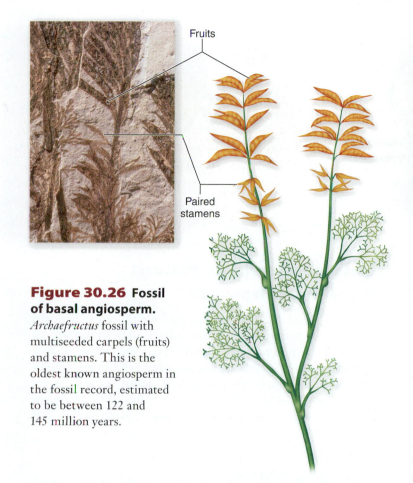

Fruits

Paired stamens

**Figure 30.26** Fossil of basal angiosperm. *Archaefructus* fossil with multiseeded carpels (fruits) and stamens. This is the oldest known angiosperm in the fossil record, estimated to be between 122 and 145 million years.

**Figure 30.27** An ancient living angiosperm, *Amborella trichopoda.* This plant is believed to be the closest living relative to the original angiosperm.

carpel

petal

sepal

*Archaefructus* fossils have both male and female reproductive structures; however, they lack the sepals and petals that evolved in later angiosperms to attract pollinators. The fossils were so well preserved that fossil pollen could be examined using scanning electron microscopy. Although *Archaefructus* is ancient, it is unlikely to be the very first angiosperm. Still, the incredibly well-preserved fossils provide valuable detail on angiosperms in the Upper Jurassic to Lower Cretaceous period, when dinosaurs roamed the Earth.

Consensus has also been growing on the most basal living angiosperm—*Amborella trichopoda* (figure 30.27). *Amborella*, with small, cream-colored flowers, is even more primitive than water lilies. This small shrub, found only on the island of New Caledonia in the South Pacific, is the last remaining species of the earliest extant lineage of the angiosperms that arose about 135 MYA.

Although *Amborella* is not the original angiosperm, it is sufficiently close that studying its reproductive biology may help us understand the early radiation of the angiosperms. The angiosperm phylogeny reflects an evolutionary hypothesis that is driving new research on angiosperm origins (figure 30.28).

extinct angiosperm family, Archaefructaceae, with two species: *Archaefructus liaoningensis* and *A. sinensis. Archaefructus* was an herbaceous, aquatic plant. This family is proposed to be the sister clade to all other angiosperms, but there is a lively debate about the validity of this claim.

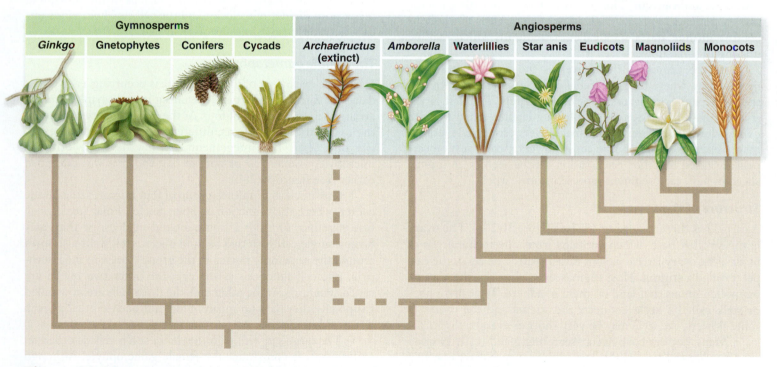

| Gymnosperms | | | | Angiosperms | | | | | | | |
|---|---|---|---|---|---|---|---|---|---|---|---|
| *Ginkgo* | Gnetophytes | Conifers | Cycads | *Archaefructus* (extinct) | *Amborella* | Waterlillies | Star anis | Eudicots | Magnoliids | Monocots |

**Figure 30.28** *Archaefructus* **may be the sister clade to all other angiosperms.** All members of the *Archaefructus* lineage are extinct, leaving *Amborella* as the most basal, living angiosperm. Gymnosperms species labels are shaded green.

**Figure 30.29** Diagram of an angiosperm flower. *a.* The main structures of the flower are labeled. *b.* Details of an ovule. The ovary as it matures will become a fruit; as the ovule's outer layers (integuments) mature, they will become a seed coat.

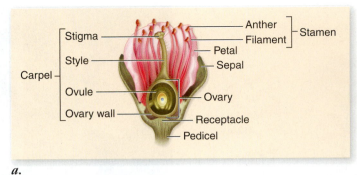

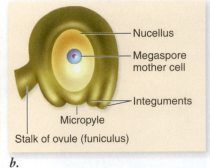

## Flowers house the gametophyte generation of angiosperms

Flowers are considered to be modified stems bearing modified leaves. Regardless of their size and shape, they all share certain features (figure 30.29). Each flower originates as a **primordium** that develops into a bud at the end of a stalk called a pedicel. The pedicel expands slightly at the tip to form the receptacle, to which the remaining flower parts are attached.

### Flower morphology

The other flower parts typically are attached in circles called **whorls.** The outermost whorl is composed of **sepals.** Most flowers have three to five sepals, which are green and somewhat leaflike. The next whorl consists of **petals** that are often colored, attracting pollinators such as insects, birds, and some small mammals. The petals, which also commonly number three to five, may be separate, fused together, or missing altogether in wind-pollinated flowers.

The third whorl consists of **stamens** and is collectively called the androecium. This whorl is where the male gametophytes, pollen, are produced. Each stamen consists of a pollen-bearing **anther** and a stalk called a **filament,** which may be missing in some flowers.

At the center of the flower is the fourth whorl, the **gynoecium,** where the small female gametophytes are housed; the gynoecium consists of one or more **carpels.** The first carpel is believed to have been formed from a leaflike structure with ovules along its margins. Primitive flowers can have several to many separate carpels, but in most flowers, two to several carpels are fused together. Such fusion can be seen in an orange sliced in half; each segment represents one carpel.

### Structure of the carpel

A carpel has three major regions (see figure 30.29*a*). The **ovary** is the swollen base, which contains from one to hundreds of ovules; the ovary later develops into a **fruit.** The tip of the carpel is called a **stigma.** Most stigmas are sticky or feathery, causing pollen grains that land on them to adhere. Typically, a neck or stalk called a **style** connects the stigma and the ovary; in some flowers, the style may be very short or even missing.

Many flowers have nectar-secreting glands called *nectaries,* often located toward the base of the ovary. Nectar is a fluid containing sugars, amino acids, and other molecules that attracts insects, birds, and other animals to flowers.

## Most species use flowers to attract pollinators and reproduce

Eudicots (about 175,000 species) include the great majority of familiar angiosperms—almost all kinds of trees and shrubs, snapdragons, mints, peas, sunflowers, and other plants. Monocots (about 65,000 species) include the lilies, grasses, cattails, palms, agaves, yuccas, orchids, and irises and share a common ancestor with the eudicots (see figure 30.28). Some of the monocots, including maize, rely on wind rather than pollinators to reproduce.

## The angiosperm life cycle includes double fertilization

During development of a flower bud, a single megaspore mother cell in the ovule undergoes meiosis, producing four megaspores (figure 30.30). In most flowering plants, three of the megaspores soon disappear; the nucleus of the remaining megaspore divides mitotically, and the cell slowly expands until it becomes many times its original size.

### The female gametophyte

While the expansion of the megaspore is occurring, each of the daughter nuclei divides twice, resulting in eight haploid nuclei arranged in two groups of four. At the same time, two layers of the ovule, the integuments, differentiate and become the *seed coat* of a seed. The integuments, as they develop, form the micropyle, a small gap or pore at one end that was described earlier (see figure 30.29b).

One nucleus from each group of four migrates toward the center, where they function as polar nuclei. Polar nuclei may fuse together, forming a single diploid nucleus, or they may form a single cell with two haploid nuclei. Cell walls also form around the remaining nuclei. In the group closest to the micropyle, one cell functions as the egg; the other two nuclei are called synergids. At the other end, the three cells are now called antipodals; they have no apparent function and eventually break down and disappear.

The large sac with eight nuclei in seven cells is called an embryo sac; it constitutes the female gametophyte. Although it is completely dependent on the sporophyte for nutrition, it is a multicellular, haploid individual.

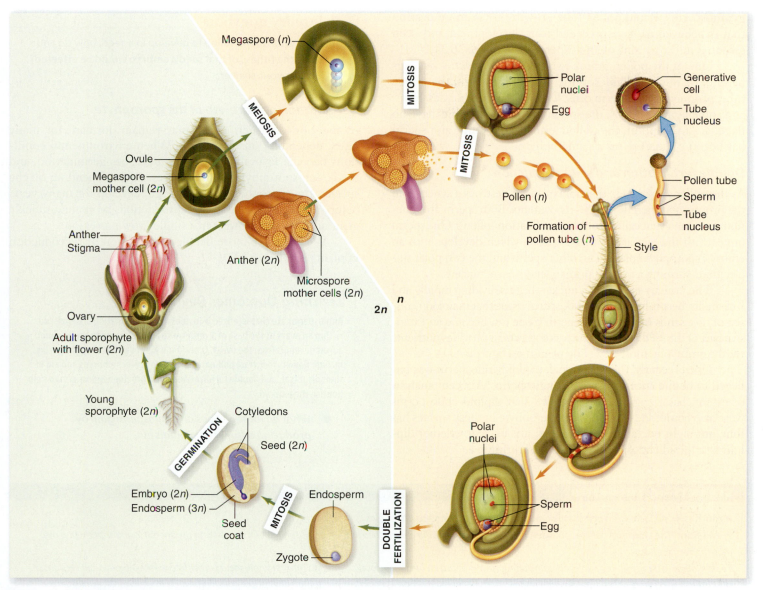

**Figure 30.30 Life cycle of a typical angiosperm.** As in pines, external water is no longer required for fertilization. In most species of angiosperms, animals carry pollen to the carpel. The outer wall of the carpel forms the fruit, which often entices animals to disperse the seed.

### Pollen production

While the female gametophyte is developing, a similar but less complex process takes place in the anthers (see figure 30.30). Most anthers have patches of tissue (usually four) that eventually become chambers lined with nutritive cells. The tissue in each patch is composed of many diploid microspore mother cells that undergo meiosis more or less simultaneously, each producing four microspores.

The four microspores at first remain together as a quartet, or tetrad, and the nucleus of each microspore divides once; in most species, the microspores of each quartet then separate. At the same time, a two-layered wall develops around each microspore. As the microspore-containing anther continues to mature, the wall between adjacent pairs of chambers breaks down, leaving two larger sacs. At this point, the binucleate microspores have become pollen grains.

The outer pollen grain wall layer often becomes beautifully sculptured, and it contains chemicals that may react with others in a stigma to signal whether development of the male gametophyte should proceed to completion. The pollen grain has areas called *apertures*, through which a pollen tube may later emerge.

### Pollination and the male gametophyte

**Pollination** is simply the mechanical transfer of pollen from its source (an anther) to a receptive area (the stigma of a flowering plant). Most pollination takes place between flowers of different plants and is brought about by insects, wind, water, gravity, bats, and other animals. In as many as one-quarter of all angiosperms, however, a pollen grain may be deposited directly on the stigma of its own flower, and self-pollination occurs. Pollination may or may not be followed by *fertilization*, depending on the genetic compatibility of the pollen grain and the flower on whose stigma it has landed.

If the stigma is receptive, the pollen grain's dense cytoplasm absorbs substances from the stigma and bulges through an aperture. The bulge develops into a pollen tube that responds to chemical and mechanical stimuli that guide it to the embryo sac. It follows a diffusion gradient of the chemicals and grows down through the style and into the micropyle. The pollen tube usually takes several hours to two days to reach the micropyle, but in a few instances, the journey may take up to a year. Pollen tube growth is more rapid in angiosperms than gymnosperms. Rapid pollen tube growth rate is an innovation that is believed to have preceded fruit development and been essential in the origins of angiosperms (see figure 30.31)

One of the pollen grain's two cells, the *generative cell*, lags behind. Its nucleus divides in the pollen grain or in the pollen tube, producing two sperm cells. Unlike sperm in mosses, ferns, and some gymnosperms, the sperm of flowering plants have no flagella. At this point, the pollen grain with its tube and sperm has become a mature male gametophyte.

## Double fertilization and seed production

As the pollen tube enters the embryo sac, it destroys a synergid in the process and then discharges its contents. Both sperm are functional, and an event called **double fertilization** follows. One sperm unites with the egg and forms a zygote, which develops into an embryo sporophyte plant. The other sperm and the two polar nuclei unite, forming a triploid primary endosperm nucleus.

The primary endosperm nucleus begins dividing rapidly and repeatedly, becoming triploid endosperm tissue that may soon consist of thousands of cells. Endosperm tissue can become an extensive part of the seed in grasses such as corn, and it provides nutrients for the embryo in most flowering plants (see figure 37.11).

Until recently, the nutritional, triploid endosperm was believed to be the ancestral state in angiosperms. A recent analysis of extant, basal angiosperms revealed that diploid endosperms were also common. The female gametophyte in these species has four, not eight nuclei. At the moment, it is unclear whether diploid or triploid endosperms are the most primitive.

## Inquiry question

**?** If the endosperm failed to develop in a seed, how do you think the fitness of that seed's embryo would be affected? Explain your answer.

### Germination and growth of the sporophyte

As mentioned earlier, a seed may remain dormant for many years, depending on the species. When environmental conditions become favorable, the seed undergoes germination, and the young sporophyte plant emerges. Again depending on the species, the sporophyte may grow and develop for many years before becoming capable of reproduction, or it may quickly grow and produce flowers in a single growing season.

We present a more detailed description of reproduction in plants in chapter 42.

### Learning Outcomes Review 30.9

Angiosperms are characterized by ovules that at pollination are enclosed within an ovary at the base of a carpel, a structure unique to the phylum; a fruit develops from the ovary. Evolutionary innovations of angiosperms include flowers to attract pollinators, fruits to protect embryos and aid in their dispersal, and double fertilization, which provides endosperm to help nourish the embryo.

■ *What advantage does an angiosperm gain by producing a fruit that animals eat?*

---

## SCIENTIFIC THINKING

**Hypothesis:** *An increase in pollen tube growth accompanied angiosperm origins.*

**Prediction:** *The time from pollination to fertilization will be greater in gymnosperms than angiosperms that are sister to the ancestral angiosperm and also more derived angiosperms.*

**Test:** *Pollinate three angiosperm species, including Amborella, that are most closely related to the first angiosperm. At different time intervals, cut sections of the carpel and observe pollen tube position under a fluorescent microscope. Calculate and compare the rate of pollen tube growth with results published for gymnosperms and more derived angiosperms.*

| Species | Pollen Tube Growth Rate (μm/hour) |
|---|---|
| **Close relatives of ancestral angiosperm** | |
| *Amborella trichopoda* | 80 |
| *Nuphar polysepala* | 589 |
| *Austrobaileya scandens* | 271 |
| **Derived angiosperms** | |
| *Petunia inflata* | 900 |
| *Zea mays* (maize) | 10,000 |
| **Gymnosperms** | |
| *Gnetum gnemon* | 6 |
| *Ginkgo biloba* | 0.31 |

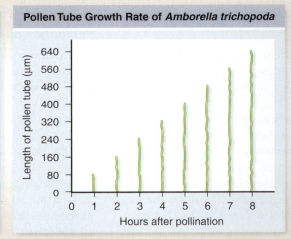

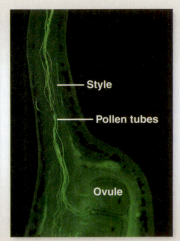

**Conclusion:** *An increase in pollen tube growth rate is found in angiosperms most closely related to the ancestral angiosperm, supporting the hypothesis.*

**Further Experiments:** *Develop a hypothesis to explain the difference in pollen tube growth rates among the tested angiosperms. Is there a correlation between the distance a pollen tube must travel to fertilize an egg and the rate of growth? How could you test your hypothesis?*

**Figure 30.31 Rapid pollen tube growth accompanied the origin of angiosperms.**

# Chapter Review

## 30.1 Defining Plants

**Land plants evolved from freshwater algae.**

All green plants arose from a single freshwater green algal species (see figure 30.1). The charophytes are the sister clade of the land plants.

Green algae and the land plants are placed in the kingdom Viridiplantae.

**Land plants have adapted to terrestrial life.**

Land plants have two major characteristics: protected embryos and multicellular haploid and diploid phases. A waxy cuticle, stomata, and specialized cells for transport of water and minerals enhance survival.

Most multicellular Viridiplantae have haplodiplontic life cycles.

Plants have a haplodiplontic life cycle with multicellular diploid sporophytes and haploid gametophytes (see figure 30.2).

**The haplodiplontic cycle produces alternation of generations.**

**The relative sizes of haploid and diploid generations vary.**

As some plants became more complex, the sporophyte stage became the dominant phase.

## 30.2 Chlorophytes and Charophytes: Green Algae
(see figure 30.5)

The chlorophytes gave rise to aquatic algae; the streptophytes include the group that gave rise to land plants.

**Chlorophytes can be unicellular.**

Unicellular chlorophytes include *Chlamydomonas*, which has two flagella, and *Chlorella*, which has no flagella and reproduces asexually.

**Colonial chlorophytes have some cell specialization.**

*Volvox* is an example of a colonial green alga; some cells specialize for producing gametes or for asexual reproduction.

**Multicellular chlorophytes can have haplodiplontic life cycles.**

*Ulva* has sporophyte and gametophyte generations; however, the chlorophytes did not give rise to land plants.

**Charophytes are the closest relatives to land plants.**

Both candidate Streptophyta clades—Charales and Coleochaetales—exhibit plasmodesmata, cytoplasmic links between cells. They also undergo mitosis and cytokinesis like terrestrial plants.

## 30.3 Bryophytes: Dominant Gametophyte Generation

**Bryophytes are unspecialized but successful in many environments.**

Bryophytes consist of three distinct clades: liverworts, mosses, and hornworts. Bryophytes do not have true roots or tracheids, but do have conducting cells for movement of water and nutrients.

In liverworts and mosses, the nonphotosynthetic sporophyte is nutritionally dependent on the gametophyte.

**Liverworts are an ancient phylum.**

The gametophyte of some liverworts is flattened and has lobes that resemble those of the liver. They produce upright structures that contain the gametangia.

**Mosses have rhizoids and water-conducting tissue.**

Mosses exhibit alternation of generations and have widespread distribution. Many are able to withstand droughts.

**Hornworts developed stomata.**

Stomata in the sporophyte can open and close to regulate gas exchange. The sporophyte is also photosynthetic.

## 30.4 Tracheophyte Plants: Roots, Stems, and Leaves (see table 30.1)

**Vascular tissue allows for distribution of nutrients.**

The evolution of tracheids allowed more efficient vascular systems to develop. This vascular tissue develops in the sporophyte.

Vascular plants have a much reduced gametophyte.

**Tracheophytes include seven extant phyla grouped in three clades.**

The vascular plants found today exist in three clades: lycophytes, pterophytes, and seed plants.

**Stems evolved prior to roots.**

**Roots provide structural support and transport capability.**

**Leaves evolved more than once.**

Lycophytes have small leaves called lycophylls that lack vascularization.

True leaves (euphylls) are found only in ferns and seed plants and have origins different from lycophylls.

**Seeds are another innovation in some phyla.**

Seeds are resistant structures that protect the embryo from desication and to some extent from predators.

## 30.5 Lycophytes: Dominant Sporophyte Generation and Vascular Tissue

Lycophyte ancestors were the earliest vascular plants and were among the first plants to have a dominant sporophyte generation.

## 30.6 Pterophytes: Ferns and Their Relatives
(see figure 30.17)

Ancestors of the pterophytes gave rise to two clades: one line of ferns and horsetails, and a second line of ferns and whisk ferns.

Pterophytes require water for fertilization and are seedless.

**Whisk ferns lost their roots and leaves secondarily.**

The sporophyte of a whisk fern consists of evenly forking green stems without roots.

**Horsetails have jointed stems with brushlike leaves.**

Scalelike leaves of horsetail sporophytes emerge in a whorl. The stems have silica deposits in epidermal cells of their ribs.

**Ferns have fronds that bear sori.**

The leaves of ferns, called fronds, develop as tightly rolled coils that unwind to expand. Sporangia called sori develop on the underside of the fronds. The gametophyte is often heart shaped and can live independently.

## 30.7 The Evolution of Seed Plants

**The seed protects the embryo.**

An extra layer of sporophyte tissue surrounds the embryo, creating the ovule, which later hardens. The seed protects the embryo, helps it resist drying out, and allows a dormant stage that pauses the life cycle until environmental conditions are favorable.

**A pollen grain is the male gametophyte.**

The gametophytes of seed plants consist of only a few cells. Pollen grains are male gametophytes; each pollen grain contains sperm cells. Water is not required for fertilization. The female gametophyte develops within an ovule that forms the seed.

## 30.8 Gymnosperms: Plants with "Naked Seeds"
(see figure 30.23)

Gymnosperms have ovules that are not completely enclosed in sporophyte (diploid) tissue at the time of pollination.

The four groups of gymnosperms are coniferophytes, cycadophytes, gnetophytes, and ginkgophytes; all lack flowers and true fruits.

### Conifers are the largest gymnosperm phylum.

Conifers include pines, spruces, firs, cedars, and many other groups. Both the tallest and the oldest vascular plants are conifers.

### Pines are an exemplary conifer genus.

Pines have tough, needlelike leaves in clusters of two to five. They produce male and female cones.

In the male cones, microspore mother cells in the microsporangia give rise to microspores that then develop into four-celled pollen grains, the male gametophytes.

In the female cones, a megasporangium (nucellus) produces a single megaspore mother cell that becomes four megaspores; three of these break down, and the remaining one develops into a female gametophyte, which produces archegonia that carry eggs.

Upon fertilization, a pollen tube emerges from the pollen grain and grows through the nucellus. Eventually two sperm cells migrate through the tube, and one unites with the egg; the other disintegrates.

### Cycads resemble palms, but are not flowering plants.

Most cycads can reach heights of 15 m or more. Cycads, unlike palms, produce cones; in some species the female cones are huge. Their life cycle is like that of conifers.

### Gnetophytes have xylem vessels.

Xylem vessels, a common feature in angiosperms, are highly efficient conducting cells. Gnetophytes are the only gymnosperms that have them.

This group includes the strange *Welwitschia* genus of southwestern Africa and the numerous worldwide *Ephedra* species.

### Only one species of the ginkgophytes remains extant.

*Ginkgo biloba* is a gymnosperm with broad leaves that it sheds in the fall. It is dioecious, and the fleshy seeds of the female tree have a foul odor.

## 30.9 Angiosperms: The Flowering Plants
(see figure 30.28)

Angiosperms are distinct from gymnosperms and other plants because their ovules are enclosed within diploid tissue called the ovary at the time of fertilization, and they form fruits.

### Angiosperm origins are a mystery.

No one is certain how the angiosperms arose, although the extinct family Archaefructaceae may have been a sister clade. The earliest extant angiosperm appears to be *Amborella trichopoda*, found on the island of New Caledonia.

### Flowers house the gametophyte generation of angiosperms.

Flowers are considered to be modified stems that bear modified leaves. Flower parts are organized into four whorls: sepals, petals, androecium, and gynoecium (see figure 30.29*a*).

The male androecium consists of the stamens where haploid pollen, the male gametophyte, is produced.

The female gynoecium consists of one or more carpels that contain the female gametophyte. The carpel has three major regions: the ovary, which later becomes the fruit; the stigma, which is the tip of the carpel; and the style, a stalk that connects the stigma and ovary.

### Most species use flowers to attract pollinators and reproduce.

Many angiosperm flowers have nectaries near the base of the ovary that produce nectar containing nutrients and other molecules. Nectar and scent attracts animal pollinators, which carry pollen from one flower to another; some angiosperms are wind pollinated, however.

### The angiosperm life cycle includes double fertilization.

The megaspore produces eight haploid nuclei. The female gametophyte consists of a large embryo sac with the eight nuclei in seven cells. The egg and the two polar nuclei (in a single cell) are most important.

After landing on a receptive stigma, a pollen grain develops a pollen tube that grows toward the embryo sac. Eventually, two sperm pass through this tube. One fuses with the egg to form a zygote, and the other unites with the polar bodies to form a triploid endosperm nucleus that develops into endosperm to nourish the embryo.

## Review Questions

### UNDERSTAND

1. Which of the following plant structures is not matched to its correct function?

   a. Stomata—allow gas transfer
   b. Tracheids—allow the movement of water and minerals
   c. Cuticle—prevents desication
   d. All of the above are matched correctly.

2. Which of the following genera most likely directly gave rise to the land plants?

   a. *Volvox*          c. *Ulva*
   b. *Chlamydomonas*   d. *Chara*

3. Which of the following would not be found in a bryophytes?

   a. Mycorrhizal associations
   b. Rhizoids
   c. Tracheid cells
   d. Photosynthetic gametophytes

4. Which of the following statements is correct regarding the bryophytes?

   a. The bryophytes represent a monophyletic clade.
   b. The sporophyte stage of all bryophytes is photosynthetic.
   c. Archegonium and antheridium represent haploid structures that produce reproductive cells.
   d. Stomata are common to all bryophytes.

5. The lack of seeds is a characteristic of all
   a. lycophytes.
   b. conifers.
   c. tracheophytes.
   d. gnetophytes.

6. Which of the following adaptations allows plants to pause their life cycle until environmental conditions are optimal?
   a. Stomata
   b. Phloem and xylem
   c. Seeds
   d. Flowers

7. Which of the following gymnosperms possesses a form of vascular tissue that is similar to that found in the angiosperms?
   a. Cycads
   b. Gnetophytes
   c. Ginkgophytes
   d. Conifers

8. In a pine tree, the microspores and megaspores are produced by the process of
   a. fertilization.
   b. mitosis.
   c. fusion.
   d. meiosis.

9. Which of the following terms is *not* associated with a male portion of a plant?
   a. Megaspore
   b. Antheridium
   c. Pollen grains
   d. Microspore

10. Which of the following potentially represents the oldest known living species of angiosperm?
    a. *Cooksonia*
    b. *Chlamydomonas*
    c. *Archaefructus*
    d. *Amborella*

## APPLY

1. Compare what happens to a spore mother cell as it gives rise to a spore with what happens to a spore as it gives rise to a gametophyte.
   a. The spore mother cell and the spore both go through meiosis.
   b. The spore mother cell and the spore both go through mitosis.
   c. The spore mother cell goes through mitosis and the spore goes through meiosis.
   d. The spore mother cell goes through meiosis and the spore goes through mitosis.

2. How could a plant without roots obtain sufficient nutrients from the soil?
   a. It cannot, all land plants have roots.
   b. Mychorrizal fungi associate with the plant and assist with the transfer of nutrients.
   c. Charophytes associate with the plant and assist with the transfer of nutrients.
   d. It relies on its xylem in the absence of a root.

3. A major innovation of land plants is embryo protection. How is a moss embryo protected from desication?
   a. By the seed
   b. By the antheridium
   c. By the archegonium
   d. By the lycophyll

4. Reproduction in angiosperms can occur more quickly than in gymnosperms because
   a. gymnosperm sperm requires water to swim to the egg.
   b. flowers always increase the rate of reproduction.

   c. angiosperm pollen tubes grow more quickly than gymnosperm pollen tubes.
   d. angiosperms have nectaries.

5. In double fertilization, one sperm produces a diploid _____, and the other produces a triploid _____.
   a. zygote; primary endosperm
   b. primary endosperm; microspore
   c. antipodal; zygote
   d. polar nuclei; zygote

6. Apply your understanding of angiosperms to identify which innovations likely contributed to the tremendous success of angiosperms.
   a. Homospory in angiosperms
   b. Fruits that attract animal dispersers
   c. Cones that protect the seed
   d. Dominant gametophyte generation

7. Comparing stems of two plant specimens under the microscope, you identify vessels in one sample and conclude the specimen
   a. with vessels must be an angiosperm.
   b. with vessels is either *Ephedra* or a cycad.
   c. without vessels is a pterophyte.
   d. without vessels must be a tracheophyte.

8. In a flower after fertilization, the following tissues are diploid:
   a. carpel, integuments, and megaspore mother cell.
   b. carpel, integuments, and megaspore.
   c. carpel, megaspore, and zygote.
   d. carpel, megaspore mother cell, and endosperm.

## SYNTHESIZE

1. You have access to the sequenced genomes for moss and the lycophyte *Selaginella*. Your goal in analyzing the data is to write a ground-breaking paper that answers an important question about the evolution of plants. What question would you try to answer?

2. You have been hired as a research assistant to investigate the origins of the angiosperms, specifically the boundary between a gymnosperm and an angiosperm. Which characteristics would you use to clearly define a new fossil as a gymnosperm? An angiosperm?

3. Assess the benefits and drawbacks of self-pollination for a flowering plant? Explain your answer.

4. The relationship between flowering plants and pollinators is often used as an example of coevolution. Many flowering plant species have flower structures that are adaptive to a single species of pollinator. Evaluate the benefits and drawbacks of using such a specialized relationship.

## ONLINE RESOURCE

**www.ravenbiology.com**

Understand, Apply, and Synthesize—enhance your study with animations that bring concepts to life and practice tests to assess your understanding. Your instructor may also recommend the interactive eBook, individualized learning tools, and more.

*Chapter* 31

# *Fungi*

## Chapter Outline

## Introduction

*The fungi, an often overlooked group of unicellular and multicellular organisms, have a profound influence on ecology and human health. Along with bacteria, they are important decomposers and disease-causing organisms. Fungi are found everywhere—from the tropics to the tundra and in both terrestrial and aquatic environments. Fungi made it possible for plants to colonize land by associating with rootless stems and aiding in the uptake of nutrients and water. Mushrooms and toadstools are the multicellular spore-producing part of fungi that grow rapidly under proper conditions. A single Armillaria fungus can cover 15 hectares underground and weigh 100 tons, making it the largest organism in the world based on area. Some puffball fungi are almost a meter in diameter and may contain 7 trillion spores—enough to circle the Earth's equator!*

*Yeasts are used to make bread and beer, but other fungi cause disease in plants and animals. These fungal killers are particularly problematic because fungi are animals' closest relatives. Drugs that can kill fungi often have toxic effects on animals, including humans. In this chapter we present the major groups of this intriguing life form.*

## 31.1  *Defining Fungi*

### Learning Outcomes

1. *Identify characteristics that distinguish fungi from other eukaryotes.*
2. *Compare mitosis in fungi and animals.*
3. *Explain why fungi are useful for bioremediation.*

Mycologists, scientists who study fungi as well as fungi-like protists, believe there may be as many as 1.5 million fungal species. Fungi exist either as single-celled yeasts or in multicellular form with several different cell types. Their reproduction may be either sexual or asexual, and they exhibit an unusual form of mitosis. They are specialized to extract and absorb nutrients from their surroundings through external secretion of enzymes. Recent phylogenetic analysis of DNA sequences and protein sequences indicates that fungi are more closely related to animals than to plants. Fossils and molecular data indicate that animals and fungi last shared a common ancestor at least 460 MYA, but inconsistencies remain. The oldest

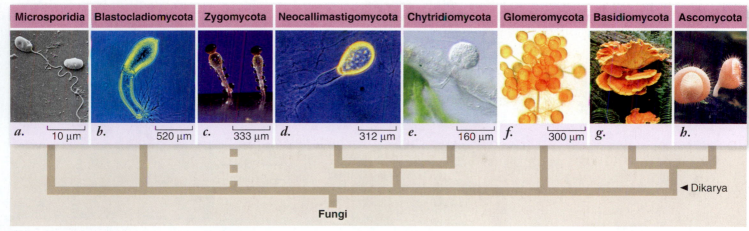

**Figure 31.1** **Seven major phyla of fungi.** All phyla, except Zygomycota, are monophyletic. *a.* Microsporidia, including *Encephalitozoon cuniculis*, are animal parasites. *b.* *Allomyces arbuscula*, a water mold, is a blastocladiomycete. *c.* *Pilobolus*, a zygomycete, grows on animal dung and also on culture medium. Stalks about 10 mm long contain dark, spore-bearing sacs. *d.* Neocallimastigales, including *Piromyces communis*, decompose cellulose in the rumens of herbivores. *e.* Some chytrids, including members of the genus *Rhizophydium*, parasitize green algae. *f.* Spores of *Glomus intraradices*, a glomeromycete associated with roots. *g.* *Amanita muscaria*, the fly agaric, is a toxic basidiomycete. *h.* The cup fungus *Cookeina tricholoma* is an ascomycete from the rain forest of Costa Rica. In the cup fungi, the spore-producing structures line the cup; in basidiomycetes that form mushrooms such as *Amanita*, they line the gills beneath the cap of the mushroom. All visible structures of fungi, including the ones shown here, arise from an extensive network of filamentous hyphae that penetrates and is interwoven with the substrate on which they grow.

fossil resembles extant members of the genus *Glomus* that arose within the Glomeromycota. One DNA analysis placed the animal/fungal divergence at 1.5500 bya. This latter estimate is not generally accepted, but many researchers believe that the last common ancestor existed around close to 670 mya based on an analysis of multiple genes. The last common ancestor with animals was a single cell, and unique solutions to multicellularity evolved both in fungi and in animals.

The phylogenetic relationships among fungi have been the cause of much debate. Traditionally, four fungal phyla were recognized, based primarily on characteristics of the cells undergoing meiosis: Chytridiomycota ("chytrids"), Zygomycota ("zygomycetes"), Ascomycota ("ascomycetes"), and Basidiomycota ("basidiomycetes"). The chytrids and zygomycetes are not monophyletic.

The understanding of fungal phylogeny is going through rapid and exciting changes, aided by increasing molecular sequence data (figure 31.1 and table 31.1). In 2007, mycologists agreed on seven monophyletic phyla: Microsporidia, Blastocladiomycota, Neocallismastigomycota, Chytridiomycota, Glomeromycota, Basidiomycota, and Ascomycota (see figure 31.1). Blastomycetes and neocallistmastigamycetes were formerly grouped with the chytrids. The Microsporidia are sister to all other fungi, but there is disagreement as to whether or not they are true fungi.

In reading the chapter you will find that phyla with common characteristics are sometimes grouped under one heading. Phylogenies are included as reminders of the evolutionary relationships among phyla. Not all fungi are currently assigned to a monophyletic clade, yet their biology is fascinating.

| TABLE 31.1 | Fungi | | |
|---|---|---|---|
| **Group** | **Typical Examples** | **Key Characteristics** | **Approximate Number of Living Species** |
| Chytridiomycota | *Allomyces* | Aquatic, flagellated fungi that produce haploid gametes in sexual reproduction or diploid zoospores in asexual reproduction. | 1000 |
| Zygomycota | *Rhizopus, Pilobolus* | Multinucleate hyphae lack septa, except for reproductive structures; fusion of hyphae leads directly to formation of a zygote in zygosporangium, in which meiosis occurs just before it germinates; asexual reproduction is most common. | 1050 |
| Glomeromycota | *Glomus* | Form arbuscular mycorrhizae. Multinucleate hyphae lack septa. Reproduce asexually. | 150 |
| Ascomycota | Truffles, morels | In sexual reproduction, ascospores are formed inside a sac called an ascus; asexual reproduction is also common. | 45,000 |
| Basidiomycota | Mushrooms, toadstools, rusts | In sexual reproduction, basidiospores are borne on club-shaped structures called basidia; asexual reproduction occurs occasionally. | 22,000 |

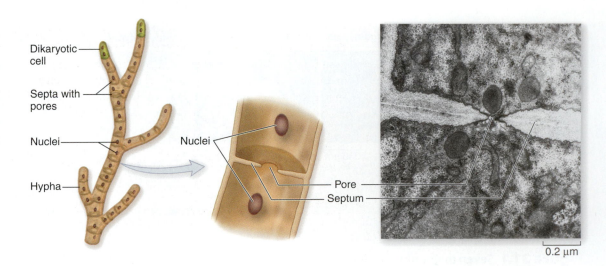

**Figure 31.2 A septum.** This transmission electron micrograph of a section through a hypha of an ascomycete shows a pore through which the cytoplasm streams.

Dikaryotic cell

Septa with pores

Nuclei

Hypha

Nuclei

Pore

Septum

0.2 μm

## The body of a fungus is a mass of connected hyphae

Some hyphae are continuous or branching tubes filled with cytoplasm and multiple nuclei. Other hyphae are typically made up of long chains of cells joined end-to-end and divided by cross-walls called septa (singular, *septum*). The septa rarely form a complete barrier, except when they separate the reproductive cells. Even fungi with septa can be considered one long cell.

Cytoplasm characteristically flows or streams freely throughout the hyphae, passing through major pores in the septa (figure 31.2). Because of this streaming, proteins synthesized throughout the hyphae may be carried to their actively growing tips. As a result, fungal hyphae may grow very rapidly when food and water are abundant and the temperature is optimum. For example, you may have seen mushrooms suddenly appear in a lawn overnight after a rain in summer.

### The mycelium

A mass of connected hyphae is called a **mycelium** (plural, *mycelia*). (This word and the term mycology, the study of fungi, are both derived from the Greek word *mykes*, meaning fungi.) The mycelium of a fungus (figure 31.3) constitutes a system that may, in the aggregate, be many meters long. This mycelium grows into the soil, wood, or other material and digestion of the material begins quickly. In two of the four major groups of fungi, reproductive structures formed of interwoven hyphae, such as mushrooms, puffballs, and morels, are produced at certain stages of the life cycle. These structures expand rapidly because of rapid inflation of the hyphae.

### Cell walls with chitin

The cell walls of fungi are formed of polysaccharides, including chitin. In contrast, cell walls of plants and many protists contain cellulose, not chitin. Chitin is a modified cellulose consisting of linked glucose units to which nitrogen groups have been added; this polymer is then cross-linked with proteins. Chitin is the same material that makes up the major portion of the hard shells, or exoskeletons, of arthropods, a group of animals that includes insects and crustaceans (chapter 34). Chitin is one of

the shared traits that has led scientists to believe that fungi and animals are more closely related than fungi and plants.

## Fungal cells may have more than one nucleus

Fungi are different from most animals and plants in that each cell (or hypha) can house one, two, or more nuclei. A hypha that has only one nucleus is called **monokaryotic;** a cell with two nuclei is **dikaryotic.** In a dikaryotic cell, the two haploid nuclei exist independently. Dikaryotic hyphae have some of the genetic properties of diploids, because both genomes are transcribed.

Sometimes, many nuclei intermingle in the common cytoplasm of a fungal mycelium, which can lack distinct cells. If a dikaryotic or multinucleate hypha has nuclei that are derived from two genetically distinct individuals, the hypha is called **heterokaryotic.** Hyphae whose nuclei are genetically similar to one another are called **homokaryotic.**

## Mitosis is not followed by cell division

Mitosis in multicellular fungi differs from that in most other organisms. Because of the linked nature of the cells, the cell

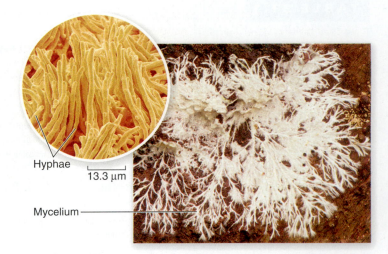

Hyphae

13.3 μm

Mycelium

**Figure 31.3 Fungal mycelium.** This mycelium, composed of hyphae, is growing through leaves on the forest floor in Maryland.

**Figure 31.4**
**Fungal spores.**
Scanning electron micrograph of fungal spores from *Aspergillus*.

9.5 μm

itself is not the relevant unit of reproduction; instead, the nucleus is. The nuclear envelope does not break down and reform; instead, the spindle apparatus is formed *within* it.

Centrioles are absent in all fungi except chytrids; instead, fungi regulate the formation of microtubules during mitosis with small, relatively amorphous structures called *spindle plaques*. This unique combination of features strongly suggests that fungi originated from some unknown group of single-celled eukaryotes with these characteristics.

## Fungi can reproduce both sexually and asexually

Many fungi are capable of producing both sexual and asexual spores. When a fungus reproduces sexually, two haploid hyphae of compatible mating types may come together and fuse.

### The dikaryon stage

In animals, plants, and some fungi, the fusion of two haploid cells during reproduction immediately results in a diploid cell (2*n*). But in other fungi, namely basidiomycetes and ascomycetes, an intervening dikaryotic stage (1*n* + 1*n*) occurs before the parental nuclei fuse and form a diploid nucleus. In ascomycetes, this dikaryon stage is brief, occurring in only a few cells of the sexual reproductive structure. In basidiomycetes, however, it can last for most of the life of the fungus, including both the feeding and sexual spore-producing structures.

### Reproductive structures

Some fungal species produce specialized mycelial structures to house the production of spores. Examples are the mushrooms we see above ground, the "shelf" fungus that appears on the trunks of dead trees, and puffballs, which can house billions of spores.

As noted previously, the cytoplasm in fungal hyphae normally flows through perforated septa or moves freely in their absence. Reproductive structures are an important exception to this general pattern. When reproductive structures form, they are cut off by complete septa that lack perforations or that have perforations that soon become blocked.

### Spores

Spores are the most common means of reproduction among fungi. They may form as a result of either asexual or sexual processes, and they are often dispersed by the wind. When spores land in a suitable place, they germinate, giving rise to a new fungal mycelium.

Because the spores are very small, between 2 and 75 μm in diameter (figure 31.4), they can remain suspended in the air for a long time. Unfortunately, many of the fungi that cause diseases in plants and animals are spread rapidly by such means. The spores of other fungi are routinely dispersed by insects or other small animals. A few fungal phyla retain the ancestral flagella and have motile zoospores.

Biologists had believed for a long time that the worldwide presence of fungal species could be accounted for, on an evolutionary timescale, by the almost limitless, long-distance dispersal of fungal spores. Recent biogeographic studies, however, have examined the phylogenetic relationships among fungi in distant parts of the world and disproved this long-held assumption.

## Fungi are heterotrophs that absorb nutrients

All fungi obtain their food by secreting digestive enzymes into their surroundings and then absorbing the organic molecules produced by this external digestion. The fungal body plan reflects this approach. Unicellular fungi have the greatest surface area-to-volume ratio of any fungus, maximizing the surface area for absorption. Extensive networks of hyphae also provide an enormous surface area for absorptive nutrition in a fungal mycelium.

Many fungi are able to break down the cellulose in wood, cleaving the linkages between glucose subunits and then absorbing the glucose molecules as food. Most fungi also digest lignin, an insoluble organic compound that strengthens plant cell walls. The specialized metabolic pathways of fungi allow them to obtain nutrients from dead trees and from an extraordinary range of organic compounds, including tiny roundworms called nematodes (figure 31.5*a*).

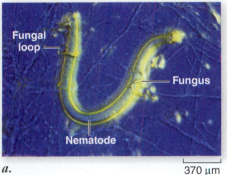

Fungal loop — Fungus — Nematode

*a.*  370 μm

*b.*

**Figure 31.5 Carnivorous fungi.** *a.* Fungus obtaining nutrients from a nematode. *b.* The oyster mushroom *Pleurotus ostreatus* not only decomposes wood but also immobilizes nematodes, which the fungus uses as a source of nitrogen.

The mycelium of the edible oyster mushroom *Pleurotus ostreatus* (figure 31.5*b*) excretes a substance that paralyzes nematodes that feed on the fungus. When the worms become sluggish and inactive, the fungal hyphae envelop and penetrate their bodies. Then the fungus secretes digestive juices and absorbs the nematode's nutritious contents, just like it would from a plant source.

This fungus usually grows within living trees or on old stumps, obtaining the bulk of its glucose through the enzymatic digestion of cellulose and lignin from plant cell walls. The nematodes it consumes apparently serve mainly as a source of nitrogen—a substance almost always in short supply in biological systems. Other fungi are even more active predators than *Pleurotus*, snaring, trapping, or firing projectiles into nematodes, rotifers, and other small animals on which they prey.

Because of their ability to break down almost any carbon-containing compound—even jet fuel—fungi are of interest for use in bioremediation, using organisms to clean up soil or water that is environmentally contaminated. As one example, some fungal species can remove selenium, an element that is toxic in high accumulations, from soils by combining it with other harmless volatile compounds.

## Learning Outcomes Review 31.1

Fungi are more closely related to animals than to plants. Many, but not all, fungi form seven monophyletic phyla. A fungus consists of a mass of hyphae (cells) termed a mycelium; cell walls contain the polysaccharide chitin. Mitosis in fungi divides the nucleus but not the hypha itself. Sexual reproduction may occur when hyphae of two different mating types fuse. Haploid nuclei from each type may persist separately in some groups, termed a dikaryon stage. Spores are produced sexually or asexually and are spread by wind or animals. Fungi secrete digestive enzymes externally and then absorb the products of the digestion. Fungi can break down almost any organic compound.

- **What differentiates fungi from animals, since both are heterotrophs?**
- **What protects hyphae from being digested by the fungus's own secreted enzymes?**

## 31.2 Microsporidia: Unicellular Parasites

### Learning Outcomes

1. **Explain characteristics that led microsporidians to be classified as protists.**
2. **Describe evidence for placing microsporidians with fungi.**

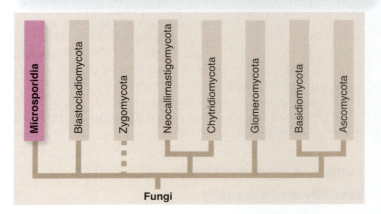

Microsporidia are obligate, intracellular, animal parasites, long thought to be protists. The lack of mitochondria led biologists to believe that microsporidians were in a deep branch of protists that diverged before endosymbiosis led to mitochondria. Genome sequencing of the microsporidian *Encephalitozoon cuniculi* revealed genes related to mitochondrial functions within the tiny 2.9-Mb genome. Finding mitochondrial genes led to the hypothesis that microsporidia ancestors had mitochondria, and that greatly reduced, mitochondrion-derived organelles exist in microsporidia. Coupled with phylogenies derived from analyses of new sequence data, microsporidia have been tentatively moved from the protists to the fungi.

*E. cuniculi* and other microsporidia commonly cause disease in immunosuppressed patients, such as those with AIDS and people who have received organ transplants. Microsporidians infect hosts with their spores, which contain a polar tube (figure 31.6). The polar tube extrudes the contents of the spore

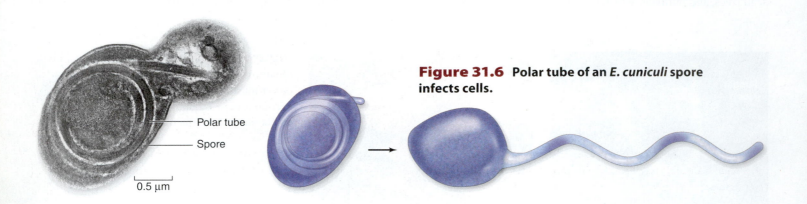

0.5 µm

Polar tube
Spore

**Figure 31.6** Polar tube of an *E. cuniculi* spore infects cells.

into the cell and the parasite sets up housekeeping in a vacuole. *E. cuniculi* infects intestinal and neuronal cells, leading to diarrhea and neurodegenerative disease. Understanding the phylogenetic placement of the microsporidia is important in identifying effective disease treatments.

### Learning Outcomes Review 31.2

Microsporidia lack mitochondria; however, the presence of mitochondrial genes indicates that at one time an ancestral form possessed them. As obligate parasites, microsporidia cause diseases in animals, including humans.

■ *How would you distinguish a microsporidian from the parasitic protistan* Plasmodium?

## 31.3 Chytridiomycota and Relatives: Fungi with Flagellated Zoospores

### Learning Outcomes

1. *Distinguish between blastocladiomycetes and microsporidians.*
2. *Explain the meaning of "chytrid."*
3. *Discuss possible uses of neocallimastigomycetes.*

Members of phylum Chytridiomycota, the **chitridiomycetes** or **chytrids,** are aquatic, flagellated fungi that are closely related to ancestral fungi. Motile zoospores are a distinguishing character of this fungal group. Chytrid has its origins in the Greek word *chytridion,* meaning "little pot," referring to the structure that releases the flagellated zoospores (figure 31.7).

Chytrids include *Batrachochytrium dendrobatidis,* which has been implicated in the die-off of amphibians. Other chytrids have been identified as plant pathogens (figure 31.8). Traditionally the blastocladiomycetes and the neocallismastigomycetes have been grouped with the chytrids. Recent phylogenetic inferences have accorded the two groups their own phyla. Both proposed phyla are discussed here because of their many similarities with the chytrids.

### Blastocladiomycota have single flagella

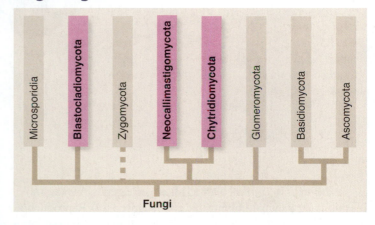

Blastocladiomycetes have uniflagellated zoospores. Blastocladiomycetes, neocallismastigomycetes, and chytridiomycetes were originally grouped as a single phylum because they all have flagella that have been lost in other groups, except the microsporidians. Inclusion of multiple genes in phylogenetic analyses has established that the three groups form three separate, monophyletic phyla.

**Figure 31.7 Zoospore release.** The potlike structure (*chytridion* in Greek) containing the zoospores gives chytrids their name.

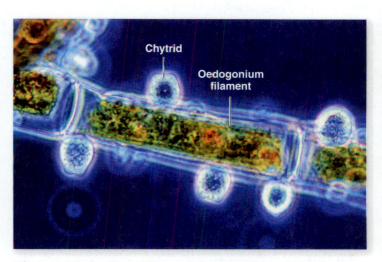

**Figure 31.8 Chytridiomycota can be plant pathogens.** *Rhizophydium granulosporum* sporangia on a filament of the green algae *Oedogonium.*

## Figure 31.9

**Allomyces, a blastocladiomycete that grows in the soil.** *a.* The spherical sporangia can produce either diploid zoospores via mitosis or haploid zoospores via meiosis. *b.* Life cycle of *Allomyces*, which has both haploid and diploid multicellular stages (alternation of generations).

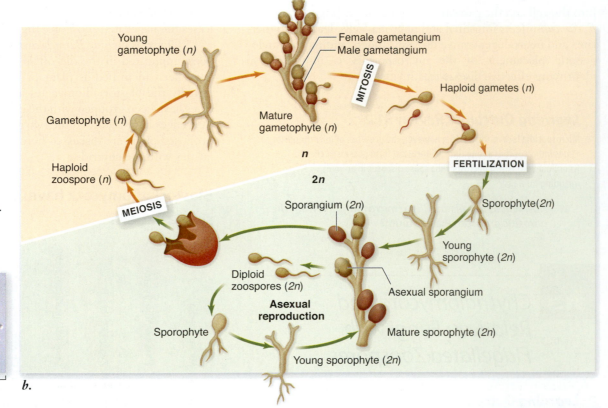

a.                100 μm   b.

*Allomyces* is a typical blastocladiomycete genus. A water mold, it exhibits a true haplodiplontic life cycle (figure 31.9). Reproduction in *Allomyces* species is enhanced by the secretion of a pheromone, a long-distance chemical signal, from the female gametes that attracts male gametes. Pheromones are similar to hormones, but work between organisms, rather than within organisms. The *Allomyces* pheromone is called sirenin (after the Sirens in Greek mythology) and was the first fungal sex hormone to be identified chemically.

Unlike microsporidia, which lack mitochondria, *A. macrogynus* has giant mitochondria in its zoospores. Each flagellated zoospore contains a single giant mitochondrion that is fragmented into several normal-sized organelles in vegetative cells.

## Neocallimastigomycota digest cellulose in ruminant herbivores

Within the rumens of mammalian herbivores, **neocallimastigomycetes** enzymatically digest the cellulose and lignin of the plant biomass in their grassy diet. Sheep, cows, kangaroos, and elephants all depend on these fungi to obtain sufficient calories. These anaerobic fungi have greatly reduced mitochondria that lack cristae. Their zoospores have multiple flagella. "Mastig" in Neocallimas*tigo*mycota is Latin for "whips," referencing the multiple flagella.

The genus *Neocallimastix* can survive on cellulose alone. Genes encoding digestive enzymes such as cellulase made their way into the *Neocallimastix* genomes via horizontal gene transfer from bacteria. Horizontal gene transfer is covered in chapter 26.

The many enzymes that neocallimastigamycetes use to digest cellulose and lignin in plant cell walls may be useful in biofuel production from cellulose. Although it is possible to obtain ethanol from cellulose, breaking down the cellulose is a major technical hurdle. The use of neocallimastigamycetes fungi to produce cellulosic ethanol is a promising, cost-effective approach.

## 31.4 Zygomycota: Fungi That Produce Zygotes

**Zygomycetes** (phylum Zygomycota) include only about 1050 named species, but they are incredibly diverse. The zygomycota are not monophyletic, but are included in this chapter as a group while research on their evolutionary history continues. Among them are some of the more common bread molds, which have been assigned to the monophyletic subphylum Mucoromycotina (figure 31.10), as well as a variety of others

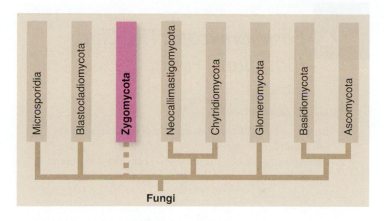

found on decaying organic material, including strawberries and other fruits. A few human pathogens are in this group.

## In sexual reproduction, zygotes form inside a zygosporangium

The zygomycetes lack septa in their hyphae except when they form sporangia or gametangia (structures in which spores or gametes are produced). The group is named after a characteristic feature of the sexual phase of the life cycle, the formation of diploid zygote nuclei.

Sexual reproduction begins with the fusion of gametangia, which contain numerous nuclei. The gametangia are cut off from the hyphae by complete septa. These gametangia may be formed on hyphae of different mating types or on a single hypha.

The haploid nuclei fuse to form a diploid zygote nucleus, a process called karyogamy. The area where the fusion has taken place develops into a zygosporangium (figure 31.10b), within which a **zygospore** develops. The zygospore, which may contain one or more diploid nuclei, acquires a thick coat that helps the fungus survive conditions not favorable for growth.

Meiosis, followed by mitosis, occurs during the germination of the zygospore, which releases haploid spores. Haploid hyphae grow when these haploid spores germinate. Except for the zygote nuclei, all nuclei of the zygomycetes are haploid.

## Asexual reproduction is more common

Asexual reproduction occurs much more frequently than sexual reproduction in the zygomycetes. During asexual reproduction, hyphae produce clumps of erect stalks, called **sporangiophores.** The tips of the sporangiophores form sporangia, which are separated by septa. Thin-walled haploid spores are produced within the sporangia. These spores are shed above the food substrate, in a position where they may be picked up by the wind and dispersed to a new food source.

### Learning Outcomes Review 31.4

Zygomycetes are named for the production of diploid zygote nuclei by fusion of haploid nuclei, a process called karyogamy. The hyphae of zygomycetes are multinucleate, with septa only where gametangia or sporangia are separated. Many zygomycetes form characteristic resting structures called zygosporangia, which contain zygospores that are able to withstand harsh conditions.

■ *Under what conditions would you expect a zygomycete to produce zygospores rather than haploid spores?*

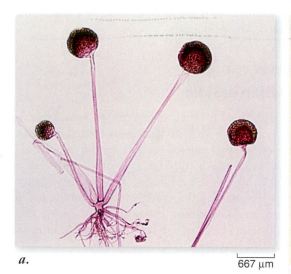

*a.*

667 μm

**Figure 31.10** *Rhizopus,* **a zygomycete that grows on simple sugars.** This fungus is often found on moist bread or fruit. *a.* The dark, spherical, spore-producing sporangia are on hyphae about 1 cm tall. The rootlike hyphae (rhizoids) anchor the sporangia. *b.* Life cycle of *Rhizopus.* The Zygomycota group is named for the zygosporangia characteristic of *Rhizopus.* The (+) and (-) denote mating types.

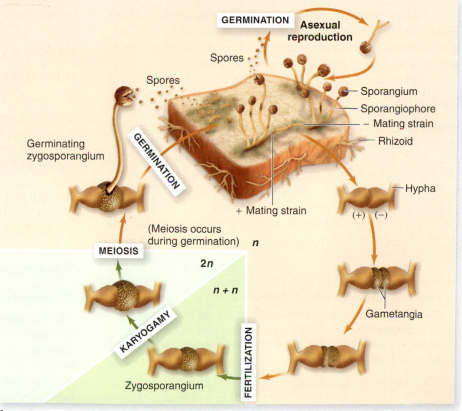

*b.*

## 31.5 Glomeromycota: Asexual Plant Symbionts

### Learning Outcome

1. **Explain why Glomeromycota is now considered separate from Zygomycota.**

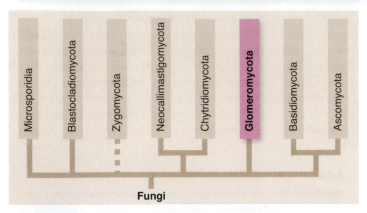

The glomeromycetes, a tiny group of fungi with approximately 150 described species, likely made the evolution of terrestrial plants possible. Tips of hyphae grow within the root cells of most trees and herbaceous plants, forming a branching structure that allows nutrient exchange. The intracellular associations with plant roots are called **arbuscular mycorrhizae.** The specifics of arbuscular mycorrhizal associations and other forms of mycorrhizal interactions are detailed in section 31.8.

Glomeromycetes cannot survive in the absence of a host plant. The symbiotic relationship is mutualistic, with the glomeromycetes providing essential minerals, especially phosphorous, and the plants providing carbohydrates.

The glomeromycetes are challenging to characterize, in part, because there is no evidence of sexual reproduction. These fungi exemplify our emerging understanding of fungal phylogeny. Like zygomycetes, glomeromycetes lack septae in their hyphae and were once grouped with the zygomycetes. However, comparisons of DNA sequences of small-subunit rRNAs reveal that glomeromycetes are a monophyletic clade that is phylogenetically distinct from zygomycetes. Unlike zygomycetes, glomeromycetes lack zygospores. Glomeromycota originated at least 600 to 620 MYA, well before the split of the Ascomycota and Basidiomycota, which we will consider next.

### Learning Outcome Review 31.5

Glomeromycetes are a monophyletic fungal lineage based on analysis of small-subunit rRNAs. Their obligate symbiotic relationship with the roots of many plants appears to be ancient and may have made it possible for terrestrial plants to evolve.

■ *Why do glomeromycetes require a host plant?*

## 31.6 Basidiomycota: The Club (Basidium) Fungi

### Learning Outcomes

1. **Explain which cells in the life cycle of a basidiomycete are diploid.**
2. **Distinguish between primary and secondary mycelium in basidiomycetes.**

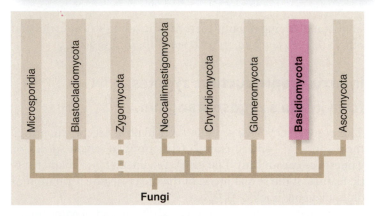

The basidiomycetes (phylum Basidiomycota) include some of the most familiar fungi. Among the basidiomycetes are not only the mushrooms, toadstools, puffballs, jelly fungi, and shelf fungi, but also many important plant pathogens, including rusts and smuts (figure 31.11a). Rust infections resemble rusting metals, and smut infections appear black and powdery due to the spores. Many mushrooms are used as food, but others are hallucinogenic or deadly poisonous.

### Basidiomycetes sexually reproduce within basidia

Basidiomycetes are named for their characteristic sexual reproductive structure, the club-shaped **basidium** (plural, *basidia*). Karyogamy (fusion of two nuclei) occurs within the basidium, giving rise to the only diploid cell of the life cycle (figure 31.11b). Meiosis occurs immediately after karyogamy. In the basidiomycetes, the four haploid products of meiosis are incorporated into **basidiospores.** In most members of this phylum, the basidiospores are borne at the end of the basidia on slender projections (sterigmata).

### The secondary mycelium of basidiomycetes is heterokaryotic

The life cycle of a basidiomycete continues with the production of monokaryotic hyphae after spore germination. These hyphae lack septa early in development. Eventually, septa form between the nuclei of the monokaryotic hyphae. A basidiomycete mycelium made up of monokaryotic hyphae is called a *primary mycelium*.

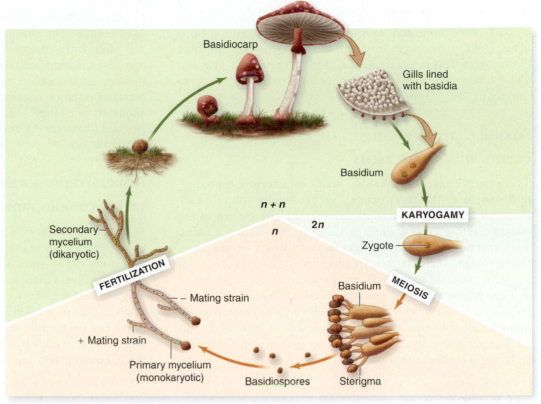

**Figure 31.11** **Basidiomycetes.**
*a.* The death cap mushroom, *Amanita phalloides.* When eaten, these mushrooms are usually fatal. *b.* Life cycle of a basidiomycete. The basidium is the reproductive structure.

Different mating types of monokaryotic hyphae may fuse, forming a dikaryotic mycelium, or *secondary mycelium*. Such a mycelium is heterokaryotic, with two nuclei representing the two different mating types, between each pair of septa. This stage is the dikaryon stage described earlier as being a distinguishing feature of fungi. It is found in both the ascomycetes and the basidiomycetes. The two phyla are grouped as the subkingdom Dikarya because of this commonality. The maintenance of two genomes in the heterokaryon allows for more genetic plasticity than in a diploid cell with one nucleus. One genome may compensate for mutations in the other.

The **basidiocarps,** or mushrooms, are formed entirely of secondary (dikaryotic) mycelium. Gills, sheets of tissue on the undersurface of the cap of a mushroom, produce vast numbers of minute spores. It has been estimated that a mushroom with a cap measuring 7.5 cm in diameter produces as many as 40 million spores per hour!

### Learning Outcomes Review 31.6

Basidiomycetes undergo karyogamy, after which meiosis occurs within club-shaped basidia. The primary mycelium consists of monokaryotic hyphae resulting from spore germination. The secondary mycelium of basidiomycetes is the dikaryon stage, in which two nuclei exist within a single hyphal segment.

■ *What distinguishes a dikaryotic cell from a diploid cell?*

## 31.7 Ascomycota: The Sac (Ascus) Fungi

### Learning Outcomes

1. *Compare the ascomycetes and the basidiomycetes*
2. *List the ways ascomycetes affect humans.*

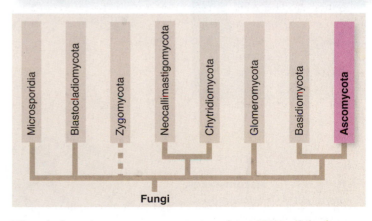

The phylum **Ascomycota** contains about 75% of the known fungi. Among the ascomycetes are such familiar and economically important fungi as bread yeasts, common molds, morels (figure 31.12*a*), cup fungi (figure 31.12*b*), and truffles. Also included in this phylum are many serious plant pathogens, including those that produce chestnut blight, *Cryphonectria parasitica*, and Dutch elm disease, *Ophiostoma ulmi*. Penicillin-producing ascomycetes are in the genus *Penicillium*.

## Sexual reproduction occurs within the ascus

The ascomycetes are named for their characteristic reproductive structure, the microscopic, saclike **ascus** (plural, *asci*). Karyogamy, the production of the only diploid nucleus of the ascomycete life cycle (figure 31.12*c*), occurs within the ascus. The structure of an ascus differs from that of a basidium, although functionally the two are identical.

Asci are differentiated within a structure made up of densely interwoven hyphae, corresponding to the visible portions of a morel or cup fungus, called the **ascocarp**. Meiosis immediately follows karyogamy, forming four haploid daughter nuclei. These usually divide again by mitosis, producing eight haploid nuclei that become walled **ascospores**. The as-

cospores of the ascomycetes are borne internally in asci instead of externally as in basidiospores.

In many ascomycetes, the ascus becomes highly turgid at maturity and ultimately bursts, often at a preformed area. When this occurs, the ascospores may be thrown as far as 31 cm, an amazing distance considering that most ascospores are only about 10 μm long. This would be equivalent to throwing a baseball (diameter 7.5 cm) 1.25 km—about 10 times the length of a home run!

## Asexual reproduction occurs within conidiophores

Asexual reproduction is very common in the ascomycetes. It takes place by means of **conidia** (singular, *conidium*), asexual spores cut off by septa at the ends of modified hyphae called conidiophores. Conidia allow for the rapid colonization of a new food source. Many conidia are multinucleate. The hyphae of ascomycetes are divided by septa, but the septa are perforated, and the cytoplasm flows along the length of each hypha. The septa that cut off the asci and conidia are initially perforated, but later become blocked.

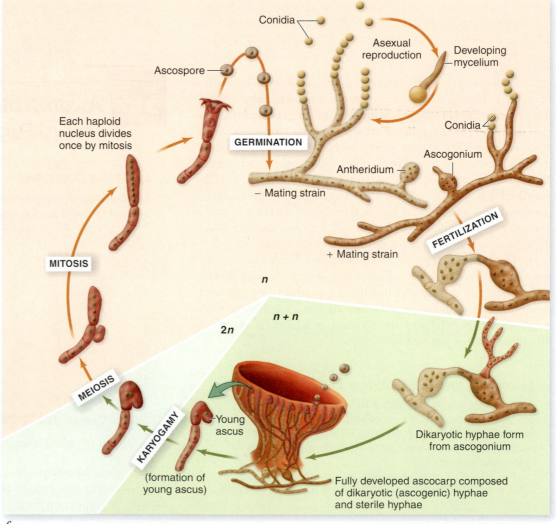

**Figure 31.12 Ascomycetes.**
*a.* This morel, *Morchella esculenta*, is a delicious edible ascomycete that appears in early spring. *b.* A cup fungus. *c.* Life cycle of an ascomycete. Haploid ascospores form within the ascus.

*a.*

*b.*

*c.*

## Some ascomycetes have yeast morphology

Most yeasts are ascomycetes with a single-celled lifestyle. Most of yeasts' reproduction is asexual and takes place by cell fission or budding, when a smaller cell forms from a larger one (figure 31.13). Sometimes two yeast cells fuse, forming one cell containing two nuclei. This cell may then function as an ascus, with karyogamy followed immediately by meiosis. The resulting ascospores function directly as new yeast cells.

The ability of yeasts to ferment carbohydrates, breaking down glucose to produce ethanol and carbon dioxide, is fundamental in the production of bread, beer, and wine. About four billion of these tiny, powerful organisms can fit in a teaspoon. Many different strains of yeast have been domesticated and selected for these processes, using the sugars in rice, barley, wheat, and corn. Wild yeasts—ones that occur naturally in the areas where wine is made—were important in wine making historically, but domesticated cultured yeasts are normally used now.

Wild yeast, often *Candida milleri*, is still important in making sourdough bread. Unlike most breads that are made with pure cultures of yeast, sourdough uses an active culture of wild yeast and bacteria that generate acid. This culture is maintained, and small amounts—"starter" cultures—are used for each batch of bread. The combination of yeast and acid-producing bacteria is needed for fermentation and gives sourdough bread its unique flavor.

The most important yeast in baking, brewing, and wine making is *Saccharomyces cerevisiae*. This yeast has been used by humans throughout recorded history. Yeast is also employed as a nutritional supplement because it contains high levels of B vitamins and because about 50% of yeast is protein.

## Ascomycete genetics and genomics have practical applications

Yeast is a long-standing model system for genetic research. It was the first eukaryote to be manipulated extensively by the techniques of genetic engineering, and they still play the lead-ing role as models for research in eukaryotic cells. In 1996, the genome sequence of *S. cerevisiae*, the first eukaryote to be sequenced entirely, was completed. The yeast two-hybrid system has been an important component of research on protein interactions (see chapter 17).

The fungal genome initiative is now under way to provide sequence information on other fungi. More than 25 fungi have been or are being sequenced. These fungi were selected based on their effects on human health, including plant pathogens that threaten our food supply.

The ascomycetes *Coccidioides posadasii* and its relative *C. immitis* were included because they are endemic in soil in the southwestern portion of the United States, can cause a fatal infection called coccidioidomycosis ("valley fever"), and have been considered a possible bioterrorism threat. In the United States the annual infection rate is about 100,000 individuals, although only a small percentage of infected individuals die.

A second important criterion in selecting which fungi to sequence was the potential to provide information on fungal evolution. This new information will complement and expand our understanding of the diverse fungal kingdom.

### Learning Outcomes Review 31.7

Ascomycetes undergo karyogamy within a characteristic saclike structure, the ascus. The function of the ascus is therefore identical to that of the basidium, although they are structurally different. Meiosis follows, resulting in the production of ascospores. Yeasts within this group generally reproduce asexually by budding. Ascomycetes include both beneficial forms used as foods, and in the production of foods, and harmful forms responsible for diseases and spoilage. Many ascomycetes are employed in scientific research.

■ *Coccidioidomycosis is caused by inhaling spores; it often occurs in farmworkers in the Southwest United States. What would help prevent this disease?*

## 31.8 Ecology of Fungi

### Learning Outcomes

1. *Identify a trait that contributes to the value of fungi in symbiotic relationships.*
2. *Describe the living components of a lichen.*
3. *List examples of fungal associations with different organisms.*

Fungi, together with bacteria, are the principal decomposers in the biosphere. They break down organic materials and return the substances locked in those molecules to circulation in the ecosystem. Fungi can break down cellulose and lignin, an insoluble organic compound that is one of the major constituents of wood. By breaking down such substances, fungi release carbon,

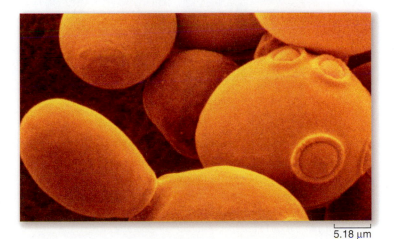

5.18 μm

**Figure 31.13 Budding in *Saccharomyces*.** As shown in this scanning electron micrograph, the cells tend to hang together in chains, a feature that calls to mind the derivation of single-celled yeasts from multicellular ancestors.

nitrogen, and phosphorus from the bodies of living or dead organisms and make them available to other organisms.

In addition to their role as decomposers, fungi have entered into fascinating relationships with a variety of life forms. Interactions between different species are described in chapter 57 where we discuss community ecology, but we cover fungal relationships briefly here because of their unique character.

## Fungi have a range of symbioses

The interactions, or symbioses, between fungi and other living organisms fall into a broad range of categories. In some cases, the symbiosis is an **obligate symbiosis** (essential for survival), and in other cases it is a **facultative symbiosis** (the fungus can survive without the host). Within a group of closely related fungi, several different types of symbiosis can be found.

First, here is a summary of ways in which living things can interact. **Pathogens** and **parasites** gain resources from their host, but they have a negative effect on the host that can even lead to death. The difference between pathogens and parasites is that pathogens cause disease, but parasites do not, except in extreme cases.

**Commensal** relationships benefit one partner but do not harm the other. Fungi that are in a **mutualistic** relationship benefit both themselves and their hosts. Many of these relationships are described in the discussion that follows.

## Endophytes live inside plants and may protect plants from parasites

Endophytic fungi live inside plants, actually in the intercellular spaces. Found throughout the plant kingdom, many of these relationships may be examples of parasitism or commensalism.

There is growing evidence that some of these fungi protect their hosts from herbivores by producing chemical toxins or deterrents. Most often, the fungus synthesizes alkaloids that protect the plant. As you will learn in chapter 40, plants also synthesize a wide range of alkaloids, many of which serve to defend the plant.

One way to assess whether an endophyte is enhancing the health of its host plant is to grow plots of plants with and without the same endophyte. An experiment with perennial ryegrass, *Lolium perenne*, demonstrated that it is more resistant to aphid feeding when an endophytic fungus, *Neotyphodium*, is present (figure 31.14).

## Lichens are an example of symbiosis between different kingdoms

**Lichens** (figure 31.15) are symbiotic associations between a fungus and a photosynthetic partner. Although many lichens are excellent examples of mutualism, some fungi are parasitic on their photosynthetic host.

### Composition of a lichen

Ascomycetes are the fungal partners in all but about 20 of the approximately 15,000 species of lichens estimated to exist. Most of the visible body of a lichen consists of its fungus, but between

**SCIENTIFIC THINKING**

**Hypothesis:** *Endophytic fungi can protect their host from herbivory.*
**Prediction:** *There will be fewer aphids (Rhopalosiphum padi, an herbivore) on perennial ryegrass (Lolium perenne) infected with endophytic fungi than on uninfected ryegrass.*
**Test:** *Place five adult aphids on each pot of 2-week-old grass plants with and without endophytic fungi. Place pots in perforated bags and grow for 36 days. Count the number of aphids in each pot.*

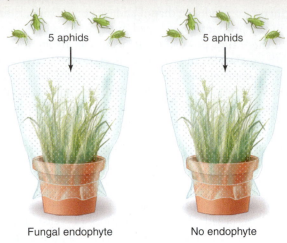

5 aphids                    5 aphids

Fungal endophyte              No endophyte

**Result:** *Significantly more aphids were found on the uninfected grass plants.*

**Conclusion:** *Endophytic fungi protect host plants from herbivory.*
**Further Experiments:** *How do you think the fungi protect the plants from herbivory? If they secrete chemical toxins, could you use this basic experimental design to test specific fungal compounds?*

**Figure 31.14** **Effect of the fungal endophyte *Neotyphodium* on the aphid population living on perennial ryegrass (*Lolium perenne*).**

| Fruticose Lichen | Foliose Lichen | Crustose Lichen |
|---|---|---|

*a.*  *b.*  *c.*

**Figure 31.15** **Lichens are found in a variety of habitats.** *a.* A fruticose lichen, growing in the soil. *b.* A foliose ("leafy") lichen, growing on the bark of a tree in Oregon. *c.* A crustose lichen, growing on rocks leading to the breakdown of rock into soil.

the filaments of that fungus are cyanobacteria, green algae, or sometimes both (figure 31.16).

Specialized fungal hyphae penetrate or envelop the photosynthetic cell walls within them and transfer nutrients directly to the fungal partner. Note that although fungi penetrate the cell wall, they do not penetrate the plasma membrane. Biochemical signals sent out by the fungus apparently direct its cyanobacterial or green algal component to produce metabolic substances that it does not produce when growing independently of the fungus.

The fungi in lichens are unable to grow normally without their photosynthetic partners, and the fungi protect their partners from strong light and desiccation. When fungal components of lichens have been experimentally isolated from their photosynthetic partner, they survive, but grow very slowly.

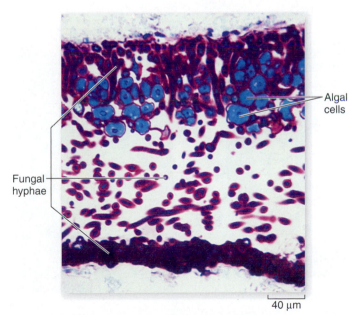

**Figure 31.16** **Stained section of a lichen.** This section shows fungal hyphae *(purple)* more densely packed into a protective layer on the top and, especially, the bottom layer of the lichen. The blue cells near the upper surface of the lichen are those of a green alga. These cells supply carbohydrate to the fungus.

Algal cells

Fungal hyphae

40 µm

### Ecology of lichens

The durable construction of the fungus combined with the photosynthetic properties of its partner have enabled lichens to invade the harshest habitats—the tops of mountains, the farthest northern and southern latitudes, and dry, bare rock faces in the desert. In harsh, exposed areas, lichens are often the first colonists, breaking down the rocks and setting the stage for the invasion of other organisms.

Lichens are often strikingly colored because of the presence of pigments that probably play a role in protecting the photosynthetic partner from the destructive action of the sun's rays. These same pigments may be extracted from the lichens and used as natural dyes. The traditional method of manufacturing Scotland's famous Harris tweed used fungal dyes.

Lichens vary in sensitivity to pollutants in the atmosphere, and some species are used as bioindicators of air quality. Their sensitivity results from their ability to absorb substances dissolved in rain and dew. Lichens are generally absent in and around cities because of automobile traffic and industrial activity, but some are adapted to these conditions. As pollution decreases, lichen populations tend to increase.

## Mycorrhizae are fungi associated with roots of plants

The roots of about 90% of all plant families have species that are involved in mutualistic symbiotic relationships with certain kinds of fungi. It has been estimated that these fungi probably amount to 15% of the total weight of the world's plant roots. Associations of this kind are termed **mycorrhizae,** from the Greek words for fungus and root.

The fungi in mycorrhizal associations function as extensions of the root system. The fungal hyphae dramatically increase the amount of soil contact and total surface area for absorption. When mycorrhizae are present, they aid in the direct transfer of phosphorus, zinc, copper, and other mineral nutrients from the soil into the roots. The plant, on the other hand, supplies organic carbon to the fungus, so the system is an example of mutualism.

There are two principal types of mycorrhizae (figure 31.17). In arbuscular mycorrhizae, the fungal hyphae penetrate the outer cells of the plant root, forming coils, swellings, and minute branches; they also extend out into the surrounding soil. In **ectomycorrhizae**, the hyphae surround but do not penetrate the cell walls of the roots. In both kinds of mycorrhizae, the mycelium extends far out into the soil. A single root may associate with many fungal species, dividing the root at a millimeter-by-millimeter level.

### Arbuscular mycorrhizae

Arbuscular mycorrhizae are by far the more common of the two types, involving roughly 70% of all plant species (figure 31.17*a*). The fungal component in them are glomeromycetes, a monophyletic group that arose within one of the zygomycete lineages. The glomeromycetes are associated with more than 200,000 species of plants.

Unlike mushrooms, none of the glomeromycetes produce aboveground fruiting structures, and as a result, it is difficult to arrive at an accurate count of the number of extant species. Arbuscular mycorrhizal fungi are being studied intensively because they are potentially capable of increasing crop yields with lower phosphate and energy inputs.

The earliest fossil plants often show arbuscular mycorrhizal roots. Such associations may have played an important role in allowing plants to colonize land. The soils available at such times would have been sterile and lacking in organic matter. Plants that form mycorrhizal associations are particularly successful in infertile soils; considering the fossil evidence, it seems reasonable that mycorrhizal associations helped the earliest plants succeed on such soils. In addition, the closest living relatives of early vascular plants surviving today continue to depend strongly on mycorrhizae.

Some nonphotosynthetic plants also have mycorrhizal associations, but the symbiosis is one-way because the plant has no photosynthetic resources to offer. Instead of a two-partner symbiosis, a tripartite symbiosis is established. The fungal mycelium extends between a photosynthetic plant and a nonphotosynthetic, parasitic plant. This third, nonphotosynthetic member of the symbiosis is called an *epiparasite*. Not only does it obtain phosphate from the fungus, but it uses the fungus to channel carbohydrates from the photosynthetic plant to itself. Epiparasitism also occurs in ectomycorrhizal symbiosis.

### Ectomycorrhizae

Ectomycorrhizae (see figure 31.17*b*) involve far fewer kinds of plants than do arbuscular mycorrhizae—perhaps a few thousand. Most ectomycorrhizal hosts are forest trees, such as pines, oaks, birches, willows, eucalyptus, and many others. The fungal components in most ectomycorrhizae are basidiomycetes, but some are ascomycetes.

Most ectomycorrhizal fungi are not restricted to a single species of plant, and most ectomycorrhizal plants form associations with many ectomycorrhizal fungi. Different combinations have different effects on the physiological characteristics of the plant and its ability to survive under different environmental conditions. At least 5000 species of fungi are involved in ectomycorrhizal relationships.

## Fungi also form mutual symbioses with animals

A range of mutualistic fungal–animal symbioses has been identified. Ruminant animals host neocallimastigomycete fungi in

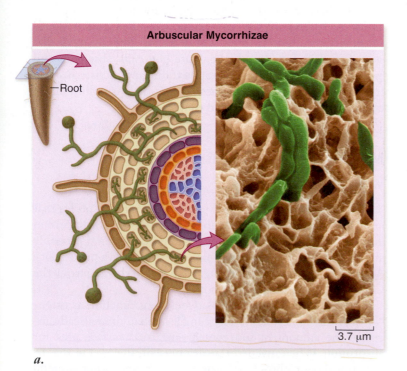

Arbuscular Mycorrhizae

—Root

3.7 μm

*a.*

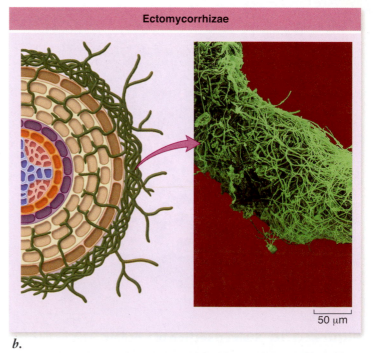

Ectomycorrhizae

50 μm

*b.*

**Figure 31.17 Arbuscular mycorrhizae and ectomycorrhizae.** *a.* In arbuscular mycorrhizae, fungal hyphae penetrate the root cell wall of plants but not the plant membranes. *b.* Ectomycorrhizae on the roots of a *Eucalyptus* tree do not penetrate root cells, but grow around and extend between the cells.

**Figure 31.18** **Ant–fungal symbiosis.** Ants farming their fungal garden.

their gut. The fungus gains a nutrient-rich environment in exchange for releasing nutrients from grasses with high cellulose and lignin content.

One tripartite symbiosis involves ants, plants, and fungi. Leaf-cutter ants are the dominant herbivore in the New World tropics. These ants, members of the phylogenetic tribe Attini, have an obligate symbiosis with specific fungi that they have domesticated and maintain in an underground garden. The ants provide fungi with leaves to eat and protection from pathogens and other predators (figure 31.18). The fungi are the ants' food source.

Depending on the species of ant, the ant nest can be as small as a golf ball or as large as 50 cm in diameter and many feet deep. Some nests are inhabited by millions of leaf-cutter ants that maintain fungal gardens. These social insects have a caste system, and different ants have specific roles. Traveling on trails as long as 200 m, leaf-cutter ants search for foliage for their fungi. A colony of ants can defoliate an entire tree in a day. This ant farmer–fungi symbiosis has evolved multiple times and may have occurred as early as 50 MYA.

### Learning Outcomes Review 31.8

Fungi are the primary decomposers in ecosystems. A range of symbiotic relationships have evolved between fungi and plants. Endophytes live inside tissues of a plant and may protect it from parasites. Lichens are a complex symbiosis between fungal species and cyanobacteria or green algae. Mycorrhizal associations between fungi and plant roots are mutually beneficial and in some cases are obligate symbioses. Fungi have also coevolved with animals in mutualistic relationships.

■ *How might the symbiosis between fungi and ants have evolved?*

## 31.9 Fungal Parasites and Pathogens

### Learning Outcomes

1. Review the pathogenic effects of fungi and the targets they affect.
2. Explain why treating fungal disease in animals is particularly difficult.

Fungi can destroy a crop of plants and create significant problems for human health. A major problem in treatment and prevention is that fungi are eukaryotes, as are plants and animals. Understanding how fungi are distinct from these other two eukaryotic kingdoms may lead to safer and more efficient means of treating diseases caused by fungal parasites and pathogens.

### Fungal infestation can harm plants and those who eat them

Fungal species cause many diseases in plants (figure 31.19), and they are responsible for billions of dollars in agricultural losses

**Figure 31.19** **World's largest organism?**
*a. Armillaria*, a pathogenic fungus shown here afflicting three discrete regions of coniferous forest in Montana, grows out from a central focus as a single, circular clone. The large patch at the bottom of the picture is almost 8 hectares. *b.* Closeup of tree destroyed by *Armillaria*. *c. Armillaria* growing on a tree.

*a.*

*c.*

every year. Not only are fungi among the most harmful pests of living plants, but they also spoil food products that have been harvested and stored. In addition, fungi often secrete substances into the foods they are infesting that make these foods unpalatable, carcinogenic, or poisonous.

Pathogenic fungal–plant symbioses are numerous, and fungal pathogens of plants can also harm the animals that consume the plants. *Fusarium* species growing on spoiled food produce highly toxic substances, including vomitoxin, which has been implicated in brain damage in humans and animals in the southwestern United States.

Aflatoxins, which are among the most carcinogenic compounds known, are produced by some *Aspergillus flavus* strains growing on corn, peanuts, and cotton seed (figure 31.20). Aflatoxins can also damage the kidneys and the nervous system of animals, including humans. Most developed countries have legal limits on the concentration of aflatoxin permitted in different foods. More recently, aflatoxins have been considered as possible bioterrorism agents.

In contrast, corn smut is a maize fungal disease that is harmful to the plant, but not animals that consume it (figure 31.20). Corn smut is caused by the basidiomycete *Ustilago maydi* and is edible.

## Fungal infections are difficult to treat in humans and other animals

Human and animal diseases can also be fungal in origin. Some common diseases, such as ringworm (which is not a worm but a fungus), athlete's foot, and nail fungus, can be treated with topical antifungal ointments and in some cases with oral medication.

Fungi can create devastating human diseases that are often difficult to treat because of the close phylogenetic relationship between fungi and animals. Yeast ascomycetes are important pathogens that cause diseases such as thrush, an infection of the mouth; the yeast *Candida* causes common oral or vaginal infections. *Pneumocystis jiroveci* (formerly *P. carinii*) invades the lungs, disrupting breathing, and can spread to other organs. In immune-suppressed AIDS patients, this infection can lead to death.

*a.*                    *b.*         4.50 μm

**Figure 31.20 Maize (corn) fungal infections.** *a. Ustilago maydis* infections of maize are a delicacy in Hispanic cuisine. *b.* A photomicrograph of *Aspergillus flavus* conidia. *Aspergillus flavus* infects maize and can produce aflatoxins that are harmful to animals.

**Figure 31.21 Frog killed by chytridiomycosis.** Lesions formed by the chytrid can be seen on the abdomen of this frog.

Chytrid

10 μm

Mold allergies are common, and mold-infested "sick" buildings pose concerns for inhabitants. Individuals with suppressed immune systems and people undergoing steroid treatments for inflammatory disorders are particularly at risk for fungal disease.

An example of a parasitic fungal–animal symbiosis is **chytridiomycosis,** first identified in 1998 as an emerging infectious disease of amphibians. Amphibian populations have been declining worldwide for over three decades. The many possible causes for the decline in amphibian numbers are covered in chapter 60. In this chapter, a primary causative agent, fungal infection, is explored. The decline correlates with the presence of the chytrid *Batrachochytrium dendrobatidis encased in the skin* (figure 31.21), identified after extensive studies of frog carcasses. Sick and dead frogs were more likely than healthy frogs to have flasklike structures encased in their skin, which proved to be associated with chytrid spore production (see figure 31.21).

The connection with *B. dendrobatidis* has been supported by DNA sequence data, by isolating and culturing the chytrid, and by infecting healthy frogs with the organism and replicating disease symptoms. The *B. dendrobatidis* genome has now been sequenced. The infection reduces sodium and potassium transport across the skin, altering electrolyte balance which leads to cardiac arrest. Bathing frogs in antifungal drugs can halt the disease or even eliminate the chytrids.

How the disease emerged simultaneously on different continents is a yet unsolved mystery. Both environmental change and carriers are being considered.

---

### Learning Outcomes Review 31.9

Fungi can severely harm or kill both plants and animals, either by direct infection or by secretion of toxins and carcinogens. Treatment of fungal disease and parasitism in animals is made difficult by the close relationship between fungi and animals; what is damaging to the fungus may also have ill effects on the host.

■ *What is likely to be the most common mechanism for the spread of fungal disease?*

## 31.1 Defining Fungi

Fungi are more closely related to animals than to plants and form seven monophyletic phyla (see figure 31.1).

Fungi are heterotrophic and have hyphal cells; their cell walls contain chitin. They may have a dikaryon stage and undergo nuclear mitosis.

**The body of a fungus is a mass of connected hyphae.**

A mass of connected hyphae is termed a mycelium. Hyphae can be continuous and multinucleate, or they may be divided into long chains of cells separated by cross-walls called septa.

The chitin found in fungi cell walls is the same material found in the exoskeletons of arthropods.

**Fungal cells may have more than one nucleus.**

A hypha with only one nucleus is monokaryotic; a hypha with two nuclei is dikaryotic. The two haploid nuclei exist independently, but both genomes are transcribed so that some properties of diploids may be observed.

**Mitosis is not followed by cell division.**

Because cells are linked, the cell is not the relevant unit of reproduction, but rather the nucleus is. The spindle forms inside the nuclear envelope, which does not break down and re-form.

**Fungi can reproduce both sexually and asexually.**

Fungi can reproduce sexually by fusion of hyphae from two compatible mating types or hyphae from the same fungus. Spores can form either by asexual or sexual reproduction and are usually dispersed by the wind.

**Fungi are heterotrophs that absorb nutrients.**

Fungi obtain their nutrients through excreting enzymes for external digestion and then absorbing the products.

## 31.2 Microsporidia: Unicellular Parasites

Microsporidia are obligate cellular parasites that lack mitochondria but may have had them at one time; they were previously classed with the protists.

## 31.3 Chytridiomycota and Relatives: Fungi with Flagellated Zoospores

Chytrids form symbiotic relationships; they have been implicated in the decline of amphibian species.

**Blastocladiomycota have single flagella.**

*Allomyces*, a blastocladiomycete, is an example of a fungus with a haplodiplontic life cycle.

**Neocallimastigomycota digest cellulose in ruminant herbivores.**

Neocallimastigomycetes have enzymes that can digest cellulose and lignin; they may have uses in production of biofuels.

## 31.4 Zygomycota: Fungi That Produce Zygotes

**In sexual reproduction, zygotes form inside a zygosporangium.**

Zygomycetes all produce a diploid zygote. In sexual reproduction, fusion (karyogamy) of the haploid nuclei of gametangia produces diploid zygote nuclei. These become zygospores.

**Asexual reproduction is more common.**

Sporangia produce haploid spores that are airborne; bread mold is a common example of a zygomycete.

## 31.5 Glomeromycota: Asexual Plant Symbionts

Glomeromycete hyphae form intracellular associations with plant roots and are called arbuscular mycorrhizae.

The glomeromycetes show no evidence of sexual reproduction.

## 31.6 Basidiomycota: The Club (Basidium) Fungi

The basidiocarp is the visible reproductive structure of this group, which includes mushrooms, toadstools, puffballs, and others.

**Basidiomycetes sexually reproduce within basidia (see figure 31.11).**

Karyogamy occurs within the basidia, giving rise to a diploid cell. Meiosis then ultimately results in four haploid basidiospores.

**The secondary mycelium of basidiomycetes is heterokaryotic.**

Primary mycelium is monokaryotic, but different mating types may fuse to form the secondary mycelium. Maintenance of two haploid genomes allows greater genetic plasticity.

## 31.7 Ascomycota: The Sac (Ascus) Fungi

**Sexual reproduction occurs within the ascus** (see figure 31.12).

Karyogamy occurs only in the ascus and results in a diploid nucleus. Meiosis and mitosis then result in eight haploid nuclei in walled ascospores.

**Asexual reproduction occurs within conidiophores.**

Asexual reproduction is very common and occurs by means of conidia formed at the end of modified hyphae called conidiophores.

**Some ascomycetes have yeast morphology.**

Yeasts usually reproduce by cell fission or budding.

**Ascomycete genetics and genomics have practical applications.**

## 31.8 Ecology of Fungi

Fungi are organisms capable of breaking down cellulose and lignin.

**Fungi have a range of symbioses.**

Fungi can be pathogenic or parasitic, commensal or mutualistic.

**Endophytes live inside plants and may protect plants from parasites.**

**Lichens are an example of symbiosis between different kingdoms.**

A lichen is composed of a fungus, usually an ascomycete, along with cyanobacteria, green algae, or both.

**Mycorrhizae are fungi associated with roots of plants.**

Arbuscular mycorrhizae are common and involve glomeromycetes; ectomycorrhizae are primarily found in forest trees and involve basidiomycetes and a few ascomycetes.

**Fungi also form mutual symbioses with animals.**

Some ants grow "farms" of fungi by providing plant material.

## 31.9 Fungal Parasites and Pathogens

**Fungal infestation can harm plants and those who eat them.**

Fungi spread via spores and can secrete chemicals that make food unpalatable, carcinogenic, or poisonous.

**Fungal infections are difficult to treat in humans and other animals.**

Treatment of fungal diseases in animals is difficult because of the similarities between the two kingdoms.

## UNDERSTAND

1. Which of the following is not a characteristic of a fungus?
   a. Cell walls made of chitin
   b. A form of mitosis different from plants and animals
   c. Ability to conduct photosynthesis
   d. Filamentous structure

2. A fungal cell that contains two genetically different nuclei would be classified as
   a. monokaryotic.
   c. homokaryotic.
   b. bikaryotic.
   d. heterokaryotic.

3. Which of the following groups of fungi is *not* monophyletic?
   a. Zygomycota
   c. Glomeromycota
   b. Basidiomycota
   d. Ascomycota

4. Based on physical characteristics, the _____ represent the most ancient phylum of fungi.
   a. Basidiomycota
   c. Ascomycota
   b. Zygomycota
   d. Chytridiomycota

5. The early evolution of terrestrial plants was made possible by mycorrhizal relationships with the
   a. Zygomycetes.
   c. Ascomycota.
   b. Glomeromycota.
   d. Basidiomycota.

6. Symbiotic relationships occur between the fungi and
   a. plants.
   c. animals.
   b. bacteria.
   d. all of the above.

7. Which of the following species of fungi is not associated with diseases in humans?
   a. *Pneumocystis jiroveci*
   b. *Aspergillus flavus*
   c. *Candida albicans*
   d. *Batrachochytrium dendrobatidis*

## APPLY

1. In a culture of hyphae of unknown origin you notice that the hyphae lack septa and that the fungi reproduce asexually by using clumps of erect stalks. However, at times sexual reproduction can be observed. To what group of fungi would you assign it?
   a. Chytridiomycota
   c. Ascomycota
   b. Basidiomycota
   d. Zygomycota

2. Examine the life cycle of a typical basidiomycetes and determine where you would expect to find a dikaryotic cell.
   a. Primary mycelium
   c. In the basidiospores
   b. Secondary mycelium
   d. In the zygote

3. Determine which of the following is correct regarding the yeast *Saccharomyces cerevisiae*.
   a. It reproduces asexually by a process called budding.
   b. It produces an ascocarp during reproduction.
   c. It belongs in the group Zygomycota.
   d. All of the above are correct.

4. Appraise the fungal relationship between a forest tree and a basidiomycetes and determine the most suitable classification for the symbiosis.
   a. Parasitism only
   b. An arbuscular mycorrhizae
   c. Ectomycorrhizae
   d. A lichen

5. Choose which of the following best reflects the symbiotic relationships between animals and fungi.
   a. Protection from bacteria
   b. Colonization of land
   c. Protection from desiccation
   d. Exchange of nutrients

## SYNTHESIZE

1. Historically fungi have been classified as being more plantlike despite their lack of photosynthetic ability. Although we now know that fungi are more closely related to the animals than the plants, review characteristics that initially led scientists to place them closer to the plants.

2. The importance of fungi in the evolution of terrestrial life is typically understated. Evaluate the importance of fungi in the colonization of land.

3. Based on your understanding of fungi, hypothesize why antibiotics won't work in the treatment of a fungal infection.

## ONLINE RESOURCE

www.ravenbiology.com

Understand, Apply, and Synthesize—enhance your study with animations that bring concepts to life and practice tests to assess your understanding. Your instructor may also recommend the interactive eBook, individualized learning tools, and more.

Chapter **32**

# Overview of Animal Diversity

## Chapter Outline

## Introduction

*We now explore the great diversity of modern animals, the result of a long evolutionary history. Animals are among the most abundant living organisms. Found in almost every habitat, they bewilder us with their diversity in form, habitat, behavior, and lifestyle. About a million and a half species have been described, and several million more are thought to await discovery. Despite their great diversity, animals have much in common. For example, locomotion is a distinctive characteristic, although not all animals can move about. Early naturalists thought that sponges and corals were plants because the adults are attached to the surface on which they live.*

## 32.1 Some General Features of Animals

### Learning Outcome

1. *Identify three features that characterize all animals and three that characterize only some types of animals.*

Animals are so diverse that few criteria fit them all. But some, such as animals being eaters, or consumers, apply to all. Others, such as their being mobile (they can move about) have excep-

tions. Taken together, the universal characteristics and other features of major importance that have exceptions are convincing evidence that animals are monophyletic—that they descended from a common ancestor. Table 32.1 describes the general features of animals.

### Learning Outcome Review 32.1

All animals are multicellular and heterotrophic, and their cells lack cell walls. Most animals can move from place to place, can reproduce sexually, and possess unique tissues. Animals can be found in almost all habitats.

■ *What evidence is there that animals could not have been the first type of life to have evolved?*

| TABLE 32.1 | General Features of Animals |
|---|---|
| **Heterotrophy.** All animals are heterotrophs—that is, they obtain energy and organic molecules by ingesting other organisms. Unlike autotrophic plants and algae, animals cannot construct organic molecules from inorganic chemicals. Some animals (herbivores) consume autotrophs; other animals (carnivores) consume heterotrophs; some animals (omnivores) consume both autotrophs and heterotrophs; and still others (detritivores) consume decomposing organisms. |  |
| **Multicellularity.** All animals are multicellular; many have complex bodies like that of this jellyfish (phylum Cnidaria). The unicellular heterotrophic organisms called Protozoa, which were at one time regarded as simple animals, are now considered members of the large and diverse kingdom Protista, discussed in chapter 29. | 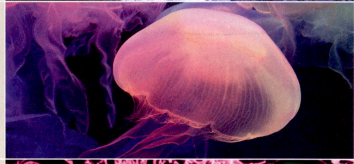 |
| **No Cell Walls.** Animal cells differ from those of other multicellular organisms: they lack rigid cell walls and are usually quite flexible. The many cells of animal bodies are held together by extracellular frames of structural proteins such as collagen. Other proteins form unique intercellular junctions between animal cells. | 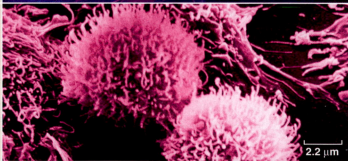<br>2.2 μm |
| **Active Movement.** Animals move more rapidly and in more complex ways than members of other kingdoms—this ability is perhaps their most striking characteristic, one directly related to the flexibility of their cells and the evolution of nerve and muscle tissues. A remarkable form of movement unique to animals is flying, a capability that is well developed among vertebrates and insects such as this butterfly (phylum Arthropoda). Many animals cannot move from place to place (they are sessile) or do so rarely or slowly (they are sedentary) although they have muscles or muscle fibers that allow parts of their bodies to move. Sponges, however, have little capacity for movement. |  |

*norigid cell wall*

**TABLE 32.1**    **General Features of Animals,** *continued*

**Diversity in Form.** Animals vary greatly in form, ranging in size from organisms too small to see with the unaided eye to enormous whales and giant squids. Almost all animals, like this millipede (phylum Arthropoda), lack a backbone—they are therefore called invertebrates. Of the million known living animal species, only 42,500 have a backbone—they are therefore referred to as **vertebrates.** Probably most of the many millions of animal species awaiting discovery are invertebrates.

*small or large*

**Diversity in Habitat.** The animal kingdom is divided into 35–40 phyla, most of which have members that occur only in the sea like this brittlestar (phylum Echinodermata). Members of fewer phyla occur in fresh water, and members of fewer still occur on land. Members of three phyla that are successful in the marine environment—Arthropoda, Mollusca, and Chordata—also dominate animal life on land. Only one animal phylum, Onychophora (velvet worms) is entirely terrestrial.

**Sexual Reproduction.** Most animals reproduce sexually; these tortoises (phylum Chordata) are engaging in the first step of that process. Animal eggs, which are nonmobile, are much larger than the small, usually flagellated sperm. In animals, cells formed in meiosis function as gametes. These haploid cells do not divide by mitosis first, as they do in plants and fungi, but rather fuse directly with each other to form the zygote. Consequently, there is no counterpart among animals to the alternation of haploid (gametophyte) and diploid (sporophyte) generations characteristic of plants. Some individuals of some species and all individuals of a very few animal species are incapable of sexual reproduction.

**Embryonic Development.** An animal zygote first undergoes a series of mitotic divisions, called *cleavage,* and like this dividing frog's egg, that produces a ball of cells, the **blastula.** In most animals, the blastula folds inward at one point to form a hollow sac with an opening at one end called the **blastopore.** An embryo at this stage is called a **gastrula.** The subsequent growth and movement of the cells of the gastrula differ from one group of animals to another, reflecting the evolutionary history of the group. Embryos of most kinds of animals develop into a larva, which looks unlike the adult of the species, lives in a different habitat, and eats different sorts of food; in most groups, it is very small. A larva undergoes metamorphosis, a radical reorganization, to transform into the adult body form.

**Tissues.** The cells of all animals except sponges are organized into structural and functional units called **tissues,** collections of cells that together are specialized to perform specific tasks. Animals are unique in having two tissues associated with movement: (1) muscle tissue, which contracts, and (2) nervous tissue, which conducts signals among cells. Neuromuscular junctions, where nerves connect with muscle tissue, are shown here.

# 32.2 Evolution of the Animal Body Plan

## Learning Outcomes

1. Differentiate between a pseudocoelom and a coelom.
2. Explain the difference between protostomes and deuterostomes.
3. Describe the advantages of segmentation.

The features described in the preceding section evolved over the course of millions of years. We can understand how the history of life has proceeded by examining the types of animal bodies and body plans present in fossils and in existence today.

Five key innovations can be noted in animal evolution:

1. The evolution of symmetry
2. The evolution of tissues, allowing specialized structures and functions
3. The evolution of a body cavity
4. The evolution of various patterns of embryonic development
5. The evolution of segmentation, or repeated body units

These innovations are explained in the sections that follow. Some innovations appear to have evolved only once, some twice or more. Scientists use an innovation that evolved once as evidence that all the animals possessing it are more closely related to one another than they are to any animal lacking the innovation. The animals with the innovation and their ancestor in which the innovation arose are said to constitute a clade—an evolutionarily coherent group (see chapter 23). On the other hand, some innovations evolve more than once in different clades. This is the phenomenon of convergent evolution (see chapter 23). Although not indicative of close evolutionary relationship, convergently evolved innovations may be important to how species have adapted to their environments.

## Most animals exhibit radial or bilateral symmetry

A typical sponge lacks definite symmetry, growing as an irregular mass. Virtually all other animals have a definite shape and symmetry that can be defined along an imaginary axis drawn through the animal's body. The two main types of symmetry are radial and bilateral.

### Radial symmetry

The body of a member of phylum Cnidaria (jellyfish, sea anemones, and corals: the C of Cnidaria is silent; see chapter 34) exhibits **radial symmetry.** Its parts are arranged in such a way that any longitudinal plane passing through the central axis divides the organism into halves that are approximate mirror images (figure 32.1a). A pie, for example, is radially symmetrical. In cnidarians such as corals and sea anemones, the mouth is not circular, but oval, because it opens into a sort of throat that is like a flattened sleeve. Thus there are two planes that divide the body into mirror-

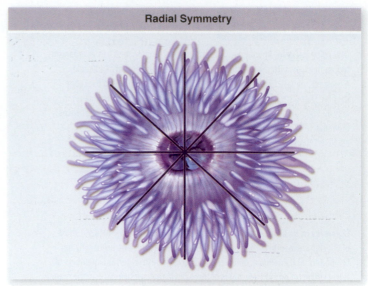

**Radial Symmetry**

*a.*

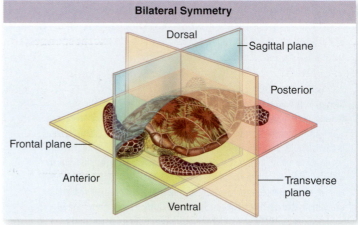

**Bilateral Symmetry**

*b.*

**Figure 32.1  A comparison of radial and bilateral symmetry.** *a.* Radially symmetrical animals, such as this sea anemone (phylum Cnidaria), can be bisected into equal halves by any longitudinal plane that passes through the central axis. *b.* Bilaterally symmetrical animals, such as this turtle (phylum Chordata), can only be bisected into equal halves in one plane (the sagittal plane).

image halves, one along the mouth and one perpendicular to it; these animals are actually biradially symmetrical (figure 32.1b).

### Bilateral symmetry

The bodies of most animals other than sponges and cnidarians exhibit **bilateral symmetry,** in which the body has right and left halves that are mirror images of each other. Animals with this body plan are collectively termed the Bilateria. The sagittal plane defines these halves. A bilaterally symmetrical body has, in addition to left and right halves, dorsal and ventral portions, which are divided by the frontal plane, and anterior (front) and posterior (rear) ends, which are divided by the transverse plane (in an animal that walks on all fours, dorsal is the top side). In echinoderms (sea stars and their relatives), adults are radially symmetrical (actually pentaradially symmetrical, because the body has five clear sections), but the larvae are bilaterally symmetrical.

Bilateral symmetry constitutes a major evolutionary advance in the animal body plan. Bilaterally symmetrical animals have the ability to move through the environment in a consistent direction (typically with the anterior end leading)—a feat that is difficult for radially symmetrical animals. Associated with directional movement is the grouping of nerve cells into a brain, and sensory structures, such as eyes and ears, at the anterior end of the body. This concentration of nervous tissue at the anterior end, which appears to have occurred early in evolution, is called **cephalization.** Much of the layout of the nervous system in bilaterally symmetrical animals is centered on one or more major longitudinal nerve cords that transmit information from the anterior sense organs and brain to the rest of the body. Cephalization is often considered a consequence of the development of bilateral symmetry.

## The evolution of tissues allowed for specialized structures and functions

The zygote (a fertilized egg), has the capability to give rise to all the kinds of cells in an animal's body. That is, it is totipotent (all powerful). During embryonic development, cells specialize to carry out particular functions. In all animals except sponges, the process is irreversible: once a cell differentiates to serve a function, it and its descendants can never serve any other.

A sponge cell that had specialized to serve one function (such as lining the cavity where feeding occurs) can lose the special attributes that serve that function and change to serve another function (such as being a gamete). Thus a sponge cell can dedifferentiate and redifferentiate. Cells of all other animals are organized into tissues, each of which is characterized by cells of particular morphology and capability. But their competence to dedifferentiate prevents sponge cells from forming clearly defined tissues (and therefore, of course, organs, which are composed of tissues).

Because cells differentiate irreversibly in all animals except sponges, scientists infer that bodies containing cells specialized to serve particular functions have an advantage compared to those with cells that potentially have multiple functions. Judging by the relative diversity of animals with specialized tissues and those lacking them, tissues are a favorable adaptation. Presumably the advantage to the animal is embodied in the old adage "Jack of all trades, master of none."

## A body cavity made possible the development of advanced organ systems

In the process of embryonic development, the cells of animals of most groups organize into three layers (called germ layers): an outer **ectoderm,** an inner **endoderm,** and an intermediate **mesoderm.** Animals with three embryonic cell layers are said to be triploblastic. Part of the maturation from the embryo is that certain organs and organ systems develop from each germ layer. The ectoderm gives rise to the outer covering of the body and the nervous system; the endoderm gives rise to the digestive system, including the intestine; and the skeleton and muscles develop from the mesoderm. Cnidarians have only two layers (thus they are diploblastic), the endoderm and the ectoderm, and lack organs. Sponges lack germ layers altogether; they, of course, have no tissues or organs. All triploblastic animals are members of the Bilateria.

A key innovation in the body plan of some bilaterians was a body cavity isolated from the exterior of the animal. This is different from the digestive cavity, which is open to the exterior at least through the mouth, and in most animals at the opposite end as well, via the anus. The evolution of efficient organ systems within the animal body was not possible until a body cavity evolved for accommodating and supporting organs (such as our heart and lungs), distributing materials, and fostering complex developmental interactions. The cavity is filled with fluid: in most animals, the fluid is liquid, but in vertebrates, it is gas—the body cavity of humans filling with liquid is a life-threatening condition. A very few types of bilaterians have no body cavity, the space between tissues that develop from the mesoderm and those that develop from the endoderm being filled with cells and connective tissue. These are the so-called acoelomate animals (figure 32.2).

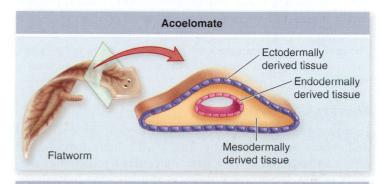

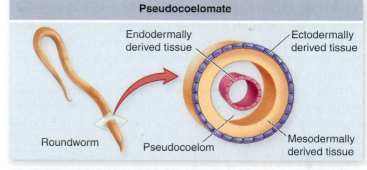

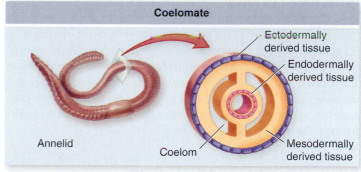

**Figure 32.2** **Three body plans for bilaterally symmetrical animals.** Acoelomates, such as flatworms, have no body cavity between the digestive tract (derived from the endoderm) and the musculature layer (derived from the mesoderm). Pseudocoelomates have a body cavity, the pseudocoelom, between tissues derived from the endoderm and those derived from the mesoderm. Coelomates have a body cavity, the coelom, that develops entirely within tissues derived from the mesoderm, and so is lined on both sides by tissue derived from the mesoderm.

## Body cavities

Body cavities appear to have evolved multiple times in the Bilateria (see figure 32.2). A body cavity called the **pseudocoelom** develops embryologically between mesoderm and endoderm, so occurs in the adult between tissues derived from the mesoderm and those derived from endoderm; animals with this type of body cavity are termed pseudocoelomates. Although the word *pseudocoelom* means "false coelom," this is a true body space and characterizes many successful groups of animals. A **coelom** is a cavity that develops entirely within the mesoderm. The coelom is surrounded by a layer of epithelial cells derived from the mesoderm and termed the peritoneum.

Zoologists previously inferred that the first animals were acoelomate, that some of their descendants evolved a pseudocoelom, and that some pseudocoelomate descendants evolved the coelom. However, as you saw in chapter 21, evolution rarely occurs in such a linear and directional way. Rather, pseudocoeloms seem to have evolved several times, and some animals have lost the body space, becoming acoelomate secondarily. However, a coelom appears to have evolved just once. Thus, species possessing a coelom form a clade, but those with a pseudocoelom do not.

## The circulatory system

In many small animals, nutrients and oxygen are distributed and wastes are removed by fluid in the body cavity. Most larger animals, in contrast, have a **circulatory system,** a network of vessels that carry fluids to and from the parts of the body distant from the sites of digestion (gut) and gas exchange (gills or lungs). The circulating fluid carries nutrients and oxygen to the tissues and removes wastes, including carbon dioxide, by diffusion between the circulatory fluid and the other cells of the body.

In an **open circulatory system,** the blood passes from vessels into sinuses, mixes with body fluid that bathes the cells of tissues, then reenters vessels in another location. In a **closed circulatory system,** the blood is entirely confined to blood vessels, so is physically separated from other body fluids. Blood moves through a closed circulatory system faster and more efficiently than it does through an open system; open systems are typical of animals that are relatively inactive and so do not have a high demand for oxygen. In small animals, blood can be pushed through a closed circulatory system by movement of the animal. In larger animals, the body musculature does not provide enough force, so the blood must be propelled by contraction of one or more hearts, which are specialized, muscular parts of the blood vessels.

# Bilaterians have two main types of development

The processes of embryonic development in animals is discussed fully in chapter 54. Briefly, development of a bilaterally symmetrical animal begins with mitotic cell divisions (called cleavages) of the egg that lead to the formation of a hollow ball of cells, which subsequently indents to form a two-layered ball. The internal space that is created through such indentation (figure 54.11) is the **archenteron** (literally the "primitive gut"); it communicates with the outside by a **blastopore.**

In a protostome, the mouth of the adult animal develops from the blastopore or from an opening near the blastopore (protostome means "first mouth"—the first opening becomes the mouth). **Protostomes** include most bilaterians, including flatworms, nematodes, mollusks, annelids, and arthropods. In some protostomes, both mouth and anus form from the embryonic blastopore; in other protostomes, the anus forms later in another region of the embryo. Two outwardly dissimilar groups, the echinoderms and the chordates, together with a few other small phyla, constitute the **deuterostomes,** in which the mouth of the adult animal does not develop from the blastopore. The deuterostome blastopore gives rise to the organism's anus, and the mouth develops from a second pore that arises later in development (deuterostome means "second mouth"). Protostomes and deuterostomes differ in several other aspects of embryology too, as discussed later.

## Cleavage patterns

The cleavage pattern relative to the embryo's polar axis determines how the resulting cells lie with respect to one another. In some protostomes, each new cell cleaves off at an angle oblique to the polar axis. As a result, a new cell nestles into the space between the older ones in a closely packed array. This pattern is called **spiral cleavage** because a line drawn through a sequence of dividing cells spirals outward from the polar axis (figure 32.3 top). Spiral cleavage is characteristic of annelids, mollusks, nemerteans, and related phyla; the clade of animals with this cleavage pattern is therefore known as the Spiralia.

In all deuterostomes, by contrast, the cells divide parallel to and at right angles to the polar axis. As a result, the pairs of cells from each division are positioned directly above and below one another, a process that gives rise to a loosely packed ball. This pattern is called **radial cleavage** because a line drawn through a sequence of dividing cells describes a radius outward from the polar axis (figure 32.3 bottom).

## Determinate versus indeterminate development

Many protostomes exhibit **determinate development,** in which the type of tissue each embryonic cell will form in the adult is determined early, in many lineages even before cleavage begins, when the molecules that act as developmental signals are localized in different regions of the egg. Consequently, the cell divisions that occur after fertilization segregate molecular signals into different daughter cells, specifying the fate of even the very earliest embryonic cells. Each embryonic cell is destined to occur only in particular parts of the adult body, so if the cells are separated, development cannot proceed.

Deuterostomes, on the other hand, display **indeterminate development.** The first few cell divisions of the zygote produce identical daughter cells. If the cells are separated, any one can develop into a complete organism because the molecules that signal the embryonic cells to develop differently are not segregated in different cells until later in the embryo's development. (This is how identical twins are formed.) Thus, each cell remains totipotent and its fate is not determined for several cleavages.

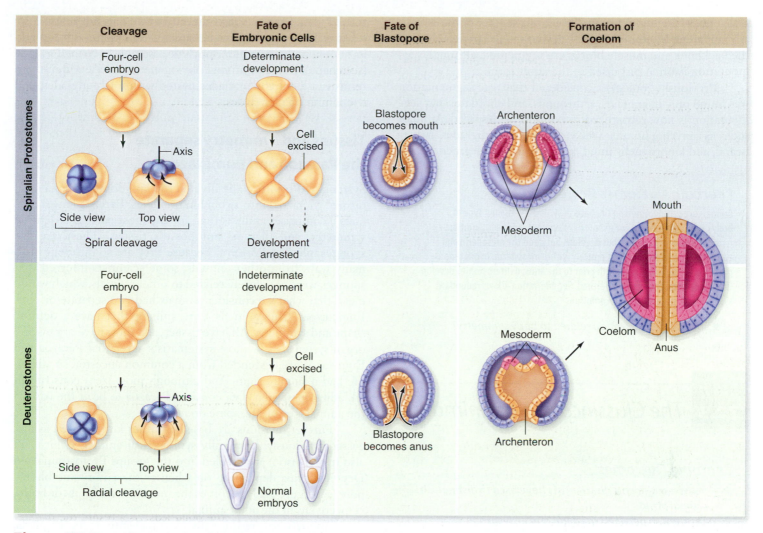

| | Cleavage | Fate of Embryonic Cells | Fate of Blastopore | Formation of Coelom |
|---|---|---|---|---|

**Spiralian Protostomes**

Four-cell embryo — Side view / Top view — Axis — Spiral cleavage

Determinate development — Cell excised — Development arrested

Blastopore becomes mouth

Archenteron — Mesoderm — Mouth — Mesoderm — Coelom — Anus

**Deuterostomes**

Four-cell embryo — Side view / Top view — Axis — Radial cleavage

Indeterminate development — Cell excised — Normal embryos

Blastopore becomes anus

Mesoderm — Archenteron

**Figure 32.3** **Embryonic development in protostomes and deuterostomes.** In spiralian protostomes, embryonic cells cleave in a spiral pattern and exhibit determinate development; the blastopore becomes the animal's mouth, and the coelom originates from a split among endodermal cells. In deuterostomes, embryonic cells cleave radially and exhibit indeterminate development; the blastopore becomes the animal's anus, and the coelom originates from an invagination of the archenteron.

### Formation of the coelom

The coelom arises within the mesoderm. In protostomes, cells simply move apart from one another to create an expanding coelomic cavity within the mass of mesodermal cells. In deuterostomes, groups of cells pouch off the end of the archenteron, which you will recall is the primitive gut—the hollow in the center of the developing embryo that is lined with endoderm.

The consistency of deuterostome development and its distinctiveness from that of the protostomes suggest that it evolved once, in the ancestor of the deuterostome phyla. The mode of development in protostomes is more diverse, but because of the distinctiveness of spiral development, scientists infer it also evolved once, in the common ancestor to all spiralian phyla.

### Segmentation allowed for redundant systems and improved locomotion

Segmented animals consist of a series of linearly arrayed compartments that typically look alike (see figure 34.14), at least early in development, but that may have specialized functions. Development of segmentation is mediated at the molecular level by *Hox* genes (see chapters 19 and 25, and in section 32.4). During early development, segments first are obvious in the mesoderm but later are reflected in the ectoderm and endoderm. Two advantages result from early embryonic segmentation:

1. In highly segmental animals, such as earthworms (phylum Annelida), each segment may develop a more or less complete set of adult organ systems. Because these are redundant systems, damage to any one segment need not be fatal because other segments duplicate the damaged segment's functions.

2. Locomotion is more efficient when individual segments can move semi-independently. Because partitions isolate the segments, each can contract or expand autonomously. Therefore, a long body can move in ways that are often quite complex.

**Segmentation** underlies the organization of body plans of the most morphologically complex animals. In some adult arthropods, the segments are fused, but segmentation is usually apparent in embryological development. In vertebrates, the backbone and muscle blocks are segmented, although segmentation is often disguised in the adult form.

Previously, zoologists considered that true segmentation was found only in annelids, arthropods, and chordates, but segmentation is now recognized to be more widespread. Animals such as onychophorans (velvet worms), tardigrades (water bears), and kinorhynchs (mud dragons) are also segmented.

---

### Learning Outcomes Review 32.2

Animals are distinguished on the basis of symmetry, tissues, type of body cavity, sequence of embryonic development, and segmentation. A pseudocoelom is a space that develops between the mesoderm and endoderm; a coelom develops entirely within mesoderm. In bilaterians, protostomes develop the mouth prior to the anus; deuterostomes develop the mouth after the anus has formed. Segmentation allows redundant systems and more efficient locomotion.

■ *How is cephalization related to body symmetry?*

---

## 32.3 The Classification of Animals

### Learning Outcomes

1. List the major criteria scientists have used to distinguish animal phyla.
2. Distinguish between spiralian and ecdysozoan organisms.
3. Identify the placement of humans among the animal phyla.

---

Multicellular animals, or metazoans, are traditionally divided into 35 to 40 phyla (singular, *phylum*). There is little disagreement among biologists about the placement of most animals in phyla, although zoologists disagree on the status of some, particularly those with few members or recently discovered ones. The diversity of animals is obvious in tables 32.2 and 32.3, which describe key characteristics of 20 of the phyla.

Traditionally, the phylogeny of animals has been inferred using features of anatomy and aspects of embryological development, as discussed earlier, from which a broad consensus emerged over the last century concerning the main branches of the animal tree of life. In the past 30 years, data derived from molecular features have been added, leading to some rethinking of classification schemes. Depending on the features compared, biologists may draw quite different family trees—although, of course, there is only one way that evolution actually occurred, and the goal of phylogeny is to detect that history.

Whether morphological or molecular characters (or both) are used, the underlying principle is the same: systematists use features they assume to have evolved only once, so the animals sharing such a feature are inferred to be more closely

related to one another than they are to animals not sharing the feature. The shared derived characters unique to a group and its ancestors define a monophyletic assemblage termed a clade (see chapter 23). The animal phylogenetic tree viewed in these terms is a hierarchy of clades nested within larger clades, and containing smaller clades.

### Tissues and symmetry separate the Parazoa and Eumetazoa

Systematists traditionally divided the kingdom Animalia (also termed Metazoa) into two main branches. Parazoa ("near animals") comprises animals that, for the most part, lack definite symmetry, and that do not possess tissues. These are the sponges, phylum Porifera. Because they are so different in so many ways from other animals, some scientists inferred that sponges were not closely related to other animals, which would mean that what we consider animals had two separate origins. Eumetazoa ("true animals") are animals that have a definite shape and symmetry. All have tissues, and most have organs and organ systems. Now most systematists agree that Parazoa and Eumetazoa are descended from a common ancestor, so animal life had a single origin. And although most trees constructed including molecular data consider Parazoa to be at the base of the animal tree of life, some do not.

Further divisions are based on other key features, as discussed previously. Bilaterally symmetrical animals (which are also triploblastic) are divided into the groups Protostomia and Deuterostomia depending on whether the embryonic blastopore (see figure 32.3) becomes the mouth or the anus (or both), respectively, in the adult animal.

Animals are traditionally classified into 35 to 40 phyla. The evolutionary relationships among the animal phyla are based on the inference that phyla sharing certain fundamental morphological and molecular characters are more closely related to one another than they are to phyla not sharing those characters. Phylogenetically informative characters are inferred to have arisen only once.

### Molecular data help reveal evolutionary relationships

Gene sequence data are accumulating at an accelerating pace for all animal groups. Phylogenies developed from different molecules sometimes suggest quite different evolutionary relationships among the same groups of animals. However, combining data from multiple genes has resolved the relationships of most phyla. Current studies are using sequences from hundreds of genes to try to fully resolve the animal tree of life.

Molecular data are helping to resolve some problems with the traditional phylogeny, such as puzzling groups that did not fit well into the widely accepted phylogeny. These data may be especially helpful in clarifying relationships that conventional data cannot, as, for example, in animals such as parasites. Through dependence on their host, the anatomy, physiology, and behavior of parasites tends to be greatly altered, so features that may reveal the phylogenetic affinities of free-living animals can be highly modified or lost.

| TABLE 32.2 | Animal Phyla with the Most Species | | | |
|---|---|---|---|---|
| **Phylum** | **Typical Examples** | | **Key Characteristics** | **Approximate Number of Named Species** |
| **Arthropoda** (arthropods) | Beetles, other insects, crabs, spiders, krill, scorpions, centipedes, millipedes | | Chitinous exoskeleton covers segmented, coelomate body. With paired, jointed appendages; many types of insects have wings. Occupy marine, terrestrial, and freshwater habitats. Most arthropods are insects (as are most animals!). | 1,000,000 |
| **Mollusca** (mollusks) | Snails, oysters, clams, octopuses, slugs | | Coelomate body of many mollusks is covered by one or more shells secreted by a part of the body termed the mantle. Many kinds possess a unique rasping tongue, a radula. Members occupy marine, terrestrial, and freshwater habitats (35,000 species are terrestrial). | 110,000 |
| **Chordata** (chordates) | Mammals, fish, reptiles, amphibians | | Each coelomate individual possesses a notochord, a dorsal nerve cord, pharyngeal slits, and a postanal tail at some stage of life. In vertebrates, the notochord is replaced during development by the spinal column. Members occupy marine, terrestrial, and freshwater habitats (20,000 species are terrestrial). | 56,000 |
| **Platyhelminthes** (flatworms) | Planarians, tapeworms, liver and blood flukes | | Unsegmented, acoelomate, bilaterally symmetrical worms. Digestive cavity has only one opening; tapeworms lack a gut. Many species are parasites of medical and veterinary importance. Members occupy marine, terrestrial, and freshwater habitats (as well as the bodies of other animals) | 20,000 |
| **Nematoda** (roundworms) | *Ascaris*, pinworms, hookworms, filarial worms | | Pseudocoelomate, unsegmented, bilaterally symmetrical worms; tubular digestive tract has mouth and anus. Members occupy marine, terrestrial, and freshwater habitats; some are important parasites of plants and animals, including humans. | 25,000 (but it is thought by some that the number of nematode species may be much greater) |
| **Annelida** (segmented worms) | Earthworms, polychaetes, tube worms, leeches | | Segmented, bilaterally symmetrical, coelomate worms with a complete digestive tract; most have bristles (chaetae) on each segment that anchor them in tubes or aid in crawling. Occupy marine, terrestrial, and freshwater habitats. | 16,000 |
| **Cnidaria** (cnidarians) | Jellyfish, *Hydra*, corals, sea anemones, sea fans | | Radially symmetrical, acoelomate body has tissues but no organs. Mouth opens into a simple digestive sac and is surrounded by tentacles armed with stinging capsules (nematocysts). In some groups, individuals are joined into colonies; some can secrete a hard exoskeleton. The very few nonmarine species live in fresh water. | 10,000 |
| **Echinodermata** (echinoderms) | Sea stars, sea urchins, sand dollars, sea cucumbers | | Adult body pentaradial (fivefold) in symmetry. Water-vascular system is a coelomic space; endoskeleton of calcium carbonate plates. Many can regenerate lost body parts. Fossils are more diverse in body plan than extant species. Exclusively marine. | 7000 |
| **Porifera** (sponges) | Barrel sponges, boring sponges, basket sponges, bath sponges | | Bodies of most asymmetrical: defining "an individual" is difficult. Body lacks tissues or organs, being a meshwork of cells surrounding channels that open to the outside through pores, and that expand into internal cavities lined with food-filtering flagellated cells (choanocytes). Most species are marine (150 species live in fresh water). | 7000 |
| **Bryozoa** (moss animals) (also called Polyzoa and Ectoprocta) | Sea mats, sea moss | | The only exclusively colonial phylum; each colony comprises small, coelomate individuals (zooids) connected by an exoskeleton (calcareous in marine species, organic in most freshwater ones). A ring of ciliated tentacles (lophophore) surrounds the mouth of each zooid; the anus lies beyond the lophophore. | 4500 |

| TABLE 32.3 | Some Important Animal Phyla with Fewer Species—and Three Recently Discovered Ones |

| Phylum | Typical Examples | | Key Characteristics | Approximate Number of Named Species |
|---|---|---|---|---|
| **Rotifera** (wheel animals) | Rotifers | | Small pseudocoelomates with a complete digestive tract including a set of complex jaws. Cilia at the anterior end beat so they resemble a revolving wheel. Some are very important in marine and freshwater habitats as food for predators such as fishes. | 2000 |
| **Nemertea** (ribbon worms) (also called Rhynchocoela) | *Lineus* | | Protostome worms notable for their fragility—when disturbed, they fragment in pieces. Long, extensible proboscis occupies a coelomic space; that of some tipped by a spearlike stylet. Most marine, but some live in fresh water, and a few are terrestrial. | 900 |
| **Tardigrada** (water bears) | *Hypsibius* | | Microscopic protostomes with five body segments and four pairs of clawed legs. An individual lives a week or less but can enter a state of suspended animation ("cryptobiosis") in which it can survive for many decades. Occupy marine, freshwater, and terrestrial habitats. | 800 |
| **Brachiopoda** (lamp shells) | *Lingula* | | Protostomous animals encased in two shells that are oriented with respect to the body differently than in bivalved mollusks. A ring of ciliated tentacles (lophophore) surrounds the mouth. More than 30,000 fossil species are known. | 300 |
| **Onychophora** (velvet worms) | *Peripatus* | | Segmented protostomous worms resembling tardigrades; with a chitinous soft exoskeleton and unsegmented appendages. Related to arthropods. The only exclusively terrestrial phylum, but what are interpreted as their Cambrian ancestors were marine. | 110 |
| **Ctenophora** (sea walnuts) | Comb jellies, sea walnuts | | Gelatinous, almost transparent, often bioluminescent marine animals; eight bands of cilia; largest animals that use cilia for locomotion; complete digestive tract with anal pore. | 100 |
| **Chaetognatha** (arrow worms) | *Sagitta* | | Small, bilaterally symmetrical, transparent marine worms with a fin along each side, powerful bristly jaws, and lateral nerve cords. Some inject toxin into prey and some have large eyes. It is uncertain if they are coelomates, and, if so, whether protostomes or deuterostomes. | 100 |
| **Loricifera** (loriciferans) | *Nanaloricus mysticus* | | Tiny marine pseudocoelomates that live in spaces between grains of sand. The mouth is borne on the tip of a flexible tube. Discovered in 1983. | 10 |
| **Cycliophora** (cycliophorans) | *Symbion* | | Microscopic animals that live on mouthparts of claw lobsters. Discovered in 1995. | 3 |
| **Micrognathozoa** (micrognathozoans) | *Limnognathia* | | Microscopic animals with complicated jaws. Discovered in 2000 in Greenland. | 1 |

## Morphology- and molecule-based phylogenies agree on many major groupings

Although they differ from one another in some respects, phylogenies incorporating molecular data or based entirely on them share some deep structure with the traditional animal tree of life. Figure 32.4 is a summary of animal phylogeny developed from morphological, molecular, life-history, and other types of relevant data. Some aspects of this view have been contradicted by studies based on particular characters or using particular analytical methods. It is an exciting time to be a systematist, but shifts in understanding of relationships among groups of animals can be frustrating to some! Like any scientific idea, a phylogeny is a hypothesis, open to challenge and to being revised in light of additional data.

One consistent result is that Porifera (sponges) constitutes a monophyletic group that shares a common ancestor with other animals. Some systematists had considered sponges to comprise two (or three) groups that are not particularly closely related, but molecular data support what had been the majority view, that phylum Porifera is monophyletic. And, as mentioned earlier, all animals are found to be monophyletic.

Among eumetazoans, molecular data are in accord with the traditional view that cnidarians (hydras, sea jellies, and corals) branch off the tree before the origin of animals with bilateral symmetry. Our understanding of the phylogeny of the deuterostome branch of Bilateria (discussed in chapter 34) has not changed much, but our understanding of the phylogeny of protostomes has been altered by molecular data.

Most revolutionary is that annelids and arthropods, which had been considered closely related based on the occurrence of segmentation in both, belong to separate clades. Now arthropods are grouped with protostomes that molt their cuticles at least once during their life. These are termed ecdysozoans, which means "molting animals" (see chapter 34). Molecular sequence data can help test our ideas of which morphological features reveal evolutionary relationships best; in this case, molecular data allowed us to see that, contrary to our hypothesis, segmentation seems to have evolved convergently, but molting did not.

But not all features are easy to diagnose, and molecular data do not resolve all uncertainties. The enigmatic phylum Ctenophora (comb jellies)—pronounced with a silent C—has been considered both diploblastic and triploblastic and has been thought to have both a complete gut and a blind gut. Likewise the enigmatic phylum Chaetognatha (arrow worms) has been considered both coelomate and pseudocoelomate, and if coelomate, both protostome and deuterostome (as reflected in figure 32.4). Their placement in phylogenies varies, seeming to depend on the features and methods used to construct the tree. Further research is needed to resolve these uncertainties.

Molecular data are contributing to our understanding of relationships among animal phyla. Animals are monophyletic, as are sponges—relationships that were uncertain using only morphological data. Molecular data confirm that cnidarians branched off from the rest of animals before bilateral symmetry evolved. Although the position of ctenophores has not been resolved, molecular data have significantly altered some ideas of protostome evolution.

## Morphology-based phylogeny focused on the state of the coelom

In the morphology-based animal family tree, bilaterally symmetrical animals comprised three major branches. If the body has no cavity (other than the gut), the animal is said to be acoelomate; members of phylum Platyhelminthes are acoelomates.

A body cavity not lined with tissue derived from mesoderm is a pseudocoelom; members of the phylum Nematoda are pseudocoelomate. A body cavity lined with tissue derived from mesoderm is a coelom; we and members of the phylum Annelida are coelomate. All acoelomates and pseudocoelomates are protostomes; some coelomates are protostomes and some are deuterostomes.

## Protostomes consist of spiralians and ecdysozoans

Two major clades of protostomes are recognized as having evolved independently since ancient times: the spiralians and the ecdysozoans (see figure 32.4).

### Spiralia

Spiralian animals grow by gradual addition of mass to the body. Most live in water, and propel themselves through it using cilia or contractions of the body musculature. Spiralians undergo spiral cleavage (see figure 32.3).

There are two main groups of spiralians: Lophotrochozoa and Platyzoa. Lophotrochozoa includes most coelomate protostome phyla; those animals move by muscular contractions. Most platyzoans are acoelomates; these animals are tiny or flat, and move by ciliary action. Some platyzoans (such as rotifers, gnathostomulids, and the recently discovered phylum Micrognathozoa have a set of complicated jaws. The most prominent group is phylum Platyhelminthes; a flatworm has a simple body with no circulatory or respiratory system but a complex reproductive system. This group includes marine and freshwater planarians as well as the parasitic flukes and tapeworms.

Lophotrochozoa consists of two major phyla and several smaller ones. Many of the animals have a type of free-living larva known as a **trochophore,** and some have a feeding structure termed a **lophophore,** a horseshoe-shaped crown of ciliated tentacles around the mouth used in filter-feeding. The phyla characterized by a lophophore are Bryozoa and Brachiopoda. Lophophorate animals are sessile (anchored in place).

Among the lophotrochozoans with a trochophore are phyla Mollusca and Annelida. Mollusks are unsegmented, and their coelom is reduced to a hemocoel (open circulatory space) and some other small body spaces. This phylum includes animals as diverse as octopuses, snails, and clams. Annelids are segmented coelomate worms, the most familiar of which is the earthworm, but also includes leeches and the largely marine polychaetes.

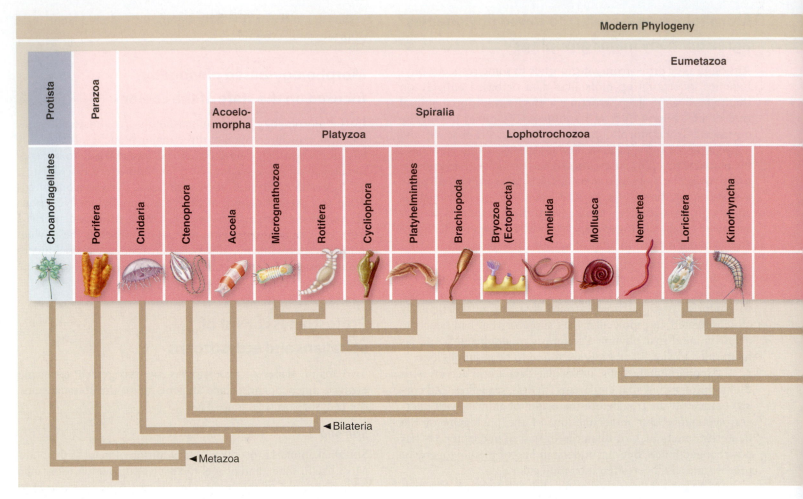

**Figure 32.4** **Proposed revision of the animal tree of life.** A phylogeny of many of the 35–40 phyla reflects the consensus as of 2005 based on interpretation of anatomical and developmental data as well as results derived from molecular phylogenetic studies. Whether Chaetognatha is a protostome or a deuterostome is unclear.

### Ecdysozoa

The other major clade of protosomes is the Ecdysozoa. Ecdysozoans are animals that molt, a phenomenon that seems to have evolved only once in the animal kingdom. When an animal grows large enough that it completely fills its hard external skeleton, it must lose that skeleton (by molting, a process also called ecdysis). While the animal grows, it forms a new exoskeleton underneath the existing one. The first step in molting is for the body to swell until the existing exoskeleton cracks open and is shed (figure 32.5). Upon molting that skeleton, the animal inflates the soft, new one, expanding it using body fluids (and, in many insects and spiders, air as well). When the new one hardens, it is larger than the molted one had been and has room for growth. Thus, rather than being continuous, as in other animals, the growth of ecdysozoans is step-wise.

Of the numerous phyla of protostomes assigned to the Ecdysozoa, Arthropoda contains the largest number of described species of any phylum. Each phylum contains one of the model organisms used in laboratory studies that have informed much of our current understanding of genetics and development: the fruit fly *Drosophila melanogaster* and the roundworm *Caenorhabditis elegans.*

Arthropods are coelomate animals with jointed appendages and segmented external skeletons composed of chitin. Ar-

thropods include insects, spiders, crustaceans, and centipedes, among many others. Arthropods have colonized almost all habitats, being found from the ocean floor to the air and in all terrestrial and freshwater environments.

Roundworms are pseudocoelomate worms that lack circulatory or gas exchange structures, and their bodies have only longitudinal muscles. Nematodes inhabit marine, freshwater, and terrestrial environments, and many species are parasitic in

**Figure 32.5**
**Blue crab undergoing ecdysis (molting).**
Members of Ecdysozoa grow step-wise because their external skeleton is rigid.

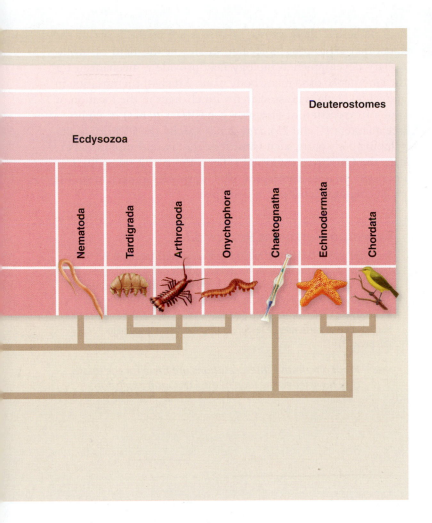

Deuterostomes

Ecdysozoa

Nematoda

Tardigrada

Arthropoda

Onychophora

Chaetognatha

Echinodermata

Chordata

plants or animals. It is said that if everything in the world except nematodes were to disappear, an outline of what had been there would be visible in the remaining nematodes!

## Deuterostomes include chordates and echinoderms

Deuterostomes consist of fewer phyla and species than protostomes, and are more uniform in many ways, despite great differences in appearance. Echinoderms such as sea stars, and chordates such as humans, share a mode of development that is evidence of their evolution from a common ancestor, and separates them clearly from other animals.

### Learning Outcomes Review 32.3

Scientists have defined phyla based on tissues, symmetry, characteristics such as presence or absence of a coelom or pseudocoelom, protostome versus deuterostome development, growth pattern and larval stages, and molecular data. Among protostomes, spiralian organisms have a growth pattern in which their body size simply increases; ecdysozoans must molt in order to grow larger. Among the deuterostome phyla are Echinodermata and Chordata, which includes humans.

■ *Why do systematists attempt to characterize each group of animals by one or more features that have evolved only once?*

## 32.4 The Roots of the Animal Tree of Life

### Learning Outcomes

1. *Explain the colonial flagellate hypothesis of metazoan origin and why it is now favored.*
2. *Describe the possible role of Hox genes in the Cambrian explosion.*

Some of the most exciting contributions of molecular systematics are being made to our understanding of the base of the animal family tree—the origins of the major clades of animals.

### Metazoans appear to have evolved from colonial protists

The ancestor to all animals was presumably a protist (see chapter 29), but it is not clear from which line of protists animals evolved. Evidence is available to support two major hypotheses.

■ The multinucleate hypothesis is that metazoans arose from a multinuclear protist similar to today's ciliates. Each nucleus became compartmentalized into a cell, resulting in the multicellular condition.

■ The **colonial flagellate hypothesis,** first proposed by Ernst Haeckel in 1874, is that metazoans descended from colonial protists. Each colony is a hollow sphere composed of flagellated cells. Some of the cells of sponges are strikingly like those of choanoflagellate protists.

Molecular data based on ribosomal RNA sequences favor the colonial flagellate hypothesis, and reject the multinucleate ciliate hypothesis based on evidence that metazoans are more closely related to eukaryotic algae than to ciliates.

### Molecular analysis may explain the Cambrian explosion

Most major animal body plans can be seen in fossils of Cambrian age, dating from 543 to 525 MYA. Although fossil cnidarians are found in rocks from the Ediacaran period, as old as 565 million years, along with what appear to be fossil mollusks and the burrows of worms, the great diversity of animals evolved quite rapidly in geological terms around the beginning of the Cambrian period—an event known as the **Cambrian explosion.** Biologists have long debated what caused this enormous expansion of animal diversity (figure 32.6). Many have argued that the emergence of new body plans was biological—the consequence of the evolution of predation, which encouraged an arms race between defenses, such as armor, and innovations that improved mobility and hunting success. Others have attributed the rapid diversification in body plans to physical factors—such as the build-up of dissolved oxygen and minerals in the oceans.

**Figure 32.6 Diversity of animals that evolved during the Cambrian explosion.** The Cambrian saw an astonishing variety of body plans, many of which gave rise to the animals we find today. The natural history of these species is open to speculation.

Whether these causes or others are at the heart of the Cambrian explosion, molecular studies in the field of evolutionary developmental biology may provide a mechanism for the emergence of so many body plans. Much of the variation in animal body plans is associated with changes in the location or time of expression of *homeobox* genes (*Hox* genes) in embryos (see chapters 19 and 25). *Hox* genes specify the identity of developing body parts, such as the legs, thorax, and antennae. Perhaps the Cambrian explosion reflects the evolution of the *Hox* developmental gene complex, which provides a mechanism for producing rapid changes in body plan.

### Learning Outcomes Review 32.4

The hypothesis of evolution of metazoans from colonial flagellates is favored because of the similarity between flagellate colonies and metazoan sponges, and because of molecular data based on ribosomal RNA sequences. Animal fossils become highly abundant in the Cambrian period in what is known as the Cambrian explosion. *Hox* genes, which control development of body shape and parts, may be responsible for the diversity found in this period.

■ *What alternative interpretations are there for the fossils that have led to the idea of the Cambrian explosion?*

## Chapter Review

### 32.1 Some General Features of Animals

Features common to all animals are multicelluarity, heterotrophic lifestyle, and lack of a cell wall. Other features include specialized tissues, ability to move, and sexual reproduction.

### 32.2 Evolution of the Animal Body Plan

**Most animals exhibit radial or bilateral symmetry.**

Most sponges are asymmetrical, but other animals are bilaterally or radially symmetrical at some time during their life. The body parts of radially symmetrical animals are arranged around a central axis. The body of a bilaterally symmetrical animal has left and right halves. Most bilaterally symmetrical organisms are cephalized and can move directionally.

**The evolution of tissues allowed for specialized structures and functions.**

Each tissue consists of differentiated cells that have characteristic forms and functions.

**A body cavity made possible the development of advanced organ systems.**

Most bilaterian animals possess a body cavity other than the gut. A coelom is a cavity that lies within tissues derived from mesoderm. A pseudocoelom lies between tissues derived from mesoderm and the gut (which develops from endoderm). The acoelomate condition and the pseudocoelom appear to have evolved more than once, but the coelom evolved only once.

A circulatory system is an example of a specialized organ system that assists with distribution of nutrients and removal of wastes.

**Bilaterians have two main types of development.**

In a protostome, the mouth develops from or near the blastopore. A protostome has determinate development, and many have spiral cleavage.

In a deuterostome, the anus develops from the blastopore. A deuterostome has indeterminate development and radial cleavage.

**Segmentation allowed for redundant systems and improved locomotion.**

Segmentation, which evolved multiple times, allows for efficient and flexible movement because each segment can move somewhat independently. Another advantage to segmentation is redundant organ systems.

### 32.3 The Classification of Animals

Animals are classified into 35 to 40 phyla based on shared characteristics. Systematists attempt to use features assumed to have evolved only once.

**Tissues and symmetry separate the Parazoa and Eumetazoa.**

With the exception of sponges, animals exhibit embryonic germ layers and differentiated cells that form tissues. These characteristics lead to most animals being termed collectively the Eumetazoa; other animals, including the sponges, are Parazoa.

### Molecular data help reveal evolutionary relationships.

By incorporating molecular data into phylogenetic analyses, major alterations have been made to the traditional view of how members of these phyla are related.

### Morphology- and molecule-based phylogenies agree on many major groupings.

Porifera (sponges) constitutes a monophyletic group that shares a common ancestor with other animals. Cnidarians (hydras, sea jellies, and corals) evolved before the origin of bilaterally symmetrical animals.

Annelids and arthropods had been considered closely related based on segmentation, but now arthropods are grouped with protostomes that molt their cuticles at least once during their life.

### Morphology-based phylogeny focused on the state of the coelom.

The two groups of bilaterally symmetrical animals (the Bilateria)—protostomes and deuterostomes—differ in embryology. All acoelomates and pseudocoelomates are protostomes; some coelomates are protostomes and some are deuterostomes.

### Protostomes consist of spiralians and ecdysozoans.

Spiralia comprises the clades Lophotrochozoa and Platyzoa. Spiralian animals grow by gradual addition of mass to the body and undergo spiral cleavage. Examples of Lophotrochozoa include annelids and mollusks. Examples of Platyzoa are rotifers and platyhelminthine worms.

Ecdysozoans grow by molting the external skeleton; Ecdysozoa includes many varied species, ranging from the pseudocoelomate, unsegmented Nematoda to the coelomate, segmented Arthropoda.

### Deuterostomes include chordates and echinoderms.

The major groups of deuterostomes are the echinoderms, which include animals such as sea stars and sea urchins, and the chordates, which include vertebrates.

Deuterostome development indicates that echinoderms and chordates evolved from a common ancestor, distinguishing them clearly from other animals.

## 32.4 The Roots of the Animal Tree of Life

### Metazoans appear to have evolved from colonial protists.

Systematics based on ribosomal RNA supports the hypothesis that the Eumetazoa are monophyletic and arose from colonial flagellates.

### Molecular analysis may explain the Cambrian explosion.

Molecular analysis suggests that the rapid diversification during the Cambrian explosion may have been due to evolution of the *Hox* genes.

## Review Questions

### UNDERSTAND

1. Which of the following characteristics is unique to all members of the animal kingdom?
   a. Sexual reproduction    c. Lack of cell walls
   b. Multicellularity       d. Heterotrophy

2. Animals are unique in the fact that they possess _____ for movement and _____ for conducting signals between cells.
   a. brains; muscles
   b. muscle tissue; nervous tissue
   c. limbs; spinal cords
   d. flagella; nerves

3. In animal sexual reproduction the gametes are formed by the process of
   a. meiosis.     c. fusion.
   b. mitosis.     d. binary fission.

4. The evolution of bilateral symmetry was a necessary precursor for the evolution of
   a. tissues.          c. a body cavity.
   b. segmentation.     d. cephalization.

5. A fluid-filled cavity that develops completely within mesodermal tissue is a characteristic of a
   a. coelomate.        c. acoelomate.
   b. pseudocoelomate.  d. all of the above

6. Which of the following statements is not true regarding segmentation?
   a. Segmentation allows the evolution of redundant systems.
   b. Segmentation is a requirement for a closed circulatory system.
   c. Segmentation enhances locomotion.
   d. Segmentation represents an example of convergent evolution.

7. Which of the following characteristics is used to distinguish between a parazoan and a eumetazoan?
   a. Presence of a true coelom
   b. Segmentation
   c. Cephalization
   d. Tissues

8. With regard to classification in the animals, the study of which of the following is changing our understanding of the organization of the kingdom?
   a. Molecular systematics
   b. Origin of tissues
   c. Patterns of segmentation
   d. Evolution of morphological characteristics

9. The _____ contain the greatest number of known species.
   a. Chordata      c. Porifera
   b. Arthropoda    d. Mollusca

10. The evolution of which of the following occurred after the Cambrian explosion?
    a. Cephalization   c. Segmentation
    b. Coelom          d. None of the above

11. A coelomate organism may have which of the following characteristics?
    a. Circulatory system
    b. Internal skeleton
    c. Larger size than a pseudocoelomate
    d. All of the above

## APPLY

1. The following diagram is of the blastopore stage of embryonic development. Based on the information in the diagram, which of the following statements is correct?

   a. It is a diagram of a protostome.
   b. It would have formed by radial cleavage.
   c. It would exhibit determinate development.
   d. All of the above are correct.

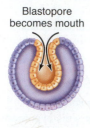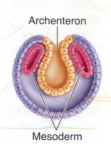

Blastopore becomes mouth    Archenteron

Mesoderm

2. Which of the following characteristics would not apply to a species in the Ecdysozoa?

   a. Bilateral
   b. Indeterminate cleavage
   c. Molt at least once in their life cycle
   d. Metazoan

3. In the rain forest you discover a new species that is terrestrial, has determinate development, molts during its lifetime, and possesses jointed appendages. To which phylum of animals should it be assigned?

## SYNTHESIZE

1. Worm evolution represents an excellent means of understanding the evolution of a body cavity. Using the phyla of worms Nematoda, Annelida, Platyhelminthes, and Nemetera, construct a phylogenetic tree based only on the form of body cavity (refer to figure 32.2 and table 32.2 for assistance). How does this relate to the material in figure 32.4? Should body cavity be used as the sole characteristic for classifying a worm?

2. Most students find it hard to believe that Echinodermata and Chordata are closely related phyla. If it were not for how their members form a body cavity, where would you place Echinodermata in the animal kingdom? Defend your answer.

## ONLINE RESOURCE

**www.ravenbiology.com**

Understand, Apply, and Synthesize—enhance your study with animations that bring concepts to life and practice tests to assess your understanding. Your instructor may also recommend the interactive eBook, individualized learning tools, and more.

Chapter **33**

# Noncoelomate Invertebrates

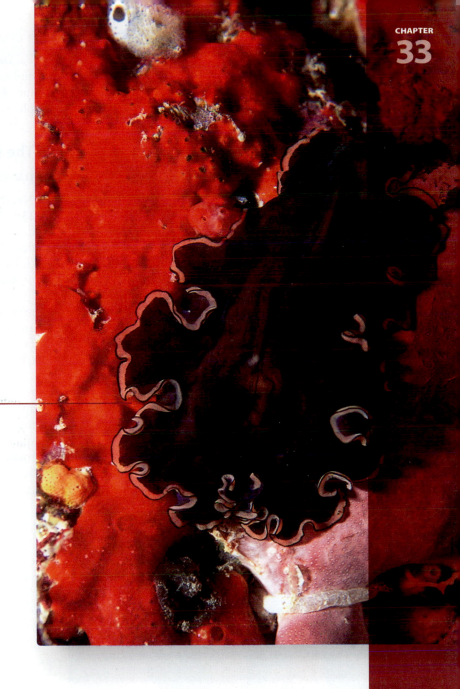

## Chapter Outline

## Introduction

*Our exploration of the great diversity of animals starts with the morphologically simplest members of the animal kingdom—sponges, jellyfish, and some of the worms (fully a third of animal phyla are based on a "wormy" body plan!). Despite their simplicity, these animals can carry out all the essential functions of life, just as do more morphologically complex animals—eating, respiring, reproducing, and protecting themselves. These animals lack a coelom, so we refer to them as noncoelomates, but many have a body space called a pseudocoelom. The major organization of the animal body first evolved in these animals, the basic body plan from which that of all the rest of animals evolved. In chapter 34, we consider the invertebrate animals that have a coelom, and in chapter 35 the vertebrates. You will see that all animals, despite their great variation, have much in common.*

# 33.1 Parazoa: Animals That Lack Specialized Tissues

Parazoans are animals lacking tissues (and therefore organs) and a definite symmetry. The major group of parazoans is phylum **Porifera**, the sponges. Despite their morphological simplicity, like all animals, sponges are truly multicellular.

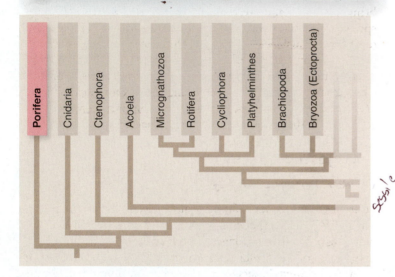

## The sponges, phylum Porifera, have a loose body organization

Nearly 7000 species of sponges live in the sea, and perhaps 150 species live in fresh water. Marine sponges occur at all depths, and may be among the most abundant animals in the deepest part of the oceans. Although some sponges are small (no more than a few millimeters across), some may reach 2 m or more in diameter.

A few small sponges are radially symmetrical, but most members of this phylum lack symmetry. Some have a low and encrusting form and grow covering various sorts of surfaces; others are erect and lobed, some in complex patterns (figure 33.1*a*).

As is true of many marine invertebrate animals, larval sponges are free-swimming. After a sponge larva attaches to an appropriate surface, it metamorphoses into an adult and remains attached to that surface for the rest of its life. Thus adult sponges are sessile; that is, they are anchored, immobile, on rocks or other submerged objects. Sponges defend themselves by producing chemicals that repel potential predators and organisms that might overgrow them.

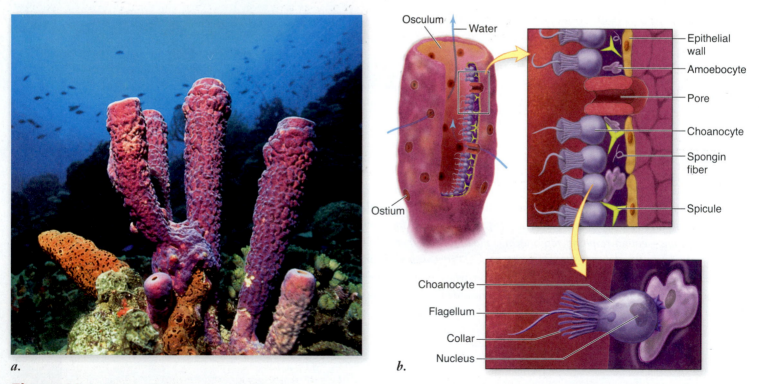

**Figure 33.1  Phylum Porifera: Sponges.** *a. Aplysina longissima.* This beautiful, bright orange and purple elongated sponge is found on deep coral reefs. *b.* Diagrammatic drawing of the simplest type of sponge. Sponges are composed of several distinct cell types, the activities of which are coordinated. The sponge body has no organized tissues, and most are not symmetrical.

As a result, pharmaceutical companies are interested in possibly using these chemicals for human applications.

## The sponge body is composed of several cell types

Lacking head or appendages, mouth or anus, and the organized internal structure characteristic of all other animals, at first sight a sponge seems to be little more than a mass of cells embedded in a gelatinous matrix. In fact, a sponge contains several cell types (figure 33.1b), each with specialized functions. If a sponge is put through a fine sieve or coarse cloth so that the cells are separated, they will seek one another out and reassemble the entire sponge—a phenomenon that does not occur in any other animal.

As mentioned in chapter 32, a unique feature of sponge cells is their ability to differentiate from one type to another, and to dedifferentiate from a specialized state to an unspecialized one. Activities of the cells are loosely coordinated to perform functions such as synchronizing reproduction and building the complex skeletal meshwork. This distinguishes sponges as truly multicellular, by contrast with colonial protists, which may form aggregates of cells, but all are functionally identical (except for the reproductive cells).

A small, anatomically simple sponge has a vaselike shape. The walls of the "vase" have three functional layers. Facing the internal cavity are flagellated cells called **choanocytes,** or collar cells (see figure 33.1b). A larger and more complex sponge has many small chambers connected by channels rather than a single chamber. Once water has passed through a flagellated chamber, it travels through channels that converge at a large opening called an **osculum** (plural, oscula), through which water is expelled from the sponge.

The body of a sponge is bounded by an outer epithelium consisting of flattened cells somewhat like those that make up the outer layers of animals in other phyla. Pores on the sponge allow water to enter the channels that course through its body, leading to and from the flagellated chambers. The name of the phylum, Porifera, refers to these pores, the ostia (singular, ostium); a large sponge has multiple oscula, but they are far, far fewer than the number of ostia.

Some epithelial cells are specialized to surround the ostia; they can contract when touched or exposed to appropriate stimuli, causing the ostia to close and thereby protecting the delicate inner cells from the entry of potentially harmful substances such as sand and noxious chemicals. Cells surrounding individual ostia operate independently of one another; because a sponge has no nervous system, actions cannot be coordinated across large distances.

Between the outer and inner layers of cells, sponges consist mainly of a gelatinous, protein-rich matrix called the **mesohyl,** which contains various types of amoeboid cells (and eggs). In many kinds of sponges, some of these cells secrete needles of calcium carbonate or silica known as **spicules,** or fibers of a tough protein called **spongin.** Spicules and spongin form the skeleton of the sponge, strengthening its body. The siliceous spicules of some deep-sea sponges can reach a meter in length! A genuine bath sponge is the spongin skeleton of a marine sponge; artificial sponges made of cellulose or plastic are modeled on the body design of this animal, with a porous body

adapted to contain large amounts of water. The three classes of sponges—Hexactinellida, Demospongiae, and Calcarea—are distinguished in part by the mineral form of their spicules.

## Choanocytes help circulate water through the sponge

Each choanocyte resembles a protist with a single flagellum (plural, flagella) (see figure 33.1b), a similarity that may reflect its evolutionary derivation. The pressure created by the beating flagella in the cavity contributes to circulating the water that brings in food and oxygen and carries out wastes. In large sponges, the inner wall of the body interior is convoluted, increasing the surface area and, therefore, the number of flagella. In such a sponge, 1 cm³ of sponge can propel more than 20 L of water per day. Choanocytes also capture food particles from the passing water, engulfing and digesting them. Obviously, this arrangement restricts a sponge to feeding on particles considerably smaller than choanocytes—largely bacteria. *suspension feeding*

## Sponges reproduce both asexually and sexually

Some sponges can reproduce asexually simply by breaking into fragments. Each fragment is able to continue growing as a new individual. Whether a sponge should be considered colonial is an illustration of the limitations of human language. A colony of invertebrate animals, such as coral, is generally defined as a group of individuals that are physically connected (and may be physiologically connected as well), all having been produced by asexual reproduction (such as budding or dividing) from a single progenitor that arose by sexual reproduction. Nearly all sponges grow by multiplying the number of flagellated chambers connected to a single osculum, but whether these units can be considered "individuals" is debatable.

Sponge sperm are created by the transformation of choanocytes, which are then released into the water where they may be carried into another sponge of the same species. When a sperm is captured by a choanocyte, it is carried to an egg cell, which is in the mesohyl (and in some sponges is also a transformed choanocyte). In many sponges, development of the externally ciliated larva occurs within the mother. In sponges of other species, the fertilized egg is released into the water, where development occurs. Whether a fertilized egg or a ciliated larva is released, after a short planktonic (drifting) stage, the larva settles on a suitable substrate where it transforms into an adult.

### Learning Outcomes Review 33.1

Sponges possess multicellularity but have neither tissue-level development nor body symmetry. Cells that compose a sponge include a layer of choanocytes, a layer of epithelial cells, and amoeboid cells in the mesohyl between the two layers. Choanocytes have flagella that beat to circulate water through the sponge body.

■ *What features of a sponge make it seem to be a colony, and what features make it seem to be a single organism?*

*Eumetazoa: Animals with True Tissues*

### Learning Outcomes

1. *Explain the defining feature of cnidarians.*
2. *Differentiate between cnidarians and ctenophores.*
3. *Discuss the question of symmetry of ctenophores.*

The Eumetazoa contains animals that evolved the first key transition in the animal body plan: distinct tissues. The embryonic cell layers differentiate into the tissues of the adult body, giving rise to the body plan characteristic of each group of animals.

Recall that the outer covering of the body (the epidermis) and the nervous system develop from the embryonic ectoderm, and the digestive tissue (called the **gastrodermis**) develops from the embryonic endoderm. In the Bilateria, the embryonic mesoderm, which lies between endoderm and ectoderm, forms the muscles.

Eumetazoans also evolved body symmetry. Metazoans living sessile on the ocean floor or free-living in the water may be radially symmetrical. One phylum consisting of penta-radially symmetrical animals (those with fivefold symmetry), the Echinodermata, are dealt with in chapter 34. Some animals of the phylum Cnidaria, comprising hydroids, jellyfish, sea anemones, and corals, are clearly radially symmetrical and some are biradially symmetrical (see chapter 32). Members of the phylum Ctenophora, the comb jellies, are considered by some people to be radially symmetrical but by others to be bilaterally symmetrical.

## All cnidarians, phylum Cnidaria, are carnivores

Most of the 10,000 species of cnidarians are marine; a very few live in fresh water. The bodies of these fascinating and simply constructed diploblastic animals are made of distinct tissues, although they do not have organs. Despite having no reproductive, circulatory, digestive, or excretory systems, cnidarians reproduce, exchange gas, capture and digest prey, and distribute the resulting organic molecules to all their cells. A cnidarian has no concentration of nervous tissue that could be considered a brain or even a ganglion. Rather, its nervous system is a latticework, the cells having junctions like those of bilaterians. All cnidarians have nervous receptors sensitive to touch, and some have gravity and light receptors, which include, in a few species, image-forming eyes.

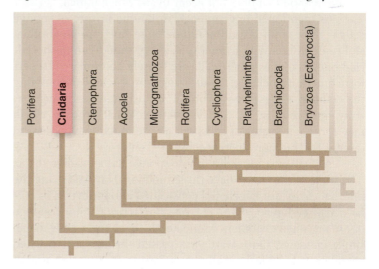

Cnidarians capture their prey (which includes fishes, crustaceans, and many other kinds of animals) with nematocysts (figure 33.2), microscopic intracellular structures unique

**Figure 33.2 Phylum Cnidaria: Cnidarians.** The cells of a cnidarian such as this *Hydra* are organized into specialized tissues. The interior gut cavity is specialized for extracellular digestion—that is, digestion begins within the gut cavity rather than within a cell. The epidermis contains nematocysts for defense and for capturing prey. This *Hydra* is undergoing asexual reproduction—budding off a new individual.

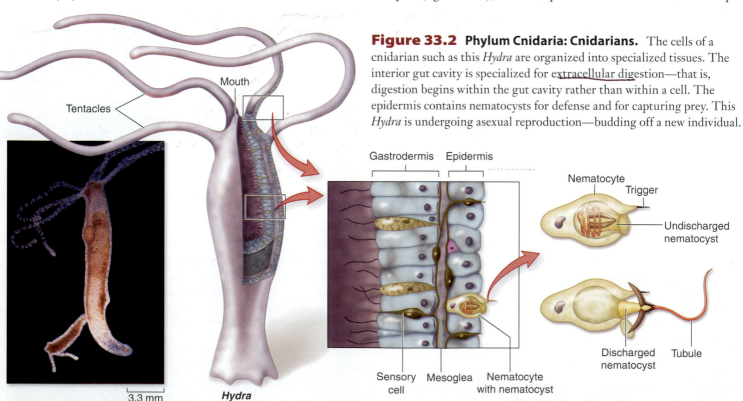

to the phylum. Food captured by a cnidarian is brought to the mouth by the tentacles that ring the mouth.

### Basic body plans

A cnidarian exhibits one of two body forms: the polyp and the medusa (figure 33.3). A **polyp** is cylindrical, with a mouth surrounded by tentacles at the end of the cylinder opposite where it is attached. Attachment in most solitary polyps is to a firm substratum, but in those that are part of a colony, it is to the mass of common colonial tissue. A **medusa** is discoidal or umbrella-shaped, with a mouth surrounded by tentacles on one side; most live free in the water. These two seemingly quite different body forms share the same morphology—the mouth opens into a sac-like gastrovascular cavity and is surrounded by tentacles.

The cnidarian body plan has a single opening leading to the gastrovascular space, which is the site of digestion, most gas exchange, waste discharge, and, in many cnidarians, formation of gametes. The body wall is composed of two layers: the epidermis, which covers the surfaces in contact with the outside environment, and the gastrodermis, which covers the gastrovascular cavity. Between these two layers is the **mesoglea,** which varies from acellular, being no more than a glue holding gastrodermis to epidermis in *Hydra*, to thick and rubbery with many cells in large medusae called jellyfish (see figures 33.2, 33.3).

The gastrovascular space also serves as a hydrostatic skeleton (see chapter 47). A hydrostatic skeleton serves two of the roles that a skeleton made of bone or shells does: it provides a rigid structure against which muscles can operate, and it gives the animal shape. For muscles to operate against it, the fluid-filled space must be closed sufficiently tightly so the fluid is under pressure and does not escape when muscles contract around the space. Think of the gastrovascular space of a cnidarian full of water like an inflated, elongated, air-filled balloon. Because it is firm, muscles that shorten it cause it to broaden, and muscles that decrease its diameter lengthen it. However, if you inflate the balloon with air, but then do not hold the opening closed, the air will escape and the balloon will become flaccid. Similarly, when a cnidarian contracts greatly, it must open its mouth so water can escape. However, the mouth can close sufficiently tightly to retain water in the gastrovascular cavity, so the animal is turgid and can bend and extend its tentacles.

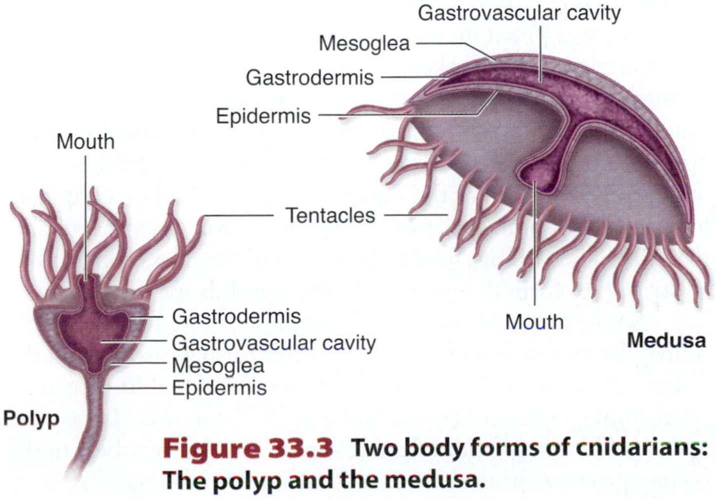

In addition to the hydrostatic skeleton of all polyps, those of many species build an exoskeleton of chitin or calcium carbonate around themselves; in many colonial species, the skeleton links the members of the colony. The polyps of a smaller number of species secrete internal skeletal elements. Polyps of some groups of cnidarians, such as sea anemones, have no skeleton at all. All medusae are solitary (that is, they do not form colonies) and form no skeleton.

### The cnidarian life cycle

Some cnidarians occur only as polyps, and others exist only as medusae, but many alternate between these two phases (see figure 33.3); both phases consist of diploid individuals. In general, in species having both polyp and medusa in the life cycle, the medusa forms gametes. The sexes are separate; this condition, known as gonochorism, means an individual is either male or female. An egg and a sperm unite to form a zygote, which develops into a planktonic ciliated **planula** larva that metamorphoses into a polyp. The polyp produces medusae asexually. Dispersal occurs in both medusa and larvae. In most species with such a life cycle, a polyp may also produce other polyps asexually; if they remain attached to one other, the resulting group is referred to as a colony.

In a small number of species, the planula produced by medusae may develop directly or indirectly into another medusa without passing through the polyp stage. More commonly, there is a polyp but no medusa in the life cycle. In such cnidarians, the polyp can form gametes, and the resulting planula will develop into another polyp. In some, but by no means all, of these species, the polyp can also produce other polyps asexually, by dividing, budding, or breaking off bits of itself that regenerate (grow the missing parts).

### Digestion

A major evolutionary innovation in cnidarians is extracellular digestion of food inside the animal. Recall that in a sponge, digestion occurs within choanocytes, so food particles must be small enough to be engulfed by a choanocyte. In a cnidarian, digestion takes place partly in the gastrovascular cavity. Digestive enzymes, released from cells lining the cavity, partially break down food. Other cells lining the space engulf those food fragments by phagocytosis. This allows a cnidarian to feed on prey larger than a sponge can handle.

### Nematocysts

Cnidarians capture food with the aid of **nematocysts,** microscopic stinging capsules unique to the phylum (see figure 33.2). Although often referred to as "stinging cells," they are capsules, each secreted within a cell called a nematocyte. Cnidarians may be morphologically simple, but nematocysts are the most complex structures secreted by single animal cells. When appropriately stimulated, the closure at the end of the capsule springs open, and a tubule is emitted. Nematocyst discharge is one of the fastest cellular processes in nature. The mechanism of discharge of a nematocyst is unknown—several hypotheses for it have been proposed. Although the action of a nematocyst is often described as harpoon-like, the tubule actually everts (turns inside-out). It may penetrate or wrap around an object; the tubules of some nematocysts are barbed and some carry

**Figure 33.3** **Two body forms of cnidarians: The polyp and the medusa.**

Gastrovascular cavity
Mesoglea
Gastrodermis
Epidermis
Mouth
Tentacles
Gastrodermis
Gastrovascular cavity
Mesoglea
Epidermis
Polyp
Mouth
**Medusa**

venom. In a very few species, the venoms are strong enough to kill a human.

Many thousand nematocytes typically are part of the epidermis of each tentacle. Each one can be used only once. In some types of cnidarians, nematocysts occur in parts of the body other than the tentacles, including in the gastrovascular cavity, where they may aid in digestion. In addition to being used offensively, nematocysts are the only defense of cnidarians—they are the reason jellyfish and fire coral sting. Some cnidarians have stinging capsules of types other than nematocysts, which are termed cnidae—hence the name of the phylum, Cnidaria.

## Cnidarians are grouped into four—or five—classes

Traditionally, three classes of Cnidaria were recognized: Anthozoa (sea anemones, corals, sea fans), Hydrozoa (hydroids, Hydra, Portuguese man-of-war), and Scyphozoa (jellyfish). Now nearly all biologists accept that some scyphozoans are sufficiently distinct in life cycle and morphology that they constitute their own class, Cubozoa (box jellies), some of which have a sting sufficiently toxic to kill humans. Less widely accepted is the separation of some other scyphozoans into their own class, Staurozoa (star jellies).

### Class Anthozoa: Sea anemones and corals

The largest class of Cnidaria is **Anthozoa,** consisting of approximately 6200 species of solitary and colonial polyps. They include stony corals (figure 33.4), soft-bodied sea anemones (figure 33.5), and other groups known by such fanciful names as sea pens, sea pansies, sea fans, and sea whips. Many of these names reflect the plantlike appearance of the individual polyps or colonies.

**Figure 33.5**
**Class Anthozoa.**
Crimson anemone, *Cribrinopsis fernaldi.*

An anthozoan polyp differs from a polyp of the other classes in its gastrovascular cavity being compartmentalized by radially arrayed, longitudinal sheets of tissue called mesenteries. The way they are arranged imparts the biradial symmetry to these animals mentioned in chapter 32. The gametes of an anthozoan develop in the mesenteries. The tentacles of an anthozoan are hollow, whereas those of many other cnidarians are solid.

Sea anemones (see figure 33.5) constitute a group of just over 1000 species of highly muscular and relatively complex soft-bodied anthozoans. Living in waters of all depths throughout the world, they range from a few millimeters to over a meter in diameter, and many are equally long.

Most corals are anthozoans, and most hard corals (about 1400 species, see figure 33.4) are closely related to sea anemones. The polyp of a coral secretes an exoskeleton of calcium carbonate around and under itself (this is the same material of which chalk is composed); as the individual or colony grows upward, dead skeleton accumulates below it. In shallow water of the tropics, these accumulations form coral reefs. Most waters in which coral reefs develop are nutrient-poor, but the corals are able to grow well because they contain within their cells symbiotic dinoflagellates (zooxanthellae) that photosynthesize and provide energy for the animals. Obviously coral reefs are restricted to water sufficiently shallow for sunlight to reach the living animals (typically no more than 100 m), but corals that do not form reefs can grow deeper—to about 5000 m. Only about half the species of hard corals participate in forming reefs.

Coral reefs are economically important, serving as refuges for the young of many species of crustaceans and fishes that are eaten by humans, as well as protecting coasts of many tropical islands. But they are threatened by global climate change. Water warmer than usual can cause the symbiosis with zooxanthellae to break down, a phenomenon known as "coral bleaching" because the underlying white skeleton of the animal becomes visible through its body in the absence of the symbionts. Bleaching does not always kill a coral, but it is stressful. As carbon dioxide in the atmosphere rises, it dissolves in water, forming carbonic acid, which lowers the pH of the water. This makes calcium carbonate less available; some species of calcifying marine plants and animals, including corals, have been shown to form less robust skeletons, and to form them more slowly, as pH drops.

Some "soft corals" secrete needles of calcium carbonate much like sponge spicules; these sclerites form a case around the polyp or are embedded in their tissues, presumably providing protection against predation. Some of these animals also secrete a horny rod that provides flexible support to the members of the colony growing around it (sea fans are such colonies).

**Figure 33.4 Stony corals.** *Tubastraea aurea,* a non-reef building species from Malaysia.

**Figure 33.6**
**Class Cubozoa.**
*Chironex fleckeri,*
a box jelly.

**Figure 33.8**
**Class Scyphozoa.**
*Aurelia aurita,* a
jellyfish.

## Class Cubozoa: The box jellies

As their name implies, medusae of class **Cubozoa** are box-shaped, with a tentacle or group of tentacles hanging from each corner of the box (figure 33.6). Most of the 40 or so species are only a few centimeters in height, although some reach 25 cm. Box jellies are strong swimmers and voracious predators of fish in tropical and subtropical waters; both of these facts are related to some cubozoans having image-forming eyes! The stings of some species can be fatal to humans. The polyp stage is inconspicuous and in many cases unknown.

## Class Hydrozoa: The hydroids

Most of the approximately 2700 species of class **Hydrozoa** have both polyp and medusa stages in their life cycle (see figure 33.3). The polyp stage of most species is colonial. The polyps of a colony may not be identical in structure or function: some may be specialized to feed but be unable to reproduce, whereas the opposite may be true of others (they are nourished by material transported from feeding polyps through the gastrovascular space connecting members of the colony). The Portuguese man-of-war (figure 33.7) is not a jellyfish, but is a floating colony of highly integrated polypoid and medusoid individuals! Some marine hydroids and medusae are bioluminescent.

Hydrozoa is the only class of Cnidaria with freshwater members. A well-known hydroid is the freshwater *Hydra,* which is exceptional not only in its habitat, but in having no medusa stage and being solitary (see figure 33.2). Each polyp attaches by a basal disk, on which it can glide, aided by mucous

secretions. It can also somersault—by bending over and attaching to the substrate by its tentacles, then looping over to a new location. If the polyp detaches from the substrate, it can float to the surface.

## Class Scyphozoa: The jellyfish

In the approximately 200 species of class **Scyphozoa,** the medusa is much more conspicuous and complex than the polyp. Although many scyphomedusae are essentially colorless (figure 33.8), some are a striking orange, blue, or pink. The polyp is small, inconspicuous, simple in structure, and typically white in color, but is entirely lacking in a few scyphozoans that live in the open ocean.

The epithelium around the margin of a jellyfish contains a ring of muscle cells that can contract rhythmically to propel the animal through the water by jetting water from the gastrovascular cavity or space beneath it; by contracting those on just one side, the animal can steer. A scyphomedusa (*Cyanea capilata*) was the killer in the Sherlock Holmes tale "The Lion's Mane," but, although some can inflict pain on humans, they are unlikely to be capable of killing.

## Class Staurozoa: The star jellies

Among the reasons the 50 species of this group were separated from the Scyphozoa and placed in their own class (Staurozoa) is that the animal resembles a medusa in most ways but is attached to the substratum by a sort of stalk that emerges from the side opposite the mouth (figure 33.9). In addition, in all staurozoans known, the planula larva creeps rather than swims or drifts.

**Figure 33.7**
**Portuguese man-of-war**
**(Physalia physalis).** This species has a very painful sting.

**Figure 33.9**
**Star jelly.** Stalked jellyfish (*Haliclystus auricula*).

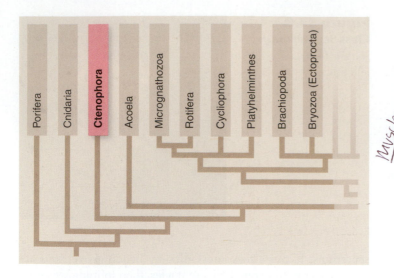

## The comb jellies, phylum Ctenophora, use cilia for movement

Pelagic members of the small marine phylum **Ctenophora** range from spherical to ribbon-like and are known as comb jellies, sea walnuts, or sea gooseberries. Abundant in the open ocean, most of these animals are transparent and only a few centimeters long, but rare ones are deeply pigmented and reach 1 m in length. They propel themselves through the water with eight rows of comblike plates of fused cilia that beat in a coordinated fashion, scattering light so they appear like rainbows (figure 33.10). Ctenophores are the largest animals that use cilia for locomotion. Many ctenophores are bioluminescent, giving off bright flashes of light that are particularly evident in the deep sea or on the surface of the ocean at night. Most ctenophores have two long, retractable tentacles used in prey capture. The epithelium of the tentacles contains **colloblasts,** a type of cell that bursts to discharge a strong adhesive material on contact with animal prey.

**Figure 33.10**
**A comb jelly (phylum Ctenophora).** Note the iridescent rows of comblike plates of fused cilia.

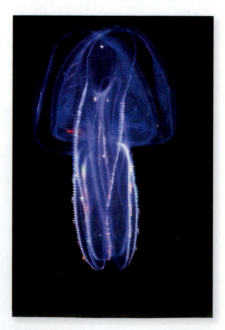

The phylogenetic position of Ctenophora is unclear. It was formerly considered closely related to Cnidaria because of the gelatinous, medusa-like form of most species. However, ctenophores lack nematocysts and are structurally more complex than cnidarians. They have anal pores through which water and other substances can exit the body. Although ctenophores have been considered diploblasts with radial symmetry, recent developmental studies have demonstrated them to have muscle cells derived from mesoderm, which means they should be considered triploblasts, like bilaterians. The two tentacles placed on opposite sides of a ctenophore's body impart some bilaterality to them, but whether their symmetry should be considered biradial, like that of sea anemones, is unclear. A recent molecular phylogeny places ctenophores at the base of the animal tree of life, as the sister group to all other metazoans. If this is borne out, it implies that the ancestral animal was triploblastic and bilaterally symmetrical.

### Learning Outcomes Review 33.2

Members of phylum Cnidaria have nematocysts, capsules used in defense and prey capture, and are radially symmetrical. Members of phylum Ctenophora lack nematocysts; they propel themselves by means of eight rows of comblike plates of fused cilia. Ctenophores have cells called colloblasts that assist in prey capture. The symmetry of ctenophores is a subject of debate.

■ *Why would triploblasty be important to phylogeny?*

## 33.3 *The Bilaterian Acoelomates*

### Learning Outcomes

1. *List the distinguishing features of bilaterian flatworms.*
2. *Explain why the scolex of a tapeworm is not a head.*

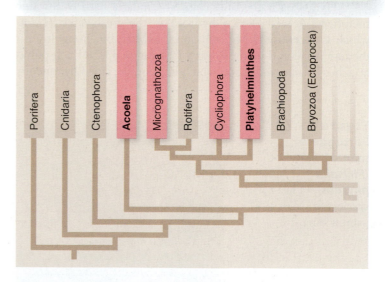

The Bilateria is characterized by a key transition in the animal body plan—bilateral symmetry—which allowed animals to achieve high levels of specialization within parts of their bodies, such as the concentration of sensory structures at the anterior. (Even if ctenophores are truly bilateral as just mentioned, they lack these other specializations.)

As discussed in chapter 32, bilaterians are traditionally divided into acoelomates, pseudocoelomates, and coelomates. The acoelomate and pseudocoelomate conditions appear to have evolved multiple times; thus these conditions are convergent and not homologous and do not necessarily indicate close evolutionary relationship among the animals sharing that anatomy. Nonetheless, the state of the internal part of the animal's body does provide information about how the animals are constructed and how they live. In this chapter, we cover acoelomates and pseudocoelomates; in the next chapter we cover coelomates, which are probably monophyletic.

Structurally, the simplest bilaterians are the acoelomates, which lack an internal cavity other than the digestive tract. The largest phylum of the group is the Platyhelminthes.

## The flatworms, phylum Platyhelminthes, have an incomplete gut

The phylum Platyhelminthes consists of some 20,000 species. These ciliated, soft-bodied animals are flattened dorsoventrally, the anatomy that gives them the name flatworms. Flatworm bodies are solid aside from an incomplete digestive cavity (figure 33.11). Although among the morphologically simplest of bilaterally symmetrical animals, they have some complex structures, like their reproductive apparatus, and they have the most complex life cycles among animals.

Free-living flatworms occur in a wide variety of marine, freshwater, and even moist terrestrial habitats. They are carnivores and scavengers, eating small animals and bits of organic debris. They move around by means of ciliated epithelial cells, which are particularly concentrated on their ventral surfaces, but they also have well-developed musculature. By contrast, many species of flatworms are parasitic, living inside the bodies of other animals. Flatworms range in length from 1 mm or less to many meters (some tapeworms).

### Digestion in flatworms

Most flatworms have only a single opening for their digestive cavity, a mouth located on the bottom side of the animal at midbody. A flatworm ingests its food and tears it into small bits using muscular contractions in the upper end of the gut, the pharynx.

Like sponges, cnidarians, and ctenophores, a flatworm lacks a circulatory system for the transport of oxygen and food molecules. The thin body of a flatworm allows gas to diffuse between its cells and the air (oxygen diffuses in and carbon dioxide diffuses out). Branches of the gut extend throughout the body, so the gut functions in both digestion and distribution of food. Cells that line the gut engulf most of the food particles by phagocytosis and digest them; but, as in cnidarians and most bilaterians, some particles are partly digested extracellularly. Tapeworms, which are parasitic, have a mouth at the front of their body and no digestive cavity at all; they absorb food directly through the body wall.

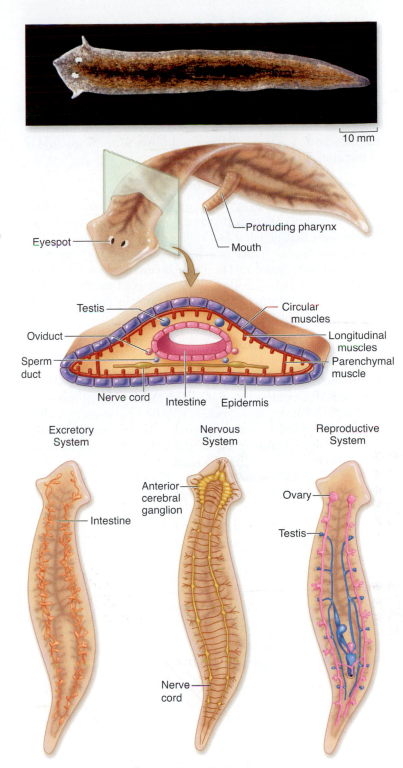

**Figure 33.11 Architecture of a flatworm.** A photo and an idealized diagram of the genus *Dugesia*, the familiar freshwater planarian of ponds and rivers. Upper schematic shows a whole animal and a transverse section through the anterior part of the body. Schematics below show the digestive, central nervous, and reproductive systems.

### Excretion and osmoregulation

Unlike cnidarians and ctenophores, flatworms have an excretory system, which consists of a network of fine tubules that run throughout the body. Bulblike **flame cells,** so named because of the flickering movements of the flagella beating inside them, are located on the side branches of the tubules. Flagella in the flame cells move water and excretory substances into the tubules and then to pores located between the epidermal cells through which the liquid is expelled. Flame cells primarily regulate water balance of the organism; the excretory function appears to be secondary, and much of the metabolic waste of a flatworm diffuses into the gut and is eliminated through the mouth.

### Nervous system and sensory organs

The flatworm nervous system comprises an anterior cerebral ganglion and nerve cords that run down the body, with cross-connections that give it a ladder-like shape (see figure 33.11). Free-living flatworms are poorly cephalized, with eyespots on their heads (see figure 33.11). These inverted, pigmented cups, which contain light-sensitive cells connected to the nervous system, enable a worm to distinguish light from dark: most flatworms tend to move away from strong light.

### Flatworm reproduction

The reproductive systems of flatworms are complex. Most are **hermaphroditic,** each individual containing both male and female sexual structures (see figure 33.11). In many of members of Platyhelminthes, copulation is required between two individuals, and fertilization is internal, each partner depositing sperm in the copulatory sac of the other. The sperm travel along special tubes to reach the eggs.

In most freshwater flatworms, fertilized eggs are laid in cocoons strung in ribbons and hatch into miniature adults. In contrast, some marine species develop indirectly, the fertilized egg undergoing spiral cleavage, and the embryo giving rise to a larva that swims or drifts until metamorphosing, when it settles in an appropriate habitat.

Flatworms are known for their regenerative capacity: when a single individual of some species is divided into two or more parts, an entirely new flatworm can regrow what is missing from each bit.

## Flatworms comprise two major groups

Most flatworms are parasitic; those that are not are referred to as free-living. There is strong morphological and molecular evidence that the parasitic lifestyle evolved only once in platyhelminths, from free-living ancestors.

### Turbellaria: Free-living flatworms

Flatworm phylogeny is in a state of flux. The group of free-living flatworms, Turbellaria, has been considered a class, but recent studies show it is not monophyletic so it is likely to be divided into several classes. One of the most familiar members of this group are freshwater members of the genus *Dugesia*, the common planarian used in biology laboratories.

### Neodermata: Parasitic flatworms

All parasitic flatworms are placed in the subphylum Neodermata. That name means "new skin" and refers to the animal's outer surface. All neodermatans live as ectoparasites or endoparasites on or in the bodies of other animals for some period of their lives. The neodermis is resistant to the digestive enzymes and immune defenses produced by the animals parasitized by these flatworms. These animals also lack other features of free-living flatworms such as eyespots, which are of no adaptive value to an organism living inside the body of another animal. Neodermata contains two subgroups: Trematoda, the flukes, and Cercomeromorpha, the tapeworms and their relatives.

### Trematoda: The flukes

There are more than 10,000 named species of flukes, ranging in length from less than 1 mm to more than 8 cm. Flukes attach themselves within the bodies of their hosts by means of suckers, anchors, or hooks. A fluke takes in food (cells or fluids of the host) through its mouth, like its free-living relatives. The life cycle of some species involves only one host, usually a fish, but the life cycle of most flukes involves two or more hosts. The first intermediate host is almost always a snail, and the final host (in which the adult fluke lives and reproduces sexually) is almost always a vertebrate; in between there may be other intermediate hosts. Although the life of a parasite is secure within a host, which provides food and shelter, getting from one host to another is extremely risky, and most individuals die in the transition.

### Flukes that cause disease in humans

The oriental liver fluke, *Clonorchis sinensis*, is an example of a flatworm that parasitizes humans, living in the bile duct of the liver (as well as that of cats, dogs, and pigs) (figure 33.12). It is especially common in Asia. Each worm is 1 to 2 cm long and, like all flukes, has a complex life cycle. A fertilized egg containing a ciliated first-stage larva, the **miracidium,** is passed in the feces. If the larva reaches water, it may be ingested by an aquatic snail (but most do not reach water and most that do are not ingested. The prodigious number of eggs a parasitic flatworm produces is an adaptation to this life-cycle full of risks). Within the snail, the ciliated larva transforms into a **sporocyst,** a bag-like structure containing embryonic germ cells, each of which develops into a **redia** (plural, *rediae*), an elongated, nonciliated larva. Each of these larvae grows within the snail, then gives rise to several individuals of the next larval stage, the tadpole-like **cercaria** (plural, *cercariae*).

Cercariae escape into the water, where they swim about freely. When one encounters a fish of the family Cyprinidae—the family that includes carp and goldfish—it bores into the muscles, loses its tail, and encysts, transforming into a metacercaria. If a human or other mammal eats raw fish containing metacercariae, the cyst dissolves in the intestine, and the young fluke migrates to the bile duct, where it matures, thereby completing the cycle. Even if infected fish is cooked, the parasite can be transmitted if metacercariae stuck to cutting boards or the hands of a person handling the raw fish flesh are ingested. An individual fluke may live for 15 to 30 years in the liver; a heavy infection of liver flukes may cause cirrhosis of the liver and death in humans.

Perhaps the most important trematodes to human health are blood flukes of the genus *Schistosoma*. They afflict about 5%

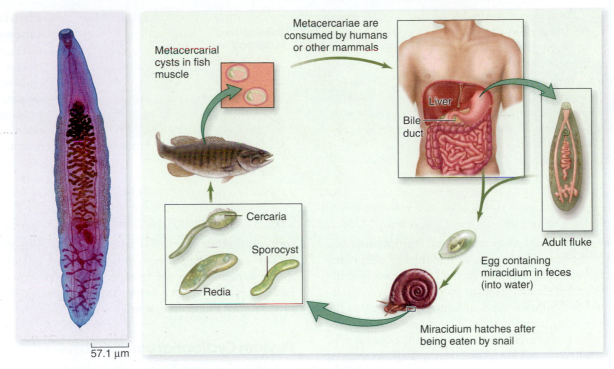

57.1 μm

**Figure 33.12** Life cycle of the oriental liver fluke, *Clonorchis sinensis.*

of the world's population, or more than 200 million people, in tropical Asia, Africa, Latin America, and the Middle East. About 800,000 people die each year from the disease called **schisto-somiasis,** or bilharzia.

Schistosomes live in blood vessels associated with the intestine or the urinary bladder, depending on the species (figure 33.13). Thus if the worm is killed, it cannot be washed out of the host, unlike parasites that live in the gut or associated organs such as the liver. Nor do its fertilized eggs have that easy route out of the body. Instead, a fertilized egg must break through the wall of the blood vessel to get into either the intestine or the urinary bladder (depending on the species). The damage done to the blood vessels and gut or bladder wall is considerable, especially considering that an individual worm may release 300 to 3000 eggs per day and live for many years.

Great effort is being made to control schistosomiasis. The worms protect themselves from the body's immune system in part by coating themselves with some of the host's own antigens that effectively render the worm immunologically invisible (see chapter 52). The search is on for a vaccine that would cause the host to develop antibodies to one of the antigens of young worms before they can protect themselves.

### Cercomeromorpha: The tapeworms and their relatives

An adult tapeworm hangs onto the inner wall of its host's intestine by means of a terminal attachment structure. It lacks a digestive cavity as well as digestive enzymes, absorbing food from the host's gut through its outer surface. Most species of tape-

worm occur in the intestines of vertebrates; about a dozen of them regularly occur in humans.

The long, flat body of a tapeworm is divided into three zones: the **scolex,** or attachment structure; the neck; and a series of repetitive sections, the **proglottids** (figure 33.14). The scolex of many species bears four suckers and may also have hooks. The scolex is not a head: it has neither concentrated nervous tissue nor a mouth. Each proglottid is a complete hermaphroditic unit, containing both male and female

125 μm

**Figure 33.13** **Schistosomes.** The male lies within the groove on the female's ventral side, with its front and hind ends protruding.

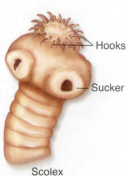

500 μm

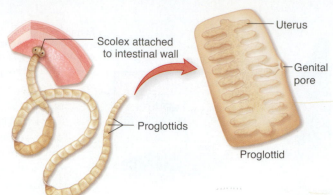

Hooks

Sucker

Scolex

Scolex attached to intestinal wall

Proglottids

Uterus

Genital pore

Proglottid

reproductive organs. Proglottids are formed continuously in a growth zone at the base of the neck, with maturing ones being pushed posteriorly as new ones are formed. The gonads in the proglottids progressively mature away from the neck, fertilization occurs, and the embryos form, the proglottids nearer the end of the body being more mature. The most terminal proglottid, filled with embryonated eggs, breaks off; either it ruptures and the embryos, each surrounded by a shell, are carried out with the host's feces, or the entire proglottid is carried out, where the embryos emerge from it through a pore or the ruptured body wall. Embryos are scattered in the environment, on leaves, in water, or in other places where they may be picked up by another animal.

The beef tapeworm, *Taenia saginata*, occurs as a juvenile in the intermuscular tissue of cattle; as an adult, it inhabits the intestines of human beings, where a mature worm may reach a length of 10 m or more. A worm attaches itself to the intestinal wall of the host by a scolex with four suckers. Shed proglottids pass from the human in the feces and may crawl onto vegetation, a favorable place to be picked up by cattle; they may remain viable for up to five months. If one is ingested by cattle, the larva burrows through the wall of the intestine and ultimately reaches muscle tissues through the blood or lymph vessels. About 1% of cattle in the United States are infected, and because some 20% of the beef consumed is not federally inspected, when humans eat infected beef that is cooked "rare," infection by these tapeworms can occur. As a result, the beef tapeworm is a frequent parasite of humans.

## Acoel flatworms appear to be distinct from Platyhelminthes: A case study

An acoel flatworm (figure 33.15) has a nervous system that consists of a simple network of nerves with a minor concentration of neurons in the anterior body end. It lacks a permanent digestive cavity, so the mouth leads to a solid digestive syncytium (a mass of cells that have no cell membranes separating them).

These characteristics had been used to place the acoels at the base of phylum Platyhelminthes and that phylum at the base of the Bilateria. However, based on molecular evidence, scientists have concluded that acoels are not closely related to members of phylum Platyhelminthes—similarities between the two groups are convergent. They belong in their own phylum, Acoela, or are members of the phylum Acoelomorpha, which includes another group of simple bilaterians once considered to be flatworms. Their precise position in the phylogenetic tree differs depending on the features used to construct it; one hypothesis is they evolved before the phylogenetic split between protostomes and deuterostomes.

## Phylum Cycliophora was discovered relatively recently

In December 1995, Danish biologists Peter Funch and Reinhardt Kristensen reported the discovery of a strange new kind of acoelomate creature about the size of a period on a printed page. The tiny organism has a striking circular mouth surrounded by a ring of cilia, and its anatomy and life cycle are so unusual that their discoverers assigned it to an entirely new phylum, Cycliophora (figure 33.16).

The newest phylum to be named before Cycliophora, the Loricifera, was discovered also by Reinhardt Kristensen in 1983, and he and Peter Funch discovered yet another new phylum in 2000, the Micrognathozoa.

Cycliophorans live on the mouthparts of claw lobsters on both sides of the North Atlantic. When the lobster to which they are attached starts to molt, the tiny cycliophoran undergoes sexual reproduction. Each male, which consists of nothing but brains and reproductive organs, seeks out a female on the molting lobster and fertilizes her eggs, generating free-swimming larvae that can seek out another lobster and continue the life cycle.

**Figure 33.15  Phylum Acoela.**  An acoel flatworm of the genus *Waminoa*. These flatworms, long thought to be relatives of the Platyhelminthes, have a primitive nervous system and lack a permanent digestive cavity.

100 μm

**Figure 33.16**
**Phylum Cycliophora.**
About the size of the period at the end of this sentence, these acoelomates live on the mouthparts of claw lobsters. One feeding stage (and part of a second one) of *Symbion pandora* are shown attached to the mouthpart of a lobster.

---

**Learning Outcomes Review 33.3**

The acoelomates, typified by flatworms, are compact, bilaterally symmetrical animals. Most have a blind digestive cavity with only one opening; they also have an excretory system consisting of flame cells within tubules that run throughout the body. Many are free-living, but some cause human diseases. The scolex of a tapeworm is not a head, but simply an anchoring device to hold the animal in the intestine where it acts as a parasite.

■ *How does the anatomy of a tapeworm relate to its way of life?*

## 33.4 *The Pseudocoelomates*

**Learning Outcomes**

1. Describe the distinguishing features of pseudocoelomates.
2. Describe the musculature of a nematode that allows it to wriggle in a highly characteristic manner.
3. Explain why rotifers are referred to as "wheel animals."

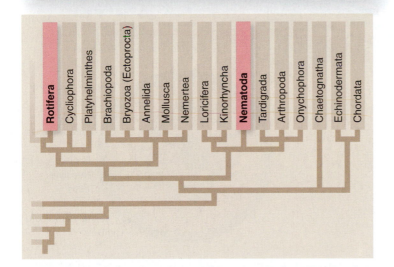

All bilaterians except acoelomates possess an internal body cavity. One type of cavity is a pseudocoelom, which, you will

recall, lies between tissues derived from the mesoderm and those derived from the endoderm (chapter 32; see figure 32.2). The pseudocoelomic fluid performs the functions carried out by a circulatory system in most coelomate animals. The pseudocoelom also serves as a hydrostatic skeleton. The hydrostatic skeleton of both pseudocoelomates and coelomates is an improvement on the one supporting cnidarian polyps and medusae because, not being the digestive cavity, it is entirely isolated from the environment. The movement of these animals with a hydrostatic skeleton is more efficient than that of the solid acoelomates.

Recall that pseudocoelomates are not monophyletic. Most belong to the Ecdysozoa, which includes phyla Nematoda, Kinorhyncha, and Loricifera. Other pseudocoelomates, such as the rotifers, belong to the Platyzoa. In this section, we focus on two significant pseudocoelomate phyla.

### The roundworms, phylum Nematoda, are ecdysozoans comprising many species

Vinegar eels, eelworms, and other roundworms constitute a large phylum, **Nematoda**, with some 20,000 recognized species; scientists estimate that the actual number might approach 100 times that many. Nematodes are abundant and diverse in marine and freshwater habitats, and many members of this phylum are parasites of animals (figure 33.17) and plants. Many nematodes are microscopic and live in soil. A spadeful of fertile soil may contain, on the average, a million nematodes.

#### Nematode structure

Nematodes are bilaterally symmetrical, unsegmented worms covered by a flexible, thick cuticle that is molted as they grow— parasitic nematodes molt four times. Lacking specialized respiratory organs, nematodes exchange oxygen and carbon dioxide through their cuticles. Muscles beneath the epidermis, which underlies the cuticle, extend longitudinally, from anterior to posterior. Nematodes are unusual among worms in that they lack circular musculature, so they can shorten but not change

50 μm

**Figure 33.17** *Trichinella* **nematode encysted in pork.**
The serious disease trichinosis can result from eating undercooked pork or bear meat containing such cysts.

diameter. The pulling of these longitudinal muscles against both the cuticle and the pseudocoelom produces the characteristic wriggling motion of nematodes.

Nematodes possess a well-developed digestive system and feed on a diversity of food sources. Near the mouth, at the anterior end, are hairlike sensory structures. The mouth may be equipped with piercing organs called **stylets**. Food passes into the mouth as a result of the sucking action produced by the rhythmic contraction of a muscular pharynx and continues through the intestine; waste is eliminated through the anus (figure 33.18).

### Reproduction and development

Reproduction in nematodes is sexual; most nematodes are gonochoric. Nematode males and females differ in form, a state known as **sexual dimorphism** (meaning "two bodies"): the tail end of the smaller male is hooked (see figure 33.18), whereas that of a female is straight. Fertilization is internal, the male using its hooked end and associated structure to help inseminate the female. Development is indirect, meaning that an egg hatches into a larva, which does not grow directly into an adult, but must pass through several molts and, in parasitic species, transfer from one host to another.

The adults of some species consist of a fixed number of cells, a phenomenon known as eutely. For this reason, nematodes have become extremely important subjects for genetic and developmental studies (see chapter 19). The 1 mm long *Caenorhabditis elegans* matures in three days; its body is transparent, and it has precisely 959 cells. It is the only animal whose complete developmental cellular anatomy is known.

### Nematode lifestyles

Many nematodes are active hunters, preying on protists and other small animals. Many are parasites of plants or live within the bodies of larger animals. Almost every species of plant and animal that has been studied has been found to have at least one parasitic species of nematode. The largest known nematode, which can attain a length of 9 m, parasitizes the placenta of sperm whales.

### Nematode-caused human diseases

About 50 species of nematodes, including several that are rather common in the United States, regularly parasitize human beings. Hookworms, most of the genus *Necator*, can be common in southern states. By sucking blood through the intestinal wall, they can produce anemia.

The most serious and common nematode-caused disease in temperate regions is trichinosis. Worms of the genus *Trichinella* (see figure 33.17) live in the small intestine of some mammals, especially pigs and bears, where fertilized females burrow through the intestinal wall and release live young (as many as 1500 per female). The young enter the lymph channels, which transport them to muscles throughout the body. There they mature and form highly resistant, calcified cysts. Eating undercooked or raw pork or bear in which cysts are present transmits the worm. Fatal infections, which can occur if the worms are abundant, are rare: in the United States, only about 20 deaths have been attributed to trichinosis during the past decade.

It is estimated that pinworms, *Enterobius vermicularis*, infect about 30% of children and 16% of adults in the United States. Adult pinworms live in the human rectum where they

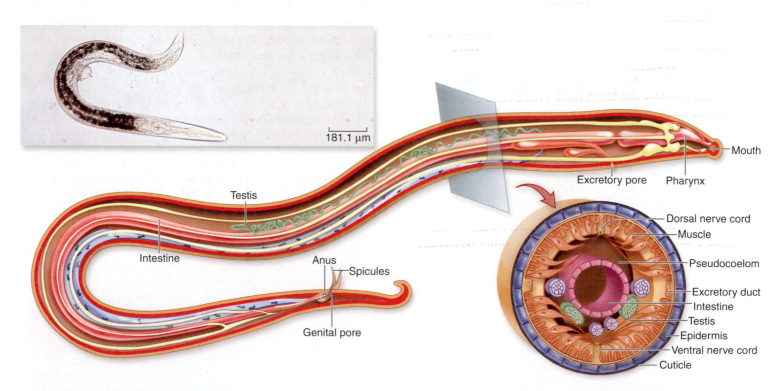

Testis
Intestine
Anus
Spicules
Genital pore

Mouth
Excretory pore    Pharynx
Dorsal nerve cord
Muscle
Pseudocoelom
Excretory duct
Intestine
Testis
Epidermis
Ventral nerve cord
Cuticle

181.1 μm

**Figure 33.18 Phylum Nematoda: Roundworms.** Roundworms such as this male nematode possess a body cavity between the gut and the body wall called the pseudocoelom. It allows nutrients to circulate throughout the body and prevents organs from being deformed by muscle movements.

usually cause nothing more serious than itching of the anus; large numbers, however, can lead to prolapse of the rectum. The worms can easily be killed by drugs.

The intestinal roundworm *Ascaris lumbricoides* infects approximately one of six people worldwide, but is rare in areas with modern plumbing. An adult female, which can be as much as 30 cm long, can release as many as 20,000 fertilized eggs each day into the gut of its host. The eggs, are carried from the body in the host's feces, and can remain viable for years in the soil; dust may carry them onto food, eating implements, or lips. Because the embryo has developed in each egg before it is shed, once it is ingested, it hatches. The larva follows a circuitous path through the body, and metamorphoses into an adult, which lives in the human intestine.

Some nematode-caused diseases are extremely serious in the tropics. Filariasis is caused by several species of nematodes that infect at least 250 million people worldwide. Filarial worms of some species live in the circulatory system. Infection by *Wuchereria bancrofti* may produce the condition known as elephantiasis, in which the lower extremities may swell to disfiguring proportions. This occurs because worms clog the lymph nodes, causing severe inflammation and resulting in swelling by preventing the lymph from circulating. The larval filarial worms are transmitted by an intermediate host, typically a blood-sucking insect such as a mosquito.

## The rotifers, phylum Rotifera, are tiny

Rotifers (phylum **Rotifera**) are bilaterally symmetrical, unsegmented pseudocoelomates (figure 33.19) that look nothing like nematodes. Several features suggest their ancestors may have resembled flatworms, with which they are classified in the spiralian Platyzoa.

At 50 to 500 μm long, rotifers are smaller than some ciliate protists. But they have complex bodies with three cell layers, highly developed internal organs, and a complete gut. An extensive pseudocoelom acts as a hydrostatic skeleton; the cytoskeleton provides rigidity. A rotifer has a rigid external covering, but its body can lengthen and shorten greatly because the posterior part is tapered so it can fold up like a telescope. Many have adhesive toes used for clinging to vegetation and other such objects.

### Diversity and distribution

About 1800 species are known, most of which occur in fresh water; a few rotifers live in soil, the capillary water in cushions of mosses, and the ocean. The lifespan of a rotifer is typically no longer than 1 or 2 weeks, but some species can survive in a des-

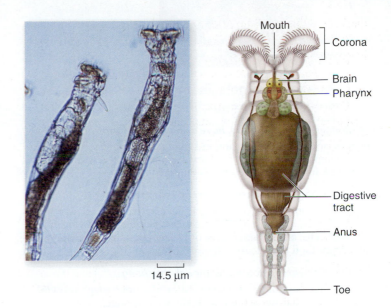

14.5 μm

**Figure 33.19 Phylum Rotifera.** Microscopic in size, rotifers are smaller than some ciliate protists, and yet have complex internal organs.

iccated, inactive state on the leaves of plants; when rain falls, the rotifers become active and feed in the film of water that temporarily covers the leaf.

### Food gathering

The corona, a conspicuous ring of cilia at the anterior end (see figure 33.19), is the source of the common name "wheel animals" for rotifers because its beating cilia make it appear that a wheel is rotating around the head of the animal. The corona is used for locomotion, but its cilia also sweep food into the rotifer's mouth. Once food is swallowed, it is crushed with a complex jaw in the pharynx.

---

### Learning Outcomes Review 33.4

Pseuodocoelomates have fluid-filled body cavities lined by endoderm and mesoderm. Nematodes are bilaterally symmetrical, unsegemented worms that have longitudinal muscle, but not muscle in a circle around the body. Aside from the many free-living species, some nematodes are parasites of animals and plants. Rotifers are extremely small but with highly complex body structure; the name "wheel animals" comes from the apparent motion of their beating cilia.

■ *What modern development is most effective in combating the spread of intestinal roundworms?*

## 33.1 Parazoa: Animals That Lack Specialized Tissues

**The sponges, phylum Porifera, have a loose body organization.**

Sponges lack tissues and organs and a definite symmetry, but they do have a complex multicellularity. Larval sponges are free-swimming, and the adults are anchored onto submerged objects.

**The sponge body is composed of several cell types.**

Sponges are composed of three layers: an external protective epithelial layer; a central protein-rich matrix called mesohyl with amoeboid cells; and an inner layer of choanocytes that circulate water and capture food particles (see figure 33.1*b*).

**Choanocytes help circulate water though the sponge.**

The mesohyl may contain spicules and/or fibers of a tough protein called spongin that strengthen the body of the sponge.

**Sponges reproduce both asexually and sexually.**

Fragments of a sponge are able to grow into complete individuals. Sperm and eggs may be produced by mature individuals; these undergo fertilization to form zygotes that develop into free-swimming larvae that eventually become sessile adults.

## 33.2 Eumetazoa: Animals with True Tissues

**All cnidarians, phylum Cnidaria, are carnivores.**

Members of the carnivorous and radially (or biradially) symmetrical Cnidaria have distinct tissues but no organs. They are diploblastic and have two body forms: a sessile, cylindrical polyp and a free-floating medusa (see figure 33.3).

Cnidarians are distinguished by capsules called nematocysts that are used in offense and defense.

Cnidarians have no circulatory, excretory, or respiratory systems. They have a latticework of nerve cells and are sensitive to touch; some have gravity receptors and light receptors.

**Cnidarians are grouped into four—or five—classes.**

The five classes of Cnidaria are the Anthozoa (sea anemones, corals, seafans); Cubozoa (box jellies); Hydrozoa (hydroids, Hydra), Scyphozoa (jellyfish); and Staurozoa (star jellies). The Staurozoa class is not accepted by all scientists.

**The comb jellies, phylum Ctenophora, use cilia for movement.**

Ctenophora (comb jellies) is a small phylum of medusa-like animals that propel themselves with bands of fused cilia. They may be triploblastic. They capture prey with colloblasts, cells that release an adhesive.

## 33.3 The Bilaterian Acoelomates

The Bilateria are characterized by bilateral symmetry, which allows for functional specialization such as having nerve receptors at the anterior end of the body.

**The flatworms, phylum Platyhelminthes, have an incomplete gut.**

Free-living flatworms, phylum Platyhelminthes, move by muscles and ciliated epithelial cells. They also exhibit a head and an incomplete gut (see figure 33.11).

Flatworms have an excretory system containing a fine network of tubules with flame cells. The primary function of this system is water balance.

Flatworms reproduce sexually and are hermaphroditic. They also have the capacity for asexual regeneration.

**Flatworms comprise two major groups.**

Free-living flatworms belong to the groups Turbellaria, which is likely not to be monophyletic.

Parasitic flatworms belong to the group Neodermata, of which there are two groups: the flukes (Trematoda), and the tapeworms and their relatives (Cercomeromorpha). Flukes and tapeworms can cause disease in humans.

**Acoel flatworms appear to be distinct from Platyhelminthes: A case study.**

Acoel flatworms, phylum Acoela, were once considered basal to the phylum Platyhelminthes, but they may have evolved before the split between protostomes and deuterostomes.

**Phylum Cycliophora was discovered relatively recently.**

Cycliophorans are tiny organisms that live on the mouthparts of claw lobsters. They undergo sexual reproduction that coincides with the lobsters' molts.

## 33.4 The Pseudocoelomates

A pseudocoelom is a cavity between tissues derived from mesoderm and tissues derived from endoderm. The pseudocoelomate animals do not represent a clade.

**The roundworms, phylum Nematoda, are ecdysozoans comprising many species.**

Nematodes, which are ecdysozoans, reproduce sexually and exhibit sexual dimorphism. More species of nematodes may exist than species of arthropods.

Some important human, veterinary, and plant diseases are caused by nematodes, including hookworm, pinworm, trichinosis, intestinal roundworm, and filariasis.

**The rotifers, phylum Rotifera, are tiny.**

The tiny rotiferans are spiralian, and belong to the Platyzoa.

Rotifers propel themselves and gather food with cilia and break down food with a complex jaw located in the pharynx. They are either free-swimming or sessile.

## Review Questions

### UNDERSTAND

1. In modern phylogenetic analysis of the animals, the protostomes are divided into two major groups based on what characteristic?
   a. Their symmetry
   b. Having a head
   c. Their ability to molt
   d. The presence or absence of vertebrae

2. Which of the following cell types of a sponge possesses a flagellum?
   a. Choanocyte        c. Epithelial
   b. Amoebocyte        d. Spicules

3. Spicules and spongin are found _____ of a sponge.
   a. within the osculum
   b. within the mesohyl
   c. within the choanocytes
   d. outside of the epithelial cells

4. The larval stage of a cnidarian is known as a
   a. medusa.           c. polyp.
   b. planula.          d. cnidocyte.

5. In the flatworm, flame cells are involved in what metabolic process?
   a. Reproduction      c. Locomotion
   b. Digestion         d. Osmoregulation

6. Which of the following nematodes cause disease?
   a. Filarial worms    c. Trichina worms
   b. Pinworms          d. All of the above

7. Which of the following have a complete gut?
   a. Tapeworms         c. Nematodes
   b. Medusae           d. None of the above

### APPLY

1. All animals have which of the following characteristics?
   a. Body symmetry     c. Multicellularity
   b. Tissues           d. Body cavity

2. Which of the following cell layers is not necessary to be considered a eumetazoan?
   a. Ectoderm
   b. Endoderm
   c. Mesoderm
   d. All of the above are found in all eumetazoans.

3. Which of the following would be considered a neodermatan?
   a. Earthworm         c. Tapeworm
   b. Fluke             d. Both b and c

### SYNTHESIZE

1. What do the phyla Acoela and Cycliophora tell you about our understanding of noncoelomate invertebrates? Do you think that the phylogeny presented in section 33.2 is complete? Explain your answer.

2. What benefit would being a hermaphrodite confer on a parasitic species?

3. Does the lack of a digestive system in tapeworms indicate that it is a primitive, ancestral form of platyhelminthes? Explain your answer.

### ONLINE RESOURCE

www.ravenbiology.com

Understand, Apply, and Synthesize—enhance your study with animations that bring concepts to life and practice tests to assess your understanding. Your instructor may also recommend the interactive eBook, individualized learning tools, and more.

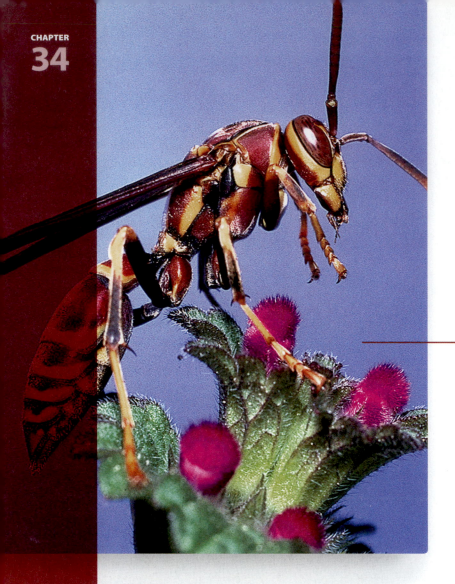

Chapter 34

# Coelomate Invertebrates

## Chapter Outline

## Introduction

*The body cavity of some animals is a coelom. As described in chapter 32, a coelom is an internal space lined with tissue derived from mesoderm. Clades of coelomate animals can be recognized by details of how the coelom develops and other features such as whether the body is segmented or the skeleton is internal or external. Some animals with a coelom are protostomes; all deuterostomes have a coelom. Among coelomate protostomes are mollusks, annelids, and arthropods. Deuterostomes include echinoderms, which are exclusively marine animals, and chordates (the subject of chapter 35).*

## 34.1 Phylum Mollusca: The Mollusks

### Learning Outcomes

1. *List the defining features of phylum Mollusca.*
2. *Describe representatives of the four best-known groups of mollusks.*
3. *Explain the distinguishing features of cephalopods.*

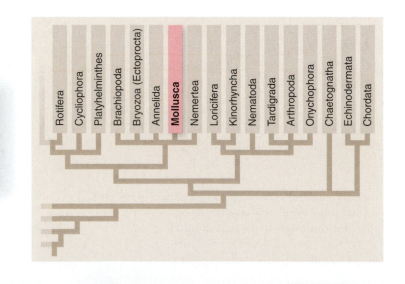

Mollusks (phylum Mollusca) are diverse morphologically and live in many types of environments. With more than 110,000 described species, the phylum is second only to arthropods. Mollusks include snails, slugs, clams, scallops,

a.   b.   c.   d.

**Figure 34.1  Mollusk diversity.**  Mollusks exhibit a broad range of variation. *a.* The flame scallop, *Lima scabra*, is a filter feeder. *b.* The blue-ringed octopus, *Hapalochlaena maculosa*, is one of the few mollusks dangerous to humans. Strikingly beautiful, it is equipped with a sharp beak that can deliver a  poisonous bite! *c.* Nautiluses, such as this chambered nautilus, *Nautilus pompilius*, have been around since before the age of the dinosaurs. *d.* The banana slug, *Ariolimax columbianus*, native to the Pacific Northwest, is the second largest slug in the world, attaining a length of 25 cm.

oysters, cuttlefish, octopuses, and many other familiar animals (figures 34.1 and 34.2). The shells of many mollusks are beautiful and elegant; they have long been collected, preserved, and studied by professional scientists and amateurs. Some mollusks, however, lack a shell.

## Mollusks are extremely diverse— and important to humans

Mollusks range in size from almost microscopic to huge. Although most measure a few millimeters to centimeters in their largest dimension, the giant squid may grow to more than 15 m

**Figure 34.2  Giant clam.**  Second only to the arthropods in number of described species, members of the phylum Mollusca occupy almost every habitat on Earth. This giant clam, *Tridacna maxima*, contains symbiotic dinoflagellates (zooxanthellae) as do reef-forming corals. Through photosynthesis, the dinoflagellates probably contribute to the food of the clam, although it is a filter feeder like most bivalves. Some individual giant clams may be nearly 1.5 m long and weigh as much as 270 kg.

long and weigh as much as 250 kg. It is therefore one of the heaviest invertebrates (although nemerteans can be longer, as discussed later). Other large mollusks are the giant clams of the genus *Tridacna*, which may be as long as 1.5 m and may weigh as much as 270 kg (see figure 34.2).

Like all major animal groups, mollusks evolved in the oceans, and most groups have remained there. Marine mollusks are widespread and many are abundant. Snails and slugs have invaded freshwater and terrestrial habitats, and freshwater mussels live in lakes and streams (the flat foot of a snail or slug allows it to crawl, but the foot of clams, mussels, and other bivalved mollusks is adapted to digging, so they cannot move about on land). Some places where terrestrial mollusks live, such as crevices of desert rocks, may appear dry, but if mollusks live there, the habitat has at least a temporary supply of water.

Mollusks—including oysters, clams, scallops, mussels, octopuses, and squids—are an important source of food for humans. They are also economically significant in other ways. For example, the material called mother-of-pearl (nacre), which is used for jewelry and other decorative objects, and formerly for buttons, comes from mollusk shells, most notably that of the abalone. Mollusks can also be pests. Bivalves called ship-worms burrow through wood exposed to the sea, damaging boats, docks, and pilings. The zebra mussel (*Dreissena polymorpha*) (see figure 60.16) has recently invaded many North American freshwater ecosystems. Many slugs and snails damage flowers, vegetable gardens, and crops. Other mollusks serve as hosts to the larval stages of many serious parasites, as discussed in chapter 33.

## The mollusk body plan is complex and varied

Some mollusk body plans are illustrated in figure 34.3. The **mantle,** a thick epidermal sheet, covers the dorsal side of the body, and bounds the mantle cavity. The mantle secretes the calcium carbonate of the shell in those mollusks with a shell. The muscular foot is the primary means of locomotion in mollusks other than cephalopods (octopuses, squid, and

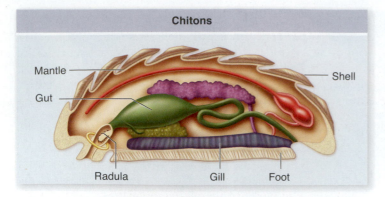

**Chitons**

Mantle · Shell · Gut · Radula · Gill · Foot

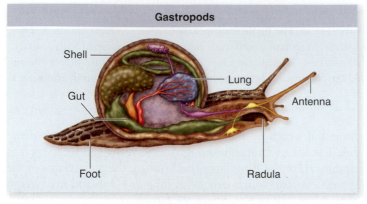

**Gastropods**

Shell · Lung · Gut · Antenna · Foot · Radula

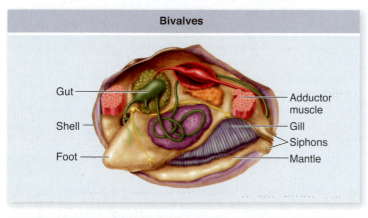

**Bivalves**

Gut · Adductor muscle · Shell · Gill · Siphons · Foot · Mantle

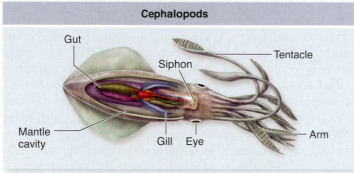

**Cephalopods**

Gut · Tentacle · Siphon · Mantle cavity · Gill · Eye · Arm

**Figure 34.3 Body plans of some mollusks.**

chambered nautilus). The head may be well developed or not. Like all coelomates, mollusks are bilaterally symmetrical, but this symmetry is modified during development of many gastropods (snails and their relatives), which undergo torsion (a twisting of the body discussed in detail later on).

The muscular foot is variously adapted for locomotion, attachment, food capture, digging, or combinations of these

functions. The foot of slugs and snails secretes mucus, forming a path that it glides along. In cephalopods, the foot is divided into tentacles and, in some cephalopods, arms. Clams burrow into mud and sand using their hatchet-shaped foot. In some mollusks that live in the open ocean, the foot is modified into winglike projections, the large surface area of which serves to slow its sinking. The feet of these mollusks can beat like wings.

### Internal organs

In all mollusks, the coelom is highly reduced, being limited to small spaces around the excretory organs, heart, and part of the intestine. An important role of the coelom in some other invertebrates (that is, forming the hydrostatic skeleton) is served in mollusks by the shell. The digestive, excretory, and reproductive organs are concentrated in a **visceral mass.**

In aquatic mollusks, the **ctenidia** (or gills, the respiratory structures) project into the mantle cavity (see figure 34.3). They consist of filaments rich in blood vessels that greatly increase the surface area and capacity for gas exchange. The continuous stream of water that passes through the mantle cavity, propelled by cilia on the gills of all mollusks except cephalopods, carries oxygen in and carbon dioxide away. Mollusk ctenidia are so efficient that they can extract 50% or more of the dissolved oxygen from the water that passes through the mantle cavity. In addition to extracting oxygen from incoming water, the gills of most bivalves filter out food. Because the outlets from the excretory, reproductive, and digestive organs open into the mantle cavity, wastes and gametes are carried away from a mollusk's body with the exiting water stream.

### Shells

One of the best known characters of the phylum is the shell. A mollusk shell, which is secreted by the outer surface of the mantle, protects against predators and adverse environmental conditions. However, a shell is clearly not essential: reduction, internalization, and loss of the shell have evolved repeatedly. Examples of shell-less mollusks are cuttlefish, squids, and octopuses (cephalopods) as well as slugs (gastropods).

A typical mollusk shell consists of two layers of calcium carbonate, which is precipitated extracellularly. The outer layer consists of densely packed crystals. In some species, the inner layer is pearly in appearance, and is called mother-of-pearl or nacre. Particularly in freshwater mollusks, the mineralic layers are covered by a thin organic coating rich in the protein conchiolin that protects the shell from dissolving. Pearls are formed when a foreign object, such as a grain of sand, becomes lodged between the mantle and the inner shell layer. The mantle coats the object with layer upon layer of nacre to reduce the irritation caused by the object. The most beautiful and highly valued pearls are produced by oysters.

### Feeding and prey capture: Radula

A characteristic feature of most mollusks is the **radula** (plural, *radulae*), a rasping, tonguelike structure used in feeding. It consists of dozens to hundreds of microscopic, chitinous teeth arranged in rows on an underlying membrane and lies in a chamber at the anterior end of the gut (figure 34.4). The

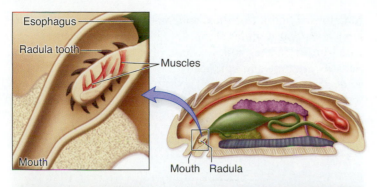

**Figure 34.4 Structure of the radular apparatus in a chiton.** The radula consists of rows of teeth made of chitin. As the animal feeds, its mouth opens, and the radula is thrust out to scrape food off surfaces.

membrane wraps around a muscular support structure so the radula can be protruded through the mouth and move something like a sanding belt over what is being rasped. Benthic mollusks use their radulae to scrape up algae and other food materials.

In some predatory gastropods (such as moon snails), the radula is modified to drill through clam shells so the snail can eat the clams. In snails of the genus *Conus*, the radula has been transformed into a harpoon that is associated with a venom gland; cone snails use this harpoon to capture prey such as fish, and some cone snails can harm—or even kill—humans.

Bivalves are the only mollusks that have no radula. The gills of most bivalves are adapted to filter food particles from the water, although primitive bivalves pick up bits of food from soft sediments (this is, they are deposit feeders) using appendages around the mouth.

### Removal of wastes

Nitrogenous wastes are removed from the mollusk body by the **nephridium** (plural, *nephridia*), a sort of kidney. A typical nephridium has an open funnel, the nephrostome, which is lined with cilia. A coiled tubule runs from the **nephrostome** into a bladder, which in turn connects to an excretory pore. Wastes are gathered by the nephridia from the coelomic cavity and discharged into the mantle cavity. Sugars, salts, water, and other materials are reabsorbed by the walls of the nephridia and returned to the animal's body as needed to maintain osmotic balance.

### The circulatory system

The main coelomic cavity of a mollusk is a hemocoel, which comprises several sinuses and a network of vessels in the gills, where gas exchange takes place. Except for cephalopods, all mollusks have such an open circulatory system; blood (technically termed "hemolymph") is propelled by a heart through the aorta vessel that empties to the hemocoel. The blood moves through the hemocoel being recaptured by other venous vessels before re-entering the heart (see chapter 50). The heart of most, but not all mollusks has three chambers, two that collect aerated blood from the gills, and a third that pumps it into the hemocoel. The blood of the closed circulatory system of cephalopods is contained in a continuous system of vessels, so it does not contact other tissues directly.

### Reproduction

Most mollusks have separate sexes although a few bivalves and many freshwater and terrestrial gastropods are hermaphroditic. Most hermaphroditic mollusks engage in cross-fertilization. Some oysters are able to change sex.

As is typical of animals living in the sea, many marine mollusks have external fertilization: gametes are released by males and females into the water where fertilization occurs. Most gastropods, however, have internal fertilization, with the male inserting sperm directly into the female's body (not, that is, into a preformed channel). Internal fertilization, a foot, and an efficient excretory system that prevents desiccation are some of the key adaptations that allowed gastropods to colonize the land.

A mollusk zygote undergoes spiral cleavage (thus Mollusca is part of the Spiralia; see chapter 32). The embryo develops into a free-swimming larva called a trochophore (figure 34.5a) that closely resembles the larval stage of many marine annelids and other lophotrochozoans. A trochophore swims by means of cilia that encircle the middle of its body.

In most marine snails and in bivalves, the trochophore develops into a second free-swimming stage, the **veliger**. The veliger forms the beginnings of a foot, shell, and mantle (figure 35.5b). Trochophores and veligers drift widely in the ocean, dispersing these otherwise sedentary mollusks.

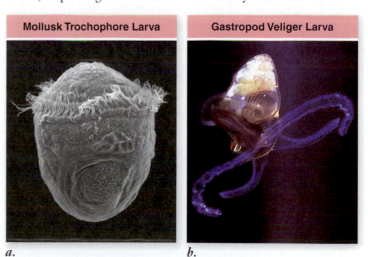

**Figure 34.5 Stages in the molluskan life cycle.** *a.* The trochophore larva. Similar larvae are characteristic of some annelid worms as well as a few other phyla. *b.* The veliger stage of a gastropod.

## Four classes of mollusks show the diversity of the phylum

We examine four of the seven or eight recognized classes of mollusks: (1) Polyplacophora—chitons; (2) Gastropoda—limpets, snails, slugs, and their relatives; (3) Bivalvia—clams, oysters, scallops, and their relatives; and (4) Cephalopoda—squids, octopuses, cuttlefishes, and the chambered nautilus.

By studying living mollusks and the fossil record, some scientists have deduced that the ancestral mollusk was probably a bilateral, dorsoventrally flattened, unsegmented, wormlike animal that glided on its ventral surface. This animal may have had a chitinous cuticle that secreted calcareous spicules. Other scientists infer that mollusks arose from segmented ancestors and became unsegmented secondarily.

### Class Polyplacophora: Chitons

Chitons are exclusively marine; there are perhaps 1000 species. The oval body is covered dorsally with eight overlapping dorsal calcareous plates (figure 34.6). The body is not segmented, but chitons do have eight sets of dorsoventral pedal retractor muscles and serially repeated gills. The broad, flat ventral foot, on which the animal creeps, is surrounded by a groove, the mantle cavity, in which the gills are suspended. Most chitons are grazing herbivores, and live in shallow marine habitats, but chitons occur to depths of more than 7000 m.

### Class Gastropoda: Snails and slugs

The 40,000 or so species of limpets, snails and slugs belong to this class, which is primarily marine. However, this group contains many freshwater species and the only terrestrial mollusks (figure 34.7). Most gastropods have a single shell, but some, such as slugs and nudibranchs (or sea slugs), have lost the shell through the course of evolution. Most gastropods creep on a foot, but in some it is modified for swimming.

The head of most gastropods has a pair of tentacles, which serve as chemo- or mechanoreceptors, with eyes at the base. A typical garden snail may have two sets of tentacles, one of them bearing eyes at the ends (see figure 34.7).

Uniquely among animals, gastropods undergo torsion during larval life. **Torsion** involves twisting of the body so the

**Figure 34.7  A Gastropod mollusk.** The terrestrial Oregon forest snail *Allogona townsendiana*.

mantle cavity and anus are moved from a posterior location to the front of the body. Torsion may lead to the reduction or disappearance of the nephridium, gonad, or other internal organs on one side. Most adult gastropods are therefore not bilaterally symmetrical. Torsion should not be confused with coiling, the spiral winding of the shell. Coiling also occurs in cephalopods. The fossil record suggests that the first gastropods were coiled but did not undergo torsion.

Like many gastropods, nudibranchs (sea slugs) are active predators. Nudibranchs get their name from their gills, which, instead of being enclosed within the mantle cavity, are exposed along the dorsal surface (figure 34.8). Nudibranchs would seem vulnerable to predation, but many secrete distasteful chemicals. They prey on animals that are avoided by other predators. Some are specialist feeders on sponges, most species of which form spicules and noxious chemicals. Other nudibranchs specialize in feeding on cnidarians, which are protected from most predators by their nematocysts. Some of these nudibranchs have the extraordinary ability to extract the

**Figure 34.6  The noble chiton, *Eudoxochiton nobilis*, from New Zealand.** The foot of the chiton can grip the substrate very strongly, making chitons hard to dislodge by waves or predators.

**Figure 34.8  A nudibranch (or sea slug).** The bright colors of many nudibranchs such as this alert predators to their repulsive taste.

nematocysts undischarged, transfer them through their digestive tract to the surface of their bodies, and use them for their own protection.

In terrestrial gastropods, the mantle cavity, which is occupied by gills in aquatic snails, is extremely rich in blood vessels and serves as a lung. This lung absorbs oxygen from the air much more effectively than a gill could; however, a snail will drown if its lung fills with water; for this reason, terrestrial gastropods can close the opening of the lung to the outside.

### Class Bivalvia: Clams, mussels, and cockles

Most of the 10,000 species of bivalves are marine, but some live in fresh water. More than 500 species of pearly freshwater mussels, or naiads, occur in the rivers and lakes of North America.

Unlike other mollusks, a bivalve does not have a radula or distinct head (figure 34.9). The foot of most is wedge-shaped, adapted for burrowing or anchoring the animal in its burrow. Some species of clams can dig into sand or mud very rapidly by means of muscular contractions of their foot. Some species of scallops and file clams can move swiftly by clapping their shells rapidly together (although they cannot control the direction of their movement); the adductor muscle that allows this clapping is the part of a scallop eaten by humans. Projecting from the edge of a scallop's mantle are tentacle-like projections having complex eyes between them.

Bivalves, as their name implies, have two shells (valves) that are hinged dorsally so the shells are oriented laterally (left and right). A ligament lying along the hinge is structured so it causes the shells to gape open. One or two large adductor muscles link the shells internally (see figure 34.9), and when they contract, they counteract the hinge ligament to draw the shells together. The mantle covers the internal surface of the shells, enveloping the visceral mass on its inner side and secreting the shells on its outer side. As is typical of mollusks, the respiratory structures, a set of complexly folded gills on each side of the visceral mass, lie in the mantle cavity.

The edges of the mantle may be partly fused. In bivalves in which this is the case, typically two areas are not fused, and may be drawn out to form tubes called siphons (see figure 34.9). Water enters the mantle chamber through the **inhalant siphon** bringing oxygen and food, and water exits through the **exhalant siphon,** taking wastes and gametes with it. In bivalves that live buried deeply in mud or burrow into rock, the siphons allow the animals to eat and breathe, functioning essentially as snorkels.

### Class Cephalopoda: Octopuses, squids, and nautiluses

The more than 600 species of cephalopods are strictly marine. They are active predators that swim, often swiftly, and they are the only mollusks with a closed circulatory system. The foot has evolved into a series of arms equipped with suction cups, adhesive structures, or hooks that seize prey. Octopuses, as their name suggests, have eight arms; squids have eight arms and two tentacles; and the chambered nautilus has 80 to 90 tentacles (which lack suckers). After snaring prey with its arms, a cephalopod bites the prey with its strong, beak-like jaws, then pulls it into its mouth by the action of the radula. The salivary gland of many cephalopods secretes a toxin that can be injected into prey; the tiny blue-ringed octopus of Australia (see figure 34.1b) can kill a human with its deadly bite.

Cephalopods have the largest relative brain sizes among invertebrates and highly developed nervous systems. Many exhibit complex patterns of behavior and are highly intelligent (figure 34.10); octopuses can be easily trained to distinguish

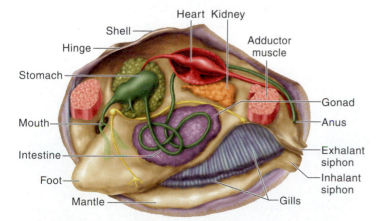

**Figure 34.9 Diagram of a clam.** The left shell and mantle are removed to show the internal organs and the foot. Bivalves such as this clam circulate water across their gills and filter out food particles.

**Figure 34.10 Problem-solving by an octopus.** This two-month-old common octopus (*Octopus vulgaris*) was presented with a crab in a jar. It tried to unscrew the lid to get to the crab. Although it failed in this attempt, in some cases it was successful.

among classes of objects and are capable of leaving one tank to seize prey in another, then returning to their original one. Cephalopod eyes are much like those of vertebrates, although they evolved independently (see chapter 45).

Aside from the chambered nautiluses, living cephalopods lack an external shell. Shelled cephalopods were formerly far more diverse, as evidenced by the many fossil cephalopods such as ammonites and belemnites. These cephalopods were extraordinarily successful because they could move in open water instead of on the sea bottom like other mollusks. However, once the more maneuverable fishes evolved, shelled mollusks declined, some dying out, others experiencing evolutionary reduction and eventual loss of their heavy shells. The cuttlebone of cuttlefish and the pen of squids are internal shells that support these animals and give them some buoyancy. Even the internal shell has disappeared in the lineage that gave rise to octopuses.

As in other mollusks, water passes through the mantle cavity. In a cephalopod, it is pumped in by muscles and exits through a siphon, which allows the animal to move by jet propulsion, and which can be directed to steer. The ink sac of cephalopods, which typically contains a purplish fluid, can eject its contents through the siphon as a cloud that may hide the cephalopod and confuse predators (figure 34.11).

Most octopuses and squids are capable of changing skin color and texture to match their background or to communicate with one another. They do so using chromatophores, epithelial cells that contain pigments. Some deep-sea squids harbor symbiotic luminescent bacteria. These may be emitted with the ink to produce a glimmering cloud (ink would not be seen at depths where sunlight cannot penetrate) or they may inhabit cells like chromatophores so they can light up the surface of the animal.

Another difference with many other mollusks is that cephalopods have direct development, that is, they lack a larval stage, hatching as miniature adults.

### Learning Outcomes Review 34.1

Mollusks are coelomates with a coelom surrounding the heart. Most have efficient excretory systems, ctenidia for respiration, and a rasping structure, the radula, for gathering food. The mantle of mollusks not only secretes their protective shell but also forms structures essential to body functions. Chitons, gastropods, bivalves, and cephalopods are the four best-known groups. Cephalopods lack cilia on their ctenidia and have a closed circulatory system.

■ *Why might a closed circulatory system be necessary in a cephalopod?*

## 34.2 Phylum Nemertea: The Ribbon Worms

### Learning Outcome

1. *Describe the two characteristics that place nemerteans with mollusks in the lophotrochozoa.*

Nemerteans (phylum Nemertea) consist of about 900 species of cylindrical to flattened very long worms (figure 34.12). Most nemerteans are marine; a few species live in fresh water and humid terrestrial habitats. An individual may reach 10 to 20 cm in length, although the animals are difficult to measure because they can stretch, and many species break into pieces when disturbed or handled. The species *Lineus longissimus* has been reported to measure 60 m in length—the longest animal known!

The nemertean body plan resembles that of a flatworm (see chapter 33), with networks of fine tubules constituting the excretory system, and with internal organs not lying in a body cavity. A bit of cephalization is present, with two lateral nerve cords extending posteriorly from an anterior ganglion; some animals have eyespots on the head. But, by contrast with a platyhelminth, a nemertean has a complete gut, with both mouth and anus, connected by a straight tube. Nemerteans also possess a fluid-filled cavity called a rhynchocoel. This sac serves

**Figure 34.11 Ink defense by a giant Pacific octopus (*Octopus dofleini*).** When threatened, octopuses and squids expel a dark cloudy liquid.

**Figure 34.12 Phylum Nemertea: A ribbon worm of the genus *Lineus*.** Some nemerteans can stretch to several meters in length.

as a hydraulic power source for the proboscis, a long muscular tube that can be thrust out quickly from a sheath to capture animal prey.

Nemerteans are gonochoric, and all reproduce sexually. Some are capable of asexual reproduction by fragmentation. However, in most species, most fragments resulting from disturbance die, so nemertean regenerative powers may not be as great as is sometimes stated.

Blood of nemerteans flows entirely in vessels that are derived from the coelom. That and the rhynchocoel are good evidence that nemerteans are not related to flatworms, which they resemble superficially, but belong to the Lophotrochozoa, along with mollusks.

### Learning Outcome Review 34.2

Nemerteans are very long worms that have a coelomic cavity and blood vessels derived from the coelom. They capture prey with a muscular proboscis. Unlike the acoelomate flatworms, nemerteans have a complete gut with mouth and anus.

■ **What would be some advantages of a flow-through digestive tract?**

## 34.3 Phylum Annelida: The Annelids

### Learning Outcomes

1. Explain how circular and longitudinal muscles in a segmented body facilitate movement.
2. Distinguish between the classes Polychaeta and Clitellata.
3. Describe adaptations in leeches for feeding on the blood of animals.

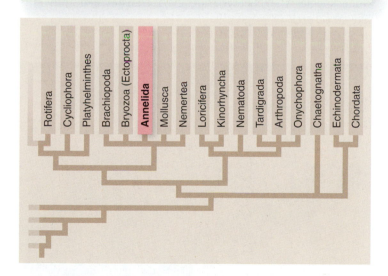

An important innovation in the animal body plan was segmentation, the building of a body from a series of repeated units (see chapter 32), which has evolved multiple times. Worms of the phylum Annelida (figure 34.13) are segmented. One advan-

**Figure 34.13** **A polychaete annelid.** *Nereis virens* is a wide-ranging, predatory, marine polychaete worm equipped with feathery parapodia for movement and respiration, as well as jaws for hunting. You may have purchased *Nereis* as fishing bait!

tage of a segmented body is that the development and function of individual segments or groups of segments can differ. For example, some segments may be specialized for reproduction, whereas others are adapted for locomotion or excretion.

All animals that have been regarded as annelids are segmented, so the animals were considered to constitute a natural group, but the monophyly of Annelida is being reconsidered because some unsegmented worms may belong to this clade.

### The annelid body is composed of ringlike segments

The head, which contains a well-developed cerebral ganglion, or brain, and sensory organs occurs at the anterior end (front) of a series of ringlike segments that resemble a stack of coins (figure 34.14). Many species have eyes, which in some species have lenses and retinas. Technically the head is not a segment,

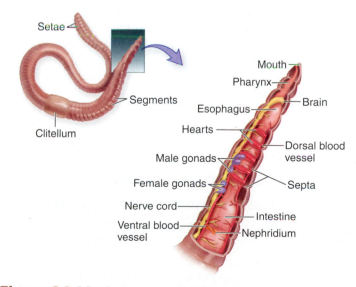

**Figure 34.14** **Phylum Annelida: An oligochaete.** The earthworm body plan is based on repeated body segments. Segments are separated internally from each other by septa.

nor is the posterior end of the worm, the pygidium. In embryonic development, the head and tail form first, and then segments form between them; if a worm is cut in pieces, generally only those parts containing either head or tail can regenerate the missing parts and the middle bits just die.

Internally, the segments are divided from one another by partitions called septa, just as bulkheads separate the compartments of a submarine. Each segment has a pair of excretory organs, a ganglion, and locomotory structure; in most marine annelids, each also has a set of reproductive organs.

Although septa separate the segments, materials and biological signals do pass between segments. A closed circulatory system carries blood the length of the animal, anteriorly in the dorsal vessel and posteriorly in the ventral one. Connections from ventral to dorsal vessel in each segment bring the blood near enough to each cell so oxygen and food molecules diffuse from the blood into the cells of the body wall, and carbon dioxide and other wastes diffuse from the cells into the blood. A ventral nerve cord connects the ganglia in each segment with one another and with the brain. These neural connections allow the worm to function as a unified and coordinated organism.

## Annelids move by contracting their segments

The basic annelid body plan is a tube within a tube, the digestive tract—extending from mouth to anus—passing through the septa, and suspended within the spacious coelom, which is surrounded by the body wall. Each portion of the digestive tract—pharynx, esophagus, crop, gizzard, and intestine—is specialized for a different function.

The coelomic fluid creates a hydrostatic skeleton that gives each segment rigidity, like an inflated balloon (see chapter 47). Annelid locomotion is effected by contraction of the circular and longitudinal muscles against the hydrostatic skeleton. When circular muscles are contracted around a segment, the segment decreases in diameter, so the coelomic fluid causes the segment to elongate. When longitudinal muscles are contracted, the segment shortens, so the coelomic fluid causes the segment to increase in diameter. Alternating these contractions and confining them to only some segments allows the worms to move in complex ways.

In most annelid groups, each segment possesses bristles of chitin called **chaetae** (or setae—singular, seta or chaeta). By extending the chaetae in some segments so that they protrude into the substrate and retracting them in other segments, the worm can extend its body, but not slip (see figure 47.1).

## Annelids have a common, closed circulatory system but a segmented excretory system

Unlike arthropods and mollusks, except for cephalopods, annelids have a closed circulatory system. Annelids exchange oxygen and carbon dioxide with the environment through their body surfaces, although some nonterrestrial ones have gills along the sides of the body or at the anterior end. Gases (and food molecules) are distributed throughout the body in blood vessels. Some of the vessels at the anterior end of the body are enlarged and heavily muscular, serving as hearts that pump the blood. An earthworm has five pulsating blood vessels on each side that help to move blood from the main dorsal vessel, the major pumping structure, to the ventral vessel.

The excretory system of annelids consists of ciliated, funnel-shaped nephridia like those of mollusks. Each segment has a pair of nephridia that collect wastes and transport them out of the body by way of excretory tubes. Some polychaetes have protonephridia like the flame cells of planarians.

## Annelida comprises two—or three—classes

The roughly 12,000 described species of annelids occur in many habitats. They range in length from as little as 0.5 mm to giant Australian earthworms more than 3 m long. Although traditionally annelids have been classified into classes Polychaeta (mostly marine worms), Oligochaeta (mostly terrestrial worms, including earthworms), and Hirudinea (leeches), the monophyly of polychaetes is not well established. The classification of annelids may change in the near future, but we adopt the current two-class system of Polychaeta and Clitellata (which combines Oligochaeta and Hirudinea).

### Class Polychaeta: Polychaetes

Polychaetes include clamworms, scaleworms, lugworms, sea mice, tubeworms, and many others. Polychaetes are a crucial part of many marine food chains, and are extremely abundant in particular habitats. Some of these worms are beautiful, with unusual forms and iridescent colors (figure 34.15).

On most segments, a polychaete has paired, fleshy, paddle-like lateral projections called **parapodia** (see figures 34.13, 34.15). The parapodia bear chaetae; the word *polychaeta* means "many chaetae." Parapodia are used in swimming, burrowing, or crawling, and those of polychaetes that live in burrows or tubes may have chaetae with hooks that help anchor the worm. Parapodia can also play an important role in gas exchange because they greatly increase the surface area of the body, and in some species they bear or are even transformed into gill-like structures.

**Figure 34.15 A polychaete.** The shiny bristleworm *Oenone fulgida*. Notice chaete extending from the iridescent parapodia.

**Figure 34.16** Giant tubeworms *(Riftia pachyptila)* living in deep-sea hydrothermal vents near the Galápagos. These tubeworms and associated animals (notice the small white crab) are an example of a community dependent on hydrogen sulfide, rather than the Sun, as an energy source.

Polychaetes can swim or crawl, and some are active predators with powerful jaws. Other polychaetes live in tubes or burrows of hardened mud, sand, mucuslike secretions, or calcium carbonate. Sedentary polychaetes may project feathery tentacles that sweep the water for food, filter feeding; the tentacles may also serve as gills, exchanging gas. Some deep-sea tubeworms such as *Riftia* (figure 34.16) are gutless as adults. Projections from the body of these worms house sulfur-oxidizing bacteria that synthesize organic compounds used by the worm. These worms aggregate near hydrothermal vents where sulfur is plentiful and can grow to more than a meter in length.

Most polychaetes are gonochoric. Gametes typically are released into the water, where fertilization occurs externally. Many polychaetes have gonads in most segments, but in some groups, gonads are confined to certain segments. In palolo worms and their relatives, these segments are at the end of the body; spawning involves the end of the worm breaking off and swimming to the surface of the sea, where it ruptures, releasing the gametes. The gamete-filled terminal parts of palolo worms are considered delicacies by some people in the South Pacific.

Fertilization results in spiral cleavage followed by the production of ciliated, mobile trochophore larvae similar to that of mollusks. Metamorphosis of a trochophore involves differentiation of a head and tail end, with development of segments in between, from a posterior growth zone.

### Class Clitellata: Earthworms and leeches

Some authorities still consider earthworms to belong to class Oligochaeta and leeches to class Hirudinea, but most now put earthworms and leeches into a single class, although, confusingly, it sometimes may be called Oligochaeta. More often it is called Clitellata, because of the feature that unites these seemingly quite different animals, the clitellum—a thickened band on the body, which is the familiar "saddle" of an earthworm (see figure 34.14).

**Earthworms.** The body of a typical earthworm consists of 100 to 175 similar segments. The head is not well differentiated. An earthworm has no parapodia, and its chaetae (which are fewer than in polychaetes—the word *oligochaeta* means "few chaetae") project directly from the body wall.

Earthworms eat their way through the soil, ingesting it by muscular action of their strong pharynx; organic material is ground in the gizzard. What passes through an earthworm is deposited outside the opening of its burrow as castings that form irregular mounds. In this way, earthworms contribute to loosening, aeration, and enrichment of the soil. In view of their underground lifestyle, it is not surprising that earthworms have no eyes. But they do have light-, chemo-, and touch-sensitive cells, most concentrated in segments near each end of the body—those regions most likely to encounter light or other stimuli.

Earthworms are hermaphroditic, another way in which they differ from most polychaetes, but they cross-fertilize through mating (figure 34.17). The clitellum secretes mucus that holds the worms together during copulation, their anterior ends pointing in opposite directions, their ventral surfaces touching. Sperm cells are released from pores in specialized segments of one partner into the sperm receptacles of the other, the process going in both directions simultaneously. Several days after the worms separate, the clitellum of each worm secretes a mucus cocoon, surrounded by a protective layer of chitin. As the worm moves, this sheath passes over the female pores of the body, receiving eggs and incorporating the deposited sperm so that fertilization takes place within the cocoon. When the cocoon passes over the end of the worm, its edges pinch together. Within the cocoon, the fertilized eggs develop directly into young worms similar to adults.

**Leeches.** Most leeches live in fresh water, although a few are marine and some tropical leeches occupy terrestrial habitats. Dorsoventrally flattened, most leeches are 2 to 6 cm long, but one tropical species reaches 30 cm. Like earthworms, leeches are hermaphroditic, but the clitellum develops only during the breeding season. Leeches also cross-fertilize.

Unlike that of earthworms and polychaetes, the coelom of a leech is reduced and not divided into segments. The suckers at one or both ends of a leech's body are used for locomotion and to attach to prey. A leech with suckers at both ends moves by attaching first one and then the other end to the substrate, looping along. Many species are also capable of swimming. Except for one species, leeches have no chaetae.

**Figure 34.17** Earthworms mating. The anterior ends are pointing in opposite directions.

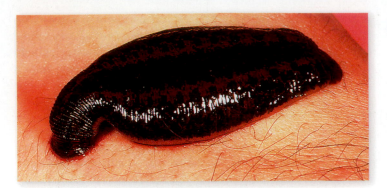

**Figure 34.18 A leech.** *Hirudo medicinalis*, the medicinal leech, feeding on a human arm. Leeches use chitinous, bladelike jaws to make an incision to access blood; they secrete an anticoagulant to keep the blood from clotting. Both the anticoagulant and the leech itself have made important contributions to modern medicine.

About half the known species of leeches eat detritus or devour small animals. The others suck blood or other fluids from their hosts (figure 34.18). Such a leech secretes an anticoagulant into the wound to prevent the blood from clotting, and vasodilators to keep the blood flowing; the leech's powerful pharynx pumps the blood out quickly once a hole has been opened. Anesthetics injected into the prey prevent the leech from being noticed while piercing the skin; they are usually detected only after detaching, when blood starts to flow from the wound. Freshwater parasitic leeches may remain on their hosts for long periods, sucking the host's blood from time to time. Leeches detect prey by sensing gradients of carbon dioxide in the environment. In some tropical forests, a few seconds after you stop on a trail, you can see dozens of leeches approaching you from all directions!

One of the best-known species, the medicinal leech *Hirudo medicinalis* (see figure 34.18), reaches 10 to 12 cm long, and has bladelike, chitinous jaws that can rasp through an animal's skin. Leeches were used in medicine for hundreds of years to treat patients whose diseases were mistakenly believed to be caused by an excess of blood. Today, leeches are used to remove excess blood after surgery or to keep blood from coagulating in severed appendages that have been reattached. Accumulations of blood can cause the tissue to die; when leeches remove such blood, new capillaries form in about a week, and the tissues remain healthy. The anticoagulant and anesthetic properties of the leech are also being investigated by pharmaceutical companies.

### Learning Outcomes Review 34.3

Annelids generally exhibit segmentation. Each segment has its own excretory and locomotor elements; circular and longitudinal muscles in segments cause the body to extend and contract, respectively. Worms of class Polychaeta, which are mostly marine, have parapodia on their segments. Leeches and earthworms were formerly in separate classes, but a major morphological similarity, the clitellum, has been used to group them into a single class, Clitellata.

■ *What would be the advantages of having nervous and circulatory systems that serve the entire body instead of segmented systems?*

## 34.4 The Lophophorates: Bryozoa and Brachiopoda

### Learning Outcomes

1. Describe the lophophore and its function.
2. Distinguish between bryozoans and brachiopods.

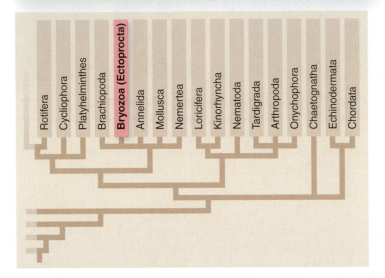

Two phyla of mostly marine animals—Bryozoa and Brachiopoda—are characterized by a lophophore, a circular or U-shaped ridge around the mouth bearing one or two rows of ciliated tentacles into which the coelom extends. The lophophore functions as a surface for gas exchange, and the cilia of the lophophore serve to guide organic detritus and plankton on which the animal feeds to the mouth. Because of the lophophore, bryozoans and brachiopods have been considered related to one another, but some recent data indicate that the structures may have evolved convergently.

Brachiopods share some features with protostomes and others with deuterostomes. Cleavage in both brachiopods and bryozoans is mostly radial, as in deuterostomes. The formation of the coelom varies. In phoronids (once considered a phylum on their own but now considered part of Brachiopoda), the mouth forms from the blastopore (a feature of protostomes), whereas in the rest of brachiopods and in the bryozoans, it forms from the end of the embryo opposite the blastopore (a feature of deuterostomes). Molecular evidence allies lophophorates with protostomes. Because of the discrepancies between anatomical and developmental characters and molecular characters, the phylogeny of these animals continues to be a fascinating puzzle.

### The bryozoans, phylum Bryozoa, are the only exclusively colonial animals

Bryozoans (phylum Bryozoa or Ectoprocta) are small—usually less than 0.5 mm long—and live in colonies that look like patches of moss on the surfaces of submerged objects (figure 34.19).

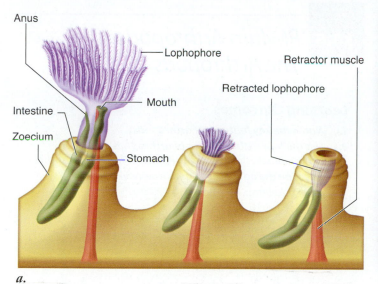

Anus
Lophophore
Retractor muscle
Retracted lophophore
Intestine
Mouth
Zoecium
Stomach

a.

b.

**Figure 34.19** Bryozoans (phylum Bryozoa). *a.* This drawing depicts a small portion of a colony of the freshwater bryozoan genus *Plumatella*, which grows on rocks. The individual at the left has a fully extended lophophore. The tiny individuals disappear into the zoecium when disturbed. *b. Plumatella repens,* another freshwater bryozoan.

Their common name, "moss-animals," is a direct translation of the Latin word *bryozoa*. The digestive system is U-shaped, with the anus opening near the mouth, as in many sessile animals. The alternative name Ectoprocta refers to the location of the anus (proct) outside the ring of the lophophore.

The 4000 species of bryozoans include both marine and freshwater forms. Each individual bryozoan—a zooid—secretes a tiny chitinous chamber called a zoecium (plural, *zoecia*) that is attached to rocks or other substrates such as the leaves of marine plants and algae. Calcium carbonate is deposited in the wall of a zoecium in many marine bryozoans, and in early geological times, bryzoans formed reefs just as corals do today. A zooid can divide or bud to create asexually another zooid beside the existing one so one wall of the new zooid's zoecium is shared with that of the existing one; this expanding group of zoecia constitutes a colony. Individuals in the colony communicate chemically through pores between the zoecia. Not all zoecia of a colony may be identical; some are specialized for functions such as feeding, reproduction, or defense.

## The brachiopods and phoronids, phylum Brachiopoda, are solitary lophophorates

Brachiopods, or lamp shells, superficially resemble clams because they have two calcified valves (figure 34.20). Recall that the shells of bivalves are lateral, but in brachiopods, the valves are dorsal and ventral. Many species attach to rocks or sand by the pedicle (a stalk) that protrudes through an opening in one shell, whereas in others one valve is cemented to the substrate and the animal lacks a pedicle. The lophophore lies on the body, between the shells. The gut in some brachiopods is U-shaped, as in bryozoans, whereas in others there is no anus at all.

Slightly more than 300 species of brachiopods exist today, but more than 30,000 fossil species are known. Because brachiopods were common in the Earth's oceans for millions of years and because their shells fossilize readily, many are used as index fossils, defining a particular geological period or sediment type.

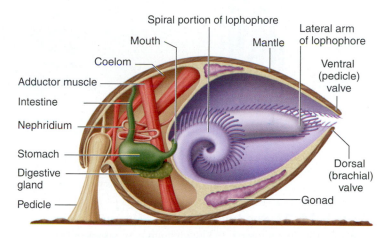

Spiral portion of lophophore
Mouth
Mantle
Lateral arm of lophophore
Coelom
Adductor muscle
Ventral (pedicle) valve
Intestine
Nephridium
Stomach
Digestive gland
Dorsal (brachial) valve
Pedicle
Gonad

a.

b.

**Figure 34.20** Brachiopods (phylum Brachiopoda). *a.* All the body structures except the pedicle lay within two calcified shells, or valves. *b.* The brachiopod *Terebratulina septentrionalis* is slightly opened so the lophophore is visible.

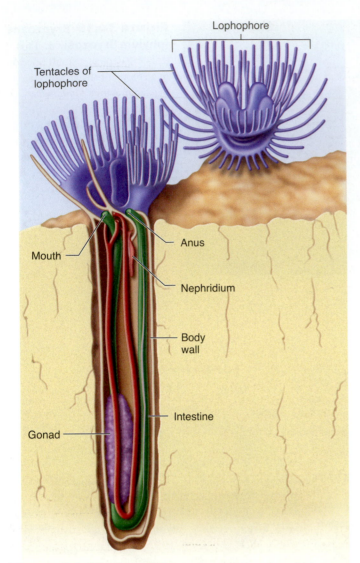

**Figure 34.21 Phoronids.** A phoronid lives in a chitinous tube that the animal secretes. The lophophore consists of two horseshoe-shaped ridges of tentacles and can be withdrawn into the tube when the animal is disturbed.

Each **phoronid** (figure 34.21) secretes a chitinous tube around itself from which it can extend its lophophore to feed. The animal quickly withdraws into the tube when disturbed, as some polychaete worms do. Only about 10 phoronid species are known, ranging in length from a few millimeters to 30 cm. Individuals of some species lie buried in sand; others are attached to rocks, either singly or in groups, forming loose colonies.

## Learning Outcomes Review 34.4

The two phyla of lophophorates probably share a common ancestor, and they show a mixture of protostome and deuterostome characteristics. The lophophore is a characteristic feeding and exchange structure with ciliated tentacles. Bryozoans are exclusively colonial, whereas brachiopods and phoronids are solitary. Brachiopods have two shells with dorsal and ventral valves, not lateral.

■ *How is a U-shaped digestive tract an advantage to bryozoans and brachipods?*

# 34.5 Phylum Arthropoda: The Arthropods

### Learning Outcomes

1. Name the key features of arthropods.
2. List the four extant classes of arthropods and a characteristic that distinguishes them from one another.
3. Describe the advantages and drawbacks of an exoskeleton.

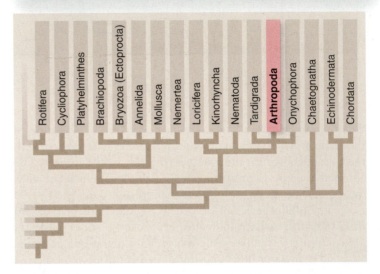

Arthropods are by far the most successful of all animals (table 34.1). Well over 1,000,000 species—about two-thirds of all the named species on Earth— are members of the phylum Arthropoda (figure 34.22). One scientist recently estimated that insects alone may comprise as many as 30 million species. About 200 million individual insects are alive at any time for each human! Insects (see figure 34.22) and other arthropods abound in every habitat on the planet, but there are few marine insects. Members of the phylum are small, generally a few millimeters in length, but adults range in size from about 80 μm long (some parasitic mites) to 3 m across (Japanese spider crabs).

Arthropods are of enormous economic importance, affecting all aspects of human life. They pollinate crops and are valuable as food for humans and other animals, but they also compete with humans for food and damage crops. Diseases spread by insects and ticks strike every kind of plant and animal, including human beings. Insects are by far the most important herbivores in terrestrial ecosystems: virtually every kind of plant is eaten by one or more species.

Although our understanding of the phylogenetic relationships among the groups of arthropods and their relationships to other animals may shift with new findings, taxonomists currently recognize four extant classes (a fifth, the trilobites, is extinct): chelicerates, crustaceans, hexapods, and myriapods. Mouthparts of chelicerates are chelicerae (pincers), whereas those of the other three classes are **mandibles** (biting jaws). Mandibles are inferred to have arisen (probably from a pair of limbs) in the common ancestor of crustaceans, hexapods, and

| TABLE 34.1 | Major Groups of the Phylum Arthropoda | | |
|---|---|---|---|
| **Class** | | **Characteristics** | **Members** |
| Chelicerata |  | Mouthparts are chelicerae (pincers or fangs). | Spiders, mites, ticks, scorpions, daddy long-legs, horseshoe crabs |
| Crustacea |  | Mouthparts are mandibles; appendages are biramous ("two-branched"); the head has two pairs of antennae. | Lobsters, crabs, shrimps, isopods, barnacles |
| Hexapoda |  | Mouthparts are mandibles; the body consists of three regions: a head with one pair of antennae, a thorax, and an abdomen; appendages are uniramous ("single-branched"). | Insects (beetles, bees, flies, fleas, true bugs, grasshoppers, butterflies, termites), springtails |
| Myriapoda |  | Mouthparts are mandibles; the body consists of a head with one pair of antennae, and numerous segments, each bearing paired uniramous appendages. | Centipedes, millipedes |

myriapods, which means that these groups are more closely related to one another than any of them is to chelicerates.

## Arthropods exhibit key features and organ systems

Part of arthropod success is explained by the modularity of the segmented body, the **exoskeleton,** and the jointed appendages. The advantages of segmentation were discussed in the section on annelids. A hard exoskeleton confers protection against predators, but it acts something like a straight-jacket, restricting motion. Joints in the appendages maintain protection while providing some flexibility. With this system, arthropods have developed many efficient modes of locomotion, both in the oceans, where they originated, and on land, which they colonized early in the Devonian period.

### Segmentation

In members of some classes of arthropods, many body segments look alike. In others, the segments are specialized into functional groups, or **tagmata** (singular, *tagma*), such as the head, thorax, and abdomen of an insect (figure 34.23). The fusion of segments, known as tagmatization, is of central importance in the evolution of arthropods. Typically, the segments can be distinguished during larval development, but fusion in development obliterates them. All arthropods have a distinct head; in many crustaceans and chelicerates, head and thorax fuse to form the cephalothorax, or **prosoma.**

### An exoskeleton

The rigid external skeleton, or exoskeleton, is made of chitin and protein. In any animal, the skeleton provides antagonism for muscles (and in many animals, a surface for muscle attachment), support for the body, and protection against physical forces. The arthropod exoskeleton protects against water loss,

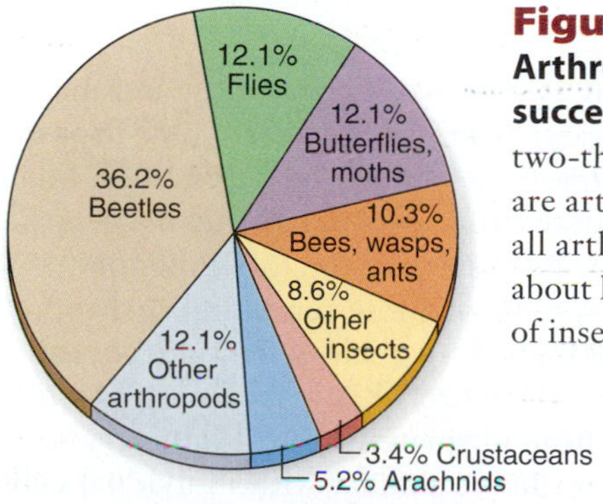

**Figure 34.22**
**Arthropods are a successful group.** About two-thirds of all named species are arthropods. About 80% of all arthropods are insects, and about half of the named species of insects are beetles.

*Pie chart:*
- 12.1% Flies
- 12.1% Butterflies, moths
- 10.3% Bees, wasps, ants
- 8.6% Other insects
- 36.2% Beetles
- 12.1% Other arthropods
- 3.4% Crustaceans
- 5.2% Arachnids

**Figure 34.23 Phylum Arthropoda.** This bee, like all insects and other arthropods, has a segmented body and jointed appendages. An insect body is composed of three tagmata: head, thorax, and abdomen. All arthropods have an exoskeleton made of chitin. Some insects evolved wings that permit them to fly.

*Labels:* Head, Thorax, Air sac, Malpighian tubules, Compound eye, Abdomen, Antenna, Rectum, Mouthparts, Sting, Spiracles, Midgut, Poison sac

which was a powerful advantage in insects colonizing land. As you learned in chapter 3, chitin is chemically similar to cellulose, the dominant structural component of plants, and shares with it properties of toughness and flexibility. The chitin and protein of an arthropod exoskeleton provide a covering that is very strong while being capable of flexing in response to the contraction of muscles attached to it.

An exoskeleton has inherent limitations. As arthropods increase in size, their exoskeletons must get disproportionately thick to bear the pull of the muscles. If beetles were as large as eagles, or crabs the size of cows, the exoskeleton would be so thick that the animal would be unable to move its great weight. Few terrestrial arthropods weigh more than a few grams, but aquatic ones can be heavier because water, being denser than air, provides more support. Another limitation is that, because the body is encased in a rigid skeleton, arthropods periodically must undergo **ecdysis,** or molting. Controlled by ecdysteroid hormones (chapter 46), molting was explained in chapter 32. The anterior and posterior regions of the digestive tract as well as the **compound eyes** are covered with cuticle and therefore are also shed at ecdysis. The animal is especially vulnerable during molting while the exoskeleton is soft, and it may hide from predators until the new exoskeleton hardens.

### Jointed appendages

The name *arthropod* means "jointed feet"; all arthropods have jointed appendages. Appendages may be modified into antennae, mouthparts of various kinds, or legs.

One advantage of jointed appendages is that they can be extended and retracted by bending. Imagine how difficult life would be if your arms and legs could not bend! In addition, joints serve as a fulcrum, or stable point, for appendage movement, so leverage is possible. A small muscle force on a lever can produce a large movement; for example, extending your lower arm takes advantage of the fulcrum of the elbow. A small contraction distance in your muscles moves your hand through a large arc.

### Circulatory system

The circulatory system of arthropods is open. The principal component of an insect's circulatory system is a longitudinal muscular vessel called the heart, which is near the dorsal surface of the thorax and abdomen (figure 34.24). When the heart contracts, blood is pumped anteriorly. From there it gradually flows through the spaces between the tissues toward the posterior end. When the heart relaxes, blood returns to it from those spaces through one-way valves in the posterior region of the heart.

### Nervous system

The central feature of the arthropod nervous system is a double chain of segmented ganglia along the animal's ventral surface (see figure 34.24). At the anterior end of the animal are three fused pairs of dorsal ganglia, which constitute the brain; however, ventral ganglia (generally a pair per segment) control much of the animal's activities. Therefore, an arthropod can carry out functions such as eating, moving, and copulating even if the brain has been removed. The brain seems to be a control

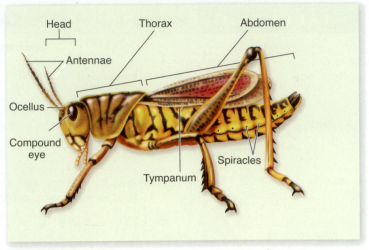

a.

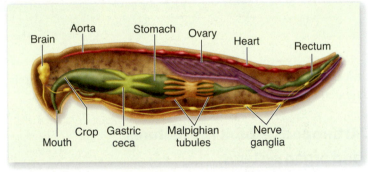

b.

**Figure 34.24 A Grasshopper (order Orthoptera).** This grasshopper illustrates the major structural features of the insects, the arthropod group with the greatest number of species. *a.* External anatomy. *b.* Internal anatomy.

point, or inhibitor, for various actions, rather than a stimulator, as it is in vertebrates.

Compound eyes (figure 34.25) occur in many insects, crustaceans, centipedes, and the extinct trilobites. They are composed of hundreds or more independent visual units called **ommatidia** (singular, *ommatidium*), each covered with a lens and including a complex of eight retinular cells and a light-sensitive central core, the rhabdom. Simple eyes, or **ocelli** (singular, *ocellus*) with single lenses, occur in some arthropods including those with compound eyes. Ocelli distinguish light from darkness. The ocelli of locusts and dragonflies function as horizon detectors to help the insect visually stabilize flight.

### Respiratory system

Marine arthropods such as crustaceans have gills, and marine chelicerates (such as horseshoe crabs) have book gills, flaps under the prosoma that appear to have evolved from legs. Some tiny arthropods lack any structures for exchanging oxygen, and their outer epithelium or gut have a respiratory function.

The respiratory system of most terrestrial arthropods consists of small, branched, cuticle-lined ducts called **tracheae** (singular, *trachea*) (figure 34.26) (the lining of which is shed at ecdysis). Tracheae ultimately branch into very small **tracheoles,** which are in direct contact with individual cells,

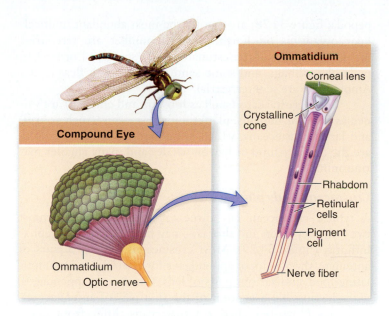

**Figure 34.25 The compound eye.** The compound eyes in insects are complex structures composed of many independent visual units called ommatidia.

Labels in figure: Ommatidium; Compound Eye; Ommatidium; Optic nerve; Corneal lens; Crystalline cone; Rhabdom; Retinular cells; Pigment cell; Nerve fiber

allowing oxygen and carbon dioxide to diffuse across the plasma membranes. Because insects depend on the respiratory system rather than the circulatory system to carry oxygen to their tissues, all parts of the body must be near a respiratory passage. Along with the weight of the exoskeleton, this places severe limitations on arthropod size.

Air passes into the tracheae through openings in the exoskeleton called **spiracles** (see figures 34.23, 34.24, and 34.26), which, in most insects, can be opened and closed by valves. The ability to prevent water loss by closing the spiracles was a key adaptation that facilitated the arthropod invasion of land.

Many spiders have book lungs instead of or in addition to tracheae. A **book lung** is a series of leaflike plates within a chamber into which air is drawn and from which it is expelled by muscular contraction.

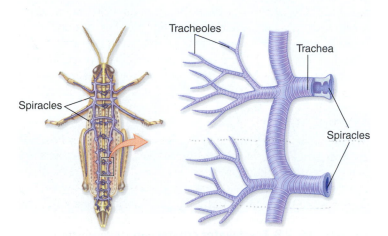

**Figure 34.26 Tracheae and tracheoles.** Tracheae and tracheoles are connected to the exterior by openings called spiracles and carry oxygen to all parts of a terrestrial insect's body.

Labels in figure: Tracheoles; Trachea; Spiracles; Spiracles

### Excretory system

Various kinds of excretory systems occur in arthropods. In aquatic arthropods, much of the waste may diffuse from the blood in the gills.

**Malpighian tubules,** which occur in terrestrial insects, myriapods, and chelicerates, are slender projections from the digestive tract attached at the junction of the midgut and hindgut (see figures 34.23, 34.24). Fluid passes through the walls of the Malpighian tubules to and from the blood in which the tubules are bathed. Nitrogenous wastes are precipitated as concentrated uric acid or guanine, emptied into the hindgut, and eliminated. Most of the water and salts in the fluid are re-absorbed by the hindgut and rectum to be returned to the arthropod's body. This efficient conservation of water by Malpighian tubules was another key adaptation facilitating invasion of the land by arthropods.

## Class Chelicerata includes spiders, mites, ticks, and horseshoe crabs

In the class Chelicerata, with some 57,000 species, the most anterior appendages, called **chelicerae** (singular, *chelicera*), may function as fangs or pincers. The body of a chelicerate is divided into two tagmata: the anterior prosoma, which bears all the appendages, and the posterior **opisthosoma,** which contains the reproductive organs. Chelicerates include familiar largely terrestrial arthropods such as spiders, ticks, mites, scorpions, and daddy long-legs. However, 4000 known species of mites and one species of spider live in freshwater habitats, and a few mites live in the sea. Exclusively marine groups of chelicerates are horseshoe crabs and sea spiders.

In addition to a pair of chelicerae, a chelicerate has a pair of **pedipalps,** and four pairs of walking legs on its prosoma. The pedipalps (often simply called palps) resemble legs but have one fewer segment and are not used for locomotion. In male spiders, the pedipalps are copulatory organs; in scorpions, they are large pincers; and in most other chelicerates, they are sensorial, acting like the antennae of other arthropods.

Most chelicerates are carnivorous, but mites are largely herbivorous. Aside from the daddy long-legs, which can ingest small particles, most cannot consume solid food. They subsist on liquids, including solid food that they liquefy by injecting with digestive enzymes and then suck up with the muscular pharynx.

Horseshoe crabs comprise four species that live off the North American Atlantic coast and in Southeast Asia. Sea spiders are such strange marine animals that some authorities exclude them from the Chelicerata. Most are small, but some can reach 150 mm or so across; many live in association with other marine animals, such as hydroids.

### Order Araneae: Spiders

The 35,000 named species of spiders (order Araneae) play a major role in virtually all terrestrial ecosystems. They are particularly important as predators of insects and other small animals. Spiders hunt their prey or catch it in silk webs of remarkable diversity. Silk is formed from a fluid protein that is forced out of **spinnerets** on the posterior portion of the spider's abdomen. Trap-door spiders construct silk-lined burrows with lids, seizing their prey as it passes by. Spiders such as the familiar wolf spiders and tarantulas hunt rather than spin webs.

All spiders have poison glands with channels through their chelicerae, which are pointed and are used to bite and paralyze prey. The bites of some, such as the western black widow (*Latrodectus hesperus*) and brown recluse (*Loxosceles reclusa*) (figure 34.27), can be fatal to humans and other large mammals.

### Order Acari: Mites and ticks

The order Acari is the most diverse of the chelicerates. About 30,000 species of mites and ticks have been named, but scientists estimate that more than a million members of this order may exist. Acarines are found in virtually every habitat; they feed on a variety of organisms as predators and parasites.

Most mites are less than 1 mm long, but adults range from 100 nm to 2 cm. In most mites, the cephalothorax and abdomen are fused into an unsegmented, ovoid body. Respiration is by means of tracheae or directly through the body surface. Many mites pass through several stages during their life cycle. In most, an inactive eight-legged prelarva gives rise to an active six-legged larva, which, in turn, produces a succession of three eight-legged stages, and, finally, the adult.

Ticks are parasites that attach to the surface of humans and other animals, causing discomfort by sucking blood. Ticks, which are larger than most other members of the order, can carry disease-causing agents. For example, Rocky Mountain spotted fever is caused by bacteria; Lyme disease is caused by spirochaetes; and red-water fever, or Texas fever, is an important tick-borne protozoan disease of cattle, horses, sheep, and dogs.

## Class Crustacea includes crabs, shrimps, lobsters, and pill bugs

The crustaceans (class Crustacea) comprise some 35,000 species of largely marine organisms, such as crabs, shrimps, lobsters, and barnacles. However, some groups, such as crayfish, occur in freshwater, and some crabs and copepods (order Co-pepoda; figure 34.28) are among the most abundant multicellular organisms on Earth. A small number are terrestrial, including about half the estimated 4500 species of order Isopoda, the pillbugs; and some sand fleas or beach fleas (order Amphipoda) are semiterrestrial.

Some crustaceans (such as lobsters and crayfish) are valued as food for humans; planktonic crustaceans (such as krill) and larval crustaceans, which are abundant in the plankton, are the primary food of baleen whales and many smaller marine animals.

### Crustacean body plans

A typical crustacean has three tagmata; the anteriormost two—the cephalon and thorax—may fuse to form the cephalothorax (figure 34.29). Most crustaceans have two pairs of antennae, three pairs of appendages for chewing and manipulating food, and various pairs of legs. Crustacean appendages, with the possible exception of the first pair of antennae, are biramous ("two-branched"). Crustaceans differ from hexapods, but resemble myriopods, in having appendages on their abdomen as well as their thorax. They are the only arthropods with two pairs of antennae.

Large crustaceans have feathery gills for respiration near the bases of their legs (see figure 34.29). Oxygen extracted from the gills is distributed through the circulatory system. In smaller crustaceans, gas exchange takes place directly through the thinner areas of the cuticle or the entire body.

### Crustacean reproduction

Nearly all crustaceans except barnacles are gonochoric. Many kinds of copulation occur, and the members of some groups carry their eggs, either singly or in egg pouches, until they hatch. Crustaceans develop through a **nauplius** (plural, *nauplii*) stage (figure 34.30). The nauplius hatches with three pairs of appendages and undergoes metamorphosis through several stages before reaching maturity. In many groups, this nauplius stage is passed in the egg, and the hatchling resembles a miniature adult.

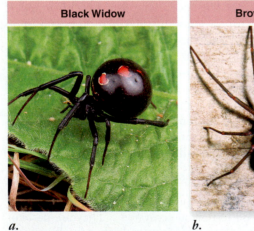

**Figure 34.27 Two common poisonous spiders.** *a.* The southern black widow, *Latrodectus mactans*. *b.* The brown recluse spider, *Loxosceles reclusa*. Both species are common throughout temperate and subtropical North America.

**Figure 34.28 Freshwater crustacean.** A copepod with attached eggs. Members of the marine and freshwater order Copepoda are important components of the plankton. Most are a few millimeters long.

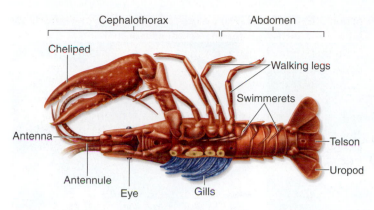

Figure 34.29 **Decapod crustacean.** Ventral view of a lobster, *Homarus americanus*, with some of its principal features labeled.

The nauplius larva is characteristic of Crustacea, providing evidence that all members of this diverse group descended from a common ancestor that had a nauplius in its life cycle. The sessile barnacles, with their shell-like exoskeleton, had been thought to be related to mollusks until they were discovered to have a nauplius larva. More recently, the wormy pentastomids, which parasitize the respiratory tracts of vertebrates, were determined to be crustaceans in part through their nauplii (recall from chapter 32 that parasites may become morphologically simplified and so can be difficult to place phylogenetically).

### Decapod crustaceans: Shrimps, lobsters, crabs, and crayfish

Large, primarily marine crustaceans such as shrimps, lobsters, and crabs, along with their freshwater relatives, the crayfish, belong to order Decapoda (see figure 34.29), which means "ten-footed" because of their five pairs of thoracic appendages. The exoskeleton of most is reinforced with calcium carbonate. The cephalothorax is covered by a dorsal shield, or carapace, which arises from the head. The pincers of many decapod crustaceans are used in obtaining food—for example, by crushing mollusk shells.

In lobsters and crayfish, appendages called **swimmerets** that occur along the ventral surface of the abdomen are used in reproduction and swimming. At the posterior end of the abdomen, paired flattened appendages known as **uropods** form a kind of paddle between which is a **telson,** a tail spine (see

Figure 34.31 **Cephalothorax.** The cephalothorax of a Chesapeake Bay blue crab *(Callinectes sapidus).*

figure 34.29). When a lobster or crayfish contracts its abdominal muscle, the uropods and telson push water anteriorly, propelling the animal posteriorly through the water rapidly and forcefully. It is this very large muscle that constitutes the "lobster tail" so valued by human diners!

One difference between crabs and lobsters is that the crab carapace is relatively much broader and the abdomen is just a small vestige tucked under the cephalothorax. The abdomen of a male crab is much narrower than that of a female of the same species and size (figure 34.31): the female carries her eggs attached to appendages of the abdomen between it and the thorax. A female with eggs is said to be "in berry."

### Sessile crustaceans: Barnacles

Barnacles (order Cirripedia; figure 34.32) are sessile as adults. At the end of its larval life, a barnacle nauplius attaches by its

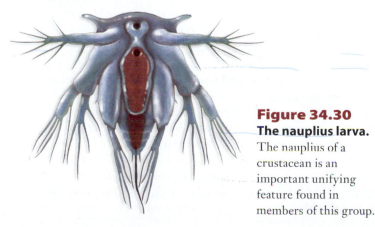

Figure 34.30
**The nauplius larva.**
The nauplius of a crustacean is an important unifying feature found in members of this group.

Figure 34.32 **Gooseneck barnacles,** *Lepas anatifera.* These barnacles are filter feeding, which they do by sweeping their jointed legs through the water, gathering small particles of food. These are stalked barnacles; others lack a stalk.

**Figure 34.33** **Insect diversity.** *a.* Luna moth, *Actias luna.* Luna moths and their relatives are among the most spectacular insects (order Lepidoptera). *b.* A thorn-shaped treehopper, *Umbonia crassicornis* (order Homoptera). *c.* Boll weevil, *Anthonomus grandis.* Weevils are one of the largest groups of beetles (order Coleoptera). *d.* Soldier fly, *Ptecticus trivittatus* (order Diptera). *e.* Lubber grasshopper, *Romalea guttata* (order Orthoptera). *f.* Termites, like ants, have several castes with individuals specialized for different tasks. The individual on the left is a soldier; its large jaws aid in defending the colony.

head to a piling, rock, or other submerged object, metamorphoses, grows calcareous plates around it, and spends the rest of its life capturing food with its jointed, feathery legs. The hermaphroditic state of barnacles is thought to be related to their sessility. Barnacles have the longest penis in the animal kingdom, relative to their size, which enables these sessile animals to cross-fertilize.

## Class Hexapoda comprises the insects

The insects, members of class Hexapoda, are by far the largest group of animals on Earth, in terms of number of species and number of individuals. Insects live in every habitat on land and in fresh water, but very few have invaded the sea. More than half of named animal species are insects, and the actual proportion may be higher because millions of forms await detection, classification, and naming.

Approximately 90,000 described species occur in the United States and Canada; the actual number probably approaches 125,000. A hectare of lowland tropical forest is estimated to be inhabited by as many as 41,000 species of insects, and many suburban gardens may have 1500 or more species. It has been estimated that approximately a billion billion ($10^{18}$)

individual insects are alive at any one time. A glimpse into the enormous diversity of insects is presented in figure 34.33 and table 34.2.

### External features

Insects are primarily terrestrial, and aquatic insects probably had terrestrial ancestors. Most are small, ranging from 0.1 mm to about 30 cm in length or wingspan. Insect mouthparts all have the same basic structure; modifications reflect feeding habits (figure 34.34). Most insects have compound eyes, and many also have ocelli.

An insect body has three regions: the head, thorax, and abdomen (see figures 34.23, 34.24). The thorax consists of three segments, each with a pair of legs, which accounts for the name of the group, hexa (six) and poda (legs). Legs are absent in the larvae of certain groups—for example, most flies (order Diptera) and mosquitoes (figure 34.35). In addition, an insect may have one or two pairs of wings, which are not homologous to the other appendages, and which attach to the middle and posterior segments of the thorax (see figure 34.23). The wings, which consist of chitin and protein, arise as saclike outgrowths of the body wall; wings of moths and butterflies are covered with detachable scales that provide most of their bright colors

| TABLE 34.2 | Major Orders of Insects | | | |
|---|---|---|---|---|
| **Order** | **Typical Examples** | | **Key Characteristics** | **Approximate Number of Named Species** |
| Coleoptera | Beetles | | Two pairs of wings, the front one hard, protecting the rear one; heavily armored exoskeleton; biting and chewing mouthparts. Complete metamorphosis. The most diverse animal order. | 350,000 |
| Diptera | Flies | | Front flying wings transparent; hindwings reduced to knobby balancing organs called halteres. Sucking, piercing, or lapping mouthparts; some bite people and other mammals. Complete metamorphosis. | 120,000 |
| Lepidoptera | Butterflies, moths | | Two pairs of broad, scaly, flying wings, often brightly colored. Hairy body; tubelike, sucking mouthparts. Complete metamorphosis. | 120,000 |
| Hymenoptera | Bees, wasps, ants | | Two pairs of transparent flying wings; mobile head and well-developed compound eyes; often possess stingers; chewing and sucking mouthparts. Many social. Complete metamorphosis. | 100,000 |
| Hemiptera and Homoptera | True bugs, bedbugs, leafhoppers, aphids, cicadas | | Wingless or with two pairs of wings; piercing, sucking mouthparts, with which some draw blood, some feed on plants. Simple metamorphosis. | 60,000 |
| Orthoptera | Grasshoppers, crickets | | Wingless or with two pairs of wings; among the largest insects; biting and chewing mouthparts in adults. Third pair of legs modified for jumping. Simple metamorphosis. | 20,000 |
| Odonata | Dragonflies | | Two pairs of transparent flying wings that cannot fold back; large, long, and slender body; chewing mouthparts. Simple metamorphosis. | 5000 |
| Isoptera | Termites | | Two pairs of wings, but some stages wingless; chewing mouthparts; simple metamorphosis. Social organization: labor divided among several body types. Some are among the few types of animals able to digest wood. Complete metamorphosis. | 2000 |
| Siphonaptera | Fleas | | Wingless; flattened body with jumping legs; piercing and sucking mouthparts. Small; known for irritating bites. Complete metamorphosis. | 1200 |

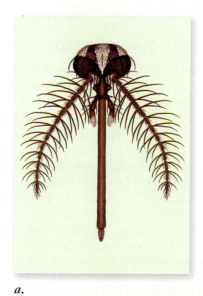

*a.*

*b.*

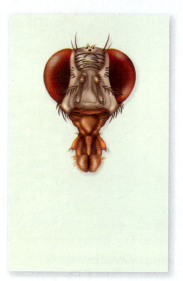

*c.*

**Figure 34.34**

**Mouthparts in three kinds of insects.** Mouthparts are modified for *(a)* piercing in this mosquito of the genus *Culex;* *(b)* sucking nectar from flowers in the alfalfa butterfly of the genus *Colias;* and *(c)* sopping up liquids in the housefly, *Musca domestica.*

## Figure 34.35 Larva of a mosquito, *Culex pipiens.*

The aquatic larvae of mosquitoes are quite active. They breathe through tubes at the surface of the water, as shown here. Covering the water with a thin film of oil suffocates them.

(figure 34.36). Veins strengthen wings. An insect's thorax is almost entirely filled with muscles that operate the legs and wings. Fleas and lice are considered secondarily wingless, having descended from ancestors with wings. However, the ancestors of springtails and silverfish evolved before wings did, so those hexapods are considered primarily wingless.

### Internal organization

The internal features of insects resemble those of other arthropods in many ways. The digestive tract is a tube about the same length as the body in some groups. However, in insects that feed on juices and so have sucking mouthparts, such as leafhoppers, cicadas, and many flies, the greatly coiled digestive tube may be several times longer than the body. Digestion takes place primarily in the stomach, or midgut, and excretion takes place through Malpighian tubules. Digestive enzymes are mainly secreted from the cells that line the midgut, although some are contributed by the salivary glands near the mouth.

**Figure 34.36 Scales on the wing of *Parnassius imperator*, a butterfly from China.** Scales of this sort account for most of the colored patterns on the wings of butterflies and moths.

In many winged insects, tracheae are dilated in various parts of the body, forming air sacs, which are surrounded by muscles to form a kind of bellows system that forces air deep into the body. The spiracles through which air enters the tracheal system are located on or between the segments along the sides of the thorax and abdomen. In most insects, the spiracles can be opened by muscular action. In some parasitic and aquatic groups of insects, the spiracles are permanently closed. In these groups, the tracheae are just below the surface of the insect, and gas exchange takes place by diffusion.

### Sensory receptors

In addition to eyes, insects have several characteristic kinds of sense receptors. **Sensory setae** are hairlike structures that are widely distributed over the body. They are sensitive to mechanical and chemical stimulation and are linked to nerve cells. They are particularly abundant on the antennae and legs, the parts of the insect most likely to come into contact with other objects.

Sound, which may be of vital importance to insects such as grasshoppers, crickets, cicadas, and some moths, is detected by a thin membrane, each called a **tympanum** (see figure 34.24), associated with the tracheal air sacs. In other groups of insects, sound waves are detected by sensory hairs. Male mosquitoes use thousands of sensory hairs on their antennae to detect sounds made by the vibrating wings of female mosquitoes.

In addition to sound, nearly all insects communicate by means of chemicals known as pheromones. These extremely diverse compounds are sent forth into the environment, where they convey a variety of messages, including mating signals and trail markers.

### Insect life histories

During the course of their development, many insects undergo metamorphosis. For those such as grasshoppers, in which immature individuals are quite similar to adults, a series of molts results in an individual gradually getting bigger and more developed; this is termed simple metamorphosis. Those such as moths and butterflies have a life history involving a wormlike larval stage, a resting stage called a **pupa** or **chrysalis,** during which metamorphosis occurs, and then a final molt into the adult form or imago; this is termed complete metamorphosis.

## Myriapoda includes centipedes and millipedes

The body of a centipede (subclass Chilopoda) and millipede (subclass Diplopoda) consists of a head region posterior to which are numerous, more or less similar segments. Nearly all segments of a centipede have one pair of appendages (figure 34.37*a*), and nearly all segments of a millipede have two pairs of appendages (figure 34.37*b*). Each segment of a millipede is a simple tagma derived evolutionarily from two ancestral segments, which explains why millipedes have twice as many legs per segment as centipedes. Although the name *centipede* would imply an animal with 100 legs and the name *millipede* one with 1000, an adult centipede usually has fewer than 100 legs (most have 15, 21, or 23 pairs of legs); an adult millipede never reaches 1000 legs, most having 100 or fewer.

Both centipedes and millipedes are gonochoric; fertilization is internal, and all lay eggs. Young millipedes usually hatch with three pairs of legs; they add segments and legs as they pass

Centipede

a.

Millipede

b.

**Figure 34.37** **Myriapods.** *a.* Centipedes, such as this member of the genus *Scolopendra*, are active predators. *b.* Millipedes, such as this member of the genus *Sigmoria*, are important herbivores and detritivores. Centipedes have one pair of legs per body segment, millipedes have two pairs per segment.

through growth stages, but they do not change in general appearance. Centipedes have several types of development, young of some species hatching with their final number of legs and others adding legs after hatching. Centipedes that do not add legs as they grow tend to take care of their young, a behavior rather uncommon among invertebrates.

Centipedes, of which some 3000 species are known, are carnivorous, feeding mainly on insects. The appendages of the first trunk segment are modified into a pair of poison fangs. The poison may be toxic to humans, and although extremely painful, centipede bites are never fatal. In contrast, most millipedes are herbivores, feeding mainly on decaying vegetation such as leaf litter and rotting logs (which are typical habitats for the animals). Many millipedes can roll their bodies into a flat coil or sphere to defend themselves. More than 12,000 species of millipedes have been named, but this is estimated to be no more than one-sixth of the number of species that exists.

In each segment of their body, many millipedes have a pair of complex glands that produce a bad-smelling fluid, which they exude for defense through openings along the sides of the body. The chemistry of this material interests biologists because of the diversity of the compounds involved and their effectiveness in protecting millipedes from attack. Some species produce cyanide gas from segments near their head.

### Learning Outcomes Review 34.5

Arthropods are segmented animals with exoskeletons and jointed appendages. The four living classes of arthropods are Chelicerata, with mouthparts (chelicerae) that function as fangs or pincers; Crustacea, in which all members have a nauplius developmental stage; Hexapoda, the insects, having three pairs of legs attached to fused segments of the thorax as adults; and Myriopoda, with one or two pairs of appendages on every body segment. An exoskeleton provides protection and muscle attachment, but growth requires molting. In some cases, larvae undergo metamorphosis into an adult with very different appearance.

■ *What would explain why the largest arthropods are found in marine environments?*

## 34.6 Phylum Echinodermata: The Echinoderms

### Learning Outcomes

1. Explain what is meant by pentaradial symmetry.
2. Describe the five extant classes of echinoderms.

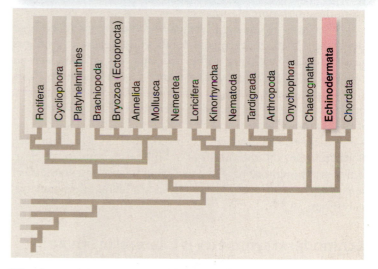

Members of the exclusively marine phylum Echinodermata are characterized by deuterostome development (see chapter 32) and an endoskeleton. The endoskeleton is composed of hard, calcium carbonate plates that lie just beneath the delicate skin. The term *echinoderm*, which means "spiny skin," refers to the spines or bumps that occur on these plates in many species. Echinoderms, including sea stars (figure 34.38), brittle stars, sea urchins, sand dollars, and sea cucumbers are some of the most familiar animals on the seashore. All have five axes of symmetry (that is, you could draw lines through their body in five different places that produced mirror images on each side) and thus are said to be **pentaradially symmetrical.**

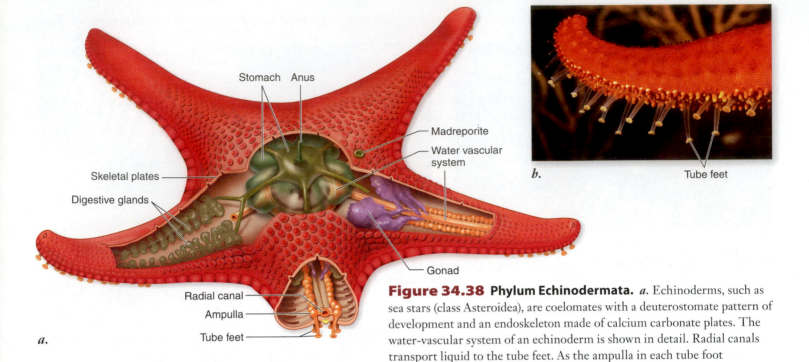

Stomach  Anus

Madreporite

Water vascular system

Skeletal plates

Digestive glands

*b.*

Tube feet

Gonad

Radial canal

Ampulla

Tube feet

*a.*

**Figure 34.38 Phylum Echinodermata.** *a.* Echinoderms, such as sea stars (class Asteroidea), are coelomates with a deuterostomate pattern of development and an endoskeleton made of calcium carbonate plates. The water-vascular system of an echinoderm is shown in detail. Radial canals transport liquid to the tube feet. As the ampulla in each tube foot contracts, the tube foot extends and can attach to the substrate. When the muscles in the tube feet contract, the tube foot bends, pulling the animal forward. *b.* Extended nonsuckered tube feet of the sea star *Luidia magnifica*.

## Echinoderms are ancient and unmistakable

Echinodermata is an ancient group of marine animals that appeared nearly 600 MYA and that comprise about 6000 living species. As with other deuterostomes, the mouth does not form from the embryonic blastopore.

Because the skeletal elements of echinoderms are covered by living tissue, they constitute an endoskeleton. A unique feature of echinoderms is the hydraulic system that aids in movement or feeding called a **water-vascular system.** This fluid-filled system, which is a modification of one of several coelomic spaces, is composed of a central ring canal from which **radial canals** extend.

Although an excellent fossil record extends back into the Cambrian period, the origin of echinoderms remains unclear. They are thought to have evolved from bilaterally symmetrical ancestors because echinoderm larvae are bilaterally symmetrical (figure 34.39).

## Echinoderm symmetry is bilateral in larvae but pentaradial in adults

The body of echinoderms undergoes a fundamental shift during development, from bilaterally symmetrical larvae (see figure 34.39) to pentaradially symmetrical adults (see figure 34.38). Dorsal, ventral, anterior, and posterior have no meaning without a head or tail for orientation. Thus, orientation of the body of an adult echinoderm is described in reference to the mouth, which defines the **oral surface.** All systems of an adult echinoderm are organized with branches radiating from a center. For example, the nervous system consists of a central nerve ring from which branches arise; although the animals are capable of complex behavior patterns, there is no centralization of function.

In many echinoderms, the oral surface faces the substratum, although in sea cucumbers, the animal's axis is horizontal, so the animal crawls oral surface foremost, and in crinoids (sea lilies and feather stars), the oral surface is located opposite to the substrate.

### The endoskeleton

Echinoderms have a delicate epidermis that stretches over an endoskeleton composed of calcium carbonate (calcite) plates called **ossicles.** In echinoderms such as asteroids (sea stars), the individual skeletal elements are loosely joined to

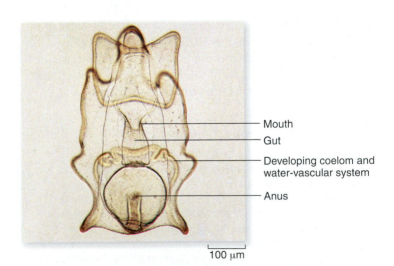

Mouth

Gut

Developing coelom and water-vascular system

Anus

100 μm

**Figure 34.39 The free-swimming larva of the common sea star, *Asterias rubens*.** Such bilaterally symmetrical larvae suggest that the ancestors of the echinoderms may not have been radially symmetrical.

one another. In others, especially echinoids (sea urchins and sand dollars), the ossicles abut one another tightly, forming a rigid shell (called a test). In sea cucumbers, by contrast, the ossicles are widely scattered, so the body wall is flexible. The ossicles in certain portions of the body of some echinoderms are perforated by pores. Through these pores extend tube feet, part of the water-vascular system that is a unique feature of this phylum.

Members of this phylum have mutable collagenous tissue, which can change in texture from tough and rubbery to weak and fluid. This amazing tissue accounts for attributes of echinoderms such as the ability to autotomize (cast off) parts. This tissue is also responsible for a sea cucumber being able to change from almost rigid to flaccid in a matter of seconds.

### The water-vascular system

The water-vascular system is radially organized. From the ring canal, which encircles the animal's esophagus, a radial canal extends into each branch of the body (see figure 34.38). Water enters the water-vascular system through a **madreporite**, a sievelike plate that, in most echinoderms, is on the animal's surface, and flows to the ring canal through a stone canal, so named because it is reinforced by calcium carbonate. Each radial canal, in turn, extends through short side branches into the hollow tube feet (see figure 34.38*b*). In some echinoderms, each tube foot has a sucker at its end; in others, suckers are absent. At the base of each tube foot in most types of echinoderms is a muscular sac, the ampulla. When the ampulla contracts, the fluid, prevented from entering the radial canal by a one-way valve, is forced into the tube foot, thus extending it. Contraction of longitudinal muscles on one side of the tube foot wall causes the tube foot to bend; relaxation of the muscles in the ampulla and contraction of all the longitudinal muscles in the tube foot forces the fluid back into the ampulla.

In asteroids and echinoids, concerted action of a very large number of small, individually weak tube feet causes the animal to move across the sea floor. The tube feet around the mouth of a holothurian are used in feeding. In crinoids, tube feet that arise from the branches of the arms, which extend from the margins of an upward-directed cup, are used in capturing food from the surrounding water. Ophiuroid tube feet are pointed and specialized for feeding.

Gas exchange in most echinoderms is through the body surface and tube feet. In addition, a holothurian has paired respiratory trees, which branch off the hindgut. Water is drawn into them and exits from them through the anus. In an asteroid, one of the coelomic spaces other than the water-vascular system has branches into protrusions from the epidermis called papulae through which gas exchange also occurs.

### Regeneration and reproduction

Many echinoderms are able to regenerate lost parts. Some asteroids and especially ophiuroids can autotomize an arm. When a holothurian of some species is disturbed, it can cast out its entire digestive system. Some echinoderms can reproduce asexually by splitting.

However, most reproduction in echinoderms is sexual. As a rule, echinoderms are gonochoric. Gametes are generally released into the water, where fertilization occurs, and free-swimming

bilaterally symmetrical larvae develop (see figure 34.39). Each class of echinoderms has a characteristic type of larva. These larvae develop in the plankton until they metamorphose into the sedentary adults.

## Echinodermata comprises five extant classes

There are five classes of living echinoderms, but more than 20 others have gone extinct. Living ones are: (1) Asteroidea, sea stars, or starfish, and sea daisies; (2) Crinoidea, sea lilies and feather stars; (3) Echinoidea, sea urchins and sand dollars; (4) Holothuroidea, sea cucumbers; and (5) Ophiuroidea, brittle stars (figure 34.40).

**Class: Asteroidea**

*a.*

**Class: Holothuroidea**

*b.*

**Class: Echinoidea**

*c.*

**Class: Crinoidea**

*d.*

**Class: Ophiuroidea**

*e.*

**Figure 34.40 Diversity in echinoderms. *a.*** Sea star, *Oreaster occidentalis* (class Asteroidea), in the Gulf of California, Mexico. *b.* Warty sea cucumber, *Parastichopus parvimensis* (class Holothuroidea), Philippines. *c.* Sea urchin of the genus *Echinometra* (class Echinoidea). *d.* Feather star (class Crinoidea) of the genus *Comatheria*, from Indonesia. *e.* Gaudy brittle star, *Ophioderma ensiferum* (class Ophiuroidea).

Adults of all classes exhibit a five-part body plan. Even sea cucumbers, which are shaped like their fruit namesake, have five longitudinal grooves along their bodies. Here we discuss three of the living classes.

### Class Asteroidea: Sea stars

Sea stars are perhaps the most familiar echinoderms. Important predators in many marine ecosystems, they range in size from a centimeter to a meter across. They are abundant in the intertidal zone, but also occur at the greatest depths of the ocean—10,000 m. Around 1500 species of sea stars are known.

A sea star consists of tapering arms that gradually merge into a central disk. Most sea stars have five arms, but some have many more, typically in multiples of five. The digestive space and gonads extend into the arms. The body is somewhat flattened, flexible, and covered with a pigmented epidermis. Asteroidea includes sea daisies, which were discovered in 1986 and were once considered to constitute their own class.

### Class Ophiuroidea: Brittle stars

Brittle stars constitute the largest class of echinoderms, with about 2000 species, and are probably the most abundant also. They resemble asteroids, but differ morphologically in several ways. The arms, which are of nearly equal diameter their entire length, tapering only slightly from base to tip, merge abruptly into the central disk. They are nearly solid and can easily be autotomized (the source of the name "brittle"). The tube feet lack ampullae and suckers, being used for feeding, not locomotion. The animal has no anus.

The most mobile of echinoderms, brittle stars move by pulling themselves along by "rowing" over the substrate by moving their slender arms, often in pairs or groups, from side to side. Some brittle stars use their arms to swim, an unusual habit among echinoderms. A brittle star has five arms, but in some larger ones (the basket stars), each arm may bifurcate several times. Brittle stars avoid light and are more active at night.

### Class Echinoidea: Sea urchins and sand dollars

Sand dollars and sea urchins lack arms. Five double rows of tube feet protrude through the plates of the calcareous skeleton. The protective, moveable spines that are attached to the skeleton by muscles and connective tissue, are also arrayed pentamerally.

About 950 living species constitute the class Echinoidea. Their calcareous plates preserve well, so sea urchins and sand dollars are well represented in the fossil record, with more than 5000 extinct species described. Sand dollars are essentially flattened sea urchins; heart urchins are intermediate between the two.

Like holothurians, sea urchins are eaten by humans. The gonads, known as *uni* in Japan, are the part considered edible.

---

### Learning Outcomes Review 34.6

Echinoderms are marine deuterostomes with endoskeletons. They are characterized by pentaradial symmetry in the adult, in which a line drawn in five directions produces mirror images. The water-vascular system and tube feet that act as suction cups aid in movement and feeding. The five living classes of echinoderms are Asteroidea (sea stars), Crinoidea (sea lilies), Echinoidea (sea urchins and sand dollars), Holothuroidea (sea cucumbers), and Ophiuroidea (brittle stars).

■ *What is the significance of the bilateral larval form of echinoderms?*

---

## Chapter Review

### 34.1 Phylum Mollusca: The Mollusks

*Mollusks are extremely diverse—and important to humans.*
Mollusks range from microscopic to huge and exhibit many different forms. They all have a coelom surrounding the heart.

*The mollusk body plan is complex and varied.*
Mollusks are generally bilaterally symmetrical, at least at some point in their lives (see figure 34.3). They use a muscular foot (podium) for locomotion, attachment, food capture, or a combination.

The mantle is a thick epidermal sheet that forms the mantle cavity. It houses the respiratory structures (ctenidia or gills), and digestive, excretory, and reproductive products are discharged into it.

The outer mantle secretes a protective calcium carbonate shell. Some mollusks have internal or reduced shells, or none at all.

All mollusks except bivalves have a radula, a rasplike structure used in feeding (see figure 34.4). Most have an open circulatory system, but cephalopods have a closed circulatory system.

In many mollusks, an embryo develops into a free-swimming trochophore larva (see figure 34.5a). In some bivalves and gastropods, the embryo becomes a free-swimming veliger larva (see figure 34.5b).

*Four classes of mollusks show the diversity of the phylum.*
The four best-known classes are Polyplacophora (chitons), Gastropoda (snails and slugs), Bivalvia (clams, mussels, and cockles), and Cephalopoda (octopuses and squids).

### 34.2 Phylum Nemertea: The Ribbon Worms

Nemerteans superficially resemble acoelomate flatworms, but they have a closed circulatory system and a complete digestive tract.

### 34.3 Phylum Annelida: The Annelids

*The annelid body is composed of ringlike segments.*
The segments of the annelid body are separated by septa. Each segment contains a pair of excretory organs, a ganglion, and, in most

marine annelids, a set of reproductive organs. Anterior and posterior segments contain light-, chemo-, and touch receptors.

Segments are connected by a ventral nerve cord that includes an anterior brain region, and by a closed circulatory system.

### Annelids move by contracting their segments.

The fluid-filled coelom acts as a hydrostatic skeleton. Each segment typically possesses chaetae, chitin bristles that help anchor the worm.

### Annelids have a common, closed circulatory system but a segmented excretory system.

Annelids have a closed circulatory system; the dorsal vessel is connected to the ventral vessel by smaller vessels in the body wall.

Each segment contains a pair of nephridia that excrete wastes out of the body via the coelom and excretory tubes.

### Annelids comprise two—or three—classes.

Annelids have been grouped into three classes, but the currently accepted classification recognizes two: the Polychaeta, which exhibit parapodia and are mostly marine; and the Clitellata, which includes earthworms and leeches.

## 34.4 The Lophophorates: Bryozoa and Brachiopoda

Bryozoa and Brachiopoda are characterized by a lophophore, a U-shaped ridge around the mouth bearing ciliated tentacles.

### The bryozoans, phylum Bryozoa, are the only exclusively colonial animals.

Each individual zooid produces a chitinous chamber called a zoecium that attaches to substrates and other colony members. They have deuterostome development.

### The brachiopods and phoronids, phylum Brachiopoda, are solitary lophophorates.

The body of brachiopods is enclosed between two calcified shells that are dorsal and ventral, not lateral as in bivalves (see figure 34.20). They also are deuterostomes.

The phoronids, tube worms, are included with bryozoans because they are solitary lophophorates; however, they are protostomes.

## 34.5 Phylum Arthropoda: The Arthropods

### Arthropods exhibit key features and organ systems.

Arthropods are segmented and exhibit an exoskeleton with muscles attached to the inside. The exoskeleton is molted during ecdysis, allowing the arthropod to grow. In some species, segments are fused into units called tagmata.

Arthropods' jointed appendages may be modified into mouth parts, antennae, or legs.

An open circulatory system includes a muscular heart. The respiratory system in terrestrial arthropods comprises spiracles, tracheae, and tracheoles (see figure 34.26). The main components of the nervous system are an inhibitory brain and a ventral nerve cord.

Many arthropods have compound eyes composed of ommatidia (figure 34.25); others have simple eyes (ocelli).

The excretory system of terrestrial hexapods, myriapods, and chelicerates consists of Malpighian tubules that eliminate uric acid or guanine.

### Class Chelicerata includes spiders, mites, and horseshoe crabs.

Chelicerates have specialized anterior appendages, the chelicerae, that function as fangs or pincers.

### Class Crustacea includes crabs, shrimps, lobsters, and pill bugs.

Crustaceans have three tagmata, and the two anterior ones fused to form a cephalothorax (see figure 34.29). Crustacea is characterized by a nauplius larva (see figure 34.30).

### Class Hexapoda comprises the insects.

The hexapods are extraordinarily diverse. Insects have three pairs of legs attached to the thorax and may have wings. They have highly developed sensory systems.

### Myriapoda includes centipedes and millipedes.

Centipedes have one pair of appendages per segment, whereas millipedes have two pairs.

## 34.6 Phylum Echinodermata: The Echinoderms

### Echinoderms are ancient and unmistakable.

Echinoderms are characterized by deuterostome development, pentameral symmetry, an endoskeleton covered by a delicate epidermis, and a water-vascular system.

### Echinoderm symmetry is bilateral in larvae but pentaradial in adults.

The larvae of echinoderms are bilateral, but the adult is pentaradial.

The water-vascular system, which is one of several coelomic compartments, aids in movement, feeding, circulation, respiration, and excretion.

### Echinodermata comprises five extant classes.

The five classes of echinoderms are Asteroidea (sea stars), Crinoidea (sea lilies), Echinoidea (sea urchins and sand dollars), Holothuroidea (sea cucumbers), and Ophiuroidea (brittle stars).

## Review Questions

### UNDERSTAND

1. The _____ of a mollusk is a highly efficient respiratory structure.
   a. nephridium
   b. radula
   c. ctenidium
   d. veliger

2. Torsion is a unique characteristic of the
   a. bivalves.
   b. gastropods.
   c. chitons.
   d. cephalopods.

3. Intelligence and complex behaviors are characteristics of the
   a. cephalopods.
   b. polychaetes.
   c. brachiopods.
   d. echinoderms.

4. Serial segmentation is a key characteristic of which of the following phyla?
   a. Mollusca
   b. Brachiopoda
   c. Bryozoa
   d. Annelida

5. The distinguishing feature of the Bryozoa and Brachiopoda is
   a. coelom.
   b. segmentation.
   c. chaetae.
   d. a lophophore.

6. In terms of numbers of species, the most successful phylum on the planet is the
   a. Mollusca.
   b. Arthropoda.
   c. Echinodermata.
   d. Annelida.

7. Which of the following characteristics is not found in the arthropods?
   a. Jointed appendages
   b. Segmentation
   c. Closed circulatory system
   d. Segmented ganglia

8. Which of the following classes of arthropod possess chelicerae?
   a. Chilopoda
   b. Crustacea
   c. Hexapoda
   d. Chelicerata

9. Examples of decapods are
   a. centipedes and millipedes.
   b. barnacles.
   c. ticks and mites.
   d. lobsters and crayfish.

10. What characteristic separates the Diptera, Lepidoptera, and Hymenoptera?
    a. Type of wings
    b. Type of mouthparts
    c. Type of legs
    d. Method of reproduction

11. Which of the following structures is not a component of the water-vascular system of an echinoderm?
    a. Ossicles
    b. Ampullae
    c. Radial canals
    d. Madreporites

## APPLY

1. The fact that Arthropods molt means that they are considered
   a. spiralians.
   b. ecdysozoans.
   c. deuterostomes.
   d. parazoans.

2. Based on embryonic development, which of the following phyla is the closest to the chordates?
   a. Annelida
   b. Arthropoda
   c. Echinodermata
   d. Mollusca

3. To which of the following groups would a species that does not molt, possesses a coelom, and has a trochophore larva belong?
   a. Ecdysozoa
   b. Parazoa
   c. Platyzoa
   d. Lophotrochozoa

4. Nematodes once were thought to be closely related to rotifers due to the presence of a pseudocoelom, but are now considered closer to the arthropods due to
   a. molting.
   b. jointed appendages.
   c. wings.
   d. a coelom.

## SYNTHESIZE

1. Scientists studying the Chesapeake Bay have discovered that the decline in populations of clams and scallops has led to a drastic increase in the levels of pollution. What characteristic of this group could be attributed to this observation?

2. Chitin is present in a number of invertebrate coelomates, as well as the fungi. What does this tell you about the origin and importance of this substance?

## ONLINE RESOURCE

www.ravenbiology.com

Understand, Apply, and Synthesize—enhance your study with animations that bring concepts to life and practice tests to assess your understanding. Your instructor may also recommend the interactive eBook, individualized learning tools, and more.

*Chapter* 35

# Vertebrates

## Chapter Outline

## Introduction

*Members of the phylum Chordata exhibit great changes in the endoskeleton from what is seen in echinoderms. As you saw in chapter 34, the endoskeleton of echinoderms is functionally similar to the exoskeleton of arthropods—a hard shell with muscles attached to its inner surface. Chordates employ a very different kind of endoskeleton, one that is truly internal. Members of the phylum Chordata are characterized by a flexible rod that develops along the back of the embryo. Muscles attached to this rod allowed early chordates to swing their bodies from side to side, swimming through the water. This key evolutionary advance, attaching muscles to an internal element, started chordates along an evolutionary path that led to the vertebrates—and, for the first time, to truly large animals.*

# 35.1 The Chordates

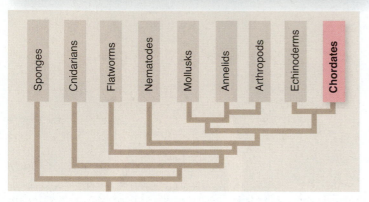

**Chordates** (phylum Chordata) are deuterostome coelomates; their nearest relatives in the animal kingdom are the echinoderms, the only other major phylum of deuterostomes. There are some 56,000 species of chordates, a phylum that includes fishes, amphibians, reptiles, birds, and mammals.

Four features characterize the chordates and have played an important role in the evolution of the phylum (figure 35.1):

1. A single, hollow **nerve cord** runs just beneath the dorsal surface of the animal. In vertebrates, the dorsal nerve cord differentiates into the brain and spinal cord.
2. A flexible rod, the **notochord,** forms on the dorsal side of the primitive gut in the early embryo and is present at some developmental stage in all chordates. The notochord is located just below the nerve cord. The notochord may persist in some chordates; in others it is replaced during embryonic development by the vertebral column that forms around the nerve cord.

3. **Pharyngeal slits** connect the **pharynx,** a muscular tube that links the mouth cavity and the esophagus, with the external environment. In terrestrial vertebrates, the slits do not actually connect to the outside and are better termed **pharyngeal pouches.** Pharyngeal pouches are present in the embryos of all vertebrates. They become slits, open to the outside in animals with gills, but leave no external trace in those lacking gills. The presence of these structures in all vertebrate embryos provides evidence of their aquatic ancestry.
4. Chordates have a **postanal tail** that extends beyond the anus, at least during their embryonic development. Nearly all other animals have a terminal anus.

All chordates have all four of these characteristics at some time in their lives. For example, humans as embryos have pharyngeal pouches, a dorsal nerve cord, a postanal tail, and a notochord. As adults, the nerve cord remains, and the notochord is replaced by the vertebral column. All but one pair of pharyngeal pouches are lost; this remaining pair forms the Eustachian tubes that connect the throat to the middle ear. The postanal tail regresses, forming the tail bone (coccyx).

A number of other characteristics also fundamentally distinguish the chordates from other animals. Chordate muscles are arranged in segmented blocks that affect the basic organization of the chordate body and can often be clearly seen in embryos of this phylum (figure 35.2). Most chordates have an internal skeleton against which the muscles work. Either this internal skeleton or the notochord (figure 35.3) makes possible the extraordinary powers of locomotion characteristic of this group.

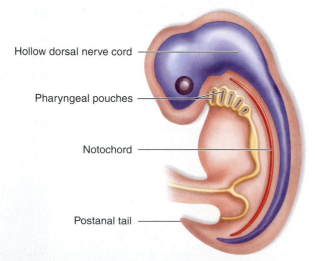

**Figure 35.1** The four principal features of the chordates, as shown in a generalized embryo.

Hollow dorsal nerve cord

Pharyngeal pouches

Notochord

Postanal tail

**Figure 35.2**
**A mouse embryo.**
At 11.5 days of development, the mesoderm is already divided into segments called somites (stained dark in this photo), reflecting the fundamentally segmented nature of all chordates.

500 μm

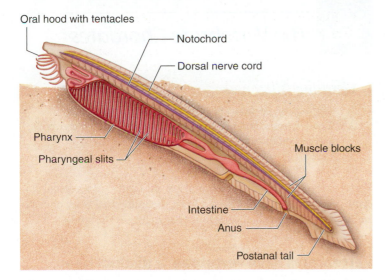

**Figure 35.3 Phylum Chordata: Chordates.** Vertebrates, tunicates, and lancelets are chordates (phylum Chordata), coelomate animals with a flexible rod, the notochord, that provides resistance to muscle contraction and permits rapid lateral body movements. Chordates also possess pharyngeal pouches or slits (reflecting their aquatic ancestry and present habitat in some) and a hollow dorsal nerve cord. In nearly all vertebrates, the notochord is replaced during embryonic development by the vertebral column.

## 35.2 The Nonvertebrate Chordates

### Learning Outcome

1. **Describe the nonvertebrate chordates and their characteristics.**

Phylum Chordata can be divided into three subphyla. Two of these, Urochordata and Cephalochordata, are nonvertebrate; the third subphylum is Vertebrata. The nonvertebrate chordates do not form vertebrae or other bones, and in the case of the urochordates, their adult form is greatly different from what we expect chordates to look like.

### Tunicates have chordate larval forms

The tunicates and salps (subphylum Urochordata) are a group of about 1250 species of marine animals. Most of them are immobile as adults, with only the larvae having a notochord and nerve cord. As adults, they exhibit neither a major body cavity nor visible signs of segmentation (figure 35.4*a*, *b*). Most species occur in shallow waters, but some are found at great depths. In some tunicates, adults are colonial, living in masses on the ocean floor. The pharynx is lined with numerous cilia; beating of the cilia draws a stream of water into the pharynx, where microscopic food particles become trapped in a mucous sheet secreted from a structure called an *endostyle*.

The tadpolelike larvae of tunicates plainly exhibit all of the basic characteristics of chordates and mark the tunicates as having the most primitive combination of features found in any chordate (figure 35.4*c*). The larvae do not feed and have a poorly developed gut. They remain free-swimming for only a few days before settling to the bottom and attaching themselves to a suitable substrate by means of a sucker.

Tunicates change so much as they mature and adjust developmentally to an immobile, filter-feeding existence that it would be difficult to discern their evolutionary relationships solely by examining an adult. Many adult tunicates secrete a tunic, a tough sac composed mainly of cellulose, a substance frequently found in the cell walls of plants and algae but rarely found in animals. The tunic surrounds the animal and gives the subphylum its name. Colonial tunicates may have a common sac and a common opening to the outside.

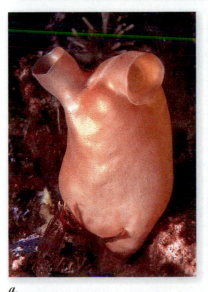

*a.*

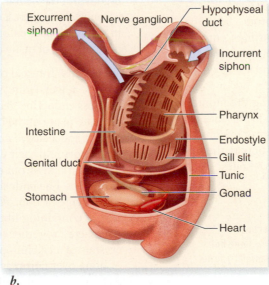

*b.*

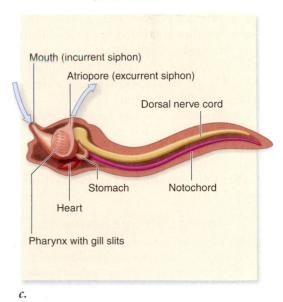

*c.*

**Figure 35.4 Tunicates (phylum Chordata, subphylum Urochordata).** *a.* The sea peach, *Halocynthia auranthium*, like other tunicates, does not move as an adult, but rather is firmly attached to the sea floor. *b.* Diagram of the structure of an adult tunicate. *c.* Diagram of the structure of a larval tunicate, showing the characteristic tadpolelike form. Larval tunicates resemble the postulated common ancestor of the chordates.

**Figure 35.5**

**Lancelets.** Two lancelets, *Branchiostoma lanceolatum* (phylum Chordata, subphylum Cephalochordata), partly buried in shell gravel, with their anterior ends protruding. The muscle segments are clearly visible.

One group of Urochordates, the Larvacea, retains the tail and notochord into adulthood. One theory of vertebrate origins involves a larval form, perhaps that of a tunicate, which acquired the ability to reproduce.

## Lancelets are small marine chordates

Lancelets (subphylum Cephalochordata) were given their English name because they resemble a lancet—a small, two-edged surgical knife. These scaleless chordates, a few centimeters long, occur widely in shallow water throughout the oceans of the world. There are about 23 species of this subphylum. Most of them belong to the genus *Branchiostoma*, formerly called *Amphioxus*, a name still used widely. In lancelets, the notochord runs the entire length of the dorsal nerve cord and persists throughout the animal's life.

Lancelets spend most of their time partly buried in sandy or muddy substrates, with only their anterior ends protruding (figure 35.5). They can swim, although they rarely do so. Their muscles can easily be seen through their thin, transparent skin as a series of discrete blocks, called myomeres. Lancelets have many more pharyngeal gill slits than fishes do. They lack pigment in their skin, which has only a single layer of cells, unlike the multilayered skin of vertebrates. The lancelet body is pointed at both ends. There is no distinguishable head or sensory structure other than pigmented light receptors.

Lancelets feed on microscopic plankton, using a current created by beating cilia that line the oral hood, pharynx, and gill slits. The gill slits provide an exit for the water and are an adaptation for filter feeding. The oral hood projects beyond the mouth and bears sensory tentacles, which also ring the mouth.

The recent discovery of fossil forms similar to living lancelets in rocks 550 million years old argues for the antiquity of this group. Recent studies by molecular systematists further support the hypothesis that lancelets are the closest relatives of vertebrates.

### Learning Outcome Review 35.2

Nonvertebrate chordates have notochords but no vertebrae or bones. Urochordates, such as tunicates, have obviously chordate larval forms but drastically different adult forms. Cephalochordates, such as lancelets, do not change body form as adults.

■ *How do lancelets and tunicates differ from each other, and from vertebrates?*

## 35.3 The Vertebrate Chordates

### Learning Outcomes

1. Distinguish vertebrates from other chordates.
2. Explain how cartilage and bone contributed to increased size in vertebrates.

Vertebrates (subphylum Vertebrata) are chordates with a spinal column. The name *vertebrate* comes from the individual bony or cartilaginous segments called vertebrae that make up the spine.

## Vertebrates have vertebrae, a distinct head, and other features

Vertebrates differ from the tunicates and lancelets in two important respects:

**Vertebral column.** In all vertebrates except the earliest diverging fishes, the notochord is replaced during embryonic development by a vertebral column (figure 35.6). The column is a series of bony or cartilaginous vertebrae that enclose and protect the dorsal nerve cord like a sleeve.

**Head.** Vertebrates have a distinct and well-differentiated head with three pairs of well-developed sensory organs; the brain is encased within a protective box, the skull, or cranium, made of bone or cartilage.

In addition to these two key characteristics, vertebrates differ from other chordates in other important respects (figure 35.7):

**Neural crest.** A unique group of embryonic cells called the **neural crest** contributes to the development of many vertebrate structures. These cells develop on the crest of the neural tube as it forms by invagination and pinching together of the neural plate (see chapter 54 for a detailed account). Neural crest cells then migrate to various locations in the developing embryo, where they participate in the development of many different structures.

**Internal organs.** Internal organs characteristic of vertebrates include a liver, kidneys, and endocrine glands. The ductless endocrine glands secrete hormones that help regulate many of the body's functions. All vertebrates have a heart and a closed circulatory system. In both their circulatory and their excretory functions, vertebrates differ markedly from other animals.

**Endoskeleton.** The endoskeleton of most vertebrates is made of cartilage or bone. Cartilage and bone are specialized tissues containing fibers of the protein collagen compacted together (see chapter 47). Bone also contains crystals of a calcium phosphate salt. The great advantage of bone over chitin as a structural material is that bone is a dynamic, living tissue that is strong without being brittle. The vertebrate endoskeleton makes possible the great size and extraordinary powers of movement that characterize this group.

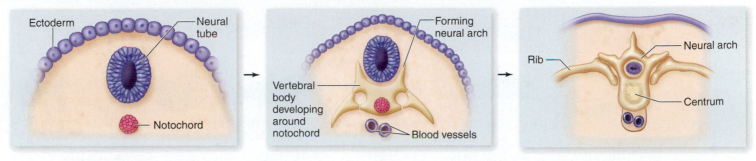

**Figure 35.6 Embryonic development of a vertebra.** During the evolution of animal development, the flexible notochord is surrounded and eventually replaced by a cartilaginous or bony covering, the centrum. The neural tube is protected by an arch above the centrum. The vertebral column functions as a strong, flexible rod that the muscles pull against when the animal swims or moves.

## Vertebrates evolved half a billion years ago: An overview

The first vertebrates evolved in the oceans about 545 MYA, during the Cambrian period. Many of them looked like a flattened hot dog, with a mouth at one end and a fin at the other. The appearance of a hinged jaw was a major advance, opening up new food-gathering options, and jawed fishes became the dominant creatures in the sea. Their descendants, the amphibians, invaded the land. Amphibians, in turn, gave rise to the first reptiles about 300 MYA. Within 50 million years, reptiles, better suited to living out of water, replaced amphibians as the dominant land vertebrates.

With the success of reptiles, vertebrates truly came to dominate the surface of the Earth. Many kinds of reptiles evolved, ranging in size from smaller than a chicken to bigger than a truck, and including some that flew and others that swam. Among them evolved reptiles that gave rise to the two remaining great lines of terrestrial vertebrates: birds and mammals.

Dinosaurs and mammals appear at about the same time in the fossil record, 220 MYA. For over 150 million years, dinosaurs dominated the face of the Earth. Over all these million-and-a-half centuries, the largest mammal was no bigger than a medium-sized dog. Then, in the Cretaceous mass extinction, about 65 MYA, the dinosaurs abruptly disappeared. In their absence, mammals and birds quickly took their place, becoming abundant and diverse.

The history of vertebrates has been a series of evolutionary advances that have allowed vertebrates to first invade the land and then the air. In this chapter, we examine the key evolutionary advances that permitted vertebrates to invade the land successfully. As you will see, this invasion was a staggering evolutionary achievement, involving fundamental changes in many body systems.

While considering vertebrate evolution, keep in mind that two vertebrate groups—fish and reptiles—are paraphyletic (figure 35.8). Some fish are more closely related to other vertebrates than they are to some other fish. Similarly, some reptiles are more closely related to birds than they are to other reptiles. Biologists are currently divided about how to handle situations like this, as we discussed in chapter 23 (see figure 23.5). For the time being, we continue to use the traditional classification of vertebrates, bearing in mind the evolutionary implications of the paraphyly of fish and reptiles.

### Learning Outcomes Review 35.3

Vertebrates are characterized by a vertebral column and a distinct head. Other distinguishing features are the development of a neural crest, a closed circulatory system, specialized organs, and a bony or cartilaginous endoskeleton that has the strength to support larger body size and powerful movements.

- ■ *In what ways would an exoskeleton limit the size of an organism?*

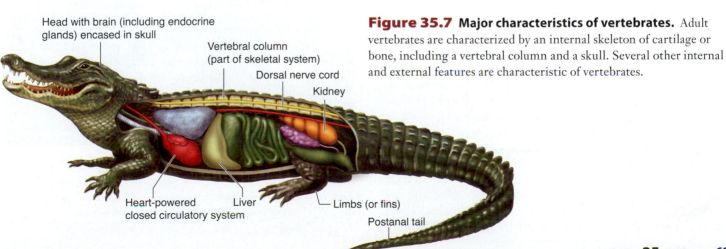

**Figure 35.7 Major characteristics of vertebrates.** Adult vertebrates are characterized by an internal skeleton of cartilage or bone, including a vertebral column and a skull. Several other internal and external features are characteristic of vertebrates.

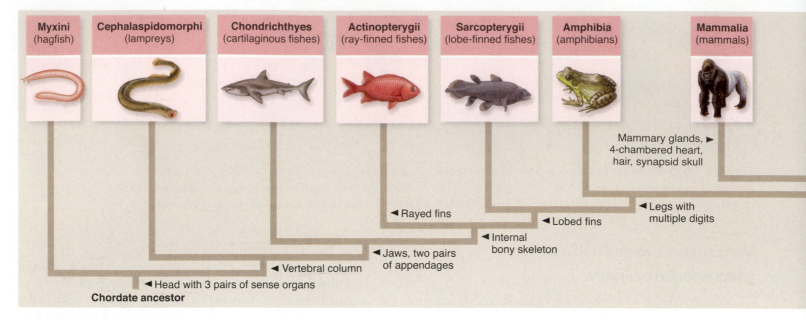

Myxini (hagfish) | Cephalaspidomorphi (lampreys) | Chondrichthyes (cartilaginous fishes) | Actinopterygii (ray-finned fishes) | Sarcopterygii (lobe-finned fishes) | Amphibia (amphibians) | Mammalia (mammals)

Mammary glands, ► 4-chambered heart, hair, synapsid skull

◄ Legs with multiple digits

◄ Rayed fins

◄ Lobed fins

◄ Internal bony skeleton

◄ Jaws, two pairs of appendages

◄ Vertebral column

◄ Head with 3 pairs of sense organs

**Chordate ancestor**

**Figure 35.8 Phylogeny of the living vertebrates.** Some of the key characteristics that evolved among the vertebrate groups are shown in this phylogeny.

## 35.4 Fishes

### Learning Outcomes

1. *Describe the major groups of fishes.*
2. *List the evolutionary innovations of fishes.*

Over half of all vertebrates are fishes. The most diverse vertebrate group, fishes provided the evolutionary base for invasion of land by amphibians. In many ways, amphibians can be viewed as transitional—"fish out of water."

The story of vertebrate evolution started in the ancient seas of the Cambrian period (545 to 490 MYA). Figure 35.8 shows the key vertebrate characteristics that evolved subsequently. Wriggling through the water, jawless and toothless, the first fishes sucked up small food particles from the ocean floor like miniature vacuum cleaners. Most were less than a foot long, respired with gills, and had no paired fins or vertebrae (although some had rudimentary vertebrae); they did have a head and a primitive tail to push them through the water.

For 50 million years, during the Ordovician period (490 to 438 MYA), these simple fishes were the only vertebrates. By the end of this period, fish had developed primitive fins to help them swim and massive shields of bone for protection. Jawed fishes first appeared during the Silurian period (438 to 408 MYA), and along with them came a new mode of feeding.

### Fishes exhibit five key characteristics

From whale sharks 18 m long to tiny gobies no larger than your fingernail, fishes vary considerably in size, shape, color, and appearance (figure 35.9). Some live in freezing arctic seas, others in warm, freshwater lakes, and still others spend a lot of time

entirely out of water. However varied, all fishes have important characteristics in common:

1. **Vertebral column.** Fish have an internal skeleton with a bony or cartilaginous spine surrounding the dorsal nerve cord, and a bony or cartilaginous skull encasing the brain. Exceptions are the jawless hagfish and lampreys. In hagfish, a cartilaginous skull is present, but vertebrae are not; the notochord persists and provides support. In lampreys, a cartilaginous skeleton and notochord are

**Figure 35.9 Fish.** Fish are the most diverse vertebrates and include more species than all other kinds of vertebrates combined. Top, ribbon eel, *Rhinomuraena quaesita;* bottom left, leafy seadragon, *Phycodurus eques;* bottom right, yellowfin tuna, *Thunnus albacares.*

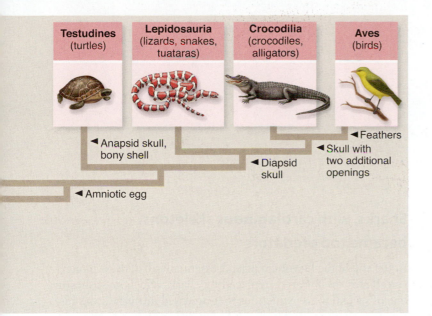

Testudines (turtles) | Lepidosauria (lizards, snakes, tuataras) | Crocodilia (crocodiles, alligators) | Aves (birds)

◄ Anapsid skull, bony shell
◄ Diapsid skull
◄ Skull with two additional openings
◄ Feathers
◄ Amniotic egg

this by directing a flow of water through their mouths and across their gills (see chapter 49). The gills are composed of fine filaments of tissue that are rich in blood vessels.

4. **Single-loop blood circulation.** Blood is pumped from the heart to the gills. From the gills, the oxygenated blood passes to the rest of the body, and then returns to the heart. The heart is a muscular tube-pump made of two chambers that contract in sequence.

5. **Nutritional deficiencies.** Fishes are unable to synthesize the aromatic amino acids (phenylalanine, tryptophan, and tyrosine; see chapter 3), and they must consume them in their foods. This inability has been inherited by all of their vertebrate descendants.

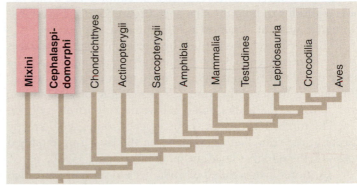

Mixini | Cephalaspidomorphi | Chondrichthyes | Actinopterygii | Sarcopterygii | Amphibia | Mammalia | Testudines | Lepidosauria | Crocodilia | Aves

### The first fishes

The first fishes did not have jaws, and instead had only a mouth at the front end of the body that could be opened to take in food. Two groups survive today as hagfish (class Myxini; table 35.1) and lampreys (class Cephalaspidomorphi).

present, but rudimentary cartilaginous vertebrae also surround the notochord in places.

2. **Jaws and paired appendages.** Fishes other than lampreys and hagfish all have jaws and paired appendages, features that are also seen in tetrapods (see figure 35.8). Jaws allowed these fish to capture larger and more active prey. Most fishes have two pairs of fins: a pair of pectoral fins at the shoulder, and a pair of pelvic fins at the hip. In the lobe-finned fish, these pairs of fins became jointed.

3. **Internal gills.** Fishes are water-dwelling creatures and must extract oxygen dissolved in the water around them. They do

| TABLE 35.1 | Major Classes of Fishes | | |
|---|---|---|---|
| **Class** | **Typical Examples** | **Key Characteristics** | **Approximate Number of Living Species** |
| Sarcopterygii | Lobe-finned fishes | Largely extinct group of bony fishes; ancestral to amphibians; paired lobed fins | 8 |
| Actinopterygii | Ray-finned fishes | Most diverse group of vertebrates; swim bladders and bony skeletons; paired fins supported by bony rays | 30,000 |
| Chondrichthyes | Sharks, skates, rays | Cartilaginous skeletons; no swim bladders; internal fertilization | 750 |
| Cephalaspidomorphi | Lampreys | Largely extinct group of jawless fishes with no paired appendages; parasitic and nonparasitic types; all breed in fresh water | 35 |
| Myxini | Hagfishes | Jawless fishes with no paired appendages; scavengers; mostly blind, but having a well-developed sense of smell | 30 |
| Placodermi | Armored fishes | Jawed fishes with heavily armored heads; many were quite large | Extinct |
| Acanthodii and Ostracoderms | Spiny fishes | Fishes with (acanthodians) or without (placoderms) jaws; paired fins supported by sharp spines; head shields made of bone; rest of skeleton cartilaginous | Extinct |

Another group were the *ostracoderms* (a word meaning "shell-skinned"). Only their head-shields were made of bone; their elaborate internal skeletons were constructed of cartilage. Many ostracoderms were bottom-dwellers, with a jawless mouth underneath a flat head, and eyes on the upper surface. Ostracoderms thrived in the Ordovician and Silurian periods (490 to 408 MYA), only to become almost completely extinct at the close of the Devonian period (408 to 360 MYA).

### Evolution of the jaw

A fundamentally important evolutionary advance that occurred in the late Silurian period was the development of jaws. Jaws evolved from the most anterior of a series of arch-supports made of cartilage, which were used to reinforce the tissue between gill slits to hold the slits open (figure 35.10). This transformation was not as radical as it might at first appear.

Each gill arch was formed by a series of several cartilages (which later evolved to become bones) arranged somewhat in the shape of a V turned on its side, with the point directed outward. Imagine the fusion of the front pair of arches at top and bottom, with hinges at the points, and you have the primitive vertebrate jaw. The top half of the jaw is not attached to the skull directly except at the rear. Teeth developed on the jaws from modified scales on the skin that lined the mouth (see figure 35.10).

Armored fishes called placoderms and spiny fishes called acanthodians both had jaws. Spiny fishes were very common during the early Devonian period, largely replacing ostracoderms, but they became extinct themselves at the close of the Permian. Like ostracoderms, they had internal skeletons made of cartilage, but their scales contained small plates of bone, foreshadowing the much larger role bone would play in the future of vertebrates. Spiny fishes were jawed predators and far better swimmers than ostracoderms, with as many as seven fins to aid their swimming. All of these fins were reinforced with strong spines, giving these fishes their name.

By the mid-Devonian period, the heavily armored placoderms became common. A very diverse and successful group, seven orders of placoderms dominated the seas of the late Devonian, only to become extinct at the end of that period. The placoderm jaw was much improved over the primitive jaw of spiny fishes, with the upper jaw fused to the skull and the skull hinged on the shoulder. Many of the placoderms grew to enormous sizes, some over 30 feet long, with 2-foot skulls that had an enormous bite.

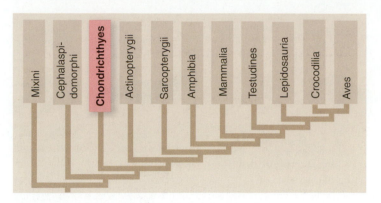

## Sharks, with cartilaginous skeletons, became top predators

At the end of the Devonian period, essentially all of these pioneer vertebrates disappeared, replaced by sharks and bony fishes in one of several mass extinctions that occurred during Earth's history (see chapter 22). Sharks and bony fishes first evolved in the early Devonian, 400 MYA. In these fishes, the jaw was improved even further, with the upper part of the first gill arch behind the jaws being transformed into a supporting strut or prop, joining the rear of the lower jaw to the rear of the skull. This allowed the mouth to open much wider than was previously possible.

During the Carboniferous period (360 to 280 MYA), sharks became the dominant predators in the sea. Sharks, as well as skates and rays (all in the class Chondrichthyes), have a skeleton made of cartilage, like primitive fishes, but it is "calcified," strengthened by granules of calcium carbonate deposited in the outer layers of cartilage. The result is a very light and strong skeleton.

Streamlined, with paired fins and a light, flexible skeleton, sharks are superior swimmers (figure 35.11). Their pectoral fins are particularly large, jutting out stiffly like airplane wings—and that is how they function, adding lift to compensate for the downward thrust of the tail fin. Sharks are very aggressive predators, and some early sharks reached enormous size.

### The evolution of teeth

Sharks were among the first vertebrates to develop teeth. These teeth evolved from rough scales on the skin and are not set into the jaw as human teeth are, but rather sit atop it. They are not firmly anchored and are easily lost. In a shark's mouth, the teeth are arrayed in up to 20 rows; the teeth in front do the biting and cutting, and behind them other teeth grow and wait their turn.

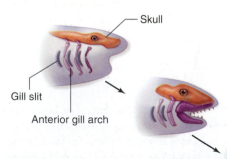

**Figure 35.10 Evolution of the jaw.** Jaws evolved from the anterior gill arches of ancient, jawless fishes.

**Figure 35.11 Chondrichthyes.** Members of the class Chondrichthyes, such as this blue shark, *Prionace glauca*, are mainly predators or scavengers.

When a tooth breaks or is worn down, a replacement from the next row moves forward. A single shark may eventually use more than 20,000 teeth in its lifetime.

A shark's skin is covered with tiny, toothlike scales, giving it a rough "sandpaper" texture. Like the teeth, these scales are constantly replaced throughout the shark's life.

### The lateral line system

Sharks, as well as bony fishes, possess a fully developed lateral line system. The **lateral line system** consists of a series of sensory organs that project into a canal beneath the surface of the skin. The canal runs the length of the fish's body and is open to the exterior through a series of sunken pits. Movement of water past the fish forces water through the canal. The pits are oriented so that some are stimulated no matter what direction the water moves. Details of the lateral line system's function are described in chapter 45. In a very real sense, the lateral line system is a fish's equivalent of hearing and therefore is an additional means of mechanoreception.

### Reproduction in cartilaginous fishes

Reproduction in the class Chondrichthyes differs from that of most other fishes. Shark eggs are fertilized internally. During mating, the male grasps the female with modified fins called claspers, and sperm run from the male into the female through grooves in the claspers. Although a few species lay fertilized eggs, the eggs of most species develop within the female's body, and the pups are born alive.

In recent times, this reproductive system has worked to the detriment of sharks. Because of their long gestation periods and relatively few offspring, shark populations are not able to recover quickly from population declines. Unfortunately, in recent times sharks have been fished very heavily because shark fin soup has become popular in Asia and elsewhere. As a result, shark populations have declined greatly, and there is concern that many species may soon face extinction.

### Shark evolution

Many of the early evolutionary lines of sharks died out during the great extinction at the end of the Permian period (248 MYA). The survivors thrived and underwent a burst of diversification during the Mesozoic era (248 to 65 MYA), when most of the modern groups of sharks appeared. Skates and rays, which are dorsoventrally flattened relatives of sharks, evolved at this time, some 200 million years after the sharks first appeared.

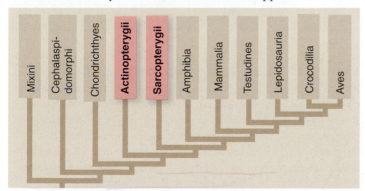

## Bony fishes dominate the waters

Bony fishes evolved at the same time as sharks, some 400 MYA, but took quite a different evolutionary road. Instead of gaining speed through lightness, as sharks did, bony fishes adopted a heavy internal skeleton made completely of bone.

Bone is very strong, providing a base against which very strong muscles can pull. Not only is the internal skeleton ossified, but so is the outer covering of plates and scales. Most bony fishes have highly mobile fins, very thin scales, and completely symmetrical tails (which keep the fish on a straight course as it swims through the water). Bony fishes are the most species-rich group of fishes, indeed of all vertebrates. There are several dozen orders containing more than 30,000 living species.

The remarkable success of the bony fishes has resulted from a series of significant adaptations that have enabled them to dominate life in the water. These include the swim bladder and the gill cover (figure 35.12).

### Swim bladder

Although bones are heavier than cartilaginous skeletons, most bony fishes are still buoyant because they possess a **swim bladder,** a gas-filled sac that allows them to regulate their buoyant density and so remain suspended at any depth in the water effortlessly. Sharks, by contrast, must move through the water or sink because, lacking a swim bladder, their bodies are denser than water.

In primitive bony fishes, the swim bladder is a dorsal outpocketing of the pharynx behind the throat, and these species fill the swim bladder by simply gulping air at the surface of the water. In most of today's bony fishes, the swim bladder is an independent organ that is filled and drained of gases, mostly nitrogen and oxygen, internally.

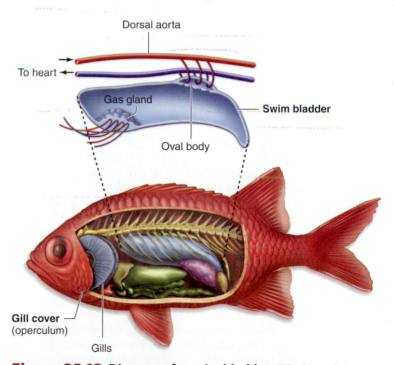

**Figure 35.12 Diagram of a swim bladder.** The bony fishes use this structure, which evolved as a dorsal outpocketing of the pharynx, to control their buoyancy in water. The swim bladder can be filled with or drained of gas to allow the fish to control buoyancy. Gases are taken from the blood, and the gas gland secretes the gases into the swim bladder; gas is released from the bladder by a muscular valve, the oval body.

How do bony fishes manage this remarkable trick? It turns out that the gases are harvested from the blood by a unique gland that discharges the gases into the bladder when more buoyancy is required. To reduce buoyancy, gas is reabsorbed into the bloodstream through a structure called the oval body. A variety of physiological factors control the exchange of gases between the bloodstream and the swim bladder.

### Gill cover

Most bony fishes have a hard plate called the **operculum** that covers the gills on each side of the head. Flexing the operculum permits bony fishes to pump water over their gills. The gills are suspended in the pharyngeal slits that form a passageway between the pharynx and the outside of the fish's body. When the operculum is closed, it seals off the exit.

When the mouth is open, closing the operculum increases the volume of the mouth cavity, so that water is drawn into the mouth. When the mouth is closed, opening the operculum decreases the volume of the mouth cavity, forcing water past the gills to the outside. Using this very efficient bellows, bony fishes can pass water over the gills while remaining stationary in the water. That is what a goldfish is doing when it seems to be gulping in a fish tank.

## The evolutionary path to land ran through the lobe-finned fishes

Two major groups of bony fish are the ray-finned fishes (class Actinopterygii; figure 35.13a) and lobe-finned fishes (class Sarcopterygii). The groups differ in the structure of their fins (figure 35.13b). In ray-finned fishes, the internal skeleton of the fin is composed of parallel bony rays that support and stiffen each fin. There are no muscles within the fins; rather, the fins are moved by muscles within the body.

By contrast, lobe-finned fishes have paired fins that consist of a long fleshy muscular lobe (hence their name), supported by a central core of bones that form fully articulated joints with one another. There are bony rays only at the tips of each lobed fin. Muscles within each lobe can move the fin rays independently of one another, a feat no ray-finned fish could match.

Lobe-finned fishes evolved 390 MYA, shortly after the first bony fishes appeared. Only eight species survive today, two species of coelacanth (figure 35.13b) and six species of lungfish. Although rare today, lobe-finned fishes played an important part in the evolutionary story of vertebrates. Amphibians almost certainly evolved from the lobe-finned fishes.

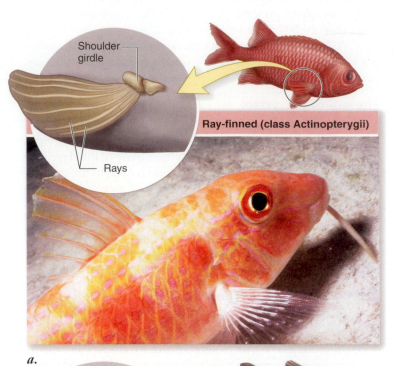

Ray-finned (class Actinopterygii)

_a._

Lobe-finned (class Sarcopterygii)

_b._

**Figure 35.13 Ray-finned and lobe-finned fishes.**
_a._ The ray-finned fishes, such as this Koi carp (_Cyprinus carpio_), are characterized by fins of only parallel bony rays. _b._ By contrast, the fins of lobe-finned fish have a central core of bones as well as rays. The coelacanth, _Latimeria chalumnae_, a lobe-finned fish (class Sarcopterygii), was discovered in the western Indian Ocean in 1938. This coelacanth represents a group of fishes thought to have been extinct for about 70 million years. Scientists who studied living individuals in their natural habitat at depths of 100–200 m observed them drifting in the current and hunting other fishes at night. Some individuals are nearly 3 m long; they have a slender, fat-filled swim bladder.

---

### Learning Outcomes Review 35.4

Fishes are generally characterized by the possession of a vertebral column, jaws, paired appendages, a lateral line system, internal gills, and single-loop circulation. Cartilaginous fishes have lightweight skeletons and were among the first vertebrates to develop teeth. The very successful bony fishes have unique characteristics such as swim bladders and gill covers, as well as ossified skeletons. One type of bony fish, the lobe-finned fish, gave rise to the ancestors of amphibians.

■ **What advantages do lobed fins have over ray fins?**

Amphibians

### Learning Outcomes

1. **Describe the characteristics and major groups of amphibians.**
2. **Explain the challenges of moving from an aquatic to a terrestrial environment.**

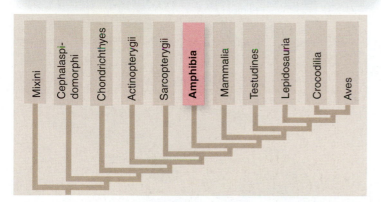

Frogs, salamanders, and caecilians, the damp-skinned vertebrates, are direct descendants of fishes. They are the sole survivors of a very successful group, the amphibians (class Amphibia), the first vertebrates to walk on land. Most present-day amphibians are small and live largely unnoticed by humans, but they are among the most numerous of terrestrial vertebrates. Throughout the world, amphibians play key roles in terrestrial food chains.

## Living amphibians have five distinguishing features

Biologists have classified living species of amphibians into three orders (table 35.2): 5000 species of frogs and toads in 22 fami-

lies make up the order Anura ("without a tail"); 500 species of salamanders and newts in 9 families make up the order Caudata ("visible tail"); and 170 species (6 families) of wormlike, nearly blind organisms called caecilians that live in the tropics make up the order Apoda ("without legs"). These amphibians have several key characteristics in common:

1. **Legs.** Frogs and most salamanders have four legs and can move about on land quite well. Legs were one of the key adaptations to life on land. Caecilians have lost their legs during the course of adapting to a burrowing existence.
2. **Lungs.** Most amphibians possess a pair of lungs, although the internal surfaces have much less surface area than do reptilian or mammalian lungs. Amphibians breathe by lowering the floor of the mouth to suck in air, and then raising it back to force the air down into the lungs (see chapter 49).
3. **Cutaneous respiration.** Frogs, salamanders, and caecilians all supplement the use of lungs by respiring through their skin, which is kept moist and provides an extensive surface area.
4. **Pulmonary veins.** After blood is pumped through the lungs, two large veins called pulmonary veins return the aerated blood to the heart for repumping. In this way aerated blood is pumped to the tissues at a much higher pressure.
5. **Partially divided heart.** A dividing wall helps prevent aerated blood from the lungs from mixing with nonaerated blood being returned to the heart from the rest of the body. The blood circulation is thus divided into two separate paths: pulmonary and systemic. The separation is imperfect, however, because no dividing wall exists in one chamber of the heart, the ventricle (see chapter 49).

Several other specialized characteristics are shared by all present-day amphibians. In all three orders, there is a zone of weakness between the base and the crown of the teeth. They also have a peculiar type of sensory rod cell in the retina of the eye called a "green rod." The function of this rod is unknown.

| TABLE 35.2 | Orders of Amphibians | | | |
|---|---|---|---|---|
| Order | Typical Examples | | Key Characteristics | Approximate Number of Living Species |
| Anura | Frogs, toads | | Compact, tailless body; large head fused to the trunk; rear limbs specialized for jumping | 5000 |
| Caudata | Salamanders, newts | | Slender body; long tail and limbs set out at right angles to the body | 500 |
| Apoda | Caecilians | | Tropical group with a snakelike body; no limbs; little or no tail | 170 |

## Amphibians overcame terrestrial challenges

The word *amphibia* means "double life," and it nicely describes the essential quality of modern-day amphibians, reflecting their ability to live in two worlds—the aquatic world of their fish ancestors and the terrestrial world they first invaded. Here, we review the checkered history of this group, almost all of whose members have been extinct for the last 200 million years. Then we examine in more detail what the few kinds of surviving amphibians are like.

The successful invasion of land by vertebrates posed a number of major challenges:

- Because amphibian ancestors had relatively large bodies, supporting the body's weight on land as well as enabling movement from place to place was a challenge (figure 35.14). Legs evolved to meet this need.
- Even though far more oxygen is available to gills in air than in water, the delicate structure of fish gills requires the buoyancy of water to support them, and they will not function in air. Therefore, other methods of obtaining oxygen were required.
- Delivering great amounts of oxygen to the larger muscles needed for movement on land required modifications to the heart and circulatory system.
- Reproduction still had to be carried out in water so that eggs would not dry out.
- Most importantly, the body itself had to be prevented from drying out.

### The first amphibian

Amphibians solved these problems only partially, but their solutions worked well enough that amphibians have survived for 350 million years. Evolution does not insist on perfect solutions, only workable ones.

Paleontologists agree that amphibians evolved from lobe-finned fish. *Ichthyostega*, one of the earliest amphibian fossils (figure 35.15), was found in a 370-million-year-old rock in Greenland. At that time, Greenland was part of what is now the North American continent and lay near the equator. All amphibian fossils from the next 100 million years are found in North America. Only when Asia and the southern continents merged with North America to form the supercontinent Pangaea did amphibians spread throughout the world.

*Ichthyostega* was a strongly built animal, with sturdy forelegs well supported by shoulder bones. Unlike the bone structure of fish, the shoulder bones were no longer attached to the skull, so the limbs could support the animal's weight. Because the hindlimbs were flipper-shaped, *Ichthyostega* probably moved like a seal, with the forelimbs providing the propulsive force for locomotion and the hindlimbs being dragged along with the rest of the body. To strengthen the backbone further, long, broad ribs that overlap each other formed a solid cage for the lungs and heart. The rib cage was so solid that it probably couldn't expand and contract for breathing. Instead, *Ichthyostega* probably obtained oxygen as many amphibians do today, by lowering the floor of the mouth to draw air in, and then raising it to push air down the windpipe into the lungs.

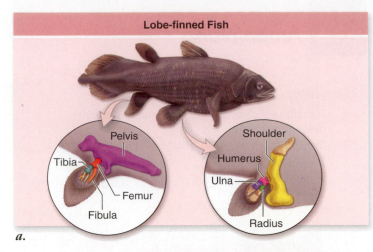

a.

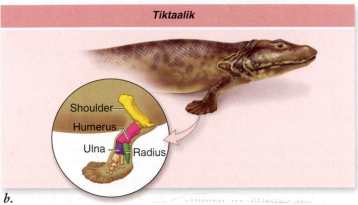

b.

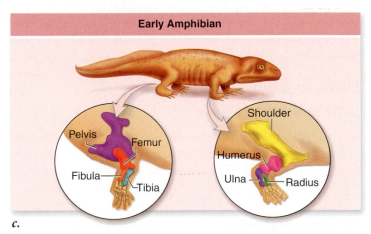

c.

**Figure 35.14** **A comparison between the limbs of a lobe-finned fish, *Tiktaalik,* and a primitive amphibian.** *a.* A lobe-finned fish. Some of these animals could probably move on land. *b. Tiktaalik.* The shoulder and limb bones are like those of an amphibian, but the fins are like those of a lobe-finned fish. The fossil of *Tiktaalik* did not contain the hindlimbs. *c.* A primitive amphibian. As illustrated by their skeletal structure, the legs of such an animal clearly could function better than those of its ancestors for movement on land.

In 2006, an important transitional fossil between fish and *Ichthyostega* was discovered in northern Canada. *Tiktaalik,* which lived 375 MYA, had gills and scales like a fish, but a neck like an amphibian. Particularly significant, however, was the form of its forelimbs (see figure 35.14): its shoulder, forearm, and wrist bones were like those of amphibians, but at the end of the limb

**Figure 35.15 Amphibians were the first vertebrates to walk on land.** *Ichthyostega*, one of the first amphibians, had efficient limbs for crawling on land, an improved olfactory sense associated with a lengthened snout and a relatively advanced ear structure for picking up airborne sounds. Despite these features, *Ichthyostega*, which lived about 350 MYA, was still quite fishlike in overall appearance and may have spent much of its life in water.

was a lobed fin, rather than the toes of an amphibian. Ecologically, the 3-m long *Tiktaalik* was probably also intermediate between fish and amphibians, spending most of its time in the water, but capable of hauling itself out onto land to capture food or escape predators.

### The rise and fall of amphibians

By moving onto land, amphibians were able to utilize many resources and to access many habitats. Amphibians first became common during the Carboniferous period (360 to 280 MYA). Fourteen families of amphibians are known from the early Carboniferous, nearly all of them aquatic or semiaquatic, like *Ichthyostega* (see figure 35.15). By the late Carboniferous, much of North America was covered by low-lying tropical swamplands, and 34 families of amphibians thrived in this wet terrestrial environment, sharing it with pelycosaurs and other early reptiles.

In the early Permian period that followed (280 to 248 MYA), a remarkable change occurred among amphibians—they began to leave the marshes for dry uplands. Many of these terrestrial amphibians had bony plates and armor covering their bodies and grew to be very large, some as big as a pony. Both their large size and the complete covering of their bodies indicate that these amphibians did not use the skin respiratory system of present-day amphibians, but rather had an impermeable leathery skin to prevent water loss. Consequently, they must have relied entirely on their lungs for respiration. By the mid-Permian period, there were 40 families of amphibians. Only 25% of them were still semiaquatic like *Ichthyostega;* 60% of the amphibians were fully terrestrial, and 15% were semiterrestrial. This was the peak of amphibian success, sometimes called the Age of Amphibians.

By the end of the Permian period, reptiles had evolved from amphibians. One group, therapsids, had become common and ousted the amphibians from their newly acquired niche on land. Following the mass extinction event at the end of the Permian, therapsids were the dominant land vertebrate, and most amphibians were aquatic. This trend continued in the following Triassic period (248 to 213 MYA), which saw the virtual extinction of amphibians from land.

## Modern amphibians belong to three groups

All of today's amphibians descended from the three families of amphibians that survived the Age of the Dinosaurs. During the Tertiary period (65 to 2 MYA), these moist-skinned amphibians accomplished a highly successful invasion of wet habitats all over the world, and today there are over 5600 species of amphibians in 37 different families, comprising the orders Anura, Caudata, and Apoda.

### Order Anura: Frogs and toads

Frogs and toads, amphibians ~~without~~ tails, live in a variety of environments, from deserts and mountains to ponds and puddles (figure 35.16*a*). Frogs have smooth, moist skin, a broad body, and long hind legs that make them excellent jumpers.

a.

b.

c.

**Figure 35.16 Class Amphibia.** *a.* Red-eyed tree frog, *Agalychnis callidryas* (order Anura). *b.* An adult tiger salamander, *Ambystoma tigrinum* (order Caudata). *c.* A caecilian, *Caecilia tentaculata* (order Apoda).

Most frogs live in or near water and go through an aquatic tadpole stage before metamorphosing into frogs; however, some tropical species that don't live near water bypass this stage and hatch out as little froglets.

Unlike frogs, toads have a dry, bumpy skin and short legs, and are well adapted to dry environments. Toads do not form a monophyletic group; that is, all toads are not more closely related to each other than they are to some other frogs. Rather, the term *toad* is applied to those anurans that have adapted to dry environments by evolving a suite of adaptive characteristics; this convergent evolution has occurred many times among distantly related anurans.

Most frogs and toads return to water to reproduce, laying their eggs directly in water. Their eggs lack watertight external membranes and would dry out quickly on land. Eggs are fertilized externally and hatch into swimming larval forms called tadpoles. Tadpoles live in the water, where they generally feed on algae. After considerable growth, the body of the tadpole gradually undergoes metamorphosis into that of an adult frog.

### Order Caudata: Salamanders

Salamanders have elongated bodies, long tails, and smooth, moist skin (figure 35.16*b*). They typically range in length from a few inches to a foot, although giant Asiatic salamanders of the genus *Andrias* are as much as 1.5 m long and weigh up to 33 kg. Most salamanders live in moist places, such as under stones or logs, or among the leaves of tropical plants. Some salamanders live entirely in water.

Salamanders lay their eggs in water or in moist places. Most species practice a type of internal fertilization in which the female picks up sperm packets deposited by the male. Like anurans, many salamanders go through a larval stage before metamorphosing into adults. However, unlike anurans, in which the tadpole is strikingly different from the adult frog, larval salamanders are quite similar to adults, although most live in water and have external gills and gill slits that disappear at metamorphosis.

### Order Apoda: Caecilians

Caecilians, members of the order Apoda (also called Gymnophiona), are a highly specialized group of tropical burrowing amphibians (figure 35.16*c*). These legless, wormlike creatures average about 30 cm long, but can be up to 1.3 m long. They have very small eyes and are often blind. They resemble worms but have jaws with teeth. They eat worms and other soil invertebrates. Fertilization is internal.

#### Learning Outcomes Review 35.5

Amphibians, which includes frogs and toads, salamanders, and caecilians, are generally characterized by legs, lungs, cutaneous respiration, and a more complex and divided circulatory system. All of these developed as adaptations to life on land. Most species rely on a water habitat for reproduction. Although some early forms reached the size of a pony, modern amphibians are generally quite small.

■ *What challenges did amphibians overcome to make the transition to living on land?*

## 35.6 Reptiles

### Learning Outcomes

1. **Describe the characteristics and major groups of reptiles.**
2. **Distinguish between synapsids and diapsids.**
3. **Explain the significance of the evolution of the amniotic egg.**

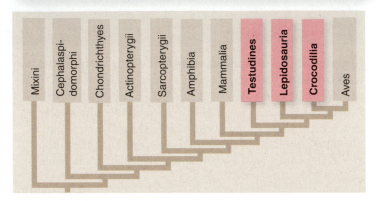

If we think of amphibians as a first draft of a manuscript about survival on land, then reptiles are the finished book. For each of the five key challenges of living on land, reptiles improved on the innovations of amphibians. The arrangement of legs evolved to support the body's weight more effectively, allowing reptile bodies to be bigger and to run. Lungs and heart became more efficient. The skin was covered with dry plates or scales to minimize water loss, and watertight coverings evolved for eggs.

Over 7000 species of reptiles (class Reptilia) now live on Earth (table 35.3). They are a highly successful group in today's world; there are more living species of snakes and lizards than there are of mammals.

### Reptiles exhibit three key characteristics

All living reptiles share certain fundamental characteristics, features they retain from the time when they replaced amphibians as the dominant terrestrial vertebrates. Among the most important are:

1. **Amniotic eggs.** Amphibians' eggs must be laid in water or a moist setting to avoid drying out. Most reptiles lay watertight eggs that contain a food source (the yolk) and a series of four membranes: the yolk sac, the amnion, the allantois, and the chorion (figure 35.17). Each membrane plays a role in making the egg an independent life-support system. All modern reptiles, as well as birds and mammals, show exactly this same pattern of membranes within the egg. These three classes are called **amniotes.**

   The outermost membrane of the egg is the **chorion,** which lies just beneath the porous shell. It allows exchange of respiratory gases but retains water. The **amnion** encases the developing embryo within a fluid-filled cavity. The **yolk sac** provides food from the yolk for the embryo via blood vessels connecting to the embryo's gut. The **allantois** surrounds a cavity into which waste products from the embryo are excreted.

| Order | Typical Examples | | Key Characteristics | Approximate Number of Living Species |
|---|---|---|---|---|
| **TABLE 35.3** | **Major Orders of Reptiles** | | | |
| Squamata, suborder Sauria | Lizards | | Limbs set at right angles to body; anus is in transverse (sideways) slit; most are terrestrial | 3800 |
| Squamata, suborder Serpentes | Snakes | | No legs; move by slithering; scaly skin is shed periodically; most are terrestrial | 3000 |
| Rhynchocephalia | Tuataras | | Sole survivors of a once successful group that largely disappeared before dinosaurs; fused, wedgelike, socketless teeth; primitive third eye under skin of forehead | 2 |
| Chelonia | Turtles, tortoises, sea turtles | | Armored reptiles with shell of bony plates to which vertebrae and ribs are fused; sharp, horny beak without teeth | 250 |
| Crocodylia | Crocodiles, alligators | | Advanced reptiles with four-chambered heart and socketed teeth; anus is a longitudinal (lengthwise) slit; closest living relatives to birds | 25 |
| Ornithischia | Stegosaur | | Dinosaurs with two pelvic bones facing backward, like a bird's pelvis; herbivores; legs under body | Extinct |
| Saurischia | Tyrannosaur | | Dinosaurs with one pelvic bone facing forward, the other back, like a lizard's pelvis; both plant- and flesh-eaters; legs under body; birds evolved from Saurischian dinosaurs. | Extinct |
| Pterosauria | Pterosaur | | Flying reptiles; wings were made of skin stretched between fourth fingers and body; wingspans of early forms typically 60 cm, later forms nearly 8 m | Extinct |
| Plesiosaura | Plesiosaur | | Barrel-shaped marine reptiles with sharp teeth and large, paddle-shaped fins; some had snakelike necks twice as long as their bodies | Extinct |
| Ichthyosauria | Ichthyosaur | | Streamlined marine reptiles with many body similarities to sharks and modern fishes | Extinct |

2. **Dry skin.** Most living amphibians have moist skin and must remain in moist places to avoid drying out. Reptiles have dry, watertight skin. A layer of scales covers their bodies, preventing water loss. These scales develop as surface cells fill with keratin, the same protein that forms claws, fingernails, hair, and bird feathers.

3. **Thoracic breathing.** Amphibians breathe by squeezing their throat to pump air into their lungs; this limits their breathing capacity to the volume of their mouths. Reptiles developed pulmonary breathing, expanding and contracting the rib cage to suck air into the lungs and then force it out. The capacity of this system is limited only by the volume of the lungs.

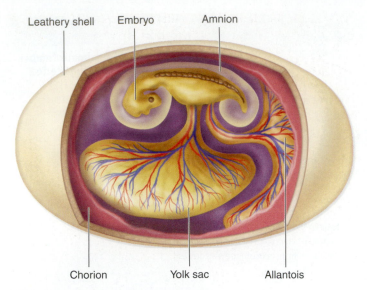

Leathery shell    Embryo    Amnion

Chorion    Yolk sac    Allantois

**Figure 35.17  The watertight egg.**  The amniotic egg is perhaps the most important feature that allows reptiles to live in a wide variety of terrestrial habitats.

## Reptiles dominated the Earth for 250 million years

During the 250 million years that reptiles were the dominant large terrestrial vertebrates, a series of different reptile groups appeared and then disappeared.

### Synapsids

An important feature of reptile classification is the presence and number of openings behind the eyes (figure 35.18). Reptiles' jaw muscles were anchored to these holes, which allowed them to bite more powerfully. The first group to rise to dominance were the **synapsids,** whose skulls had a pair of temporal holes behind the openings for the eyes.

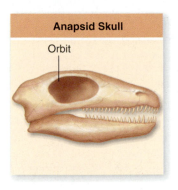

**Anapsid Skull**

Orbit

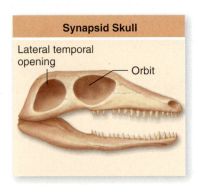

**Synapsid Skull**

Lateral temporal opening

Orbit

**Figure 35.18  Skulls of reptile groups.**  Reptile groups are distinguished by the number of holes on the side of the skull behind the eye orbit: 0 (anapsids), 1 (synapsids), or 2 (diapsids). Turtles are the only living anapsids, although several extinct groups also had this condition.

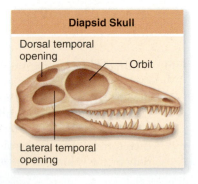

**Diapsid Skull**

Dorsal temporal opening

Orbit

Lateral temporal opening

**Figure 35.19  A pelycosaur.**  *Dimetrodon*, a carnivorous pelycosaur, had a dorsal sail that is thought to have been used to regulate body temperature by dissipating body heat or gaining it by basking.

Pelycosaurs, an important group of early synapsids, were dominant for 50 million years and made up 70% of all land vertebrates; some species weighed as much as 200 kg. With long, sharp, "steak knife" teeth, these pelycosaurs were the first land vertebrates to kill beasts their own size (figure 35.19).

About 250 MYA, pelycosaurs were replaced by another type of synapsid, the therapsids (figure 35.20). Some evidence indicates that they may have been endotherms, able to produce heat internally, and perhaps even possessed hair. This would have permitted therapsids to be far more active than other vertebrates of that time, when winters were cold and long.

For 20 million years, therapsids (also called "mammal-like reptiles") were the dominant land vertebrate, until they were largely replaced 230 MYA by another group of reptiles, the diapsids. Most therapsids became extinct 170 MYA, but one group survived and has living descendants today—the mammals.

**Figure 35.20  A therapsid.**  This small, weasel-like cynodont therapsid, *Megazostrodon*, may have had fur. Living in the late Triassic period, this therapsid is so similar to modern mammals that some paleontologists consider it the first mammal.

**Figure 35.21 An early archosaur.** *Euparkeria* had rows of bony plates along the sides of the backbone, as seen in modern crocodiles and alligators.

## Archosaurs

**Diapsids** have skulls with two pairs of temporal holes, and like amphibians and early reptiles, they were ectotherms. A variety of different diapsids occurred in the Triassic period (213 to 248 MYA), but one group, the archosaurs, were of particular evolutionary significance because they gave rise to crocodiles, pterosaurs, dinosaurs, and birds (figure 35.21).

Among the early archosaurs were the largest animals the world had seen, up to that point, and the first land vertebrates to be bipedal—to stand and walk on two feet. By the end of the Triassic period, however, one archosaur group rose to prominence: the dinosaurs.

Dinosaurs evolved about 220 MYA. Unlike previous bipedal diapsids, their legs were positioned directly underneath their bodies (figure 35.22). This design placed the weight of the body directly over the legs, which allowed dinosaurs to run with great speed and agility. Subsequently, a number of types of dinosaur evolved enormous size and reverted to a four-legged

**Figure 35.22 Mounted skeleton of *Afrovenator*.** This bipedal carnivore was about 30 feet long and lived in Africa about 130 MYA.

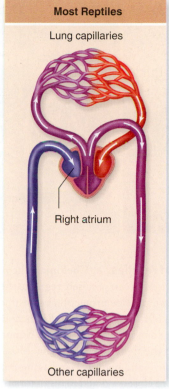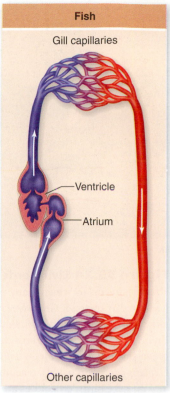

| Most Reptiles | Fish |
|---|---|
| Lung capillaries | Gill capillaries |

*a.*                          *b.*

**Figure 35.23 A comparison of reptile and fish circulation.** *a.* In most reptiles, oxygenated blood (red) is repumped after leaving the lungs, and circulation to the rest of the body remains vigorous. *b.* The blood in fishes flows from the gills directly to the rest of the body, resulting in slower circulation.

posture to support their massive weight. Other types—the therapods—became the most fearsome predators the earth has ever seen, and one theropod line evolved to become birds. Dinosaurs went on to become the most successful of all land vertebrates, dominating for more than 150 million years. All dinosaurs, except their bird descendants, became extinct rather abruptly 65 MYA, apparently as a result of an asteroid's impact.

### Important characteristics of modern reptiles

As you might imagine from the structure of the amniotic egg, reptiles and other amniotes do not practice external fertilization as most amphibians do. Sperm would be unable to penetrate the membrane barriers protecting the egg. Instead, the male places sperm inside the female, where sperm fertilizes the egg before the protective membranes are formed. This is called internal fertilization.

The circulatory system of reptiles is an improvement over that of fish and amphibians, providing oxygen to the body more efficiently (figure 35.23; see chapter 50). The improvement is achieved by extending the septum within the heart from the atrium partway across the ventricle. This septum creates a partial wall that tends to lessen mixing of oxygen-poor blood with oxygen-rich blood within the ventricle. In crocodiles, the septum completely divides the ventricle, creating a four-chambered heart, just as it does in birds and mammals (and probably did in dinosaurs).

| Order Chelonia | Order Rhynchocephalia |

  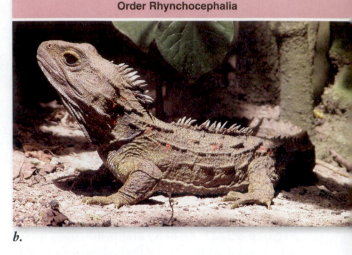

*a.*      *b.*

**Figure 35.24 Living orders of reptiles**. *a.* **Chelonia.** The red-bellied turtle, *Pseudemys rubriventris* (left) is shown basking, an effective means by which many ectotherms can precisely regulate their body temperature. The domed shells of tortoises, such as this Sri Lankan star tortoise, *Geochelone elegans*, provide protection against predators for these entirely terrestrial chelonians. *b.* **Tuatara (*Sphenodon punctatus*).** The sole living members of the ancient group Rhynchocephalia. Although they look like lizards, the common ancestor of rhynchocephalians and lizards diverged more than 250 MYA. *c.* **Squamata.** A collared lizard, *Crotaphytus collaris*, is shown left, and a smooth green snake, *Liochlorophis vernalis*, on the right. *d.* **Crocodylia.** Most crocodilians, such as the crocodile, *Crocodylus acutus*, and the gharial, *Gavialis gangeticus* (right), resemble birds and mammals in having four-chambered hearts; all other living reptiles have three-chambered hearts. Like birds, crocodiles are more closely related to dinosaurs than to any of the other living reptiles.

All living reptiles are **ectothermic**, obtaining their heat from external sources. In contrast, **endothermic** animals are able to generate their heat internally (see chapter 43). Although they are ectothermic, that does not mean that reptiles cannot control their body temperature. Many species are able to precisely regulate their temperature by moving in and out of sunlight. In this way, some desert lizards can keep their bodies at a constant temperature throughout the course of an entire day. Of course, on cloudy days, or for species that live in shaded habitats, such thermoregulation is not possible, and in these cases, body temperature is the same as the temperature of the surrounding environment.

## Modern reptiles belong to four groups

The four surviving orders of reptiles contain about 7000 species. Reptiles occur worldwide except in the coldest regions, where it is impossible for ectotherms to survive. Reptiles are among the most numerous and diverse of terrestrial vertebrates.

### Order Chelonia: Turtles and tortoises

The order Chelonia (figure 35.24*a*) consists of about 250 species of turtles (most of which are aquatic) and tortoises (which are terrestrial). Turtles and tortoises lack teeth but have sharp beaks. They differ from all other reptiles because their bodies are encased within a protective shell. Many of them can pull their head and legs into the shell as well, for total protection from predators.

The shell consists of two basic parts. The carapace is the dorsal covering, and the plastron is the ventral portion. In a fundamental commitment to this shell architecture, the vertebrae and ribs of most turtle and tortoise species are fused to the inside of the carapace. All of the support for muscle attachment comes from the shell.

Whereas most tortoises have a dome-shaped shell into which they can retract their head and limbs, water-dwelling turtles have a streamlined, disc-shaped shell that permits rapid turning in water. Freshwater turtles have webbed toes; in marine turtles, the forelimbs have evolved into flippers.

Although marine turtles spend their lives at sea, they must return to land to lay their eggs. Many species migrate long distances to do this. Atlantic green turtles (*Chelonia mydas*) migrate from their feeding grounds off the coast of Brazil to Ascension Island in the middle of the South Atlantic—a distance of more than 2000 km—to lay their eggs on the same beaches where they themselves hatched.

### Order Rhynchocephalia: Tuataras

Today, the order Rhynchocephalia contains only two species of tuataras, large, lizard-like animals about half a meter long (figure 35.24*b*). The only place in the world where these endangered species are found is a cluster of small islands off the coast of New Zealand. The limited diversity of modern rhynchocephalians belies their rich evolutionary past: In the Triassic period, rhynchocephalians experienced a great adaptive radiation, producing many species that differed greatly in size and habitat.

An unusual feature of the tuatara (and some lizards) is the inconspicuous "third eye" on the top of its head, called a parietal eye. Concealed under a thin layer of scales, the eye has a lens and a retina and is connected by nerves to the brain. Why have an eye, if it is covered up? The parietal eye may function to alert the tuatara when it has been exposed to too much sunlight, protecting it against overheating. Unlike most reptiles, tuataras are most active at low temperatures. They burrow during the day and feed at night on insects, worms, and other small animals.

Rhynchocephalians are the closest relatives of snakes and lizards, with whom they form the group Lepidosauria.

| Order Squamata | Order Crocodylia |
|---|---|

c.      d.

### Order Squamata: Lizards and snakes

The order Squamata (figure 35.24c) includes 3800 species of lizards and about 3000 species of snakes. A distinguishing characteristic of this order is the presence of paired copulatory organs in the male. In addition, changes to the morphology of the head and jaws allow greater strength and mobility. Most lizards and snakes are carnivores, preying on insects and small animals, and these improvements in jaw design have made a major contribution to their evolutionary success.

Snakes, which evolved from a lizard ancestor, are characterized by the lack of limbs, movable eyelids, and external ears, as well as a great number of vertebrae (sometimes more than 300). Limblessness has actually evolved more than a dozen times in lizards; snakes are simply the most extreme case of this evolutionary trend.

Common lizards include iguanas, chameleons, geckos, and anoles. Most are small, measuring less than a foot in length. The largest lizards belong to the monitor family. The largest of all monitor lizards is the Komodo dragon of Indonesia, which reaches 3 m in length and can weigh more than 100 kg. Snakes also vary in length from only a few inches to more than 10 m.

Many lizards and snakes rely on agility and speed to catch prey and elude predators. Only two species of lizard are venomous, the Gila monster of the southwestern United States and the beaded lizard of western Mexico. Similarly, most species of snakes are nonvenomous. Of the 13 families of snakes, only 4 contain venomous species: the elapids (cobras, kraits, and coral snakes); the sea snakes; the vipers (adders, bushmasters, rattlesnakes, water moccasins, and copperheads); and some colubrids (African boomslang and twig snake).

Many lizards, including anoles, skinks, and geckos, have the ability to lose their tails and then regenerate a new one. This ability allows these lizards to escape from predators.

### Order Crocodylia: Crocodiles and alligators

The order Crocodylia is composed of 25 species of large, primarily aquatic reptiles (figure 35.24d). In addition to crocodiles and alligators, the order includes two less familiar animals: the caimans and the gavials. Although all crocodilians are fairly similar in appearance today, much greater diversity existed in the past, including species that were entirely terrestrial and others that achieved a total length in excess of 50 feet.

Crocodiles are largely nocturnal animals that live in or near water in tropical or subtropical regions of Africa, Asia, and the Americas. The American crocodile (*Crocodylus acutus*) is found in southern Florida, Cuba, and throughout tropical Central America. Nile crocodiles (*Crocodylus niloticus*) and estuarine crocodiles (*Crocodylus porosus*) can grow to enormous size and are responsible for many human fatalities each year.

There are only two species of alligators: one living in the southern United States (*Alligator mississippiensis*) and the other a rare endangered species living in China (*Alligator sinensis*). Caimans, which resemble alligators, are native to Central America. Gharials, or gavials, are a group of fish-eating crocodilians with long, slender snouts that live only in India and Burma.

All crocodilians are carnivores. They generally hunt by stealth, waiting in ambush for prey, and then attacking ferociously. Their bodies are well adapted for this form of hunting with eyes on top of their heads and their nostrils on top of their snouts, so they can see and breathe while lying quietly submerged in water. They have enormous mouths, studded with sharp teeth, and very strong necks. A valve in the back of the mouth prevents water from entering the air passage when a crocodilian feeds underwater.

In many ways, crocodiles resemble birds far more than they do other living reptiles. For example, crocodiles build nests and care for their young (traits they share with at least some dinosaurs), and they have a four-chambered heart, as birds do. Why are crocodiles more similar to birds than to other living reptiles? Most biologists agree that birds are in fact the direct descendants of dinosaurs. Both crocodiles and birds are more closely related to dinosaurs, and to each other, than they are to lizards and snakes.

---

### Learning Outcomes Review 35.6

Reptiles have a hard, scaly skin that minimizes water loss, thoracic breathing, and an enclosed, amniotic egg that does not need to be laid in water. Synapsids had a single hole in the skull behind the eyes, and included ancestors of mammals; diapsids had two holes and are ancestors of modern reptiles and birds. The four living orders of reptiles include the turtles and tortoises, tuataras, lizards and snakes, and crocodiles.

■ *How do reptile eggs differ from those of amphibians?*

## 35.7 Birds

### Learning Outcomes

1. *Name the key characteristics of birds.*
2. *Explain why some consider birds to be one type of reptile.*

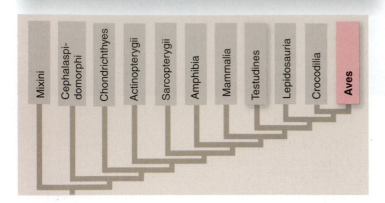

The success of birds lies in the development of a structure unique in the animal world—the feather. Developed from reptilian scales, feathers are the ideal adaptation for flight, serving as lightweight airfoils that are easily replaced if damaged (unlike the vulnerable skin wings of bats and the extinct pterosaurs). Today, birds (class **Aves**) are the most diverse of all terrestrial vertebrates, with 28 orders containing a total of 166 families and about 8600 species (table 35.4).

## Key characteristics of birds are feathers and a lightweight skeleton

Modern birds lack teeth and have only vestigial tails, but they still retain many reptilian characteristics. For instance, birds lay amniotic eggs. Also, reptilian scales are present on the feet and lower legs of birds. Two primary characteristics distinguish birds from living reptiles:

1. **Feathers.** Feathers are modified reptilian scales made of keratin, just like hair and scales. Feathers serve two functions: providing lift for flight and conserving heat. The structure of feathers combines maximum flexibility and strength with minimum weight (figure 35.25).

   Feathers develop from tiny pits in the skin called follicles. In a typical flight feather, a shaft emerges from the follicle, and pairs of vanes develop from its opposite sides. At maturity, each vane has many branches called barbs. The barbs, in turn, have many projections called barbules that are equipped with microscopic hooks. These hooks link the barbs to one another, giving the feather a continuous surface and a sturdy but flexible shape.

   Like scales, feathers can be replaced. Among living animals, feathers are unique to birds. Recent fossil finds suggest that some dinosaurs may have had feathers.

2. **Flight skeleton.** The bones of birds are thin and hollow. Many of the bones are fused, making the bird skeleton more rigid than a reptilian skeleton. The fused sections of

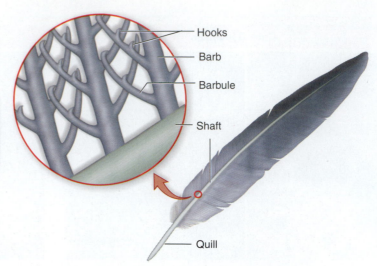

**Figure 35.25 A feather.** The enlargement shows how the secondary branches and barbs of the vanes are linked together by microscopic barbules.

backbone and of the shoulder and hip girdles form a sturdy frame that anchors muscles during flight. The power for active flight comes from large breast muscles that can make up 30% of a bird's total body weight. They stretch down from the wing and attach to the breastbone, which is greatly enlarged and bears a prominent keel for muscle attachment. Breast muscles also attach to the fused collarbones that form the so-called wishbone. No other living vertebrates have a fused collarbone or a keeled breastbone.

### Birds arose about 150 MYA

A 150-million-year-old fossil of the first known bird, *Archaeopteryx* (see figures 21.11 and 35.26) was found in 1862 in a limestone quarry in Bavaria, the impression of its feathers stamped clearly into the rocks. The skeleton of *Archaeopteryx* shares many features with small theropod dinosaurs. About the size of a crow, *Archeopteryx* had a skull with teeth, and very few of its bones were fused to one another. Its bones are thought to have been solid, not hollow like a bird's. Also, it had a long, reptilian tail and no enlarged breastbone such as modern birds use to anchor flight muscles. Finally, the skeletal structure of the forelimbs were nearly identical to those of theropods.

Because of its many dinosaur features, several *Archaeopteryx* fossils were originally classified as *Compsognathus*, a small theropod dinosaur of similar size—until feathers were discovered on

**Figure 35.26 *Archaeopteryx*.** Closely related to its ancestors among the bipedal dinosaurs, the crow-sized *Archaeopteryx* lived in the forests of central Europe 150 MYA. The true feather colors of *Archaeopteryx* are not known.

TABLE 35.4 **Major Orders of Birds**

| Order | Typical Examples | Key Characteristics | Approximate Number of Living Species |
|---|---|---|---|
| Passeriformes | Crows, mockingbirds, robins, sparrows, starlings, warblers | *Songbirds*<br>Well-developed vocal organs; perching feet; dependent young | 5276 (largest of all bird orders; contains over 60% of all species) |
| Apodiformes | Hummingbirds, swifts | *Fast fliers*<br>Short legs; small bodies; rapid wing beat | 428 |
| Piciformes | Honeyguides, toucans, woodpeckers | *Woodpeckers or toucans*<br>Grasping feet; chisel-like, sharp bills can break down wood | 383 |
| Psittaciformes | Cockatoos, parrots | *Parrots*<br>Large, powerful bills for crushing seeds; well-developed vocal organs | 340 |
| Charadriiformes | Auks, gulls, plovers, sandpipers, terns | *Shorebirds*<br>Long, stiltlike legs; slender, probing bills | 331 |
| Columbiformes | Doves, pigeons | *Pigeons*<br>Perching feet; rounded, stout bodies | 303 |
| Falconiformes | Eagles, falcons, hawks | *Diurnal birds of prey*<br>Carnivorous; keen vision; sharp, pointed beaks for tearing flesh; active during the day | 288 |
| Galliformes | Chickens, grouse, pheasants, quail | *Gamebirds*<br>Often limited flying ability; rounded bodies | 268 |
| Gruiformes | Bitterns, coots, cranes, rails | *Marsh birds*<br>Long, stiltlike legs; diverse body shapes; marsh-dwellers | 209 |
| Anseriformes | Ducks, geese, swans | *Waterfowl*<br>Webbed toes; broad bill with filtering ridges | 150 |
| Strigiformes | Barn owls, screech owls | *Owls*<br>Nocturnal birds of prey; strong beaks; powerful feet | 146 |
| Ciconiiformes | Herons, ibises, storks | *Waders*<br>Long-legged; large bodies | 114 |
| Procellariformes | Albatrosses, petrels | *Seabirds*<br>Tube-shaped bills; capable of flying for long periods of time | 104 |
| Sphenisciformes | Emperor penguins, crested penguins | *Penguins*<br>Marine; modified wings for swimming; flightless; found only in southern hemisphere; thick coats of insulating feathers | 18 |
| Dinornithiformes | Kiwis | *Kiwis*<br>Flightless; small; confined to New Zealand | 2 |
| Struthioniformes | Ostriches | *Ostriches*<br>Powerful running legs; flightless; only two toes; very large | 1 |

**Figure 35.27**
**The evolutionary path to the birds.** Almost all paleontologists now accept the theory that birds are the direct descendants of theropod dinosaurs.

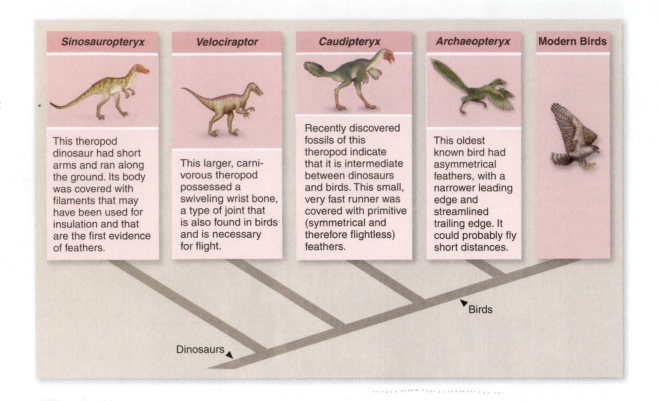

**Sinosauropteryx**
This theropod dinosaur had short arms and ran along the ground. Its body was covered with filaments that may have been used for insulation and that are the first evidence of feathers.

**Velociraptor**
This larger, carnivorous theropod possessed a swiveling wrist bone, a type of joint that is also found in birds and is necessary for flight.

**Caudipteryx**
Recently discovered fossils of this theropod indicate that it is intermediate between dinosaurs and birds. This small, very fast runner was covered with primitive (symmetrical and therefore flightless) feathers.

**Archaeopteryx**
This oldest known bird had asymmetrical feathers, with a narrower leading edge and streamlined trailing edge. It could probably fly short distances.

**Modern Birds**

Dinosaurs

Birds

the fossils. What makes *Archaeopteryx* distinctly avian is the presence of feathers on its wings and tail.

The remarkable similarity of *Archaeopteryx* to *Compsognathus* has led almost all paleontologists to conclude that *Archaeopteryx* is the direct descendant of dinosaurs—indeed, that today's birds are "feathered dinosaurs." Some even speak flippantly of "carving the dinosaur" at Thanksgiving dinner. The recent discovery of fossils of a feathered dinosaur in China lends strong support to this inference. The dinosaur *Caudipteryx*, for example, is clearly intermediate between *Archaeopteryx* and dinosaurs, having large feathers on its tail and arms but also many features of dinosaurs like *Velociraptor* (figure 35.27). Because the arms of *Caudipteryx* were too short to use as wings, feathers probably didn't evolve for flight, but instead served as insulation, much as fur does for mammals.

Flight is an ability certain kinds of dinosaurs achieved as they evolved longer arms. We call these dinosaurs birds. Despite their close affinity to dinosaurs, birds exhibit three evolutionary novelties: feathers, hollow bones, and physiological mechanisms such as superefficient lungs that permit sustained, powered flight.

By the early Cretaceous period, only a few million years after *Archaeopteryx* lived, a diverse array of birds had evolved, with many of the features of modern birds. Fossils in Mongolia, Spain, and China discovered within the last few years reveal a diverse collection of toothed birds with the hollow bones and breastbones necessary for sustained flight (figure 35.28). Other fossils reveal highly specialized, flightless diving birds. These diverse birds shared the skies with pterosaurs for 70 million years until the flying reptiles went extinct at the end of the Cretaceous.

Because the impression of feathers is rarely fossilized and modern birds have hollow, delicate bones, the fossil record of birds is incomplete. Relationships among the 166 families of modern birds are mostly inferred from studies of the anatomy and degree of DNA similarity among living birds.

**Figure 35.28 A fossil bird from the early cretaceous.**
*Confuciornis* had long tail feathers. Some fossil specimens of this species lack the long tail feathers, suggesting that this trait was present in only one sex, as in some modern birds.

## Modern birds are diverse but share several characteristics

The most ancient living birds appear to be the flightless birds, such as the ostrich. Ducks, geese, and other waterfowl evolved next, in the early Cretaceous, followed by a diverse group of woodpeckers, parrots, swifts, and owls. The largest of the bird orders, Passeriformes, evolved in the mid-Cretaceous and comprise 60% of species alive today. Overall, there are 28 orders of birds, the largest consisting of over 5000 species (figure 35.29).

You can tell a great deal about the habits and food of a bird by examining its beak and feet. For instance, carnivorous birds such as owls have curved talons for seizing prey and sharp beaks for tearing apart their meal. The beaks of ducks are flat for shoveling through mud, and the beaks of finches are short, thick seed-crushers.

Many adaptations enabled birds to cope with the heavy energy demands of flight, including respiratory and circulatory adaptations and endothermy.

### Efficient respiration

Flight muscles consume an enormous amount of oxygen during active flight. The reptilian lung has a limited internal surface area, not nearly enough to absorb all the oxygen needed. Mammalian lungs have a greater surface area, but bird lungs satisfy this challenge with a radical redesign.

When a bird inhales, the air goes past the lungs to a series of air sacs located near and within the hollow bones of the back; from there, the air travels to the lungs and then to a set of anterior air sacs before being exhaled. Because air passes all the way through the lungs in a single direction, gas exchange is highly efficient. Respiration in birds is described in more detail in chapter 49.

### Efficient circulation

The revved-up metabolism needed to power active flight also requires very efficient blood circulation, so that the oxygen cap-tured by the lungs can be delivered to the flight muscles quickly. In the heart of most living reptiles, oxygen-rich blood coming from the lungs mixes with oxygen-poor blood returning from the body because the wall dividing the ventricle into two chambers is not complete. In birds, the wall dividing the ventricle is complete, and the two blood circulations do not mix—so flight muscles receive fully oxygenated blood (see chapter 50).

In comparison with reptiles and most other vertebrates, birds have a rapid heartbeat. A hummingbird's heart beats about 600 times a minute, and an active chickadee's heart beats 1000 times a minute. In contrast, the heart of the large, flightless ostrich averages 70 beats per minute—the same rate as the human heart.

### Endothermy

Birds, like mammals, are endothermic (an example of convergent evolution). Many paleontologists believe the dinosaurs from which birds evolved were endothermic as well. Birds maintain body temperatures significantly higher than those of most mammals, ranging from 40° to 42°C (human body temperature is 37°C). Feathers provide excellent insulation, helping to conserve body heat.

The high temperatures maintained by endothermy permit metabolism in the bird's flight muscles to proceed at a rapid pace, to provide the ATP necessary to drive rapid muscle contraction.

---

### Learning Outcomes Review 35.7

Birds have the greatest diversity of species of all terrestrial vertebrates. *Archaeopteryx,* the oldest fossil bird, exhibited many traits shared with theropod dinosaurs. Key features of birds are feathers and a lightweight, hollow skeleton; additional features include auxiliary air sacs and a four-chambered heart.

■ **What traits do birds share with reptiles?**

---

**Order: Passeriformes**

*a.*  *b.*  *c.*  *d.*

**Figure 35.29 Diversity of *Passeriformes,* the largest order of birds.** *a.* Summer tanager, *Piranga rubra;* (b) Indigo bunting, *Passerina cyanea;* (c) Stellar's jay, *Cyanositta stelleri;* (d) Bobolink, *Dolichonyx oryzivorus.*

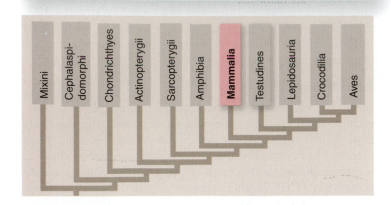

There are about 4500 living species of mammals (class Mammalia), fewer than the number of fishes, amphibians, reptiles or birds. Most large, land-dwelling vertebrates are mammals. When we look out over an African plain, we see the big mammals—the lions, zebras, gazelles, and antelope. But the typical mammal is not that large. Of the 4500 species of mammals, 3200 are rodents, bats, shrews, or moles.

## Mammals have hair, mammary glands, and other characteristics

Mammals are distinguished from all other classes of vertebrates by two fundamental characteristics—hair and mammary glands—and are marked by several other notable features:

1. **Hair.** All mammals have hair. Even apparently hairless whales and dolphins grow sensitive bristles on their snouts. The evolution of fur and the ability to regulate body temperature enabled mammals to invade colder climates that ectothermic reptiles do not inhabit. Mammals are endothermic animals, and typically maintain body temperatures higher than the temperature of their surroundings. The dense undercoat of many mammals reduces the amount of body heat that escapes.

   Another function of hair is camouflage. The coloration and pattern of a mammal's coat usually matches its background. A little brown mouse is practically invisible against the brown leaf litter of a forest floor, and the orange and black stripes of a Bengal tiger disappear against the orange-brown color of the tall grass in which it hunts. Hairs also function as sensory structures. The whiskers of cats and dogs are stiff hairs that are very sensitive to touch. Mammals that are active at night or live underground often rely on their whiskers to locate prey or to avoid colliding with objects. Finally, hair can serve as a defensive weapon. Porcupines and hedgehogs protect themselves with long, sharp, stiff hairs called quills.

Unlike feathers, which evolved from modified reptilian scales, mammalian hair is a completely different form of skin structure. An individual mammalian hair is a long, protein-rich filament that extends like a stiff thread from a bulblike foundation beneath the skin known as a hair follicle. The filament is composed mainly of dead cells filled with the fibrous protein keratin.

2. **Mammary glands.** All female mammals possess mammary glands that can secrete milk. Newborn mammals, born without teeth, suckle this milk as their primary food. Even baby whales are nursed by their mother's milk. Milk is a very high-calorie food (human milk has 750 kcal per liter), important because of the high energy needs of a rapidly growing newborn mammal. About 50% of the energy in the milk comes from fat.

3. **Endothermy.** As stated previously, mammals are endothermic, a crucial adaptation that has allowed them to be active at any time of the day or night and to colonize severe environments, from deserts to ice fields. Also, more efficient blood circulation provided by the four-chambered heart (see chapter 50) and more efficient respiration provided by the *diaphragm* (a special sheet of muscles below the rib cage that aids breathing; see chapter 49) make possible the higher metabolic rate on which endothermy depends.

4. **Placenta.** In most mammal species, females carry their developing young internally in a uterus, nourishing them through the placenta, and give birth to live young. The **placenta** is a specialized organ that brings the bloodstream of the fetus into close contact with the bloodstream of the mother (figure 35.30). Food, water, and oxygen can pass across from mother to child, and wastes can pass over to the mother's blood and be carried away.

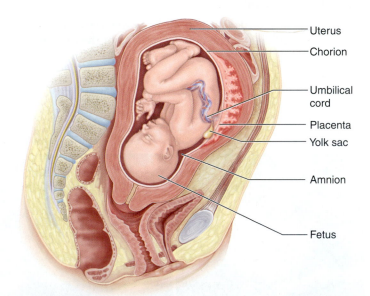

Uterus
Chorion
Umbilical cord
Placenta
Yolk sac
Amnion
Fetus

**Figure 35.30 The placenta.** The placenta is characteristic of the largest group of mammals, the placental mammals. It evolved from membranes in the amniotic egg. The umbilical cord evolved from the allantois. The chorion, or outermost part of the amniotic egg, forms most of the placenta itself. The placenta serves as the provisional lungs, intestine, and kidneys of the fetus, without ever mixing maternal and fetal blood.

In addition to these main characteristics, the mammalian lineage gave rise to several other adaptations in certain groups. These include specialized teeth, the ability of grazing animals to digest plants, hooves and horns made of keratin, and adaptations for flight in the bats.

### Specialized teeth

Mammals have different types of teeth that are highly specialized to match particular eating habits (figure 35.31). It is usually possible to determine a mammal's diet simply by examining its teeth. A dog's long canine teeth, for example, are well suited for biting and holding prey, and some of its premolar and molar teeth are triangular and sharp for ripping off chunks of flesh.

In contrast, large herbivores such as deer lack canine teeth; instead, deer clip off mouthfuls of plants with flat, chisel-like incisors on its lower jaw. The deer's molars are large and covered with ridges to effectively grind and break up tough plant tissues.

### Digestion of plants

Most mammals are herbivores, eating mostly or only plants. Cellulose forms the bulk of a plant's body and is a major source of food for mammalian herbivores. Mammals do not have the enzymes, however, that break the links between glucose molecules in cellulose. Herbivorous mammals rely on a mutualistic partnership with bacteria in their digestive tracts that have the necessary cellulose-splitting enzymes.

Mammals such as cows, buffalo, antelopes, goats, deer, and giraffes have huge, four-chambered fermentation vats derived from the esophagus and stomach. The first chamber is the largest and holds a dense population of cellulose-digesting bacteria. Chewed plant material passes into this chamber, where the bacteria attack the cellulose. The material is then digested further in the other three chambers.

Rodents, horses, rabbits, and elephants, by contrast, have relatively small stomachs, and instead digest plant material in their large intestine, like a termite. The bacteria that actually carry out the digestion of the cellulose live in a pouch called the cecum that branches from the end of the small intestine.

Even with these complex adaptations for digesting cellulose, a mouthful of plant is less nutritious than a mouthful of meat. Herbivores must consume large amounts of plant material to gain sufficient nutrition. An elephant eats 135 to 150 kg (300 to 330 pounds) of plant foods each day.

### Development of hooves and horns

Keratin, the protein of hair, is also the structural building material in claws, fingernails, and hooves. Hooves are specialized keratin pads on the toes of horses, cows, sheep, and antelopes. The pads are hard and horny, protecting the toe and cushioning it from impact.

The horns of cattle, sheep, and antelope are composed of a core of bone surrounded by a sheath of keratin. The bony core is attached to the skull, and the horn is not shed.

Deer antlers are made not of keratin, but of bone. Male deer grow and shed a set of antlers each year. While growing during the summer, antlers are covered by a thin layer of skin known as velvet.

### Flying mammals: Bats

Bats are the only mammals capable of powered flight (figure 35.32). Like the wings of birds and pterosaurs, bat wings are modified forelimbs. The bat wing is a leathery membrane of skin and muscle stretched over the bones of four fingers. The edges of the membrane attach to the side of the body and to the

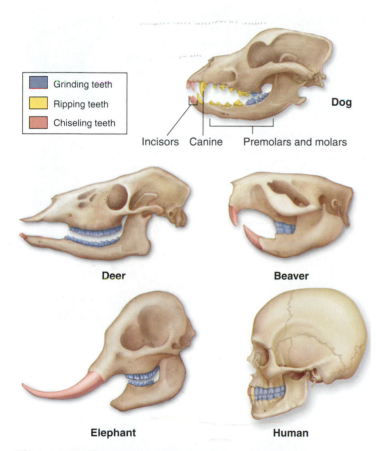

**Legend:**
- Grinding teeth
- Ripping teeth
- Chiseling teeth

Dog

Incisors  Canine  Premolars and molars

Deer

Beaver

Elephant

Human

**Figure 35.31 Mammals have different types of specialized teeth.** Carnivores, such as dogs, have canine teeth that are able to rip food; some of the premolars and molars in dogs are also ripping teeth. Herbivores, such as deer, have incisors to chisel off vegetation and molars designed to grind up the plant material. In the beaver, the chiseling incisors dominate. In the elephant, the incisors have become specialized weapons, and molars grind up vegetation. Humans are omnivores; we have all three types: grinding, ripping, and chiseling teeth.

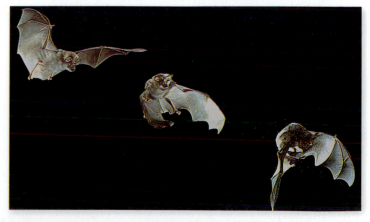

**Figure 35.32 Greater horseshoe bat, *Rhinolophus ferrumequinum.*** Bats are the only mammal capable of true flight.

hind leg. When resting, most bats prefer to hang upside down by their toe claws.

After rodents, bats are the second largest order of mammals. They have been a particularly successful group because many species have been able to utilize a food resource that most birds do not use—night-flying insects.

How do bats navigate in the dark? Late in the eighteenth century, the Italian biologist Lazzaro Spallanzani showed that a blinded bat could fly without crashing into things and still capture insects. Clearly another sense other than vision was being used by bats to navigate in the dark. When Spallanzani plugged the ears of a bat, it was unable to navigate and collided with objects. Spallanzani concluded that bats "hear" their way through the night world.

## Mammals diverged about 220 MYA

Mammals have been around since the time of the dinosaurs, about 220 MYA. Tiny, shrewlike creatures that lived in trees eating insects, the earliest mammals were only a minor element in a land that quickly came to be dominated by dinosaurs. Fossils reveal that these early mammals had large eye sockets, evidence that they may have been active at night. Early mammals also had a single lower jawbone. The fossil record shows a change in therapsids (the ancestors of mammals) from the reptile lower jaw, having several bones, to a jaw closer to the mammalian type. Two of the bones forming the therapsid jaw joint moved into the middle ear of mammals, linking with a bone already there to produce a three-bone structure that amplifies sound better than the reptilian ear.

### The age of mammals

At the end of the Cretaceous period, 65 MYA, the dinosaurs and numerous other land and marine animals became extinct, but mammals survived, possibly because of the insulation their fur provided. In the Tertiary period (lasting from 65 MYA to 2 MYA), mammals rapidly diversified, taking over many of the ecological roles once dominated by dinosaurs.

Mammals reached their maximum diversity late in the Tertiary period, about 15 MYA. At that time, tropical conditions existed over much of the world. During the last 15 million years, world climates have changed, and the area covered by tropical habitats has decreased, causing a decline in the total number of mammalian species (table 35.5).

## Modern mammals are placed into three groups.

For 155 million years, while the dinosaurs flourished, mammals were a minor group of small insectivores and herbivores. The most primitive mammals were members of the subclass Prototheria. Most prototherians were small and resembled modern shrews. All prototherians laid eggs, as did their synapsid ancestors. The only prototherians surviving today are the monotremes.

The other major mammalian group is the subclass **Theria**. Therians are viviparous (that is, their young are born alive). The two living therian groups are marsupials, or pouched mammals (including kangaroos, opossums, and koalas), and the placental mammals (dogs, cats, humans, horses, and most other mammals).

| TABLE 35.5 | Some Groups of Extinct Mammals |
|---|---|
| **Group** | **Description** |
| Cave bears | Numerous in the ice ages; this enormous bear had a largely vegetarian diet and slept through the winter in large groups. |
| Irish elk | Neither Irish nor an elk (it is a kind of deer), *Megaloceros* was the largest deer that ever lived, with horns spanning 12 feet. Seen in French cave paintings, they became extinct about 2500 years ago. |
| Mammoths | Although only two species of elephants survive today, the elephant family was far more diverse during the late Tertiary. Many were cold-adapted mammoths with long, shaggy fur. |
| Giant ground sloths | *Megatherium* was a giant, 20-foot ground sloth that weighed 3 tons and was as large as a modern elephant. |
| Sabertooth cats | The jaws of these large, lionlike cats opened an incredible 120° to allow the animal to drive its huge upper pair of saber teeth into prey. |

### Monotremes: Egg-laying mammals

The duck-billed platypus (*Ornithorhynchus anatinus*) and two species of echidna are the only living **monotremes** (figure 35.33a). Among living mammals, only monotremes lay shelled eggs. The structure of their shoulder and pelvis is more similar to that of the early reptiles than to any other living mammal. Also like reptiles, monotremes have a cloaca, a single opening through which feces, urine, and reproductive products leave the body.

**Monotremes**

*a.*

**Marsupials**

*b.*

**Placental Mammals**

*c.*

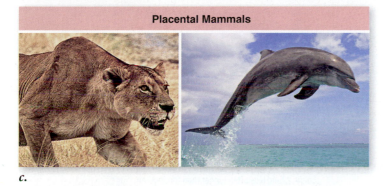

**Figure 35.33 Today's mammals.** *a.* Monotremes, the short-nosed echidna, *Tachyglossus aculeatus* (left), and the duck-billed platypus, *Ornithorhynchus anatinus* (right); *(b)* Marsupials, the red kangaroo, *Macropus rufus* (left) and the opossum, *Didelphis virginiana*, (right); *(c)* Placental mammals, the lion, *Panthera leo* (left) and the bottle-nosed dolphin, *Tursiops truncatus* (right).

Despite the retention of some reptilian features, monotremes have the diagnostic mammalian characters: a single bone on each side of the lower jaw, fur, and mammary glands. Young monotremes drink their mother's milk after they hatch from eggs. Females lack well-developed nipples; instead, the milk oozes onto the mother's fur, and the babies lap it off with their tongues.

The platypus, found only in Australia, lives much of its life in the water and is a good swimmer. It uses its bill much as a duck does, rooting in the mud for worms and other soft-bodied animals. Echidnas of Australia (*Tachyglossus aculeatus*, the short-nosed echidna) and New Guinea (*Zaglossus bruijni*, the long-nosed echidna) have very strong, sharp claws, which they use for burrowing and digging. The echidna probes with its snout for insects, especially ants and termites.

### Marsupials: Pouched mammals

The major difference between **marsupials** (figure 35.33*b*) and other mammals is their pattern of embryonic development. In marsupials, a fertilized egg is surrounded by chorion and amniotic membranes, but no shell forms around the egg as it does in monotremes. During most of its early development, the marsupial embryo is nourished by an abundant yolk within the egg. Shortly before birth, a short-lived placenta forms from the chorion membrane. Soon after, sometimes within eight days of fertilization, the embryonic marsupial is born. It emerges tiny and hairless, and crawls into the marsupial pouch, where it latches onto a mammary-gland nipple and continues its development.

Marsupials evolved shortly before placental mammals, about 125 MYA. Today, most species of marsupials live in Australia and South America, areas that have undergone long periods of geographic isolation. Marsupials in Australia and New Guinea have diversified to fill ecological positions occupied by placental mammals elsewhere in the world (see figure 21.18). The placental mammals in Australia and New Guinea today arrived relatively recently and include some introduced by humans. The only marsupial found in North America is the Virginia opossum (*Didelphis virginiana*), which has migrated north from Central America within the last three million years.

### Placental mammals

A placenta that nourishes the embryo throughout its entire development forms in the uterus of placental mammals (figure 35.33*c*). Most species of mammals living today, including humans, are in this group. Of the 19 orders of living mammals, 17 are placental mammals (although some scientists recognize four orders of marsupials, rather than one). Table 35.6 shows some of these orders. They are a very diverse group, ranging in size from 1.5-g pygmy shrews to 100,000-kg whales.

Early in the course of embryonic development, the placenta forms. Both fetal and maternal blood vessels are abundant in the placenta, and substances can be exchanged efficiently between the bloodstreams of mother and offspring (see figure 35.30). The fetal placenta is formed from the membranes of the chorion and allantois. In placental mammals, unlike in marsupials, the young undergo a considerable period of development before they are born.

---

#### Learning Outcomes Review 35.8

Mammals are the only animals with hair and mammary glands. Other mammalian specializations include endothermy, the placenta, a tooth design suited to diet, and specialized sensory systems. Today three subgroups of mammals are recognized: monotremes, which lay eggs; marsupials, which feed embryonic young in a marsupial pouch; and placental mammals, in which the placenta nourishes the embryo throughout its development.

■ *What features found in both mammals and birds are examples of convergent evolution?*

TABLE 35.6

## Major Orders of Placental Mammals

| Order | Typical Examples | Key Characteristics | Approximate Number of Living Species |
|---|---|---|---|
| Rodentia | Beavers, mice, porcupines, rats | *Small plant-eaters*<br>Chisel-like incisor teeth | 1814 |
| Chiroptera | Bats | *Flying mammals*<br>Primarily fruit- or insect-eaters; elongated fingers; thin wing membrane; mostly nocturnal; navigate by sonar | 986 |
| Insectivora | Moles, shrews | *Small, burrowing mammals*<br>Insect-eaters; the most primitive placental mammals; spend most of their time underground | 390 |
| Carnivora | Bears, cats, raccoons, weasels, dogs | *Carnivorous predators*<br>Teeth adapted for shearing flesh; no native families in Australia | 274 |
| Primates | Apes, humans, lemurs, monkeys | *Tree-dwellers*<br>Large brain size; binocular vision; opposable thumb; group that evolved from a line that branched off early from other mammals | 233 |
| Artiodactyla | Cattle, deer, giraffes, pigs | *Hoofed mammals with two or four toes*<br>Most species are herbivorous ruminants | 211 |
| Cetacea | Dolphins, porpoises, whales | *Fully marine mammals*<br>Streamlined bodies; front limbs modified into flippers; no hindlimbs; blowholes on top of head; no hair except on muzzle | 79 |
| Lagomorpha | Rabbits, hares, pika | *Rodentlike jumpers*<br>Four upper incisors (rather than the two seen in rodents); hind legs often longer than forelegs, an adaptation for jumping | 69 |
| Edentata | Anteaters, armadillos, sloths | *Toothless insect-eaters*<br>Many are toothless, but some have degenerate, peglike teeth | 30 |
| Perissodactyla | Horses, rhinoceroses, tapirs | *Hoofed mammals with odd number of toes*<br>Herbivorous teeth adapted for chewing | 17 |
| Proboscidea | Elephants | *Long-trunked herbivores*<br>Two upper incisors elongated as tusks; largest living land animal | 2 |

## 35.9 Evolution of the Primates

### Learning Outcomes

1. Describe the characteristics and major groups of primates.
2. List the distinguishing characteristics of hominids.
3. Explain the variations that form the basis for human races and why races do not reflect speciation.

**Primates** are the mammalian group that gave rise to our own species. Primates evolved two distinct features that allowed them to succeed as arboreal (tree-dwelling) insectivores.

1. **Grasping fingers and toes.** Unlike the clawed feet of tree shrews and squirrels, primates have grasping hands and feet that enable them to grip limbs, hang from branches, seize food, and in some primates, use tools. The first digit in many primates, namely the thumb, is opposable, and at least some, if not all, of the digits have nails.
2. **Binocular vision.** Unlike the eyes of shrews and squirrels, which sit on each side of the head, the eyes of primates are shifted forward to the front of the face. This produces overlapping binocular vision that lets the brain judge distance precisely—important to an animal moving through the trees and trying to grab or pick up food items.

Other mammals have binocular vision—for example, carnivorous predators—but only primates have both binocular vision and grasping hands, making them particularly well adapted to their arboreal environment.

### The anthropoid lineage led to the earliest humans

About 40 MYA, the earliest primates split into two groups: the prosimians and the anthropoids. The **prosimians** ("before monkeys") looked something like a cross between a squirrel and a cat and were common in North America, Europe, Asia, and Africa. Only a few prosimians survive today—lemurs, lorises, and tarsiers (figure 35.34). In addition to grasping digits and binocular

**Figure 35.34** A prosimian. This tarsier, *Tarsius*, a prosimian native to tropical Asia, shows the characteristic features of primates: grasping fingers and toes and binocular vision.

vision, prosimians have large eyes with increased visual acuity. Most prosimians are nocturnal, feeding on fruits, leaves, and flowers, and many lemurs have long tails for balancing.

### Anthropoids

Anthropoids include monkeys, apes, and humans. Anthropoids are almost all diurnal—that is, active during the day—feeding mainly on fruits and leaves. Natural selection favored many changes in eye design, including color vision, that were adaptations to daytime foraging. An expanded brain governs the improved senses, with the braincase forming a larger portion of the head.

Anthropoids, like the relatively few diurnal prosimians, live in groups with complex social interactions. They tend to care for their young for prolonged periods, allowing for a long childhood of learning and brain development.

About 30 MYA, some anthropoids migrated to South America. Their descendants, known as the New World monkeys (figure 35.35a), are easy to identify: All are arboreal; they have flat, spreading noses; and many of them grasp objects with long, prehensile tails.

Anthropoids that remained in Africa gave rise to two lineages: the Old World monkeys (figure 35.35b) and the hominoids (apes and humans, figure 35.35c). Old World monkeys include ground-dwelling as well as arboreal species. None of them have prehensile tails, their nostrils are close together, their noses point downward, and some have toughened pads of skin on their rumps for prolonged sitting.

| New World Monkeys | Old World Monkeys | Hominoids |
|---|---|---|
|  |  |  |
| *a.* | *b.* | *c.* |

**Figure 35.35**
**Anthropoids.** *a.* New World Monkey, the squirrel monkey, *Saimiri oerstedii*; **(b)** Old World Monkey, the mandrill, *Mandrillus sphinx*; **(c)** hominoids, gorilla, *Gorilla gorilla* (left) and human, *Homo sapiens* (right).

### Hominoids

The **hominoids** include the apes and the **hominids** (humans and their direct ancestors). The living apes consist of the gibbon (genus *Hylobates*), orangutan (*Pongo*), gorilla (*Gorilla*), and chimpanzee (*Pan*). Apes have larger brains than monkeys, and they lack tails. With the exception of the gibbon, which is small, all living apes are larger than any monkey. Apes exhibit the most adaptable behavior of any mammal except human beings. Once widespread in Africa and Asia, apes are rare today, living in relatively small areas. No apes ever occurred in North or South America.

Studies of ape DNA have explained a great deal about how the living apes evolved. The Asian apes evolved first. The line of apes leading to gibbons diverged from other apes about 15 MYA, whereas orangutans split off about 10 MYA (figure 35.36). Neither group is closely related to humans.

The African apes evolved more recently, between 6 and 10 MYA. These apes are the closest living relatives to humans. The taxonomic group "apes" is a paraphyletic group; some apes are more closely related to hominids than they are to other apes. For this reason, some taxonomists have advocated placing humans and the African apes in the same zoological family, the Hominidae.

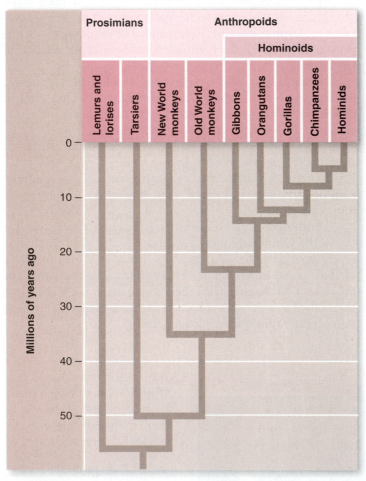

**Figure 35.36 A primate evolutionary tree.** Prosimians diverged early in primate evolution, whereas hominids diverged much more recently. Apes constitute a paraphyletic group because some apes are more closely related to nonape species (hominids) than they are to other apes.

Fossils of the earliest hominids (humans and their direct ancestors), described later in this section, suggest that the common ancestor of the hominids was more like a chimpanzee than a gorilla. Based on genetic differences, scientists estimate that gorillas diverged from the line leading to chimpanzees and humans some 8 MYA.

Soon after the gorilla lineage diverged, the common ancestor of all hominids split off from the chimpanzee line to begin the evolutionary journey leading to humans. Because this split was so recent, few genetic differences between humans and chimpanzees have had time to evolve. For example, a human hemoglobin molecule differs from its chimpanzee counterpart in only a single amino acid. In general, humans and chimpanzees exhibit a level of genetic similarity normally found between closely related species of the same genus!

#### Comparing apes with hominids

The common ancestor of apes and hominids is thought to have been an arboreal climber. Much of the subsequent evolution of the hominoids reflected different approaches to locomotion. Hominids became bipedal, walking upright; in contrast, the apes evolved knuckle-walking, supporting their weight on the dorsal sides of their fingers. (Monkeys, by contrast, walk using the palms of their hands.)

Humans depart from apes in several areas of anatomy related to bipedal locomotion. Because humans walk on two legs, their vertebral column is more curved than an ape's, and the human spinal cord exits from the bottom rather than the back of the skull. The human pelvis has become broader and more bowl-shaped, with the bones curving forward to center the weight of the body over the legs. The hip, knee, and foot have all changed proportions.

Being bipedal, humans carry much of the body's weight on the lower limbs, which comprise 32 to 38% of the body's weight and are longer than the upper limbs; human upper limbs do not bear the body's weight and make up only 7 to 9% of human body weight. African apes walk on all fours, with the upper and lower limbs both bearing the body's weight; in gorillas, the longer upper limbs account for 14 to 16% of body weight, the somewhat shorter lower limbs for about 18%.

### Australopithecines were early hominids

Five to 10 MYA, the world's climate began to get cooler, and the great forests of Africa were largely replaced with savannas and open woodland. In response to these changes, a new kind of hominoid was evolving, one that was bipedal. These new hominoids are classified as hominids—that is, of the human line.

The major groups of hominids include three to seven species of the genus *Homo* (depending how you count them), seven species of the older, smaller-brained genus *Australopithecus*, and several even older lineages (figure 35.37). In every case where the fossils allow a determination to be made, the hominids are bipedal, the hallmark of hominid evolution.

In recent years, anthropologists have found a remarkable series of early hominid fossils extending as far back as 6 to 7 million years. Often displaying a mixture of primitive and modern traits, these fossils have thrown the study of early hominids into turmoil. Although the inclusion of these fossils

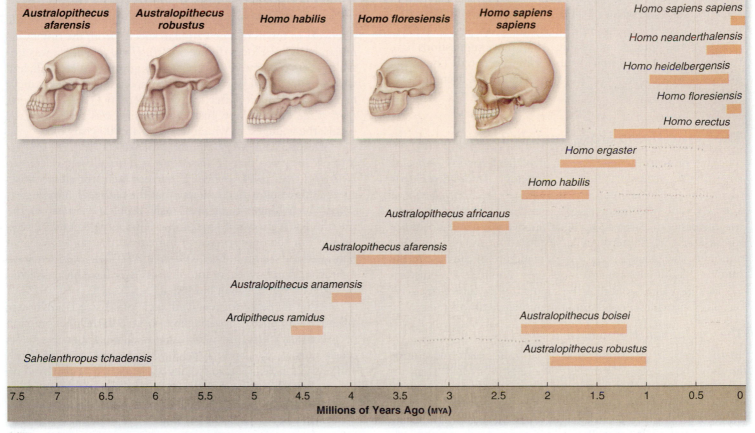

**Figure 35.37 Hominid fossil history.** Most, but not all, fossil hominoids are indicated here. New species are regularly being discovered, though great debate sometimes exists about whether a particular specimen represents a new species.

among the hominids seems warranted, only a few specimens have been discovered, and they do not provide enough information to determine with certainty their relationships to australopithecines and humans. The search for additional early hominid fossils continues.

### Early australopithecines

Our knowledge of australopithecines is based on hundreds of fossils, all found in South and East Africa (except for one specimen from Chad in West Africa). Australopithecines may have lived over a much broader area of Africa, but rocks of the proper age that might contain fossils are not exposed elsewhere. The evolution of hominids seems to have begun with an initial radiation of numerous species. The seven species identified so far provide ample evidence that australopithecines were a diverse group.

These early hominids weighed about 18 kg and were about 1 m tall. Their dentition was distinctly hominid, but their brains were no larger than those of apes, generally 500 cubic centimeters (cm³) or less. *Homo* brains, by comparison, are usually larger than 600 cm³; modern *H. sapiens* brains average 1350 cm³.

The structure of australopithecine fossils clearly indicates that they walked upright. Evidence of bipedalism includes a set of some 69 hominid footprints found at Laetoli, East Africa. Two individuals, one larger than the other, walked upright side-by-side for 27 m, their footprints preserved in a layer of 3.7-million-year-old volcanic ash. Importantly, the big toe is not splayed out to the side as in a monkey or ape, indicating that these footprints were clearly made by hominids.

### Bipedalism

The evolution of bipedalism marks the beginning of hominids. Bipedalism seems to have evolved as australopithecines left dense forests for grasslands and open woodland.

Whether larger brains or bipedalism evolved first was a matter of debate for some time. One school of thought proposed that hominid brains enlarged first, and then hominids became bipedal. Another school of thought saw bipedalism as a precursor to larger brains, arguing that bipedalism freed the forelimbs to manufacture and use tools, leading to the evolution of bigger brains. Recently, fossils unearthed in Africa have settled the debate. These fossils demonstrate that bipedalism extended back 4 million years; knee joint, pelvis, and leg bones all exhibit the hallmarks of an upright stance. Substantial brain expansion, on the other hand, did not appear until roughly 2 MYA. In hominid evolution, upright walking clearly preceded large brains.

The reason bipedalism evolved in hominids remains a matter of controversy. No tools appeared until 2.5 MYA, so tool-making seems an unlikely cause. Alternative ideas suggest that walking upright is faster and uses less energy than walking on four legs; that an upright posture permits hominids to pick fruit from trees and see over tall grass; that being upright reduces the body surface exposed to the Sun's rays; that an upright stance aided the wading of semiaquatic hominids; and that bipedalism frees the forelimbs of males to carry food back to females, encouraging pair-bonding. All of these suggestions have their proponents, and none is universally accepted. The origin of bipedalism, the key event in the evolution of hominids, remains a mystery.

## The genus *Homo* arose roughly 2 MYA

The first humans (genus *Homo*) evolved from australopithecine ancestors about 2 MYA. The exact ancestor has not been clearly identified, but is commonly thought to be *Australopithecus afarensis*. Only within the last 30 years have a significant number of fossils of early *Homo* been uncovered. An explosion of interest has fueled intensive field exploration, and new finds are announced regularly; every year, our picture of the base of the human evolutionary tree grows clearer. The following historical account will undoubtedly be supplanted by future discoveries, but it provides a good example of science at work.

### The first human: Homo habilis

In the early 1960s, stone tools were found scattered among hominid bones close to the site where *A. boisei* had been unearthed. Although the fossils were badly crushed, painstaking reconstruction of the many pieces suggested a skull with a brain volume of about 680 cm³, larger than the australopithecine range of 400 to 550 cm³. Because of its association with tools, this early human was called *Homo habilis*, meaning "handy man." Partial skeletons discovered in 1986 indicate that *H. habilis* was small in stature, with arms longer than its legs and a skeleton much like that of *Australopithecus*. Because of its general similarity to australopithecines, many researchers at first questioned whether this fossil was human.

### Out of Africa: Homo erectus

Our picture of what early *Homo* was like lacks detail because it is based on only a few specimens. We have much more information about the species that replaced it, *Homo erectus* and *H. ergaster*, which are sometimes considered a single species.

These species were a lot larger than *Homo habilis*—about 1.5 m tall. They had a large brain, about 1000 cm³, and walked erect. Their skull had prominent brow ridges and, like modern humans, a rounded jaw. Most interesting of all, the shape of the skull interior suggests that *H. erectus* was able to talk.

Far more successful than *H. habilis*, *H. erectus* quickly became widespread and abundant in Africa, and within 1 million years had migrated into Asia and Europe. A social species, *H. erectus* lived in tribes of 20 to 50 people, often dwelling in caves. They successfully hunted large animals, butchered them using flint and bone tools, and cooked them over fires—a site in China contains the remains of horses, bears, elephants, and rhinoceroses.

*Homo erectus* survived for over a million years, longer than any other species of human. These very adaptable humans only disappeared in Africa about 500,000 years ago, as modern humans were emerging. Interestingly, they survived even longer in Asia, until 250,000 years ago.

## A new addition to the human family: Homo floresiensis

The world was stunned in 2004 with the announcement of the discovery of fossils of a new human species from the tiny Indonesian island of Flores (figure 35.38). *Homo floresiensis* was notable for its diminutive stature; standing only a meter tall, and with a brain size of just 380 cm³, the species was quickly nicknamed "the Hobbit" after the characters in J. R. R. Tolkien's *Lord of the Rings* trilogy. Just as surprising was the age of the fossils, the youngest of which was only 15,000 years old.

Despite its recency, a number of skeletal features suggest to most scientists that *H. floresiensis* is more closely related to *H. erectus* than to *H. sapiens*. If correct (and not all scientists agree), this result would indicate that the *H. erectus* lineage persisted much longer than previously thought—almost to the present day. It also would mean that until very recently, *H. sapiens* was not the only species of human on the planet. We can only speculate about how *H. sapiens* and *H. floresiensis* may have interacted, and how these interactions may have been affected by the great difference in body size.

Why *H. floresiensis* evolved such small size is unknown, although a number of experts have pointed to the phenomenon of "island dwarfism," in which mammal species evolve to be much smaller on islands. Indeed, *H. floresiensis* coexisted with and preyed on a miniature species of elephant that also lived on Flores, but which also has gone extinct. These findings have rekindled interest in explaining why island dwarfism occurs.

**Figure 35.38** *Homo floresiensis.* This diminutive species (compare the modern human female on the right with the female *H. floresiensis* on the left) occurred on the small island of Flores in what is now Indonesia. *H. floresiensis* preyed upon a dwarf species of elephant, *Stegodon sondaari*, which also occurred on Flores (compare with the larger African elephant, *Loxodonta african*, in gray).

## Modern humans

The evolutionary journey entered its final phase when modern humans first appeared in Africa about 600,000 years ago. Investigators who focus on human diversity denote three species of modern humans: *Homo heidelbergensis*, *H. neanderthalensis*, and *H. sapiens*. Other investigators lump the three species into one, *H. sapiens* ("wise man").

The oldest modern human, *Homo heidelbergensis*, is known from a 600,000-year-old fossil from Ethiopia. Although it coexisted with *H. erectus* in Africa, *H. heidelbergensis* has more advanced anatomical features, including a bony keel running along the midline of the skull, a thick ridge over the eye sockets, and a large brain. Also, its forehead and nasal bones are very much like those of *H. sapiens*.

As *H. erectus* was becoming rarer, about 130,000 years ago, a new species of human arrived in Europe from Africa. *Homo neanderthalensis* likely branched off the ancestral line leading to modern humans as long as 500,000 years ago. Compared with modern humans, Neanderthals were short, stocky, and powerfully built; their skulls were massive, with protruding faces, heavy, bony ridges over the brows, and larger braincases.

## Cro-Magnons and Neanderthals

The Neanderthals (classified by many paleontologists as a separate species, *Homo neanderthalensis*) were named after the Neander Valley of Germany where their fossils were first discovered in 1856. Rare at first outside of Africa, they became progressively more abundant in Europe and Asia, and by 70,000 years ago had become common.

The Neanderthals made diverse tools, including scrapers, spearheads, and hand axes. They lived in huts or caves. Neanderthals took care of their injured and sick and commonly buried their dead, often placing food, weapons, and even flowers with the bodies. Such attention to the dead strongly suggests that they believed in a life after death. This is the first evidence of the symbolic thinking characteristic of modern humans.

Fossils of *H. neanderthalensis* abruptly disappear from the fossil record about 34,000 years ago and are replaced by fossils of *H. sapiens* called the Cro-Magnons (named after the valley in France where their fossils were first discovered). We can only speculate why this sudden replacement occurred, but it was complete all over Europe in a short period.

A variety of evidence indicates that Cro-Magnons came from Africa—fossils of essentially modern aspect but as much as 100,000 years old have been found there. Cro-Magnons seem to have replaced the Neanderthals completely in the Middle East by 40,000 years ago, and then spread across Europe, coexisting with the Neanderthals for several thousand years. Recent analyses of Neanderthal DNA reveal it to be quite distinct from Cro-Magnon DNA, indicating the two species did not interbreed, although not all scientists agree on this point. Neanderthals are our cousins, not our ancestors. The Cro-Magnons that replaced the Neanderthals had a complex social organization and are thought to have had full language capabilities. Elaborate and often beautiful cave paintings made by Cro-Magnons can be seen throughout Europe (figure 35.39).

Humans of modern appearance eventually spread across Siberia to North America, where they arrived at least 13,000

**Figure 35.39 Cro-Magnon art.** Rhinoceroses are among the animals depicted in this remarkable cave painting found in 1995 near Vallon-Pont d'Arc, France.

years ago, after the ice had begun to retreat and a land bridge still connected Siberia and Alaska. By 10,000 years ago, about 5 million people inhabited the entire world (compared with more than 6 billion today).

## Our own species: Homo sapiens

*Homo sapiens* is the only surviving species of the genus *Homo*, and indeed the only surviving hominid. Some of the best fossils of *H. sapiens* are 20 well-preserved skeletons with skulls found in a cave near Nazareth in Israel. Modern dating techniques estimate these humans to be between 90,000 and 100,000 years old. The skulls are modern in appearance and size, with high, short braincases, vertical foreheads with only slight brow ridges, and a cranial capacity of roughly 1550 cm³. Our evolution has been marked by a progressive increase in brain size, distinguishing us from other animals in several ways. First, humans are able to make and use tools more effectively than any other animal—a capability that, more than any other factor, has been responsible for our dominant position in the world. Second, although not the only animal capable of conceptual thought, humans have refined and extended this ability until it has become the hallmark of our species. Finally, we use symbolic language and can, with words, shape concepts out of experience and transmit that accumulated experience from one generation to another.

Humans have undergone what no other animal ever has: extensive cultural evolution. Through culture, we have found ways to change and mold our environment, rather than changing evolutionarily in response to the environment's demands. We control our biological future in a way never before possible—an exciting potential and a frightening responsibility.

**Figure 35.40 Patterns of genetic variation in human populations differ from patterns of skin color variation.**
*a.* Genetic variation among *Homo sapiens*. The more similar areas are in color, the more similar they are genetically based on many enzyme and blood group genetic loci.
*b.* Similarity among *Homo sapiens* based on skin color. The color of an area represents the skin pigmentation of the people native to that region.

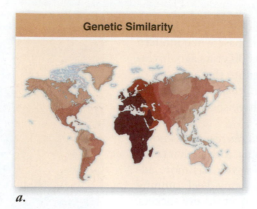

Genetic Similarity

*a.*

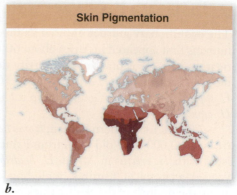

Skin Pigmentation

*b.*

## Human races

Human beings, like all other species, have differentiated in their characteristics as they have spread throughout the world. Local populations in one area often appear significantly different from those that live elsewhere. For example, northern Europeans often have blond hair, fair skin, and blue eyes, whereas Africans often have black hair, dark skin, and brown eyes. These traits may play a role in adapting the particular populations to their environments. Blood groups may be associated with immunity to diseases more common in certain geographical areas, and dark skin shields the body from the damaging effects of ultraviolet radiation, which is much stronger in the tropics than in temperate regions.

All human beings are capable of mating with one another and producing fertile offspring. The reasons that they do or do not choose to associate with one another are purely psychological and behavioral (cultural).

The number of groups into which the human species might logically be divided has long been a point of contention. Some contemporary anthropologists divide people into as many as 30 "races," others as few as three: Caucasoid, Negroid, and Oriental. American Indians, Bushmen, and Aborigines are examples of particularly distinctive subunits that are sometimes regarded as distinct groups.

The problem with classifying people or other organisms into races in this fashion is that the characteristics used to define the races are usually not well correlated with one another, and so the determination of race is always somewhat arbitrary. Humans are visually oriented; consequently, we have relied on visual cues—primarily skin color—to define races. However, when other types of characteristics, such as blood groups, are examined, patterns of variation correspond very poorly with visually determined racial classes. Indeed, if one were to break the human species into subunits based on overall genetic similarity, the groupings would be very different from those based on skin color or other visual features (figure 35.40).

In human beings, it is simply not possible to delimit clearly defined races that reflect biologically differentiated and well-defined groupings. The reason is simple: Different groups of people have constantly intermingled and interbred with one another during the entire course of history. This constant gene flow has prevented the human species from fragmenting into highly differentiated subspecies. Those characteristics that are differentiated among populations, such as skin color, represent classic examples of the antagonism between gene flow and natural selection. As you saw in chapter 20, when selection is strong enough, as it is for dark coloration in tropical regions, populations can differentiate even in the presence of gene flow. However, even in cases such as this, gene flow will still ensure that populations are relatively homogeneous for genetic variation at other loci.

For this reason, relatively little of the variation in the human species represents differences between the described races. Indeed, one study calculated that only 8% of all genetic variation among humans could be accounted for as differences that exist among racial groups; in other words, the human racial categories do a very poor job in describing the vast majority of genetic variation that exists in humans. For this reason, most modern biologists reject human racial classifications as reflecting patterns of biological differentiation in the human species. This is a sound biological basis for dealing with each human being on his or her own merits and not as a member of a particular "race."

### Learning Outcomes Review 35.9

Primates include prosimians, monkeys, apes, and humans (hominids). Primates have grasping fingers and toes and binocular vision. Hominids diverged from other primates by developing bipedal locomotion that led to a number of additional adaptations, including modification of the spine, pelvis, and limbs. Several species of *Homo* evolved in Africa, and some migrated from there to Europe and Asia. Our own species, *Homo sapiens*, is proficient at conceptual thought and tool use and is the only animal that uses symbolic language. Considerable variation occurs among human populations, but the recognized races, which are based primarily on skin color, do not reflect significant biological differences.

■ *Which of these groups is monophyletic: prosimians, monkeys, apes, hominids?*

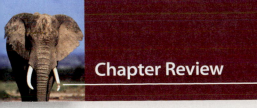

## 35.1 The Chordates

Chordates share four features at some time during development: a single, hollow nerve cord; a flexible rod, the notochord; pharyngeal slits or pouches; and a postanal tail (see figure 35.1).

## 35.2 The Nonvertebrate Chordates

**Tunicates have chordate larval forms.**
Tunicates have a swimming larval form exhibiting all the features of a chordate, but their adult form is sessile and baglike.

**Lancelets are small marine chordates.**
Lancelets have chordate features throughout life, but as adults they lack bones and have no distinct head (see figure 35.3).

## 35.3 The Vertebrate Chordates

**Vertebrates have vertebrae, a distinct head, and other features.**
In vertebrates, a vertebral column encloses and protects the dorsal nerve cord. The distinct and well-differentiated head carries sensory organs. Vertebrates also have specialized internal organs and a bony or cartilaginous endoskeleton.

**Vertebrates evolved half a billion years ago: An overview.**
In fishes, evolution of a hinged jaw was a major advance. Other changes allowed a move into the terrestrial environment, giving rise to amphibians, reptiles, birds, and mammals (see figure 35.8).

## 35.4 Fishes

**Fishes exhibit five key characteristics.**
The key characteristics of fishes are a vertebral column of bone or cartilage, jaws, paired appendages, internal gills, and a closed circulatory system.

**Sharks, with cartilaginous skeletons, became top predators.**
Sharks, rays, and skates are cartilaginous fishes. Sharks were streamlined for fast swimming, and they evolved teeth that enabled them to readily grab, kill, and devour prey.
The lateral line system of sharks and bony fishes is a sensory system that detects changes in pressure waves.

**Bony fishes dominate the waters.**
Bony fishes belong either to the ray-finned fishes (Actinopterygii), or the lobe-finned fishes (Sarcopterygii). Ray-finned fishes have fins stiffened with bony parallel rays.

**The evolutionary path to land ran through the lobe-finned fishes.**
The lobe-finned fishes have muscular lobes with bones connected by joints (see figure 35.13). These structures could evolve into limbs capable of movement on land.

## 35.5 Amphibians

**Living amphibians have five distinguishing features.**
Amphibian adaptations include legs, lungs, cutaneous respiration, pulmonary veins, and a partially divided heart.

**Amphibians overcame terrestrial challenges.**
Terrestrial adaptations included being able to support large bodies against gravity, to breathe out of water, and to avoid dessication.

**Modern amphibians belong to three groups.**
The Anura (frogs and toads) lack tails as adults; many have a larval tadpole stage. The Caudata (salamanders) have tails as adults and larvae similar to the adult form. The Apoda (caecilians) are legless.

## 35.6 Reptiles

**Reptiles exhibit three key characteristics.**
Reptiles posses a watertight amniotic egg; dry, watertight skin; and thoracic breathing (see figure 35.17).
Modern reptiles practice internal fertilization and are ectothermic.

**Reptiles dominated the Earth for 250 million years.**
Synapsids gave rise to the therapsids that became the mammalian line. Diapsids gave rise to modern reptiles and the birds.

**Modern reptiles belong to four groups.**
The four groups of reptiles are Chelonia (turtles and tortoises); Rhynchocephalia (tuataras); Squamata (lizards and snakes); and Crocodylia (crocodiles and alligators).

## 35.7 Birds

**Key characteristics of birds are feathers and a lightweight skeleton.**
The feather is a modified reptilian scale. Feathers provide lift in gliding or flight and conserve heat (see figure 35.25).
The lightweight skeleton of birds is an adaptation to flight.

**Birds arose about 150 MYA.**
Birds evolved from theropod dinosaurs. Feathers probably first arose to provide insulation, only later being modified for flight.

**Modern birds are diverse but share several characteristics.**
In addition to the key characteristics, birds have efficient respiration and circulation and are endothermic.

## 35.8 Mammals

**Mammals have hair, mammary glands, and other characteristics.**
Mammals are distinguished by fur and by mammary glands, which provide milk to feed the young. Mammals are also endothermic.

**Mammals diverged about 220 MYA.**
Mammals evolved from therapsids (synapsids) and reached maximum diversity about 15 MYA.

**Modern mammals are placed into three groups.**
The monotremes lay shelled eggs. In marsupials, an embryo completes development in a pouch. Placental mammals produce a placenta in the uterus to nourish the embryo.

## 35.9 Evolution of the Primates (see figure 35.36)

Primates share two innovations: grasping fingers and toes, and binocular vision.

**The anthropoid lineage led to the earliest humans.**
The earliest primates were the prosimians; anthropoids, which include monkeys, apes, and humans, evolved later. Hominoids include the apes and the hominids, or humans.

**Austrolopithecines were early hominids.**
The distinguishing characteristics of hominids are upright posture and bipedal locomotion.

**The genus Homo arose roughly 2 MYA.**
Common features of early *Homo* species include a larger body and brain size. *Homo sapiens* is the only extant species. Humans exhibit conceptual thought, tool use, and symbolic language.

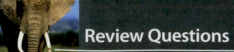
## UNDERSTAND

1. Which of the following statements regarding all species of chordates is false?
   a. Chordates are deuterostomes.
   b. A notochord is present in the embryo.
   c. The notochord is surrounded by bone or cartilage.
   d. All possess a postanal tail during embryonic development.

2. In the following figure, item A is the _____ and item B is the _____.
   a. complete digestive system; notochord
   b. spinal cord; nerve cord
   c. notochord; nerve cord
   d. pharyngeal slits; notochord

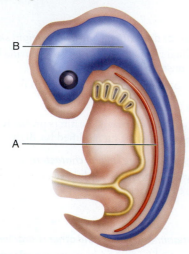

3. During embryonic development, a neural crest would be found in all of the following chordates, except
   a. cephalochordates.     c. birds.
   b. reptiles.              d. mammals.

4. The _____ of the bony fish evolved to counter the effects of increased bone density.
   a. gills                 c. swim bladder
   b. jaws                  d. teeth

5. Why was the evolution of the pulmonary veins important for amphibians?
   a. To move oxygen to and from the lungs
   b. To increase the metabolic rate
   c. For increased blood circulation to the brain
   d. None of the above

6. Which of the following groups lacks a four-chambered heart?
   a. Birds                 c. Mammals
   b. Crocodilians          d. Amphibians

7. All of the following are characteristics of reptiles, except
   a. cutaneous respiration.
   b. amniotic egg.
   c. thoracic breathing.
   d. dry, watertight skin.

8. Which of the following evolutionary adaptations allows the birds to become efficient at flying?
   a. Structure of the feather
   b. High metabolic temperatures
   c. Increased respiratory efficiency
   d. All of the above

## APPLY

1. The reason that birds and crocodilians both build nests might be because they
   a. are both warm-blooded.
   b. both eat fish.
   c. both inherited the trait from a common ancestor.
   d. both lay eggs.

2. Which of the following is the closest relative of lungfish?
   a. Hagfish               c. Ray-finned fish
   b. Sharks                d. Mammals

3. The fact that monotremes lay eggs
   a. indicates that they are more closely related to some reptiles than they are to some mammals.
   b. is a plesiomorphic trait.
   c. demonstrates that the amniotic egg evolved multiple times.
   d. is a result of ectothermy.

## SYNTHESIZE

1. Some scientists believe the feathers did not evolve initially for flight, but rather for insulation. What benefits would this have had for early flightless birds?

2. Some people state that the dinosaurs have not "gone extinct," they are with us today. What evidence can be used to support this statement?

3. In what respect is the evolutionary diversification of hominids similar to that of horses discussed in chapter 21?

## ONLINE RESOURCE

www.ravenbiology.com

Understand, Apply, and Synthesize—enhance your study with animations that bring concepts to life and practice tests to assess your understanding. Your instructor may also recommend the interactive eBook, individualized learning tools, and more.

# Notes

# Notes

# Notes

Part **VIII** Ecology and Behavior

*Chapter* **55**

# *Behavioral Biology*

## Chapter Outline

## Introduction

*The study of behavior is at the center of many disciplines of biology. Observing behavior provides important insights into the workings of the brain and nervous system, the influences of genes and the environment, when and how animals reproduce, and how they adapt to their environment. Behavior is shaped by natural selection and is controlled by internal mechanisms involving genes, hormones, neurotransmitters, and neural circuits. In this chapter, we explore how behavioral biology integrates approaches from several branches of biological science to provide a detailed understanding of the mechanisms that underscore behavior and its evolution.*

## 55.1 The Natural History of Behavior

### Learning Outcomes

1. Contrast the proximate and ultimate causation of behavior.
2. Explain instinct theory.
3. Describe the physiological factors that might be the basis for innate behaviors.

Observing animal behavior and making inferences about what one sees is at once simple and profound. Behavior is what an animal does. It is the most immediate way an animal responds adaptively to its environment by tracking environmental cues and signals such as odors, sounds, or visual signals associated with food, predators, or mates. Behavior also concerns thinking and cognition, monitoring one's social environment, and making decisions as to whether or not to cooperate or act altruistically. Behavior allows animals to survive and reproduce and is thus critical to the evolutionary process. The work of behavioral biologists has provided important insights into animal behavior, including the very meaning of human behavior.

### Behavior can be analyzed in terms of mechanisms (cause) and evolutionary origin (adaptive nature)

Why does an animal behave in a particular way? Consider hearing a bird sing. We could ask how it vocalizes or determine the time of the year it sings most frequently. We could also ask about the function of the song, that is, ask why it sings. Answers to questions about how birds sing consider the role of internal factors such as hormones and nerve cells and other physiological processes. Such questions concern proximate causation: the mechanisms that are the reason for behavior. To analyze the proximate cause of bird song, we could measure hormone levels or study the development of brain regions and neural circuits associated with singing. For example, a male songbird may sing during the breeding season because of an increased level of the steroid sex hormone testosterone, which binds to receptors in the brain and triggers the production of song. Additionally, neural connections between the brain and the syrinx (the bird's vocal organ) must develop to allow songs to be produced. These explanations describe the proximate cause of bird song.

Asking about the function of a behavior (once again, bird song) is to ask why it evolved. To answer this question, we would determine how it influenced survival or reproductive success. A male bird sings to defend a territory from other males and to attract a female with which to reproduce. This is the ultimate, or evolutionary, explanation for the male's vocalization. Now we can understand its ultimate causation, or adaptive value. Researchers often study behavior from both perspectives to fully appreciate its mechanisms and ecological function, and thus its role in evolution. Behavior can be analyzed at four levels: (1) physiology (how it is influenced by hormones, nerve cells, and other internal factors); (2) ontogeny (how it develops in an individual), (3) phylogeny (its origin in groups of related species), and (4) adaptive significance (its role in survival and fitness). We'll begin by tracing the history of the study of mechanisms of behavior by focusing on the work of ethologists—biologists who first began to study behavior at the turn of the 20th century.

### Ethology emphasizes the study of instinct and its origins

*Ethology* is the study of the natural history of behavior, with an emphasis on behaviors that form an animal's instincts, or programmed behaviors. Ethologists observed that individuals of a given species behaved in stereotyped ways, showing the same pattern of behavior in response to a particular stimulus. Because their behavior seemed reflexive, they considered it to be instinctive, or *innate*. Behaviors were thought to be programmed by the nervous system, which in turn was designed by genes, and responses would occur without experience. Ethologists based their instinct model on observations and experiments of simple behaviors such as egg retrieval by geese. Geese incubate their eggs in a nest. If an egg falls out of the nest, the goose will roll the egg back into the nest with a side-to-side motion of its neck while the egg is tucked beneath its bill (figure 55.1). Even if the egg is removed during retrieval, the goose will still complete the egg-retrieval sequence, as if driven by a program activated by the initial sight of the egg outside the nest.

This example is one paradigm of instinct theory and illustrates the way ethologists conceptualized the mechanisms of behavior. Egg retrieval behavior is triggered by a *key stimulus* (sometimes called a *sign stimulus*); this is the egg out of the nest. Early ethologists thought the nervous system regulated behavior via the *innate releasing mechanism*, a neural circuit involved

Sign stimulus

Fixed action pattern

**Figure 55.1  Innate egg-rolling response in geese.** The series of movements used by a goose to retrieve an egg is a fixed action pattern. Once it detects the sign stimulus (in this case, an egg outside the nest), the goose goes through the entire set of movements: It will extend its neck toward the egg, get up, and roll the egg back into the nest with a side-to-side motion of its neck while the egg is tucked beneath its bill.

in the perception of the key stimulus and the triggering of a motor program, the *fixed action pattern*, in this case the act of guiding the egg back to the nest. Ethologists generalized that the key stimulus is a cue or signal in the environment that initiates neural events that cause behavior. The innate releasing mechanism involves the sensory apparatus that detects the signal and the neural circuit controlling muscles to generate the fixed action pattern.

### Learning Outcomes Review 55.1

Proximate causation of behavior involves the immediate mechanisms that bring about an action; ultimate causation refers to the adaptive value of a behavior. Ethology is the study of the nature of behavior, emphasizing instinct and the regulation of behavior by internal factors such as genes, nerve cells, and hormones. Ethologists are also interested in the origins of behavior.

■ *Why is it important to understand the phylogeny (evolutionary origins) of behavior?*

## 55.2 Nerve Cells, Neurotransmitters, Hormones, and Behavior

### Learning Outcomes

1. Relate the structure of neural circuits to their function.
2. Describe the role of hormones and neurotransmitters in behavior.

Although early ethologists had little understanding of neurobiology, they hypothesized elements of the nervous system (the innate releasing mechanism) controlled behavior. Today, neuroethologists—researchers who examine the neurobiology of behavior—can describe in detail how information in the environment is processed by sensory cells and how nerve impulses are transmitted to other neurons and muscles to form neural circuits that regulate behaviors important to survival. Behavior reflects the organization of the peripheral and central nervous system, and studying behavior can help us understand how neurons function individually and in combination with other neurons in circuits (see chapters 44 and 45).

Behaviors that must occur rapidly, like those used to capture prey or flee predators, involve neural mechanisms that enable such functions. Some moths have an earlike sensory organ equipped with sensory neurons designed to detect the ultrasonic cries of bats, the first step in evading predation. Specialized cells in the frog's retina detect moving objects like insects and release the tongue in fractions of a second once suitable prey is sighted. Likewise, the jaws of a predatory ant snap shut when prey trigger sensory hairs between the mandibles. Rapid responses to predators or prey often involve large nerve cell axons that can quickly transmit impulses to muscles. In the example of "trap jaw" ants, large axons of the mandibular motor neuron—the fastest neuron yet identified—fire nerve impulses

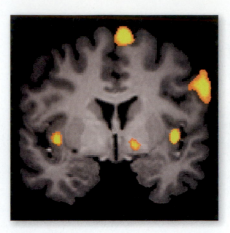

**Figure 55.2**
**Functional Magnetic Resonance Imaging (fMRI).** MRIs reveal neural activity in specific regions of the brain. In this case, activity in part of the brain called the nucleus accumbens is associated with viewing images of food.

that close the jaws in only 33 msec. Neural circuits that enable quick responses often are made up of few sensory and motor neurons, and their connecting nerve cells.

Behavioral biologists examine the relationship of hormones to behavior to understand the endocrine mechanisms that are the foundation of reproduction, parental care, aggression, and stress (see chapter 46). In this way, the effects of the steroid sex hormones estrogen and testosterone on behavior have been determined. Testosterone in the male, for example, regulates territorial behavior and courtship, whereas estrogen in the female controls her mating behavior. Glucocorticoid hormones are involved in stress.

Neuroscientists may measure levels of neurotransmitters such as serotonin and dopamine in the nervous system or blood and associate these chemicals with behavior (see chapter 44). These chemicals are released by nerve cells and can affect activity in different brain regions. Serotonin has been shown to influence aggression in an incredibly wide range of animals including lobsters, mice, and humans. Researchers may inject a neurotransmitter or pharmacologically change its level in the brain to examine how it affects behavior.

The techniques of neuroethology include identifying and mapping individual neurons, their dendrites and connections to other neurons, and how their impulses and neurochemicals regulate behavior. Today, techniques such as functional magnetic resonance imaging (fMRI) are generating exciting data on the specialized functions of different regions of the human brain. One striking example concerns how the brain responds to images of food (figure 55.2). In contrast to expectation, the brain's response does not occur in the visual cortex, the region associated with object recognition, but in a circuit in the nucleus accumbens in the forebrain, normally involved in reward and pleasure.

### Learning Outcomes Review 55.2

Instinctive behaviors appear to involve programmed circuits in the nervous system that are likely to be genetically controlled. Research in neuroethology supports the instinct concept of behavior by describing the organization of neural circuits governing behavior. Chemical signals provided by hormones and by neurotransmitters such as serotonin and dopamine cause behaviors to occur.

■ *If a male songbird is injected with testosterone two weeks earlier than when these birds normally start to sing in the spring, what would you expect to happen?*

## 55.3 Behavioral Genetics

### Learning Outcomes

1. *Discuss the types of studies that have provided evidence to link genes and behavior.*
2. *Explain how single genes can influence behavior.*
3. *Describe the role of genes in complex behaviors such as aggression, parental care, and pair bonding.*

Instinct theory assumed that genes play a role in behavior, but ethologists did not conclusively demonstrate the role genes can play. The study of genes and behavior has often been highly controversial, as ethologists and social scientists engaged in a seemingly endless debate over whether behavior is determined more by an individual's genes (nature) or by its learning and experience (nurture). One problem with this nature/nurture controversy is that the question is framed as an "either/or" proposition, which fails to consider that both instinct and experience can have significant roles, often interacting in complex ways to shape behavior.

**Behavioral genetics** deals with the contribution that heredity makes to behavior. It is obvious that genes, the units of heredity, are passed from one generation to the next and guide the development of the nervous system and potentially the behavioral responses it regulates. But animals may also develop in a rich social environment and have experiences that guide behavior. The importance of "nature" and "nurture" to behavior can be seen by first reviewing the history of studies in behavioral genetics and next examining the importance of experience and development. We'll then consider their interaction.

### Artificial selection and hybrid studies link genes and behavior

Pioneering research indicated that behavioral differences among individuals result from genetic differences. Research on a variety of animals demonstrated that hybrids showed behaviors involved in nest building and courtship that were intermediate between those of parents. These early efforts to define the role of genes in behavior demonstrated that behavior can have a heritable component, but fell short of identifying the genes involved. With the development of molecular biology, far greater precision was added to the analysis of the genetics of behavior.

Learning itself can be influenced by genes. In one classic study, rats had to find their way through a maze of blind alleys and only one exit, where a reward of food awaited them. Some rats quickly learned to zip through the maze to the food, making few mistakes, but other rats made more errors in learning the correct path. Researchers bred rats that made few errors with one another to establish a "maze-bright" group, and error-prone rats were interbred, forming a "maze-dull" group. Offspring in each group were then tested for their maze-learning ability. The offspring of maze-bright rats learned to negotiate the maze with fewer errors than their parents, while the offspring of maze-dull parents performed more poorly. Repeating this artificial selection method for several generations led to two behaviorally distinct types of rat with very different maze-learning abilities (figure 55.3). This type of study suggests the ways in which natural selection could shape behavior over time, making genes for certain abilities more prevalent.

**? Inquiry question**

What would happen if, after the seventh generation, rats were randomly assigned mates regardless of their ability to learn the maze?

### Some behaviors appear to be controlled by a single gene

Artificial selection and hybrid studies only suggested a role for genes in behavior. Subsequent research took advantage of advances in molecular biology and identified the genes involved. Fruit flies, *Drosophila*, have traditionally provided a useful model system in which the effect of single genes have been identified.

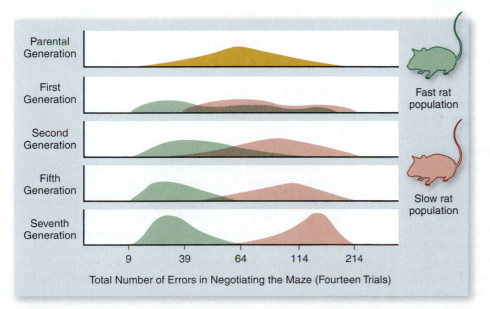

**Figure 55.3  The genetics of learning.** Rats that made the fewest errors in the parental population were interbred to select for rats that had improved maze-learning ability (green), and rats that made the most errors were interbred to select for rats that were error prone (red).

**? Inquiry question**

What would happen if, after the seventh generation, rats were randomly assigned mates regardless of their ability to learn the maze?

Total Number of Errors in Negotiating the Maze (Fourteen Trials)

Single genes have also been shown to influence behavior in animals ranging from mice to humans.

In fruit flies, individuals that possess alternative alleles for a particular gene differ greatly in their feeding behavior as larvae: Larvae with one allele move around a great deal as they eat, whereas individuals with the alternative allele move hardly at all. A wide variety of experimentally induced mutations at other genes affect courtship behavior in males and females. For example, *fru* is a regulatory gene whose transcription products govern the design of the courtship center of the fruit fly brain. This gene turns on other genes involved in the neural circuitry of courtship.

Single genes in mice are associated with spatial memory and parenting. For example, some mice with a particular mutation have trouble remembering recently learned information about where objects are located. This is apparently because they lack the ability to produce the enzyme α-calcium-calmodulin-dependent kinase II, which plays an important role in the functioning of the hippocampus, a part of the brain important for spatial learning.

It is particularly interesting that genes are involved in behavior as complex as maternal care: The presence or absence of *fosB* determines whether female mice nurture their young in particular ways. Females with both *fosB* alleles disabled initially investigate their newborn babies, but then ignore them, in stark contrast to the caring and protective maternal behavior displayed by normal females (figure 55.4). The cause of this inattentiveness appears to result from a chain reaction. When mothers of new babies initially inspect them, information from their auditory, olfactory, and tactile senses is transmitted to the hypothalamus, where *fosB* alleles are activated. The *fosB* alleles produce a protein, which in turn activates other enzymes and genes that affect the neural circuitry of the hypothalamus. These modifications in the brain cause the female to behave maternally. If mothers lack the *fosB* alleles, this process is stopped midway. No protein is activated, the brain's neural circuitry is not rewired, and maternal behavior does not result. The "maternal instincts" of mice can thus be defined genetically!

Another fascinating example of the genetic basis of behavior concerns prairie and montane voles, two closely related species of North American rodents that differ profoundly in their social behavior. Male and female prairie voles form monogamous pair bonds and share parental care, whereas montane voles are promiscuous (meaning they mate with multiple partners and go their separate ways). The act of mating leads to the release of the neuropeptides vasopressin and oxytocin, and the response to these peptides differs dramatically in each species. Injection of either peptide into prairie voles leads to pair bonding even without mating. Conversely, injecting a chemical that blocks the action of these neuropeptides causes prairie voles not to form pair bonds after mating. By contrast, montane voles are unaffected by either of these manipulations.

These different responses have been traced to interspecific differences in brain structure (figure 55.5). The prairie vole has many receptors for these peptides in a particular part of the brain, the nucleus accumbens, which seems to be involved in the expression of pair-bonding behavior. By contrast, few such receptors occur in the same brain region in the montane vole. In laboratory experiments with prairie voles, blocking these receptors tends to prevent pair-bonding, whereas stimulating them

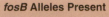

**fosB Alleles Present**

*a.*

**fosB Alleles Inactivated**

*b.*

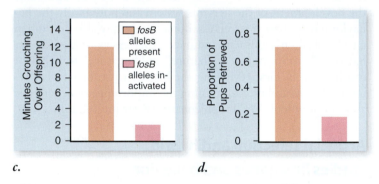

*c.*　　　　　　　　　　　　　　　　*d.*

**Figure 55.4 Genetically caused defect in maternal care.**
*a.* In mice, normal mothers take very good care of their offspring, retrieving them if they move away and crouching over them.
*b.* Mothers with the mutant *fosB* allele perform neither of these behaviors, leaving their pups exposed. *c.* Amount of time female mice were observed crouching in a nursing posture over offspring.
*d.* Proportion of pups retrieved when they were experimentally moved.

### Inquiry question

**?** Why does the lack of *fosB* alleles lead to maternal inattentiveness?

leads to pair-bonding behavior. The gene that codes for the peptide receptors has also been identified, and a difference in the DNA structure between the species has been discovered. To test the hypothesis that this genetic difference was responsible for the differences in behavior, scientists created transgenic mice with the prairie vole version of the gene, and sure enough, when injected with vasopressin, the transgenic mice exhibited pair-bonding behavior very similar to that of prairie voles, whereas normal mice showed no response (see figure 55.5). The

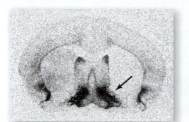 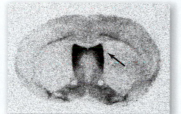

*a.* Prairie vole    *b.* Montane vole

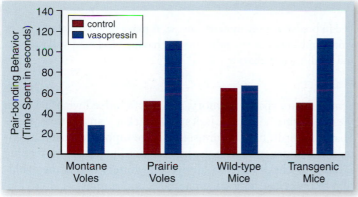

*c.*

**Figure 55.5 Genetic basis of differences in pair-bonding behavior in two rodent species.** *a.* and *b.* The prairie (*Microtus ochrogaster*) and montane (*M. montanus*) voles differ in the distribution of one type of vasopressin receptor in the brain. *c.* Transgenic mice created with the prairie-vole version of the receptor genes respond to injections of vasopressin by exhibiting heightened levels of pair-bonding behavior in 5-min trials compared with their response to a control injection. By contrast, normal wild-type mice (control) show no increase in such behaviors.

vasopressin receptor gene varies in structure among primate species that vary in degree of pair bonding. In human males, the gene has recently been found to be associated with the strength of marital bonds and satisfaction in marriage.

The production of monoamine oxidases (MAOs), enzymes that degrade neurotransmitters such as serotonin and dopamine, are controlled by single genes. Transgenic mice that lack MAOA (monoamine oxidase-A) are highly aggressive. In humans, a single point mutation results in the lack of the ability to produce MAOA, resulting in antisocial behavior and violence. MAO abnormalities are also associated with mood disorders in humans.

---

### Learning Outcomes Review 55.3

A relationship between genes and behavior has been demonstrated in many ways, including artificial selection experiments and studies on the effects of single genes. Genes can regulate behavior by producing molecular factors that influence the function of the nervous system; mutations altering these factors have been found to affect behavior.

- ■ *What would you infer about the role of genes in pair-bonding in prairie voles if you learned that males sometimes seek to copulate with females other than their own mate?*

---

**Learning Outcomes**

1. *Describe the mechanisms of learning.*
2. *Define learning preparedness.*
3. *Explain how instinct influences learning preparedness.*

Instincts can guide an animal's actions, but behavior can also develop from previous experiences, a process termed learning. Traditionally, psychologists studied the mechanisms of learning using laboratory rodents, but today both proximate and ultimate causes of learning are understood by integrating learning into an ecological and evolutionary framework.

## Learning mechanisms include habituation and association

Habituation is a simple form of learning defined as a decrease in response to a repeated stimulus that has no positive or negative consequences. Initially, the stimulus may evoke a strong response, but the response declines with repeated exposure. For example, young birds see many types of objects moving overhead. At first, they may respond by crouching and remaining still. But frequently seen objects, such as falling leaves or members of their own species flying overhead, have no positive or negative consequence to the nestlings. Over time, the young birds may habituate to such stimuli and stop responding. Thus, habituation can be thought of as learning not to respond to a stimulus.

One ecological context in which habituation has adaptive value is prey defense. Birds that feed on insects search for suitable prey in a visually complex environment. Insects that have camouflaged bodies appear to be twigs or leaves, which are commonly encountered as birds search for prey. Because birds see these objects very frequently, they habituate to their appearance. Insects that look like twigs or leaves are therefore protected because they do not trigger an attack, and they survive to reproduce.

More complex forms of learning concern changes in behavior through an association between two stimuli or between a stimulus and a response. In associative learning, for example, (figure 55.6) a behavior is modified, or conditioned, through the association. The two major types of associative learning—classical conditioning and operant conditioning—differ in the way the associations are established. In **classical conditioning,** the paired presentation of two different kinds of stimuli causes the animal to form an association between the stimuli. Classical conditioning is also called **Pavlovian conditioning,** after the Russian psychologist Ivan Pavlov, who first described it.

Pavlov presented meat powder, an unconditioned stimulus, to a dog and noted that the dog responded by salivating, an unconditioned response. If an unrelated stimulus, such as the ringing of a bell, was repeatedly presented at the same time as the meat powder, the dog would soon salivate in response to the sound of the bell alone. The dog had learned to associate the unrelated sound stimulus with the meat powder stimulus. Its

a.          b.          c.

**Figure 55.6** **Learning what is edible.** Associative learning is involved in predator–prey interactions. *a.* A naive toad is offered a bumblebee as food. *b.* The toad is stung, and *(c)* subsequently avoids feeding on bumblebees or any other insects having black-and-yellow coloration. The toad has associated the appearance of the insect with pain and modifies its behavior.

response to the sound stimulus was, therefore, conditioned, and the sound of the bell is referred to as a conditioned stimulus.

In **operant conditioning,** an animal learns to associate its behavioral response with a reward or punishment. American psychologist B. F. Skinner studied operant conditioning in rats by placing them in an apparatus that came to be called a "Skinner box." As the rat explored the box, it would occasionally press a lever by accident, causing a pellet of food to appear. Soon it learned to associate pressing the lever (the behavioral response) with obtaining food (the reward). This sort of trial-and-error learning is of major importance to most vertebrates. Learning provides flexibility that allows behavior to be fine-tuned to an environment.

## Instinct governs learning preparedness

Psychologists once believed that any two stimuli could be linked through learning and that animals could be conditioned to perform any learnable behavior. This view has changed. Today, researchers believe that instinct guides learning by determining what type of information can be learned. Animals may have innate predispositions toward forming certain associations. For example, if a rat is offered a food pellet at the same time it is exposed to X-rays (which later produce nausea), the rat remembers the taste of the food pellet but not its size, and in the future will avoid food with that taste, but will readily eat pellets of the same size if they have a different taste. Similarly, pigeons can learn to associate food with colors, but not with sounds. In contrast, they can associate danger with sounds, but not with colors.

These examples of learning preparedness demonstrate that what an animal can learn is biologically influenced—that is, learning is possible only within the boundaries set by evolution. Innate programs for learning have evolved because they lead to adaptive responses. In nature, food that is toxic to a rat is likely to have a particular taste; thus, it is adaptive to be able to associate a taste with a feeling of sickness that may develop hours later. The seed a pigeon eats may have a distinctive color that the pigeon can see, but it makes no sound the pigeon can hear.

An animal's ecology is key to understanding its learning capabilities. Some species of birds, such as Clark's nutcracker, feed on seeds. When seeds are abundant, these birds store them in buried caches so they will have food during the winter. Seed caches (up to 2000!) may be buried and then recovered as long as nine months later. One would expect these birds to have an

extraordinary spatial memory, and this is indeed what has been found (figure 55.7). Clark's nutcracker, and other seed-hoarding birds, have an unusually large hippocampus, the center for memory storage in the brain. This illustrates how feeding ecology (caching seeds to survive the winter) affects the evolution of brain anatomy (an enlarged hippocampus).

### Learning Outcomes Review 55.4

Habituation is a diminishing response to a repeated stimulus that is neither positive nor negative. Association may occur as either classical conditioning or operant conditioning. Animals can change their behavior through learning in a variety of ways. Although learning mechanisms may be similar across species, animals also differ in their learning abilities according to their ecology.

■ *In some rodents, males travel far while females remain close to the nest. Do males or females have greater spatial memory? What experiment could you conduct to test your hypothesis?*

**Figure 55.7** **The Clark's nutcracker has an extraordinary memory.** A Clark's nutcracker (*Nucifraga columbiana*) can remember the locations of up to 2000 seed caches months after hiding them. After conducting experiments, scientists have concluded that the birds use features of the landscape and other surrounding objects as spatial references to memorize the locations of the caches.

# *The Development of Behavior*

## Learning Outcomes

1. *Discuss the role of the critical period in imprinting.*
2. *Explain how social contact can influence growth and development.*
3. *Explain how the study of song learning in white-crowned sparrows illustrates the interaction of instinct and learning.*

Behavioral biologists recognize that behavior has both genetic and learned components. Thus far in this chapter, we have discussed the influence of genes and learning separately. But as you will see, these factors interact during development to shape behavior.

## Parent–offspring interactions influence how behavior develops

As an animal matures, it may form social attachments to other individuals or develop preferences that will influence behavior later in life. This process of behavioral development is called **imprinting.** The success of imprinting is highest during a critical period (roughly 13 to 16 hours after hatching in geese). During this time, information required for normal development must be acquired. In **filial imprinting,** social attachments form between parents and offspring. For example, young birds like ducks and geese begin to follow their mother within a few hours after hatching, and their following response results in a social bond between mother and young. The young birds' initial experience, through imprinting, can determine how social behavior develops later in life. The ethologist Konrad Lorenz showed that geese will follow the first object they see after hatching and direct their social behavior toward that object, even if it is not their mother! Lorenz raised geese from eggs, and when he offered himself as a model for imprinting, the goslings treated him as if he were their parent, following him dutifully (figure 55.8).

Interactions between parents and offspring are key to the normal development of social behavior. The psychologist Harry Harlow gave orphaned rhesus monkey infants the opportunity to form social attachments with two surrogate "mothers," one made of soft cloth covering a wire frame and the other made only of wire (figure 55.9). The infants chose to spend time with the cloth mother, even if only the wire mother provided food, indicating that texture and tactile contact, rather than provision of food, may be among the key qualities in a mother that promote infant social attachment. If infant monkeys are deprived of normal social contact, their development is abnormal. Greater degrees of deprivation lead to greater abnormalities in social behavior during childhood and adulthood. Studies of orphaned human infants similarly suggest that a constant "mother figure" is required for normal growth and psychological development.

**Figure 55.8 An unlikely parent.** The eager goslings follow Konrad Lorenz as if he were their mother. He is the first object they saw when they hatched, and they have used him as a model for imprinting. Lorenz won the 1973 Nobel Prize in medicine or physiology for this work.

Recent research has revealed a biological need for the stimulation that occurs during parent–offspring interactions early in life. Female rats lick their pups after birth, and this stimulation inhibits the release of a brain peptide that can block normal growth. Pups that receive normal tactile stimulation also have more brain receptors for glucocorticoid hormones, thus a greater tolerance for stress, and longer-lived brain cells. Premature human infants who are massaged gain weight rapidly. These studies indicate that the need for normal social interaction is based in the brain, and that touch and

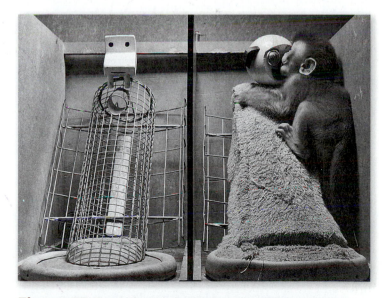

**Figure 55.9 Choice trial on infant monkeys.** Given a choice between a wire frame that provided food and a similar frame covered with cloth and given a monkey-like head, orphaned rhesus monkeys (*Macaca mulatta*) chose the monkeylike figure over the food.

other aspects of contact between parents and offspring are important for physical as well as behavioral development.

## Instinct and learning may interact as behavior develops

We began this chapter by considering the proximate and ultimate causation of bird song. Let's continue with the classic studies by Peter Marler on song learning in white-crowned sparrows to examine how innate programs and experience each contribute to the development of behavior.

Mature male white-crowned sparrows sing a species-specific courtship song during the mating season. Through a series of elegant experiments, Peter Marler asked if the song was the result of an instinctive program, learning, or both. Marler reared male birds in soundproof incubators equipped with speakers and microphones to control what a bird heard as it matured, and then recorded the song it produced as an adult. Males that heard no song at all during development sang a poorly developed song as adults (figure 55.10), indicating that instinct alone did not guide song production. In a second study, males were played only the song of a different species, the song sparrow. These males sang a poorly structured song as well. This experiment showed that males would not imitate any song they heard to learn to sing. But birds that heard the song of their own species, or that heard the songs of both the white-crowned sparrow and the song sparrow, sang a fully developed, white-crowned sparrow song as adults.

These results suggest males have a selective **genetic template,** or innate program, that guides them to learn the appropriate song. During a critical period in development, the template will accept the white-crowned sparrow song as a model. Thus, song acquisition depends on learning, but only the song of the correct species can be learned; the genetic template limits what can be learned.

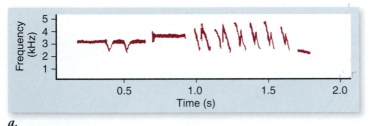

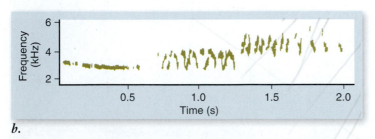

b.

**Figure 55.10 Song development in birds.** *a.* The sonograms of songs produced by male white-crowned sparrows (*Zonotrichia leucophrys*) that had been exposed to their own species' song during development are different from (*b*) those of male sparrows that heard no song during rearing. This difference indicates that the genetic program itself is insufficient to produce a normal song.

**Figure 55.11 Brood parasite.** Cuckoos lay their eggs in the nests of other species of birds. Because the young cuckoos (large bird to the right) are raised by a different species (such as this meadow pipit, smaller bird to the left), they have no opportunity to learn the cuckoo song; the cuckoo song they later sing is innate.

But learning plays a prominent role as well. If a young male becomes deaf after it hears its species' song during the critical period, it will sing a poorly developed song as an adult. Therefore, the bird must hear the correct song at the right time, and then "practice" listening to himself sing, matching what he hears to the model his genetic template has accepted.

Although this explanation of song development stood unchallenged for many years, white-crowned sparrow males can learn another species' song under certain conditions. If a live male strawberry finch is placed in a cage next to a young male sparrow, the young sparrow will learn to sing the strawberry finch's song. This finding indicates that social stimuli—in this case, being able to see, hear, and interact with another bird—is more effective than a tape-recorded song in altering the innate template that guides song development.

The males of some bird species may have no opportunity to hear the song of their own species. In such cases, it appears that the males instinctively "know" their own species' song. For example, cuckoos are **brood parasites;** females lay their eggs in the nest of another species of bird, and the young that hatch are reared by the foster parents (figure 55.11). When the cuckoos become adults, they sing the song of their own species rather than that of their foster parents. Because male brood parasites would most likely hear the song of their host species during development, it is adaptive for them to ignore such "incorrect" stimuli. They hear no adult males of their own species singing, so no correct song models are available. In these species, natural selection has produced a completely genetically guided song. Other birds can also sing a correct species-typical song, even if reared in isolation.

### Inquiry question

? Imagine there is only one bird species on an island. Do you think instinct, learning, or both will guide song development?

## Studies on twins reveal a role for both genes and environment in human behavior

The interaction of genes and the environment can be seen in humans by comparing the behavior of identical twins (which are genetically the same), raised in the same environment or separated at birth and raised apart in different environments. Data on human twins raised together or raised apart allows researchers to determine whether similarities in behavior result from their genetic similarity or from shared environmental experiences. Twins studies indicate many similarities in a wide range of personality traits even though twins were raised in very different environments. Other studies show that antisocial behavior in humans, for which genetic factors such as MAOA deficiencies are known in individuals in the study sample, results from a combination of genes and experience during childhood. These similarities indicate that genetics plays a role in behavior even in humans, although the relative importance of genetics versus environment is still debated.

### Learning Outcomes Review 55.5

During the critical period, offspring must engage in certain social interactions for normal behavioral development. Parent–offspring contact stimulates the release of physiological factors, such as hormones and brain receptors, crucial to growth and brain development. In white-crowned sparrows, young males must hear their species' song to sing it correctly, indicating that both instinct and learning affect song development.

- **Some researchers have tried to link IQ and genes in humans. Why would this research be seen as controversial?**

## 55.6 Animal Cognition

### Learning Outcome

1. Explain why behavioral biologists today are more open to considering that animals can think.

For many decades, students of animal behavior flatly rejected the notion that nonhuman animals can think. Now serious attention is given to animal awareness. The central question of whether animals show **cognitive behavior**—that is, they process information and respond in a manner that suggests thinking—is widely supported (figure 55.12).

In a series of classic experiments conducted in the 1920s, a chimpanzee was left in a room with bananas hanging from the ceiling out of reach. Also in the room were several boxes lying on the floor. After some unsuccessful attempts to jump up and grab the bananas, the chimp stacked the boxes beneath the suspended bananas, and climbed up to claim its prize (figure 55.13). Field researchers have observed that Japanese macaques learned

*a.*  *b.*

**Figure 55.12  Animal thinking?** *a.* This chimpanzee is stripping the leaves from a twig, which it will then use to probe a termite nest. This behavior strongly suggests that the chimpanzee is consciously planning ahead, with full knowledge of what it intends to do. *b.* This sea otter is using a rock as an "anvil," against which it bashes a clam to break it open. A sea otter will often keep a favorite rock for a long time, as though it has a clear idea of its future use of the rock. Behaviors such as these suggest that animals have cognitive abilities.

to wash sand off potatoes and to float grain to separate it from sand. Chimpanzees pull leaves off a tree branch and then stick the branch into the entrance of a termite nest to "fish" for food. Chimps also crack open nuts using pieces of wood in a "hammer and anvil" technique. Even more remarkable is that parents appear to teach nut cracking to their offspring!

Recent studies have found that chimpanzees and other primates show amazing behaviors that provide strong evidence of cognition. Chimpanzees will eat the leaves of medicinal plants when infected with certain parasites. Chimps also cooperate with other chimps in ways that suggest an understanding of past success. Cognitive ability is not limited to primates: Ravens and other corvid birds also show extraordinary insight and problem-solving ability (figure 55.14).

**Figure 55.13  Problem solving by a chimpanzee.** Unable to get the bananas by jumping, the chimpanzee devises a solution.

**Figure 55.14 Problem solving by a raven.** Confronted with a problem it has never previously faced, the raven figures out how to get the meat at the end of the string by repeatedly pulling up a bit of string and stepping on it.

**Learning Outcome Review 55.6**

Research has provided compelling evidence that some nonhuman animals are able solve problems and use reasoning, cognitive abilities once thought uniquely human.

■ *How could you determine whether a chimpanzee had the ability to count objects?*

## 55.7 Orientation and Migratory Behavior

**Learning Outcomes**

1. Define migration.
2. Distinguish between orientation and navigation.
3. Describe different systems for navigation.

Monarch butterflies and many birds travel thousands of miles over continents to overwintering sites in the tropics. Many animals travel away from a nest and then return. To do so, they track cues in the environment, often showing exceptional skill at orientation. Animals with a homing instinct, such as pigeons, recognize complex features of the environment to return to their home. Despite decades of study, our understanding of animal orientation is far from complete.

### Migration often involves populations moving large distances

Long-range, two-way movements are known as migrations. Each fall, ducks, geese, and many other birds migrate south along flyways from Canada across the United States, heading as far as South America, and then returning each spring.

Monarch butterflies also migrate each fall from central and eastern North America to their overwintering sites in several small, geographically isolated areas of coniferous forest in the mountains of central Mexico (figure 55.15). Each August, the butterflies begin a flight southward and at the end of winter, the monarchs begin the return flight to their summer breeding ranges. Two to five generations may be produced as the butterflies fly north: butterflies that migrate in the autumn to the precise locations in Mexico have never been there before!

Recent geographic range expansions by some migrating birds have revealed how migratory patterns change. When colonies of bobolinks became established in the western United States, far from their normal range in the Midwest and East, they did not migrate directly to their winter range in South America. Instead, they migrated east to their ancestral range, and then south along the original flyway (figure 55.16). Rather than changing the original migration pattern, they simply added a new segment. Scientists continue to study the western bobolinks to learn whether, in time, a more efficient migration path will evolve or

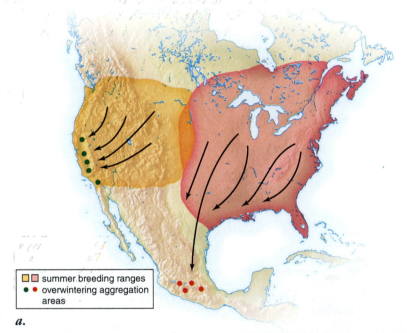

a.

b.                                         c.

**Figure 55.15 Migration of monarch butterflies (Danaus plexippus).** *a.* Monarchs from western North America overwinter in areas of mild climate along the Pacific coast. Those from eastern North America migrate over 3000 kilometers to Mexico. *b.* Monarch butterflies arrive at the remote forests of the overwintering grounds in Mexico, where they *(c)* form aggregations on the tree trunks.

whether the birds will always follow their ancestral course. The behavior of butterflies and birds accentuate the mysteries of the mechanism employed during migration.

## Migrating animals must be capable of orientation and navigation

To get from one place to another, animals must have a "map" (that is, know where to go) and a "compass" (use environmental cues to guide their journey). Orientation requires following a bearing such as a source of light, but navigation is the ability to set or adjust a bearing, and then follow it. The former is analogous to using a compass, while the latter is like using a compass in conjunction with a map. The nature of the "map" animals use is unclear.

Birds and other animals navigate by looking at the sun during the day and the stars at night. The indigo bunting is a short-distance nocturnal migrant bird. It flies during the day using the Sun as a guide, and compensates for the movement of the Sun in the sky as the day progresses. These birds use the positions of constellations around the North Star in the night sky as a compass.

Many migrating birds also have the ability to detect Earth's magnetic field and to orient themselves with respect

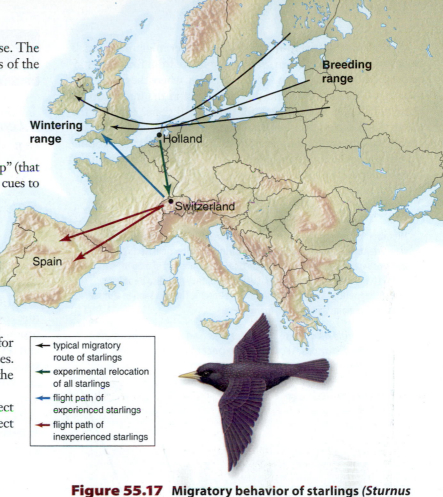

typical migratory
route of starlings
experimental relocation
of all starlings
flight path of
experienced starlings
flight path of
inexperienced starlings

**Figure 55.17 Migratory behavior of starlings (*Sturnus vulgaris*).** The navigational abilities of inexperienced birds differ from those of adults that have made the migratory journey before. Starlings were captured in Holland, halfway along their full migratory route from Baltic breeding grounds to wintering grounds in the British Isles; these birds were transported to Switzerland and released. Experienced older birds compensated for the displacement and flew toward the normal wintering grounds (blue arrow). Inexperienced young birds kept flying in the same direction, on a course that took them toward Spain (red arrows). These observations imply that inexperienced birds fly by orientation, but experienced birds learn true navigation.

to it when cues from the Sun or stars are not available. In an indoor cage, they will attempt to move in the correct geographic direction, even though there are no visible external cues. However, the placement of a magnet near the cage can alter the direction in which the birds attempt to move. Researchers have found magnetite, a magnetized iron ore, in the eyes and upper beaks of some birds, but how these sensory organs function is not known.

The first migration of a bird appears to be innately guided by both celestial cues (the birds fly mainly at night) and Earth's magnetic field. When the two cues are experimentally manipulated to give conflicting directions, the information provided by the stars seems to override the magnetic information. Recent studies, however, indicate that celestial cues indicate the general direction for migration, whereas magnetic cues indicate the specific migratory path (perhaps a turn the bird must make midroute). Experiments on starlings indicate that inexperienced birds migrate by orientation, but older birds that have migrated previously use true navigation (figure 55.17).

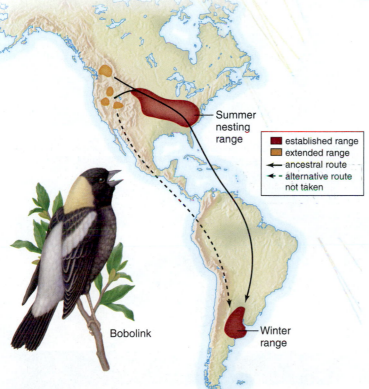

established range
extended range
ancestral route
alternative route
not taken

**Figure 55.16 Birds on the move.** The summer range of bobolinks (*Dolichonyx oryzivorus*) recently extended to the far western United States from their established range in the Midwest. When birds in these newly established populations migrate to South America in the winter, they do not fly directly to the winter range; instead, they first fly to the Midwest and then use the ancestral flyway, going much farther than if they flew directly to their winter range.

We know relatively little about how other migrating animals navigate. For instance, green sea turtles migrate from Brazil halfway across the Atlantic Ocean to Ascension Island, where the females lay their eggs. How do they find this tiny island in the middle of the ocean, which they haven't seen for perhaps 30 years? How do the young that hatch on the island know how to find their way to Brazil? Newly hatched turtles use wave action as a cue to head to sea. Some sea turtles use the Earth's magnetic field to maintain position in the North Atlantic, but turtle migration is still largely a mystery.

### Learning Outcomes Review 55.7

Migration is the long-distance movement of a population, often in a cyclic way. Orientation refers to following a bearing or a direction; navigation involves setting a bearing or direction based on some sort of map or memory. Many species use celestial navigation; they may also be able to detect magnetic fields when those cues are absent. The precision of animal migration remains a mystery in many species.

■ *Animals as diverse as butterflies and birds migrate over long distances. Would you expect them to use different navigation systems? Why or why not?*

## 55.8 Animal Communication

### Learning Outcomes

1. *Explain the nature of signals used in mate attraction.*
2. *Explain the role of courtship signals in reproductive isolation.*
3. *Describe how honeybees communicate information about the location of new food sources.*

Communication is central to species recognition and reproductive isolation, and to the interactions that are essential to social behavior. Much research in behavior analyzes the nature of communication signals, determining how they are produced and received, and identifies their ecological roles and evolutionary origins. Communication involves several signal modalities, including visual, acoustic, chemical, electric, and vibrational signals.

**Figure 55.18** **A stimulus–response chain.** Stickleback courtship involves a sequence of behaviors leading to the fertilization of eggs.

1. Female gives head-up display to male

2. Male swims zigzag to female and then leads her to nest

3. Male shows female entrance to nest

4. Female enters nest and spawns while male stimulates tail

5. Male enters nest and fertilizes eggs

## Successful reproduction depends on appropriate signals and responses

During courtship, animals produce signals to communicate with potential mates and with other members of their own sex. A stimulus–response chain sometimes occurs, in which the behavior of the male in turn releases a behavior in the female, resulting in mating (figure 55.18). These signals are usually highly species-specific. Many studies on communication involve designing experiments to determine which key stimuli associated with an animal's visual appearance, sounds, or odors convey information about the nature of the signals produced by the sender. One classical study analyzed territorial defense and courtship communication in stickleback fish (figure 55.19).

### Finding a mate: Communicating information about species identity

Courtship signals often restrict communication to members of the same species and in doing so serve a key function in reproductive isolation (see chapter 22). The flashes of fireflies (which are actually beetles) are species-specific signals: females recognize conspecific males by their flash pattern (figure 55.20), and

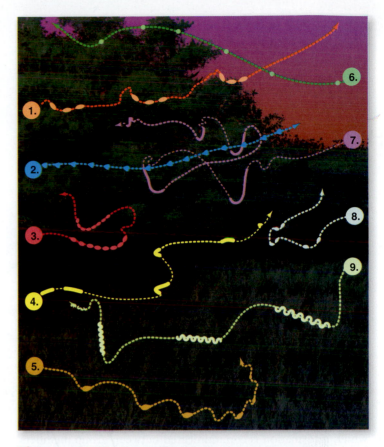

**Figure 55.20 Firefly fireworks.** The bioluminescent displays of these lampyrid beetles are species-specific and serve as behavioral mechanisms of reproductive isolation. Each number represents the flash pattern of a male of a different species.

### SCIENTIFIC THINKING

**Hypothesis:** *The red underside of male stickleback is the key stimulus that releases an aggressive response by a territory-holding male.*

**Prediction:** *Models with red coloration will trigger an attack by a resident male.*

**Test:** *Construct plastic models, some of which accurately resemble a stickleback male, but lack the red underside. Construct other models that vary in their fishlike appearance, but have red-colored undersides. Expose a territorial male to the models one at a time, and record the number of attacks.*

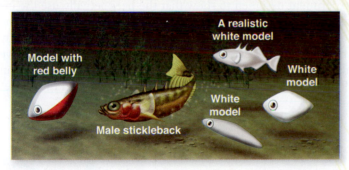

**Result:** *Realistic models lacking red elicit no response. Odd-shape models trigger an attack if they have red undersides, even if they poorly resemble fish.*

**Conclusion:** *The red underside of a male stickleback is the key stimulus that triggers aggressive behavior.*

**Further Experiments:** *How would you determine if the color of a male stickleback was a releaser of aggressive behavior? How would you know if sound was important? Could you determine if stimuli have additive effects? How? Why do you think the color red is important in territorial defense? Might it also be a courtship signal? What information might the color red encode for a female looking for a mate? (see also figure 55.18)*

**Figure 55.19 Key stimulus in stickleback fish.**

males recognize conspecific females by their flash response. This series of reciprocal responses provides a continuous "check" on the species identity of potential mates.

Pheromones, chemical messengers used for communication between individuals of the same species, serve as sex attractants in many animals. Female silk moths (*Bombyx mori*) produce a sex pheromone called bombykol in a gland associated with the reproductive system. The male's antennae contain numerous highly sensitive sensory receptors, and neurophysiological studies show they specifically detect bombykol. In some moth species, males can detect extremely low concentrations of sex pheromone and locate females from as far as 7 km away!

Many insects, amphibians, and birds produce species-specific acoustic signals to attract mates. Bullfrog males call by inflating and discharging air from their vocal sacs, located beneath the lower jaw. Females can distinguish a conspecific male's call from those of other frogs that may be in the same habitat and calling at the same time. As mentioned earlier, male birds sing to advertise their presence and to attract females. In many species, variations in the males' songs identify individual males in a population. In these species, the song is individually specific as well as species-specific. Vibrations, like sound signals, are a form of mechanical communication used by insects, amphibians, and other animals.

Courtship behaviors play a major role in sexual selection, which we discuss later in this chapter.

**Figure 55.21 Alarm calling by a prairie dog (*Cynomys ludovicianus*).** When a prairie dog sees a predator, it stands on its hind legs and gives an alarm call, which causes other prairie dogs to rapidly return to their burrows.

## Communication enables information exchange among group members

Many insects, fish, birds, and mammals live in social groups in which information is communicated between group members. For example, some individuals in mammalian societies serve as sentinels, vigilantly on the lookout for danger. When a predator appears, they give an alarm call, and group members respond by seeking shelter (figure 55.21). Social insects such as ants and honeybees produce alarm pheromones that trigger attack behavior. Ants also deposit trail pheromones between the nest and a food source to lead other colony members to food. Honeybees have an extremely complex dance language that directs hivemates to nectar sources.

### The dance language of the honeybee

The European honeybee lives in colonies of tens of thousands of individuals whose behaviors are integrated into a complex,

cooperative society. Worker bees may forage miles from the hive, collecting nectar and pollen from a variety of plants and switching between plant species depending on their energetic rewards. Food sources used by bees tend to occur in patches, and each patch offers much more food than a single bee can transport to the hive. A colony is able to exploit the resources of a patch because of the behavior of scout bees, which locate patches and communicate their location to hivemates through a dance language. Over many years, Nobel laureate Karl von Frisch (who shared the 1973 prize with Tinbergen and Lorenz), together with generations of students and colleagues, was able to unravel the details of dance language communication.

When a scout bee returns after finding a distant food source, she performs a remarkable behavior pattern called a waggle dance on a vertical comb in the darkness of the hive. The path of the bee during the dance resembles a figure-eight. On the straight part of the path (indicated with dashes in figure 55.22), the bee vibrates ("waggles") her abdomen while producing bursts of sound. The bee may stop periodically to give her hivemates a sample of the nectar carried in her crop. As she dances, she is followed closely by other bees, which soon appear at the new food source to assist in collecting food.

Von Frisch and his colleagues performed experiments to show that hivemates use information in the waggle dance to locate new food sources. The scout bee indicates the direction of the food source by representing the angle between the food source, the hive, and the Sun as the deviation from vertical of the straight run of the dance performed on the hive comb. Thus if the bee danced with the straight run pointing directly up, then the food source would be in the direction of the Sun. If the food is at a 30° angle to the right of the Sun's position, then the straight run would be oriented upward at a 30° angle to the right of vertical) (figure 55.22*a*). The distance to the food source is indicated by the duration of the straight run. One ingenious experiment designed to show that the bees actually use the information in the dance tricked bees that were unaware of the location of food into misinterpreting the directions given by the scout bee's dance. Computer-controlled robot bees have also been used to give hivemates incorrect information, again demonstrating that bees use the directions coded in the dance!

**Figure 55.22 The waggle dance of honeybees (*Apis mellifera*). *a*.** The angle between the food source, the nest, and the Sun is represented by a dancing bee as the angle between the straight part of the dance and vertical. The food is 30° to the right of the Sun, and the straight part of the bee's dance on the hive is 30° to the right of vertical. *b*. A scout bee dances on a comb in the hive.

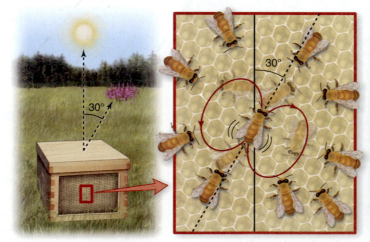

*a.*

*b.*

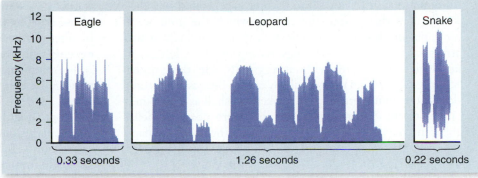

a.

b.

**Figure 55.23** **Primate semantics.** Vervet monkeys (*Cercopithecus aethiops*) give different alarm calls (*a*) when troop members sight an eagle, leopard, or snake. *b.* Each distinctive call elicits a different and adaptive escape behavior.

### Language in nonhuman primates and humans

Evolutionary biologists have sought the origins of human language in the communication systems of monkeys and apes. Some nonhuman primates have a "vocabulary" that allows individuals to signal the identity of specific predators. Different vocalizations of African vervet monkeys, for example, indicate eagles, leopards, or snakes, among other threats (figure 55.23).

The complexity of human language would at first appear to defy biological explanation, but closer examination suggests that the differences are in fact superficial—all languages share many basic similarities. All of the roughly 3000 languages draw from the same set of 40 consonant and vowel sounds (English uses two dozen of them), and humans of all cultures can acquire and learn them. Researchers believe these similarities reflect the way our brains handle abstract information. The discovery of *FoxP2*, the so-called "language gene," supports the idea that human language has a hereditary basis.

### Learning Outcomes Review 55.8

Animal communication involves production and reception of signals, in the form of sounds, chemicals, or movements, that primarily have an ecological function. Courtship signals are highly species-specific and serve as a mechanism of reproductive isolation. Animals living in social groups, such as honeybees, may use complex systems of communication to exchange information about food and predators.

■ *Two species of moth use the same sex pheromone to locate mates. Explain how these species could nevertheless be reproductively isolated.*

## 55.9 Behavioral Ecology

### Learning Outcomes

1. *Describe behavioral ecology.*
2. *Discuss the economic analysis of behaviors.*

Niko Tinbergen pioneered the study of the adaptive function of behavior. Stated simply, this is how behavior allows an animal to stay alive and keep its offspring alive. For example, Tinbergen observed that after gull nestlings hatch, the parents remove the eggshells from the nest. To understand why (ultimate causation), he painted chicken eggs to resemble gull eggs (figure 55.24), which had camouflage coloration to allow them

**Figure 55.24** **The adaptive value of egg coloration.** Niko Tinbergen, a winner of the 1973 Nobel Prize in physiology or medicine, painted chicken eggs to resemble the mottled brown camouflage of gull eggs. The eggs were used to test the hypothesis that camouflaged eggs are more difficult for predators to find and thus increase the young's chances of survival.

to be inconspicuous against the natural background. He distributed them throughout the area in which the gulls were nesting, placing broken eggshells with their prominent white interiors next to some of the eggs. As a control, he left other camouflaged eggs alone without eggshells. He then noted which eggs were found more easily by crows. Because the crows could use the white interior of a broken eggshell as a cue, they ate more of the camouflaged eggs that were near eggshells. Tinbergen concluded that eggshell removal behavior is adaptive: it reduces predation and thus increases the offspring's chances of survival.

Tinbergen is credited with being one of the founders of **behavioral ecology,** the study of how natural selection shapes behavior. This branch of ecology examines the adaptive significance of behavior, or how behavior may increase survival and reproduction. Current research in behavioral ecology focuses on how behavior contributes to an animal's reproductive success, or fitness. As we saw in section 55.3, differences in behavior among individuals often result from genetic differences. Therefore, natural selection operating on behavior has the potential to produce evolutionary change.

Consequently, the field of behavioral ecology is concerned with two questions. First, is behavior adaptive? Although it is tempting to assume that behavior must in some way represent an adaptive response to the environment, this need not be the case. As you saw in chapter 20, traits can appear for many reasons other than natural selection, such as genetic drift, gene flow, or the correlated consequences of selection on other traits. Moreover, traits may be present in a population because they evolved as adaptations in the past, but are no longer useful. These possibilities hold true for behavioral traits as much as for any other kind of trait.

If behavior is adaptive, the next question is: How is it adaptive? Although the ultimate criterion is reproductive success, behavioral ecologists are interested in how behavior can lead to greater reproductive success. Does a behavior enhance energy intake, thus increasing the number of offspring produced? Does it increase mating success? Does it decrease the chance of predation? The job of a behavioral ecologist is to determine the effect of a behavioral trait—for example, foraging efficiency—on each of these activities and then to discover whether increases translate into increased fitness. Benefits and costs of behaviors, estimated in terms of energy or offspring, are often used to analyze the adaptive nature of behavior.

## Foraging behavior can directly influence energy intake and individual fitness

A useful way to understand the approach of behavioral ecology is by focusing on foraging behavior. For many animals, food comes in a variety of sizes. Larger foods may contain more energy but may be harder to capture and less abundant. In addition, animals may forage for some types of food that are farther away than other types. For these animals foraging involves a trade-off between a food's energy content and the cost of obtaining it. The net energy (estimated in calories or joules) gained by feeding on prey of each size is simply the energy content of the prey minus the energy costs of pursuing and handling it. According to

optimal foraging theory, natural selection favors individuals whose foraging behavior is as energetically efficient as possible. In other words, animals tend to feed on prey that maximize their net energy intake per unit of foraging time.

A number of studies have demonstrated that foragers do prefer prey that maximize energy return. Shore crabs, for example, tend to feed primarily on intermediate-sized mussels, which provide the greatest energy return; larger mussels yield more energy, but also take considerably more energy to crack open (figure 55.25).

This optimal foraging approach assumes natural selection will favor behavior that maximizes energy acquisition if the increased energy reserves lead to increases in reproductive success. In both Colombian ground squirrels and captive zebra finches, a direct relationship exists between net energy intake and the number of offspring raised; similarly, the reproductive success of orb-weaving spiders is related to how much food they can capture.

Animals have other needs besides energy, however, and sometimes these needs conflict. One obvious need is the avoidance of predators: Often, the behavior that maximizes energy intake is not the one that minimizes predation risk. In this case, the behavior that maximizes fitness often may reflect a trade-off between obtaining the most energy at the least risk of being eaten. Not surprisingly, many studies have shown that a wide variety of animal species alter their foraging behavior— becoming less active, spending more time watching for predators, or staying nearer to cover—when predators are present. Compromises, in this case a trade-off between vigilance and feeding, may thus be made during foraging.

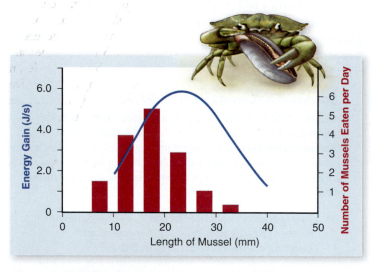

**Figure 55.25 Optimal diet.** The shore crab selects a diet of energetically profitable prey. The curve describes the net energy gain (equal to energy gained minus energy expended) derived from feeding on different sizes of mussels. The bar graph shows the numbers of mussels of each size in the diet. Shore crabs tend to feed on those mussels that provide the most energy.

**Inquiry question**

? What factors might be responsible for the slight difference in peak prey length relative to the length optimal for maximum energy gain?

Optimal foraging theory assumes that energy-maximizing behavior has evolved by natural selection. Therefore, it must have a genetic basis. For example, female zebra finches particularly successful in maximizing net energy intake tend to have similarly successful offspring. In this study, young birds were removed from their mothers before they were able to leave the nest, so this similarity indicates that foraging behavior probably has a genetic component. Studies on other animals show that age, experience, and learning are also important to the development of efficient foraging.

## Territorial behavior evolves if the benefits of holding a territory exceed the costs

Animals often move over a large area, or home range, during their course of activity. In many species, the home range of several individuals overlaps in time or in space, but each individual defends a portion of its home range and uses it and its resources exclusively. This behavior is called **territoriality** (figure 55.26).

The defining characteristic of territorial behavior is defense against intrusion and resource use by other individuals. Territories are defended by displays advertising that territories are occupied, and by overt aggression. A bird sings from its perch within a territory to prevent take-over by a neighboring bird. If a potential usurper is not deterred by the song, the territory owner may attack and try to drive it away. But territorial defense has its costs. Singing is energetically expensive, and attacks can lead to injury. Using a signal (a song or visual display) to advertise occupancy can reveal a bird's position to a predator.

Why does an animal bear the costs of territorial defense? Energetic benefits of territoriality may take the form of increased food intake due to exclusive use of resources, access to mates, or access to refuges from predators. Studies of nectar-feeding birds such as hummingbirds and sunbirds provide an example (figure 55.27). A bird benefits from having the exclusive use of a patch of flowers because it can efficiently harvest the nectar the flowers produce. To maintain exclusive use, the bird

**Figure 55.27** **The benefit of territoriality.** Sunbirds (on the left), found in Africa and ecologically similar to New World hummingbirds (on the right), protect their food source by attacking other sunbirds that approach flowers in their territory.

must actively defend the patch. The benefits of exclusive use outweigh the costs of defense only under certain conditions.

Sunbirds, for example, expend 3000 calories per hour chasing intruders from a territory. Whether the benefit of defending a territory will exceed this cost depends on the amount of nectar in the flowers and how efficiently the bird can collect it. When flowers are very scarce or nectar levels are very low, a nectar-feeding bird may not gain enough energy to balance the energy used in defense. Under these conditions, it is not energetically advantageous to be territorial. Similarly, when flowers are very abundant, a bird can efficiently meet its daily energy requirements without behaving territorially and adding the costs of defense. Again, from an energetic standpoint, defending abundant resources isn't worth the cost, either. Territoriality therefore only occurs at intermediate levels of flower availability and nectar production, when the benefits of defense outweigh the costs.

In many species, access to females is a more important determinant of territory size for males than is food availability. In some lizards, for example, males maintain enormous territories during the breeding season. These territories, which encompass the territories of several females, are much larger than would be required to supply enough food, and they are defended vigorously. In the nonbreeding season, by contrast, male territory size decreases dramatically, as does aggressive territorial behavior.

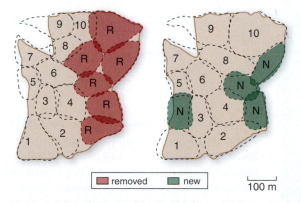

removed | new | 100 m

**Figure 55.26** **Competition for space.** Territory size in birds is adjusted according to the number of competitors. When six pairs of great tits (*Parus major*) were removed from their territories (indicated by R in the left figure), their territories were taken over by other birds in the area and by four new pairs (indicated by N in the right figure). Numbers correspond to the birds present before and after.

### Learning Outcomes Review 55.9

Behavioral ecology is the study of the adaptive significance of behavior—that is, how it affects survival and reproductive success. An economic approach estimates the energy benefits and costs of a behavior and assumes that animals gain more from a behavior than they expend, obtaining a fitness advantage. Foraging behavior and defense of a territory can be analyzed in this way. Apart from energy gains, considerations such as avoiding predators are also important to fitness.

■ *The Hawaiian honeycreeper, a nectar-feeding bird, fails to defend flowers that are either infrequently encountered or very abundant. Why?*

## 55.10 Reproductive Strategies and Sexual Selection

### Learning Outcomes

1. Explain parental investment and the prediction it makes about mate choice.
2. Describe how sexual selection leads to the evolution of secondary sexual characteristics.
3. Explain why some species are generally monogamous and other are polygynous.

During the breeding season, animals make several important life-history "decisions" concerning their choice of mates, how many mates to have, and how much time and energy to devote to rearing offspring. These decisions are all aspects of an animal's **reproductive strategy,** a set of behaviors that presumably have evolved to maximize reproductive success. Energetic costs of reproduction appear to have been critically important to behavioral differences between females and males. Ecological factors such as the way food resources, nest sites, and members of the opposite sex are spatially distributed in the environment, as well as disease, are important in the evolution of reproductive decisions.

### The sexes often have different reproductive strategies

Males and females have the common goal of improving the quantity and quality of offspring they produce, but usually differ in the way they attempt to maximize fitness. Such a difference in reproductive behavior is clearly seen in mate choice. Darwin was the first to observe that females often do not mate with the first male they encounter, but instead seem to evaluate a male's quality and then decide whether to mate. Peahens prefer to mate with peacocks that have more eyespots on their elaborate tail feathers (figure 55.28b, c). Similarly, female frogs prefer to mate with males having more acoustically complex, and thus attractive, calls. This behavior, called mate choice, is well known in many invertebrate and vertebrate species.

Males are selective in choosing a mate much less frequently than females. Why should this be? Many of the differences in reproductive strategies between the sexes can be understood by comparing the parental investment made by males and females. **Parental investment** refers to the energy and time each sex makes ("invests") in producing and rearing offspring; it is, in effect, an estimate of the energy expended by males and females in each reproductive event.

Numerous studies have shown that females generally have a higher parental investment. One reason is that eggs are much larger than sperm—195,000 times larger in humans! Eggs contain proteins and lipids in the yolk and other nutrients for the developing embryo, but sperm are little more than mobile DNA packages. In some groups of animals (mammals, for example), females are responsible for gestation and lactation, costly reproductive functions only they can carry out.

The consequence of such inequalities in reproductive investment is that the sexes face very different selective pressures. Because any single reproductive event is relatively inexpensive for males, they can best increase their fitness by mating with as many females as possible. This is because

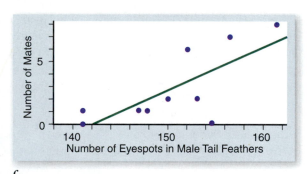

c.

**Figure 55.28 Products of sexual selection.**
Attracting mates with long feathers is common in bird species such as **(a)** the African paradise whydah (*Vidua paradisaea*), and **(b)** the peacock (*Pavo cristatus*) which show pronounced sexual dimorphism. **c.** Female peahens prefer to mate with males having greater numbers of eyespots in their tail feathers.

### Inquiry question

**?** Why do females prefer males with more spots?

male fitness is likely limited by the amount of sperm they can produce. By contrast, each reproductive event for females is much more costly, and the number of eggs that can be produced often limits reproductive success. For this reason, a female should be choosy, trying to pick the male that can provide the greatest benefit to her offspring and thus improve her fitness.

These conclusions hold only when female reproductive investment is much greater than that of males. In species with biparental care, males may contribute equally to the cost of raising young; in this case, the degree of mate choice should be more equal between the sexes.

In some cases, male investment exceeds that of females. For example, male Mormon crickets transfer a protein-containing packet (a spermatophore) to females during mating. Almost 30% of a male's body weight is made up by the spermatophore, which provides nutrition for the female and helps her develop her eggs. As we might expect from our model of mate choice, in this case it is the females that compete with one another for access to males, which are the choosy sex. Indeed, males are quite selective, favoring heavier females. Heavier females have more eggs; thus, males that choose larger females leave more offspring (figure 55.29).

Males care for eggs and developing young in many species, including seahorses and a number of birds and insects. As with Mormon crickets, these males are often choosy, and females compete for mates.

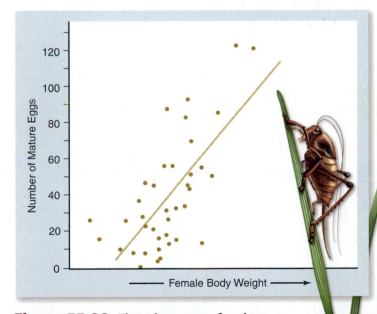

**Figure 55.29  The advantage of male mate choice.** Male Mormon crickets (*Anabrus simplex*) choose heavier females as mates, and larger females have more eggs. Thus, male mate selection increases fitness.

### Inquiry question

 Is there a benefit to females for mating with large males?

## Sexual selection occurs through mate competition and mate choice

As discussed in chapter 20, the reproductive success of an individual is determined by how long the individual lives, how frequently it mates, and how many offspring it produces per mating. The second of these factors, competition for mates, is termed **sexual selection.** Some people consider sexual selection to be distinctive from natural selection, but others see it as a subset of natural selection, just one of the many factors affecting an organism's fitness.

Sexual selection involves both **intrasexual selection,** or competitive interactions between members of one sex ("the power to conquer other males in battle," as Darwin put it), and **intersexual selection,** which is another name for mate choice ("the power to charm"). Sexual selection leads to the evolution of structures used in combat with other males, such as a deer's antlers and a ram's horns, as well as ornaments used to "persuade" members of the opposite sex to mate, such as long tail feathers and bright plumage (see figure 55.28a, b). These traits are called **secondary sexual characteristics.**

Selection strongly favors any trait that confers greater ability in mate competition. Larger body size is a great advantage if dominance is important, as it is in territorial species. Males may thus be considerably larger than females. Such differences between the sexes are referred to as sexual dimorphism. In other species, structures used for fighting, such as horns, antlers, and large canine teeth, have evolved to be larger in males because of the advantage they give in intrasexual competition.

Sometimes **sperm competition** occurs between the sperm of different males if females mate with multiple males. This type of competition, which occurs after mating, has selected for sperm-transfer organs designed to remove the sperm of a prior mating, large testes to produce more sperm per mating, and sperm that hook themselves together to swim more rapidly. These traits enhance the likelihood of fertilizing an egg.

### Intrasexual selection

In many species, individuals of one sex—usually males—compete with one another for the opportunity to mate. Competition can occur for a territory in which females feed or bear young. Males may also directly compete for the females themselves. A few successful males may engage in an inordinate number of matings, while most males do not mate at all. For example, elephant seal males control territories on breeding beaches and a few dominant males do most of the breeding (figure 55.30). On one beach, for example, eight males impregnated 348 females, while the remaining males mated rarely, if at all.

### Intersexual selection

Intersexual selection concerns the active choice of a mate. Mate choice has both direct and indirect benefits.

**Direct benefits of mate choice.** In some cases, the benefits of mate choice are obvious. If males help raise offspring, females benefit by choosing the male that can provide the best

**Figure 55.30 Female defense polygyny in northern elephant seals (*Mirounga angustirostris*).** Male elephant seals fight with one another for possession of territories. Only the largest males can hold territories, which contain many females.

care—the better the parent, the more offspring she is likely to rear. In other species, males provide no care, but maintain territories that provide food, nesting sites, and predator refuges. In red deer, males that hold territories with the highest quality grasses mate with the most females. In this case, there is a direct benefit of a female mating with such a territory owner: She feeds with little disturbance on quality food.

**Indirect benefits of mate choice.** In many species, however, males provide no direct benefits of any kind to females. In such cases, it is not intuitively obvious what females have to gain by being "choosy." Moreover, what could be the possible benefit of choosing a male with an extremely long tail or a complex song?

A number of theories have been proposed to explain the evolution of such preferences. One idea is that females choose the male that is the healthiest or oldest. Large males, for example, have probably been successful at living long, acquiring a lot of food, and resisting parasites and disease. In other species, features other than size may indicate a male's condition. In guppies and some birds, the brightness of a male's color reflects the quality of his diet and overall health. Females may gain two benefits from mating with the healthiest males. First, healthy males are less likely to be carrying diseases, which might be transmitted to the female during mating. Second, to the extent that the males' success in living long and prospering is the re-

sult of his genetic makeup, the female will be ensuring that her offspring receive good genes from their father.

Several experimental studies in fish and moths have examined whether female mate choice leads to greater reproductive success. In these experiments, females in one group were allowed to choose males, whereas males were randomly mated to a different group of females. Offspring of females that chose their mates were more vigorous and survived better than offspring from females given no choice, which suggests that females preferred males with a better genetic makeup.

A variant of this theory goes one step further. In some cases, females prefer mates with traits that appear to be detrimental to survival (see figure 55.28c). The long tail of the peacock is a hindrance in flying and makes males more vulnerable to predators. Why should females prefer males with such traits? The **handicap hypothesis** states that only genetically superior mates can survive with such a handicap. By choosing a male with the largest handicap, the female is ensuring that her offspring will receive these quality genes. Of course, the male offspring will also inherit the genes for the handicap. For this reason, evolutionary biologists are still debating the merit of this hypothesis.

**Alternative theories about the evolution of mate choice.** Some courtship displays appear to have evolved from a predisposition in the female's sensory system to respond to certain stimuli. For example, females may be better able to detect particular colors or sounds at a certain frequency, and thus be attracted to such signals. **Sensory exploitation** involves the evolution in males of a signal that "exploits" these preexisting biases. For example, if females are particularly adept at detecting red objects, then red coloration may evolve in males as part of a courtship display.

To understand the evolution of courtship calls, consider the vocalizations of the Túngara frog (figure 55.31). Unlike related species, males include a short burst of sound, termed a "chuck," at the end of their calls. Recent research suggests that not only are females of this species particularly attracted to calls of this sort, but so are females of related species, even though males of these species do not produce "chucks."

A great variety of other hypotheses have been proposed to explain the evolution of mating preferences. Many of these hypotheses may be correct in some circumstances, but none seems capable of explaining all of the variation in mating behavior in the animal world. This is an area of vibrant research, with new discoveries appearing regularly.

**Figure 55.31**
**Male Túngara frog (*Physalaemus pustulosus*) calling.** Female frogs of several species in the genus *Physalaemus* prefer males that include a "chuck" in their call. However, only males of the Túngaru frog (*a*) produce such calls (*b*); males of other species do not (*c*).

*a.*

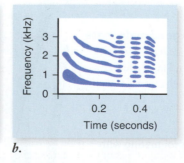

*b.*

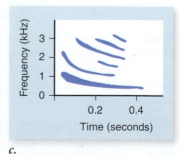

*c.*

## Mating systems reflect the ability of parents to care for offspring and are influenced by ecology

The number of individuals with which an animal mates during the breeding season varies among species. Mating systems include monogamy (one male mates with one female), polygyny (one male mates with more than one female; see figure 55.30), and polyandry (one female mates with more than one male). Only monogamous mating includes a pair bond (like prairie voles). Like mate choice, mating systems have evolved to allow females and males to maximize fitness.

The option of having more than one mate may be constrained by the need for offspring care. If females and males are able to care for young, then the presence of both parents may be necessary for young to be reared successfully. Monogamy may thus be favored. Generally this is the case for birds, in which over 90% of all species appear to be monogamous. A male may either remain with his mate and provide care for the offspring or desert that mate to search for others; both strategies may increase his fitness. The strategy that natural selection will favor depends on the requirement for male assistance in feeding or defending the offspring. In some species (like humans!), offspring are **altricial**—they require prolonged and extensive care. In these species, the need for care by two parents reduces the tendency for the male to desert his mate and seek other matings. In species in which the young are **precocial** (requiring little parental care), males may be more likely to be polygynous because the need for their parenting is lower. In mammals, only females lactate, freeing males from feeding offspring. It follows that most mammals are polygynous.

Mating systems are strongly influenced by ecology. A male may defend a territory that holds nest sites or food sources sufficient for more than one female. If territories vary in quality or quantity of resources, a female's fitness is maximized if she mates with a male holding a high-quality territory, even if he has mated. Although a male may already have a mate, it is still more advantageous for the female to breed with a mated male holding a high-quality territory than with an unmated male holding a low-quality territory. This favors the evolution of polygyny.

Polyandry is relatively rare, but the evolution of multiple mating by females is becoming better understood. It is best known in birds like spotted sandpipers and jacanas living in highly productive environments such as marshes and wetlands. Here, females take advantage of the increased resources available to rear offspring by laying clutches of eggs with more than one male. Males provide all incubation and parenting, and females mate and leave eggs with two or more males.

Females may also mate with several males to genetically diversify their offspring, which in turn increases disease resistance. This appears to be the case in honey bees, for example, in which a queen may mate with many males.

### Extra-pair copulations

The "monogamy" of many bird species has been re-evaluated as DNA fingerprinting (see chapter 15) has become commonly used to determine paternity and precisely quantify the reproductive success of individual males (figure 55.32a). In red-winged blackbirds (figure 55.32b), researchers established that

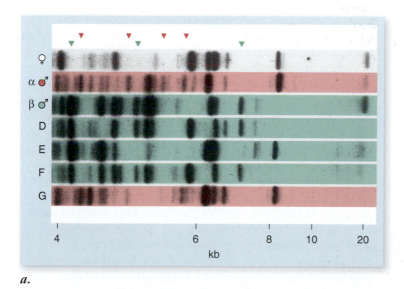

*a.*

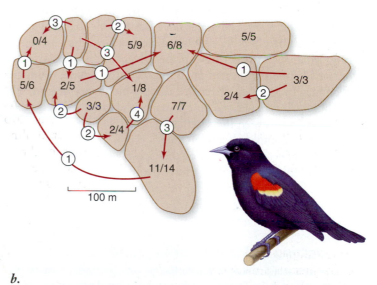

*b.*

**Figure 55.32 The study of paternity.** *a.* A DNA fingerprinting gel from the dunnock *(Prunella modularis)*. The bands represent fragments of DNA of different lengths. The four nestlings (D–G) were in the nest of the female. By comparing the bands present in the two males and the female, we can determine which male fathered which offspring. The triangles point to the bands that are diagnostic for one male and not the other. In this case, the β-male fathered three (D, E, F, but not G) of the four offspring. *b.* Results of a DNA fingerprinting study in red-winged blackbirds *(Agelaius phoeniceus)*. Fractions indicate the proportion of offspring fathered by the male in whose territory the nest occurred. Arrows indicate how many offspring were fathered by particular males outside of each territory. Nests on some territories were not sampled.

half of all nests contained at least one hatchling fertilized by a male other than the territory owner; overall, 20% of the offspring were the result of such **extra-pair copulations (EPCs)**.

What is the evolutionary advantage of EPCs? For males, the answer is obvious: increased reproductive success. Females, on the other hand, may mate with genetically superior individuals even if already paired with a male, thus enhancing the genes passed on to their offspring. The female doesn't produce more offspring, but offpring of better genetic quality. In some birds and other animals, EPCs may help females increase the amount of care they get from males to raise their offspring. This is exactly what happens in a common English bird, the dunnock. Females mate not only with the territory owner, but also with subordinate males that hang around the edge of the territory. If these subordinates mate a sufficient number of times with a female, they will help raise her young, presumably because they may have fathered some of these young.

### Alternative mating strategies

Natural selection has led to the evolution of many ways of increasing reproductive success. For example, in many species of fish, there are two genetic classes of males. One group is large and defends territories to obtain matings. The other group is small and adopts a completely different strategy. These males do not maintain territories, but loiter at the edge of the territories of large males. Just at the end of a male's courtship, when the female is laying her eggs and the territorial male is depositing sperm, the smaller male darts in and releases its own sperm into the water, thus fertilizing some of the eggs. If this strategy is successful, natural selection will favor the evolution of these two different male reproductive strategies.

Similar patterns are seen in other organisms. In some dung beetles, territorial males have large horns that they use to guard the chambers in which females reside, whereas genetically small males don't have horns. Instead, the smaller males dig side tunnels and attempt to intercept the female inside her chamber. In Isopods, there are three genetic size classes. The medium-sized males pass for females and enter a large male's territory in this way; the smallest class are so tiny, they are able to sneak in completely undetected.

This is just a glimpse of the rich diversity in mating systems and mating tactics that have evolved. The bottom line is: If there is a way of increasing reproductive success, natural selection will favor its evolution.

### Learning Outcomes Review 55.10

The sex that invests more in reproduction (parental investment) tends to exhibit mate choice. Females or males can be selective, depending on the energy and time they devote to parental care. Sexual selection governs evolution of secondary sex characteristics in that mates are chosen on the basis of phenotype and competitive success. Reproductive success influences whether males and females mate monogamously or with multiple partners.

■ *Pipefish males incubate young in a brood pouch. Which sex would you expect to show mate choice? Why?*

## 55.11 Altruism

### Learning Outcomes

1.  **Explain altruism and its benefits.**
2.  **Explain kin selection and inclusive fitness.**
3.  **Discuss how haplodiploidy influences kin selection in eusocial insects.**

Understanding the evolution of altruism has been a particular challenge to evolutionary biologists, including Darwin himself. Why should an individual decrease his or her own fitness to help another? How could genes for altruism be favored by natural selection, given that the frequency of such genes should decrease in populations through time?

In fact, there can be great benefits to being an altruist, even if the altruism leads an individual to forego reproduction or even sacrifice its own life. Let's examine how this can work.

**Altruism** is behavior that benefits another individual at a cost to the actor. Humans sacrificing themselves in times of war or placing themselves in jeopardy to help their children are examples, but altruism also has been described in an extraordinary variety of organisms. In many bird species, for example, there are "helpers at the nest"—birds other than parents who assist in raising their young. In both mammals and birds, individuals that spy a predator may give an alarm call, alerting other members of their group to allow them to escape, even though such an act might call the predator's attention to the caller. And in social insects like ants, workers are sterile offspring that help their mother, the colony's queen, to reproduce.

A number of explanations have been put forward to explain the evolution of altruism. Once it was thought that altruism evolved for the "good of the species." Individuals that fail to mate, for example, have been called "altruists" because their lack of success in competition has been misinterpreted as a willingness to forego reproduction so that the population or species does not increase in size, exhaust its resources, and go extinct. This group selection explanation (selection acting on a population or species) is simply incorrect because individuals that fail to secure mates and not breed will not leave any offspring. Therefore, their "altruism" would not be favored by selection.

Current studies of altruism note that seemingly altruistic acts are in fact selfish. For example, helpers at the nest are often young birds that gain valuable parenting experience by assisting established breeders; this may give them an advantage when they breed. Moreover, they may have limited opportunities to reproduce on their own, and by hanging around breeding pairs, may inherit the territory when established breeders die.

### Reciprocity theory explains altruism between unrelated individuals

One explanation of altruism proposes that genetically unrelated individuals may form "partnerships" in which mutual exchanges of altruistic acts occur because they benefit both participants.

Partners are willing to give aid at one time and delay "repayment" for the good deed to a time in the future when they themselves are in need. In **reciprocal altruism,** the partnerships are stable because "cheaters" (nonreciprocators) are discriminated against and do not receive future aid. According to this hypothesis, if the altruistic act is relatively inexpensive, the small benefit a cheater receives by not reciprocating is far outweighed by the potential cost of not receiving future aid. Under these conditions, cheating behavior should be eliminated by selection.

Vampire bats roost in hollow trees, caves, and mines in groups of 8 to 12 individuals (figure 55.33). Because bats have a high metabolic rate, individuals that have not fed recently may die. Bats that have found a host imbibe a great deal of blood, so giving up a small amount to keep a roostmate from starvation presents no great energy cost to the donor. Vampire bats tend to share blood with past reciprocators that are not necessarily relatives. If an individual fails to give blood to a bat from which it received blood in the past, it will be excluded from future bloodsharing. Reciprocity routinely occurs in many primates, including humans (obviously!).

## Kin selection theory proposes a direct genetic advantage to altruism

The great population geneticist J. B. S. Haldane once passionately said in a pub that he would willingly lay down his life for two brothers or eight first cousins.

Evolutionarily speaking, this sacrifice makes sense, because for each allele Haldane received from his parents, his brothers each had a 50% chance of receiving the same allele (figure 55.34). Statistically, it is expected that two of his brothers would pass on as many of Haldane's particular combination

**Figure 55.33 Truth is stranger than fiction: Reciprocal altruism in vampire bats (Desmodus rotundus).** Vampire bats do feed on the blood of large mammals, but they don't transform into people and sleep in coffins. Vampires live in groups and share blood meals. They remember which bats have provided them with blood in the past and are more likely to share with those bats that have shared with them previously. The bats here are feeding on cattle in Brazil.

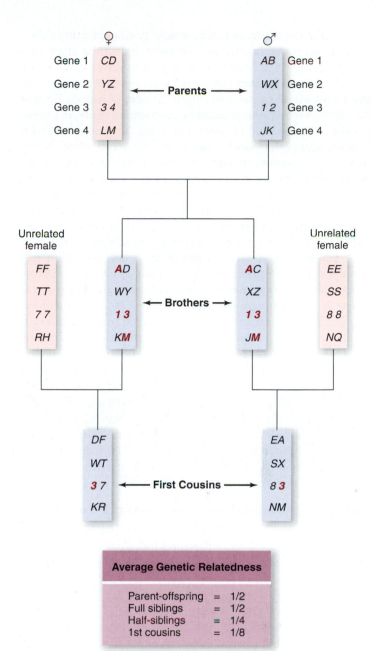

**Figure 55.34 Hypothetical example of genetic relationships.** On average, full siblings share half of their alleles. By contrast, cousins only share one-eighth of their alleles on average. Each letter and number represents a different allele.

of alleles to the next generation as Haldane himself would. Similarly, Haldane and a first cousin would share an eighth of their alleles (see figure 55.34). Their parents, who are siblings, would each share half their alleles, and each of their children would receive half of these, of which half on the average would be in common: $1/2 \times 1/2 \times 1/2 = 1/8$. Eight first cousins would therefore pass on as many of those alleles to the next generation as Haldane himself would.

The most compelling explanation for the kin-related origin of altruism was presented by one of the most influential evolutionary biologists of our time, William D. Hamilton, in 1964. Hamilton understood Haldane's point: Natural selection will favor any behavior, including the sacrifice of life, that increases the propagation of an individual's alleles.

Hamilton mathematically showed that by directing aid toward close genetic relatives, an altruist may increase the reproductive success of its relatives enough to not only compensate for the reduction in its own fitness, but even increase its fitness beyond what would be possible without assisting relatives. Because the altruist's behavior increases the propagation of alleles in relatives, it will be favored by natural selection. Selection that favors altruism directed toward relatives is called kin selection. Although the behaviors are altruistic, the genes are actually "behaving selfishly," because they encourage the organism to favor the success of copies of themselves in relatives. In other words, if an individual has a dominant allele that causes altruism, any action that increases the frequency of this allele in future generations will be favored, even if that action is detrimental to the actor.

Hamilton then defined reproductive success with a new concept—inclusive fitness. Inclusive fitness considers gene propagation through both direct (personal fitness) and indirect (the fitness of relatives) reproduction. Hamilton's kin selection model predicts that altruism is likely to be directed toward close relatives. The more closely related two individuals are, the greater the potential genetic payoff, and the greater inclusive fitness. This is described by Hamilton's rule, which states that altruistic acts are favored when $rb > c$. In this expression, $b$ and $c$ are the benefits and costs of the altruistic act, respectively, and $r$ is the coefficient of relatedness, the proportion of alleles shared by two individuals through common descent. For example, an individual should be willing to have one less child ($c = 1$) if such actions allow a half-sibling, which shares one-quarter of its genes ($r = 0.25$), to have five or more additional offspring ($b = 5$).

### Haplodiploidy and altruism in ants, bees, and wasps

The relationship between genetic relatedness, kin selection, and altruism can be best understood using social insects as an example. A hive of honeybees consists of a single queen, who is the sole egg-layer, and tens of thousands of her offspring, female workers with nonfunctional ovaries (figure 55.35). Honeybees are eusocial ("truly" social): their societies are defined by reproductive division of labor (only the queen reproduces), cooperative care of the brood (workers nurse, clean, and forage), and overlap of generations (the queen lives with several generations of her offspring).

Darwin was perplexed by eusociality. How could natural selection favor the evolution of sterile workers that left no offspring? It remained for Hamilton to explain the origin of eusociality in hymenopterans (bees, wasps, and ants) using his kin selection model. In these insects, males are haploid (produced from unfertilized eggs) and females are diploid. This system of sex determination and parthenogenesis, called haplodiploidy, leads to unusual genetic relatedness among colony members. If the queen is fertilized by a single male, then all female offspring will inherit exactly the same alleles from their father (because he is haploid and has only one copy of each allele). Female offspring (workers and future queens) will also share among themselves, on average, half of the alleles they get from their mother, the queen. Consequently, they will share, on average, 75% of their alleles with each sister (to verify this, rework figure 55.34, but allow the father to only have one allele for each gene).

Now recall Haldane's statement of commitment to family while you read this section. If a worker should have offspring of

**Figure 55.35** **Reproductive division of labor in honeybees.** The queen (center) is the sole egg-layer. Her daughters are sterile workers.

her own, she would share only half of her alleles with her young (the other half would come from their father). Thus, because of this close genetic relatedness due to haplodiploidy, workers would propagate more of their own alleles by giving up their own reproduction to assist their mother in rearing their sisters, some of whom will be new queens, start new colonies, and reproduce.

In this way, the unusual haplodiploid system may have set the "genetic stage" for the evolution of eusociality. Indeed, eusociality has evolved at least 12 separate times in the Hymenoptera. One wrinkle in this theory, however, is that eusocial systems have evolved in other insects (thrips, weevils, and termites), and mammals (naked mole rats). Although thrips are also haplodiploid, termites and naked mole rats are not. Thus, although haplodiploidy may have facilitated the evolution of eusociality, other factors can influence social evolution.

### Other examples of kin selection

Kin selection may explain altruism in other animals. Belding's ground squirrels give alarm calls when they spot a predator such as a coyote or a badger. Such predators may attack a calling squirrel, so giving the signal places the caller at risk. A ground squirrel colony consists of a female and her daughters, sisters, aunts, and nieces. When males mature, they disperse long distances from where they are born, so adult males in the colony are not genetically related to the females. By marking all squirrels in a colony with an individual dye pattern on their fur and by recording which individuals gave calls and the social circumstances of their calling, researchers found that females who have relatives living nearby are more likely to give alarm calls than females with no kin nearby. Males tend to call much less frequently, as would be expected because they are not related to most colony members.

Another example of kin selection is provided by the white-fronted bee-eater, a bird which lives along river banks in Africa in colonies of 100 to 200 individuals (figure 55.36). In contrast to ground squirrels, the male bee-eaters usually remain in the colony in which they were born, and the females disperse to join new colonies. Many bee-eaters do not raise their own offspring, but instead help others. Most helpers are young birds,

**Figure 55.36 Kin selection in the white-fronted bee-eater (*Merops bullockoides*).** Bee-eaters are small insectivorous birds that live in Africa in large colonies. Bee-eaters often help others raise their young; helpers usually choose to help close relatives.

but older birds whose nesting attempts have failed may also be helpers. The presence of a single helper, on average, doubles the number of offspring that survive. Two lines of evidence support the idea that kin selection is important in determining helping behavior in this species. First, helpers are normally males, which are usually related to other birds in the colony, and not females, which are not related. Second, when birds have the choice of helping different parents, they almost invariably choose the parents to which they are most closely related.

### Learning Outcomes Review 55.11

Genetic and ecological factors have contributed to evolution of altruism, a behavior that benefits another individual at a cost to the actor. Individuals may benefit directly if cooperative acts are reciprocated among unrelated interactants. Kin selection explains how altruistic acts directed toward relatives, which share alleles, increase an individual's inclusive fitness. Haplodiploidy has resulted in eusociality among some insects by increasing genetic relatedness; it is not found in vertebrates.

■ *Imagine that you witness older group members rescuing infants in a troupe of monkeys when a predator appears. How would you test whether the altruistic act you see is reciprocity or kin selection?*

## 55.12 The Evolution of Group Living and Animal Societies

### Learning Outcomes

1. Explain the possible advantages of group living.
2. Contrast the nature of insect and vertebrate societies.
3. Discuss social organization in African weaver birds and how it is influenced by ecology.

Organisms from cnidarians and insects to fish, whales, chimpanzees, and humans live in social groups. To encompass the

wide variety of social phenomena, we can broadly define a society as a group of organisms of the same species that are organized in a cooperative manner.

Why have individuals in some species given up a solitary existence to become members of a group? One hypothesis is that individuals in groups benefit directly from social living. For example, a bird in a flock may be better protected from predators. As flock size increases, the risk of predation decreases because there are more individuals to scan the environment for predators (figure 55.37).

A member of a flock may also increase its feeding success if it can acquire information from other flock members about the location of new, rich food sources. In some predators, hunting in groups can increase success and allow the group to tackle prey too large for any one individual.

### Insect societies form efficient colonies containing specialized castes

We've already discussed the origin of eusociality in the insect order Hymenoptera (ants, bees, and wasps). Additionally, all termites (order Isoptera) are also eusocial, and a few other insect and arthropod species are eusocial. Social insect colonies are composed of different *castes*, groups of individuals that differ in reproductive ability (queens vs. workers), size, and morphology and perform different tasks. Workers nurse, maintain the nest, and forage; soldiers are large and have powerful jaws specialized for defense.

The structure of an insect society is illustrated by leafcutters, which form colonies of as many as several million individuals. These ants cut leaves and use it to grow crops of fungi beneath the ground. Workers divide the tasks of leaf cutting, defense, mulching the fungus garden, and implanting fungal hyphae according to their body size (figure 55.38).

### The structure of a vertebrate society is related to ecology

In contrast to the highly structured and integrated insect societies and their remarkable forms of altruism, vertebrate social

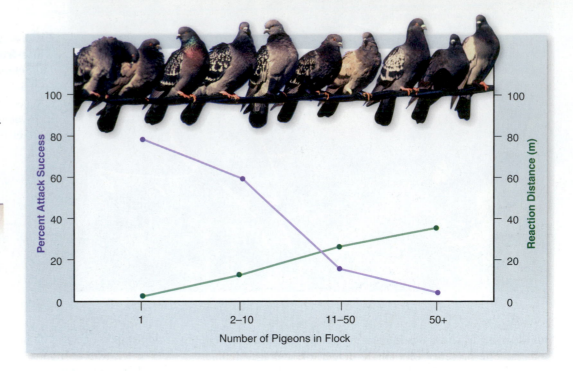

**Figure 55.37** **Flocking behavior decreases predation.** When more pigeons are present in the flock, they can detect hawks at greater distances, thus allowing more time for the pigeons to escape. As a result, as the size of a pigeon flock increases, hawks are less successful at capturing pigeons.

**Inquiry question**

**?** How would living in a flock affect the time available for foraging by individual pigeons?

groups are usually less rigidly organized and less cohesive. It seems paradoxical that vertebrates, which have larger brains and are capable of more complex behaviors, are generally less altruistic than insects (the exception, of course, is humans). Reciprocity and kin-selected altruism are common in vertebrate societies, although there is often more conflict and aggression among group members. Conflicts generally center on access to food and mates and occur because a vertebrate society is a made up of individuals striving to improve their own fitness.

Social groups of vertebrates have a size, stability of members, number of breeding males and females, and type of mating system characteristic of a given species. Diet and predation are important factors in shaping social groups. For example, meerkats take turns watching for predators while other group members forage for food (figure 55.39).

African weaver birds, which construct nests from vegetation, provide an excellent example of the relationship between ecology and social organization. Their roughly 90 species can be divided according to the type of social group they form. One group of species lives in the forest and builds camouflaged, solitary nests. Males and females are monogamous; they forage for insects to feed their young. The second group of species nests in colonies in trees on the savanna. They are polygynous and feed in flocks on seeds.

The feeding and nesting habits of these two groups of species are correlated with their mating systems. In the forest, insects are hard to find, and both parents must cooperate in feeding the young. The camouflaged nests do not call the attention of predators to their brood. On the open savanna, building a hidden nest is not an option. Rather, savanna-dwelling weaver birds protect their young from predators by nesting in trees, which are not very abundant. This shortage of safe nest sites means that birds must nest together in colonies. Because seeds occur abundantly, a female can acquire all the food needed to rear young without a male's help. The male, free from the duties of parenting, spends his time courting many females—a polygynous mating system.

One exception to the general rule that vertebrate societies are not organized like those of insects is the naked mole rat, a small, hairless rodent that lives in and near East Africa. Unlike other kinds of mole rats, which live alone or in small family groups, naked mole rats form large underground colonies with a far-ranging system of tunnels and a central nesting area. It is not unusual for a colony to contain 80 individuals.

Naked mole rats feed on bulbs, roots, and tubers, which they locate by constant tunneling. As in insect societies, there is a division of labor among the colony members, with some individuals working as tunnelers while others perform different

**Figure 55.38** **Castes of ants.** These leaf-cutter ants are members of different castes. The large ant is a worker carrying leaves to the nest, whereas the smaller ants are protecting the worker from attack.

**Figure 55.39 Foraging and predator avoidance.** A meerkat sentinel on duty. Meerkats (*Suricata suricata*) are a species of highly social mongoose living in the semiarid sands of the Kalahari Desert in southern Africa. This meerkat is taking its turn to act as a lookout for predators. Under the security of its vigilance, the other group members can focus their attention on foraging.

tasks, depending on the size of their bodies. Large mole rats defend the colony and dig tunnels.

Naked mole rat colonies have a reproductive division of labor similar to the one normally associated with the eusocial insects. All of the breeding is done by a single female, or "queen," who has one or two male consorts. The workers, consisting of both sexes, keep the tunnels clear and forage for food.

### Learning Outcomes Review 55.12

Advantages of group living include protection from predators and increased feeding success. Eusocial insects form complex, highly altruistic societies that increase the fitness of the colony. The members of vertebrate societies exhibit more conflict and competition, but also cooperate and behave altruistically, especially toward kin. African weaver birds have developed different types of societies depending on the ecology of their habitat, particularly the safety of nesting sites.

- **What are the benefits and costs associated with living in social groups?**
- **Why is altruism directed toward kin considered to be selfish behavior?**
- **Is a human army more like an insect society or a vertebrate society? Explain your answer.**

## Chapter Review

### 55.1 The Natural History of Behavior

*Behavior can be analyzed in terms of mechanisms (cause) and evolutionary origin (adaptive nature).*
Proximate causation refers to the mechanisms of behavior. Ultimate causation examines a behavior's evolutionary significance.

*Ethology emphasizes the study of instinct and its origins.*
Innate, or instinctive, behavior is a response to an environmental stimulus or trigger that does not require learning (see figure 55.1).

### 55.2 Nerve Cells, Neurotransmitters, Hormones, and Behavior

Instinctive behaviors are accomplished by neural circuits, which develop under genetic control. Hormones and neurotransmitters can act to regulate behavior.

### 55.3 Behavioral Genetics

*Artificial selection and hybrid studies link genes and behavior.*
Breeding fast-learning and slow-learning rats among each other for several generations produced two distinct behavioral populations (see figure 55.3).

*Some behaviors appear to be controlled by a single gene.*

### 55.4 Learning

*Learning mechanisms include habituation and association.*
Habituation, a form of nonassociative learning, is a decrease in response to repeated nonessential stimuli. Associative learning is a change in behavior by association of two stimuli or of a behavior and a response (conditioning).

Classical (Pavlovian) conditioning occurs when two stimuli are associated with each other. Operant conditioning occurs when an animal associates a behavior with reward or punishment.

***Instinct governs learning preparedness.***
What an animal can learn is biologically influenced—that is, learning is possible only within the boundaries set by evolution.

## 55.5 The Development of Behavior

***Parent–offspring interactions influence how behavior develops.***
In imprinting, a young animal forms an attachment to other individuals or develops preferences that influence later behavior.

***Instinct and learning may interact as behavior develops.***
Animals may have an innate genetic template that guides their learning as behavior develops, such as song development in birds.

***Studies on twins reveal a role for both genes and environment in human behavior.***

## 55.6 Animal Cognition

Some animals exhibit cognitive behavior and can respond to novel situations using logic (see figures 55.12, 55.13).

## 55.7 Orientation and Migratory Behavior

***Migration often involves populations moving large distances.***

***Migrating animals must be capable of orientation and navigation (see figure 55.16).***
Orientation is the mechanism by which animals move by tracking environmental stimuli such as celestial clues or Earth's magnetic field. Navigation is following a route based on orientation and some sort of "map." The nature of the map in animals is not known.

## 55.8 Animal Communication

***Successful reproduction depends on appropriate signals and responses.***
Courtship signals are usually species-specific and help to ensure reproductive isolation (see figure 55.19).

***Communication enables information exchange among group members (see figures 55.20, 55.21).***

## 55.9 Behavioral Ecology

***Foraging behavior can directly influence energy intake and individual fitness.***
Natural selection favors optimal foraging strategies in which energy acquisition (cost) is minimized and reproductive success (benefit) is maximized.

Territorial behavior evolves if the benefits of holding a territory exceed the costs.

## 55.10 Reproductive Strategies and Sexual Selection

***The sexes often have different reproductive strategies.***
One sex may be choosier than the other, and which one often depends on the degree of parental investment.

***Sexual selection occurs through mate competition and mate choice.***
Intrasexual selection involves competition among members of the same sex for the chance to mate. Intersexual selection is one sex choosing a mate.

Mate choice may provide direct benefits (increased resource availability or parental care) or indirect benefits (genetic quality of the mate).

***Mating systems reflect the ability of parents to care for offspring and are influenced by ecology.***
Mating systems include monogamy, polygyny, and polyandry; they are influenced by ecology and constrained by needs of offspring.

## 55.11 Altruism

***Reciprocity theory explains altruism between unrelated individuals.***
Mutual exchanges benefit both participants; a participant that does not reciprocate would not receive future aid.

***Kin selection theory proposes a direct genetic advantage to altruism.***
Kin selection increases the reproductive success of relatives and increased frequency of alleles shared by kin, and thus increases an individual's inclusive fitness.

Ants, bees, and wasps have haplodiploid reproduction, and therefore high degree of gene sharing.

## 55.12 The Evolution of Group Living and Animal Societies

A social system is a group organized in a cooperative manner.

***Insect societies form efficient colonies containing specialized castes (see figure 55.38).***
Social insect societies are composed of different castes that are specialized to reproduce or to perform certain colony maintenance tasks.

***The structure of a vertebrate society is related to ecology.***
Vertebrate social systems are less rigidly organized and cohesive and are influenced by food availability and predation.

## Review Questions

### UNDERSTAND

1. A key stimulus, innate releasing mechanism, and fixed action pattern
   a. are mechanisms associated with behaviors that are learned.
   b. are components of behaviors that are innate.
   c. involve behaviors that cannot be explained in terms of ultimate causation.
   d. involve behaviors that are not subject to natural selection.

2. In operant conditioning
   a. an animal learns that a particular behavior leads to a reward or punishment.
   b. an animal associates an unconditioned stimulus with a conditioned response.
   c. learning is unnecessary.
   d. habituation is required for an appropriate response.

3. The study of song development in sparrows showed that
   a. the acquisition of a species-specific song is innate.
   b. there are two components to this behavior: a genetic template and learning.
   c. song acquisition is an example of associative learning.
   d. All of these are correct.

4. The difference between following a set of driving directions given to you by somebody on the street (for example ". . . take a right at the next light, go four blocks and turn left . . .") and using a map to find your destination is
   a. the difference between navigation and orientation, respectively.
   b. the difference between learning and migration, respectively.
   c. the difference between orientation and navigation, respectively.
   d. why birds are not capable of orientation.

5. In courtship communication
   a. the signal itself is always species-specific.
   b. the sign communicates species identity.
   c. it involves a stimulus–response chain.
   d. courtship signals are produced only by males.

6. Behavioral ecology assumes
   a. that all behavioral traits are innate.
   b. learning is the dominant determinant of behavior.
   c. behavioral traits are subject to natural selection.
   d. behavioral traits do not affect fitness.

7. According to optimal foraging theory
   a. individuals minimize energy intake per unit of time.
   b. energy content of a food item is the only determinant of a forager's food choice.
   c. time taken to capture a food item is the only determinant of a forager's food choice.
   d. a higher energy item might be less valuable than a lower energy item if it takes too much time to capture the larger item.

8. The elaborate tail feathers of a male peacock evolved because they
   a. improve reproductive success of males and females.
   b. improve male survival.
   c. reduce survival.
   d. None of the above.

9. From the perspective of females, extra-pair copulations (EPCs)
   a. are always disadvantageous to females.
   b. can be associated with receiving male aid.
   c. are too rare to affect female fitness.
   d. can only be of benefit if the EPC male has elaborate secondary sexual traits.

10. In the haplodiploidy system of sex determination, males are
    a. haploid.
    b. diploid.
    c. sterile.
    d. not present because bees exist as single-sex populations.

11. According to kin selection, saving the life of your _____ would do the least for increasing your inclusive fitness.
    a. mother            c. sister-in-law
    b. brother           d. niece

12. Altruism
    a. is only possible through reciprocity.
    b. is only possible through kin selection.
    c. can only be explained by group selection.
    d. will only occur when the fitness benefit of a given act is greater than the fitness cost.

## APPLY

1. Refer to figure 55.25. Data on size of mussels eaten by shore crabs suggest they eat sizes smaller than expected by an optimal foraging model. Suggest a hypothesis for why and describe an experiment to test your hypothesis.

2. Refer to figure 55.26. Six pairs of birds were removed but only four pairs moved in. Where did the new pairs come from? Additionally, it appears that many of the birds that were not removed expanded their territories and that the new residents ended up with smaller territories than the pairs they replaced. Explain.

3. Refer to figure 55.28. Peahens prefer to mate with peacocks that have more eyespots in their tail feathers (that is, longer tail feathers). It has also been suggested that the longer the tail feathers, the more impaired the flight of the males. One possible hypothesis to explain such a preference by females is that the males with the longest tail feathers experience the most severe handicap, and if they can nevertheless survive, it reflects their "vigor." Suggest some studies that would allow you to test this idea. Your description should include the kinds of traits that you would measure and why.

4. An altruistic act is defined as one that benefits another individual at a cost to the actor. There are two theories to explain how such behavior evolves: reciprocity and kin selection. How would you distinguish between the two in a field study? In the context of natural selection, is an altruistic act "costly" to an individual who performs it?

## SYNTHESIZE

1. Insects that sting or contain toxic chemicals often have black and yellow coloration and consequentially are not eaten by predators. How could you determine if a predator has an innate avoidance of insects that are colored this way, or if the avoidance is learned? If avoidance is learned, how would you determine the learning mechanism involved? How would you measure the adaptive significance of the black and yellow coloration to the prey insect?

2. Behavioral genetics has made great advances from detailed studies of a single animal such as the fruit fly as a model system to develop general principles of how genes regulate behavior. What are advantages and disadvantages of this "model system" approach? How would you determine how broadly applicable the results of such studies are to other animals?

3. If a female bird chooses to live in the territory of a particular male, why might she mate with a male other than the territory owner?

## ONLINE RESOURCE

www.ravenbiology.com

Mc Graw Hill connect™ | BIOLOGY

Understand, Apply, and Synthesize—enhance your study with animations that bring concepts to life and practice tests to assess your understanding. Your instructor may also recommend the interactive eBook, individualized learning tools, and more.

Chapter 56

# Ecology of Individuals and Populations

## Chapter Outline

## Introduction

*Ecology, the study of how organisms relate to one another and to their environments, is a complex and fascinating area of biology that has important implications for each of us. In our exploration of ecological principles, we first consider how organisms respond to the abiotic environment in which they exist and how these responses affect the properties of populations, emphasizing population dynamics. In chapter 57, we discuss communities of coexisting species and the interactions that occur among them. In subsequent chapters, we discuss the functioning of entire ecosystems and of the biosphere, concluding with a consideration of the problems facing our planet and our fellow species.*

## 56.1 The Environmental Challenges

### Learning Outcomes

1. *List some challenges that organisms face in their environments.*
2. *Describe ways in which individuals respond to environmental changes.*
3. *Explain how species adapt to environmental conditions.*

The nature of the physical environment in large measure determines which organisms live in a particular climate or region. Key elements of the environment include:

**Temperature.** Most organisms are adapted to live within a relatively narrow range of temperatures and will not thrive if temperatures are colder or warmer. The growing season of plants, for example, is importantly influenced by temperature.

**Water.** All organisms require water. On land, water is often scarce, so patterns of rainfall have a major influence on life.

**Figure 56.1 Meeting the challenge of obtaining moisture.** On the dry sand dunes of the Namib Desert in southwestern Africa, the fog-basking beetle (*Onymacris unguicularis*) collects moisture from the fog by holding its abdomen up at the crest of a dune to gather condensed water; water condenses as droplets and trickles down to the beetle's mouth.

**Sunlight.** Almost all ecosystems rely on energy captured by photosynthesis; the availability of sunlight influences the amount of life an ecosystem can support, particularly below the surface in marine communities.

**Soil.** The physical consistency, pH, and mineral composition of the soil often severely limit terrestrial plant growth, particularly the availability of nitrogen and phosphorus.

An individual encountering environmental variation may maintain a "steady-state" internal environment, a condition known as *homeostasis*. Many animals and plants actively employ physiological, morphological, or behavioral mechanisms to maintain homeostasis. The beetle in figure 56.1 is using a behavioral mechanism to cope with drastic changes in water availability. Other animals and plants are known as conformers because they conform to the environment in which they find themselves, their bodies adopting the temperature, salinity, and other physical aspects of their surroundings.

Responses to environmental variation can be seen over both the short and the long term. In the short term, spanning periods of a few minutes to an individual's lifetime, organisms have a variety of ways of coping with environmental change. Over longer periods, natural selection can operate to make a population better adapted to the environment.

## Organisms are capable of responding to environmental changes that occur during their lifetime

During the course of a day, a season, or a lifetime, an individual organism must cope with a range of living conditions. They do so through the physiological, morphological, and behavioral abilities they possess. These abilities are a product of natural selection acting in a particular environmental setting over time, which explains why an individual organism that is moved to a different environment may not survive.

| TABLE 56.1 | Physiological Changes at High Elevation |
|---|---|
| Increased rate of breathing | |
| Increased erythrocyte production, raising the amount of hemoglobin in the blood | |
| Decreased binding capacity of hemoglobin, increasing the rate at which oxygen is unloaded in body tissues | |
| Increased density of mitochondria, capillaries, and muscle myoglobin | |

### Physiological responses

Many organisms are able to adapt to environmental change by making physiological adjustments. For example, you sweat when it is hot, increasing evaporative heat loss and thus preventing overheating. Similarly, people who visit high altitudes may initially experience altitude sickness—the symptoms of which include heart palpitations, nausea, fatigue, headache, mental impairment, and in serious cases, pulmonary edema—because of the lower atmospheric pressure and consequent lower oxygen availability in the air. After several days, however, the same people usually feel fine, because a number of physiological changes have increased the delivery of oxygen to their body tissues (table 56.1).

Some insects avoid freezing in the winter by adding glycerol "antifreeze" to their blood; others tolerate freezing by converting much of their glycogen reserves into alcohols that protect their cell membranes from freeze damage.

### Morphological capabilities

Animals that maintain a constant internal temperature (endotherms) in a cold environment have adaptations that tend to minimize energy expenditure. For example, many mammals grow thicker coats during the winter, their fur acting as insulation to retain body heat. In general, the thicker the fur, the greater the insulation (figure 56.2). Thus, a wolf's fur is about three times thicker in winter than in summer and insulates more than twice as well.

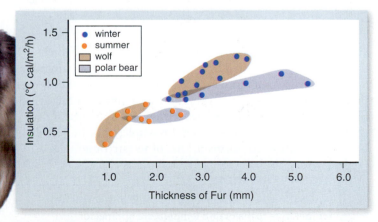

**Figure 56.2 Morphological adaptation.** Fur thickness in North American mammals has a major effect on the degree of insulation the fur provides.

### Behavioral responses

Many animals deal with variation in the environment by moving from one patch of habitat to another, avoiding areas that are unsuitable. The tropical lizard in figure 56.3 manages to maintain a fairly uniform body temperature in an open habitat by basking in patches of sunlight and then retreating to the shade when it becomes too hot. By contrast, in shaded forests, the same lizard does not have the opportunity to regulate its body temperature through behavioral means. Thus, it becomes a conformer and adopts the temperature of its surroundings.

Behavioral adaptations can be extreme. Spadefoot toads (genus *Scaphiophus*), which live in the deserts of North America, can burrow nearly a meter below the surface and remain there for as long as nine months of each year, their metabolic rates greatly reduced as they live on fat reserves. When moist, cool conditions return, the toads emerge and breed. The young toads mature rapidly and burrow underground.

## Natural selection leads to evolutionary adaptation to environmental conditions

The ability of an individual to alter its physiology, morphology, or behavior is itself an evolutionary adaptation, the result of natural selection. The results of natural selection can also be detected by comparing closely related species that live in different environments. In such cases, species often have evolved striking adaptations to the particular environment in which they live.

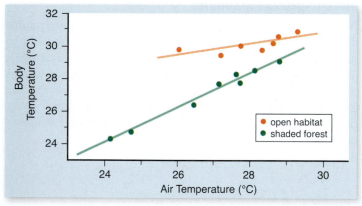

**Figure 56.3 Behavioral adaptation.** In open habitats, the Puerto Rican crested lizard (*Anolis cristatellus*) maintains a relatively constant temperature by seeking out and basking in patches of sunlight; as a result, it can maintain a relatively high temperature even when the air is cool. In contrast, in shaded forests, this behavior is not possible, and the lizard's body temperature conforms to that of its surroundings.

### Inquiry question

**?** When given the opportunity, lizards regulate their body temperature to maintain a temperature optimal for physiological functioning. Would lizards in open habitats exhibit different escape behaviors from lizards in shaded forest?

For example, animals that live in different climates show many differences. Mammals from colder climates tend to have shorter ears and limbs—a phenomenon termed *Allen's rule*—which reduces the surface area across which animals lose heat. Lizards that live in different climates exhibit physiological adaptations for coping with life at different temperatures. Desert lizards are unaffected by high temperatures that would kill a lizard from northern Europe, but the northern lizards are capable of running, capturing prey, and digesting food at cooler temperatures at which desert lizards would be completely immobilized.

Many species also exhibit adaptations to living in areas where water is scarce. Everyone knows of the camel and other desert animals that can go extended periods without drinking water. Another example of desert adaptation is seen in frogs. Most frogs have moist skins through which water permeates readily. Such animals could not survive in arid climates because they would rapidly dehydrate and die. However, some frogs have solved this problem by evolving a greatly reduced rate of water loss through the skin. One species, for example, secretes a waxy substance from specialized glands that waterproofs its skin and reduces rates of water loss by 95%.

Adaptation to different environments can also be studied experimentally. For example, when strains of *E. coli* were grown at high temperatures (42°C), the speed at which the bacteria utilized resources improved through time. After 2000 generations, this ability increased 30% over what it had been when the experiment started. The means by which efficiency of resource use increased is unknown and is the focus of current research.

### Learning Outcomes Review 56.1

Environmental conditions include temperature, water and light availability, and soil characteristics. When the environment changes, individual organisms use a variety of physiological, morphological, and behavioral mechanisms to adjust. Over time, adaptations to different environments may evolve in populations.

- *How might a species respond if its environment grew steadily warmer over time?*

## 56.2 Populations: Groups of a Single Species in One Place

### Learning Outcomes

1. **Distinguish between a population and a metapopulation.**
2. **Understand what causes a species' geographic ranges to change through time.**

Organisms live as members of populations, groups of individuals that occur together at one place and time. In the rest of this chapter, we consider the properties of populations, focusing on factors that influence whether a population grows or shrinks, and at what rate. The explosive growth of the world's human population in the last few centuries provides a focus for our inquiry.

The term *population* can be defined narrowly or broadly. This flexibility allows us to speak in similar terms of the world's human population, the population of protists in the gut of a termite, or the population of deer that inhabit a forest. Sometimes the boundaries defining a population are sharp, such as the edge of an isolated mountain lake for trout, and sometimes they are fuzzier, as when deer readily move back and forth between two forests separated by a cornfield.

Three characteristics of population ecology are particularly important: (1) population range, the area throughout which a population occurs; (2) the pattern of spacing of individuals within that range; and (3) how the population changes in size through time.

### A population's geographic distribution is termed its range

No population, not even one composed of humans, occurs in all habitats throughout the world. Most species, in fact, have relatively limited geographic ranges, and the range of some species is miniscule. For example, the Devil's Hole pupfish lives in a single spring in southern Nevada (figure 56.4), and the Socorro isopod (*Thermosphaeroma thermophilus*) is known from a single spring system in New Mexico. At the other extreme, some species are widely distributed. The common dolphin (*Delphinus delphis*), for example, is found throughout all the world's oceans.

As discussed earlier, organisms must be adapted for the environment in which they occur. Polar bears are exquisitely adapted to survive the cold of the Arctic, but you won't find them in the tropical rain forest. Certain prokaryotes can live in the near-boiling waters of Yellowstone's geysers, but they do not occur in cooler streams nearby. Each population has its own requirements—temperature, humidity, certain types of food, and a host of other factors—that determine where it can live and reproduce and where it can't. In addition, in places that are otherwise suitable, the presence of predators, competitors, or parasites may prevent a population from occupying an area, a topic we will take up in chapter 57.

**Figure 56.4** **The Devil's Hole pupfish (*Cyprinodon diabolis*).** This fish has the smallest range of any vertebrate species in the world.

### Ranges undergo expansion and contraction

Population ranges are not static but change through time. These changes occur for two reasons. In some cases, the environment changes. As the glaciers retreated at the end of the last ice age, approximately 10,000 years ago, many North American plant and animal populations expanded northward. At the same time, as climates warmed, species experienced shifts in the elevation at which they could live (figure 56.5).

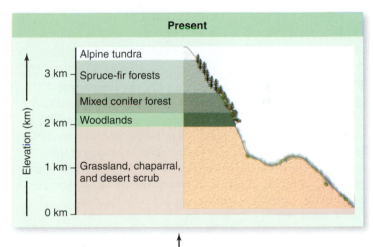

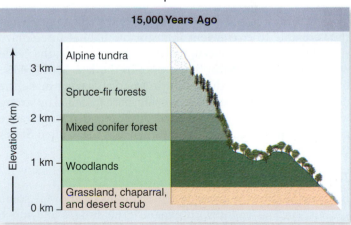

**Figure 56.5** **Altitude shifts in altitudinal distributions of trees in the mountains of southwestern North America.** During the glacial period 15,000 years ago, conditions were cooler than they are now. As the climate warmed, tree species that require colder temperatures shifted their range upward in altitude so that they live in the climatic conditions to which they are adapted.

**Figure 56.6 Range expansion of the cattle egret (*Bubulcus ibis*).** The cattle egret—so named because it follows cattle and other hoofed animals, catching any insects or small vertebrates it disturbs—first arrived in South America from Africa in the late 1800s. Since the 1930s, the range expansion of this species has been well documented, as it has moved northward into much of North America, as well as southward along the western side of the Andes to near the southern tip of South America.

In addition, populations can expand their ranges when they are able to circumvent inhospitable habitat to colonize suitable, previously unoccupied areas. For example, the cattle egret is native to Africa. Some time in the late 1800s, these birds appeared in northern South America, having made the nearly 3500-km transatlantic crossing, perhaps aided by strong winds. Since then, they have steadily expanded their range and now can be found throughout most of the United States (figure 56.6).

### The human effect

By altering the environment, humans have allowed some species, such as coyotes, to expand their ranges and move into areas they previously did not occupy. Moreover, humans have served as an agent of dispersal for many species. Some of these transplants have been widely successful, as is discussed in greater detail in chapter 60. For example, 100 starlings were introduced into New York City in 1896 in a misguided attempt to establish every species of bird mentioned by Shakespeare. Their population steadily spread so

that by 1980, they occurred throughout the United States. Similar stories could be told for countless plants and animals, and the list increases every year. Unfortunately, the success of these invaders often comes at the expense of native species.

### Dispersal mechanisms

Dispersal to new areas can occur in many ways. Lizards have colonized many distant islands, as one example, probably due to individuals or their eggs floating or drifting on vegetation. Bats are the only mammals on many distant islands because they can fly to them.

Seeds of plants are designed to disperse in many ways (figure 56.7). Some seeds are aerodynamically designed to be blown long distances by the wind. Others have structures that stick to the fur or feathers of animals, so that they are carried long distances before falling to the ground. Still others are enclosed in fleshy fruits. These seeds can pass through the digestive systems of mammals or birds and then germinate where they are defecated. Finally, seeds of mistletoes (*Arceuthobium*) are violently propelled from the base of the fruit in an explosive discharge. Although the probability of long-distance dispersal events leading to successful establishment of new populations is low, over millions of years, many such dispersals have occurred.

**Figure 56.7 Some of the many adaptations of seeds.** Seeds have evolved a number of different means of facilitating dispersal from their maternal plant. Some seeds can be transported great distances by the wind, whereas seeds enclosed in adherent or fleshy fruits can be transported by animals.

## Individuals in populations exhibit different spacing patterns

Another key characteristic of population structure is the way in which individuals of a population are distributed. They may be randomly spaced, uniformly spaced, or clumped.

### Random spacing

Random spacing of individuals within populations occurs when they do not interact strongly with one another and when they are not affected by nonuniform aspects of their environment. Random distributions are not common in nature. Some species of trees, however, appear to exhibit random distributions in Panamanian rain forests.

### Uniform spacing

Uniform spacing within a population may often, but not always, result from competition for resources. This spacing is accomplished, however, in many different ways

In animals, uniform spacing often results from behavioral interactions, as described in chapter 55. In many species, individuals of one or both sexes defend a territory from which other individuals are excluded. These territories provide the owner with exclusive access to resources, such as food, water, hiding refuges, or mates, and tend to space individuals evenly across the habitat. Even in nonterritorial species, individuals often maintain a defended space into which other animals are not allowed to intrude.

Among plants, uniform spacing is also a common result of competition for resources. Closely spaced individual plants compete for available sunlight, nutrients, or water. These contests can be direct, as when one plant casts a shadow over another, or indirect, as when two plants compete by extracting nutrients or water from a shared area. In addition, some plants, such as the creosote bush, produce chemicals in the surrounding soil that are toxic to other members of their species. In all of these cases, only plants that are spaced an adequate distance from each other will be able to coexist, leading to uniform spacing.

### Clumped spacing

Individuals clump into groups or clusters in response to uneven distribution of resources in their immediate environments. Clumped distributions are common in nature because individual animals, plants, and microorganisms tend to occur in habitats defined by soil type, moisture, or other aspects of the environment to which they are best adapted.

Social interactions also can lead to clumped distributions. Many species live and move around in large groups, which go by a variety of names (for example, flock, herd, pride). These groupings can provide many advantages, including increased awareness of and defense against predators, decreased energy cost of moving through air and water, and access to the knowledge of all group members.

On a broader scale, populations are often most densely populated in the interior of their range and less densely distributed toward the edges. Such patterns usually result from the manner in which the environment changes in different areas.

Populations are often best adapted to the conditions in the interior of their distribution. As environmental conditions change, individuals are less well adapted, and thus densities decrease. Ultimately, the point is reached at which individuals cannot persist at all; this marks the edge of a population's range.

## A metapopulation comprises distinct populations that may exchange members

Species often exist as a network of distinct populations that interact with one another by exchanging individuals. Such networks, termed **metapopulations,** usually occur in areas in which suitable habitat is patchily distributed and is separated by intervening stretches of unsuitable habitat.

### Dispersal and habitat occupancy

The degree to which populations within a metapopulation interact depends on the amount of dispersal; this interaction is often not symmetrical: Populations increasing in size tend to send out many dispersers, whereas populations at low levels tend to receive more immigrants than they send off. In addition, relatively isolated populations tend to receive relatively few arrivals.

Not all suitable habitats within a metapopulation's area may be occupied at any one time. For a number of reasons, some individual populations may become extinct, perhaps as a result of an epidemic disease, a catastrophic fire, or the loss of genetic variation following a population bottleneck (see chapter 60). Dispersal from other populations, however, may eventually recolonize such areas. In some cases, the number of habitats occupied in a metapopulation may represent an equilibrium in which the rate of extinction of existing populations is balanced by the rate of colonization of empty habitats.

### Source–sink metapopulations

A species may also exhibit a metapopulation structure in areas in which some habitats are suitable for long-term population maintenance, but others are not. In these situations, termed **source–sink metapopulations,** the populations in the better areas (the sources) continually send out dispersers that bolster the populations in the poorer habitats (the sinks). In the absence of such continual replenishment, sink populations would have a negative growth rate and would eventually become extinct.

Metapopulations of butterflies have been studied particularly intensively. In one study, researchers sampled populations of the Glanville fritillary butterfly at 1600 meadows in southwestern Finland (figure 56.8). On average, every year, 200 populations became extinct, but 114 empty meadows were colonized. A variety of factors seemed to increase the likelihood of a population's extinction, including small population size, isolation from sources of immigrants, low resource availability (as indicated by the number of flowers on a meadow), and lack of genetic variation within the population.

The researchers attribute the greater number of extinctions than colonizations to a string of very dry summers. Because none of the populations is large enough to survive on its own, continued survival of the species in southwestern Finland would appear to require the continued existence of a metapopulation network in which new populations are continually

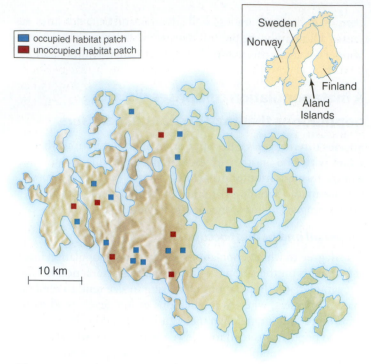

Sweden
Norway
Finland
Åland
Islands

10 km

**Figure 56.8 Metapopulations of butterflies.**
The Glanville fritillary butterfly (*Melitaea cinxia*) occurs in metapopulations in southwestern Finland on the Åland Islands. None of the populations is large enough to survive for long on its own, but continual immigration of individuals from other populations allows some populations to survive. In addition, continual establishment of new populations tends to offset extinction of established populations, although in recent years, extinctions have outnumbered colonizations.

created and existing populations are supplemented by immigrants. Continued bad weather thus may doom the species, at least in this part of its range.

Metapopulations, where they occur, can have two important implications for the range of a species. First, through continuous colonization of empty patches, metapopulations prevent long-term extinction. If no such dispersal existed, then each population might eventually perish, leading to disappearance of the species from the entire area. Moreover, in source–sink metapopulations, the species occupies a larger area than it otherwise might, including marginal areas that could not support a population without a continual influx of immigrants. For these reasons, the study of metapopulations has become very important in conservation biology as natural habitats become increasingly fragmented.

### Learning Outcomes Review 56.2

A population is a group of individuals of a single species existing together in an area. A population's range, the area it occupies, changes over time. Populations, in turn, may form a network, or metapopulation, connected by individuals that move from one group to another. Within a population, the distribution of individuals can be random, uniform, or clumped, and the distribution is determined in part by the availability of resources.

■ *How might the geographic range of a species change if populations could not exchange individuals with each other?*

# 56.3 Population Demography and Dynamics

### Learning Outcomes

1. Define demography.
2. Describe the factors that influence a species' demography.
3. Explain the significance of survivorship curves.

The dynamics of a population—how it changes through time—are affected by many factors. One important factor is the age distribution of individuals—that is, what proportion of individuals are adults, juveniles, and young.

**Demography** is the quantitative study of populations. How the size of a population changes through time can be studied at two levels: as a whole or broken down into parts. At the most inclusive level, we can study the whole population to determine whether it is increasing, decreasing, or remaining constant. Put simply, populations grow if births outnumber deaths and shrink if deaths outnumber births. Understanding these trends is often easier, however, if we break the population into smaller units composed of individuals of the same age (for example, 1-year-olds) and study the factors affecting birth and death rates for each unit separately.

## Sex ratio and generation time affect population growth rates

Population growth can be influenced by the population's sex ratio. The number of births in a population is usually directly related to the number of females; births may not be as closely related to the number of males in species in which a single male can mate with several females. In many species, males compete for the opportunity to mate with females, as you learned in the preceding chapter; consequently, a few males have many matings, and many males do not mate at all. In such species, the sex ratio is female-biased and does not affect population growth rates; reduction in the number of males simply changes the identities of the reproductive males without reducing the number of births. By contrast, among monogamous species, pairs may form long-lasting reproductive relationships, and a reduction in the number of males can then directly reduce the number of births.

**Generation time** is the average interval between the birth of an individual and the birth of its offspring. This factor can also affect population growth rates. Species differ greatly in generation time. Differences in body size can explain much of this variation—mice go through approximately 100 generations during the course of one elephant generation (figure 56.9). But small size does not always mean short generation time. Newts, for example, are smaller than mice, but have considerably longer generation times.

In general, populations with short generations can increase in size more quickly than populations with long generations. Conversely, because generation time and life span are

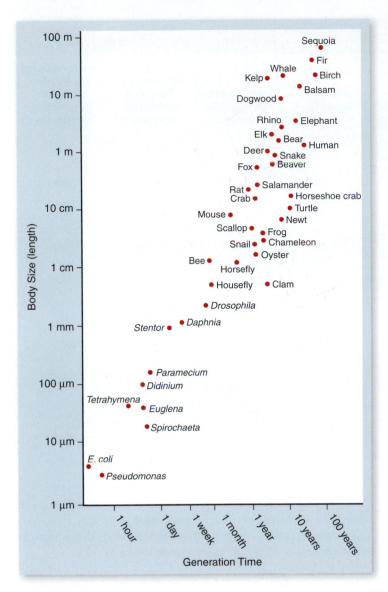

**Figure 56.9** **The relationship between body size and generation time.** In general, larger organisms have longer generation times, although there are exceptions.

**Inquiry question**

? If resources became more abundant, would you expect smaller or larger species to increase in population size more quickly?

usually closely correlated, populations with short generation times may also diminish in size more rapidly if birth rates suddenly decrease.

## Age structure is determined by the numbers of individuals in different age groups

A group of individuals of the same age is referred to as a cohort. In most species, the probability that an individual will reproduce or die varies through its life span. As a result, within a population, every cohort has a characteristic birth rate, or **fecundity**, defined as the number of offspring produced in a standard time (for example, per year), and death rate, or **mortality**, the number of individuals that die in that period.

The relative number of individuals in each cohort defines a population's **age structure.** Because different cohorts have different fecundity and death rates, age structure has a critical influence on a population's growth rate. Populations with a large proportion of young individuals, for example, tend to grow rapidly because an increasing proportion of their individuals are reproductive. Human populations in many developing countries are an example, as will be discussed later in this chapter. Conversely, if a large proportion of a population is relatively old, populations may decline. This phenomenon now characterizes Japan and some countries in Europe.

## Life tables show probability of survival and reproduction through a cohort's life span

To assess how populations in nature are changing, ecologists use a **life table,** which tabulates the fate of a cohort from birth until death, showing the number of offspring produced and the number of individuals that die each year. Table 56.2 shows an example of a life table analysis from a study of the meadow grass *Poa annua*. This study follows the fate of 843 individuals through time, charting how many survive in each interval and how many offspring each survivor produces.

In table 56.2, the first column indicates the age of the cohort (that is, the number of 3-month intervals from the start of the study). The second and third columns indicate the number of survivors and the proportion of the original cohort still alive at the beginning of that interval. The fifth column presents the **mortality rate,** the proportion of individuals that started that interval alive but died by the end of it. The seventh column indicates the average number of seeds produced by each surviving individual in that interval, and the last column shows the number of seeds produced relative to the size of the original cohort.

Much can be learned by examining life tables. In the case of *P. annua*, we see that both the probability of dying and the number of offspring produced per surviving individual steadily increases with age. By adding up the numbers in the last column, we get the total number of offspring produced per individual in the initial cohort. This number is almost 2, which means that for every original member of the cohort, on average two new individuals have been produced. A figure of 1.0 would be the break-even number, the point at which the population was neither growing nor shrinking. In this case, the population appears to be growing rapidly.

In most cases, life table analysis is more complicated than this. First, except for organisms with short life spans, it is difficult to track the fate of a cohort until the death of the last individual. An alternative approach is to construct a cross-sectional study, examining the fate of cohorts of different ages in a single period. In addition, many factors—such as offspring

| TABLE 56.2 | Life Table of the Meadow Grass (*Poa annua*) for a Cohort Containing 843 Seedlings | | | | | | |
|---|---|---|---|---|---|---|---|
| Age (in 3-month intervals) | Number Alive at Beginning of Time Interval | Proportion of Cohort Alive at Beginning of Time Interval (survivorship) | Deaths During Time Interval | Mortality Rate During Time Interval | Seeds Produced During Time Interval | Seeds Produced per Surviving Individual (fecundity) | Seeds Produced per Member of Cohort (fecundity × survivorship) |
| 0 | 843 | 1.000 | 121 | 0.143 | 0 | 0.00 | 0.00 |
| 1 | 722 | 0.857 | 195 | 0.271 | 303 | 0.42 | 0.36 |
| 2 | 527 | 0.625 | 211 | 0.400 | 622 | 1.18 | 0.74 |
| 3 | 316 | 0.375 | 172 | 0.544 | 430 | 1.36 | 0.51 |
| 4 | 144 | 0.171 | 90 | 0.626 | 210 | 1.46 | 0.25 |
| 5 | 54 | 0.064 | 39 | 0.722 | 60 | 1.11 | 0.07 |
| 6 | 15 | 0.018 | 12 | 0.800 | 30 | 2.00 | 0.04 |
| 7 | 3 | 0.004 | 3 | 1.000 | 10 | 3.33 | 0.01 |
| 8 | 0 | 0.000 | — | | Total = 1665 | | Total = 1.98 |

reproducing before all members of their parents' cohort have died—complicate the interpretation of whether populations are growing or shrinking.

## Survivorship curves demonstrate how survival probability changes with age

The percentage of an original population that survives to a given age is called its **survivorship.** One way to express some aspects of the age distribution of populations is through a *survivorship curve.* Examples of different survivorship curves are shown in figure 56.10. Oysters produce vast numbers of offspring, only a few of which live to reproduce. However, once they become established and grow into reproductive individuals, their mortality rate is extremely low (type III survivorship curve). Note that in this type of curve, survival and mortality rates are inversely related. Thus, the rapid decrease in the proportion of oysters surviving indicates that few individuals survive, thus producing a high mortality rate. In contrast, the relatively flat line at older ages indicates high survival and low mortality.

In hydra, animals related to jellyfish, individuals are equally likely to die at any age. The result is a straight survivorship curve (type II).

Finally, mortality rates in humans, as in many other animals and in protists, rise steeply later in life (type I survivorship curve).

Of course, these descriptions are just generalizations, and many organisms show more complicated patterns. Examination of the data for *P. annua*, for example, reveals that it is most similar to a type II survivorship curve (figure 56.11).

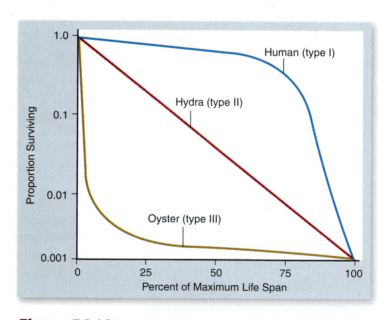

**Figure 56.10 Survivorship curves.** By convention, survival (the vertical axis) is plotted on a log scale. Humans have a type I life cycle, hydra (an animal related to jellyfish) type II, and oysters type III.

**Figure 56.11** **Survivorship curve for a cohort of the meadow grass.** After several months of age, mortality increases at a constant rate through time.

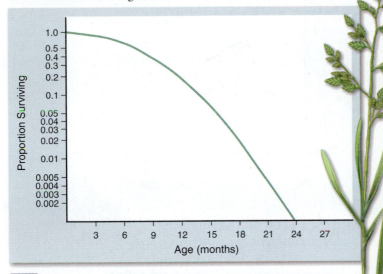

**Inquiry question**

**?** Suppose you wanted to keep meadow grass in your room as a houseplant. Suppose, too, that you wanted to buy an individual plant that was likely to live as long as possible. What age plant would you buy? How might the shape of the survivorship curve affect your answer?

### Learning Outcomes Review 56.3

Demography is the quantitative study of populations. Demographic characteristics include age structure, life span, sex ratio, generation time, and birth and mortality rates. The age structure of a population and the manner in which mortality and birth rates vary among different age cohorts, determine whether a population will increase or decrease in size.

■  *Will populations with higher survivorship rates always have higher population growth rates than populations with lower survivorship rates?*

## 56.4 Life History and the Cost of Reproduction

### Learning Outcomes

1. Describe reproductive trade-offs in an organism's life history.
2. Compare the costs and benefits of allocating resources to reproduction.

Natural selection favors traits that maximize the number of surviving offspring left in the next generation by an individual organism. Two factors affect this quantity: how long an individual lives, and how many young it produces each year.

Why doesn't every organism reproduce immediately after its own birth, produce large families of offspring, care for them intensively, and perform these functions repeatedly throughout a long life, while outcompeting others, escaping predators, and capturing food with ease? The answer is that no one organism can do all of this, simply because not enough resources are available. Consequently, organisms allocate resources either to current reproduction or to increasing their prospects of surviving and reproducing at later life stages.

The complete life cycle of an organism constitutes its life history. All life histories involve significant trade-offs. Because resources are limited, a change that increases reproduction may decrease survival and reduce future reproduction. As one example, a Douglas fir tree that produces more cones increases its current reproductive success—but it also grows more slowly. Because the number of cones produced is a function of how large a tree is, this diminished growth will decrease the number of cones it can produce in the future. Similarly, birds that have more offspring each year have a higher probability of dying during that year or of producing smaller clutches the following year (figure 56.12). Conversely, individuals that delay reproduction may grow faster and larger, enhancing future reproduction.

In one elegant experiment, researchers changed the number of eggs in the nests of a bird, the collared flycatcher (figure 56.13). Birds whose clutch size (the number of eggs produced in one breeding event) was decreased expended less energy raising their young and thus were able to lay more eggs the next year, whereas those given more eggs worked harder and consequently produced fewer eggs the following year. Ecologists refer to the reduction in future reproductive potential resulting from current reproductive efforts as the **cost of reproduction.**

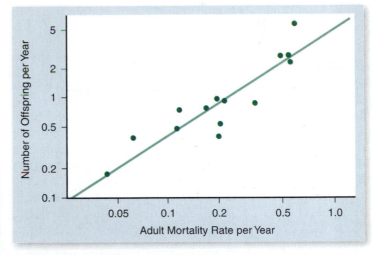

**Figure 56.12** **Reproduction has a price.** Data from many bird species indicate that increased fecundity in birds correlates with higher mortality, ranging from the albatross (lowest) to the sparrow (highest). Birds that raise more offspring per year have a higher probability of dying during that year.

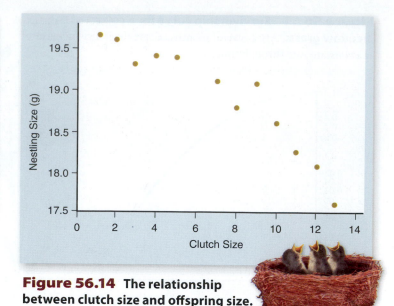

**Figure 56.13 Reproductive events per lifetime.** Adding eggs to nests of collared flycatchers *(Ficedula albicollis)*, which increases the reproductive efforts of the female rearing the young, decreases clutch size the following year; removing eggs from the nest increases the next year's clutch size. This experiment demonstrates the trade-off between current reproductive effort and future reproductive success.

**Figure 56.14 The relationship between clutch size and offspring size.** In great tits *(Parus major)*, the size of the nestlings is inversely related to the number of eggs laid. The more mouths they have to feed, the less the parents can provide to any one nestling.

**Inquiry question**

? Would natural selection favor producing many small young or a few large ones?

Natural selection favors the life history that maximizes lifetime reproductive success. When the cost of reproduction is low, individuals should produce as many offspring as possible because there is little cost. Low costs of reproduction may occur when resources are abundant and may also be relatively low when overall mortality rates are high. In the latter case, individuals may be unlikely to survive to the next breeding season anyway, so the incremental effect of increased reproductive efforts may have little effect on future survival.

Alternatively, when costs of reproduction are high, lifetime reproductive success may be maximized by deferring or minimizing current reproduction to enhance growth and survival rates. This situation may occur when costs of reproduction significantly affect the ability of an individual to survive or decrease the number of offspring that can be produced in the future.

## A trade-off exists between number of offspring and investment per offspring

In terms of natural selection, the number of offspring produced is not as important as how many of those offspring themselves survive to reproduce. Assuming that the amount of energy to be invested in offspring is limited, a balance must be reached between the number of offspring produced and the size of each offspring (figure 56.14). This trade-off has been experimentally demonstrated in the side-blotched lizard, which normally lays between four and five eggs at a time. When some of the eggs are removed surgically early in the reproductive cycle, the female lizard produces only one to three eggs, but supplies each of these eggs with greater amounts of yolk, producing eggs and, subsequently, hatchlings that are much larger than normal (figure 56.15). Alternatively, by removing yolk from eggs, scientists have demonstrated that smaller young would be produced.

**Figure 56.15 Variation in the size of baby side-blotched lizards *(Uta stansburiana)* produced by experimental manipulations.** In clutches in which some developing eggs were surgically removed, the remaining offspring were larger (center) than lizards produced in control clutches in which all the eggs were allowed to develop (right). In experiments in which some of the yolk was removed from the eggs, smaller lizards hatched (left).

In the side-blotched lizard and many other species, the size of offspring is critical—larger offspring have a greater chance of survival. Producing many offspring with little chance of survival might not be the best strategy, but producing only a single, extraordinarily robust offspring also would not maximize the number of surviving offspring. Rather, an intermediate situation, in which several fairly large offspring are produced, should maximize the number of surviving offspring.

## Reproductive events per lifetime represent an additional trade-off

The trade-off between age and fecundity plays a key role in many life histories. Annual plants and most insects focus all their reproductive resources on a single large event and then die. This life history adaptation is called **semelparity.** Organisms that produce offspring several times over many seasons exhibit a life history adaptation called **iteroparity.**

Species that reproduce yearly must avoid overtaxing themselves in any one reproductive episode so that they will be able to survive and reproduce in the future. Semelparity, or "big bang" reproduction, is usually found in short-lived species that have a low probability of staying alive between broods, such as plants growing in harsh climates. Semelparity is also favored when fecundity entails large reproductive cost, exemplified by Pacific salmon migrating upriver to their spawning grounds. In these species, rather than investing some resources in an unlikely bid to survive until the next breeding season, individuals put all their resources into one reproductive event.

## Age at first reproduction correlates with life span

Among mammals and many other animals, longer-lived species put off reproduction longer than short-lived species, relative to expected life span. The advantage of delayed reproduction is that juveniles gain experience before expending the high costs of reproduction. In long-lived animals, this advantage outweighs the energy that is invested in survival and growth rather than reproduction.

In shorter-lived animals, on the other hand, time is of the essence; thus, quick reproduction is more critical than juvenile training, and reproduction tends to occur earlier.

### Learning Outcomes Review 56.4

Life history adaptations involve many trade-offs between reproductive cost and investment in survival. These trade-offs take a variety of forms, from laying fewer than the maximum possible number of eggs to putting all energy into a single bout of reproduction. Natural selection favors maximizing reproductive success, but number of offspring produced must be tempered by available resources.

■ *How might the life histories of two species differ if one was subject to high levels of predation and the other had few predators?*

# 56.5 Environmental Limits to Population Growth

### Learning Outcomes

1. Explain exponential growth.
2. Discuss why populations cannot grow exponentially forever.
3. Define carrying capacity.

Populations often remain at a relatively constant size, regardless of how many offspring are born. As you saw in chapter 1, Darwin based his theory of natural selection partly on this seeming contradiction. Natural selection occurs because of checks on reproduction, with some individuals producing fewer surviving offspring than others. To understand populations, we must consider how they grow and what factors in nature limit population growth.

## The exponential growth model applies to populations with no growth limits

The rate of population increase, *r*, is defined as the difference between the birth rate, *b*, and the death rate, *d*, corrected for movement of individuals in or out of the population (*e*, rate of movement out of the area; *i*, rate of movement into the area). Thus,

$$r = (b - d) + (i - e)$$

Movements of individuals can have a major influence on population growth rates. For example, the increase in human population in the United States during the closing decades of the 20th century was mostly due to immigration.

The simplest model of population growth assumes that a population grows without limits at its maximal rate and also that rates of immigration and emigration are equal. This rate, called the **biotic potential,** is the rate at which a population of a given species increases when no limits are placed on its rate of growth. In mathematical terms, this is defined by the following formula:

$$\frac{dN}{dt} = r_i N$$

where *N* is the number of individuals in the population, *dN/dt* is the rate of change in its numbers over time, and $r_i$ is the intrinsic rate of natural increase for that population—its innate capacity for growth.

The biotic potential of any population is exponential (red line in figure 56.16). Even when the *rate* of increase remains constant, the actual *number* of individuals accelerates rapidly as the size of the population grows. The result of unchecked exponential growth is a population explosion.

A single pair of houseflies, laying 120 eggs per generation, could produce more than 5 trillion descendants in a year. In 10 years, their descendants would form a swarm more than 2 m thick over the entire surface of the Earth! In practice, such patterns of unrestrained growth prevail only for short periods, usually when an organism reaches a new habitat with abundant

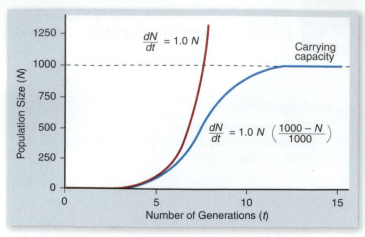

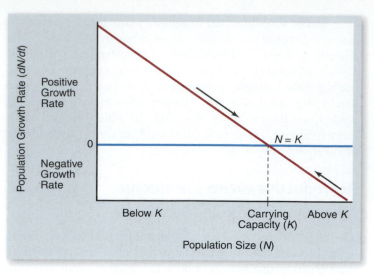

**Figure 56.16  Two models of population growth.** The red line illustrates the exponential growth model for a population with an *r* of 1.0. The blue line illustrates the logistic growth model in a population with *r* = 1.0 and *K* = 1000 individuals. At first, logistic growth accelerates exponentially; then, as resources become limited, the death rate increases and growth slows. Growth ceases when the death rate equals the birth rate. The carrying capacity *(K)* ultimately depends on the resources available in the environment.

**Figure 56.17  Relationship between population growth rate and population size.** Populations far from the carrying capacity (*K*) have high growth rates—positive if the population is below *K*, and negative if it is above *K*. As the population approaches *K*, growth rates approach zero.

**Inquiry question**

**?**  Why does the growth rate converge on zero?

resources. Natural examples of such short period of unrestrained growth include dandelions arriving in the fields, lawns, and meadows of North America from Europe for the first time; algae colonizing a newly formed pond; or cats introduced to an island with many birds, but previously lacking predators.

### Carrying capacity

No matter how rapidly populations grow, they eventually reach a limit imposed by shortages of important environmental factors, such as space, light, water, or nutrients. A population ultimately may stabilize at a certain size, called the **carrying capacity** of the particular place where it lives. The carrying capacity, symbolized by *K*, is the maximum number of individuals that the environment can support.

## The logistic growth model applies to populations that approach their carrying capacity

As a population approaches its carrying capacity, its rate of growth slows greatly, because fewer resources remain for each new individual to use. The growth curve of such a population, which is always limited by one or more factors in the environment, can be approximated by the following logistic growth equation:

$$\frac{dN}{dt} = rN \left( \frac{K - N}{K} \right)$$

In this model of population growth, the growth rate of the population *(dN/dt)* is equal to its intrinsic rate of natural increase (*r* multiplied by *N*, the number of individuals present at any one time), adjusted for the amount of resources available. The adjust-

ment is made by multiplying *rN* by the fraction of *K*, the carrying capacity, still unused [*(K – N)/K*]. As *N* increases, the fraction of resources by which *r* is multiplied becomes smaller and smaller, and the rate of increase of the population declines.

Graphically, if you plot *N* versus *t* (time), you obtain a **sigmoidal growth curve** characteristic of many biological populations. The curve is called "sigmoidal" because its shape has a double curve like the letter **S**. As the size of a population stabilizes at the carrying capacity, its rate of growth slows, eventually coming to a halt (blue line in figure 56.16).

In mathematical terms, as *N* approaches *K*, the *rate* of population growth *(dN/dt)* begins to slow, reaching 0 when *N = K* (figure 56.17). Conversely, if the population size exceeds the carrying capacity, then *K – N* will be negative, and the population will experience a negative growth rate. As the population size then declines toward the carrying capacity, the magnitude of this negative growth rate will decrease until it reaches 0 when *N = K*.

Notice that the population tends to move toward the carrying capacity regardless of whether it is initially above or below it. For this reason, logistic growth tends to return a population to the same size. In this sense, such populations are considered to be in equilibrium because they would be expected to be at or near the carrying capacity at most times.

In many cases, real populations display trends corresponding to a logistic growth curve. This is true not only in the laboratory, but also in natural populations (figure 56.18*a*). In some cases, however, the fit is not perfect (figure 56.18*b*), and as we shall see shortly, many populations exhibit other patterns.

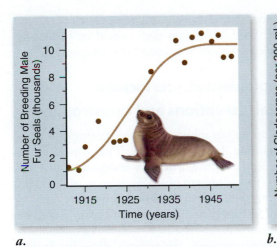

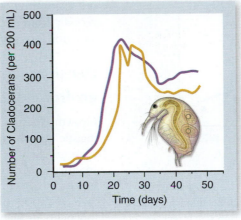

**Figure 56.18  Many populations exhibit logistic growth.** *a.* A fur seal (*Callorhinus ursinus*) population on St. Paul Island, Alaska. *b.* Two laboratory populations of the cladoceran *Bosmina longirostris*. Note that the populations first exceeded the carrying capacity, before decreasing to a size that was then maintained.

*a.*

*b.*

---

### Learning Outcomes Review 56.5

Exponential growth refers to population growth in which the number of individuals accelerates even when the rate of increase remains constant; it results in a population explosion. Exponential growth is eventually limited by resource availability. The size at which a population in a particular location stabilizes is defined as the carrying capacity of that location for that species. Populations often grow to the carrying capacity of their environment.

■ **What might cause a population's carrying capacity to change, and how would the population respond?**

## 56.6  Factors That Regulate Populations

### Learning Outcomes

1. **Compare density-dependent and density-independent factors.**
2. **Evaluate why the size of some populations cycle.**
3. **Consider how the life history adaptations of species may differ depending on how often populations are at their carrying capacity.**

A number of factors may affect population size through time. Some of these factors depend on population size and are therefore termed *density-dependent*. Other factors, such as natural disasters, affect populations regardless of size; these factors are termed *density-independent*. Many populations exhibit cyclic fluctuations in size that may result from complex interactions of factors.

### Density-dependent effects occur when reproduction and survival are affected by population size

The reason population growth rates are affected by population size is that many important processes have **density-dependent effects.** That is, as population size increases, either reproductive rates decline or mortality rates increase, or both, a phenomenon termed *negative feedback* (figure 56.19).

Populations can be regulated in many different ways. When populations approach their carrying capacity, competition for resources can be severe, leading both to a decreased birth rate and an increased risk of death (figure 56.20). In addition, predators often focus their attention on a particularly common prey species, which also results in increasing rates of mortality as populations increase. High population densities can also lead to an accumulation of toxic wastes in the environment.

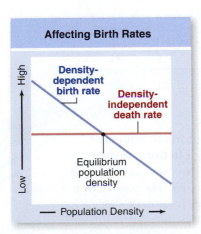

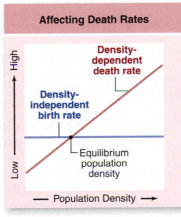

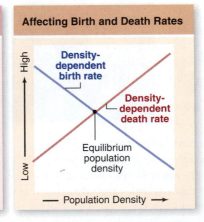

**Figure 56.19  Density-dependent population regulation.** Density-dependent factors can affect birth rates, death rates, or both.

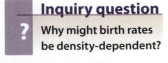

**Inquiry question**

**Why might birth rates be density-dependent?**

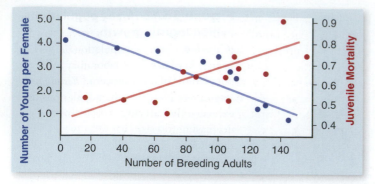

**Figure 56.20 Density dependence in the song sparrow (Melospiza melodia) on Mandarte Island.** Reproductive success decreases and mortality rates increase as population size increases.

> **Inquiry question**
>
> **?** What would happen if researchers supplemented the food available to the birds?

Behavioral changes may also affect population growth rates. Some species of rodents, for example, become antisocial, fighting more, breeding less, and generally acting stressed-out. These behavioral changes result from hormonal actions, but their ultimate cause is not yet clear; most likely, they have evolved as adaptive responses to situations in which resources are scarce. In addition, in crowded populations, the population growth rate may decrease because of an increased rate of emigration of individuals attempting to find better conditions elsewhere (figure 56.21).

However, not all density-dependent factors are negatively related to population size. In some cases, growth rates increase with population size. This phenomenon is referred to as the **Allee effect** (after Warder Allee, who first described it), and is an example of *positive feedback*. The Allee effect can take several forms. Most obviously, in populations that are too sparsely distributed, individuals may have difficulty finding mates. Moreover, some species may rely on large groups to deter predators or to provide the necessary stimulation for breeding activities. The Allee effect

is a major threat for many endangered species, which may never recover from decreased population sizes caused by habitat destruction, overexploitation, or other causes (see chapter 60).

## Density-independent effects include environmental disruptions and catastrophes

Growth rates in populations sometimes do not correspond to the logistic growth equation. In many cases, such patterns result because growth is under the control of **density-independent effects.** In other words, the rate of growth of a population at any instant is limited by something unrelated to the size of the population.

A variety of factors may affect populations in a density-independent manner. Most of these are aspects of the external environment, such as extremely cold winters, droughts, storms, or volcanic eruptions. Individuals often are affected by these occurrences regardless of the size of the population.

Populations in areas where such events occur relatively frequently display erratic growth patterns in which the populations increase rapidly when conditions are benign, but exhibit large reductions whenever the environment turns hostile (figure 56.22). Needless to say, such populations do not produce the sigmoidal growth curves characteristic of the logistic equation.

## Population cycles may reflect complex interactions

In some populations, density-dependent effects lead not to an equilibrium population size but to cyclic patterns of increase and decrease. For example, ecologists have studied cycles in hare

**Figure 56.21 Density-dependent effects.** Migratory locusts (*Locusta migratoria*) are a legendary plague of large areas of Africa and Eurasia. At high population densities, the locusts have different hormonal and physical characteristics and take off as a swarm.

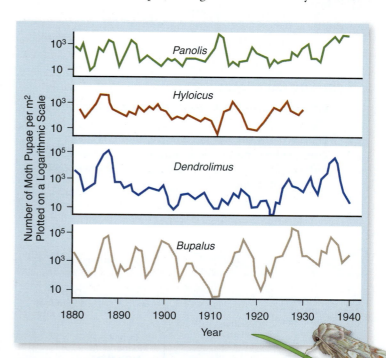

**Figure 56.22 Fluctuations in the number of pupae of four moth species in Germany.** The population fluctuations suggest that density-independent factors are regulating population size. The concordance in trends through time suggests that the same factors are regulating population size in all four species.

populations since the 1820s. They have found that the North American snowshoe hare *(Lepus americanus)* follows a "10-year cycle" (in reality, the cycle varies from 8 to 11 years). Hare population numbers fall 10-fold to 30-fold in a typical cycle, and 100-fold changes can occur (figure 56.23). Two factors appear to be generating the cycle: food plants and predators.

**Food plants.** The preferred foods of snowshoe hares are willow and birch twigs. As hare density increases, the quantity of these twigs decreases, forcing the hares to feed on high-fiber (low-quality) food. Lower birthrates, low juvenile survivorship, and low growth rates follow. The hares also spend more time searching for food, an activity that increases their exposure to predation. The result is a precipitous decline in willow and birch twig abundance, and a corresponding fall in hare abundance. It takes 2 to 3 years for the quantity of mature twigs to recover.

**Predators.** A key predator of the snowshoe hare is the Canada lynx. The Canada lynx shows a "10-year" cycle of abundance that seems remarkably entrained to the hare abundance cycle (see figure 55.23). As hare numbers increase, lynx numbers do too, rising in response to the increased availability of the lynx's food. When hare numbers fall, so do lynx numbers, their food supply depleted.

Which factor is responsible for the predator–prey oscillations? Do increasing numbers of hares lead to overharvesting of plants (a hare–plant cycle), or do increasing numbers of lynx lead to overharvesting of hares (a hare–lynx cycle)? Field experiments carried out by Charles Krebs and coworkers in 1992 provide an answer.

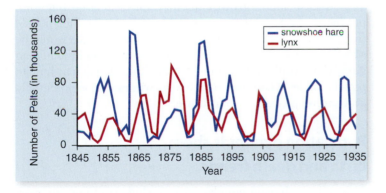

**Figure 56.23 Linked population cycles of the snowshoe hare *(Lepus americanus)* and the northern lynx *(Lynx canadensis).*** These data are based on records of fur returns from trappers in the Hudson Bay region of Canada. The lynx population carefully tracks that of the snowshoe hare, but lags behind it slightly.

### Inquiry question

**?** Suppose experimenters artificially kept the hare population at a high and constant level; what would happen to the lynx population? Conversely, if experimenters artificially kept the lynx population at a high and constant level, what would happen to the hare population?

In Canada's Yukon, Krebs set up experimental plots that contained hare populations. If food is added (no food shortage effect) and predators are excluded (no predator effect) in an experimental area, hare numbers increase 10-fold and stay there—the cycle is lost. However, the cycle is retained if either of the factors is allowed to operate alone: exclude predators but don't add food (food shortage effect alone), or add food in the presence of predators (predator effect alone). Thus, both factors can affect the cycle, which in practice seems to be generated by the interaction between the two.

Population cycles traditionally have been considered to occur rarely. However, a recent review of nearly 700 long-term (25 years or more) studies of trends within populations found that cycles were not uncommon; nearly 30% of the studies—including birds, mammals, fish, and crustaceans—provided evidence of some cyclic pattern in population size through time, although most of these cycles are nowhere near as dramatic in amplitude as the hare–lynx cycles. In some cases, such as that of the snowshoe hare and lynx, density-dependent factors may be involved, whereas in other cases, density-independent factors, such as cyclic climatic patterns, may be responsible.

## Resource availability affects life history adaptations

As you have seen, some species usually maintain stable population sizes near the carrying capacity, whereas in other species population sizes fluctuate markedly and are often far below carrying capacity. The selective factors affecting such species differ markedly. Individuals in populations near their carrying capacity may face stiff competition for limited resources; by contrast, individuals in populations far below carrying capacity have access to abundant resources.

We have already described the consequences of such differences. When resources are limited, the cost of reproduction often will be very high. Consequently, selection will favor individuals that can compete effectively and utilize resources efficiently. Such adaptations often come at the cost of lowered reproductive rates. Such populations are termed **K-selected** because they are adapted to thrive when the population is near its carrying capacity (*K*). Table 56.3 lists some of the typical features of *K*-selected populations. Examples of *K*-selected species include coconut palms, whooping cranes, whales, and humans.

By contrast, in populations far below the carrying capacity, resources may be abundant. Costs of reproduction are low, and selection favors those individuals that can produce the maximum number of offspring. Selection here favors individuals with the highest reproductive rates; such populations are termed *r*-selected. Examples of organisms displaying *r*-selected life history adaptations include dandelions, aphids, mice, and cockroaches.

Most natural populations show life history adaptations that exist along a continuum ranging from completely *r*-selected traits to completely *K*-selected traits. Although these tendencies hold true as generalities, few populations are purely *r*- or *K*-selected and show all of the traits listed in table 56.3. These attributes should be treated as generalities, with the recognition that many exceptions exist.

| TABLE 56.3 | r-Selected and K-Selected Life History Adaptations | |
|---|---|---|
| Adaptation | r-Selected Populations | K-Selected Populations |
| Age at first reproduction | Early | Late |
| Life span | Short | Long |
| Maturation time | Short | Long |
| Mortality rate | Often high | Usually low |
| Number of offspring produced per reproductive episode | Many | Few |
| Number of reproductions per lifetime | Few | Many |
| Parental care | None | Often extensive |
| Size of offspring or eggs | Small | Large |

### Learning Outcomes Review 56.6

Density-dependent factors such as resource availability come into play particularly when population size is larger; density-independent factors such as natural disasters operate regardless of population size. Population density may be cyclic due to complex interactions such as resource cycles and predator effects. Populations with density-dependent regulation often are near their carrying capacity; in species with populations well below carrying capacity, natural selection may favor high rates of reproduction when resources are abundant.

■ **Can a population experience both positive and negative density-dependent effects?**

## 56.7 Human Population Growth

### Learning Outcomes

1. Explain how the rate of human population growth has changed through time.
2. Describe the effects of age distribution on future growth.
3. Evaluate the relative importance of rapid population growth and resource consumption as threats to the biosphere and human welfare.

Humans exhibit many K-selected life history traits, including small brood size, late reproduction, and a high degree of parental care. These life history traits evolved during the early history of hominids, when the limited resources available from the environment controlled population size. Throughout most of human history, our populations have been regulated by food availability, disease, and predators. Although unusual disturbances, including floods, plagues, and droughts, no doubt affected the pattern of human population growth, the overall size of the human population grew slowly during our early history.

Two thousand years ago, perhaps 130 million people populated the Earth. It took a thousand years for that number to double, and it was 1650 before it had doubled again, to about 500 million. In other words, for over 16 centuries, the human population was characterized by very slow growth. In this respect, human populations resembled many other species with predominantly K-selected life history adaptations.

### Human populations have grown exponentially

Starting in the early 1700s, changes in technology gave humans more control over their food supply, enabled them to develop superior weapons to ward off predators, and led to the development of cures for many diseases. At the same time, improvements in shelter and storage capabilities made humans less vulnerable to climatic uncertainties. These changes allowed humans to expand the carrying capacity of the habitats in which they lived and thus to escape the confines of logistic growth and re-enter the exponential phase of the sigmoidal growth curve.

Responding to the lack of environmental constraints, the human population has grown explosively over the last 300 years. Although the birth rate has remained unchanged at about 30 per 1000 per year over this period, the death rate has fallen dramatically, from 20 per 1000 per year to its present level of 13 per 1000 per year. The difference between birth and death rates meant that the population grew as much as 2% per year, although the rate has now declined to 1.2% per year.

A 1.2% annual growth rate may not seem large, but it has produced a current human population of nearly 7 billion people (figure 56.24). At this growth rate, 78 million people would be added to the world population in the next year, and the human population would double in 58 years. Both the current human population level and the projected growth rate have potentially grave consequences for our future.

### Population pyramids show birth and death trends

Although the human population as a whole continues to grow rapidly at the beginning of the 21st century, this growth is not occurring uniformly over the planet. Rather, most of the population growth is occurring in Africa, Asia, and Latin America (figure 56.25). By contrast, populations are actually decreasing in some countries in Europe.

The rate at which a population can be expected to grow in the future can be assessed graphically by means of a **population pyramid**, a bar graph displaying the numbers of people in each age category (figure 56.26). Males are conventionally shown to the left of the vertical age axis, females to the right. A human population pyramid thus displays the age composition of a population by sex. In most human population pyramids, the number of older females is disproportionately large compared with the

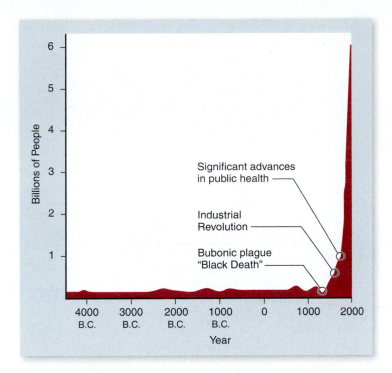

**Figure 56.24 History of human population size.**
Temporary increases in death rate, even a severe one such as that occurring during the Black Death of the 1300s, have little lasting effect. Explosive growth began with the Industrial Revolution in the 1800s, which produced a significant, long-term lowering of the death rate. The current world population is 6.9 billion, and at the present rate, it will double in 58 years.

**? Inquiry question**

Based on what we have learned about population growth, what do you predict will happen to human population size?

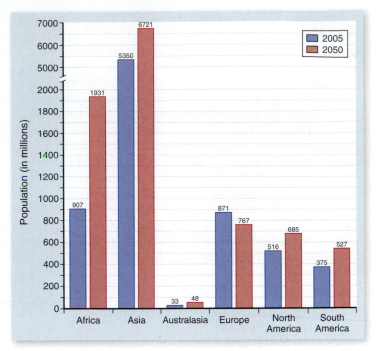

**Figure 56.25 Projected population growth in 2050.**
Developed countries are predicted to grow little; almost all of the population increase will occur in less-developed countries.

number of older males, because females in most regions have a longer life expectancy than males.

Viewing such a pyramid, we can predict demographic trends in births and deaths. In general, a rectangular pyramid is characteristic of countries whose populations are stable, neither growing nor shrinking. A triangular pyramid is characteristic of a country that will exhibit rapid future growth because most of

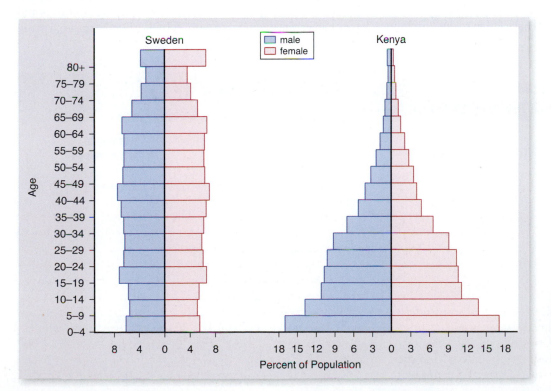

**Figure 56.26 Population pyramids from 2008.** Population pyramids are graphed according to a population's age distribution. Kenya's pyramid has a broad base because of the great number of individuals below childbearing age. When the young people begin to bear children, the population will experience rapid growth. The Swedish pyramid exhibits a slight bulge among middle-aged Swedes, the result of the "baby boom" that occurred in the middle of the 20th century, and many postreproductive individuals resulting from Sweden's long average life span.

**? Inquiry question**

What will the population distributions look like in 20 years?

its population has not yet entered the childbearing years. Inverted triangles are characteristic of populations that are shrinking, usually as a result of sharply declining birth rates.

Examples of population pyramids for Sweden and Kenya in 2008 are shown in figure 56.26. The two countries exhibit very different age distributions. The nearly rectangular population pyramid for Sweden indicates that its population is not expanding because birth rates have decreased and average life span has increased. The very triangular pyramid of Kenya, by contrast, results from relatively high birthrates and shorter average life spans, which can lead to explosive future growth. The difference is most apparent when we consider that only 16% of Sweden's population is less than 15 years old, compared with nearly half of all Kenyans. Moreover, the fertility rate (offspring per woman) in Sweden is 1.7; in Kenya, it is 4.7. As a result, Kenya's population could double in less than 35 years, whereas Sweden's will remain stable.

## Humanity's future growth is uncertain

Earth's rapidly growing human population constitutes perhaps the greatest challenge to the future of the biosphere, the world's interacting community of living things. Humanity is adding 78 million people a year to its population—over a million every 5 days, 150 every minute! In more rapidly growing countries, the resulting population increase is staggering (table 56.4). India, for example, had a population of 1.05 billion in 2002; by 2050, its population likely will exceed 1.6 billion.

A key element in the world's population growth is its uneven distribution among countries. Of the billion people added to the world's population in the 1990s, 90% live in developing countries (figure 56.27). The fraction of the world's population that lives in industrialized countries is therefore diminishing. In 1950, fully one-third of the world's population lived in industrialized countries; by 1996, that proportion had fallen to one-quarter; and in 2020, the proportion will have fallen to one-sixth.

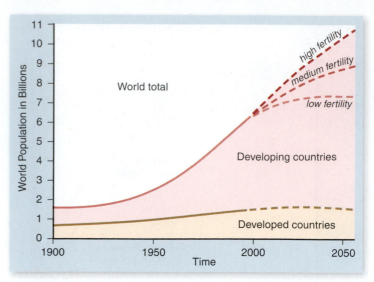

**Figure 56.27 Distribution of population growth.** Most of the worldwide increase in population since 1950 has occurred in developing countries. The age structures of developing countries indicate that this trend will increase in the near future. World population in 2050 likely will be between 7.3 and 10.7 billion, according to a recent United Nations study. Depending on fertility rates, the population at that time will either be increasing rapidly or slightly, or in the best case, declining slightly.

In the future, the world's population growth will be centered in the parts of the world least equipped to deal with the pressures of rapid growth.

Rapid population growth in developing countries has had the harsh consequence of increasing the gap between rich and poor. Today, the 19% of the world's population that lives in the industrialized world have a per capita income of $22,060, but 81% of the world's population lives in developing countries and has a per capita income of only $3,580. Furthermore, of the

| TABLE 56.4 | A Comparison of 2005 Population Data in Developed and Developing Countries | | |
|---|---|---|---|
| | United States (highly developed) | Brazil (moderately developed) | Ethiopia (poorly developed) |
| Fertility rate | 2.1 | 1.9 | 5.3 |
| Doubling time at current rate (years) | 75 | 65 | 29 |
| Infant mortality rate (per 1000 births) | 6.5 | 30 | 95 |
| Life expectancy at birth (years) | 78 | 72 | 49 |
| Per capita GDP (U.S. $)* | $40,100 | $8100 | $800 |
| Population < 15 years old (%) | 21 | 26 | 44 |

*GDP, gross domestic product.

people in the developing world, about one-quarter of the population gets by on $1 per day. Eighty percent of all the energy used today is consumed by the industrialized world, but only 20% is used by developing countries.

No one knows whether the world can sustain today's population of 6.9 billion people, much less the far greater numbers expected in the future. As chapter 58 outlines, the world ecosystem is already under considerable stress. We cannot reasonably expect to expand its carrying capacity indefinitely, and indeed we already seem to be stretching the limits.

Despite using an estimated 45% of the total biological productivity of Earth's landmasses and more than one-half of all renewable sources of fresh water, between one-fourth and one-eighth of all people in the world are malnourished. Moreover, as anticipated by Thomas Malthus in his famous 1798 work, *Essay on the Principle of Population*, death rates are beginning to rise in some areas. In sub-Saharan Africa, for example, population projections for the year 2025 have been scaled back from 1.33 billion to 1.05 billion (21%) because of the effect of AIDS. Similar decreases are projected for Russia as a result of higher death rates due to disease.

If we are to avoid catastrophic increases in the death rate, birth rates must fall dramatically. Faced with this grim dichotomy, significant efforts are underway worldwide to lower birth rates.

## The population growth rate has declined

The world population growth rate is declining, from a high of 2.0% in the period 1965–1970 to 1.2% in 2008. Nonetheless, because of the larger population, this amounts to an increase of 78 million people per year to the world population, compared with 53 million per year in the 1960s.

The United Nations attributes the growth rate decline to increased family planning efforts and the increased economic power and social status of women. The United States has led the world in funding family planning programs abroad, but some groups oppose spending money on international family planning. The opposition believes that money is better spent on improving education and the economy in other countries, leading to an increased awareness and lowered fertility rates. The U.N. certainly supports the improvement of education programs in developing countries, but interestingly, it has reported increased education levels *following* a decrease in family size as a result of family planning.

Most countries are devoting considerable attention to slowing the growth rate of their populations, and there are genuine signs of progress. For example, from 1984 to 2008, family planning programs in Kenya succeeded in reducing the fertility rate from 8.0 to 4.7 children per couple, thus lowering the population growth rate from 4.0% per year to 2.8% per year. Because of these efforts, the global population may stabilize at about 8.9 billion people by the middle of the current century. How many people the planet can support sustainably depends on the quality of life that we want to achieve; there are already more people than can be sustainably supported with current technologies.

## Consumption in the developed world further depletes resources

Population size is not the only factor that determines resource use; per capita consumption is also important. In this respect, we in the industrialized world need to pay more attention to lessening the impact each of us makes because, even though the vast majority of the world's population is in developing countries, the overwhelming percentage of consumption of resources occurs in the industrialized countries. Indeed, the wealthiest 20% of the world's population accounts for 86% of the world's consumption of resources and produces 53% of the world's carbon dioxide emissions, whereas the poorest 20% of the world is responsible for only 1.3% of consumption and 3% of carbon dioxide emissions. Looked at another way, in terms of resource use, a child born today in the industrialized world will consume many more resources over the course of his or her life than a child born in the developing world.

One way of quantifying this disparity is by calculating what has been termed the **ecological footprint**, which is the amount of productive land required to support an individual at the standard of living of a particular population through the course of his or her life. This figure estimates the acreage used for the production of food (both plant and animal), forest products, and housing, as well as the area of forest required to absorb carbon dioxide produced by the combustion of fossil fuels. As figure 56.28 illustrates, the

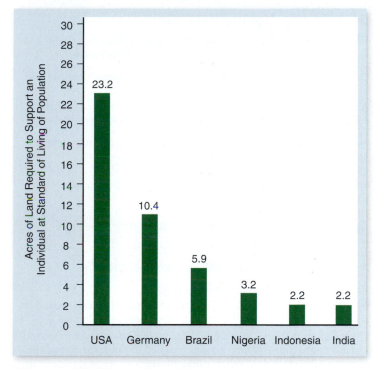

**Figure 56.28 Ecological footprints of individuals in different countries.** An ecological footprint calculates how much land is required to support a person through his or her life, including the acreage used for production of food, forest products, and housing, in addition to the forest required to absorb the carbon dioxide produced by the combustion of fossil fuels.

**Inquiry question**

? **Which is a more important cause of resource depletion, overpopulation or overconsumption?**

ecological footprint of an individual in the United States is more than 10 times greater than that of someone in India.

Based on these measurements, researchers have calculated that resource use by humans is now one-third greater than the amount that nature can sustainably replace. Moreover, consumption is increasing rapidly in parts of the developing world; if all humans lived at the standard of living in the industrialized world, two additional planet Earths would be needed.

Building a sustainable world is the most important task facing humanity's future. The quality of life available to our children will depend to a large extent on our success in limiting both population growth and the amount of per capita resource consumption.

### Learning Outcomes Review 56.7

For most of its history, the *K*-selected human population increased gradually. In the last 400 years, with resource control, the human population has grown exponentially; at the current rate, it would double in 58 years. A population pyramid shows the number of individuals in different age categories. Pyramids with a wide base are undergoing faster growth than those that are uniform from top to bottom. Growth rates overall are declining, but consumption per capita in the developed world is still a significant drain on resources.

■ *Which is more important, reducing global population growth or reducing resource consumption levels in developed countries?*

# Chapter Review

## 56.1 The Environmental Challenges

Key environmental factors include temperature, water, sunlight, and soil type. Individuals seek to maintain internal homeostasis.

**Organisms are capable of responding to environmental changes that occur during their lifetime.**

Most individuals can cope with variations in their natural habitat, such as short-term changes in temperature and water availability.

**Natural selection leads to evolutionary adaptation to environmental conditions.**

Over evolutionary time, physiological, morphological, or behavioral adaptations evolve that make organisms better suited to the environment in which they live.

## 56.2 Populations: Groups of a Single Species in One Place

**A population's geographic distribution is termed its range.**

**Ranges undergo expansion and contraction.**

Most populations have limited geographic ranges that can expand or contract through time as the environment changes.

Dispersal mechanisms may allow some species to cross a barrier and expand their range. Human actions have led to range expansion of some species, often with detrimental effects.

**Individuals in populations exhibit different spacing patterns.**

Within a population, individuals are distributed randomly, uniformly, or are clumped . Nonrandom distributions may reflect resource distributions or competition for resources.

**A metapopulation comprises distinct populations that may exchange members.**

The degree of exchange between populations in a metapopulation is highest when populations are large and more connected.

Metapopulations may act as a buffer against extinction by permitting recolonization of vacant areas or marginal areas.

## 56.3 Population Demography and Dynamics

**Sex ratio and generation time affect population growth rates.**

Abundant females, a short generation time, or both can be responsible for more rapid population growth.

**Age structure is determined by the numbers of individuals in different age groups.**

Every age cohort has a characteristic fecundity and death rate, and so the age structure of a population affects growth.

**Life tables show probability of survival and reproduction through a cohort's life span.**

**Survivorship curves demonstrate how survival probability changes with age (see figures 56.11, 56.12).**

In some populations, survivorship is high until old age, whereas in others, survivorship is lowest among the youngest individuals.

## 56.4 Life History and the Cost of Reproduction

Because resources are limited, reproduction has a cost. Resources allocated toward current reproduction cannot be used to enhance survival and future reproduction (see figure 56.13).

**A trade-off exists between number of offspring and investment per offspring.**

When reproductive cost is high, fitness can be maximized by deferring reproduction, or by producing a few large-sized young that have a greater chance of survival.

**Reproductive events per lifetime represent an additional trade-off.**

Semelparity is reproduction once in a single large event. Iteroparity is production of offspring several times over many seasons.

**Age at first reproduction correlates with life span.**

Longer-lived species delay first reproduction longer compared with short-lived species, in which time is of the essence.

## 56.5 Environmental Limits to Population Growth

***The exponential growth model applies to populations with no growth limits.***

The rate of population increase, $r$, is defined as the difference between birth rate, $b$, and death rate, $d$.

Exponential growth occurs when a population is not limited by resources or by other species (see figure 56.16).

***The logistic model applies to populations that approach their carrying capacity.***

Logistic growth is observed as a population reaches its carrying capacity. Usually, a population's growth rate slows to a plateau. In some cases the population overshoots and then drops back to the carrying capacity.

## 56.6 Factors That Regulate Populations

***Density-dependent effects occur when reproduction and survival are affected by population size.***

Density-dependent factors include increased competition and disease. To stabilize a population size, birth rates must decline, death rates must increase, or both.

***Density-independent effects include environmental disruptions and catastrophes.***

Density-independent factors are not related to population size and include environmental events that result in mortality.

***Population cycles may reflect complex interactions.***

In some cases, population size is cyclic because of the interaction of factors such as food supply and predation (see figure 56.23).

***Resource availability affects life history adaptations.***

Populations at carrying capacity have adaptations to compete for limited resources; populations well below carrying capacity exhibit a high reproductive rate to use abundant resources.

## 56.7 Human Population Growth

***Human populations have grown exponentially.***

Technology and other innovations have simultaneously increased the carrying capacity and decreased mortality in the past 300 years.

***Population pyramids show birth and death trends.***

Populations with many young individuals are likely to experience high growth rates as these individuals reach reproductive age.

***Humanity's future growth is uncertain.***

The human population is unevenly distributed. Rapid growth in developing countries has resulted in poverty, whereas most resources are utilized by the industrialized world.

***The population growth rate has declined.***

Even at lower growth rates, the number of individuals on the planet is likely to plateau at 7 to 10 billion.

***Consumption in the developed world further depletes resources.***

Resource consumption rates in the developed world are very high; a sustainable future requires limits both to population growth and to per capita resource consumption.

## Review Questions

### UNDERSTAND

1. Source–sink metapopulations are distinct from other types of metapopulations because
   a. exchange of individuals only occurs in the former.
   b. populations with negative growth rates are a part of the former.
   c. populations never go extinct in the former.
   d. all populations eventually go extinct in the former.

2. The potential for social interactions among individuals should be maximized when individuals
   a. are randomly distributed in their environment.
   b. are uniformly distributed in their environment.
   c. have a clumped distribution in their environment.
   d. None of the above

3. When ecologists talk about the cost of reproduction they mean
   a. the reduction in future reproductive output as a consequence of current reproduction.
   b. the amount of calories it takes for all the activity used in successful reproduction.
   c. the amount of calories contained in eggs or offspring.
   d. None of the above

4. A life history trade-off between clutch size and offspring size
   a. means that as clutch size increases, offspring size increases.
   b. means that as clutch size increases, offspring size decreases.
   c. means that as clutch size increases, adult size increases.
   d. means that as clutch size increases, adult size decreases.

5. The difference between exponential and logistic growth rates is
   a. exponential growth depends on birth and death rates and logistic does not.
   b. in logistic growth, emigration and immigration are unimportant.
   c. that both are affected by density, but logistic growth is slower.
   d. that only logistic growth reflects density-dependent effects on births or deaths.

6. The logistic population growth model, $dN/dt = rN[(K - N)/K]$, describes a population's growth when an upper limit to growth is assumed. As $N$ approaches (numerically) the value of $K$
   a. $dN/dt$ increases rapidly.
   b. $dN/dt$ approaches 0.
   c. $dN/dt$ increases slowly.
   d. the population becomes threatened by extinction.

7. Which of the following is an example of a density-dependent effect on population growth?

    a. An extremely cold winter

    b. A tornado

    c. An extremely hot summer in which cool burrow retreats are fewer than number of individuals in the population

    d. A drought

## APPLY

1. If the size of a population is reduced due to a natural disaster such as a flood

    a. population growth rates may increase because the population is no longer near its carrying capacity.

    b. population growth rates may decrease because individuals have trouble finding mates.

    c. both effects a. and b. may occur and whether population rates increase or decrease cannot be predicted.

    d. All of the above

2. In populations subjected to high levels of predation

    a. individuals should invest little in reproduction so as to maximize their survival.

    b. individuals should produce few offspring and invest little in any of them.

    c. individuals should invest greatly in reproduction because their chance of surviving to another breeding season is low.

    d. individuals should stop reproducing altogether.

3. In a population in which individuals are uniformly distributed

    a. the population is probably well below its carrying capacity.

    b. natural selection should favor traits that maximize the ability to compete for resources.

    c. immigration from other populations is probably keeping the population from going extinct.

    d. None of the above

4. The elimination of predators by humans

    a. will cause its prey to experience exponential growth until new predators arrive or evolve.

    b. will lead to an increase in the carrying capacity of the environment.

    c. may increase the population size of a prey species if that prey's population was being regulated by predation from the predator.

    d. will lead to an Allee effect.

## SYNTHESIZE

1. Refer to figure 56.8. What are the implications for evolutionary divergence among populations that are part of a metapopulation versus populations that are independent of other populations?

2. Refer to figure 56.13. Given a trade-off between current reproductive effort and future reproductive success (the so-called cost of reproduction), would you expect old individuals to have the same "optimal" reproductive effort as young individuals?

3. Refer to figure 56.14. Because the number of offspring that a parent can produce is often a trade-off with the size of individual offspring, many circumstances lead to an intermediate number and size of offspring being favored. If the size of an offspring was completely unrelated to the quality of that offspring (its chances of surviving until it reaches reproductive age), would you expect parents to fall on the left or right side of the x-axis (clutch size)? Explain.

4. Refer to figure 56.26. Would increasing the mean generation time have the same kind of effect on population growth rate as reducing the number of children that an individual female has over her lifetime? Which effect would have a bigger influence on population growth rate? Explain.

## ONLINE RESOURCE

**www.ravenbiology.com**

Understand, Apply, and Synthesize—enhance your study with animations that bring concepts to life and practice tests to assess your understanding. Your instructor may also recommend the interactive eBook, individualized learning tools, and more.

# Chapter 57

# Community Ecology

## Chapter Outline

## Introduction

*All the organisms that live together in a place are members of a community. The myriad of species that inhabit a tropical rain forest are a community. Indeed, every inhabited place on Earth supports its own particular array of organisms. Over time, the different species that live together have made many complex adjustments to community living, evolving together and forging relationships that give the community its character and stability. Both competition and cooperation have played key roles; in this chapter, we look at these and other factors in community ecology.*

## 57.1 Biological Communities: Species Living Together

**Learning Outcomes**

1. Define community.
2. Describe how community composition may change across a geographic landscape.

Almost any place on Earth is occupied by species, sometimes by many of them, as in the rain forests of the Amazon, and sometimes by only a few, as in the near-boiling waters of Yellowstone's geysers (where a number of microbial species live). The term **community** refers to the species that occur at any particular locality (figure 57.1). Communities can be characterized either by their constituent species or by their properties, such as **species richness** (the number of species present) or **primary productivity** (the amount of energy produced).

Interactions among community members govern many ecological and evolutionary processes. These interactions, such as predation and mutualism, affect the population biology of particular species—whether a population increases or decreases in abundance, for example—as well as the ways in which energy and nutrients cycle through the ecosystem. Moreover, the community context affects the patterns of natural selection faced by a species, and thus the evolutionary course it takes.

Scientists study biological communities in many ways, ranging from detailed observations to elaborate, large-scale experiments. In some cases, studies focus on the entire community, whereas in other cases only a subset of species that are likely to interact with one another are studied. Although scientists sometimes refer to such subsets as communities (for example, the "spider community"), the term **assemblage** is more appropriate to connote that the species included are only a portion of those present within the entire community.

### Communities have been viewed in different ways

Two views exist on the structure and functioning of communities. The *individualistic concept* of communities holds that a community is simply an aggregation of species that happen to occur together at one place.

By contrast, the **holistic concept** of communities views communities as an integrated unit. In this sense, the community could be viewed as a superorganism whose constituent species have coevolved to the extent that they function as part of a greater whole, just as the kidneys, heart, and lungs all function together within an animal's body. In this view, then, a community would amount to more than the sum of its parts.

These two views make differing predictions about the integrity of communities across space and time. If, as the individualistic view implies, communities are nothing more than a combination of species that occur together, then moving geographically across the landscape or back through time, we would not expect to see the same community. That is, species should appear and disappear independently, as a function of each species' own unique ecological requirements. By contrast, if a community is an integrated whole, then we would make the opposite prediction: Communities should stay the same through space or time, until being replaced by completely different communities when environmental differences are sufficiently great.

**Figure 57.1 An African savanna community.** A community consists of all the species—plants, animals, fungi, protists, and prokaryotes—that occur at a locality, in this case Etosha National Park in Namibia.

## Communities change over space and time

Most ecologists today favor the individualistic concept. For the most part, species seem to respond independently to changing environmental conditions. As a result, community composition changes gradually across landscapes as some species appear and become more abundant, while others decrease in abundance and eventually disappear.

A famous example of this pattern is the abundance of tree species in the Santa Catalina Mountains of Arizona along a geographic gradient running from very dry to very moist. Figure 57.2 shows that species can change abundance in patterns that are for the most part independent of one another. As a result, tree communities at different localities in these mountains fall on a continuum, one merging into the next, rather than representing discretely different sets of species.

Similar patterns through time are seen in paleontological studies. For example, a very good fossil record exists for the trees and small mammals that occurred in North America over the past 20,000 years. Examination of prehistoric communities shows little similarity to those that occur today. Many species that occur together today were never found together in the past. Conversely, species that used to occur in the same communities often do not overlap in their geographic ranges today. These findings suggest that as climate has changed during the waxing and waning of the Ice Ages, species have responded independently, rather than shifting their distributions together, as would be expected if the community were an integrated unit.

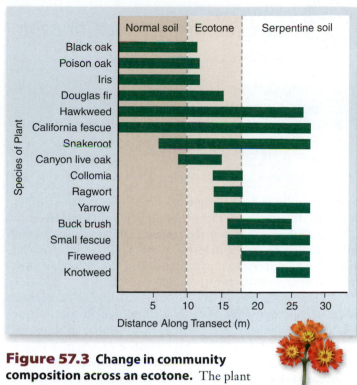

**Figure 57.3 Change in community composition across an ecotone.** The plant assemblages on normal and serpentine soils are greatly different, and the transition from one community to another occurs over a short distance.

### Inquiry question

**?** Why is there a sharp transition between the two community types?

Nonetheless, in some cases the abundance of species in a community does change geographically in a synchronous pattern. Often, this occurs at **ecotones,** places where the environment changes abruptly. For example, in the western United States, certain patches of habitat have serpentine soils. This soil differs from normal soil in many ways—for example, high concentrations of nickel, chromium, and iron; low concentrations of copper and calcium. Comparison of the plant species that occur on different soils shows that distinct communities exist on each type, with an abrupt transition from one to the other over a short distance (figure 57.3). Similar transitions are seen wherever greatly different habitats come into contact, such as at the interface between terrestrial and aquatic habitats or where grassland and forest meet.

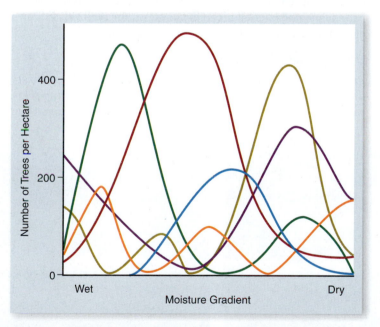

**Figure 57.2 Abundance of tree species along a moisture gradient in the Santa Catalina Mountains of southeastern Arizona.** Each line represents the abundance of a different tree species. The species' patterns of abundance are independent of one another. Thus, community composition changes continually along the gradient.

### Inquiry question

**?** Why do species exhibit different patterns of response to change in moisture?

### Learning Outcomes Review 57.1

A community comprises all species that occur at one site. In most cases, the abundance of community members appears to vary independently across space and through time. Community composition also changes gradually depending on environmental factors when moving from one location to another, such as from a very dry area to a very moist area.

■ *In a community, would you expect greater variation over time in abundance of animal life or plant life? Why?*

## 57.2 The Ecological Niche Concept

### Learning Outcomes

1. *Define niche and resource partitioning.*
2. *Differentiate between fundamental and realized niches.*
3. *Explain how the presence of other species can affect a species' realized niche.*

Each organism in a community confronts the challenge of survival in a different way. The **niche** an organism occupies is the total of all the ways it uses the resources of its environment. A niche may be described in terms of space utilization, food consumption, temperature range, appropriate conditions for mating, requirements for moisture, and other factors.

Sometimes species are not able to occupy their entire niche because of the presence or absence of other species. Species can interact with one another in a number of ways, and these interactions can either have positive or negative effects. One type of interaction, **interspecific competition,** occurs when two species attempt to use the same resource and there is not enough of the resource to satisfy both. Physical interactions over access to resources—such as fighting to defend a territory or displacing an individual from a particular location—are referred to as **interference competition;** consuming the same resources is called **exploitative competition.**

### Fundamental niches are potential; realized niches are actual

The entire niche that a species is capable of using, based on its physiological tolerance limits and resource needs, is called the **fundamental niche.** The actual set of environmental conditions, including the presence or absence of other species, in which the species can establish a stable population is its **realized niche.** Because of interspecific interactions, the realized niche of a species may be considerably smaller than its fundamental niche.

### Competition between species for niche occupancy

In a classic study, Joseph Connell of the University of California, Santa Barbara, investigated competitive interactions between two species of barnacles that grow together on rocks along the coast of Scotland. Of the two species Connell studied, *Chthamalus stellatus* lives in shallower water, where tidal action often exposes it to air, and *Semibalanus balanoides* (called *Balanus balanoides* prior to 1995) lives lower down, where it is rarely exposed to the atmosphere (figure 57.4). In these areas, space is at a premium. In the deeper zone, *S. balanoides* could always outcompete *C. stellatus* by crowding it off the rocks, undercutting it, and replacing it even where it had begun to grow, an example of interference competition.

When Connell removed *S. balanoides* from the area, however, *C. stellatus* was easily able to occupy the deeper zone, indicating that no physiological or other general obstacles prevented it from becoming established there. In contrast, *S. balanoides* could not survive in the shallow-water habitats where *C. stellatus* normally occurs; it does not have the physiological adaptations to warmer temperatures that allow *C. stellatus* to occupy this zone. Thus, the fundamental niche of *C. stellatus* includes both shallow and deeper zones, but its realized niche is much narrower because *C. stellatus* can be outcompeted by *S. balanoides* in parts of its fundamental niche. By contrast, the realized and fundamental niches of *S. balanoides* appear to be identical.

### Other causes of niche restriction

Processes other than competition can also restrict the realized niche of a species. For example, the plant St. John's wort (*Hypericum perforatum*) was introduced and became widespread in

---

**Figure 57.4**

**Competition among two species of barnacles.** The fundamental niche of *Chthamalus stellatus* includes both deep and shallow zones, but *Semibalanus balanoides* forces *C. stellatus* out of the part of its fundamental niche that overlaps the realized niche of *Semibalanus.*

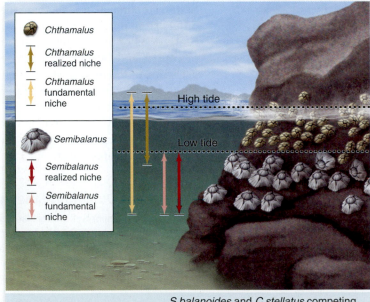

Legend:
- *Chthamalus*
- *Chthamalus* realized niche
- *Chthamalus* fundamental niche
- *Semibalanus*
- *Semibalanus* realized niche
- *Semibalanus* fundamental niche

High tide
Low tide

*S. balanoides* and *C. stellatus* competing

*C. stellatus* fundamental and realized niches are identical when *S. balanoides* is removed.

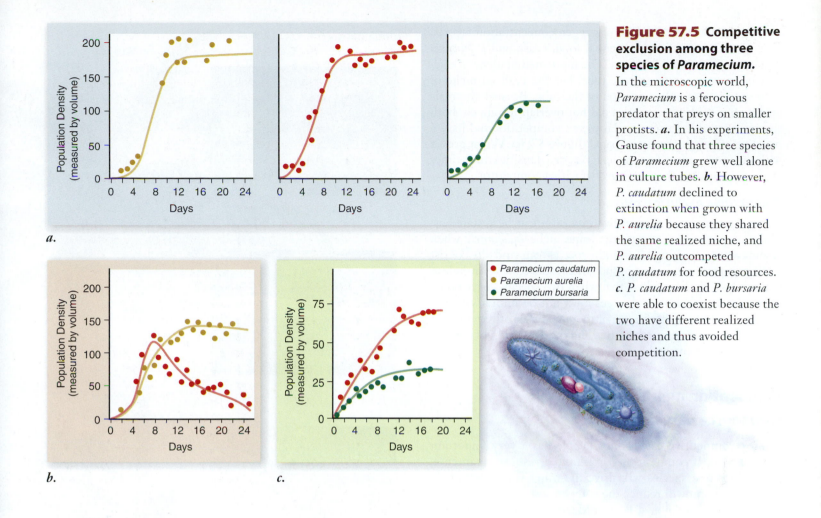

**Figure 57.5** Competitive exclusion among three species of *Paramecium*. In the microscopic world, *Paramecium* is a ferocious predator that preys on smaller protists. *a.* In his experiments, Gause found that three species of *Paramecium* grew well alone in culture tubes. *b.* However, *P. caudatum* declined to extinction when grown with *P. aurelia* because they shared the same realized niche, and *P. aurelia* outcompeted *P. caudatum* for food resources. *c. P. caudatum* and *P. bursaria* were able to coexist because the two have different realized niches and thus avoided competition.

● *Paramecium caudatum*
● *Paramecium aurelia*
● *Paramecium bursaria*

open rangeland habitats in California until a specialized beetle was introduced to control it. Population size of the plant quickly decreased, and it is now only found in shady sites where the beetle cannot thrive. In this case, the presence of a predator limits the realized niche of a plant.

In some cases, the absence of another species leads to a smaller realized niche. Many North American plants depend on insects for pollination; indeed, the value of insect pollination for American agriculture has been estimated as more than $2 billion per year. However, pollinator populations are currently declining for several reasons. Conservationists are concerned that if these insects disappear from some habitats, the realized niche of many plant species will decrease or even disappear entirely. In this case, the absence—rather than the presence—of another species will be the cause of a relatively small realized niche.

## Competitive exclusion can occur when species compete for limited resources

In classic experiments carried out in 1934 and 1935, Russian ecologist Georgii Gause studied competition among three species of *Paramecium*, a tiny protist. Each of the three species grew well in culture tubes by themselves, preying on bacteria and yeasts that fed on oatmeal suspended in the culture fluid (figure 57.5*a*). However, when Gause grew *P. aurelia* together

with *P. caudatum* in the same culture tube, the numbers of *P. caudatum* always declined to extinction, leaving *P. aurelia* the only survivor (figure 57.5*b*). Why did this happen? Gause found that *P. aurelia* could grow six times faster than its competitor *P. caudatum* because it was able to better utilize the limited available resources, an example of exploitative competition.

From experiments such as this, Gause formulated what is now called the principle of **competitive exclusion**. This principle states that if two species are competing for a limited resource such as food or water, the species that uses the resource more efficiently will eventually eliminate the other locally. In other words, no two species with the same niche can coexist when resources are limiting.

### Niche overlap and coexistence

In a revealing experiment, Gause challenged *Paramecium caudatum*—the defeated species in his earlier experiments—with a third species, *P. bursaria*. Because he expected these two species to also compete for the limited bacterial food supply, Gause thought one would win out, as had happened in his previous experiments. But that's not what happened. Instead, both species survived in the culture tubes, dividing the food resources.

The explanation for the species' coexistence is simple. In the upper part of the culture tubes, where the oxygen concentration and bacterial density were high, *P. caudatum* dominated because it was better able to feed on bacteria. In the lower part of the tubes, however, the lower oxygen concentration favored the growth of a different potential food, yeast, and *P. bursaria* was better able to eat this food. The fundamental niche of each species was the whole culture tube, but the realized niche of each species was only a portion of the tube. Because the realized niches of the two species did not overlap too much, both species were able to survive. However, competition did have a negative effect on the participants (figure 57.5c). When grown without a competitor, both species reached densities three times greater than when they were grown with a competitor.

### Competitive exclusion refined

Gause's principle of competitive exclusion can be restated as: No two species can occupy the same niche *indefinitely* when resources are limiting. Certainly species can and do coexist while competing for some of the same resources. Nevertheless, Gause's hypothesis predicts that when two species coexist on a long-term basis, either resources must not be limited or their niches will always differ in one or more features; otherwise, one species will outcompete the other, and the extinction of the second species will inevitably result.

## Competition may lead to resource partitioning

Gause's competitive exclusion principle has a very important consequence: If competition for a limited resource is intense, then either one species will drive the other to extinction, or natural selection will reduce the competition between them.

When the ecologist Robert MacArthur studied five species of warblers, small insect-eating forest songbirds, he discovered that they appeared to be competing for the same resources. But when he studied them more carefully, he found that each species actually fed in a different part of spruce trees and so ate different subsets of insects. One species fed on insects near the tips of branches, a second within the dense foliage, a third on the lower branches, a fourth high on the trees, and a fifth at the very apex of the trees. Thus, each species of warbler had evolved so as to utilize a different portion of the spruce tree resource. They had *subdivided the niche* to avoid direct competition with one another. This niche subdivision is termed **resource partitioning**.

Resource partitioning is often seen in similar species that occupy the same geographic area. Such sympatric species often avoid competition by living in different portions of the habitat or by using different food or other resources (figure 57.6). This pattern of resource partitioning is thought to result from the process of natural selection causing initially similar species to diverge in resource use to reduce competitive pressures.

Whether such evolutionary divergence occurs can be investigated by comparing species whose ranges only partially overlap. Where the two species occur together, they often tend to exhibit greater differences in morphology (the form and structure of an organism) and resource use than do allopatric populations of the same species that do not occur with the other species. Called *character displacement*, the differences evident between sympatric species are thought to have been favored by

a.

b.

c.

d.

**Figure 57.6 Resource partitioning among sympatric lizard species.** Species of *Anolis* lizards on Caribbean islands partition their habitats in a variety of ways. *a.* Some species occupy leaves and branches in the canopy of trees, (*b*) others use twigs on the periphery, and (*c*) still others are found at the base of the trunk. In addition, (*d*) some use grassy areas in the open. When two species occupy the same part of the tree, they either utilize different-sized insects as food or partition the thermal microhabitat; for example, one might only be found in the shade, whereas the other would only bask in the sun.

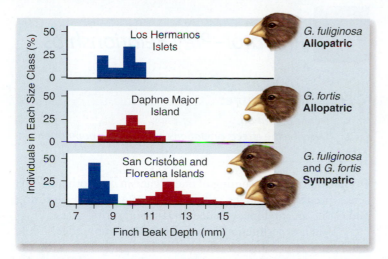

**Figure 57.7 Character displacement in Darwin's finches.** These two species of finches (genus *Geospiza*) have beaks of similar size when allopatric, but different size when sympatric.

natural selection as a means of partitioning resources and thus reducing competition.

As an example, the two Darwin's finches in figure 57.7 have bills of similar size where the finches are allopatric (that is, each living on an island where the other does not occur). On islands where they are sympatric (that is, occur together), the two species have evolved beaks of different sizes, one adapted to larger seeds and the other to smaller ones. Character displacement such as this may play an important role in adaptive radiation, leading new species to adapt to different parts of the environment, as discussed in chapter 22.

## Detecting interspecific competition can be difficult

It is not simple to determine when two species are competing. The fact that two species use the same resources need not imply competition if that resource is not in limited supply. Even if the population sizes of two species are negatively correlated, such that where one species has a large population, the other species has a small population and vice versa, the two species may not be competing for the same limiting resource. Instead, the two species might be independently responding to the same feature of the environment—perhaps one species thrives best in warm conditions and the other where it's cool.

### Experimental studies of competition

Some of the best evidence for the existence of competition comes from experimental field studies. By setting up experiments in which two species occur either alone or together, scientists can determine whether the presence of one species has a negative effect on a population of the second species.

For example, a variety of seed-eating rodents occur in North American deserts. In 1988, researchers set up a series of 50-m × 50-m enclosures to investigate the effect of kangaroo rats on smaller, seed-eating rodents. Kangaroo rats were removed from half of the enclosures, but not from the others. The walls of all of the enclosures had holes that allowed rodents to come and go, but in the plots in which the kangaroo

rats had been removed, the holes were too small to allow the kangaroo rats to reenter.

Over the course of the next 3 years, the researchers monitored the number of the smaller rodents present in the plots. As figure 57.8 illustrates, the number of other rodents was substantially higher in the absence of kangaroo rats, indicating that kangaroo rats compete with the other rodents and limit their population sizes.

A great number of similar experiments have indicated that interspecific competition occurs between many species of plants and animals. The effects of competition can be seen in aspects of population biology other than population size, such

**SCIENTIFIC THINKING**

**Question:** *Does interspecific interaction occur between rodent species?*

**Hypothesis:** *The larger kangaroo rat will have a negative effect on other species.*

**Experiment:** *Build large cages in desert areas. Remove kangaroo rats from some cages, leaving them present in others.*

**Result:** *In the absence of kangaroo rats, the number of other rodents increases quickly and remains higher than in the control cages throughout the course of the experiment.*

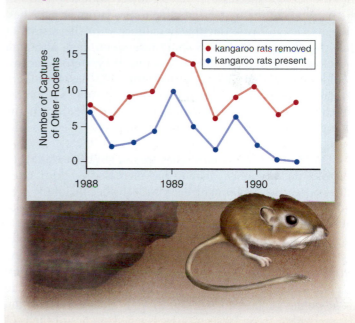

**Interpretation:** *Why do you think population sizes rise and fall in synchrony in the two cages?*

**Figure 57.8 Detecting interspecific competition.** This experiment tested how removal of kangaroo rats affected the population size of other rodents. Immediately after kangaroo rats were removed, the number of other rodents increased relative to the enclosures that still contained kangaroo rats. Notice that population sizes (as estimated by number of captures) changed in synchrony in the two treatments, probably reflecting changes in the weather.

**Inquiry question**

? **Why are there more individuals of other rodent species when kangaroo rats are excluded?**

as behavior and individual growth rates. For example, two species of *Anolis* lizards occur on the Caribbean island of St. Maarten. When one of the species, *A. gingivinus*, is placed in 12-m × 12-m enclosures without the other species, individual lizards grow faster and perch lower than do lizards of the same species when placed in enclosures in which *A. pogus*, a species normally found near the ground, is also present.

### Limitations of experimental studies

Experimental studies are a powerful means of understanding interactions between coexisting species and are now commonly conducted by ecologists. Nonetheless, they have their limitations.

First, care is necessary in interpreting the results of field experiments. Negative effects of one species on another do not automatically indicate the existence of competition. For example, many similarly sized fish have a negative effect on one another, but it results not from competition, but from the fact that adults of each species prey on juveniles of the other species.

In addition, the presence of one species may attract predators or parasites, which then also prey on the second species. In this case, even if the two species are not competing, the second species may have a lower population size in the presence of the first species due to predators or parasites. Indeed, we can't rule out this possibility with the results of the kangaroo rat exclusion study just mentioned, although the close proximity of the enclosures (they were adjacent) would suggest that the same predators and parasites were present in all of them. Thus, experimental studies are most effective when combined with detailed examination of the ecological mechanisms causing the observed effect of one species on another.

Second, experimental studies are not always feasible. For example, the coyote population has increased in the United States in recent years concurrently with the decline of the grey wolf. Is this trend an indication that the species compete? Because of the size of the animals and the large geographic areas occupied by each individual, manipulative experiments involving fenced areas with only one or both species—with each experimental treatment replicated several times for statistical analysis—are not practical. Similarly, studies of slow-growing trees might require many centuries to detect competition between adult trees. In such cases, detailed studies of the ecological requirements of each species are our best bet for understanding interspecific interactions.

## 57.3 Predator–Prey Relationships

**Predation** is the consuming of one organism by another. In this sense, predation includes everything from a leopard capturing and eating an antelope, to a deer grazing on spring grass.

When experimental populations are set up under simple laboratory conditions, as illustrated in figure 57.9 with the predatory protist *Didinium* and its prey *Paramecium*, the predator often exterminates its prey and then becomes extinct itself, having nothing left to eat. If refuges are provided for the *Paramecium*, however, its population drops to low levels but not to extinction. Low prey population levels then provide inadequate food for the *Didinium*, causing the predator population to decrease. When this occurs, the prey population can recover.

## Predation strongly influences prey populations

In nature, predators often have large effects on prey populations. As the previous example indicates, however, the interaction is a two-way street: prey can also affect the dynamics of predator populations. The outcomes of such interactions are complex and depend on a variety of factors.

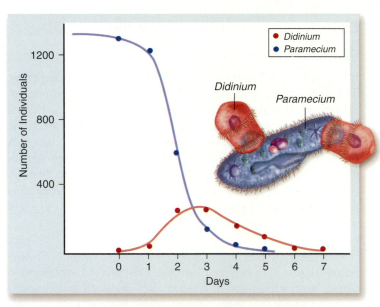

**Figure 57.9 Predator–prey in the microscopic world.** When the predatory *Didinium* is added to a *Paramecium* population, the numbers of *Didinium* initially rise, and the numbers of *Paramecium* steadily fall. When the *Paramecium* population is depleted, however, the *Didinium* individuals also die.

### Inquiry question

**?** Can you think of any ways this experiment could be changed so that Paramecium might not go extinct?

### Prey population explosions and crashes

Some of the most dramatic examples of the interconnection between predators and their prey involve situations in which humans have either added or eliminated predators from an area. For example, the elimination of large carnivores from much of the eastern United States has led to population explosions of white-tailed deer, which strip the habitat of all edible plant life within their reach. Similarly, when sea otters were hunted to near extinction on the western coast of the United States, populations of sea urchins, a principal prey item of the otters, exploded.

Conversely, the introduction of rats, dogs, and cats to many islands around the world has led to the decimation of native fauna. Populations of Galápagos tortoises on several islands are endangered by introduced rats, pigs, dogs, and cats, which eat the eggs and the young tortoises. Similarly, in New Zealand, several species of birds and reptiles have been eradicated by rat predation and now only occur on a few offshore islands that the rats have not reached. On Stephens Island, near New Zealand, every individual of the now-extinct Stephens Island wren was killed by a single lighthouse keeper's cat.

A classic example of the role predation can play in a community involves the introduction of prickly pear cactus to Australia in the 19th century. In the absence of predators, the cactus spread rapidly, so that by 1925 it occupied 12 million hectares of rangeland in an impenetrable morass of spines that made cattle ranching difficult. To control the cactus, a predator from its natural habitat in Argentina, the moth *Cactoblastis cactorum*, was introduced, beginning in 1926. By 1940, cactus populations had been greatly reduced and it now usually occurs in small populations.

### Predation and coevolution

Predation provides strong selective pressures on prey populations. Any feature that would decrease the probability of capture should be strongly favored. In turn, the evolution of such features causes natural selection to favor counteradaptations in predator populations. The process by which these adaptations are selected in lockstep fashion in two or more interacting species is termed **coevolution.** A coevolutionary "arms race" may ensue in which predators and prey are constantly evolving better defenses and better means of circumventing these defenses. In the sections that follow, you'll learn more about these defenses and responses.

## Plant adaptations defend against herbivores

Plants have evolved many mechanisms to defend themselves from herbivores. The most obvious are morphological defenses: Thorns, spines, and prickles play an important role in discouraging large plant eaters, and plant hairs, especially those that have a glandular, sticky tip, deter insect herbivores. Some plants, such as grasses, deposit silica in their leaves, both strengthening and protecting themselves. If enough silica is present, these plants are simply too tough to eat.

### Chemical defenses

As significant as morphological adaptations are, the chemical defenses that occur so widely in plants are even more widespread. Plants exhibit some amazing chemical adaptations to combat herbivores. For example, recent work demonstrates that when attacked by caterpillars, wild tobacco plants emit a chemical into the air that attracts a species of bug that feeds on that caterpillar (discussed in greater detail in chapter 40).

The best known and perhaps most important of the chemical defenses of plants against herbivores are *secondary chemical compounds*. These chemicals are distinguished from primary compounds, which are the components of a major metabolic pathway, such as respiration. Many plants, and apparently many algae as well, contain structurally diverse secondary compounds that are either toxic to most herbivores or disturb their metabolism greatly, preventing, for example, the normal development of larval insects. Consequently, most herbivores tend to avoid the plants that possess these compounds.

The mustard family (Brassicaceae) produces a group of chemicals known as mustard oils. These substances give the pungent aromas and tastes to plants such as mustard, cabbage, watercress, radish, and horseradish. The flavors we enjoy indicate the presence of chemicals that are toxic to many groups of insects. Similarly, plants of the milkweed family (Asclepiadaceae) and the related dogbane family (Apocynaceae) produce a milky sap that deters herbivores from eating them. In addition, these plants usually contain cardiac glycosides, molecules that can produce drastic deleterious effects on the heart function of vertebrates.

### The coevolutionary response of herbivores

Certain groups of herbivores are associated with each family or group of plants protected by a particular kind of secondary compound. These herbivores are able to feed on these plants without harm, often as their exclusive food source.

For example, cabbage butterfly caterpillars (subfamily Pierinae) feed almost exclusively on plants of the mustard and caper families, as well as on a few other small families of plants that also contain mustard oils (figure 57.10). Similarly, caterpillars of

*a.*

*b.*

**Figure 57.10**
**Insect herbivores well suited to their plant hosts.** *a.* The green caterpillars of the cabbage white butterfly (*Pieris rapae*) are camouflaged on the leaves of cabbage and other plants on which they feed. Although mustard oils protect these plants against most herbivores, the cabbage white butterfly caterpillars are able to break down the mustard oil compounds. *b.* An adult cabbage white butterfly.

monarch butterflies and their relatives (subfamily Danainae) feed on plants of the milkweed and dogbane families. How do these animals manage to avoid the chemical defenses of the plants, and what are the evolutionary precursors and ecological consequences of such patterns of specialization?

We can offer a potential explanation for the evolution of these particular patterns. Once the ability to manufacture mustard oils evolved in the ancestors of the caper and mustard families, the plants were protected for a time against most or all herbivores that were feeding on other plants in their area. At some point, certain groups of insects—for example, the cabbage butterflies—evolved the ability to break down mustard oils and thus feed on these plants without harming themselves. Having developed this new capability, the butterflies were able to use a new resource without competing with other herbivores for it. As we saw in chapter 22, exposure to an underutilized resource often leads to evolutionary diversification and adaptive radiation.

## Animal adaptations defend against predators

Some animals that feed on plants rich in secondary compounds receive an extra benefit. For example, when the caterpillars of monarch butterflies feed on plants of the milkweed family, they do not break down the cardiac glycosides that protect these plants from herbivores. Instead, the caterpillars concentrate and store the cardiac glycosides in fat bodies; they then pass them through the chrysalis stage to the adult and even to the eggs of the next generation.

The incorporation of cardiac glycosides protects all stages of the monarch life cycle from predators. A bird that eats a monarch butterfly quickly regurgitates it (figure 57.11) and in the future avoids the conspicuous orange-and-black pattern that characterizes the adult monarch. Some bird species have

**Figure 57.12 Vertebrate chemical defenses.** Frogs of the family Dendrobatidae, abundant in the forests of Central and South America, are extremely poisonous to vertebrates; 80 different toxic alkaloids have been identified from different species in this genus. Dendrobatids advertise their toxicity with bright coloration. As a result of either instinct or learning, predators avoid such brightly colored species that might otherwise be suitable prey.

evolved the ability to tolerate the protective chemicals; these birds eat the monarchs.

### Chemical defenses

Animals also manufacture and use a startling array of defensive substances. Bees, wasps, predatory bugs, scorpions, spiders, and many other arthropods use chemicals to defend themselves and to kill their own prey. In addition, various chemical defenses have evolved among many marine invertebrates, as well as a variety of vertebrates, including frogs, snakes, lizards, fishes, and some birds.

The poison-dart frogs of the family Dendrobatidae produce toxic alkaloids in the mucus that covers their brightly colored skin; these alkaloids are distasteful and sometimes deadly to animals that try to eat the frogs (figure 57.12). Some of these toxins are so powerful that a few micrograms will kill a person if injected into the bloodstream. More than 200 different alkaloids have been isolated from these frogs, and some are playing important roles in neuromuscular research. Similarly intensive investigations of marine animals, venomous reptiles, algae, and flowering plants are underway in search of new drugs to fight cancer and other diseases, or to use as sources of antibiotics.

### Defensive coloration

Many insects that feed on milkweed plants are brightly colored; they advertise their poisonous nature using an ecological strategy known as warning coloration.

Showy coloration is characteristic of animals that use poisons and stings to repel predators; organisms that lack specific chemical defenses are seldom brightly colored. In fact, many have cryptic coloration—color that blends with the surroundings and thus hides the individual from predators (figure 57.13). Camouflaged animals usually do not live together in groups because a predator that discovers one individual gains a valuable clue to the presence of others.

*a.*                                    *b.*

**Figure 57.11 A blue jay learns not to eat monarch butterflies.** *a.* This cage-reared jay had never seen a monarch butterfly before it tried eating one. *b.* The same jay regurgitated the butterfly a few minutes later. This bird will probably avoid trying to capture all orange-and-black insects in the future.

**Figure 57.13 Cryptic coloration and form.** An inchworm caterpillar (*Nacophora quernaria*) closely resembles the twig on which it is hanging..

## Mimicry allows one species to capitalize on defensive strategies of another

During the course of their evolution, many species have come to resemble distasteful ones that exhibit warning coloration. The mimic gains an advantage by looking like the distasteful model. Two types of mimicry have been identified: Batesian mimicry and Müllerian mimicry.

### Batesian mimicry

**Batesian mimicry** is named for Henry Bates, the British naturalist who first brought this type of mimicry to general attention in 1857. In his journeys to the Amazon region of South America, Bates discovered many instances of palatable insects that resembled brightly colored, distasteful species. He reasoned that the mimics would be avoided by predators, who would be fooled by the disguise into thinking the mimic was the distasteful species.

Many of the best-known examples of Batesian mimicry occur among butterflies and moths. Predators of these insects must use visual cues to hunt for their prey; otherwise, similar color patterns would not matter to potential predators. Increasing evidence indicates that Batesian mimicry can involve nonvisual cues, such as olfaction, although such examples are less obvious to humans.

The kinds of butterflies that provide the models in Batesian mimicry are, not surprisingly, members of groups whose caterpillars feed on only one or a few closely related plant families. The plant families on which they feed are strongly protected by toxic chemicals. The model butterflies incorporate the poisonous molecules from these plants into their bodies. The mimic butterflies, in contrast, belong to groups in which the feeding habits of the caterpillars are not so restricted. As caterpillars, these butterflies feed on a number of different plant families that are unprotected by toxic chemicals.

One often-studied mimic among North American butterflies is the tiger swallowtail, whose range occurs throughout the eastern United States and into Canada (figure 57.14*a*). In areas in which the poisonous pipevine swallowtail occurs, female tiger swallowtails are polymorphic and one color form is extremely similar in appearance to the pipevine swallowtail.

The caterpillars of the tiger swallowtail feed on a variety of trees, including tulip, aspen, and cherry, and neither caterpillars nor adults are distasteful to birds. Interestingly, the Batesian mimicry seen in the adult tiger swallowtail butterfly does not extend to the caterpillars: Tiger swallowtail caterpillars are camouflaged on leaves, resembling bird droppings, but the pipevine swallowtail's distasteful caterpillars are very conspicuous.

### Müllerian mimicry

Another kind of mimicry, **Müllerian mimicry,** was named for the German biologist Fritz Müller, who first described it in 1878. In Müllerian mimicry, several unrelated but protected animal species come to resemble one another (figure 57.14*b*). If animals that resemble one another are all poisonous or dangerous, they gain an advantage because a predator will learn more quickly to avoid them. In some cases, predator populations even evolve an innate avoidance of species; such evolution may occur more quickly when multiple dangerous prey look alike.

*Battus philenor*    *Papilio glaucus*

*a.* **Batesian mimicry:** Pipevine swallowtail butterfly (*Battus philenor*) is poisonous; Tiger swallowtail (*Papilio glaucus*) is a palatable mimic.

*Heliconius erato*    *Heliconius melpomene*

*Heliconius sapho*    *Heliconius cydno*

*b.* **Müllerian mimicry:** Two pairs of mimics; all are distasteful.

**Figure 57.14 Mimicry.** *a.* Batesian mimicry. Pipevine swallowtail butterflies (*Battus philenor*) are protected from birds and other predators by the poisonous compounds they derive from the food they eat as caterpillars and store in their bodies. Adult pipevine swallowtails advertise their poisonous nature with warning coloration. Tiger swallowtails (*Papilio glaucus*) are Batesian mimics of the poisonous pipevine swallowtail and are not chemically protected. *b.* Pairs of Müllerian mimics. *Heliconius erato* and *H. melpomene* are sympatric, and *H. sapho* and *H. cydno* are sympatric. All of these butterflies are distasteful. They have evolved similar coloration patterns in sympatry to minimize predation; predators need only learn one pattern to avoid.

In both Batesian and Müllerian mimicry, mimic and model must not only look alike but also act alike. For example, the members of several families of insects that closely resemble wasps behave surprisingly like the wasps they mimic, flying often and actively from place to place.

### Learnings Outcomes Review 57.3

Predation is the consuming of one organism by another. High predation can drive prey populations to extinction; conversely, in the absence of predators, prey populations often explode and exhaust their resources. Defensive adaptations may evolve in prey species, such as becoming distasteful or poisonous, or having defensive structures, appearance, or capabilities.

■ *A nonpoisonous scarlet king snake has red, black, and yellow bands of color similar to that of the poisonous eastern coral snake. What type of mimicry is being exhibited?*

## 57.4 The Many Types of Species Interactions

### Learning Outcomes

1. *Explain the different forms of symbiosis.*
2. *Describe how coevolution occurs between mutualistic partners.*
3. *Explain how the occurrence of one ecological process may affect the outcome of another occurring at the same time.*

**Figure 57.15 Pollination by a bat.** Many flowers have coevolved with other species to facilitate pollen transfer. Insects are widely known as pollinators, but they're not the only ones: birds, bats, and even small marsupials and lizards serve as pollinators for some species. Notice the cargo of pollen on the bat's snout.

The plants, animals, protists, fungi, and prokaryotes that live together in communities have changed and adjusted to one another continually over millions of years. We have already discussed competition and predation, but other types of ecological interactions commonly occur. For example, many features of flowering plants have evolved in relation to the dispersal of the plant's gametes by animals (figure 57.15). These animals, in turn, have evolved a number of special traits that enable them to obtain food or other resources efficiently from the plants they visit, often from their flowers. While doing so, the animals pick up pollen, which they may deposit on the next plant they visit, or seeds, which may be left elsewhere in the environment, sometimes a great distance from the parent plant.

### Symbiosis involves long-term interactions

In symbiosis, two or more kinds of organisms interact in often elaborate and more-or-less permanent relationships. All symbiotic relationships carry the potential for coevolution between the organisms involved, and in many instances the results of this coevolution are fascinatingly complex.

Examples of symbiosis include lichens, which are associations of certain fungi with green algae or cyanobacteria. Another important example are mycorrhizae, associations between fungi and the roots of most kinds of plants. The fungi expedite the plant's absorption of certain nutrients, and the plants in turn provide the fungi with carbohydrates (both mycorrhizae and lichens are discussed in greater detail in chapter 31). Similarly, root nodules that occur in legumes and certain other kinds of plants contain bacteria that fix atmospheric nitrogen and make it available to their host plants.

In the tropics, leaf-cutter ants are often so abundant that they can remove a quarter or more of the total leaf surface of the plants in a given area in a single year (see figure 31.18). They do not eat these leaves directly; rather, they take them to underground nests, where they chew them up and inoculate them with the spores of particular fungi. These fungi are cultivated by the ants and brought from one specially prepared bed to another, where they grow and reproduce. In turn, the fungi constitute the primary food of the ants and their larvae. The relationship between leaf-cutter ants and these fungi is an excellent example of symbiosis. Recent phylogenetic studies using DNA and assuming a molecular clock (see chapter 23) suggest that these symbioses are ancient, perhaps originating more than 50 mya.

The major kinds of symbiotic relationships include (1) commensalism, in which one species benefits and the other neither benefits nor is harmed; (2) mutualism, in which both participating species benefit; and (3) **parasitism,** in which one species benefits but the other is harmed. Parasitism can also be viewed as a form of predation, although the organism that is preyed on does not necessarily die.

## Commensalism benefits one species and is neutral to the other

In commensalism, one species benefits and the other is neither hurt nor helped by the interaction. In nature, individuals of one species are often physically attached to members of another. For example, epiphytes are plants that grow on the branches of other plants. In general, the host plant is unharmed, and the epiphyte that grows on it benefits. An example is Spanish moss, which hangs on trees in the southern United States. This plant and other members of its genus, which is in the pineapple family, grow on trees to gain access to sunlight; they generally do not harm the trees (figure 57.16).

Similarly, various marine animals, such as barnacles, grow on other, often actively moving sea animals, such as whales, and thus are carried passively from place to place. These "passengers" presumably gain more protection from predation than they would if they were fixed in one place, and they also reach new sources of food. The increased water circulation that these animals receive as their host moves around may also be of great importance, particularly if the passengers are filter feeders. Unless the number of these passengers gets too large, the host species is usually unaffected.

### When commensalism may not be commensalism

One of the best known examples of symbiosis involves the relationships between certain small tropical fishes (clownfish) and sea anemones, shown in the first figure of this chapter. The fish have evolved the ability to live among the stinging tentacles of sea anemones, even though these tentacles would quickly paralyze other fishes that touched them. The clownfish feed on food particles left from the meals of the host anemone, remaining uninjured under remarkable circumstances.

On land, an analogous relationship exists between birds called oxpeckers and grazing animals such as cattle or ante-

**Figure 57.17  Commensalism, mutualism, or parasitism?** In this symbiotic relationship, oxpeckers definitely receive a benefit in the form of nutrition from the ticks and other parasites they pick off their host (in this case, an impala, *Aepyceros melampus*). But the effect on the host is not always clear. If the ticks are harmful, their removal benefits the host, and the relationship is mutually beneficial. If the oxpeckers also pick at scabs, causing blood loss and possible infection, the relationship may be parasitic. If the hosts are unharmed by either the ticks or the oxpeckers, the relationship may be an example of commensalism.

lopes (figure 57.17). The birds spend most of their time clinging to the animals, picking off parasites and other insects, carrying out their entire life cycles in close association with the host animals.

No clear-cut boundary exists between commensalism and mutualism; in each of these casees, it is difficult to be certain whether the second partner receives a benefit or not. A sea anemone may benefit by having particles of food removed from its tentacles because it may then be better able to catch other prey. Similarly, although often thought of as commensalism, the association of grazing mammals and gleaning birds is actually an example of mutualism. The mammal benefits by having parasites and other insects removed from its body, but the birds also benefit by gaining a dependable source of food.

On the other hand, commensalism can easily transform itself into parasitism. Oxpeckers are also known to pick not only parasites, but also scabs off their grazing hosts. Once the scab is picked, the birds drink the blood that flows from the wound. Occasionally, the cumulative effect of persistent attacks can greatly weaken the herbivore, particularly when conditions are not favorable, such as during droughts.

**Figure 57.16  An example of commensalism.** Spanish moss *(Tillandsia usneoides)* benefits from using trees as a substrate, but the trees generally are not affected positively or negatively.

## Mutualism benefits both species

Mutualism is a symbiotic relationship between organisms in which both species benefit. Mutualistic relationships are of fundamental importance in determining the structure of biological communities.

### Mutualism and coevolution

Some of the most spectacular examples of mutualism occur among flowering plants and their animal visitors, including insects, birds, and bats. During the course of flowering-plant evolution, the characteristics of flowers evolved in relation to the characteristics of the animals that visit them for food and, in the process, spread their pollen from individual to individual. At the same time, characteristics of the animals have changed, increasing their specialization for obtaining food or other substances from particular kinds of flowers.

Another example of mutualism involves ants and aphids. Aphids are small insects that suck fluids from the phloem of living plants with their piercing mouthparts. They extract a certain amount of the sucrose and other nutrients from this fluid, but they excrete much of it in an altered form through their anus. Certain ants have taken advantage of this—in effect, domesticating the aphids. Like ranchers taking cattle to fresh fields to graze, the ants carry the aphids to new plants and then consume as food the "honeydew" that the aphids excrete.

### Ants and acacias: A prime example of mutualism

A particularly striking example of mutualism involves ants and certain Latin American tree species of the genus *Acacia*. In these species, certain leaf parts, called stipules, are modified as paired, hollow thorns. The thorns are inhabited by stinging ants of the genus *Pseudomyrmex*, which do not nest anywhere else (figure 57.18). Like all thorns that occur on plants, the acacia thorns serve to deter herbivores.

At the tip of the leaflets of these acacias are unique, protein-rich bodies called Beltian bodies, named after the 19th-century British naturalist Thomas Belt. Beltian bodies do not occur in species of *Acacia* that are not inhabited by ants, and their role is clear: they serve as a primary food for the ants. In addition, the plants secrete nectar from glands near the bases of their leaves. The ants consume this nectar as well, feeding it and the Beltian bodies to their larvae.

Obviously, this association is beneficial to the ants, and one can readily see why they inhabit acacias of this group. The ants and their larvae are protected within the swollen thorns, and the trees provide a balanced diet, including the sugar-rich nectar and the protein-rich Beltian bodies. What, if anything, do the ants do for the plants?

Whenever any herbivore lands on the branches or leaves of an acacia inhabited by ants, the ants, which continually patrol the acacia's branches, immediately attack and devour the herbivore. The ants that live in the acacias also help their hosts compete with other plants by cutting away any encroaching branches that touch the acacia in which they are living. They create, in effect, a tunnel of light through which the acacia can grow, even in the lush tropical rain forests of lowland Central America. In fact, when an ant colony is experimentally removed

**Figure 57.18 Mutualism: Ants and acacias.** Ants of the genus *Pseudomyrmex* live within the hollow thorns of certain species of acacia trees in Latin America. The nectaries at the bases of the leaves and the Beltian bodies at the ends of the leaflets provide food for the ants. The ants, in turn, supply the acacias with organic nutrients and protect the acacias from herbivores and shading from other plants.

from a tree, the acacia is unable to compete successfully in this habitat. Finally, the ants bring organic material into their nests. The parts they do not consume, together with their excretions, provide the acacias with an abundant source of nitrogen.

### When mutualism may not be mutualism

As with commensalism, however, things are not always as they seem. Ant–acacia associations also occur in Africa; in Kenya, several species of acacia ants occur, but only a single species is found on any one tree. One species, *Crematogaster nigriceps*, is competitively inferior to two of the other species. To prevent invasion by these other ant species, *C. nigriceps* prunes the branches of the acacia, preventing it from coming into contact with branches of other trees, which would serve as a bridge for invaders.

Although this behavior is beneficial to the ant, it is detrimental to the tree because it destroys the tissue from which flowers are produced, essentially sterilizing the tree. In this case, what initially evolved as a mutualistic interaction has instead become a parasitic one.

## Parasitism benefits one species at the expense of another

Parasitism is harmful to the prey organism and beneficial to the parasite. In many cases, the parasite kills its host, and thus the ecological effects of parasitism can be similar to those of predation. In the past parasitism was studied mostly in terms of its effects on individuals and the populations in which they live, but in recent years researchers have realized that parasitism can be an important factor affecting community structure.

### External parasites

Parasites that feed on the exterior surface of an organism are external parasites, or ectoparasites (figure 57.19). Many instances of external parasitism are known in both plants and animals. **Parasitoids** are insects that lay eggs in or on living hosts. This behavior is common among wasps, whose larvae feed on the body of the unfortunate host, often killing it.

### Internal parasites

Parasites that live within the body of their hosts, termed **endoparasites,** occur in many different phyla of animals and protists. Internal parasitism is generally marked by much more extreme specialization than external parasitism, as shown by the many protist and invertebrate parasites that infect humans.

   The more closely the life of the parasite is linked with that of its host, the more its morphology and behavior are likely to have been modified during the course of its evolution (the same is true of symbiotic relationships of all sorts). Conditions within the body of an organism are different from those encountered outside and are apt to be much more constant. Consequently, the structure of an internal parasite is often simplified, and unnecessary armaments and structures are lost as it evolves (for example, see descriptions of tapeworms in chapter 33).

### Parasites and host behaviors

Many parasites have complex life cycles that require several different hosts for growth to adulthood and reproduction. Recent research has revealed the remarkable adaptations of certain parasites that alter the behavior of the host and thus facilitate transmission from one host to the next. For example, many parasites cause their hosts to behave in ways that make them more vulnerable to their predators; when the host is ingested, the parasite is able to infect the predator.

**Figure 57.20**
**Parasitic manipulation of host behavior.** Due to a parasite in its brain, an ant climbs to the top of a grass blade, where it may be eaten by a grazing herbivore, thus passing the parasite from insect to mammal.

Infected ant

   One of the most famous examples involves a parasitic flatworm, *Dicrocoelium dendriticum*, which lives in ants as an intermediate host, but reaches adulthood in large herbivorous mammals such as cattle and deer. Transmission from an ant to a cow might seem difficult because cows do not normally eat insects. The flatworm, however, has evolved a remarkable adaptation. When an ant is infected, one of the flatworms migrates to the brain and causes the ant to climb to the top of vegetation and lock its mandibles onto a grass blade at the end of the day, just when herbivores are grazing (figure 57.20). The result is that the ant is eaten along with the grass, leading to infection of the grazer.

## Ecological processes have interactive effects

We have seen the different ways in which species can interact with one another. In nature, however, more than one type of interaction often occurs at the same time. In many cases, the outcome of one type of interaction is modified or even reversed when another type of interaction is also occurring.

### Predation reduces competition

When resources are limiting, a superior competitor can eliminate other species from a community through competitive exclusion. However, predators can prevent or greatly reduce exclusion by lowering the numbers of individuals of competing species.

   A given predator may often feed on two, three, or more kinds of plants or animals in a given community. The predator's choice depends partly on the relative abundance of the prey options. In other words, a predator may feed on species A when it is abundant and then switch to species B when A is rare. Similarly, a given prey species may become a primary source of food for increasing numbers of species as it becomes more abundant. In this way, superior competitors may be prevented from competitively excluding other species.

**Figure 57.19  An external parasite.** The yellow vines are the flowering plant dodder *(Cuscuta)*, a parasite that has lost its chlorophyll and its leaves in the course of its evolution. Because it is heterotrophic (unable to manufacture its own food), dodder obtains its food from the host plants it grows on.

Such patterns are often characteristic of communities in marine intertidal habitats. For example, in preying selectively on bivalves, sea stars prevent bivalves from monopolizing a habitat, opening up space for many other organisms (figure 57.21). When sea stars are removed from a habitat, species diversity falls precipitously, and the seafloor community comes to be dominated by a few species of bivalves.

Predation tends to reduce competition in natural communities, so it is usually a mistake to attempt to eliminate a major predator, such as wolves or mountain lions, from a community. The result may be a decrease in biological diversity.

### Parasitism may counter competition

Parasites may affect sympatric species differently and thus influence the outcome of interspecific interactions. One classic experiment investigated interactions between two sympatric flour beetles, *Tribolium castaneum* and *T. confusum*, with and without a parasite, *Adelina*. In the absence of the parasite, *T. castaneum* is dominant, and *T. confusum* normally becomes extinct. When the parasite is present, however, the outcome is reversed, and *T. castaneum* perishes.

Similar effects of parasites in natural systems have been observed in many species. For example, in the *Anolis* lizards of St. Maarten mentioned previously, the competitively inferior species is resistant to lizard malaria (a disease related to human malaria), whereas the other species is highly susceptible. In places where the parasite occurs, the competitively inferior species can hold its own and the two species coexist; elsewhere, the competitively dominant species outcompetes and eliminates it.

### Indirect effects

In some cases, species may not directly interact, yet the presence of one species may affect a second by way of interactions with a third. Such effects are termed indirect effects.

The desert rodents described earlier in the experiment with kangaroo rats eat seeds, and so do the ants in their community; thus, we might expect them to compete with each other. But when all rodents were removed from experimental enclosures and not allowed back in (unlike the previous experiment, no holes were placed in the enclosure walls), ant populations first increased but then declined (figure 57.22).

The initial increase was the expected result of removing a competitor. Why did it then reverse? The answer reveals the intricacies of natural ecosystems. Rodents prefer large seeds, whereas ants prefer smaller ones. Furthermore, in this system, plants with large seeds are competitively superior to plants with small seeds. The removal of rodents therefore led to an increase in the number of plants with large seeds, which reduced the number of small seeds available to ants, which in turn led to a decline in ant populations. In summary, the effect

---

## SCIENTIFIC THINKING

**Question:** *Does predation affect the outcome of interspecific competitive interactions?*

**Hypothesis:** *In the absence of predators, prey populations will increase until resources are limiting, and some species will be competitively excluded.*

**Experiment:** *Remove predatory sea stars (Pisaster ochraceus) from some areas of rocky intertidal shoreline and monitor populations of species the sea stars prey upon. In control areas, pick up sea stars, but replace them where they were found.*

*a.*

*b.*

**Result:** *In the absence of sea stars, the population of the mussel* Mytilus californianus *exploded, occupying all available space and eliminating many other species from the community.*

**Interpretation:** *What would happen if sea stars were returned to the experimental plots?*

---

**Figure 57.21 Predation reduces competition.** *a.* In a controlled experiment in a coastal ecosystem, Robert Paine of the University of Washington removed a key predator, sea stars *(Pisaster)*. *b.* In response, fiercely competitive mussels, a type of bivalve mollusk, exploded in population growth, effectively crowding out seven other indigenous species.

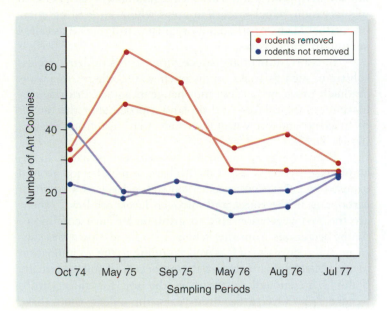

a.

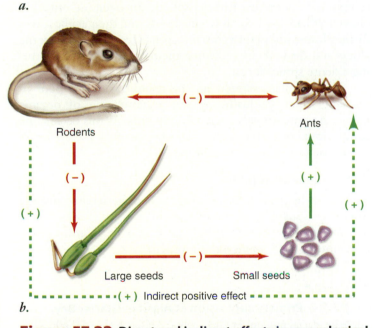

b.

**Figure 57.22 Direct and indirect effects in an ecological community.** *a.* In the enclosures in which kangaroo rats had been removed, ants initially increased in population size relative to the ants in the control enclosures, but then these ant populations declined. *b.* Rodents and ants both eat seeds, so the presence of rodents has a direct negative effect on ants, and vice versa. However, the presence of rodents has a negative effect on large seeds. In turn, the number of plants with large seeds has a negative effect on plants that produce small seeds, which the ants eat. Hence, the presence of rodents should increase the number of small seeds. In turn, the number of small seeds has a positive effect on ant populations. Thus, indirectly, the presence of rodents has a positive effect on ant population size.

**? Inquiry question**

How would you test the hypothesis that plant competition mediates the positive effect of kangaroo rats on ants?

of rodents on ants is complicated: a direct, negative effect of resource competition and an indirect, positive effect mediated by plant competition.

## Keystone species have major effects on communities

Species whose effects on the composition of communities are greater than one might expect based on their abundance are termed **keystone species.** Predators, such as the sea star described earlier, can often serve as keystone species by preventing one species from outcompeting others, thus maintaining high levels of species richness in a community.

A wide variety of other types of keystone species also exist. Some species manipulate the environment in ways that create new habitats for others. Beavers, for example, change running streams into small impoundments, altering the flow of water and flooding areas (figure 57.23). Similarly, alligators excavate deep holes at the bottoms of lakes. In times of drought, these holes are the only areas where water remains, thus allowing aquatic species that otherwise would perish to persist until the drought ends and the lake refills.

---

### Learning Outcomes Review 57.4

The types of symbiosis include mutualism, in which both participants benefit; commensalism, in which one benefits and the other is neutrally affected; and parasitism, in which one benefits at the expense of the other. Mutualistic species often undergo coevolution, such as the shape of flowers and the features of animals that feed on and pollinate them. Ecological interactions can affect many processes in a community; for example, predation and parasitism may lessen resource competition.

■ *How could the presence of a predator positively affect populations of a species on which it preys?*

---

**Figure 57.23 Example of a keystone species.** Beavers, by constructing dams and transforming flowing streams into ponds, create new habitats for many plant and animal species.

# Ecological Succession, Disturbance, and Species Richness

### Learning Outcomes

1. *Define succession and distinguish primary versus secondary.*
2. *Describe how early colonizers may affect subsequent occurrence of other species.*
3. *Explain how disturbance can either positively or negatively affect species richness.*

Even when the climate of an area remains stable year after year, communities have a tendency to change from simple to complex in a process known as **succession.** This process is familiar to anyone who has seen a vacant lot or cleared woods slowly become occupied by an increasing number of species.

## Succession produces a change in species composition

If a wooded area is cleared or burned and left alone, plants will slowly reclaim the area. Eventually, all traces of the clear-ing will disappear, and the area will again be woods. This kind of succession, which occurs in areas where an existing community has been disturbed but organisms still remain, is called **secondary succession.**

In contrast, **primary succession** occurs on bare, lifeless substrate, such as rocks, or in open water, where organisms gradually move into an area and change its nature. Primary succession occurs in lakes and on land exposed after the retreat of glaciers, and on volcanic islands that rise from the sea (figure 57.24).

Primary succession on glacial moraines provides an example (see figure 57.24). On the bare, mineral-poor ground exposed when glaciers recede, soil pH is basic as a result of carbonates in the rocks, and nitrogen levels are low. Lichens are the first vegetation able to grow under such conditions. Acidic secretions from the lichens help break down the substrate and reduce the pH, as well as adding to the accumulation of soil. Mosses then colonize these pockets of soil, eventually building up enough nutrients in the soil for alder shrubs to take hold. Over a hundred years, the alders, which have symbiotic bacteria that fix atmospheric nitrogen (described in chapter 28), increase soil nitrogen levels, and their acidic leaves further lower soil pH. Eventually, spruce trees grow above the alders and shade them, crowding them out entirely and forming a dense spruce forest.

In a similar example, an *oligotrophic* lake—one poor in nutrients—may gradually, by the accumulation of organic matter, become *eutrophic*—rich in nutrients. As this occurs, the composition of communities will change, first increasing in species richness and then declining.

### Why succession happens

Succession happens because species alter the habitat and the resources available in it in ways that favor other species. Three dynamic concepts are of critical importance in the process: establishment, facilitation, and inhibition.

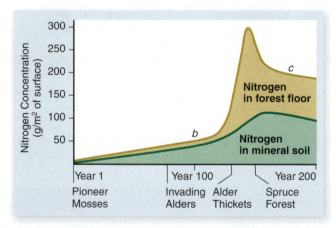

a.

**Figure 57.24 Primary succession at Alaska's Glacier Bay.**
*a.* Initially, the glacial moraine at Glacier Bay, Alaska, had little soil nitrogen *b.* The first invaders of these exposed sites are pioneer moss species with nitrogen-fixing, mutualistic microbes. *c.* Within 20 years, young alder shrubs take hold. Rapidly fixing nitrogen, they soon form dense thickets. *d.* Eventually spruce overgrow the mature alders, forming a forest.

b.

c.

d.

1. **Establishment.** Early successional stages are characterized by weedy, *r*-selected species that are tolerant of the harsh, abiotic conditions in barren areas (the preceding chapter discussed *r*-selected and *K*-selected species).
2. **Facilitation.** The weedy early successional stages introduce local changes in the habitat that favor other, less weedy species. Thus, the mosses in the Glacier Bay succession convert nitrogen to a form that allows alders to invade (see figure 57.24). Similarly, the nitrogen build-up produced by the alders, though not necessary for spruce establishment, leads to more robust forests of spruce better able to resist attack by insects.
3. **Inhibition.** Sometimes the changes in the habitat caused by one species, while favoring other species, also inhibit the growth of the original species that caused the changes. Alders, for example, do not grow as well in acidic soil as the spruce and hemlock that replace them.

Over the course of succession, the number of species typically increases as the environment becomes more hospitable. In some cases, however, as ecosystems mature, more *K*-selected species replace *r*-selected ones, and superior competitors force out other species, leading ultimately to a decline in species richness.

### Succession in animal communities

The species of animals present in a community also change through time in a successional pattern. As the vegetation changes during succession, habitat disappears for some species and appears for others.

A particularly striking example occurred on the Krakatau islands, which were devastated by an enormous volcanic eruption in 1883. Initially composed of nothing but barren ashfields, the three islands of the group experienced rapid successional change as vegetation became reestablished. A few blades of grass appeared the next year, and within 15 years the coastal vegetation was well established and the interior was covered with dense grasslands. By 1930, the islands were almost entirely forested (figure 57.25).

The fauna of Krakatau changed in synchrony with the vegetation. Nine months after the eruption, the only animal found was a single spider, but by 1908, 200 animal species were found in a 3-day exploration. For the most part, the first animals were grassland inhabitants, but as trees became established, some of these early colonists, such as the zebra dove and the long-tailed shrike (a type of predatory bird), disappeared and were replaced by forest-inhabiting species, such as fruit bats and fruit-eating birds.

Although patterns of succession of animal species have typically been caused by vegetational succession, changes in the composition of the animal community in turn have affected plant occurrences. In particular, many plant species that are animal-dispersed or pollinated could not colonize Krakatau until their dispersers or pollinators had become established. For example, fruit bats were slow to colonize Krakatau, and until they appeared, few bat-dispersed plant species were present.

## Disturbances can play an important role in structuring communities

Traditionally, many ecologists considered biological communities to be in a state of equilibrium, a stable condition that resisted change and fairly quickly returned to its original state if disturbed by humans or natural events. Such stability was usually attributed to the process of interspecific competition.

In recent years, this viewpoint has been reevaluated. Increasingly, scientists are recognizing that communities are constantly changing as a result of climatic changes, species invasions, and disturbance events. As a result, many ecologists now invoke nonequilibrium models that emphasize change, rather than stability. A particular focus of ecological research concerns the role that disturbances play in determining the structure of communities.

Disturbances can be widespread or local. Severe disturbances, such as forest fires, drought, and floods, may affect large areas. Animals may also cause severe disruptions. Gypsy moths can devastate a forest by consuming all of the leaves on its trees. Unregulated deer populations may grow explosively, the deer

*a.*                    *b.*

**Figure 57.25 Succession after a volcanic eruption.**
A major volcanic explosion in 1883 on the island of Krakatau destroyed all life on the island. *a.* This photo shows a later, much less destructive eruption of the volcano. *b.* Krakatau, forested and populated by animals.

overgrazing and so destroying the forest in which they live. On the other hand, local disturbances may affect only a small area, as when a tree falls in a forest or an animal digs a hole and up-roots vegetation.

### Intermediate disturbance hypothesis

In some cases, disturbance may act to increase the species richness of an area. According to the *intermediate disturbance hypothesis*, communities experiencing moderate amounts of disturbance will have higher levels of species richness than communities experiencing either little or great amounts of disturbance.

Two factors could account for this pattern. First, in communities where moderate amounts of disturbance occur, patches of habitat exist at different successional stages. Within the area as a whole, then, species diversity is greatest because the full range of species—those characteristic of all stages of succession—are present. For example, a pattern of intermittent episodic disturbance that produces gaps in the rain forest (as when a tree falls) allows invasion of the gap by other species (figure 57.26). Eventually, the species inhabiting the gap will go through a successional sequence, one tree replacing another, until a canopy tree species comes again to occupy the gap. But if there are many gaps of different ages in the forest, many different species will be coexisting, some in young gaps and others in older ones.

Second, moderate levels of disturbance may prevent communities from reaching the final stages of succession, in which a few dominant competitors eliminate most of the other species. In contrast, too much disturbance might leave the community continually in the earliest stages of succession, when species richness is relatively low.

Ecologists are increasingly realizing that disturbance is common, rather than exceptional, in many communities. As a result, the idea that communities inexorably move along a successional trajectory culminating in the development of a predictable end-state, or "climax," community is no longer widely accepted. Rather, predicting the state of a community in the future may be difficult because the unpredictable occurrence of disturbances will often counter successional changes. Understanding the role that disturbances play in structuring communities is currently an important area of investigation in ecology.

**Figure 57.26 Intermediate disturbance.** A single fallen tree created a small light gap in the tropical rain forest of Panama. Such gaps play a key role in maintaining the high species diversity of the rain forest. In this case, a sunlight-loving plant is able to sprout up among the dense foliage of trees in the forest.

### Learning Outcomes Review 57.5

Communities change through time by a process termed succession. Primary succession occurs on bare, lifeless substrate; secondary succession occurs where an existing community has been disturbed. Early-arriving species alter the environment in ways that allow other species to colonize, and new colonizers may have negative effects on species already present. Sometimes, moderate levels of disturbance can lead to increased species richness because species characteristic of all levels of succession may be present.

■ *From a community point of view, would clear-cutting a forest be better than selective harvest of individual trees? Why or why not?*

## Chapter Review

### 57.1 Biological Communities: Species Living Together

A community is a group of different species that occupy a given location.

**Communities have been viewed in different ways.**
The individualistic concept of a community is a random assemblage of species that happen to occur in a given place. The holistic concept of a community is an integrated unit composed of species that work together as part of a functional whole.

**Communities change over space and time.**
In accordance with the individualistic view, species generally respond independently to environmental conditions, and community composition gradually changes over space and time. However, in locations where conditions rapidly change, species composition may change greatly over short distances.

## 57.2 The Ecological Niche Concept

**Fundamental niches are potential; realized niches are actual.**

A niche is the total of all the ways a species uses environmental resources. The fundamental niche is the entire niche a species is capable of using if there are no intervening factors. The realized niche is the set of actual environmental conditions that allow establishment of a stable population.

Realized niches are usually smaller than fundamental niches because interspecific interactions limit a species' use of some resources.

**Competitive exclusion can occur when species compete for limited resources.**

The principle of competitive exclusion states that if resources are limiting, two species cannot simultaneously occupy the same niche; rather, one species will be eliminated.

**Competition may lead to resource partitioning.**

By using different resources (partitioning), sympatric species can avoid competing with each other and can coexist with reduced realized niches.

**Detecting interspecific competition can be difficult.**

Although experimentation is a powerful means of testing the hypothesis that species compete, practical limitations exist. Detailed knowledge of the ecology of species is important to evaluate the results of experiments and possible interactions.

## 57.3 Predator–Prey Relationships

**Predation strongly influences prey populations.**

Predation is the consuming of one organism by another, and includes not only one animal eating another, but also an animal eating a plant.

Natural selection strongly favors adaptations of prey species to prevent predation. In turn, sometimes predators evolve counter-adaptations, leading to an evolutionary "arms race."

**Plant adaptations defend against herbivores.**

Plants produce secondary chemical compounds that deter herbivores. Sometimes the herbivores evolve an ability to ingest the compounds and use them for their own defense.

**Animal adaptations defend against predators.**

Animal adaptations include chemical defenses and defensive coloration such as warning coloration or camouflage.

**Mimicry allows one species to capitalize on defensive strategies of another.**

In Batesian mimicry, a species that is edible or nontoxic evolves warning coloration similar to that of an inedible or poisonous species.

In Müllerian mimicry, two species that are both toxic evolve similar warning coloration.

## 57.4 The Many Types of Species Interactions

**Symbiosis involves long-term interactions.**

Many symbiotic species have coevolved and have permanent relationships.

**Commensalism benefits one species and is neutral to the other.**

Examples of commensal relationships include epiphytes growing on large plants and barnacles growing on sea animals.

**Mutualism benefits both species.**

One example is the case of ants and acacias, in which *Acacia* plants provide a home and food for a species of stinging ants that protect them from herbivores.

**Parasitism benefits one species at the expense of another.**

Many organisms have parasitic lifestyles, living on or inside one or more host species and causing damage or disease as a result.

**Ecological processes have interactive effects.**

Because many processes may occur simultaneously, species may affect one another not only through direct interactions but also through their effects on other species in the community.

**Keystone species have major effects on communities.**

Keystone species are those that maintain a more diverse community by reducing competition between species or by altering the environment to create new habitats.

## 57.5 Ecological Succession, Disturbance, and Species Richness

**Succession produces a change in species composition.**

Primary succession begins with a barren, lifeless substrate, whereas secondary succession occurs after an existing community is disrupted by fire, clearing, or other events.

**Disturbances can play an important role in structuring communities.**

Community composition changes as a result of local and global disturbances that "reset" succession.

Intermediate levels of such disturbance may maximize species richness in two ways: by creating a patchwork of different habitats harboring different species, and by preventing communities from reaching the final stage of succession, which may be dominated by only a few, competitively superior species.

## Review Questions

### UNDERSTAND

1. Studies that demonstrate that species living in an ecological community change independently of one another in space and time
   a. support the individualistic concept of ecological communities.
   b. support the holistic concept of ecological communities.
   c. suggest species interactions are the sole determinant of which species coexist in a community.
   d. None of the above

2. If two species have very similar realized niches and are forced to coexist and share a limiting resource indefinitely,
   a. both species would be expected to coexist.
   b. both species would be expected to go extinct.
   c. the species that uses the limiting resource most efficiently should drive the other species extinct.
   d. both species would be expected to become more similar to one another.

3. According to the idea of coevolution between predator and prey, when a prey species evolves a novel defense against a predator

   a. the predator is expected to always go extinct.
   b. the prey population should increase irreversibly out of control of the predator.
   c. the predator population should increase.
   d. evolution of a predator response should be favored by natural selection.

4. In order for mimicry to be effective in protecting a species from predation, it must

   a. occur in a palatable species that looks like a distasteful species.
   b. have cryptic coloration.
   c. occur such that mimics look and act like models.
   d. occur in only poisonous or dangerous species.

5. Which of the following is an example of commensalism?

   a. A tapeworm living in the gut of its host
   b. A clownfish living among the tentacles of a sea anemone
   c. An acacia tree and acacia ants
   d. Bees feeding on nectar from a flower

6. A species whose effect on the composition of a community is greater than expected based on its abundance can be called a

   a. predator.
   b. primary succession species.
   c. secondary succession species.
   d. keystone species.

7. When a predator preferentially eats the superior competitor in a pair of competing species

   a. the inferior competitor is more likely to go extinct.
   b. the superior competitor is more likely to persist.
   c. coexistence of the competing species is more likely.
   d. None of the above

8. Species that are the first colonists in a habitat undergoing primary succession

   a. are usually the fiercest competitors.
   b. help maintain their habitat constant so their persistence is ensured.
   c. may change their habitat in a way that favors the invasion of other species.
   d. must first be successful secondary succession specialists.

## APPLY

1. Which of the following can cause the realized niche of a species to be smaller than its fundamental niche?

   a. Predation          c. Parasitism
   b. Competition        d. All of the above

2. The presence of a predatory species

   a. always drives a prey species to extinction.
   b. can positively affect a prey species by having a detrimental effect on competing species.
   c. indicates that the climax stage of succession has been reached.
   d. None of the above

3. Resource partitioning by sympatric species

   a. always occurs when species have identical niches.
   b. may not occur in the presence of a predator, which reduces prey population sizes.

   c. results in the fundamental and realized niches being the same.
   d. is more common in herbivores than carnivores.

4. Parasitism differs from predation because

   a. the presence of parasitism doesn't lead to selection for defensive adaptations in parasitized species.
   b. parasites and the species they parasitize never engage in an evolutionary "arms race."
   c. parasites don't have strong effects on the populations of the species they parasitize.
   d. None of the above

5. The presence of one species (A) in a community may benefit another species (B) if

   a. a commensualistic relationship exists between the two.
   b. The first species (A) preys on a predator of the second species (B).
   c. The first species (A) preys on a species that competes with a species that is eaten by the second species (B).
   d. All of the above

## SYNTHESIZE

1. Competition is traditionally indicated by documenting the effect of one species on the population of another. Are there alternative ways to study the potential effects of competition on organisms that are impractical to study with experimental manipulations because they are too big or live too long?

2. Refer to figure 57.9. If the single prey species of *Paramecium* was replaced by several different potential prey species that varied in their palatability or ease of subduing by the predator (leading to different levels of preference by the predator) what would you expect the dynamics of the system to look like; that is, would the system be more or less likely to go to extinction?

3. Refer to figure 57.22. Are there alternative hypotheses that might explain the increase followed by the decrease in ant colony numbers subsequent to rodent removal in the experiment described in figure 57.22? If so, how would you test the mechanism hypothesized in the figure?

4. Refer to figure 57.7. Examine the pattern of beak size distributions of two species of finches on the Galápagos Islands. One hypothesis that can be drawn from this pattern is that character displacement has taken place. Are there other hypotheses? If so, how would you test them?

5. Is it possible that some species function together as an integrated, holistic community, whereas other species at the same locality behave more individualistically? If so, what factors might determine which species function in which way?

### ONLINE RESOURCE

www.ravenbiology.com

Understand, Apply, and Synthesize—enhance your study with animations that bring concepts to life and practice tests to assess your understanding. Your instructor may also recommend the interactive eBook, individualized learning tools, and more.

Chapter 58

# Dynamics of Ecosystems

## Chapter Outline

## Introduction

*The Earth is a relatively closed system with respect to chemicals. It is an open system in terms of energy, however, because it receives energy at visible and near-visible wavelengths from the Sun and steadily emits thermal energy to outer space in the form of infrared radiation. The organisms in ecosystems interact in complex ways as they participate in the cycling of chemicals and as they capture and expend energy. All organisms, including humans, depend on the specialized abilities of other organisms—plants, algae, animals, fungi, and prokaryotes—to acquire the essentials of life, as explained in this chapter. In chapters 58 and 59, we consider the many different types of ecosystems that constitute the biosphere and discuss the threats to the biosphere and the species it contains.*

# Biogeochemical Cycles

An ecosystem includes all the organisms that live in a particular place, plus the abiotic (nonliving) environment in which they live—and with which they interact—at that location. Ecosystems are intrinsically dynamic in a number of ways, including their processing of matter and energy. We start with matter.

## The atomic constituents of matter cycle within ecosystems

During the biological processing of matter, the atoms of which it is composed, such as the atoms of carbon or oxygen, maintain their integrity even as they are assembled into new compounds and the compounds are later broken down. The Earth has an essentially fixed number of each of the types of atoms of biological importance, and the atoms are recycled.

Each organism assembles its body from atoms that previously were in the soil, the atmosphere, other parts of the abiotic environment, or other organisms. When the organism dies, its atoms are released unaltered to be used by other organisms or returned to the abiotic environment. Because of the cycling of the atomic constituents of matter, your body is likely during

your life to contain a carbon or oxygen atom that once was part of Julius Caesar's body or Cleopatra's.

The atoms of the various chemical elements are said to move through ecosystems in biogeochemical cycles, a term emphasizing that the cycles of chemical elements involve not only biological organisms and processes, but also geological (abiotic) systems and processes. Biogeochemical cycles include processes that occur on many spatial scales, from cellular to planetary, and they also include processes that occur on multiple timescales, from seconds (biochemical reactions) to millennia (weathering of rocks).

Biogeochemical cycles usually cross the boundaries of ecosystems to some extent, rather than being self-contained within individual ecosystems. For example, one ecosystem might import or export carbon to others.

In this section, we consider the cycles of some major elements along with the compound water. We also present an example of biogeochemical cycles in a forest ecosystem.

## Carbon, the basis of organic compounds, cycles through most ecosystems

Carbon is a major constituent of the bodies of organisms because carbon atoms help form the framework of all organic compounds (see chapter 3); almost 20% of the weight of the human body is carbon. From the viewpoint of the day-to-day dynamics of ecosystems, carbon dioxide ($CO_2$) is the most significant carbon-containing compound in the abiotic environments of organisms. It makes up 0.03% of the volume of the atmosphere, meaning the atmosphere contains about 750 billion metric tons of carbon. In aquatic ecosystems, $CO_2$ reacts spontaneously with the water to form bicarbonate ions ($HCO_3^-$).

**Figure 58.1** **The carbon cycle.** Photosynthesis by plants and algae captures carbon in the form of organic chemical compounds. Aerobic respiration by organisms and fuel combustion by humans return carbon to the form of carbon dioxide ($CO_2$) or bicarbonate ($HCO_3^{2}$). Microbial methanogens living in oxygen-free microhabitats, such as the mud at the bottom of the pond, might produce methane ($CH_4$), a gas that would enter the atmosphere and then gradually be oxidized abiotically to carbon dioxide (shown in green circled inset).

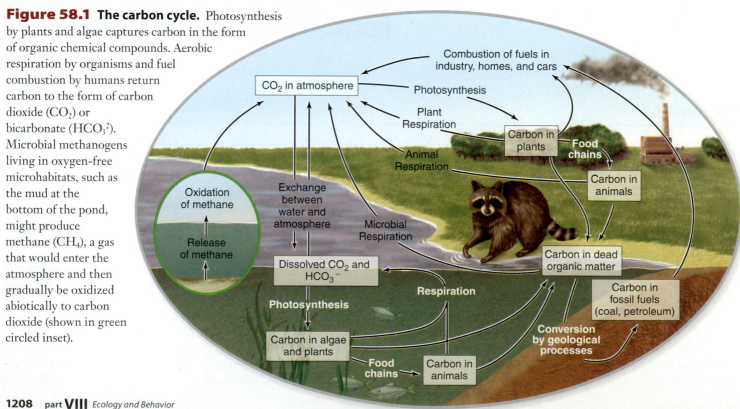

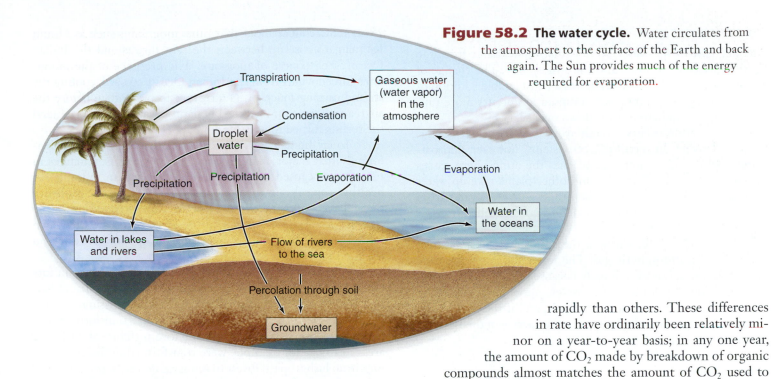

**Figure 58.2 The water cycle.** Water circulates from the atmosphere to the surface of the Earth and back again. The Sun provides much of the energy required for evaporation.

### The basic carbon cycle

The carbon cycle is straightforward, as shown in figure 58.1. In terrestrial ecosystems, plants and other photosynthetic organisms take in $CO_2$ from the atmosphere and use it in photosynthesis to synthesize the carbon-containing organic compounds of which they are composed (see chapter 8). The process is sometimes called *carbon fixation*; fixation refers to metabolic reactions that make nongaseous compounds from gaseous ones.

Animals eat the photosynthetic organisms and build their own tissues by making use of the carbon atoms in the organic compounds they ingest. Both the photosynthetic organisms and the animals obtain energy during their lives by breaking down some of the organic compounds available to them, through aerobic cellular respiration (see chapter 7). When they do this, they produce $CO_2$. Decaying organisms also produce $CO_2$. Carbon atoms returned to the form of $CO_2$ are available once more to be used in photosynthesis to synthesize new organic compounds.

In aquatic ecosystems, the carbon cycle is fundamentally similar, except that inorganic carbon is present in the water not only as dissolved $CO_2$, but also as $HCO_3^-$ ions, both of which act as sources of carbon for photosynthesis by algae and aquatic plants.

### Methane producers

Microbes that break down organic compounds by anaerobic cellular respiration (see chapter 7) provide an additional dimension to the global carbon cycle. Methanogens, for example, are microbes that produce methane ($CH_4$) instead of $CO_2$. One major source of $CH_4$ is wetland ecosystems, where methanogens live in the oxygen-free sediments. Methane that enters the atmosphere is oxidized abiotically to $CO_2$, but $CH_4$ that remains isolated from oxygen can persist for great lengths of time.

### The rise of atmospheric carbon dioxide

Another dimension of the global carbon cycle is that over long stretches of time, some parts of the cycle may proceed more rapidly than others. These differences in rate have ordinarily been relatively minor on a year-to-year basis; in any one year, the amount of $CO_2$ made by breakdown of organic compounds almost matches the amount of $CO_2$ used to synthesize new organic compounds.

Small mismatches, however, can have large consequences if continued for many years. The Earth's present reserves of coal were built up over geologic time. Organic compounds such as cellulose accumulated by being synthesized faster than they were broken down, and then they were transformed by geological processes into the fossil fuels. Most scientists believe that the world's petroleum reserves were created in the same way.

Human burning of fossil fuels today is creating large contemporary imbalances in the carbon cycle. Carbon that took millions of years to accumulate in the reserves of fossil fuels is being rapidly returned to the atmosphere, driving the concentration of $CO_2$ in the atmosphere upward year by year and helping to spur fears of global warming (see chapter 59).

## The availability of water is fundamental to terrestrial ecosystems

The water cycle, seen in figure 58.2, is probably the most familiar of all biogeochemical cycles. All life depends on the presence of water; even organisms that can survive without water in resting states require water to regain activity. The bodies of most organisms consist mainly of water. The adult human body, for example, is about 60% water by weight. The amount of water available in an ecosystem often determines the nature and abundance of the organisms present, as illustrated by the difference between forests and deserts (see chapter 59).

Each type of biogeochemical cycle has distinctive features. A distinctive feature of the water cycle is that water is a compound, not an element, and thus it can be synthesized and broken down. It is synthesized during aerobic cellular respiration (see chapter 7) and chemically split during photosynthesis (see chapter 8). The rates of these processes are ordinarily about equal, and therefore a relatively constant amount of water cycles through the biosphere.

### The basic water cycle

One key part of the water cycle is that liquid water from the Earth's surface evaporates into the atmosphere. The change of water from a liquid to a gas requires a considerable addition of thermal energy, explaining why evaporation occurs more rapidly when solar radiation beats down on a surface.

Evaporation occurs directly from the surfaces of oceans, lakes, and rivers. In terrestrial ecosystems, however, approximately 90% of the water that reaches the atmosphere passes through plants. Trees, grasses, and other plants take up water from soil via their roots, and then the water evaporates from their leaves and other surfaces through a process called transpiration (see chapter 38).

Evaporated water exists in the atmosphere as a gas, just like any other atmospheric gas. The water can condense back into liquid form, however, mostly because of cooling of the air. Condensation of gaseous water (water vapor) into droplets or crystals causes the formation of clouds, and if the droplets or crystals are large enough, they fall to the surface of the Earth as precipitation (rain or snow).

### Groundwater

Less obvious than surface water, which we see in rivers and lakes, is water under ground—termed groundwater. Groundwater occurs in **aquifers,** which are permeable, underground layers of rock, sand, and gravel that are often saturated with water. Groundwater is the most important reservoir of water on land in many parts of the world, representing over 95% of all fresh water in the United States, for example.

Goundwater consists of two subparts. The upper layers of the groundwater constitute the water table, which is unconfined in the sense that it flows into streams and is partly accessible to the roots of plants. The lower, confined layers of the groundwater are generally out of reach to streams and plants, but can be tapped by wells. Groundwater is recharged by water that percolates downward from above, such as from precipitation. Water in an aquifer flows much more slowly than surface water, anywhere from a few millimeters to a meter or so per day.

In the United States, groundwater provides about 25% of the water used by humans for all purposes, and it supplies about 50% of the population with drinking water. In the Great Plains states, the deep Ogallala Aquifer is tapped extensively as a water source for agricultural and domestic needs. The aquifer is being depleted faster than it is recharged—a local imbalance in the water cycle—posing an ominous threat to the agricultural production of the area. Similar threats exist in many of the drier portions of the globe.

### Changes in ecosystems brought about by changes in the water cycle

Water is so crucial for life that changes in its supply in an ecosystem can radically alter the nature of the ecosystem. Such changes have occurred often during the Earth's geological history.

Consider, for example, the ecosystem of the Serengeti Plain in Tanzania, famous for its seemingly endless grasslands occupied by vast herds of antelopes and other grazing animals. The semiarid grasslands of today's Serengeti were rain forests

25 MYA. Starting at about that time, mountains such as Mount Kilimanjaro rose up between the rain forests and the Indian Ocean, their source of moisture. The presence of the mountains forced winds from the Indian Ocean upward, cooling the air and causing much of its moisture to precipitate before the air reached the rain forests. The land became much drier, and the forests turned to grasslands.

Today, human activities can alter the water cycle so profoundly that major changes occur in ecosystems. Changes in rain forests caused by deforestation provide an example. In healthy tropical rain forests, more than 90% of the moisture that falls as rain is taken up by plants and returned to the air by transpiration. Plants, in a very real sense, create their own rain: The moisture returned to the atmosphere falls back on the forests.

When human populations cut down or burn the rain forests in an area, the local water cycle is broken. Water that falls as rain thereafter drains away in rivers instead of rising to form clouds and fall again on the forests. Just such a transformation is occurring today in many tropical rain forests (figure 58.3). Large areas in Brazil, for example, were transformed in the 20th century from lush tropical forest to semiarid desert, depriving many unique plant and animal species of their native habitat.

## The nitrogen cycle depends on nitrogen fixation by microbes

Nitrogen is a component of all proteins and nucleic acids and is required in substantial amounts by all organisms; proteins are 16% nitrogen by weight. In many ecosystems, nitrogen is the chemical element in shortest supply relative to the needs of organisms. A paradox is that the atmosphere is 78% nitrogen by volume.

**Figure 58.3 Deforestation disrupts the local water cycle.** Tropical deforestation can have severe consequences, such as the extensive erosion in this area in the Amazon region of Brazil.

### Nitrogen availability

How can nitrogen be in short supply if the atmosphere is so rich with it? The answer is that the nitrogen in the atmosphere is in its elemental form—molecules of nitrogen gas ($N_2$)—and the vast majority of organisms, including all plants and animals, have no way to use nitrogen in this chemical form.

For animals, the ultimate source of nitrogen is nitrogen-containing organic compounds synthesized by plants or by algae or other microbes. Herbivorous animals, for example, eat plant or algal proteins and use the nitrogen-containing amino acids in them to synthesize their own proteins.

Plants and algae use a number of simple nitrogen-containing compounds as their sources of nitrogen to synthesize proteins and other nitrogen-containing organic compounds in their tissues. Two commonly used nitrogen sources are ammonia ($NH_3$) and nitrate ions ($NO_3^-$). As described in chapter 39, certain prokaryotic microbes can synthesize ammonia and nitrate from $N_2$ in the atmosphere, thereby constituting a part of the nitrogen cycle that makes atmospheric nitrogen accessible to plants and algae (figure 58.4). Other prokaryotes turn $NH_3$ and $NO_3^-$ into $N_2$, making the nitrogen inaccessible. The balance of the activities of these two sets of microbes determines the accessibility of nitrogen to plants and algae.

### Microbial nitrogen fixation, nitrification, and denitrification

The synthesis of nitrogen-containing compounds from $N_2$ is known as **nitrogen fixation.** The first step in this process is the synthesis of $NH_3$ from $N_2$, and biochemists sometimes use the term *nitrogen fixation* to refer specifically to this step. After $NH_3$ has been synthesized, other prokaryotic microbes oxidize part of it to form $NO_3^-$, a process called **nitrification.**

Certain genera of prokaryotes have the ability to accomplish nitrogen fixation using a system of enzymes known as the nitrogenase complex (the *nif* gene complex; see chapter 28). Most of the microbes are free-living, but on land some are found in symbiotic relationships with the roots of legumes (plants of the pea family, Fabaceae), alders, myrtles, and other plants.

Additional prokaryotic microbes (including both bacteria and archaea) are able to convert the nitrogen in $NO_3^-$ into $N_2$ (or other nitrogen gases such as $N_2O$), a process termed **denitrification.** Ammonia can be subjected to denitrification indirectly by being converted first to $NO_3^-$ and then to $N_2$.

### Nitrogenous wastes and fertilizer use

Most animals, when they break down proteins in their metabolism, excrete the nitrogen from the proteins as $NH_3$. Humans and other mammals excrete nitrogen as urea in their urine (see chapter 51); a number of types of microbes convert the urea to $NH_3$. The $NH_3$ from animal excretion can be picked up by plants and algae as a source of nitrogen.

Human populations are radically altering the global nitrogen cycle by the use of fertilizers on lawns and agricultural fields. The fertilizers contain forms of fixed nitrogen that crops can use, such as ammonium ($NH_4$) salts manufactured industrially from atmospheric $N_2$. Partly because of the production of fertilizers, humans have already doubled the rate of transfer of $N_2$ in usable forms into soils and waters.

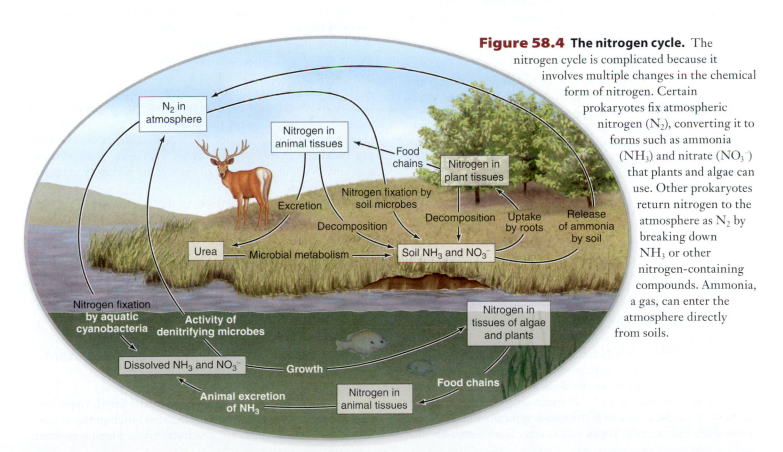

**Figure 58.4 The nitrogen cycle.** The nitrogen cycle is complicated because it involves multiple changes in the chemical form of nitrogen. Certain prokaryotes fix atmospheric nitrogen ($N_2$), converting it to forms such as ammonia ($NH_3$) and nitrate ($NO_3^-$) that plants and algae can use. Other prokaryotes return nitrogen to the atmosphere as $N_2$ by breaking down $NH_3$ or other nitrogen-containing compounds. Ammonia, a gas, can enter the atmosphere directly from soils.

**Figure 58.5** **The phosphorus cycle.** In contrast to carbon, water, and nitrogen, phosphorus occurs only in the liquid and solid states and thus does not enter the atmosphere.

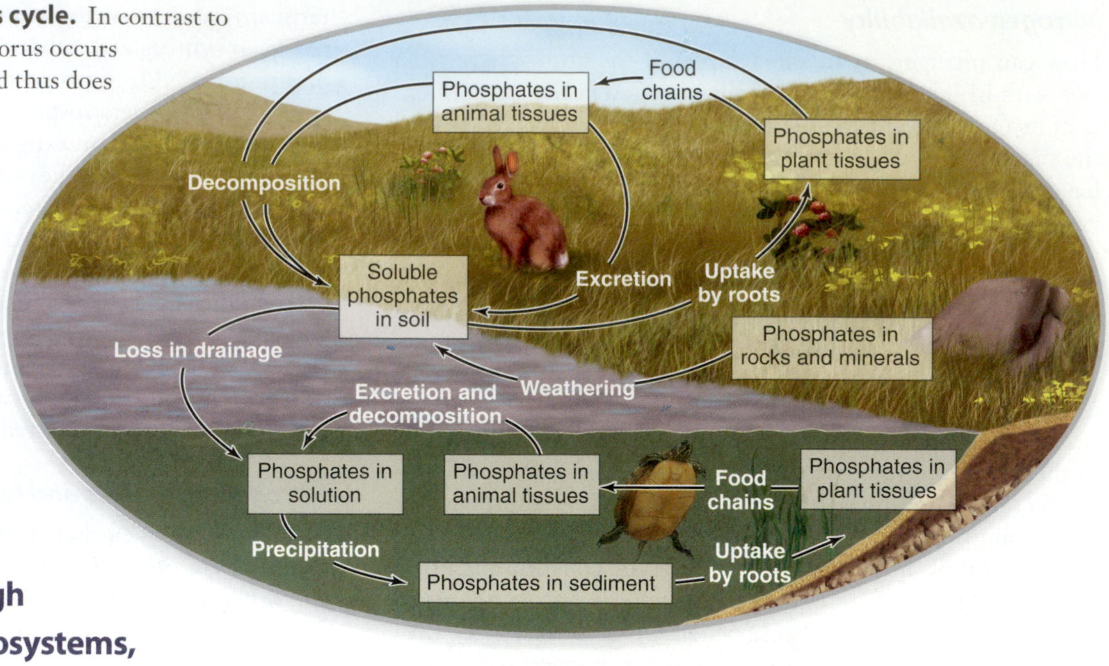

## Phosphorus cycles through terrestrial and aquatic ecosystems, but not the atmosphere

Phosphorus is required in substantial quantities by all organisms; it occurs in nucleic acids, membrane phospholipids, and other essential compounds, such as adenosine triphosphate (ATP).

Unlike carbon, water, and nitrogen, phosphorus has no significant gaseous form and does not cycle through the atmosphere (figure 58.5). In this respect, the phosphorus cycle exemplifies the sorts of cycles also exhibited by calcium, silicon, and many other mineral elements. Another feature that greatly simplifies the phosphorus cycle compared with the nitrogen cycle is that phosphorus exists in ecosystems in just a single oxidation state, phosphate ($PO_4^{3-}$).

### Phosphate availability

Plants and algae use free inorganic $PO_4^{3-}$ in the soil or water for synthesizing their phosphorus-containing organic compounds. Animals then tap the phosphorus in plant or algal tissue compounds to build their own phosphorus compounds. When organisms die, decay microbes—in a process called phosphate remineralization—break up the organic compounds in their bodies, releasing phosphorus as inorganic $PO_4^{3-}$ that plants and algae again can use.

The phosphorus cycle includes critical abiotic chemical and physical processes. Free $PO_4^{3-}$ exists in soil in only low concentrations both because it combines with other soil constituents to form insoluble compounds and because it tends to be washed away by streams and rivers. Weathering of many sorts of rocks releases new $PO_4^{3-}$ into terrestrial systems, but then rivers carry the $PO_4^{3-}$ into the ocean basins. There is a large one-way flux of $PO_4^{3-}$ from terrestrial rocks to deep-sea sediments.

### Phosphates as fertilizers

Human activities have greatly modified the global phosphorus cycle since the advent of crop fertilization. Fertilizers are typically designed to provide $PO_4^{3-}$ because crops might otherwise be short of it; the $PO_4^{3-}$ in fertilizers is typically derived from crushed phosphate-rich rocks and bones. Detergents are an-

other potential culprit in adding $PO_4^{3-}$ to ecosystems, but laws now mandate low-phosphate detergents in much of the world.

## Limiting nutrients in ecosystems are those in short supply relative to need

A chain is only as strong as its weakest link. For the plants and algae in an ecosystem to grow—and to thereby provide food for animals—they need many different chemical elements. The simplest theory is that in any particular ecosystem, one element will be in shortest supply relative to the needs for it by the plants and algae. That element is the limiting nutrient—the weak link—in the ecosystem.

The cycle of a limiting nutrient is particularly important because it determines the rate at which the nutrient is made available for use. We gave the nitrogen and phosphorus cycles close attention precisely because those elements are the limiting nutrients in many ecosystems. Nitrogen is the limiting nutrient in about two-thirds of the oceans and in many terrestrial ecosystems.

Oceanographers have discovered in just the last 15 years that iron is the limiting nutrient for algal populations (phytoplankton) in about one-third of the world's oceans. In these waters, wind-borne soil dust seems often to be the chief source of iron. When wind brings in iron-rich dust, algal populations proliferate, provided the iron is in a usable chemical form. In this way, sand storms in the Sahara Desert, by increasing the dust in global winds, can increase algal productivity in Pacific waters (figure 58.6).

## Biogeochemical cycling in a forest ecosystem has been studied experimentally

An ongoing series of studies at the Hubbard Brook Experimental Forest in New Hampshire has yielded much of the available information about the cycling of nutrients in forest ecosystems.

**Figure 58.6 One world.** Every year, millions of metric tons of iron-rich dust is carried westward by the trade winds from the Sahara Desert and neighboring Sahel area. A working hypothesis of many oceanographers is that this dust fertilizes parts of the ocean, including parts of the Pacific Ocean, where iron is the limiting nutrient. Land use practices in Africa, which are increasing the size of the north African desert, can thus affect ecosystems on the other side of the globe.

Hubbard Brook is the central stream of a large watershed that drains the hillsides of a mountain range covered with temperate deciduous forest. Multiple tributary streams carry water off the hillsides into Hubbard Brook.

Six tributary streams, each draining a particular valley, were equipped with measurement devices when the study was started. All of the water that flowed out of each valley had to pass through the measurement system, where the flow of water and concentrations of nutrients was quantified.

The undisturbed forests around Hubbard Brook are efficient at retaining nutrients. In a year, only small quantities of nutrients enter a valley from outside, doing so mostly as a result of precipitation. The quantities carried out in stream waters are small also. When we say "small," we mean the influxes and outfluxes represent just minor fractions of the total amounts of nutrients in the system—about 1% in the case of calcium, for example.

In 1965 and 1966, the investigators felled all the trees and cleared all shrubs in one of the six valleys and prevented regrowth (figure 58.7a). The effects were dramatic. The amount of water running out of that valley increased by 40%, indicating that water previously taken up by vegetation and evaporated into the atmosphere was now running off. The amounts of a number of nutrients running out of the system also greatly increased. For example, the rate of loss of calcium increased ninefold. Phosphorus, on the other hand, did not increase in the stream water; it apparently was locked up in insoluble compounds in the soil.

The change in the status of nitrogen in the disturbed valley was especially striking (figure 58.7b). The undisturbed forest in this valley had been accumulating $NO_3^-$ at a rate of about 5 kg per hectare per year, but the deforested ecosystem lost $NO_3^-$ at a rate of about 53 kg per hectare per year. The $NO_3^-$ concentration in the stream water rapidly increased. The fertility of the valley decreased dramatically, while the run-off of nitrate generated massive algal blooms downstream, and the danger of downstream flooding greatly increased.

This experiment is particularly instructive at the start of the 21st century because forested land continues to be cleared worldwide (see chapter 59).

*a.*

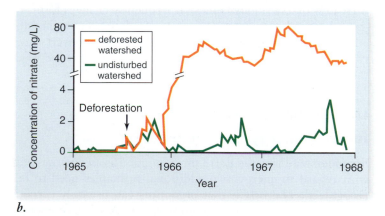

*b.*

**Figure 58.7 The Hubbard Brook experiment.** *a.* A 38-acre watershed was completely deforested, and the runoff monitored for several years. *b.* Deforestation greatly increased the loss of nutrients in runoff water from the ecosystem. The orange curve shows the nitrate concentration in the runoff water from the deforested watershed; the green curve shows the nitrate concentration in runoff water from an undisturbed neighboring watershed.

chapter **58** *Dynamics of Ecosystems*

# 58.2 The Flow of Energy in Ecosystems

## Learning Outcomes

1. *Describe the different trophic levels.*
2. *Distinguish between energy and heat.*
3. *Explain how energy moves through trophic levels.*

The dynamic nature of ecosystems includes the processing of energy as well as that of matter. Energy, however, follows very different principles than does matter. Energy is never recycled. Instead, radiant energy from the Sun that reaches the Earth makes a one-way pass through our planet's ecosystems before being converted to heat and radiated back into space, signifying that the Earth is an open system for energy.

## Energy can neither be created nor destroyed, but changes form

Why is energy so different from matter? A key part of the answer is that energy exists in several different forms, such as light, chemical-bond energy, motion, and heat. Although energy is neither created nor destroyed in the biosphere (the First Law of Thermodynamics), it frequently changes form.

A second key point is that organisms cannot convert heat to any of the other forms of energy. Thus, if organisms convert some chemical-bond or light energy to heat, the conversion is one-way; they cannot cycle that energy back into its original form.

## Living organisms can use many forms of energy, but not heat

To understand why the Earth must function as an open system with regard to energy, two additional principles need to be recognized. The first is that organisms can use only certain forms of energy. For animals to live, they must have energy specifically as chemical-bond energy, which they acquire from their foods. Plants must have energy as light. Neither animals nor plants (nor any other organisms) can use heat as a source of energy.

The second principle is that whenever organisms use chemical-bond or light energy, some of it is converted to heat; the Second Law of Thermodynamics states that a partial conversion to heat is inevitable. Put another way, animals and plants require chemical-bond energy and light to stay alive, but as they use these forms of energy, they convert them to heat, which they cannot use to stay alive and which they cannot cycle back into the original forms.

Fortunately for organisms, the Earth functions as an open system for energy. Light arrives every day from the Sun. Plants and other photosynthetic organisms use the newly arrived light to synthesize organic compounds and stay alive. Animals then eat the photosynthetic organisms, making use of the chemical-bond energy in their organic molecules to stay alive. Light and chemical-bond energy are partially converted to heat at every step. In fact, the light and chemical-bond energy are ultimately converted completely to heat. The heat leaves the Earth by being radiated into outer space at invisible, infrared wavelengths of the electromagnetic spectrum. For life to continue, new light energy is always required.

The Earth's incoming and outgoing flows of radiant energy must be equal for global temperature to stay constant. One concern is that human activities are changing the composition of the atmosphere in ways that impede the outgoing flow—the so-called *greenhouse effect*, which is described in the following chapter. Heat may be accumulating on Earth, causing global warming (see chapter 59).

## Energy flows through trophic levels of ecosystems

In chapter 7, we introduced the concepts of autotrophs ("self-feeders") and heterotrophs ("fed by others"). **Autotrophs** synthesize the organic compounds of their bodies from inorganic precursors such as $CO_2$, water, and $NO_3^-$ using energy from an abiotic source. Some autotrophs use light as their source of energy and therefore are **photoautotrophs;** they are the photosynthetic organisms, including plants, algae, and cyanobacteria. Other autotrophs are **chemoautotrophs** and obtain energy by means of inorganic oxidation reactions, such as the microbes that use hydrogen sulfide available at deep water vents (see chapter 59). All chemoautotrophs are prokaryotic. The photoautotrophs are of greatest importance in most ecosystems, and we focus on them in the remainder of this chapter.

Heterotrophs are organisms that cannot synthesize organic compounds from inorganic precursors, but instead live by taking in organic compounds that other organisms have made. They obtain the energy they need to live by breaking up some of the organic compounds available to them, thereby liberating chemical-bond energy for metabolic use (see chapter 7). Animals, fungi, and many microbes are heterotrophs.

When living in their native environments, species are often organized into chains that eat each other sequentially. For example, a species of insect might eat plants, and then a species of shrew might eat the insect, and a species of hawk might eat the shrew. Food passes through the four species in the sequence: plants $\longrightarrow$ insect $\longrightarrow$ shrew $\longrightarrow$ hawk. A sequence of species like this is termed a food chain.

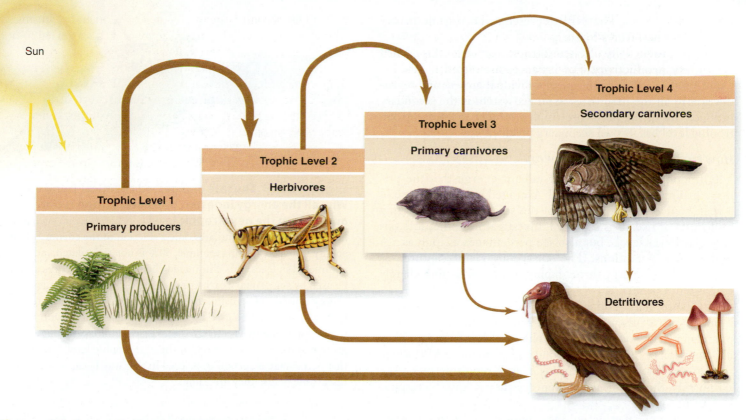

**Figure 58.8 Trophic levels within an ecosystem.** Primary producers such as plants obtain their energy directly from the Sun, placing them in trophic level 1. Animals that eat plants, such as plant-eating insects, are herbivores and are in trophic level 2. Animals that eat the herbivores, such as shrews, are primary carnivores and are in trophic level 3. Animals that eat the primary carnivores, such as owls, are secondary carnivores in trophic level 4. Each trophic level, although illustrated here by a particular species, consists of all the species in the ecosystem that function in a similar way in terms of what they eat. The organisms in the detritivore trophic level consume dead organic matter they obtain from all the other trophic levels.

In a whole ecosystem, many species play similar roles; there is typically not just a single species in each role. For example, the animals that eat plants might include not just a single insect species, but perhaps 30 species of insects, plus perhaps 10 species of mammals. To organize this complexity, ecologists recognize a limited number of feeding, or **trophic, levels** (figure 58.8).

### Definitions of trophic levels

The first trophic level in an ecosystem, called the **primary producers,** consists of all the autotrophs in the system. The other trophic levels consist of the heterotrophs—the **consumers.** All the heterotrophs that feed directly on the primary producers are placed together in a trophic level called the **herbivores.** In turn, the heterotrophs that feed on the herbivores (eating them or being parasitic on them) are collectively termed **primary carnivores,** and those that feed on the primary carnivores are called **secondary carnivores.**

Advanced studies of ecosystems need to take into account that organisms often do not line up in simple linear sequences in terms of what they eat; some animals, for example, eat both primary producers and other animals. A linear sequence of trophic levels is a useful organizing principle for many purposes, however.

An additional consumer level is the **detritivore** trophic level. Detritivores differ from the organisms in the other

trophic levels in that they feed on the remains of already-dead organisms; detritus is dead organic matter. A subcategory of detritivores is the **decomposers,** which are mostly microbes and other minute organisms that live on and break up dead organic matter.

### Concepts to describe trophic levels

Trophic levels consist of whole populations of organisms. For example, the primary-producer trophic level consists of the whole populations of all the autotrophic species in an ecosystem. Ecologists have developed a special set of terms to refer to the properties of populations and trophic levels.

The **productivity** of a trophic level is the rate at which the organisms in the trophic level collectively synthesize new organic matter (new tissue substance). **Primary productivity** is the productivity of the primary producers. An important complexity in analyzing the primary producers is that not only do they synthesize new organic matter by photosynthesis, but they also break down some of the organic matter to release energy by means of aerobic cellular respiration (see chapter 7). The **respiration** of the primary producers, in this context, is the rate at which they break down organic compounds. **Gross primary productivity (GPP)** is simply the raw rate at which the primary producers synthesize new organic matter; **net primary productivity (NPP)** is the GPP minus the respiration of the primary producers. The NPP represents the organic matter available for herbivores to use as food.

The productivity of a heterotroph trophic level is termed **secondary productivity.** For instance, the rate that new organic matter is made by means of individual growth and reproduction in all the herbivores in an ecosystem is the secondary productivity of the herbivore trophic level. Each heterotroph trophic level has its own secondary productivity.

### How trophic levels process energy

The fraction of incoming solar radiant energy that the primary producers capture is small. Averaged over the course of a year, something around 1% of the solar energy impinging on forests or oceans is captured. Investigators sometimes observe far lower levels, but also see percentages as high as 5% under some conditions. The solar energy not captured as chemical-bond energy through photosynthesis is immediately converted to heat.

The primary producers, as noted before, carry out respiration in which they break down some of the organic compounds in their bodies to release chemical-bond energy. They use a portion of this chemical-bond energy to make ATP, which they in turn use to power various energy-requiring processes. Ultimately, the chemical-bond energy they release by respiration turns to heat.

Remember that organisms cannot use heat to stay alive. As a result, whenever energy changes form to become heat, it loses much or all of its usefulness for organisms as a fuel source. What we have seen so far is that about 99% of the solar energy impinging on an ecosystem turns to heat because it fails to be used by photosynthesis. Then some of the energy captured by photosynthesis also becomes heat because of respiration by the primary producers. All the heterotrophs in an ecosystem must live on the chemical-bond energy that is left.

### An example of energy loss between trophic levels

As chemical-bond energy is passed from one heterotroph trophic level to the next, a great deal of the energy is diverted all along the way. This principle has dramatic consequences. It means that, over any particular period of time, the amount of chemical-bond energy available to primary carnivores is far less than that available to herbivores, and the amount available to secondary carnivores is far less than that available to primary carnivores.

Why does the amount of chemical-bond energy decrease as energy is passed from one trophic level to the next? Consider the use of energy by the herbivore trophic level as an example (figure 58.9). After an herbivore such as a leaf-eating insect ingests some food, it produces feces. The chemical-bond energy in the compounds in the feces is not passed along to the primary carnivore trophic level. The chemical-bond energy of the food that is assimilated by the herbivore is used for a number of functions. Part of the assimilated energy is liberated by cellular respiration to be used for tissue repair, body movements, and other such functions. The energy used in these ways turns to heat and is not passed along to the carnivore trophic level. Some chemical-bond energy is built into the tissues of the herbivore and can serve as food for a carnivore. However, some herbivore individuals die of disease or accident rather than being eaten by predators.

17% growth

33% cellular respiration

50% feces

**Figure 58.9** **The fate of ingested chemical-bond energy: Why all the energy ingested by a heterotroph is not available to the next trophic level.** A heterotroph such as this herbivorous insect assimilates only a fraction of the chemical-bond energy it ingests. In this example, 50% is not assimilated and is eliminated in feces; this eliminated chemical-bond energy cannot be used by the primary carnivores. A third (33%) of the ingested energy is used to fuel cellular respiration and thus is converted to heat, which cannot be used by the primary carnivores. Only 17% of the ingested energy is converted into insect biomass through growth and can serve as food for the next trophic level, but not even that percentage is certain to be used in that way because some of the insects die before they are eaten.

In the end, of course, some of the initial chemical-bond energy acquired from the leaf is built into the tissues of herbivore individuals that are eaten by primary carnivores. Much of the initial chemical-bond energy, however, is diverted into heat, feces, and the bodies of herbivore individuals that carnivores do not get to eat. The same scenario is repeated at each step in a series of trophic levels (figure 58.10).

Ecologists figure as a rule of thumb that the amount of chemical-bond energy available to a trophic level over time is about 10% of that available to the preceding level over the same period of time. In some instances the percentage is higher, even as high as 30%.

### Heat as the final energy product

Essentially all of the chemical-bond energy captured by photosynthesis in an ecosystem eventually becomes heat as the chemical-bond energy is used by various trophic levels. To see this important point, recognize that when the detritivores in the ecosystem metabolize all the dead bodies, feces, and other materials made available to them, they produce heat just like the other trophic levels do.

### Productive ecosystems

Ecosystems vary considerably in their NPP. Wetlands and tropical rain forests are examples of particularly productive ecosystems (figure 58.11); in them, the NPP, measured as dry weight of new organic matter produced, is often around 2000 g/m²/ year. By contrast, the corresponding figures for some other types of ecosystems are 1200 to 1300 for temperate forests, 900 for savanna, and 90 for deserts. (These general ecosystem types, termed *biomes*, are described in the following chapter.)

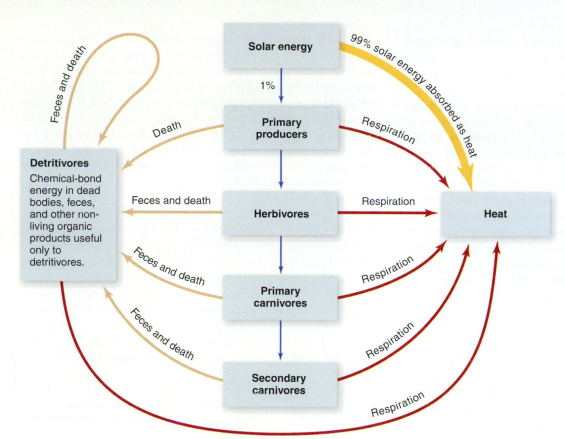

**Figure 58.10** The flow of energy through an ecosystem. Blue arrows represent the flow of energy that enters the ecosystem as light and is then passed along as chemical-bond energy to successive trophic levels. At each step energy is diverted, meaning that the chemical-bond energy available to each trophic level is less than that available to the preceding trophic level. Red arrows represent diversions of energy into heat. Tan arrows represent diversions of energy into feces and other organic materials useful only to the detritivores. Detritivores may be eaten by carnivores, so some of the chemical-bond energy returns to higher trophic levels.

## The number of trophic levels is limited by energy availability

The rate at which chemical-bond energy is made available to organisms in different trophic levels decreases exponentially as energy makes its way from primary producers to herbivores and then to various levels of carnivores. To envision this critical point, assume for simplicity that the primary producers in an ecosystem gain 1000 units of chemical-bond energy over a period of time. If the energy input to each trophic level is 10% of the input to the preceding level, then the input of chemical-bond energy to the herbivore trophic level is 100 units, to the

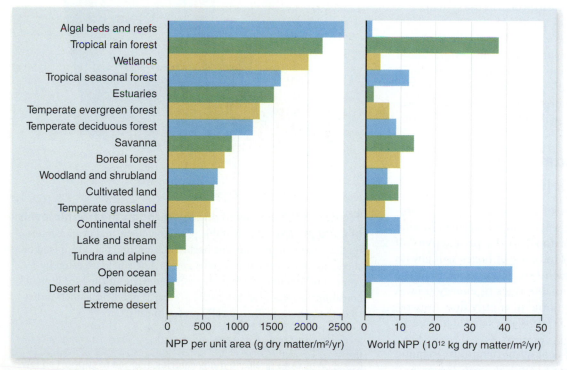

**Figure 58.11** Ecosystem productivity per year. The first column of data shows the average net primary productivity (NPP) per square meter per year. The second column of data factors in the area covered by the ecosystem type; it is the product of the productivity per square meter per year times the number of square meters occupied by the ecosystem type worldwide. Note that an ecosystem type that is very productive on a square-meter basis may not contribute much to global productivity if it is an uncommon type, such as wetlands. On the other hand, a very widespread ecosystem type, such as the open ocean, can contribute greatly to global productivity even if its productivity per square meter is low.

*Source:* Data in: Begon, M., J.L. Harper, and C.R. Townsend, *Ecology* 3/e, Blackwell Science, 1996, page 715. Original source: Whittaker, R.H. *Communities and Ecosystems*, 2/e, Macmillan, London, 1975.

primary carnivores, 10 units, and to the secondary carnivores, 1 unit over the same period of time.

### Limits on top carnivores

The exponential decline of chemical-bond energy in a trophic chain limits the lengths of trophic chains and the numbers of top carnivores an ecosystem can support. According to our model calculations, if an ecosystem includes secondary carnivores, only about one-thousandth of the energy captured by photosynthesis passes all the way through the series of trophic levels to reach these animals as usable chemical-bond energy. Tertiary carnivores would receive only one ten-thousandth. This helps explain why no predators subsist solely on eagles or lions.

The decline of available chemical-bond energy also helps explain why the numbers of individual top-level carnivores in an ecosystem tend to be low. The whole trophic level of top carnivores receives relatively little energy, and yet such carnivores tend to be big: They have relatively large individual body sizes and great individual energy needs. Because of these two factors, the population numbers of top predators tend to be small.

The longest trophic chains probably occur in the oceans. Some tunas and other top-level ocean predators probably function as third- and fourth-level carnivores at times. The challenge of explaining such long trophic chains is obvious, but the solutions are not well understood presently.

### Humans as consumers: A case study

The flow of energy in Cayuga Lake in upstate New York (figure 58.12) helps illustrate how the energetics of trophic levels can affect the human food supply. Researchers calculated from the actual properties of this ecosystem that about 150 of each 1000 calories of chemical-bond energy captured by primary producers in the lake were transferred into the bodies of herbivores. Of these calories, about 30 were transferred into the bodies of smelt, small fish that were the principal primary carnivores in the system.

If humans ate the smelt, they gained about 6 of the 1000 calories that originally entered the system. If trout ate the smelt and humans ate the trout, the humans gained only about 1.2 calories. For human populations in general, more energy is available if plants or other primary producers are eaten than if animals are eaten—and more energy is available if herbivores rather than carnivores are consumed.

## Ecological pyramids illustrate the relationship of trophic levels

Imagine that the trophic levels of an ecosystem are represented as boxes stacked on top of each other. Imagine also that the width of each box is proportional to the productivity of the trophic level it represents. The stack of boxes will always have the shape of a pyramid; each box is narrower than the one under it because of the inviolable rules of energy flow. A diagram of this sort is called a pyramid of energy flow or pyramid of productivity (figure 58.13a). It is an example of an ecological pyramid.

There are several types of ecological pyramids. Pyramid diagrams can be used to represent standing crop biomass or numbers of individuals, as well as productivity.

In a **pyramid of** biomass, the widths of the boxes are drawn to be proportional to standing crop biomass. Usually, trophic levels that have relatively low productivity also have relatively little biomass present at a given time. Thus, pyramids of biomass are usually upright, meaning each box is narrower than the one below it (figure 58.13b). An upright pyramid of biomass is not mandated by fundamental and inviolable rules like an upright pyramid of productivity is, however. In some ecosystems, the pyramid of biomass is **inverted,** meaning that at least one trophic level has greater biomass than the one below it (figure 58.13c).

How is it possible for the pyramid of biomass to be inverted? Consider a common sort of aquatic system in which the primary producers are single-celled algae (phytoplankton), and the herbivores are rice grain-sized animals (such as copepods) that feed directly on the algal cells. In such a system, the turnover of the algal cells is often very rapid: The cells multiply rapidly, but the animals consume them equally rapidly. In these circumstances, the algal cells never develop a large population size or large biomass. Nonetheless, because the algal cells are very productive, the ecosystem can support a substantial

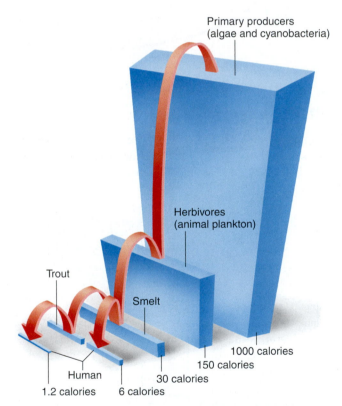

**Figure 58.12 Flow of energy through the trophic levels of Cayuga Lake.** Autotrophic plankton (algae and cyanobacteria) fix the energy of the Sun, the herbivores (animal plankton) feed on them, and both are consumed by smelt. The smelt are eaten by trout. The amount of fish flesh produced per unit time for human consumption is at least five times greater if people eat smelt rather than trout, but people typically prefer to eat trout.

### Inquiry question

? Why does it take so many calories of algae to support so few calories of humans?

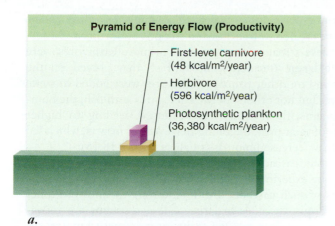

**Pyramid of Energy Flow (Productivity)**

First-level carnivore
(48 kcal/m²/year)

Herbivore
(596 kcal/m²/year)

Photosynthetic plankton
(36,380 kcal/m²/year)

*a.*

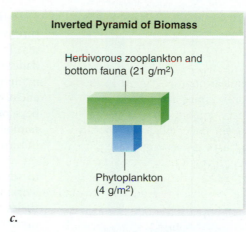

**Inverted Pyramid of Biomass**

Herbivorous zooplankton and
bottom fauna (21 g/m²)

Phytoplankton
(4 g/m²)

*c.*

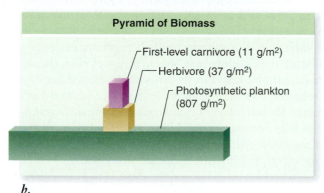

**Pyramid of Biomass**

First-level carnivore (11 g/m²)

Herbivore (37 g/m²)

Photosynthetic plankton
(807 g/m²)

*b.*

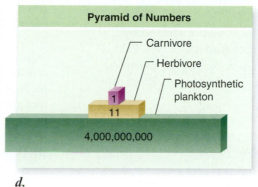

**Pyramid of Numbers**

Carnivore

Herbivore

Photosynthetic
plankton

1

11

4,000,000,000

*d.*

**Figure 58.13 Ecological pyramids.** In an ecological pyramid, successive trophic levels in an ecosystem are represented as stacked boxes, and the widths of the boxes represent the magnitude of an ecological property in the various trophic levels. Ecological pyramids can represent several different properties. *a.* Pyramid of energy flow (productivity). *b.* Pyramid of biomass of the ordinary type. *c.* Inverted pyramid of biomass. *d.* Pyramid of numbers.

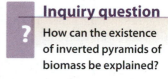

**Inquiry question**

? How can the existence of inverted pyramids of biomass be explained?

biomass of the animals, a biomass larger than that ever observed in the algal population.

In a pyramid of numbers, the widths of the boxes are proportional to the numbers of individuals present in the various trophic levels (figure 58.13*d*). Such pyramids are usually, but not always, upright.

---

### Learning Outcomes Review 58.2

Trophic levels in an ecosystem include primary producers, herbivores, primary carnivores, and secondary carnivores. Detritivores consume dead or waste matter from all levels. As energy passes from one level to another, some is inevitably lost as heat, which cannot be reclaimed. Photosynthetic primary producers capture about 1% of solar energy as chemical-bond energy. As this energy is passed through the other trophic levels, some is diverted at each step into heat, feces, and dead matter; only about 10% is available to the next level.

■ *Describe the different ways that matter, such as carbon atoms, and energy move through ecosystems?*

---

## 58.3 Trophic-Level Interactions

### Learning Outcomes

1. *Explain the meaning of trophic cascade.*
2. *Distinguish between top-down and bottom-up effects.*

The existence of food chains creates the possibility that species in any one trophic level may have effects on more than one trophic level. Primary carnivores, for example, may have effects not only on the animals they eat, but also, indirectly, on the plants or algae eaten by their prey. Conversely, increases in primary productivity may provide more food not just to herbivores, but also, indirectly, to carnivores.

The process by which effects exerted at an upper trophic level flow down to influence two or more lower levels is termed a **trophic cascade**. The effects themselves are called **top-down effects**. When an effect flows up through a trophic chain, such as from primary producers to higher trophic levels, it is termed a **bottom-up effect**.

### Top-down effects occur when changes in the top trophic level affect primary producers

The existence of top-down effects has been confirmed by controlled experiments in some types of ecosystems, particularly freshwater ones. For example, in one study, sections of a stream were enclosed with a mesh that prevented fish from entering. Brown trout—predators on invertebrates—were added to some enclosures but not others. After 10 days, the numbers of invertebrates in the enclosures with trout were only two-thirds as great as the numbers in the no-fish enclosures (figure 58.14). In turn, the biomass of algae, which the invertebrates ate, was five times greater in the trout enclosures than the no-fish ones.

The logic of the trophic cascade just described leads to the expectation that if secondary carnivores are added to

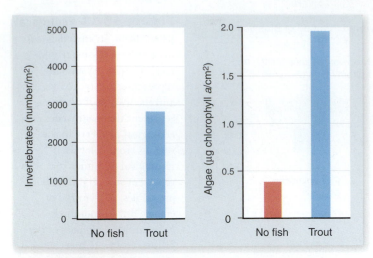

**Figure 58.14 Top-down effects demonstrated by experiment in a simple trophic cascade.** In a New Zealand stream, enclosures with trout had fewer herbivorous invertebrates (see the left-hand panel) and more algae (see the right-hand panel) than ones without trout.

**Inquiry question**

**?** Why do streams with trout have more algae?

enclosures, they would also cause cascading effects. The secondary carnivores would be predicted to keep populations of primary carnivores in check, which would lead to a profusion of herbivores and a scarcity of primary producers.

In an experiment similar to the one just described, enclosures were created in free-flowing streams in northern California. In these streams, the principal primary carnivores were damselfly larvae (termed *nymphs*). Fish that preyed on the nymphs and on other primary carnivores were added to some enclosures but not others. In the enclosures with fish, the numbers of damselfly nymphs were reduced, leading to higher numbers of their prey, including herbivorous insects, which led in turn to a decreased biomass of algae (figure 58.15).

Trophic cascades in large-scale ecosystems are not as easy to verify by experiment as ones in stream enclosures, and the workings of such cascades are not thoroughly known. Nonetheless, certain cascades in large-scale ecosystems are recognized by most ecologists. One of the most dramatic involves sea otters, sea urchins, and kelp forests along the West Coast of North America (figure 58.16).

The otters eat the urchins, and the urchins eat young kelps, inhibiting the development of kelp forests. When the otters are abundant, the kelp forests are well developed because there are relatively few urchins in the system. But when the otters are sparse, the urchins are numerous and impair development of the kelp forests. Orcas (killer whales) also enter the picture because in recent years they have started to prey intensively on the otters, driving otter populations down.

## Human removal of carnivores produces top-down effects

Human activities are believed to have had top-down effects in a number of ecosystems, usually by the removal of top-level

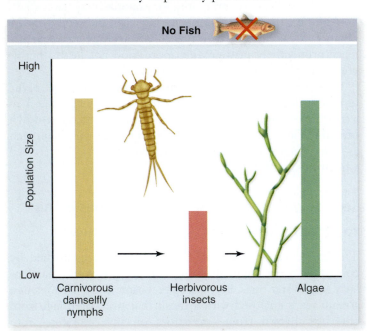
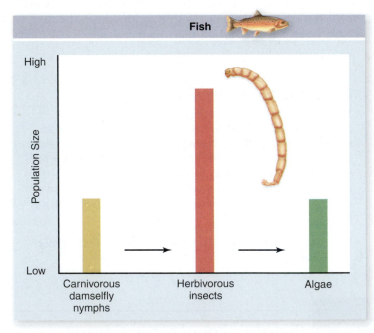

**Figure 58.15 Top-down effects demonstrated by an experiment in a four-level trophic cascade.** Stream enclosures with large, carnivorous fish *(on right)* have fewer primary carnivores, such as damselfly nymphs, more herbivorous insects (exemplified here by the number of chironomids, a type of aquatic insect), and lower levels of algae.

**Inquiry question**

**?** What might be the effect if snakes that prey on fish were added to the enclosures?

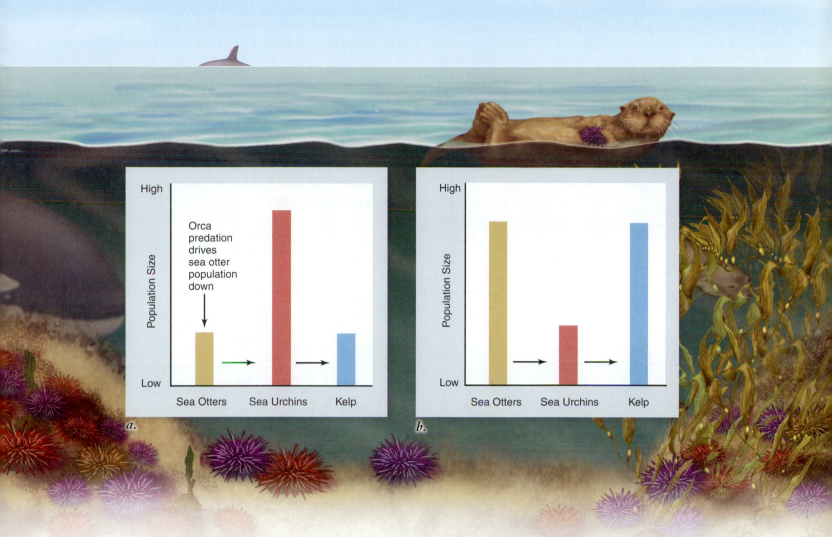

**Figure 58.16 A trophic cascade in a large-scale ecosystem.** Along the West Coast of North America, the sea otter/sea urchin/kelp system exists in two states: In the state shown in panel *a*, low populations of sea otters permit high populations of urchins, which suppress kelp populations; in the state shown in panel *b*, high populations of otters keep urchins in check, permitting profuse kelp growth. According to a recent hypothesis, a switch of orcas to preying on otters rather than other mammals is leading the ecosystem today to be mostly in the state represented on the left.

carnivores. The great naturalist Aldo Leopold posited such effects long before the trophic cascade hypothesis had been scientifically articulated when he wrote in *Sand County Almanac:*

"I have lived to see state after state extirpate its wolves. I have watched the face of many a new wolfless mountain, and seen the south-facing slopes wrinkle with a maze of new deer trails. I have seen every edible bush and seedling browsed, first to anemic desuetude, and then to death. I have seen every edible tree defoliated to the height of a saddle horn."

Many similar examples exist in which the removal of predators has led to cascading effects on lower trophic levels. Large predators such as jaguars and mountain lions are absent on Barro Colorado Island, a hilltop turned into an island by the construction of the Panama Canal at the beginning of the last century. As a result, smaller predators whose populations are normally held in check—including monkeys, peccaries (a relative of the pig), coatimundis, and armadillos—have become extraordinarily abundant. These animals eat almost anything they

find. Ground-nesting birds are particularly vulnerable, and many species have declined; at least 15 bird species have vanished from the island entirely.

Similarly, in the world's oceans, large predatory fish such as billfish and cod have been reduced by overfishing to an average of 10% of their previous numbers in virtually all parts of the world's oceans. In some regions, the prey of cod—such as certain shrimp and crabs—have become many times more abundant than they were before, and further cascading effects are evident at still lower trophic levels.

## Bottom-up effects occur when changes to primary producers affect higher trophic levels

In predicting bottom-up effects, ecologists must take account of the life histories of the organisms present. A model of bottom-up effects thought to apply to a number of types of ecosystems is diagrammed in figure 58.17.

According to the model, when primary productivity is low, producer populations cannot support significant herbivore populations. As primary productivity increases, herbivore populations become a feature of the ecosystem. Increases in primary productivity are then entirely devoured by the herbivores, the populations of which increase in size while keeping the populations of primary producers from increasing.

As primary productivity becomes still higher, herbivore populations become large enough that primary carnivores can be supported. Further increases in primary productivity then does not lead to increases in herbivore populations, but rather to increases in carnivore populations.

Experimental evidence for the bottom-up effects predicted by the model was provided by a study conducted in enclosures on a river (figure 58.18). The enclosures excluded large fish (secondary carnivores). A roof was placed above each enclosure. Some roofs were clear, whereas others were tinted to various degrees, so that the enclosures differed in the amount of sunlight entering them.

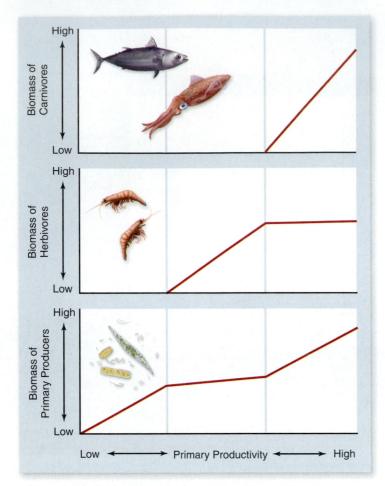

**Figure 58.17 A model of bottom-up effects.** At low levels of primary productivity, herbivore populations cannot obtain enough food to be maintained; without herbivory, the standing crop biomass of the primary producers such as these diatoms increases as their productivity increases. Above some threshold, increases in primary productivity lead to increases in herbivore populations and herbivore biomass; the biomass of the primary producers then does not increase as primary productivity increases because the increasing productivity is cropped by the herbivores. Above another threshold, populations of primary carnivores can be sustained. As primary productivity increases above this threshold, the carnivores consume the increasing productivity of the herbivores, so the biomass of the herbivore populations remains relatively constant while the biomass of the carnivore populations increases. The biomass of the primary producers is no longer constrained by increases in the herbivore populations and thus also increases with increasing primary productivity. A key to understanding the model is to maintain a distinction between the concepts of productivity and standing crop biomass.

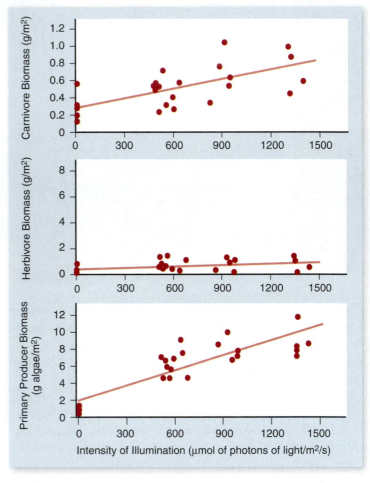

**Figure 58.18 An experimental study of bottom-up effects in a river ecosystem.** This system, studied on the Eel River in northern California, exhibited the patterns modeled by the red graphs of figure 58.17. Increases in the intensity of illumination led to increases in primary productivity and in the biomass of the primary producers. The biomass of the carnivore populations also increased. However, herbivore biomass did not increase much with increasing primary productivity because increases in herbivore productivity were consumed by the carnivores.

**Inquiry question**

**?** How is it possible for the biomass of the primary producers to stay relatively constant as the primary productivity increases?

**Inquiry question**

**?** Why is the amount of light an important determinant of carnivore biomass?

The primary productivity was highest in the enclosures with clear roofs and lowest in the ones with darkly tinted roofs. As primary productivity increased in parallel with illumination, the biomass of the primary producers increased, as did the biomass of the carnivores. However, the biomass of the trophic level sandwiched in between, the herbivores, did not increase much, as predicted by the model in figure 58.17 (see red graph lines).

### Learning Outcomes Review 58.3

Populations of species at different trophic levels affect one another, and these effects can propagate through the levels. Top-down effects, termed trophic cascades, are observed when changes in carnivore populations affect lower trophic levels. Bottom-up effects are observed when changes in primary productivity affect the higher trophic levels.

■ *Could top-down and bottom-up effects occur simultaneously?*

## 58.4 Biodiversity and Ecosystem Stability

### Learning Outcomes

1. *Define ecosystem stability.*
2. *Describe the effects of species richness on ecosystem function.*
3. *Name possible factors that contribute to species richness in the tropics.*

In the preceding chapter, we discussed *species richness*—the number of species present in a community. Ecologists have long debated the consequences of differences in species richness between communities. One theory is that species-rich communities are more stable—that is, more constant in composition and better able to resist disturbance. This hypothesis has been elegantly studied by David Tilman and colleagues at the University of Minnesota's Cedar Creek Natural History Area.

### Species richness may increase stability: The Cedar Creek studies

Workers monitored 207 small rectangular plots of land (8–16 m²) for 11 years (figure 58.19a). In each plot, they counted the number of prairie plant species and measured the total amount of plant biomass (that is, the mass of all plants on the plot). Over the course of the study, plant species richness was related to community stability—plots with more species showed less year-to-year variation in biomass. Moreover, in two drought years, the decline in biomass was negatively related to species richness—that is, plots with more species were less affected by drought.

These findings were subsequently confirmed by an experiment in which plots were seeded with different numbers of

**Question:** *Does species richness affect the invasibility of a community?*

**Hypothesis:** *The rate of successful invasion will be lower in communities with greater richness.*

**Experiment:** *Add seeds from the same number of non-native plants to experimental plots that differ in the number of plant species.*

*a.*

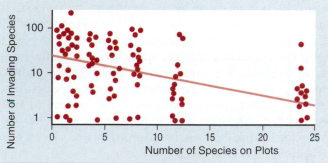

*b.*

**Result:** *Although the number of successful invasive species is highly variable, more species-rich plots on average are invaded by fewer species.*

**Interpretation:** *What might explain why so much variation exists in the number of successful invading species in communities with the same species richness?*

**Figure 58.19** **Effect of species richness on ecosystem stability.** *a.* One of the Cedar Creek experimental plots. *b.* Community stability can be assessed by looking at the effect of species richness on community invasibility. Each dot represents data from one experimental plot in the Cedar Creek experimental fields. Plots with more species are harder to invade by nonnative species.

 **Inquiry question**

How could you devise an experiment on invasibility that didn't rely on species from surrounding areas?

species. Again, more species-rich plots had greater year-to-year stability in biomass over a 10-year period.

In a related experiment, when seeds of other plant species were added to different plots, the ability of these species to become established was negatively related to species richness (figure 58.19b). More diverse communities, in other words, are more resistant to invasion by new species, which is another measure of community stability.

Species richness may also affect other ecosystem processes. Tilman and colleagues monitored 147 experimental plots that varied in number of species to estimate how much growth was occurring and how much nitrogen the growing plants were taking up from the soil. They found that the more species a plot had, the greater the nitrogen uptake and total amount of biomass produced. In his study, increased biodiversity clearly appeared to lead to greater productivity.

Laboratory studies on artificial ecosystems have provided similar results. In one elaborate study, ecosystems covering 1 m$^2$ were constructed in growth chambers that controlled temperature, light levels, air currents, and atmospheric gas concentrations. A variety of plants, insects, and other animals were introduced to construct ecosystems composed of 9, 15, or 31 species, with the lower diversity treatments containing a subset of the species in the higher diversity enclosures. As with Tilman's experiments, the amount of biomass produced was related to species richness, as was the amount of carbon dioxide consumed, another measure of the productivity of the ecosystem.

Tilman's conclusion that healthy ecosystems depend on diversity is not accepted by all ecologists, however. Critics question the validity and relevance of these biodiversity studies, arguing that the more species are added to a plot, the greater the probability that one species will be highly productive. To show that high productivity results from high species richness per se, rather than from the presence of particular highly productive species, experimental plots have to exhibit "overyielding"; in other words, plot productivity has to be greater than that of the single most productive species grown in isolation.

Although this point is still debated, recent work at Cedar Creek and elsewhere has provided evidence of overyielding, supporting the claim that species richness of communities enhances community productivity and stability.

## Species richness is influenced by ecosystem characteristics

A number of factors are known or hypothesized to affect species richness in a community. We discussed some in chapter 57, such as loss of keystone species and moderate physical disturbance. Here we discuss three more: primary productivity, habitat heterogeneity, and climatic factors.

### Primary productivity

Ecosystems differ substantially in primary productivity (see figure 58.11). Some evidence indicates that species richness is related to primary productivity, but the relationship between them is not linear. In a number of cases, for example, ecosystems with intermediate levels of productivity tend to have the greatest number of species (figure 58.20*a*).

Why this is so is debated. One possibility is that levels of productivity are linked with numbers of consumers. Applying this concept to plant species richness, the argument is that at low productivity, there are few herbivores, and superior competitors among the plants are able to eliminate most other plant species. In contrast, at high productivity so many herbivores are present that only the plant species most resistant to grazing survive, reducing species diversity. As a result, the greatest numbers of plant species coexist at intermediate levels of productivity and herbivory.

### Habitat heterogeneity

Spatially heterogeneous abiotic environments are those that consist of many habitat types—such as soil types, for example. These heterogeneous environments can be expected to accommodate more species of plants than spatially homogeneous environments. What's more, the species richness of animals can be expected to reflect the species richness of plants present. An

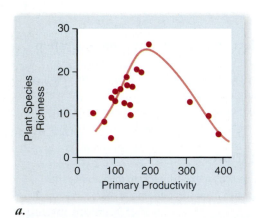

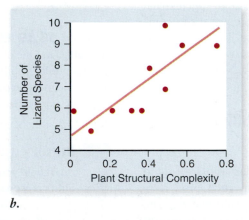

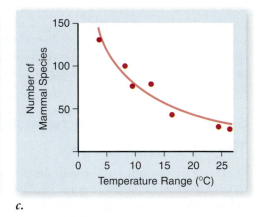

*a.*        *b.*        *c.*

**Figure 58.20 Factors that affect species richness.** *a. Productivity:* In plant communities of mountainous areas of South Africa, species richness of plants peaks at intermediate levels of productivity (biomass). *b. Spatial heterogeneity:* The species richness of desert lizards is positively correlated with the structural complexity of the plant cover in desert sites in the American Southwest. *c. Climate:* The species richness of mammals is inversely correlated with monthly mean temperature range along the West Coast of North America.

**Inquiry question**

? **(a.) Why is species richness greatest at intermediate levels of productivity? (b.) Why do more structurally complex areas have more species? (c.) Why do areas with less variation in temperature have more species?**

example of this latter effect is seen in figure 58.20*b:* The number of lizard species at various sites in the American Southwest mirrors the local structural diversity of the plants.

### Climatic factors

The role of climatic factors is more difficult to predict. On the one hand, more species might be expected to coexist in a seasonal environment than in a constant one because a changing climate may favor different species at different times of the year. On the other hand, stable environments are able to support specialized species that would be unable to survive where conditions fluctuate. The number of mammal species at locations along the West Coast of North America is inversely correlated with the amount of local temperature variation—the wider the variation, the fewer mammalian species—supporting the latter line of argument (figure 58.20*c*).

## Tropical regions have the highest diversity, although reasons are unclear

Since before Darwin, biologists have recognized that more different kinds of animals and plants inhabit the tropics than the temperate regions. For many types of organisms, there is a steady increase in species richness from the arctic to the tropics. Called a **species diversity cline,** this biogeographic gradient in numbers of species correlated with latitude has been reported for plants and animals, including birds (figure 58.21), mammals, and reptiles.

For the better part of a century, ecologists have puzzled over the species diversity cline from the arctic to the tropics. The difficulty has not been in forming a reasonable hypothesis of why more species exist in the tropics, but rather in sorting through these many reasonable hypotheses. Here, we consider five of the most commonly discussed suggestions.

### Evolutionary age of tropical regions

Scientists have frequently proposed that the tropics have more species than temperate regions because the tropics have existed over long, uninterrupted periods of evolutionary time, whereas temperate regions have been subject to repeated glaciations. The greater age of tropical communities would have allowed complex population interactions to coevolve within them, fostering a greater variety of plants and animals.

Recent work suggests that the long-term stability of tropical communities has been greatly exaggerated, however. An examination of pollen within undisturbed soil cores reveals that during glaciations, the tropical forests contracted to a few small refuges surrounded by grassland. This suggests that the tropics have not had a continuous record of species richness over long periods of evolutionary time.

### Increased productivity

A second often-advanced hypothesis is that the tropics contain more species because this part of the Earth receives more solar radiation than do temperate regions. The argument is that more solar energy, coupled to a year-round growing season, greatly increases the overall photosynthetic activity of tropical plants.

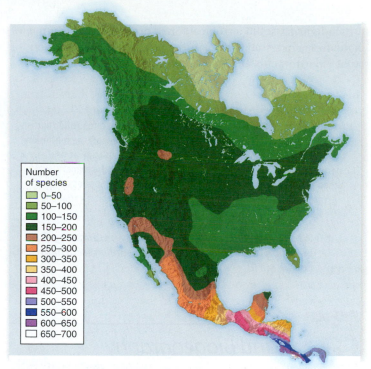

**Number of species**
- 0–50
- 50–100
- 100–150
- 150–200
- 200–250
- 250–300
- 300–350
- 350–400
- 400–450
- 450–500
- 500–550
- 550–600
- 600–650
- 650–700

**Figure 58.21** **A latitudinal cline in species richness.** Among North and Central American birds, a marked increase in the number of species occurs moving toward the tropics. Fewer than 100 species are found at arctic latitudes, but more than 600 species live in southern Central America.

If we visualize the tropical forest's total resources as a pie, and its species niches as slices of the pie, we can see that a larger pie accommodates more slices. But as noted earlier, many field studies have indicated that species richness is highest at intermediate levels of productivity. Accordingly, increasing productivity would be expected to lead to lower, not higher, species richness.

### Stability/constancy of conditions

Seasonal variation, though it does exist in the tropics, is generally substantially less than in temperate areas. This reduced seasonality might encourage specialization, with niches subdivided to partition resources and so avoid competition. The expected result would be a larger number of more specialized species in the tropics, which is what we see. Many field tests of this hypothesis have been carried out, and almost all support it, reporting larger numbers of narrower niches in tropical communities than in temperate areas.

### Predation

Many reports indicate that predation may be more intense in the tropics. In theory, more intense predation could reduce the importance of competition, permitting greater niche overlap and thus promoting greater species richness.

### Spatial heterogeneity

As noted earlier, spatial heterogeneity promotes species richness. Tropical forests, by virtue of their complexity, create a variety of microhabitats and so may foster larger numbers of species. Perhaps the long vertical column of vegetation through which light passes in a tropical forest produces a wide range of light frequencies and intensities, creating a greater variety of light environments and so promoting species diversity.

### Learning Outcomes Review 58.4

An ecosystem is stable if it remains relatively constant in composition and is able to resist disturbance. Experimental field studies support the conclusion that species-rich communities are better able to resist invasion by new species, as well as have increased biomass production at the primary level, although not all ecologists agree with these conclusions. Species richness is greatest in the tropics, and the reasons may include habitat variation, increased sunlight, and long-term climate and seasonal stability.

■ **What might be the effects on primary productivity if air pollution decreased the amount of sunlight reaching Earth's surface?**

## 58.5 Island Biogeography

### Learning Outcomes

1. Describe the species–area relationship.
2. Explain how area and isolation affect rates of colonization and extinction.

One of the most reliable patterns in ecology is the observation that larger islands contain more species than do smaller islands. In 1967, Robert MacArthur of Princeton University and Edward O. Wilson of Harvard University proposed that this species–area relationship was a result of the effect of geographic area and isolation on the likelihood of species extinction and colonization.

## The equilibrium model proposes that extinction and colonization reach a balance point

MacArthur and Wilson reasoned that species are constantly being dispersed to islands, so islands have a tendency to accumulate more and more species. At the same time that new species are added, however, other species are lost by extinction. As the number of species on an initially empty island increases, the rate of colonization must decrease as the pool of potential colonizing species not already present on the island becomes depleted. At the same time, the rate of extinction should increase—the more species on an island, the greater the likelihood that any given species will perish.

As a result, at some point, the number of extinctions and colonizations should be equal, and the number of species should then remain constant. Every island of a given size, then, has a characteristic equilibrium number of species that tends to persist through time (the intersection point in figure 58.22a)—though the species composition will change as some species become extinct and new species colonize.

MacArthur and Wilson's equilibrium model proposes that island species richness is a dynamic equilibrium between colonization and extinction. Both island size and distance from the mainland would affect colonization and extinction. We would expect smaller islands to have higher rates of extinction because their population sizes would, on average, be smaller. Also, we would expect fewer colonizers to reach islands that lie farther from the mainland. Thus, small islands far from the mainland would have the fewest species; large islands near the mainland would have the most (figure 58.22b).

The predictions of this simple model bear out well in field data. Asian Pacific bird species (figure 58.22c) exhibit a positive correlation of species richness with island size, but a negative correlation of species richness with distance from the source of colonists.

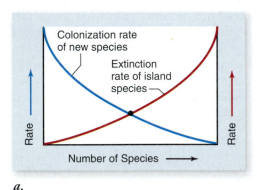

a.

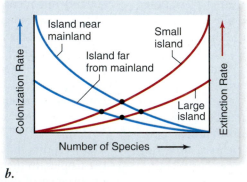

b.

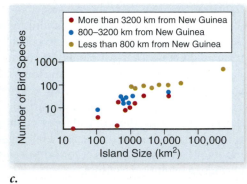

c.

**Figure 58.22 The equilibrium model of island biogeography.** *a.* Island species richness reaches an equilibrium (black dot) when the colonization rate of new species equals the extinction rate of species on the island. *b.* The equilibrium shifts depending on the rate of colonization, the size of an island, and its distance to sources of colonists. Species richness is positively correlated with island size and inversely correlated with distance from the mainland. Smaller islands have higher extinction rates, shifting the equilibrium point to the left. Similarly, more distant islands have lower colonization rates, again shifting the equilibrium point leftward. *c.* The effect of distance from a larger island, which can be the source of colonizing species, is readily apparent. More distant islands have fewer Asian Pacific bird species than do nearer islands of the same size.

## The equilibrium model is still being tested

Wilson and Dan Simberloff, then a graduate student, performed initial studies in the mid-1960s on small mangrove islands in the Florida keys. These islands were censused, cleared of animal life by fumigation, and then allowed to recolonize, with censuses being performed at regular intervals. These and other such field studies have tended to support the equilibrium model.

Long-term experimental field studies, however, are suggesting that the situation is more complicated than MacArthur and Wilson envisioned. Their model predicts a high level of species turnover as some species perish and others arrive. But studies of island birds and spiders indicate that very little turnover occurs from year to year. Those species that do come and go, moreover, comprise a subset of species that never attain high populations. A substantial proportion of the species appear to maintain high populations and rarely go extinct.

These studies have been going on for a relatively short period of time. It is possible that over periods of centuries, the equilibrium model is a good description of what determines island species richness.

### Learning Outcomes Review 58.5

The species–area relationship is an observation that an island of larger area contains more species. Species richness on islands appears to be a dynamic equilibrium between colonization and extinction. Distance from a mainland also affects the rates of colonization and extinction, and therefore fewer species would be found on small, isolated islands far from a mainland.

■ *Under what circumstances would a smaller island be expected to have more species than a larger island?*

# Chapter Review

## 58.1 Biogeochemical Cycles

**The atomic constituents of matter cycle within ecosystems.**
The atoms of chemical elements move through ecosystems in biogeochemical cycles.

**Carbon, the basis of organic compounds, cycles through most ecosystems.**
The carbon cycle usually involves carbon dioxide, which is fixed through photosynthesis and released by respiration. Carbon is also present as bicarbonate ions and as methane. Burning of fossil fuels has created an imbalance in the carbon cycle (see figure 58.1).

**The availability of water is fundamental to terrestrial ecosystems.**
Water enters the atmosphere via evaporation and transpiration and returns to the Earth's surface as precipitation. It is broken down during photosynthesis and also produced during cellular respiration. Much of the Earth's water, including the groundwater in aquifers, is polluted, and human activities alter the water supply of ecosystems (see figure 58.2).

**The nitrogen cycle depends on nitrogen fixation by microbes.**
Nitrogen is usually the element in shortest supply even though $N_2$ makes up 78% of the atmosphere. Nitrogen must be converted into usable forms by nitrogen-fixing microorganisms. Human use of nitrates in fertilizers has doubled the available nitrogen (see figure 58.4).

**Phosphorus cycles through terrestrial and aquatic ecosystems, but not the atmosphere.**
Phosphorus, another limiting nutrient, is released by weathering of rocks; it flows into the oceans where it is deposited in deep-sea sediments. Humans also use phosphates as fertilizers (see figure 58.5).

**Limiting nutrients in ecosystems are those in short supply relative to need.**
The cycle of a limiting nutrient, such as nitrogen, determines the rate at which the nutrient is made available for use.

**Biogeochemical cycling in a forest ecosystem has been studied experimentally.**
Ongoing experiments indicate that severe disturbance of an ecosystem results in mineral depletion and runoff of water.

## 58.2 The Flow of Energy in Ecosystems

**Energy can neither be created nor destroyed, but changes form.**
Energy exists in forms such as light, stored chemical-bond energy, motion, and heat. In any conversion, some energy is lost.

**Living organisms can use many forms of energy, but not heat.**
The Second Law of Thermodynamics states that whenever organisms use chemical-bond or light energy, some of it is inevitably converted to heat and cannot be retrieved.

**Energy flows through trophic levels of ecosystems.**
Organic compounds are synthesized by autotrophs and are utilized by both autotrophs and heterotrophs. As energy passes from organism to organism, each level is termed a trophic level, and the sequence through progressive trophic levels is called a food chain (see figure 58.8).

The base trophic level includes the primary producers; herbivores that consume primary producers are the next level. They in turn are eaten by primarily carnivores, which may be consumed by secondary carnivores. Detritivores feed on waste and the remains of dead organisms.

Only about 1% of the solar energy that impinges on the Earth is captured by photosynthesis. As energy moves through each trophic level, very little (approximately 10%) remains from the preceding trophic level (see figure 58.10).

**The number of trophic levels is limited by energy availability.**
The exponential decline of energy between trophic levels limits the length of food chains and the numbers of top carnivores that can be supported.

**Ecological pyramids illustrate the relationship of trophic levels.**
Ecological pyramids based on energy flow, biomass, or numbers of organisms are usually upright. Inverted pyramids of biomass or numbers are possible if at least one trophic level has a greater biomass or more organisms than the level below it (see figure 58.13).

## 58.3 Trophic-Level Interactions

**Top-down effects occur when changes in the top trophic level affect primary producers.**
A trophic cascade, or top-down effect, occurs when a change exerted at an upper trophic level affects a lower level (see figure 58.15).

**Human removal of carnivores produces top-down effects.**
Removal of carnivores causes an increase in the abundance of species in lower trophic levels, such as an increase in deer populations when wolves or other predators are destroyed.

**Bottom-up effects occur when changes to primary producers affect higher trophic levels.**
An increase of producers may lead to the appearance or increase of herbivores; however, further increase in producers may then lead to increase in carnivores, without a comparable increase in herbivores (see figure 58.17).

## 58.4 Biodiversity and Ecosystem Stability

**Species richness may increase stability: The Cedar Creek studies.**
The Cedar Creek studies indicate that higher species richness results in less year-to-year variation in biomass and in greater resistance to drought and invasion by non-native species.

**Species richness is influenced by ecosystem characteristics.**
Primary production, habitat heterogeneity, and climatic factors all affect the number of species in an ecosystem (see figure 58.20).

**Tropical regions have the highest diversity, although the reasons are unclear.**
The higher diversity of tropical regions may reflect long evolutionary time, higher productivity from increased sunlight, less seasonal variation, greater predation that reduces competition, or spatial heterogeneity (see figure 58.21).

## 58.5 Island Biogeography

The species–area relationship reflects that larger islands contain more species than do smaller ones.

**The equilibrium model proposes that extinction and colonization reach a balance point (see figure 58.22).**
Smaller islands have fewer species because of higher rates of extinction. Islands near a mainland have more species than distant islands because of higher rates of colonization. An equilibrium is reached when the extinction rate balances the colonization rate.

**The equilibrium model is still being tested.**
Long-term studies are needed to clarify all the factors involved.

# Review Questions

## UNDERSTAND

1. Which of the statements about groundwater is *not* accurate?
   a. In the United States, groundwater provides 50% of the population with drinking water.
   b. Groundwaters are being depleted faster than they can be recharged.
   c. Groundwaters are becoming increasingly polluted.
   d. Removal of pollutants from groundwaters is easily achieved.

2. Photosynthetic organisms
   a. fix carbon dioxide.
   b. release carbon dioxide.
   c. fix oxygen.
   d. (a) and (b)
   e. (a) and (c)

3. Some bacteria have the ability to "fix" nitrogen. This means
   a. they convert ammonia into nitrites and nitrates.
   b. they convert atmospheric nitrogen gas into biologically useful forms of nitrogen.
   c. they break down nitrogen-rich compounds and release ammonium ions.
   d. they convert nitrate into nitrogen gas.

4. Which of the following statements about the phosphorus cycle is correct?
   a. Phosphorus is fixed by plants and algae.
   b. Most phosphorus released from rocks is carried to the oceans by rivers.
   c. Animals cannot get their phosphorus from eating plants and algae.
   d. Fertilizer use has not affected the global phosphorus budget.

5. As a general rule, how much energy is lost in the transmission of energy from one trophic level to the one immediately above it?
   a. 1%          c. 90%
   b. 10%         d. 50%

6. Inverted ecological pyramids of real systems usually involve
   a. energy flow.
   b. biomass.
   c. energy flow and biomass.
   d. None of the above

7. Bottom-up effects on trophic structure result from
   a. a limitation of energy flowing to the next higher trophic level.
   b. actions of top predators on lower trophic levels.

c. climatic disruptions on top consumers.

d. stability of detritivores in ecosystems.

8. Species diversity

   a. increases with latitude as you move away from the equator to the arctic.

   b. decreases with latitude as you move away from the equator to the arctic.

   c. stays the same as you move away from the equator to the arctic.

   d. increases with latitude as you move north of the equator and decreases with latitude as you move south of the equator.

9. The equilibrium model of island biogeography suggests all of the following *except*

   a. larger islands have more species than smaller islands.

   b. the species richness of an island is determined by colonization and extinction.

   c. smaller islands have lower rates of extinction.

   d. islands closer to the mainland will have higher colonization rates.

## APPLY

1. Nitrogen is often a limiting nutrient in many ecosystems because

   a. there is much less nitrogen in the atmosphere than carbon.

   b. elemental nitrogen is very rapidly used by most organisms.

   c. nitrogen availability is being reduced by pollution due to fertilizer use.

   d. most organisms cannot use nitrogen in its elemental form.

2. Based on results from studies at Hubbard Brook Experimental Forest, what would be the predicted effect of clearing trees from a watershed?

   a. Increased loss of water and nutrients from a watershed

   b. Decreased loss of water and nutrients from a watershed

   c. Increased availability of phosphorus

   d. Increased availability of nitrate

3. According to the trophic cascade hypothesis, the removal of carnivores from an ecosystem may result in

   a. a decline in the number of herbivores and a decline in the amount of vegetation.

   b. a decline in the number of herbivores and an increase in the amount of vegetation.

   c. an increase in the number of herbivores and an increase in the amount of vegetation.

   d. an increase in the number of herbivores and a decrease in the amount of vegetation.

4. At Cedar Creek Natural History Area, experimental plots showed reduced numbers of invaders as species diversity of plots increased

   a. suggesting that low species diversity increases stability of ecosystems.

   b. suggesting that ecosystem stability is a function of primary productivity only.

   c. consistent with the theory that intermediate disturbance results in the highest stability.

   d. None of the above

## SYNTHESIZE

1. Given that ectotherms do not utilize a large fraction of ingested food energy to maintain a high and constant body temperature (generate heat), how would you expect the food chains of systems dominated by ectothermic herbivores and carnivores to compare with systems dominated by endothermic herbivores and carnivores?

2. Given that, in general, energy input is greatest at the bottom trophic level (primary producers) and decreases with increasing transfers across trophic levels, how is it possible for many lakes to show much greater standing biomass in herbivorous zooplankton than in the phytoplankton they consume?

3. Ecologists often worry about the potential effects of the loss of species (e.g., due to pollution, habitat degradation, or other human-induced factors) on an ecosystem for reasons other than just the direct loss of the species. Using figure 58.17 explain why.

4. Explain several detailed ways in which increasing plant structural complexity could lead to greater species richness of lizards (figure 58.20*b*). Could any of these ideas be tested? How?

## ONLINE RESOURCE

**www.ravenbiology.com**

Understand, Apply, and Synthesize—enhance your study with animations that bring concepts to life and practice tests to assess your understanding. Your instructor may also recommend the interactive eBook, individualized learning tools, and more.

Chapter 59

# The Biosphere

## Chapter Outline

## Introduction

*The biosphere includes all living communities on Earth, from the profusion of life in the tropical rain forests to the planktonic communities in the world's oceans. In a very general sense, the distribution of life on Earth reflects variations in the world's abiotic environments, such as the variations in temperature and availability of water from one terrestrial environment to another. The figure on this page is a satellite image of the Americas, based on data collected over 8 years. The colors are keyed to the relative abundance of chlorophyll, an indicator of the richness of biological communities. Green and dark green areas on land are areas with high primary productivity (such as thriving forests), whereas yellow areas include the deserts of the Americas and the tundra of the far north, which have lower productivity.*

## 59.1 Ecosystem Effects of Sun, Wind, and Water

### Learning Outcomes

1. *Describe changes in wind and current direction with latitude.*
2. *Explain the Coriolis effect.*
3. *Describe how temperature changes with altitude and latitude.*

The great global patterns of life on Earth are heavily influenced by (1) the amount of solar radiation that reaches different parts of the Earth and seasonal variations in that radiation; and (2) the patterns of global atmospheric circulation and the resulting patterns of oceanic circulation. Local characteristics, such as soil types and the altitude of the land, interact with the global patterns in sunlight, winds, and water currents to determine the conditions under which life exists and thus the distributions of ecosystems.

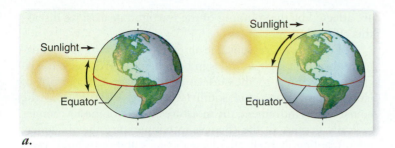

a.

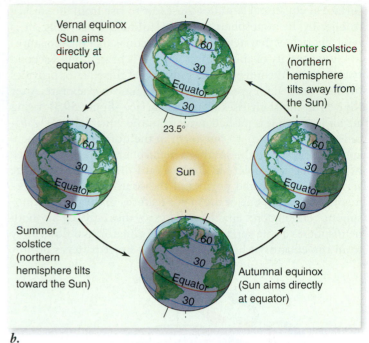

b.

**Figure 59.1   Relationships between the Earth and the Sun are critical in determining the nature and distribution of life on Earth.** *a.* A beam of solar energy striking the Earth in the middle latitudes of the northern hemisphere (or the southern) spreads over a wider area of the Earth's surface than an equivalent beam striking the Earth at the equator. *b.* The fact that the Earth orbits the Sun each year has a profound effect on climate. In the northern and southern hemispheres, temperature changes in an annual cycle because the Earth's axis is not perpendicular to its orbital plane and, consequently, each hemisphere tilts toward the Sun in some months but away from the Sun in others.

## Solar energy and the Earth's rotation affect atmospheric circulation

The Earth receives energy from the Sun at a high rate in the form of electromagnetic radiation at visible and near-visible wavelengths. Each square meter of the upper atmosphere receives about 1400 joules per second (J/sec), which is equivalent to the output of fourteen 100-watt (W) lightbulbs.

As the solar radiant energy passes through the atmosphere, its intensity and wavelength composition are modified. About half of the energy is absorbed within the atmosphere, and half reaches the Earth's surface. The gases in the atmosphere absorb some wavelengths strongly while allowing other wavelengths to pass freely through. As a result, the wavelength composition of the solar energy that reaches the Earth's surface is different from that emitted by the Sun. For example, the band of ultraviolet wavelengths known as UV-B is strongly absorbed by ozone ($O_3$) in the atmosphere, and thus this wavelength is greatly reduced in the solar energy that reaches the Earth's surface.

### How solar radiation affects climate

Some parts of the Earth's surface receive more energy from the Sun than others. These differences have a great effect on climate.

A major reason for differences in solar radiation from place to place is the fact that Earth is a sphere, or nearly so (figure 59.1*a*). The tropics are particularly warm because the Sun's rays arrive almost perpendicular to the surface of the Earth in regions near the equator. Closer to the poles, the angle at which the Sun's rays strike, called the *angle of incidence*, spreads the solar energy out over more of the Earth's surface, providing less energy per unit of surface area. As figure 59.2 shows, the highest annual mean temperatures occur near the equator (0° latitude).

The Earth's annual orbit around the Sun and its daily rotation on its own axis are also important in determining patterns of solar radiation and their effects on climate (figure 59.1*b*). The axis of rotation of the Earth is not perpendicular to the plane in which the earth orbits the Sun. Because the axis is tilted by approximately 23.5°, a progression of seasons occurs on all parts of the Earth, especially at latitudes far from the equator. The northern hemisphere, for example, tilts toward the Sun during some months but away during others, giving rise to summer and winter.

### Global circulation patterns in the atmosphere

Hot air tends to rise relative to cooler air because the motion of molecules in the air increases as temperature increases, making it less dense. Accordingly, the intense solar heating of the Earth's

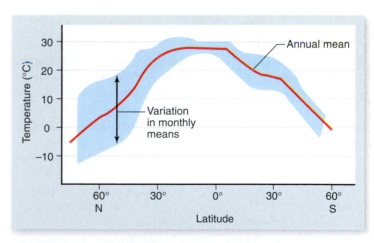

**Figure 59.2   Annual mean temperature varies with latitude.** The red line represents the annual mean temperature at various latitudes, ranging from near the North Pole at the left to near Antarctica at the right; the equator is at 0° latitude. At each latitude, the upper edge of the blue zone is the highest mean monthly temperature observed in all the months of the year, and the lower edge is the lowest mean monthly temperature.

surface at equatorial latitudes causes air to rise from the surface to high in the atmosphere at these latitudes. This rising air is typically rich with water vapor; one reason is that the moisture-holding capacity of air increases when it is heated, and a second reason is that the intense solar radiation at the equator provides the heat needed for great quantities of water to evaporate. After the warm, moist air rises from the surface (figure 59.3), rising air underneath it is pushed away from the equator at high altitudes (above 10 km), to the north in the northern hemisphere and to the south in the southern hemisphere. To take the place of the rising air, cooler air flows toward the equator along the surface from both the north and the south. These air movements give rise to one of the major features of the global atmospheric circulation: air flows toward the equator in both hemispheres at the surface, rises at the equator, and flows away from the equator at high altitudes. The exact patterns of flow are affected by the spinning of the Earth on its axis; we discuss this effect shortly.

For complex reasons, the air circulating up from the equator and away at high altitudes in both hemispheres tends to circulate back down to the surface of the Earth at about 30° of latitude, both north and south (see figure 59.3). During the course of this movement, the moisture content of the air changes radically because of the changes in temperature the air undergoes. Cooling dramatically decreases air's ability to hold water vapor. Consequently, much of the water vapor in the air rising from the equator condenses to form clouds and rain as the air moves upward. This rain falls in the latitudes near the equator, latitudes that experience the greatest precipitation on Earth.

By the time the air starts to descend back to the Earth's surface at latitudes near 30°, it is cold and thus has lost most of its water vapor. Although the air rewarms as it descends, it does not gain much water vapor on the way down. Many of the greatest deserts occur at latitudes near 30° because of the steady descent of dry air to the surface at those latitudes. The Sahara Desert is the most dramatic example.

The air that descends at latitudes near 30° flows only partly toward the equator after reaching the surface of the Earth. Some of it flows toward the poles, helping to give rise in each hemisphere to winds that blow over the Earth's surface from 30° toward 60° latitude. At latitudes near 60° air tends to rise from the surface toward high altitudes.

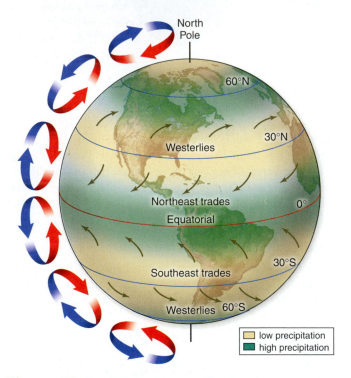

### Inquiry question

**?** Why is it hotter at latitudes near 0°?

## The Coriolis effect

If Earth did not rotate on its axis, global air movements would follow the simple patterns already described. Air currents—the winds—move across a rotating surface, however. Because the solid Earth rotates under the winds, the winds move in curved paths across the surface, rather than straight paths. The curvature of the paths of the winds due to Earth's rotation is termed the **Coriolis effect,** after the 19th-century French mathematician, Gaspard-Gustave Coriolis, who described it.

If you were standing on the North Pole, the Earth would appear to be rotating counterclockwise on its axis, but if you were at the South Pole, the Earth would appear to be rotating clockwise. This property of a rotating sphere, that its direction of rotation is opposite when viewed from its two poles, explains why the direction of the Coriolis effect is opposite in the two hemispheres. In the northern hemisphere, winds always curve to the right of their direction of motion; in the southern hemisphere, they always curve to the left.

The reason for these wind patterns is that the circumference of a sphere, the Earth, changes with latitude. It is zero at the poles and 38,000 km at the equator. Thus, land surface speed changes from about 0 to 1500 km per hour going from the poles to the equator. Air descending at 30° north latitude may be going roughly the same speed as the land surface below it. As it moves toward the equator, however, it is moving more slowly than the surface below it, so it is deflected to its right in the northern hemisphere and to its left in the southern hemisphere. In other words, in both the northern and southern

**Figure 59.3 Global patterns of atmospheric circulation.** The diagram shows the patterns of air circulation that prevail on average over weeks and months of time (on any one day the patterns might be dramatically different from these average patterns). Rising air that is cooled creates bands of relatively high precipitation near the equator and at latitudes near 60°N and 60°S. Air that has lost most of its moisture at high altitudes tends to descend to the surface of the Earth at latitudes near 30°N and 30°S, creating bands of relatively low precipitation. The red arrows show the winds blowing at the surface of the Earth; the blue arrows show the direction the winds blow at high altitude. The winds travel in curved paths relative to the Earth's surface because the Earth is rotating on its axis under them (the Coriolis effect). A terminological problem to recognize is that the formal names given to winds refer to the directions from which they come, rather than the directions toward which they go; thus, the winds between 30° and 60° are called Westerlies because they come out of the west. Unfortunately, oceanographers use the opposite approach, naming water currents for the directions in which they go.

hemispheres, the winds blow westward as well as toward the equator. The result (see figure 59.3) is that winds on both sides of the equator—called the Trade Winds—blow out of the east and toward the west.

Conversely, air masses moving north from 30° are moving more rapidly than underlying land surfaces and thus are deflected again to their right, which in this case is eastward. Similarly, in the southern hemisphere, air masses between 30° and 60° are deflected eastward, to the left. In both hemispheres, therefore, winds between 30° and 60° blow out of the west and toward the east; these winds are called Westerlies.

## Global currents are largely driven by winds

The major ocean currents are driven by the winds at the surface of the Earth, which means that indirectly the currents are driven by solar energy. The radiant input of heat from the Sun sets the atmosphere in motion as already described, and then the winds set the ocean in motion.

In the north Atlantic Ocean (figure 59.4), the global winds follow this pattern: Surface winds tend to blow out of the east and toward the west near the equator, but out of the west and toward the east at midlatitudes (between 30° and 60°). Consequently, surface waters of the north Atlantic Ocean tend to move in a giant closed curve—called a **gyre**—flowing from North America toward Europe at midlatitudes, then re-

turning from Europe and Africa to North America at latitudes near the equator.

Water currents are affected by the Coriolis effect. Thus, the Coriolis effect contributes to this clockwise closed-curve motion. Water flowing across the Atlantic toward Europe at midlatitudes tends to curve to the right and enters the flow from east to west near the equator. This latter flow also tends to curve to its right and enters the flow from west to east at midlatitudes. In the south Atlantic Ocean, the same processes occur in a sort of mirror image, and similar clockwise and counterclockwise gyres occur in the north and south Pacific Ocean as well.

## Regional and local differences affect terrestrial ecosystems

The environmental conditions at a particular place are affected by regional and local effects of solar radiation, air circulation, and water circulation, not just the global patterns of these processes. In this section we look at just a few examples of regional and local effects, focusing on terrestrial systems. These include rain shadows, monsoon winds, elevation, and presence of microclimate factors.

### Rain shadows

Deserts on land sometimes occur because mountain ranges intercept moisture-laden winds from the sea. When air flowing

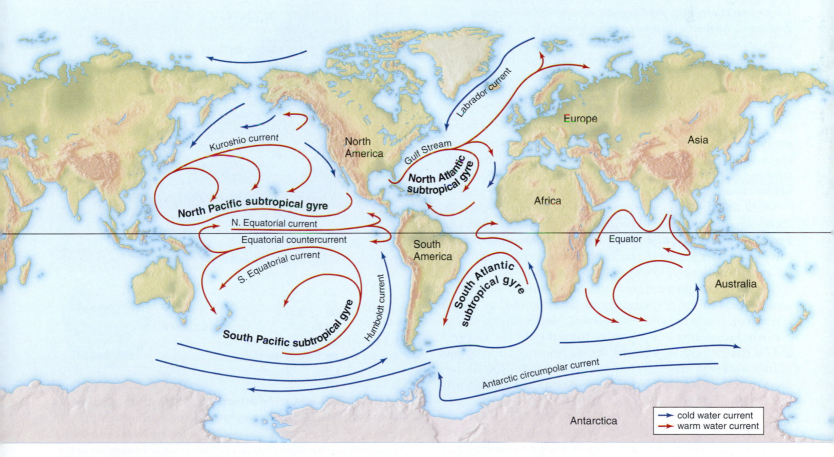

**Figure 59.4 Ocean circulation.** In the centers of several of the great ocean basins, surface water moves in great closed-curve patterns called gyres. These water movements affect biological productivity in the oceans and sometimes profoundly affect the climate on adjacent landmasses, as when the Gulf Stream brings warm water to the region of the British Isles.

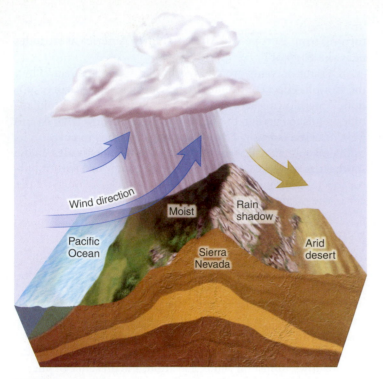

**Figure 59.5 The rain shadow effect exemplified in California.** Moisture-laden winds from the Pacific Ocean rise and are cooled when they encounter the Sierra Nevada Mountains. As the moisture-holding capacity of the air decreases at colder, higher altitudes, precipitation occurs, making the seaward-facing slopes of the mountains moist; tall forests occur on those slopes, including forests that contain the famous giant sequoias *(Sequoiadendron giganteum)*. As the air descends on the eastern side of the mountain range, its moisture-holding capacity increases again, and the air picks up moisture from its surroundings. As a result, the eastern slopes of the mountains are arid, and rain shadow deserts sometimes occur.

landward from the oceans encounters a mountain range (figure 59.5), the air rises, and its moisture-holding capacity decreases because it becomes cooler at higher altitude, causing precipitation to fall on the mountain slopes facing the sea.

As the air—stripped of much of its moisture—then descends on the other side of the mountain range, it remains dry even as it is warmed, and as it is warmed its moisture-holding capacity increases, meaning it can readily take up moisture from soils and plants.

One consequence is that the two slopes of a mountain range often differ dramatically in how moist they are; in California, for example, the eastern slopes of the Sierra Nevada Mountains—facing away from the Pacific Ocean—are far drier than the western slopes. Another consequence is that a desert may develop on the dry side, the Mojave Desert being an example. The mountains are said to produce a rain shadow.

### Monsoons

The continent of Asia is so huge that heating and cooling of its surface during the passage of the seasons causes massive regional shifts in wind patterns. During summer, the surface of the Asian landmass heats up more than the surrounding oceans,

but during winter the landmass cools more than the oceans. The consequence is that winds tend to blow off the water into the interior of the Asian continent in summer, particularly in the region of the Indian Ocean and western tropical Pacific Ocean. These winds reverse to flow off the continent out over the oceans in winter. These seasonally shifting winds are called the monsoons. They affect rainfall patterns, and their duration and strength can spell the difference between food sufficiency and starvation for hundreds of millions of people in the region each year.

### Elevation

Another significant regional pattern is that in mountainous regions, temperature and other conditions change with elevation. At any given latitude, air temperature falls about 6°C for every 1000-m increase in elevation. The ecological consequences of the change of temperature with elevation are similar to those of the change of temperature with latitude (figure 59.6).

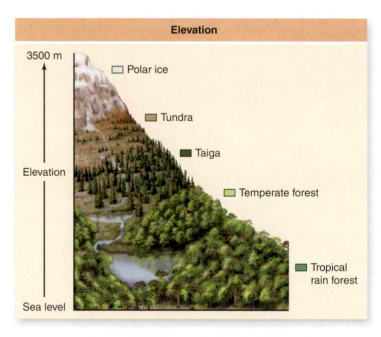

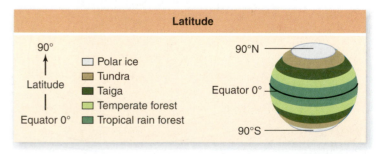

**Figure 59.6 Elevation affects the distribution of biomes in much the same manner as latitude does.** Biomes that normally occur far north of the equator at sea level also occur in the tropics at high mountain elevations. Thus, on a tall mountain in the tropics, one might see a sequence of biomes like the one illustrated above. In North America, a 1000-m increase in elevation results in a temperature drop equal to that of an 880-km increase in latitude.

## Microclimates

Conditions also vary in significant ways on very small spatial scales. For example, in a forest, a bird sitting in an open patch may experience intense solar radiation, a high air temperature, and a low humidity, even while a mouse hiding under a log 10 feet away may experience shade, a cool temperature, and air saturated with water vapor. Such highly localized sets of climatic conditions are called microclimates.

In some cases, species avoid competing by adapting to use different microclimates. Sympatric salamanders, for example, may be specialized for the different levels of moisture found in different parts of the habitat.

### Learning Outcomes Review 59.1

More intense solar heating of some global regions relative to others sets up global patterns of atmospheric circulation, which in turn cause global patterns of water circulation in the oceans. The Coriolis effect is caused by the Earth's spin beneath the moving air masses of the atmosphere. These patterns—plus seasonal changes—strongly affect the conditions that exist for living organisms in different parts of the world. In general, temperature declines as altitude or latitude increases.

■ *How would global air movement patterns be different if the Earth turned in the opposite direction?*

## 59.2 Earth's Biomes

### Learning Outcomes

1.  Define biome.
2.  Explain the primary factors that determine which type of biome is found in a particular place.

**Biomes** are major types of ecosystems on land. Each biome has a characteristic appearance and is distributed over wide areas of land defined largely by sets of regional climatic conditions. Biomes are named according to their vegetational structures, but they also include the animals that are present.

As you might imagine from the broad definition given for biomes, there are a number of ways to classify terrestrial ecosystems into biomes. Here we recognize eight principal biomes: (1) tropical rain forest, (2) savanna, (3) desert, (4) temperate grassland, (5) temperate deciduous forest, (6) temperate evergreen forest, (7) taiga, (8) tundra.

Six additional biomes recognized by some ecologists are: polar ice, mountain zone, chaparral, warm moist evergreen forest, tropical monsoon forest, and semidesert. Other ecologists lump these six with the eight major ones. Figure 59.7 shows the distributions of all 14 biomes.

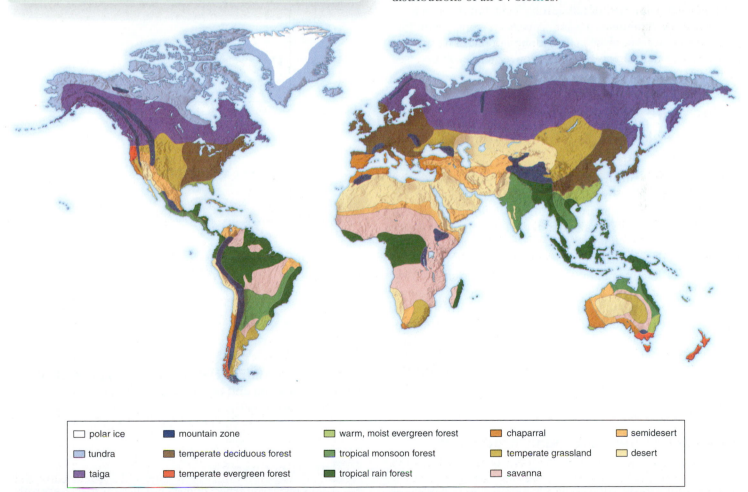

| | | | | |
|---|---|---|---|---|
| ☐ polar ice | ■ mountain zone | ■ warm, moist evergreen forest | ■ chaparral | ■ semidesert |
| ☐ tundra | ■ temperate deciduous forest | ■ tropical monsoon forest | ■ temperate grassland | ☐ desert |
| ■ taiga | ■ temperate evergreen forest | ■ tropical rain forest | ■ savanna | |

**Figure 59.7  The distributions of biomes.** Each biome is similar in vegetational structure and appearance wherever it occurs.

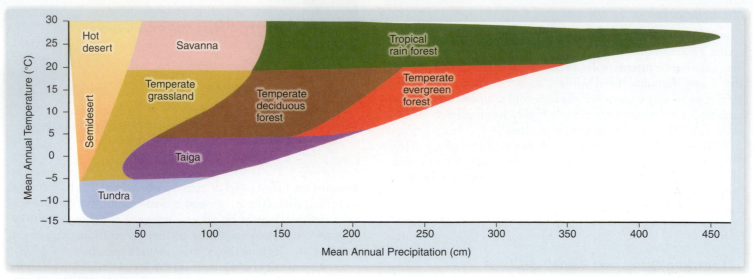

**Figure 59.8 Predictors of biome distribution.** Temperature and precipitation are quite useful predictors of biome distribution, although other factors sometimes also play critical roles.

Biomes are defined by their characteristic vegetational structures and associated climatic conditions, rather than by the presence of particular plant species. Two regions assigned to the same biome thus may differ in the species that dominate the landscape. Tropical rain forests around the world, for example, are all composed of tall, lushly vegetated trees, but the tree species that dominate a South American tropical rain forest are different from those in an Indonesian one. The similarity between such forests results from convergent evolution (see chapter 21).

## Temperature and moisture often determine biomes

In determining which biomes are found where, two key environmental factors are temperature and moisture. As seen in figure 59.8, if you know the mean annual temperature and mean annual precipitation in a terrestrial region, you often can predict the biome that dominates. Temperature and moisture affect ecosystems in a number of ways. One reason they are so influential is that primary productivity is strongly correlated with them, as described in the preceding chapter (figure 59.9).

Different places that are similar in mean annual temperature and precipitation sometimes support different biomes, indicating that temperature and moisture are not the only factors that can be important. Soil structure and mineral composition (see chapter 39) are among the other factors that can be influential. The biome that is present may also depend on whether the conditions of temperature and precipitation are strongly seasonal or relatively constant.

## Tropical rain forests are highly productive equatorial systems

**Tropical rain forests,** which typically require 140 to 450 cm of rain per year, are the richest ecosystems on land (figure 59.10).

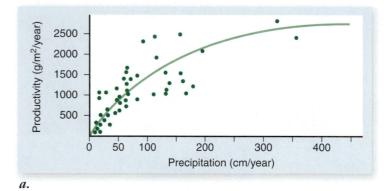

*a.*

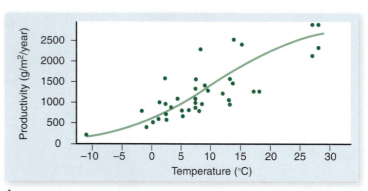

*b.*

**Figure 59.9 The correlations of primary productivity with precipitation and temperature.** The net primary productivity of ecosystems at 52 locations around the globe correlates significantly with (*a*) mean annual precipitation and (*b*) mean annual temperature.

**Inquiry question**

? Why might you expect primary productivity to increase with increasing precipitation and temperature?

**Figure 59.10**
Tropical rainforest.

They are very productive because they enjoy the advantages of both high temperature and high precipitation (see figure 59.9). They also exhibit very high biodiversity, being home to at least half of all the species of terrestrial plants and animals—over 2 million species! In a single square mile of Brazilian rain forest, there can be 1200 species of butterflies—twice the number found in all of North America. Tropical rain forests recycle nutrients rapidly, so their soils often lack great reservoirs of nutrients.

## Savannas are tropical grasslands with seasonal rainfall

The **savannas** are tropical or subtropical grasslands, often dotted with widely spaced trees or shrubs. On a global scale, savannas often occur as transition ecosystems between tropical rain forests and deserts; they are characteristic of warm places where annual rainfall (50–125 cm) is too little to support rain forest, but not so little as to produce desert conditions.

Rainfall is often highly seasonal in savannas. The Serengeti ecosystem in East Africa is probably the world's most famous example of the savanna biome. In most of the Serengeti, no rain falls for many months of the year, but during other months rain is abundant. The huge herds of grazing animals in the ecosystem respond to the seasonality of the rain; a number of species migrate away from permanently flowing rivers only during the months when rain falls.

## Deserts are regions with little rainfall

**Deserts** are dry places where rain is both sparse (annual rainfall often less than 25–40 cm) and unpredictable. The unpredictability means that plants and animals cannot depend on experiencing rain even once each year. As mentioned earlier, many of the largest deserts occur at latitudes near 30°N and 30°S because of global air circulation patterns (see figure 59.3). Other deserts result from rain shadows (see figure 59.5).

Vegetation is sparse in deserts, and survival of both plants and animals depends on water conservation. Many desert organisms enter inactive stages during rainless periods. To avoid extreme temperatures, small desert vertebrates often live in deep, cool, and sometimes even somewhat moist burrows. Some emerge only at night. Among large desert animals, camels drink large quantities of water when it is available and then conserve it so well that they can survive for weeks without drinking. Oryxes (large, desert-dwelling antelopes) survive opportunistically on moisture in leaves or roots that they dig up, as well as drinking water when possible.

## Temperate grasslands have rich soils

Halfway between the equator and the poles are temperate regions where rich temperate grasslands grow. These grasslands, also called **prairies,** once covered much of the interior of North America, and they were widespread in Eurasia and South America as well.

The roots of perennial grasses characteristically penetrate far into the soil, and grassland soils tend to be deep and fertile. Temperate grasslands are often highly productive when converted to agricultural use, and vast areas have been transformed in this way. In North America prior to this change in land use, huge herds of bison and pronghorn antelope inhabited the temperate grasslands, migrating seasonally as resources changed over the course of the year. Natural temperate grasslands are one of the biomes adapted to periodic fire and therefore need fires to prosper.

## Temperate deciduous forests are adapted to seasonal change

Mild but seasonal climates (warm summers and cold winters), plus plentiful rains, promote the growth of temperate deciduous forests in the eastern United States, eastern Canada, and Eurasia (figure 59.11). A deciduous tree is one that drops its leaves in the winter. Deer, bears, beavers, and raccoons are familiar animals of these forests.

## Temperate evergreen forests are coastal

**Temperate evergreen forests** occur along coastlines with temperate climates, such as in the northwest of the United States. The dominant vegetation includes trees, such as spruces, pines, and redwoods, that do not drop their leaves (thus, they are *ever green*).

## Taiga is the northern forest where winters are harsh

Taiga and tundra (described next) differ from other biomes in that both stretch in great unbroken circles around the entire globe (see figure 58.7). The taiga consists of a great band of northern forest dominated by coniferous trees (spruce, hemlock, and fir) that retain their needle-like leaves all year long.

**Figure 59.11  Temperate deciduous forest.**

The taiga is one of the largest biomes on Earth. The winters where taiga occurs are severely long and cold, and most of the limited precipitation falls in the summer. Many large herbivores, including elk, moose, and deer, plus carnivores such as wolves, bears, lynx, and wolverines, are characteristic of the taiga.

## Tundra is a largely frozen treeless area with a short growing season

In the far north, at latitudes above the taiga but south of the polar ice, few trees grow. The landscape that occurs in this band, called tundra, is open, windswept, and often boggy. This enormous biome covers one-fifth of the Earth's land surface. Little rain or snow falls. **Permafrost**—soil ice that persists throughout all seasons—usually exists within a meter of the ground surface.

What trees can be found are small and mostly confined to the margins of streams and lakes. Large grazing mammals, including musk-oxen and reindeer (caribou), and carnivores such as wolves, foxes, and lynx, live in the tundra. Populations of lemmings (a small rodent native to the Arctic) rise and fall dramatically, with important consequences for the animals that prey on them.

### Learning Outcomes Review 59.2

Major types of ecosystems called biomes can be distinguished in different climatic regions on land. These biomes are much the same wherever they are found on the Earth. Annual mean temperature and precipitation are effective predictors of biome type; however, the range of seasonal variation and the soil characteristics of a region also come into play.

■ *Why do different biomes occur at different latitudes?*

## 59.3  Freshwater Habitats

### Learning Outcomes

1. *Define photic zone.*
2. *Explain what causes spring and fall overturns in lakes.*
3. *Distinguish between eutrophic and oligotrophic lakes.*

Of the major habitats, fresh water covers by far the smallest percentage of the Earth's surface: Only 2%, compared with 27% for land and 71% for ocean. The formation of fresh water starts with the evaporation of water into the atmosphere, which removes most dissolved constituents, much like distillation does. When water falls back to the Earth's surface as rain or snow, it arrives in an almost pure state, although it may have picked up biologically significant dissolved or particulate matter from the atmosphere.

Freshwater wetlands—marshes, swamps, and bogs—represent intermediate habitats between the freshwater and terrestrial realms. Wetlands are highly productive (see figure 58.11).

They also play key additional roles, such as acting as water storage basins that moderate flooding.

Primary production in freshwater bodies is carried out by single-celled algae (phytoplankton) floating in the water, by algae growing as films on the bottom, and by rooted plants such as water lilies. In addition, a considerable amount of organic matter—such as dead leaves—enters some bodies of fresh water from plant communities growing on the land nearby.

## Life in freshwater habitats depends on oxygen availability

The concentration of dissolved oxygen ($O_2$) is a major determinant of the properties of freshwater communities. Oxygen dissolves in water just like sugar or salt does. Fish and other aquatic organisms obtain the oxygen they need by taking it up from solution. The solubility of oxygen is therefore critically important.

In reality, oxygen is not very soluble in water. Consequently, even when fresh water is fully aerated and at equilibrium with the atmosphere, the amount of oxygen it contains per liter is only 5%, or less, of that in air. This means that, in terms of acquiring the oxygen they need, freshwater organisms have a far smaller margin of safety than air-breathing ones.

Oxygen is constantly added to and removed from any body of fresh water. Oxygen is added by photosynthesis and by aeration from the atmosphere, and it is removed by animals and other heterotrophs. If a lot of decaying organic matter is present in a body of water, the oxygen demand of the decay microbes can be high and affect other life forms. Under conditions in which the rate of oxygen removal from water exceeds the rate of addition, the concentration of dissolved oxygen can fall so low that many aquatic animals cannot survive in it.

## Lake and pond habitats change with water depth

Bodies of relatively still fresh water are called lakes if large and ponds if small. Water absorbs light passing through it, and the intensity of sunlight available for photosynthesis decreases sharply with increasing depth. In deep lakes, only water relatively near the surface receives enough light for phytoplankton to exhibit a positive net primary productivity (figure 59.12). Those waters are described as the photic zone.

### The photic zone

The thickness of the photic zone depends on how much particulate matter is in the water. Water that is relatively free of particulate matter and clear allows light to penetrate to a depth of 10 m at sufficient intensity to support phytoplankton. Water that is thick with surface algal cells or soil from erosion may not allow light to penetrate very far before its intensity becomes too diminished for algal growth.

The supply of dissolved oxygen to the deep waters of a lake can be a problem because all oxygen enters any aquatic system near its surface. In the still waters of a lake, mixing between the surface and deeper layers may not occur except occasionally. When photosynthesis produces oxygen, it adds it to the photic zone of the lake near the surface. Thermal stratifica-

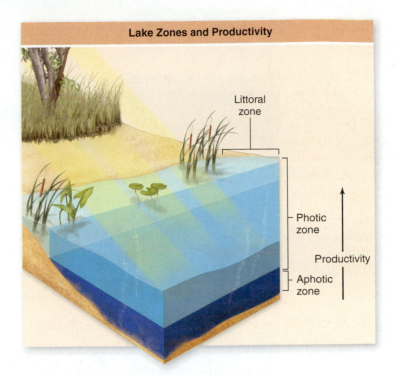

**Figure 59.12  Light in a lake.** The intensity of the sunlight available for photosynthesis decreases with depth in a lake. Consequently, only some of the upper waters—termed the photic zone—receive sufficient light for the net primary productivity of phytoplankton to be positive. The depth of the photic zone depends on how cloudy the water is. The shallows at the edge of a lake are called the littoral zone. They are well-illuminated to the bottom, so rooted plants and bottom algae can thrive there.

tion commonly affects how readily oxygen enters the deep waters from the surface waters.

### Thermal stratification

**Thermal stratification** is characteristic of many lakes and large ponds. In summer, as shown at the bottom of figure 59.13, water warmed by the Sun forms a layer known as the *epilimnion* at the surface—because warm water is less dense than cold water and tends to float on top. Colder, denser water, called the *hypolimnion*, lies below. Between the warm and cold layers is a transitional layer, the thermocline. Although here we are focusing on fresh water, a similar thermal structuring of the water column occurs also in many parts of the ocean.

In a lake, thermal stratification tends to cut off the oxygen supply to the bottom waters; a consequence of the stratification is that the upper waters that receive oxygen do not mix with the bottom waters. The concentration of oxygen at the bottom may then gradually decline over time as the organisms living there use oxygen faster than it is replaced. If the rate of oxygen use is high, the bottom waters may run out of oxygen and become oxygen-free before summer is over. Oxygen-free conditions, if they occur, kill most (although not all) animals.

In autumn, the temperature of the upper waters in a stratified lake drops until it is about the same as the temperature of the deep waters. The densities of the two water layers become similar, and the tendency for them to stay apart is weakened.

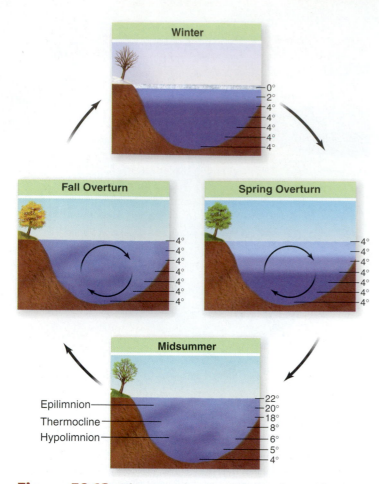

**Figure 59.13** **The annual cycle of thermal stratification in a temperate-zone lake.** During the summer (lower diagram), water warmed by the Sun (the epilimnion) floats on top of colder, denser water (the hypolimnion). The lake is also thermally stratified in winter (upper diagram) when water that is near freezing or frozen floats on top of water that is at 4°C (the temperature of greatest density for fresh water). Stratification is disrupted in the spring and fall overturns, when the lake is at an approximately uniform temperature and winds mix it from top to bottom.

Winds can then force the layers to mix, a phenomenon called the fall overturn (see figure 59.13). High oxygen concentrations are then restored in the bottom waters.

Chapter 2 discussed the unique properties of water. Fresh water is densest when its temperature is 4°C, and ice, at 0°, floats on top of this dense water. As a lake is cooled toward the freezing point with the onset of winter, the whole lake first reaches 4°C. Then, some water cools to an even lower temperature, and when it does, it becomes less dense and rises to the top. Further cooling of this surface water causes it to freeze into a layer of ice covering the lake. In spring, the ice melts, the surface water warms up, and again winds are able to mix the whole lake—the spring overturn.

Because temperature changes less over the course of the year in the tropics, many lakes there do not experience turnover. As a result, tropical lakes can have a permanent thermocline with depletion of oxygen near the bottom.

## Lakes differ in oxygen and nutrient content

Bodies of fresh water that are low in algal nutrients (such as nitrate or phosphate) and low in the amount of algal material per unit of volume are termed *oligotrophic*. Such waters are often crystal clear. Oligotrophic streams and rivers tend to be high in dissolved oxygen because the movement of the flowing water aerates them; the small amount of organic matter in the water means that oxygen is used at a relatively low rate. Similarly, oligotrophic lakes and ponds tend to be high in dissolved oxygen at all depths all year because they also have a low rate of oxygen use. Because the water is relatively clear, light can penetrate the waters readily, allowing photosynthesis to occur through much of the water column, from top to bottom (figure 59.14).

**Eutrophic** bodies of water are high in algal nutrients and often populated densely with algae. They are more likely to be low in dissolved oxygen, especially in summer. In a eutrophic body of water, decay microbes often place high demands on the

*a.*  *b.*

**Figure 59.14** **Oligotrophic and eutrophic lakes.** *a.* Oligotrophic lakes are low in algal nutrients, have high levels of dissolved oxygen, and are clear. *b.* Eutrophic lakes have high levels of algal nutrients and low levels of dissolved oxygen. Light does not penetrate deeply in such lakes.

oxygen available because when thick populations of algae die, large amounts of organic matter are made available for decomposition. Moreover, light does not penetrate eutrophic waters well because of all the organic matter in the water; photosynthetic oxygen addition is therefore limited to just a relatively thin layer of water at the top.

Human activities have often transformed oligotrophic lakes into eutrophic ones. For example, when people overfertilize their lawns or fields, nitrate and phosphate from the fertilizers wash off into local water systems. Lakes that receive these nutrients become more eutrophic. A consequence is that the bottom waters are more likely to become oxygen-free during the summer. Many species of fish that are characteristic of oligotrophic lakes, such as trout, are very sensitive to oxygen deprivation. When lakes become eutrophic, these species of fish disappear and are replaced with species like carp that can better tolerate low oxygen concentrations. Lakes can return toward an oligotrophic state over time if steps are taken to eliminate the addition of excess nitrates, phosphates, and foreign organic matter such as sewage.

### Learning Outcomes Review 59.3

The photic zone is the layer near the surface into which light penetrates. Photosynthesis can occur only in the photic zone. Thermal stratification is a major determinant of oxygen levels. In temperate lakes, mixing of different layers occurs when the layers reach the same temperature in spring and fall, and winds can cause the layers to mix. This overturn prevents oxygen depletion near the lake bottom. Eutrophic lakes are high in nutrients for algae but are low in dissolved oxygen; oligotrophic lakes are low in nutrients but high in dissolved oxygen at all depths.

■ *Why do tropical lakes often not experience seasonal turnover, and what effect is this likely to have on the ecosystems of these lakes?*

## 59.4 Marine Habitats

### Learning Outcomes

1. *Know the different marine habitats.*
2. *Explain why El Niño events occur.*

About 71% of the Earth's surface is covered by ocean. Near the coastlines of the continents are the continental shelves, where the water is not especially deep (figure 59.15); the shelves, in essence, represent the submerged edges of the continents. Worldwide, the shelves average about 80 km wide, and the depth of the water over them increases from 1 m to about 130 m as one travels from the coast toward the open ocean.

Beyond the continental shelves, the depth suddenly becomes much greater. The average depth of the open ocean is 4000 to 5000 m, and some parts—called trenches—are far deeper, reaching 11,000 m in the Marianas Trench in the western Pacific Ocean.

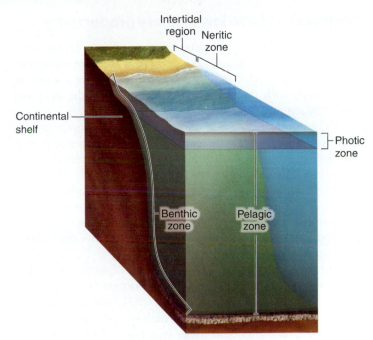

**Figure 59.15  Basic concepts and terminology used in describing marine ecosystems.** The continental shelf is the submerged edge of the continent. The waters over it are termed neritic and, on a worldwide average basis, are only 130 m deep at their deepest. The region where the tides rise and fall along the shoreline is called the intertidal region. The bottom is called the benthic zone, whereas the water column in the open ocean is called the pelagic zone. The photic zone is the part of the pelagic zone in which enough light penetrates for the phytoplankton to have a positive net primary productivity. The vertical scale of this drawing is highly compressed; whereas the outer edge of the continental shelf is 130 m deep, the open ocean in fact averages 35 times deeper (4000–5000 m deep).

In most of the ocean, the principal primary producers are phytoplankton floating in the well-lit surface waters. A revolution is currently underway in scientific understanding of the limiting nutrients for ocean phytoplankton (see chapter 58). Primary production by the phytoplankton is presently understood to be nitrogen-limited in about two-thirds of the world's ocean, but iron-limited in about one-third. The principal known iron-limited areas are the great Southern Ocean surrounding Antarctica, parts of the equatorial Pacific Ocean, and parts of the subarctic, northeast Pacific Ocean. Where the water is shallow along coastlines, primary production is carried out not just by phytoplankton but also by rooted plants such as seagrasses and by bottom-dwelling algae, including seaweeds.

The world's ocean is so vast that it includes many different types of ecosystems. Some, such as coral reefs and estuaries, are high in their net primary productivity per unit of area (see figure 58.11), but others are low in productivity per unit area. Ocean ecosystems are of four major types: open oceans, continental shelf ecosystems, upwelling regions, and deep sea.

## Open oceans have low primary productivity

In speaking of the open oceans, we mean the waters far from land (beyond the continental shelves) that are near enough to the surface to receive sunlight or to interact on a daily or weekly basis with those waters. We will discuss the deep sea separately later on.

The intensity of solar illumination in the open oceans drops from being high at the surface to being essentially zero at 200 m of depth; photosynthesis is limited to this level of the ocean. However, nutrients for phytoplankton, such as nitrate, tend to be present at low concentrations in the photic zone because over eons of time in the past, ecological processes have exported nitrate and other nutrients from the upper waters to the deep waters, and no vigorous forces exist in the open ocean to return the nutrients to the sunlit waters.

Because of the low concentrations of nutrients in the photic zone, large parts of the open oceans are low in primary productivity per unit area (see figure 58.11) and aptly called a "biological desert." These parts—which correspond to the centers of the great midocean gyres (see figure 59.4)—are often collectively termed the *oligotrophic ocean* (figure 59.16) in reference to their low nutrient levels and low productivity.

People fish the open oceans today for only a few species, such as tunas and some species of squids and whales. Fishing in the open oceans is limited to relatively few species for two reasons. First, because of the low primary productivity per unit of area, animals tend to be thinly distributed in the open oceans. The only ones that are commercially profitable to catch are those that are individually large or tend to gather together in tight schools. Second, costs for travelling far from land are high. All authorities agree that as we turn to the sea to help feed the burgeoning human population, we cannot expect the open ocean regions to supply great quantities of food.

## Continental shelf ecosystems provide abundant resources

Many of the ecosystems on the continental shelves are relatively high in productivity per unit area. An important reason is that the waters over the shelves—termed the **neritic waters** (see figure 59.15)—tend to have relatively high concentrations of nitrate and other nutrients, averaged over the year.

Because the waters over the shelves are shallow, they have not been subject, over the eons of time, to the loss of nutrients into the deep sea, as the open oceans have. Over the shelves, nutrient-rich materials that sink hit the shallow bottom, and the nutrients they contain are stirred back into the water column by stormy weather. In addition, nutrients are continually replenished by run-off from nearby land.

Around 99% of the food people harvest from the ocean comes from continental shelf ecosystems or nearby upwelling regions. The shelf ecosystems are also particularly important to humankind in other ways. Mineral resources taken from the ocean, such as petroleum, come almost exclusively from the shelves. In addition, almost all recreational uses of the ocean, from sailing to scuba diving, take place on the shelves. The

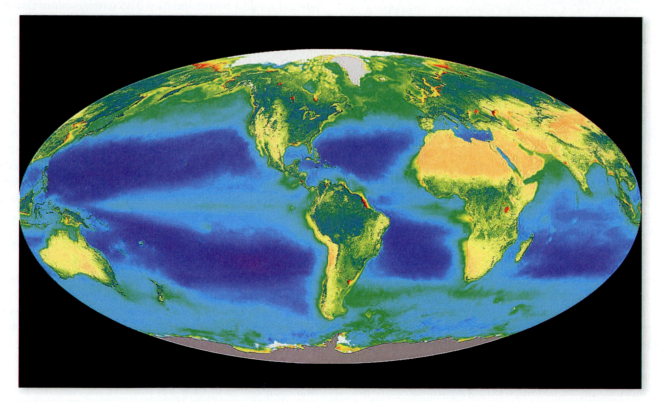

**Figure 59.16** **Major functional regions of the ocean.** The regions classed as oligotrophic ocean (*colored dark blue*) are "biological deserts" with low productivity per unit area. Continental shelf ecosystems (*green at the edge of continents*) are typically medium to high in productivity. Upwelling regions (*yellow at the edge of continents*) are the highest in productivity per unit area and rank with the most productive of all ecosystems on Earth.

shelves feature prominently in these ways because they are close to coastlines and relatively shallow.

## Estuaries

Estuaries are one of the types of shelf ecosystems. An estuary is a place along a coastline, such as a bay, that is partially surrounded by land and in which fresh water from streams or rivers mixes with ocean water, creating intermediate (brackish) salinities.

Estuaries, besides being bodies of water, include intertidal marshes or swamps. An **intertidal** habitat is an area that is exposed to air at low tide but under water at high tide. The marshes of the intertidal zone are called **salt marshes.** Intertidal swamps called **mangrove swamps** (dominated by trees and bushes) occur in tropical and subtropical parts of the world.

Estuaries are a vital and highly productive ecosystem—they provide shelter and food for many aquatic animals, especially the larvae and young, that people harvest for food. Estuaries are also important to a very large number of other animal species, such as migrating birds.

## Banks and coral reefs

Other types of shelf ecosystems include banks and coral reefs. **Banks** are local shallow areas on the shelves, often extremely important as fishing grounds; Georges Bank, 100 km off the shore of Massachusetts, was formerly one of the most productive and famous; much of this area has been closed to fishing since the mid-1990s because of overexploitation.

**Coral reef** ecosystems occur in subtropical and tropical latitudes. Their defining feature is that in them, stony corals—corals that secrete a solid, calcified type of skeleton—build three-dimensional frameworks that form a unique habitat in which many other distinctive organisms live, including reef fish and soft corals (figure 59.17).

**Figure 59.17  A coral reef ecosystem.** Reef-building corals, which consist of symbioses between cnidarians and algae, construct the three-dimensional structure of the reef and carry out considerable primary production. Fish and many other kinds of animals find food and shelter, making these ecosystems among the most diverse. About 20% of all fish species occur specifically in coral reef ecosystems.

All the 700 or so species of reef-building corals are animal–algal symbioses; the animals are cnidarians, and dino-flagellate symbionts live within the cells of their inner cell layer (the gastrodermis). These corals depend on photosynthesis by the algal symbionts, and thus require clear waters through which sunlight can readily penetrate. Reef-building corals are threatened worldwide, as described later in this chapter.

## Upwelling regions experience mixing of nutrients and oxygen

The upwelling regions of the ocean are localized places where deep water is drawn consistently to the surface because of the action of local forces such as local winds. The deep water is often rich in nitrate and other nutrients. Upwelling therefore steadily brings nutrients into the well-lit surface layers. Phytoplankton respond to the abundance of nutrients and light with prolific growth and reproduction. Upwelling regions have the highest primary productivity per unit area in the world's ocean.

The most famous upwelling region (see figure 59.16) is found along the coast of Peru and Ecuador, where upwelling occurs year-round. Another important upwelling region is the coastline of California, along which upwelling occurs during about half the year in the summer, explaining why swimmers find cold water at the beaches even in July and August.

Upwelling regions support prolific but vulnerable fisheries. Sardine fishing in the California upwelling region crashed a few decades ago, but previously was enormously important to the region, as Nobel Prize–winning author John Steinbeck chronicled in a number of his books, most notably *Cannery Row.*

### El Niño Southern Oscillation (ENSO)

The phenomenon named El Niño first came to the attention of science in studies of the Peru–Ecuador upwelling region. In that region, every 2 to 7 years on an irregular and relatively unpredictable basis, the water along the coastline becomes profoundly warm, and simultaneously the primary productivity becomes unusually low.

Because of the low primary productivity, the ordinarily prolific fish populations weaken, and populations of seabirds and sea mammals that depend on the fish are stressed or plummet. The local people had named a mild annual warming event, which occurred around Christmas each year, "El Niño" (literally, "the child," after the Christ Child). Scientists adopted the term El Niño Southern Oscillation (ENSO) to refer to those dramatic warming events.

The immediate cause of El Niño took several decades to figure out, but research ultimately showed that the cause is a weakening of the east-to-west Trade Winds in the region. The Trade Winds ordinarily blow warm surface water to the west, away from the Peru–Ecuador coast. This thins the warm surface layer of water along the coast, so that deep water—cold but highly rich in nutrients—is drawn to the surface, leading to high primary production.

Weakening of the Trade Winds allows the warm surface layer to become thicker. Upwelling continues, but under such circumstances it merely recirculates the thick warm surface layer, which is nutrient-depleted.

After these fundamentals had been discovered, researchers in the 1980s realized that the weakening of the Trade Winds is actually part of a change in wind circulation patterns that recurs irregularly. One reason the Trade Winds blow east-to-west in ordinary times is that the surface waters in the western equatorial Pacific are warmer than those in the eastern equatorial Pacific; air rises from the warm western areas, creating low pressure at the surface there, and air blows out of the east into the low pressure. During an El Niño, the warmer the eastern ocean gets, the more similar it becomes to the western ocean, reducing the difference in pressure across the ocean. Thus, once the Trade Winds weaken a bit, the pressure difference that makes them blow is lessened, weakening the Trade Winds further. Warm water ordinarily kept in the west by the Trade Winds creeps progressively eastward at equatorial latitudes because of this self-reinforcing series of events. Ultimately, effects of El Niño occur across large parts of the world's weather systems, affecting sea temperatures in California, rainfall in the southwestern United States, and even systems as far distant as Africa.

One specific result is to shift the weather systems of the western Pacific Ocean 6000 km eastward. The tropical rainstorms that usually drench Indonesia and the Philippines occur when warm seawater abutting these islands causes the air above it to rise, cool, and condense its moisture into clouds. When the warm water moves east, so do the clouds, leaving the previously rainy areas in drought. Conversely, the western edge of Peru and Ecuador, which usually receives little precipitation, gets a soaking.

El Niño can wreak havoc on ecosystems. During an El Niño event, plankton can drop to 1/20 of their normal abundance in the waters of Peru and Ecuador, and because of the drop in plankton productivity, commercial fish stocks virtually disappear (figure 59.18). In the Galápagos Islands, for example, seabird and sea lion populations crash as animals starve due to the lack of fish. By contrast, on land, the heavy rains produce a

*a.*     *b.*

**Figure 59.19  Life in the deep sea.** *a.* The luminous spot below the eye of this deep-sea fish results from the presence of a symbiotic colony of bioluminescent bacteria. Bioluminescence is a fairly common feature of mobile animals in the parts of the ocean that are so deep as to be dark. It is more common among species living part way down to the bottom than in ones living at the bottom. *b.* These large worms live along vents where hot water containing hydrogen sulfide rises through cracks in the seafloor crust. Much of the body of each worm is devoted to a colony of symbiotic sulfur-oxidizing bacteria. The worms transport sulfide and oxygen to the bacteria, which oxidize the sulfur and use the energy thereby obtained for primary production of new organic compounds, which they share with their worm hosts.

bumper crop of seeds, and land birds flourish. In Chile, similar effects on seed abundance propagate up the food chain, leading first to increased rodent populations and then to increased predator populations, a nice example of a bottom-up trophic cascade, as was discussed in chapter 58.

## The deep sea is a cold, dark place with some fascinating communities

The deep sea is by far the single largest habitat on Earth, in the sense that it is a huge region characterized by relatively uniform conditions throughout the globe. The deep sea is seasonless, cold (2–5°C), totally dark, and under high pressure (400–500 atmospheres where the bottom is 4000–5000 m deep).

In most regions of the deep sea, food originates from photosynthesis in the sunlit waters far above. Such food—in the form of carcasses, fecal pellets, and mucus—can take as much as a month to drift down from the surface to the bottom, and along the way about 99% of it is eaten by animals living in the water column. Thus, the bottom communities receive only about 1% of the primary production and are food-poor. Nonetheless, a great many species of animals—most of them small-bodied and thinly distributed—are now known to live in the deep sea. Some of the animals are bioluminescent (figure 59.19a) and thereby able to communicate or attract prey by use of light.

### Hydrothermal vent communities

The most astounding communities in the deep sea are the hydrothermal vent communities. Unlike most parts of the deep

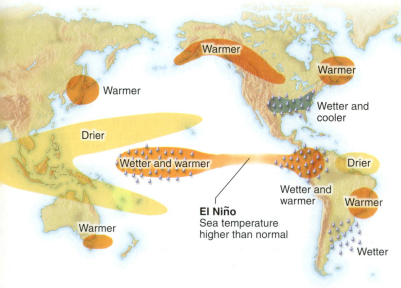

**Figure 59.18  An El Niño winter.** This diagram shows just some of the worldwide alterations of weather that are often associated with the El Niño phenomenon.

sea, these communities are thick with life (figure 59.19b), including large-bodied animals such as worms the size of baseball bats. The reason such a profusion of life can be supported is that these communities live on vigorous, local primary production rather than depending on the photic zone far above.

The hydrothermal vent communities occur at places where tectonic plates are moving apart, and seawater—circulating through porous rock—is able to come into contact with very hot rock under the seafloor. This water is heated to temperatures in excess of 350°C and, in the process, becomes rich in hydrogen sulfide.

As the water rises up out of the porous rock, free-living and symbiotic bacteria oxidize the sulfide, and from this reaction they obtain energy, which, in a manner analogous to photosynthesis, they use to synthesize their own cellular substance, grow, and reproduce. These sulfur-oxidizing bacteria are chemoautotrophs (see chapter 58). Animals in the communities either survive on the bacteria or eat other animals that do. The hydrothermal vent communities are among the few communities on Earth that do not depend on the Sun's energy for primary production.

### Learning Outcomes Review 59.4

The oligotrophic ocean includes the open ocean and the deep sea, where little primary productivity occurs. Continental shelf ecosystems tend to be moderate to high in productivity; they include estuaries, salt marshes, fishing banks, and coral reefs. The highest levels of productivity are found in upwelling regions, such as those along the west coasts of North and South America, where prolific but vulnerable fisheries can be found. Periodic weakening of the Trade Winds in this region can prevent the upwelling of cold water and subsequently cause weather changes in an event termed El Niño.

■ **What sort of population cycles would you expect to see in regions that are affected by the ENSO?**

## 59.5 Human Impacts on the Biosphere: Pollution and Resource Depletion

### Learning Outcomes

1. Name the major human threats to ecosystems.
2. Differentiate between point-source pollution and diffuse pollution.
3. Explain the effect of deforestation.

We all know that human activities can cause adverse changes in ecosystems. In discussing these, it is important to recognize that creative people can often come up with rational solutions to such problems.

An outstanding example is provided by the history of DDT in the United States. DDT is a highly effective insecti-

cide that was sprayed widely in the decades following World War II, often on wetlands to control mosquitoes. During the years of heavy DDT use, populations of ospreys, bald eagles, and brown pelicans—all birds that catch large fish—plummeted. Ultimately, the use of DDT was connected with the demise of these birds.

Scientists established that DDT and its metabolic products became more and more concentrated in the tissues of animals as the compounds were passed along food chains (figure 59.20). Animals at the bottom of food chains accumulated relatively low concentrations in their fatty tissues. But the primary carnivores that preyed on them accumulated higher concentrations from eating great numbers, and the secondary carnivores accumulated higher concentrations yet. Top-level carnivores, such as the birds that eat large fish, were dramatically affected by the DDT. In these birds, scientists found that metabolic products of DDT disrupted the formation of eggshells. The birds laid eggs with such thin shells that they often cracked before the young could hatch.

Researchers concluded that the demise of the fish-eating birds could be reversed by a rational plan to clean ecosystems of DDT, and laws were passed banning its use. Now, three decades later, populations of ospreys, eagles, and pelicans are rebounding dramatically. For some people, a major reason to study science is the opportunity to be part of success stories of this sort.

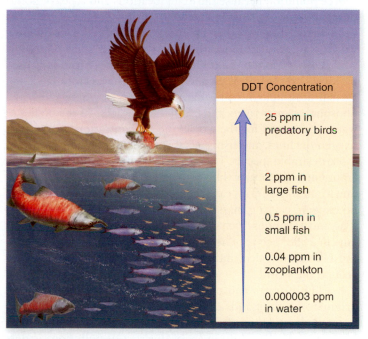

DDT Concentration

25 ppm in predatory birds

2 ppm in large fish

0.5 ppm in small fish

0.04 ppm in zooplankton

0.000003 ppm in water

**Figure 59.20 Biological magnification of DDT concentration.** Because all the DDT an animal eats in its food tends to accumulate in its fatty tissues, DDT becomes increasingly concentrated in animals at higher levels of the food chain. The concentrations at the right are in parts per million (ppm). Before DDT was banned in the United States, bird species that eat large fish underwent drastic population declines because metabolic products of DDT made their eggshells so thin that the shells broke during incubation.

## Freshwater habitats are threatened by pollution and resource depletion

Fresh water is not just the smallest of the major habitats, but also the most threatened. One of the simplest yet most ominous threats to fresh water is that burgeoning human populations often extract excessive amounts of water from rivers, lakes, or streams. The Colorado River, for example, is one of the greatest rivers in North America, originating with snow melt in the Rocky Mountains and flowing through Utah, Arizona, Nevada, California, and northern Mexico before emptying into the ocean. Today, water is pumped out of the river all along its way to meet the water needs of cities (even ones as distant as Los Angeles) and to irrigate crops. The river now frequently runs out of water and dries up in the desert, never reaching the sea. Worldwide, many crises in the supply of fresh water loom on the horizon.

### Pollution: Point source versus diffuse

Pollution of fresh water is a global problem. Point-source pollution comes from an identifiable location—such as easily identified factories or other facilities that add pollutants at defined locations, such as an outfall pipe. Examples include sewage-treatment plants, which discharge treated effluents at specific spots on rivers, and factories that sometimes discharge water contaminated with heavy metals or chemicals. Laws and technologies can readily be brought to bear to moderate point-source pollution because the exact locations and types of pollution are well defined. In many countries, great progress has been made, but in other countries, often in the developing world, water pollution is still a major problem.

Diffuse pollution is exemplified by eutrophication caused by excessive run-off of nitrates and phosphates from lawn and agricultural field fertilization. When excessive nitrates and phosphates enter rivers and lakes, the character of the bodies of water is changed for the worse; the concentration of dissolved oxygen declines, and fish species such as carp take the place of more desirable species. The problem is exacerbated when rivers empty into the ocean. The eutrophication caused by the accumulation of chemicals can lead to enormous areas of water with no oxygen, causing massive die-offs of fish and other animals. The most famous such area, covering approximately 20,000 km² in 2008, occurs where the Mississippi River empties into the Gulf of Mexico, but other "dead zones" occur in places around the world.

The nitrates and phosphates that cause these problems originate on thousands of farms and lawns spread over whole watersheds, and they often enter fresh waters at virtually countless locations. The diffuseness of this sort of pollution renders it difficult to modify by simple technical fixes. Instead, solutions often depend on public education and political action.

### Pollution from coal burning: Acid precipitation

A type of pollution that has properties intermediate between the point-source and diffuse types is the pollution that can arise from burning of coal for power generation. Although each smokestack is a point source, there are many stacks, and the smoke and gases from these stacks spread over wide areas.

Acid precipitation is one aspect of this problem. When coal is burned, sulfur in the coal is oxidized. The sulfur oxides, unless controlled, are spewed into the atmosphere in the stack smoke, and there they combine with water vapor to produce sulfuric acid. Falling rain or snow picks up the acid and is excessively acidic when it reaches the surface of the Earth (figure 59.21).

Mercury emitted in stack smoke is a second potential problem. Burning of coal can be one of the major sources of environmental mercury, a serious public health issue because just small amounts of mercury can interfere with brain development in human fetuses and infants.

Acid precipitation and mercury pollution affect freshwater ecosystems. At pH levels below 5.0, many fish species and other aquatic animals die, unable to reproduce. Thousands of lakes and ponds around the world no longer support fish because of pH shifts induced by acid precipitation. Mercury that falls from atmospheric emissions into lakes and ponds accumulates in the tissues of food fish. In the Great Lakes region of the United States, people—especially pregnant women—are advised to eat little or no locally caught fish because of its mercury content.

## Forest ecosystems are threatened in tropical and temperate regions

Probably the single greatest problem for terrestrial habitats worldwide is deforestation by cutting or burning. There are many reasons for deforestation. In poverty-stricken countries, deforestation is often carried out diffusely by the general population; people burn wood to cook or stay warm, and they collect it from the local forests.

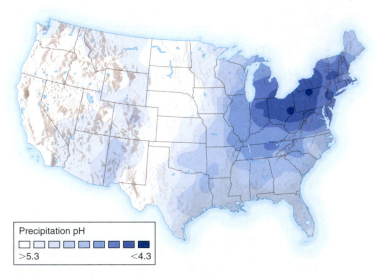

Precipitation pH

>5.3          <4.3

**Figure 59.21  pH values of rainwater in the United States.** pH values of less than 7 represent acid conditions; the lower the values, the greater the acidity. Precipitation in parts of the United States, especially in the Northeast, is commonly more acidic than natural rainwater, which has a pH of 5.6 or higher.

At the other extreme, corporations still cut large tracts of virgin forests in an industrialized fashion, often shipping the wood halfway around the world to buyers. Tropical hardwoods, such as mahogany, from Southeast Asian rain forests are shipped to the United States for use in furniture, and softwood logs are shipped from Alaska to East Asia for pulping and paper production. Forests are sometimes simply burned to open up land for farming or ranching (figure 59.22*a*).

### Loss of habitat

The loss of forest habitat can have dire consequences. Particularly diverse sets of species depend on tropical rain forests for their habitat, for example. Thus, when rain forests are cleared, the loss of biodiversity can be extreme. Many tropical forest regions have been severely degraded, and recent estimates suggest that less than half of the world's tropical rain forests remain in pristine condition. All of the world's tropical rain forests will be degraded or gone in about 30 years at present rates of destruction.

Besides loss of habitat, deforestation can have numerous secondary consequences, depending on local contexts. In the Sahel region, South of the Sahara Desert in Africa, deforestation has been a major contributing factor in increased desertification. In the forests of the northeastern United States, as the Hubbard Brook experiment shows (see figure 58.7), deforestation can lead to both a loss of nutrients from forest soils and a simultaneous nutrient enrichment of bodies of water downstream.

### Disruption of the water cycle

As discussed in chapter 58, cutting of a tropical rain forest often interrupts the local water cycle in ways that permanently alter the landscape. After an area of tropical rain forest is cleared, rain water often runs off the land to distant places, rather than being returned to the atmosphere immediately above by transpiration. This change may render conditions unsuitable for the rain forest trees that originally lived there. Then the poorly vegetated land—exposed and no longer stabilized by thick root systems—may be ravaged by erosion (figure 59.22*b*).

### Acid rain

Deforestation can be a problem in temperate regions, as well as in the tropics. In addition, acid rain affects forests as well as lakes and streams; large tracts of trees in temperate regions have been adversely affected by acid rain. By changing the acidity of the soil, acid rain can lead to widespread tree mortality (figure 59.23).

## Marine habitats are being depleted of fish and other species

Overfishing of the ocean has risen to crisis proportions in recent decades and probably represents the single greatest current problem in the ocean realm. The ocean is so huge that it has tended to be more immune than fresh water or terrestrial ecosystems to global human alteration. Nonetheless, the total world fish catch has been pushed to its maximum for over two decades, even as demand for fish has continued to rise. Fishing pressure is so excessive that 25% to 30% of the world's ocean

*a.* *b.*

**Figure 59.22** **Destroying the tropical rain forests.** *a.* These fires are destroying a tropical rain forest in Brazil to clear it for cattle pasture. *b.* The consequences of deforestation can be seen on these middle-elevation slopes in Madagascar, which once supported tropical rain forest, but now support only low-grade pastures and permit topsoil to erode into the rivers (note the color of the water, stained brown by high levels of soil erosion). This sort of picture is seen in a number of places around the world, including Ecuador and Haiti as well as Madagascar.

fish stocks are presently officially rated as being overexploited, depleted, or in recovery; another 40% to 50% are rated as being maximally exploited.

Major cod fisheries in waters off of Nova Scotia, Massachusetts, and Great Britain have been closed to fishing in the past 15 years because of collapse (figure 59.24). Overfishing can

**Figure 59.23**
**Damage to trees by acid precipitation at Clingman's Dome, Tennessee.** Acid precipitation weakens trees and makes them more susceptible to pests and predators.

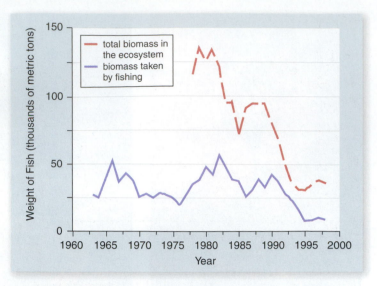

**Figure 59.24   The collapse of a fishery.** The red line shows the biomass of cod (*Gadus morhua*) in the Georges Bank ecosystem as estimated by the U.S. National Marine Fisheries Service based on data collected by scientific sampling. The biomass declined steeply between the 1970s and 1990s because of fishing pressure. As the years passed, commercial landings of cod (*blue line*) remained fairly constant, in part because ships worked harder and harder to catch cod, until catches fell precipitously toward zero and the fishery collapsed in the mid-1990s. Regulatory agencies closed the fishery in the mid-1990s to permit the cod to recover, but even in 2009 recovery of cod was weak at best, and production from the fishery was far below historical norms.

have disturbing indirect effects. In impoverished parts of Africa, poaching on primates and other wild mammals in national parks increases when fish catches decline.

### Aquaculture: At present only a quick fix

Production of fish by aquaculture has grown steadily in the last two decades, and it is often viewed as a straightforward solution to the fisheries problem. But the dietary protein needs of many aquacultured fish, such as salmon, are met largely with wild-caught fish. In this case, exploitation has simply shifted to different species.

In addition, current aquaculture practices often damage natural ocean ecosystems. One example is the clearing of mangrove swamps along coasts to create shrimp and fish ponds, which are abandoned when their productivity declines. Research is needed to ameliorate these problems.

### Pollution effects

As large as the ocean is, enough pollutants are being added that at the start of the 21st century, polluting materials are easily detectable on a global basis. An expedition to some of the most remote, uninhabited islands in the vast Pacific Ocean recently reported, for example, that considerable amounts of plastic could be found washed up on the beaches. Similarly, even the waters of the Arctic are laced with toxic chemicals; biopsy samples of tissue from Arctic killer whales (*Orcinus orca*) revealed extremely high levels of many chemicals, including pesticides

and a flame-retardant chemical often used in carpets. Nonetheless, because of the ocean's vastness, concentrations of pollutants are not at crisis levels in the ocean at large.

### Destruction of coastal ecosystems

Second to overfishing, the greatest problem in the ocean realm is deterioration of coastal ecosystems. Estuaries along coastlines are often subject to severe eutrophication; since about 1970, for example, the bottom waters of the Chesapeake Bay near Washington, DC, have become oxygen-free each summer because of the decay of excessive amounts of organic matter.

Another coastal problem is destruction of salt marshes, which (like freshwater wetlands) are often perceived as disposable. Most authorities believe that the loss of salt marshes in the 20th century was a major contributing factor to the destruction of New Orleans by Hurricane Katrina in 2005; had the salt marshes and cypress swamps been present at their full extent, they would have absorbed a great deal of the flooding water and buffered the city from some of the storm's violence.

## Stratospheric ozone depletion has led to an ozone "hole"

The colors of the satellite photo in figure 59.25*a* represent different concentrations of ozone ($O_3$) located 20 to 25 km above the Earth's surface in the stratosphere. Stratospheric ozone is depleted over Antarctica (purple region in the figure) to between one-half and one-third of its historically normal concentration, a phenomenon called the ozone hole.

Although depletion of stratospheric ozone is most dramatic over Antarctica, it is a worldwide phenomenon. Over the United States, the ozone concentration has been reduced by about 4%, according to the U.S. Environmental Protection Agency.

### Stratospheric ozone and UV-B

Stratospheric ozone is important because it absorbs ultraviolet (UV) radiation—specifically the wavelengths called **UV-B**—from incoming solar radiation. UV-B is damaging to living organisms in a number of ways; for instance, it increases risks of cataracts and skin cancer in people. Depletion of stratospheric ozone permits more UV-B to reach the Earth's surface and therefore increases the risks of UV-B damage. Every 1% drop in stratospheric ozone is estimated to lead to a 6% increase in the incidence of skin cancer, for example. UV exposure also may be detrimental to many types of animals, such as amphibians (figure 59.26)

### Ozone depletion and CFCs

The major cause of the depletion of stratospheric ozone is the addition of industrially produced chlorine- and bromine-containing compounds to the atmosphere. Of particular concern are chlorofluorocarbons (CFCs), used until recently as refrigerants in air conditioners and refrigerators, and in manufacturing. CFCs released into the atmosphere can ultimately liberate free chlorine atoms, which in the stratosphere catalyze the breakdown of ozone molecules ($O_3$) to form ordinary oxygen ($O_2$). Ozone is continually being made and broken down,

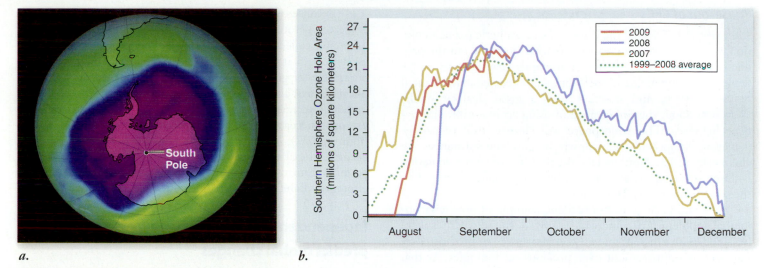

a.  b.

**Figure 59.25  The ozone hole over Antarctica.** NASA satellites currently track the extent of ozone depletion in the stratosphere over Antarctica each year. Every year since about 1980, an area of profound ozone depletion, called the ozone hole, has appeared in August (early spring in the southern hemisphere) when sunlight triggers chemical reactions in cold air trapped over the South Pole during the Antarctic winter. The hole intensifies during September before tailing off as temperature rises in November–December. *a.* In September, 2006, the 11.4 million-square-mile hole (*purple* in the satellite image shown) covered an area larger than the United States, Canada, and Mexico combined, the largest hole ever recorded. *b.* Concentrations of ozone-depleting chemical compounds in the atmosphere have probably peaked in the last few years and are expected to decline slowly over the decades ahead.

and free chlorine atoms tilt the balance toward a faster rate of breakdown.

The extreme depletion of ozone seen in the ozone hole is a consequence of the unique weather conditions that exist over Antarctica. During the continuous dark of the Antarctic winter, a strong stratospheric wind, the polar-night jet, develops and, blowing around the full circumference of the Earth, isolates the stratosphere over Antarctica from the rest of the atmosphere.

The Antarctic stratosphere stays extremely cold (–80°C or lower) for many weeks as a consequence, permitting unique types of ice clouds to form. Reactions associated with the particles in these clouds lead to accumulation of diatomic chlorine, $Cl_2$. When sunlight returns in the early Antarctic spring, the diatomic chlorine is photochemically broken up to form free chlorine atoms in great abundance, and the ozone-depleting reactions ensue.

## SCIENTIFIC THINKING

**Question:** *Does exposure to UV radiation affect the survival of amphibian eggs?*

**Hypothesis:** *Direct UV exposure is detrimental to eggs.*

**Experiment:** *Fertilized eggs from several frog species are placed into enclosures in full sunlight. All enclosures have screens, some of which filter out UV radiation, whereas others do not affect UV transmission. Eggs are monitored to see whether they survive to hatching or whether they die.*

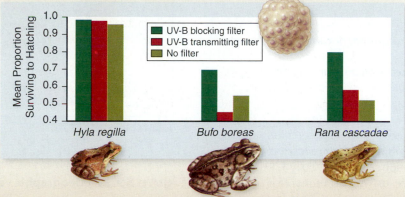

**Result:** *Egg survival was greatly decreased in two of three species in the enclosures where UV radiation was not filtered out, as compared to survival in the filtered enclosures. Therefore, the hypothesis is confirmed: UV exposure is detrimental to amphibian eggs.*

**Further Questions:** *What factors might explain why some species are affected by UV exposure and others are not? How could your hypotheses be tested?*

**Figure 59.26  The effect of UV radiation on amphibian eggs.**

### Phase-out of CFCs

After research revealed the causes of stratospheric ozone depletion, worldwide agreements were reached to phase out the production of CFCs and other compounds that lead to ozone depletion. Manufacture of such compounds ceased in the United States in 1996, and there is now a great deal of public awareness about the importance of using "ozone-safe" alternative chemicals. The atmosphere will cleanse itself of ozone-depleting compounds only slowly because the substances are chemically stable. Nonetheless, the problem of ozone depletion is diminishing and is expected to be substantially corrected by the second half of the 21st century.

The CFC story is an excellent example of how environmental problems arise and can be solved. Initially, CFCs were heralded as an efficient and cost-effective way to provide cooling, a clear improvement over previous technologies. At that time, their harmful consequences were unknown. Once the problems were identified, international agreements led to an effective solution, and creative technological advances led to replacements that solved the problem at little cost.

---

**Learning Outcomes Review 59.5**

Pollution and resource depletion are the major human effects on the environment, with freshwater habitats being most threatened. Point-source pollution comes from identifiable locations, such as factories, whereas diffuse pollution comes from numerous sources, such as fertilized lawns. Deforestation is a major problem in that it destroys habitat, disrupts communities, depletes resources, and changes the local water cycle and weather patterns. Overfishing is the greatest problem in the oceans.

- ■ *Were CFCs an example of point-source or diffuse pollution? In general, how do efforts to combat pollution depend on their source?*

---

## 59.6 Human Impacts on the Biosphere: Climate Change

**Learning Outcomes**

1. *Explain the link between atmospheric carbon dioxide and global warming.*
2. *Describe the consequences of global warming on ecosystems and human health.*

By studying the Earth's history and making comparisons with other planets, scientists have determined that concentrations of gases in our atmosphere, particularly $CO_2$, maintain the average temperature on Earth about 25°C higher than it would be if these gases were absent. This fact emphasizes that the composition of our atmosphere is a key consideration for life on Earth. Unfortunately, human activities are now changing the composition of the atmosphere in ways that most authorities conclude will be damaging or, in the long run, disastrous.

Because of changes in atmospheric composition, the average temperature of the Earth's surface is increasing, a phenomenon called global warming. As you might imagine from what we said at the beginning of this chapter, changes in temperature alter global wind and water-current patterns in complicated ways. This means that as the average global temperature increases, some particular regions of the world warm to a lesser extent, whereas other regions heat up to a greater extent (figure 59.27). It also means that rainfall patterns are altered because global precipitation patterns depend on global wind patterns. Enormous computer models are used to calculate the effects predicted in all parts of the world.

### Independent computer models predict global changes

The Intergovernmental Panel on Climate Change, which shared the 2007 Nobel Peace Prize with Al Gore for their work on global climate change, recently released its fourth assessment report. Based on a variety of different scenarios, computer models predicted that global temperatures would increase 1.1°C to 6.4°C (2.0–11.5°F) by the end of this century.

More ominous perhaps than temperature are some of the predictions for precipitation. For example, although northern Europe is expected to receive more precipitation than today, another recent studied predicted that parts of southern Europe will receive about 20% less, disrupting natural ecosystems, agriculture, and human water supplies. Some European countries may come out ahead economically, but others will come out behind, and political relationships among countries will likely change as some shift from being food exporters to the more tenuous role of requiring food imports.

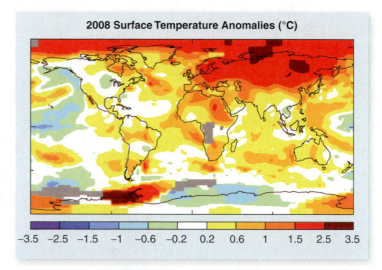

**2008 Surface Temperature Anomalies (°C)**

–3.5  –2.5  –1.5  –1  –0.6  –0.2  0.2  0.6  1  1.5  2.5  3.5

**Figure 59.27 Geographic variation in global warming.**
The 10 warmest years since record keeping began in 1880 all occur within the 12-year period 1997–2008, but some areas of the globe heated up more than others. Colors indicate how much warming occurred in 2008 relative to the mean temperature during a reference period (1951–1980) prior to full onset of the modern greenhouse effect.

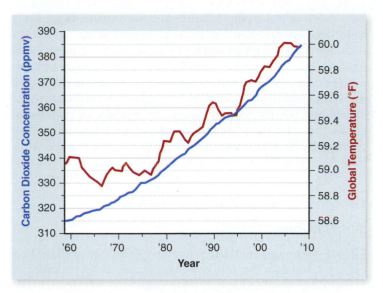

**Figure 59.28 The greenhouse effect.** The concentration of carbon dioxide in the atmosphere has increased steadily since the 1950s, as shown by the blue line. The red line shows the change in average global temperature over the same period.

## Carbon dioxide is a major greenhouse gas

Carbon dioxide is the gas usually emphasized in discussing the cause of global warming (figure 59.28), although other atmospheric gases are also involved. A monitoring station on the top of the 13,700-foot (4200-m) Mauna Loa volcano on the island of Hawaii has monitored the concentration of atmospheric $CO_2$ since the 1950s. This station is particularly important because it is in the middle of the Pacific Ocean, far from the great continental landmasses where most people live, and it is therefore able to monitor the state of the global atmosphere without confounding influences of local events.

In 1958, the atmosphere was 0.031% $CO_2$. By 2004, the concentration had risen to 0.038%. All authorities agree that the cause of this steady rise in atmospheric $CO_2$ is the burning of coal and petroleum products by the increasing (and increasingly energy-demanding) human population.

### How carbon dioxide affects temperature

The atmospheric concentration of $CO_2$ affects global temperature because carbon dioxide strongly absorbs electromagnetic radiant energy at some of the wavelengths that are critical for the global heat budget. As stressed in chapter 58, the Earth not only receives radiant energy from the Sun, but also emits radiant energy into outer space. The Earth's temperature will be constant only if the rates of these two processes are equal.

The incoming solar energy is at relatively short wavelengths of the electromagnetic spectrum: Wavelengths that are visible or near-visible. The outgoing energy from the Earth is at different, longer wavelengths. Carbon dioxide absorbs energy at certain of the important long-wave infrared wavelengths. This means that although carbon dioxide does not interfere with the arrival of radiant energy at short wavelengths, it retards the rate at which energy travels away from the Earth at long wavelengths into outer space.

Carbon dioxide is often called a greenhouse gas because its effects are analogous to those of a greenhouse. The reason that a glass greenhouse gets warm inside is that window glass is transparent to light but only slightly transparent to long-wave infrared radiation. Energy that strikes a greenhouse as light enters the greenhouse freely. Once inside, the energy is absorbed as heat and then re-radiated as long-wave infrared radiation. The infrared radiation cannot easily get out through the glass, and therefore energy accumulates inside.

### Other greenhouse gases

Carbon dioxide is not the only greenhouse gas. Others include methane and nitrous oxide. The effect of any particular greenhouse gas depends on its molecular properties and concentration. For example, molecule-for-molecule, methane has about 20 times the heat-trapping effect of carbon dioxide; on the other hand, methane is less concentrated and less long-lived in the atmosphere than carbon dioxide.

Methane is produced in globally significant quantities in anaerobic soils and in the fermentation reactions of ruminant mammals, such as cows. Huge amounts of methane are presently locked up in Arctic permafrost. Melting of the permafrost could cause a sudden and large perturbation in global temperature by releasing methane rapidly.

Agricultural use of fertilizers is the largest source of nitrous oxide emissions, with energy consumption second and industrial use third.

## Global temperature change has affected ecosystems in the past and is doing so now

Evidence for warming can be seen in many ways. For example, on a worldwide statistical basis, ice on lakes and rivers forms later and melts sooner than it used to; on average, ice-free seasons are now 2.5 weeks longer than they were a century ago. Also, the extent of ice at the North Pole has decreased substantially, and glaciers are retreating around the world (figure 59.29).

**Figure 59.29 Disappearing glaciers.** Mount Kilimanjaro in Tanzania in 1970 (*top*) and 2000 (*bottom*). Note the decrease in glacier coverage over three decades.

Global warming—and cooling—have occurred in the past, most recently during the ice ages and intervening warm periods. Species often responded by shifting their geographic ranges, tracking their environments. For example, a number of cold-adapted North American tree species that are now found only in the far north, or at high elevations, lived much farther south or at substantially lower elevations 10,000–20,000 years ago, when conditions were colder. Present-day global warming is having similar effects. For example, many butterfly and bird species have shifted northward in recent decades (figure 59.30).

Many migratory birds arrive earlier at their summer breeding grounds than they did decades ago. Many insects and amphibians breed earlier in the year, and many plants flower earlier. In Australia, recent research shows that wild fruit fly populations have undergone changes in gene frequencies in the past 20 years, such that populations in cool parts of the country now genetically resemble ones in warm parts.

Reef-building corals seem to have narrow margins of safety between the sea temperatures to which they are accustomed and the maximum temperatures they can survive. Global warming seems already to be threatening some corals by inducing mass "bleaching," a disruption of the normal and necessary symbiosis between the cnidarians and algal cells.

There are reasons to think that the effects of global warming on natural ecosystems today may, overall, be more severe than those of warming events in the distant past. One concern is that the rate of warming today is rapid, and therefore evolutionary adaptations would need to occur over relatively few generations to aid the survival of species. Another concern is that natural areas no longer cover the whole landscape but often take the form of parks that are completely surrounded by cities or farms. The parks are at fixed geographic locations and in general cannot be moved. If climatic conditions in a park become unsuitable for its inhabitants, the park will cease to perform its function. Moreover, the areas in which the park in-

habitants might then find suitable climatic conditions are likely to be developed, rather than being protected parks.

Similarly, as temperatures increase, many montane species have shifted to higher altitudes to find their preferred habitat. However, eventually they can shift no higher because they reach the mountain's peak. As the temperature continues to increase, the species' habitat disappears entirely. A number of Costa Rican frog species are thought to have become extinct for this reason. The same fate may befall many Arctic species as their habitat melts away.

## Global warming affects human populations as well

Global warming could affect human health and welfare in a variety of ways. Some of these changes may be beneficial, but even if they are detrimental, some countries—particularly the wealthier ones—will be able to adjust. But poorer countries may not be able to transform as quickly, and some changes will require extremely costly countermeasures that even wealthy countries will be hard-pressed to afford.

### Rising sea levels

During the second half of the 20th century, sea level rose at 2 to 3 cm per decade. The U.S. Environmental Protection Agency predicts that sea level is likely to rise two or three times faster in the 21st century because of two effects of global warming: (1) the melting of polar ice and glaciers, adding water to the ocean, and (2) the increase of average ocean temperature, causing an increase in volume because water expands as it warms. Such an increase would cause increased erosion and inundation of low-lying land and coastal marshes, and other habitats would also be imperiled. As many as 200 million people would be affected by increased flooding. Should sea levels continue to rise, coastal cities and some entire islands, such as the Maldives in the Indian Ocean, would be in danger of becoming submerged.

### Other climatic effects

Global warming is predicted to have a variety of effects besides increased temperatures. In particular, the frequency or severity of extreme meteorological events—such as heat waves, droughts, severe storms, and hurricanes—is expected to increase, and El Niño events, with their attendant climatic effects, may become more common.

In addition, rainfall patterns are likely to shift, and those geographic areas that are already water-stressed, which are currently home to nearly 2 billion people, will likely face even graver water shortage problems in the years to come. Some evidence suggests that these effects are already evident in the increase in powerful storms, hurricanes, and the frequency of El Niño events over the past few years.

### Effects on agriculture

Global warming may have both positive and negative effects on agriculture. On the positive side, warmer temperatures and increased atmospheric carbon dioxide tend to increase growth of some crops and thus may increase agricultural yields. Other crops, however, may be negatively affected. Furthermore, most

**Figure 59.30 Butterfly range shift.** The distribution of the speckled wood butterfly, *Pararge aegeria*, in Great Britain in 1970–1997 (green) included areas far to the north of the distribution in 1915–1939 (black).

crops will be affected by increased frequencies of droughts. Moreover, although crops in north temperate regions may flourish with higher temperatures, many tropical crops are already growing at their maximal temperatures, so increased temperatures may lead to reduced crop yields.

Also on the negative side, changes in rainfall patterns, temperature, pest distributions, and various other factors will require many adjustments. Such changes may come relatively easily for farmers in the developed world, but the associated costs may be devastating for those in the developing countries.

### Effects on human health

Increasingly frequent storms, flooding, and drought will have adverse consequences on human health. Aside from their direct effect, such events often disrupt the fragile infrastructure of developing countries, leading to the loss of safe drinking water and other problems. As a result, epidemics of cholera and other diseases may be expected to occur more often.

In addition, as temperatures rise, areas suitable for tropical organisms will expand northward. Of particular concern are those organisms that cause human diseases. Many diseases currently limited to tropical areas may expand their range and become problematic in nontropical countries. Diseases transmitted by mosquitoes, such as malaria (see chapter 29), dengue fever, and several types of encephalitis, are examples. The distribution of mosquitoes is limited by cold; winter freezes kill many mosquitoes and their eggs. As a result, malaria only occurs in areas where temperatures are usually above 16°C, and yellow fever and dengue fever, transmitted by a different mosquito species from malaria, occur in areas where temperatures are normally above 10°C. Moreover, at higher temperatures, the malaria pathogen matures more rapidly.

Malaria already kills 1 million people every year; some projections suggest that the percentage of the human population at risk for malaria may increase by 33% by the end of the 21st century. Moreover, as predicted, malaria already appears to be on the move. By 1980, malaria had been eradicated from all of the United States except California, but in recent years it has appeared in a variety of southern, and even a few northern, states.

Dengue fever (sometimes called "breakbone fever" because of the pain it causes) is also spreading. Previously a disease restricted to the tropics and subtropics, where it infects 50 to 100 million people a year, it now occurs in the United States, southern South America, and northern Australia.

One of the most alarming aspects of these diseases is that no vaccines are available. Drug treatment is available (for malaria), but the parasites are rapidly evolving resistance and rendering the drugs ineffective. There is no drug treatment for dengue fever.

### Solving the problem

The release of the IPCC's fourth assessment in 2007 may come to be seen as a turning point in humanity's response to climate change. Global warming is now recognized, even by former skeptics, as an ongoing phenomenon caused in large part by human actions. Even formerly recalcitrant governments now seem poised to take action, and corporations are recognizing the opportunities provided by the need to reverse human impacts. The resulting "green" technologies and practices are becoming increasingly common. With concerted efforts from citizens, corporations, and governments, the more serious consequences of global climate change hopefully can be averted, just as ozone depletion was reversed in the last century.

---

#### Learning Outcomes Review 59.6

Carbon dioxide is a significant greenhouse gas, meaning that it prevents heat from escaping the Earth so that temperatures rise. Global warming caused by changes in atmospheric composition—most notably $CO_2$ accumulation—may increase desertification and cause some habitats and species to disappear. Global warming may also melt ice caps and glaciers, altering coastlines as water levels rise. Violent weather events, disruption of water availability, and flooding of low-lying areas, as well as increased incidence of tropical diseases, may also occur.

■ *In what ways does global climate change pose different questions from those posed by ozone depletion?*

---

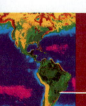

## Chapter Review

### 59.1 Ecosystem Effects of Sun, Wind, and Water

**Solar energy and the Earth's rotation affect atmospheric circulation.**

The amount of solar radiation reaching the Earth's surface has a great effect on climate. The seasons result from changes in the Earth's position relative to the Sun (see figure 59.1). Hot air with its increased water content rises at the equator, then cools and loses its moisture, creating the equatorial rain forests (see figure 59.3).

As the drier cool air of the upper atmosphere moves away from the equator and then descends to Earth, it removes moisture from the Earth's surface and creates deserts on its way back to the equator.

Winds travel in curved paths relative to the Earth's surface because the Earth rotates on its axis (the Coriolis effect; see figure 59.3).

**Global currents are largely driven by winds (see figure 59.4).**

Four large circular gyres in ocean currents can be found, driven by wind direction. These also are influenced by the Coriolis effect.

**Regional and local differences affect terrestrial ecosystems.**

A rain shadow occurs when a range of mountains removes moisture from air moving over it from the windward side, creating a drier environment on the opposite side (see figure 59.5).

For every 1000-m increase in elevation, temperature drops approximately 6°C (see figure 59.6).

Microclimates are small-scale differences in conditions.

## 59.2 Earth's Biomes

**Temperature and moisture often determine biomes.**
Average annual temperature and rainfall, as well as the range of seasonal variation, determine different biomes. Eight major types of biomes are recognized.

**Tropical rain forests are highly productive equatorial systems.**

**Savannas are tropical grasslands with seasonal rainfall.**

**Deserts are regions with little rainfall.**

**Temperate grasslands have rich soils.**

**Temperate deciduous forests are adapted to seasonal change.**

**Temperate evergreen forests are coastal.**

**Taiga is the northern forest where winters are harsh.**

**Tundra is a largely frozen treeless area with a short growing season.**

## 59.3 Freshwater Habitats

**Life in freshwater habitats depends on oxygen availability.**
Oxygen is not very soluble in water. Oxygen is constantly added by photosynthesis of aquatic plants and removed by heterotrophs.

**Lake and pond habitats change with water depth.**
The photic zone, near the surface, is the zone of primary productivity; its depth varies with water clarity (see figure 59.12).

In the summer, the warmer water (epilimnion) floats on top of the colder water (hypolimnion). Freshwater lakes turn over twice a year as the temperature at the surface and at depth become the same, and the layers are set in motion by wind (see figure 59.13).

**Lakes differ in oxygen and nutrient content.**
Oligotrophic lakes have high oxygen and low nutrients, whereas eutrophic lakes are the opposite.

## 59.4 Marine Habitats

The ocean is divided into several zones: intertidal, neritic, photic, benthic, and pelagic zones (see figure 59.15).

**Open oceans have low primary productivity.**
Phytoplankton is the primary producer in open waters, and primary production is low due to low nutrient levels.

**Continental shelf ecosystems provide abundant resources.**
Neritic waters are found over continental shelves and have higher nutrient levels (see figure 59.15). Estuaries frequently contain rich

intertidal zones. Other ecosystems include productive banks on continental shelves and symbiotic coral reef ecosystems.

**Upwelling regions experience mixing of nutrients and oxygen.**
In upwelling regions, local winds bring up nutrient-rich deep waters, creating the highest rates of primary production. El Niño events occur when Trade Winds weaken, restricting upwelling to surface waters rather than to the deeper nutrient-rich waters.

**The deep sea is a cold, dark place with some fascinating communities.**
The deep sea is the single largest habitat. Hydrothermal vent communities occur where tectonic plates are moving apart; chemoautotrophs living there obtain energy from oxidation of sulfur.

## 59.5 Human Impacts on the Biosphere: Pollution and Resource Depletion

Dangerous chemicals like DDT are biomagnified as energy moves up the food chain (see figure 59.20).

**Freshwater habitats are threatened by pollution and resource depletion.**
Point-source and diffuse pollution, acid precipitation, and overuse threaten freshwater habitats (see figure 59.21).

**Forest ecosystems are threatened in tropical and temperate regions.**
Deforestation leads to loss of habitat, disruption of the water cycle, and loss of nutrients. Acid rain has a major detrimental effect on forests as well as on lakes and streams (see figure 59.23).

**Marine habitats are being depleted of fish and other species.**
Many fisheries, such as the Georges Bank ecosystem, have collapsed and have not recovered.

**Stratospheric ozone depletion has led to an ozone "hole."**
Increased transmission of UV-B radiation is harmful to life. Global regulation of CFCs seems to be reversing ozone depletion.

## 59.6 Human Impacts on the Biosphere: Climate Change

**Independent computer models predict global changes.**

**Carbon dioxide is a major greenhouse gas.**
Carbon dioxide allows solar radiation to pass through the atmosphere but prevents heat from leaving the Earth, creating warmer conditions.

**Global temperature change has affected ecosystems in the past and is doing so now.**
If temperatures change rapidly, natural selection cannot occur rapidly enough to prevent many species from becoming extinct.

**Global warming affects human populations as well.**
Changing sea levels, increased frequency of extreme climatic events, direct and indirect effects on agriculture, and the expansion of tropical diseases can all affect human life.

## UNDERSTAND

1. The Coriolis effect
   a. drives the rotation of the Earth.
   b. is responsible for the relative lack of seasonality at the equator.
   c. drives global wind circulation patterns.
   d. drives global wind and ocean circulation patterns.

2. What two factors are most important in biome distribution?
   a. Temperature and latitude
   b. Rainfall and temperature
   c. Latitude and rainfall
   d. Temperature and soil type

3. In a rain shadow, air is cooled as it rises and heated as it descends, often producing a wet and dry side because the water-holding capacity of the air
   a. is directly related to air temperature.
   b. is inversely related to air temperature.
   c. is unaffected by air temperature.
   d. produces changes in air temperature.

4. Thermal stratification in a lake
   a. is not modified by fall and spring overturn.
   b. leads to higher oxygen in deep versus surface waters.
   c. leads to higher oxygen in surface versus deep waters.
   d. is reduced when ice forms on the surface of the lake.

5. Oligotrophic lakes have
   a. low oxygen, and high nutrient availability.
   b. high oxygen, and high nutrient availability.
   c. high oxygen, and low nutrient availability.
   d. low oxygen, and low nutrient availability.

6. Deep-sea hydrothermal vent communities
   a. get their energy from photosynthesis in the photic zone near the surface.
   b. use bioluminescence to generate food.
   c. are built on the energy produced by the activity of chemoautotrophs that oxidize sulfur.
   d. contain only bacteria and other microorganisms.

7. Biological magnification occurs when
   a. pollutants increase in concentration in tissues at higher trophic levels.
   b. the effect of a pollutant is magnified by chemical interactions within organisms.
   c. an organism is placed under a dissecting scope.
   d. a pollutant has a greater than expected effect once ingested by an organism.

8. Which of the following is a point source of pollution?
   a. Lawns
   b. Smokestacks of coal-fired power plants
   c. Factory effluent pipe draining into a river
   d. Acid rain

## APPLY

1. If the Earth were not tilted on its axis of rotation, the annual cycle of seasons in the northern and southern hemispheres
   a. would be reversed.     c. would be reduced.
   b. would stay the same.   d. would not exist.

2. Oligotrophic lakes can be turned into eutrophic lakes as a result of human activities such as
   a. overfishing of sensitive species, which disrupts fish communities.
   b. introducing nutrients into the water, which stimulates plant and algal growth.
   c. disrupting terrestrial vegetation near the shore, which causes soil to run into the lake.
   d. spraying pesticides into the water to control aquatic insect populations.

3. If a pesticide is harmless at low concentrations (such as, DDT) and used properly, how can it become a threat to nontarget organisms?
   a. Because after exposure to DDT, some species develop allergic reactions even at low levels of exposure
   b. Because DDT molecules can combine so that their concentration increases through time
   c. Because the concentration of chemicals such as DDT is increasingly concentrated at higher trophic levels
   d. Because global warming and exposure to UV-B radiation renders molecules such as DDT increasingly potent

4. If there are many greenhouse gases, why is only carbon dioxide considered a cause of global warming?
   a. The other gases do not cause global warming.
   b. Scientists are concerned about other causes; for example, release of methane from melting permafrost could have significant effects on global warming.
   c. Other gases occur in such low quantities that they have little effect on the climate.
   d. Carbon dioxide is the only gas that absorbs long-wavelength infrared radiation.

## SYNTHESIZE

1. Discuss how figure 59.1 explains the pattern observed in figure 59.2.

2. Why are most of the Earth's deserts found at approximately 30° latitude?

3. If the world has experienced global warming many times in the past, why should we be concerned about it happening again now?

## ONLINE RESOURCE

**www.ravenbiology.com**

Understand, Apply, and Synthesize—enhance your study with animations that bring concepts to life and practice tests to assess your understanding. Your instructor may also recommend the interactive eBook, individualized learning tools, and more.

Chapter 60

# Conservation Biology

## Chapter Outline

**60.1** Overview of the Biodiversity Crisis

**60.2** The Value of Biodiversity

**60.3** Factors Responsible for Extinction

**60.4** Approaches for Preserving Endangered Species and Ecosystems

## Introduction

*Among the greatest challenges facing the biosphere is the accelerating pace of species extinctions. Not since the end of the Cretaceous period 65 MYA have so many species become extinct in so short a time span. This challenge has led to the emergence of the discipline of conservation biology. Conservation biology is an applied science that seeks to learn how to preserve species, communities, and ecosystems. It studies the causes of declines in species richness and attempts to develop methods for preventing such declines. In this chapter, we first examine the biodiversity crisis and its importance. Then, using case histories, we identify and study factors that have played key roles in many extinctions. We finish with a review of recovery efforts at the species and community levels.*

## Overview of the Biodiversity Crisis

Extinction is a fact of life. Most species—probably all—become extinct eventually. More than 99% of species known to science (most from the fossil record) are now extinct. Current rates of extinction are alarmingly high, however. Taking into account the current rapid and accelerating loss of habitat, especially in the tropics, it has been calculated that as much as 20% of the world's biodiversity may be lost by the middle of this century. In addition, many of these species may be lost before we are even aware of their existence. Scientists estimate that no more than 15% of the world's eukaryotic organisms have been discovered and given scientific names, and this proportion is probably much lower for tropical species.

These losses will affect more than poorly known groups. As many as 50,000 species of the world's total of 250,000 species of plants, 4000 of the world's 20,000 species of butterflies, and nearly 2000 of the world's 8600 species of birds could be lost during this period. Considering that the human species has been in existence for less than 200,000 years of the world's 4.5-billion-year history, and that our ancestors developed agriculture only about 10,000 years ago, this is an astonishing—and dubious—accomplishment.

### Prehistoric humans were responsible for local extinctions

A great deal can be learned about current rates of extinction by studying the past. In prehistoric times, members of *Homo sapiens* wreaked havoc whenever they entered a new area. For example, at the end of the last Ice Age, approximately 12,000 years ago, the fauna of North America was composed of a diversity of large mammals similar to those living in Africa today: mammoths and mastodons, horses, camels, giant ground sloths, saber-toothed cats, and lions, among others (figure 60.1).

Shortly after humans arrived, 74% to 86% of the megafauna (that is, animals weighing more than 100 lb) became extinct. These extinctions are thought to have been caused by hunting and, indirectly, by burning and clearing of forests. (Some scientists attribute these extinctions to climate change, but that hypothesis doesn't explain why the ends of earlier Ice Ages were not associated with mass extinctions, nor does it explain why extinctions occurred primarily among larger animals, with smaller species being relatively unaffected.)

Around the globe, similar results have followed the arrival of humans. Forty thousand years ago, Australia was occupied by a wide variety of large animals, including marsupials

**Figure 60.1  North America before human inhabitants.** Animals found in North America prior to the arrival of humans included birds and large mammals, such as the ancient North American camel, saber-toothed cat, giant ground sloth, and teratorn vulture.

similar in size and ecology to hippos and leopards, a kangaroo 9 ft tall, and a 20-ft-long monitor lizard. These all disappeared at approximately the same time as humans arrived.

Smaller islands have also been devastated. Madagascar has seen the extinction of at least 15 species of lemurs, including one the size of a gorilla; a pygmy hippopotamus; and the flightless elephant bird, *Aepyornis*, the largest bird to ever live (more than 3 m tall and weighing 450 kg). On New Zealand, 30 species of birds went extinct, including all 13 species of moas, another group of large, flightless birds. Interestingly, one continent that seems to have been spared these megafaunal extinctions is Africa. Scientists speculate that this lack of extinction in prehistoric Africa may have resulted because much of human evolution occurred in Africa. Consequently, African species had been coevolving with humans for several million years and thus had evolved counteradaptations to human predation.

## Extinctions have continued in historical time

Historical extinction rates are best known for birds and mammals because these species are conspicuous—that is, relatively large and well studied. Estimates of extinction rates for other species are much rougher. The data presented in table 60.1, based on the best available evidence, show recorded extinctions from 1600 to the present. These estimates indicate that about 85 species of mammals and 113 species of birds have become extinct since the year 1600. That is about 2.1% of known mammal species and 1.3% of known birds.

The majority of extinctions have occurred in the last 150 years: one species every year during the period from 1850 to 1950, and four species per year between 1986 and 1990. This increase in the rate of extinction is the heart of the biodiversity crisis.

Unfortunately, the situation is worsening. For example, the number of bird species recognized as "critically endangered" increased 8% from 1996 to 2000, and a recent report suggested that as many as half of Earth's plant species may be threatened with extinction. Some researchers predict that two-thirds of all vertebrate species could perish by the end of this century.

The majority of historic extinctions—though by no means all of them—have occurred on islands. For example, of the 85 species of mammals that have gone extinct in the last 400 years, 60% lived on islands. The particular vulnerability of island species probably results from a number of factors: Such species have often evolved in the absence of predators, and so have lost their ability to escape both humans and introduced predators such as rats and cats. In addition, humans have introduced competitors and diseases; malaria, for example, has devastated the bird fauna of the Hawaiian Islands. Finally, island populations are often relatively small, and thus particularly vulnerable to extinction, as we shall see later in this chapter.

In recent years, the extinction crisis has moved from islands to continents. Most species now threatened with extinction occur on continents, and these areas will bear the brunt of the extinction crisis in this century.

Some people have argued that we should not be concerned, because extinctions are a natural event and mass extinctions have occurred in the past. Indeed, mass extinctions have taken place several times over the past half-billion years (see figure 22.18). However, the current mass extinction event is notable in several respects. First, it is the only such event triggered by a single species (us!). Moreover, although species diversity usually recovers after a few million years (as discussed in chapter 22), this is a long time to deny our descendants the benefits and joys of biodiversity.

In addition, it is not clear that biodiversity will rebound this time. After previous mass extinctions, new species have evolved to utilize resources newly available due to extinctions of the species that previously used them. Today, however, such resources are unlikely to be available, because humans are destroying the habitats and taking the resources for their own use.

## Endemic species hotspots are especially threatened

A species found naturally in only one geographic area and no place else is said to be endemic to that area. The area over which an endemic species is found may be very large. For example, the black cherry tree (*Prunus serotina*) is endemic to all of temperate North America. More typically, however, endemic species occupy restricted ranges. The Komodo dragon (*Varanus*

| TABLE 60.1 | Recorded Extinctions Since 1600 | | | | | |
|---|---|---|---|---|---|---|
| | RECORDED EXTINCTIONS | | | | Approximate Number of Species | Percent of Taxon Extinct |
| Taxon | Mainland | Island | Ocean | Total | | |
| Mammals | 30 | 51 | 4 | 85 | 4,000 | 2.1 |
| Birds | 21 | 92 | 0 | 113 | 8,600 | 1.3 |
| Reptiles | 1 | 20 | 0 | 21 | 6,300 | 0.3 |
| Fish | 22 | 1 | 0 | 23 | 24,000 | 0.1 |
| Invertebrates* | 49 | 48 | 1 | 98 | 1,000,000+ | 0.01 |
| Flowering plants | 245 | 139 | 0 | 384 | 250,000 | 0.2 |

*Number of extinct invertebrates is probably greatly underestimated due to lack of knowledge for many species (other groups are probably underestimated to a lesser extent for the same reason).

*komodoensis)* lives only on a few small islands in the Indonesian archipelago, and the Mauna Kea (*Argyroxiphium sandwicense*) and Haleakala silverswords (*A. s. macrocephalum*) each lives in a single volcano crater on the island of Hawaii (figure 60.2). Isolated geographic areas, such as oceanic islands, lakes, and mountain peaks, often have high percentages of endemic species, many in significant danger of extinction.

The number of endemic plant species can vary greatly from one place to another. In the United States, for example, 379 plant species are found in Texas and nowhere else, whereas New York has only one endemic plant species. California, with its varied array of habitats, including deserts, mountains, seacoast, old-growth forests, and grasslands, is home to more endemic plant species than any other state.

## Species hotspots

Worldwide, notable concentrations of endemic species occur in particular regions. Conservationists have recently identified areas, termed hotspots, that have high endemism and are disappearing at a rapid rate. Such hotspots include Madagascar, a variety of tropical rain forests, the eastern Himalayas, areas with Mediterranean climates such as California, South Africa, and Australia, and several other areas (figure 60.3 and table 60.2). Overall, 25 such hotspots have been identified,

**Figure 60.2  Mauna Kea silversword (*Argyroxiphium sandwicense*).**  Many species of silverswords are endemic to very small areas. This photo illustrates two stages in the plant's life cycle.

which in total contain nearly half of all the terrestrial species in the world.

Why these areas contain so many endemic species is a topic of active scientific research. Some of these hotspots occur in areas of high species diversity; for these hotspots, the explanations for high species diversity in general, such as high productivity, probably apply (see chapter 58). In addition, some hotspots occur

**Figure 60.3  Hotspots of high endemism.**  These areas are rich in endemic species under threat of imminent extinction.

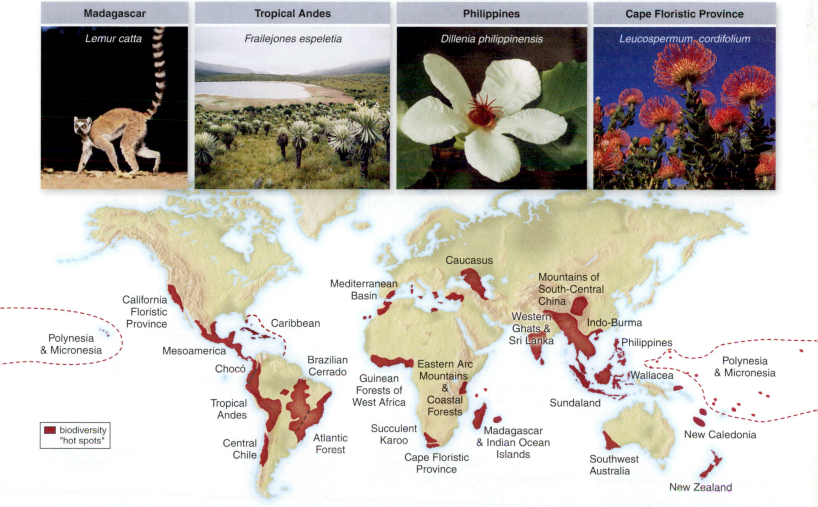

chapter **60** *Conservation Biology*

| TABLE 60.2 | Numbers of Endemic Species in Some Hotspot Areas | | | |
|---|---|---|---|---|
| **Region** | **Mammals** | **Reptiles** | **Amphibians** | **Plants** |
| Atlantic coastal forest (Brazil) | 160 | 60 | 253 | 6,000 |
| South American Chocó | 60 | 63 | 210 | 2,250 |
| Philippines | 115 | 159 | 65 | 5,832 |
| Tropical Andes | 68 | 218 | 604 | 20,000 |
| Southwestern Australia | 7 | 50 | 24 | 4,331 |
| Madagascar | 84 | 301 | 187 | 9,704 |
| Cape region (South Africa) | 9 | 19 | 19 | 5,682 |
| California Floristic Province | 30 | 16 | 17 | 2,125 |
| New Caledonia | 6 | 56 | 0 | 2,551 |
| South-Central China | 75 | 16 | 51 | 3,500 |

on isolated islands, such as New Zealand, New Caledonia, and the Hawaiian Islands, where evolutionary diversification over long periods has resulted in rich biotas composed of plant and animal species found nowhere else in the world.

## Human population growth in hotspots

Because of the great number of endemic species that hotspots contain, conserving their biological diversity must be an important component of efforts to safeguard the world's biological heritage. Or, to look at it another way, by protecting just 1.4% of the world's land surface, 44% of the world's vascular plants and 35% of its terrestrial vertebrates can be preserved.

Unfortunately, hotspots contain not only many endemic species, but also growing human populations. In 1995, these areas contained 1.1 billion people—20% of the world's population—sometimes at high densities (figure 60.4a). More important, human populations were growing in all but one of these hotspots both because birth rates are much higher than

**Figure 60.4**
**Human populations in hotspots.**
*a.* Human population density and **(b)** population growth rate in biodiversity hotspots.

**Inquiry question**

? Why do population density and growth rates differ among hotspots?

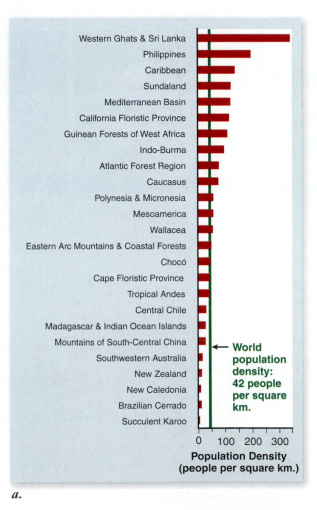

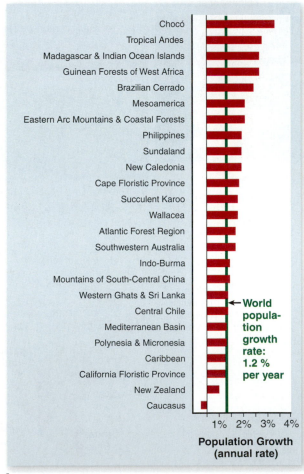

*a.*

*b.*

death rates and because rates of immigration into these areas are often high. Overall, the rate of growth exceeded the global average in 19 hotspots (figure 60.4b). In some hotspots, the rate of growth is nearly twice that of the rest of the world.

Not surprisingly, many of these areas are experiencing high rates of habitat destruction as land is cleared for agriculture, housing, and economic development. More than 70% of the original area of each hotspot has already disappeared, and in 14 hotspots, 15% or less of the original habitat remains. In Madagascar, it is estimated that 90% of the original forest has already been lost—this on an island where 85% of the species are found nowhere else in the world. In the forests of the Atlantic coast of Brazil, the extent of deforestation is even higher: 95% of the original forest is gone.

Population pressure is not the only cause of habitat destruction in hotspots. Commercial exploitation to meet the demands of more affluent people in the developed world also plays an important role. For example, large-scale logging of tropical rain forests occurs in countries around the world to provide lumber, most of which ends up in the United States, western Europe, and Japan. Similarly, many forests in Central and South America are cleared to make way for cattle ranches that produce cheap meat for fast-food restaurants. Hotspots in more affluent countries are often at risk because they occur in areas where land has great value for real estate and commercial purposes, such as in Florida and California in the United States.

### Learning Outcomes Review 60.1

The most recent losses of biodiversity have resulted from human activities, in both prehistoric and historical times. Endemic species are found in only a single region on Earth; regions with a high number of endemic species, known as hotspots, are particularly threatened by human encroachment and their preservation is critical.

- ■ *Why does so much resource exploitation occur in areas that are biodiversity hotspots?*

## 60.2 The Value of Biodiversity

### Learning Outcomes

1. *Distinguish between the direct and indirect economic value of biodiversity.*
2. *Explain what is meant by the aesthetic value of biodiversity.*

Why should we worry about loss of biodiversity? The reason is that biodiversity is valuable to us in a number of ways:

- ■ *Direct economic value* of products we obtain from species of plants, animals, and other groups
- ■ *Indirect economic value* of benefits produced by species without our consuming them
- ■ *Ethical and aesthetic values*

## The direct economic value of biodiversity includes resources for our survival

Many species have direct value as sources of food, medicine, clothing, biomass (for energy and other purposes), and shelter. Most of the world's food crops, for example, are derived from a small number of plants that were originally domesticated from wild plants in tropical and semiarid regions. As a result, many of our most important crops, such as corn, wheat, and rice, contain relatively little genetic variation (equivalent to a founder effect; see chapter 20), whereas their wild relatives have great diversity.

In the future, genetic variation from wild strains of these species may be needed if we are to improve yields or find a way to breed resistance to new pests. In fact, recent agricultural breeding experiments have illustrated the value of conserving wild relatives of common crops. For example, by breeding commercial varieties of tomato with a small, oddly colored wild tomato species from the mountains of Peru, scientists were able to increase crop yields by 50%, while increasing both nutritional content and color.

About 70% of the world's population depends directly on wild plants as their source of medicine. In addition, about 40% of the prescription and nonprescription drugs used today have active ingredients extracted from plants or animals. Aspirin, the world's most widely used drug, was first extracted from the leaves of the tropical willow, *Salix alba*. The rosy periwinkle from Madagascar has yielded potent drugs for combating childhood leukemia (figure 60.5), and drugs effective in treating

*a.*                                    *b.*

**Figure 60.5** **Plants of pharmaceutical importance.**
*a.* Two drugs extracted from the rosy periwinkle (*Catharanthus roseus*), vinblastine and vincristine, effectively treat common forms of childhood leukemia, increasing chances of survival from 20% to over 95%. *b.* Cancer-fighting drugs, such as taxol, have been developed from the bark of the Pacific yew (*Taxus brevifolia*).

several forms of cancer and other diseases have been produced from the Pacific yew. Overall, 62% of cancer drugs were developed from products derived from plants and animals.

Only recently have biologists perfected the techniques that make possible the transfer of genes from one species to another. We are just beginning to use genes obtained from other species to our advantage (see chapter 15). So-called "gene prospecting" of the genomes of plants and animals for useful genes has only begun. We have been able to examine only a minute proportion of the world's organisms to see whether any of their genes have useful properties for humans.

By conserving biodiversity, we maintain the option of finding useful benefits in the future. Unfortunately, many of the most promising species occur in habitats, such as tropical rain forests, that are being destroyed at an alarming rate.

## Indirect economic value is derived from ecosystem services

Diverse biological communities are of vital importance to healthy ecosystems. They help maintain the chemical quality of natural water, buffer ecosystems against storms and drought, preserve soils and prevent loss of minerals and nutrients, moderate local and regional climate, absorb pollution, and promote the breakdown of organic wastes and the cycling of minerals.

In chapter 58, we discussed the evidence that the stability and productivity of ecosystems is related to species richness. By destroying biodiversity, we are creating conditions of instability and lessened productivity and promoting desertification, waterlogging, mineralization, and many other undesirable outcomes throughout the world.

### The value of intact habitats

Economists have recently been able to compare the societal value, in monetary terms, of intact habitats compared with the value of destroying those habitats. Surprisingly, in most studies conducted so far, intact ecosystems are more valuable than the products derived by destroying them. In Thailand, as one example, coastal mangrove habitats are commonly cleared so that shrimp farms can be established. Although the shrimp produced are valuable, their value is vastly outweighed by the benefits in timber, charcoal production, offshore fisheries, and storm protection provided by the mangroves (figure 60.6a).

Similarly, intact tropical rain forest in Cameroon, West Africa, provides fruit and other forest materials. Clearing the forest for agriculture or palm plantations leads to stream-polluting erosion as well as increased flooding. Combining all the costs and benefits of the three options, maintaining intact forests has the highest economic value (figure 60.6b).

### Case study: New York City watersheds

Probably the most famous example of the value of intact ecosystems is provided by the watersheds of New York City. Ninety percent of the water for the New York area's 9 million residents comes from the Catskill Mountains and the nearby headwaters of the Delaware River (figure 60.7). Water that runs off from over 4000 km² of rural, mountainous areas is collected into reservoirs and then transported by aqueduct more than 136.8 km to New York City at a rate of 4.9 billion liters per day.

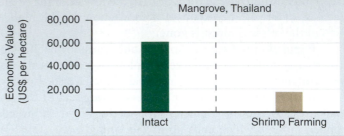

*a.*

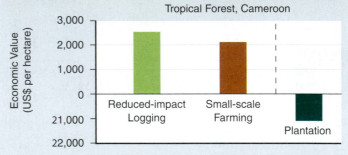

*b.*

**Figure 60.6** **The economic value of maintaining habitats.** *a.* Mangroves in Thailand are more valuable than shrimp farms. *b.* Rain forests in Cameroon provide more economic benefits if they are left standing than if they are destroyed and the land used for other purposes.

### Inquiry question

**?** If shrimp farms established on cleared mangrove habitats make money, how can clearing mangroves not be an economic plus?

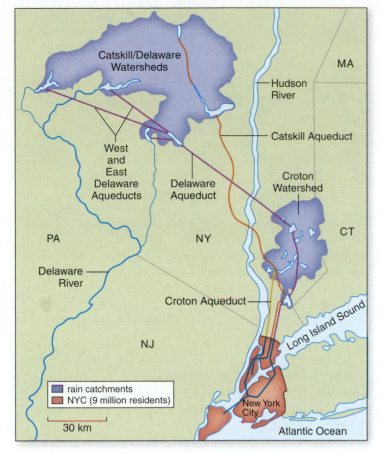

**Figure 60.7** **New York City's water source.** New York gets its water from distant rain catchments. Preserving the ecological integrity of these areas is cheaper than building new water treatment plants.

In the 1990s, New York City faced a dilemma. New federal water regulations were requiring ever cleaner water, even as development and pollution in the source areas of the water were threatening to compromise water quality. The city had two choices: either work to protect the functioning ecosystem so that it could produce clean water, or construct filtration plants to clean it on arrival. Economic analysis made the choice clear: Building the plants would cost $6 billion, with annual operating costs of $300 million, whereas spending a billion dollars over 10 years could preserve the ecosystem and maintain water purity. The decision was easy.

### Economic trade-offs

These examples provide some idea of the value of the services that ecosystems provide. But maintaining ecosystems is not always more valuable than converting them to other uses. Certainly, when the United States was being settled and land was plentiful, ecosystem conversion was beneficial. Even today, habitat destruction sometimes is economically desirable. Nonetheless, we still have only a rudimentary knowledge of the many ways intact ecosystems provide services. Often, it is not until they are lost that the value becomes clear, as unexpected negative effects, such as increased flooding and pollution, decreased rainfall, or vulnerability to hurricanes become apparent.

The same argument can be made for preserving particular species within ecosystems. Given how little we know about the biology of most species, particularly in the tropics, it is impossible to predict all the consequences of removing a species.

Imagine taking a parts list for an airplane and randomly changing a digit in one of the part numbers. You might change a seat cushion into a roll of toilet paper—or you might just as easily change a key bolt holding up a wing into a pencil. By removing biodiversity, we are gambling with the future of the ecosystems on which we depend and whose functioning we understand very little.

In recent years, the field of ecological economics has developed to study how the societal benefits provided by species and ecosystems can be appropriately valued. The problem is twofold. First, until recently, we have not had a good estimate of the monetary value of services provided by ecosystems, a situation which, as you've just seen, is now changing.

The second problem, however, is that the people who gain the benefits of environmental degradation are often not the same as the people who pay the costs. For instance, in the Thai mangrove example, the shrimp farmers reap the financial rewards, while the local people bear the costs. The same is true of factories that produce air or water pollution. Environmental economists are devising ways to appropriately value and regulate the use of the environment in ways that maximize the benefits relative to the costs to society as a whole.

## Ethical and aesthetic values are based on our conscience and our consciousness

Many people believe that preserving biodiversity is an ethical issue because every species is of value in its own right, even if humans are not able to exploit or benefit from it. These people feel that along with the power to exploit and destroy other species comes responsibility: As the only organisms capable of eliminating large numbers of species and entire ecosystems, and as the only organisms capable of reflecting on what we are doing, humans should act as guardians or stewards for the diversity of life around us.

Almost no one would deny the aesthetic value of biodiversity—a wild mountain range, a beautiful flower, or a noble elephant—but how do we place a value on beauty or on the renewal many of us feel when we are in natural surroundings? Perhaps the best we can do is to consider the deep sense of loss we would feel if it no longer existed.

> ### Learning Outcomes Review 60.2
> The direct value of biodiversity includes resources for our survival, such as natural products and medicines that enhance our lives and can be used in a sustainable way. Indirect value includes economic benefits provided by healthy ecosystems, such as availability of clean water and recreational benefits. The aesthetic value of biodiversity refers to our sense of beauty and peace when experiencing a natural environment.
>
> ■ *What arguments could you use to convince shrimp farmers to stop operations and remediate the area they are using?*

## 60.3 Factors Responsible for Extinction

### Learning Outcomes

1. List the major causes of habitat destruction.
2. Explain how these causes can interact to bring about extinction.

A variety of causes, independently or in concert, are responsible for extinctions (table 60.3). Historically, overexploitation was the major cause of extinction; although it is still a factor, habitat loss is the major problem for most groups today, and introduced species rank second. Many other factors can contribute to species extinctions as well, including disruption of ecosystem interactions, pollution, loss of genetic variation, and catastrophic disturbances, either natural or human-caused.

More than one of these factors may affect a species. In fact, a chain reaction is possible in which the action of one factor predisposes a species to be more severely affected by another factor. For example, habitat destruction may lead to decreased birth rates and increased mortality rates. As a result, populations become smaller and more fragmented, making them more vulnerable to disasters such as floods or forest fires, which may eliminate populations. Also, as the habitat becomes more fragmented, populations become isolated, so that genetic interchange ceases and areas devastated by disasters are not recolonized. Finally, as populations become very small, inbreeding increases, and genetic variation is lost through genetic drift, further decreasing population fitness. Which factor acts as the final coup de grace may be irrelevant; many factors, and the interactions between them, may have contributed to a species' eventual extinction.

**Figure 60.8 An extinct species.** A breeding assemblage of the golden toad (*Bufo periglenes*) which was last seen in the wild in 1989.

### Amphibians are on the decline: A case study

In 1963, herpetologist Jay Savage was hiking through pristine cloud forest in Costa Rica. Reaching a windswept ridge, he couldn't believe his eyes. Before him was a huge aggregation of breeding toads. What was so amazing was the color of the toads: bright, eye-dazzling orange, unlike anything he had ever seen before (figure 60.8).

The color of the toads was so amazing and unexpected that Savage briefly considered the possibility that his colleagues had played a practical joke, getting to the clearing before him and somehow coloring normal toads orange. Realizing that this could not be, he went on to study the toads, eventually describing a species new to science, the golden toad, *Bufo periglenes*.

For the next 24 years, large numbers of toads were seen during the breeding season each spring. Their home was legally recognized as the Monteverde Cloud Forest Reserve, a well-protected, intact, and functioning ecosystem, seemingly

| TABLE 60.3 | Causes of Extinctions | | | | |
|---|---|---|---|---|---|
| | *PERCENTAGE OF SPECIES INFLUENCED BY A GIVEN FACTOR** | | | | |
| **Group** | **Habitat Loss** | **Overexploitation** | **Species Introduction** | **Other** | **Unknown** |
| EXTINCTIONS | | | | | |
| Mammals | 19 | 23 | 20 | 2 | 36 |
| Birds | 20 | 11 | 22 | 2 | 45 |
| Reptiles | 5 | 32 | 42 | 0 | 21 |
| Fish | 35 | 4 | 30 | 4 | 48 |
| THREATENED EXTINCTIONS | | | | | |
| Mammals | 68 | 54 | 6 | 20 | — |
| Birds | 58 | 30 | 28 | 2 | — |
| Reptiles | 53 | 63 | 17 | 9 | — |
| Fish | 78 | 12 | 28 | 2 | — |

*Some species may be influenced by more than one factor; thus, some rows may exceed 100%.

| Venezuela | Panama | Madagascar | Australia |
|---|---|---|---|
| *Dendrobates leucomelas* | *Atelopus zeteki* | *Mantella aurantiaca* | *Litoria caerulea* |

**Figure 60.9 Amphibian extinction crisis.** Boxes indicate the number of threatened species around the world. These numbers are rapidly being revised upward as scientists focus their attention on little-known species, many of which turn out to be in grave danger.

a successful model of conservation. Then, in 1988, few toads were seen, and in 1989, only a single male was observed. Since then, despite exhaustive efforts, no more golden toads have been found.

Despite living in a well-protected ecosystem, with no obvious threats from pollution, introduced species, overexploitation, or any other factor, the species appears to have gone extinct, right under the eyes of watchful scientists and conservationists. How could this happen?

### Frogs in trouble

At the first World Herpetological Congress in 1989 in Canterbury, England, frog experts from around the world met to discuss conservation issues relating to frogs and toads. At this meeting, it became clear that the golden toad story was not unique. Experts reported case after case of similar losses: Frog populations that had once been abundant were now decreasing or entirely gone.

Since then, scientists have devoted a great deal of time and effort to determining whether frogs and other amphibian species truly are in trouble and, if so, why. Unfortunately, the situation appears to be even worse than originally suspected. Amphibian experts recently reported that 43% of all amphibian

species have experienced decreases in population size, and one third of all amphibian species are threatened with extinction in countries as different as Ecuador, Venezuela, Australia, and the United States (figure 60.9).

Moreover, these numbers are probably underestimates; little information exists from many areas of the world, such as Southeast Asia and central Africa. Indeed researchers think that as many as 100 species from the island nation of Sri Lanka have recently gone extinct, perhaps not surprisingly because 95% of that nation's rain forests have also disappeared in recent times.

### Cause for concern

Amphibian declines are worrisome for several reasons. First, many of the species—including the golden toad—have declined in pristine, well-protected habitats. If species are becoming extinct in such areas, it brings into question our ability to preserve global biological diversity.

Second, many amphibian species are particularly sensitive to the state of the environment because of their moist skin, which allows chemicals from the environment to pass into the body, and their use of aquatic habitats for larval stages, which requires unpolluted water. In other words, amphibians may be analogous to the canaries formerly used in coal mines to detect problems with air quality: If the canaries keeled over, the miners knew they had to get out.

Third, no single cause for amphibian declines is apparent. Although a single cause would be of concern, it would also suggest that a coordinated global effort could reverse the trend, as happened with chlorofluorocarbons and decreasing ozone levels (see chapter 59). However, different species are afflicted by different problems, including habitat destruction, the effects of global warming, pollution, decreased stratospheric ozone levels, disease epidemics, and introduced species.

The implication is that the global environment is deteriorating in many different ways. Could amphibians be global "canaries," serving as indicators that the world's environment is in serious trouble?

## Habitat loss devastates species richness

As table 60.3 indicates, habitat loss is the most important cause of modern-day extinction. Given the tremendous amounts of ongoing destruction of all types of habitat, from rain forest to ocean floor, this should come as no surprise. Natural habitats may be adversely affected by humans in four ways:

1. **destruction,**
2. **pollution,**
3. **disruption,** and
4. **habitat fragmentation.**

In addition to these causes, global climate change, discussed in the previous chapter, is an insidious threat that combines many of these factors. As climate changes, habitats will change—or disappear entirely, as is the case for polar bears (*Thalarctos maritimus*), which require ice floes on which to hunt their seal prey. Some studies estimate that as many as 30% of all species may be imperiled by global warming.

### Destruction of habitat

A proportion of the habitat available to a particular species may simply be destroyed. This destruction is a common occurrence in the "clear-cut" harvesting of timber, in the burning of tropical forest to produce grazing land, and in urban and industrial development. Deforestation has been, and continues to be, by far the most pervasive form of habitat disruption (figure 60.10). Many tropical forests are being cut or burned at a rate of 1% or more per year.

To estimate the effect of reductions in habitat available to a species, biologists often use the well-established observation that larger areas support more species (see figure 58.22). Although this relationship varies according to geographic area, type of organism, and type of area, in general a 10-fold increase in area leads to approximately a doubling in the number of species. This relationship suggests, conversely, that if the area of a habitat is reduced by 90%, so that only 10% remains, then half of all species will be lost. Evidence for this hypothesis comes from a study in Finland of extinction rates of birds on habitat islands (that is, islands of a particular type of habitat surrounded by unsuitable habitat) where the population extinction rate was found to be inversely proportional to island size (figure 60.11).

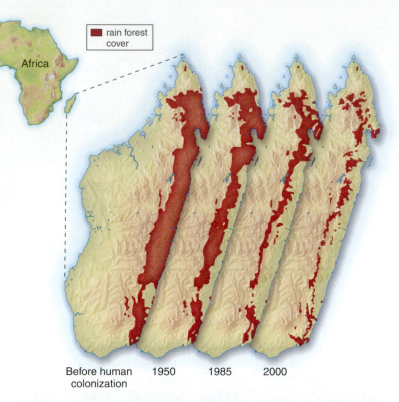

Before human colonization    1950    1985    2000

**Figure 60.10  Extinction and habitat destruction.**
The rain forest covering the eastern coast of Madagascar, an island off the coast of East Africa, has been progressively destroyed and fragmented as the island's human population has grown. Ninety percent of the eastern coast's original forest cover is now gone. Many species have become extinct, and many others are threatened, including 16 of Madagascar's 31 primate species.

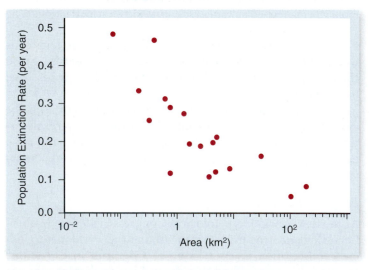

**Figure 60.11  Extinction and island area.**  The data present percent extinction rates for populations as a function of habitat area for birds on a series of Finnish habitat islands. Smaller islands experience far greater extinction rates.

**Inquiry question**

**?**  Why does extinction rate increase with decreasing island size?

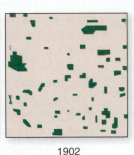

1831      1882      1902      1950

**Figure 60.12 Fragmentation of woodland habitat.** From the time of settlement of Cadiz Township, Wisconsin, the forest has been progressively reduced from a nearly continuous cover to isolated woodlots covering less than 1% of the original area.

## Pollution

Habitat may be degraded by pollution to the extent that some species can no longer survive there. Degradation occurs as a result of many forms of pollution, from acid rain to pesticides. Aquatic environments are particularly vulnerable; for example, many northern lakes in both Europe and North America have been essentially sterilized by acid rain (see chapter 59).

## Disruption

Human activities may disrupt a habitat enough to make it untenable for some species. For example, visitors to caves in Alabama and Tennessee caused significant population declines in bats over an 8-year period, some as great as 100%. When visits were fewer than one per month, less than 20% of bats were lost, but caves having more than four visits per month suffered population declines of 86% to 95%.

More generally, humans often alter the interactions that occur among species, such as the predator–prey or symbiotic relationships discussed in chapter 57. These disruptions can have far-ranging effects throughout an ecosystem. For example, when pollinating insects are killed off by insecticides, many plants do not reproduce, thus affecting all the animals that depend on the plants and their seeds for food.

## Habitat fragmentation

Loss of habitat by a species frequently results not only in lowered population numbers, but also in fragmentation of the population into unconnected patches (figure 60.12). A habitat also may become fragmented in nonobvious ways, as when roads and habitation intrude into forest. The effect is to carve the populations living in the habitat into a series of smaller populations, often with disastrous consequences because of the relationship between range size and extinction rate. Although detailed data

are not available, fragmentation of wildlife habitat in developed temperate areas is thought to be very substantial.

As habitats become fragmented and shrink in size, the relative proportion of the habitat that occurs on the boundary, or edge, increases. **Edge effects** can significantly degrade a population's chances of survival. Changes in microclimate (such as temperature, wind, humidity) near the edge may reduce appropriate habitat for many species more than the physical fragmentation suggests. In isolated fragments of rain forest, for example, trees on the edge are exposed to direct sunlight. As a result, these trees experience hotter and drier conditions than those normally encountered in the cool, moist forest interior, leading to negative effects on their survival and growth. In one study, the biomass of trees within 100 m of the forest edge decreased by 36% in the first 17 years after fragment isolation.

Also, increasing habitat edges opens up opportunities for some parasite and predator species that are more effective at edges. As fragments decrease in size, the proportion of habitat that is distant from any edge decreases, and consequently, more and more of the habitat is within the range of these species. Habitat fragmentation is blamed for local extinctions in a wide range of species.

The impact of habitat fragmentation can be seen clearly in a study conducted in Manaus, Brazil, where the rain forest was commercially logged. Landowners agreed to preserve patches of rain forest of various sizes, and censuses of these patches were taken before the logging started, while they were still part of a continuous forest. After logging, species began to disappear from the now-isolated patches (figure 60.13). First to go were the monkeys, which have large home ranges. Birds that prey on the insects flushed out by marching army ants followed, disappearing from patches too small to maintain enough army ant colonies to support them. As expected, the

**Figure 60.13 A study of habitat fragmentation.** Landowners in Manaus, Brazil, agreed to preserve patches of rain forest of different sizes to examine the effect of patch size on species extinction. Biodiversity was monitored in the isolated patches before and after logging. Fragmentation led to significant species loss within patches. Army ants were one of the species that disappeared from smaller patches.

extinction rate was negatively related to patch size, but even the largest patches (100 hectares) lost half of their bird species in less than 15 years.

Because some species, such as monkeys, require large patches, large fragments are indispensable if we wish to preserve high levels of biodiversity. The take-home lesson is that preservation programs will need to provide suitably large habitat fragments to avoid this effect.

### Case study: Songbird declines

Every year since 1966, the U.S. Fish and Wildlife Service has organized thousands of amateur ornithologists and birdwatchers in an annual bird count called the Breeding Bird Survey. In recent years, a shocking trend has emerged. While year-round residents that prosper around humans, such as robins, starlings, and blackbirds, have increased their numbers and distribution over the last 30 years, forest songbirds have declined severely. The decline has been greatest among long-distance migrants such as thrushes, orioles, tanagers, vireos, buntings, and warblers. These birds nest in northern forests in the summer, but spend their winters in South or Central America or the Caribbean Islands.

In many areas of the eastern United States, more than three-quarters of the tropical migrant bird species have declined significantly. Rock Creek Park in Washington, D.C., for example, has lost 90% of its long-distance migrants in the past 20 years. Nationwide, American redstarts declined about 50% in the single decade of the 1970s. Studies of radar images from National Weather Service stations in Texas and Louisiana indicate that only about half as many birds fly over the Gulf of Mexico each spring as did in the 1960s. This suggests a total loss of about half a billion birds.

The culprit responsible for this widespread decline appears to be habitat fragmentation and loss. Fragmentation of breeding habitat and nesting failures in the summer nesting grounds of the United States and Canada have had a major negative effect on the breeding of woodland songbirds. Many of the most threatened species are adapted to deep woods and need an area of 25 acres or more per pair to breed and raise their young. As woodlands are broken up by roads and developments, it is becoming increasingly difficult for them to find enough contiguous woods to nest successfully.

A second and perhaps even more important factor is the availability of critical winter habitat in Central and South America. Studies of the American redstart clearly indicate that birds with better winter habitat have a superior chance of successfully migrating back to their breeding grounds in the spring. In a recent study, scientists were able to determine the quality of the habitat that particular birds used during the winter by examining levels of the stable carbon isotope $^{13}C$ in their blood. Plants growing in the best habitats in Jamaica and Honduras (mangroves and wetland forests) have low levels of $^{13}C$, and so do the redstarts that feed on the insects that live in them. Of these wet-forest birds, 65% maintained or gained weight over the winter.

By contrast, plants growing in substandard dry scrub have high levels of $^{13}C$, and so do the redstarts that feed in those habitats. Scrub-dwelling birds lost up to 11% of their body mass over the winter. Now here's the key: Birds that winter in the substandard scrub leave later in the spring on the long flight to northern breeding grounds, arrive later at their summer homes, and have fewer young (figure 60.14).

The proportion of $^{13}C$ in birds arriving in New Hampshire breeding grounds increases as spring wears on and scrub-overwintering stragglers belatedly arrive. Thus, loss of mangrove habitat in the neotropics is having a quantifiable negative influence. As the best habitat disappears, overwintering birds fare poorly, and this leads to decreased reproduction and population declines.

Unfortunately, the Caribbean lost about 10% of its mangroves in the 1980s, and continues to lose about 1% per year. This loss of key habitat appears to be a driving force in the looming extinction of some songbirds.

## Overexploitation wipes out species quickly

Species that are hunted or harvested by humans have historically been at grave risk of extinction, even when the species is initially very abundant. A century ago, the skies of North America were darkened by huge flocks of passenger pigeons, but after being hunted as free and tasty food, they were driven to extinction. The bison that used to migrate in enormous herds

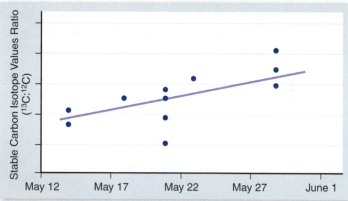

**Figure 60.14** **The American redstart (*Setophaga ruticilla*) a migratory songbird.** The numbers of this species are in serious decline. The graph presents data on the ratio of $^{13}C$ to $^{12}C$ in male redstarts arriving at summer breeding grounds. Early arrivals, which have higher reproductive success, have lower proportions of $^{13}C$ to $^{12}C$, indicating they wintered in more favorable mangrove–wetland forest habitats.

across the central plains of North America only narrowly escaped the same fate.

## Commercial motivation for exploitation

The existence of a commercial market often leads to overexploitation of a species. The international trade in furs, for example, has severely reduced the numbers of chinchilla, vicuña, otter, and many cat species. The harvesting of commercially valuable trees provides another example: Almost all West Indies mahogany trees (*Swietenia mahogani*) have been logged, and the extensive cedar forests of Lebanon, once widespread at high elevations, now survive in only a few isolated groves.

A particularly telling example of overexploitation is the commercial harvesting of fish in the North Atlantic. During the 1980s, fishing fleets continued to harvest large amounts of cod off the coast of Newfoundland, even as the population numbers declined precipitously. By 1992, the cod population had dropped to less than 1% of its original numbers. The American and Canadian governments have closed the fishery, but no one can predict whether the fish populations will recover. The Atlantic bluefin tuna has experienced a 90% population decline in the past 10 years. The swordfish has declined even further. In both cases, the drop has led to even more intense fishing of the remaining populations.

## Case study: Whales

Whales, the largest living animals that ever evolved, are rare in the world's oceans today, their numbers driven down by commercial whaling. Before the advent of cheap, high-grade oils manufactured from petroleum in the early 20th century, oil made from whale blubber was an important commercial product in the worldwide marketplace. In addition, the fine, lattice-like structure termed "baleen" used by baleen whales to filter-feed plankton from seawater was used in women's undergarments. Because a whale is such a large animal, each individual captured is of significant commercial value.

In the 18th century, right whales were the first to bear the brunt of commercial whaling. They were called "right" whales because they were slow, easy to capture, did not sink when killed and provided up to 150 barrels of blubber oil and abundant baleen, making them the right whale for a commercial whaler to hunt.

As the right whale declined, whalers turned to the gray, humpback, and bowhead whales. As their numbers declined, whalers turned to the blue, the largest of all whales, and when those were decimated, to the fin, then the Sei, and then the sperm whales. As each species of whale became the focus of commercial whaling, its numbers began a steep decline (figure 60.15).

Hunting of right whales was made illegal in 1935. By then, they had been driven to the brink of extinction, their numbers less than 5% of what they had been. Although protected ever since, their numbers have not recovered in either the North Atlantic or the North Pacific. By 1946, several other whale species faced imminent extinction, and whaling nations formed the International Whaling Commission (IWC) to regulate commercial whale hunting. Like a fox guarding the henhouse, the IWC for decades did little to limit whale harvests, and whale numbers continued to decline steeply.

Finally, in 1974, when the numbers of all but the small minke whales had been driven down, the IWC banned hunting of blue, gray, and humpback whales, and instituted partial bans on other species. The rule was violated so often, however, that the IWC in 1986 instituted a worldwide moratorium on all commercial killing of whales. Although some commercial whaling continues, often under the guise of harvesting for scientific studies, annual whale harvests have dropped dramatically in the last 20 years.

Some species appear to be recovering, but others are not. Humpback numbers have more than doubled since the early 1960s, increasing nearly 10% annually, and Pacific gray whales have fully recovered to their previous numbers of about 20,000 animals, after having been hunted to fewer than 1000. Right, sperm, fin, and blue whales have not recovered, and no one knows whether they ever will.

## Introduced species threaten native species and habitats

Colonization, a natural process by which a species expands its geographic range, occurs in many ways: A flock of birds gets blown off course, a bird eats a fruit and defecates its seed miles away, or lowered sea levels connect two previously isolated landmasses, allowing species to freely move back and forth. Such events—particularly those leading to successful establishment of a new population—probably occur rarely, but when they do, the resulting change to natural communities can be large. The reason is that colonization brings together species with no history of interaction. Consequently, ecological interactions may

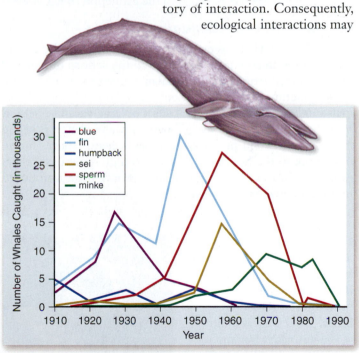

**Figure 60.15 World catch of some whale species in the 20th century.** Each species is hunted in turn until its numbers fall so low that hunting it becomes commercially unprofitable.

### Inquiry question

**?** Why might whale populations fail to recover once hunting is stopped?

**Figure 60.16** **Zebra mussels** *(Dreissena polymorpha)* **clogging a pipe.** These mussels were introduced from Europe, and are now a major problem in North American rivers.

be particularly strong because the species have not evolved ways of adjusting to the presence of one another, such as adaptations to avoid predation or to minimize competitive effects.

The paleontological record documents many cases in which geologic changes brought previously isolated species together, such as when the Isthmus of Panama emerged above the sea approximately 3 MYA, connecting the previously isolated fauna and flora of North and South America. In some cases, the result has been an increase in species diversity, but in other cases, invading species have led to the extinction of natives.

### Human influence on colonization

Unfortunately, what was naturally a rare process has become all too common in recent years, thanks to the actions of humans. Species introductions due to human activities occur in many ways, sometimes intentionally, but usually not. Plants and animals can be transported in the ballast of large ocean vessels; in nursery plants; as stowaways in boats, cars, and planes; as beetle larvae within wood products—even as seeds or spores in the mud stuck to the bottom of a shoe. Overall, some researchers estimate that as many as 50,000 species have been introduced into the United States.

The effects of introductions on humans have been enormous. In the United States alone, nonnative species cost the economy an estimated $140 billion per year. For example, dozens of foreign weeds in Colorado have covered more than a million acres. Just three of these species cost wheat farmers tens of millions of dollars. At the same time, leafy spurge, a plant from Europe, outcompetes native grasses, ruining rangeland for cattle at a price tag of $144 million per year.

The zebra mussel, a mollusk native to the Black Sea region, is a huge problem throughout much of the eastern and central United States, where it can attain densities as high as 700,000/m², clogging pipes, including those for water and power plants, and causing an estimated $3 to $5 billion damage a year (figure 60.16).

Introduced species can also affect human health. For example, West Nile fever was probably introduced from Africa or the Middle East to the United States in the late 1990s.

The effect of species introductions on native ecosystems is equally dramatic. Islands have been particularly affected. For example, as mentioned in chapter 57, a single lighthouse keeper's cat wiped out an entire species, the Stephens Island wren. Rats had a devastating effect throughout the South Pacific where bird species nested on the ground and had no defense against the voracious predators to which they were evolutionarily naive. More recently, the brown tree snake, introduced to the island of Guam, essentially eliminated all species of forest birds.

In Hawaii, the problem has been slightly different: Introduced mosquitoes brought with them malaria, to which the native species had evolved no resistance. The result is that more than 100 species (>70% of the native fauna) either became extinct or are now restricted to higher and cooler elevations where the mosquitoes don't occur (figure 60.17).

The effects of introduced species are not always direct, but instead may reverberate throughout an ecosystem. For example, the Argentine ant has spread through much of the southern United States, greatly reducing populations of most native ant species with which it comes in contact. The extinction of these ant species has had a dramatic negative effect on the coast horned lizard (*Phrynosoma coronatum*), which feeds on the larger native species. In their absence, the lizards have shifted to less-preferred prey species. In addition, the native ant species consume seeds, and in the process, play an important

**Figure 60.17** **The akiapolaau** *(Hemignathus munroi)* **and the Palila** *(Loxioides bailleui),* **endangered Hawaiian birds.** More than two-thirds of Hawaii's native bird species are now extinct or have been greatly reduced in population size. Bird faunas on islands around the world have experienced similar declines after human arrival.

role in seed dispersal. Argentine ants, by contrast, do not eat seeds. In South Africa, where the Argentine ant has also appeared, at least one plant species has experienced decreased reproductive success due to the loss of its dispersal agent.

The most dramatic effects of introduced species, however, occur when entire ecosystems are transformed. Some plant species can completely overrun a habitat, displacing all native species and turning the area into a monoculture (that is, an area occupied by a single species). In California, the yellow star thistle now covers 4 million hectares of what was once highly productive grassland. In Hawaii, a small tree native to the Canary Islands, *Myrica faya*, has spread widely. Because it is able to fix nitrogen at high rates, it has caused a 90-fold increase in the nitrogen content of the soil, thus allowing other, nitrogen-requiring species to invade.

### Efforts to combat introduced species

Once an introduced species becomes established, eradicating it is often extremely difficult, expensive, and time-consuming. Some efforts—such as the removal of goats and rabbits from certain small islands—have been successful, but many other efforts have failed. The best hope for stopping the ravages of introduced species is to prevent them from being introduced in the first place. Although easier said than done, government agencies are now working strenuously to put into place procedures that can intercept species in transit, before they have the opportunity to become established.

### Case study: Lake Victoria cichlids

Lake Victoria, an immense, shallow, freshwater sea about the size of Switzerland in the heart of equatorial East Africa, used to be home to an incredibly diverse collection of over 300 species of cichlid fishes (see figure 22.15). These small, perchlike fish range from 5 to 13 cm in length, with males having endless varieties of color. Today, most of these cichlid species are threatened, endangered, or extinct.

What happened to bring about the abrupt loss of so many endemic cichlid species? In 1954, the Nile perch, a commercial fish with a voracious appetite, was purposely introduced on the Ugandan shore of Lake Victoria. Nile perch, which grow to over a meter in length, were to form the basis of a new fishing industry (figure 60.18). For decades, these perch did not seem to have a significant effect; over 30 years later, in 1978, Nile perch still made up less than 2% of the fish harvested from the lake.

Then something happened to cause the Nile perch population to explode and to spread rapidly through the lake, eating their way through the cichlids. By 1986, Nile perch constituted nearly 80% of the total catch of fish from the lake and the endemic cichlid species were virtually gone. Over 70% of cichlid species disappeared, including all open-water species.

So what happened to kick-start the mass extinction of the cichlids? The trigger seems to have been eutrophication. Before 1978, Lake Victoria had high oxygen levels at all depths, down to the bottom layers more than 60 m deep. However, by 1989 high inputs of nutrients from agricultural runoff and sewage from towns and villages had led to algal blooms that severely depleted oxygen levels in deeper parts of the lake. Cichlids feed on algae, and initially their population numbers are thought to

**Figure 60.18 Nile perch (Lates niloticus).** This predatory fish, which can reach a length of 2 m and a mass of 200 kg, was introduced into Lake Victoria as a potential food source. It is responsible for the virtual extinction of hundreds of species of cichlid fishes.

have risen in response to this increase in their food supply, but unlike the conditions during similar algal blooms of the past, the Nile perch was present to take advantage of the situation. With a sudden increase in its food supply (cichlids), the numbers of Nile perch exploded, and they simply ate all available cichlids.

Since 1990, the situation has been compounded by the introduction into Lake Victoria of a floating water weed from South America, the water hyacinth *Eichhornia crassipes*. Reproducing quickly under eutrophic conditions, thick mats of water hyacinth soon covered entire bays and inlets, choking off the coastal habitats of non-open-water cichlids.

## Disruption of ecosystems can cause an extinction cascade

Species often become vulnerable to extinction when their web of ecological interactions becomes seriously disrupted. Because of the many relationships linking species in an ecosystem (see chapter 58), human activities that affect one species can have ramifications throughout an ecosystem, ultimately affecting many other species.

A recent case in point involves the sea otters that live in the cold waters off Alaska and the Aleutian Islands. Otter populations have declined sharply in recent years. In a 500-mile stretch of coastline, otter numbers have dropped from 53,000 in the 1970s to an estimated 6000, a plunge of nearly 90%. Investigating this catastrophic decline, marine ecologists uncovered a chain of interactions among the species of the ocean and kelp forest ecosystems, a falling-domino series of lethal effects that illustrates the concepts of both top-down and bottom-up trophic cascades discussed in chapter 58.

### Case study: Alaskan near-shore habitat

The first in a series of events leading to the sea otter's decline seems to have been the heavy commercial harvesting of whales, described earlier in this chapter. Without whales to keep their numbers in check, ocean zooplankton thrived, leading in turn to proliferation of a species of fish called pollock that feeds on the abundant zooplankton. Given this ample food supply, the pollock proved to compete very successfully with other northern Pacific fish, such as herring and ocean perch, so that levels of these other fish fell steeply in the 1970s.

Then the falling chain of dominoes began to accelerate. The decline in the nutritious forage fish led to an ensuing crash in Alaskan populations of sea lions and harbor seals, for which pollock did not provide sufficient nourishment. This decline may also have been hastened by orcas (also called killer whales) switching from feeding on the less-available whales to feeding on seals and sea lions; the numbers of these pinniped species have fallen precipitously since the 1970s.

When pinniped numbers crashed, some orcas, faced with a food shortage, turned to the next best thing: sea otters. In one bay where the entrance from the sea was too narrow and shallow for orcas to enter, only 12% of the sea otters have disappeared, while in a similar bay that orcas could enter easily, two-thirds of the otters disappeared in a year's time.

Without otters to eat them, the population of sea urchins exploded, eating the kelp and thus "deforesting" the kelp forests and denuding the ecosystem (figure 60.19). As a result, fish species that live in the kelp forest, such as sculpins and greenlings, are declining.

### Loss of keystone species

As discussed in chapter 57, a keystone species is a species that exerts a greater influence on the structure and functioning of an ecosystem than might be expected solely on the basis of its abundance. The sea otters of figure 60.19 are a keystone species of the kelp forest ecosystem, and their removal can have disastrous consequences.

No hard-and-fast line allows us to clearly identify keystone species. Rather, it is a qualitative concept, a statement that indicates a species plays a particularly important role in its community. Keystone species are usually characterized by the strength of their effect on their community.

### Case study: Flying foxes

The severe decline of many species of "flying foxes," a type of bat (figure 60.20), in the Old World tropics is an example of how the loss of a keystone species can dramatically affect the other species living within an ecosystem, sometimes even leading to a cascade of further extinctions.

These bats have very close relationships with important plant species on the islands of the Pacific and Indian Oceans. The family Pteropodidae contains nearly 200 species, approximately one-quarter of them in the genus *Pteropus*, and is widespread on the islands of the South Pacific, where they are the most important—and often the only—pollinators and seed dispersers.

**Figure 60.19** **Disruption of the kelp forest ecosystem.** Overharvesting by commercial whalers altered the balance of fish in the ocean ecosystem, inducing killer whales to feed on sea otters, a keystone species of the kelp forest ecosystem.

**1. Whales**
Overharvesting of plankton-eating whales may have caused an increase in plankton-eating pollock populations.

**2. Nutritious fish**
Populations of nutritious fish like ocean perch and herring declined, likely due to competition with pollock.

**3. Sea lions and harbor seals**
Sea lion and harbor seal populations drastically declined in Alaska, probably because the less-nutritious pollock could not sustain them.

**4. Killer whales**
With the decline in their prey populations of sea lions and seals, killer whales turned to a new source of food: sea otters.

**5. Sea otters**
Sea otter populations declined so dramatically that they disappeared in some areas.

**6. Sea urchins**
Usually the preferred food of sea otters, sea urchin populations now exploded and fed on kelp.

**7. Kelp forests**
Severely thinned by the sea urchins, the kelp beds no longer support a diversity of fish species, which may lead to a decline in populations of eagles that feed on the fish.

**Figure 60.20 The importance of keystone species.**
Flying foxes, a type of fruit-eating bat, are keystone species on many Old World tropical islands. It pollinates many plants and is a key disperser of seeds. Its elimination due to hunting and habitat loss is having a devastating effect on the ecosystems of many South Pacific Islands.

A study in Samoa found that 80% to 100% of the seeds landing on the ground during the dry season were deposited by flying foxes, which eat the fruits and defecate the seeds, often moving them great distances in the process. Many species are entirely dependent on these bats for pollination. Some have evolved features such as night-blooming flowers that prevent any other potential pollinators from taking over the role of the fruit bats.

In Guam, the two local species of flying fox have recently been driven extinct or nearly so, with a substantial impact on the ecosystem. Botanists have found that some plant species are not fruiting or are doing so only marginally, producing fewer fruits than normal. Fruits are not being dispersed away from parent plants, so seedlings are forced to compete, usually unsuccessfully, with adult trees.

Flying foxes are being driven to extinction by human hunters who kill them for food and for sport, and by orchard farmers who consider them pests. Flying foxes are particularly vulnerable because they live in large and obvious groups of up to a million individuals. Because they move in regular and predictable patterns and can be easily tracked to their home roost, hunters can easily kill thousands at a time.

Programs aimed at preserving particular species of flying foxes are only just beginning. One particularly successful example is the program to save the Rodrigues fruit bat, *Pteropus rodricensis*, which occurs only on Rodrigues Island in the Indian Ocean near Madagascar. The population dropped from about 1000 individuals in 1955 to fewer than 100 by 1974, largely due to the loss of the fruit bat's forest habitat to farming. Since 1974, the species has been legally protected, and the forest area of the island is being increased through a tree-planting program. Eleven captive-breeding colonies have been established, and the bat population is now increasing rapidly. The combination of legal protection, habitat restoration, and captive breeding has in this instance produced a very effective preservation program.

## Small populations are particularly vulnerable

Because of the factors just discussed, populations of many species are fragmented and reduced in size. Such populations are particularly prone to extinction.

### Demographic factors

Small populations are vulnerable to events that decrease survival or reproduction. For example, by nature of their size, small populations are ill-equipped to withstand catastrophes, such as a flood, forest fire, or disease epidemic. One example is provided by the history of the heath hen. Although the species was once common throughout the eastern United States, hunting pressure in the 18th and 19th centuries eventually eliminated all but one population, on the island of Martha's Vineyard near Cape Cod, Massachusetts. Protected in a nature preserve, the population was increasing in number until a fire destroyed most of the preserve's habitat. The small surviving population was then ravaged the next year by an unusual congregation of predatory birds, followed shortly thereafter by a disease epidemic. The last sighting of a heath hen, a male, was in 1932 (figure 60.21*a*) .

When populations become extremely small, bad luck can spell the end. For example, the dusky seaside sparrow (figure 60.21*b*), a now-extinct subspecies that was found on the east coast of Florida, dwindled to a population of five individuals, all of which happened to be males. In a large population, the probability that all individuals will be of one sex is infinitesimal. But in small populations, just by the luck of the draw, it is possible that 5 or 10 or even 20 consecutive births will all be individuals of one sex, and that can be enough to send a species to extinction. In addition, when populations are small, individuals may have trouble finding each other (the Allee effect discussed in chapter 56), thus leading the population into a downward spiral toward extinction.

**Figure 60.21 Alive no more.** *a.* A museum specimen of the heath hen (*Tympanuchus cupido cupido*) which went extinct in 1932. *b.* This male was one of the last dusky seaside sparrows (*Ammodramus maritimus nigrescens*).

## Lack of genetic variability

Small populations face a second dilemma. Because of their low numbers, such populations are prone to the loss of genetic variation as a result of genetic drift (figure 60.22). Indeed, many small populations contain little or no genetic variability. The result of such genetic homogeneity can be catastrophic. Genetic variation is beneficial to a population both because of heterozygote advantage (see chapter 20) and because genetically variable individuals tend not to have two copies of deleterious recessive alleles. Populations lacking variation are often composed of sickly, unfit, or sterile individuals. Laboratory groups of rodents and fruit flies that are maintained at small population sizes often perish after a few generations as each generation becomes less robust and fertile than the preceding one.

Although it is difficult to demonstrate that a species has gone extinct because of lack of genetic variation, studies of both zoo and natural populations clearly reveal that more genetically variable individuals have greater fitness. Furthermore, in the longer term, populations with limited genetic variation have diminished ability to adapt to changing environments.

### Interaction of demographic and genetic factors

As populations decrease in size, demographic and genetic factors combine to cause what has been termed an "extinction vortex." That is, as a population gets smaller, it becomes more vulnerable to demographic catastrophes. In turn, genetic variation starts to be lost, causing reproductive rates to decline and population numbers to decline even further, and so on. Eventually, the population disappears entirely, but attributing its demise to one particular factor would be misleading.

### Case study: Prairie chickens

The greater prairie chicken, a close relative of the now-extinct heath hen, is a showy, 2-lb bird renowned for its flamboyant mating rituals (figure 60.23). Abundant in many midwestern states, the prairie chickens in Illinois have in the past six decades undergone a population collapse.

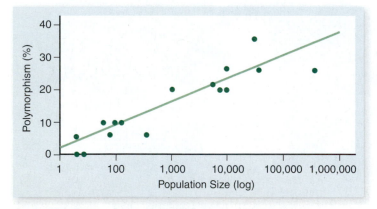

**Figure 60.22 Loss of genetic variability in small populations.** The percentage of genes that are polymorphic in isolated populations of the tree *Halocarpus bidwillii* in the mountains of New Zealand is a sensitive function of population size.

### Inquiry question

**?** Why do small populations lose genetic variation?

**Figure 60.23 A mating ritual.** The male greater prairie chicken (*Tympanuchus cupido pinnatus*) inflates bright orange air sacs, part of his esophagus, into balloons on each side of his head. As air is drawn into the sacs, it creates a three-syllable low frequency "boom-boom-boom" that can be heard for kilometers.

Once, enormous numbers of birds occurred throughout the state, but with the 1837 introduction of the steel plow, the first that could slice through the deep, dense root systems of prairie grasses, the Illinois prairie began to be replaced by farmland. By the turn of the 20th century, the prairie had all but vanished, and by 1931, the heath hen had become locally extinct in Illinois. The greater prairie chicken fared little better, its numbers falling to 25,000 statewide in 1933 and then to 2000 by 1962. In surrounding states with less intensive agriculture, it continued to prosper.

In 1962 and 1967, sanctuaries were established in Illinois to attempt to preserve the greater prairie chicken. But privately owned grasslands kept disappearing, along with their prairie chickens, and by the 1980s the birds were extinct in Illinois except for two preserves, and even there, their numbers kept falling. By 1990, the egg hatching rate, which at one time had averaged between 91% and 100%, had dropped to an extremely low 38%. By the mid-1990s, the count of males had dropped to as low as six in each sanctuary.

What was wrong with the sanctuary populations? One suggestion was that because of very small population sizes and a mating ritual whereby one male may dominate a flock, the Illinois prairie chickens had lost so much genetic variability as to create serious genetic problems. To test this idea, biologists at the University of Illinois compared DNA from frozen tissue samples of birds that had died in Illinois between 1974 and 1993, and found that in recent years Illinois birds had indeed become genetically less diverse.

The researchers then extracted DNA from tissue in the roots of feathers from stuffed birds collected in the 1930s from the same population. They found that Illinois birds had lost fully one-third of the genetic diversity of birds living in the same place before the population collapse of the 1970s. By contrast, prairie chicken populations in other states still contained much of the genetic variation that had disappeared from Illinois populations.

Now the stage was set to halt the Illinois prairie chicken's race toward extinction in Illinois. Wildlife managers began to transplant birds from genetically diverse populations of Minnesota, Kansas, and Nebraska to Illinois. Between 1992 and 1996, a total of 518 out-of-state prairie chickens were brought in to interbreed with the Illinois birds, and hatching rates were back up to 94% by 1998. It looks as though the prairie chickens have been saved from extinction in Illinois.

The key lesson here is the importance of not allowing things to go too far—not to drop down to a single isolated population. Without the outlying genetically different populations, the prairie chickens in Illinois could not have been saved. When the last population of the dusky seaside sparrow lost its last female, there was no other source of females, and the subspecies went extinct.

> ### Learning Outcomes Review 60.3
>
> Habitat factors responsible for extinction include habitat destruction, pollution, disruption, and fragmentation. Overexploitation can reduce populations to low levels or eliminate them entirely. Introduced species can wreak havoc on native communities. Finally, small populations have less ability to rebound from catastrophes and are vulnerable to loss of genetic variation. Interaction of all these factors can hasten species' decline into extinction.
>
> ■ *Does it make sense to take endangered species out of the wild to preserve them if their habitat is allowed to disappear? Explain.*

## 60.4 Approaches for Preserving Endangered Species and Ecosystems

> ### Learning Outcomes
>
> 1. *Distinguish between restoration of species and restoration of ecosystem functioning.*
> 2. *List the strategies for habitat restoration.*
> 3. *Explain the rationale for captive breeding programs.*

Once the cause of a species' endangerment is known, it becomes possible to design a recovery plan. If the cause is commercial overharvesting, regulations can be issued to restrict harvesting and protect the threatened species. If the cause is habitat loss, plans can be instituted to restore the habitat. Loss of genetic variability in isolated subpopulations can be countered by transplanting individuals from genetically different populations. Populations in immediate danger of extinction can be captured, introduced into a captive-breeding program, and later reintroduced to other suitable habitat.

All of these solutions are extremely expensive. But as Bruce Babbitt, Secretary of the Interior in the Clinton administration, noted, it is much more economical to prevent "environmental trainwrecks" from occurring than to clean them up afterward. Preserving ecosystems and monitoring species before they are threatened is the most effective means of protecting the environment and preventing extinctions.

## Destroyed habitats can sometimes be restored

Conservation biology typically concerns itself with preserving populations and species in danger of decline or extinction. Conservation, however, requires that there be something left to preserve; in many situations, conservation is no longer an option. Species, and in some cases whole communities, have disappeared or been irretrievably modified. The clear-cutting of the temperate forests of Washington State leaves little behind to conserve, as does converting a piece of land into a wheat field or an asphalt parking lot. Redeeming these situations requires restoration rather than conservation.

Three quite different sorts of habitat restoration programs might be undertaken, depending on the cause of the habitat loss.

### Pristine restoration

In ecosystems where all species have been effectively removed, conservationists might attempt to restore the plants and animals that are the natural inhabitants of the area, if these species can be identified. When abandoned farmland is to be restored to prairie, as in figure 60.24, how would conservationists know what to plant?

*a.*

*b.*

**Figure 60.24 Habitat restoration.** The University of Wisconsin–Madison Arboretum has pioneered restoration ecology. *a.* The restoration of the prairie was at an early stage in November 1935. *b.* The prairie as it looks today. This picture was taken at approximately the same location as the 1935 photograph.

Although it is in principle possible to reestablish each of the original species in their original proportions, rebuilding a community requires knowing the identities of all the original inhabitants and the ecologies of each of the species. We rarely have this much information, so no restoration is ever truly pristine.

Increasingly, restoration biologists are working on restoring the functioning of an ecosystem, rather than trying to recreate the same community composition. This approach shifts the focus from restoring species to reconstructing the processes that operated in the natural habitat.

### Removing introduced species

Sometimes the habitat has been destroyed by a single introduced species. In such a case, habitat restoration involves removing the introduced species. Restoration of the once-diverse cichlid fishes to Lake Victoria will require more than breeding and restocking the endangered species. The introduced water hyacinth and Nile perch populations will have to be brought under control or removed, and eutrophication will have to be reversed.

It is important to act quickly if an introduced species is to be removed. When aggressive African bees (the so-called "killer bees") were inadvertently released in Brazil, they remained confined to the local area for only one season. Now they occupy much of the western hemisphere.

### Cleanup and rehabilitation

Habitats seriously degraded by chemical pollution cannot be restored until the pollution is cleaned up. The successful restoration of the Nashua River in New England is one example of how a concerted effort can succeed in restoring a heavily polluted habitat to a relatively pristine condition.

Once so heavily polluted by chemicals from dye manufacturing plants that it was different colors in different places, the river is now clean and used for many recreational activities.

## Captive breeding programs have saved some species

Recovery programs, particularly those focused on one or a few species, must sometimes involve direct intervention in natural populations to avoid an immediate threat of extinction.

### Case study: The peregrine falcon

American populations of birds of prey, such as the peregrine falcon, began an abrupt decline shortly after World War II. Of the approximately 350 breeding pairs east of the Mississippi River in 1942, all had disappeared by 1960. The culprit proved to be the chemical pesticide DDT (Chapter 59).

The use of DDT was banned by federal law in 1972, causing levels in the eastern United States to fall quickly. However, no peregrine falcons were left in the eastern United States to reestablish a natural population. Falcons from other parts of the country were used to establish a captive-breeding program at Cornell University in 1970, with the intent of reestablishing the peregrine falcon in the eastern United States by releasing offspring of these birds. By the end of 1986, over 850 birds had been released in 13 eastern states, producing an astonishingly strong recovery (figure 60.25).

### Case study: The California condor

The number of California condors (*Gymnogyps californianus*), a large, vulture-like bird with a wingspan of nearly 3 m, has been declining gradually for the past 200 years. By 1985, condor numbers had dropped so low that the bird was on the verge of extinction. Six of the remaining 15 wild birds disappeared in that year alone. The entire breeding population of the species consisted of the birds remaining in the wild and an additional 21 birds in captivity.

In a last-ditch attempt to save the condor from extinction, the remaining birds were captured and placed in a captive-breeding population. The breeding program was set up in zoos, with the goal of releasing offspring on a large, 5300-hectare ranch in prime condor habitat. Birds were isolated from human contact as much as possible, and closely related individuals were prevented from breeding.

By early 2009, the captive population of California condors had reached over 160 individuals. After extensive pre-release training to avoid power poles and people, captive-reared condors have been released successfully in California at two sites in the mountains north of Los Angeles, as well as at the Grand Canyon. Many of the released birds are doing well, and the wild population now numbers nearly 200 birds. Biologists are particularly

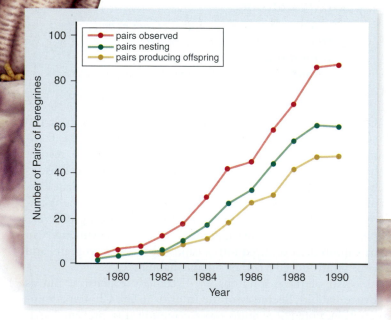

**Figure 60.25 Success of captive breeding.** The peregrine falcon (*Falco peregrinus*) has been reestablished in the eastern United States by releasing captive-bred birds over a period of 10 years.

excited by breeding activities that resulted in the first-ever offspring produced in the wild by captive-reared parents in both California and Arizona.

### Case study: Yellowstone wolves

The ultimate goal of captive-breeding programs is not simply to preserve interesting species, but rather to restore ecosystems to a balanced, functional state. Yellowstone Park has been an ecosystem out of balance, due in large part to the systematic extermination of the gray wolf (*Canis lupus*) in the park early in the 20th century. Without these predators to keep their numbers in check, herds of elk and deer expanded rapidly, damaging vegetation so that the elk themselves starve in time of scarcity.

In an attempt to restore the park's natural balance, two complete wolf packs from Canada were released into the park in 1995 and 1996. The wolves adapted well, breeding so successfully that by 2002 the park contained 16 free-ranging packs and more than 200 wolves.

Although ranchers near the park have been unhappy about the return of the wolves, little damage to livestock has been noted, and the ecological equilibrium of Yellowstone Park seems well on the way to being regained. Elk are congregating in larger herds and are avoiding areas near rivers where they are vulnerable. As a result, riverside trees such as willows are increasing in number, in turn providing food for beavers, whose dams lead to the creation of ponds, a habitat type that had become rare in Yellowstone. This newly restored habitat, in turn, has led to increases in some species of birds such as the redstart that had been in decline for decades or disappeared entirely.

## Current conservation approaches are multidimensional

Historically, conservationists strived to solve the problems of habitat fragmentation by focusing solely on preserving as much land as possible in a pristine state in national parks and reserves. Increasingly, however, it has become apparent that the amount of land that can be preserved in such a state is limited; moreover, many areas that are not completely protected nonetheless provide suitable habitat for many species.

As a result, conservation plans are becoming multidimensional, including not only pristine areas, but also surrounding areas in which some level of human disturbance is permitted. As discussed previously, isolated patches of habitat lose species far more rapidly than large preserves do. By including these other, less pristine areas, the total amount of area available for many species is increased.

The key to managing such large tracts of land successfully over a long time is to operate them in a way compatible with local land use. For example, although no economic activity is allowed in the core pristine area, the remainder of the land may be used for nondestructive harvesting of resources. Even areas in which hunting of some species is allowed provide protection for many other species.

Corridors of dispersal are also being provided that link the pristine areas, thus effectively increasing population sizes and allowing recolonization if a population disappears in one area due to a catastrophe. Corridors can also provide protection to species that move over great distances during the course of a year. Corridors in East Africa have protected the migration routes of ungulates. In Costa Rica, a corridor linking the lowland rain forest at the La Selva Biological Station to the montane rain forest in Braulio Carrillo National Park permits the altitudinal migration of many species of birds, mammals, and butterflies (figure 60.26).

**Figure 60.26 Corridor connecting two reserves.** *a.* The Organization of Tropical Studies' La Selva Biological Station in Costa Rica is connected to Braulio Carrillo National Park. *b.* The corridor allows migration of birds, mammals, butterflies, and other animals from La Selva at 35 m above sea level to mountainous habitats up to 2900 m elevation.

In addition to this focus on maintaining large enough reserves, in recent years conservation biologists also have recognized that the best way to preserve biodiversity is to focus on preserving intact ecosystems, rather than particular species. For this reason, attention in many cases is turning to identifying those ecosystems most in need of preservation and devising the means to protect not only the species within the ecosystem, but the functioning of the ecosystem itself. This entails making sure that reserves are not only large enough, but also that they protect elements such as watersheds so that activities outside the reserve won't threaten the ecosystem within it.

### Learning Outcomes Review 60.4

Restoration of species may prevent extinction, but only if restoration of habitat or an entire ecosystem is also undertaken. Removal of introduced species and cleanup of pollutants are primary strategies for habitat restoration. In cases where extinction appears imminent, removal of individuals from the wild and preservation in captive breeding programs may be necessary while habitat is restored.

■ *Can habitat restoration ever approach a pristine state? Why or why not?*

# Chapter Review

## 60.1 Overview of the Biodiversity Crisis

### Prehistoric humans were responsible for local extinctions.

Shortly after humans arrived in North America after the last Ice Age, at least 75% of large mammals became extinct. The same pattern has been observed in other parts of the world.

### Extinctions have continued in historical time.

The majority of historical extinctions have occurred within the last 150 years and on islands. The current mass extinction is the only such event triggered by one species, *Homo sapiens*, and the only one in which resources will not be widely available for evolutionary recovery afterward.

### Endemic species hotspots are especially threatened.

Endemic species are found in one restricted range and are thus vulnerable to extinction. Hotspots are areas with many endemic species; many hotspots are the site of large human population growth and high rates of extinction.

## 60.2 The Value of Biodiversity

### The direct economic value of biodiversity includes resources for our survival.

Many products are obtained from different species and ecosystems, including food, materials for clothing and shelter, and medicines.

### Indirect economic value is derived from ecosystem services.

Intact ecosystems provide services such as maintaining water quality, preserving soils and nutrients, moderating local climates, and recycling nutrients. The value of intact ecosystems is often not apparent until they are lost.

### Ethical and aesthetic values are based on our conscience and our consciousness.

Humans can and should make ethical decisions to protect the esthetic, ecological, and economic values of ecosystems.

## 60.3 Factors Responsible for Extinction

### Amphibians are on the decline: A case study.

Almost half of all amphibian species have experienced decreases in population size. No single cause has been identified, which implies that global environmental changes may be responsible.

### Habitat loss devastates species richness.

Habitat may be destroyed, polluted, disrupted, or fragmented. As habitats become more fragmented, the relative proportion of the remaining habitat that occurs on the boundary or edge increases rapidly, exposing species to parasites, nonnative invasive species, and predators (see figure 60.11).

### Overexploitation wipes out species quickly.

Hunting and harvesting of wild species pose a risk of extinction. The collapse of the cod fisheries of the North Atlantic and the decline of whale species are only two of many examples.

### Introduced species threaten native species and habitats.

Natural or accidental introductions of new species results in large and often negative changes to a community because of lack of checks and balances on introduced species' growth in the form of species interactions.

### Disruption of ecosystems can cause an extinction cascade.

Extinction cascades may occur either top-down or bottom-up through the trophic levels. Loss of a keystone species may increase competition and greatly alter ecosystem structure and function.

### Small populations are particularly vulnerable.

Catastrophes, lack of mates, and loss of genetic variability all make reduced populations more likely to become extinct (see figure 60.22).

## 60.4 Approaches for Preserving Endangered Species and Ecosystems

### Destroyed habitats can sometimes be restored.

Restoration by removal of introduced species is very difficult and is most successful if done very soon after a new species is introduced. Severely polluted or damaged habitats sometimes cannot be restored to original conditions, but they may be restored to provide different environmental services.

### Captive breeding programs have saved some species.

Species may be bred in captivity and returned to the wild when the factors that caused their endangerment are no longer a threat. Preservation of habitat may be a key in successful reintroduction.

### Current conservation approaches are multidimensional.

The best way to preserve biodiversity is to preserve intact ecosystems rather than individual species. The key to management of large tracts of land is to operate them in a way compatible with local human needs.

Corridors of dispersal can link habitat fragments with one another and with larger habitats, allowing for increased population size, genetic exchange, and recolonization.

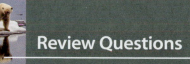

## UNDERSTAND

1. Conservation hotspots are best described as
   a. areas with large numbers of endemic species, in many of which species are disappearing rapidly.
   b. areas where people are particularly active supporters of biological diversity.
   c. islands that are experiencing high rates of extinction.
   d. areas where native species are being replaced with introduced species.

2. The economic value of indirect ecosystem services
   a. is unlikely to exceed the economic value derived from uses after ecosystem conversion.
   b. has never been carefully determined.
   c. can greatly exceed the value derived after ecosystem conversion.
   d. is entirely aesthetic.

3. The amphibian decline is best described as
   a. global disappearance of amphibian populations due to the pervasiveness of local habitat destruction.
   b. global shrinkage of amphibian populations due to global climate change.
   c. the unexplained disappearance of golden toads in Costa Rica.
   d. None of the above

4. Habitat fragmentation can negatively affect populations by
   a. restricting gene flow among areas that were previously continuous.
   b. increasing the relative amount of edge in suitable habitat patches.
   c. creating patches that are too small to support a breeding population.
   d. all of the above.

5. When populations are drastically reduced in size, genetic diversity and heterozygosity
   a. are likely to increase, enhancing the probability of extinction.
   b. are likely to decrease, enhancing the probability of extinction.
   c. are usually not factors that influence the probability of extinction.
   d. automatically respond in a way that protects populations from future changes.

6. A captive-breeding program followed by release to the wild
   a. is very likely, all by itself, to save a species threatened by extinction.
   b. is only likely to succeed when genetic variation of wild populations is very low.
   c. may be successful when combined with proper regulations and habitat restoration.
   d. None of the above

## APPLY

1. Historically, island species have tended to become extinct faster than species living on a mainland. Which of the following reasons can be used to explain this phenomenon?
   a. Island species have often evolved in the absence of predators and have no natural avoidance strategies.
   b. Humans have introduced diseases and competitors to islands, which negatively affect island populations.
   c. Island populations are usually smaller than mainland populations.
   d. All of the above

2. Ninety-nine percent of all the species that ever existed have gone extinct,
   a. serving as evidence that current extinction rates are not higher than normal.
   b. but most of these losses have occurred in the last 400 years.
   c. which argues that the world just had too many species.
   d. None of the above

3. To effectively address the biodiversity crisis, the protection of individual species
   a. must be used in concert with a principle of ecosystem management and restoration.
   b. is a sufficient management approach that merely needs to be expanded to more species.
   c. has no role to play in addressing the biodiversity crisis.
   d. usually conflicts with the principle of ecosystem management.

4. The introduction of a non-native predator to an ecosystem could cause extinction by
   a. causing a top-down trophic cascade (see chapter 58).
   b. outcompeting a native carnivore (see chapter 57).
   c. transmitting parasites to which the native species are not adapted.
   d. all of the above.

## SYNTHESIZE

1. If 99% of the species that ever existed are now extinct, why is there such concern over the extinction rates over the last several centuries?

2. Ecosystem conversion always has a cost and a benefit. Usually the benefit flows to a segment of society (a business or one group of people, for instance), but the costs are borne by all of society. That is what makes decisions about how and when to convert ecosystems difficult. However, is that a problem unique to conversion of ecosystems in the way we understand it today (for example, the conversion of the mangrove to a shrimp farm)? Are there other examples we can look to for guidance in how to make these decisions?

3. There is concern and evidence that amphibian populations are declining worldwide as a consequence of factors acting globally. Given that we know that species extinction is a natural process, how do we determine if there is a global decline that is different from normal species extinction?

4. Given what you learned in chapter 57 about interactions between species and in chapter 58 about interactions among trophic levels, how can the extinction of one species have far-ranging effects on an ecosystem? Is it possible to predict which species would be particularly likely to affect many other species if they were to go extinct?

5. All populations become small before going extinct. Is small population size really a cause of extinction, or just something that happens as a result of other factors that cause extinction?

# Appendix A

# Answer Key

## CHAPTER 1

### LEARNING OUTCOME QUESTIONS

**1.1** No. The study of biology encompasses information/tools from chemistry, physics, geology, literally all of the "natural sciences."

**1.2** A scientific theory has been tested by experimentation. A(n) hypothesis is a starting point to explain a body of observations. When predictions generated using the hypothesis have been tested it gains the confidence associated with a theory. A theory still cannot be "proved" however as new data can always force us to re-evaluate a theory.

**1.3** No. Natural selection explains the patterns of living organisms we see at present, and allows us to work back in time, but it is not intended to explain how life arose. This does not mean that we can never explain this, but merely that natural selection does not do this.

**1.4** Viruses do not fit well into our definition of living systems. It is a matter of controversy whether viruses should be considered "alive." They lack the basic cellular machinery, but they do have genetic information. Some theories for the origin of cells view viruses as being a step from organic molecules to cell, but looking at current organisms, they do not fulfill our definition of life.

### INQUIRY QUESTIONS

**Page 10** Reducing the factor by which the geometric progression increases (lowering the value of the exponent) reduces the difference between numbers of people and amount of food production. It can be achieved by lowering family size or delaying childbearing.

**Page 11** A snake would fall somewhere near the bird, as birds and snakes are closely related.

### UNDERSTAND

1. b  2. c  3. a  4. b  5. d  6. b  7. c  8. c

### APPLY

1. d  2. d  3. c  4. d  5. d  6. d  7. a

### SYNTHESIZE

1. For something to be considered living it would demonstrate organization, possibly including a cellular structure. The organism would gain and use energy to maintain homeostasis, respond to its environment, and to grow and reproduce. These latter properties would be difficult to determine if the evidence of life from other planets comes from fossils. Similarly, the ability of an alien organism to evolve could be difficult to establish.

2. a. The variables that were held the same between the two experiments include the broth, the flask, and the sterilization step.

b. The shape of the flask influences the experiment because any cells present in the air can enter the flask with the broken neck, but they are trapped in the neck of the other flask.

c. If cells can arise spontaneously, then cell growth will occur in both flasks. If cells can only arise from preexisting cells (cells in the air), then only the flask with the broken neck will grow cells. Breaking the neck exposes the broth to a source of cells.

d. If the sterilization step did not actually remove all cells, then growth would have occurred in both flasks. This result would seem to support the hypothesis that life can arise spontaneously.

## CHAPTER 2

### LEARNING OUTCOME QUESTIONS

**2.1** If the number of proton exceeds neutrons, there is no effect on charge; if the number of protons exceeds electrons, then the charge is (+).

**2.2** Atoms are reactive when their outer electron shell is not filled with electrons. The noble gases have filled outer electrons shells, and are thus unreactive.

**2.3** An ionic bond results when there is a transfer of electrons resulting in positive and negative ions that are attracted to each other. A covalent bond is the result of two atoms sharing electrons. Polar covalent bonds involve unequal sharing of electrons. This produces regions of partial charge, but not ions.

**2.4** C and H have about the same electronegativity, and thus form nonpolar covalent bonds. This would not result in a cohesive or adhesive fluid.

**2.5** Since ice floats, a lake will freeze from the top down, not the bottom up. This means that water remains fluid on the bottom of the lake allowing living things to overwinter.

**2.6** Since pH is a log scale, this would be a change of 100 fold in [H$^+$].

### INQUIRY QUESTION

**Page 30** The buffer works over a broad range because it ionizes more completely as pH increases; in essence, there is more acid to neutralize the greater amount of base you are adding. At pH4 none of the buffer is ionized. Thus below that pH, base raises the pH without the ameliorating effects of the ionization of the buffer.

### UNDERSTAND

1. b  2. d  3. b  4. a  5. c  6. d  7. b

### APPLY

1. c  2. b  3. a  4. c  5. d  6. Chemical reactions involve changes in the electronic configuration of atoms. Radioactive decay involves the actual decay of the nucleus producing another atom and emitting radiation.

### SYNTHESIZE

1. A cation is an element that tends to lose an electron from its outer energy level, leaving behind a net positive charge due to the presence of the protons in the atomic nucleus. Electrons are only lost from the outer energy level if that loss is energetically favorable, that is, if it makes the atom more stable by virtue of obtaining a filled outer energy level (the octet rule). You can predict which elements are likely to function as cations by calculating which of the elements will possess one (or two) electrons in their outer energy level. Recall that each orbital surrounding an atomic nucleus can only hold two electrons. Energy level K is a single *s* orbital and can hold two electrons. Energy level L consists of another *s* orbital plus three *p* orbitals—holding a total of eight electrons. Use the atomic number of each element to predict the total number of electrons present. Examples of other cations would include: hydrogen (H), lithium (Li), magnesium (Mg), and beryllium (Be).

2. Silicon has an atomic number of 14. This means that there are four unpaired electrons in its outer energy level (comparable to carbon). Based on this fact, you can conclude that silicon, like carbon, could form four covalent bonds. Silicon also falls within the group of elements with atomic masses less than 21, a property of the elements known to participate in the formation of biologically important molecules. Interestingly, silicon is much more prevalent than carbon on Earth. Although silicon dioxide is found in the cell walls of plants and single-celled organisms called diatoms, silicon-based life has not been identified on this planet. Given the abundance of silicon on Earth you can conclude that some other aspect of the chemistry of this atom makes it incompatible with the formation of molecules that make up living organisms.

3. Water is considered to be a critical molecule for the evolution of life on Earth. It is reasonable to assume that water on other planets could play a similar role. The key properties of water that would support its role in the evolution of life are:

- The ability of water to acts as a solvent. Molecules dissolved in water could move and interact in ways that would allow for the formation of larger, more complex molecules such as those found in living organisms.

- The high specific heat of water. Water can modulate and maintain its temperature, thereby protecting the molecules or organisms within it from temperature extremes—an important feature on other planets.

- The difference in density between ice and liquid water. The fact that ice floats is a simple, but important feature of water environments since it allows living organisms to remain in a liquid environment protected under a surface of ice. This possibility is especially intriguing given recent evidence of ice-covered oceans on Europa, a moon of the planet Jupiter.

## CHAPTER 3

### LEARNING OUTCOME QUESTIONS

**3.1** Hydrolysis is the reverse reaction of dehydration. Dehydration is a synthetic reaction involving the loss of water and hydrolysis is cleavage by addition of water.

**3.2** Starch and glycogen are both energy storage molecules. Their highly branched nature allows the formation of droplets, and the similarity in the bonds holding adjacent glucoses together mean that the enzyme we have to break down glycogen allow us to break down starch. The same enzymes do not allow us to break down cellulose. The structure of cellulose leads to the formation of tough fibers.

**3.3** The sequence of bases would be complementary. Wherever there is an A in the DNA there would be a U in the RNA, wherever there is a G in the DNA there would be a C in the RNA.

**3.4** If an unknown protein has sequence similarity to a known protein, we can infer its function is also similar. If an unknown protein has known functional domains or motifs we can also use these to help predict function.

**3.5** Phospholipids have a charged group replacing one of the fatty acids in a triglyceride. This leads to an amphipathic molecule that has both hydrophobic and hydrophilic regions. This will spontaneously form bilayer membranes in water.

### UNDERSTAND

1. b   2. a   3. d   4. c   5. b   6. b   7. c   8. b

### APPLY

1. c   2. d   3. b   4. d   5. b   6. b   7. d

### SYNTHESIZE

1. The four biological macromolecules all have different structure and function. In comparing carbohydrates, nucleic acids and proteins, we can think of these as being polymers with different monomers. In the case of carbohydrates, the polymers are all polymers of the simple sugar glucose. These are energy storage molecules (with many C-H bonds) and structural molecules such as cellulose that make tough fibers.

    Nucleic acids are formed of nucleotide monomers, each of which consists of ribose, phosphate, and a nitrogenous base. These molecules are informational molecules that encode information in the sequence of bases. The bases interact in specific ways: A base pairs with T and G base pairs with C. This is the basis for their informational storage.

    Proteins are formed of amino acid polymers. There are 20 different amino acids, and thus an incredible number of different proteins. These can have an almost unlimited number of functions. These functions arise from the amazing flexibility in structure of protein chains.

2. *Nucleic Acids*—Hydrogen bonds are important for complementary base-pairing between the two strands of nucleic acid that make up a molecule of DNA. Complementary base-pairing can also occur within the single nucleic acid strand of a RNA molecule.

    *Proteins*—Hydrogen bonds are involved in both the secondary and tertiary levels of protein structure. The α helices and β-pleated sheets of secondary structure are stabilized by hydrogen bond formation between the amino and carboxyl groups of the amino acid backbone. Hydrogen bond formation between R-groups helps stabilize the three-dimensional folding of the protein at the tertiary level of structure.

    *Carbohydrates*—Hydrogen bonds are less important for carbohydrates; however, these bonds are responsible for the formation of the fibers of cellulose that make up the cell walls of plants.

    *Lipids*—Hydrogen bonds are not involved in the structure of lipid molecules. The inability of fatty acids to form hydrogen bonds with water is key to their hydrophobic nature.

3. We have enzymes that can break down glycogen. Glycogen is formed from alpha-glucose subunits. Starch is also formed from alpha-glucose units, but cellulose is formed from beta-glucose units. The enzymes that break the alpha-glycosidic linkages cannot break the beta-glycosidic linkages. Thus we can degrade glycogen and starch but not cellulose.

## CHAPTER 4

### LEARNING OUTCOME QUESTIONS

**4.1** The statement about all cells coming from preexisting cells might need to be modified. It would really depend on whether these Martian life forms were based on a similar molecular/cellular basis as terrestrial life.

**4.2** Bacteria and archaea both tend to be single cells that lack a membrane-bounded nucleus, and extensive internal endomembrane systems. They both have a cell wall, although the composition is different. They do not undergo mitosis, although the proteins involved in DNA replication and cell division are not similar.

**4.3** Part of what gives different organs their unique identities are the specialized cell types found in each. That does not mean that there will not be some cell types common to all (epidermal cells for example) but that organs tend to have specialized cell types.

**4.4** They don't!

**4.5** The nuclear genes that encode organellar proteins moved from the organelle to the nucleus. There is evidence for a lot of "horizontal gene transfer" across domains; this is an example of how that can occur.

**4.6** It provides structure and support for larger cells, especially in animal cells that lack a cell wall.

**4.7** Microtubules and microfilaments are both involved in cell motility, and in movement of substance around cells. Intermediate filaments do not have this dynamic role, but are more structural.

**4.8** Cell junctions help to put together cells into higher level structures that are organized and joined in different ways. Different kinds of junctions can be used for different functional purposes.

### INQUIRY QUESTIONS

*Page 64* Stretch, dent, convolute, fold, add more than one nuclei, anything which would increase the amount of diffusion between the cytoplasm and the external environment.

*Page 75* Both the cristae of mitochondria and the thylakoids of chloroplasts, where many of the reactions take place leading to the production of ATP, are highly folded. The convolutions allow for a large surface area increasing the efficiency of the mechanisms of oxidative phosphorylation.

*Page 80* Ciliated cell in the trachea help to remove particulate matter from the respiratory tact where it can be expelled or swallowed and processed in the digestive tract.

### UNDERSTAND

1. d   2. d   3. c   4. a   5. c   6. d   7. b

### APPLY

1. c   2. b   3. b   4. b   5. c   6. b   7. a

### SYNTHESIZE

1. Your diagram should start at the SER and then move to the RER, Golgi apparatus, and finally to the plasma membrane. Small transport vesicles are the mechanism that would carry a phospholipids molecule between two membrane compartments. Transport vesicles are small "membrane bubbles" composed of a phospholipid bilayer.

2. If these organelles were free-living bacteria, they would have the features found in bacteria. Mitochondria and chloroplasts do both have DNA but no nucleus, and they lack the complex organelles found in eukaryotes. At first glance, the cristae may seem to be an internal membrane system, but they are actually infoldings of the inner membrane. If endosymbiosis occurred, this would be the plasma membrane of the endosymbiont, and the outer membrane would be the plasma membrane of the engulfing cell. Another test would be to compare DNA in these organelles with current bacteria. This has actually shown similarities that make us confident of the identity of the endosymbionts.

3. The prokaryotic and eukaryotic flagella are examples of an analogous trait. Both flagella function to propel the cell through its environment by converting chemical energy into mechanical force. The key difference is in the structure of the flagella. The bacterial flagellum is composed of a single protein emerging from a basal body anchored within the cell's plasma membrane and using the potential energy of a proton gradient to cause a rotary movement. In contrast, the flagellum of the eukaryote is composed of

many different proteins assembled into a complex axoneme structure that uses ATP energy to cause an undulating motion.

4. Eukaryotic cells are distinguished from prokaryotic cells by the presence of a system of internal membrane compartments and membrane-bounded organelles such as mitochondria and chloroplasts. As outlined in Figure 4.19, the first step in the evolution of the eukaryotic cell was the infolding of the plasma membrane to create separate internal membranes such as the nuclear envelope and the endoplasmic reticulum. The origins of mitochondria and chloroplasts are hypothesized to be the result of a bit of cellular "indigestion" where aerobic or photosynthetic prokaryotes were engulfed, but not digested by the larger ancestor eukaryote. Given this information, there are two possible scenarios for the origin of *Giardia*. In the first scenario, the ancestor of *Giardia* split off from the eukaryotic lineage after the evolution of the nucleus, but before the acquisition of mitochondria. In the second scenario, the ancestor of *Giardia* split off after the acquisition of mitochondria, and subsequently lost the mitochondria. At present, neither of these two scenarios can be rejected. The first case was long thought to be the best explanation, but recently it has been challenged by evidence for the second case.

# CHAPTER 5

## LEARNING OUTCOME QUESTIONS

**5.1**  Cells would not be able to control their contents. Nonpolar molecules would be able to cross the membrane by diffusion, as would small polar molecules, but without proteins to control the passage of specific molecules, it would not function as a semipermeable membrane.

**5.2**  No. The nonpolar interior of the bilayer would not be soluble in the solvent. The molecules will organize with their nonpolar tails in the solvent, but the negative charge on the phosphates would repel other phosphates.

**5.3**  Transmembrane domains anchor protein in the membrane. They associate with the hydrophobic interior, thus they must be hydrophobic as well. If they slide out of the interior, they are repelled by water.

**5.4**  The concentration of the IV will be isotonic with your blood cell. If it were hypotonic, your blood cells would take on water and burst; if it were hypertonic, your blood cells would lose water and shrink.

**5.5**  Channel proteins are aqueous pores that allow facilitated diffusion. They cannot actively transport ions. Carrier proteins bind to their substrates and couple transport to some form of energy for active transport.

**5.6**  In all cases, there is recognition and specific binding of a molecule by a protein. In each case this binding is necessary for biological function.

## INQUIRY QUESTIONS

**Page 94**  As the name suggests for the fluid mosaic model, cell membranes have some degree of fluidity. The degree of fluidity varies with the composition of the membrane, but in all membranes, phospholipids are able to move about within the membrane. Also, due to the hydrophobic and hydrophilic opposite ends of phospholipid molecules, phospholipid bilayers form spontaneously. Therefore, if stressing forces happen to damage a membrane, adjacent phospholipids automatically move to fill in the opening.

**Page 95**  Integral membrane proteins are those that are embedded within the membrane structure and provide passageways across the membrane. Because integral membrane proteins must pass through both polar and nonpolar regions of the phospholipid bilayer, the protein portion held within the nonpolar fatty acid interior of the membrane must also be nonpolar. The amino acid sequence of an integral protein would have polar amino acids at both ends, with nonpolar amino acids comprising the middle portion of the protein.

## UNDERSTAND

1. d   2. a   3. d   4. d   5. b   6. d   7. a

## APPLY

1. c   2. b   3. d   4. c   5. d

## SYNTHESIZE

1. Since the membrane proteins become intermixed in the absence of the energy molecule, ATP, one can conclude that chemical energy is not required for their movement. Since the proteins do not move and intermix when the temperature is cold, one can also conclude that the movement is temperature-sensitive. The passive diffusion of molecules also depends on tempera-

ture and does not require chemical energy; therefore, it is possible to conclude that membrane fluidity occurs as a consequence of passive diffusion.

2. The inner half of the bilayer of the various endomembranes becomes the outer half of the bilayer of the plasma membrane.

3. Lipids can be inserted into one leaflet to produce asymmetry. When lipids are synthesized in the SER, they can be assembled into asymmetric membranes. There are also enzymes that can flip lipids from one leaflet to the other.

# CHAPTER 6

## LEARNING OUTCOME QUESTIONS

**6.1**  At the bottom of the ocean, light is not an option as it does not penetrate that deep. However, there is a large source of energy in the form of reduced minerals, such as sulfur compounds, that can be oxidized. These are abundant at hydrothermal vents found at the junctions of tectonic plates. This supports whole ecosystems dependent on bacteria that oxidize reduced minerals available at the hydrothermal vents.

**6.2**  In a word: No. Enzymes only alter the rate of a reaction; they do not change the thermodynamics of the reaction. The action of an enzyme does not change the $\Delta G$ for the reaction.

**6.3**  In the text, it stated that the average person turns over approximately their body weight in ATP per day. This gives us enough information to determine approximately the amount of energy released:

$100 \text{ kg} = 1.0 \times 10^5 \text{ g}$
$(1.0 \times 10^5 \text{ g})/(507.18 \text{ g/mol})=197.2 \text{ mol}$
$(197.2 \text{ mol})(7.3 \text{ kcal/mol})=1{,}439 \text{ kcal}$

**6.4**  This is a question that cannot be definitely answered, but we can give some reasonable conjectures. First, DNA's location is in the nucleus and not the cytoplasm, where most enzymes are found. Second, the double stranded structure of DNA is works well for information storage, but would not necessarily function well as an enzyme. Each base interacts with a base on the opposite strand, which makes for a very stable linear molecule, but does not encourage folding into the kind of complex 3-D shape found in enzymes.

**6.5**  Feedback inhibition is common in pathways that synthesize metabolites. In these anabolic pathways, when the end product builds up, it feeds back to inhibit its own production. Catabolic pathways are involved in the degradation of compounds. Feedback inhibition makes less biochemical sense in a pathway that degrades compounds as these are usually involved in energy metabolism, or recycling or removal of compounds. Thus the end product is destroyed or removed and cannot feed back.

## INQUIRY QUESTION

**Page 113**  If ATP hydrolysis supplies more energy than is needed to drive the endergonic reaction, the overall process is exergonic. The reactions result in a net release of energy, so the $\Delta G$ for the overall process is therefore negative.

## UNDERSTAND

1. b   2. a   3. b   4. a   5. d   6. b   7. d

## APPLY

1. b   2. c   3. d   4. c   5. c   6. c

## SYNTHESIZE

1. a. At 40°C the enzyme is at it optimum. The rate of the reaction is at its highest level.

   b. Temperature is a factor that influences enzyme function. This enzyme does not appear to function at either very cold or very hot temperatures. The shape of the enzyme is affected by temperature, and the enzyme's structure is altered enough at extreme temperatures that it no longer binds substrate. Alternatively, the enzyme may be denatured—that is a complete loss of normal three-dimensional shape at extreme temperatures. Think about frying an egg: What happens to the proteins in the egg?

   c. Everyone's body is slightly different. If the temperature optimum was very narrow, then the cells that make up a body would be vulnerable. Having a broad range of temperature optimums keeps the enzyme functioning.

2. a. The reaction rate would be slow because of the low concentration of the substrate ATP. The rate of reaction depends on substrate concentration.

b. ATP acts like a noncompetitive, allosteric inhibitor when ATP levels are very high. If ATP binds to the allosteric site, then the reaction should slow down.

c. When ATP levels are high, the excess ATP molecules bind to the allosteric site and inhibit the enzyme. The allosteric inhibitor functions by causing a change in the shape of the active site in the enzyme. This reaction is an example of feedback regulation because ATP is a final product of the overall series of reactions associated with glycolysis. The cell regulates glycolysis by regulating this early step catalyzed by phosphofructokinase; the allosteric inhibitor is the "product" of glycolysis (and later stages) ATP.

## CHAPTER 7

### LEARNING OUTCOME QUESTIONS

**7.1** Cells require energy for a wide variety of functions. The reactions involved in the oxidation of glucose are complex and linking these to the different metabolic functions that require energy would be inefficient. Thus cells make and use ATP as a reusable source of energy.

**7.2** The location of glycolysis does not argue for or against the endosymbiotic origin of mitochondria. If could have been located in the mitochondria previously and moved to the cytoplasm, or could have always been located in the cytoplasm in eukaryotes.

**7.3** For an enzyme like pyruvate decarboxylase the complex reduces the distance for the diffusion of substrates for the different stages of the reaction. If there are any unwanted side reactions they are prevented. Finally the reactions occur within a single unit and thus can be controlled in a coordinated fashion. The main disadvantage is that since the enzymes are all part of a complex their evolution is more constrained than if they were independent.

**7.4** At the end of the Krebs cycle, the electrons removed from glucose are all carried by soluble electron carriers. Most of these are in NADH and a few are in $FADH_2$. All of these are all fed into the electron transport chain under aerobic conditions where they are used to produce a proton gradient.

**7.5** A hole in the outer membrane would allow protons in the intermembrane space to leak out. This would destroy the proton gradient across the inner membrane, stopping the phosphorylation of ADP by ATP synthase.

**7.6** The inner membrane actually allows a small amount of leakage of protons back into the matrix, reducing the yield per NADH. The proton gradient can also be used to power other functions, such as the transport of pyruvate. The actual yield is also affected by the relative concentrations ADP, Pi, and ATP as the equilibrium constant for this reaction depends on this.

**7.7** Glycolysis, which is the starting point for respiration from sugars is regulated at the enzyme phosphofructokinase. This enzyme is just before the 6-C skeleton is split into two 3-C molecules. The allosteric effectors for this enzyme include ATP and citrate. Thus the "end product" ATP, and an intermediate from the Krebs cycle, both feedback to inhibit the first part of this process.

**7.8** The first obvious point is that the most likely type of ecosystem would be one where oxygen is nonexistent or limiting. This includes marine, aquatic, and soil environments. Any place where oxygen is in short supply is expected to be dominated by anaerobic organisms and respiration produces more energy than fermentation.

**7.9** The short answer is no. The reason is two-fold. First the oxidation of fatty acids feeds acetyl units into the Krebs cycle. The primary output of the Krebs cycle is electrons that are fed into the electron transport chain to eventually produce ATP by chemiosmosis. The second reason is that the process of beta-oxidation that produces the acetyl units is oxygen dependent as well. This is because beta-oxidation uses FAD as a cofactor for an oxidation, and the $FADH_2$ is oxidized by the electron transport chain.

**7.10** The evidence for the origins of metabolism is indirect. The presence of $O_2$ in the atmosphere is the result of photosynthesis, so the record of when we went from a reducing to an oxidizing atmosphere chronicles the rise of oxygenic photosynthesis. Glycolysis is a universal pathway that is found in virtually all types of cells. This indicates that it is an ancient pathway that likely evolved prior to other types of energy metabolism. Nitrogen fixation probably evolved in the reducing atmosphere that preceded oxygenic photosynthesis as it is poisoned by oxygen, and aided by the reducing atmosphere.

### INQUIRY QUESTION

**Page 142** During the catabolism of fats, each round of 2-oxidation uses one molecule of ATP and generates one molecule each of $FADH_2$ and NADH. For a 16-carbon fatty acid, seven rounds of 2-oxidation would convert the fatty acid into eight molecules of acetyl-CoA. The oxidation of each acetyl-CoA in the Krebs

cycle produces 10 molecules of ATP. The overall ATP yield from a 16-carbon fatty acid would be: a net gain of 21 ATP from 7 rounds of 2-oxidation [gain of 4 ATP per round minus 1 per round to prime reactions] + 80 ATP from the oxidation of 8 acetyl-CoAs = 101 molecules of ATP.

### UNDERSTAND

1. d   2. d   3. c   4. c   5. a   6. d   7. c

### APPLY

1. b   2. b   3. d   4. b   5. a   6. b   7. b

### SYNTHESIZE

1.

| Molecules | Glycolysis | Cellular Respiration |
|---|---|---|
| Glucose | *Is the starting material for the reaction* | *Does not directly use glucose; however, does use pyruvate derived from glucose* |
| Pyruvate | *The end product of glycolysis* | *The starting material for cellular respiration* |
| Oxygen | *Not required* | *Required for aerobic respiration, but not for anaerobic respiration* |
| ATP | *Produced through substrate-level phosphorylation* | *Produced through oxidative phosphorylation. More produced than in glycolysis* |
| $CO_2$ | *Not produced* | *Produced during pyruvate oxidation and Krebs cycle* |

2. The electron transport chain of the inner membrane of the mitochondria functions to create a hydrogen ion concentration gradient by pumping protons into the intermembrane space. In a typical mitochondrion, the protons can only diffuse back down their concentration gradient by moving through the ATP synthase and generating ATP. If protons can move through another transport protein then the potential energy of the hydrogen ion concentration gradient would be "lost" as heat.

3. If brown fat persists in adults, then the uncoupling mechanism to generate heat described above could result in weight loss under cold conditions. There is now some evidence to indicate that this may be the case.

## CHAPTER 8

### LEARNING OUTCOME QUESTIONS

**8.1** Both chloroplasts and mitochondria have an outer membrane and an inner membrane. The inner membrane in both forms an elaborate structure. These inner membrane systems have electron transport chains that move protons across the membrane to allow for the synthesis of ATP by chemiosmosis. They also both have a soluble compartment in which a variety of enzymes carry out reactions.

**8.2** All of the carbon in your body comes from carbon fixation by autotrophs. Thus, all of the carbon in your body was once $CO_2$ in the atmosphere, before it was fixed by plants.

**8.3** The action spectrum for photosynthesis refers to the most effective wavelengths. The absorption spectrum for an individual pigment shows how much light is absorbed at different wavelengths.

**8.4** Before the discovery of photosystems, we assumed that each chlorophyll molecule absorbed photons resulting in excited electrons.

**8.5** Without a proton gradient, synthesis of ATP by chemiosmosis would be impossible. However, NADPH could still be synthesized because electron transport would still occur as long as photons were still being absorbed to begin the process.

**8.6** A portion of the Calvin cycle is the reverse of glycolysis (the reduction of 3-phosphoglycerate to glyceraldehyde-3-phosphate).

**8.7** Both $C_4$ plants and CAM plants fix carbon by incorporating $CO_2$ into the 4-carbon malate, then use this to produce high local levels of $CO_2$ for the Calvin cycle. The main difference is that in $C_4$ plants, this occurs in different cells, and in CAM plants this occurs at different times.

### INQUIRY QUESTIONS

**Page 150** Light energy is used in light-dependent reactions to reduce NADP⁺ and to produce ATP. Molecules of chlorophyll absorb photons of light energy, but only within narrow energy ranges (specific wavelengths of light). When all chlorophyll molecules are in use, no additional increase in light intensity will increase the rate at which they can absorb light energy.

**Page 154** Saturation levels should be higher when light intensity is greater, up to a maximum level. If it were possible to minimize the size of photosystems by reducing the number of chlorophyll molecules in each, then the saturation level would also increase.

**Page 157** You could conclude that the two photosystems do not function sequentially.

## UNDERSTAND

1. c   2. a   3. a   4. b   5. c   6. c   7. a   8. b

## APPLY

1. d   2. b   3. c   4. c   5. d   6. b   7. a   8. a

## SYNTHESIZE

1. In $C_3$ plants $CO_2$ reacts with ribulose 1,5-bisphosphate (RuBP) to yield 2 molecules of PGA. This reaction is catalyzed by the enzyme rubisco. Rubisco also catalyzes the oxidation of RuBP. Which reaction predominates depends on the relative concentrations of reactants. The reactions of the Calvin cycle reduce the PGA to G3P, which can be used to make a variety of sugars including RuBP. In $C_4$ and CAM plants, an initial fixation reaction incorporates $CO_2$ into malate. The malate then can be decarboxylated to pyruvate and $CO_2$ to produce locally high levels of $CO_2$. The high levels of $CO_2$ get around the oxidation of RuBP by rubisco. In $C_4$ plants malate is produced in one cell, then shunted into an adjacent cell that lacks stomata to produce high levels of $CO_2$. CAM plants fix carbon into malate at night when their stomata are open, then use this during the day to fuel the Calvin cycle. Both are evolutionary innovations that have arisen in hot dry climates that allow plants to more efficiently fix carbon and prevent desiccation.

2. Figure 8.19 diagrams this relationship. The oxygen produced by photosynthesis is used as a final electron acceptor for electron transport in respiration. The $CO_2$ that results from the oxidation of glucose (or fatty acids) is incorporated into organic compounds via the Calvin cycle. Respiration also produces water, while photosynthesis consumes water.

3. Yes. Plants use their chloroplasts to convert light energy into chemical energy. During light reactions ATP and NADPH are created, but these molecules are consumed during the Calvin cycle and are not available for the cell's general use. The G3P produced by the Calvin cycle stores the chemical energy from the light reactions within its chemical bonds. Ultimately, this energy is stored in glucose and retrieved by the cell through the process of glycolysis and cellular respiration.

# CHAPTER 9

## LEARNING OUTCOME QUESTIONS

**9.1** Ligands bind to receptors based on complementary shapes. This interaction based on molecular recognition is similar to how enzymes interact with their ligands.

**9.2** Hydrophobic molecule can cross the membrane and are thus more likely to have an internal receptor.

**9.3** Intracellular receptors have direct effects on gene expression. This generally leads to effects with longer duration.

**9.4** Ras protein occupies a central role in signaling pathways involving growth factors. A number of different kinds of growth factors act through Ras. So it is not surprising that this is mutated in a number of different cancers.

**9.5** GPCRs are a very ancient and flexible receptor/signaling pathway. The genes encoding these receptors have been duplicated and then have diversified over evolutionary time so now there are many members of this gene family.

## UNDERSTAND

1. b   2. b   3. c   4. d   5. b   6. d   7. c   8. a

## APPLY

1. b   2. c   3. b   4. d   5. d   6. c

## SYNTHESIZE

1. All signaling events start with a ligand binding to a receptor. The receptor initiates a chain of events that ultimately leads to a change in cellular

behavior. In some cases the change is immediate—for example, the opening of an ion channel. In other cases the change requires more time before it occurs, such as when the MAP kinase pathway becomes activated multiple different kinases become activated and deactivated. Some signals only affect a cell for a short time (the channel example), but other signals can permanently change the cell by changing gene expression, and therefore the number and kind of proteins found in the cell.

2. a. This system involves *both* autocrine and paracrine signaling because Netrin-1 can influence the cells within the crypt that are responsible for its production and the neighboring cells.

   b. The binding of Netrtin-1 to its receptor produces the signal for cell growth. This signal would be strongest in the regions of the tissue with the greatest amount of Netrin-1—that is, in the crypts. A concentration gradient of Netrin-1 exists such that the levels of this ligand are lowest at the tips of the villi. Consequently, the greatest amount of cell death would occur at the villi tips.

   c. Tumors occur when cell growth goes on unregulated. In the absence of Netrin-1, the Netrin-1 receptor can trigger cell death—controlling the number of cells that make up the epithelial tissue. Without this mechanism for controlling cell number, tumor formation is more likely.

# CHAPTER 10

## LEARNING OUTCOME QUESTIONS

**10.1** The concerted replication and segregation of chromosomes works well with one small chromosome, but would likely not work as well with many chromosomes.

**10.2** No.

**10.3** The first irreversible step is the commitment to DNA replication.

**10.4** Loss of cohesins would mean that the products of DNA replication would not be kept together. This would make normal mitosis impossible, and thus lead to aneuploid cells and probably be lethal.

**10.5** The segregation of chromatids that lose cohesin would be random as they could not longer be held at metaphase attached to opposite poles. This would likely lead to gain and loss of this chromosome in daughter cells due to improper partitioning.

**10.6** Tumor suppressor genes are genetically recessive, while proto-oncogenes are dominant. Loss of function for a tumor suppressor gene leads to cancer while inappropriate expression or gain of function lead to cancer with proto-oncogenes.

## UNDERSTAND

1. d   2. b   3. b   4. b   5. a   6. c   7. b

## APPLY

1. d   2. a   3. c   4. b   5. d   6. c   7. d

## SYNTHESIZE

1. If Wee-1 were absent then there would be no way for the cell to phosphorylate Cdk. If Cdk is not phosphorylated, then it cannot be inhibited. If Cdk is not inhibited, then it will remain active. If Cdk remains active, then it will continue to signal the cell to move through the $G_2/M$ checkpoint, but now in an unregulated manner. The cells would undergo multiple rounds of cell division without the growth associated with $G_2$. As a consequence, the daughter cells will become smaller and smaller with each division—hence the name of the protein!

2. Growth factor = ligand

   1. Ligand binds to receptor (the growth factor will bind to a growth factor receptor).

   2. A signal is transduced (carried) into the cytoplasm.

   3. A signal cascade is triggered. Multiple intermediate proteins or second messengers will be affected.

   4. A transcription factor will be activated to bind to a specific site on the DNA.

   5. Transcription occurs and the mRNA enters the cytoplasm.

   6. The mRNA is translated and a protein is formed.

   7. The protein functions within the cytoplasm—possibly triggering S phase.

   If you study Figure 10.22 you will see a similar pathway for the formation of S phase proteins following receptor–ligand binding by a growth factor. In this diagram various proteins in the signaling pathway become phosphorylated and then dephosphorylated. Ultimately, the Rb protein that regulated the transcription factor E2F becomes phosphorylated. This releases the E2F and allows it to bind to the gene for S phase proteins and cyclins.

3. Proto-oncogenes tend to encode proteins that function in signal transduction pathways that control cell division. When the regulation of these proteins is aberrant, or they are stuck in the "on" state by mutation, it can lead to cancer. Tumor suppressor genes, on the other hand, tend to be in genes that encode proteins that suppress instead of activate cell division. Thus loss of function for a tumor suppressor gene leads to cancer.

## CHAPTER 11

### LEARNING OUTCOME QUESTIONS

**11.1** Stem cells divide by mitosis to produce one cell that can undergo meiosis, and another stem cell.

**11.2** No. Keeping sister chromatids together at the first division is key to this is reductive division. Homologues segregate at the first division, reducing the number of chromosomes by half.

**11.3** An improper disjunction at anaphase I would result in 4 aneuploid gametes: 2 with an extra chromosome and 2 that are missing a chromosome. Nondisjunction at anaphase II would result in 2 normal gametes and 2 aneuploid gametes: 1 with an extra chromosome and 1 missing a chromosome.

**11.4** The independent alignment of homologous pairs at metaphase I and the process of crossing over. The first shuffles the genome at the level of entire chromosomes, and the second shuffles the genome at the level of individual chromosomes.

### INQUIRY QUESTION

**Page 217** No, at the conclusion of meiosis I each cell has a single copy of each homologue. So, even if the attachment of sister chromatids were lost after a meiosis I division, the results would not be the same as mitosis.

### UNDERSTAND

1. c  2. d  3. a  4. b  5. b  6. a  7. b

### APPLY

1. c  2. b  3. b  4. d  5. b  6. a

### SYNTHESIZE

1. Compare your figure with Figure 11.8.
   a. There would be three homologous pairs of chromosomes for an organism with a diploid number of six.
   b. For each pair of homologues, you should now have a maternal and paternal pair.
   c. Many possible arrangements are possible. The key to your image is that it must show the homologues aligned pairwise—not single-file along the metaphase plate. The maternal and paternal homologues *do not* have to align on the same side of the cell. Independent assortment means that the pairs can be mixed.
   d. A diagram of metaphase II would not include the homologous pairs. The pairs have separated during anaphase of meiosis I. Your picture should diagram the haploid number of chromosomes, in this case three, aligned single-file along the metaphase plate. Remember that meiosis II is similar to mitosis.

2. The diploid chromosome number of a mule is 63. The mule receives 32 chromosomes from its horse parent (diploid 64: haploid 32) and another 31 chromosomes from its donkey parent (diploid 61: haploid 31). 32 + 31 = 63. The haploid number for the mule would be one half the diploid number $63 \div 2 = 31.5$. Can there be a 0.5 chromosome? Even if the horse and donkey chromosomes can pair (no guarantee of that) there will be one chromosome without a partner. This will lead to aneuploid gametes that are not viable.

3. Independent assortment involves the random distribution of maternal versus paternal homologues into the daughter cells produced during meiosis I. The number of possible gametes is equal to $2^n$, where $n$ is the haploid number of chromosomes. Crossing over involves the physical exchange of genetic material between homologous chromosomes, creating new combinations of genes on a single chromosome. Crossing over is a relatively rare event that affects large blocks of genetic material, so independent assortment likely has the greatest influence on genetic diversity.

4. Aneuploid gametes are cells that contain the wrong number of chromosomes. Aneuploidy occurs as a result of *nondisjunction*, or lack of separation of the chromosomes during either phase of meiosis.

a. Nondisjunction occurs at the point when the chromosomes are being pulled to opposite poles. This occurs during anaphase.

b. Use an image like Figure 11.8 and illustrate nondisjunction at anaphase I versus anaphase II

Anaphase I nondisjunction:

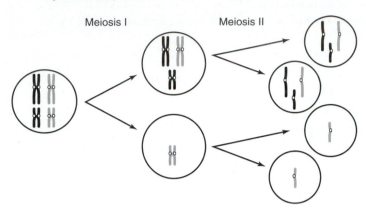

Meiosis I          Meiosis II

## CHAPTER 12

### LEARNING OUTCOME QUESTIONS

**12.1** Both had an effect, but the approach is probably the most important. In theory, his approach would have worked for any plant, or even animal he chose. In practice, the ease of both cross and self-fertilization was helpful.

**12.2** $\frac{1}{3}$ of tall $F_2$ plants are true-breeding.

**12.3** The events of meiosis I are much more important in explaining Mendel's laws. During anaphase I homologues separate and are thus segregated, and the alignment of different homologous pairs at metaphase I is independent.

**12.4** Assuming independent assortment of all three genes, the cross is Aa Bb Cc × Aa Bb Cc and the prob(A_ B_ C_)=($\frac{3}{4}$) ($\frac{3}{4}$) ($\frac{3}{4}$)=27/64.

**12.5** 1:1:1:1 dom dom:dom rec:rec dom:rec rec.

**12.6** 6/16.

### INQUIRY QUESTIONS

**Page 223** The ability to control whether the plants self-fertilized or cross-fertilized was of paramount importance in Mendel's studies. Results due to cross-fertilization would have had confounding influences on the predicted number of offspring with a particular phenotype.

**Page 227** Each of the affected females in the study had one unaffected parent, which means that each is heterozygous for the dominant trait. If each female marries an unaffected (recessive) male, each could produce unaffected offspring. The chance of having unaffected offspring is 50% in each case.

**Page 228** Genetic defects that remain hidden or dormant as heterzygotes in the recessive state are more likely to be revealed in homozygous state among closely related individuals.

**Page 235** Almost certainly, differences in major phenotypic traits of twins would be due to environmental factors such as diet.

### UNDERSTAND

1. b  2. c  3. c  4. c  5. b  6. d

### APPLY

1. b  2. c  3. b  4. a  5. c  6. d

### SYNTHESIZE

1. The approach to solving this type of problem is to identify the possible gametes. Separate the possible gamete combinations into the boxes along the top and side. Fill in the Punnet square by combining alleles from each parent.

   a. A monohybrid cross between individuals with the genotype *Aa* and *Aa*

|   | *A* | *a* |
|---|-----|-----|
| *A* | AA | Aa |
| *a* | aA | aa |

Phenotypic ratio: 3 dominant to 1 recessive

b. A dihybrid cross between two individuals with the genotype *AaBb*

|     | AB   | Ab   | aB   | ab   |
| --- | ---- | ---- | ---- | ---- |
| AB  | AABB | AABb | AaBB | AaBb |
| Ab  | AAbB | AAbb | AabB | Aabb |
| aB  | aABB | aABb | aaBB | aaBb |
| ab  | aAbB | aAbb | aabB | aabb |

Phenotypic ratio: 9 dominant dominant to 3 dominant recessive to 3 recessive dominant to 1 recessive recessive

Using Product Rule:
Prob(A_ B_) = (¾)(¾) = 9/16
Prob(A_ bb) = (¾)(¼) = 3/16
Prob(aa B_) = (¼)(¾) = 3/16
Prob(aa bb) = (¼)(¼) = 1/16

c. A dihybrid cross between individuals with the genotype *AaBb* and *aabb*

|     | AB   | Ab   | aB   | ab   |
| --- | ---- | ---- | ---- | ---- |
| ab  | aAbB | aAbb | aabB | aabb |

Using Product Rule:
Prob(A_ B_) = (¼)(1) = 1/16
Prob(A_ bb) = (¼)(1) = 1/16
Prob(aa B_) = (¼)(1) = 1/16
Prob(aa bb) = (¼)(1) = 1/16

2. The segregation of different alleles for any gene occurs due to the pairing of homologous chromosomes, and the subsequent separation of these homologues during anaphase I. The independent assortment of traits, more accurately the independent segregation of different allele pairs, is due to the independent alignment of chromosomes during metaphase I of meiosis.

3. There seems to be the loss of a genotype as there are only 3 possible outcomes (2 yellow and 1 black). If the yellow gene has a dominant effect on coat color, but also causes lethality when homozygous, then this could explain the observations. So, a yellow mouse is heterozygous and crossing two yellow mice yields 1 homozygous yellow (dead):2 heterozygous (appears yellow):1 black. You could test this by crossing the yellow to homozygous black. You should get 1 yellow:1 black, and all black offspring should be true breeding, and all yellow should behave as above.

4. There are two genes involved, one of which is epistatic to the other. At one gene, there are two alleles: black and brown; at the other gene, there are two alleles: albino and colored. The albino gene is epistatic to the brown gene so when you are homozygous recessive for albino, you are albino regardless of whether you are black or brown at the other locus. This leads to the 4 albino in a Mendelian kind of crossing scheme.

# CHAPTER 13

## LEARNING OUTCOME QUESTIONS

**13.1** Females would be all wild type; males would be all white eyed.

**13.2** Yes, should be viable and appear female.

**13.3** The mt-DNA could be degraded by a nuclease similar to how bacteria deal with invading viruses. Alternatively, the mt-containing mitochondria could be excluded from the zygote.

**13.4** No, not by genetic crosses.

**13.5** Yes. First division nondisjunction yields four aneuploid gametes while second division yields only two aneuploid gametes.

## INQUIRY QUESTIONS

**Page 244** There would probably be very little if any recombination so the expected assortment ratios would have been skewed from the expected 9:3:3:1.

**Page 247** About 10% of the progeny would have been recombinants, based on the relationship of 1 cM (map unit or centimorgan) equals 1% recombination frequency. When gene loci are separated by greater distances, the frequency of recombination between them increases to the extent that the number of recombinant gametes roughly equals the number of parental gametes. In that instance, the genes would exhibit independent assortment. With a recombination frequency of only 10%, it is doubtful that it would have led Mendel to the concept of independent assortment.

**Page 250** What has changed is the mother's age. The older the woman, the higher the risk she has of nondisjunction during meiosis. Thus, she also has a much greater risk of producing a child with Down syndrome.

**Page 251** XY egg is fertilized by an X sperm. A normal X egg is fertilized by an XY sperm.

**Page 253** Advanced maternal age, a previous child with birth defects, or a family history of birth defects.

## UNDERSTAND

1. c   2. d   3. d   4. a   5. c   6. c   7. c

## APPLY

1. c   2. b   3. c   4. b   5. c   6. b

## SYNTHESIZE

1. Theoretically, 25% of the children from this cross will be color blind. All of the color blind children will be male and 50% of the males will be color blind.

2. Parents of heterozygous plant were: green wrinkled X yellow round
Frequency of recombinants is 36+29/1300=0.05
Map distance = 5 cM

3. Male calico cats are very rare. The coloration that is associated with calico cats is the product of X inactivation. X inactivation only occurs in females as a response to dosage levels of the X-linked genes. The only way to get a male calico is to be heterozygous for the color gene and to be the equivalent of a Klinefelters male (*XXY*).

# CHAPTER 14

## LEARNING OUTCOME QUESTIONS

**14.1** The 20 different amino acid building blocks offers chemical complexity. This appears to offer informational complexity as well.

**14.2** The proper tautomeric forms are necessary for proper base pairing, which is critical to DNA structure.

**14.3** Prior to replication in light N there would be only one band. After one round of replication, there would be two bands with denatured DNA: one heavy and one light.

**14.4** The 5′ to 3′ activity is used to remove RNA primers. The 3′ to 5′ activity is used to removed mispaired bases (proofreading).

**14.5** A shortening of chromosome ends would eventually affect DNA that encodes important functions.

**14.6** No. The number of DNA damaging agents, in addition to replication errors, would cause lethal damage (this has been tested in yeast).

## INQUIRY QUESTIONS

**Page 262** Because adenine always forms bonds with only thymine, and guanine forms bonds with only cytosine, adenine and thymine will always have the same proportions, and likewise with guanine and cytosine.

**Page 265** The covalent bonds create a strong backbone for the molecule making it difficult to disrupt. Individual hydrogen bonds are more easily broken allowing enzymes to separate the two strands without disrupting the inherent structure of the molecule.

**Page 269** DNA ligase is important in connecting Okazaki fragments during DNA replication. Without it, the lagging strand would not be complete.

**Page 273** The linear structure of chromosomes creates the end problem discussed in the text. It is impossible to finish the ends of linear chromosomes using unidirectional polymerases that require RNA primers. The size of eukaryotic genomes also means that the time necessary to replicate the genome is much greater than in prokaryotes with smaller genomes. Thus the use of multiple origins of replication.

**Page 275** Cells have a variety of DNA repair pathways that allow them to restore damaged DNA to its normal constitution. If DNA repair pathways are compromised, the cell will have a higher mutation rate. This can lead to higher rates of cancer in a multicellular organism such as humans.

## UNDERSTAND

1. d   2. a   3. c   4. a   5. c   6. b   7. b

## APPLY

1. c  2. b  3. c  4. c  5. a  6. b  7. d  8. c

## SYNTHESIZE

1.  a. If both bacteria are heat-killed, then the transfer of DNA will have no effect since pathogenicity requires the production of proteins encoded by the DNA. Protein synthesis will not occur in a dead cell.

    b. The nonpathogenic cells will be transformed to pathogenic cells. Loss of proteins will not alter DNA.

    c. The nonpathogenic cells remain nonpathogenic. If the DNA is digested, it will not be transferred and no transformation will occur.

2.  The region could be an origin of replication. Origins of replication are adenine- and thymine-rich regions since only these nucleotides form two hydrogen bonds versus the three hydrogen bonds formed between guanine and cytosine, making it easier to separate the two strands of DNA.

    The RNA primer sequences would be 5′-ACUAUUGCUUUAUAA-3′. The sequence is antiparallel to the DNA sequence (review Figure 14.16) meaning that the 5′ end of the RNA is matching up with the 3′ end of the DNA. It is also important to remember that in RNA the thymine nucleotide is replaced by uracil (U). Therefore, the adenine in DNA will form a complementary base-pair with uracil.

3.  a. *DNA gyrase* functions to relieve torsional strain on the DNA. If DNA gyrase were not functioning, the DNA molecule would undergo supercoiling, causing the DNA to wind up on itself, preventing the continued binding of the polymerases necessary for replication.

    b. *DNA polymerase III* is the primary polymerase involved in the addition of new nucleotides to the growing polymer and in the formation of the phosphodiester bonds that make up the sugar–phosphate backbone. If this enzyme were not functioning, then no new DNA strand would be synthesized and there would be no replication.

    c. *DNA ligase* is involved in the formation of phosphodiester bonds between Okazaki fragments. If this enzyme was not functioning, then the fragments would remain disconnected and would be more susceptible to digestion by nucleases.

    d. *DNA polymerase I* functions to remove and replace the RNA primers that are required for DNA polymerase III function. If DNA polymerase I was not available, then the RNA primers would remain and the replicated DNA would become a mix of DNA and RNA.

## CHAPTER 15

### LEARNING OUTCOME QUESTIONS

**15.1**  There is no molecular basis for recognition between amino acids and nucleotides. The tRNA is able to interact with nucleic acid by base pairing and an enzyme can covalently attach amino acids to it.

**15.2**  There would be no specificity to the genetic code. Each codon must specify a single amino acid, although amino acids can have more than one codon.

**15.3**  Transcription translation coupling cannot exist in eukaryotes where the two processes are separated in both space and time.

**15.4**  No. This is a result of the evolutionary history of eukaryotes but is not necessitated by genome complexity.

**15.5**  Alternative splicing offers flexibility in coding information. One gene can encode multiple proteins.

**15.6**  This tRNA would be able to "read" STOP codons. This could allow nonsense mutations to be viable, but would cause problems making longer than normal proteins. Most bacterial genes actually have more than one STOP at the end of the gene.

**15.7**  Attaching amino acids to tRNAs, bringing charged tRNAs to the ribosome, and ribosome translocation all require energy.

**15.8**  No. It depends on where the breakpoints are that created the inversion, or duplication. For duplications it also depends on the genes that are duplicated.

### INQUIRY QUESTIONS

**Page 281**  One would expect higher amounts of error in transcription over DNA replication. Proofreading is important in DNA replication because errors in DNA replication will be passed on to offspring as mutations. However, RNA's have very short life spans in the cytoplasm therefore mistakes are not permanent.

**Page 284**  The very strong similarity among organisms indicates a common ancestry of the code.

**Page 285**  The promoter acts a binding site for RNA polymerase. The structure of the promoter provides information as to both where to bind, but also the direction of transcription. If the two sites were identical, the polymerase would need some other cue for the direction of transcription.

**Page 289**  Splicing can produce multiple transcripts from the same gene.

**Page 297**  Wobble not only explains the number of tRNAs that are observed due to the increased flexibility in the 5′ position, it also accounts for the degeneracy that is observed in the Genetic Code. The degenerate base is the one in the wobble position.

### UNDERSTAND

1. d  2. c  3. d  4. b  5. c  6. b  7. c

### APPLY

1. d  2. c  3. b  4. b  5. c  6. b  7. b

### SYNTHESIZE

1.  the predicted sequence of the mRNA for this gene
    5′–GCAAUGGGCUCGGCAUGCUAAUCC–3′
    the predicted amino acid sequence of the protein
    5′–GCA AUG GGC UCG GCA UGC UAA UCC–3′
    Met-Gly-Ser-Ala-Cys-STOP

2.  A frameshift essentially turns the sequence of bases into a "random" sequence. If you consider the genetic code, 3 of the 64 codons are STOP, so the probability of hitting a STOP in a random sequence is 3/64 or about 1 every 20 codons.

3.  a. mRNA = 5′–GCA AUG GGC UCG GCA UUG CUA AUC C–3′
    The amino acid sequence would then be: Met-Gly-Ser-Ala-Leu-Leu-Iso-.
    There is no stop codon. This is an example of a frameshift mutation. The addition of a nucleotide alters the "reading frame," resulting in a change in the type and number of amino acids in this protein.

    b. mRNA = 5′–GCA AUG GGC UAG GCA UGC UAA UCC–3′
    The amino acid sequence would then be: Met-Gly-STOP.
    This is an example of a nonsense mutation. A single nucleotide change has resulted in the early termination of protein synthesis by altering the codon for Ser into a stop codon.

    c. mRNA = 5′–GCA AUG GGC UCG GCA AGC UAA UCC –3′
    The amino acid sequence would then be: Met-Gly-Ser-Ala-Ser-STOP.
    This base substitution has affected the codon that would normally encode Cys (UGC) and resulted in the addition of Ser (AGC).

4.  The split genes of eukaryotes offers the opportunity to control the splicing process, which does not exist in prokaryotes. This is also true for poly adenylation in eukaryotes. In prokaryotes, transcription/translation coupling offers the opportunity for the process of translation to have an effect on transcription.

## CHAPTER 16

### LEARNING OUTCOME QUESTIONS

**16.1**  The control of gene expression would be more like humans (fellow eukaryote) than E. coli.

**16.2**  The two helices both interact with DNA, so the spacing between the helices is important for both to be able to bind to DNA.

**16.3**  The operon would be on all of the time (constitutive expression).

**16.4**  The loss of a general transcription factor would likely be lethal as it would affect all transcription. The loss of a specific factor would affect only those genes controlled by the factor.

**16.5**  These genes are necessary for the ordinary functions of the cell. That is, the role of these genes is in ordinary housekeeping and not in any special functions.

**16.6**  RNA interference offers a way to specifically affect gene expression using drugs made of siRNAs.

**16.7**  As there are many proteins in a cell doing a variety of functions, uncontrolled degradation of proteins would be devastating to the cell.

### INQUIRY QUESTIONS

**Page 308**  The presence more than one gene in the operon allows for increased control over the elements of the pathway and therefore the product. A single regulatory system can regulate several adjacent genes.

**Page 315** Regulation occurs when various genes have the same regulatory sequences, which bind the same proteins.

**Page 324** Ubiquitin is added to proteins that need to be removed because they are nonfunctional or those that are degraded as part of a normal cellular cycle.

## UNDERSTAND

1. c  2. d  3. a  4. c  5. b  6. c  7. b

## APPLY

1. c  2. c  3. b  4. d  5. c  6. a  7. c

## SYNTHESIZE

1. Mutations that affect binding sites for proteins on DNA will control the expression of genes covalently linked to them. Introducing a wild type binding site on a plasmid will not affect this. We call this being cis-dominant. Mutations in proteins that bind to DNA would be recessive to a wild type gene introduced on a plasmid.

2. Negative control of transcription occurs when the ability to initiate transcription is reduced. Positive control occurs when the ability to initiate transcription is enhanced. The *lac* operon is regulated by the presence or absence of lactose. The proteins encoded within the operon are specific to the catabolism (breakdown) of lactose. For this reason, operon expression is only required when there is lactose in the environment. Allolactose is formed when lactose is present in the cell. The allolactose binds to a repressor protein, altering its conformation and allowing RNA polymerase to bind. In addition to the role of lactose, there is also a role for the activator protein CAP in regulation of *lac*. When cAMP levels are high then CAP can bind to DNA and make it easier for RNA polymerase to bind to the promoter. The *lac* operon is an example of both positive and negative control.

   The *trp* operon encodes protein manufacture of tryptophan in a cell. This operon must be expressed when cellular levels of tryptophan are low. Conversely, when tryptophan is available in the cell, there is no need to transcribe the operon. The tryptophan repressor must bind tryptophan before it can take on the right shape to bind to the operator. This is an example of negative control.

3. Forms that control gene expression that are unique to eukaryotes include alternative splicing, control of chromatin structure, control of transport of mRNA from the nucleus to the cytoplasm, control of translation by small RNAs, and control of protein levels by ubiquitin- directed destruction. Of these, most are obviously part of the unique features of eukaryotic cells. The only mechanisms that could work in prokaryotes would be translational control by small RNAs and controlled destruction of proteins.

4. Mutation is a permanent change in the DNA. Regulation is a short-term change controlled by the cell. Like mutations, regulation can alter the number of proteins in a cell, change the size of a protein, or eliminate the protein altogether. The key difference is that gene regulation can be reversed in response to changes in the cell's environment. Mutations do not allow for this kind of rapid response.

## CHAPTER 17

### LEARNING OUTCOME QUESTIONS

**17.1** *Eco*RI is a restriction enzyme that can be used to cut DNA at specific places. Ligase is used to "glue" together pieces of DNA that have been cut with the same restriction enzyme. The two enzymes make it possible to add foreign DNA into an *E. coli* plasmid.

**17.2** A cDNA library is constructed from mRNA. Unlike the gene itself, cDNA does not include the introns or regulatory elements.

**17.3** Multiple rounds of DNA replication allow for an exponential increase in copies of the DNA. A heat-stable DNA polymerase makes this possible.

**17.4** The gene coding for a functional protein must be mutated. Recombination allows for the "knockout" gene to be specifically targeted.

**17.5** The protein must be completely pure so that the patient does not have an immune response to proteins from another organism.

   It is important that the protein have exactly the same structure when it is produced in a bacterial cell as in a human cell. Because post-translational modification is specific to eukaryotes, the human DNA may need to be modified before it is inserted in a bacterial genome to ensure the protein structure in identical to the human protein.

The protein may not be produced in every cell in a human. It is difficult to target the manufactured protein to only the cells where it is produced or needed. The protein could have unintended consequences in other cells in the patient's body.

**17.6** The pollen from the plant with the recombinant gene might fertilize a closely related wild plant. If the offspring are viable, the recombinant gene will be introduced into the wild population.

### INQUIRY QUESTIONS

**Page 331** A bacterial artificial chromosome or a yeast artificial chromosome would be the best way to go as a plasmid vector only can stably hold up to 10 kb.

**Page 332** No, cDNA is created using mRNA as a template, therefore, intron sequences would not be expressed.

**Page 340** Yes, if you first used reverse transcriptase to make cDNA to amplify. This is called RT PCR.

### UNDERSTAND

1. b  2. b  3. d  4. d  5. c  6. c  7. b  8. d  9. a

### APPLY

1. d  2. c  3. d

### SYNTHESIZE

1. Genes coding for each of the subunits would need to be inserted into different plasmids that are integrated into different bacteria. The cultures would need to be grown separately and the different protein subunits would then need to be isolated and purified. If the subunits can self assemble in vitro, then the protein could be functional. It could be difficult to establish just the right conditions for the assembly of the multiple subunits.

2. 5′–CTGATAGTCAGCTG–3′

## CHAPTER 18

### LEARNING OUTCOME QUESTIONS

**18.1** Banding sites on karyotypes depend on dyes binding to the condensed DNA that is wrapped around protein. The dyes bind to some regions, but not all and are therefore not evenly spaced along the genome in the way that sequential base-pairs are evenly spaced.

**18.2** Sequencing is not a perfect process and a small number of errors would occur. Also, the number of base-pairs that can be sequenced in an individual sequencing reaction is limited. Multiple copies of the genome need to be cut in different places and sequenced so that the overlapping pieces can be assembled into an overall genome sequence. If there were not multiple, overlapping sequences, it would not be possible to determine the order of the smaller pieces that are sequenced.

**18.3** One possibility is that transposable elements can move within the genome and create new genetic variability, subject to natural selection.

**18.4** From the transcriptome, it is possible to predict the proteins that may be translated and available for use in part of an organism at a specific time in development.

**18.5** Yes. Additional protein could enhance the nutritional value of the potato for human consumption. One caveat would be that the increased level of protein not change the texture or flavor of potatoes that a consumer is expecting.

### INQUIRY QUESTIONS

**Page 354** Repetitive elements are one of the main obstacles to assembling the DNA sequences in proper order. There is one copy of *bcr* (see with green probe) and one copy of *abl* (seen with red probe).

   The other *bcr* and *abl* genes are fused and the yellow color is the result of red plus green fluorescence combined).

**Page 361** Repetitive elements are one of the main obstacles to assembling the DNA sequences in proper order because it is difficult to determine which sequences are overlapping.

**Page 366** Proteins exhibit post-translational modification and the formation of protein complexes. Additionally a single gene can code for multiple proteins using alternative splicing.

**Page 367** A proteome is all the proteins coded for by the genome, and the transcriptome is all the RNA present in a cell or tissue at a specific time.

**Page 369** You may be able to take advantage of synteny between the rice and corn genome (see Figure 18.14). Let's assume that a drought-tolerance gene has already been identified and mapped in rice. Using what is known about synteny between the rice and corn genomes, you could find the region of the corn genome that corresponds to the rice drought-tolerance gene. This would narrow down the region of the corn genome that you might want to sequence to find your gene. A subsequent step might be to modify the corn gene that corresponds to the rice gene to see if you can increase drought tolerance.

## UNDERSTAND

1.b   2.a   3.c   4.d   5.b   6.c   7.b   8.d

## APPLY

1.b   2.a   3.d   4.b   5.c   6.d   7.d

## SYNTHESIZE

1. The STSs represent unique sequences in the genome. They can be used to align the clones into one contiguous sequence of the genome based on the presence or absence of an STS in a clone. The contig, with aligned clones, would look like this:

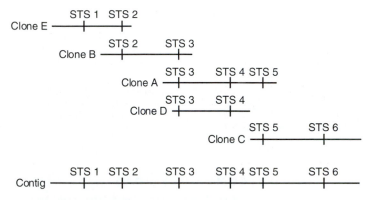

2. The anthrax genome has been sequenced. Investigators would look for differences in the genome between existing natural strains and those collected from a suspected outbreak. The genome of an infectious agent can be modified, or "weaponized," to make it more deadly. Also, single-nucleotide polymorphisms could be used to identify the source of the anthrax. In the case of the Florida anthrax outbreak it was determined that the source was a research laboratory.

# CHAPTER 19

## LEARNING OUTCOME QUESTIONS

**19.2**   The early cell divisions are very rapid and do not involve an increase in size between divisions. Interphase is greatly reduced allowing very fast cell divisions.

**19.3**   This requires experimentation to isolate cell from contact, which would prevent induction, or to follow a particular cells lineage.

**19.4**   The nucleus must be reprogrammed. What this means exactly on the molecular level is not clear, but probably involves changes in chromatin structure and methylation patterns.

**19.5**   Homeotic genes seem to have arisen very early in the evolutionary history of bilaterians. These have been duplicated and they have diversified with increasing morphological complexity.

**19.6**   Cell death can be a patterning mechanism. Your fingers were sculpted from a paddle-like structure by cell death.

## INQUIRY QUESTION

**Page 378** The *macho-1* gene product is a transcription factor that can activate the expression of several muscle-specific genes. Whether or not the fibroblast growth factor (FGF) signal is received from underlying endoderm precursor cells in the embryo determines how *macho-1* acts. If the FGF signal is present, it activates a Ras/MAP kinase pathway which, together with *macho-1*, either suppresses muscle genes or activates the transcription of mesenchyme genes. Without the FGF signal, *macho-1* alone triggers the transcription of muscle genes.

## UNDERSTAND

1.b   2.d   3.c   4.d   5.b   6.c   7.b

## APPLY

1.d   2.a   3.b   4.a   5.c   6.c   7.c

## SYNTHESIZE

1. The horizontal lines of the fate map represent cell divisions. Starting with the egg, four cell divisions are required to establish a population of cells that will become nervous tissue. It takes another eight to nine divisions to produce the final number of cells that will make up the nervous system of the worm. It takes seven to eight rounds of cell division to generate the population of cells that will become the gonads. Once established, another seven to eight cell divisions are required to produce the actual gonad cells.

2. Not every cell in a developing embryo will survive. The process of apoptosis is responsible for eliminating cells from the embryo. In *C. elegans*, the process of apoptosis is regulated by three genes: *ced-3*, *ced-4*, and *ced-9*. Both *ced-3 and ced-4* encode proteases, enzymes that degrade proteins. Interestingly, the *ced-3* protease functions to activate gene expression of the *ced-4* protease. Together, these proteases will destroy the cell from the inside-out. The *ced-9* gene functions to repress the activity of the protease-encoding genes, thereby preventing apoptosis.

3. a. N-cadherin plays a specific role in differentiating cells of the nervous system from ectodermal cells. Ectodermal cells express E-cadherin, but neural cells express N-cadherin. The difference in cell-surface cadherins means that the neural cells lose their contact with the surrounding ectodermal cells and establish new contacts with other neural cells. In the absence of N-cadherin, the nervous system would not form. If you assume that E-cadherin expression is also lost (as would occur normally in development) then these cells would lose all cell–cell contacts and would probably undergo apoptosis.

   b. Integrins mediate the connection between a cell and its surrounding environment, the extracellular matrix (ECM). The loss of integrins would result in the loss of cell adhesion to the ECM. These cells would not be able to move and therefore, gastrulation and other developmental processes would be disrupted.

   c. Integrins function by linking the cell's cytoskeleton to the ECM. This connection is critical for cell movement. The deletion of the cytoplasmic domain of the integrin would not affect the ability of integrin to attach to the ECM, but it would prevent the cytoskeleton from getting a "grip." This deletion would likely result in a disruption of development similar to the complete loss of integrin.

4. Adult cells from the patient would be cultured with factors that reprogram the nucleus into pluripotent cells. These cells would then be grown in culture with factors necessary to induce differentiation into a specific cell type that could be transplanted into the patient. This would be easiest for tissue like a liver that regenerates, but could in theory be used for a variety of cell types.

# CHAPTER 20

## LEARNING OUTCOME QUESTIONS

**20.1**   Natural selection occurs when some individuals are better suited to their environment than others. These individuals live longer and reproduce more, leaving more offspring with the traits that enabled their parents to thrive. In essence, genetic variation within a population provides the raw material on which natural selection can act.

**20.2**   To determine if a population is in Hardy Weinberg equilibrium, one would first need to determine the actual allele frequencies, which can be calculated based on the actual genotype frequencies. After assigning variables $p$ and $q$ to the actual allele frequencies, one would then use the Hardy Weinberg equation, $p^2 + 2pq + q^2 = 1$ in order to determine the expected genotype frequencies. If the actual and expected genotype frequencies are the same (or, at least not significantly different) then it is safe to say that the population is in Hardy Weinberg equilibrium.

**20.3**   There are five mechanisms of evolution—natural selection, mutation, gene flow (migration), genetic drift, and nonrandom mating. Any of these mechanisms can alter allele frequencies within a population, although usually a change in allele frequency results from more than one mechanism working in concert (for example, mutation will introduce a beneficial new allele into the population, and natural selection will select for that allele such that its frequency increases over the course of two or more generations). Natural selection, the first mechanism and probably the most influential in bringing about evolutionary change, is also the only mechanism to produce adaptive change, that is, change that results in the population being better adapted to its environment. Mutation is the only way in which new alleles can be introduced—it is the ultimate source of all variation. Because it is a relatively rare event, mutation by itself is not a strong agent of allele frequency change; however, in concert with other mechanisms, especially natural selection, it can drastically change the allele frequencies in a population. Gene flow can introduce new alleles into a population from another population of the same species, thus changing the allele frequency within both the recipient and donor populations. Genetic drift is the random, chance factor of evolution—while the results of genetic drift can be negligible in a large population, small populations can see drastic changes in allele frequency due to this agent. Finally, nonrandom mating results in populations varying from Hardy Weinberg equilibrium not by changing allele frequencies but by changing genotype frequencies—nonrandom mating reduces the proportion of heterozygotes in a population.

**20.4**  Reproductive success relative to other individuals within an organism's population is referred to as that organism's fitness. Its fitness is determined by its longevity, mating frequency, and the number of offspring it produces for each mating. None of these factors is always the most important in determining reproductive success—instead it is the cumulative effects of all three factors that determines an individual's reproductive success. For example, an individual that has a very long life span but mates only infrequently might have lower fitness than a conspecific that lives only half as long but mates more frequently and with greater success. As seen with the water strider example in this section, traits that are favored for one component of fitness, say, for example, longevity, may be disadvantageous for other components of fitness, say, lifetime fecundity.

**20.5**  The dynamics among the different evolutionary mechanisms are very intricate, and it is often difficult, if not impossible, to discern which direction each process is operating within a population—it is much easier to simply see the final cumulative effects of the various agents of evolutionary change. However, there are cases in which more than one evolutionary process will operate in the same direction, with the resulting population changing, or evolving, more rapidly than it would have under only one evolutionary mechanism. For example, mutation may introduce a beneficial allele into a population; gene flow could then spread the new allele to other populations. Natural selection will favor this allele within each population, resulting in relatively rapid evolutionary adaptation of a novel phenotype.

**20.6**  In a population wherein heterozygotes had the lowest fitness, natural selection should favor both homozygous forms. This would result in disruptive selection, and a bimodal distribution of traits within the population. Over enough time, it could lead to a speciation event.

**20.7**  Directional selection occurs when one phenotype has an adaptive advantage over other phenotypes in the population, regardless of its relative frequency within the population. Frequency-dependent selection, on the other hand, results when either a common (positive frequency-dependent selection) or rare (negative frequency-dependent selection) has a selective advantage simply by virtue of its commonality or rarity. In other words, if a mutation introduces a novel allele into a population, directional selection may result in evolution because the allele is advantageous, not because it is rare.

**20.8**  Wild guppies have to balance natural selection, which, in the presence of a predator such as the pike cichlid, would tend to favor drab coloration, with sexual selection, wherein females prefer brightly colored males. Thus, in low-predation environments the male guppies tend to be brightly colored whereas in high-predation environments they are drably colored. Background color matching is a form of camouflage used by many species to avoid predation; again, however, in many cases this example of natural selection runs counter to sexual selection—males want to be inconspicuous to predators but attractive to potential mates. For example, to test the effects of predation on background color matching in a species of butterfly, one might raise captive populations of butterflies with a normal variation in coloration. After a few generations, add natural predators to half of the enclosures. After several generations, one would expect the butterflies in the predatory environment to have a high degree of background color matching in order to avoid predation, while the non-predatory environment would have promoted brightly-colored individuals where color would correlate with mating success.

**20.9**  Pleiotropic effects occur with many genes; in other words, a single gene has multiple effects on the phenotype of the individual. Whereas natural selection might favor a particular aspect of the pleiotropic gene, it might select against another aspect of the same gene; thus, pleiotropy often limits the degree to which a phenotype can be altered by natural selection. Epistasis occurs when the expression of one gene is controlled or altered by the existence or expression of another gene. Thus, the outcome of natural selection will depend not just on the genotype of one gene, but the other genotype as well.

## INQUIRY QUESTIONS

***Page 399***  In the example of Figure 20.3, the frequency of the recessive white genotype is 0.16. The remaining 84 cats (out of 100) in the population are ho-

mozygous or heterozygous black. If the 16 white cats died, they will not contribute recessive white genes to the next generation. Only heterozygous black cats will produce white kittens in a 3:1 ratio of black to white. Homozygous × homozygous black and homozygous × heterozygous black cats will have all black kittens. Since there are 36 homozygous black cats and 48 heterozygous black cats, with a new total of 84 cats, the new frequency of homozygous black cats is 36/84 or 43%, with the heterozygous black cats now comprising 57% of the population. If $p^2 = 0.43$, then $p = 0.65$ (approximately), then $1-p = q$, and $q = 0.35$. The frequency of white kittens in the next generation, $q^2$, is 0.12 or 12%.

***Page 405***  Differential predation might favor brown toads over green toads, green toads might be more susceptible to disease, or green toads might be less able to tolerate variations in climate, among other possibilities.

***Page 406***  Since the intermediate-sized water strider has the highest level of fitness, it would be expected that the intermediate size would become more prevalent in the population. If the number of eggs laid per day was not affected by body size, the small water striders would be favored because of their tendency to live longer than their larger counterparts.

***Page 407***  Yes. The frequency of copper tolerance will decrease as distance from the mine increases.

***Page 411***  The proportion of flies moving toward light (positive phototropism) would again begin to increase in successive generations.

***Page 411***  The distribution of birth weights in the human population would expand somewhat to include more babies of higher and lower birth weights.

***Page 413***  Guppy predators evidently locate their prey using visual cues. The more colorful the guppy, the more likely it is to be seen and thus the more likely it will become prey.

***Page 414***  Thoroughbred horse breeders have been using selective breeding for certain traits over many decades, effectively removing variation from the population of thoroughbred horses. Unless mutation produces a faster horse, it remains unlikely that winning speeds will improve.

## UNDERSTAND

1. a  2. b  3. d  4. a  5. d  6. a  7. d

## APPLY

1. d  2. d  3. a

## SYNTHESIZE

1.  The results depend on coloration of guppies increasing their conspicuousness to predators such that an individual's probability of survival is lower than if it was a drab morph. In the laboratory it may be possible to conduct trials in simulated environments; we would predict, based on the hypothesis of predation, that the predator would capture more of the colorful morph than the drab morph when given access to both. Design of the simulated environment would obviously be critical, but results from such an experiment, if successful, would be a powerful addition to the work already accomplished.

2.  On the large lava flows, where the background is almost entirely black, those individuals with black coloration within a population will have a selective advantage because they will be more cryptic to predators. On the other hand, on small flows, which are disrupted by light sand and green plants, dark individuals would be at an adaptive disadvantage for the same reason. You can read more about this in chapter 21 (21.2); the black peppered moths had an advantage on the trees lacking lichen, but a disadvantage on lichen-covered trees.

3.  Ultimately, genetic variation is produced by the process of mutation. However, compared with the speed at which natural selection can reduce variation in traits that are closely related to fitness, mutation alone cannot account for the persistence of genetic variation in traits that are under strong selection. Other processes can account for the observation that genetic variation can persist under strong selection. They include gene flow. Populations are often distributed along environmental gradients of some type. To the extent that different environments favor slightly different variants of phenotypes that have a genetic basis, gene flow among areas in the habitat gradient can introduce new genetic variation or help maintain existing variation. Similarly, just as populations frequently encounter different selective environments across their range (think of the guppies living above and below the waterfalls in Trinidad), a single population also encounters variation in selective environments across time (oscillating selection). Traits favored this year may not be the same as those favored next year, leading to a switching of natural selection and the maintenance of genetic variation.

# CHAPTER 21

## LEARNING OUTCOME QUESTIONS

**21.1** No. If eating hard seeds caused individuals to develop bigger beaks, then the phenotype is a result of the environment, not the genotype. Natural selection can only act upon those traits with a genetic component. Just as a body builder develops large muscles in his or her lifetime but does not have well-muscled offspring, birds that develop large beaks in their lifetime will not necessarily have offspring with larger beaks.

**21.2** An experimental design that would test this hypothesis could be as simple as producing enclosures for the moths and placing equal numbers of both morphs into each enclosure and then presenting predatory birds to each enclosure. One enclosure could be used as a control. One enclosure would have a dark background while the other would have a light background. After several generations, measuring the phenotype frequency of the moths should reveal very clear trends—the enclosure with the dark background should consist of mostly dark moths, the enclosure with the light background mostly light moths, and the neutral enclosure should have an approximately equal ratio of light to dark moths.

**21.3** If the trait that is being artificially selected for is due to the environment rather than underlying genotype, then the individuals selected that have that trait will not necessarily pass it on to their offspring.

**21.4** The major selective agent in most cases of natural selection is the environment; thus, climatic changes, major continental shifts, and other major geological changes would result in dramatic changes in selective pressure; during these times the rate and direction of evolutionary change would likely be affected in many, if not most, species. On the other hand, during periods of relative environmental stability, the selective pressure does not change and we would not expect to see many major evolutionary events.

**21.5** The only other explanation that could be used to explain homologous characteristics and vestigial structures could be mutation. Especially in the case of vestigial structures, if one resulted from a mutation that had pleiotropic effects, and the other effects of the genetic anomaly were selected for, then the vestigial structure would also be selected for, much like a rider on a Congressional Bill.

**21.6** Convergence occurs when distantly related species experience similar environmental pressures and respond, through natural selection, in similar ways. For example, penguins (birds), sharks (fish), sea lions (mammals) and even the extinct ichthyosaur (reptile) all exhibit the fusiform shape. Each of these animals has similar environmental pressures in that they are all aquatic predators and need to be able to move swiftly and agilely through the water. Clearly their most recent common ancestor does not have the fusiform body shape; thus the similarities are due to convergence (environment) rather than homology (ancestry). However, similar environmental pressures will not always result in convergent evolution. Most importantly, in order for a trait to appear for the first time in a lineage, there must have been a mutation; however, mutations are rare events, and even rarer is a beneficial mutation. There may also be other species that already occupy a particular niche; in these cases it would be unlikely that natural selection would favor traits that would increase the competition between two species.

**21.7** It is really neither a hypothesis nor a theory. Theories are the building blocks of scientific knowledge, they have withstood the most rigorous testing and review. Hypotheses, on the other hand, are tentative answers to a question. Unfortunately, a good hypothesis must be testable and falsifiable, and stating that humans came from Mars is not realistically testable or falsifiable; thus, it is, in the realm of biological science, a nonsense statement.

## INQUIRY QUESTIONS

**Page 419** The figure demonstrates that the beak depth of offspring can be predicted by the average beak depth of the parent's bills. Thus, one would expect the offspring to have the same beak depth if their parents' mean beak depth is the same. This is only correct if males and females do not differ in beak depth. In species for which the sexes differ (such as height in humans), then one would need to know both the depth and the sex of the parents and the calculation would be more complicated.

**Page 421** Such a parallel trend would suggest that similar processes are operating in both localities. Thus, one would conduct a study to identify similarities. In this case, both areas have experienced coincident reductions in air pollution, which most likely is the cause of the parallel evolutionary trends.

**Page 422** Assuming that small and large individuals would breed with each other, then middle-sized offspring would still be born (the result of matings between small and large flies). Nonetheless, there would also be many small and large individuals (the result of small × small and large × large matings). Thus, the

frequency distribution of body sizes would be much broader than the distributions in the figures.

**Page 426** This evolutionary decrease could occur for many reasons. For example, maybe *Nannippus* adapted to forested habitats and thus selection favored smaller size, as it had in the ancestral horses, before horses moved into open, grassland habitats. Another possibility is that there were many species of horses present at that time, and different sized horses ate different types of food. By evolving small size, *Nannippus* may have been able to eat a type of food not eaten by the others.

## UNDERSTAND

1. d   2. b   3. b   4. a   5. b   6. b   7. b

## APPLY

1. a   2. d   3. d

## SYNTHESIZE

1. Briefly, they are:

    A. There must be variation among individuals within a population.

    B. Variation among individuals must be related to differences among individuals in their success in producing offspring over their lifetime.

    C. Variation related to lifetime reproductive success must have a genetic (heritable) basis.

2. Figure 21.2a shows in an indirect way that beak depth varies from year to year. Presumably this is a function of variation among individuals in beak size. However, the most important point of 21.2a is that it shows the result of selection. That is, if the three conditions hold, we might expect to see average beak depth change accordingly as precipitation varies from year to year. Figure 21.2b is more directly relevant to the conditions noted for natural selection to occur. The figure shows that beak size varies among individuals, *and* that it tends to be inherited.

3. The relationship would be given by a cloud of points with no obvious linear trend in any direction different from a zero slope. In other words, it would be a horizontal line through an approximately circular cloud of points. Such data would suggest that whether a parent(s) has a large or small beak has no bearing on the beak size of its offspring.

4. Assuming that small and large individuals would breed with each other, then middle-sized offspring would still be born (the result of matings between small and large flies). Nonetheless, there would also be many small and large individuals (the result of small × small and large × large matings). Thus, the frequency distribution of body sizes would be much broader than the distributions in the figures. In some experiments, reproductive isolation evolves in which small and large individuals evolve mating preferences that prevent them from interbreeding, leading to the production of two different-sized species. This would be a laboratory example of sympatric speciation. Most studies, however, have failed to produce such reproductive isolation; rather, a single population remains through time with great variation.

5. The evolution of horses was not a linear event; instead it occurred over 55 million years and included descendents of 34 different genera. By examining the fossil record, one can see that horse evolution did not occur gradually and steadily; instead several major evolutionary events occurred in response to drastic changes in environmental pressures. The fossil record of horse evolution is remarkably detailed, and shows that while there have been trends toward certain characteristics, change has not been fluid and constant over time, nor has it been entirely consistent across all of the horse lineages. For example, some lineages experienced rapid increases in body size over relatively short periods of geological time, while other lineages actually saw decreases in body size.

# CHAPTER 22

## LEARNING OUTCOME QUESTIONS

**22.1** The Biological Species Concept states that different species are capable of mating and producing viable, fertile offspring. If sympatric species are unable to do so, they will remain reproductively isolated and thus distinct species. Along the same lines, gene flow between populations of the same species allow for homogenization of the two populations such that they remain the same species.

**22.2** In order for reinforcement to occur and complete the process of speciation, two populations must have some reproductive barriers in place prior to sympatry. In the absence of this initial reproductive isolation we would expect rapid exchange of genes and thus homogenization resulting from gene flow. On the other hand, if two populations are already somewhat reproductively isolated (due to hybrid infertility or a prezygotic barrier such as behavioral isolation), then we would expect natural selection to continue improving the fitness of the non-hybrid offspring, eventually resulting in speciation.

**22.3** Reproductive isolation that occurs due to different environments is a factor of natural selection; the environmental pressure favors individuals best suited for that environment. As isolated populations continue to develop, they accumulate differences due to natural selection that eventually will result in two populations so different that they are reproductively isolated. Reinforcement, on the other hand, is a process that specifically relates to reproductive isolation. It occurs when natural selection favors non-hybrids because of hybrid infertility or are simply less fit than their parents. In this way, populations that may have been only partly reproductively isolated become completely reproductively isolated.

**22.4** Polyploidy occurs instantaneously; in a single generation, the offspring of two different parental species may be reproductively isolated; however, if it is capable of self-fertilization then it is, according to the Biological Species Concept, a new species. Disruptive selection, on the other hand, requires many generations as reproductive barriers between the two populations must evolve and be reinforced before the two would be considered separate species.

**22.5** In the archipelago model, adaptive radiation occurs as each individual island population adapts to its different environmental pressures. In sympatric speciation resulting from disruptive selection, on the other hand, traits are selected for that are not necessarily best suited for a novel environment but are best able to reduce competition with other individuals. It is in the latter scenario wherein adaptive radiation due to a key innovation is most likely to occur.

**22.6** It depends on what species concept you are using to define a given species. Certainly evolutionary change can be punctuated, but in times of changing environmental pressures we would expect adaptation to occur. The adaptations, however, do not necessarily have to lead to the splitting of a species—instead one species could simply change in accordance with the environmental changes to which it is subjected. This would be an example of non-branching, as opposed to branching, evolution; but again, whether the end-result organism is a different species from its ancestral organism that preceded the punctuated event is subject to interpretation.

**22.7** Unlike the previous major mass extinction events, the current mass extinction is largely attributable to human activity, including but not limited to habitat degradation, pollution, and hunting.

## INQUIRY QUESTIONS

**Page 447** Speciation can occur under allopatric conditions because isolated populations are more likely to diverge over time due to drift or selection. Adaptive radiation tends to occur in places inhabited by only a few other species or where many resources in a habitat are unused. Different environmental conditions typical of adaptive radiation tend to favor certain traits within a population. Allopatric conditions would then generally favor adaptive radiation.

In character displacement, natural selection in each species favors individuals able to use resources not used by the other species. Two species might have evolved from two populations of the same species located in the same environment (sympatric species). Individuals at the extremes of each population are able to resources not used by the other group. Competition for a resource would be reduced for these individuals, possibly favoring their survival and leading to selection for the tendency to use the new resource. Character displacement tends to compliment sympatric speciation.

**Page 452** If one area experiences an unfavorable change in climate, a mobile species can move to another area where the climate was like it was before the change. With little environmental change to drive natural selection within that species, stasis would be favored.

## UNDERSTAND

1. a  2. c  3. a  4. b  5. a  6. a  7. d  8. b

## APPLY

1. b  2. a  3. d  4. a  5. b  6. b

## SYNTHESIZE

1. If hybrids between two species have reduced viability or fertility, then natural selection will favor any trait that prevents hybrid matings. The reason is that individuals that don't waste time, energy, or resources on such matings will have greater fitness if they instead spend the time, energy, and resources on mating with members of their own species. For this reason, natural selection

will favor any trait that decreases the probability of hybridization. By contrast, once hybridization has occurred, the time, energy, and resources have already been expended. Thus, there is no reason that less fit hybrids would be favored over more fit ones. The only exception is for species that invest considerable time and energy in incubating eggs and rearing the young; for those species, selection may favor reduced viability of hybrids because parents of such individuals will not waste further time and energy on them.

2. The biological species concept, despite its limitations, reveals the continuum of biological processes and the complexity and dynamics of organic evolution. At the very least, the biological species concept provides a mechanism for biologists to communicate about taxa and know that they are talking about the same thing! Perhaps even more significantly, discussion and debate about the meaning of "species" fuels a deeper understanding about biology and evolution in general. It is unlikely that we will ever have a single unifying concept of species given the vast diversity of life, both extinct and extant.

3. The principle is the same as in character displacement. In sympatry, individuals of the two species that look alike may mate with each other. If the species are not completely interfertile, then individuals hybridizing will be at a selective disadvantage. If a trait appears in one species that allows that species to more easily recognize members of its own species and thus avoid hybridization, then individuals bearing that trait will have higher fitness and that trait will spread through the population.

4. I would expect the two species to have more similar morphology when they are found alone (allopatry) than when they are found together (sympatry), assuming that food resources were the same from one island to the next. This would be the result of character displacement expected under a hypothesis of competition for food when the two species occur in sympatry. A species pair that is more distantly related might not be expected to show the pattern of character displacement since they show greater differences in morphology (and presumably in ecology and behavior as well), which should reduce the potential for competition to drive character divergence.

## CHAPTER 23

### LEARNING OUTCOME QUESTIONS

**23.1** Because of convergent evolution; two distantly related species subjected to the same environmental pressures may be more phenotypically similar than two species with different environmental pressures but a more recent common ancestor. Other reasons for the possible dissimilarity between closely related species include oscillating selection and rapid adaptive radiations in which species rapidly adapt to a new available niche.

**23.2** In some cases wherein characters diverge rapidly relative to the frequency of speciation, it can be difficult to construct a phylogeny using cladistics because the most parsimonious phylogeny may not be the most accurate. In most cases, however, cladistics is a very useful tool for inferring phylogenetic relationships among groups of organisms.

**23.3** Yes, in some instances this is possible. For example, assume two populations of a species become geographically isolated from one another in similar environments, and each population diverges and speciation occurs, with one group retaining its ancestral traits and the other deriving new traits. The ancestral group in each population may be part of the same biological species but would be considered polyphyletic because to include their common ancestor would also necessitate including the other, more derived species (which may have diverged enough to be reproductively isolated).

**23.4** Not necessarily; it is possible that the character changed since the common ancestor and is present in each group due to convergence. While the most recent common ancestor possessing the character is the most parsimonious, and thus the most likely, explanation, it is possible, especially for small clades, that similar environmental pressures resulted in the emergence of the same character state repeatedly during the course of the clade's evolution.

**23.5** Hypothetically it is possible; however, the viral analyses and phylogenetic analyses have provided strong evidence that HIV emergence was the other way around; it began as a simian disease and mutated to become a human form, and that this has occurred several times.

### INQUIRY QUESTIONS

**Page 461** In parsimony analyses of phylogenies, the least complex explanation is favored. High rates of evolutionary change and few character states complicate matters. High rates of evolutionary change, such as occur when mutations arise in noncoding portions of DNA, can be misleading when constructing phylogenies. Mutations arising in noncoding DNA are not eliminated by natural selection in the same manner as mutations in coding (functional) DNA. Also, evolution of new character states can be very high in nonfunctional DNA and this can lead to genetic drift. Since DNA has only four nucleotides (four character states) it is highly likely that two species could evolve the same derived character at a particular base position. This leads to a violation of the assumptions of parsimony—that the fewest evolutionary events lead to the best hypothesis of phylogenetic relationships—and resulting phylogenies are inaccurate.

**Page 462** The only other hypothesis is that the most recent common ancestor of birds and bats was also winged. Of course, this scenario is much less parsimonious (and thus much more unlikely) than the convergence hypothesis, especially given the vast number of reptiles and mammals without wings. Most phylogenies are constructed based on the rule of parsimony; in the absence of fossil evidence of other winged animals and molecular data supporting a closer relationship between birds and bats than previously thought, there is no way to test the hypothesis that bird and bat wings are homologous rather than analogous.

**Page 471** If the victim had contracted HIV from a source other than the patient, the most recent common ancestor of the two strains would be much more distant. As it is, the phylogeny shows that the victim and patient strains share a relatively recent ancestor, and that the victim's strain is derived from the patient's strain.

## UNDERSTAND

1. d   2. b   3. a   4. b   5. a   6. d   7. b   8. c

## APPLY

1. c   2. d   3. d   4. a

## SYNTHESIZE

1. Naming of groups can be variable; names provided here are just examples. Jaws—shark, salamander, lizard, tiger, gorilla, human (jawed vertebrates); lungs—salamander, lizard, tiger, gorilla, human (terrestrial tetrapods); amniotic membrane—lizard, tiger, gorilla, human (amniote tetrapods); hair—tiger, gorilla, human (mammals); no tail—gorilla, human (humanoid primate); bipedal—human (human).

2. It would seem to be somewhat of a conundrum, or potentially circular; choosing a closely related species as an outgroup when we do not even know the relationships of the species of interest. One way of guarding against a poor choice for an outgroup is to choose several species as outgroups and examine how the phylogenetic hypothesis for the group of interest changes as a consequence of using different outgroups. If the choice of outgroup makes little difference, then that might increase one's confidence in the phylogenetic hypotheses for the species of interest. On the other hand, if the choice makes a big difference (different phylogenetic hypotheses result when choosing different outgroups), that might at least lead to the conclusion that one cannot be confident in inferring a robust phylogenetic hypothesis for the group of interest without collecting more data.

3. Recognizing that birds are reptiles potentially provides insight to the biology of both birds and reptiles. For example, some characteristics of birds are clearly of reptilian origin, such as feathers (modified scales), nasal salt secreting glands, and strategies of osmoregulation/excretion (excreting nitrogenous waste products as uric acid) representing ancestral traits, that continue to serve birds well in their environments. On the other hand, some differences from other reptiles (again, feathers) seem to have such profound significance biologically, that they overwhelm similarities visible in shared ancestral characteristics. For example, no extant nonavian reptiles can fly, or are endothermic and these two traits have created a fundamental distinction in the minds of many biologists. Indeed, many vertebrate biologists prefer to continue to distinguish birds from reptiles rather than emphasize their similarities even though they recognize the power of cladistic analysis in helping to shape classification. Ultimately, it may be nothing much more substantial than habit which drives the preference of some biologists to traditional classification schemes.

4. In fact, such evolutionary transitions (the loss of the larval mode, and the re-evolution of a larval mode from direct development) are treated with equal weight under the simplest form of parsimony. However, if it is known from independent methods (for example, developmental biology) that one kind of change is less likely than another (loss versus a reversal), these should and can be taken into account in various ways. The simplest way might be to assign weights based on likelihoods; two transitions from larval development to direct development is equal to one reversal from direct development back to a larval mode. In fact, there are such methods, and they are similar in spirit to the statistical approaches used to build specific models of evolutionary change rather than rely on simple parsimony.

5. The structures are both homologous, as forelimbs, and convergent, as wings. In other words, the most recent common ancestor of birds, pterosaurs and bats had a forelimb similar in morphology to that which these organisms possess—it has similar bones and articulations. Thus, the forelimb itself among these organisms is homologous. The wing, however, is clearly convergent; the most recent common ancestor surely did not have wings (or all other mammals and reptiles would have had to have lost the wing, which violates the rule of parsimony). The wing of flying insects is purely convergent with the vertebrate wing, as the forelimb of the insect is not homologous with the vertebrate forelimb.

6. The biological species concept focuses on processes, in particular those which result in the evolution of a population to the degree that it becomes reproductively isolated from its ancestral population. The process of speciation as utilized by the biological species concept occurs through the interrelatedness of evolutionary mechanisms such as natural selection, mutation, and genetic drift. On the other hand, the phylogenetic species concept focuses not on process but on history, on the evolutionary patterns that led to the divergence between populations. Neither species concept is more right or more wrong; species concepts are, by their very nature, subjective and potentially controversial.

## CHAPTER 24

### LEARNING OUTCOME QUESTIONS

**24.1** There should be a high degree of similarity between the two genomes because they are relatively closely related. There could be differences in the relative amounts of non-coding DNA. Genes that are necessary for bony skeletal development might be found in the bony fish. The cartilaginous fish might lack those genes or have substantial sequences in the genes needed for skeletal development in bony fish.

**24.2** There would now be three copies of the chromosome from the same species. This would cause a problem for the cell during meiosis I as there would not be an even number of homologs of the chromosome to pair up and segregate.

**24.3** Compare the sequence of the pseudogene with other species. If, for example, it is a pseudogene of an olfactory gene that is found in mice or chimps, the sequences will be much more similar than in a more distantly related species. If horizontal gene transfer explains the origins of the gene, there may not be a very similar gene in closely related species. You might use the BLAST algorithm discussed in chapter 18 to identify similar sequences and then construct a phylogenetic tree to compare the relationships among the different species.

**24.4** A SNP can change a single amino acid in the coded peptide. If the new R group is very different, the protein may fold in a different way and not function effectively. SNPs in the *FOXP2* gene may, in part, explain why humans have speech and chimps do not. Other examples that you may remember from earlier in the text include cystic fibrosis and sickle cell anemia.

**24.5** One approach would be to create a mutation in the non-coding gene and ask whether or not this changes the phenotype. You would need to be sure that both copies of the nonprotein-coding gene were "knocked out."

**24.6** Much of the non-coding DNA could contain retrotransposons that replicate and insert the new DNA into the genome, enlarging the genome. Since the number of genes does not change, polyploidy is not a good explanation.

**24.7** An effective drug might bind only to the region of the pathogen protein that is distinct from the human protein. The drug could render the pathogen protein ineffective without making the human ill. If the seven amino acids that differ are scattered throughout the genome, they might have a minimal effect on the protein and it would be difficult to develop a drug that could detect small differences. It's possible that the drug could inadvertently affect other areas of the protein as well.

**24.8** One approach would be to create transgenic soy with additional protein coding genes.

### INQUIRY QUESTIONS

**Page 478** Meiosis in a 3n cell would be impossible because three sets of chromosomes cannot be divided equally between two cells. In a 3n cell, all three homologous chromosomes would pair in prophase I, then align during anaphase I. As the homologous chromosomes separate, two of a triplet might go to one cell while the third chromosome would go to the other cell. The same would be true for each set of homologues. Daughter cells would have an unpredictable number of chromosomes.

**Page 479** Polyploidization seems to induce the elimination of duplicated genes. Duplicate genes code for the same gene product. It is reasonable that duplicate genes would be eliminated to decrease the redundancy arising from the translation of several copies of the same gene.

**Page 484** Ape and human genomes show very different patterns of gene transcription activity, even though genes encoding proteins are over 99% similar between chimps and humans. Different genes would be transcribed when comparing apes with humans, and the levels of transcription would vary widely.

## UNDERSTAND

1. c  2. d  3. d  4. b  5. b  6. a

## APPLY

1. a  2. d  3. d  4. a

## SYNTHESIZE

1. The two amino acid difference between the FOXP2 protein in humans and closely related primates must alter the way the protein functions in the brain. The protein affects motor function in the brain allowing coordination of larynx, mouth and brain for speech in humans. For example, if the protein affects transcription, there could be differences in the genes that are regulated by FOXP2 in humans and chimps.

2. Human and chimp DNA is close to 99% similar, yet our phenotypes are conspicuously different in many ways. This suggests that a catalogue of genes is just the first step to identifying the mechanisms underlying genetically influenced diseases like cancer or cystic fibrosis. Clearly, gene expression, which might involve the actions of multiple noncoding segments of the DNA and other potentially complex regulatory mechanics, are important sources of how phenotypes are formed, and it is likely that many genetically determined diseases result from such complex underlying mechanisms, making the gene identification of genomics just the first step; a necessary but not nearly sufficient strategy. What complete genomes do offer is a starting point to correlating sequence differences among humans with genetic disease, as well as the opportunity to examine how multiple genes and regulatory sequences interact to cause disease.

3. Phylogenetic analysis usually assumes that most genetic and phenotypic variation arises from descent with modification (vertical inheritance). If genetic and phenotypic characteristics can be passed horizontally (that is, not vertically through genetic lineages) then using patterns of shared character variation to infer genealogical relationships will be subject to potentially significant error. We might expect that organisms with higher rates of HGT will have phylogenetic hypotheses that are less reliable or at least are not resolved as a neatly branching tree.

## CHAPTER 25

### LEARNING OUTCOME QUESTIONS

**25.1** A change in the promoter of a gene necessary for wing development might lead to the repression of wing development in a second segment of a fly in a species that has double wings.

**25.2** No. This cichlid would need to reproduce and over time give rise to a line of cichlid's with extra-long jaws. Perhaps they would populate a different part of the lake and not reproduce with other cichlids. Over time they could become a new species. The extra-long jaw would have to offer some selective advantage or the trait would not persist in the population.

**25.3** Yes, although this is not the only explanation. The coding regions could be identical but the promoter or other regulatory regions could have been altered by mutation, leading to altered patterns of gene expression. To test this hypothesis, the pitx1 gene should be sequenced in both fish and compared.

**25.4** The pectoral fins are homoplastic because sharks and whales are only distantly related and pectoral fins are not found in whales' more recent ancestors.

**25.5** The duplication could persist if a mutation in the duplicated gene prevented its expression or altered the coding region, and either a regulatory or a coding change could lead to a new function.

**25.6** A phylogenetic analysis of paleoAP3 and its gene duplicates demonstrated that the presence of AP3 correlates with petal formation. The specific domain of AP3 that is necessary for petal development was identified by making gene constructs of the AP3 gene where the C terminus of the protein was eliminated or was replaced with the C terminus from the duplicate gene. The C terminus was shown to be essential for petal formation.

**25.7** There is no need for eyes in the dark. Perhaps the fish expend less energy when eyes are not produced and that offered a selective advantage in cavefish. In a habitat with light, a mutation that resulted in a functional Pax6 would likely be selected for and over time more of the fish would have eyes. Keep in mind that the probability of a mutation restoring Pax6 function is very low, but real.

## INQUIRY QUESTIONS

**Page 495** Because there is a stop codon located in the middle of the CAL (cauliflower) gene coding sequence, the wild-type function of CAL must be concerned with producing branches rather than leaves. The wild type of *Brassica oleracea* consists of compact plants that add leaves rather than branches; branches are typical of the flowering heads of broccoli and cauliflower. Additional evolutionary events possibly include large flower heads, unusual head coloration, protective leaves covering flower heads, or head size variants, among other possibilities.

**Page 501** Functional analysis involves the use of a variety of experiments designed to test the function of a specific gene in different species. By mixing and matching parts of the *AP3* and *PI* genes and introducing them into *ap3* mutant plants, it was found that the C terminus sequence of the *AP3* protein is essential for specifying petal function. Without the 3 region of the *AP3* gene, the *Arabidopsis* plant cannot make petals.

## UNDERSTAND

1. c  2. b  3. a  4. a  5. b  6. d  7. b  8. c  9. c  10. d

## APPLY

1. b  2. a  3. d  4. b

## SYNTHESIZE

1. Mutations in the promoter region of other genes allowed them to be recognized by Tbx5, which led to transcriptional control of these genes by Tbx5.

2. Development is a highly conserved and constrained process; small perturbations can have drastic consequences, and most of these are negative. Given the thousands or hundreds of thousands of variables that can change in even a simple developmental pathway, most perturbations lead to negative outcomes. Over millions of years, some of these changes will arise under the right circumstances to produce a benefit. In this way, developmental perturbations are not different from what we know about mutations in general. Beneficial mutations are rare, but with enough time they will emerge and spread under specific circumstances.

   Not all mutations provide a selective advantage. For example, reduced body armor increases the fitness of fish in freshwater, but it was not selected for in a marine environment where the armor was important for protection from predators. The new trait can persist at low levels for a very long time until a change in environmental conditions results in an increase in fitness for individuals exhibiting the trait.

3. The latter view represents our current understanding. There are many examples of small gene families (such as, *Hox*, *MADS*) whose apparent role in generating phenotypic diversity among major groupings of organisms is in altering the expression of other genes. Alterations in timing (heterochrony) or spatial pattern of expression (homeosis) can lead to shifts in developmental events, giving rise to new phenotypes. Many examples are presented in the chapter, such as the developmental variants of two species of sea urchins, one with a normal larval phase, and another with direct development. In this case the two species do not have different sets of developmental genes, rather the expression of those genes differ. Another example that makes the same point is the evolution of an image forming eye. Recent studies suggest, in contrast to the view that eyes across the animal kingdom evolved independently multiple times, that image-forming eyes from very distantly related taxa (such as, insects and vertebrates) may trace back to the common origin of the *Pax6* gene. If that view is correct, then genes controlling major developmental patterns would seem to be highly conserved across long periods of time, with expression being the major form of variation.

4. Unless the Pax6 gene was derived multiple times, it is difficult to hypothesize multiple origins of eyes. Pax6 initiates eye development in many species. The variation in eyes among animals is a result of which genes are expressed and when after Pax6 initiates eye development.

5. Maize relies on paleoAP3 and PI for flower development while tomato has three genes because of a duplication of paleoAP3. This duplication event in the ancestor of tomato, but not maize, is correlated with independent petal origin.

6. The direct developing sea urchin has an ancestor that had one or more mutations in genes that were needed to regulate the expression of other genes needed for larval stage development. When those genes were not expressed, there was no larval development and the genes necessary for adult development were expressed.

# CHAPTER 26

## LEARNING OUTCOME QUESTIONS

**26.1**  The evidence would be that the organism reproduces and posses a system to pass on information from generation to generation (heredity), regulates its internal processes and can maintain homeostasis, grows and develops, has some sort of cellular organization, and can respond to some stimuli.

**26.2**  You can infer that both a squirrel and fox are in the class Mammalia but are in different orders. Thus they share many, but not all traits. They likely shared a common ancestor. However the taxonomic hierarchy does not show the evolutionary relationships among organisms the way a phylogeny would.

**26.3**  The viral genome would now be part of the infected cell's genome and the viral genes could be expressed. One example of this is the chicken pox virus.

**26.4**  Without atmospheric oxygen, organisms would still be anaerobic. There would be no cellular respiration and no mitochondria in cells. Organisms would not be as effective at producing energy and they may not have evolved to be as large as some life forms today because they couldn't meet the energy demands of the cells.

**26.5**  Insect vectors might carry DNA from moss to a flowering plant.

**26.6**  Closely related living organisms might have diverged from a common ancestor millions of years ago. Even though they are the closest living relatives, much evolutionary change could have occurred during the intervening years.

## INQUIRY QUESTIONS

**Page 515**  A clade is an evolutionary unit consisting of a common ancestor and all of its descendants. Evidence suggests that the Archaea are very different from all other organisms, which justifies including the Archaea in a separate domain. Phylogenetically, each domain forms a clade.

**Page 522**  Comparisons of a single gene could result in an inaccurate phylogenetic tree because it fails to take into account the effects of horizontal gene transfer. For example, the clade of *Amborella trichopoda* is a sister clade to all other flowering plants, but roughly ⅔ of its mitochondrial genes are present due to horizontal gene transfer from other land plants, including more distantly-related mosses.

**Page 522**  To determine if a moss gene had a function you would employ functional analysis, using a variety of experiments, to test for possible functions of the moss gene in *Amborella*.

## UNDERSTAND

1. b   2. c   3. c   5. The protists are a bit of a catchall and are not monophyletic. Organisms that were clearly eukaryotic but did not fit with plants, fungi, or animals were placed in the protists   6. c   7. c   8. d

## APPLY

1. Kindgom Fungi because some fungi have flagella and cell walls made of chitin. Fungi lack a nervous system   2. a   3. c   4. d   5. b   6. d

## SYNTHESIZE

1. If the life is biochemically the same on one of these moons and Earth, then it is possible that life originated in one place and was moved to the other location by the action of meteorites and comets. As you have seen with convergent evolution, panspermia would still not be proven by such a finding. However, if the life was biochemically different it would suggest that life originated independently on the moons and Earth.

2.

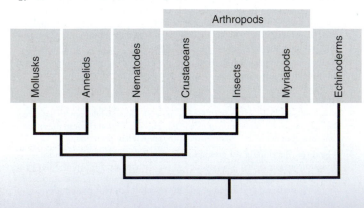

3. The most logical choice would be a species from the domain Archae. These are considered to be the oldest forms of life on our planet, and are known to have evolved to survive harsh environmental condition.

4. Morphology may be influenced by processes such as convergent evolution. However, DNA acts as a molecular record of a species' past. Combining what is being learned from both morphological and molecular data leads to more robust evolutionary hypotheses.

# CHAPTER 27

## LEARNING OUTCOME QUESTIONS

**27.1**  Viruses use cellular machinery for replication. They do not make all of the proteins necessary for complete replication.

**27.2**  A prophage carrying such a mutation could not be induced to undergo the lytic cycle.

**27.3**  This therapy, at present, does not remove all detectable viruses. This cannot be considered a true cure.

**27.4**  In addition to a high mutation rate, the influenza genome consists of multiple RNA segments that can recombine during infection. This causes the main antigens for the immune system to shift rapidly.

**27.5**  Prions carry information in their three-dimensional structure. This 3-D information is different from the essentially one-dimensional genetic information in DNA.

## UNDERSTAND

1. c   2. b   3. c   4. d   5. b   6. d   7. b

## APPLY

1. c   2. b   3. c   4. d   5. b   6. c   7. c   8. a

## SYNTHESIZE

1. A set of genes that are involved in the response to DNA damage are normally induced by the same system. The protein involved destroys a repressor that keeps DNA repair genes unexpressed. Lambda has evolved to use this system to its advantage.

2. Since viruses require the replication machinery of a host cell to replicate, it is unlikely that they existed before the origin of the first cells.

3. This is a complex situation. Factors that act include the high mutation rate of the virus and the fact that the virus targets the very cells that mount an immune response. The influenza virus also requires a new vaccine every year due to rapids changes in the virus. The smallpox virus was a DNA virus that had antigenic determinants that did not change rapidly making a vaccine possible.

4. Emerging viruses are those that jump species and thus are new to humans. Recent examples include SARS and Ebola.

5. If excision of the lambda prophage is imprecise, then the phage produced will carry E. coli genes adjacent to the integration site.

# CHAPTER 28

## LEARNING OUTCOME QUESTIONS

**28.1**  Evidence would take the form of microfossils, evidence for altered isotopic ratios, or biomarkers such as hydrocarbons that do not arise by abiotic processes.

**28.2**  Archaea have ether linked instead of ester linked phospholipids; their cell wall is made of unique material.

**28.3**  Compare their DNA. The many metabolic tests we have used for years have been supplanted by DNA analysis.

**28.4**  Transfer of genetic information in bacteria is directional: from donor to recipient and does not involve fusion of gametes.

**28.5**  Prokaryotes do not have a lot of morphological features, but do have diverse metabolic functions.

**28.6**  Pathogens tend to evolve to be less virulent. If they are too good at killing, their lifestyle is an evolutionary dead end.

**28.7**  Rotating a crop that has a symbiotic association with nitrogen fixing bacteria will return nitrogen to the soil depleted by other plants.

# INQUIRY QUESTION

**Page 562** The simplest explanation is that the two STDs are occurring in different populations, and one population has rising levels of sexual activity, while the other has falling levels. However, the rise in incidence of an STD can reflect many parameters other than level of sexual activity. The virulence or infectivity of one or both disease agents may be changing, for example, or some aspect of exposed people may be changing in such a way as to alter susceptibility. Only a thorough public health study can sort this out.

## UNDERSTAND

1. b   2. a   3. c   4. c   5. d   6. a   7. b

## APPLY

1. c   2. b   3. b   4. c   5. d   6. b   7. a

## SYNTHESIZE

1. The study of carbon signatures in rocks using isotopic data assumes that ancient carbon fixation involves one of two pathways that each show a bias towards incorporation of carbon 12. If this bias were not present, it is not possible to infer early carbon fixation by this pathway. This pathway could have arisen even earlier and we would have no way to detect it.

2. The heat killing of the virulent S strain of *Streptococcus* released the genome of the virulent smooth strain into the environment. These strains of *Streptococcus* bacteria are capable of natural transformation. At least some of the rough strain cells took up smooth strain genes that encoded the polysaccharide coat from the environment. These genes entered into the rough strain genome by recombination, and then were expressed. These transformed cells were now smooth bacteria.

3. The multiple antibiotics are not a bad idea if all of the bacteria are killed. In the case of some persistent infections, this is an effective strategy. However, it does provide very strong selective pressure for rare genetic events that produce multiple resistances in a single bacteria species. For this reason, it is not a good idea for it to be the normal practice. The more bacteria that undergo this selection for multiple resistance, the more likely it will arise. This is helped by patients not taking the entire course as bacteria may survive by chance and proliferate with each generation providing the opportunity for new mutations. This is also complicated by the horizontal transfer of resistance via resistance plasmids, and the existence of transposable genetic elements that can move genes from one piece of DNA to another.

4. Most species on the planet are incapable of fixing nitrogen without the assistance of bacteria. Without nitrogen, amino acids and other compounds cannot be synthesized. Thus a loss of the nitrogen fixing bacteria due to increased UV radiation levels would reduce the ability of plants to grow, severely limiting the food sources of the animals.

# CHAPTER 29

## LEARNING OUTCOME QUESTIONS

**29.1** Mitochondria and chloroplasts contain their own DNA. Mitochondrial genes are transcribed within the mitochondrion, using mitochondrial ribosomes that are smaller than those of eukaryotic cells and quite similar to bacterial ribosomes. Antibiotics that inhibit protein translation in bacteria also inhibit protein translation in mitochondria. Also, both chloroplasts and mitochondria divide using binary fission like bacteria.

**29.2** There are distinct clades in the Protista that do not share a common ancestor. The group of organisms commonly referred to as protists are actually a collection of a number of monophyletic clades.

Pseudopodia provide a large surface area and substantial traction for stable movement.

**29.3** Undulating membranes would be effective on surfaces with curvature that may not always be smooth, including intestinal walls.

**29.4** Contractile vacuoles collect and remove excess water from within the *Euglena*.

**29.5** The *Plasmodium* often becomes resistant to new poisons and drugs.

**29.6** While the gametophytes are often much smaller than the sporophytes, you could be most confident in your answer if you counted the chromosomes in the cells of each. The diploid sporophyte will have twice as many chromosomes as the haploid gametophyte.

**29.7** Both the red and green algae obtained their chloroplasts through endosymbiosis, possibly of the same lineage of photosynthetic bacteria. The red and green algae had diverged before the endosymbiotic events and the history recorded in their nuclear DNA is a different evolutionary history than that recorded in the plastids derived through emdosymbiosis.

**29.8** Comparative genomic studies of choanoflagellates and sponges would be helpful. Considering the similarities among a broader range of genes than just the conserved tyrosine kinase receptor would provide additional evidence.

**29.9** It is unlikely that cellular and plasmodial slime molds are closely related. They both appear in the last section of this chapter because they have yet to be assigned to clades. The substantial differences in their cell biology are inconsistent with a close phylogenetic relationship.

## INQUIRY QUESTION

**Page 570** Red and green algae obtained chloroplasts by engulfing photosynthetic bacteria by primary endosymbiosis; chloroplasts in these cells have two membranes. Brown algae obtained chloroplasts by engulfing cells of red algae through secondary endosymbiosis; chloroplasts in cells of brown algae have four membranes. Counting the number of cell membranes of chloroplasts indicates primary or secondary endosymbiosis.

## UNDERSTAND

1. b   2. a   3. b   4. c   5. d   6. b   7. a   8. c   9. b, c   10. a, d
11. d   12. a

## APPLY

1. d   2. a   3. a

## SYNTHESIZE

1. Cellular and plasmodial slime molds both exhibit group behavior and can produce mobile slime mold masses. However, these two groups are very distantly related phylogenetically.

2. The development of a vaccine, though challenging, will be the most promising in the long run. It is difficult to eradicate all the mosquito vectors and many eradication methods can be harmful to the environment. Treatments to kill the parasites are also difficult because the parasite is likely to become resistant to each new poison or drug. A vaccine would provide long-term protection without the need to use harmful pesticides or drugs where drug resistance is a real possibility.

3. For the first experiment, plate the cellular slime molds on a plate that has no bacteria. Spot cyclic-AMP and designated places on the plate and determine if the bacteria aggregate around the cAMP.

    For the second experiment, repeat the first experiment using plates that have a uniform coating of bacteria as well as plates with no bacteria. If the cellular slime molds aggregate on both plates, resource scarcity is not an issue. If the cells aggregate only in the absence of bacteria, you can conclude that the attraction to cAMP occurs only under starvation conditions.

# CHAPTER 30

## LEARNING OUTCOME QUESTIONS

**30.1** Make sections and examine them under the microscope to look for tracheids. Only the tracheophytes will have tracheids.

Gametes in plants are produced by mitosis. Human gametes are produced directly by meiosis.

**30.2** Chlorophytes have chloroplasts which are not found in choanoflagellates.

The lack of water is the major barrier for sperm that move through water to reach the egg. It is more difficult for sperm to reach the egg on land.

**30.3** Moss are extremely desiccation tolerant and can withstand the lack of water. Also, freezing temperatures at the poles are less damaging when moss have a low water content.

**30.4** The sporophyte generation has evolved to be the larger generation and therefore an effective means to transporting water and nutrients over greater distances would be advantageous.

**30.5** There was substantial climate change during that time period. Glaciers had spread, then melted and retreated. Drier climates could have contributed to the extinction of large club mosses. Refer to chapter 26 for more information on changes in Earth's climate over geological time.

**30.6** The silica can increase the strength of the hollow-tube stems and would also deter herbivores.

**30.7** The pollen tube grows towards the egg, carrying the sperm within the pollen tube.

**30.8** The ovule rests, exposed on the scale (a modified leaf).

**30.9** Animals that consume the fruit disperse the seed over longer distances than wind can disperse seed. The species can colonize a larger territory more rapidly.

## INQUIRY QUESTIONS

**Page 592** The diploid sporophyte of *Ulva* produces sporangia in which meiosis occurs. The resultant haploid spores develop into either plus or minus strains of multicellular gametophytes which, in turn, produce haploid gametangia. The gametangia produce haploid gametes. Meiosis is involved in the formation of *Ulva* gametes, but not directly.

**Page 596** Tracheophytes developed vascular tissue, enabling them to have efficient water- and food-conducting systems. Vascular tissue allowed tracheophytes to grow larger, possibly then able to out-compete smaller, nonvascular land plants. A protective cuticle and stomata that can close during dry conditions also conferred a selective advantage.

**Page 610** Endosperm provides nutrients for the developing embryo in most flowering plants. The embryo cannot derive nutrition from soil prior to root development, therefore without endosperm, the embryo is unlikely to survive.

## UNDERSTAND

1. d   2. d, c   4. c   5. a   6. c   7. b   8. d   9. a   10. d

## APPLY

2. d   3. b   4. c   5. c   6. a   7. b   8. a   9. a

## SYNTHESIZE

1. Moss has a dominant gametophyte generation while lycophytes have a dominant sporophyte generation. Perhaps a comparison of the two genomes would provide insight into the genomic differences associated with the evolutionary shift from dominant gametophyte to dominant sporophyte.

2. Answers to this question may vary. However, gymnosperms are defined as "naked" seed plants. Therefore, an ovule that is not completely protected by sporophyte tissue would be characteristic of a gymnosperm. To be classified as an angiosperm, evidence of flower structures and double fertilization are key characteristics, although double fertilization has been observed in some gnetophytes.

3. The purpose of pollination is to bring together the male and female gametes for sexual reproduction. Sexual reproduction is designed to increase the genetic variability of a species. If a plant allows self-pollination, then the amount of genetic diversity will be reduced, but this is a better alternative than not reproducing at all. This would be especially useful in species in which the individuals are widely dispersed.

4. The benefit is that by developing a relationship with a specific pollinator, the plant species increases the chance that its pollen will be brought to another member of its species for pollination. If the pollinator is a generalist, then the pollinator might not travel to another member of the same species, and pollination would not occur. The drawback is that if something happens to the pollinator (extinction or drop in population size) then the plant species would be left with either a reduced or nonexistent means of pollination.

# CHAPTER 31

## LEARNING OUTCOME QUESTIONS

**31.1** In fungi mitosis results in duplicated nuclei, but the nuclei remain within a single cell. This lack of cell division following mitosis is very unusual in animals.
Hyphae are protected by chitin, which is not digested by fungal enzymes.

**31.2** Microsporidians lack mitochondria which are found in *Plasmodium*.

**31.3** Blastocladiomycetes are free-living and have mitochondria. Microsporidians are obligate parasites and lack mitochondria.

**31.4** Zygospores are more likely to be produced when environmental conditions are not favorable. Sexual reproduction increases the chances of offspring with new combinations of genes that will have an advantage in a changing environment. Also, the zygospore can stay dormant until conditions improve.

**31.5** Parasitism is a subset of symbiotic relationships. Symbiotic relationships refer to two or more organisms of different species living in close relationship to each other to the benefit of one, both or neither. In parasitism, only one member of the symbiosis benefits and that is at the expense of the other.

**31.6** A dikaryotic cell has two nuclei, each with a single set of chromosomes. A diploid cell has a single nucleus with two sets of chromosomes.

**31.7** Preventing the spread of the fungal infection using fungicides and good cultivation practices could help. If farmworkers must tend to infected fields, masks that filter out the spores could protect the workers.

**31.8** The fungi that ants consumed may have originally been growing on leaves. Over evolutionary time, mutations that altered ant behavior so the ants would bring leaves to a stash of fungi would have been favored and the tripartite symbiosis evolved.

**31.9** Wind can spread spores over large distances, resulting in the spread of fungal disease.

## UNDERSTAND

1. c   2. d   3. a   4. d   5. b   6. d   7. d

## APPLY

1. d   2. b   3. a   4. c   5. d

## SYNTHESIZE

1. Fungi possess cell walls. Although the composition of these cell walls differs from that of the plants, cell walls are completely absent in animals. Fungi are also immobile (except for chytrids), and mobility is a key characteristic of the animals.

2. The mycorrhizal relationships between the fungi and plants allow plants to make use of nutrient poor soil. Without the colonization of land by plants, it is unlikely that animals would have diversified to the level they have achieved today. Lichens are important organisms in the colonization of land. Early land masses would have been composed primarily of barren rock, with little or no soil for plant colonization. As lichens colonize an area they begin the process of soil formation, which allows other plant

3. Antibiotics are designed to combat prokaryotic organisms and fungi are eukaryotic. In addition, fungi possess a cell wall that has a different chemical constitution (chitin) from that of prokaryotes.

# CHAPTER 32

## LEARNING OUTCOME QUESTIONS

**32.1** The rules of parsimony state that the simplest phylogeny is most likely the true phylogeny. As there are living organisms that are both multicellular and unicellular, it stands to reason that the first organisms were unicellular, and multicellularity followed. Animals are also all heterotrophs; if they were the first type of life to have evolved, there would not have been any autotrophs on which they could feed.

**32.2** Cephalization, the concentration of nervous tissue in a distinct head region, is intrinsically connected to the onset of bilateral symmetry. Bilateral symmetry promotes the development of a central nerve center, which in turn favors the nervous tissue concentration in the head. In addition, the onset of both cephalization and bilateral symmetry allows for the marriage of directional movement (bilateral symmetry) and the presence of sensory organs facing the direction in which the animal is moving (cephalization).

**32.3** This allows systematists to classify animals based solely on derived characteristics. Using features that have only evolved once implies that the species that have that characteristic are more closely related to each other than they are to species that do not have the characteristic.

**32.4** One hypothesis is that the rapid diversification in body plan was a biological response to the evolution of predation—the adaptation of traits that enabled predators to better find prey and prey to better elude predators. Another hypothesis is that the explosion of new body forms resulted from changes in the physical environment such as oxygen and mineral build up in the oceans.

## UNDERSTAND

1. c   2. b   3. a   4. d   5. a   6. b   7. d   8. a   9. b   10. d   11. d

## APPLY

1. d   2. b   3. Determinate development indicates that it is a protostome and the fact that it molts places it within the Ecdysozoa. The presence of jointed appendages makes it an arthropod.

## SYNTHESIZE

1. The tree should contain platyhelminthes and nemetera on one branch, a second branch should contain nematodes, and a third branch should contain the annelids and the hemichordates. This does not coincide with the information in Figure 32.4. Therefore, some of the different types of body cavities have evolved multiple times, and the body cavities are not good characteristics to infer phylogenetic relationships.

2. Answers may vary depending on the classification used. Many students will place the Echinoderms near the Cnidaria due to radial symmetry; others will place them closer to the Annelids.

# CHAPTER 33

## LEARNING OUTCOME QUESTIONS

**33.1** The cells of a truly colonial organism, such as a colonial protist, are all structurally and functionally identical; however, sponge cells are differentiated and these cells coordinate to perform functions required by the whole organism. Unlike all other animals, however, sponges do appear much like colonial organisms in that they are not comprised of true tissues, and the cells are capable of differentiating from one type to another.

**33.2** The importance of triploblasty relates to the placement of ctenophores on the animal phylogenetic tree. Until recently, ctenophores have been considered diploblasts, with platyhelminthes as the first triploblasts. New evidence, however, indicates that ctenophores are actually triploblastic. In addition, molecular evidence suggests that this phylum belongs at the base of the animal phylogeny—thus implying that the ancestor to all animals was triploblastic.

**33.3** Tapeworms are parasitic platyhelminthes that live in the digestive system of their host. Tapeworms have a scolex, or head, with hooks for attaching to the wall of their host's digestive system. Another way in which the anatomy of a tapeworm relates to its way of life is their dorsoventrally flattened body and corresponding lack of a digestive system. Tapeworms live in their food; as such they absorb their nutrients directly through the body wall, and their flat bodies facilitate this form of nutrient delivery.

**33.4** *Ascaris lumbricoides*, the intestinal roundworm, infects humans when the human swallows food or water contaminated with roundworm eggs. The most effective ways of preventing the spread of intestinal roundworms is to increase sanitation, especially those in food handling, education, and cease using human feces as fertilizer. Not surprisingly, infection by these parasites is most common in areas without modern plumbing.

## UNDERSTAND

1. c  2. a  3. b  4. b  5. d  6. d  7. c

## APPLY

1. c  2. c  3. d

## SYNTHESIZE

1. Answers may vary. Phylum Acoela represents a reclassification of the platyhelminthes and phylum Cycliophora represents an entirely new kingdom. Since we have most likely not discovered all of the noncoelomate invertebrate species on the planet, and we are utilizing new molecular tools to examine the relationships of existing phyla, it is unlikely that the modern phylogeny presented in section 33.2 is complete.

2. Since the population size of a parasitic species may be very small (just a few individuals), possessing both male and female reproductive structures would allow the benefits of sexual reproduction.

3. Answers may vary. However, it is known that the tapeworm is not the ancestral form of platyhelminthes; instead it has lost its digestive tract due to its role as an intestinal parasite. As an intestinal parasite, the tapeworm relies on the digestive system of its host to break down nutrients into their building blocks for absorption.

# CHAPTER 34

## LEARNING OUTCOME QUESTIONS

**34.1** Cephalopods are the most active of all mollusks, and this increased level of activity necessitates a more efficient oxygen delivery system. The extensive series of blood vessels, and thus more efficient gas exchange, in the cephalopod circulatory system allows the animal to move more rapidly and over longer periods of time.

**34.2** With a flow-through digestive tract, food moves in only one direction. This allows for specialization within the tract; sections may be specialized for

mechanical and chemical digestion, some for storage, and yet others for absorption. Overall, the specialization yields greater efficiency than does a gastrovascular cavity.

**34.3** The main advantage is coordination. A nervous system that serves the entire body allows for coordinated movement and coordinated physiological activities such as reproduction and excretion, even if those systems themselves are segmented. Likewise, a body-wide circulatory system enables efficient oxygen delivery to all of the body cells regardless of the nature of the organism's individual segments.

**34.4** Lophophorates are sessile suspension-feeding animals. Much of their body also remains submerged in the ocean floor. Thus, a traditional tubular digestive system would require either the mouth or the anus to be inaccessible to the water column—meaning the animal either could not feed or would have to excrete waste into a closed environment. The U-shaped gut allows them to both acquire nutrients from and excrete waste into their environment.

**34.5** One of the defining features of the arthropods is the presence of a chitinous exoskeleton. As arthropods increase in size, the exoskeleton must increase in thickness disproportionately, in order to bear the pull of the animal's muscles. This puts a limit on the size a terrestrial arthropod can reach, as the increased bulk of the exoskeleton would prohibit the animal's ability to move. Water is denser than air and thus provides more support; for this reason aquatic arthropods are able to be larger than terrestrial arthropods.

**34.6** Bilateral symmetry evolved relatively early in animal phylogeny, with the platyhelminthes. Echinoderms clearly branched off later in evolutionary history, as evidenced by their deuterostome development, and yet, as adults they exhibit radial (or, more accurately, pentaradial) symmetry. This might be a confusing factor when determining the phylogeny of animals, if not for the bilateral form the echinoderm larvae take. The bilaterally symmetrical larvae suggest that the echinoderm ancestor is in fact bilaterally symmetrical, rather than radially symmetrical.

## UNDERSTAND

1. c  2. b  3. a  4. d  5. d  6. b  7. c  8. d  9. d  10. a  11. a

## APPLY

1. b  2. c  3. d  4. a

## SYNTHESIZE

1. Clams and scallops are bivalves, which are filter feeders that siphon large amounts of water through their bodies to obtain food. They act as natural pollution-control systems for bays and estuaries. A loss of bivalves (from overfishing, predation, or toxic chemicals) would upset the aquatic ecosystem and allow pollution levels to rise.

2. Chitin is an example of convergent evolution since these organisms do not share a common chitin-equipped ancestor. Chitin is often used in structures that need to withstand the rigors of stress (chaetae, exoskeletons, zoecium, etc.).

# CHAPTER 35

## LEARNING OUTCOME QUESTIONS

**35.1** Chordates have a truly internal skeleton (an endoskeleton), compared to the endoskeleton on echinoderms, which is functionally similar to the exoskeleton of arthropods. Whereas an echinoderm uses tube feet attached to an internal water vascular system for locomotion, a chordate has muscular attachments to its endoskeleton. Finally, chordates have a suite of four characteristics that are unique to the phylum—a nerve chord, a notochord, pharyngeal slits, and a postanal tail.

**35.2** While mature and immature lancelets are similar in form, the tadpole-like tunicate larvae are markedly different from the sessile, vase-like adult form. Both tunicates and lancelets are chordates, but they differ from vertebrates in that they do not have vertebrae or internal bony skeletons.

**35.3** The functions of an exoskeleton include protection and locomotion—arthropod exoskeletons, for example, provide a fulcrum to which the animals' muscles attach. In order to resist the pull of increasingly large muscles, the exoskeleton must dramatically increase in thickness as the animal grows larger. There is thus a limit on the size of an organism with an exoskeleton—if it gets too large it will be unable to move due to the weight and heft of its exoskeleton.

**35.4** Lobe-finned fish are able to move their fins independently, whereas ray-finned fish must move their fins simultaneously. This ability to "walk" with their fins indicates that lobe-finned fish are most certainly the ancestors of amphibians.

**35.5** The challenges of moving onto land were plentiful for the amphibians. First, amphibians needed to be able to support their body weight and locomote on land; this challenge was overcome by the evolution of legs. Second, amphibians needed to be able to exchange oxygen with the atmosphere; this was accomplished by the evolution of more efficient lungs than their lungfish ancestors as well as cutaneous respiration. Third, since movement on land requires more energy than movement in the water, amphibians needed a more efficient oxygen delivery system to supply their larger muscles; this was accomplished by the evolution of double-loop circulation and a partially divided heart. Finally, the first amphibians needed to develop a way of staying hydrated in a non-aquatic environment, and these early amphibians developed leathery skin that helped prevent desiccation.

**35.6** Amphibians remain tied to the water for their reproduction; their eggs are jelly-like and if laid on the land will quickly desiccate. Reptile eggs, on the other hand, are amniotic eggs—they are watertight and contain a yolk, which nourishes the developing embryo, and a series of four protective and nutritive membranes.

**35.7** There are two primary traits shared between birds and reptiles. First, both lay amniotic eggs. Second, they both possess scales (which cover the entire reptile body but solely the legs and feet of birds). Birds also share characteristics only with one group of reptiles—the crocodilians, such as a four-chambered heart.

**35.8** The most striking convergence between birds and mammals is endothermy, the ability to regulate body temperature internally. Less striking is flight; found in most birds and only one mammal, the ability to fly is another example of convergent evolution.

**35.9** Only the hominids comprise a monophyletic group. Prosimians, monkeys, and apes are all paraphyletic—they include the common ancestor but not all descendents: the clade that prosimians share with the common prosimian ancestor excludes all anthropoids, the clade that monkeys share with the common monkey ancestor excludes hominoids, and the clade that apes share with the common ape ancestor excludes hominids.

## UNDERSTAND

1. c  2. c  3. a  4. c  5. a  6. d  7. a  8. d

## APPLY

1. c  2. c  3. b

## SYNTHESIZE

1. Increased insulation would have allowed birds to become endothermic and thus to be active at times that ectothermic species could not be active. High body temperature may also allow flight muscles to function more efficiently.

2. Birds evolved from one type of dinosaurs. Thus, in phylogenetic terms, birds are a type of dinosaur.

3. Like the evolution of modern day horses, the evolution of hominids was not a straight and steady progression to today's *Homo sapiens*. Hominid evolution started with an initial radiation of numerous species. From this group, there was a evolutionary trend of increasing size, similar to what is seen in the evolution of horses. However, like in horse evolution, there are examples of evolutionary decreases in body size as seen in *Homo floresiensis*. Hominid evolution also reveals the coexistence of related species, as seen with *Homo neaderthalensis* and *Homo sapiens*. Hominid evolution, like horse evolution, was not a straight and steady progression to the animal that exists today.

# CHAPTER 36
## LEARNING OUTCOME QUESTIONS

**36.1** Primary growth contributes to the increase in plant height, as well as branching. Secondary growth makes substantial contributions to the increase in girth of the plant, allowing for a much larger sporophyte generation.

**36.2** Vessels transport water and are part of the xylem. The cells are dead with only the walls remaining. Cylinders of stacked vessels move water from the roots to the leaves of plants. Sieve tube members are part of the phloem and transport nutrients. Sieve tube members are living cells, but they lack a nucleus. The rely on neighboring companion cells to carry out some metabolic functions. Like vessels, sieve tube members are stacked to form a cylinder.

**36.3** The energy of the cell is used primarily to elongate the cell. It would be difficult for a root hair to form in the region of elongation because its base would be pulled apart by the elongation of the cell wall.

**36.4** Roots are constantly growing through soil where cells are damaged and sloughed off. The tips of stems do not encounter the same barriers and do not require the additional protection.

**36.5** Both sides of the leaf are equally exposed to sunlight. In contrast, horizontal leaves have a top and a bottom. Palisade layers are tightly packed with minimum airspace between the cells which maximizes photosynthetic surface area.

## INQUIRY QUESTION

**Page 736** Three dermal tissue traits that are adaptive for a terrestrial lifestyle include: guard cells, trichomes, and root hairs. Guard cells flank an epidermal opening called a stoma and regulate its opening and closing. Stomata are closed when water is scarce, thus conserving water. Trichomes are hairlike outgrowths of the epidermis of stems, leaves, and reproductive organs. Trichomes help to cool leaf surfaces and reduce evaporation from stomata. Root hairs are epidermal extensions of certain cells in young roots and greatly increase the surface area for absorption.

## UNDERSTAND

1. d  2. d  3. c  4. b  5. a  6. c  7 a  8. b

## APPLY

1. a  2. c  3. d  4. c

## SYNTHESIZE

1. Roots lack leaves with axillary buds at nodes, although there may be lateral roots that originated from deep within the root. The vascular tissue would have a different pattern in roots and stems. If there is a vascular stele at the core with a pericycle surrounded by a Casparian strip, you are looking at a root.

2. Lenticels increase gas exchange. In wet soil, the opportunity for gas exchange decreases. Lenticels could compensate for decreased gas exchange, which would be adaptive.

3. The tree is likely to die because the phloem and vascular cambium is located near the surface. Removing a ring of bark results in the loss of the vascular cambium and phloem, leading to starvation and death.

# CHAPTER 37
## LEARNING OUTCOME QUESTIONS

**37.1** Only angiosperms have an endosperm which results from double fertilization. The endosperm is the nutrient source in angiosperms. Gymnosperm embryos rely on megagametophytic tissue sources for nutrients.

**37.2** These seeds might be sensitive to temperature and require a period of cold before germinating.

**37.3** Fruits with fleshy coverings, often shiny black or bright blue or red, normally are favored by birds or other vertebrates.

**37.4** Retaining the seed in the ground might provide greater stability for the seedling until its root system is established.

## INQUIRY QUESTIONS

**Page 758** The root meristem never forms, although the shoot meristem is fully functional. This plant is missisng the HOBBIT protein which normally allows auxin to induce the expression of a gene or genes needed for correct cell division to make a root meristem. Without the correct cell divisions, the meristem fails to form.

**Page 758** The *MONOPTEROS* (*MP*) gene product cannot act as a transcription factor when it is bound by its repressor. With a *MP* protein that can no longer bind to its repressor, *MP* acts as a transcription factor and activates a root development gene. The phenotype of a plant with a mutation in the *MP* gene has roots.

**Page 761** A monocot has a solitary cotyledon. Two cotyledons are illustrated here, thus the embryo is a eudicot.

**Page 762** The prior sporophyte generation, as part of the ovary, is diploid. The degenerating gametophyte generation is haploid. The next sporophyte generation, the embryo, is diploid.

## UNDERSTAND

1. c  2. a  3. d  4. a  5. d  6. b  7. a  8. c  9. c

## APPLY

1. c  2. c  3. b  4. d  5. c

## SYNTHESIZE

1. Place *Fucus* zygotes on a screen and shine a light from the bottom. If light is more important, the rhizoid will form towards the light, even though that is the opposite direction gravity would dictate. If gravity is more important, the rhizoid will form away from the direction of the light.

2. The endosperm has three times as many copies of each gene. If transcription occurs at a constant rate in both nutritive tissues, more will be produced in the endosperm because of the extra copies of the genes.

3. The seeds may need to be chilled before they can germinate. You can store them in the refrigerator for several weeks or months and try again. The surface of the seed may need to be scarified (damaged) before it can germinate. Usually this would happen from the effects of weather or if the seed goes through the digestive track of an animal where the seed coat is weakened by acid in the gut of the animal. You could substitute for natural scarification by rubbing your seeds on sand paper before germinating them. It is possible that your seed needs to be exposed to light or received insufficient water when you first planted it. You may need to soak your seed in water for a bit to imbibe it. Exposing the imbibed seed to sunlight might also increase the chances of germination.

# CHAPTER 38

## LEARNING OUTCOME QUESTIONS

**38.1** Physical pressures include gravity and transpiration, as well as turgor pressure as an expanding cell presses against its cell wall. Increases in turgor pressure and other physical pressures are associated with increases water potential. Solute concentration determines whether water enters or leaves a cell via osmosis. The smallest amount of pressure on the side of the cell membrane with the greater solute concentration that is necessary to stop osmosis is the solute potential. Water potential is the sum of the pressure from physical forces and from the solute potential.

**38.2** Proteins in the cell membrane allow diffusion to be selective. Other protein channels are involved in active transport across the membrane. Water moves through channels called aquaporins. For a review of membrane properties, see chapter 5.

**38.3** The driving force for transpiration is the gradient between 100% humidity inside the leaf and the external humidity. When the external humidity is low, the rate of transpiration is high, limited primarily by the amount of water available for uptake through the root system.
The minerals are used for metabolic activities. Some minerals can move into the phloem and be transported to metabolically active areas of the plants, but others, including calcium, cannot be relocated after they leave the xylem.

**38.4** Once carbon dioxide is dissolved in water, it can be transported to photosynthetically active cells where it is used in carbon fixation in the Calvin Cycle (see chapter 8 for a review of photosynthesis).

**38.5** Physical changes in the roots in response to oxygen deprivation may prevent further transport of water in the xylem. Although the leaves may be producing oxygen, it is not available to the roots.

**38.6** Phloem liquid is rich in organic compounds including sucrose and plant hormones dissolved in water. Fluid in the xylem consists of minerals dissolved in water.

## INQUIRY QUESTIONS

**Page 773** Before equilibrium, the solute potential of the solution is –0.5 MPa, and that of the cell is –0.2 MPa. Since the solution contains more solute than does the cell, water will leave the cell to the point that the cell is plasmolyzed. Initial turgor pressure ($\Psi_p$) of the cell = 0.05 MPa, while that of the solution is 0 MPa. At equilibrium, both the solution and the cell will have the same $\Psi_w$. $\Psi_{cell}$ = –0.2 MPa + 0.5 MPa = 0.3 MPa before equilibrium is reached. At equilibrium, $\Psi_{cell} = \Psi_{solution}$ = –0.5 MPa, thus $\Psi_{w\ cell}$ = –0.5 MPa. At equilibrium, the plasmolyzed cell $\Psi_p$ = 0 MPa. Finally, using the relationship $\Psi_{W(cell)} = \Psi_p + \Psi_s$ and $\Psi_{W(cell)}$ = –0.5 MPa, $\Psi_{P(cel)}$ = 0 MPa, then $\Psi_{s(cell)}$ = –0.5 MPa.

**Page 775** The fastest route for water movement through cells has the least hindrance, and thus is the symplast route. The route that exerts the most control over what substances enter and leave the cell is the transmembrane route, which is then the best route for moving nutrients into the plant.

**Page 777** If a mutation increases the radius, r, of a xylem vessel threefold, then the movement of water through the vessel would increase 81-fold ($r^4 = 3^4 = 81$). A plant with larger diameter vessels can move much more water up its stems.

## UNDERSTAND

1. a   2. c   3. d   4. a   5. c   6. d   7. b   8. a   9. b   10. b

## APPLY

1. b   2. c   3. b   4. c   5. b

## SYNTHESIZE

1. The solute concentration outside the root cells is greater than inside the cells. Thus the solute potential is more negative outside the cell and water moves out of the root cells and into the soil. Without access to water, your plant wilts.

2. Look for wilty plants since the rate of water movement across the membrane would decrease in the aquaporin mutants.

3. At the level of membrane transport, plants and animals are very similar. Plant cell walls allow plant cells to take up more water than most animal cells, which rupture without the supportive walls. At the level of epidermal cells there is substantial variation among animals. Amphibians exchange water across the skin. Plants have waterproof epidermal tissue but lose water through stomata. Humans sweat, but dogs do not. Some animals have adaptations for living in aquatic or high saline environment, as do plants. Vascular plants move vast amounts of water through the plant body via the xylem, using evaporation to fuel the transport. Animals with closed circulatory systems can move water throughout the organism and also excrete excess water through the urinary system, which is responsible for osmoregulation.

4. The rate of transpiration is greater during the day than the night. Since water loss first occurs in the upper part of the tree where more leaves with stomata are located, the decrease in water volume in the xylem would first be observed in the upper portion, followed by the lower portion of the tree.

5. Spring year 1—The new carrot seedling undergoes photosynthesis in developing leaves and the sucrose moves towards the growing tip.
Summer year 1—The developing leaves are sources of carbohydrate, which now moves to the developing root and also the growing young tip.
Fall year 1—The carrot root is now the sink for all carbohydrates produced by the shoot.
Spring year 2—Stored carbohydrate in the root begins to move upwards into the shoot.
Summer year 2—The shoot is flowering and the developing flowers are the primary sink for carbohydrates from the root and also from photosynthesis in the leaves.
Fall year 2—Seeds are developing and they are the primary sink. The root reserves have been utilized and any remaining carbohydrates from photosynthesis are transported to developing seeds.

# CHAPTER 39

## LEARNING OUTCOME QUESTIONS

**39.1** Alkaline soil can affect the availability of nutrients in the soil for uptake by a plant.

**39.2** Magnesium is found in the center of the chlorophyll molecule. Without sufficient magnesium, chlorophyll deficiencies will result in decreased photosynthesis and decreased yield per acre.

**39.3** Nitrogen is essential for all amino acids, the building blocks of protein. Without sufficient levels of proteins that function as enzymes, membrane transporters, transcription factors, and structural components, plant growth and reproduction will be limited.

**39.4** Increasing the amount of available nitrogen in the soil is one strategy. This can be accomplished with chemically produced ammonia for fertilizing, intercropping with nitrogen-fixing legumes, or using organic matter rich in nitrogen for enriching the soil. Efforts to reduce the relative amounts of atmospheric carbon dioxide would also be helpful.

**39.5** Large poplar trees that are not palatable to animals offer a partial solution. Fencing in areas that are undergoing phytoremediation is another possibility, but it would be difficult to isolate all animals, especially birds. Plants that naturally deter herbivores with secondary compounds, including some mustard species (*Brassica* species) could be effective for phytoremediation.

## INQUIRY QUESTION

**Page 797** At low and high temperature extremes, enzymes involved in plant respiration are denatured. Plants tend to acclimate to slower long-term changes in temperature, and rates of respiration are able to adjust. Short-term more dramatic changes might slow or halt respiration, especially if a temperature change is large enough to cause enzymes to denature.

## UNDERSTAND

1. b   2. a   3. c   4. d   5. a   6. b   7. c   8. a

## APPLY

1. c   2. a   3. a   4. d   5. The macronutrient potassium constitutes 0.5–6% of the dry weight. Let's assume that the potato is 90% water. The dry weight would be 10% of 1000 kg, or 100 kg. Next you calculate 0.5% of 100, which is 0.5 kg. You would do the same type of calculation for 6%.
The micronutrient problems would also use the estimate of 100 kg dry weight. The conversion you need to use is that 1 ppm is the same as 1 mg/kg. So, 4 ppm of copper is the same as 4 mg/kg. Multiply this by 100 kg of dry weight potato and

you have 400 mg of copper. Since there are 1000 mg in a gram, 400 mg × 1 g/1000 mg = 0.4 g of copper in a ton of potato. The other micronutrient problems would be calculated in a similar manner.

## SYNTHESIZE

1. Bacteria that are important for nitrogen fixation could be destroyed. Other microorganisms that make nutrients available to plants could also be destroyed.

2. Grow the tomatoes hydroponically in a complete nutrient solution minus boron and complete nutrient solution with varying concentrations of boron. Compare the coloration of the leaves, the rate of growth (number of new leaves per unit time), and number and size of fruits produced on plants in each treatment group. It would also be helpful to compare the dry weights of plants from each treatment group at the end of the study.

3. Other inputs include both the macronutrients and micronutrients. Nitrogen, potassium, and phosphorous are common macronutrients in fertilizers. Of course the plants also need to be watered.

## CHAPTER 40

### LEARNING OUTCOME QUESTIONS

**40.1** The lipid-based compounds help to create a water impermeable layer on the leaves.

**40.2** A drug prepared from a whole plant or plant tissue would contain a number of different compounds, in addition to the active ingredient. Chemically synthesized or purified substances contain one or more known substances in known quantities.

**40.3** It is unlikely that wasps will kill all the caterpillars. When attacked by a caterpillar, the plant releases a volatile substance that attracts the wasp. But, the wasp has to be within the vicinity of the signal when the plant releases the signal. As a result, some caterpillars will escape detection by wasps.

**40.4** The local death of cells creates a barrier between the pathogen and the rest of the plant.

### INQUIRY QUESTION

**Page 808** Ricin functions as a ribosome-binding protein that limits translation. A very small quantity of rice was injected into Markov's thigh from the modified tip of his assassin's umbrella. Without translation of proteins in cells, enzymes and other gene products are no longer produced, causing the victim's metabolism to shut down leading to death.

### UNDERSTAND

1. d  2. b  3. b  4. d  5. c  6. a  7. c  8. a  9. d

### APPLY

1. c  2. d  3. d  4. b  5. c  6. a

### SYNTHESIZE

1. Humans learn quickly and plants with toxins that made people ill would not become a dietary mainstay. If there was variation in the levels of toxin in the same species in different areas, humans would likely have continued to harvest plants from the area where plants had reduced toxin levels. As domestication continued, seeds would be collected from the plants with reduced toxin levels and grown the following year.

2. For parasitoid wasps to effectively control caterpillars, sufficiently large populations of wasps would need to be maintained in the area where the infestation occurred. As wasps migrate away from the area, new wasps would need to be introduced. The density of wasps is critical because the wasp has to be in the vicinity of the plant being attacked by the caterpillar when the plant releases its volatile signal. Maintaining sufficient density is a major barrier to success.

3. If a plant is flowering or has fruits developing, the systemin will move towards the fruit or flowers, providing protection for the developing seed. If the plant is a biennial, such as a carrot plant, in its first year of growth, systemin will likely be diverted to the root or other storage organ that will reserve food stores for the plant for the following year.

## CHAPTER 41

### LEARNING OUTCOME QUESTIONS

**41.1** Chlorphyll is essential for photosynthesis. Phytochromes regulate plant growth and development using light as a signal. Phytochrome mediated responses

align the plant with the light environment so photosynthesis is maximized which is advantageous for the plant.

**41.2** The plant would not have normal gravitropic responses. Other environmental signals, including light, would determine the direction of plant growth.

**41.3** Folding leaves can startle an herbivore that lands on the plant. The herbivore leaves and the plant is protected.

**41.4** During the winter months the leaves would cease photosynthesis except on a few warm days. If the weather warmed briefly, water would move into the leaves and photosynthesis would begin. Unfortunately, the minute the temperature dropped, the leaves would freeze and be permanently damaged. Come the spring, the leaves would not be able to function and the tree would die. It is to the trees advantage to shed it's leaves and grow new, viable leaves in the spring when the danger of freezing is past.

**41.5** Abscisic acid could be isolated from root caps of several plants. The isolated abscisic acid could then be applied to the buds on stems of other plants of the same species. The growth of these buds (or lack of growth) could be compared with untreated controls to determine whether or not the abscisic acid had an effect.

### INQUIRY QUESTIONS

**Page 816** A number of red-light-mediated responses are linked to phytochrome action alone, including seed germination, shoot elongation, and plant spacing. Only some of the red-light-mediated responses leading to gene expression are dependent on the action of protein kinases. When phytochrome converts to the Pfr form, a protein kinase triggers phosphorylation that, in turn, initiates a signaling cascade that triggers the translation of certain light-regulated genes. Not all red-light-mediated responses are disrupted in a plant with a mutation in the protein kinase domain of phytochrome.

**Page 819** Auxin is involved in the phototropic growth responses of plants, including the bending of stems and leaves toward light. Auxin increases the plasticity of plants cells and signals their elongation. The highest concentration of auxin would most likely occur at the tips of stems where sun exposure is maximal.

**Page 827** A chemical substance, such as the hormone auxin, could trigger the elongation of cells on the shaded side of a stem, causing the stem to bend toward the light.

### UNDERSTAND

1. c  2. a  3. d  4. d  5. b  6. d

### APPLY

1. b  2. a  3. b  4. c  5. c  6. b  7. d

### SYNTHESIZE

1. You are observing etiolation. Etiolation is an energy conservation strategy to help plants growing in the dark reach the light before they die. They don't green up until light becomes available, and they divert energy to internode elongation. This strategy is useful for potato shoots. The sprouts will be long so they can get to the surface more quickly. They will remain white until exposed to sunlight which will signal the production of chlorophyll.

2. Tropism refers to the growth of an organism in response to an environmental signal such as light. Taxis refers to the movement of an organism in response to an environmental signal. Since plants cannot move, they will not exhibit taxis, but they do exhibit tropisms.

3. Auxin accumulates on the lower side of a stem in a gravitropism, resulting in elongation of cells on the lower side. If auxin or vesicles containing auxin responded to a gravitational field, it would be possible to have a gravitropic response without amyloplasts.

4. Farmers are causing a thigmotropic response. In response to touch, the internodes of the seedlings will increase in diameter. The larger stems will be more resistant to wind and rain once they are moved to the field. The seedlings will be less likely to snap once they are moved to the more challenging environment.

## CHAPTER 42

### LEARNING OUTCOME QUESTIONS

**42.1** Without flowering in angiosperms, sexual reproduction is not possible and the fitness of a plant drops to zero.

**42.2** Set up an experiment in a controlled growth chamber with a day/night light regiment that promotes flowering. Then interrupt the night length with a brief exposure to light. If day length is the determining factor, the brief flash of light will not affect flowering. If night length is the determining factor, the light flash may affect the outcome. For example, if the plant requires a long night, interrupting the night will prevent flowering. If the plant flowers whether or not you interrupt the night with light, it may be a short night plant. In that case, you would want to set up a second experiment where you lengthen the night length. That should prevent the plant from flowering.

**42.3** Flowers can attract pollinators, enhancing the probability of reproduction.

**42.4** No because the gametes are formed by meiosis which allows for new combinations of alleles to combine. You may want to review Mendel's law of independent assortment.

**42.5** When conditions are uniform and the plant is well adapted to those constant conditions, genetic variation would not be advantageous. Rather, vegetative reproduction will ensure that the genotypes that are well adapted to the current conditions are maintained.

**42.6** A biennial life cycle allows an organism to store up substantial reserves to be used to support reproduction during the second season. The downside to this strategy is that the plant might not survive the winter between the two growing seasons and its fitness would be reduced to zero.

## INQUIRY QUESTIONS

***Page 843*** Strict levels of CONSTANS (CO) gene protein are maintained according to the circadian clock. Phytochrome, the pigment that perceives photoperiod, regulates the transcription of CO. By examining posttranslational regulation of CO, it might be possible to determine whether protein levels are modulated by means other than transcription. An additional level of control might be needed to ensure that the activation of floral meristem genes coincides with the activation of genes that code for individual flower organs.

***Page 846*** Flower production employs up to four genetically-regulated pathways. These pathways ensure than the plant flowers when it has reached adult size, when temperature and light regimes are optimal, and when nutrition is sufficient to support flowering. All of these factors combine to ensure the success of flowering and the subsequent survival of the plant species.

***Page 846*** Once vernalization occurred and nutrition was optimal, flowering could occur in the absence of flower-repressing genes, even if the plant had not achieved adult size. Thus flowering might occur earlier than normal.

## UNDERSTAND

1. a  2. c  3. a  4. d  5. d  6. c  7. d  8. c  9. b  10. c  11. a

## APPLY

1. b  2. c  3. b  4. d  5. b

## SYNTHESIZE

1. Pointsettias are short day plants. The lights from the cars on the new highway interrupt the long night and prevent flowering.

2. Spinach is a long day plant and you want to harvest the vegetative, not the reproductive parts of the plant. Spinach will flower during the summer as the days get longer. Only leaves will be produced during the spring. If you grow and harvest your spinach in the early spring, you will be able to harvest the leaves before the plant flowers and begins to senesce.

3. Cross-pollination increases the genetic diversity of the next generation. But, self-pollination is better than no pollination. The floral morphology of columbine favors cross-pollination, but self-pollination is a backup option. Should this back up option be utilized, there is still one more opportunity for cross-pollination to override self-pollination because the pollen tube from the other plant can still grow through the style more rapidly than the pollen tube from the same plant.

4. Potatoes grown from true seed take longer to produce new potatoes than potatoes grown from tubers. Seeds are easier to store between growing seasons and require much less storage space than whole potatoes. The seed-grown potatoes will have greater genetic diversity than the asexually propagated potato tubers. If environmental conditions vary from year to year, the seed grown potatoes may have a better yield because different plants will have an advantage under different environmental conditions. The tuber-grown potatoes will be identical. If conditions are optimal for that genotype, the tuber-grown potatoes will outperform the more variable seed-grown potatoes. But, if conditions are not optimal for the asexually propagated potatoes, the seed-grown potatoes may have the higher yield.

# CHAPTER 43

## LEARNING OUTCOME QUESTIONS

**43.1** Organs may be made of multiple tissue types. For example, the heart contains muscle, connective tissue and epithelial tissue.

**43.2** The epithelium in glandular tissue produces secretions, the epithelium has microvilli on the apical surface that increase surface area for absorption.

**43.3** Blood is a form of connective tissue because it contains abundant extracellular material: the plasma.

**43.4** The function of heart cell requires their being electrically connected. The gap junctions allow the flow of ions between cells.

**43.5** Neurons may be a meter long, but this is a very thin projection that still can allow diffusion of materials along its length. They do require specialized transport along microtubules to move proteins from the cell body to the synapse.

**43.6** The organ systems may overlap. Consider the respiratory and circulatory systems. These systems are interdependent.

**43.7** Yes.

**43.8** The distinction should be between the ability to generate metabolic heat to modulate temperature, and the lack of that ability. Thus ectotherms and endotherms have replaced cold-blooded and warm-blooded.

## INQUIRY QUESTIONS

***Page 880*** After two minutes of shivering, the thoracic muscles have warmed up enough to engage in full contractions. The muscle contractions that allow the full range of motion of the wings utilize kinetic energy in the movement of the wings, rather than releasing the energy as heat, which occurred in the shivering response.

***Page 882*** Small mammals, with a proportionately larger surface area, dissipate heat readily, which is helpful in a warm environment, but detrimental in a cold environment. In cold conditions, small mammals must seek shelter or have adaptations, such as insulating hair, to maintain body temperature. Because of a greater volume and proportionately less surface area, large mammals are better adapted to cold environments since it takes much longer for them to lose body heat. Hot environments pose a greater challenge for them for the same reason.

## UNDERSTAND

1. a  2. c  3. c  4. d  5. a  6. d  7. b  8. b

## APPLY

1. b  2. b  3. c  4. c  5. d  6. a  7. c

## SYNTHESIZE

1. Yes, both the gut and the skin include epithelial tissue. A disease that affects epithelial cells could affect both the digestive system and the skin. For example, cystic fibrosis affects the ion transport system in epithelial membranes. It is manifested in the lungs, gut, and sweat glands.

2. The digestive, circulatory, and respiratory systems are grouped together because they all provide necessary nutrients for the body. The digestive system is responsible for the acquisition of nutrients from food; the respiratory system provides oxygen and removes waste (carbon monoxide). The circulatory system transports nutrients to the cells of the body and removes metabolic wastes.

3. Hunger is a negative feedback stimulus. Hunger stimulates an individual to eat which in turn causes a feeling of fullness that removes hunger. Hunger is the stimulus; eating is the response that removes the stimulus.

4. The internal environment is constantly changing. As you move through your day, muscle activity raises your body temperature, but when you sit down to eat or rest, your temperature cools. The body must constantly adjust to changes in activity or the environment.

# CHAPTER 44

## LEARNING OUTCOME QUESTIONS

**44.1** The somatic nervous system is under conscious control.

**44.2** A positive current inwards (influx of $Na^+$) depolarizes the membrane while a positive current outward (efflux of $K^+$) repolarizes the membrane.

**44.3** Tobacco contains the compound nicotine, which can bind some acetylcholine receptors. This leads to the classic symptoms of addiction due to underlying habituation involving changes to receptor numbers and responses.

**44.4** Reflex arcs allow you to respond to a stimulus that is damaging before the information actually arises at your brain.

**44.5** These two systems work in opposition. This may seem counterintuitive, but is the basis for much of homeostasis.

## UNDERSTAND

1. a  2. c  3. a  4. a  5. d  6. d  7. a

## APPLY

1. d  2. b  3. c  4. a  5. a  6. c  7. d

## SYNTHESIZE

1. TEA blocks K$^+$ channels so that they will not permit the passage of K$^+$ out of the cell, thereby not allowing the cell to return to the resting potential. Voltage-gated Na$^+$ channels would still be functional and Na$^+$ would still flow into the cell but there would be no repolarization. Na$^+$ would continue to flow into the cell until an electrochemical equilibrium was reached for Na$^+$, which is + 60 mV. After the membrane potential reached + 60 mV, there would be no net movement of Na$^+$, but the membrane would also not be able to repolarize back to the resting membrane potential. The neuron would no longer be able to function.

   The effects on the postsynaptic cell would be somewhat similar if TEA were applied to the presynaptic cell. The presynaptic cell would depolarize and would continue to release neurotransmitter until it had exhausted its store of synaptic vesicles. As a result, the postsynaptic cell would be bombarded with neurotransmitters and would be stimulated continuously until the stores of presynaptic neurotransmitter were depleted. The postsynaptic cell however would recover, being able to repolarize its membrane, and return to the resting membrane potential.

2. Rising: Na$^+$ gates open, K$^+$ closed
   Falling: Na$^+$ inactivation gate closes, K$^+$ open
   Undershoot: Na$^+$ activation gate closed, inactivation gate open, K$^+$ gate closing.

3. Action potential arrives at the end of the axon.
   Ca$^{2+}$ channels open.
   Ca$^{2+}$ causes synaptic vesicles to fuse with the axon membrane at the synapse.
   Synaptic vesicles release their neurotransmitter.
   Neurotransmitter molecules diffuse across synaptic cleft.
   Postsynaptic receptor proteins bind neurotransmitter.
   Postsynaptic membrane depolarizes.
   If this were an inhibitory synapse, the binding of receptor protein and neurotransmitter would cause the postsynaptic membrane to hyperpolarize.

4. Cells exposed to a stimulus repeatedly may lose their ability to respond. This is known as habituation. Karen's postsynaptic cells may have decreased the number of receptor proteins they produce because the stimulatory signal is so abundant. The result is that it now takes more stimuli to achieve the same result.

# CHAPTER 45

## LEARNING OUTCOME QUESTIONS

**45.1** When the log values of the intensity of the stimulus and the frequency of the resulting action potentials are plotted against each other, a straight line results; this is referred to as a logarithmic relationship.

**45.2** Proprioceptors detect the stretching of muscles and subsequently relay information about the relative position and movement of different parts of the organism's body to the central nervous system. This knowledge is critical for the central nervous system; it must be able to respond to these data by signaling the appropriate muscular responses, allowing for balance, coordinated locomotion, and reflexive responses.

**45.3** The lateral line system supplements the sense of hearing in fish and amphibian larvae by allowing the organism to detect minute changes in the pressure and vibrations of its environment. This is facilitated by the density of water; without an aquatic environment the adult, terrestrial amphibian will no longer be able to make use of this system. On land, sound waves are more easily detectable by the sense of hearing than are vibratory or pressure waves by the similar structures of a lateral line.

**45.4** Many insects, such as the housefly, have chemoreceptors on their feet with which they can detect the presence of edible materials as they move through their environment. These insects can thus "taste" what they are walking on, and when they encounter an edible substrate they can then descend their proboscis and consume the food.

**45.5** Individuals with complete red-green color blindness (those who have no red cones or no green cones, as opposed to those who lack only some red or green cones) would be highly unlikely to be able to learn to distinguish these colors. In order for an individual to perceive the colors in the red-green area of the spectrum, both red and green cones are required; without both cones there is no reference point by which individuals could compare the signals between the retina and the brain. If there are other cues available, such as color saturation or object shape and size, individuals with a less severe form of color blindness may be able to learn to distinguish these colors. In the absence of other references, however, it would be very difficult for individuals with even partial red-green color blindness to distinguish these colors.

**45.6** The body temperature of an ectothermic organism is not necessarily the same as the ambient temperature; for example, other reptiles may bask in the sun, wherein on a chilly day the sun may warm the animal's body temperature above the ambient temperature. In this situation, the heat-sensing organs of, for example, a pit viper would still be effective in hunting as it would be able to distinguish the differences between the environment and its ectothermic prey.

## INQUIRY QUESTIONS

***Page 921*** As the injured fish thrashed around, it would produce vibrations, rapid changes in the pressure of the water. The lateral line system in fish consists of canals filled with sensory cells that send a signal to the brain in response to the changes in water pressure.

***Page 927*** Both taste and smell utilize chemoreceptors as sensory receptors, wherein the binding of specific proteins to the receptor induces an action potential which is sent as a sensory signal to the brain. The chemicals detected by both systems must first be dissolved in extracellular fluid before they can be detected. One major difference between the two systems is that the olfactory system does not route a signal through the thalamus; instead, action potentials are routed directly to the olfactory cortex. Another difference is that olfactory receptors occur in larger numbers—tens of millions, as opposed to tens or hundreds of thousands for taste receptors.

***Page 929*** In humans, the ganglion cells attach to the front of the retinal cells, thus forcing the optic nerve to disrupt the continuity of the retina, leading to the formation of a "blind spot". In mollusks, however, the ganglion cells attach to the back of the retina and thus the retina is uninterrupted, eliminating the blind spot.

## UNDERSTAND

1. d  2. b  3. d  4. b  5. a  6. c  7. b  8. d  9. a

## APPLY

1. c  2. a  3. c  4. b

## SYNTHESIZE

1. When blood pH becomes acidic, chemoreceptors in the circulatory and the nervous systems notify the brain and the body responds by increasing the breathing rate. This causes an increase in the release of carbon dioxide through the lungs. Decreased carbon dioxide levels in the blood cause a decrease in carbonic acid, which, in turn, causes the pH to rise.

2. In order to reach the retina and generate action potentials on the optic nerve, light must first pass through the ganglion and bipolar cells to reach the rods and cones that synapse with the bipolar cells. The bipolar cells then synapse with ganglion cells. These in turn send action potentials to the brain. Because the retina comprises three layers, with the rods and cones located farthest from the pupil, light must travel to the deepest level to set off reactions that move up through the more superficial levels and result in optic signals.

3. Without gravity to force the otoliths down toward the hair cells, the otolith organ will not function properly. The otolith membrane would not rest on the hair cells and would not move in response to movement of the body parallel or perpendicular to the pull of gravity. Consequently, the hair cell would not bend and so would not produce receptor potentials. Because the astronauts can see, they would have an impression of motion—they can see themselves move in relation to objects around them—but with their eyes closed, they would not know if they were moving in relation to their surroundings. Because their proprioceptors would still function, they would be able to sense when they moved their arms or legs, but they would not have the sensation of their enter body moving through space.

   The semicircular canals would not function equally well in zero-gravity conditions. Although the fluid in the semicircular canals is still able to move around, some sensation of angular movement would most likely occur, but the full function of the semicircular canals requires the force of gravity to aid in the directional movement of the fluid in the canals.

# CHAPTER 46

## LEARNING OUTCOME QUESTIONS

**46.1** Neurotransmitters are released at a synapse and act on the post synaptic membrane. Hormones enter the circulatory system and are thus delivered to the entire body.

**46.2** The response of a particular tissue depends first on the receptors on its surface, and second on the response pathways active in a cell. There can be different receptor subtypes that bind the same hormone, and the same receptor can stimulate different response pathways.

**46.3** This might lower the amount of GH in circulation. As a treatment, it may have unwanted side effects.

**46.4** With two hormones that have antagonistic effects, the body can maintain a fine level of blood sugar.

**46.5** Reducing blood volume should also reduce blood pressure.

## UNDERSTAND

1. b   2. d   3. c   4. b   5. d   6. b   7. a

## APPLY

1. a   2. c   3. c   4. b   5. b   6. b   7. b

## SYNTHESIZE

1. If the target cell for a common hormone or paracrine becomes cancerous, it may become hypersensitive to the messenger. This may in turn cause over production of cells, which would result in tumor formation. By blocking the production of the hormone specific to that tissue (for example, breast or prostate tissue and sex steroids), it would be possible to slow the growth rate and decrease the size of the tumor.

2. The same hormone can affect two different organs in different ways because the second messengers triggered by the hormone have different targets inside the cell because the cells have different functions. Epinephrine affects the cells of the heart by increasing metabolism so that their contractions are faster and stronger. However, liver cells do not contract and so the second messenger in liver cells triggers the conversion of glycogen into glucose. That is why hormones are so valuable but also economical to the body. One hormone can be produced, one receptor can be made, and one second-messenger system can be used, but there can be two different targets inside the cell.

3. With hormones such as thyroxine, whose effects are slower and have a broader range of activity, a negative feedback system using one hormone adequately controls the system. However, for certain parameters that have a very narrow range and change constantly within that range, a regulatory system that uses up-and-down regulation is desirable. Too much or too little $Ca^{2+}$ or glucose in the blood can have devastating effects on the body and so those levels must be controlled within a very narrow range. To rely on negative feedback loops would restrict the quick "on" and "off" responses needed to keep the parameters in a very narrow range.

# CHAPTER 47

## LEARNING OUTCOME QUESTIONS

**47.1** There are three limitations terrestrial invertebrates experience due to an exoskeleton. First, animals with an exoskeleton can only grow by shedding, or molting, the exoskeleton, leaving them vulnerable to predation. Second, muscles that act upon the exoskeleton cannot strengthen and grow as they are confined within a defined space. Finally, the exoskeleton, in concert with the respiratory system of many terrestrial invertebrates, limits the size to which these animals can grow. In order for the exoskeleton of a terrestrial animal to be strong, it has to have a sufficient surface area, and thus it has to increase in thickness as the animal gets larger. The weight of a thicker exoskeleton would impose debilitating constraints on the animal's ability to move.

**47.2** Vitamin D is important for the absorption of dietary calcium as well as the deposition of calcium phosphate in bone. Children undergo a great deal of skeletal growth and development; without sufficient calcium deposition their bones can become soft and pliable, leading to a condition known as rickets, which causes a bending or bowing of the lower limbs. In the elderly, bone remodeling without adequate mineralization of the bony tissue can lead to brittle bones, a condition known as osteoporosis.

**47.3** First, unlike the chitinous exoskeleton, a bony endoskeleton is made of living tissue; thus, the endoskeleton can grow along with the organism. Second, because the muscles that act upon the bony endoskeleton are not confined within a rigid structure, they are able to strengthen and grow with increased use. Finally, the size limitations imposed by a heavy exoskeleton that covers the entire organism

are overcome by the internal bony skeleton, which can support a greater size and weight without itself becoming too cumbersome.

**47.4** Slow-twitch fibers are found primarily in muscles adapted for endurance rather than strength and power. Myoglobin provides oxygen to the muscles for the aerobic respiration of glucose, thus providing a higher ATP yield than anaerobic respiration. Increased mitochondria also increases the ATP productivity of the muscle by increasing availability of cellular respiration and thus allows for sustained aerobic activity.

**47.5** Locomotion via alternation of legs requires a greater degree of nervous system coordination and balance; the animal needs to constantly monitor its center of gravity in order to maintain stability. In addition, a series of leaps will cover more ground per unit time and energy expenditure than will movement by alternation of legs.

## INQUIRY QUESTIONS

**Page 969** The idea is very similar; both quadrupeds and insects such as grasshoppers have flexors and extensors that exert antagonistic control over many of their muscles. The main different is in the structure rather than function—in a grasshopper, the muscles are covered by the skeletal elements, while in organisms with an endoskeleton, the muscles overlie the bony skeleton.

**Page 974** Increasing the frequency of stimulation to a maximum rate will yield the maximum amplitude of a summated muscle contraction. The strength of a contraction increases because little or no relaxation time occurs between successive twitches.

**Page 974** A rough estimate of the composition of calf muscle could be obtained by measuring the amount of time the calf muscle takes to reach maximum tension and compare that amount with the contraction speed of muscles of known fiber composition. Alternatively, a small sample of muscle could be extracted and examined for histological differences in fiber composition.

## UNDERSTAND

1. d   2. b   3. c   4. a   5. c   6. a   7. b   8. a

## APPLY

1. d   2. b   3. d   4. b   5. b   6. b

## SYNTHESIZE

1. Although a hydrostatic skeleton might have advantages in terms of ease of transport and flexibility of movement, the exoskeleton would probably do a better job at protecting the delicate instruments within. This agrees with our observations of these support systems on Earth. Worms and marine invertebrates use hydrostatic skeletons, although arthropods ("hard bodies") use an exoskeleton. Worms are very flexible, but easily crushed.

2. The first 90 seconds of muscle activity are anaerobic in which the cells utilize quick sources of energy (creatine phosphate, lactic acid fermentation) to generate ATP. After that, the respiratory and circulatory systems will catch up and begin delivering more oxygen to the muscles which allows them to use aerobic respiration, which is a much more efficient method of generating ATP from glucose.

3. If acetylcholinesterase is inhibited, acetylcholine will continue to stimulate muscles to contract. As a result, muscle twitching, and eventually paralysis, will occur. In March 1995, canisters of Sarin were released into a subway system in Tokyo. Twelve people were killed and hundreds injured.

4. Natural selection is not goal-oriented. In other words, evolution does not anticipate environmental pressures and the structures that result from evolution by natural selection are those most well-suited the previous generations' environment. Since vertebrate wing development occurred several times during evolution, it is probable that the animals in question—birds, pterosaurs, and bats—all encountered different evolutionary pressures during wing evolution.

# CHAPTER 48

## LEARNING OUTCOME QUESTIONS

**48.1** The cells and tissues of a one-way digestive system are specialized such that ingestion, digestion, and elimination can happen concurrently, making it more efficient in terms of food processing and energy utilization. With a gastrovascular cavity, however, all of the cells are exposed to all aspects of digestion.

**48.2** Voluntary processes include bringing food into the mouth (food capture), mastication, and the initiation of swallowing. Salivation and the swallowing reflex are involuntary.

**48.3** The sandwich represents carbohydrate (bread), protein (chicken), and fat (mayonnaise). The breakdown of carbohydrates begins with salivary amylase in the mouth. The breakdown of proteins begins in the stomach with pepsinogen, and the emulsification of fats begins in the duodenum with the introduction of bile. So—it is the chicken that will begin its breakdown in the stomach.

**48.4** Fats are broken down, by emulsification, into fatty acids and monoglycerides, both of which are nonpolar molecules. Nonpolar molecules are able to enter the epithelial cells by simple diffusion.

**48.5** The success of any mutation depends upon the selective pressures that species is subjected to. Thus, if two different species are subjected to similar environmental conditions and undergo the same mutation, then, yes, the mutation should be similarly successful. If two species undergo the same mutation but are under different selective pressures, then the mutation may not be successful in both species.

**48.6** The sight, taste, and, yes, smell of food are the triggers the digestive system needs to release digestive enzymes and hormones. The saliva and gastric secretions that are required for proper digestion and are triggered by the sense of smell would be affected by anosmia.

**48.7** Any ingested compounds that might be dangerous are metabolized first by the liver, thus reducing the risk to the rest of the body.

**48.8** Even with normal leptin levels, individuals with reduced sensitivity in the brain to the signaling molecule may still become obese.

## INQUIRY QUESTIONS

**Page 985** If the epiglottis does not properly seal off the larynx and trachea, food can accidentally become lodged in the airway, causing choking.

**Page 986** The digestive system secretes a mucus layer that helps to protect the delicate tissues of the alimentary canal from acidic secretions.

**Page 992** The amino acid sequences for lysozyme evolved convergently among ruminants and langur monkeys. Thus, if a phylogeny was constructed using solely the lysozyme molecular data, these species—ruminants and langur monkeys—would be adjacent to each other on the phylogenetic tree.

**Page 997** GIP and CCK send inhibitory signals to the hypothalamus upon food intake. If the hypothalamus sensors did not work properly, leptin levels would increase; increased leptin levels would result in a loss of appetite.

## UNDERSTAND

1. b 2. c 3. c 4. b 5. d 6. d 7. c

## APPLY

1. d 2. b 3. c 4. c

## SYNTHESIZE

1. Birds feed their young with food they acquire from the environment. The adult bird consumes the food but stores it in her crop. When she returns to the nest, she regurgitates the food into the mouths of the fledglings. Mammals on the other hand feed their young with milk that is produced in the mother's mammary glands. Young feed by latching onto the mother's nipples and sucking the milk. Mammals have no need for a crop in their digestive system because they don't feed their young in the same way as birds.

2. Leptin is produced by the adipose cells and serves as a signal for feeding behavior. Since low blood leptin levels signal the brain to initiate feeding, a treatment for obesity would need to raise leptin levels, thereby decreasing appetite.

3. The liver plays many important roles in maintaining homeostasis. Two of those roles are detoxifying drugs and chemicals and producing plasma proteins. A drop in plasma protein levels is indicative of liver disease, which in turn could be caused by abuse of alcohol or other drugs.

4. The selective pressures that guide the adaptation of mutated alleles within a population were the same in these two groups of organisms. Both ruminants and langur monkeys eat tough, fibrous plant materials which are broken down by intestinal bacteria. The ruminants and langurs then absorb the nutrients from the cellulose by digesting those bacteria; this is accomplished through the use of these adapted lysozymes. Normal lysozymes, found in saliva and other secretions, work in a relatively neutral pH environment. These intestinal lysozymes, however, needed to adapt to an acidic environment, which explains the level of convergence.

5. Whereas mammalian dentition is adapted to process different food types, birds are able to process different types of food by breaking up food particles

in the gizzard. Bird diets are comparably diverse to mammalian diets; some birds are carnivores, others are insectivores or frugivores, still others omnivores.

## CHAPTER 49

### LEARNING OUTCOME QUESTIONS

**49.1** Fick's law states that the rate of diffusion (R) can be increased by increasing the surface area of a respiratory surface, increase the concentration difference between respiratory gases, and decreasing the distance the gases must diffuse: $R = \frac{DA \, \Delta p}{d}$. Continually beating cilia increase the concentration difference ($\Delta p$).

**49.2** Countercurrent flow systems maximize the oxygenation of the blood by increasing $\Delta p$, thus maintaining a higher oxygen concentration in the water than in the blood throughout the entire diffusion pathway. The lamellae, found within a fish's gill filaments, facilitate this process by allowing water to flow in only one direction, counter to the blood flow within the capillary network in the gill.

**49.3** Birds have a more efficient respiratory system than other terrestrial vertebrates. Birds that live or fly at high altitudes are subjected to lower oxygen partial pressure and thus have evolved a respiratory system that is capable of maximizing the diffusion and retention of oxygen in the lungs. In addition, efficient oxygen exchange is crucial during flight; flying is more energetically taxing than most forms of locomotion and without efficient oxygen exchange birds would be unable to fly even short distances safely.

**49.4** There are both structural and functional differences in bird and mammalian respiration. Both mammals and birds have lungs, but only birds also have air sacs, which they use to move air in and out of the respiratory system, while only mammals have a muscular diaphragm used to move air and in and out of the lungs. Mammalian lungs are pliable, and gas exchange occurs within small closed-ended sacs in the mammalian lung called alveoli. In contrast, bird lungs are rigid, and gas exchange occurs in the unidirectional parabronchi. In addition, because air flow in mammals is bi-directional, there is a mixing of oxygenated and deoxygenated air, while the unidirectional air flow in birds increases the purity of the oxygen entering the capillaries. Mammalian respiration is less efficient than avian respiration; birds transfer more oxygen with each breath than do mammals. Finally, mammals only have one respiratory cycle whereas birds have two complete cycles.

**49.5** Most oxygen is transported in the blood bound to hemoglobin (forming oxyhemoglobin) while only a small percentage is dissolved in the plasma. Carbon dioxide, on the other hand, is predominantly transported as bicarbonate (having first been combined with water to form carbonic acid and then dissociated into bicarbonate and hydrogen ions). Carbon dioxide is also transported dissolved in the plasma and bound to hemoglobin.

### INQUIRY QUESTIONS

**Page 1002** Capillaries, the tiniest of the cardiovascular vessels, are located near every cell of the body. Because of their small size and large number, the surface area for gas exchange through them is maximized. This capillary arrangement also works well with the tiny alveoli of the lungs which also provide a large surface area for gas exchange. Since capillaries are in intimate contact with alveoli, rapid gas exchange is enhanced.

**Page 1012** Fick's law of diffusion states that for a dissolved gas, the rate of diffusion is directly proportional to the pressure difference between the two sides of the membrane and to the area over which the diffusion occurs. In emphysema, alveolar walls break down and alveoli increase in size, effectively reducing the surface area for gas exchange. Emphysema thus reduces the diffusion of gases.

**Page 1013** Most veins have a bluish color and function to return oxygen-depleted blood to the heart. The pulmonary veins, however, are bright red because they return fully oxygenated blood from the lungs to the left atrium of the heart.

**Page 1013** The difference in oxygen content between arteries and veins during rest and exercise shows how much oxygen was unloaded to the tissues.

**Page 1014** Not really. A healthy individual still has a substantial oxygen reserve in the blood even after intense exercise.

**Page 1014** It increases it. At any pH or temperature, the percentage of $O_2$ saturation falls (e.g. more $O_2$ is delivered to tissues) as pressure increases.

### UNDERSTAND

1. c 2. d 3. d 4. d 5. b 6. a 7. d 8. c

## APPLY

1. d   2. c   3. a   4. c   5. a   6. c

## SYNTHESIZE

1. Fish gills have not only a large respiratory surface area but also a countercurrent flow system, which maintains an oxygen concentration gradient throughout the entire exchange pathway, thus providing the most efficient system for the oxygenation of blood. Amphibian respiratory systems are not very efficient. They practice positive pressure breathing. Bird lungs are quite effective, in that they have a large surface area and one-way air flow; mammals, on the other hand, have only a large surface area but no mechanism to ensure the maintenance of a strong concentration gradient.

2. During exercise, cellular respiration increases the amount of carbon dioxide released, thus decreasing the pH of the blood. In addition, the increased cellular respiration increases temperature, as heat is released during glucose metabolism. Decreased pH and increased temperature both facilitate an approximately 20% increase in oxygen unloading in the peripheral tissues.

3. Unicellular prokaryotic organisms, protists, and many invertebrates are small enough such that gas exchange can occur over the body surface directly from the environment. Only larger organisms, where most cells are not in direct contact with the environment with which gases must be exchanged, require specialized structures for gas exchange.

## CHAPTER 50

### LEARNING OUTCOME QUESTIONS

**50.1** Following an injury to a vessel, vasoconstriction is followed by the accumulation of platelets at the site of injury and the subsequent formation of a platelet plug. This triggers a positive feedback enzyme cascade, attracting more platelets, clotting factors, and other chemicals, each of which continually attract additional clotting molecules until the clot is formed. The enzyme cascade also causes fibrinogen to come out of solution as fibrin, forming a fibrin clot that will eventually replace the platelet plug.

**50.2** When the insect heart contracts, it forces hemolymph out through the vessels and into the body cavities. When it relaxes, the resulting negative pressure gradient, combined with muscular contractions in the body, draws the blood back to the heart.

**50.3** The primary advantage of having two ventricles rather than one is the separation of oxygenated from deoxygenated blood. In fish and amphibians, oxygenated and deoxygenated blood mix, leading to less oxygen being delivered to the body's cells.

**50.4** The delay following auricular allows the atrioventricular valves to close prior to ventricular contraction. Without that delay, the contraction of the ventricles would force blood back up through the valves into the atria.

**50.5** During systemic gas exchange, only about 90% of the fluid that diffuses out of the capillaries returns to the blood vessels; the rest moves into the lymphatic vessels, which then return the fluid to the circulatory system via the left and right subclavian veins.

**50.6** Breathing rate is regulated to ensure ample oxygen is available to the body. However, the heart rate must be regulated to ensure efficient delivery of the available oxygen to the body cells and tissues. For example, during exertion, respiratory rates will increase in order to increase oxygenation and allow for increased aerobic cellular respiration. But simply increasing the oxygen availability is not enough—the heart rate must also increase so that the additional oxygen can be quickly delivered to the muscles undergoing cellular respiration.

### INQUIRY QUESTION

**Page 1021** Erythropoietin is a hormone that stimulates the production of erythrocytes from the myeloid stem cells. If more erythrocytes are produced, the oxygen-carrying capacity of the blood is increased. This could potentially enhance athletic performance and is why erythropoietin is banned from use during the Olympics and other sporting events.

### UNDERSTAND

1. a   2. b   3. c   4. a   5. c   6. d   7. c

### APPLY

1. a   2. b   3. a   4. c   5. a

## SYNTHESIZE

1. Antidiuretic hormone (ADH) is secreted by the posterior pituitary but has its target cells in the kidney. In response to the presence of ADH, the kidneys increase the amount of water reabsorbed. This water eventually returns to the plasma where it causes an increase in volume and subsequent increase in blood pressure. Another hormone, aldosterone, also causes an increase in blood pressure by causing the kidney to retain Na$^+$, which sets up a concentration gradient that also pulls water back into the blood.

2. Blood includes plasma (comprised primarily of water with dissolved proteins) and formed elements (red blood cells, white blood cells, and platelets). Lymph is comprised of interstitial fluid and found only within the lymphatic vessels and organs. Both blood and lymph are found in organisms with closed circulatory systems. Hemolymph is both the circulating fluid and the interstitial fluid found in organisms with open circulatory systems.

3. Many argue that the evolution of endothermy was less an adaptation to maintain a constant internal temperature and more an adaptation to function in environments low in oxygen. If this is the case, then yes, it makes sense that the evolution of the four-chambered heart, an adaptation that increases the availability of oxygen in the body tissues and which would be highly beneficial in an oxygen-poor environment, and the evolution of endothermy were related. These two adaptations can also be looked at as related in that the more efficient heart would be able to provide the oxygen necessary for the increased metabolic activity that accompanies endothermy.

4. The SA node acts as a natural pacemaker. If it is malfunctioning, one would expect a slow or irregular heartbeat or irregular electrical activity between the atria and the ventricles.

## CHAPTER 51

### LEARNING OUTCOME QUESTIONS

**51.1** Water moves towards regions of higher osmolarity.

**51.2** The are both involved in water conservation.

**51.3** This may have arisen independently in both the mammalian and avian lineages, or lost from the reptilian lineage.

**51.4** Nitrogenous waste is a problem because it is toxic, and it is a result of degrading old proteins.

**51.5** This would increase the osmolarity within the tubule system, and thus should decrease reabsorption of water. This would lead to loss of water.

**51.6** Blocking aquaporin channels would prevent reabsorption of water from the collecting duct.

### UNDERSTAND

1. d   2. a   3. c   4. c   5. d   6. d   7. d

### APPLY

1. d   2. c   3. b   4. b   5. c   6. b

### SYNTHESIZE

1a. Antidiuretic hormone (ADH) is produced in the hypothalamus and is secreted by the posterior pituitary. ADH targets the collecting duct of the nephron and stimulates the reabsorption of water from the urine by increasing the permeability of water in the walls of the duct. The primary stimulus for ADH secretion is an increase in the osmolarity of blood.

1b. Aldosterone is produced and secreted by the adrenal cortex in response to a drop in blood Na$^+$ concentration. Aldosterone stimulates the distal convoluted tubules to reabsorb Na$^+$, decreasing the excretion of Na$^+$ in the urine. The reabsorption of Na$^+$ is followed by Cl$^-$ and water, and so aldosterone has the net effect of retaining both salt and water. Aldosterone secretion however, is not stimulated by a decrease in blood osmolarity, but rather by a decrease in blood volume. A group of cells located at the base of the glomerulus, called the juxtaglomerular apparatus, detect drops in blood volume that then stimulates the renin-angiotensin-aldosterone system.

1c. Atrial natriuretic hormone (ANH) is produced and secreted by the right atrium of the heart, in response to an increase in blood volume. The secretion of ANH results in the reduction of aldosterone secretion. With the secretion of ANH, the distal convoluted tubules reduce the amount of Na$^+$ that is reabsorbed, and likewise reduces the amount of Cl$^-$ and water that is reabsorbed. The final result is the reduction in blood volume.

His normal renal blood flow rate would be 21% of cardiac output, or 7.2 L/min × 0.21 = 1.5 L/min.

If John's kidneys are not affected by his circulatory condition, his renal blood flow rate should be about 1.5 L/min.

# CHAPTER 52

## LEARNING OUTCOME QUESTIONS

**52.1** No, innate immunity shows some specificity for classes of molecules common to pathogens.

**52.2** Hematopoetic stem cells.

**52.3** T-cell receptors are rearranged to generate a large number of different receptors with specific binding abilities. Toll-like receptors are not rearranged, and recognize specific classes of molecules, not specific molecules.

**52.4** Ig receptors are rearranged to generate many different specificities. TLR innate receptors are not rearranged and bind to specific classes of molecules.

**52.5** Allergies are a case of the immune system overreacting while autoimmune disorders involve the immune system being compromised.

**52.6** Diagnostic kits use monoclonal antibodies because they are against a single specific epitope of an antigen. They also use cells that can be grown in culture, and do not require immunizing an animal, bleeding them and then isolating the antibodies from their sera.

**52.7** The main difference between Polio and influenza is the rate at which the viruses can change. The Polio virus is a RNA virus with a genome that consists of a single RNA. The viral surface proteins do not change rapidly allowing immunity via a vaccine. Influenza is an RNA virus with a high mutation rate, which means that surface proteins change rapidly. Influenza has a genome that consists of multiple RNAs, which allows recombination of the different viral RNA's during infection with different strains.

## INQUIRY QUESTIONS

**Page 1059** The viruses would be liberated into the body where they could infect numerous additional cells.

**Page 1063** The antigenic properties of the two viruses must be similar enough that immunity to cowpox also enables protection against smallpox.

**Page 1074** The common structure and mechanism of formation of B cell immunoglobulins (Igs) and T-cell receptors (TCRs) suggests a common ancestral form of adaptive immunity gave rise to the two cell lines existing today.

**Page 1078** A high level of HCG in a urine sample will block the binding of the antibody to HCG-coated particles and prevent any agglutination.

**Page 1079** Influenza frequently alters its surface antigens making it impossible to produce a vaccine with a long-term effect. Smallpox virus has a considerably more stable structure.

## UNDERSTAND

1. b   2. a   3. b   4. c   5. c   6. b   7. c

## APPLY

1. d   2. c   3. c   4. a. b., then d., then c   5. c   6. b   7. a

## SYNTHESIZE

1. It would be difficult to advertise this lotion as immune-enhancing. The skin serves as a barrier to infection because it is oily and acidic. Applying a lotion that is watery and alkaline will dilute the protective effects of the skin secretions, thereby inhibiting the immune functions. Perhaps it is time to look for another job.

2. The scratch has caused an inflammatory response. Although it is very likely that some pathogens entered her body through the broken skin, the response is actually generated by the injury to her tissue. The redness is a result of the increased dilation of blood vessels caused by the release of histamine. This also increases the temperature of the skin by bringing warm blood closer to the surface. Leakage of fluid from the vessels causes swelling in the area of the injury, which can cause pressure on the pain sensors in the skin. All of these serve to draw defensive cells and molecules to the injury site, thereby helping to defend her against infection.

3. There are a number of ways that this could be done. However, one method would be to show that viral genetic material never appears within the cells of those who claim immunity. Another method would involve testing for the presence of interferon, which is released by cells in response to viral infection.

4. These data imply that innate immunity is a very ancient defense mechanism. The presence of these proteins in Cnidarians indicates that they arose soon after multicellularity.

# CHAPTER 53

## LEARNING OUTCOME QUESTIONS

**53.1** Genetic sex determination essentially guarantees equal sex ratios; when sex ratios are not equal, the predominant sex is selected against because those individuals have more competition for mates. Temperature-dependent sex-determination can result in skewed sex ratios in which one sex or the other is selected against. Genetic sex determination, on the other hand, can provide much greater stability within the population, and consequently the genetic characteristics that provide that stability are selected for.

**53.2** Estrous cycles occur in most mammals, and most mammalian species have relatively complex social organizations and mating behaviors. The cycling of sexual receptivity allows for these complex mating systems. Specifically, in social groups where male infanticide is a danger, synchronized estrous among females may be selected for as it would eliminate the ability of the male to quickly impregnate the group females. Physiologically, estrous cycles result in the maturation of the egg accompanying the hormones that promote sexual receptivity.

**53.3** In mating systems where males compete for mates, sperm competition, a form of sexual selection, is very common. In these social groups, multiple males may mate with a given female, and thus those individuals who produced the highest number of sperm would have a reproductive advantage—a higher likelihood of siring the offspring.

**53.4** The answer varies depending upon the circumstances. In a species that is very r-selected, in other words, one that reproduces early in life and often but does not invest much in the form of parental care, multiple offspring per pregnancy would definitely be favored by natural selection. In K-selected species where parental care is very high, on the other hand, single births might be favored because the likelihood of offspring survival is greater if the parental resources are not divided among the offspring.

**53.5** The birth control pill works by hormonally controlling the ovulation cycle in women. By releasing progesterone continuously the pill prevents ovulation. Ovulation is a cyclical event and under hormonal control, thus it is easy for the process to be controlled artificially. In addition, the female birth control pill only has to halt the release of a single ovum. An analogous male birth control pill, on the other hand, would have to completely cease sperm production (and men produce millions of sperm each day), and such hormonal upheaval in the male could lead to infertility or other intolerable side effects.

## INQUIRY QUESTIONS

**Page 1085** The ultimate goal of any organism is to maximize its relative fitness. Small females are able to reproduce but once they become very large they would be better able to maximize their reproductive success by becoming male, especially in groups where only a few males mate with all of the females. Protandry might evolve in species where there is a limited supply of mates and relatively little space; a male of such a species in close proximity to another male would have higher reproductive success by becoming female and mating with the available male than by waiting for a female (and then having to compete for her with the other male).

**Page 1088** The evolutionary progression from oviparity to viviparity is a complex process; requiring the development of a placenta or comparable structure. Once a complex structure evolves, it is rare for an evolutionary reversal to occur. Perhaps more importantly, there are several advantages to viviparity over oviparity, especially in cold environments where eggs are vulnerable to mortality due to cold weather (and predation). In aquatic reptiles such as sea snakes, viviparity allows the female to remain at sea and avoid coming ashore, where both she and her eggs would be exposed to predators.

**Page 1094** Under normal circumstances, the testes produce hormones, testosterone and inhibin, which exert negative feedback inhibition on the hormones produced and secreted by the anterior pituitary (luteinizing hormone and follicle-stimulating hormone). Following castration, testosterone and inhibin are no longer produced and thus the brain will overproduce LH and FSH. For this reason, hormone therapy is usually prescribed following castration.

## UNDERSTAND

1. c   2. d   3. d   4. d   5. b   6. c   7. a   8. c   9. a

## APPLY

1. a   2. b   3. d   4. a

## SYNTHESIZE

1. A mutation that makes *SRY* nonfunctional would mean that the embryo would lack the signal to form male structures during development. Therefore, the embryo would have female genitalia at birth.

2. Amphibians and fish that rely on external fertilization also have access to water. Lizards, birds, and mammals have adaptations that allow them to reproduce away from a watery environment. These adaptations include eggs that have protective shells or internal development, or both.

3. FSH and LH are produced by the anterior pituitary in both males and females. In both cases they play roles in the production of sex hormones and gametogenesis. However, FSH stimulates spermatogenesis in males and oogenesis in females, whereas LH promotes the production of testosterone in males and estradiol in females.

4. It could indeed work. The hormone hCG is produced by the zygote to prevent menstruation, which would in turn prevent implantation in the uterine lining. Blocking the hormone receptors would prevent implantation and therefore pregnancy.

5. Parthenogenic species reproduce from gametes that remain diploid. Sperm are haploid, whereas eggs do not complete meiosis (becoming haploid) until after fertilization. Therefore, only eggs could develop without DNA from an outside source. In addition, only eggs have the cellular structures needed for development. Therefore only females can undergo parthenogenesis.

# CHAPTER 54

## LEARNING OUTCOME QUESTIONS

**54.1** Ca²⁺ ions act as second messengers and bring about changes in protein activity that result in blocking polyspermy and increasing the rate of protein synthesis within the egg.

**54.2** In a mammal, the cells at the four-cell stage are still uncommitted and thus separating them will still allow for normal development. In frogs, on the other hand, yolk distribution results in displaced cleavage; thus, at the four-cell stage the cells do not each contain a nucleus which contains the genetic information required for normal development.

**54.3** The cellular behaviors necessary for gastrulation differ across organisms; however, some processes are necessary for any gastrulation to occur. Specifically, cells must rearrange and migrate throughout the developing embryo.

**54.4** No—neural crest cell fate is determined by its migratory pathway.

**54.5** Marginal zone cells in both the ventral and dorsal regions express bone morphogenetic protein 4 (BMP4). The fate of these cells is determined by the number of receptors on the cell membrane to bind to BMP4; greater BMP4 binding will induce a ventral mesodermal fate. The organizer cells, which previously were thought to activate dorsal development, have been found to actually inhibit ventral development by secreting one of many proteins that block the BMP4 receptors on the dorsal cells.

**54.6** Most of the differentiation of the embryo, in which the initial structure formation occurs, happens during the first trimester; the second and third trimesters are primarily times of growth and organ maturation, rather than the actual development and differentiation of structures. Thus, teratogens are most potent during this time of rapid organogenesis.

## INQUIRY QUESTION

**Page 1127** High levels of estradiol and progesterone in the absence of pregnancy would still affect the body in the same way. High levels of both hormones would inhibit the release of FSH and LH, thereby preventing ovulation. This is how birth control pills work. The pills contain synthetic forms of either both estradiol and progesterone or just progesterone. The high levels of these hormones in the pill trick the body into thinking that it is pregnant and so the body does not ovulate.

## UNDERSTAND

1. d  2. b  3. d  4. c  5. d  6. b

## APPLY

1. c  2. b  3. a  4. a  5. d  6. b  7. c

## SYNTHESIZE

1. By starting with a series of embryos at various stages, you could try removing cells at each stage. Embryos that failed to compensate for the removal (evidenced by missing structures at maturity) would be those that lost cells after they had become committed; that is, when their fate has been determined.

2. Homeoboxes are sequences of conserved genes that play crucial roles in development of both mammals (Fifi) and *Drosophila* (the fruit fly). In fact, we know that they are more similar than dissimilar; research has demonstrated that both groups use the same transcription factors during organogenesis. The major difference between them is in the genes that are transcribed. Homeoboxes in mammals turn on genes that cause the development of mammalian structures, and those in insects would generate insect structures.

3. After fertilization, the zygote produces hCG, which inhibits menstruation and maintains the corpus luteum. At 10 weeks gestation, the placenta stops releasing hCG but it does continue to release estradiol and progesterone, which maintain the uterine lining and inhibit the pituitary production of FSH and LH. Without FSH and LH no ovulation and no menstruation occur.

4. Spemann and Mangold removed cells from the dorsal lip of one amphibian embryo and transplanted them to a different location on a second embryo. The transplanted cells caused cells that would normally form skin and belly to instead form somites and the structures associated with the dorsal area. Because of this and because the secondary dorsal structures contained both host and transplanted cells, Spemann and Mangold concluded that the transplanted cells acted as organizers for dorsal development.

# CHAPTER 55

## LEARNING OUTCOME QUESTIONS

**55.1** Just as with morphological characteristics that enhance an individual's fitness, behavioral characteristics can also affect an individual's survivability and reproductive success. Understanding the evolutionary origins of many behaviors allows biologists insights into animal behavior, including that of humans.

**55.2** A male songbird injected with testosterone prior to the usual mating season would likely begin singing prior to the usual mating season. However, since female mating behavior is largely controlled by hormones (estrogen) as well, most likely that male will not have increased fitness (and may actually have decreased fitness, if the singing stops before the females are ready to mate, or if the energetic expenditure from singing for two additional weeks is compensated by reduced sperm production).

**55.3** The genetic control over pair-bonding in prairie voles has been fairly well-established. The fact that males sometimes seek extra-pair copulations indicates that the formation of pair-bonds is under not only genetic control but also behavioral control.

**55.4** In species where males travel farther from the nest (and thus have larger range sizes), there should be significant sex differences in spatial memory. However, in species without sexual differences in range sizes should not express sex differences in spatial memory. To test the hypothesis you could perform maze tests on males and females of species with sex differences in range size as well as those species without range size differences between the sexes. (NOTE: such experiments have been performed and do support the hypothesis that there is a significant correlation between range size and spatial memory, so in species with sex differences in range size there are indeed sex differences in spatial memory. See Jones, CM et al., 2003. "The Evolution of Sex Differences in Spatial Ability." *Behavioral Neuroscience*. 117(3): 403-411)

**55.5** Although there may be a link between IQ and genes in humans, there is most certainly also an environmental component to IQ. The danger of assigning a genetic correlation to IQ lies in the prospect of selective "breeding" and the emergence of "designer babies."

**55.6** One experiment that has been implemented in testing counting ability among different primate and bird species is to present the animal with a number and have him match the target number to one of several arrays containing that number of objects. In another experiment, the animal may be asked to select the appropriate number of individual items within an array of items that equals the target number.

**55.7** Butterflies and birds have extremely different anatomy and physiology and thus most likely use very different navigation systems. Birds generally migrate bi-directionally; moving south during the cold months and back north during the warmer months. Usually, then, migrations are multi-generational events and it could be argued that younger birds can learn migratory routes from older generations. Butterflies, on the other hand, fly south to breed and die. Their offspring must then fly north having never been there before.

**55.8** In addition to chemical reproductive barriers, many species also employ behavioral and morphological reproductive barriers, such that even if a female moth is attracted by the pheromones of a male of another species, the two may be behaviorally or anatomically incompatible.

**55.9** The benefits of territorial behavior must outweigh the potential costs, which may include physical danger due to conflict, energy expenditure, and the loss of foraging or mating time. In a flower that is infrequently encountered, the honeycreeper would lose more energy defending the resource than it could gain by utilizing the resource. On the other hand, there is usually low competitive pressure for highly abundant resources, thus the bird would expend unnecessary energy defending a resource to which its access is not limited.

**55.10** The males should exhibit mate choice, as they are the sex with the greater parental investment and energy expenditure; thus, like females of most species, they should be the "choosier" sex.

**55.11** Generally, reciprocal behaviors are low-cost while behaviors due to kin selection may be low- or high-cost. Protecting infants from a predator is definitely a high-risk / potentially high-cost behavior; thus it would seem that the behavior is due to kin selection. The only way to truly test this hypothesis, however, is to conduct genetic tests or, in a particularly well-studied population, consult a pedigree.

Living in a group is associated with both costs and benefits. The primary cost is increased competition for resources, while the primary benefit is protection from predation. Altruism toward kin is considered selfish because helping individuals closely related to you will directly affect your inclusive fitness. Most armies more closely resemble insect societies than vertebrate societies. Insect societies consist of multitudes of individuals congregated for the purpose of supporting and defending a select few individuals. One could think of these few protected and revered individuals as the society the army is charged with protecting. These insect societies, like human armies, are composed of individuals each "assigned" to a particular task. Most vertebrate societies, on the other hand, are less altruistic and express increased competition and aggression between group members. In short, vertebrate societies are comprised of individuals whose primary concern is usually their own fitness, while insect societies are comprised of individuals whose primary concern is the colony itself.

## INQUIRY QUESTIONS

**Page 1135** Selection for learning ability would cease, and thus change from one generation to the next in maze learning ability; would only result from random genetic drift.

**Page 1136** Normal *fosB* alleles produce a protein that in turn affects enzymes that affect the brain. Ultimately, these enzymes trigger maternal behavior. In the absence of the enzymes, normal maternal behavior does not occur.

**Page 1140** Peter Marler's experiments addressed this question and determined that both instinct and learning are instrumental in song development in birds.

**Page 1148** Many factors affect the behavior of an animal other than its attempts to maximize energy intake. For example, avoiding predation is also important. Thus, it may be that larger prey take longer to subdue and ingest, thus making the crabs more vulnerable to predators. Hence, the crabs may trade off decreased energy gain for decreased vulnerability for predators. Many other similar explanations are possible.

**Page 1150** A question that is the subject of much current research. Ideas include the possibility that males with longer tails are in better condition (because males in poor condition couldn't survive the disadvantage imposed by the tail). The advantage to a female mating with a male in better condition might be either that the male is less likely to be parasitized, and thus less likely to pass that parasite on to the female, or the male may have better genes, which in turn would be passed on to the offspring. Another possibility is that the visual system for some reason is better able to detect males with long tails, and thus long-tailed males are preferred by females simply because the longer tails are more easily detected and responded to.

**Page 1151** Yes, the larger the male, the larger the prenuptial gift, which provides energy that the female converts into egg production.

**Page 1158** If more birds are present, then each one can spend less time watching for predators, and thus have more time for foraging.

## UNDERSTAND

1. b  2. a  3. a  4. c  5. a  6. c  7. d  8. a  9. b  10. a
11. c  12. d

## APPLY

1. Presumably, the model is basic, taking into account only size and energetic value of mussels. However, it may be that larger mussels are in places where shore crabs would be exposed to higher levels of predation or greater physiological stress. Similarly, it could be that the model underestimated time costs or energy returns as a function of mussel size. In the case of large mussels being in a place where shore crabs are exposed to costs not considered by the model, one could test the hypothesis in several ways. First, how are the sizes of mussels distributed in space? If they are completely interspersed that would tend to reject the hypothesis. Alternatively, if the mussels were differentially distributed such that the hypothesis was

reasonable, mussels could be experimentally relocated (change their distribution in space) and the diets would be expected to shift to match more closely the situation predicted by the model.

2. The four new pairs may have been living in surrounding habitat that was of lower quality, or they may have been individuals that could not compete for a limited number of suitable territories for breeding. Often, the best territories are won by the most aggressive or largest or otherwise best competitors, meaning that the new territory holders would likely have been less fierce competitors. If new residents were weaker competitors (due to aggression or body size), then the birds not removed would have been able to expand their territories to acquire even more critical resources.

3. The key here is that if the tail feathers are a handicap, then by reducing the handicap in these males should enhance their survival compared with males with naturally shorter tail feathers. The logic is simple. If the mail with long tail feathers is superior such that it can survive the negative effect of the long tail feathers, then that superior phenotype should be "exposed" with the removal or reduction of the tail feathers. Various aspects of performance could be measured since it is thought that the tail feathers hinder flying. Can males with shorter tails fly faster? Can males with shorter tails turn better? Ultimately, whether males with shorter tails survive better than males with un-manipulated tails can be measured.

4. Both reciprocity and kin selection explain the evolution of altruistic acts by examining the hidden benefits of the behavior. In both cases, altruism actually *benefits* the individual performing the act in terms of its fitness effects. If it didn't, it would be very hard to explain how such behavior could be maintained because actions that reduce the fitness of an individual should be selected against. Definition of the behavior reflects the apparent paradox of the behavior because it focuses on the cost and not the benefit that also accrues to the actor.

## SYNTHESIZE

1. The best experiment for determining whether predatory avoidance of certain coloration patterns would involve rearing a predator without an opportunity to learn avoidance and subsequently presenting the predator with prey with different patterns. If the predator avoids the black and yellow coloration more frequently than expected then the avoidance is most likely innate. If the predator does not express any preference but upon injury from a prey with the specific coloration does begin to express a preference, then the avoidance is most likely learned. In this case, the learning would be operant conditioning; the predator has learned to associate the coloration with pain and thus subsequently avoids prey with that coloration. To measure the adaptive significance of black and yellow coloration, both poisonous (or stinging) and harmless prey species with the coloration and without the coloration pattern could be presented to predators; if predators avoid both the harmful and the harmless prey, the coloration is evolutionary significant.

2. In many cases the organisms in question are unavailable for or unrealistic to study in a laboratory setting. Model organisms allow behavioral geneticists to overcome this obstacle by determining general patterns and then applying these patterns and findings to other, similar organisms. The primary disadvantage of the model system is, of course, the vast differences that are usually found between groups of taxa; however, when applying general principles, in particular those of genetic behavioral regulation, the benefits of using a model outweigh the costs. Phylogenetic analysis is the best way to determine the scale of applicability when using model organisms.

3. Extra-pair copulations and mating with males that are outside a female's territory are, by and large, more beneficial than costly to the female. By mating with males outside her territory, she reduces the likelihood that a male challenging the owner of her territory would target her offspring; males of many species are infanticidal but would not likely attack infants that could be their own. Historical data have actually shown that in many cases, females are more attracted to infanticidal males if those males win territory prior to their infanticidal behavior.

## CHAPTER 56

### LEARNING OUTCOME QUESTIONS

**56.1** It depends upon the type of species in question. Conformers are able to adapt to their environment by adjusting their body temperature and making other physiological adjustments. Over a longer period of time, individuals within a non-conforming species might not adjust to the changing environment but we would expect the population as a whole to adapt due to natural selection.

**56.2** If the populations in question comprised a source-sink metapopulations, then the lack of immigration into the sink populations would, most likely, eventually result in the extinction of those populations. The source populations would likely then increase their geographic ranges.

**56.3** It depends upon the initial sizes of the populations in question; a small population with a high survivorship rate will not necessarily grow faster than a large population with a lower survivorship rate.

**56.4** A species with high levels of predation would likely exhibit an earlier age at first reproduction and shorter inter-birth intervals in order to maximize its fitness under the selective pressure of the predation. On the other hand, species with few predators have the luxury of waiting until they are more mature before reproducing and can increase the inter-birth interval (and thus invest more in each offspring) because their risk of early mortality is decreased.

**56.5** Many different factors might affect the carrying capacity of a population. For example, climate changes, even on a relatively small scale, could have large effects on carrying capacity by altering the available water and vegetation, as well as the phenology and distribution of the vegetation. Regardless of the type of change in the environment, however, most populations will move toward carrying capacity; thus, if the carrying capacity is lowered, the population should decrease, and if the carrying capacity is raised, the population should increase.

**56.6** A given population can experience both positive and negative density-dependent effects, but not at the same time. Negative density-dependent effects, such as low food availability or high predation pressure, would decrease the population size. On the other hand, positive density-dependent effects, such as is seen with the Allee effect, results in a rapid increase in population size. Since a population cannot both increase and decrease at the same time, the two cannot occur concurrently. However, the selective pressures on a population are on a positive-negative continuum, and the forces shaping population size can not only vary in intensity but can also change direction from negative to positive or positive to negative.

**56.7** The two are closely tied together, and both are extremely important if the human population is not to exceed the Earth's carrying capacity. As population growth increases, the human population approaches the planet's carrying capacity; as consumption increases, the carrying capacity is lowered—thus, both trends must be reversed.

## INQUIRY QUESTIONS

**Page 1164** Very possibly. How fast a lizard runs is a function of its body temperature. Researchers have shown that lizards in shaded habitats have lower temperatures and thus lower maximal running speeds. In such circumstances, lizards often adopt alternative escape tactics that rely less on rapidly running away from potential predators.

**Page 1169** Because of their shorter generation times, smaller species tend to reproduce more quickly, and thus would be able to respond more quickly to increased resources in the environment.

**Page 1171** Based on the survivorship curve of meadow grass, the older the plant, the less likely it is to survive. It would be best to choose a plant that is very young to ensure the longest survival as a house plant. A survivorship curve that is shaped like a Type I curve, in which most individuals survive to an old age and then die would also lead you to select a younger plant. A type III survivorship curve, in which only a few individuals manage to survive to an older age, would suggest the selection of a middle-aged plant that had survived the early stages of life since it would also be more likely to survive to old age.

**Page 1172** It depends on the situation. If only large individuals are likely to reproduce (as is the case in some territorial species, in which only large males can hold a territory), then a few large offspring would be favored; alternatively, if body size does not affect survival or reproduction, then producing as many offspring as possible would maximize the representation of an individual's genes in subsequent generations. In many cases, intermediate values are favored by natural selection.

**Page 1174** Because when the population is below carrying capacity, the population increases in size. As it approaches the carrying capacity, growth rate slows down either from increased death rates, decreased birthrates, or both, becoming zero as the population hits the carrying capacity. Similarly, populations well above the carrying capacity will experience large decreases in growth rate, resulting either from low birthrates or high death rates, that also approach zero as the population hits the carrying capacity.

**Page 1175** There are many possible reasons. Perhaps resources become limited, so that females are not able to produce as many offspring. Another possibility is that space is limited so that, at higher populations, individuals spend more time in interactions with other individuals and squander energy that otherwise could be invested in producing and raising more young.

**Page 1176** The answer depends on whether food is the factor regulating population size. If it is, then the number of young produced at a given population size would increase and the juvenile mortality rate would decrease. However, if other factors, such as the availability of water or predators, regulated population size, then food supplementation might have no effect.

**Page 1177** If hare population levels were kept high, then we would expect lynx populations to stay high as well because lynx populations respond to food availability. If lynx populations were maintained at a high level, we would expect hare populations to remain low because increased reproduction of hares would lead to increased food for the lynxes.

**Page 1179** If human populations are regulated by density-dependent factors, then as the population approaches the carrying capacity, either birthrates will decrease or death rates will increase, or both. If populations are regulated by density-independent factors, then if environmental conditions change, then either both rates will decline, death rates will increase, or both.

**Page 1179** The answer depends on whether age-specific birth and death rates stay unchanged. If they do, then the Swedish distribution would remain about the same. By contrast, because birthrates are far outstripping death rates, the Kenyan distribution will become increasingly unbalanced as the bulge of young individuals enter their reproductive years and start producing even more offspring.

**Page 1181** Both are important causes and the relative importance of the two depends on which resource we are discussing. One thing is clear: The world cannot support its current population size if everyone lived at the level of resource consumption of people in the United States.

## UNDERSTAND
1. b  2. c  3. a  4. b  5. d  6. b  7. c

## APPLY
1. d  2. c  3. b  4. c

## SYNTHESIZE

1. The genetic makeup of isolated populations will change over time based on the basic mechanisms of evolutionary change; for example, natural selection, mutation, assortative mating, and drift. These same processes affect the genetic makeup of populations in a metapopulation, but the outcomes are likely to be much more complicated. For example, if immigration between a source and a sink population is very high, then local selection in a sink population may be swamped by the regular flow of individuals carrying alleles of lower fitness from a source population where natural selection may not be acting against those alleles; divergence might be slowed or even stopped under some circumstances. On the other hand, if sinks go through repeated population declines such that they often are made up of a very small number of individuals, then they may lose considerable genetic diversity due to drift. If immigration from source populations is greater than zero but not large, these small populations might begin to diverge substantially from other populations in the metapopulation due to drift. The difference is that in the metapopulation, such populations might actually be able to persist and diverge, rather than just going extinct due to small numbers of individuals and no ability to be rescued by neighboring sources.

2. The probability that an animal lives to the next year should decline with age (Note that in Figure 55.11, all the curves decrease with age) so the cost of reproduction for an old animal would, all else being equal, be lower than for a young animal. The reason is that the cost of reproduction is measured by changes in fitness. Imagine a very old animal that has almost no chance in surviving to another reproductive event; it should spend all its effort on a current reproductive effort since its future success is likely to be zero anyway.

3. If offspring size does not affect offspring quality, then it is in the parent's interest to produce absolutely as many small offspring as possible. In doing so, it would be maximizing its fitness by increasing the number of related individuals in the next generation.

4. By increasing the mean generation time (increasing the age at which an individual can begin reproducing; age at first reproduction), keeping all else equal, one would expect that the population growth rate would be reduced. That comes simply from the fact of reducing the number of individuals that are producing offspring in the adult age classes; lower population birth rates would lead to a reduced population growth rate. As to which would have a larger influence, that is hard to say. If the change in generation time (increased age at first reproduction) had an overall larger effect on the total number of offspring an individual female had than a reduced fecundity at any age, then population growth rate would probably be more sensitive to the

change in generation time. Under different scenarios, the comparison of these two effects could become more complicated, however. Suffice it to say that population growth control can come from more than one source: fecundity and age at first reproduction.

# CHAPTER 57

## LEARNING OUTCOME QUESTIONS

**57.1**   The answer depends upon the habitat of the community in question. Some habitats are more hospitable to animals, and others to plants. The abundance of plants and animals in most habitats is also closely tied; thus the variation in abundance of one would affect the variation in abundance of the other.

**57.2**   It depends upon whether we are talking about fundamental niche or realized niche. Two species can certainly have identical fundamental niches and coexist indefinitely, because they could develop different realized niches within the fundamental niche. In order for two species with identical realized niches to coexist indefinitely, the resources within the niche must not be limited.

**57.3**   This is an example of Batesian mimicry, in which a non-poisonous species evolves coloration similar to a poisonous species.

**57.4**   In an ecosystem with limited resources and multiple prey species, one prey species could out-compete another to extinction in the absence of a predator. In the presence of the predator, however, the prey species that would have otherwise be driven to extinction by competitive exclusion is able to persist in the community. The predators that lower the likelihood of competitive exclusion are known as keystone predators.

**57.5**   Selective harvesting of individual trees would be preferable from a community point of view. According to the Intermediate Disturbance Hypothesis, moderate degrees of disturbance, as in selective harvesting, increase species richness and biodiversity more than severe disturbances, such as clear-cutting.

## INQUIRY QUESTIONS

**Page 1187**   The different soil types require very different adaptations, and thus different species are adapted to each soil type.

**Page 1191**   The kangaroo rats competed with all the other rodent species for resources, keeping the size of other rodent populations smaller. In the absence of competition when the kangaroo rats were removed, there were more resources available which allowed the other rodent populations to increase in size.

**Page 1192**   This could be accomplished in a variety of ways. One option would be to provide refuges to give some *Paramecium* a way of escaping the predators. Another option would be to include predators of the *Didinium*, which would limit their populations (see Ecosystem chapter).

**Page 1201**   By removing the kangaroo rats from the experimental enclosures and measuring the effects on both plants and ants. At first, the number of small seeds available to ants increases due to the absence of rodents. However, over time, plants that produce large seeds outcompete plants that produce small seeds, and thus fewer small seeds are produced and available to ants; hence, ant populations decline.

## UNDERSTAND

1. a   2. a   3. d   4. a   5. b   6. d   7. c   8. c

## APPLY

1. d   2. b   3. d   4. d   5. d

## SYNTHESIZE

1. Experiments are useful means to test hypotheses about ecological limitations, but they are generally limited to rapidly reproducing species that occur in relatively small areas. Alternative means of studying species' interactions include detailed studies of the mechanisms by which species might interact; sometimes, for long-lived species, instead of monitoring changes in population size, which may take a very long time, other indices can be measured, such as growth or reproductive rate. Another means of assessing interspecific interactions is to study one species in different areas, in only some of which a second species occurs. Such studies must be interpreted cautiously, however, because there may be many important differences between the areas in addition to the difference in the presence or absence of the second species.

2. Adding differentially preferred prey species might have the same effect as putting in a refuge for prey in the single species system. One way to think about it is that if a highly preferred species becomes rare due to removal by the predator, then a predator might switch to a less desirable species, even if it

doesn't taste as good or is harder to catch, simply because it is still provides a better return than chasing after a very rare preferred species. While the predator has switched, there might be enough time for the preferred species to rebound. All of these dynamics will depend upon the time it takes a predator to reduce the population size of its prey relative to the time it takes for those prey populations to rebound once the predator pressure is removed.

3. Although the mechanism might be known in this system, hidden interactions might affect interpretations in many ways because ecological systems are complex. For example, what if some other activity of the rodents besides their reduction of large seeds leading to an increase in the number of small seeds was responsible for the positive effect of rodents on ants? One way to test the specific mechanism would be to increase the abundance of small seeds experimentally independent of any manipulation of rodents. Under the current hypothesis, an increase in ant population size would be expected and should be sustained, unlike the initial increase followed by a decrease seen when rodents are removed.

4. By itself, the pattern shown in Figure 56.7 suggests character displacement, but alternative hypotheses are possible. For example, what if the distribution of seeds available on the two islands where the species are found alone is different from that seen where they are found in sympatry? If there were no large and small seeds seen on Los Hermanos or Daphne, just medium-sized ones, then it would be hard to conclude that the bill size on San Cristobal has diverged relative to the other islands just due to competition. This is a general criticism of inferring the process of character displacement with just comparing the size distributions in allopatry and sympatry. In this case, however, the Galápagos system has been very well studied. It has been established that the size distribution of seeds available is not measurably different. Furthermore, natural selection-induced changes seen in the bill size of birds on a single island, in response to drought-induced changes in seed size lend further support to the role of competition in establishing and maintaining these patterns.

5. It is possible, as the definition of an ecosystem depends upon scale. In some ecosystems, there may be other, smaller ecosystems operating within it. For example, within a rainforest ecosystem, there are small aquatic ecosystems, ecosystems within the soil, ecosystems upon an individual tree. Research seems to indicate that most species behave individualistically, but there are some instances where groups of species do depend upon one another and do function holistically. We would expect this kind of dual community structure especially in areas of overlap between distinct ecosystems, where ecotones exist.

# CHAPTER 58

## LEARNING OUTCOME QUESTIONS

**58.1**   Yes, fertilization with natural materials such as manure is less disruptive to the ecosystem than is chemical fertilization. Many chemical fertilizers, for example, contain higher levels of phosphates than does manure and thus chemical fertilization has disrupted the natural global phosphorus cycle.

**58.2**   Both matter and energy flow through ecosystems by changing form, but neither can be created or destroyed. Both matter and energy also flow through the trophic levels within an ecosystem. The flow of matter such as carbon atoms is more complex and multi-leveled than is energy flow, largely because it is truly a cycle. The atoms in the carbon cycle truly cycle through the ecosystem, with no clear beginning or end. The carbon is changed during the process of cycling from a solid to a gaseous state and back again. On the other hand, energy flow is unidirectional. The ultimate source of the energy in an ecosystem is the sun. The solar energy is captured by the primary producers at the first trophic level and is changed in form from solar to chemical energy. The chemical energy is transferred from one trophic level to another, until only heat, low quality energy, remains.

**58.3**   Yes, there are certainly situations in ecosystems in which the top predators in one trophic chain affect the lower trophic levels, while within the same ecosystem the primary producers affect the higher trophic levels within another trophic chain.

**58.4**   It depends on whether the amount of sunlight captured by the primary producers was affected. Currently, only approximately 1% of the solar energy in Earth's atmosphere is captured by primary producers for photosynthesis. If less sunlight reached Earth's surface, but a correlating increase in energy capture accompanied the decrease in sunlight, then the primary productivity should not be affected.

**58.5**   The equilibrium model of island biogeography describes the relationship between species richness and not only island size but also distance from the mainland. A small island closer to the mainland would be expected to have more species than would a larger island that is farther from the mainland.

## INQUIRY QUESTIONS

***Page 1218*** At each link in the food chain, only a small fraction of the energy at one level is converted into mass of organisms at the next level. Much energy is dissipated as heat or excreted.

***Page 1219*** In the inverted pyramid, the primary producers reproduce quickly and are eaten quickly, so that at any given time, a small population of primary producers exist relative to the heterotroph population.

***Page 1220*** Because the trout eat the invertebrates which graze the algae. With fewer grazers, there is more algae.

***Page 1220*** The snakes might reduce the number of fish, which would allow an increase in damselflies, which would reduce the number of chironomids and increase the algae. In other words, lower levels of the food chain would be identical for the "snake and fish" and "no fish and no snake" treatments. Both would differ from the enclosures with only fish.

***Page 1222*** Herbivores consume much of the algal biomass even as primary productivity increases. Increases in primary productivity can lead to increased herbivore populations. The additional herbivores crop the biomass of the algae even while primary productivity increases.

***Page 1222*** More light means more photosynthesis. More plant material means more herbivores, which translates into more predator biomass.

***Page 1223*** Introduce them yourself. For example, each spring, you could place a premeasured number of seeds of a particular invasive species in each plot. Such an experiment would have the advantage of more precisely controlling the opportunity for invasion, but also would be less natural, which is one of the advantages of the Cedar Creek study site: the plots are real ecosystems, interacting with their surrounding environment in natural ways.

***Page 1224*** (*a*) Perhaps because an intermediate number of predators is enough to keep numbers of superior competitors down. (*b*) Perhaps because there are more habitats available and thus more different ways of surviving in the environment. (*c*) Hard to say. Possibly more stable environments permit greater specialization, thus permitting coexistence of more species.

## UNDERSTAND

1. d  2. d  3. b  4. a  5. a  6. b  7. a  8. a  9. c

## APPLY

1. d  2. a  3. d  4. d

## SYNTHESIZE

1. Because the length of food chains appears to be ultimately limited by the amount of energy entering a system, and the characteristic loss of usable energy (about 90%) as energy is transferred to each higher level, it would be reasonable to expect that the ectotherm-dominated food chains would be longer than the endotherm-dominated chains. In fact, there is some indirect evidence for this from real food chains, and it is also predicted by some advanced ecological models. However, whether in reality such is the case, is difficult to determine due to all of the complex factors that determine food chain length and structure. Moreover, there are many practical difficulties associated with measuring actual food chain length in natural systems.

2. It is critical to distinguish, as this chapter points out, between energy and mass transfer in trophic dynamics of ecosystems. The standing biomass of phytoplankton is not necessarily a reliable measure of the energy contained in the trophic level. If phytoplankton are eaten as quickly as they are produced, they may contribute a tremendous amount of energy, which can never be directly measured by a static biomass sample. The standing crop therefore, is an incomplete measure of the productivity of the trophic level.

3. As Figure 58.17 suggests, trophic structure and dynamics are interrelated and are primary determinants of ecosystem characteristics and behavior. For example, if a particularly abundant herbivore is threatened, energy that is abundant at the level of primary productivity in an ecosystem may be relatively unavailable to higher trophic levels (e.g., carnivores). That is, the herbivores are an important link in transducing energy through an ecosystem. Cascading effects, whether they are driven from the bottom up or from the top down are a characteristic of energy transfer in ecosystems, and that translates into the reality that effects on any particular species are unlikely to be limited to that species itself.

4. There are many ways to answer this question, but the obvious place to start is to think about the many ways plant structural diversity potentially affects animals that are not eating the plants directly. For example, plants may provide shelter, refuges, food for prey, substrate for nesting, among other

things. Therefore, increasing complexity might increase the ability of lizards to partition the habitat in more ways, allow more species to escape their predators or seek refuge from harsh physical factors (such as, cold or hot temperatures), provide a greater substrate for potential prey in terms of food resources, for instance. If we want to know the exact mechanisms for the relationship, we would need to conduct experiments to test specific hypotheses. For example, if we hypothesize that some species that require greater structural complexity in order to persist in a particular habitat, we could modify the habitat (reduce plant structure) and test whether species originally present were reduced in numbers or became unable to persist.

# CHAPTER 59

## LEARNING OUTCOME QUESTIONS

**59.1** If the Earth rotated in the opposite direction, the Coriolis Effect would be reversed. In other words, winds descending between 30° north or 30° south and the equator would still be moving more slowly than the underlying surface so it would be deflected; however, they would be deflected to the left in the northern hemisphere and to the right in the southern hemisphere. The pattern would be reversed between 30° and 60° because the winds would be moving more rapidly than the underlying surface, and would thus be deflected again in the opposite directions from normal—to the left in the northern hemisphere and to the right in the southern hemisphere. All of this would result in Trade Winds that blew from west to east and "Westerlies" that were actually "Easterlies," blowing east to west.

**59.2** As with elevation, latitude is a primary determinant of climate and precipitation, which together largely determine the vegetational structure of a particular area, which in turn defines biomes.

**59.3** The spring and fall overturns that occur in freshwater lakes found in temperate climates result in the oxygen-poor water near the bottom of the lake getting re-mixed with the oxygen-rich water near the top of the lake, essentially eliminating, at least temporarily, the thermocline layer. In the tropics, there is less temperature fluctuation; thus the thermocline layer is more permanent and the oxygen depletion (and resulting paucity of animal life) is sustained.

**59.4** Regions affected by the ENSO, or El Niño Southern Oscillation events, experience cyclical warming events in the waters around the coastline. The warmed water lowers the primary productivity, which stresses and subsequently decreases the populations of fish, seabirds, and sea mammals.

**59.5** CFCs, or chlorofluorocarbons, are an example of point-source pollution. CFCs and other types of point-source pollutants are, in general, easier to combat because their sources are more easily identified and thus the pollutants more easily eliminated.

**59.6** Global climate change and ozone depletion may be interconnected. However, while climate change and ozone depletion are both global environmental concerns due to the impact each has on human health, the environment, economics, and politics, there are some different approaches to combating and understanding each dilemma. Ozone depletion results in an increase in the ultraviolet radiation reaching the earth's surface. Global climate change, on the other hand, results in long-term changes in sea level, ice flow, and storm activity.

## INQUIRY QUESTIONS

***Page 1232*** Because of the tilt of the Earth's axis and the spherical shape of the planet, the light (and heat) from the sun hits the equator and nearby latitudes more directly than it does at the poles.

***Page 1236*** Increased precipitation and temperature allows for the sustainability of a larger variety and biomass of vegetation, and primary productivity is a measure of the rate at which plants convert solar energy into chemical energy.

## UNDERSTAND

1. d  2. b  3. a  4. c  5. c  6. c  7. a  8. c

## APPLY

1. d  2. b  3. c  4. b

## SYNTHESIZE

1. The Earth is tilted on its axis such that regions away from the equator receive less incident solar radiation per unit surface area (because the angle of incidence is oblique). The northern and southern hemispheres alternate between angling towards vs. away from the Sun on the Earth's annual orbit. These two facts mean that the annual mean temperature will decline as you move away from the equator, and that variation in the mean temperatures of

the northern and southern hemispheres will be complementary to each other; when one is hot, the other will be cold.

2. Energy absorbed by the Earth is maximized at the equator because of the angle of incidence. Because there are large expanses of ocean at the equator, warmed air picks up moisture and rises. As it rises, equatorial air, now saturated with moisture, cools and releases rain, the air falling back to Earth's surface displaced north and south to approximately 30°. The air, warming as it descends, absorbs moisture from the land and vegetation below, resulting in desiccation in the latitudes around 30°.

3. Even though there have been global climate changes in the past, conservation biologists are concerned about the current warming trend for two reasons. First, the warming rate is rapid, thus the selective pressures on the most vulnerable organisms may be too strong for the species to adapt. Second, the natural areas that covered most of the globe during past climatic changes are now in much more limited, restricted areas, thus greatly impeding the ability of organisms to migrate to more suitable habitats.

4. Two characteristics can lead to a phenomenon known as biological magnification. First, if a pesticide actually persists in the bodies of target species (that is, it doesn't degrade after having its effect), then depending on its chemical composition, it might actually be sequestered in the bodies of animals that eat the target species. Because large numbers of prey are consumed at each trophic level (due to the 10% rate of transfer of energy), large amounts of the pesticide may be passed up the food chain. So, persistence and magnification can lead to toxic exposures at the top of food chains.

## CHAPTER 60

### LEARNING OUTCOME QUESTIONS

**60.1**  Unfortunately, most of the Earth's biodiversity hotspots are also areas of the greatest human population growth; human population growth is accompanied by increased resource utilization and exploitation.

**60.2**  I would tell the shrimp farmers that if they were to shut down the shrimp farm and remediate the natural mangrove swamp on which their property sits, other, more economically lucrative businesses could be developed, such as timber, charcoal production, and offshore fishing.

**60.3**  Absolutely. The hope of conservation biologists is that even if a species is endangered to the brink of extinction due to habitat degradation, the habitat may someday be restored. The endangered species can be bred in captivity (which also allows for the maintenance of genetic diversity within the species) and either re-introduced to a restored habitat, or even introduced to another suitable habitat.

**60.4**  It depends upon the reason for the degradation of the habitat in the first place, but yes, in some cases, habitat restoration can approach a pristine state. For example, the Nashau River in New England was heavily polluted, but habitat restoration efforts returned it to a relatively pristine state. However, because habitat degradation affects so many species within the ecosystem, and the depth and complexity of the trophic relationships within the ecosystem are difficult if not impossible to fully understand, restoration is rarely if ever truly pristine.

### INQUIRY QUESTIONS

**Page 1260**  Many factors affect human population trends, including resource availability, governmental support for settlement in new areas or for protecting natural areas, and the extent to which governments attempt to manage population growth.

**Page 1262**  The mangroves provide many economic services. For example, without them, fisheries become less productive and storm damage increases. However, because the people who benefit from these services do not own the mangroves, governmental action is needed to ensure that the value of what are economists call "common goods" is protected.

**Page 1266**  On smaller islands, populations tend to be smaller. As we discuss later in this chapter, small populations are vulnerable to many problems, which individually or in concert can heighten the risk of extinction.

**Page 1269**  As discussed in this chapter, populations that are small face many problems that can reinforce one another and eventually cause extinction.

**Page 1274**  As we discussed in chapter 21, allele frequencies change randomly in a process called genetic drift. The smaller the population size, the greater these random fluctuations will be. Thus, small populations are particularly prone to one allele being lost from a population due to these random changes.

### UNDERSTAND
1. a   2. c   3. d   4. d   5. b   6. c

### APPLY
1. d   2. d   3. a   4. d

### SYNTHESIZE

1. Although it is true that extinction is a natural part of the existence of a species, several pieces of evidence suggest that current rates of extinction are much elevated over the natural background level and the disappearance is associated with human activities (which many of the most pronounced extinction events in the history of the Earth were not). It is important to appreciate the length of time over which the estimate of 99% is made. The history of life on Earth extends back billions of years. Certainly, clear patterns of the emergence and extinction of species in the fossil record extend back many hundreds of millions of years. Since the average time of species' existence is short relative to the great expanse of time over which we can estimate the percentage of species that have disappeared, the perception might be that extinction rates have always been high, when in fact the high number is driven by the great expanse of time of measurement. We have very good evidence that modern extinction rates (over human history) are considerably elevated above background levels. Furthermore, the circumstances of the extinctions may be very different because they are also associated with habitat and resource removal; thus potentially limiting the natural processes that replace extinct species.

2. The problem is not unique and not new. It represents a classic conflict that is the basic source of societal laws and regulations, especially in the management of resources. For example, whether or not to place air pollution scrubbers on the smoke stacks of coal-fired power plants is precisely the same issue. In this case, it is not ecosystem conversion, per se, but the fact that the businesses that run the power plants benefit from their operation, but the public "owns" and relies on the atmosphere is a conflict between public and private interests. Some of the ways to navigate the dilemma is for society to create regulations to protect the public interest. The problem is difficult and clearly does not depend solely on economic valuation of the costs and benefits because there can be considerable debate about those estimates. One only has to look at the global climate change problem to suggest how hard it will be to make progress in an expedient manner.

3. This is not a trivial undertaking, which is why, since the first concerns were raised in the late 1980s, it has taken nearly 15 years to collect evidence showing a decline is likely. Although progress has been made on identifying potential causes, much work remains to be done. Many amphibians are secretive, relatively long-lived, and subject to extreme population fluctuations. Given those facts about their biology, documenting population fluctuations (conducting censuses of the number of individuals in populations) for long periods of time is the only way to ultimately establish the likely fate of populations, and that process is time-consuming and costly.

4. Within an ecosystem, every species is dependent upon and depended upon by any number of other species. Even the smallest organisms, bacteria, are often specific about the species they feed upon, live within, parasitize, etc. So, the extinction of a single species anywhere in the ecosystem will affect not only the organisms it directly feeds upon and that directly feed upon it, but also those related more distantly. In the simplest terms, if, for example, a species of rodent goes extinct, the insects and vegetation upon which it feeds would no longer be under the same predation pressure and thus could grow out of control, outcompeting other species and leading to their demise. In addition, the predators of the rodent would have to find other prey, which would result in competition with those species' predators. And so on, and so on. The affects could be catastrophic to the entire ecosystem. By looking at the trophic chains in which a particular organism is involved, one could predict the affects its extinction would have on other species.

5. Population size is not necessarily a direct cause of extinction, but it certainly is an indirect cause. Smaller populations have a number of problems that themselves can lead directly to extinction, such as loss of diversity (and thus increased susceptibility to pathogens) and greater vulnerability to natural catastrophes.

# A

**ABO blood group** A set of four phenotypes produced by different combinations of three alleles at a single locus; blood types are A, B, AB, and O, depending on which alleles are expressed as antigens on the red blood cell surface.

**abscission** In vascular plants, the dropping of leaves, flowers, fruits, or stems at the end of the growing season, as the result of the formation of a layer of specialized cells (the abscission zone) and the action of a hormone (ethylene).

**absorption spectrum** The relationship of absorbance vs. wavelength for a pigment molecule. This indicates which wavelengths are absorbed maximally by a pigment. For example, chlorophyll *a* absorbs most strongly in the violet-blue and red regions of the visible light spectrum.

**acceptor stem** The 3′ end of a tRNA molecule; the portion that amino acids become attached to during the tRNA charging reaction.

**accessory pigment** A secondary light-absorbing pigment used in photosynthesis, including chlorophyll *b* and the carotenoids, that complement the absorption spectrum of chlorophyll *a*.

**aceolomate** An animal, such as a flatworm, having a body plan that has no body cavity; the space between mesoderm and endoderm is filled with cells and organic materials.

**acetyl-CoA** The product of the transition reaction between glycolysis and the Krebs cycle. Pyruvate is oxidized to acetyl-CoA by $NAD^+$, also producing $CO_2$, and NADH.

**achiasmate segregation** The lining up and subsequent separation of homologues during meiosis I without the formation of chiasmata between homologues; found in *Drosophila* males and some other species.

**acid** Any substance that dissociates in water to increase the hydrogen ion ($H^+$) concentration and thus lower the pH.

**actin** One of the two major proteins that make up vertebrate muscle; the other is myosin.

**action potential** A transient, all-or-none reversal of the electric potential across a membrane; in neurons, an action potential initiates transmission of a nerve impulse.

**action spectrum** A measure of the efficiency of different wavelengths of light for photosynthesis. In plants it corresponds to the absorption spectrum of chlorophylls.

**activation energy** The energy that must be processed by a molecule in order for it to undergo a specific chemical reaction.

**active site** The region of an enzyme surface to which a specific set of substrates binds, lowering the activation energy required for a particular chemical reaction and so facilitating it.

**active transport** The pumping of individual ions or other molecules across a cellular membrane from a region of lower concentration to one of higher concentration (i.e., against a concentration gradient); this transport process requires energy, which is typically supplied by the expenditure of ATP.

**adaptation** A peculiarity of structure, physiology, or behavior that promotes the likelihood of an organism's survival and reproduction in a particular environment.

**adapter protein** Any of a class of proteins that acts as a link between a receptor and other proteins to initiate signal transduction.

**adaptive radiation** The evolution of several divergent forms from a primitive and unspecialized ancestor.

**adenosine triphosphate (ATP)** A nucleotide consisting of adenine, ribose sugar, and three phosphate groups; ATP is the energy currency of cellular metabolism in all organisms.

**adherins junction** An anchoring junction that connects the actin filaments of one cell with those of adjacent cells or with the extracellular matrix.

**ATP synthase** The enzyme responsible for producing ATP in oxidative phosphorylation; it uses the energy from a proton gradient to catalyze the reaction $ADP + P_i \longrightarrow ATP$.

**adenylyl cyclase** An enzyme that produces large amounts of cAMP from ATP; the cAMP acts as a second messenger in a target cell.

**adhesion** The tendency of water to cling to other polar compounds due to hydrogen bonding.

**adipose cells** Fat cells, found in loose connective tissue, usually in large groups that form adipose tissue. Each adipose cell can store a droplet of fat (triacylglyceride).

**adventitious** Referring to a structure arising from an unusual place, such as stems from roots or roots from stems.

**aerenchyma** In plants, loose parenchymal tissue with large air spaces in it; often found in plants that grow in water.

**aerobic** Requiring free oxygen; any biological process that can occur in the presence of gaseous oxygen.

**aerobic respiration** The process that results in the complete oxidation of glucose using oxygen as the final electron acceptor. Oxygen acts as the final electron acceptor for an electron transport chain that produces a proton gradient for the chemiosmotic synthesis of ATP.

**aleurone** In plants, the outer layer of the endosperm in a seed; on germination, the aleurone produces α-amylase that breaks down the carbohydrates of the endosperm to nourish the embryo.

**alga**, pl. **algae** A unicellular or simple multicellular photosynthetic organism lacking multicellular sex organs.

**allantois** A membrane of the amniotic egg that functions in respiration and excretion in birds and reptiles and plays an important role in the development of the placenta in most mammals.

**allele** One of two or more alternative states of a gene.

**allele frequency** A measure of the occurrence of an allele in a population, expressed as proportion of the entire population, for example, an occurrence of 0.84 (84%).

**allometric growth** A pattern of growth in which different components grow at different rates.

**allelopathy** The release of a substance from the roots of one plant that block the germination of nearby seeds or inhibits the growth of a neighboring plant.

**allopatric speciation** The differentiation of geographically isolated populations into distinct species.

**allopolyploid** A polyploid organism that contains the genomes of two or more different species.

**allosteric activator** A substance that binds to an enzyme's allosteric site and keeps the enzyme in its active configuration.

**allosteric inhibitor** A noncompetitive inhibitor that binds to an enzyme's allosteric site and prevents the enzyme from changing to its active configuration.

**allosteric site** A part of an enzyme, away from its active site, that serves as an on/off switch for the function of the enzyme.

**alpha (α) helix** A form of secondary structure in proteins where the polypeptide chain is wound into a spiral due to interactions between amino and carboxyl groups in the peptide backbone.

**alternation of generations** A reproductive cycle in which a haploid (*n*) phase (the gametophyte), gives rise to gametes, which, after fusion to form a zygote, germinate to produce a diploid (*2n*) phase (the sporophyte). Spores produced by meiotic division from the sporophyte give rise to new gametophytes, completing the cycle.

**alternative splicing** In eukaryotes, the production of different mRNAs from a single primary transcript by including different sets of exons.

**altruism** Self-sacrifice for the benefit of others; in formal terms, the behavior that increases the fitness of the recipient while reducing the fitness of the altruistic individual.

**alveolus**, pl. **alveoli** One of many small, thin-walled air sacs within the lungs in which the bronchioles terminate.

**amino acid** The subunit structure from which proteins are produced, consisting of a central carbon atom with a carboxyl group (—COOH), an amino group (—NH₂), a hydrogen, and a side group (R group); only the side group differs from one amino acid to another.

**aminoacyl-tRNA synthetase** Any of a group of enzymes that attach specific amino acids to the correct tRNA during the tRNA-charging reaction. Each of the 20 amino acids has a corresponding enzyme.

**amniocentesis** Indirect examination of a fetus by tests on cell cultures grown from fetal cells obtained from a sample of the amniotic fluid or tests on the fluid itself.

**amnion** The innermost of the extraembryonic membranes; the amnion forms a fluid-filled sac around the embryo in amniotic eggs.

**amniote** A vertebrate that produces an egg surrounded by four membranes, one of which is the amnion; amniote groups are the reptiles, birds, and mammals.

**amniotic egg** An egg that is isolated and protected from the environment by a more or less impervious shell during the period of its development and that is completely self-sufficient, requiring only oxygen.

**ampulla** In echinoderms, a muscular sac at the base of a tube foot that contracts to extend the tube foot.

**amyloplast** A plant organelle called a plastid that specializes in storing starch.

**anabolism** The biosynthetic or constructive part of metabolism; those chemical reactions involved in biosynthesis.

**anaerobic** Any process that can occur without oxygen, such as anaerobic fermentation or $H_2S$ photosynthesis.

**anaerobic respiration** The use of electron transport to generate a proton gradient for chemiosmotic synthesis of ATP using a final electron acceptor other than oxygen.

**analogous** Structures that are similar in function but different in evolutionary origin, such as the wing of a bat and the wing of a butterfly.

**anaphase** In mitosis and meiosis II, the stage initiated by the separation of sister chromatids, during which the daughter chromosomes move to opposite poles of the cell; in meiosis I, marked by separation of replicated homologous chromosomes.

**anaphase-promoting complex (APC)** A protein complex that triggers anaphase; it initiates a series of reactions that ultimately degrades cohesin, the protein complex that holds the sister chromatids together. The sister chromatids are then released and move toward opposite poles in the cell.

**anchoring junction** A type of cell junction that mechanically attaches the cytoskeleton of a cell to the cytoskeletons of adjacent cells or to the extracellular matrix.

**androecium** The floral whorl that comprises the stamens.

**aneuploidy** The condition in an organism whose cells have lost or gained a chromosome; Down syndrome, which results from an extra copy of human chromosome 21, is an example of aneuploidy in humans.

**angiosperms** The flowering plants, one of five phyla of seed plants. In angiosperms, the ovules at the time of pollination are completely enclosed by tissues.

**animal pole** In fish and other aquatic vertebrates with asymmetrical yolk distribution in their eggs, the hemisphere of the blastula comprising cells relatively poor in yolk.

**anion** A negatively charged ion.

**annotation** In genomics, the process of identifying and making note of "landmarks" in a DNA sequence to assist with recognition of coding and transcribed regions.

**anonymous markers** Genetic markers in a genome that do not cause a detectable phenotype, but that can be detected using molecular techniques.

**antenna complex** A complex of hundreds of pigment molecules in a photosystem that collects photons and feeds the light energy to a reaction center.

**anther** In angiosperm flowers, the pollen-bearing portion of a stamen.

**antheridium, pl. antheridia** A sperm-producing organ.

**anthropoid** Any member of the mammalian group consisting of monkeys, apes, and humans.

**antibody** A protein called immunoglobulin that is produced by lymphocytes in response to a foreign substance (antigen) and released into the bloodstream.

**anticodon** The three-nucleotide sequence at the end of a transfer RNA molecule that is complementary to, and base-pairs with, an amino-acid–specifying codon in messenger RNA.

**antigen** A foreign substance, usually a protein or polysaccharide, that stimulates an immune response.

**antiporter** A carrier protein in a cell's membrane that transports two molecules in opposite directions across the membrane.

**anus** The terminal opening of the gut; the solid residues of digestion are eliminated through the anus.

**aorta** (Gr. *aeirein*, to lift) The major artery of vertebrate systemic blood circulation; in mammals, carries oxygenated blood away from the heart to all regions of the body except the lungs.

**apical meristem** In vascular plants, the growing point at the tip of the root or stem.

**apoplast route** In plant roots, the pathway for movement of water and minerals that leads through cell walls and between cells.

**apoptosis** A process of programmed cell death, in which dying cells shrivel and shrink; used in all animal cell development to produce planned and orderly elimination of cells not destined to be present in the final tissue.

**aposematic coloration** An ecological strategy of some organisms that "advertise" their poisonous nature by the use of bright colors.

**aquaporin** A membrane channel that allows water to cross the membrane more easily than by diffusion through the membrane.

**aquifers** Permeable, saturated, underground layers of rock, sand, and gravel, which serve as reservoirs for groundwater.

**archegonium, pl. archegonia** The multicellular egg-producing organ in bryophytes and some vascular plants.

**archenteron** The principal cavity of a vertebrate embryo in the gastrula stage; lined with endoderm, it opens up to the outside and represents the future digestive cavity.

**arteriole** A smaller artery, leading from the arteries to the capillaries.

**artificial selection** Change in the genetic structure of populations due to selective breeding by humans. Many domestic animal breeds and crop varieties have been produced through artificial selection.

**ascomycetes** A large group comprising part of the "true fungi." They are characterized by separate hyphae, asexually produced conidiospores, and sexually produced ascospores within asci.

**ascus, pl. asci** A specialized cell, characteristic of the ascomycetes, in which two haploid nuclei fuse to produce a zygote that divides immediately by meiosis; at maturity, an ascus contains ascospores.

**asexual reproduction** The process by which an individual inherits all of its chromosomes from a single parent, thus being genetically identical to that parent; cell division is by mitosis only.

**A site** In a ribosome, the aminoacyl site, which binds to the tRNA carrying the next amino acid to be added to a polypeptide chain.

**assembly** The phase of a virus's reproductive cycle during which the newly made components are assembled into viral particles.

**assortative mating** A type of nonrandom mating in which phenotypically similar individuals mate more frequently.

**aster** In animal cell mitosis, a radial array of microtubules extending from the centrioles toward the plasma membrane, possibly serving to brace the centrioles for retraction of the spindle.

**atom** The smallest unit of an element that contains all the characteristics of that element. Atoms are the building blocks of matter.

**atrial peptide** Any of a group of small polypeptide hormones that may be useful in treatment of high blood pressure and kidney failure; produced by cells in the atria of the heart.

**atrioventricular (AV) node** A slender connection of cardiac muscle cells that receives the heartbeat impulses from the sinoatrial node and conducts them by way of the bundle of His.

**atrium** An antechamber; in the heart, a thin-walled chamber that receives venous blood and passes it on to the thick-walled ventricle; in the ear, the tympanic cavity.

**autonomic nervous system** The involuntary neurons and ganglia of the peripheral nervous system of vertebrates; regulates the heart, glands, visceral organs, and smooth muscle.

**autopolyploid** A polyploid organism that contains a duplicated genome of the same species; may result from a meiotic error.

**autosome** Any eukaryotic chromosome that is not a sex chromosome; autosomes are present in the same number and kind in both males and females of the species.

**autotroph** An organism able to build all the complex organic molecules that it requires as its own food source, using only simple inorganic compounds.

**auxin** (Gr. *auxein*, to increase) A plant hormone that controls cell elongation, among other effects.

**auxotroph** A mutation, or the organism that carries it, that affects a biochemical pathway causing a nutritional requirement.

**avirulent pathogen** Any type of normally pathogenic organism or virus that utilizes host resources but does not cause extensive damage or death.

**axil** In plants, the angle between a leaf's petiole and the stem to which it is attached.

**axillary bud** In plants, a bud found in the axil of a stem and leaf; an axillary bud may develop into a new shoot or may become a flower.

**axon** A process extending out from a neuron that conducts impulses away from the cell body.

# B

*b6–f* complex *See* cytochrome *b6–f* complex.

**bacteriophage** A virus that infects bacterial cells; also called a *phage*.

**Barr body** A deeply staining structure, seen in the interphase nucleus of a cell of an individual with more than one X chromosome, that is a condensed and inactivated X. Only one X remains active in each cell after early embryogenesis.

**basal body** A self-reproducing, cylindrical, cytoplasmic organelle composed of nine triplets of microtubules from which the flagella or cilia arise.

**base** Any substance that dissociates in water to absorb and therefore decrease the hydrogen ion ($H^+$) concentration and thus raise the pH.

**base-pair** A complementary pair of nucleotide bases, consisting of a purine and a pyrimidine.

**basidium, pl. basidia** A specialized reproductive cell of the basidiomycetes, often club-shaped, in which nuclear fusion and meiosis occur.

**basophil** A leukocyte containing granules that rupture and release chemicals that enhance the inflammatory response. Important in causing allergic responses.

**Batesian mimicry** A survival strategy in which a palatable or nontoxic organism resembles another kind of organism that is distasteful or toxic. Both species exhibit warning coloration.

**B cell** A type of lymphocyte that, when confronted with a suitable antigen, is capable of secreting a specific antibody protein.

**behavioral ecology** The study of how natural selection shapes behavior.

**biennial** A plant that normally requires two growing seasons to complete its life cycle. Biennials flower in the second year of their lives.

**bilateral symmetry** A single plane divides an organism into two structural halves that are mirror images of each other.

**bile salts** A solution of organic salts that is secreted by the vertebrate liver and temporarily stored in the gallbladder; emulsifies fats in the small intestine.

**binary fission** Asexual reproduction by division of one cell or body into two equal or nearly equal parts.

**binomial distribution** The distribution of phenotypes seen among the progeny of a cross in which there are only two alternative alleles.

**binomial name** The scientific name of a species that consists of two parts, the genus name and the specific species name, for example, *Apis mellifera*.

**biochemical pathway** A sequence of chemical reactions in which the product of one reaction becomes the substrate of the next reaction. The Krebs cycle is a biochemical pathway.

**biodiversity** The number of species and their range of behavioral, ecological, physiological, and other adaptations, in an area.

**bioenergetics** The analysis of how energy powers the activities of living systems.

**biofilm** A complex bacterial community comprising different species; plaque on teeth is a biofilm.

**biogeography** The study of the geographic distribution of species.

**biological community** All the populations of different species living together in one place; for example, all populations that inhabit a mountain meadow.

**biological species concept (BSC)** The concept that defines species as groups of populations that have the potential to interbreed and that are reproductively isolated from other groups.

**biomass** The total mass of all the living organisms in a given population, area, or other unit being measured.

**biome** One of the major terrestrial ecosystems, characterized by climatic and soil conditions; the largest ecological unit.

**bipolar cell** A specialized type of neuron connecting cone cells to ganglion cells in the visual system. Bipolar cells receive a hyperpolarized stimulus from the cone cell and then transmit a depolarization stimulus to the ganglion cell.

**biramous** Two-branched; describes the appendages of crustaceans.

**blade** The broad, expanded part of a leaf; also called the lamina.

**blastocoel** The central cavity of the blastula stage of vertebrate embryos.

**blastodisc** In the development of birds, a disclike area on the surface of a large, yolky egg that undergoes cleavage and gives rise to the embryo.

**blastomere** One of the cells of a blastula.

**blastopore** In vertebrate development, the opening that connects the archenteron cavity of a gastrula stage embryo with the outside.

**blastula** In vertebrates, an early embryonic stage consisting of a hollow, fluid-filled ball of cells one layer thick; a vertebrate embryo after cleavage and before gastrulation.

**Bohr effect** The release of oxygen by hemoglobin molecules in response to elevated ambient levels of $CO_2$.

**bottleneck effect** A loss of genetic variability that occurs when a population is reduced drastically in size.

**Bowman's capsule** In the vertebrate kidney, the bulbous unit of the nephron, which surrounds the glomerulus.

**β-oxidation** The oxygen-dependent reactions where 2-carbon units of fatty acids are cleaved and combined with CoA to produce acetyl-CoA, which then enters the Krebs cycle. This occurs cyclically until the entire fatty acid is oxidized.

**β sheet** A form of secondary structure in proteins where the polypeptide folds back on itself one or more times to form a planar structure stabilized by hydrogen bonding between amino and carboxyl groups in the peptide backbone. Also known as a β-pleated sheet.

**book lung** In some spiders, a unique respiratory system consisting of leaflike plates within a chamber over which gas exchange occurs.

**bronchus, pl. bronchi** One of a pair of respiratory tubes branching from the lower end of the trachea (windpipe) into either lung.

**bud** An asexually produced outgrowth that develops into a new individual. In plants, an embryonic shoot, often protected by young leaves; buds may give rise to branch shoots.

**buffer** A substance that resists changes in pH. It releases hydrogen ions ($H^+$) when a base is added and absorbs $H^+$ when an acid is added.

# C

**$C_3$ photosynthesis** The main cycle of the dark reactions of photosynthesis, in which $CO_2$ binds to ribulose 1,5-bisphosphate (RuBP) to form two 3-carbon phosphoglycerate (PGA) molecules.

**$C_4$ photosynthesis** A process of $CO_2$ fixation in photosynthesis by which the first product is the 4-carbon oxaloacetate molecule.

**cadherin** One of a large group of transmembrane proteins that contain a $Ca^{2+}$-mediated binding between cells; these proteins are responsible for cell-to-cell adhesion between cells of the same type.

**callus** Undifferentiated tissue; a term used in tissue culture, grafting, and wound healing.

**Calvin cycle** The dark reactions of $C_3$ photosynthesis; also called the Calvin–Benson cycle.

**calyx** The sepals collectively; the outermost flower whorl.

**CAM plant** Plants that use $C_4$ carbon fixation at night, then use the stored malate to generate $CO_2$ during the day to minimize dessication.

**Cambrian explosion** The huge increase in animal diversity that occurred at the beginning of the Cambrian period.

**cAMP response protein (CRP)** *See* catabolite activator protein (CAP)

**cancer** The unrestrained growth and division of cells; it results from a failure of cell division control.

**capillary** The smallest of the blood vessels; the very thin walls of capillaries are permeable to many molecules, and exchanges between blood and the tissues occur across them; the vessels that connect arteries with veins.

**capsid** The outermost protein covering of a virus.

**capsule** In bacteria, a gelatinous layer surrounding the cell wall.

**carapace** (Fr. from Sp. *carapacho*, shell) Shieldlike plate covering the cephalothorax of decapod crustaceans; the dorsal part of the shell of a turtle.

**carbohydrate** An organic compound consisting of a chain or ring of carbon atoms to which hydrogen and oxygen atoms are attached in a ratio of approximately 2:1; having the generalized formula $(CH_2O)_n$; carbohydrates include sugars, starch, glycogen, and cellulose.

**carbon fixation** The conversion of $CO_2$ into organic compounds during photosynthesis; the first stage of the dark reactions of photosynthesis, in which carbon dioxide from the air is combined with ribulose 1,5-bisphosphate.

**carotenoid** Any of a group of accessory pigments found in plants; in addition to absorbing light energy, these pigments act as antioxidants, scavenging potentially damaging free radicals.

**carpel** A leaflike organ in angiosperms that encloses one or more ovules.

**carrier protein** A membrane protein that binds to a specific molecule that cannot cross the membrane and allows passage through the membrane.

**carrying capacity** The maximum population size that a habitat can support.

**cartilage** A connective tissue in skeletons of vertebrates. Cartilage forms much of the skeleton of embryos, very young vertebrates, and some adult vertebrates, such as sharks and their relatives.

**Casparian strip** In plants, a band that encircles the cell wall of root endodermal cells. Adjacent cells' strips connect, forming a layer through which water cannot pass; therefore, all water entering roots must pass through cell membranes and cytoplasm.

**catabolism** In a cell, those metabolic reactions that result in the breakdown of complex molecules into simpler compounds, often with the release of energy.

**catabolite activator protein (CAP)** A protein that, when bound to cAMP, can bind to DNA and activate transcription. The level of cAMP is inversely related to the level of glucose, and CAP/cAMP in *E. coli* activates the *lac* (lactose) operon. Also called *cAMP response protein* (*CRP*).

**catalysis** The process by which chemical subunits of larger organic molecules are held and positioned by enzymes that stress their chemical bonds, leading to the disassembly of the larger molecule into its subunits, often with the release of energy.

**cation** A positively charged ion.

**cavitation** In plants and animals, the blockage of a vessel by an air bubble that breaks the cohesion of the solution in the vessel; in animals more often called embolism.

**CD4⁺ cell** A subtype of helper T cell that is identified by the presence of the CD4 protein on its surface. This cell type is targeted by the HIV virus that causes AIDS.

**cecum** In vertebrates, a blind pouch at the beginning of the large intestine.

**cell cycle** The repeating sequence of growth and division through which cells pass each generation.

**cell determination** The molecular "decision" process by which a cell becomes destined for a particular developmental pathway. This occurs before overt differentiation and can be a stepwise process.

**cell-mediated immunity** Arm of the adaptive immune system mediated by T cells, which includes cytotoxic cells and cells that assist the rest of the immune system.

**cell plate** The structure that forms at the equator of the spindle during early telophase in the dividing cells of plants and a few green algae.

**cell-surface marker** A glycoprotein or glycolipid on the outer surface of a cell's membrane that acts as an identifier; different cell types carry different markers.

**cell-surface receptor** A cell surface protein that binds a signal molecule and converts the extracellular signal into an intracellular one.

**cellular blastoderm** In insect embryonic development, the stage during which the nuclei of the syncitial blastoderm become separate cells through membrane formation.

**cellular respiration** The metabolic harvesting of energy by oxidation, ultimately dependent on molecular oxygen; carried out by the Krebs cycle and oxidative phosphorylation.

**cellulose** The chief constituent of the cell wall in all green plants, some algae, and a few other organisms; an insoluble complex carbohydrate formed of microfibrils of glucose molecules.

**cell wall** The rigid, outermost layer of the cells of plants, some protists, and most bacteria; the cell wall surrounds the plasma membrane.

**central nervous system (CNS)** That portion of the nervous system where most association occurs; in vertebrates, it is composed of the brain and spinal cord; in invertebrates, it usually consists of one or more cords of nervous tissue, together with their associated ganglia.

**central vacuole** A large, membrane-bounded sac found in plant cells that stores proteins, pigments, and waste materials, and is involved in water balance.

**centriole** A cytoplasmic organelle located outside the nuclear membrane, identical in structure to a basal body; found in animal cells and in the flagellated cells of other groups; divides and organizes spindle fibers during mitosis and meiosis.

**centromere** A visible point of constriction on a chromosome that contains repeated DNA sequences that bind specific proteins. These proteins make up the kinetochore to which microtubules attach during cell division.

**cephalization** The evolution of a head and brain area in the anterior end of animals; thought to be a consequence of bilateral symmetry.

**cerebellum** The hindbrain region of the vertebrate brain that lies above the medulla (brainstem) and behind the forebrain; it integrates information about body position and motion, coordinates muscular activities, and maintains equilibrium.

**cerebral cortex** The thin surface layer of neurons and glial cells covering the cerebrum; well developed only in mammals, and particularly prominent in humans. The cerebral cortex is the seat of conscious sensations and voluntary muscular activity.

**cerebrum** The portion of the vertebrate brain (the forebrain) that occupies the upper part of the skull, consisting of two cerebral hemispheres united by the corpus callosum. It is the primary association center of the brain. It coordinates and processes sensory input and coordinates motor responses.

**chaetae** Bristles of chitin on each body segment that help anchor annelid worms during locomotion.

**channel protein (ion channel)** A transmembrane protein with a hydrophilic interior that provides an aqueous channel allowing diffusion of species that cannot cross the membrane. Usually allows passage of specific ions such as $K^+$, $Na^+$, or $Ca^{2+}$ across the membrane.

**chaperone protein** A class of enzymes that help proteins fold into the correct configuration and can refold proteins that have been misfolded or denatured.

**character displacement** A process in which natural selection favors individuals in a species that use resources not used by other species. This results in evolutionary change leading to species dissimilar in resource use.

**character state** In cladistics, one of two or more distinguishable forms of a character, such as the presence or absence of teeth in amniote vertebrates.

**charging reaction** The reaction by which an aminoacyl-tRNA synthetase attaches a specific amino acid to the correct tRNA using energy from ATP.

**chelicera**, pl. **chelicerae** The first pair of appendages in horseshoe crabs, sea spiders, and arachnids—the chelicerates, a group of arthropods. Chelicerae usually take the form of pincers or fangs.

**chemical synapse** A close association that allows chemical communication between neurons. A chemical signal (neurotransmitter) released by the first neuron binds to receptors in the membrane of the second neurons.

**chemiosmosis** The mechanism by which ATP is generated in mitochondria and chloroplasts; energetic electrons excited by light (in chloroplasts) or extracted by oxidation in the Krebs cycle (in mitochondria) are used to drive proton pumps, creating a proton concentration gradient; when protons subsequently flow back across the membrane, they pass through channels that couple their movement to the synthesis of ATP.

**chiasma** An X-shaped figure that can be seen in the light microscope during meiosis; evidence of crossing over, where two chromatids have exchanged parts; chiasmata move to the ends of the chromosome arms as the homologues separate.

**chitin** A tough, resistant, nitrogen-containing polysaccharide that forms the cell walls of certain fungi, the exoskeleton of arthropods, and the epidermal cuticle of other surface structures of certain other invertebrates.

**chlorophyll** The primary type of light-absorbing pigment in photosynthesis. Chlorophyll *a* absorbs light in the violet-blue and the red ranges of the visible light spectrum; chlorophyll *b* is an accessory pigment to chlorophyll *a*, absorbing light in the blue and red-orange ranges. Neither pigment absorbs light in the green range, 500–600 nm.

**chloroplast** A cell-like organelle present in algae and plants that contains chlorophyll (and usually other pigments) and carries out photosynthesis.

**choanocyte** A specialized flagellated cell found in sponges; choanocytes line the body interior.

**chorion** The outer member of the double membrane that surrounds the embryo of reptiles, birds, and mammals; in placental mammals, it contributes to the structure of the placenta.

**chorionic villi sampling** A technique in which fetal cells are sampled from the chorion of the placenta rather than from the amniotic fluid; this less invasive technique can be used earlier in pregnancy than amniocentesis.

**chromatid** One of the two daughter strands of a duplicated chromosome that is joined by a single centromere.

**chromatin** The complex of DNA and proteins of which eukaryotic chromosomes are composed; chromatin is highly uncoiled and diffuse in interphase nuclei, condensing to form the visible chromosomes in prophase.

**chromatin-remodeling complex** A large protein complex that has been found to modify histones and DNA and that can change the structure of chromatin, moving or transferring nucleosomes.

**chromosomal mutation** Any mutation that affects chromosome structure.

**chromosome** The vehicle by which hereditary information is physically transmitted from one generation to the next; in a bacterium, the chromosome consists of a single naked circle of DNA; in eukaryotes, each chromosome consists of a single linear DNA molecule and associated proteins.

**chromosomal theory of inheritance** The theory stating that hereditary traits are carried on chromosomes.

**cilium** A short cellular projection from the surface of a eukaryotic cell, having the same internal structure of microtubules in a 9 + 2 arrangement as seen in a flagellum.

**circadian rhythm** An endogenous cyclical rhythm that oscillates on a daily (24-hour) basis.

**circulatory system** A network of vessels in coelomate animals that carries fluids to and from different areas of the body.

**cisterna** A small collecting vessel that pinches off from the end of a Golgi body to form a transport vesicle that moves materials through the cytoplasm.

**cisternal space** The inner region of a membrane-bounded structure. Usually used to describe the interior of the endoplasmic reticulum; also called the *lumen*.

**clade** A taxonomic group composed of an ancestor and all its descendents.

**cladistics** A taxonomic technique used for creating hierarchies of organisms that represent true phylogenetic relationship and descent.

**class** A taxonomic category between phyla and orders. A class contains one or more orders, and belongs to a particular phylum.

**classical conditioning** The repeated presentation of a stimulus in association with a response that causes the brain to form an association between the stimulus and the response, even if they have never been associated before.

**clathrin** A protein located just inside the plasma membrane in eukaryotic cells, in indentations called clathrin-coated pits.

**cleavage** In vertebrates, a rapid series of successive cell divisions of a fertilized egg, forming a hollow sphere of cells, the blastula.

**cleavage furrow** The constriction that forms during cytokinesis in animal cells that is responsible for dividing the cell into two daughter cells.

**climax vegetation** Vegetation encountered in a self-perpetuating community of plants that has proceeded through all the stages of succession and stabilized.

**cloaca** In some animals, the common exit chamber from the digestive, reproductive, and urinary system; in others, the cloaca may also serve as a respiratory duct.

**clone-by-clone sequencing** A method of genome sequencing in which a physical map is constructed first, followed by sequencing of fragments and identifying overlap regions.

**clonal selection** Amplification of a clone of immune cells initiated by antigen recognition.

**cloning** Producing a cell line or culture all of whose members contain identical copies of a particular nucleotide sequence; an essential element in genetic engineering.

**closed circulatory system** A circulatory system in which the blood is physically separated from other body fluids.

**coacervate** A spherical aggregation of lipid molecules in water, held together by hydrophobic forces.

**coactivator** A protein that functions to link transcriptional activators to the transcription complex consisting of RNA polymerase II and general transcription factors.

**cochlea** In terrestrial vertebrates, a tubular cavity of the inner ear containing the essential organs for hearing.

**coding strand** The strand of a DNA duplex that is the same as the RNA encoded by a gene. This strand is not used as a template in transcription, it is complementary to the template.

**codominance** Describes a case in which two or more alleles of a gene are each dominant to other alleles but not to each other. The phenotype of a heterozygote for codominant alleles exhibit characteristics of each of the homozygous forms. For example, in human blood types, a cross between an AA individual and a BB individual yields AB individuals.

**codon** The basic unit of the genetic code; a sequence of three adjacent nucleotides in DNA or mRNA that codes for one amino acid.

**coelom** In animals, a fluid-filled body cavity that develops entirely within the mesoderm.

**coenzyme** A nonprotein organic molecule such as NAD that plays an accessory role in enzyme-catalyzed processes, often by acting as a donor or acceptor of electrons.

**coevolution** The simultaneous development of adaptations in two or more populations, species, or other categories that interact so closely that each is a strong selective force on the other.

**cofactor** One or more nonprotein components required by enzymes in order to function; many cofactors are metal ions, others are organic coenzymes.

**cohesin** A protein complex that holds sister chromatids together during cell division. The loss of cohesins at the centromere allow the anaphase movement of chromosomes.

**collenchyma cell** In plants, the cells that form a supporting tissue called collenchyma; often found in regions of primary growth in stems and in some leaves.

**colloblast** A specialized type of cell found in members of the animal phylum Ctenophora (comb jellies) that bursts on contact with zooplankton, releasing an adhesive substance to help capture this prey.

**colonial flagellate hypothesis** The proposal first put forth by Haeckel that metazoans descended from colonial protists; supported by the similarity of sponges to choanoflagellate protists.

**commensalism** A relationship in which one individual lives close to or on another and benefits, and the host is unaffected; a kind of symbiosis.

**community** All of the species inhabiting a common environment and interacting with one another.

**companion cell** A specialized parenchyma cell that is associated with each sieve-tube member in the phloem of a plant.

**competitive exclusion** The hypothesis that two species with identical ecological requirements cannot exist in the same locality indefinitely, and that the more efficient of the two in utilizing the available scarce resources will exclude the other; also known as Gause's principle.

**competitive inhibitor** An inhibitor that binds to the same active site as an enzyme's substrate, thereby competing with the substrate.

**complementary** Describes genetic information in which each nucleotide base has a complementary partner with which it forms a base-pair.

**complementary DNA (cDNA)** A DNA copy of an mRNA transcript; produced by the action of the enzyme reverse transcriptase.

**complement system** The chemical defense of a vertebrate body that consists of a battery of proteins that become activated by the walls of bacteria and fungi.

**complete digestive system** A digestive system that has both a mouth and an anus, allowing unidirectional flow of ingested food.

**compound eye** An organ of sight in many arthropods composed of many independent visual units called ommatidia.

**concentration gradient** A difference in concentration of a substance from one location to another, often across a membrane.

**condensin** A protein complex involved in condensation of chromosomes during mitosis and meiosis.

**cone** (1) In plants, the reproductive structure of a conifer. (2) In vertebrates, a type of light-sensitive neuron in the retina concerned with the perception of color and with the most acute discrimination of detail.

**conidia** An asexually produced fungal spore.

**conjugation** Temporary union of two unicellular organisms, during which genetic material is transferred from one cell to the other; occurs in bacteria, protists, and certain algae and fungi.

**consensus sequence** In genome sequencing, the overall sequence that is consistent with the sequences of individual fragments; computer programs are used to compare sequences and generate a consensus sequence.

**conservation of synteny** The preservation over evolutionary time of arrangements of DNA segments in related species.

**contig** A contiguous segment of DNA assembled by analyzing sequence overlaps from smaller fragments.

**continuous variation** Variation in a trait that occurs along a continuum, such as the trait of height in human beings; often occurs when a trait is determined by more than one gene.

**contractile vacuole** In protists and some animals, a clear fluid-filled vacuole that takes up water from within the cell and then contracts, releasing it to the outside through a pore in a cyclical manner; functions primarily in osmoregulation and excretion.

**conus arteriosus** The anteriormost chamber of the embryonic heart in vertebrate animals.

**convergent evolution** The independent development of similar structures in organisms that are not directly related; often found in organisms living in similar environments.

**cork cambium** The lateral meristem that forms the periderm, producing cork (phellem) toward the surface (outside) of the plant and phelloderm toward the inside.

**cornea** The transparent outer layer of the vertebrate eye.

**corolla** The petals, collectively; usually the conspicuously colored flower whorl.

**corpus callosum** The band of nerve fibers that connects the two hemispheres of the cerebrum in humans and other primates.

**corpus luteum** A structure that develops from a ruptured follicle in the ovary after ovulation.

**cortex** The outer layer of a structure; in animals, the outer, as opposed to the inner, part of an organ; in vascular plants, the primary ground tissue of a stem or root.

**cotyledon** A seed leaf that generally stores food in dicots or absorbs it in monocots, providing nourishment used during seed germination.

**crassulacean acid metabolism (CAM)** A mode of carbon dioxide fixation by which $CO_2$ enters open leaf stomata at night and is used in photosynthesis during the day, when stomata are closed to prevent water loss.

**crista** A folded extension of the inner membrane of a mitochondrion. Mitochondria contain numerous cristae.

**cross-current flow** In bird lungs, the latticework of capillaries arranged across the air flow, at a 90° angle.

**crossing over** In meiosis, the exchange of corresponding chromatid segments between homologous chromosomes; responsible for genetic recombination between homologous chromosomes.

**ctenidia** Respiratory gills of mollusks; they consist of a system of filamentous projections of the mantle that are rich in blood vessels.

**cuticle** A waxy or fatty, noncellular layer (formed of a substance called cutin) on the outer wall of epidermal cells.

**cutin** In plants, a fatty layer produced by the epidermis that forms the cuticle on the outside surface.

**cyanobacteria** A group of photosynthetic bacteria, sometimes called the "blue-green algae," that contain the chlorophyll pigments most abundant in plants and algae, as well as other pigments.

**cyclic AMP (cAMP)** A form of adenosine monophosphate (AMP) in which the atoms of the phosphate group form a ring; found in almost all organisms, cAMP functions as an intracellular second messenger that regulates a diverse array of metabolic activities.

**cyclic photophosphorylation** Reactions that begin with the absorption of light by reaction center chlorophyll that excites an electron. The excited electron returns to the photosystem, generating ATP by chemiosmosis in the process. This is found in the single bacterial photosystem, and can occur in plants in photosystem I.

**cyclin** Any of a number of proteins that are produced in synchrony with the cell cycle and combine with certain protein kinases, the cyclin-dependent kinases, at certain points during cell division.

**cyclin-dependent kinase (Cdk)** Any of a group of protein kinase enzymes that control progress through the cell cycle. These enzymes are only active when complexed with cyclin. The cdc2 protein, produced by the *cdc2* gene, was the first Cdk enzyme discovered.

**cytochrome** Any of several iron-containing protein pigments that serve as electron carriers in transport chains of photosynthesis and cellular respiration.

**cytochrome *b6–f* complex** A proton pump found in the thylakoid membrane. This complex uses energy from excited electrons to pump protons from the stroma into the thylakoid compartment.

**cytokinesis** Division of the cytoplasm of a cell after nuclear division.

**cytokine** Signaling molecules secreted by immune cells that affect other immune cells.

**cytoplasm** The material within a cell, excluding the nucleus; the protoplasm.

**cytoskeleton** A network of protein microfilaments and microtubules within the cytoplasm of a eukaryotic cell that maintains the shape of the cell, anchors its organelles, and is involved in animal cell motility.

**cytosol** The fluid portion of the cytoplasm; it contains dissolved organic molecules and ions.

**cytotoxic T cell** A special T cell activated during cell-mediated immune response that recognizes and destroys infected body cells.

# D

**deamination** The removal of an amino group; part of the degradation of proteins into compounds that can enter the Krebs cycle.

**deductive reasoning** The logical application of general principles to predict a specific result. In science, deductive reasoning is used to test the validity of general ideas.

**dehydration reaction** A type of chemical reaction in which two molecules join to form one larger molecule, simultaneously splitting out a molecule of water; one molecule is stripped of a hydrogen atom, and another is stripped of a hydroxyl group (—OH), resulting in the joining of the two molecules, while the H and —OH released may combine to form a water molecule.

**dehydrogenation** Chemical reaction involving the loss of a hydrogen atom. This is an oxidation that combines loss of an electron with loss of a proton.

**deletion** A mutation in which a portion of a chromosome is lost; if too much information is lost, the deletion can be fatal.

**demography** The properties of the rate of growth and the age structure of populations.

**denaturation** The loss of the native configuration of a protein or nucleic acid as a result of excessive heat, extremes of pH, chemical modification, or changes in solvent ionic strength or polarity that disrupt hydrophobic interactions; usually accompanied by loss of biological activity.

**dendrite** A process extending from the cell body of a neuron, typically branched, that conducts impulses toward the cell body.

**deoxyribonucleic acid (DNA)** The genetic material of all organisms; composed of two complementary chains of nucleotides wound in a double helix.

**dephosphorylation** The removal of a phosphate group, usually by a phosphatase enzyme. Many proteins can be activated or inactivated by dephosphorylation.

**depolarization** The movement of ions across a plasma membrane that locally wipes out an electrical potential difference.

**derived character** A characteristic used in taxonomic analysis representing a departure from the primitive form.

**dermal tissue** In multicellular organisms, a type of tissue that forms the outer layer of the body and is in contact with the environment; it has a protective function.

**desmosome** A type of anchoring junction that links adjacent cells by connecting their cytoskeletons with cadherin proteins.

**derepression** Seen in anabolic operons where the operon that encodes the enzymes for a biochemical pathway is repressed in the presence of the end product of the pathway and derepressed in the absence of the end product. This allows production of the enzymes only when they are necessary.

**determinate development** A type of development in animals in which each embryonic cell has a predetermined fate in terms of what kind of tissue it will form in the adult.

**deuterostome** Any member of a grouping of bilaterally symmetrical animals in which the anus develops first and the mouth second; echinoderms and vertebrates are deuterostome animals.

**diacylglycerol (DAG)** A second messenger that is released, along with inositol-1,4,5-trisphosphate ($IP_3$), when phospholipase C cleaves $PIP_2$. DAG can have a variety of cellular effects through activation of protein kinases.

**diaphragm** (1) In mammals, a sheet of muscle tissue that separates the abdominal and thoracic cavities and functions in breathing. (2) A contraceptive device used to block the entrance to the uterus temporarily and thus prevent sperm from entering during sexual intercourse.

**diapsid** Any of a group of reptiles that have two pairs of temporal openings in the skull, one lateral and one more dorsal; one lineage of this group gave rise to dinosaurs, modern reptiles, and birds.

**diastolic pressure** In the measurement of human blood pressure, the minimum pressure between heartbeats (repolarization of the ventricles). *Compare with* systolic pressure.

**dicer** An enzyme that generates small RNA molecules in a cell by chopping up double-stranded RNAs; dicer produces miRNAs and siRNAs.

**dicot** Short for dicotyledon; a class of flowering plants generally characterized as having two cotyledons, net-veined leaves, and flower parts usually in fours or fives.

**dideoxynucleotide** A nucleotide lacking —OH groups at both the 2′ and 3′ positions; used as a chain terminator in the enzymatic sequencing of DNA.

**differentiation** A developmental process by which a relatively unspecialized cell undergoes a progressive change to a more specialized form or function.

**diffusion** The net movement of dissolved molecules or other particles from a region where they are more concentrated to a region where they are less concentrated.

**dihybrid** An individual heterozygous at two different loci; for example *A/a B/b*.

**dihybrid cross** A single genetic cross involving two different traits, such as flower color and plant height.

**dikaryotic** In fungi, having pairs of nuclei within each cell.

**dioecious** Having the male and female elements on different individuals.

**diploid** Having two sets of chromosomes (2n); in animals, twice the number characteristic of gametes; in plants, the chromosome number characteristic of the sporophyte generation; in contrast to haploid (n).

**directional selection** A form of selection in which selection acts to eliminate one extreme from an array of phenotypes.

**disaccharide** A carbohydrate formed of two simple sugar molecules bonded covalently.

**disruptive selection** A form of selection in which selection acts to eliminate rather than favor the intermediate type.

**dissociation** In proteins, the reversible separation of protein subunits from a quaternary structure without altering their tertiary structure. Also refers to the dissolving of ionic compounds in water.

**disassortative mating** A type of nonrandom mating in which phenotypically different individuals mate more frequently.

**diurnal** Active during the day.

**DNA-binding motif** A region found in a regulatory protein that is capable of binding to a specific base sequence in DNA; a critical part of the protein's DNA-binding domain.

**DNA fingerprinting** An identification technique that makes use of a variety of molecular techniques to identify differences in the DNA of individuals.

**DNA gyrase** A topoisomerase involved in DNA replication; it relieves the torsional strain caused by unwinding the DNA strands.

**DNA library** A collection of DNAs in a vector (a plasmid, phage, or artificial chromosome) that taken together represent a complex mixture of DNAs, such as the entire genome, or the cDNAs made from all of the mRNA in a specific cell type.

**DNA ligase** The enzyme responsible for formation of phosphodiester bonds between adjacent nucleotides in DNA.

**DNA microarray** An array of DNA fragments on a microscope slide or silicon chip, used in hybridization experiments with labeled mRNA or DNA to identify active and inactive genes, or the presence or absence of particular sequences.

**DNA polymerase** A class of enzymes that all synthesize DNA from a preexisting template. All synthesize only in the 5′-to-3′ direction, and require a primer to extend.

**DNA vaccine** A type of vaccine that uses DNA from a virus or bacterium that stimulates the cellular immune response.

**domain** (1) A distinct modular region of a protein that serves a particular function in the action of the protein, such as a regulatory domain or a DNA-binding domain. (2) In taxonomy, the level higher than kingdom. The three domains currently recognized are Bacteria, Archaea, and Eukarya.

**Domain Archaea** In the three-domain system of taxonomy, the group that contains only the Archaea, a highly diverse group of unicellular prokaryotes.

**Domain Bacteria** In the three-domain system of taxonomy, the group that contains only the Bacteria, a vast group of unicellular prokaryotes.

**Domain Eukarya** In the three-domain system of taxonomy, the group that contains eukaryotic organisms including protists, fungi, plants, and animals.

**dominant** An allele that is expressed when present in either the heterozygous or the homozygous condition.

**dosage compensation** A phenomenon by which the expression of genes carried on sex chromosomes is kept the same in males and females, despite a different number of sex chromosomes. In mammals, inactivation of one of the X chromosomes in female cells accomplishes dosage compensation.

**double fertilization** The fusion of the egg and sperm (resulting in a 2n fertilized egg, the zygote) and the simultaneous fusion of the second male gamete with the polar nuclei (resulting in a primary endosperm nucleus, which is often triploid, 3n); a unique characteristic of all angiosperms.

**double helix** The structure of DNA, in which two complementary polynucleotide strands coil around a common helical axis.

**duodenum** In vertebrates, the upper portion of the small intestine.

**duplication** A mutation in which a portion of a chromosome is duplicated; if the duplicated region does not lie within a gene, the duplication may have no effect.

# E

**ecdysis** Shedding of outer, cuticular layer; molting, as in insects or crustaceans.

**ecdysone** Molting hormone of arthropods, which triggers when ecdysis occurs.

**ecology** The study of interactions of organisms with one another and with their physical environment.

**ecosystem** A major interacting system that includes organisms and their nonliving environment.

**ecotype** A locally adapted variant of an organism; differing genetically from other ecotypes.

**ectoderm** One of the three embryonic germ layers of early vertebrate embryos; ectoderm gives rise to the outer epithelium of the body (skin, hair, nails) and to the nerve tissue, including the sense organs, brain, and spinal cord.

**ectomycorrhizae** Externally developing mycorrhizae that do not penetrate the cells they surround.

**ectotherms** Animals such as reptiles, fish, or amphibians, whose body temperature is regulated by their behavior or by their surroundings.

**electronegativity** A property of atomic nuclei that refers to the affinity of the nuclei for valence electrons; a nucleus that is more electronegative has a greater pull on electrons than one that is less electronegative.

**electron transport chain** The passage of energetic electrons through a series of membrane-associated electron-carrier molecules to proton pumps embedded within mitochondrial or chloroplast membranes. *See* chemiosmosis.

**elongation factor (Ef-Tu)** In protein synthesis in *E. coli*, a factor that binds to GTP and to a charged tRNA to accomplish binding of the charged tRNA to the A site of the ribosome, so that elongation of the polypeptide chain can occur.

**embryo** A multicellular developmental stage that follows cell division of the zygote.

**embryonic stem cell (ES cell)** A stem cell derived from an early embryo that can develop into different adult tissues and give rise to an adult organism when injected into a blastocyst.

**emergent properties** Novel properties arising from the way in which components interact. Emergent properties often cannot be deduced solely from knowledge of the individual components.

**emerging virus** Any virus that originates in one organism but then passes to another; usually refers to transmission to humans.

**endergonic** Describes a chemical reaction in which the products contain more energy than the reactants, so that free energy must be put into the reaction from an outside source to allow it to proceed.

**endocrine gland** Ductless gland that secretes hormones into the extracellular spaces, from which they diffuse into the circulatory system.

**endocytosis** The uptake of material into cells by inclusion within an invagination of the plasma membrane; the uptake of solid material is phagocytosis, and that of dissolved material is pinocytosis.

**endoderm** One of the three embryonic germ layers of early vertebrate embryos, destined to give rise to the epithelium that lines internal structures and most of the digestive and respiratory tracts.

**endodermis** In vascular plants, a layer of cells forming the innermost layer of the cortex in roots and some stems.

**endomembrane system** A system of connected membranous compartments found in eukaryotic cells.

**endometrium** The lining of the uterus in mammals; thickens in response to secretion of estrogens and progesterone and is sloughed off in menstruation.

**endomycorrhizae** Mycorrhizae that develop within cells.

**endonuclease** An enzyme capable of cleaving phosphodiester bonds between nucleotides located internally in a DNA strand.

**endoplasmic reticulum (ER)** Internal membrane system that forms a netlike array of channels and interconnections within the cytoplasm of eukaryotic cells. The ER is divided into rough (RER) and smooth (SER) compartments.

**endorphin** One of a group of small neuropeptides produced by the vertebrate brain; like morphine, endorphins modulate pain perception.

**endosperm** A storage tissue characteristic of the seeds of angiosperms, which develops from the union of a male nucleus and the polar nuclei of the embryo sac. The endosperm is digested by the growing sporophyte either before maturation of the seed or during its germination.

**endospore** A highly resistant, thick-walled bacterial spore that can survive harsh environmental stress, such as heat or dessication, and then germinate when conditions become favorable.

**endosymbiosis** Theory that proposes that eukaryotic cells evolved from a symbiosis between different species of prokaryotes.

**endotherm** An animal capable of maintaining a constant body temperature. *See* homeotherm.

**energy level** A discrete level, or quantum, of energy that an electron in an atom possesses. To change energy levels, an electron must absorb or release energy.

**enhancer** A site of regulatory protein binding on the DNA molecule distant from the promoter and start site for a gene's transcription.

**enthalpy** In a chemical reaction, the energy contained in the chemical bonds of the molecule, symbolized as *H;* in a cellular reaction, the free energy is equal to the enthalpy of the reactant molecules in the reaction.

**entropy** A measure of the randomness or disorder of a system; a measure of how much energy in a system has become so dispersed (usually as evenly distributed heat) that it is no longer available to do work.

**enzyme** A protein that is capable of speeding up specific chemical reactions by lowering the required activation energy.

**enzyme–substrate complex** The complex formed when an enzyme binds with its substrate. This complex often has an altered configuration compared with the nonbound enzyme.

**epicotyl** The region just above where the cotyledons are attached.

**epidermal cell** In plants, a cell that collectively forms the outermost layer of the primary plant body; includes specialized cells such as trichomes and guard cells.

**epidermis** The outermost layers of cells; in plants, the exterior primary tissue of leaves, young stems, and roots; in vertebrates, the nonvascular external layer of skin, of ectodermal origin; in invertebrates, a single layer of ectodermal epithelium.

**epididymis** A sperm storage vessel; a coiled part of the sperm duct that lies near the testis.

**epistasis** Interaction between two nonallelic genes in which one of them modifies the phenotypic expression of the other.

**epithelium** In animals, a type of tissue that covers an exposed surface or lines a tube or cavity.

**equilibrium** A stable condition; the point at which a chemical reaction proceeds as rapidly in the reverse direction as it does in the forward direction, so that there is no further net change in the concentrations of products or reactants. In ecology, a stable condition that resists change and fairly quickly returns to its original state if disturbed by humans or natural events.

**erythrocyte** Red blood cell, the carrier of hemoglobin.

**erythropoiesis** The manufacture of blood cells in the bone marrow.

**E site** In a ribosome, the exit site that binds to the tRNA that carried the previous amino acid added to the polypeptide chain.

**estrus** The period of maximum female sexual receptivity, associated with ovulation of the egg.

**ethology** The study of patterns of animal behavior in nature.

**euchromatin** That portion of a eukaryotic chromosome that is transcribed into mRNA; contains active genes that are not tightly condensed during interphase.

**eukaryote** A cell characterized by membrane-bounded organelles, most notably the nucleus, and one that possesses chromosomes whose DNA is associated with proteins; an organism composed of such cells.

**eutherian** A placental mammal.

**eutrophic** Refers to a lake in which an abundant supply of minerals and organic matter exists.

**evolution** Genetic change in a population of organisms; in general, evolution leads to progressive change from simple to complex.

**excision repair** A nonspecific mechanism to repair damage to DNA during synthesis. The damaged or mismatched region is excised, and DNA polymerase replaces the region removed.

**exergonic** Describes a chemical reaction in which the products contain less free energy than the reactants, so that free energy is released in the reaction.

**exhalant siphon** In bivalve mollusks, the siphon through which outgoing water leaves the body.

**exocrine gland** A type of gland that releases its secretion through a duct, such as a digestive gland or a sweat gland.

**exocytosis** A type of bulk transport out of cells in which a vacuole fuses with the plasma membrane, discharging the vacuole's contents to the outside.

**exon** A segment of DNA that is both transcribed into RNA and translated into protein. *See* intron.

**exonuclease** An enzyme capable of cutting phosphodiester bonds between nucleotides located at an end of a DNA strand. This allows sequential removal of nucleotides from the end of DNA.

**exoskeleton** An external skeleton, as in arthropods.

**experiment** A test of one or more hypotheses. Hypotheses make contrasting predictions that can be tested experimentally in control and test experiments where a single variable is altered.

**expressed sequence tag (EST)** A short sequence of a cDNA that unambiguously identifies the cDNA.

**expression vector** A type of vector (plasmid or phage) that contains the sequences necessary to drive expression of inserted DNA in a specific cell type.

**exteroceptor** A receptor that is excited by stimuli from the external world.

**extremophile** An archaean organism that lives in extreme environments; different archaean species may live in hot springs (thermophiles), highly saline environments (halophiles), highly acidic or basic environments, or under high pressure at the bottom of oceans.

# F

**5′ cap** In eukaryotes, a structure added to the 5′ end of an mRNA consisting of methylated GTP attached by a 5′ to 5′ bond. The cap protects this end from degradation and is involved in the initiation of translation.

**facilitated diffusion** Carrier-assisted diffusion of molecules across a cellular membrane through specific channels from a region of higher concentration to one of lower concentration; the process is driven by the concentration gradient and does not require cellular energy from ATP.

**family** A taxonomic grouping of similar species above the level of genus.

**fat** A molecule composed of glycerol and three fatty acid molecules.

**feedback inhibition** Control mechanism whereby an increase in the concentration of some molecules inhibits the synthesis of that molecule.

**fermentation** The enzyme-catalyzed extraction of energy from organic compounds without the involvement of oxygen.

**fertilization** The fusion of two haploid gamete nuclei to form a diploid zygote nucleus.

**fibroblast** A flat, irregularly branching cell of connective tissue that secretes structurally strong proteins into the matrix between the cells.

**first filial ($F_1$) generation** The offspring resulting from a cross between a parental generation (P); in experimental crosses, these parents usually have different phenotypes.

**First Law of Thermodynamics** Energy cannot be created or destroyed, but can only undergo conversion from one form to another; thus, the amount of energy in the universe is unchangeable.

**fitness** The genetic contribution of an individual to succeeding generations. relative fitness refers to the fitness of an individual relative to other individuals in a population.

**fixed action pattern** A stereotyped animal behavior response, thought by ethologists to be based on programmed neural circuits.

**flagellin** The protein composing bacterial flagella, which allow a cell to move through an aqueous environment.

**flagellum** A long, threadlike structure protruding from the surface of a cell and used in locomotion.

**flame cell** A specialized cell found in the network of tubules inside flatworms that assists in water regulation and some waste excretion.

**flavin adenine dinucleotide (FAD, $FADH_2$)** A cofactor that acts as a soluble (not membrane-bound) electron carrier (can be reversibly oxidized and reduced).

**fluorescent in situ hybridization (FISH)** A cytological method used to find specific DNA sequences on chromosomes with a specific fluorescently labeled probe.

**food security** Having access to sufficient, safe food to avoid malnutrition and starvation; a global human issue.

**foraging behavior** A collective term for the many complex, evolved behaviors that influence what an animal eats and how the food is obtained.

**founder effect** The effect by which rare alleles and combinations of alleles may be enhanced in new populations.

**fovea** A small depression in the center of the retina with a high concentration of cones; the area of sharpest vision.

**frameshift mutation** A mutation in which a base is added or deleted from the DNA sequence. These changes alter the reading frame downstream of the mutation.

**free energy** Energy available to do work.

**free radical** An ionized atom with one or more unpaired electrons, resulting from electrons that have been energized by ionizing radiation being ejected from the atom; free radicals react violently with other molecules, such as DNA, causing damage by mutation.

**frequency-dependent selection** A type of selection that depends on how frequently or infrequently a phenotype occurs in a population.

**fruit** In angiosperms, a mature, ripened ovary (or group of ovaries), containing the seeds.

**functional genomics** The study of the function of genes and their products, beyond simply ascertaining gene sequences.

**functional group** A molecular group attached to a hydrocarbon that confers chemical properties or reactivities. Examples include hydroxyl (—OH), carboxylic acid (—COOH) and amino groups (—$NH_2$).

**fundamental niche** Also referred to as the hypothetical niche, this is the entire niche an organism could fill if there were no other interacting factors (such as competition or predation).

# G

**$G_0$ phase** The stage of the cell cycle occupied by cells that are not actively dividing.

**$G_1$ phase** The phase of the cell cycle after cytokinesis and before DNA replication called the first "gap" phase. This phase is the primary growth phase of a cell.

**G₁/S checkpoint** The primary control point at which a cell "decides" whether or not to divide. Also called START and the restriction point.

**G₂ phase** The phase of the cell cycle between DNA replication and mitosis called the second "gap" phase. During this phase, the cell prepares for mitosis.

**G₂/M checkpoint** The second cell-division control point, at which division can be delayed if DNA has not been properly replicated or is damaged.

**gametangium, pl. gametangia** A cell or organ in which gametes are formed.

**gamete** A haploid reproductive cell.

**gametocytes** Cells in the malarial sporozoite life cycle capable of giving rise to gametes when in the correct host.

**gametophyte** In plants, the haploid (*n*), gamete-producing generation, which alternates with the diploid (*2n*) sporophyte.

**ganglion, pl. ganglia** An aggregation of nerve cell bodies; in invertebrates, ganglia are the integrative centers; in vertebrates, the term is restricted to aggregations of nerve cell bodies located outside the central nervous system.

**gap gene** Any of certain genes in *Drosophila* development that divide the embryo into large blocks in the process of segmentation; *hunchback* is a gap gene.

**gap junction** A junction between adjacent animal cells that allows the passage of materials between the cells.

**gastrodermis** In eumetazoan animals, the layer of digestive tissue that develops from the endoderm.

**gastrula** In vertebrates, the embryonic stage in which the blastula with its single layer of cells turns into a three-layered embryo made up of ectoderm, mesoderm, and endoderm.

**gastrulation** Developmental process that converts blastula into embryo with three embryonic germ layers: endoderm, mesoderm, and ectoderm. Involves massive cell migration to convert the hollow structure into a three-layered structure.

**gene** The basic unit of heredity; a sequence of DNA nucleotides on a chromosome that encodes a protein, tRNA, or rRNA molecule, or regulates the transcription of such a sequence.

**gene conversion** Alteration of one homologous chromosome by the cell's error-detection and repair system to make it resemble the sequence on the other homologue.

**gene expression** The conversion of the genotype into the phenotype; the process by which DNA is transcribed into RNA, which is then translated into a protein product.

**gene pool** All the alleles present in a species.

**gene-for-gene hypothesis** A plant defense mechanism in which a specific protein encoded by a viral, bacterial, or fungal pathogen binds to a protein encoded by a plant gene and triggers a defense response in the plant.

**general transcription factor** Any of a group of transcription factors that are required for formation of an initiation complex by RNA polymerase II at a promoter. This allows a basal level that can be increased by the action of specific factors.

**generalized transduction** A form of gene transfer in prokaryotes in which any gene can be transferred between cells. This uses a lytic bacteriophage as a carrier where the virion is accidentally packaged with host DNA.

**genetic counseling** The process of evaluating the risk of genetic defects occurring in offspring, testing for these defects in unborn children, and providing the parents with information about these risks and conditions.

**genetic drift** Random fluctuation in allele frequencies over time by chance.

**genetic map** An abstract map that places the relative location of genes on a chromosome based on recombination frequency.

**genome** The entire DNA sequence of an organism.

**genomic imprinting** Describes an exception to Mendelian genetics in some mammals in which the phenotype caused by an allele is exhibited when the allele comes from one parent, but not from the other.

**genomic library** A DNA library that contains a representation of the entire genome of an organism.

**genomics** The study of genomes as opposed to individual genes.

**genotype** The genetic constitution underlying a single trait or set of traits.

**genotype frequency** A measure of the occurrence of a genotype in a population, expressed as a proportion of the entire population, for example, an occurrence of 0.25 (25%) for a homozygous recessive genotype.

**genus, pl. genera** A taxonomic group that ranks below a family and above a species.

**germination** The resumption of growth and development by a spore or seed.

**germ layers** The three cell layers formed at gastrulation of the embryo that foreshadow the future organization of tissues; the layers, from the outside inward, are the ectoderm, the mesoderm, and the endoderm.

**germ-line cells** During zygote development, cells that are set aside from the somatic cells and that will eventually undergo meiosis to produce gametes.

**gill** (1) In aquatic animals, a respiratory organ, usually a thin-walled projection from some part of the external body surface, endowed with a rich capillary bed and having a large surface area. (2) In basidiomycete fungi, the plates on the underside of the cap.

**globular protein** Proteins with a compact tertiary structure with hydrophobic amino acids mainly in the interior.

**glomerular filtrate** The fluid that passes out of the capillaries of each glomerulus.

**glomerulus** A cluster of capillaries enclosed by Bowman's capsule.

**glucagon** A vertebrate hormone produced in the pancreas that acts to initiate the breakdown of glycogen to glucose subunits.

**gluconeogenesis** The synthesis of glucose from noncarbohydrates (such as proteins or fats).

**glucose** A common six-carbon sugar ($C_6H_{12}O_6$); the most common monosaccharide in most organisms.

**glucose repression** In *E. coli*, the preferential use of glucose even when other sugars are present; transcription of mRNA encoding the enzymes for utilizing the other sugars does not occur.

**glycocalyx** A "sugar coating" on the surface of a cell resulting from the presence of polysaccharides on glycolipids and glycoproteins embedded in the outer layer of the plasma membrane.

**glycogen** Animal starch; a complex branched polysaccharide that serves as a food reserve in animals, bacteria, and fungi.

**glycolipid** Lipid molecule modified within the Golgi complex by having a short sugar chain (polysaccharide) attached.

**glycolysis** The anaerobic breakdown of glucose; this enzyme-catalyzed process yields two molecules of pyruvate with a net of two molecules of ATP.

**glycoprotein** Protein molecule modified within the Golgi complex by having a short sugar chain (polysaccharide) attached.

**glyoxysome** A small cellular organelle or microbody containing enzymes necessary for conversion of fats into carbohydrates.

**glyphosate** A biodegradable herbicide that works by inhibiting EPSP synthetase, a plant enzyme that makes aromatic amino acids; genetic engineering has allowed crop species to be created that are resistant to glyphosate.

**Golgi apparatus (Golgi body)** A collection of flattened stacks of membranes in the cytoplasm of eukaryotic cells; functions in collection, packaging, and distribution of molecules synthesized in the cell.

**G protein** A protein that binds guanosine triphosphate (GTP) and assists in the function of cell-surface receptors. When the receptor binds its signal molecule, the G protein binds GTP and is activated to start a chain of events within the cell.

**G protein-coupled receptor (GPCR)** A receptor that acts through a heterotrimeric (three component) G protein to activate effector proteins. The effector proteins then function as enzymes to produce second messengers such as cAMP or $IP_3$.

**gradualism** The view that species change very slowly in ways that may be imperceptible from one generation to the next but that accumulate and lead to major changes over thousands or millions of years.

**Gram stain** Staining technique that divides bacteria into gram-negative or gram-positive based on retention of a violet dye. Differences in staining are due to cell wall construction.

**granum (pl. grana)** A stacked column of flattened, interconnected disks (thylakoids) that are part of the thylakoid membrane system in chloroplasts.

**gravitropism** Growth response to gravity in plants; formerly called geotropism.

**ground meristem** The primary meristem, or meristematic tissue, that gives rise to the plant body (except for the epidermis and vascular tissues).

**ground tissue** In plants, a type of tissue that performs many functions, including support, storage, secretion, and photosynthesis; may consist of many cell types.

**growth factor** Any of a number of proteins that bind to membrane receptors and initiate intracellular signaling systems that result in cell growth and division.

**guard cell** In plants, one of a pair of sausage-shaped cells flanking a stoma; the guard cells open and close the stomata.

**guttation** The exudation of liquid water from leaves due to root pressure.

**gymnosperm** A seed plant with seeds not enclosed in an ovary; conifers are gymnosperms.

**gynoecium** The aggregate of carpels in the flower of a seed plant.

# H

**habitat** The environment of an organism; the place where it is usually found.

**habituation** A form of learning; a diminishing response to a repeated stimulus.

**halophyte** A plant that is salt-tolerant.

**haplodiploidy** A phenomenon occurring in certain organisms such as wasps, wherein both haploid (male) and diploid (female) individuals are encountered.

**haploid** Having only one set of chromosomes (*n*), in contrast to diploid (2*n*).

**haplotype** A region of a chromosome that is usually inherited intact, that is, it does not undergo recombination. These are identified based on analysis of SNPs.

**Hardy-Weinberg equilibrium** A mathematical description of the fact that allele and genotype frequencies remain constant in a random-mating population in the absence of inbreeding, selection, or other evolutionary forces; usually stated: if the frequency of allele *a* is *p* and the frequency of allele *b* is *q*, then the genotype frequencies after one generation of random mating will always be $p_2 + 2pq + q_2 = 1$.

**Haversian canal** Narrow channels that run parallel to the length of a bone and contain blood vessels and nerve cells.

**heat** A measure of the random motion of molecules; the greater the heat, the greater the motion. Heat is one form of kinetic energy.

**heat of vaporization** The amount of energy required to change 1 g of a substance from a liquid to a gas.

**heavy metal** Any of the metallic elements with high atomic numbers, such as arsenic, cadmium, lead, etc. Many heavy metals are toxic to animals even in small amounts.

**helicase** Any of a group of enzymes that unwind the two DNA strands in the double helix to facilitate DNA replication.

**helix-turn-helix motif** A common DNA-binding motif found in regulatory proteins; it consists of two α-helices linked by a nonhelical segment (the "turn").

**helper T cell** A class of white blood cells that initiates both the cell-mediated immune response and the humoral immune response; helper T cells are the targets of the AIDS virus (HIV).

**hemoglobin** A globular protein in vertebrate red blood cells and in the plasma of many invertebrates that carries oxygen and carbon dioxide.

**hemopoietic stem cell** The cells in bone marrow where blood cells are formed.

**hermaphroditism** Condition in which an organism has both male and female functional reproductive organs.

**heterochromatin** The portion of a eukaryotic chromosome that is not transcribed into RNA; remains condensed in interphase and stains intensely in histological preparations.

**heterochrony** An alteration in the timing of developmental events due to a genetic change; for example, a mutation that delays flowering in plants.

**heterokaryotic** In fungi, having two or more genetically distinct types of nuclei within the same mycelium.

**heterosporous** In vascular plants, having spores of two kinds, namely, microspores and megaspores.

**heterotroph** An organism that cannot derive energy from photosynthesis or inorganic chemicals, and so must feed on other plants and animals, obtaining chemical energy by degrading their organic molecules.

**heterozygote advantage** The situation in which individuals heterozygous for a trait have a selective advantage over those who are homozygous; an example is sickle cell anemia.

**heterozygous** Having two different alleles of the same gene; the term is usually applied to one or more specific loci, as in "heterozygous with respect to the *W* locus" (that is, the genotype is *W/w*).

**Hfr cell** An *E. coli* cell that has a high frequency of recombination due to integration of an F plasmid into its genome.

**histone** One of a group of relatively small, very basic polypeptides, rich in arginine and lysine, forming the core of nucleosomes around which DNA is wrapped in the first stage of chromosome condensation.

**histone protein** Any of eight proteins with an overall positive charge that associate in a complex. The DNA duplex coils around a core of eight histone proteins, held by its negatively charged phosphate groups, forming a nucleosome.

**holoblastic cleavage** Process in vertebrate embryos in which the cleavage divisions all occur at the same rate, yielding a uniform cell size in the blastula.

**homeobox** A sequence of 180 nucleotides located in homeotic genes that produces a 60-amino-acid peptide sequence (the homeodomain) active in transcription factors.

**homeodomain motif** A special class of helix-turn-helix motifs found in regulatory proteins that control development in eukaryotes.

**homeosis** A change in the normal spatial pattern of gene expression that can result in homeotic mutants where a wild-type structure develops in the wrong place in or on the organism.

**homeostasis** The maintenance of a relatively stable internal physiological environment in an organism; usually involves some form of feedback self-regulation.

**homeotherm** An organism, such as a bird or mammal, capable of maintaining a stable body temperature independent of the environmental temperature. *See* endotherm.

**homeotic gene** One of a series of "master switch" genes that determine the form of segments developing in the embryo.

**hominid** Any primate in the human family, Hominidae. *Homo sapiens* is the only living representative.

**hominoid** Collectively, hominids and apes; the monkeys and hominoids constitute the anthropoid primates.

**homokaryotic** In fungi, having nuclei with the same genetic makeup within a mycelium.

**homologue** One of a pair of chromosomes of the same kind located in a diploid cell; one copy of each pair of homologues comes from each gamete that formed the zygote.

**homologous** (1) Refers to similar structures that have the same evolutionary origin. (2) Refers to a pair of the same kind of chromosome in a diploid cell.

**homoplasy** In cladistics, a shared character state that has not been inherited from a common ancestor exhibiting that state; may result from convergent evolution or evolutionary reversal. The wings of birds and of bats, which are convergent structures, are examples.

**homosporous** In some plants, production of only one type of spore rather than differentiated types. *Compare with* heterosporous.

**homozygous** Being a homozygote, having two identical alleles of the same gene; the term is usually applied to one or more specific loci, as in "homozygous with respect to the *W* locus" (i.e., the genotype is *W/W* or *w/w*).

**horizontal gene transfer (HGT)** The passing of genes laterally between species; more prevalent very early in the history of life.

**hormone** A molecule, usually a peptide or steroid, that is produced in one part of an organism and triggers a specific cellular reaction in target tissues and organs some distance away.

**host range** The range of organisms that can be infected by a particular virus.

*Hox* **gene** A group of homeobox-containing genes that control developmental events, usually found organized into clusters of genes. These genes have been conserved in many different multicellular animals, both invertebrates and vertebrates, although the number of clusters changes in lineages, leading to four clusters in vertebrates.

**humoral immunity** Arm of the adaptive immune system involving B cells that produce soluble antibodies specific for foreign antigens.

**humus** Partly decayed organic material found in topsoil.

**hybridization** The mating of unlike parents.

**hydration shell** A "cloud" of water molecules surrounding a dissolved substance, such as sucrose or $Na^+$ and $Cl^-$ ions.

**hydrogen bond** A weak association formed with hydrogen in polar covalent bonds. The partially positive hydrogen is attracted to partially negative atoms in polar covalent bonds. In water, oxygen and hydrogen in different water molecules form hydrogen bonds.

**hydrolysis reaction** A reaction that breaks a bond by the addition of water. This is the reverse of dehydration, a reaction that joins molecules with the loss of water.

**hydrophilic** Literally translates as "water-loving" and describes substances that are soluble in water. These must be either polar or charged (ions).

**hydrophobic** Literally translates as "water-fearing" and describes nonpolar substances that are not soluble in water. Nonpolar molecules in water associate with each other and form droplets.

**hydrophobic exclusion** The tendency of nonpolar molecules to aggregate together when placed in water. Exclusion refers to the action of water in forcing these molecules together.

**hydrostatic skeleton** The skeleton of most soft-bodied invertebrates that have neither an internal nor an external skeleton. They use the relative incompressibility of the water within their bodies as a kind of skeleton.

**hyperosmotic** The condition in which a (hyperosmotic) solution has a higher osmotic concentration than that of a second solution. *Compare with* hypoosmotic.

**hyperpolarization** Above-normal negativity of a cell membrane during its resting potential.

**hypersensitive response** Plants respond to pathogens by selectively killing plant cells to block the spread of the pathogen.

**hypertonic** A solution with a higher concentration of solutes than the cell. A cell in a hypertonic solution tends to lose water by osmosis.

**hypha, pl. hyphae** A filament of a fungus or oomycete; collectively, the hyphae constitute the mycelium.

**hypocotyl** The region immediately below where the cotyledons are attached.

**hypoosmotic** The condition in which a (hypoosmotic) solution has a lower osmotic concentration than that of a second solution. *Compare with* hyperosmotic.

**hypothalamus** A region of the vertebrate brain just below the cerebral hemispheres, under the thalamus; a center of the autonomic nervous system, responsible for the integration and correlation of many neural and endocrine functions.

**hypotonic** A solution with a lower concentration of solutes than the cell. A cell in a hypotonic solution tends to take in water by osmosis.

# I

**icosahedron** A structure consisting of 20 equilateral triangular facets; this is commonly seen in viruses and forms one kind of viral capsid.

**imaginal disk** One of about a dozen groups of cells set aside in the abdomen of a larval insect and committed to forming key parts of the adult insect's body.

**immune response** In vertebrates, a defensive reaction of the body to invasion by a foreign substance or organism. *See* antibody and B cell.

**immunoglobulin** An antibody molecule.

**immunological tolerance** Process where immune system learns to not react to self-antigens.

**in vitro mutagenesis** The ability to create mutations at any site in a cloned gene to examine the mutations' effects on function.

**inbreeding** The breeding of genetically related plants or animals; inbreeding tends to increase homozygosity.

**inclusive fitness** Describes the sum of the number of genes directly passed on in an individual's offspring and those genes passed on indirectly by kin (other than offspring) whose existence results from the benefit of the individual's altruism.

**incomplete dominance** Describes a case in which two or more alleles of a gene do not display clear dominance. The phenotype of a heterozygote is intermediate between the homozygous forms. For example, crossing red-flowered with white-flowered four o'clocks yields pink heterozygotes.

**independent assortment** In a dihybrid cross, describes the random assortment of alleles for each of the genes. For genes on different chromosomes this results from the random orientations of different homologous pairs during metaphase I of meiosis. For genes on

the same chromosome, this occurs when the two loci are far enough apart for roughly equal numbers of odd- and even-numbered multiple crossover events.

**indeterminate development** A type of development in animals in which the first few embryonic cells are identical daughter cells, any one of which could develop separately into a complete organism; their fate is indeterminate.

**inducer exclusion** Part of the mechanism of glucose repression in *E. coli* in which the presence of glucose prevents the entry of lactose such that the *lac* operon cannot be induced.

**induction** (1) Production of enzymes in response to a substrate; a mechanism by which binding of an inducer to a repressor allows transcription of an operon. This is seen in catabolic operons and results in production of enzymes to degrade a compound only when it is available. (2) In embryonic development, the process by which the development of a cell is influenced by interaction with an adjacent cell.

**inductive reasoning** The logical application of specific observations to make a generalization. In science, inductive reasoning is used to formulate testable hypotheses.

**industrial melanism** Phrase used to describe the evolutionary process in which initially light-colored organisms become dark as a result of natural selection.

**inflammatory response** A generalized nonspecific response to infection that acts to clear an infected area of infecting microbes and dead tissue cells so that tissue repair can begin.

**inhalant siphon** In bivalve mollusks, the siphon through which incoming water enters the body.

**inheritance of acquired characteristics** Also known as Lamarckism; the theory, now discounted, that individuals genetically pass on to their offspring physical and behavioral changes developed during the individuals' own lifetime.

**inhibitor** A substance that binds to an enzyme and decreases its activity.

**initiation factor** One of several proteins involved in the formation of an initiation complex in prokaryote polypeptide synthesis.

**initiator tRNA** A tRNA molecule involved in the beginning of translation. In prokaryotes, the initiator tRNA is charged with *N*-formylmethionine (tRNA$^{fMet}$); in eukaryotes, the tRNA is charged simply with methionine.

**inorganic phosphate** A phosphate molecule that is not a part of an organic molecule; inorganic phosphate groups are added and removed in the formation and breakdown of ATP and in many other cellular reactions.

**inositol-1,4,5-trisphosphate (IP$_3$)** Second messenger produced by the cleavage of phosphatidylinositol-4,5-bisphosphate.

**insertional inactivation** Destruction of a gene's function by the insertion of a transposon.

**instar** A larval developmental stage in insects.

**integrin** Any of a group of cell-surface proteins involved in adhesion of cells to substrates. Critical to migrating cells moving through the cell matrix in tissues such as connective tissue.

**intercalary meristem** A type of meristem that arises in stem internodes in some plants, such as corn and horsetails; responsible for elongation of the internodes.

**interferon** In vertebrates, a protein produced in virus-infected cells that inhibits viral multiplication.

**intermembrane space** The outer compartment of a mitochondrion that lies between the two membranes.

**interneuron (association neuron)** A nerve cell found only in the middle of the spinal cord that acts as a functional link between sensory neurons and motor neurons.

**internode** In plants, the region of a stem between two successive nodes.

**interoceptor** A receptor that senses information related to the body itself, its internal condition, and its position.

**interphase** The period between two mitotic or meiotic divisions in which a cell grows and its DNA replicates; includes G$_1$, S, and G$_2$ phases.

**intracellular receptor** A signal receptor that binds a ligand inside a cell, such as the receptors for NO, steroid hormones, vitamin D, and thyroid hormones.

**intron** Portion of mRNA as transcribed from eukaryotic DNA that is removed by enzymes before the mature mRNA is translated into protein. *See* exon.

**inversion** A reversal in order of a segment of a chromosome; also, to turn inside out, as in embryogenesis of sponges or discharge of a nematocyst.

**ionizing radiation** High-energy radiation that is highly mutagenic, producing free radicals that react with DNA; includes X-rays and γ-rays.

**isomer** One of a group of molecules identical in atomic composition but differing in structural arrangement; for example, glucose and fructose.

**isosmotic** The condition in which the osmotic concentrations of two solutions are equal, so that no net water movement occurs between them by osmosis.

**isotonic** A solution having the same concentration of solutes as the cell. A cell in an isotonic solution takes in and loses the same amount of water.

**isotope** Different forms of the same element with the same number of protons but different numbers of neutrons.

# J

**jasmonic acid** An organic molecule that is part of a plant's wound response; it signals the production of a proteinase inhibitor.

# K

**karyotype** The morphology of the chromosomes of an organism as viewed with a light microscope.

**keratin** A tough, fibrous protein formed in epidermal tissues and modified into skin, feathers, hair, and hard structures such as horns and nails.

**key innovation** A newly evolved trait in a species that allows members to use resources or other aspects of the environment that were previously inaccessible.

**kidney** In vertebrates, the organ that filters the blood to remove nitrogenous wastes and regulates the balance of water and solutes in blood plasma.

**kilocalorie** Unit describing the amount of heat required to raise the temperature of a kilogram of water by 1°C; sometimes called a Calorie, equivalent to 1000 calories.

**kinase cascade** A series of protein kinases that phosphorylate each other in succession; a kinase cascade can amplify signals during the signal transduction process.

**kinesis** Changes in activity level in an animal that are dependent on stimulus intensity. *See* kinetic energy.

**kinetic energy** The energy of motion.

**kinetochore** Disk-shaped protein structure within the centromere to which the spindle fibers attach during mitosis or meiosis. *See* centromere.

**kingdom** The second highest commonly used taxonomic category.

**kin selection** Selection favoring relatives; an increase in the frequency of related individuals (kin) in a population, leading to an increase in the relative frequency in the population of those alleles shared by members of the kin group.

**knockout mice** Mice in which a known gene is inactivated ("knocked out") using recombinant DNA and ES cells.

**Krebs cycle** Another name for the citric acid cycle; also called the tricarboxylic acid (TCA) cycle.

# L

**labrum** The upper lip of insects and crustaceans situated above or in front of the mandibles.

*lac* **operon** In *E. coli*, the operon containing genes that encode the enzymes to metabolize lactose.

**lagging strand** The DNA strand that must be synthesized discontinuously because of the 5′-to-3′ directionality of DNA polymerase during replication, and the antiparallel nature of DNA. Compare *leading strand*.

**larva** A developmental stage that is unlike the adult found in organisms that undergo metamorphosis. Embryos develop into larvae that produce the adult form by metamorphosis.

**larynx** The voice box; a cartilaginous organ that lies between the pharynx and trachea and is responsible for sound production in vertebrates.

**lateral line system** A sensory system encountered in fish, through which mechanoreceptors in a line down the side of the fish are sensitive to motion.

**lateral meristems** In vascular plants, the meristems that give rise to secondary tissue; the vascular cambium and cork cambium.

**Law of Independent Assortment** Mendel's second law of heredity, stating that genes located on nonhomologous chromosomes assort independently of one another.

**Law of Segregation** Mendel's first law of heredity, stating that alternative alleles for the same gene segregate from each other in production of gametes.

**leading strand** The DNA strand that can be synthesized continuously from the origin of replication. Compare *lagging strand*.

**leaf primordium, pl. primordia** A lateral outgrowth from the apical meristem that will eventually become a leaf.

**lenticels** Spongy areas in the cork surfaces of stem, roots, and other plant parts that allow interchange of gases between internal tissues and the atmosphere through the periderm.

**leucine zipper motif** A motif in regulatory proteins in which two different protein subunits associate to form a single DNA-binding site; the proteins are connected by an association between hydrophobic regions containing leucines (the "zipper").

**leucoplast** In plant cells, a colorless plastid in which starch grains are stored; usually found in cells not exposed to light.

**leukocyte** A white blood cell; a diverse array of nonhemoglobin-containing blood cells, including phagocytic macrophages and antibody-producing lymphocytes.

**lichen** Symbiotic association between a fungus and a photosynthetic organism such as a green alga or cyanobacterium.

**ligand** A signaling molecule that binds to a specific receptor protein, initiating signal transduction in cells.

**light-dependent reactions** In photosynthesis, the reactions in which light energy is captured and used in production of ATP and NADPH. In plants this involves the action of two linked photosystems.

**light-independent reactions** In photosynthesis, the reactions of the Calvin cycle in which ATP and NADPH from the light-dependent reactions are used to reduce $CO_2$ and produce organic compounds such as glucose. This involves the process of carbon fixation, or the conversion of inorganic carbon ($CO_2$) to organic carbon (ultimately carbohydrates).

**lignin** A highly branched polymer that makes plant cell walls more rigid; an important component of wood.

**limbic system** The hypothalamus, together with the network of neurons that link the hypothalamus to some areas of the cerebral cortex. Responsible for many of the most deep-seated drives and emotions of vertebrates, including pain, anger, sex, hunger, thirst, and pleasure.

**linked genes** Genes that are physically close together and therefore tend to segregate together; recombination occurring between linked genes can be used to produce a map of genetic distance for a chromosome.

**linkage disequilibrium** Association of alleles for 2 or more loci in a population that is higher than expected by chance.

**lipase** An enzyme that catalyzes the hydrolysis of fats.

**lipid** A nonpolar hydrophobic organic molecule that is insoluble in water (which is polar) but dissolves readily in nonpolar organic solvents; includes fats, oils, waxes, steroids, phospholipids, and carotenoids.

**lipid bilayer** The structure of a cellular membrane, in which two layers of phospholipids spontaneously align so that the hydrophilic head groups are exposed to water, while the hydrophobic fatty acid tails are pointed toward the center of the membrane.

**lipopolysaccharide** A lipid with a polysaccharide molecule attached; found in the outer membrane layer of gram-negative bacteria; the outer membrane layer protects the cell wall from antibiotic attack.

**locus** The position on a chromosome where a gene is located.

**long interspersed element (LINE)** Any of a type of large transposable element found in humans and other primates that contains all the biochemical machinery needed for transposition.

**long terminal repeat (LTR)** A particular type of retrotransposon that has repeated elements at its ends. These elements make up 8% of the human genome.

**loop of Henle** In the kidney of birds and mammals, a hairpin-shaped portion of the renal tubule in which water and salt are reabsorbed from the glomerular filtrate by diffusion.

**lophophore** A horseshoe-shaped crown of ciliated tentacles that surrounds the mouth of certain spiralian animals; seen in the phyla Brachiopoda and Bryozoa.

**lumen** A term for any bounded opening; for example, the cisternal space of the endoplasmic reticulum of eukaryotic cells, the passage through which blood flows inside a blood vessel, and the passage through which material moves inside the intestine during digestion.

**luteal phase** The second phase of the female reproductive cycle, during which the mature eggs are released into the fallopian tubes, a process called ovulation.

**lymph** In animals, a colorless fluid derived from blood by filtration through capillary walls in the tissues.

**lymphatic system** In animals, an open vascular system that reclaims water that has entered interstitial regions from the bloodstream (lymph); includes the lymph nodes, spleen, thymus, and tonsils.

**lymphocyte** A type of white blood cell. Lymphocytes are responsible for the immune response; there are two principal classes: B cells and T cells.

**lymphokine** A regulatory molecule that is secreted by lymphocytes. In the immune response, lymphokines secreted by helper T cells unleash the cell-mediated immune response.

**lysis** Disintegration of a cell by rupture of its plasma membrane.

**lysogenic cycle** A viral cycle in which the viral DNA becomes integrated into the host chromosome and is replicated during cell reproduction. Results in vertical rather than horizontal transmission.

**lysosome** A membrane-bounded vesicle containing digestive enzymes that is produced by the Golgi apparatus in eukaryotic cells.

**lytic cycle** A viral cycle in which the host cell is killed (lysed) by the virus after viral duplication to release viral particles.

# M

**macroevolution** The creation of new species and the extinction of old ones.

**macromolecule** An extremely large biological molecule; refers specifically to proteins, nucleic acids, polysaccharides, lipids, and complexes of these.

**macronutrients** Inorganic chemical elements required in large amounts for plant growth, such as nitrogen, potassium, calcium, phosphorus, magnesium, and sulfur.

**macrophage** A large phagocytic cell that is able to engulf and digest cellular debris and invading bacteria.

**madreporite** A sievelike plate on the surface of echinoderms through which water enters the water–vascular system.

*MADS* **box gene** Any of a family of genes identified by possessing shared motifs that are the predominant homeotic genes of plants; a small number of *MADS* box genes are also found in animals.

**major groove** The larger of the two grooves in a DNA helix, where the paired nucleotides' hydrogen bonds are accessible; regulatory proteins can recognize and bind to regions in the major groove.

**major histocompatibility complex (MHC)** A set of protein cell-surface markers anchored in the plasma membrane, which the immune system uses to identify "self." All the cells of a given individual have the same "self" marker, called an MHC protein.

**Malpighian tubules** Blind tubules opening into the hindgut of terrestrial arthropods; they function as excretory organs.

**mandibles** In crustaceans, insects, and myriapods, the appendages immediately posterior to the antennae; used to seize, hold, bite, or chew food.

**mantle** The soft, outermost layer of the body wall in mollusks; the mantle secretes the shell.

**map unit** Each 1% of recombination frequency between two genetic loci; the unit is termed a centimorgan (cM) or simply a map unit (m.u.).

**marsupial** A mammal in which the young are born early in their development, sometimes as soon as eight days after fertilization, and are retained in a pouch.

**mass extinction** A relatively sudden, sharp decline in the number of species; for example, the extinction at the end of the Cretaceous period in which the dinosaurs and a variety of other organisms disappeared.

**mass flow hypothesis** The overall process by which materials move in the phloem of plants.

**mast cells** Leukocytes with granules containing molecules that initiate inflammation.

**maternal inheritance** A mode of uniparental inheritance from the female parent; for example, in humans mitochondria and their genomes are inherited from the mother.

**matrix** In mitochondria, the solution in the interior space surrounded by the cristae that contains the enzymes and other molecules involved in oxidative respiration; more generally, that part of a tissue within which an organ or process is embedded.

**medusa** A free-floating, often umbrella-shaped body form found in cnidarian animals, such as jellyfish.

**megapascal (MPa)** A unit of measure used for pressure in water potential.

**megaphyll** In plants, a leaf that has several to many veins connecting it to the vascular cylinder of the stem; most plants have megaphylls.

**mesoglea** A layer of gelatinous material found between the epidermis and gastrodermis of eumetazoans; it contains the muscles in most of these animals.

**mesohyl** A gelatinous, protein-rich matrix found between the choanocyte layer and the epithelial layer of the body of a sponge; various types of amoeboid cells may occur in the mesohyl.

**metacercaria** An encysted form of a larval liver fluke, found in muscle tissue of an infected animal; if the muscle is eaten, cysts dissolves in the digestive tract, releasing the flukes into the body of the new host.

**methylation** The addition of a methyl group to bases (primarily cytosine) in DNA. Cytosine methylation is correlated with DNA that is not expressed.

**meiosis I** The first round of cell division in meiosis; it is referred to as a "reduction division" because homologous chromosomes separate, and the daughter cells have only the haploid number of chromosomes.

**meiosis II** The second round of division in meiosis, during which the two haploid cells from meiosis I undergo a mitosis-like division without DNA replication to produce four haploid daughter cells.

**membrane receptor** A signal receptor present as an integral protein in the cell membrane, such as GPCRs, chemically gated ion channels in neurons, and RTKs.

**Mendelian ratio** The characteristic dominant-to-recessive phenotypic ratios that Mendel observed in his genetics experiments. For example, the $F_2$ generation in a monohybrid cross shows a ratio of 3:1; the $F_2$ generation in a dihybrid cross shows a ratio of 9:3:3:1.

**menstruation** Periodic sloughing off of the blood-enriched lining of the uterus when pregnancy does not occur.

**meristem** Undifferentiated plant tissue from which new cells arise.

**meroblastic cleavage** A type of cleavage in the eggs of reptiles, birds, and some fish. Occurs only on the blastodisc.

**mesoderm** One of the three embryonic germ layers that form in the gastrula; gives rise to muscle, bone and other connective tissue, the peritoneum, the circulatory system, and most of the excretory and reproductive systems.

**mesophyll** The photosynthetic parenchyma of a leaf, located within the epidermis.

**messenger RNA (mRNA)** The RNA transcribed from structural genes; RNA molecules complementary to a portion of one strand of DNA, which are translated by the ribosomes to form protein.

**metabolism** The sum of all chemical processes occurring within a living cell or organism.

**metamorphosis** Process in which a marked change in form takes place during postembryonic development as, for example, from tadpole to frog.

**metaphase** The stage of mitosis or meiosis during which microtubules become organized into a spindle and the chromosomes come to lie in the spindle's equatorial plane.

**metastasis** The process by which cancer cells move from their point of origin to other locations in the body; also, a population of cancer cells in a secondary location, the result of movement from the primary tumor.

**methanogens** Obligate, anaerobic archaebacteria that produce methane.

**microarray** DNA sequences are placed on a microscope slide or chip with a robot. The microarray can then be probed with RNA from specific tissues to identify expressed DNA.

**microbody** A cellular organelle bounded by a single membrane and containing a variety of enzymes; generally derived from endoplasmic reticulum; includes peroxisomes and glyoxysomes.

**microevolution** Refers to the evolutionary process itself. Evolution within a species. Also called adaptation.

**micronutrient** A mineral required in only minute amounts for plant growth, such as iron, chlorine, copper, manganese, zinc, molybdenum, and boron.

**microphyll** In plants, a leaf that has only one vein connecting it to the vascular cylinder of the stem; the club mosses in particular have microphylls.

**micropyle** In the ovules of seed plants, an opening in the integuments through which the pollen tube usually enters.

**micro-RNA (miRNA)** A class of RNAs that are very short and only recently could be detected. *See also* small interfering RNAs (siRNAs).

**microtubule** In eukaryotic cells, a long, hollow protein cylinder, composed of the protein tubulin; these influence cell shape, move the chromosomes in cell division, and provide the functional internal structure of cilia and flagella.

**microvillus** Cytoplasmic projection from epithelial cells; microvilli greatly increase the surface area of the small intestine.

**middle lamella** The layer of intercellular material, rich in pectic compounds, that cements together the primary walls of adjacent plant cells.

**mimicry** The resemblance in form, color, or behavior of certain organisms (mimics) to other more powerful or more protected ones (models).

**miracidium** The ciliated first-stage larva inside the egg of the liver fluke; eggs are passed in feces, and if they reach water they may be eaten by a host snail in which they continue their life cycle.

**missense mutation** A base substitution mutation that results in the alteration of a single amino acid.

**mitochondrion** The organelle called the powerhouse of the cell. Consists of an outer membrane, an elaborate inner membrane that supports electron transport and chemiosmotic synthesis of ATP, and a soluble matrix containing Krebs cycle enzymes.

**mitogen-activated protein (MAP) kinase** Any of a class of protein kinases that activate transcription factors to alter gene expression. A mitogen is any molecule that stimulates cell division. MAP kinases are activated by kinase cascades.

**mitosis** Somatic cell division; nuclear division in which the duplicated chromosomes separate to form two genetically identical daughter nuclei.

**molar concentration** Concentration expressed as moles of a substance in 1 L of pure water.

**mole** The weight of a substance in grams that corresponds to the atomic masses of all the component atoms in a molecule of that substance. One mole of a compound always contains $6.023 \times 10^{23}$ molecules.

**molecular clock method** In evolutionary theory, the method in which the rate of evolution of a molecule is constant through time.

**molecular cloning** The isolation and amplification of a specific sequence of DNA.

**monocot** Short for monocotyledon; flowering plant in which the embryos have only one cotyledon, the floral parts are generally in threes, and the leaves typically are parallel-veined.

**monocyte** A type of leukocyte that becomes a phagocytic cell (macrophage) after moving into tissues.

**monoecious** A plant in which the staminate and pistillate flowers are separate, but borne on the same individual.

**monomer** The smallest chemical subunit of a polymer. The monosaccharide α-glucose is the monomer found in plant starch, a polysaccharide.

**monophyletic** In phylogenetic classification, a group that includes the most recent common ancestor of the group and all its descendants. A clade is a monophyletic group.

**monosaccharide** A simple sugar that cannot be decomposed into smaller sugar molecules.

**monosomic** Describes the condition in which a chromosome has been lost due to nondisjunction during meiosis, producing a diploid embryo with only one of these autosomes.

**monotreme** An egg-laying mammal.

**morphogen** A signal molecule produced by an embryonic organizer region that informs surrounding cells of their distance from the organizer, thus determining relative positions of cells during development.

**morphogenesis** The development of an organism's body form, namely its organs and anatomical features; it may involve apoptosis as well as cell division, differentiation, and changes in cell shape.

**morphology** The form and structure of an organism.

**morula** Solid ball of cells in the early stage of embryonic development.

**mosaic development** A pattern of embryonic development in which initial cells produced by cleavage divisions contain different developmental signals (determinants) from the egg, setting the individual cells on different developmental paths.

**motif** A substructure in proteins that confers function and can be found in multiple proteins. One example is the helix-turn-helix motif found in a number of proteins that is used to bind to DNA.

**motor (efferent) neuron** Neuron that transmits nerve impulses from the central nervous system to an effector, which is typically a muscle or gland.

**M phase** The phase of cell division during which chromosomes are separated. The spindle assembles, binds to the chromosomes, and moves the sister chromatids apart.

**M phase-promoting factor (MPF)** A Cdk enzyme active at the $G_2/M$ checkpoint.

**Müllerian mimicry** A phenomenon in which two or more unrelated but protected species resemble one another, thus achieving a kind of group defense.

**multidrug-resistant (MDR) strain** Any bacterial strain that has become resistant to more than one antibiotic drug; MDR *Staphylococcus* strains, for example, are responsible for many infection deaths.

**multienzyme complex** An assembly consisting of several enzymes catalyzing different steps in a sequence of reactions. Close proximity of these related enzymes speeds the overall process, making it more efficient.

**multigene family** A collection of related genes on a single chromosome or on different chromosomes.

**muscle fiber** A long, cylindrical, multinucleated cell containing numerous myofibrils, which is capable of contraction when stimulated.

**mutagen** An agent that induces changes in DNA (mutations); includes physical agents that damage DNA and chemicals that alter DNA bases.

**mutation** A permanent change in a cell's DNA; includes changes in nucleotide sequence, alteration of gene position, gene loss or duplication, and insertion of foreign sequences.

**mutualism** A symbiotic association in which two (or more) organisms live together, and both members benefit.

**mycelium, pl. mycelia** In fungi, a mass of hyphae.

**mycorrhiza, pl. mycorrhizae** A symbiotic association between fungi and the roots of a plant.

**myelin sheath** A fatty layer surrounding the long axons of motor neurons in the peripheral nervous system of vertebrates.

**myofilament** A contractile microfilament, composed largely of actin and myosin, within muscle.

**myosin** One of the two protein components of microfilaments (the other is actin); a principal component of vertebrate muscle.

# N

**natural killer cell** A cell that does not kill invading microbes, but rather, the cells infected by them.

**natural selection** The differential reproduction of genotypes; caused by factors in the environment; leads to evolutionary change.

**nauplius** A larval form characteristic of crustaceans.

**negative control** A type of control at the level of DNA transcription initiation in which the frequency of initiation is decreased; repressor proteins mediate negative control.

**negative feedback** A homeostatic control mechanism whereby an increase in some substance or activity inhibits the process leading to the increase; also known as feedback inhibition.

**nematocyst** A harpoonlike structure found in the cnidocytes of animals in the phylum Cnidaria, which includes the jellyfish among other groups; the nematocyst, when released, stings and helps capture prey.

**nephridium, pl. nephridia** In invertebrates, a tubular excretory structure.

**nephrid organ** A filtration system of many freshwater invertebrates in which water and waste pass from the body across the membrane into a collecting organ, from which they are expelled to the outside through a pore.

**nephron** Functional unit of the vertebrate kidney; one of numerous tubules involved in filtration and selective reabsorption of blood; each nephron consists of a Bowman's capsule, an enclosed glomerulus, and a long attached tubule; in humans, called a renal tubule.

**nephrostome** The funnel-shaped opening that leads to the nephridium, which is the excretory organ of mollusks.

**nerve** A group or bundle of nerve fibers (axons) with accompanying neurological cells, held together by connective tissue; located in the peripheral nervous system.

**nerve cord** One of the distinguishing features of chordates, running lengthwise just beneath the embryo's dorsal surface; in vertebrates, differentiates into the brain and spinal cord.

**neural crest** A special strip of cells that develops just before the neural groove closes over to form the neural tube in embryonic development.

**neural groove** The long groove formed along the long axis of the embryo by a layer of ectodermal cells.

**neural tube** The dorsal tube, formed from the neural plate, that differentiates into the brain and spinal cord.

**neuroglia** Nonconducting nerve cells that are intimately associated with neurons and appear to provide nutritional support.

**neuromuscular junction** The structure formed when the tips of axons contact (innervate) a muscle fiber.

**neuron** A nerve cell specialized for signal transmission; includes cell body, dendrites, and axon.

**neurotransmitter** A chemical released at the axon terminal of a neuron that travels across the synaptic cleft, binds a specific receptor on the far side, and depending on the nature of the receptor, depolarizes or hyperpolarizes a second neuron or a muscle or gland cell.

**neurulation** A process in early embryonic development by which a dorsal band of ectoderm thickens and rolls into the neural tube.

**neutrophil** An abundant type of granulocyte capable of engulfing microorganisms and other foreign particles; neutrophils comprise about 50–70% of the total number of white blood cells.

**niche** The role played by a particular species in its environment.

**nicotinamide adenine dinucleotide (NAD)** A molecule that becomes reduced (to NADH) as it carries high-energy electrons from oxidized molecules and delivers them to ATP-producing pathways in the cell.

**NADH dehydrogenase** An enzyme located on the inner mitochondrial membrane that catalyzes the oxidation by $NAD^+$ of pyruvate to acetyl-CoA. This reaction links glycolysis and the Krebs cycle.

**nitrification** The oxidization of ammonia or nitrite to produce nitrate, the form of nitrogen taken up by plants; some bacteria are capable of nitrification.

**nociceptor** A naked dendrite that acts as a receptor in response to a pain stimulus.

**nocturnal** Active primarily at night.

**node** The part of a plant stem where one or more leaves are attached. *See* internode.

**node of Ranvier** A gap formed at the point where two Schwann cells meet and where the axon is in direct contact with the surrounding intercellular fluid.

**nodule** In plants, a specialized tissue that surrounds and houses beneficial bacteria, such as root nodules of legumes that contain nitrogen-fixing bacteria.

**nonassociative learning** A learned behavior that does not require an animal to form an association between two stimuli, or between a stimulus and a response.

**noncompetitive inhibitor** An inhibitor that binds to a location other than the active site of an enzyme, changing the enzyme's shape so that it cannot bind the substrate.

**noncyclic photophosphorylation** The set of light-dependent reactions of the two plant photosystems, in which excited electrons are shuttled between the two photosystems, producing a proton gradient that is used for the chemiosmotic synthesis of ATP. The electrons are used to reduce NADP to NADPH. Lost electrons are replaced by the oxidation of water producing $O_2$.

**nondisjunction** The failure of homologues or sister chromatids to separate during mitosis or meiosis, resulting in an aneuploid cell or gamete.

**nonextreme archaea** Archaean groups that are not extremophiles, living in more moderate environments on Earth today.

**nonpolar** Said of a covalent bond that involves equal sharing of electrons. Can also refer to a compound held together by nonpolar covalent bonds.

**nonsense codon** One of three codons (UAA, UAG, and UGA) that are not recognized by tRNAs, thus serving as "stop" signals in the mRNA message and terminating translation.

**nonsense mutation** A base substitution in which a codon is changed into a stop codon. The protein is truncated because of premature termination.

**Northern blot** A blotting technique used to identify a specific mRNA sequence in a complex mixture. *See* Southern blot.

**notochord** In chordates, a dorsal rod of cartilage that runs the length of the body and forms the primitive axial skeleton in the embryos of all chordates.

**nucellus** Tissue composing the chief pair of young ovules, in which the embryo sac develops; equivalent to a megasporangium.

**nuclear envelope** The bounding structure of the eukaryotic nucleus. Composed of two phospholipid bilayers with the outer one connected to the endoplasmic reticulum.

**nuclear pore** One of a multitude of tiny but complex openings in the nuclear envelope that allow selective passage of proteins and nucleic acids into and out of the nucleus.

**nuclear receptor** Intracellular receptors are found in both the cytoplasm and the nucleus. The site of action of the hormone–receptor complex is in the nucleus where they modify gene expression.

**nucleic acid** A nucleotide polymer; chief types are deoxyribonucleic acid (DNA), which is double-stranded, and ribonucleic acid (RNA), which is typically single-stranded.

**nucleoid** The area of a prokaryotic cell, usually near the center, that contains the genome in the form of DNA compacted with protein.

**nucleolus** In eukaryotes, the site of rRNA synthesis; a spherical body composed chiefly of rRNA in the process of being transcribed from multiple copies of rRNA genes.

**nucleosome** A complex consisting of a DNA duplex wound around a core of eight histone proteins.

**nucleotide** A single unit of nucleic acid, composed of a phosphate, a five-carbon sugar (either ribose or deoxyribose), and a purine or a pyrimidine.

**nucleus** In atoms, the central core, containing positively charged protons and (in all but hydrogen) electrically neutral neutrons; in eukaryotic cells, the membranous organelle that houses the chromosomal DNA; in the central nervous system, a cluster of nerve cell bodies.

**nutritional mutation** A mutation affecting a synthetic pathway for a vital compound, such as an amino acid or vitamin; microorganisms with a nutritional mutation must be grown on medium that supplies the missing nutrient.

# O

**ocellus,** pl. **ocelli** A simple light receptor common among invertebrates.

**octet rule** Rule to describe patterns of chemical bonding in main group elements that require a total of eight electrons to complete their outer electron shell.

**Okazaki fragment** A short segment of DNA produced by discontinuous replication elongating in the 5′-to-3′ direction away from the replication.

**olfaction** The function of smelling.

**ommatidium,** pl. **ommatidia** The visual unit in the compound eye of arthropods; contains light-sensitive cells and a lens able to form an image.

**oncogene** A mutant form of a growth-regulating gene that is inappropriately "on," causing unrestrained cell growth and division.

**oocyst** The zygote in a sporozoan life cycle. It is surrounded by a tough cyst to prevent dehydration or other damage.

**open circulatory system** A circulatory system in which the blood flows into sinuses in which it mixes with body fluid and then reenters the vessels in another location.

**open reading frame (ORF)** A region of DNA that encodes a sequence of amino acids with no stop codons in the reading frame.

**operant conditioning** A learning mechanism in which the reward follows only after the correct behavioral response.

**operator** A regulatory site on DNA to which a repressor can bind to prevent or decrease initiation of transcription.

**operculum** A flat, bony, external protective covering over the gill chamber in fish.

**operon** A cluster of adjacent structural genes transcribed as a unit into a single mRNA molecule.

**opisthosoma** The posterior portion of the body of an arachnid.

**oral surface** The surface on which the mouth is found; used as a reference when describing the body structure of echinoderms because of their adult radial symmetry.

**orbital** A region around the nucleus of an atom with a high probability of containing an electron. The position of electrons can only be described by these probability distributions.

**order** A category of classification above the level of family and below that of class.

**organ** A body structure composed of several different tissues grouped in a structural and functional unit.

**organelle** Specialized part of a cell; literally, a small cytoplasmic organ.

**orthologues** Genes that reflect the conservation of a single gene found in an ancestor.

**oscillating selection** The situation in which selection alternately favors one phenotype at one time, and a different phenotype at a another time, for example, during drought conditions versus during wet conditions.

**osculum** A specialized, larger pore in sponges through which filtered water is forced to the outside of the body.

**osmoconformer** An animal that maintains the osmotic concentration of its body fluids at about the same level as that of the medium in which it is living.

**osmosis** The diffusion of water across a selectively permeable membrane (a membrane that permits the free passage of water but prevents or retards the passage of a solute); in the absence of differences in pressure or volume, the net movement of water is from the side containing a lower concentration of solute to the side containing a higher concentration.

**osmotic concentration** The property of a solution that takes into account all dissolved solutes in the solution; if two solutions with different osmotic concentrations are separated by a water-permeable membrane, water will move from the solution with lower osmotic concentration to the solution with higher osmotic concentration.

**osmotic pressure** The potential pressure developed by a solution separated from pure water by a differentially permeable membrane. The higher the solute concentration, the greater the osmotic potential of the solution; also called *osmotic potential*.

**ossicle** Any of a number of movable or fixed calcium-rich plates that collectively make up the endoskeleton of echinoderms.

**osteoblast** A bone-forming cell.

**osteocyte** A mature osteoblast.

**outcrossing** Breeding with individuals other than oneself or one's close relatives.

**ovary** (1) In animals, the organ in which eggs are produced. (2) In flowering plants, the enlarged basal portion of a carpel that contains the ovule(s); the ovary matures to become the fruit.

**oviduct** In vertebrates, the passageway through which ova (eggs) travel from the ovary to the uterus.

**oviparity** Refers to a type of reproduction in which the eggs are developed after leaving the body of the mother, as in reptiles.

**ovoviviparity** Refers to a type of reproduction in which young hatch from eggs that are retained in the mother's uterus.

**ovulation** In animals, the release of an egg or eggs from the ovary.

**ovum,** pl. **ova** The egg cell; female gamete.

**oxidation** Loss of an electron by an atom or molecule; in metabolism, often associated with a gain of oxygen or a loss of hydrogen.

**oxidation–reduction reaction** A type of paired reaction in living systems in which electrons lost from one atom (oxidation) are gained by another atom (reduction). Termed a *redox reaction* for short.

**oxidative phosphorylation** Synthesis of ATP by ATP synthase using energy from a proton gradient. The proton gradient is generated by electron transport, which requires oxygen.

**oxygen debt** The amount of oxygen required to convert the lactic acid generated in the muscles during exercise back into glucose.

**oxytocin** A hormone of the posterior pituitary gland that affects uterine contractions during childbirth and stimulates lactation.

**ozone** $O_3$, a stratospheric layer of the Earth's atmosphere responsible for filtering out ultraviolet radiation supplied by the Sun.

# P

**p53 gene** The gene that produces the p53 protein that monitors DNA integrity and halts cell division if DNA damage is detected. Many types of cancer are associated with a damaged or absent *p53* gene.

**pacemaker** A patch of excitatory tissue in the vertebrate heart that initiates the heartbeat.

**pair-rule gene** Any of certain genes in *Drosophila* development controlled by the gap genes that are expressed in stripes that subdivide the embryo in the process of segmentation.

**paleopolyploid** An ancient polyploid organism used in analysis of polyploidy events in the study of a species' genome evolution.

**palisade parenchyma** In plant leaves, the columnar, chloroplast-containing parenchyma cells of the mesophyll. Also called *palisade cells.*

**panspermia** The hypothesis that meteors or cosmic dust may have brought significant amounts of complex organic molecules to Earth, kicking off the evolution of life.

**papilla** A small projection of tissue.

**paracrine** A type of chemical signaling between cells in which the effects are local and short-lived.

**paralogues** Two genes within an organism that arose from the duplication of one gene in an ancestor.

**paraphyletic** In phylogenetic classification, a group that includes the most recent common ancestor of the group, but not all its descendants.

**parapodia** One of the paired lateral processes on each side of most segments in polychaete annelids.

**parasexuality** In certain fungi, the fusion and segregation of heterokaryotic haploid nuclei to produce recombinant nuclei.

**parasitism** A living arrangement in which an organism lives on or in an organism of a different species and derives nutrients from it.

**parenchyma cell** The most common type of plant cell; characterized by large vacuoles, thin walls, and functional nuclei.

**parthenogenesis** The development of an egg without fertilization, as in aphids, bees, ants, and some lizards.

**partial diploid (merodiploid)** Describes an *E. coli* cell that carries an F′ plasmid with host genes. This makes the cell diploid for the genes carried by the F′ plasmid.

**partial pressure** The components of each individual gas—such as nitrogen, oxygen, and carbon dioxide—that together constitute the total air pressure.

**passive transport** The movement of substances across a cell's membrane without the expenditure of energy.

**pedigree** A consistent graphic representation of matings and offspring over multiple generations for a particular genetic trait, such as albinism or hemophilia.

**pedipalps** A pair of specialized appendages found in arachnids; in male spiders, these are specialized as copulatory organs, whereas in scorpions they are large pincers.

**pelagic** Free-swimming, usually in open water.

**pellicle** A tough, flexible covering in ciliates and euglenoids.

**pentaradial symmetry** The five-part radial symmetry characteristic of adult echinoderms.

**peptide bond** The type of bond that links amino acids together in proteins through a dehydration reaction.

**peptidoglycan** A component of the cell wall of bacteria, consisting of carbohydrate polymers linked by protein cross-bridges.

**peptidyl transferase** In translation, the enzyme responsible for catalyzing the formation of a peptide bond between each new amino acid and the previous amino acid in a growing polypeptide chain.

**perianth** In flowering plants, the petals and sepals taken together.

**pericycle** In vascular plants, one or more cell layers surrounding the vascular tissues of the root, bounded externally by the endodermis and internally by the phloem.

**periderm** Outer protective tissue in vascular plants that is produced by the cork cambium and functionally replaces epidermis when it is destroyed during secondary growth; the periderm includes the cork, cork cambium, and phelloderm.

**peristalsis** In animals, a series of alternating contracting and relaxing muscle movements along the length of a tube such as the oviduct or alimentary canal that tend to force material such as an egg cell or food through the tube.

**peroxisome** A microbody that plays an important role in the breakdown of highly oxidative hydrogen peroxide by catalase.

**petal** A flower part, usually conspicuously colored; one of the units of the corolla.

**petiole** The stalk of a leaf.

**phage conversion** The phenomenon by which DNA from a virus, incorporated into a host cell's genome, alters the host cell's function in a significant way; for example, the conversion of *Vibrio cholerae* bacteria into a pathogenic form that releases cholera toxin.

**phage lambda (λ)** A well-known bacteriophage that has been widely used in genetic studies and is often a vector for DNA libraries.

**phagocyte** Any cell that engulfs and devours microorganisms or other particles.

**phagocytosis** Endocytosis of a solid particle; the plasma membrane folds inward around the particle (which may be another cell) and engulfs it to form a vacuole.

**pharyngeal pouches** In chordates, embryonic regions that become pharyngeal slits in aquatic and marine chordates and vertebrates, but do not develop openings to the outside in terrestrial vertebrates.

**pharyngeal slits** One of the distinguishing features of chordates; a group of openings on each side of the anterior region that form a passageway from the pharynx and esophagus to the external environment.

**pharynx** A muscular structure lying posterior to the mouth in many animals; aids in propelling food into the digestive tract.

**phenotype** The realized expression of the genotype; the physical appearance or functional expression of a trait.

**pheromone** Chemical substance released by one organism that influences the behavior or physiological processes of another organism of the same species. Pheromones serve as sex attractants, as trail markers, and as alarm signals.

**phloem** In vascular plants, a food-conducting tissue basically composed of sieve elements, various kinds of parenchyma cells, fibers, and sclereids.

**phoronid** Any of a group of lophophorate invertebrates, now classified in the phylum Brachiopoda, that burrows into soft underwater substrates and secretes a chitinous tube in which it lives out its life; it extends its lophophore tentacles to feed on drifting food particles.

**phosphatase** Any of a number of enzymes that removes a phosphate group from a protein, reversing the action of a kinase.

**phosphodiester bond** The linkage between two sugars in the backbone of a nucleic acid molecule; the phosphate group connects the pentose sugars through a pair of ester bonds.

**phospholipid** Similar in structure to a fat, but having only two fatty acids attached to the glycerol backbone, with the third space linked to a phosphorylated molecule; contains a polar hydrophilic "head" end (phosphate group) and a nonpolar hydrophobic "tail" end (fatty acids).

**phospholipid bilayer** The main component of cell membranes; phospholipids naturally associate in a bilayer with hydrophobic fatty acids oriented to the inside and hydrophilic phosphate groups facing outward on both sides.

**phosphorylation** Chemical reaction resulting in the addition of a phosphate group to an organic molecule. Phosphorylation of ADP yields ATP. Many proteins are also activated or inactivated by phosphorylation.

**photoelectric effect** The ability of a beam of light to excite electrons, creating an electrical current.

**photon** A particle of light having a discrete amount of energy. The wave concept of light explains the different colors of the spectrum, whereas the particle concept of light explains the energy transfers during photosynthesis.

**photoperiodism** The tendency of biological reactions to respond to the duration and timing of day and night; a mechanism for measuring seasonal time.

**photoreceptor** A light-sensitive sensory cell.

**photorespiration** Action of the enzyme rubisco, which catalyzes the oxidization of RuBP, releasing $CO_2$; this reverses carbon fixation and can reduce the yield of photosynthesis.

**photosystem** An organized complex of chlorophyll, other pigments, and proteins that traps light energy as excited electrons. Plants have two linked photosystems in the thylakoid membrane of chloroplasts. Photosystem II passes an excited electron through an electron transport chain to photosystem I to replace an excited electron passed to NADPH. The electron lost from photosystem II is replaced by the oxidation of water.

**phototropism** In plants, a growth response to a light stimulus.

**pH scale** A scale used to measure acidity and basicity. Defined as the negative log of $H^+$ concentration. Ranges from 0 to 14. A value of 7 is neutral; below 7 is acidic and above 7 is basic.

**phycobiloprotein** A type of accessory pigment found in cyanobacteria and some algae. Complexes of phycobiloprotein are able to absorb light energy in the green range.

**phycologist** A scientist who studies algae.

**phyllotaxy** In plants, a spiral pattern of leaf arrangement on a stem in which sequential leaves are at a 137.5° angle to one another, an angle related to the golden mean.

**phylogenetic species concept (PSC)** The concept that defines species on the basis of their phylogenetic relationships.

**phylogenetic tree** A pattern of descent generated by analysis of similarities and differences among organisms. Modern gene-sequencing techniques have produced phylogenetic trees showing the evolutionary history of individual genes.

**phylogeny** The evolutionary history of an organism, including which species are closely related and in what order related species evolved; often represented in the form of an evolutionary tree.

**phylum, pl. phyla** A major category, between kingdom and class, of taxonomic classifications.

**physical map** A map of the DNA sequence of a chromosome or genome based on actual landmarks within the DNA.

**phytochrome** A plant pigment that is associated with the absorption of light; photoreceptor for red to far-red light.

**phytoestrogen** One of a number of secondary metabolites in some plants that are structurally and functionally similar to the animal hormone estrogen.

**phytoremediation** The process that uses plants to remove contamination from soil or water.

**pigment** A molecule that absorbs light.

**pilus, pl. pili** Extensions of a bacterial cell enabling it to transfer genetic materials from one individual to another or to adhere to substrates.

**pinocytosis** The process of fluid uptake by endocytosis in a cell.

**pistil** Central organ of flowers, typically consisting of ovary, style, and stigma; a pistil may consist of one or more fused carpels and is more technically and better known as the gynoecium.

**pith** The ground tissue occupying the center of the stem or root within the vascular cylinder.

**pituitary gland** Endocrine gland at the base of the hypothalamus composed of anterior and posterior lobes. Pituitary hormones affect a wide variety of processes in vertebrates.

**placenta, pl. placentae** (1) In flowering plants, the part of the ovary wall to which the ovules or seeds are attached. (2) In mammals, a tissue formed in part from the inner lining of the uterus and in part from other membranes, through which the embryo (later the fetus) is nourished while in the uterus and through which wastes are carried away.

**plankton** Free-floating, mostly microscopic, aquatic organisms.

**plant receptor kinase** Any of a group of plant membrane receptors that, when activated by binding ligand, have kinase enzymatic activity. These receptors phosphorylate serine or threonine, unlike RTKs in animals that phosphorylate tyrosine.

**planula** A ciliated, free-swimming larva produced by the medusae of cnidarian animals.

**plasma** The fluid of vertebrate blood; contains dissolved salts, metabolic wastes, hormones, and a variety of proteins, including antibodies and albumin; blood minus the blood cells.

**plasma cell** An antibody-producing cell resulting from the multiplication and differentiation of a B lymphocyte that has interacted with an antigen.

**plasma membrane** The membrane surrounding the cytoplasm of a cell; consists of a single phospholipid bilayer with embedded proteins.

**plasmid** A small fragment of extrachromosomal DNA, usually circular, that replicates independently of the main chromosome, although it may have been derived from it.

**plasmodesmata** In plants, cytoplasmic connections between adjacent cells.

**plasmodium** Stage in the life cycle of myxomycetes (plasmodial slime molds); a multinucleate mass of protoplasm surrounded by a membrane.

**plasmolysis** The shrinking of a plant cell in a hypertonic solution such that it pulls away from the cell wall.

**plastid** An organelle in the cells of photosynthetic eukaryotes that is the site of photosynthesis and, in plants and green algae, of starch storage.

**platelet** In mammals, a fragment of a white blood cell that circulates in the blood and functions in the formation of blood clots at sites of injury.

**pleiotropy** Condition in which an individual allele has more than one effect on production of the phenotype.

**plesiomorphy** In cladistics, another term for an ancestral character state.

**plumule** The epicotyl of a plant with its two young leaves.

**point mutation** An alteration of one nucleotide in a chromosomal DNA molecule.

**polar body** Minute, nonfunctioning cell produced during the meiotic divisions leading to gamete formation in vertebrates.

**polar covalent bond** A covalent bond in which electrons are shared unequally due to differences in electronegativity of the atoms involved. One atom has a partial negative charge and the other a partial positive charge, even though the molecule is electrically neutral overall.

**polarity** (1) Refers to unequal charge distribution in a molecule such as water, which has a positive region and a negative region although it is neutral overall. (2) Refers to axial differences in a developing embryo that result in anterior–posterior and dorsal–ventral axes in a bilaterally symmetrical animal.

**polarize** In cladistics, to determine whether character states are ancestral or derived.

**pollen tube** A tube formed after germination of the pollen grain; carries the male gametes into the ovule.

**pollination** The transfer of pollen from an anther to a stigma.

**polyandry** The condition in which a female mates with more than one male.

**polyclonal antibody** An antibody response in which an antigen elicits many different antibodies, each fitting a different portion of the antigen surface.

**polygenic inheritance** Describes a mode of inheritance in which more than one gene affects a trait, such as height in human beings; polygenic inheritance may produce a continuous range of phenotypic values, rather than discrete either–or values.

**polygyny** A mating choice in which a male mates with more than one female.

**polymer** A molecule composed of many similar or identical molecular subunits; starch is a polymer of glucose.

**polymerase chain reaction (PCR)** A process by which DNA polymerase is used to copy a sequence of interest repeatedly, making millions of copies of the same DNA.

**polymorphism** The presence in a population of more than one allele of a gene at a frequency greater than that of newly arising mutations.

**polyp** A typically sessile, cylindrical body form found in cnidarian animals, such as hydras.

**polypeptide** A molecule consisting of many joined amino acids; not usually as complex as a protein.

**polyphyletic** In phylogenetic classification, a group that does not include the most recent common ancestor of all members of the group.

**polyploidy** Condition in which one or more entire sets of chromosomes is added to the diploid genome.

**polysaccharide** A carbohydrate composed of many monosaccharide sugar subunits linked together in a long chain; examples are glycogen, starch, and cellulose.

**polyunsaturated fat** A fat molecule having at least two double bonds between adjacent carbons in one or more of the fatty acid chains.

**population** Any group of individuals, usually of a single species, occupying a given area at the same time.

**population genetics** The study of the properties of genes in populations.

**positive control** A type of control at the level of DNA transcription initiation in which the frequency of initiation is increased; activator proteins mediate positive control.

**posttranscriptional control** A mechanism of control over gene expression that operates after the transcription of mRNA is complete.

**postzygotic isolating mechanism** A type of reproductive isolation in which zygotes are produced but are unable to develop into reproducing adults; these mechanisms may range from inviability of zygotes or embryos to adults that are sterile.

**potential energy** Energy that is not being used, but could be; energy in a potentially usable form; often called "energy of position."

**precapillary sphincter** A ring of muscle that guards each capillary loop and that, when closed, blocks flow through the capillary.

**pre-mRNA splicing** In eukaryotes, the process by which introns are removed from the primary transcript to produce mature mRNA; pre-mRNA splicing occurs in the nucleus.

**pressure potential** In plants, the turgor pressure resulting from pressure against the cell wall.

**prezygotic isolating mechanism** A type of reproductive isolation in which the formation of a zygote is prevented; these mechanisms may range from physical separation in different habitats to gametic in which gametes are incapable of fusing.

**primary endosperm nucleus** In flowering plants, the result of the fusion of a sperm nucleus and the (usually) two polar nuclei.

**primary growth** In vascular plants, growth originating in the apical meristems of shoots and roots; results in an increase in length.

**primary immune response** The first response of an immune system to a foreign antigen. If the system is challenged again with the same antigen, the memory cells created during the primary response will respond more quickly.

**primary induction** Inductions between the three primary tissue types: mesoderm and endoderm.

**primary meristem** Any of the three meristems produced by the apical meristem; primary meristems give rise to the dermal, vascular, and ground tissues.

**primary nondisjunction** Failure of chromosomes to separate properly at meiosis I.

**primary phloem** The cells involved in food conduction in plants.

**primary plant body** The part of a plant consisting of young, soft shoots and roots derived from apical meristem tissues.

**primary productivity** The amount of energy produced by photosynthetic organisms in a community.

**primary structure** The specific amino acid sequence of a protein.

**primary tissues** Tissues that make up the primary plant body.

**primary transcript** The initial mRNA molecule copied from a gene by RNA polymerase, containing a faithful copy of the entire gene, including introns as well as exons.

**primary wall** In plants, the wall layer deposited during the period of cell expansion.

**primase** The enzyme that synthesizes the RNA primers required by DNA polymerases.

**primate** Monkeys and apes (including humans).

**primitive streak** In the early embryos of birds, reptiles, and mammals, a dorsal, longitudinal strip of ectoderm and mesoderm that is equivalent to the blastopore in other forms.

**primordium** In plants, a bulge on the young shoot produced by the apical meristem; primordia can differentiate into leaves, other shoots, or flowers.

**principle of parsimony** Principle stating that scientists should favor the hypothesis that requires the fewest assumptions.

**prions** Infectious proteinaceous particles.

**procambium** In vascular plants, a primary meristematic tissue that gives rise to primary vascular tissues.

**product rule** *See* rule of multiplication.

**proglottid** A repeated body segment in tapeworms that contains both male and female reproductive organs; proglottids eventually form eggs and embryos, which leave the host's body in feces.

**prokaryote** A bacterium; a cell lacking a membrane-bounded nucleus or membrane-bounded organelles.

**prometaphase** The transitional phase between prophase and metaphase during which the spindle attaches to the kinetochores of sister chromatids.

**promoter** A DNA sequence that provides a recognition and attachment site for RNA polymerase to begin the process of gene transcription; it is located upstream from the transcription start site.

**prophase** The phase of cell division that begins when the condensed chromosomes become visible and ends when the nuclear envelope breaks down. The assembly of the spindle takes place during prophase.

**proprioceptor** In vertebrates, a sensory receptor that senses the body's position and movements.

**prosimian** Any member of the mammalian group that is a sister group to the anthropoids; prosimian means "before monkeys." Members include the lemurs, lorises, and tarsiers.

**prosoma** The anterior portion of the body of an arachnid, which bears all the appendages.

**prostaglandins** A group of modified fatty acids that function as chemical messengers.

**prostate gland** In male mammals, a mass of glandular tissue at the base of the urethra that secretes an alkaline fluid that has a stimulating effect on the sperm as they are released.

**protease** An enzyme that degrades proteins by breaking peptide bonds; in cells, proteases are often compartmentalized into vesicles such as lysosomes.

**proteasome** A large, cylindrical cellular organelle that degrades proteins marked with ubiquitin.

**protein** A chain of amino acids joined by peptide bonds.

**protein kinase** An enzyme that adds phosphate groups to proteins, changing their activity.

**protein microarray** An array of proteins on a microscope slide or silicon chip. The array may be used with a variety of probes, including antibodies, to analyze the presence or absence of specific proteins in a complex mixture.

**proteome** All the proteins coded for by a particular genome.

**proteomics** The study of the proteomes of organisms. This is related to functional genomics as the proteome is responsible for much of the function encoded by a genome.

**protoderm** The primary meristem that gives rise to the dermal tissue.

**proton pump** A protein channel in a membrane of the cell that expends energy to transport protons against a concentration gradient; involved in the chemiosmotic generation of ATP.

**proto-oncogene** A normal cellular gene that can act as an oncogene when mutated.

**protostome** Any member of a grouping of bilaterally symmetrical animals in which the mouth develops first and the anus second; flatworms, nematodes, mollusks, annelids, and arthropods are protostomes.

**pseudocoel** A body cavity located between the endoderm and mesoderm.

**pseudogene** A copy of a gene that is not transcribed.

**pseudomurien** A component of the cell wall of archaea; it is similar to peptidoglycan in structure and function but contains different components.

**pseudopod** A nonpermanent cytoplasmic extension of the cell body.

**P site** In a ribosome, the peptidyl site that binds to the tRNA attached to the growing polypeptide chain.

**punctuated equilibrium** A hypothesis about the mechanism of evolutionary change proposing that long periods of little or no change are punctuated by periods of rapid evolution.

**Punnett square** A diagrammatic way of showing the possible genotypes and phenotypes of genetic crosses.

**pupa** A developmental stage of some insects in which the organism is nonfeeding, immotile, and sometimes encapsulated or in a cocoon; the pupal stage occurs between the larval and adult phases.

**purine** The larger of the two general kinds of nucleotide base found in DNA and RNA; a nitrogenous base with a double-ring structure, such as adenine or guanine.

**pyrimidine** The smaller of two general kinds of nucleotide base found in DNA and RNA; a nitrogenous base with a single-ring structure, such as cytosine, thymine, or uracil.

**pyruvate** A three-carbon molecule that is the end product of glycolysis; each glucose molecule yields two pyruvate molecules.

# Q

**quantitative trait** A trait that is determined by the effects of more than one gene; such a trait usually exhibits continuous variation rather than discrete either–or values.

**quaternary structure** The structural level of a protein composed of more than one polypeptide chain, each of which has its own tertiary structure; the individual chains are called subunits.

# R

**radial canal** Any of five canals that connect to the ring canal of an echinoderm's water–vascular system.

**radial cleavage** The embryonic cleavage pattern of deuterostome animals in which cells divide parallel to and at right angles to the polar axis of the embryo.

**radial symmetry** A type of structural symmetry with a circular plan, such that dividing the body or structure through the midpoint in any direction yields two identical sections.

**radicle** The part of the plant embryo that develops into the root.

**radioactive isotope** An isotope that is unstable and undergoes radioactive decay, releasing energy.

**radioactivity** The emission of nuclear particles and rays by unstable atoms as they decay into more stable forms.

**radula** Rasping tongue found in most mollusks.

**reaction center** A transmembrane protein complex in a photosystem that receives energy from the antenna complex exciting an electron that is passed to an acceptor molecule.

**reading frame** The correct succession of nucleotides in triplet codons that specify amino acids on translation. The reading frame is established by the first codon in the sequence as there are no spaces in the genetic code.

**realized niche** The actual niche occupied by an organism when all biotic and abiotic interactions are taken into account.

**receptor-mediated endocytosis** Process by which specific macromolecules are transported into eukaryotic cells at clathrin-coated pits, after binding to specific cell-surface receptors.

**receptor protein** A highly specific cell-surface receptor embedded in a cell membrane that responds only to a specific messenger molecule.

**receptor tyrosine kinase (RTK)** A diverse group of membrane receptors that when activated have kinase enzymatic activity. Specifically, they phosphorylate proteins on tyrosine. Their activation can lead to diverse cellular responses.

**recessive** An allele that is only expressed when present in the homozygous condition, but being "hidden" by the expression of a dominant allele in the heterozygous condition.

**redia** A secondary, nonciliated larva produced in the sporocysts of liver flukes.

**regulatory protein** Any of a group of proteins that modulates the ability of RNA polymerase to bind to a promoter and begin DNA transcription.

**replicon** An origin of DNA replication and the DNA whose replication is controlled by this origin. In prokaryotic replication, the chromosome plus the origin consist of a single replicon; eukaryotic chromosomes consist of multiple replicons.

**replisome** The macromolecular assembly of enzymes involved in DNA replication; analogous to the ribosome in protein synthesis.

**reciprocal altruism** Performance of an altruistic act with the expectation that the favor will be returned. A key and very controversial assumption of many theories dealing with the evolution of social behavior. *See* altruism.

**reciprocal cross** A genetic cross involving a single trait in which the sex of the parents is reversed; for example, if pollen from a white-flowered plant is used to fertilize a purple-flowered plant, the reciprocal cross would be pollen from a purple-flowered plant used to fertilize a white-flowered plant.

**reciprocal recombination** A mechanism of genetic recombination that occurs only in eukaryotic organisms, in which two chromosomes trade segments; can occur between nonhomologous chromosomes as well as the more usual exchange between homologous chromosomes in meiosis.

**recombinant DNA** Fragments of DNA from two different species, such as a bacterium and a mammal, spliced together in the laboratory into a single molecule.

**recombination frequency** The value obtained by dividing the number of recombinant progeny by the total progeny in a genetic cross. This value is converted into a percentage, and each 1% is termed a map unit.

**reduction** The gain of an electron by an atom, often with an associated proton.

**reflex** In the nervous system, a motor response subject to little associative modification; a reflex is among the simplest neural pathways, involving only a sensory neuron, sometimes (but not always) an interneuron, and one or more motor neurons.

**reflex arc** The nerve path in the body that leads from stimulus to reflex action.

**refractory period** The recovery period after membrane depolarization during which the membrane is unable to respond to additional stimulation.

**reinforcement** In speciation, the process by which partial reproductive isolation between populations is increased by selection against mating between members of the two populations, eventually resulting in complete reproductive isolation.

**replica plating** A method of transferring bacterial colonies from one plate to another to make a copy of the original plate; an impression of colonies growing on a Petri plate is made on a velvet surface, which is then used to transfer the colonies to plates containing different media, such that auxotrophs can be identified.

**replication fork** The Y-shaped end of a growing replication bubble in a DNA molecule undergoing replication.

**repolarization** Return of the ions in a nerve to their resting potential distribution following depolarization.

**repression** In general, control of gene expression by preventing transcription. Specifically, in bacteria such as *E. coli* this is mediated by repressor proteins. In anabolic operons, repressors bind DNA in the absence of corepressors to repress an operon.

**repressor** A protein that regulates DNA transcription by preventing RNA polymerase from attaching to the promoter and transcribing the structural gene. *See* operator.

**reproductive isolating mechanism** Any barrier that prevents genetic exchange between species.

**residual volume** The amount of air remaining in the lungs after the maximum amount of air has been exhaled.

**resting membrane potential** The charge difference (difference in electric potential) that exists across a neuron at rest (about 70 mV).

**restriction endonuclease** An enzyme that cleaves a DNA duplex molecule at a particular base sequence, usually within or near a palindromic sequence; also called a restriction enzyme.

**restriction fragment length polymorphism (RFLP)** Restriction enzymes recognize very specific DNA sequences. Alleles of the same gene or surrounding sequences may have base-pair differences, so that DNA near one allele is cut into a different-length fragment than DNA near the other allele. These different fragments separate based on size on electrophoresis gels.

**retina** The photosensitive layer of the vertebrate eye; contains several layers of neurons and light receptors (rods and cones); receives the image formed by the lens and transmits it to the brain via the optic nerve.

**retinoblastoma susceptibility gene (*Rb*)** A gene that, when mutated, predisposes individuals to a rare form of cancer of the retina; one of the first tumor-suppressor genes discovered.

**retrovirus** An RNA virus. When a retrovirus enters a cell, a viral enzyme (reverse transcriptase) transcribes viral RNA into duplex DNA, which the cell's machinery then replicates and transcribes as if it were its own.

**reverse genetics** An approach by which a researcher uses a cloned gene of unknown function, creates a mutation, and introduces the mutant gene back into the organism to assess the effect of the mutation.

**reverse transcriptase** A viral enzyme found in retroviruses that is capable of converting their RNA genome into a DNA copy.

**Rh blood group** A set of cell-surface markers (antigens) on the surface of red blood cells in humans and rhesus monkeys (for which it is named); although there are several alleles, they are grouped into two main types: Rh-positive and Rh-negative.

**rhizome** In vascular plants, a more or less horizontal underground stem; may be enlarged for storage or may function in vegetative reproduction.

**rhynchocoel** A true coelomic cavity in ribbonworms that serves as a hydraulic power source for extending the proboscis.

**ribonucleic acid (RNA)** A class of nucleic acids characterized by the presence of the sugar ribose and the pyrimidine uracil; includes mRNA, tRNA, and rRNA.

**ribosomal RNA (rRNA)** A class of RNA molecules found, together with characteristic proteins, in ribosomes; transcribed from the DNA of the nucleolus.

**ribosome** The molecular machine that carries out protein synthesis; the most complicated aggregation of proteins in a cell, also containing three different rRNA molecules.

**ribosome-binding sequence (RBS)** In prokaryotes, a conserved sequence at the 5′ end of mRNA that is complementary to the 3′ end of a small subunit rRNA and helps to position the ribosome during initiation.

**ribozyme** An RNA molecule that can behave as an enzyme, sometimes catalyzing its own assembly; rRNA also acts as a ribozyme in the polymerization of amino acids to form protein.

**ribulose 1,5-bisphosphate (RuBP)** In the Calvin cycle, the five-carbon sugar to which $CO_2$ is attached, accomplishing carbon fixation. This reaction is catalyzed by the enzyme rubisco.

**ribulose bisphosphate carboxylase/oxygenase (rubisco)** The four-subunit enzyme in the chloroplast that catalyzes the carbon fixation reaction joining $CO_2$ to RuBP.

**RNA interference** A type of gene silencing in which the mRNA transcript is prevented from being translated; small interfering RNAs (siRNAs) have been found to bind to mRNA and target its degradation prior to its translation.

**RNA polymerase** An enzyme that catalyzes the assembly of an mRNA molecule, the sequence of which is complementary to a DNA molecule used as a template. *See* transcription.

**RNA primer** In DNA replication, a sequence of about 10 RNA nucleotides complementary to unwound DNA that attaches at a replication fork; the DNA polymerase uses the RNA primer as a starting point for addition of DNA nucleotides to form the new DNA strand; the RNA primer is later removed and replaced by DNA nucleotides.

**RNA splicing** A nuclear process by which intron sequences of a primary mRNA transcript are cut out and the exon sequences spliced together to give the correct linkages of genetic information that will be used in protein construction.

**rod** Light-sensitive nerve cell found in the vertebrate retina; sensitive to very dim light; responsible for "night vision."

**root** The usually descending axis of a plant, normally below ground, which anchors the plant and serves as the major point of entry for water and minerals.

**root cap** In plants, a tissue structure at the growing tips of roots that protects the root apical meristem as the root pushes through the soil; cells of the root cap are continually lost and replaced.

**root hair** In plants, a tubular extension from an epidermal cell located just behind the root tip; root hairs greatly increase the surface area for absorption.

**root pressure** In plants, pressure exerted by water in the roots in response to a solute potential in the absence of transpiration; often occurs at night. Root pressure can result in guttation, excretion of water from cells of leaves as dew.

**root system** In plants, the portion of the plant body that anchors the plant and absorbs ions and water.

**R plasmid** A resistance plasmid; a conjugative plasmid that picks up antibiotic resistance genes and can therefore transfer resistance from one bacterium to another.

**rule of addition** The rule stating that for two independent events, the probability of either event occurring is the sum of the individual probabilities.

**rule of multiplication** The rule stating that for two independent events, the probability of both events occurring is the product of the individual probabilities.

**rumen** An "extra stomach" in cows and related mammals wherein digestion of cellulose occurs and from which partially digested material can be ejected back into the mouth.

# S

**salicylic acid** In plants, an organic molecule that is a long-distance signal in systemic acquired resistance.

**saltatory conduction** A very fast form of nerve impulse conduction in which the impulses leap from node to node over insulated portions.

**saprobes** Heterotrophic organisms that digest their food externally (e.g., most fungi).

**sarcolemma** The specialized cell membrane in a muscle cell.

**sarcomere** Fundamental unit of contraction in skeletal muscle; repeating bands of actin and myosin that appear between two Z lines.

**sarcoplasmic reticulum** The endoplasmic reticulum of a muscle cell. A sleeve of membrane that wraps around each myofilament.

**satellite DNA** A nontranscribed region of the chromosome with a distinctive base composition; a short nucleotide sequence repeated tandemly many thousands of times.

**saturated fat** A fat composed of fatty acids in which all the internal carbon atoms contain the maximum possible number of hydrogen atoms.

**Schwann cells** The supporting cells associated with projecting axons, along with all the other nerve cells that make up the peripheral nervous system.

**sclereid** In vascular plants, a sclerenchyma cell with a thick, lignified, secondary wall having many pits; not elongate like a fiber.

**sclerenchyma cell** Tough, thick-walled cells that strengthen plant tissues.

**scolex** The attachment organ at the anterior end of a tapeworm.

**scrotum** The pouch that contains the testes in most mammals.

**scuttellum** The modified cotyledon in cereal grains.

**second filial (F₂) generation** The offspring resulting from a cross between members of the first filial (F₁) generation.

**secondary cell wall** In plants, the innermost layer of the cell wall. Secondary walls have a highly organized microfibrillar structure and are often impregnated with lignin.

**secondary growth** In vascular plants, an increase in stem and root diameter made possible by cell division of the lateral meristems.

**secondary immune response** The swifter response of the body the second time it is invaded by the same pathogen because of the presence of memory cells, which quickly become antibody-producing plasma cells.

**secondary induction** An induction between tissues that have already differentiated.

**secondary metabolite** A molecule not directly involved in growth, development, or reproduction of an organism; in plants these molecules, which include nicotine, caffeine, tannins, and menthols, can discourage herbivores.

**secondary plant body** The part of a plant consisting of secondary tissues from lateral meristem tissues; the older trunk, branches, and roots of woody plants.

**secondary structure** In a protein, hydrogen-bonding interactions between —CO and —NH groups of the primary structure.

**secondary tissue** Any tissue formed from lateral meristems in trees and shrubs.

**Second Law of Thermodynamics** A statement concerning the transformation of potential energy into heat; it says that disorder (entropy) is continually increasing in the universe as energy changes occur, so disorder is more likely than order.

**second messenger** A small molecule or ion that carries the message from a receptor on the target cell surface into the cytoplasm.

**seed bank** Ungerminated seeds in the soil of an area. Regeneration of plants after events such as fire often depends on the presence of a seed bank.

**seed coat** In plants, the outer layers of the ovule, which become a relatively impermeable barrier to protect the dormant embryo and stored food.

**segment polarity gene** Any of certain genes in *Drosophila* development that are expressed in stripes that subdivide the stripes created by the pair-rule genes in the process of segmentation.

**segmentation** The division of the developing animal body into repeated units; segmentation allows for redundant systems and more efficient locomotion.

**segmentation gene** Any of the three classes of genes that control development of the segmented body plan of insects; includes the gap genes, pair-rule genes, and segment polarity genes.

**segregation** The process by which alternative forms of traits are expressed in offspring rather than blending each trait of the parents in the offspring.

**selection** The process by which some organisms leave more offspring than competing ones, and their genetic traits tend to appear in greater proportions among members of succeeding generations than the traits of those individuals that leave fewer offspring.

**selectively permeable** Condition in which a membrane is permeable to some substances but not to others.

**self-fertilization** The union of egg and sperm produced by a single hermaphroditic organism.

**semen** In reptiles and mammals, sperm-bearing fluid expelled from the penis during male orgasm.

**semicircular canal** Any of three fluid-filled canals in the inner ear that help to maintain balance.

**semiconservative replication** DNA replication in which each strand of the original duplex serves as the template for construction of a totally new complementary strand, so the original duplex is partially conserved in each of the two new DNA molecules.

**senescent** Aged, or in the process of aging.

**sensory (afferent) neuron** A neuron that transmits nerve impulses from a sensory receptor to the central nervous system or central ganglion.

**sensory setae** In insect, bristles attached to the nervous system that are sensitive mechanical and chemical stimulation; most abundant on antennae and legs.

**sepal** A member of the outermost floral whorl of a flowering plant.

**septation** In prokaryotic cell division, the formation of a septum where new cell membrane and cell wall is formed to separate the two daughter cells.

**septum, pl. septa** A wall between two cavities.

**sequence-tagged site (STS)** A small stretch of DNA that is unique in a genome, that is, it occurs only once; useful as a physical marker on genomic maps.

**seta, pl. setae** (L., bristle) In an annelid, bristles of chitin that help anchor the worm during locomotion or when it is in its burrow.

**severe acute respiratory syndrome (SARS)** A respiratory infection with an 8% mortality rate that is caused by a coronavirus.

**sex chromosome** A chromosome that is related to sex; in humans, the sex chromosomes are the X and Y chromosomes.

**sex-linked** A trait determined by a gene carried on the X chromosome and absent on the Y chromosome.

**Sexual dimorphism** Morphological differences between the sexes of a species.

**sexual reproduction** The process of producing offspring through an alternation of fertilization (producing diploid cells) and meiotic reduction in chromosome number (producing haploid cells).

**sexual selection** A type of differential reproduction that results from variable success in obtaining mates.

**shared derived character** In cladistics, character states that are shared by species and that are different from the ancestral character state.

**shoot** In vascular plants, the aboveground portions, such as the stem and leaves.

**short interspersed element (SINE)** Any of a type of retrotransposon found in humans and other primates that does not contain the biochemical machinery needed for transposition; half a million copies of a SINE element called Alu is nested in the LINEs of the human genome.

**shotgun sequencing** The method of DNA sequencing in which the DNA is randomly cut into small fragments, and the fragments cloned and sequenced. A computer is then used to assemble a final sequence.

**sieve cell** In the phloem of vascular plants, a long, slender element with relatively unspecialized sieve areas and with tapering end walls that lack sieve plates.

**signal recognition particle (SRP)** In eukaryotes, a cytoplasmic complex of proteins that recognizes and binds to the signal sequence of a polypeptide, and then docks with a receptor that forms a channel in the ER membrane. In this way the polypeptide is released into the lumen of the ER.

**signal transduction** The events that occur within a cell on receipt of a signal, ligand binding to a receptor protein. Signal transduction pathways produce the cellular response to a signaling molecule.

**simple sequence repeat (SSR)** A one- to three-nucleotide sequence such as CA or CCG that is repeated thousands of times.

**single-nucleotide polymorphism (SNP)** A site present in at least 1% of the population at which individuals differ by a single nucleotide. These can be used as genetic markers to map unknown genes or traits.

**sinus** A cavity or space in tissues or in bone.

**sister chromatid** One of two identical copies of each chromosome, still linked at the centromere, produced as the chromosomes duplicate for mitotic division; similarly, one of two identical copies of each homologous chromosome present in a tetrad at meiosis.

**small interfering RNAs (siRNAs)** A class of micro-RNAs that appear to be involved in control of gene transcription and that play a role in protecting cells from viral attack.

**small nuclear ribonucleoprotein particles (snRNP)** In eukaryotes, a complex composed of snRNA and protein that clusters together with other snRNPs to form the spliceosome, which removes introns from the primary transcript.

**small nuclear RNA (snRNA)** In eukaryotes, a small RNA sequence that, as part of a small nuclear ribonucleoprotein complex, facilitates recognition and excision of introns by base-pairing with the 5′ end of an intron or at a branch site of the same intron.

**sodium–potassium pump** Transmembrane channels engaged in the active (ATP-driven) transport of Na+, exchanging them for K+, where both ions are being moved against their respective concentration gradients; maintains the resting membrane potential of neurons and other cells.

**solute** A molecule dissolved in some solution; as a general rule, solutes dissolve only in solutions of similar polarity; for example, glucose (polar) dissolves in (forms hydrogen bonds with) water (also polar), but not in vegetable oil (nonpolar).

**solute potential** The amount of osmotic pressure arising from the presence of a solute or solutes in water; measure by counterbalancing the pressure until osmosis stops.

**solvent** The medium in which one or more solutes is dissolved.

**somatic cell** Any of the cells of a multicellular organism except those that are destined to form gametes (germ-line cells).

**somatic cell nuclear transfer (SCNT)** The transfer of the nucleus of a somatic cell into an enucleated egg cell that then undergoes development. Can be used to make ES cells and to create cloned animals.

**somatic mutation** A change in genetic information (mutation) occurring in one of the somatic cells of a multicellular organism, not passed from one generation to the next.

**somatic nervous system** In vertebrates, the neurons of the peripheral nervous system that control skeletal muscle.

**somite** One of the blocks, or segments, of tissue into which the mesoderm is divided during differentiation of the vertebrate embryo.

**Southern blot** A technique in which DNA fragments are separated by gel electrophoresis, denatured into single-stranded DNA, and then "blotted" onto a sheet of filter paper; the filter is then incubated with a labeled probe to locate DNA sequences of interest.

**S phase** The phase of the cell cycle during which DNA replication occurs.

**specialized transduction** The transfer of only a few specific genes into a bacterium, using a lysogenic bacteriophage as a carrier.

**speciation** The process by which new species arise, either by transformation of one species into another, or by the splitting of one ancestral species into two descendant species.

**species, pl. species** A kind of organism; species are designated by binomial names written in italics.

**specific heat** The amount of heat that must be absorbed or lost by 1 g of a substance to raise or lower its temperature 1°C.

**specific transcription factor** Any of a great number of transcription factors that act in a time- or tissue-dependent manner to increase DNA transcription above the basal level.

**spectrin** A scaffold of proteins that links plasma membrane proteins to actin filaments in the cytoplasm of red blood cells, producing their characteristic biconcave shape.

**spermatid** In animals, each of four haploid (n) cells that result from the meiotic divisions of a spermatocyte; each spermatid differentiates into a sperm cell.

**spermatozoa** The male gamete, usually smaller than the female gamete, and usually motile.

**sphincter** In vertebrate animals, a ring-shaped muscle capable of closing a tubular opening by constriction (e.g., between stomach and small intestine or between anus and exterior).

**spicule** Any of a number of minute needles of silica or calcium carbonate made in the mesohyl by some kinds of sponges as a structural component.

**spindle** The structure composed of microtubules radiating from the poles of the dividing cell that will ultimately guide the sister chromatids to the two poles.

**spindle apparatus** The assembly that carries out the separation of chromosomes during cell division; composed of microtubules (spindle fibers) and assembled during prophase at the equator of the dividing cell.

**spindle checkpoint** The third cell-division checkpoint, at which all chromosomes must be attached to the spindle. Passage through this checkpoint commits the cell to anaphase.

**spinnerets** Organs at the posterior end of a spider's abdomen that secrete a fluid protein that becomes silk.

**spiracle** External opening of a trachea in arthropods.

**spiral cleavage** The embryonic cleavage pattern of some protostome animals in which cells divide at an angle oblique to the polar axis of the embryo; a line drawn through the sequence of dividing cells forms a spiral.

**spiralian** A member of a group of invertebrate animals; many groups exhibit spiral cleavage. Mollusks, annelids, and flatworms are examples of spiralians.

**spliceosome** In eukaryotes, a complex composed of multiple snRNPs and other associated proteins that is responsible for excision of introns and joining of exons to convert the primary transcript into the mature mRNA.

**spongin** A tough protein made by many kinds of sponges as a structural component within the mesohyl.

**spongy parenchyma** A leaf tissue composed of loosely arranged, chloroplast-bearing cells. *See* palisade parenchyma.

**sporangium, pl. sporangia** A structure in which spores are produced.

**spore** A haploid reproductive cell, usually unicellular, capable of developing into an adult without fusion with another cell.

**sporophyte** The spore-producing, diploid (2n) phase in the life cycle of a plant having alternation of generations.

**stabilizing selection** A form of selection in which selection acts to eliminate both extremes from a range of phenotypes.

**stamen** The organ of a flower that produces the pollen; usually consists of anther and filament; collectively, the stamens make up the androecium.

**starch** An insoluble polymer of glucose; the chief food storage substance of plants.

**start codon** The AUG triplet, which indicates the site of the beginning of mRNA translation; this codon also codes for the amino acid methionine.

**stasis** A period of time during which little evolutionary change occurs.

**statocyst** Sensory receptor sensitive to gravity and motion.

**stele** The central vascular cylinder of stems and roots.

**stem cell** A relatively undifferentiated cell in animal tissue that can divide to produce more differentiated tissue cells.

**stereoscopic vision** Ability to perceive a single, three-dimensional image from the simultaneous but slightly divergent two-dimensional images delivered to the brain by each eye.

**stigma** (1) In angiosperm flowers, the region of a carpel that serves as a receptive surface for pollen grains. (2) Light-sensitive eyespot of some algae.

**stipules** Leaflike appendages that occur at the base of some flowering plant leaves or stems.

**stolon** A stem that grows horizontally along the ground surface and may form adventitious roots, such as runners of the strawberry plant.

**stoma, pl. stomata** In plants, a minute opening bordered by guard cells in the epidermis of leaves and stems; water passes out of a plant mainly through the stomata.

**stop codon** Any of the three codons UAA, UAG, and UGA, that indicate the point at which mRNA translation is to be terminated.

**stratify** To hold plant seeds at a cold temperature for a certain period of time; seeds of many plants will not germinate without exposure to cold and subsequent warming.

**stratum corneum** The outer layer of the epidermis of the skin of the vertebrate body.

**striated muscle** Skeletal voluntary muscle and cardiac muscle.

**stroma** In chloroplasts, the semiliquid substance that surrounds the thylakoid system and that contains the enzymes needed to assemble organic molecules from $CO_2$.

**stromatolite** A fossilized mat of ancient bacteria formed as long as 2 BYA, in which the bacterial remains individually resemble some modern-day bacteria.

**style** In flowers, the slender column of tissue that arises from the top of the ovary and through which the pollen tube grows.

**stylet** A piercing organ, usually a mouthpart, in some species of invertebrates.

**suberin** In plants, a fatty acid chain that forms the impermeable barrier in the Casparian strip of root endoderm.

**subspecies** A geographically defined population or group of populations within a single species that has distinctive characteristics.

**substrate** (1) The foundation to which an organism is attached. (2) A molecule on which an enzyme acts.

**subunit vaccine** A type of vaccine created by using a subunit of a viral protein coat to elicit an immune response; may be useful in preventing viral diseases such as hepatitis B.

**succession** In ecology, the slow, orderly progression of changes in community composition that takes place through time.

**summation** Repetitive activation of the motor neuron resulting in maximum sustained contraction of a muscle.

**supercoiling** The coiling in space of double-stranded DNA molecules due to torsional strain, such as occurs when the helix is unwound.

**surface tension** A tautness of the surface of a liquid, caused by the cohesion of the molecules of liquid. Water has an extremely high surface tension.

**surface area-to-volume ratio** Relationship of the surface area of a structure, such as a cell, to the volume it contains.

**suspensor** In gymnosperms and angiosperms, the suspensor develops from one of the first two cells of a dividing zygote; the suspensor of an angiosperm is a nutrient conduit from maternal tissue to the embryo. In gymnosperms the suspensor positions the embryo closer to stored food reserves.

**swim bladder** An organ encountered only in the bony fish that helps the fish regulate its buoyancy by increasing or decreasing the amount of gas in the bladder via the esophagus or a specialized network of capillaries.

**swimmerets** In lobsters and crayfish, appendages that occur in lines along the ventral surface of the abdomen and are used in swimming and reproduction.

**symbiosis** The condition in which two or more dissimilar organisms live together in close association; includes parasitism (harmful to one of the organisms), commensalism (beneficial to one, of no significance to the other), and mutualism (advantageous to both).

**sympatric speciation** The differentiation of populations within a common geographic area into species.

**symplast route** In plant roots, the pathway for movement of water and minerals within the cell cytoplasm that leads through plasmodesmata that connect cells.

**symplesiomorphy** In cladistics, another term for a shared ancestral character state.

**symporter** A carrier protein in a cell's membrane that transports two molecules or ions in the same direction across the membrane.

**synapomorphy** In systematics, a derived character that is shared by clade members.

**synapse** A junction between a neuron and another neuron or muscle cell; the two cells do not touch, the gap being bridged by neurotransmitter molecules.

**synapsid** Any of an early group of reptiles that had a pair of temporal openings in the skull behind the eye sockets; jaw muscles attached to these openings. Early ancestors of mammals belonged to this group.

**synapsis** The point-by-point alignment (pairing) of homologous chromosomes that occurs before the first meiotic division; crossing over takes place during synapsis.

**synaptic cleft** The space between two adjacent neurons.

**synaptic vesicle** A vesicle of a neurotransmitter produced by the axon terminal of a nerve. The filled vesicle migrates to the presynaptic membrane, fuses with it, and releases the neurotransmitter into the synaptic cleft.

**synaptonemal complex** A protein lattice that forms between two homologous chromosomes in prophase I of meiosis, holding the replicated chromosomes in precise register with each other so that base-pairs can form between nonsister chromatids for crossing over that is usually exact within a gene sequence.

**syncytial blastoderm** A structure composed of a single large cytoplasm containing about 4000 nuclei in embryonic development of insects such as *Drosophila*.

**syngamy** The process by which two haploid cells (gametes) fuse to form a diploid zygote; fertilization.

**synthetic polyploidy** A polyploidy organism created by crossing organisms most closely related to an ancestral species and then manipulating the offspring.

**systematics** The reconstruction and study of evolutionary relationships.

**systemic acquired resistance (SAR)** In plants, a longer-term response to a pathogen or pest attack that can last days to weeks and allow the plant to respond quickly to later attacks by a range of pathogens.

**systemin** In plants, an 18-amino-acid peptide that is produced by damaged or injured leaves that leads to the wound response.

**systolic pressure** A measurement of how hard the heart is contracting. When measured during a blood pressure reading, ventricular systole (contraction) is what is being monitored.

# T

**3′ poly-A tail** In eukaryotes, a series of 1–200 adenine residues added to the 3′ end of an mRNA; the tail appears to enhance the stability of the mRNA by protecting it from degradation.

**T box** A transcription factor protein domain that has been conserved, although with differing developmental effects, in invertebrates and chordates.

**tagma**, pl. **tagmata** A compound body section of an arthropod resulting from embryonic fusion of two or more segments; for example, head, thorax, abdomen.

**Taq polymerase** A DNA polymerase isolated from the thermophilic bacterium *Thermus aquaticus* (Taq); this polymerase is functional at higher temperatures, and is used in PCR amplification of DNA.

**TATA box** In eukaryotes, a sequence located upstream of the transcription start site. The TATA box is one element of eukaryotic core promoters for RNA polymerase II.

**taxis**, pl. **taxes** An orientation movement by a (usually) simple organism in response to an environmental stimulus.

**taxonomy** The science of classifying living things. By agreement among taxonomists, no two organisms can have the same name, and all names are expressed in Latin.

**T cell** A type of lymphocyte involved in cell-mediated immunity and interactions with B cells; the "T" refers to the fact that T cells are produced in the thymus.

**telencephalon** The most anterior portion of the brain, including the cerebrum and associated structures.

**telomerase** An enzyme that synthesizes telomeres on eukaryotic chromosomes using an internal RNA template.

**telomere** A specialized nontranscribed structure that caps each end of a chromosome.

**telophase** The phase of cell division during which the spindle breaks down, the nuclear envelope of each daughter cell forms, and the chromosomes uncoil and become diffuse.

**telson** The tail spine of lobsters and crayfish.

**temperate (lysogenic) phage** A virus that is capable of incorporating its DNA into the host cell's DNA, where it remains for an indeterminate length of time and is replicated as the cell's DNA replicates.

**template strand** The DNA strand that is used as a template in transcription. This strand is copied to produce a complementary mRNA transcript.

**tendon** (Gr. *tendon*, stretch) A strap of cartilage that attaches muscle to bone.

**tensile strength** A measure of the cohesiveness of a substance; its resistance to being broken apart. Water in narrow plant vessels has tensile strength that helps keep the water column continuous.

**tertiary structure** The folded shape of a protein, produced by hydrophobic interactions with water, ionic and covalent bonding between side chains of different amino acids, and van der Waal's forces; may be changed by denaturation so that the protein becomes inactive.

**testcross** A mating between a phenotypically dominant individual of unknown genotype and a homozygous "tester," done to determine whether the phenotypically dominant individual is homozygous or heterozygous for the relevant gene.

**testis**, pl. **testes** In mammals, the sperm-producing organ.

**tetanus** Sustained forceful muscle contraction with no relaxation.

**thalamus** That part of the vertebrate forebrain just posterior to the cerebrum; governs the flow of information from all other parts of the nervous system to the cerebrum.

**therapeutic cloning** The use of somatic cell nuclear transfer to create stem cells from a single individual that may be reimplanted in that individual to replace damaged cells, such as in a skin graft.

**thermodynamics** The study of transformations of energy, using heat as the most convenient form of measurement of energy.

**thermogenesis** Generation of internal heat by endothermic animals to modulate temperature.

**thigmotropism** In plants, unequal growth in some structure that comes about as a result of physical contact with an object.

**threshold** The minimum amount of stimulus required for a nerve to fire (depolarize).

**thylakoid** In chloroplasts, a complex, organized internal membrane composed of flattened disks, which contain the photosystems involved in the light-dependent reactions of photosynthesis.

**Ti (tumor-inducing) plasmid** A plasmid found in the plant bacterium *Agrobacterium tumefaciens* that has been extensively used to introduce recombinant DNA into broadleaf plants. Recent modifications have allowed its use with cereal grains as well.

**tight junction** Region of actual fusion of plasma membranes between two adjacent animal cells that prevents materials from leaking through the tissue.

**tissue** A group of similar cells organized into a structural and functional unit.

**tissue plasminogen activator (TPA)** A human protein that causes blood clots to dissolve; if used within 3 hours of an ischemic stroke, TPA may prevent disability.

**tissue-specific stem cell** A stem cell that is capable of developing into the cells of a certain tissue, such as muscle or epithelium; these cells persist even in adults.

**tissue system** In plants, any of the three types of tissue; called a system because the tissue extends throughout the roots and shoots.

**tissue tropism** The affinity of a virus for certain cells within a multicellular host; for example, hepatitis B virus targets liver cells.

**tonoplast** The membrane surrounding the central vacuole in plant cells that contains water channels; helps maintain the cell's osmotic balance.

**topoisomerase** Any of a class of enzymes that can change the topological state of DNA to relieve torsion caused by unwinding.

**torsion** The process in embryonic development of gastropods by which the mantle cavity and anus move from a posterior location to the front of the body, closer to the location of the mouth.

**totipotent** A cell that possesses the full genetic potential of the organism.

**trachea**, pl. **tracheae** A tube for breathing; in terrestrial vertebrates, the windpipe that carries air between the larynx and bronchi (which leads to the lungs); in insects and some other terrestrial arthropods, a system of chitin-lined air ducts.

**tracheids** In plant xylem, dead cells that taper at the ends and overlap one another.

**tracheole** The smallest branches of the respiratory system of terrestrial arthropods; tracheoles convey air from the tracheae, which connect to the outside of the body at spiracles.

**trait** In genetics, a characteristic that has alternative forms, such as purple or white flower color in pea plants or different blood type in humans.

**transcription** The enzyme-catalyzed assembly of an RNA molecule complementary to a strand of DNA.

**transcription complex** The complex of RNA polymerase II plus necessary activators, coactivators, transcription factors, and other factors that are engaged in actively transcribing DNA.

**transcription factor** One of a set of proteins required for RNA polymerase to bind to a eukaryotic promoter region, become stabilized, and begin the transcription process.

**transcription bubble** The region containing the RNA polymerase, the DNA template, and the RNA transcript, so called because of the locally unwound "bubble" of DNA.

**transcription unit** The region of DNA between a promoter and a terminator.

**transcriptome** All the RNA present in a cell or tissue at a given time.

**transfection** The transformation of eukaryotic cells in culture.

**transfer RNA (tRNA)** A class of small RNAs (about 80 nucleotides) with two functional sites; at one site, an "activating enzyme" adds a specific amino acid, while the other site carries the nucleotide triplet (anticodon) specific for that amino acid.

**transformation** The uptake of DNA directly from the environment; a natural process in some bacterial species.

**transgenic organism** An organism into which a gene has been introduced without conventional breeding, that is, through genetic engineering techniques.

**translation** The assembly of a protein on the ribosomes, using mRNA to specify the order of amino acids.

**translation repressor protein** One of a number of proteins that prevent translation of mRNA by binding to the beginning of the transcript and preventing its attachment to a ribosome.

**translocation** (1) In plants, the long-distance transport of soluble food molecules (mostly sucrose), which occurs primarily in the sieve tubes of phloem tissue. (2) In genetics, the interchange of chromosome segments between nonhomologous chromosomes.

**transmembrane domain** Hydrophobic region of a transmembrane protein that anchors it in the membrane. Often composed of α-helices, but sometimes utilizing β-pleated sheets to form a barrel-shaped pore.

**transmembrane route** In plant roots, the pathway for movement of water and minerals that crosses the cell membrane and also the membrane of vacuoles inside the cell.

**transpiration** The loss of water vapor by plant parts; most transpiration occurs through the stomata.

**transposable elements** Segments of DNA that are able to move from one location on a chromosome to another. Also termed *transposons* or *mobile genetic elements*.

**transposition** Type of genetic recombination in which transposable elements (transposons) move from one site in the DNA sequence to another, apparently randomly.

**transposon** DNA sequence capable of transposition.

**trichome** In plants, a hairlike outgrowth from an epidermal cell; glandular trichomes secrete oils or other substances that deter insects.

**triglyceride (triacylglycerol)** An individual fat molecule, composed of a glycerol and three fatty acids.

**triploid** Possessing three sets of chromosomes.

**trisomic** Describes the condition in which an additional chromosome has been gained due to nondisjunction during meiosis, and the diploid embryo therefore has three of these autosomes. In humans, trisomic individuals may survive if the autosome is small; Down syndrome individuals are trisomic for chromosome 21.

**trochophore** A specialized type of free-living larva found in lophotrochozoans.

**trophic level** A step in the movement of energy through an ecosystem.

**trophoblast** In vertebrate embryos, the outer ectodermal layer of the blastodermic vesicle; in mammals, it is part of the chorion and attaches to the uterine wall.

**tropism** Response to an external stimulus.

**tropomyosin** Low-molecular-weight protein surrounding the actin filaments of striated muscle.

**troponin** Complex of globular proteins positioned at intervals along the actin filament of skeletal muscle; thought to serve as a calcium-dependent "switch" in muscle contraction.

*trp* **operon** In *E. coli*, the operon containing genes that code for enzymes that synthesize tryptophan.

**true-breeding** Said of a breed or variety of organism in which offspring are uniform and consistent from one generation to the next; for example. This is due to the genotypes that determine relevant traits being homozygous.

**tube foot** In echinoderms, a flexible, external extension of the water–vascular system that is capable of attaching to a surface through suction.

**tubulin** Globular protein subunit forming the hollow cylinder of microtubules.

**tumor-suppressor gene** A gene that normally functions to inhibit cell division; mutated forms can lead to the unrestrained cell division of cancer, but only when both copies of the gene are mutant.

**turgor pressure** The internal pressure inside a plant cell, resulting from osmotic intake of water, that presses its cell membrane tightly against the cell wall, making the cell rigid. Also known as *hydrostatic pressure*.

**tympanum** In some groups of insects, a thin membrane associated with the tracheal air sacs that functions as a sound receptor; paired on each side of the abdomen.

# U

**ubiquitin** A 76-amino-acid protein that virtually all eukaryotic cells attach as a marker to proteins that are to be degraded.

**unequal crossing over** A process by which a crossover in a small region of misalignment at synapsis causes two homologous chromosomes to exchange segments of unequal length.

**uniporter** A carrier protein in a cell's membrane that transports only a single type of molecule or ion.

**uniramous** Single-branched; describes the appendages of insects.

**unsaturated fat** A fat molecule in which one or more of the fatty acids contain fewer than the maximum number of hydrogens attached to their carbons.

**urea** An organic molecule formed in the vertebrate liver; the principal form of disposal of nitrogenous wastes by mammals.

**urethra** The tube carrying urine from the bladder to the exterior of mammals.

**uric acid** Insoluble nitrogenous waste products produced largely by reptiles, birds, and insects.

**urine** The liquid waste filtered from the blood by the kidney and stored in the bladder pending elimination through the urethra.

**uropod** One of a group of flattened appendages at the end of the abdomen of lobsters and crayfish that collectively act as a tail for a rapid burst of speed.

**uterus** In mammals, a chamber in which the developing embryo is contained and nurtured during pregnancy.

# V

**vacuole** A membrane-bounded sac in the cytoplasm of some cells, used for storage or digestion purposes in different kinds of cells; plant cells often contain a large central vacuole that stores water, proteins, and waste materials.

**valence electron** An electron in the outermost energy level of an atom.

**variable** A factor that influences a process, outcome, or observation. In experiments, scientists attempt to isolate variables to test hypotheses.

**vascular cambium** In vascular plants, a cylindrical sheath of meristematic cells, the division of which produces secondary phloem outwardly and secondary xylem inwardly; the activity of the vascular cambium increases stem or root diameter.

**vascular tissue** Containing or concerning vessels that conduct fluid.

**vas deferens** In mammals, the tube carrying sperm from the testes to the urethra.

**vasopressin** A posterior pituitary hormone that regulates the kidney's retention of water.

**vector** In molecular biology, a plasmid, phage or artificial chromosome that allows propagation of recombinant DNA in a host cell into which it is introduced.

**vegetal pole** The hemisphere of the zygote comprising cells rich in yolk.

**vein** (1) In plants, a vascular bundle forming a part of the framework of the conducting and supporting tissue of a stem or leaf. (2) In animals, a blood vessel carrying blood from the tissues to the heart.

**veliger** The second larval stage of mollusks following the trochophore stage, during which the beginning of a foot, shell, and mantle can be seen.

**ventricle** A muscular chamber of the heart that receives blood from an atrium and pumps blood out to either the lungs or the body tissues.

**vertebrate** A chordate with a spinal column; in vertebrates, the notochord develops into the vertebral column composed of a series of vertebrae that enclose and protect the dorsal nerve cord.

**vertical gene transfer (VGT)** The passing of genes from one generation to the next within a species.

**vesicle** A small intracellular, membrane-bounded sac in which various substances are transported or stored.

**vessel element** In vascular plants, a typically elongated cell, dead at maturity, which conducts water and solutes in the xylem.

**vestibular apparatus** The complicated sensory apparatus of the inner ear that provides for balance and orientation of the head in vertebrates.

**vestigial structure** A morphological feature that has no apparent current function and is thought to be an evolutionary relic; for example, the vestigial hip bones of boa constrictors.

**villus, pl. villi** In vertebrates, one of the minute, fingerlike projections lining the small intestine that serve to increase the absorptive surface area of the intestine.

**virion** A single virus particle.

**viroid** Any of a group of small, naked RNA molecules that are capable of causing plant diseases, presumably by disrupting chromosome integrity.

**virus** Any of a group of complex biochemical entities consisting of genetic material wrapped in protein; viruses can reproduce only within living host cells and are thus not considered organisms.

**visceral mass** Internal organs in the body cavity of an animal.

**vitamin** An organic substance that cannot be synthesized by a particular organism but is required in small amounts for normal metabolic function.

**viviparity** Refers to reproduction in which eggs develop within the mother's body and young are born free-living.

**voltage-gated ion channel** A transmembrane pathway for an ion that is opened or closed by a change in the voltage, or charge difference, across the plasma membrane.

# W

**water potential** The potential energy of water molecules. Regardless of the reason (e.g., gravity, pressure, concentration of solute particles) for the water potential, water moves from a region where water potential is greater to a region where water potential is lower.

**water–vascular system** A fluid-filled hydraulic system found only in echinoderms that provides body support and a unique type of locomotion via extensions called tube feet.

**Western blot** A blotting technique used to identify specific protein sequences in a complex mixture. *See* Southern blot.

**wild type** In genetics, the phenotype or genotype that is characteristic of the majority of individuals of a species in a natural environment.

**wobble pairing** Refers to flexibility in the pairing between the base at the 5′ end of a tRNA anticodon and the base at the 3′ end of an mRNA codon. This flexibility allows a single tRNA to read more than one mRNA codon.

**wound response** In plants, a signaling pathway initiated by leaf damage, such as being chewed by a herbivore, and lead to the production of proteinase inhibitors that give herbivores indigestion.

# X

**X chromosome** One of two sex chromosomes; in mammals and in *Drosophila*, female individuals have two X chromosomes.

**xylem** In vascular plants, a specialized tissue, composed primarily of elongate, thick-walled conducting cells, which transports water and solutes through the plant body.

# Y

**Y chromosome** One of two sex chromosomes; in mammals and in *Drosophila*, male individuals have a Y chromosome and an X chromosome; the Y determines maleness.

**yolk plug** A plug occurring in the blastopore of amphibians during formation of the archenteron in embryological development.

**yolk sac** The membrane that surrounds the yolk of an egg and connects the yolk, a rich food supply, to the embryo via blood vessels.

# Z

**zinc finger motif** A type of DNA-binding motif in regulatory proteins that incorporates zinc atoms in its structure.

**zona pellucida** An outer membrane that encases a mammalian egg.

**zone of cell division** In plants, the part of the young root that includes the root apical meristem and the cells just posterior to it; cells in this zone divide every 12–36 hr.

**zone of elongation** In plants, the part of the young root that lies just posterior to the zone of cell division; cells in this zone elongate, causing the root to lengthen.

**zone of maturation** In plants, the part of the root that lies posterior to the zone of elongation; cells in this zone differentiate into specific cell types.

**zoospore** A motile spore.

**zooxanthellae** Symbiotic photosynthetic protists in the tissues of corals.

**zygomycetes** A type of fungus whose chief characteristic is the production of sexual structures called zygosporangia, which result from the fusion of two of its simple reproductive organs.

**zygote** The diploid (2*n*) cell resulting from the fusion of male and female gametes (fertilization).

## Photo Credits

### Chapter 1
Opener: © Soames Summerhays/Natural Visions; 1.1d: © Dr. Donald Fawcett & Porter/Visuals Unlimited; 1.1e: © Lennart Nilsson/Albert Bonniers Förlag AB; 1.1f: © Ed Reschke; 1.1i-j: © Getty RF; 1.1k-l: © Volume 44/Getty RF; 1.1m: © Steve Harper/Grant Heilman Photography, Inc.; 1.1n: © Robert and Jean Pollock; 1.1o: NASA; 1.5: © Huntington Library/SuperStock; 1.11a: © Dennis Kunkel/Phototake; 1.11b: © Karl E. Deckart/Phototake; 1.12a: © Alan L. Detrick/Photo Researchers, Inc.; 1.12b: © DAVID M. DENNIS/Animals Animals - Earth Scenes; 1.12c: © Volume 46/Corbis RF; 1.12d: © Corbis RF; 1.12e: © Mediscan/Corbis; 1.12f: © Volume 15/Photodisc/Getty RF; 1.12g: © Corbis RF; 1.12h: © Tom Brakefield/Corbis; 1.12i: © Volume 44/Photodisc/Getty RF; 1.12j: © Volume 64/Corbis RF; 1.12k: © T.E. Adams/Visuals Unlimited; 1.12l: © Douglas P. Wilson/Frank Lane Picture Agency/Corbis; 1.12m: © R. Robinson/Visuals Unlimited; 1.12n: © Kari Lounatman/Photo Researchers, Inc.; 1.12o: © Dwight R. Kuhn; 1.12p: © Alfred Pasieka/Science Photo Library/Photo Researchers, Inc.

### Chapter 2
Opener: Courtesy of IBM Zurich Research Laboratory. Unauthorized use not permitted; 2.2: Image Courtesy of Veeco Instruments, Inc.; 2.10a: © Glen Allison/Getty Images RF; 2.10b: © PhotoLink/Getty RF; 2.10c: © Jeff Vanuga/Corbis; 2.13: © Hermann Eisenbeiss/National Audubon Society Collection/Photo Researchers, Inc.

### Chapter 3
Opener: © Jacob Halaska/Index Stock Imagery; 3.10b: © Asa Thoresen/Photo Researchers, Inc.; 3.10c: © J.Carson/Custom Medical Stock Photo; 3.11b: © J.D. Litvay/Visuals Unlimited; 3.12: © Scott Johnson/Animals Animals - Earth Scenes; 3.13a: © Driscoll, Youngquist & Baldeschwieler, Caltech/SPL/Photo Researchers, Inc.; 3.13b: © PhotoLink/Getty RF.

### Chapter 4
Opener: © Dr. Gopal Murti/Photo Researchers, Inc.; Table 4.1a: © David M. Phillips/Visuals Unlimited; Table 4.1b: © Mike Abbey/Visuals Unlimited; Table 4.1c: © David M. Phillips/Visuals Unlimited; Table 4.1d: © Mike Abbey/Visuals Unlimited; Table 4.1e: © DR TORSTEN WITTMANN/Photo Researchers, Inc.; Table 4.1f: © Med. Mic. Sciences, Cardiff Uni./Wellcome Images; Table 4.1g: © Microworks/Phototake; Table 4.1h: © Stanley Flegler/Visuals Unlimited; p. 62 (plasma membrane): © Dr. Don W. Fawcett/Visuals Unlimited; 4.3: © Phototake; 4.4: Courtesy of E.H. Newcomb & T.D. Pugh, University of Wisconsin; 4.5a: © Eye of Science/Photo Researchers, Inc.; 4.8b: © Dr. Richard Kessel & Dr. Gene Shih/Visuals Unlimited; 4.8c: © John T. Hansen, Ph.D/Phototake; 4.8d: Reprinted by permission from Macmillan Publishers Ltd: *Nature*, 323, 560-564, "The nuclear lamina is a meshwork of intermediate-type filaments," Ueli Aebi, Julie Cohn, Loren Buhle, Larry Gerace, © 1986; 4.10c: © R. Bolender & D. Fawcett/Visuals Unlimited; 4.11c: © Dennis Kunkel/Phototake; 4.14: From "Microbody-Like Organelles in Leaf Cells," Sue Ellen Frederick and Eldon H. Newcomb, *SCIENCE*, Vol. 163: 1353-1355 © 21 March 1969. Reprinted with permission from AAAS; 4.15: © Dr. Henry Aldrich/Visuals Unlimited; 4.16c: © Dr. Donald Fawcett & Dr. Porter/Visuals Unlimited; 4.17c: © Dr. Jeremy Burgess/Photo Researchers, Inc.; 4.23a-b: © William Dentler, University of Kansas; 4.24a-b: © SPL/Photo Researchers, Inc.; 4.25: © BioPhoto Associates/Photo Researchers, Inc.; 4.27a: Courtesy of Daniel Goodenough; 4.27b-c: © Dr. Donald Fawcett/Visuals Unlimited.

### Chapter 5
Opener: © Dr. Gopal Murti/Science Photo Library/Photo Researchers, Inc.; p. 91 (top)-5.3: © Don W. Fawcett/Photo Researchers, Inc.; 5.12a-c: © David M. Phillips/Visuals Unlimited; 5.15a: Micrograph Courtesy of the CDC/Dr. Edwin P. Ewing, Jr.; 5.15b: © BCC Microimaging, Inc., Reproduced with permission; 5.15c (top)-(bottom): © The Company of Biologists Limited; 5.16b: © Dr. Brigit Satir.

### Chapter 6
Opener: © Robert Caputo/Aurora Photos; 6.3a-b: © Spencer Grant/PhotoEdit; 6.11b: © Professor Emeritus Lester J. Reed, University of Texas at Austin.

### Chapter 7
Opener: © Creatas/PunchStock RF; 7.18a: © Wolfgang Baumeister/Photo Researchers, Inc.; 7.18b: National Park Service.

### Chapter 8
Opener: © Corbis RF; 8.1: Courtesy Dr. Kenneth Miller, Brown University; 8.8a-b: © Eric Soder; 8.20: © Dr. Jeremy Burgess/Photo Researchers, Inc.; 8.22a: © John Shaw/Photo Researchers, Inc.; 8.22b: © Joseph Nettis/National Audubon Society Collection/Photo Researchers, Inc.; 8.24: © Clyde H. Smith/Peter Arnold Inc.

### Chapter 9
Opener: RMF/Scientifica/Visuals Unlimited.

### Chapter 10
Opener: © Stem Jems/Photo Researchers, Inc.; 10.2a-b: Courtesy of William Margolin; 10.4: © BioPhoto Associates/Photo Researchers, Inc.; 10.6: © CNRI/Photo Researchers, Inc.; 10.10: Image courtesy of S. Hauf and J-M. Peters, IMP, Vienna, Austria; 10.11a-g, 10.12: © Andrew S. Bajer, University of Oregon; 10.13a-b: © Dr. Jeremy Pickett-Heaps; 10.14a: © David M. Phillips/Visuals Unlimited; 10.14b: © Guenter Albrecht-Buehler, Northwestern University, Chicago; 10.15: © B.A. Palevits & E.H. Newcomb/BPS/Tom Stack & Associates.

### Chapter 11
Opener: © Science VU/L. Maziarski/Visuals Unlimited; 11.3b: Reprinted, with permission, from the *Annual Review of Genetics*, Volume 6 © 1972 by Annual Reviews, www.annualreviews.org; 11.7a-h: © Clare A. Hasenkampf/Biological Photo Service.

### Chapter 12
Opener: © Corbis RF; 12.1: © Norbert Schaefer/Corbis; 12.2: © David Sieren/Visuals Unlimited; 12.3: © Leslie Holzer/Photo Researchers, Inc.; 12.11: From Albert F. Blakeslee "CORN AND MEN: The Interacting Influence of Heredity and Environment—Movements for Betterment of Men, or Corn, or Any Other Living Thing, One-sided Unless They Take Both Factors into Account," *Journal of Heredity*, 5: 511-518, © 1914 Oxford University Press; 12.14: © DK Limited/Corbis.

### Chapter 13
Opener: © Adrian T. Sumner/Photo Researchers, Inc.; 13.1a-b: © Cabisco/Phototake; p. 241: © BioPhoto Associates/Photo Researchers, Inc.; 13.3: © Bettmann/Corbis; p. 243(left): From Brian P. Chadwick and Huntington F. Willard, "Multiple spatially distinct types of facultative heterochromatin on the human inactive X chromosome," *PNAS* vol. 101 no. 50:17450-17455, Fig. 3 © 2004 National Academy of Sciences, U.S.A.; 13.4: © Kenneth Mason; 13.33: © Jackie Lewin, Royal Free Hospital/Photo Researchers, Inc.; 13.12: © Colorado Genetics Laboratory, University of Colorado Denver.

### Chapter 14
Opener: © Volume 29/Getty RF; 14.5a-b: Courtesy of Cold Spring Harbor Laboratory Archives; 14.6: © Barrington Brown/Photo Researchers, Inc.; 14.11: From M. Meselson and F.W. Stahl/*PNAS* 44(1958):671; 14.16a-b: From *Biochemistry* by Stryer. © 1995, 1981, 1988, 1995 by Lupert Stryer. Used with permission of W.H. Freeman and Company; 14.20: © Dr. Don W. Fawcett/Visuals Unlimited.

### Chapter 15
Opener: © Dr. Gopal Murti/Visuals Unlimited; 15.3: From R.C. Williams, *PNAS* 74(1977):2313;

Abbey/Visuals Unlimited; 29.16: © Prof. David J.P. Ferguson, Oxford University; 29.18(top right): © Brian Parker/Tom Stack & Associates; 29.19: © Michele Bahr and D. J. Patterson, used under license to MBL; 29.20: © David Fleetham/Visuals Unlimited; 29.22: © Dennis Kunkel/Phototake; 29.23: © Andrew Syred/Photo Researchers, Inc.; 29.24a: © Manfred Kage/Peter Arnold Inc.; 29.24b: © Wim van Egmond/Visuals Unlimited; 29.24c: © Runk/Schoenberger/Grant Heilman photography, Inc.; 29.25: © William Bourland, image used under license to MBL; 29.26: © Eye of Science/Photo Researchers, Inc.; 29.27: © Phil A. Harrington/Peter Arnold Inc.; 29.28: © Manfred Kage/Peter Arnold Inc.; 29.29: © Ric Ergenbright/Corbis; 29.30: © Peter Arnold Inc./Alamy; 29.31: © John Shaw/Tom Stack & Associates; 29.32: © Mark J. Grimson and Richard L. Blanton, Biological Sciences Electron Microscopy Laboratory, Texas Tech University.

## Chapter 30
Opener: © S.J. Krasemann/Peter Arnold Inc.; 30.3: © Dr. Richard Kessel & Dr. Gene Shih/Visuals Unlimited; 30.4: © Wim van Egmond/Visuals Unlimited; 30.5b: © Dr. Diane S. Littler; 30.6(left): © Dr. John D. Cunningham/Visuals Unlimited; 30.6(right): © Dr. Charles F. Delwiche, University of Maryland; 30.7: © David Sieren/Visuals Unlimited; 30.8: © Edward S. Ross; 30.11: © Lee W. Wilcox; 30.12a: Courtesy of Hans Steur, The Netherlands; 30.15: © Dr. Jody Banks, Purdue University; 30.16: © Kingsley Stern; 30.17: © Stephen P. Parker/Photo Researchers, Inc.; 30.18: © NHPA/Photoshot; 30.20(left): © Ed Reschke; 30.20(right): © Mike Zensa/Corbis; 30.21b: © Biology Media/Photo Researchers, Inc.; 30.22: © Patti Murray/Animals Animal - Earth Scenes; 30.24a: © Jim Strawser/Grant Heilman Photography, Inc.; 30.24b: © Nancy Hoyt Belcher/Grant Heilman Photography, Inc.; 30.24c: © Robert Gustafson/Visuals Unlimited; 30.25 (bottom right): © Goodshoot/Alamy RF; 30.26a: © David Dilcher and Ge Sun; 30.27: Courtesy of Sandra Floyd; 30.31: © Dr. Joseph Williams.

## Chapter 31
Opener: © Ullstein-Joker/Peter Arnold Inc.; 31.1a: © Dr. Ronny Larsson; 31.1b: Contributed by Don Barr, Mycological Society of America; 31.1c: © Carolina Biological Supply Company/Phototake; 31.1d: Contributed by Don Barr, Mycological Society of America; 31.1e: © Dr. Yuuji Tsukii; 31.1f: © Yolande Dalpe, Agriculture and Agri-Food Canada; 31.1g: © inga spence/Alamy; 31.1h: © Michael&Patricia Fogden; 31.2b: © Garry T. Cole/Biological Photo Service; 31.3(inset): © Micro Discovery/Corbis; 31.3(right): © Michael&Patricia Fogden/Corbis; 31.4: © Eye of Science/Photo Researchers, Inc.; 31.5a: © Carolina Biological Supply Company/Phototake; 31.5b: © L. West/Photo Researchers, Inc.; 31.6(left): © Daniel P. Fedorko; 31.7: Contributed by Daniel Wubah, Mycological Society of America; 31.8: Contributed by Don Barr, Mycological Society of America; 31.9a, 31.10a: © Carolina Biological Supply Company/Phototake; 31.11a: © Alexandra Lowry/The National Audubon Society Collection/Photo Researchers, Inc.; 31.12a: © Richard Kolar/Animals Animals - Earth Scenes; 31.12b: © Ed Reschke/Peter Arnold Inc.; 31.13: © David Scharf/

Photo Researchers, Inc.; 31.14(left): © Nigel Cattlin/Alamy; 31.14(right): © B. Borrell Casal/Frank Lane Picture Agency/Corbis; 31.15a: © Ken Wagner/Phototake; 31.15b: © Robert & Jean Pollock/Visuals Unlimited; 31.15c: © Robert Lee/Photo Researchers, Inc.; 31.16: © Ed Reschke; 31.17a: © Eye of Science/Photo Researchers, Inc.; 31.17b: © Dr. Gerald Van Dyke/Visuals Unlimited; 31.18: © Scott Camazine/Photo Researchers, Inc.; 31.19a: Courtesy of Ralph Williams/USDA Forest Service; 31.19b: © agefotostock/SuperStock; 31.19c: USDA Forest Service Archive, USDA Forest Service, Bugwood.org; 31.20a: © Dayton Wild/Visuals Unlimited; 31.20b: © Manfred Kage/Peter Arnold Inc.; 31.21(inset): Courtesy of Dr. Peter Daszak; 31.21: © School of Biological Sciences, University of Canterbury, New Zealand.

## Chapter 32
Opener: © Volume 53/Corbis RF; Table 32.1a: © Volume 86/Corbis RF; Table 32.1b: © Corbis RF; Table 32.1c: © David M. Phillips/Visuals Unlimited; Table 32.1d: © Corbis RF; Table 32.1e: © Edward S. Ross; Table 32.1f: © Volume 65/Corbis RF; Table 32.1g: © Cleveland P. Hickman; Table 32.1h: © Cabisco/Phototake; Table 32.1i: © Ed Reschke; 32.6: © Steven C. Zinski.

## Chapter 33
Opener: © Denise Tackett/Tackett Productions; 33.1a: © Andrew J. Martinez/Photo Researchers, Inc.; 33.2 (left): © Roland Birke/Phototake; 33.4: © VIOLA'S PHOTO VISIONS INC./Animals Animals - Earth Scenes; 33.5: © Neil G. McDaniel/Photo Researchers, Inc.; 33.6: © Kelvin Aitken/Peter Arnold Inc.; © Brandon Cole/Visuals Unlimited; 33.8: © Amos Nachoum/Corbis; 33.9: © Biosphoto/Leroy Christian/Peter Arnold Inc.; 33.10: © David Wrobel/Visuals Unlimited; 33.11(top): © Tom Adams/Visuals Unlimited; 33.12: © Dwight Kuhn; 33.13: © The Natural History Museum/Alamy; 33.14(left): © Dennis Kunkel/Phototake; 33.15: © L. Newman & A. Flowers/Photo Researchers, Inc.; 33.16: © Peter Funch, Aarhus University; 33.17: © Gary D. Gaugler/Photo Researchers, Inc.; 33.18: © Educational Images Ltd., Elmira, NY, USA. Used by Permission; 33.19: © T.E.Adams/Visuals Unlimited.

## Chapter 34
Opener: © James H. Robinson/Animals Animals - Earth Scenes; 34.1a: © Marty Snyderman/Visuals Unlimited; 34.1b: © Alex Kerstitch/Visuals Unlimited; 34.1c: © Douglas Faulkner/Photo Researchers, Inc.; 34.1d: © agefotostock/SuperStock; 34.2: © A. Flowers & L. Newman/Photo Researchers, Inc.; 34.4: © Eye of Science/Photo Researchers, Inc.; 34.5a: © Demian Koop, Kathryn Green, Daniel J. Jackson; 34.5b: © Kjell Sandved/Butterfly Alphabet; 34.6: © Kelvin Aitken/Peter Arnold Inc.; 34.7: © Rosemary Calvert/Getty Images; 34.8: © Photodisc Green/Getty Images; 34.10: © AFP/Getty Images; 34.11: © Jeff Rotman/Photo Researchers, Inc.; 34.12: © Kjell Sandved/Butterfly Alphabet; 34.13: © Ken Lucas/Visuals Unlimited; 34.15: © Ronald L. Shimek; 34.16: © Fred Grassle, Woods Hole Oceanographic Institution; 34.17: © David M. Dennis/Animals Animals - Earth Scenes; 34.18: © Pascal Goetgheluck/Photo Researchers, Inc.;

34.19b: © Robert Brons/Biological Photo Service; 34.20b: © Fred Bavendam/Minden Pictures; 34.27a: © National Geographic/Getty Images; 34.27b: © S. Camazine/K. Visscher/Photo Researchers, Inc.; 34.28: © T.E. Adams/Visuals Unlimited; 34.31: © David Liebman Pink Guppy; 34.32: © Kjell Sandved/Butterfly Alphabet; 34.33a: © Cleveland P. Hickman; 34.33b: © Valorie Hodgson/Visuals Unlimited; 34.33c: © Gyorgy Csoka, Hungary Forest Research Institute, Bugwood.org; 34.33d: © Kjell Sandved/Butterfly Alphabet; 34.33e: © Greg Johnston/Lonely Planet Images/Getty Images; 34.33f: © Nature's Images/Photo Researchers, Inc.; 34.35: © Dwight Kuhn; 34.36: © Kjell Sandved/Butterfly Alphabet; 34.37a: © Alex Kerstich/Visuals Unlimited; 34.37b: © Edward S. Ross; 34.38b: © Frederic Pacorel/Getty Images; 34.39: © Wim van Egmond/Visuals Unlimited; 34.40a: © Alex Kerstitch/Visuals Unlimited; 34.40b: © Randy Morse, GoldenStateImages.com; 34.40c: © Daniel W. Gotshall/Visuals Unlimited; 34.40d: © Reinhard Dirscherl/Visuals Unlimited; 34.40e: © Jeff Rotman/Photo Researchers, Inc.

## Chapter 35
Opener: © PHONE Ferrero J.P./Labat J.M./Peter Arnold Inc.; 35.2: © Eric N. Olson, PhD/The University of Texas MD Anderson Cancer Center; 35.4a: © Rick Harbo; 35.5: © Heather Angel/Natural Visions; 35.9(top): © agefotostock/SuperStock; 35.9(bottom left): © Corbis RF; 35.9(bottom right): © Brandon Cole/www.brandoncole.com/Visuals Unlimited; 35.11: © Volume 33/Corbis RF; 35.13a: © Federico Cabello/SuperStock; 35.13b: © Raymond Tercafs/Bruce Coleman/Photoshot; 35.16a: © John Shaw/Tom Stack & Associates; 35.16b: © Suzanne L. Collins & Joseph T. Collins/Photo Researchers, Inc.; 35.16c: © Jany Sauvanet/Photo Researchers, Inc.; 35.22: © Paul Sareno, courtesy of Project Exploration; 35.24a(left): © William J. Weber/Visuals Unlimited; 35.24a(right): © Frans Lemmens/Getty Images; 35.24b, 35.24c(left): © Jonathan Losos; 35.24c(right): © Rod Planck; 35.24d(left): © Volume 6/Corbis RF; 35.24d(right): © Zigmund Leszczynski/Animals Animals - Earth Scenes; 35.28: © Layne Kennedy/Corbis; 35.29a: © Corbis RF; 35.29b: © Arthur C. Smith III/Grant Heilman Photography, Inc.; 35.29c: © David Boyle/Animals Animals - Earth Scenes; 35.29d: © John Cancalosi/Peter Arnold Inc.; 35.32: © Stephen Dalton/National Audubon Society Collection/Photo Researchers, Inc.; 35.33a (left): © B.J Alcock/Visuals Unlimited; 35.33a(right): © Dave Watts/Alamy; 35.33b(left): © Volume 6/Corbis RF; 35.33b(right): © W. Perry Conway/Corbis; 35.33c(left): © Stephen J. Krasemann/DRK Photo; 35.33c(right): © Juergen & Christine Sohns/Animals Animals - Earth Scenes; 35.34: © Alan G. Nelson/Animals Animals - Earth Scenes; 35.35a: © Peter Arnold Inc./Alamy; 35.35b: © Martin Harvey/Peter Arnold Inc.; 35.35c (left): © Joe McDonald/Visuals Unlimited; 35.35c (right): © Dynamic Graphics Group/IT Stock Free/Alamy; 35.39: © AP/Wide World Photos.

## Chapter 36
Opener: © Susan Singer; 36.4(top left)-(top right): © Dr. Robert Lyndon; 36.4(bottom left)-(bottom right): © Biodisc/Visuals Unlimited; 36.6a: ©

## Chapter 45
Opener: © Omikron/Photo Researchers, Inc.; 45.11d: © Dr. John D. Cunningham/Visuals Unlimited; 45.21: © A. T. D. Bennett; 45.24: © Leonard Lee Rue III.

## Chapter 46
Opener: © Nature's Images/Photo Researchers, Inc.; 46.10: © John Paul Kay/Peter Arnold Inc.; 46.11: © Bettmann/Corbis.

## Chapter 47
Opener: © HAL BERAL/ Grant Heilman Photography, Inc.; 47.3a: © Ed Reschke/Peter Arnold Inc.; 47.3b: © David Scharf/Peter Arnold Inc.; 47.3c: © Dr. Holger Jastrow/http://www.uni-mainz.de/FB/Medizin/Anatomie/workshop/EM/EMAtlas.html; 47.3d: © CNRI/Photo Researchers, Inc.; 47.3e: © Dr. Kessel & Dr. Kardon/Tissue & Organs/Visuals Unlimted/Getty Images; 47.3f: © Ed Reschke/Peter Arnold Inc.; 47.3g: © Ed Reschke; 47.3h: © Ed Reschke/Peter Arnold Inc.; 47.10a-b: © Dr. H.E. Huxley; 47.21: © Treat Davidson/Photo Researchers, Inc.

## Chapter 48
Opener: © Gerlach Nature Photography/Animals Animals - Earth Scenes; 48.10: © Ron Boardman/Stone/Getty Images; 48.19: Courtesy AMGEN.

## Chapter 49
Opener: © Photodisc/Alamy RF; 49.1: © Bruce Watkins/Animals Animals - Earth Scenes; 49.3: © Juniors Bildarchiv/Alamy; 49.13a: © Clark Overton/Phototake; 49.13b: © Martin Rotker/Phototake; 49.14: © Kenneth Eward/BioGrafx/Photo Researchers, Inc.

## Chapter 50
Opener: © BioPhoto Associates/Photo Researchers, Inc.; 50.16a-b: © Ed Reschke; 50.16c: © Dr. Gladden Willis/Visuals Unlimited.

## Chapter 51
Opener: © Rick & Nora Bowers/Alamy.

## Chapter 52
Opener: © National Museum of Health and Medicine, Armed Forces Institute of Pathology/AP Photo; 52.3: © Manfred Kage/Peter Arnold Inc.; 52.6: © Wellcome Images; 52.12a-b: © Dr. Andrejs Liepins/Photo Researchers, Inc.; 52.22: © CDC/Science Source/Photo Researchers, Inc.

## Chapter 53
Opener: © Geordie Torr/Alamy; 53.1: © Dennis Kunkel Microscopy, Inc.; 53.2: © Fred McConnaughey/The National Audubon Society Collection/Photo Researchers, Inc.; 53.4: © Doug Perrine/SeaPics.com; 53.6: © Hans Pfletschinger/Peter Arnold Inc.; 53.7a: © Jonathan Losos; 53.7b: © David A. Northcott/Corbis; 53.7c-d: © Michael Fogden/OSF/Animals Animals - Earth Scenes; 53.8: © 2009 Frans Lanting/www.lanting.com; 53.9a: © Jean Phllippe Varin/Jacana/Photo Researchers, Inc.; 53.9b: © Tom McHugh/The National Audubon Society Collection/Photo Researchers, Inc.; 53.9c: © Corbis Volume 86 RF; 53.12: © David M. Phillips/Photo Researchers, Inc.; 53.17: © Ed Reschke; 53.21a: © Jonathan A. Meyers/Photo Researchers, Inc.; 53.21b: © The McGraw-Hill Companies, Inc./Jill Braaten, photographer; 53.21c: © The McGraw-Hill Companies, Inc./Bob Coyle, photographer; 53.21d: © Kumar Sriskandan/Alamy.

## Chapter 54
Opener: © Lennart Nilsson/Albert Bonniers Förlag AB, *A Child Is Born*, Dell Publishing Company; 54.1c-d: © David M. Phillips/Visuals Unlimited; 54.3a-d: Dr. Mathias Hafner (Mannheim University of Applied Sciences, Institute for Molecular Biology, Mannheim, Germany) and Dr. Gerald Schatten (Pittsburgh Development Centre Deputy Director, Magee-Woman's Research Institute Professor and Vice-Chair of Obstetrics, Gynecology & Reproductive Sciences and Professor of Cell Biology & Physiology Director, Division of Developmental and Regenerative Medicine University of Pittsburgh School of Medicine Pittsburgh, PA 15213); 54.7: © David M. Phillips/Visuals Unlimited; 54.8a: © Cabisco/Phototake; 54.9: © David M. Phillips/Visuals Unlimited; 54.11a: From "An Atlas of the Development of the Sea Urchin *Lytechinus variegatus*. Provided by Dr. John B. Morrill (left to right) Plate 20, pg 62, #I; 54.11b: From "An Atlas of the Development of the Sea Urchin *Lytechinus variegatus*. Provided by Dr. John B. Morrill (left to right) Plate 33, pg 93, #C; 54.11c: From "An Atlas of the Development of the Sea Urchin *Lytechinus variegatus*. Provided by Dr. John B. Morrill (left to right) Plate 38, pg 105, #G; 54.17a-b: © Courtesy of Manfred Frasch; 54.20c(1)-(2): © Roger Fleischman, University of Kentucky; 54.26a, 54.27a-d: © Lennart Nilsson/Albert Bonniers Förlag AB, *A Child Is Born*, Dell Publishing Company.

## Chapter 55
Opener: © K. Ammann/Bruce Coleman/Photoshot; 55.2: © Dr. Nicolette Siep; 55.4a-b: Reprinted from *Cell*, Volume 86, Issue 2, Jennifer R Brown, Hong Ye, Roderick T Bronson, Pieter Dikkes and Michael E Greenberg, "A Defect in Nurturing in Mice Lacking the Immediate Early Gene fosB," pp. 297-309, © 26 July 1996, with permission from Elsevier; 55.5a-b: Reprinted by permission from Macmillan Publishers Ltd: *Nature Neuroscience* 7, 1048-1054, "The neurobiology of pair bonding," Larry J Young, Zuoxin Wang © 2004; 55.6a-c: © Boltin Picture Library/The Bridgeman Art Library; 55.7: © William Grenfell/Visuals Unlimited; 55.8: © Thomas McAvoy, Life Magazine/Time, Inc./Getty Images; 55.9: © Harlow Primate Laboratory; 55.11: © Roger Wilmhurst/The National Audubon Society Collection/Photo Researchers, Inc.; 55.12a: © Linda Koebner/Bruce Coleman/Photoshot; 55.12b: © Jeff Foott/Tom Stack & Associates; 55.13a-c: © SuperStock; 55.14: Courtesy of Bernd Heinrich; 55.15b: Fred Breunner/Peter Arnold Inc.; 55.15c: © George Lepp/Getty Images; 55.18: © Dwight Kuhn; 55.21: © Tom Leeson; 55.22b: © Scott Camazine/Photo Researchers, Inc.; 55.23a: © Gerald Cubitt; 55.24: © Nina Leen, Life Magazine/Time, Inc./Getty Images; 55.27(left): © Peter Steyn/Getty Images; 55.27(right): © Gerald C. Kelley/Photo Researchers, Inc.; 55.28a: © Bruce Beehler/Photo Researchers, Inc.; 55.28b: © B. Chudleigh/Vireo; 55.30: © Cathy & Gordon ILLG; 55.31a: © Michael&Patricia Fogden/Minden Pictures/National Geographic Image Collection; 55.32a: Reprinted by permission from Macmillan Publishers Ltd: *Nature* 338, 249-251, "Parental care and mating behavior of polyandrous dunnocks," T. Burke, N. B. Daviest, M. W. Bruford, B. J. Hatchwell © 1989; 55.33: © Nick Gordon - Survival/OSF/Animals Animals - Earth Scenes; 55.35: © Steve Hopkin/Getty Images; 55.36: © Heinrich Van Den Berf/Peter Arnold Inc.; 55.37: © Stuart Westmorland/Getty Images; 55.38: © Mark Moffett/Minden Pictures; 55.39: © Nigel Dennis/National Audubon Society Collection/Photo Researchers, Inc.

## Chapter 56
Opener: © Volume 44/Photodisc/Getty RF; 56.1: © Michael Fogden/Animals Animals - Earth Scenes; 56.4: © Stone Nature Photography/Alamy; 56.13: © Christian Kerihuel; 56.15: Courtesy of Barry Sinervo; 56.21(left): © Juan Medina/Reuters/Corbis; 56.21(right): © Oxford Scientific/Photolibrary.

## Chapter 57
Opener: © Corbis RF; 57.1: © Daryl & Sharna Balfour/Okopia/Photo Researchers, Inc.; 57.6a-d: © Jonathan Losos; 57.10a: © Edward S. Ross; 57.10b: © Raymond Mendez/Animals Animals - Earth Scenes; 57.11a-b: © Lincoln P. Brower; 57.12: © Michael&Patricia Fogden/Corbis; 57.13: © Milton Tierney/Visuals Unlimited; 57.15: © Merlin D. Tuttle/Bat Conservation International; 57.16: © Eastcott/Momatiuk/The Image Works; 57.17: © Volume 44/Photodisc/Getty RF; 57.18: © Michael Fogden/DRK Photo; 57.19: © Charles T. Bryson, USDA Agricultural Research Service, Bugwood.org; 57.21a: © F. Stuart Westmorland/Photo Researchers, Inc.; 57.21b: © Ann Rosenfeld/Animals Animals - Earth Scenes; 57.23: © David Hosking/National Audubon Society Collection/Photo Researchers, Inc.; 57.24b-d: © Tom Bean; 57.25a-b: © Studio Carlo Dani/Animals Animals - Earth Scenes; 57.26: © Educational Images Ltd., Elmira, NY, USA. Used by Permission.

## Chapter 58
Opener: © Photodisc/Getty RF; 58.3: © Worldwide Picture Library/Alamy; 58.6: Jeff Schmaltz, MODIS Rapid Response Team, NASA/GSFC; 58.7a: U.S. Forest Service; 58.19a: © Layne Kennedy/Corbis.

## Chapter 59
Opener: GSFC/NASA; 59.10: © Andoni Canela/agefotostock; 59.11: © Image Plan/Corbis RF; 59.14a: © Art Wolfe/Photo Researchers, Inc.; 59.14b: © Bill Banaszowski/Visuals Unlimited; 59.16: Provided by the SeaWiFS Project, NASA/Goddard Space Flight Center, and ORBIMAGE; 59.17: © Digital Vision/Getty RF; 59.19a: © Jim Church; 59.19b: © Ralph White/Corbis; 59.22a: © Peter May/Peter Arnold Inc.; 59.22b: © 2009 Frans Lanting/www.lanting.com; 59.23: © Gilbert S. Grant/National Audubon Society Collection/Photo Researchers, Inc.; 59.25a: NASA/Goddard Space Flight Center Scientific Visualization Studio; 59.27: NASA Goddard Institute for Space Studies; 59.29a: © Dr. Bruno Messerli; 59.29b: © Prof. Lonnie Thompson, Ohio State University.

## Chapter 60

Boldface page numbers correspond with **boldface terms** in the text. Page numbers followed by an "f" indicate figures; page numbers followed by a "t" indicate tabular material.

# A

A band, 969
Aardvark, 525, 525f
ABC model, of floral organ
    specification, 846, 846f, 847f,
    848, 848f
ABO blood group, 90t, 230t,
    234-**235**, 235f, 1077
Abscisic acid, **779**, 779f, 826t,
    836, 836f
Abscission, **823**-824, 823f
Abscission zone, 823, 823f
Absolute dating, 424
Absorption
    in digestive tract, 982,
        989-990, 989f
    water and minerals in plants,
        771f, 773-775, 774f-775f
Absorption spectrum,
    of photosynthetic pigments,
        **152**-154, 152f, 153f
Abstinence, 1100
Acacia, mutualism with ants,
    809, 809f, 1198, 1198f
Acari (order), 682
Acceptor stem, **291**-292, 291f
Accessory digestive organs, 983f,
    988-989, 988f-989f, 994-995, 995f
Accessory pigment, **152**, 153f
Accessory sex organs
    female, 1097-1098, 1098f
    male, 1092-1093, 1093f
Acetaldehyde, 35f
Acetic acid, 35f
Acetyl-CoA
    in Krebs cycle, 131, 132, 133f,
        138, 138f
    from protein catabolism, 141f
    from pyruvate, 130, 130f
    uses of, 142
Acetylcholine, 897-898, 897f-898f,
    909t, 910, 912, 912f, 973, 1034
Acetylcholine (ACh) receptor,
    172, 893f, 912, 912f
Acetylcholinesterase (AChE), 898
Achiasmate segregation, **214**
Acid, **29**-30
Acid growth hypothesis, **830**, 831f
Acid precipitation, 1246, 1246f-1247f
Acid rain, 1247, 1247f
Acid soil, 789
Acini, **989**

Acoela, 644f, 660, 660f
Acoelomate, 637, 637f, 643, 644f,
    656-660, 657f, 659f-661f
Acoelomorpha, 644f
Acromegaly, **950**
Acrosomal process, 1106
Acrosome, **1106**
ACTH, 947-948
Actin, 970f
Actin filament, **76**, 76f, **84**, 84f
Actinobacteria, 550f
*Actinomyces*, 550f, 561
Actinopoda (phylum), 583
Action potential, 893-895
    all-or-none law of, 894
    falling phase of, 893, 894f
    generation of, 893-895, 894f-895f
    propagation of, 894-895, 895f
    rising phase of, 893, 894f,
        895, 895f
    undershoot phase of, 893, 894f
Action spectrum, **153**
    of chlorophyll, 153, 153f
Activation energy, **111**, 111f, 113-114
Activator, 117, 308, 313, 314-315,
    314f-315f, 316-317
    allosteric, **117**
Active immunity, 1063
Active site, **114**, 114f
Active transport, across plasma
    membrane, **99**-102, 104t
Acute-phase protein, 1059
ADA-SCID, 345
Adaptation, speciation and, 443, 443f
Adapter protein, **176**, 178
Adaptive radiation, **446**-447,
    446f-447f, 450, 450f
Adaptive significance,
    of behavior, 1148
Adaptive value, of egg coloration,
    1147-1148, 1147f
Addiction, drug, 900-901, 900f
Adenine, 42, 42f, 259f, 260, 262
Adenohypophysis, **946**
Adenosine diphosphate. *See* ADP
Adenosine monophosphate. *See* AMP
Adenosine triphosphate. *See* ATP
Adenovirus, 531f
Adenylyl cyclase, **179**-180, 180f, 946
ADH. *See* Antidiuretic hormone
Adherens junction, **84**
Adhesion, 27, 27f
Adipose cells, **868**
Adipose tissue, **868**, 868f
ADP, 113, 113f
Adrenal cortex, 954, 954f
Adrenal gland, **953**-954, 954f
Adrenal medulla, 953-954, 954f

Adrenocorticotropic hormone
    (ACTH), 947-948
Adsorption, of virus to host, 533
Adventitious plantlet, 858
Adventitious root, **742**, 746f, 765f
Aerenchyma, **780**, 781f
Aerial root, 742, 743f
Aerobic capacity, 974
Aerobic metabolism, 129
Aerobic respiration, **124**, 126, 126f,
    129, 136f
    ATP yield from, 137-138, 137f
    evolution of, 143
    regulation of, 138, 138f
Aesthetic value, of biodiversity, 1263
Afferent arteriole, 1046
Afferent neuron. *See* Sensory neuron
Aflatoxin, 630, 630f
African savanna, 1186f
African sleeping sickness, 574
African violet, 748f
*Afrovenator*, 709f
Age, at first reproduction, 1173
Age structure, of population, **1169**
Agent Orange, 831
Aging, telomerase and, 273
Agriculture
    applications of genetic
        engineering to, 346-349,
        346f-348f
    applications of genomics to,
        368-369, 368f-369f
    effect of global warming on,
        1252-1253
    pollution due to, 1251
*Agrobacterium tumefaciens*, 346, 346f,
    832, 833f
AIDS, 470-471, 531, 532t,
    535-538, **1079**
    deaths in United States, 535
    gene therapy for, 345, 345t
Air pollution, monitoring with
    lichens, 627
Akiapolaau, 1270f
Alanine, 35f, 46, 47f
Alaskan near-shore habitat,
    1271-1272, 1272f
Albinism, 227t, 228, 228f
Albumin, **1019**
Aldosterone, 954, **1035**, 1050,
    1051, 1052f
Aleurone, 764f, **765**
Alfalfa plant bug, 803, 803f
Alkaptonuria, 227t, 279
Allantoin, **1044**
Allantois, **706**, 708f, 1089, 1116
Allee effect, **1176**
Allee, Warder, 1176

Allele, **225**
    multiple, 233t, 233-235, 235f
    temperature-sensitive, 235, 235f
Allele frequency, 397, **399**-400
    changes in populations,
        398-400, 399f
Allelopathy, **807**, 807f
Allen's rule, 1164
Allergy, 1075, 1076f
Alligator, 707t, 711, 711f
Allometric growth, **1128**
*Allomyces*, 615t, 620, 621f
Allopatric speciation, **442**, 442f,
    444-445, 444f
Allopolyploidy, **445**, 445f, 477,
    477f, 479f
Allosteric activator, **117**
Allosteric enzymes, 117
Allosteric inhibitor, **117**, 117f
Allosteric site, **117**
Alpha helix, **48**
Alpha wave, 905
Alternate leaf, 744, 744f
Alternation of generations, 850
Alternative splicing, **290**, 320, 321f,
    322f, 361, 361f
Altricial young, **1153**
Altruism, **1154**-1157, 1155f-1157f
    reciprocal, 1154-1155, 1155f
Alveolata, 515f, 570f, 576-579,
    569f-579f
Alveoli, **1007**-1008, 1008f
Alveoli, of protists, 576, 576f
Alzheimer disease, 906-907
*Amborella*, 607, 607f
*Amborella trichopoda*, 521-522, 522f,
    607, 607f
American basswood, 836f
American woodcock
    (*Scolopax minor*), 933
Amino acid, **44**
    abbreviations for, 47f
    catabolism of, 141, 141f
    chemical classes of, 46, 47f
    as neurotransmitters, 898-899
    in proteins, 36f, 44
    structure of, 44-46, 47f
    twenty common, 47f
Amino acid derivative, 939
Amino group, 35, 35f
Aminoacyl-tRNA synthetase,
    **291**-291, 291f-292f
Ammonia, 1044, 1045f
Amniocentesis, **252**, 252f
Amnion, 1089, 1116
Amniotic egg, **706**, 708f, 1089
Amniotic fluid, 1116
Amniotic membrane, 1116

Archegonium, **594**, 594f
Archenteron, **638**, 639f, 1114
Archosaur, 709, 709f
Aristotle, 512
Armadillo, 525, 525f
*Armillaria*, 614, 629f
Arousal, state of consciousness, 905
ART. *See* Assisted reproductive technology
Arteriole, **1030**
Arteriosclerosis, **1033**
Artery, **1030**, 1030f
Arthropod, 641t, 643, 644, 678-687, 679f-687f
    body plan of, 679-681, 679f-681f
    circulatory system of, 680, 680f
    classification of, 523f, 524-525
    economic importance of, 678
    excretory system of, 680f, 681
    exoskeleton of, 679-680, 679f
    groups of, 679t
    jointed appendages of, 680
    locomotion in, 976
    molting in, 680
    nervous system of, 680, 681f, 901f, 902
    respiratory system of, 680-681, 681f, 1006
    segmentation in, 523, 523f, 639-640, 679, 679f
    taste in, 926, 926f
Arthropoda (phylum), 635, 641t, 644, 645f, 678-687, 679f-687f, 685t
Artificial selection, **10**, 403, 422-423, 422f-423f
    domestication, 422-423, 423f
    laboratory experiments, 422, 422f
Artificial transformation, 558
*Ascaris*, 208, 641t, 663
Ascocarp, **624**, 624f
Ascomycetes, 615, 615f, 624-625, 624f
Ascomycota (phylum), 615, 615f, 615t, 623-624
Ascospore, **624**, 624f
Ascus, **624**, 624f
Asexual reproduction, **572**
    in ascomycetes, 624-625
    in plants, 857-859, 858f
    in protists, 572
    in sponges, 651
    in zygomycetes, 621, 621f
Aspen, 859
*Aspergillus flavus*, 630, 630f
Aspirin, 348, 943
Assemblage, **1186**
Assembly, of virus particle, **533**
Assisted reproductive technology (ART), 1102
Assortative mating, **402**
Aster (mitosis), **195**, 196f
Asteroidea (class), 689, 689f, 690
Asthma, **1012**
Atherosclerosis, 55, **1033**, 1033f
Atmosphere
    of early earth, 509
    reducing, 509
Atmospheric circulation, 1231-1233, 1231f-1232f

Atom, 2f, **3**, **18-19**
    chemical behavior of, 20, 20f
    energy within, 21, 21f
    isotopes of, 19-20, 19f
    neutral, 19
    scanning tunneling microscopy of, 18f
    structure of, 18-20, 19f
Atomic mass, **18-19**
Atomic number, **18**
ATP, **43-44**, 44f
    energy storage molecule, 112-113
    production of , 113, 113f. *See also* ATP synthase
        in electron transport chain, 124, 124f, 135-136, 135f, 136f
        in glycolysis, 127, 127f, 129
        in Krebs cycle, 132, 131f, 133f
        in photosynthesis, 148, 149f, 151, 156-160, 156f, 158f-159f
    regulation of aerobic respiration, 138, 138f
    role in metabolism, 125
    structure of, 44f, 112, 112f
    synthesis of, 125-126, 125f, 126f
    uses of
        in active transport, 100-102, 100f, 101f
        in coupled transport, 101-102, 101f
        in endergonic reactions, 113, 113f, 125
        in muscle contraction, 971, 971f
        in protein folding, 51, 51f
        in sodium-potassium pump, 100-101, 100f
ATP cycle, 113, 113f
ATP-dependent remodeling factor, 317, 317f
ATP synthase, **126**, 126f, 136, 136f, 156, 158-160, 159f
Atrial natriuretic hormone, 956, 1051
Atrial peptide, **343**
    genetically engineered, 343
Atrioventricular (AV) node, 1027, 1028f, 1034
Atrioventricular (AV) valve, **1026**, 1027f
Atrium, **1023**, 1023f
Attachment
    in HIV infection cycle, 536-537
    of virus to host, 533
Auditory tube, 922
Australopithecine, 722-723
    early, 723
*Australopithecus*, 722
*Australopithecus afarensis*, 724
Autocrine signaling, 169-170
Autoimmune disease, 1075
Autologous blood donation, 1077
Automated DNA sequencing, 337f, 339
Autonomic nervous system, **888**, 889f, 909, 909t, 910, 910f, 911f
Autophosphorylation, 175-176, 175f
Autopolyploidy, **445**, 445f, 477, 479f

Autosome, **241**
    nondisjunction involving, 250-251, 250f
Autotroph, **123**, **558**, 559, **1214**
Aux/IAA protein, 829-830, 830f
Auxin
    cytokinin and, 832f
    discovery of, 825, 827-828, 827f-828f
    effects of, 828, 829f
    gravitropism and, 819, 820
    mechanism of action of, 828-830, 829f
    phototropism and, 829f
    synthetic, 829f, 830-831
    thigmotropism and, 821
Auxin binding protein, 829
Auxin receptor, 829
Auxin response factor (ARF), 829
AV node. *See* Atrioventricular node
AV valve. *See* Atrioventricular valve
Avascular bone, **966**
Avery, Oswald, 257
Aves (class), 699f, **712-715**, 712f, 714f-715f
Avian cholera, 1061
Avian influenza, 539, 1079
Avirulent pathogen, **811**
Axial locomotion, 975
Axil, **744**
Axillary bud, 730f, **744**, 744f, 802, 803f
Axon, 872, 873t
    conduction velocities of, 895-896, 895t
    diameter of, 895
    myelinated, 895-896, 895f, 895t, 896f
    unmyelinated, 895-896, 895f, 895t
Aznalcóllar mine spill (Spain), 799-800, 799f
*Azolla*, 599

# B

B cell, 1062t, **1063**, 1063f
B lymphocyte, 1063, **1063**
Babbitt, Bruce, 1275
Bacillary dysentery, 560
Bacillus, 550f, 552
*Bacillus anthracis*, 550f, 561t
*Bacillus thuringiensis* insecticidal protein, 347-348
Bacon, Francis, 5
Bacteria, 550f-551f. *See also* Prokaryote
    ancient, 546, 546f
    archaebacteria versus, 547
    cell wall of, 64, 548-549
    endosymbiotic, 568
    flagella of, 64f, 65, 548, **553**, 553f
    genetically engineered, 564
    Gram staining of, 552-553, 552f-553f
    intestinal, 564
    photosynthetic, 63-64, 64f, 150, 156, 156f, 547, 548, 569-570
    plasma membrane of, 63-64, 93, 548

Bacteria (domain), 13, 13f, 483, **515**, 515-516, 515f, 516t, 547, 549f
Bacteria (kingdom), **514**, 517f, 518t
Bacterial artificial chromosome (BAC), 330-331, 356
Bacterial disease
    in humans, 558, 560-563, 561t, 562f
    in plants, 560
Bacteriochlorophyll, 559
Bacteriophage, **258**, 528, 530-531, 530f, 533-534, 534f
    cloning vector, 330, 331f
    Hershey-Chase experiment with, 258-259, 258f
    induction of, 533-534
    lysogenic cycle of, 533-534, 534f
    lytic cycle of, 533, 534f
    temperate, **533**
    virulent, **533**
Bacteriophage lambda, 533
    cloning vector, 330, 331f
Bacteriophage T2, 531f
Bacteriophage T4, 530f, 533
Bacteriorhodopsin, 95, 95f
Bait protein, in DNA-binding hybrid, 341, 341f
Ball-and-socket joint, **967**, 968f
Bank (fishing on continental shelf), **1243**
Barley, genome of, 363, 476, 479f
Barnacle, 683-684, 683f
    competition among species of, 1188, 1188f
Barometer, 1006
Baroreceptor, 919, **1034**, 1035f
Barr body, **243**, 243f, 251
Barro Colorado Island, 1221
Basal body, **79**, 79f
Basal ganglia, 902t, 904
Basal metabolic rate (BMR), **995**
Basal surface, 866
Base, 29-**30**
Base-pairs, **262**, 262f
Base substitution, **299**, 300f
Basidiocarp, **623**, 623f
Basidiomycetes, 615, 615f, 622-623, 623f
Basidiomycota (phylum), 615, 615f, 615t, 622
Basidiospore, **622**, 623f
Basidium, **622**, 623f
Basophil, **1062**, 1062t
Bat, 525f, 717-718, 717f
    pollination by, 854, 1196f
    vampire, 1155, 1155f
Bates, Henry, 1195
Batesian mimicry, **1195**, 1195f, 1196
*Batrachochytrium dendrobatidis*, 619, 630
Beadle, George, 6, 279
Bean, 760, 760f, 765f, 822, 823f
Bee
    chromosome number in, 189t
    pollination by, 852, 852f-853f
    solitary, 852
Beetle, species richness in, 469-470, 469f

*index*  **I-3**